Civil Procedure

Civil Procedure

Cases, Materials, and Questions

SEVENTH EDITION

Richard D. Freer
Robert Howell Hall Professor of Law
Emory University School of Law

Wendy Collins Perdue
Dean and Professor of Law
University of Richmond School of Law

Carolina Academic Press
Durham, North Carolina

Clothbound ISBN 978-1-61163-911-7
Looseleaf ISBN 978-1-61163-953-7
LCCN 2016934808

Carolina Academic Press, LLC
700 Kent Street
Durham, NC 27701
Telephone (919) 489-7486
Fax (919) 493-5668
www.caplaw.com

Printed in the United States of America

Dedication

We dedicate this work to Sherman Cohn — model scholar, teacher, mentor, and friend — in celebration of his fifty years on the faculty at Georgetown University Law Center.

Contents

Preface

Civil Procedure is a challenging course both for students and teachers. Of all the first year subjects, it is the most alien to students' pre-law school lives. As a result, the course sometimes seems to students to be unconnected to the "real world." Ironically, of all the first year courses, Civil Procedure is the most connected to the "real world" of what lawyers do. Graduates routinely report that Civil Procedure is central to their work.

Thus one challenge for professors (and casebook authors) is to bridge the gap in student experience. The book addresses this issue by including many problems and hypotheticals which are intended to make the material more concrete. We also include notes and questions that explore the strategic and ethical choices that real lawyers face.

A second challenge is that the course includes significant amounts of detail, but at the same time raises such fundamental questions as the role of justice, fairness and efficiency in the adjudication of rights. Students sometimes miss the richness of the course because they fail to see how its various aspects fit together — they may come away with a knowledge of individual trees but not an overall sense of the forest. This book seeks to avoid that result by stressing integration. The chapters are arranged in related blocks and each chapter begins with a section called "Introduction and Integration" which provides an overview and indicates how the section fits with other topics.

In some areas, we have arranged material differently from what seems to be the common approach. We do this to facilitate the integrative function. The first part of the book addresses where litigation can proceed and includes personal jurisdiction, subject matter jurisdiction, and venue. We have also included notice and service of process in this part because of its close relationship to personal jurisdiction.

Next, the book moves to the phases of a lawsuit — pleading, discovery, and adjudication (with and without a jury). Joinder is covered later because we do not believe this topic is necessary to understanding the basic steps of litigation and, by delaying it, we can cover it with the related issues of preclusion. Covering pleading and discovery back-to-back highlights that they are both methods of information exchange. The chapter on adjudication includes both summary judgment and judgment as a matter of law. We place the *Erie* chapter after the chapter on adjudication. We believe students may better understand *Gasperini* if they have studied Rule 59.

Next are three chapters on preclusion and joinder. We view them as a unit on "packaging" of litigation. We begin with preclusion. That chapter, which explores the goals of efficiency and finality, lays the foundation for the joinder chapters. Although we introduce supplemental jurisdiction briefly in the chapter on subject matter jurisdiction, we defer detailed analysis until the joinder chapters. This seems particularly necessary because students cannot understand § 1367 without first studying the joinder rules. Following joinder, we address appeals.

This course stresses civil procedure as part of the litigation process — a publicly funded system of dispute resolution. We feel that students should consider whether the litigation system is a good way to resolve disputes. The last chapter of the book raises questions about alternative dispute resolution and comparative law. We feel that these issues are well treated at the end of the course, after the students have seen the litigation process fully.

Recent years have seen remarkable change in civil procedure. Much of this has been generated by the Supreme Court. In 2011, the Court returned to personal jurisdiction for the first time since 1990 with two major decisions: J. McIntyre Machinery Ltd. v. Nicastro, 131 S. Ct. 2780 (2011), which embraced a cramped view of specific jurisdiction, and Goodyear Dunlop Tires Operations, S.A. v. Brown, 131 S. Ct. 2846 (2011), which suggested major retrenchment in general jurisdiction. The Court confirmed the retrenchment of general jurisdiction in Daimler AG v. Bauman, 134 S. Ct. 746 (2014) and offered its first discussion since 1984 of "effects" jurisdiction with Walden v. Fiore, 134 S. Ct. 1115 (2014). In subject matter jurisdiction, the Court refined federal question jurisdiction over state-law claims in Gunn v. Minton, 133 S. Ct. 1059 (2013) and clarified removal procedure in Dart Cherokee Basin Operating Co., LLC, v. Owens, 135 S. Ct. 547 (2014). Atlantic Marine Construction Co., Inc. v. U.S. District Court, 134 S. Ct. 568 (2013), is a major decision concerning enforceability of forum selection clauses through transfer under 28 U.S.C. § 1404(a). In pleadings, the Court makes an important distinction between legal and factual sufficiency in Johnson v. City of Shelby, 134 S. Ct. 346 (2014), which may moderate the impact of *Twombly* and *Iqbal.* In Tolan v. Cotton, 134 S. Ct. 1861 (2014), the Court appears to give force to the hackneyed saying that a judge ruling on summary judgment must view evidence in the light most favorable to the nonmoving party.

The Court has continued its remarkable interest in the class action. Comcast Corp. v. Behrend, 133 S. Ct. 1426 (2013) is an important decision concerning certification of damages classes under Rule 23(b)(3). On the heels of Wal-Mart Stores, Inc. v. Dukes, 131 S. Ct. 2541 (2011), it front-loads a great deal of litigation into the certification stage. Yet, in securities fraud cases, the Court has rejected some efforts to require substantive showings at the certification stage. See, e.g., Amgen v. Connecticut Retirement Plans, 133 S. Ct. 1184 (2013). The Court has also continued its embrace of arbitration. In American Express Co. v. Italian Colors Restaurant, 133 S. Ct. 2304 (2013), it upheld a form contractual waiver of class arbitration even though the cost of pursuing individual litigation would be prohibitive. The decision, following AT&T

Mobility LLC v. Concepcion, 131 S. Ct. 1740 (2011), which reached the same conclusion in a consumer class action, raises significant questions of access to justice.

The Rules Advisory Committee has been active as well. This edition addresses the amendments going into effect December 1, 2015. Principal among these is the change to the scope of discoverability, which moves "proportionality" to center stage as part of the definition of what information may be discovered. Reflecting its increasing importance, we have expanded the discussion of discovery of electronically stored information, ESI, including the newly-promulgated version of Rule 36(e) regarding preservation of ESI.

Finally, though Congress has not been active in federal jurisdiction or procedure in recent years, its broad changes to removal jurisdiction and venue in the Jurisdiction and Venue Clarification Act of 2011 have now generated case law worthy of discussion in this edition. In particular, we note the emerging split of authority regarding whether the legislative abolition of the "local action" rule affected venue or subject matter jurisdiction.

Notes on Form

We indicate textual deletions from opinions and other materials by "* * *." We have not noted deletions of citations from opinions. Our additions to cases are enclosed in brackets. Our footnotes are denoted by asterisks. We have retained the original numbering of footnotes appearing in opinions. We have adopted a short form of citing the several classic treatises to which we refer throughout the book. With apologies to the contributing authors on the two standard multi-volume treatises, we refer to them, respectively, as MOORE'S FEDERAL PRACTICE AND WRIGHT & MILLER, FEDERAL PRACTICE AND PROCEDURE. CHARLES ALAN WRIGHT & MARY KAY KANE, LAW OF FEDERAL COURTS (7th ed. 2011) is cited WRIGHT & KANE, FEDERAL COURTS; and RICHARD D. FREER, CIVIL PROCEDURE (3d ed. 2012) is cited FREER, CIVIL PROCEDURE.

Acknowledgments

Acknowledgments by Professor Freer

My friends and Emory colleagues Tom Arthur, Robert Schapiro, and George Shepherd have contributed greatly to the development of this book. Beyond the Emory community, we are in the particular debt of Colleen Murphy, Mike Vitiello, and Jim Duane, who have gone far beyond the call of friendship in offering suggestions. And we have benefited greatly from contributions by Vince Alexander, John Beckerman, Lenni Benson, Debra Cohen, Stan Cox, Jeff Dobbins, Charlotte Goldberg, Heather Kolinsky, Glenn Koppel, Ben Madison, and Rocky Rhodes.

I acknowledge with gratitude the generosity of the late Judge Robert Howell Hall, who endowed the professorship which I am honored to hold. I am grateful for the continued support of Emory University School of Law. And, as with all my work, I remain indebted to Louise, Collin, and Courtney.

Acknowledgments by Dean Perdue

I am grateful for the support I have received from my colleagues over the years, particularly those who share my passion for procedure and have offered invaluable ideas and encouragement on this and earlier editions. That group includes Sherman Cohn, Carrie Menkel-Meadow, Naomi Mezey, Nina Pillard, Phil Schrag, and David Vladeck.

My deepest thanks go to my family, David, Bill, and Ben. Although my sons occasionally questioned my choice of topic ("Why don't you do something useful—like write a book about baseball?"), and my efficiency ("You're not done yet?"), their love and good humor were essential to keeping my sanity and perspective.

We acknowledge with gratitude the numerous helpful suggestions from users of prior editions. We also acknowledge the permission of the following copyright holders to quote material contained in the book. Any errors that occurred in editing or reprinting are our responsibility, not that of the copyright holder:

Mezibov, Marc, and H. Louis Sirkin, The Mapplethorpe Obscenity Trial, Litig., Summer 1992, at 12, 13-15, 71. Copyright © 1992 by the American Bar Association. Reprinted by permission.

Wagatsuma, Hiroshi, and Arthur Rosett, The Implications of Apology: Law and Culture in Japan and the United States, 20 Law and Society Review 461-495 (1986). Copyright © 1986 by the Law and Society Association. Reprinted by permission.

Civil Procedure

Chapter 1

An Introduction to the Civil Action and Procedure

A. The Study of Procedure

The course in civil procedure focuses on the litigation process, by which parties seek to resolve civil disputes in the courts. While it involves a significant amount of technical material, the course requires more than mastering discrete rules and doctrines. It should foster critical thinking about the principles underlying the rules and doctrines, and about the role of litigation as a method of resolving civil disputes. The stated goal of modern procedure is contained in Federal Rule 1: "to secure the just, speedy, and inexpensive determination of every action and proceeding." Throughout this course, we should consider whether that goal is achieved.

The focus of this course is on the *litigation* process through which parties seek to resolve their dispute by "going to court." Contrary to depiction in popular media, however, this process consists of far more than a trial. In addition, we should keep in mind that litigation is not the only method for resolving disputes. In Chapter 15, we will discuss alternatives to litigation. Indeed, most disputes in this country are not resolved through litigation; they are privately settled without the need for filing suit. And of all those disputes that do get filed in court, only a very small percentage (generally two to four percent) will actually go to trial; they are resolved during the litigation process, perhaps by court order or, more likely, by settlement.

Although only a small percentage of all disputes will actually end in trial, use of alternatives, including voluntary settlement, are always made "in the shadow of the law." Any negotiated settlement will be influenced by the parties' assessment of what they could obtain through formal litigation. Thus, a full understanding of the litigation option is essential even for lawyers who ultimately pursue alternatives to it.

In this course, we are concerned with civil, as opposed to criminal, cases. The major goal of criminal law is to *punish* defendants for breaches of the general order rather than to *compensate* the victim of the crime. Civil cases, on the other hand, usually involve disputes between private parties,* in which the plaintiff seeks to recover a remedy from the defendant.

For example, suppose defendant drives her car while under the influence of alcohol and runs into a car driven by plaintiff. Plaintiff is injured, and her car is destroyed. Defendant's act constituted a violation of the criminal (or penal) law, for which the government may prosecute. If the prosecution is successful, the state can punish defendant, perhaps by imprisonment, or by payment of a fine, or by an order to perform community service. Generally, however, any fine goes to the government and not to the injured person.

Defendant's act also constituted a *tort* for which the plaintiff can maintain a civil action against the defendant. The goal of that action will be to force defendant to compensate plaintiff for harm caused by her breach of a duty owed to plaintiff. The remedy may include reimbursement for the plaintiff's medical expenses and lost wages while recuperating, as well as compensation for pain and suffering and for the loss of her car.

Of course, not all civil cases involve criminal behavior. Breach of contract cases, for example, rarely involve misconduct that could constitute a crime. Similarly, the tort of negligence may be based on mere inadvertence which could not support a criminal prosecution. Civil cases play an important role in the administration of justice. They permit one party to sue another for breaching rules our society establishes governing relationships, even when those breaches fall short of criminal.

Throughout the law school curriculum, you will see procedural differences between criminal and civil cases. The prosecution must prove the criminal defendant guilty "beyond a reasonable doubt." The civil plaintiff generally must show that the defendant is liable "by a preponderance of the evidence." When charged, the criminal defendant is given warnings that the civil defendant is not. The court cannot compel the criminal defendant to testify at trial; the state must warn the criminal defendant that her statements may be used against her; the state must provide the criminal defendant with legal counsel if she cannot afford it. In short, more process is due the criminal defendant than the civil defendant.

The line between criminal and civil is not always bright. For example, in civil actions in which defendant has acted egregiously, our system may permit plaintiff to recover "punitive," or "exemplary," damages. Their purpose is expressly to punish — to "send a message" to defendant that her behavior is intolerable. To the extent that punitive damages serve a function similar to the criminal law, some observers have argued that the state should afford the defendant various heightened procedural protections given criminal defendants.

* The government can be a party to a civil action. For example, it might sue a contractor who breached an agreement to build some public work. In that instance, it is not enforcing a penal law but is vindicating its private right. In addition, the government often enforces laws through civil actions, for example, by bringing an action to enjoin violations of antitrust laws.

A civil litigant determines whether she has a claim and, if so, against whom, through the *substantive* law. In contrast, civil procedure provides the vehicle for attempting to vindicate rights created by substantive law. As we will see, however, the line between substance and procedure is sometimes ephemeral.

In many respects, procedure is the unique province of lawyers. Lawyers understand that *how* rights are vindicated can affect dramatically the scope of those rights. A claim or defense that one cannot prove is not worth much. Procedure is relatively invisible to most of the world, but seemingly technical procedural changes may bring about significant alteration in the scope of substantive rights. Changes in the allocation of which party has the burden of proof on an issue, or how notice is given, or who is bound by a judgment can alter the underlying rights. As one scholar has summarized:

> [N]eglecting the terrain of procedure is, as it always has been, a mistake. Fundamentally, that is because procedure is power, whether in the hands of lawyers or judges. Smart lawyers and judges recognize the power of procedure. * * * Substantive rights, including constitutional rights, are worth no more than the procedural mechanisms available for their realization and protection.

Stephen Burbank, *The Bitter With the Sweet: Tradition, History, and Limitations on Federal Judicial Power—A Case Study*, 75 NOTRE DAME L. REV. 1291, 1292–93 (2000). Throughout this course, you should consider whether seemingly neutral rules of procedure might have a distinctly substantive impact. For instance, Professor Madison has demonstrated the substantive impact of procedural provisions on human bias and the promotion of impartial justice. Benjamin V. Madison, III, *Color-Blind: Procedure's Quiet But Crucial Role in Achieving Racial Justice*, 78 U.M.K.C. L. REV. 617 (2010).

B. Federalism

Before there was a national government, the thirteen original states were separate sovereigns, governed by their individual constitutions and laws. Citizens concluded, however, that their interests might be better served by institution of a centralized government, at least for some purposes. After experimentation under the Articles of Confederation, the citizens undertook to create a national entity. Importantly, however, this national government did not replace or eliminate the separate state governments. The Constitution creates the United States government and cedes to it limited and enumerated powers.

In the first case in this book, Justice Stephen Field summarized these points succinctly:

> The several States of the Union are not, it is true, in every respect independent, many of the rights and powers which originally belonged to them being now vested in the government created by the Constitution. But, except as re-

> strained and limited by that instrument, they possess and exercise the authority of independent States * * *.

Pennoyer v. Neff, 95 U.S. 714, 722 (1878).

While federal power is limited to those areas enumerated in the Constitution, the Supremacy Clause of that document provides that "This Constitution, and the Laws of the United States which shall be made in Pursuance thereof; and all Treaties made, or which shall be made, under the Authority of the United States, shall be the supreme Law of the Land. * * *" U.S. Const., art. VI. Thus, where federal law exists and conflicts with state law, the federal law controls, so long as it concerns an issue properly within the purview of the federal government. Although most of the Constitution addresses the scope of federal power, it also imposes direct restrictions on the power of the states. For example, the Fourteenth Amendment provides that "No State shall * * * deprive any person of life, liberty, or property, without due process of law; * * *." Any state law violating this precept is unconstitutional and invalid.

The limited nature of the national government's power is reflected in the federal judiciary. Article III, section 2, of the Constitution sets the outer boundary of federal judicial power. Thus, as we will see in Chapter 4, litigants cannot file suit in a federal district court simply because they would like to be there. The case must be one as to which the Constitution and a congressional statute permit access to the federal courts. The two major types of cases which plaintiff can file in federal court are "diversity of citizenship" cases (in which the plaintiff and defendant are citizens of different states and in which the amount involved exceeds $75,000) and "federal question" cases (in which plaintiff's claim arises under a federal law).

What if the plaintiff has a dispute that cannot invoke one of these bases of federal subject matter jurisdiction? She can file in state court. Indeed, even the vast majority of those cases that can be filed in federal district court—all diversity of citizenship and most federal question cases—may also be filed in state court.* Thus, the existence of separate state and federal court systems will usually give the plaintiff a choice of fora. In fact, plaintiff may have a choice of filing in federal or in state court in several different states.

Although federal law can trump state law, it is important to note that the federal courts do not have general power to review actions of state courts. In most instances, a civil litigant in a state trial court can appeal an adverse judgment *only* to an appellate court of that state. Once the case is filed in one system—state or federal—it is subject to appellate review only in that system. There is one significant exception to this rule. The United States Supreme Court can review a decision of the highest court of a state. However, it can review that decision *only as to matters of federal law.*

---

* The only exception is with those federal question cases as to which federal district court jurisdiction is exclusive of the states. Such cases are rare. Examples include federal antitrust actions and patent cases.

Suppose, for example, that the supreme court of State A holds that unmarried people living together are not entitled to the same property law benefits as married people. The United States Supreme Court cannot review this holding, because it raises only a question of state law, as to which state courts are supreme. If, however, a party challenged this state law on the basis that it denied equal protection of the law as guaranteed by the United States Constitution, the Supreme Court would have the power to review the case. The reach of the Equal Protection Clause is a federal question, as to which the Supreme Court is the ultimate arbiter.

The American system of justice faces often thorny questions of federalism because American citizens are subject to regulation by both state and national governments. Few other countries have such dual governments. Interestingly, for example, England, from which we inherit so much of our law and legal tradition, is not a federal republic.*

C. Overview of the Structure of a Court System

As we have noted, the federal government has a system of courts. Each state is free to establish its own judicial system as it sees fit. The federal courts and the courts of many (but not all) states are established in a tripartite model, consisting of (1) trial courts reviewed by (2) intermediate appellate courts reviewed by (3) a supreme court.

1. Trial Courts

These are the courts in which the plaintiff initiates civil litigation, usually by filing a complaint and having it and a court order (called a summons) delivered to defendant. Trial courts have *original* (as opposed to *appellate*) jurisdiction. Some states assign jurisdiction to different trial courts based upon subject matter. For example, they may have separate trial courts for probate matters, family law cases, and general civil disputes. Other states divide jurisdiction based upon the amount in dispute. For example, one court may take cases involving $15,000 or less while another takes cases of greater amounts. States may use different names for their trial courts. Common names include superior, municipal, district, and circuit courts. The trial court in the

---

* Though this course will focus primarily on procedure in the federal courts, we will also note divergences in state practice. The vast majority of litigation in this country takes place in state courts. Scholarship increasingly has begun to reflect an emerging appreciation for the study of state-court practice.

In particular, Professor Koppel urges consideration of uniform rules. See Glenn Koppel, *Reflections on the "Chimera" of a Uniform Code of State Civil Procedure: The Virtue of Vision in Procedural Reform*, 58 DePaul L. Rev. 971 (2009); Glenn S. Koppel, *Toward a New Federalism in State Civil Justice: Developing a Uniform Code of State Civil Procedure Through a Collaborative Rule-Making Process*, 58 Vand. L. Rev. 1167 (2005). See also *Symposium on State Civil Procedure*, 35 W. St. L. Rev. 1–304 (2007). See generally Benjamin V. Madison, Civil Procedure for All States (2010).

federal judicial system is the federal district court. This book focuses almost entirely on the jurisdiction and procedure in trial courts, where the bulk of litigation is carried out.

2. Intermediate Appellate Courts

Despite a popular notion that a losing litigant can "fight to the highest court in the land," there is no federal constitutional right to appeal a judgment in a civil case. Nonetheless, most American jurisdictions do provide one. For example, in a three level court structure, states may permit an appeal of right to the intermediate appellate court.

In the federal judicial system, a litigant has a right to appeal an adverse district court judgment to the intermediate appellate court, which is known as the United States Court of Appeals. It consists of thirteen "circuits," eleven of which are grouped by geography into courts bearing a number. For example, the Fourth Circuit sits in Richmond, and hears appeals from federal district courts in Maryland, Virginia, West Virginia, North Carolina, and South Carolina. The twelfth is known as the Court of Appeals for the District of Columbia Circuit, which sits in Washington, D.C. and hears appeals from the federal district court in Washington.* The thirteenth United States Court of Appeals is for the "Federal Circuit," the jurisdiction of which is determined not by geography but by subject matter. It sits in Washington and considers appeals in specialized cases such as import transactions and patents.

Not all states have an intermediate court of appeals. In such states, a civil litigant who loses at the trial court may seek review at the state supreme court. Further, the existence of an intermediate appellate court does not guarantee a right of appeal in civil cases. In Virginia, for example, the intermediate appellate court reviews criminal and administrative matters, but not general civil cases. Here, too, then, a civil litigant losing at the trial court may seek review by the supreme court.

3. Supreme Courts

Supreme courts are appellate courts.** Most states refer to their court of last resort as the supreme court. (In New York, however, it is called the Court of Appeals.) In the federal judicial system, the highest court is the United States Supreme Court. It consists of nine justices,*** and sits only at Washington, D.C. In most states, as in the federal system, the highest court is not required to hear all cases in which its

---

* Each of these courts of appeals reviews decisions by administrative agencies. Because it is in Washington, the District of Columbia Circuit hears more of these than any other Circuit.

** Interestingly, the United States Constitution gives the United States Supreme Court original (trial) jurisdiction over certain types of cases, including those in which a state is a party. U.S. CONST., art. III, § 2.

*** The Constitution is silent on how many justices shall sit on the Supreme Court. The number is set by statute. See 28 U.S.C. § 1. The original Judiciary Act of 1789 provided the Court with only six justices.

review is sought. Indeed, in civil cases, supreme court review is almost always discretionary.* In a typical year, for instance, the United States Supreme Court agrees to hear fewer than four percent of the cases (of any sort, criminal or civil) in which a party seeks its review.

4. Appellate Practice and the Doctrine of Precedent

Appellate courts review dispositions of the case by the lower court(s). Appellate practice, however, is very different from trial practice. Appellate courts do not try cases, so they do not receive evidence or hear witnesses. Instead, they rely on the record below, briefs filed by counsel and, usually, oral argument on legal points. In intermediate courts of appeals, it is common to have a panel of three judges review each case. At the supreme court level, usually the entire panel of justices (commonly consisting of seven or nine) considers each case.

It is important to appreciate the role of appellate courts. The intermediate court (or the supreme court if it is reviewing the trial court directly) is not interested in whether it would have decided the case differently from the trial court; it does not retry the case and for the most part does not reexamine the facts. Instead its review is generally limited to errors of law. Even where there were errors, the doctrine of "harmless error" allows an appellate court to affirm a judgment even when the lower court made a mistake, if the result would have been the same anyway.

When reading any opinion, note what court is deciding it. If it is an appellate court, note the issues as to which it is particularly deferential to the trial court. Note also the disposition of the appellate court. Does it affirm or reverse outright? Does it remand with instructions? How clear are the instructions?

Most supreme courts have a limited, though critical, role. Rather than simply correcting mistakes made by lower courts, most supreme courts act principally as final arbiter of the content of the jurisdiction's law. This role is reflected in the fact that most are not required to hear all cases in which parties seek their review. Thus, a supreme court may accept cases for review in particular substantive areas because it needs to clarify the law there.

Appellate pronouncements on questions of law are binding on all lower courts in the jurisdiction through the doctrine of *precedent*, or *stare decisis*. This doctrine lends consistency and stability to the law. In addition, under the same principle, an appellate decision on a point of law binds the same court in later cases. Thus, once a state supreme court has held that a plaintiff's contributory negligence bars her recovery, that court will apply the same rule in deciding subsequent cases. Stare decisis does not, however, freeze the law forever. Responding to relevant changes, the court that rendered an opinion (or a higher one) can overrule the precedent. Although overruling

---

* In some states, a defendant in certain criminal cases, such as those involving capital punishment, has a right to review by the supreme court.

precedent is unusual, courts regularly elaborate on or modify rules announced in prior cases. This process of elaboration and gradual modification is at the heart of our common law system.

D. The Adversary System

One fundamental characteristic of American litigation is its adversarial nature. In our adversary system, each side to a dispute presents its case vigorously, in the best light possible. The parties take the initiative to bring suit, raise issues, present evidence, and persuade the factfinder. One obvious assumption of the system is that parties motivated by self-interest will only pursue worthwhile litigation and will invest the time and resources necessary to present their positions well. Another is that this clash of self-interested combatants hones the issues in such a way as to enhance the possibility of finding the truth and reaching a just result. Throughout the course, consider whether the adversary system relies too much on the notions that all lawyers are of equal ability and that all parties are of equal financial means.

The Constitution grants to federal courts jurisdiction only over "cases" or "controversies." Thus, courts may not render opinions on questions not presented in the context of an actual case. For example, assume that a legislature (federal or state) passes a statute that plainly violates the Constitution. No matter how egregious the violation, no federal court can declare the statute unconstitutional until the question is proffered in an actual case. The Founders expressly rejected a proposal that the Chief Justice sit with Congress to advise it on the constitutionality of its bills. Many (but not all) state court systems impose a similar limitation.

No plaintiff can sue unless she has "standing," which generally means that she must have suffered some injury before she can bring suit. Our system does not permit litigation simply because someone is upset over something or wants the courts to issue an advisory opinion; she has to be injured, to have a personal stake in the litigation, before the court is presented with the appropriate adversarial vehicle for resolution. Standing and similar doctrines governing "justiciability" of issues often present vexing questions; you will deal with them in detail in courses on constitutional law and federal courts.

Litigation is not unrestricted combat. Much like rules of a sporting contest, rules of procedure curb pure adversariness. For example, Federal Rule 11 imposes sanctions on litigants or counsel for various misdeeds, including documents filed "for any improper purpose, such as to harass or to cause unnecessary delay or needless increase in the cost of litigation." Rule 16 imposes sanctions for failure to cooperate in pretrial efforts to settle the case or to frame issues for trial. Rule 37 does the same for abuses in the area of discovery, through which litigants are permitted to find out contentions and evidence of opponents. In addition, rules of professional responsibility impose several important duties on counsel. Thus, a lawyer may not raise frivolous issues, conceal or destroy evidence, misrepresent facts, or offer false evidence. Counsel also must reveal controlling authority contrary to her position.

Under the traditional adversary model, the judge is usually passive and reactive. The parties, not the court, are responsible for initiating and developing the case, framing the issues, discovering the evidence and presenting it at trial. Under this model, the judge rarely intervenes unless asked by the parties. For example, one might make a *motion*,* that is, a request for an order, on any of dozens of grounds, such as a motion to dismiss the case, or to transfer the case to another venue, or to strike a pleading. In addition, at trial, the judge monitors the admissibility of evidence. Here, although her need to rule is usually dictated by objections made by the parties, she can and will intervene to protect witnesses from harassment and to shield the jury from irrelevant or prejudicial evidence. Although the court is entitled to ask questions of witnesses at trial, historically courts have been reluctant to do so. In general, then, the decision makers (judge and jury) consider issues and evidence proffered by partisan advocates.

Not all judicial systems envision such a passive judge. In most of continental Europe, for example, the courts follow an "inquisitorial" model, in which the judge is expected to make an independent investigation into the merits of the case. She routinely questions witnesses and generally takes charge of the case in a way American lawyers would find intrusive.

Increasingly, American judges, particularly in federal courts, are borrowing some aspects of the inquisitorial system. In response to a perception that there is too much litigation (particularly too much expensive pretrial litigation), judges have assumed an activist role in managing cases, rather than simply reacting to the parties' requests. Recent amendments to the Federal Rules of Civil Procedure foster this new activism, which is changing (at least to a degree) the traditional view of the judge in the adversary system. Indeed, it is not uncommon now to hear some federal district judges complain that their job has become more "bureaucratic" or "managerial" than umpireal. The primary responsibility is often "keeping the parties' feet to the fire" and facilitating settlement.

Among many questions, the adversary system raises the issue of who should bear the cost of litigation. Litigation is expensive. Although the public provides the courthouse and the judges and jurors, the adversary system puts the primary burden for expense on the parties. They pay the filing and other court fees, they pay to uncover evidence, they pay expert witnesses, and, most importantly, they pay attorney's fees. Attorneys are usually paid by the hour. Outside of small claims matters, cases do not get to trial without months, even years, of pretrial activity involving pleadings, motions, discovery, and settlement negotiations. Throughout these activities, the "meter is running."

* "Motion" is the noun. "Move" is the verb. Parties never "motion" the court. They "move" or "make a motion" for the desired order.

Under the "American Rule," each side pays her own attorney's fees.* The fact that it is called the American Rule implies that it is not followed in most other nations. Indeed, England now provides basically that the prevailing party recovers her costs *and* attorney's fees. In this country, there are exceptions to this rule (some created by courts, others by legislatures), and comentators and legislators increasingly advocate rejection of the American Rule. Still, it remains. Can you articulate policy support for the rule? Can you articulate policy reasons for rejecting the rule?

The expense of litigation — principally of attorney's fees — is an important factor in plaintiff's assessment of whether to attempt to enforce her substantive right. Suppose, for example, that D has swindled you out of $25,000; there is no question that D is liable to you for that sum. Suppose that you retain a lawyer who charges $150 per hour. If she spends only 50 hours litigating the case through trial, her fee will be $7,500. Thus, even if you go to trial and win a judgment for $25,000, you will actually recover a net of $17,500. Moreover, you will have spent several months (perhaps years) in the litigation process.

Under these circumstances, you may instruct the lawyer to invest as little time as possible and to settle the case. Suppose the lawyer invests five hours and receives an offer from the other side to settle the case for $10,000. Will you agree to the settlement? It would give you $10,000, out of which you pay your lawyer (based on the hourly rate) $750. You end up with $9,250. On the other hand, you obviate the need to go to trial, and receive the money now rather than months or years from now.

Sometimes, plaintiff's lawyer bears the risk of attorney's fees by agreeing to take a case on a contingent fee arrangement. By this, the client agrees to pay the lawyer a percentage (typically one-third) of any recovery she gains. Some observers hail this arrangement, saying that it helps plaintiff bring some actions that would never be brought if plaintiff had to pay an hourly rate. Others criticize contingent fees for this very reason, saying the arrangement tends to foment litigation.

Other critics worry that the contingent fee arrangement gives the lawyer too great an incentive to settle a case quickly, rather than to go through trials. Suppose, for example, lawyer could settle a case for $60,000 (and take a $20,000 contingent fee) after investing 30 hours. Suppose also that if the case goes to trial, plaintiff might win as much as $600,000; or, of course, plaintiff could win nothing. To go through trial will require several hundred attorney hours. It might be in the lawyer's economic interest to settle rather than litigate; critics worry that this economic incentive may color the advice the lawyer gives to her client.

Many lawyers, clients, judges, and commentators are addressing these and similar issues more seriously today than ever. Many are convinced that there is a "litigation

* It is important to distinguish between "costs" and attorney's fees. When lawyers speak of "costs" they mean "taxable" or "recoverable" costs. Generally, the prevailing party in litigation recovers her costs from the other side. These costs include such things as docket fees, court reporter fees, and clerk's costs, and usually amount to relatively little money. See 28 U.S.C. § 1920. They do not include attorney's fees, which will almost always be the most substantial cost of litigation.

crisis." Others disagree. But many observers seem to agree that litigation is too expensive and takes too long to resolve many disputes. Not surprisingly, people are looking to alternatives.

E. Alternatives to Litigation

This course focuses almost exclusively on litigation — the adversary system — to resolve disputes. That model has drawbacks. As noted, it is expensive. It relies in part on the fictive notions that all lawyers have equal ability and that all litigants have equal financial resources. Litigation, when pursued to adjudication (as opposed to settlement), is a zero-sum game; someone wins, and someone loses. It is also retrospective, forcing litigants to look back to what happened in the past rather than focus on the future. All of this suggests that litigation may be better suited to some kinds of disputes than to others. We will address these issues in more detail in Chapter 15.

Alternative dispute resolution (ADR) has become an important topic for an upper division law school course. In our course, we hope to raise awareness of the possibility that litigation may not be the most appropriate method for resolution of your client's dispute. Our goal here is to survey the major methods of ADR. None is a panacea. None will ever totally supplant litigation. But throughout your law school career, consider whether the disputes you consider in your cases might have been handled better through ADR.

For example, consider a dispute between two persons who envision an ongoing relationship. This could be a dispute between family members over something personal, such as inheritance of a family heirloom. Or it could be the continuing relationship between a wholesale distributor and a retailer who, except for this disruption, have gotten along fine for years. Or perhaps it is an employer-employee relationship. In such situations, the best resolution may focus on the future, on continuing the relationship, on working out an arrangement to keep the relationship intact. Traditional, retrospective, zero-sum litigation may not be optimal. But what other choices are there?

Negotiation is the most widely used ADR tool. In fact, the vast majority of cases filed in court end up in a negotiated settlement. When negotiation works, and results in a settlement, it avoids the zero-sum-game aspects of litigation. The parties are free to structure the settlement in any way they see fit. They may take into account future relations and can be more creative than courts in fashioning remedies. An early settlement avoids the expense and trauma of trial and appeal, and it can substantially lessen overall litigation costs. Although parties can enter settlement negotiations at any time, often they do so only after the litigation dance has progressed for awhile, perhaps to the discovery stage. At that point, the lawyers begin to understand the facts of the dispute better, and they may have a clearer idea of what the case is "worth."

At about that point as well, clients begin to realize not only the expense of protracted litigation, but that they are required to devote great time to the cause as well.

For example, the other side will undoubtedly take the deposition of your client, in which she must respond under oath to questions by counsel for other parties. The experience is often traumatizing and sobering. On the other hand, it also gives the client a chance to speak directly to the other side and to "tell her story." This process is often cathartic. Indeed, there are some data showing that some litigants, especially those not routinely involved in litigation, consider the process a success (regardless of the outcome) if they get this opportunity.

Mediation is essentially negotiation through the auspices of a third party who facilitates settlement of the dispute by helping the parties to find common ground. Like negotiation, it avoids the zero-sum game nature of litigation. The mediator and the parties are usually free to structure the mediation sessions in any appropriate way. Usually, the mediator will allow each side to "tell its story" and to exchange information. Sometimes, the mediator will suggest creative resolutions and can be especially helpful in disabusing one party of an unrealistic position.

Mediation is often voluntary, but an increasing number of courts require parties to submit to mediation sessions before continuing with litigation. Some litigants are offended by mandatory mediation; if they have a right to seek redress in the courts from a wrongdoer, why should they be made to sit down and try to negotiate a settlement?

Arbitration involves resolution of the dispute by a third party other than a court. Like litigation, someone wins and someone loses. The advantage is usually in time and expense. Because the discovery rules of civil litigation usually do not apply to arbitration, the parties tend to spend less money in preparation for the hearing. The hearing is less formal than a civil trial, there is no jury, and the court rules governing admissibility of evidence do not apply. The arbitrator takes evidence and makes a decision. Sometimes, as in major league baseball arbitration, the parties require that the arbitrator choose between their respective offers. When this is not done, the arbitrator is free to fashion what she sees as an appropriate award and may "split the difference" between the parties.

Arbitration is often consensual. Parties to a contract commonly agree that any dispute will be submitted to arbitration. They should spell out terms for selection and payment of the arbitrator(s), and for invocation of the process. Increasingly, commercial agreements include arbitration agreements for disputes. The terms of the agreements vary greatly. Under some, a party submitting to arbitration may waive significant rights, such as the right to jury trial and the right to seek some remedies, such as punitive damages, and the right to appeal. Most arbitration awards are reviewable only on very narrow grounds, which usually do *not* include the arbitrator's incorrect application of the law.

In some states, court-annexed arbitration requires parties to submit to arbitration before proceeding with litigation. For example, in several states, a plaintiff may not sue for medical malpractice until after she has gone through arbitration. Absent agreement of the parties, the arbitrator's decision is not binding. Either side can seek a trial de novo in court. Frequently, however, there are strong disincentives to this, such as provisions imposing various costs on that party unless she receives a better result at trial. As a result of collective bargaining agreements, many employees are required to submit to arbitration any grievances with their employers.

While arbitration offers advantages, it has its critics. Because the arbitrator is not a judge, and because her award is subject only to limited review, some have assailed arbitration as dispute resolution "without law." Moreover, there is a growing concern that the arbitration format favors "repeat players," particularly in the process of selecting the arbitrator.

Some disputes will involve traditional litigation and ADR. Indeed, much of ADR has found its way into the litigation process. As noted, it has long been true that parties negotiate a settlement to the vast majority of civil cases. Several Federal Rules enhance the prospects of settlement by forcing litigating parties to work together at various stages of suit. In addition, creative lawyers have used ADR techniques such as arbitration to resolve specific issues in the course of litigation. Creative judges have also been able to bring ADR techniques and benefits into the litigation stream.

F. A Brief History of Our English Judicial Roots

We inherited much of our law and legal tradition from England. It is impossible to understand the American legal system fully without some background in English legal history.

Before the Norman Conquest of England in 1066, the administration of justice in what is now Great Britain was entrusted to a myriad of local courts, run by feudal lords, and enforcing rights in accord with local custom. William the Conqueror did not replace the local courts, but augmented them by establishing three royal courts: The King's Bench, the Exchequer, and the Court of Common Pleas. Litigants wishing to sue in one of the royal courts sought a writ (order) from the chancellor (a royal officer, akin to secretary to the King). Each court heard only certain types of cases, as defined by the writs each could entertain.

In early development, the royal courts heard a limited number of cases concerning possession of land, actions on contract (ex contractu), and actions in what today would be called tort (ex delicto). Over time, however, they expanded the number of writs which would invoke their jurisdiction. The feudal barons who controlled the local courts tried to stop this expansion of the royal courts' power. Ultimately, though, their efforts failed, and the royal courts developed a series of new writs in the thirteenth and fourteenth centuries.

While expanding their jurisdiction by recognizing new forms of action, the royal courts became increasingly inflexible in their administration of justice. Their rigidity denied justice to many suitors because of their failure to dot the "i" or cross the "t" on some arcane procedural point. The royal courts routinely dismissed cases despite proof at trial that the plaintiff was entitled to relief, simply because plaintiff had chosen the wrong writ at the outset of the case.

In addition, the royal courts became increasingly unwilling to give a successful plaintiff any remedy other than damages. To this day, of course, many plaintiffs seek exactly that; they want to be compensated in money for injuries inflicted in tort or to recover the benefit of their bargain in contract. Often, however, damages do not give the plaintiff true relief.

For example, suppose defendant steals a piece of plaintiff's jewelry. The jewelry has a market value of $500, but is a sentimental treasure to the plaintiff. If money is the sole remedy available, the plaintiff cannot be made whole. What she wants is *specific* relief. She wants a court order commanding the defendant to return the jewelry. The royal courts largely refused to give this type of relief.

The hypertechnicality of royal court procedure, coupled with this limitation on remedies, led to pressure to reform the English practice. Litigants, used to petitioning the chancellor for a writ to sue in the royal courts, started to ask the King's Council (of which the chancellor was a minister) to intervene directly and to "do justice." In cases in which the remedy at law (through the royal courts) was inadequate, or in which a suitor alleged an enormous disparity of power between himself and his opponent, the chancellor started issuing orders on behalf of the Council to achieve equity. By the middle of the fourteenth century, Chancery (for the chancellor) was recognized as a separate court.

Over the next two centuries, this *equity* practice expanded. For example, the chancellor would enforce trusts (by which one could evade the common law rule that one could not devise land by will) and assignments of claims. The law courts would recognize neither. In addition — and most threatening to the royal courts — the chancellor could enjoin a party from enforcing a fraudulent judgment from a royal court. This seeming affront to the dignity of the common law judges led to a serious debate in the early seventeenth century. Francis Bacon, appointed by King James I as head of a commission addressing the matter, resolved the dispute in favor of equity practice. The commission upheld the chancellor's power to enjoin parties from enforcing royal court judgments procured by fraud. Because such orders were directed at a party, and not to the court that rendered the judgment, they did not constitute a direct infringement of the power of the royal courts.

After that, Chancery developed into a complete system of courts, procedures, and remedies. This system worked alongside the royal courts, which continued to administer the common law. Thus, England had a bifurcated system of civil justice — the royal (or "law") courts and Chancery (or "equity") courts. Law courts continued to award damages while equity developed a panoply of specific remedies, including the injunction, specific performance, rescission, and reformation of contracts and other documents. A plaintiff could invoke equity's jurisdiction only by demonstrating that the remedy at law was inadequate. In addition, equity developed the "clean-up doctrine," by which it would award damages incidental to the issuance of equitable decree. For example, a plaintiff might win an injunction against further trespasses by the defendant, as well as an award of "clean-up" damages to compensate for past trespasses.

The two systems developed different procedures and terminology. Law courts generally used a jury to determine facts, while equity courts generally did not. Consequently, the law courts usually allowed live witness testimony. Equity came to permit more introduction of evidence through sworn statements. Law courts entered "judgments," while equity courts entered "decrees." Law courts had "judges," while equity courts had "chancellors."

Law and equity also differed dramatically in their methods of enforcing judicial decisions. Law enforced its judgments *in rem*, that is, against property. If plaintiff at law won a money judgment, and defendant refused to pay, the plaintiff could obtain a writ of execution, by which the sheriff would seize property owned by the defendant and sell it at public auction to satisfy the judgment. If defendant had no property to seize, plaintiff was out of luck. Equity, on the other hand, enforced its decrees *in personam*, that is, against the person. For example, if the chancellor ordered the defendant to return property to plaintiff, or to sign a deed conveying property, or to desist from some conduct, he could order defendant jailed until he agreed to do so.

Earlier in our history, most American states and the federal courts bifurcated law and equity practice. Some did so with separate courts, others with separate divisions of the same court. In 1938, Congress adopted the Federal Rules of Civil Procedure. Among many important advances, the Federal Rules abolished separate law and equity dockets in the federal courts and provided that there is a single form of action, known as the "civil action." Federal Rule 2. Although most states have done the same, this merger is not universal.

Notwithstanding the widespread merger of law and equity, however, the distinction between the two continues to have practical importance in this country. For one, all jurisdictions differentiate between "legal" and "equitable" remedies. A plaintiff seeking equitable relief generally must demonstrate the inadequacy of a legal remedy. For another, the Seventh Amendment preserves federal court litigants a jury trial in civil "[s]uits at common law."* Thus, consistent with historic practice, there is no constitutional right to a jury at equity. In Chapter 9, we will explore what this means after procedural merger of law and equity.

In other areas, equity practice came to dominate modern procedure. For instance, the joinder rules, which determine the scope of litigation by prescribing who may be parties and what claims may be asserted borrow liberally from equity practice. See Stephen Subrin, *How Equity Conquered Common Law: The Federal Rules of Civil Procedure in Historical Perspective*, 135 U. Pa. L. Rev. 909 (1987).

---

* There are similar state constitutional or statutory provisions establishing a right to jury trial in state court in actions at law.

G. General Topics of Civil Procedure

Although fourteen chapters follow this one, it is helpful to view them as raising six groups of topics. Here we review these groups to provide a preview of the major procedural issues we will address in the course. We will do so using the facts from a case we will read in Chapter 2, World-Wide Volkswagen v. Woodson, 444 U.S. 286 (1980).

That case involved a tragic vehicular collision that seriously injured three members of a family in the process of moving from New York to Arizona. Harry and Kay Robinson had three children, Sam, Eva, and Sidney. Harry's doctors recommended that he leave his Massena, New York, home and move to a drier climate. The family decided to move to Arizona. They set out in two vehicles—one a rented truck to carry furniture and the other their Audi 100 LS. They had purchased the Audi from Seaway Volkswagen in Massena. The car was manufactured in Germany by Audi, imported to the United States by Volkswagen of America, and distributed to Seaway by World-Wide Volkswagen, which does business in New York and two neighboring states.

The trip went well until the family was driving on a freeway near Tulsa, Oklahoma. Harry and Sidney drove in the truck while Kay, Eva, and Sam followed in the Audi. Near Tulsa, a car driven by an inebriated Lloyd Hull, a citizen of Arkansas, collided with the rear of the Audi. The Audi caught fire. Kay and her two children were trapped inside the vehicle until a witness was able to smash the windows and rescue them. The three were burned horribly. Kay underwent more than thirty operations and spent 77 days in the intensive care unit of a Tulsa hospital. Each of the three was hospitalized for weeks.

The three Robinsons suffered enormous physical pain and incurred great financial loss. In inflicting this pain and loss, Lloyd Hull committed a crime. But, as we discussed above, the state's punishing him for driving while under the influence of alcohol would not compensate the Robinsons. Before commencing a civil case to seek compensation for the Robinsons, their lawyer had to review the substantive law to assess who might be liable and for what remedy. Obviously, as a matter of substantive law, the Robinsons could sue Lloyd Hull. Unfortunately, Hull had no appreciable assets from which to pay compensation. He also had no liability insurance. In short, Hull was "judgment proof"; any judgment against him would be uncollectible.

As a result, attorneys for the Robinsons had to consider whether the substantive law provided claims against any of the four corporations involved in manufacturing, importing, distributing, and selling the Audi to the Robinsons. In your torts class, you will study the development of various products liability theories. The Robinsons were injured and brought suit in the 1970s, when such theories were emerging and when the law in Oklahoma was not completely clear. Still, the Robinsons' lawyers determined that they could assert claims against all four (the manufacturer (Audi), the importer (Volkswagen of America), the distributor (World-Wide) and the retailer

(Seaway). Put generally, the claims centered on the theory that the car was defective because the gas tank was mounted so as to make it susceptible to rupture in a rear-end collision. For a complete discussion of the facts of the case, see Charles Adams, World-Wide Volkswagen v. Woodson—*The Rest of the Story*, 72 NEB. L. REV. 1122 (1993).

1. Selecting the Forum (Chapters 2–6, 10)

The first procedural issue is where to file the suit. The first group of chapters in this book addresses various constitutional and statutory limitations on plaintiff's choice of courts. It may not seem obvious at first, but the issue of where litigation takes place can be of enormous practical importance. Many plaintiffs, for instance, would like to sue "at home," without incurring the expense of travel and the inconvenience of hiring a lawyer in a distant forum. But not all plaintiffs can do this. The court must have *personal jurisdiction* over the defendants. Unless it does, the court cannot enter a valid judgment against the defendant. We will study the historical development of the constitutional and statutory limitations on a state's power to enter such binding judgments. Even in advance of that study, however, it makes some intuitive sense that the court of a state cannot enter binding orders over defendants who are not present there or who have no affiliation with the state.

Where does that leave the Robinsons? They no longer lived in New York; neither had they established a home in Arizona. Because of the lengthy hospitalization there, Oklahoma was about as convenient as anywhere else for them. Plus, the witnesses, police investigators, hospital records, and other important evidence was there. But would Oklahoma courts have personal jurisdiction over Audi, Volkswagen of America, World-Wide, or Seaway? If not, would New York? If New York had personal jurisdiction, then the Robinsons would be forced to litigate far from most of the relevant witnesses and evidence.

Remember that civil litigation takes place under the auspices of a government. Thus, whatever state has personal jurisdiction over the defendants, its court must have a method for giving notice to them that they have been sued and telling them the time in which they must respond. The court gives this notice, and manifests the state's personal jurisdiction over the defendants, by prescribing rules for *service of process* on the defendants.

Even if the Robinsons' lawyer decides that Oklahoma would have personal jurisdiction over the four defendants and that there is a mechanism for serving process on them, she may then face another choice. Should she file the case in an Oklahoma state court or in the federal district court in Oklahoma? In other words, what court—state or federal—will have *subject matter jurisdiction* over the dispute? Recall from supra Section B that federal courts can hear (among others) cases arising under federal law and cases between citizens of different states.

The Robinsons' case does not involve federal law, but it might qualify for diversity of citizenship jurisdiction. If so, their lawyer will have to choose whether to file in state or federal court. She will base this decision upon a variety of practical factors, including her experience with each court, how long it will take to get to trial, procedural mechanisms available, differences in choosing jury members, and many others. In *World-Wide Volkswagen*, the Robinsons' lawyer preferred state court because of the perception that juries in a particular county were extremely generous to plaintiffs. But should the plaintiffs' decision to eschew the federal court end the matter? As we will see, there may be a way for defendants to force the case into federal court.

Another issue that may affect one's choice of forum is an assessment of what law the different fora would apply. In Chapter 10 we address the question of what law applies in federal court.

2. Learning About the Opponent's Case (Chapters 7 & 8)

The second major block of material addresses the rules governing how litigants learn about each other's contentions. The first tool is *pleadings*, documents in which each side alleges facts underlying their claims and defenses. Like all plaintiffs, the Robinsons initiated suit by filing what most jurisdictions call a *complaint*, in which they set forth factual allegations supporting their legal claims for relief. The defendants have several options in response. They might bring a motion to dismiss for any of myriad reasons, such as lack of personal jurisdiction. Or they may challenge the sufficiency of the complaint by arguing that it is unclear or incomplete.

Rather than bring a motion, the defendants may file a pleading which most jurisdictions call an *answer*, in which they respond to the allegations of the complaint and raise affirmative defenses. For example, if the defendants felt that Mrs. Robinson contributed to her own injuries by mishandling the car in some way, they could assert that in the answer. In some jurisdictions, the plaintiff responds to such affirmative defenses with a pleading called a *reply*.

After pleading, the parties embark on the *discovery* phase of the case, in which they have the right to require each other to produce relevant information through a variety of tools. They may request production of documents, send interrogatories that must be answered under oath, or take depositions of persons by asking questions under oath and "live," transcribed by a court reporter. Indeed, parties must surrender specified information without a request by another party. Modern discovery provisions are extremely broad. This is consistent with modern theory that parties should not be required to plead facts in detail; factual detail is to be provided through discovery. What information would the Robinsons want to discover from the defendants? What sort of information would the defendants want to discover from the Robinsons?

Through the discovery process, the parties may find that they agree on certain facts, or that certain legal contentions are no longer tenable. Throughout this phase, the parties often start talking seriously about settlement. Recent developments foster such negotiations. The court can hold conferences to foster settlement and, if that fails, to narrow and clarify the issues remaining for adjudication.

3. Adjudication With or Without a Jury (Chapter 9)

After the discovery phase, counsel and the court start to focus on adjudication. Although the popular image of adjudication is plenary trial, in some instances other mechanisms can dispose of a case without the necessity of trial. If the case is tried, one important issue is whether the parties are entitled to have the case submitted to a jury. If so, counsel and the court must assess the division of labor at trial between the judge and the jury. Even after the jury has rendered its verdict, the court may have the power to change the result. Obviously, however, respect for the jury requires that this power be used narrowly.

4. Preclusion, Joinder, and Supplemental Jurisdiction (Chapters 11–13)

By the end of Chapter 10, you will have the tools to understand how a relatively simple dispute proceeds from beginning through adjudication. We then will address how a case can become more complicated. Two sets of rules foster the inclusive packaging of all related claims and parties into a single case. The first set consists of the *preclusion doctrines*, which prohibit parties from relitigating some issues already decided, and, in some instances, bar a plaintiff from raising things that she could have raised in an earlier case. These doctrines may counsel the Robinsons to raise all their claims in a single proceeding.

Against the background of the preclusion rules, litigants may make wiser use of the second set of rules promoting packaging — the joinder devices. These rules define the scope of litigation in terms of parties and claims. They delineate the plaintiffs' ability to join co-plaintiffs and multiple defendants in a single proceeding. In addition, they specify the circumstances under which the court, the defendants, and, in some instances, nonparties, can override the plaintiffs' structure of suit by adding new parties and claims. In *World-Wide Volkswagen*, these rules permitted the Robinsons to join together as co-plaintiffs and to sue the four defendants, all in a single case. In addition, the defendants may have been able to join claims against their insurance companies or, if the allegedly defective gas tank were manufactured by a subcontractor, to join the subcontractor to the pending litigation.

5. Appeal (Chapter 14)

All of the activities discussed to this point take place in a trial court. In Chapter 14, we will address appellate review. The most important restriction here is the final judgment rule, by which a party cannot appeal until the trial court has determined the entire dispute. In *World-Wide Volkswagen*, two defendants (WorldWide and Seaway) moved to dismiss on the ground that Oklahoma lacked personal jurisdiction over them. The trial judge disagreed. Unless they could invoke an exception to the final judgment rule, the defendants could not obtain appellate review of that order until after trial.

6. Litigation Alternatives (Chapter 15)

At the end of Chapter 14, we will have reviewed all major doctrines governing litigation. We will then be in a position to assess strengths and weaknesses of the litigation process by comparing it to alternatives. Such alternatives include not only mechanisms of ADR discussed in Section E, but dispute resolution mechanisms from other countries and cultures.

7. A Quick Note on Materials

In addition to this casebook, your professor probably asked you to acquire a booklet with the phrase "Federal Rules of Civil Procedure" on the cover. This booklet contains materials that will complement the cases and text in this book and which are essential to your learning Civil Procedure. Despite the title, you should realize that the booklet contains more than the Federal Rules of Civil Procedure (FRCP). Those Rules, which will be referred to and discussed throughout this casebook, are promulgated by the Supreme Court (though they are drafted by an Advisory Committee, not the Justices), and govern the procedures for the federal trial courts (known as district courts). The Rules are amended from time to time, so occasionally the language in the current version will differ from that in a case decided just a few years ago. We will note such changes in language in brackets in the cases.

Your booklet also contains statutes that are part of the Judicial Code of the United States (Title 28 of the United States Code). These statutes will be especially important in Chapters 4 and 5 of this book. For instance, 28 U.S.C. § 1332 grants subject matter jurisdiction over cases "between citizens of different states" — the so-called "diversity jurisdiction." Note that these statutes are *not* FRCP. Instead, they are legislation enacted by Congress to set the subject matter jurisdiction and venue of the federal courts. Both the FRCP and the statutes are important, but the statutes are of greater dignity in this sense — the FRCP cannot affect the jurisdiction or venue of the federal courts; only statutes can do that. See Federal Rule 82.

Chapter 2

Personal Jurisdiction

A. Introduction and Integration

Before a plaintiff can initiate any lawsuit, she must decide where to sue. In deciding where to sue, the plaintiff must first determine which court has (or which courts have) *jurisdiction*, that is, authority to decide the dispute between these parties.

When we speak of jurisdiction, we usually differentiate between two types — subject matter jurisdiction and personal jurisdiction. Subject matter jurisdiction deals with whether a court has authority to decide a particular type of case. For example, most state court systems have specialized courts such as probate courts, family law courts or small claims courts that can only hear certain types of cases. Similarly, the subject matter jurisdiction of the federal courts is limited to those areas specified in the Constitution and in federal statutes. Subject matter jurisdiction will be dealt with in a later chapter.

Personal jurisdiction is the topic of this chapter. It concerns the circumstances under which a court (state or federal) has authority to make decisions binding on these particular parties. By invoking the authority of the court, the plaintiff has consented to the power of that court to issue binding orders to her. But what about the defendant, who did not invoke or consent to the power of the court? What gives the court the power to enter binding orders against a particular defendant? At their root, concerns about personal jurisdiction are very similar to a question that has occupied political philosophers for centuries — what is it that makes the exercise of government authority legitimate? This chapter addresses this question not as an abstract philosophical one, but in the concrete context of litigation. Specifically, we will be analyzing whether particular judgments are valid or enforceable.

As a preliminary matter, you must know a little about the types of judgments available and how they are enforced. In some cases, the plaintiff gets a judgment in which the defendants are ordered by the court to do or refrain from doing something. This is called injunctive relief. For example, a school system might be ordered to desegregate, a town might be ordered to allow a group to hold a parade, or a party to a contract to sell land might be ordered to transfer the land. In these cases, a defendant who defies the court order may be held in contempt of court and fined or imprisoned until she complies.

Awarding money damages, though, is far more common than injunctive relief. Indeed courts will usually issue an injunction only if money damages are an inadequate remedy. Where the plaintiff secures a money judgment, that award does not actually order the defendant to do anything. If the defendant refuses voluntarily to pay the judgment, she cannot be held in contempt of court or put in jail. Instead, the burden is on the person who secures the judgment to seek enforcement. To enforce or "execute" a judgment, the plaintiff typically "attaches" property owned by the defendant. With respect to physical property other than real estate, the property may literally be seized by the sheriff. Real estate is "attached" by posting notice on the property and making a notation in the property records. After attachment and notice to the owner, the property is auctioned and the proceeds are given to the judgment holder. If there are any proceeds in excess of the amount of the judgment plus expenses, that amount is returned to the judgment debtor.

In our nation of 50 independent and separate states, a serious problem could arise if states refused to enforce the judgments of other states. The drafters of the Constitution anticipated this problem and addressed it in the Full Faith and Credit Clause in Article IV of the Constitution, which provides that "Full faith and credit shall be given in each State to the public Acts, Records, and judicial Proceedings of every other State." Congress has by statute extended the requirement of full faith and credit to the federal courts. See 28 U.S.C. § 1738. The Full Faith and Credit Clause and Statute have been interpreted to require that every state must enforce the judgments of every other state. The Supreme Court has been extremely rigorous in upholding the requirements of the Full Faith and Credit Clause. For example, a state that makes gambling contracts illegal and unenforceable must nonetheless enforce a judgment entered by a sister state enforcing a gambling contract. See Fauntleroy v. Lum, 210 U.S. 230 (1908). One of the few exceptions to the strict requirement of full faith and credit is where the court that rendered the judgment lacked personal jurisdiction over the defendant.

This brings us back to the question with which we began: when does a court have personal jurisdiction? This chapter sets forth a largely chronological series of Supreme Court cases, in which the Court attempts to delineate the criteria for personal jurisdiction. As you will see, the criteria change over time—sometimes abruptly, sometimes gradually—and the law in this area is still evolving.

B. Constitutional Limits on Personal Jurisdiction

1. The Fountainhead—*Pennoyer v. Neff*

Pennoyer v. Neff

95 U.S. 714, 24 L. Ed. 565, 5 Otto 714 (1878)

Justice Field delivered the opinion of the Court.

[In 1865, J.H. Mitchell sued Marcus Neff in Oregon state court. Mitchell claimed that Neff owed him $253.14 for legal services Mitchell had performed. Mitchell submitted an affidavit asserting that Neff owned land in Oregon and further stating that Neff was living somewhere in California and could not be found. Notice of the suit was published for six weeks in the Pacific Christian Advocate, a weekly church newspaper. Neff did not answer or appear in the case, and the court entered a default judgment. Six months later, Mitchell secured a writ of execution against Oregon real estate owned by Neff. The land was sold at a sheriff's sale and purchased by Mitchell himself, presumably in exchange for the amount of the judgment plus costs. Three days later, Mitchell transferred title to Sylvester Pennoyer.

[In September 1874, Neff sued Pennoyer in federal court seeking eviction. The trial court found for Neff, holding that the judgment in *Mitchell v. Neff* was invalid. Specifically, the judge concluded that Mitchell's affidavit concerning Neff's whereabouts did not adequately describe the steps Mitchell had taken to locate Neff and that the affidavit by the newspaper attesting to the publication of the notice was also inadequate. Pennoyer appealed to the Supreme Court of the United States.]

The Code of Oregon provides for such service [by publication] when an action is brought against a nonresident and absent defendant, who has property within the State. It also provides, where the action is for the recovery of money or damages, for the attachment of the property of the nonresident. And it also declares that no natural person is subject to the jurisdiction of a court of the State, "unless he appear in the court, or be found within the State, or be a resident thereof, or have property therein; and, in the last case, only to the extent of such property at the time the jurisdiction attached." Construing this latter provision to mean, that, in an action for money or damages where a defendant does not appear in the court, and is not found within the State, and is not a resident thereof, but has property therein, the jurisdiction of the court extends only over such property, the declaration expresses a principle of general, if not universal, law. The authority of every tribunal is necessarily restricted by the territorial limits of the State in which it is established. Any attempt to exercise authority beyond those limits would be deemed in every other forum, as has been said by this court, an illegitimate assumption of power, and be resisted as mere abuse. In the case against the plaintiff, the property here in controversy sold under the judgment rendered was not attached, nor in any way brought under the jurisdiction of the court. Its first connection with the case was caused by a levy of the execution. It was not, therefore, disposed of pursuant to any adjudication, but only in enforcement of a personal judgment, having no relation to the property, rendered against a nonresident without service of process upon him in the action, or his appearance therein. The court below did not consider that an attachment of the property was essential to its jurisdiction or to the validity of the sale, but held that the judgment was invalid from defects in the affidavit upon which the order of publication was obtained, and in the affidavit by which the publication was proved.

[The Court held that the deficiencies in the affidavits upon which the lower court relied could only be a basis for appeal. They were not a basis for a collateral attack, that is, a separate law suit seeking to invalidate the prior judgment.]

If, therefore, we were confined to the rulings of the court below upon the defects in the affidavits mentioned, we should be unable to uphold its decision. But it was also contended in that court, and is insisted upon here, that the judgment in the State court against the plaintiff was void for want of personal service of process on him, or of his appearance in the action in which it was rendered, and that the premises in controversy could not be subjected to the payment of the demand of a resident creditor except by a proceeding in rem; that is, by a direct proceeding against the property for that purpose. If these positions are sound, the ruling of the Circuit Court as to the invalidity of that judgment must be sustained, notwithstanding our dissent from the reasons upon which it was made. And that they are sound would seem to follow from two well established principles of public law respecting the jurisdiction of an independent State over persons and property. The several States of the Union are not, it is true, in every respect independent, many of the rights and powers which originally belonged to them being now vested in the government created by the Constitution. But, except as restrained and limited by that instrument, they possess and exercise the authority of independent States, and the principles of public law to which we have referred are applicable to them. One of these principles is, that every State possesses exclusive jurisdiction and sovereignty over persons and property within its territory. As a consequence, every State has the power to determine for itself the civil status and capacities of its inhabitants; to prescribe the subjects upon which they may contract, the forms and solemnities with which their contracts shall be executed, the rights and obligations arising from them, and the mode in which their validity shall be determined and their obligations enforced; and also to regulate the manner and conditions upon which property situated within such territory, both personal and real, may be acquired, enjoyed, and transferred. The other principle of public law referred to follows from the one mentioned; that is, that no State can exercise direct jurisdiction and authority over persons or property without its territory. STORY, CONFL. LAWS, c. 2; WHEAT. INT. LAW, pt. 2, c. 2. The several States are of equal dignity and authority, and the independence of one implies the exclusion of power from all others. And so it is laid down by jurists, as an elementary principle, that the laws of one State have no operation outside of its territory, except so far as is allowed by comity; and that no tribunal established by it can extend its process beyond that territory so as to subject either persons or property to its decisions. "Any exertion of authority of this sort beyond this limit," says Story, "is a mere nullity, and incapable of binding such persons or property in any other tribunals." STORY, CONFL. LAWS, sect. 539.

But as contracts made in one State may be enforceable only in another State, and property may be held by nonresidents, the exercise of the jurisdiction which every State is admitted to possess over persons and property within its own territory will often affect persons and property without it. To any influence exerted in this way by a State affecting persons resident or property situated elsewhere, no objection can be justly taken; whilst any direct exertion of authority upon them, in an attempt to give ex-territorial operation to its laws, or to enforce an ex-territorial jurisdiction by its tribunals, would be deemed an encroachment upon the independence of the State in which the persons are domiciled or the property is situated, and be resisted as usurpation.

Thus the State, through its tribunals, may compel persons domiciled within its limits to execute, in pursuance of their contracts respecting property elsewhere situated, instruments in such form and with such solemnities as to transfer the title, so far as such formalities can be complied with; and the exercise of this jurisdiction in no manner interferes with the supreme control over the property by the State within which it is situated.

So the State through its tribunals, may subject property situated within its limits owned by nonresidents to the payment of the demand of its own citizens against them; and the exercise of this jurisdiction in no respect infringes upon the sovereignty of the State where the owners are domiciled. Every State owes protection to its own citizens; and, when nonresidents deal with them, it is a legitimate and just exercise of authority to hold and appropriate any property owned by such nonresidents to satisfy the claims of its citizens. It is in virtue of the State's jurisdiction over the property of the nonresident situated within its limits that its tribunals can inquire into that nonresident's obligations to its own citizens, and the inquiry can then be carried only to the extent necessary to control the disposition of the property. If the nonresident have no property in the State, there is nothing upon which the tribunals can adjudicate.

* * * If, without personal service, judgments in personam, obtained ex parte against nonresidents and absent parties, upon mere publication of process, which, in the great majority of cases, would never be seen by the parties interested, could be upheld and enforced, they would be the constant instruments of fraud and oppression. Judgments for all sorts of claims upon contracts and for torts, real or pretended, would be thus obtained, under which property would be seized, when the evidence of the transactions upon which they were founded, if they ever had any existence, had perished.

Substituted service by publication, or in any other authorized form, may be sufficient to inform parties of the object of proceedings taken where property is once brought under the control of the court by seizure or some equivalent act. The law assumes that property is always in the possession of its owner, in person or by agent; and it proceeds upon the theory that its seizure will inform him, not only that it is taken into the custody of the court, but that he must look to any proceedings authorized by law upon such seizure for its condemnation and sale. Such service may also be sufficient in cases where the object of the action is to reach and dispose of property in the State, or of some interest therein, by enforcing a contract or a lien respecting the same, or to partition it among different owners, or, when the public is a party, to condemn and appropriate it for a public purpose. In other words, such service may answer in all actions which are substantially proceedings in rem. But where the entire object of the action is to determine the personal rights and obligations of the defendants, that is, where the suit is merely in personam, constructive service in this form upon a nonresident is ineffectual for any purpose. Process from the tribunals of one State cannot run into another State, and summon parties there domiciled to leave its territory and respond to proceedings against them. Publication of process or notice within the State where the tribunal sits cannot create any greater obligation upon the nonresident to appear. Process sent to him out of the State, and process published within it, are equally unavailing in proceedings to establish his personal liability.

The want of authority of the tribunals of a State to adjudicate upon the obligations of nonresidents, where they have no property within its limits, is not denied by the court below: but the position is assumed, that, where they have property within the State, it is immaterial whether the property is in the first instance brought under the control of the court by attachment or some other equivalent act, and afterwards applied by its judgment to the satisfaction of demands against its owner; or such demands be first established in a personal action, and the property of the nonresident be afterwards seized and sold on execution. But the answer to this position has already been given in the statement, that the jurisdiction of the court to inquire into and determine his obligations at all is only incidental to its jurisdiction over the property. Its jurisdiction in that respect cannot be made to depend upon facts to be ascertained after it has tried the cause and rendered the judgment. If the judgment be previously void, it will not become valid by the subsequent discovery of property of the defendant, or by his subsequent acquisition of it. The judgment, if void when rendered, will always remain void: it cannot occupy the doubtful position of being valid if property be found, and void if there be none. Even if the position assumed were confined to cases where the nonresident defendant possessed property in the State at the commencement of the action, it would still make the validity of the proceedings and judgment depend upon the question whether, before the levy of the execution, the defendant had or had not disposed of the property. If before the levy the property should be sold, then, according to this position, the judgment would not be binding. This doctrine would introduce a new element of uncertainty in judicial proceedings. The contrary is the law: the validity of every judgment depends upon the jurisdiction of the court before it is rendered, not upon what may occur subsequently. * * *

The force and effect of judgments rendered against nonresidents without personal service of process upon them, or their voluntary appearance, have been the subject of frequent consideration in the courts of the United States and of the several States, as attempts have been made to enforce such judgments in States other than those in which they were rendered, under the provision of the Constitution requiring that "full faith and credit shall be given in each State to the public acts, records, and judicial proceedings of every other State;" and the act of Congress providing for the mode of authenticating such acts, records, and proceedings, and declaring that, when thus authenticated, "they shall have such faith and credit given to them in every court within the United States as they have by law or usage in the courts of the State from which they are or shall be taken." In the earlier cases, it was supposed that the act gave to all judgments the same effect in other States which they had by law in the State where rendered. But this view was afterwards qualified so as to make the act applicable only when the court rendering the judgment had jurisdiction of the parties and of the subject-matter, and not to preclude an inquiry into the jurisdiction of the court in which the judgment was rendered, or the right of the State itself to exercise authority over the person or the subject-matter. * * *

* * * In several of the cases, the decision has been accompanied with the observation that a personal judgment thus recovered has no binding force without the State in which it is rendered, implying that in such State it may be valid and binding. But if the court has no jurisdiction over the person of the defendant by reason of his nonresidence, and, consequently, no authority to pass upon his personal rights and obligations; if the whole proceeding, without service upon him or his appearance, is *coram non judice* and void; if to hold a defendant bound by such a judgment is contrary to the first principles of justice,—it is difficult to see how the judgment can legitimately have any force within the State. The language used can be justified only on the ground that there was no mode of directly reviewing such judgment or impeaching its validity within the State where rendered; and that, therefore, it could be called in question only when its enforcement was elsewhere attempted. In later cases, this language is repeated with less frequency than formerly, it beginning to be considered, as it always ought to have been, that a judgment which can be treated in any State of this Union as contrary to the first principles of justice, and as an absolute nullity, because rendered without any jurisdiction of the tribunal over the party, is not entitled to any respect in the State where rendered.

Be that as it may, the courts of the United States are not required to give effect to judgments of this character when any right is claimed under them. Whilst they are not foreign tribunals in their relations to the State courts, they are tribunals of a different sovereignty, exercising a distinct and independent jurisdiction, and are bound to give to the judgments of the State courts only the same faith and credit which the courts of another State are bound to give to them.

Since the adoption of the Fourteenth Amendment to the Federal Constitution, the validity of such judgments may be directly questioned, and their enforcement in the State resisted, on the ground that proceedings in a court of justice to determine the personal rights and obligations of parties over whom that court has no jurisdiction do not constitute due process of law. Whatever difficulty may be experienced in giving to those terms a definition which will embrace every permissible exertion of power affecting private rights, and exclude such as is forbidden, there can be no doubt of their meaning when applied to judicial proceedings. They then mean a course of legal proceedings according to those rules and principles which have been established in our systems of jurisprudence for the protection and enforcement of private rights. To give such proceedings any validity, there must be a tribunal competent by its constitution—that is, by the law of its creation—to pass upon the subject-matter of the suit; and, if that involves merely a determination of the personal liability of the defendant, he must be brought within its jurisdiction by service of process within the State, or his voluntary appearance.

Except in cases affecting the personal status of the plaintiff, and cases in which that mode of service may be considered to have been assented to in advance, as hereinafter mentioned, the substituted service of process by publication, allowed by the law of Oregon and by similar laws in other States, where actions are brought against nonresidents, is effectual only where, in connection with process against the person for commencing the action, property in the State is brought under the control of the court, and subjected to its disposition by process adapted to that purpose, or where the judgment is sought as a means of reaching such property or affecting some interest therein; in other words, where the action is in the nature of a proceeding in rem. * * *

It is true that, in a strict sense, a proceeding in rem is one taken directly against property, and has for its object the disposition of the property, without reference to the title of individual claimants; but, in a larger and more general sense, the terms are applied to actions between parties, where the direct object is to reach and dispose of property owned by them, or of some interest therein. Such are cases commenced by attachment against the property of debtors, or instituted to partition real estate, foreclose a mortgage, or enforce a lien. So far as they affect property in the State, they are substantially proceedings in rem in the broader sense which we have mentioned.

It is hardly necessary to observe, that in all we have said we have had reference to proceedings in courts of first instance, and to their jurisdiction, and not to proceedings in an appellate tribunal to review the action of such courts. The latter may be taken upon such notice, personal or constructive, as the State creating the tribunal may provide. They are considered as rather a continuation of the original litigation than the commencement of a new action.

It follows from the views expressed that the personal judgment recovered in the State court of Oregon against the plaintiff herein, then a nonresident of the State, was without any validity, and did not authorize a sale of the property in controversy.

To prevent any misapplication of the views expressed in this opinion, it is proper to observe that we do not mean to assert, by anything we have said, that a State may not authorize proceedings to determine the status of one of its citizens towards a nonresident, which would be binding within the State, though made without service of process or personal notice to the nonresident. The jurisdiction which every State possesses to determine the civil status and capacities of all its inhabitants involve authority to prescribe the conditions on which proceedings affecting them may be commenced and carried on within its territory. The State, for example, has absolute right to prescribe the conditions upon which the marriage relation between its own citizens shall be created, and the causes for which it may be dissolved. One of the parties guilty of acts for which, by the law of the State, a dissolution may be granted, may have removed to a State where no dissolution is permitted. The complaining party would, therefore, fail if a divorce were sought in the State of the defendant; and if application could not be made to the tribunals of the complainant's domicile in such case, and proceedings be there instituted without personal service of process or personal notice to the offending party, the injured citizen would be without redress.

Neither do we mean to assert that a State may not require a nonresident entering into a partnership or association within its limits, or making contracts enforceable there, to appoint an agent or representative in the State to receive service of process and notice in legal proceedings instituted with respect to such partnership, association, or contracts, or to designate a place where such service may be made and notice given, and provide, upon their failure, to make such appointment or to designate such place that service may be made upon a public officer designated for that purpose, or in some other prescribed way, and that judgments rendered upon such service may not be binding upon the nonresidents both within and without the State. * * * Nor do we doubt that a State, on creating corporations or other institutions for pecuniary or charitable purposes, may provide a mode in which their conduct may be investigated, their obligations enforced, or their charters revoked, which shall require other than personal service upon their officers or members. Parties becoming members of such corporations or institutions would hold their interest subject to the conditions prescribed by law.

In the present case, there is no feature of this kind, and, consequently, no consideration of what would be the effect of such legislation in enforcing the contract of a nonresident can arise. The question here respects only the validity of a money judgment rendered in one State, in an action upon a simple contract against the resident of another, without service of process upon him, or his appearance therein.

Judgment affirmed.

[The dissenting opinion of Justice Hunt omitted.]

Notes and Questions

1. Justice Field distinguishes between in rem and in personam jurisdiction. "In rem" is Latin for "against the property" and "in personam" means "against the person." In an in personam case, because the court exercises jurisdiction over the person of the defendant, it can enter a judgment that creates a personal obligation to pay money or perform some act. A court can enforce an in personam judgment either by attaching and selling any of the defendant's property or by ordering a defendant to perform some act.

In an in rem case, the court's jurisdiction extends only to the particular property attached. In rem cases fall into two broad categories. The first category involves cases in which the proceeding concerns the ownership of the attached property. Examples of this type are condemnation or foreclosure proceedings. Suppose Penny and Dot each claim to own the same valuable painting. One might sue the other in personam and proceed to resolve the dispute. In the alternative, the one in possession could tender the painting to the court. The court, having jurisdiction over the property (the "res"), has the power to determine who owns it, even if the other party is not served within the jurisdiction.

This first category of in rem cases is sometimes subdivided to differentiate true in rem cases from what are called quasi-in-rem "of the first type." True in rem cases are ones which decide ownership as to the whole world. Government condemnation and certain admiralty cases fall into this category. After a condemnation proceeding, the government owns the land and no one else in the world does. Quasi-in-rem type 1 cases adjudicate ownership as between the litigants. For example, if I fail to pay my mortgage, a court may determine that as between the bank and me, the bank now owns the property. However, a third party could come along and prove that she has better title than the bank does.

What is important for our purpose is not the difference between true in rem and quasi-in-rem type 1, but the similarity between the two. In both categories of cases, the court takes jurisdiction over the property so as to adjudicate ownership of that property.

These cases should be distinguished from the second broad category of in rem jurisdiction, in which the lawsuit has nothing to do with ownership of the property. Instead, the presence of the property is simply the basis upon which the court relies to assert jurisdiction in the case. This type of in rem proceeding is called quasi-in-rem "of the second type" (or just quasi-in-rem). In *Mitchell v. Neff*, Mitchell could have used quasi-in-rem jurisdiction by attaching Neff's land at the outset of the lawsuit. If he had done this, then even though Neff was not served in Oregon, the default judgment would have been valid. Following the default judgment, Mitchell would have been entitled to the proceeds from the auction of Neff's land, up to the amount of Mitchell's judgment.

2. Justice Field holds that in rem jurisdiction is available only if the property is attached at the beginning of the litigation. Because that did not occur in *Mitchell v. Neff*, he holds that there was no valid in rem jurisdiction. Justice Hunt dissented on the grounds that the timing of the attachment was a matter of "municipal regulation," not "constitutional power." According to Justice Field, why is it essential that attachment happen at the beginning of the suit?

3. Justice Field suggests that in an in rem proceeding, "substitute service by publication," plus attachment of the property, provides sufficient notice of the proceeding to the defendant. Do you think Neff in fact would have learned of the case against him if both these steps had in fact occurred? In the next chapter, we will explore in more detail the requirements of notice.

4. In addition to discussing the prerequisites for valid in rem jurisdiction, Justice Field also discusses in personam jurisdiction. In personam jurisdiction is jurisdiction "against the person." Unlike in rem judgments, an in personam judgment is not limited by the value of any property. Field's discussion of why there is no in personam jurisdiction lays important foundations for the future of personal jurisdiction. Interestingly, the discussion was unnecessary to deciding the particular case because both parties appear to have conceded that the judgment was not binding in personam.

5. Review Justice Field's explanation as to why there is no in personam jurisdiction over Neff. How do you think Justice Field would have responded to the following hypotheticals?

(a) Suit was brought in Oregon state court, with Neff served personally in California.

(b) Mitchell learned that Neff was vacationing in Arizona. Mitchell filed suit in Arizona state court, and Neff was served with process in Arizona.

(c) At Mitchell's request, the Oregon sheriff went to California, where he knocked Neff unconscious, took him back to Oregon, and then served him with process.

6. Field's analysis of personal jurisdiction seems to derive from what he describes as "well-established principles of public law," apparently relying on an international law analogy. Does it make sense to apply the rules of international jurisdiction to the states? In what ways are states similar to independent nations? In what ways are they different?

7. Field cites the Fourteenth Amendment as a basis for invalidating a state judgment. This citation apparently refers to the Due Process Clause of that Amendment, which provides: "No State shall * * * deprive any person of life, liberty or property, without due process of law." Why does Field conclude that service in the forum state is part of due process?

8. The Fourteenth Amendment was not ratified until 1868, several years after judgment in *Mitchell v. Neff* was entered and executed. Is the discussion of the Fourteenth Amendment dicta, or is Field suggesting that the clause should be applied retroactively? Either way, the Fourteenth Amendment has become the basis for challenges to state court jurisdiction. You should note that the standards under the Fourteenth Amendment and the Full Faith and Credit Clause are interconnected. Thus, if a state enters a judgment without jurisdiction, it violates due process and the judgment is not entitled to full faith and credit.

9. In early judicial proceedings, the court's authority, both civil and criminal, was thought to depend on the consent of the litigants. In criminal cases in Medieval England, the court developed an effective though brutal method of persuading defendants to "consent"—the piling of stones on the accused until he either consented or died. In civil cases, the defendant was summoned to appear, and if he refused, the court could levy fines that were enforceable against any of the defendant's property that could be found. Later, the English courts began to base personal jurisdiction on the physical arrest of the defendant using a writ of *capias ad respondendum*. The defendant would be released only after posting sufficient bond to cover any adverse judgment. This form of civil arrest was not required in all civil cases and was never widely practiced in the United States. See Albert Ehrenzweig, *The Transient Rule of Personal Jurisdiction: The "Power" Myth and Forum Conveniens*, 65 YALE L.J. 289, 296–98 (1956). Nonetheless, courts and commentators frequently point to this procedure as proof that "[h]istorically the jurisdiction of courts to render judgment in personam is grounded on their de facto power over the defendant's person." *International Shoe Co. v. Washington*, *infra*. The classic statement of this view of jurisdiction is that of Justice Holmes:

> The foundation of jurisdiction is physical power, although in civilized times it is not necessary to maintain that power throughout proceedings properly begun * * *. We repeat also that the ground for giving subsequent effect to a judgment is that the court rendering it had acquired power to carry it out * * *.

McDonald v. Mabee, 243 U.S. 90, 91–92 (1917).

If the whole purpose of personal jurisdiction is to ensure that the rendering forum will have the physical power over the defendants or their property to enforce any judgment rendered, should that doctrine be applied to states, since states are bound by the Full Faith and Credit Clause? Put differently, isn't the whole purpose of the Full Faith and Credit Clause to ensure that judgments that are not physically enforceable in the rendering states are enforceable elsewhere?

10. Like most judicial opinions, the Supreme Court's opinion in *Pennoyer* does not begin to tell the full story of the people involved in this famous case. Marcus Neff was an illiterate homesteader and one of the earliest settlers to claim land under the Oregon Donation Act. Mitchell and Pennoyer were somewhat better known. "J.H. Mitchell" was the Oregon alias of John Hipple, a Pennsylvania lawyer who abandoned his wife and headed west with his paramour and four thousand dollars of client money. He wound up in Portland and quickly established himself as a successful lawyer specializing in land litigation. Scandal was a way of life for Mitchell. He was implicated, though never indicted, in a vote fraud scheme and an attempt to bribe the U.S. Attorney General. His private life was equally sordid. He married his second wife without bothering to divorce his first wife. Later, *The Oregonian* newspaper published a series of love letters Mitchell had written to his second wife's younger sister. None of this interfered with his political career. He was elected repeatedly to the U.S. Senate. In 1905, while serving in the Senate, he was convicted of a massive land fraud scheme and sentenced to six months in jail. He died while his appeal was pending.

Sylvester Pennoyer went on to be governor of Oregon, but he remained bitter about his defeat in *Pennoyer v. Neff.* Ten years after the decision, he used his inaugural address as a forum to decry that decision as a usurpation of state power. His attacks on the Supreme Court were so frequent and vociferous that such attacks became known as "Pennoyerism." See Wendy Perdue, *Sin, Scandal, and Substantive Due Process: Personal Jurisdiction and* Pennoyer *Reconsidered*, 62 WASH. L. REV. 479 (1987).

2. Interim Developments

Justice Field's approach to jurisdiction had the virtue of being easy to apply, at least as to people and tangible property. Societal changes, however, including changes in the role of corporations, brought this approach under increasing pressure. In the eighteenth and early nineteenth centuries, the prevailing view was that corporations could be sued in personam only in the state of incorporation. A corporation was thought to "exist" only within the boundaries of the state that created it. This view of corporate existence arose from the economic reality at that time. Most corporate activities were local, such as operating bridges, toll roads, and intrastate railroads.

Industrialization brought with it significant multistate corporate activities and the need for states to be able to assert jurisdiction over out-of-state corporations conducting in-state activities. *Pennoyer* itself suggested one approach. Justice Field asserts that states can require a corporation to appoint an agent for service of process as a condition for doing business in the state. Service could then be made on the in-state agent. This approach was premised, at least in part, on the understanding that states had the power to exclude out-of-state corporations and therefore had the power to condition entrance on consent to certain conditions. Under the Privileges and Immunities Clause of Article IV of the Constitution, one state could not exclude the citizens of another state. However, the Court held that corporations were not protected by the Privileges and Immunities Clause. See Paul v. Virginia, 75 U.S. 168, 177 (1869). As the Court explained in a pre-*Pennoyer* case, "A corporation created by Indiana can transact business in Ohio only with the consent, express or implied, of the latter state. This consent may be accompanied by such conditions as Ohio may think fit to impose * * *." Lafayette Ins. Co. v. French, 59 U.S. 404, 407 (1856).

By the early 20th century, the Court began to recognize that although the Privileges and Immunities Clause did not prohibit states from excluding out-of- state corporations, the Commerce Clause prohibited states from excluding corporations engaged solely in interstate commerce. See International Textbook Co. v. Pigg, 217 U.S. 91 (1910). Corporations were quick to exploit this limitation on state power. For example, in International Harvester Co. v. Kentucky, 234 U.S. 579 (1914), the corporation had set up activities in Kentucky very carefully so that those activities would be deemed to be in interstate commerce. The company contended that since Kentucky could not exclude it from the state, Kentucky also could not demand consent as a condition for entering the state. The Supreme Court responded by shifting its focus away from consent and upholding jurisdiction on the ground that regardless of consent, International Harvester was "present" in Kentucky. In a series of cases, the Supreme Court elaborated on what level of activity was necessary to make an out-of-state corporation "present." See, e.g., People's Tobacco Co. v. American Tobacco Co., 246 U.S. 79, 87 (1918); International Harvester Co. v. Kentucky, 234 U.S. 579 (1914); Green v. Chicago, B. & Q. Ry., 205 U.S. 530, 533–34 (1907).

The increased mobility of individuals put similar pressure on the jurisdictional doctrine. With increased travel, people were not always easy to locate for purposes of service of process. Moreover, the new mobility increased the ability of individuals to travel to distant locations and cause injuries which left victims who then had to travel to the defendant's state for any recourse.

One solution was to expand quasi-in-rem to include attachment of an intangible "res" such as a debt. As a result, a defendant was subject to quasi-in-rem type 2 jurisdiction wherever his debtors were found. See Harris v. Balk, 198 U.S. 215 (1905). This is discussed infra in Section B.6.

Another solution was to hold that an individual is subject to in personam jurisdiction in her domicile, regardless of whether she is physically served there. The Supreme Court upheld this approach in Milliken v. Meyer, 311 U.S. 457, 462–64 (1940), explaining:

> Domicile in the state is alone sufficient to bring an absent defendant within the reach of the state's jurisdiction. * * * [As] in the case of the authority of the United States over its absent citizens, the authority of a state over one of its citizens is not terminated by the mere fact of his absence from the state. The state which accords him privileges and affords protection to him and his property by virtue of his domicile may also exact reciprocal duties. * * * One such incident of domicile is amenability to suit within the state * * * where the state has provided and employed a reasonable method for apprising such an absent party of the proceedings against him.

This, however, was not a complete solution. States began to enact consent statutes for individuals that were similar to those used against corporations. The following case considers such a statute.

Hess v. Pawloski

274 U.S. 352, 47 S. Ct. 632, 71 L. Ed. 1091 (1927)

Justice Butler delivered the opinion of the Court.

This action was brought by defendant in error to recover damages for personal injuries. The declaration alleged that plaintiff in error negligently and wantonly drove a motor vehicle on a public highway in Massachusetts and that by reason thereof the vehicle struck and injured defendant in error. Plaintiff in error is a resident of Pennsylvania. No personal service was made on him and no property belonging to him was attached. The service of process was made in compliance with General Laws of Massachusetts [statutory law], the material parts of which follow:

> "The acceptance by a nonresident of the rights and privileges conferred by section three or four, as evidenced by his operating a motor vehicle thereunder, or the operation by a nonresident of a motor vehicle on a public way in the commonwealth other than under said sections, shall be deemed equivalent to an appointment by such nonresident of the registrar or his successor in office, to be his true and lawful attorney upon whom may be served all lawful processes in any action or proceeding against him, growing out of any accident or collision in which said nonresident may be involved while operating a motor vehicle on such a way, and said acceptance or operation shall be a signification of his agreement that any such process against him which is so served shall be of the same legal force and validity as if served on him personally. * * * "

Plaintiff in error appeared specially for the purpose of contesting jurisdiction and filed an answer in abatement and moved to dismiss on the ground that the service of process, if sustained, would deprive him of his property without due process of law in violation of the Fourteenth Amendment. The court overruled the answer in abatement and denied the motion. * * * The jury returned a verdict for defendant in error. The exceptions were overruled by the Supreme Judicial Court. Thereupon the Superior Court entered judgment. * * *

The question is whether the Massachusetts enactment contravenes the due process clause of the Fourteenth Amendment.

The process of a court of one State cannot run into another and summon a party there domiciled to respond to proceedings against him. Notice sent outside the State to a nonresident is unavailing to give jurisdiction in an action against him personally for money recovery. *Pennoyer v. Neff.* There must be actual service within the State of notice upon him or upon some one authorized to accept service for him. A personal judgment rendered against a nonresident who has neither been served with process nor appeared in the suit is without validity. The mere transaction of business in a State by nonresident natural persons does not imply consent to be bound by the process of its courts. The power of a State to exclude foreign corporations, although not absolute but qualified, is the ground on which such an implication is supported as to them. But a State may not withhold from nonresident individuals the right of doing business therein. The privileges and immunities clause of the Constitution, § 2, Art. IV, safeguards to the citizens of one State the right "to pass through, or to reside in any other state for purposes of trade, agriculture, professional pursuits, or otherwise." And it prohibits state legislation discriminating against citizens of other States.

Motor vehicles are dangerous machines; and, even when skillfully and carefully operated, their use is attended by serious dangers to persons and property. In the public interest the State may make and enforce regulations reasonably calculated to promote care on the part of all, residents and nonresidents alike, who use its highways. The measure in question operates to require a nonresident to answer for his conduct in the State where arise causes of action alleged against him, as well as to provide for a claimant a convenient method by which he may sue to enforce his rights. Under the statute the implied consent is limited to proceedings growing out of accidents or collisions on a highway in which the nonresident may be involved. It is required that he shall actually receive a receipt for notice of the service and a copy of the process. And it contemplates such continuances as may be found necessary to give reasonable time and opportunity for defense. It makes no hostile discrimination against nonresidents but tends to put them on the same footing as residents. Literal and precise equality in respect of this matter is not attainable; it is not required. The State's power to regulate the use of its highways extends to their use by nonresidents as well as by residents. And, in advance of the operation of a motor vehicle on its highway by a nonresident, the State may require him to appoint one of its officials as his agent on whom process may be served in proceedings growing out of such use. Kane v. New Jersey, 242 U.S. 160, 167 [1916]. That case recognizes power of the State to exclude a nonresident until the formal appointment is made. And, having the power so to exclude, the State may declare that the use of the highway by the nonresident is the equivalent of the appointment of the registrar as agent on whom process may be served. The difference between the formal and implied appointment is not substantial so far as concerns the application of the due process clause of the Fourteenth Amendment.

Judgment affirmed.

Notes and Questions

1. The facts state that the defendant "appeared specially." A special appearance is a procedure that allows the defendant to come forward in a case and contest jurisdiction without thereby consenting to jurisdiction. All states permit defendants to contest personal jurisdiction without waiving the defense. Similarly, under the Federal Rules of Civil Procedure, a defendant may raise a jurisdictional objection without thereby consenting to jurisdiction. In Chapter 6 we will explore in greater detail the procedures for challenging jurisdiction.

2. Is the theory of the Massachusetts statute that by driving into the state, a driver "consents" to the appointment of the Registrar of Motor Vehicles as her agent for service of process? Suppose that before heading to Massachusetts, Mr. Hess had sent a letter to the Registrar indicating in the strongest possible terms that he did *not* consent to the Registrar or anyone else being his agent. In such a case, could Hess still be sued in Massachusetts without personal service on him in state?

3. Although the Privileges and Immunities Clause clearly precludes a state from denying entry to citizens of other states, do *Hess* and *Kane* (discussed in *Hess*) allow a state to deny entry to people who are in cars? What other state interest might justify an implied consent theory? See Henry L. Doherty & Co. v. Goodman, 294 U.S. 623 (1935) (upholding jurisdiction over company whose agents were selling securities in forum; Court notes that selling of securities is highly regulated).

3. The Modern Era

In dealing with jurisdiction over corporations, the Court began moving away from the *Pennoyer*-based terms of "presence" and "consent" and focusing instead on whether the corporation was "doing business" in the state. Professor Kurland explained:

> The law reports became cluttered with decisions as to what constituted "doing business." * * * The myriad of cases dealing with the question of "doing business" soon substituted that shibboleth for any theory. Without looking back of the words, the courts held that jurisdiction existed if the corporate defendant was "doing business" within the jurisdiction but no jurisdiction existed if the corporate defendant was not "doing business."

Philip Kurland, *The Supreme Court, the Due Process Clause and the In Personam Jurisdiction of State Courts — From* Pennoyer *to* Denckla: *A Review*, 25 U. Chi. L. Rev. 569, 584–85 (1958). As you will see in the following case, the language of "doing business" ultimately gave way to another verbal formulation.

International Shoe Co. v. Washington

326 U.S. 310, 66 S. Ct. 154, 90 L. Ed. 95 (1945)

Chief Justice Stone delivered the opinion of the Court.

The questions for decision are (1) whether, within the limitations of the due process clause of the Fourteenth Amendment, appellant, a Delaware corporation, has by its activities in the State of Washington rendered itself amenable to proceedings in the courts of that state to recover unpaid contributions to the state unemployment compensation fund exacted by state statutes, and (2) whether the state can exact those contributions consistently with the due process clause of the Fourteenth Amendment.

The statutes in question set up a comprehensive scheme of unemployment compensation, the costs of which are defrayed by contributions required to be made by employers to a state unemployment compensation fund. The contributions are a specified percentage of the wages payable annually by each employer for his employees' services in the state. The assessment and collection of the contributions and the fund are administered by appellees. Section 14(c) of the Act authorizes appellee Commissioner to issue an order and notice of assessment of delinquent contributions upon prescribed personal service of the notice upon the employer if found within the state, or, if not so found, by mailing the notice to the employer by registered mail at his last known address. * * *

In this case notice of assessment for the years in question was personally served upon a sales solicitor employed by appellant in the State of Washington, and a copy of the notice was mailed by registered mail to appellant at its address in St. Louis, Missouri. Appellant appeared specially before the office of unemployment and moved to set aside the order and notice of assessment on the ground that the service upon appellant's salesman was not proper service upon appellant; that appellant was not a corporation of the State of Washington and was not doing business within the state; that it had no agent within the state upon whom service could be made; and that appellant is not an employer and does not furnish employment within the meaning of the statute.

The motion was heard on evidence and a stipulation of facts by the appeal tribunal which denied the motion and ruled that appellee Commissioner was entitled to recover the unpaid contributions. That action was affirmed by the Commissioner; both the Superior Court and the Supreme Court affirmed. Appellant in each of these courts assailed the statute as applied, as a violation of the due process clause of the Fourteenth Amendment, and as imposing a constitutionally prohibited burden on interstate commerce. * * *

The facts as found by the appeal tribunal and accepted by the state Superior Court and Supreme Court, are not in dispute. Appellant is a Delaware corporation, having its principal place of business in St. Louis, Missouri, and is engaged in the manufacture and sale of shoes and other footwear. It maintains places of business in several states, other than Washington, at which its manufacturing is carried on and from which its merchandise is distributed interstate through several sales units or branches located outside the State of Washington.

Appellant has no office in Washington and makes no contracts either for sale or purchase of merchandise there. It maintains no stock of merchandise in that state and makes there no deliveries of goods in intrastate commerce. During the years from 1937 to 1940, now in question, appellant employed eleven to thirteen salesmen under direct supervision and control of sales managers located in St. Louis. These salesmen resided in Washington; their principal activities were confined to that state; and they were compensated by commissions based upon the amount of their sales. The commissions for each year totaled more than $31,000. Appellant supplies its salesmen with a line of samples, each consisting of one shoe of a pair, which they display to prospective purchasers. On occasion they rent permanent sample rooms, for exhibiting samples, in business buildings, or rent rooms in hotels or business buildings temporarily for that purpose. The cost of such rentals is reimbursed by appellant.

The authority of the salesmen is limited to exhibiting their samples and soliciting orders from prospective buyers, at prices and on terms fixed by appellant. The salesmen transmit the orders to appellant's office in St. Louis for acceptance or rejection, and when accepted the merchandise for filling the orders is shipped f.o.b. from points outside Washington to the purchasers within the state. All the merchandise shipped into Washington is invoiced at the place of shipment from which collections are made. No salesman has authority to enter into contracts or to make collections.

The Supreme Court of Washington was of opinion that the regular and systematic solicitation of orders in the state by appellant's salesmen, resulting in a continuous flow of appellant's product into the state, was sufficient to constitute doing business in the state so as to make appellant amenable to suit in its courts. But it was also of opinion that there were sufficient additional activities shown to bring the case within the rule frequently stated, that solicitation within a state by the agents of a foreign corporation plus some additional activities there are sufficient to render the corporation amenable to suit brought in the courts of the state to enforce an obligation arising out of its activities there. The court found such additional activities in the salesmen's display of samples sometimes in permanent display rooms, and the salesmen's residence within the state, continued over a period of years, all resulting in a substantial volume of merchandise regularly shipped by appellant to purchasers within the state. The court also held that the statute as applied did not invade the constitutional power of Congress to regulate interstate commerce and did not impose a prohibited burden on such commerce.

Appellant's argument, renewed here, that the statute imposes an unconstitutional burden on interstate commerce need not detain us. [The Court rejects this argument, noting that Congress has by statute authorized states to establish such unemployment funds.] * * *

Appellant also insists that its activities within the state were not sufficient to manifest its "presence" there and that in its absence the state courts were without jurisdiction, that consequently it was a denial of due process for the state to subject appellant to suit. It refers to those cases in which it was said that the mere solicitation of orders for the purchase of goods within a state, to be accepted without the state and filled by shipment of the purchased goods interstate, does not render the corporation seller amenable to suit within the state. And appellant further argues that since it was not present within the state, it is a denial of due process to subject it to taxation or other money exaction. It thus denies the power of the state to lay the tax or to subject appellant to a suit for its collection.

Historically the jurisdiction of courts to render judgment in personam is grounded on their de facto power over the defendant's person. Hence his presence within the territorial jurisdiction of a court was prerequisite to its rendition of a judgment personally binding him. *Pennoyer v. Neff.* But now that the *capias ad respondendum* has given way to personal service of summons or other form of notice, due process requires only that in order to subject a defendant to a judgment in personam, if he be not present within the territory of the forum, he have certain minimum contacts with it such that the maintenance of the suit does not offend "traditional notions of fair play and substantial justice." Milliken v. Meyer, 311 U.S. 457, 463 (1940).

Since the corporate personality is a fiction, although a fiction intended to be acted upon as though it were a fact, it is clear that unlike an individual its "presence" without, as well as within, the state of its origin can be manifested only by activities carried on in its behalf by those who are authorized to act for it. To say that the corporation is so far "present" there as to satisfy due process requirements, for purposes of taxation or the maintenance of suits against it in the courts of the state, is to beg the question to be decided. For the terms "present" or "presence" are used merely to symbolize those activities of the corporation's agent within the state which courts will deem to be sufficient to satisfy the demands of due process. Those demands may be met by such contacts of the corporation with the state of the forum as make it reasonable, in the context of our federal system of government, to require the corporation to defend the particular suit which is brought there. An "estimate of the inconveniences" which would result to the corporation from a trial away from its "home" or principal place of business is relevant in this connection.

"Presence" in the state in this sense has never been doubted when the activities of the corporation there have not only been continuous and systematic, but also give rise to the liabilities sued on, even though no consent to be sued or authorization to an agent to accept service of process has been given. Conversely it has been generally recognized that the casual presence of the corporate agent or even his conduct of single or isolated items of activities in a state in the corporation's behalf are not enough to subject it to suit on causes of action unconnected with the activities there. To require the corporation in such circumstances to defend the suit away from its home or other jurisdiction where it carries on more substantial activities has been thought to lay too great and unreasonable a burden on the corporation to comport with due process.

While it has been held, in cases on which appellant relies, that continuous activity of some sorts within a state is not enough to support the demand that the corporation be amenable to suits unrelated to that activity, there have been instances in which the continuous corporate operations within a state were thought so substantial and of such a nature as to justify suit against it on causes of action arising from dealings entirely distinct from those activities.

Finally, although the commission of some single or occasional acts of the corporate agent in a state sufficient to impose an obligation or liability on the corporation has not been thought to confer upon the state authority to enforce it, Rosenberg Bros. & Co. v. Curtis Brown Co., 260 U.S. 516 (1923), other such acts, because of their nature and quality and the circumstances of their commission, may be deemed sufficient to render the corporation liable to suit. Cf. *Hess v. Pawloski.* True, some of the decisions holding the corporation amenable to suit have been supported by resort to the legal fiction that it has given its consent to service and suit, consent being implied from its presence in the state through the acts of its authorized agents. But more realistically it may be said that those authorized acts were of such a nature as to justify the fiction.

It is evident that the criteria by which we mark the boundary line between those activities which justify the subjection of a corporation to suit, and those which do not, cannot be simply mechanical or quantitative. The test is not merely, as has sometimes been suggested, whether the activity, which the corporation has seen fit to procure through its agents in another state, is a little more or a little less. Whether due process is satisfied must depend rather upon the quality and nature of the activity in relation to the fair and orderly administration of the laws which it was the purpose of the due process clause to insure. That clause does not contemplate that a state may make binding a judgment in personam against an individual or corporate defendant with which the state has no contacts, ties, or relations. Cf. *Pennoyer v. Neff.*

But to the extent that a corporation exercises the privilege of conducting activities within a state, it enjoys the benefits and protection of the laws of that state. The exercise of that privilege may give rise to obligations, and, so far as those obligations arise out of or are connected with the activities within the state, a procedure which requires the corporation to respond to a suit brought to enforce them can, in most instances, hardly be said to be undue.

Applying these standards, the activities carried on in behalf of appellant in the State of Washington were neither irregular nor casual. They were systematic and continuous throughout the years in question. They resulted in a large volume of interstate business, in the course of which appellant received the benefits and protection of the laws of the state, including the right to resort to the courts for the enforcement of its rights. The obligation which is here sued upon arose out of those very activities. It is evident that these operations establish sufficient contacts or ties with the state of the forum to make it reasonable and just, according to our traditional conception of fair play and substantial justice, to permit the state to enforce the obligations which appellant has incurred there. Hence we cannot say that the maintenance of the present suit in the State of Washington involves an unreasonable or undue procedure.

We are likewise unable to conclude that the service of the process within the state upon an agent whose activities establish appellant's "presence" there was not sufficient notice of the suit, or that the suit was so unrelated to those activities as to make the agent an inappropriate vehicle for communicating the notice. It is enough that appellant has established such contacts with the state that the particular form of substituted service adopted there gives reasonable assurance that the notice will be actual. Nor can we say that the mailing of the notice of suit to appellant by registered mail at its home office was not reasonably calculated to apprise appellant of the suit.

Affirmed.

Justice Black delivered the following opinion.

Certainly appellant cannot in the light of our past decisions meritoriously claim that notice by registered mail and by personal service on its sales solicitors in Washington did not meet the requirements of procedural due process. And the due process clause is not brought in issue any more by appellant's further conceptualistic contention that Washington could not levy a tax or bring suit against the corporation because it did not honor that State with its mystical "presence." For it is unthinkable that the vague due process clause was ever intended to prohibit a State from regulating or taxing a business carried on within its boundaries simply because this is done by agents of a corporation organized and having its headquarters elsewhere. To read this into the due process clause would in fact result in depriving a State's citizens of due process by taking from the State the power to protect them in their business dealings within its boundaries with representatives of a foreign corporation. Nothing could be more irrational or more designed to defeat the function of our federative system of government. Certainly a State, at the very least, has power to tax and sue those dealing with its citizens within its boundaries, as we have held before. Were the Court to follow this principle, it would provide a workable standard for cases where, as here, no other questions are involved. The Court has not chosen to do so, but instead has engaged in an unnecessary discussion in the course of which it has announced vague Constitutional criteria applied for the first time to the issue before us. It has thus introduced uncertain elements confusing the simple pattern and tending to curtail the exercise of State powers to an extent not justified by the Constitution.

It is true that this Court did use the terms "fair play" and "substantial justice" in explaining the philosophy underlying the holding that it could not be "due process of law" to render a personal judgment against a defendant without notice and an opportunity to be heard. * * * These cases, while giving additional reasons why notice under particular circumstances is inadequate, did not mean thereby that all legislative enactments which this Court might deem to be contrary to natural justice ought to be held invalid under the due process clause. None of the cases purport to support or could support a holding that a State can tax and sue corporations only if its action comports with this Court's notions of "natural justice." I should have thought the Tenth Amendment settled that.

I believe that the Federal Constitution leaves to each State, without any "ifs" or "buts," a power to tax and to open the doors of its courts for its citizens to sue corporations whose agents do business in those States. Believing that the Constitution gave the States that power, I think it a judicial deprivation to condition its exercise upon this Court's notion of "fair play," however appealing that term may be. Nor can I stretch the meaning of due process so far as to authorize this Court to deprive a State of the right to afford judicial protection to its citizens on the ground that it would be more "convenient" for the corporation to be sued somewhere else.

There is a strong emotional appeal in the words "fair play," "justice," and "reasonableness." But they were not chosen by those who wrote the original Constitution or the Fourteenth Amendment as a measuring rod for this Court to use in invalidating State or Federal laws passed by elected legislative representatives. No one, not even those who most feared a democratic government, ever formally proposed that courts should be given power to invalidate legislation under any such elastic standards. * * *

True, the State's power is here upheld. But the rule announced means that tomorrow's judgment may strike down a State or Federal enactment on the ground that it does not conform to this Court's idea of natural justice. * * *

Notes and Questions

1. After *International Shoe*, it is no longer necessary to fit the defendant's activities into a model of consent or presence. The new test focuses on whether the defendant's activities constitute "minimum contacts" such that jurisdiction is consistent with "traditional notions of fair play and substantial justice." Justice Stone says of his new formulation that it is not new at all but simply reiterates what courts were doing all along under the old models of consent and presence. But hasn't the shift in paradigm from presence to fairness fundamentally altered jurisdiction doctrine?

2. *International Shoe* involved a corporate defendant. Later cases made clear that the *International Shoe* test applies as well to individual defendants. See Kulko v. Superior Court, 436 U.S. 84, 92 (1978).

3. The Court differentiates between cases in which the cause of action is related to the contacts and those in which the case is unrelated. Later cases develop this distinction into two categories. See Goodyear Dunlop Tires Operations, S.A. v. Brown, 131 S. Ct. 2846 (2011), in Section B.4, *infra*. Suits in which the contacts are related to the claim are referred to as *specific jurisdiction* cases. Those in which the contacts are unrelated are called *general jurisdiction*. Which type of case is *International Shoe*? The Court suggests that if the contacts are unrelated to the claim, then there will be jurisdiction only if the defendant's contacts are "continuous and systematic." At what point do a defendant's contacts move from being "casual" to "continuous and systematic"?

4. Consider the following hypotheticals. How should they come out under the *International Shoe* test?

(a) An International Shoe delivery truck carrying shoes from Missouri to Washington drives through Colorado, where it hits a Colorado pedestrian. Can Pedestrian sue International Shoe in Colorado? Would it matter if the truck driver had not planned to go through Colorado but got lost and ended up there?

(b) Could Pedestrian sue International Shoe in Washington?

(c) Could Pedestrian sue International Shoe in Missouri, where the defendant's headquarters were located?

(d) International Shoe's headquarters were located in St. Louis, Missouri, very close to Illinois. Suppose Pedestrian has a vacation home in Illinois and hence thinks it would be very convenient to litigate in Illinois. Can Pedestrian sue International Shoe in Illinois?

(e) Suppose International Shoe operates retail shoe outlets in Washington. A customer buys a pair of shoes there, but the shoes are defective. Can the customer sue International Shoe in Washington?

(f) International Shoe operates retail outlets in Washington but not in Oregon. An Oregon citizen visits the Washington store and buys a pair of shoes, which she takes back to Oregon. She then discovers the shoes are defective. Can she sue International Shoe in Oregon?

(g) Suppose that the Oregonian had seen the shoes at the Washington store but had returned home. She then contacted International Shoe directly and ordered a pair of shoes. The shoes were sent by International Shoe to the customer in Oregon. Could she sue International Shoe in Oregon?

(h) Suppose that instead of having the shoes shipped to Oregon, the customer picked them up in Missouri while she was vacationing in St. Louis. At the time she picks up the shoes, the customer makes it very clear she is going to take the shoes back to Oregon. Can she sue in Oregon?

(i) Suppose International Shoe makes shoe components such as heels and soles. International Shoe sells its heels to a Pennsylvania company. The Pennsylvania company incorporates the heels into its shoes which it then sells in Oregon. Can a person who buys the shoes in Oregon and is injured by a defective heel sue International Shoe in Oregon?

5. Reconsider *Pennoyer v. Neff.* Under the test of *International Shoe*, would there have been in personam jurisdiction over Neff in the underlying suit of *Mitchell v. Neff*?

6. Note that the Court requires that the defendant have minimum contacts with the forum "if he be not present." Does that mean that defendant's presence in the forum continues to be an independent basis for in personam jurisdiction, even in the absence of other contacts? We will reconsider this issue in connection with Burnham v. Superior Court of California, 495 U.S. 604 (1990), in Section B.7, *infra*.

7. The shift in approach from *Pennoyer* to *International Shoe* can be understood as part of a broader jurisprudential movement from formalism to realism. The formalism of the nineteenth and early twentieth centuries viewed legal analysis as a deductive, almost mathematical process of identifying principles within an area of law and then deducing all the subordinate principles. Formalism relied heavily on classification and proper labeling. The analysis of *Pennoyer* has formal elements: the Court purports to deduce its conclusion about personal jurisdiction from broad principles about the nature of independent states and it draws sharp distinctions between categories such as in rem and in personam jurisdiction.

Legal realism, which became prominent during the 1930s, challenged the deductive and classification-based approach of formalism. Legal realists argued that law must be understood in functional terms as a means to accomplish social ends. In a famous article, Felix Cohen, a prominent legal realist, criticized the "transcendental nonsense" of trying to determine where a corporation is "present." Felix Cohen, *Transcendental Nonsense and the Functional Approach*, 35 Colum. L. Rev. 809 (1935). Cohen accused courts of attempting to "thingify" corporations and argued that asking where a corporation "is" is the modern equivalent of asking how many angels can dance on the head of a pin. Notice that Justice Stone in *International Shoe* similarly rejects presence as a meaningful test. Cohen offered the following analysis of the issue of personal jurisdiction:

> If a competent legislature had considered the problem of when a corporation incorporated in another State should be subject to suit, it would probably have made some factual inquiry into the practice of modern corporations in choosing their sovereigns and into the actual significance of the relationship between a corporation and the state of its incorporation. It might have considered the difficulties that injured plaintiffs may encounter if they have to bring suit against corporate defendants in the state of incorporation. It might have balanced, against such difficulties, the possible hardship to corporations of having to defend actions in many states, considering the legal facilities available to corporate defendants. On the basis of the *facts* revealed by such an inquiry, and on the basis of certain political or ethical *value judgments* as to the propriety of putting financial burdens upon corporations, a competent legislature would have attempted to formulate some rule as to when a foreign corporation should be subject to suit.

35 Colum. L. Rev. at 810. Do you think the approach Cohen describes is what the Court had in mind in *International Shoe*? For more on formalism and the realist response, see Joseph Singer, *Legal Realism Now*, 76 Cal. L. Rev. 465 (1988).

Note on McGee, Hanson, *and* Gray

During the 1950s, the Court decided a handful of personal jurisdiction cases. Two cases of note were McGee v. International Life Ins. Co., 355 U.S. 220 (1957), and Hanson v. Denckla, 357 U.S. 235 (1958).

In *McGee*, a California citizen purchased a life insurance policy from an Arizona insurance company. A Texas insurance company later took over the Arizona company. When it took over, the Texas company mailed a reinsurance certificate to the California insured. The insured in turn sent his premiums from California. The insured died in California, and a dispute arose concerning the policy. (The insurance company asserted that the policy was void because the insured had committed suicide.) The beneficiaries sued the Texas insurance company in California state court. Although there was no evidence that the defendant had ever solicited or done any insurance business in California apart from this particular policy, the Supreme Court found that there was jurisdiction. The Court explained:

> Turning to this case we think it apparent that the Due Process Clause did not preclude the California court from entering a judgment binding on respondent. It is sufficient for purposes of due process that the suit was based

> on a contract which had substantial connection with that State. The contract was delivered in California, the premiums were mailed from there and the insured was a resident of that State when he died. It cannot be denied that California has a manifest interest in providing effective means of redress for its residents when their insurers refuse to pay claims. These residents would be at a severe disadvantage if they were forced to follow the insurance company to a distant State in order to hold it legally accountable. When the claims were small or moderate individual claimants frequently could not afford the cost of bringing an action in a foreign forum—thus in effect making the company judgment proof. Often the crucial witnesses—as here on the company's defense of suicide—will be found in the insured's locality. Of course there may be inconvenience to the insurer if it is held amenable to suit in California where it had this contract but certainly nothing which amounts to a denial of due process. There is no contention that respondent did not have adequate notice of the suit or sufficient time to prepare its defenses and appear.

355 U.S. at 223–24.

A year later, *Hanson* undercut the seemingly expansive approach of *McGee. Hanson* arose out of a family inheritance dispute. At issue was the validity of a trust. Dora Donner created the trust while she was domiciled in Pennsylvania. The trust instrument was executed in Delaware, naming a Delaware bank as trustee. Donner reserved the trust income to herself and retained the power to designate who would receive the principal. Donner later moved to Florida and designated the recipients of the trust. Following her death, a dispute arose between those family members who inherited money through Donner's will and the trust beneficiaries.

Donner's will was probated in Florida, and under Florida law, the Delaware bank was a necessary party to that litigation. The issue then arose whether Florida had personal jurisdiction over the Delaware bank. The Supreme Court held that Florida did not. In reaching this conclusion, the Court noted that when the trust was created, there was no connection with Florida. In addition, the Court found that Donner's later move to Florida was not sufficient to create jurisdiction.

> The unilateral activity of those who claim some relationship with a nonresident defendant cannot satisfy the requirement of contact with the forum State. The application of that rule will vary with the quality and nature of the defendant's activity, but it is essential in each case that there be some act by which the defendant purposefully avails itself of the privilege of conducting activities within the forum State, thus invoking the benefits and protections of its laws.

357 U.S. at 253. The Court distinguished *McGee*, explaining: "From Florida Mrs. Donner carried on several bits of trust administration that may be compared to the mailing of premiums in *McGee*. But the record discloses no instance in which the *trustee* performed any acts in Florida that bear the same relationship to the agreement as the solicitation in *McGee*." Id. at 252.

For 18 years following *Hanson*, the Supreme Court paid little attention to personal jurisdiction. During this period, state courts interpreted *McGee* expansively and largely ignored *Hanson.* A typical case is Gray v. American Radiator & Standard Sanitary Corp., 176 N.E.2d 761 (Ill. 1961). In *Gray*, the plaintiff sued the Titan Valve Co. alleging that it had negligently constructed a safety valve, and as a result of its negligence, a water heater had exploded. Plaintiff sued in Illinois, and Titan, an Ohio corporation, challenged personal jurisdiction. Titan had manufactured the valve in Ohio, then sold it to a Pennsylvania company which had incorporated it into the water heater. The water heater "in the course of commerce" was sold to the Illinois consumer. There was no evidence in the record that Titan had done any other business in Illinois either directly or indirectly. The Supreme Court of Illinois upheld jurisdiction stating:

> In the case at bar defendant does not claim that the present use of its product in Illinois is an isolated instance. While the record does not disclose the volume of Titan's business or the territory in which appliances incorporating its valves are marketed, it is a reasonable inference that its commercial transactions, like those of other manufacturers, result in substantial use and consumption in this State. To the extent that its business may be directly affected by transactions occurring here it enjoys benefits from the laws of this State, and it has undoubtedly benefited, to a degree, from the protection which our law has given to the marketing of hot water heaters containing its valves. Where the alleged liability arises, as in this case, from the manufacture of products presumably sold in contemplation of use here, it should not matter that the purchase was made from an independent middleman or that someone other than the defendant shipped the product into this State.
>
> With the increasing specialization of commercial activity and the growing interdependence of business enterprises it is seldom that a manufacturer deals directly with consumers in other States. The fact that the benefit he derives from its laws is an indirect one, however, does not make it any the less essential to the conduct of his business; and it is not unreasonable, where a cause of action arises from alleged defects in his product, to say that the use of such products in the ordinary course of commerce is sufficient contact with this State to justify a requirement that he defend here.
>
> As a general proposition, if a corporation elects to sell its products for ultimate use in another State, it is not unjust to hold it answerable there for any damage caused by defects in those products. Advanced means of distribution and other commercial activity have made possible these modern methods of doing business, and have largely effaced the economic significance of State lines. By the same token, today's facilities for transportation and communication have removed much of the difficulty and inconvenience formerly encountered in defending lawsuits brought in other States.

176 N.E.2d at 766. Notice the court's rationale. You should reconsider this rationale after you have read the next case.

In 1976, the Court began hearing personal jurisdiction cases again. In the fourteen years from 1976 to 1990, the Supreme Court decided twelve personal jurisdiction cases. The Court's major decisions during this period are considered below.

World-Wide Volkswagen v. Woodson

444 U.S. 286, 100 S. Ct. 559, 62 L. Ed. 2d 490 (1980)

Justice White delivered the opinion of the Court.

The issue before us is whether, consistently with the Due Process Clause of the Fourteenth Amendment, an Oklahoma court may exercise in personam jurisdiction over a nonresident automobile retailer and its wholesale distributor in a products-liability action, when the defendants' only connection with Oklahoma is the fact that an automobile sold in New York to New York residents became involved in an accident in Oklahoma.

I

Respondents Harry and Kay Robinson purchased a new Audi automobile from petitioner Seaway Volkswagen, Inc. (Seaway), in Massena, N.Y., in 1976. The following year the Robinson family, who resided in New York, left that State for a new home in Arizona. As they passed through the State of Oklahoma, another car struck their Audi in the rear, causing a fire which severely burned Kay Robinson and her two children.[1]

The Robinsons subsequently brought a products-liability action in the District Court for Creek County, Okla., claiming that their injuries resulted from defective design and placement of the Audi's gas tank and fuel system. They joined as defendants the automobile's manufacturer, Audi NSU Auto Union Aktiengesellschaft (Audi); its importer, Volkswagen of America, Inc. (Volkswagen); its regional distributor, petitioner World-Wide Volkswagen Corp. (World-Wide); and its retail dealer, petitioner Seaway. Seaway and World-Wide entered special appearances,[3] claiming that Oklahoma's exercise of jurisdiction over them would offend the limitations on the State's jurisdiction imposed by the Due Process Clause of the Fourteenth Amendment.

The facts presented to the District Court showed that World-Wide is incorporated and has its business office in New York. It distributes vehicles, parts, and accessories, under contract with Volkswagen, to retail dealers in New York, New Jersey, and Con-

1. The driver of the other automobile does not figure in the present litigation.

3. Volkswagen also entered a special appearance in the District Court, but unlike World-Wide and Seaway did not seek review in the Supreme Court of Oklahoma and is not a petitioner here. Both Volkswagen and Audi remain as defendants in the litigation pending before the District Court in Oklahoma.

necticut. Seaway, one of these retail dealers, is incorporated and has its place of business in New York. Insofar as the record reveals, Seaway and World-Wide are fully independent corporations whose relations with each other and with Volkswagen and Audi are contractual only. Respondents adduced no evidence that either World-Wide or Seaway does any business in Oklahoma, ships or sells any products to or in that State, has an agent to receive process there, or purchases advertisements in any media calculated to reach Oklahoma. In fact, as respondents' counsel conceded at oral argument there was no showing that any automobile sold by World-Wide or Seaway has ever entered Oklahoma with the single exception of the vehicle involved in the present case.

Despite the apparent paucity of contacts between petitioners and Oklahoma, the District Court rejected their constitutional claim and reaffirmed that ruling in denying petitioners' motion for reconsideration. Petitioners then sought a writ of prohibition in the Supreme Court of Oklahoma to restrain the District Judge, respondent Charles S. Woodson, from exercising in personam jurisdiction over them. They renewed their contention that, because they had no "minimal contacts" with the State of Oklahoma, the actions of the District Judge were in violation of their rights under the Due Process Clause.

The Supreme Court of Oklahoma denied the writ holding that personal jurisdiction over petitioners was authorized by Oklahoma's "long-arm" statute, Okla. Stat., Tit. 12, § 1701.03(a)(4) (1971).[7] Although the court noted that the proper approach was to test jurisdiction against both statutory and constitutional standards, its analysis did not distinguish these questions, probably because § 1701.03(a)(4) has been interpreted as conferring jurisdiction to the limits permitted by the United States Constitution. The court's rationale was contained in the following paragraph:

> "In the case before us, the product being sold and distributed by the petitioners is by its very design and purpose so mobile that petitioners can foresee its possible use in Oklahoma. This is especially true of the distributor, who has the exclusive right to distribute such automobile in New York, New Jersey and Connecticut. The evidence presented below demonstrated that goods sold and distributed by the petitioners were used in the State of Oklahoma, and under the facts we believe it reasonable to infer, given the retail value of the automobile, that the petitioners derive substantial income from automobiles which from time to time are used in the State of Oklahoma. This being the case, we hold that under the facts presented, the trial court

---

7. This subsection provides:

"A court may exercise personal jurisdiction over a person, who acts directly or by an agent, as to a cause of action or claim for relief arising from the person's ... causing tortious injury in this state by an act or omission outside this state if he regularly does or solicits business or engages in any other persistent course of conduct, or derives substantial revenue from goods used or consumed or services rendered, in this state...." * * *

was justified in concluding that the petitioners derive substantial revenue from goods used or consumed in this State."

We granted certiorari to consider an important constitutional question with respect to state-court jurisdiction and to resolve a conflict between the Supreme Court of Oklahoma and the highest courts of at least four other States. We reverse.

II

The Due Process Clause of the Fourteenth Amendment limits the power of a state court to render a valid personal judgment against a nonresident defendant. Kulko v. California Superior Court, 436 U.S. 84, 91 (1978). A judgment rendered in violation of due process is void in the rendering State and is not entitled to full faith and credit elsewhere. *Pennoyer v. Neff.* Due process requires that the defendant be given adequate notice of the suit, Mullane v. Central Hanover Trust Co., 339 U.S. 306, 313–314 (1950), and be subject to the personal jurisdiction of the court, *International Shoe Co. v. Washington.* In the present case, it is not contended that notice was inadequate; the only question is whether these particular petitioners were subject to the jurisdiction of the Oklahoma courts.

As has long been settled and as we reaffirm today, a state court may exercise personal jurisdiction over a nonresident defendant only so long as there exist "minimum contacts" between the defendant and the forum State. *International Shoe.* The concept of minimum contacts, in turn, can be seen to perform two related, but distinguishable, functions. It protects the defendant against the burdens of litigating in a distant or inconvenient forum. And it acts to ensure that the States, through their courts, do not reach out beyond the limits imposed on them by their status as coequal sovereigns in a federal system.

The protection against inconvenient litigation is typically described in terms of "reasonableness" or "fairness." We have said that the defendant's contacts with the forum State must be such that maintenance of the suit "does not offend 'traditional notions of fair play and substantial justice.'" *International Shoe*, quoting Milliken v. Meyer, 311 U.S. 457, 463 (1940). The relationship between the defendant and the forum must be such that it is "reasonable ... to require the corporation to defend the particular suit which is brought there." Implicit in this emphasis on reasonableness is the understanding that the burden on the defendant, while always a primary concern, will in an appropriate case be considered in light of other relevant factors, including the forum State's interest in adjudicating the dispute, see *McGee v. International Life Ins. Co.*; the plaintiff's interest in obtaining convenient and effective relief, see *Kulko v. California Superior Court*, at least when that interest is not adequately protected by the plaintiff's power to choose the forum, cf. Shaffer v. Heitner, 433 U.S. 186, 211, n.37 (1977); the interstate judicial system's interest in obtaining the most efficient resolution of controversies; and the shared interest of the several States in furthering fundamental substantive social policies. See *Kulko v. California Superior Court.*

The limits imposed on state jurisdiction by the Due Process Clause, in its role as a guarantor against inconvenient litigation, have been substantially relaxed over the years. As we noted in *McGee*, this trend is largely attributable to a fundamental transformation in the American economy:

> "Today many commercial transactions touch two or more States and may involve parties separated by the full continent. With this increasing nationalization of commerce has come a great increase in the amount of business conducted by mail across state lines. At the same time modern transportation and communication have made it much less burdensome for a party sued to defend himself in a State where he engages in economic activity."

The historical developments noted in *McGee*, of course, have only accelerated in the generation since that case was decided.

Nevertheless, we have never accepted the proposition that state lines are irrelevant for jurisdictional purposes, nor could we, and remain faithful to the principles of interstate federalism embodied in the Constitution. The economic interdependence of the States was foreseen and desired by the Framers. In the Commerce Clause, they provided that the Nation was to be a common market, a "free trade unit" in which the States are debarred from acting as separable economic entities. But the Framers also intended that the States retain many essential attributes of sovereignty, including, in particular, the sovereign power to try causes in their courts. The sovereignty of each State, in turn, implied a limitation on the sovereignty of all of its sister States—a limitation express or implicit in both the original scheme of the Constitution and the Fourteenth Amendment.

Hence, even while abandoning the shibboleth that "[t]he authority of every tribunal is necessarily restricted by the territorial limits of the State in which it is established," *Pennoyer v. Neff*, we emphasized that the reasonableness of asserting jurisdiction over the defendant must be assessed "in the context of our federal system of government," *International Shoe*, and stressed that the Due Process Clause ensures not only fairness, but also the "orderly administration of the laws." As we noted in *Hanson v. Denckla*:

> "As technological progress has increased the flow of commerce between the States, the need for jurisdiction over nonresidents has undergone a similar increase. At the same time, progress in communications and transportation has made the defense of a suit in a foreign tribunal less burdensome. In response to these changes, the requirements for personal jurisdiction over nonresidents have evolved from the rigid rule of *Pennoyer v. Neff*, to the flexible standard of *International Shoe*. But it is a mistake to assume that this trend heralds the eventual demise of all restrictions on the personal jurisdiction of state courts. Those restrictions are more than a guarantee of immunity from inconvenient or distant litigation. They are a consequence of territorial limitations on the power of the respective States."

Thus, the Due Process Clause "does not contemplate that a state may make binding a judgment in personam against an individual or corporate defendant with which the state has no contacts, ties, or relations." *International Shoe*. Even if the defendant would suffer minimal or no inconvenience from being forced to litigate before the tribunals of another State; even if the forum State has a strong interest in applying its law to the controversy; even if the forum State is the most convenient location for litigation, the Due Process Clause, acting as an instrument of interstate federalism, may sometimes act to divest the State of its power to render a valid judgment. *Hanson v. Denckla.*

III

Applying these principles to the case at hand, we find in the record before us a total absence of those affiliating circumstances that are a necessary predicate to any exercise of state-court jurisdiction. Petitioners carry on no activity whatsoever in Oklahoma. They close no sales and perform no services there. They avail themselves of none of the privileges and benefits of Oklahoma law. They solicit no business there either through salespersons or through advertising reasonably calculated to reach the State. Nor does the record show that they regularly sell cars at wholesale or retail to Oklahoma customers or residents or that they indirectly, through others, serve or seek to serve the Oklahoma market. In short, respondents seek to base jurisdiction on one, isolated occurrence and whatever inferences can be drawn therefrom: the fortuitous circumstance that a single Audi automobile, sold in New York to New York residents, happened to suffer an accident while passing through Oklahoma.

It is argued, however, that because an automobile is mobile by its very design and purpose it was "foreseeable" that the Robinsons' Audi would cause injury in Oklahoma. Yet "foreseeability" alone has never been a sufficient benchmark for personal jurisdiction under the Due Process Clause. In *Hanson v. Denckla*, it was no doubt foreseeable that the settlor of a Delaware trust would subsequently move to Florida and seek to exercise a power of appointment there; yet we held that Florida courts could not constitutionally exercise jurisdiction over a Delaware trustee that had no other contacts with the forum State. In *Kulko v. California Superior Court*, it was surely "foreseeable" that a divorced wife would move to California from New York, the domicile of the marriage, and that a minor daughter would live with the mother. Yet we held that California could not exercise jurisdiction in a child-support action over the former husband who had remained in New York.

If foreseeability were the criterion, a local California tire retailer could be forced to defend in Pennsylvania when a blowout occurs there, see Erlanger Mills, Inc. v. Cohoes Fibre Mills, Inc., 239 F.2d 502, 507 (4th Cir. 1956); a Wisconsin seller of a defective automobile jack could be haled before a distant court for damage caused in New Jersey, Reilly v. Phil Tolkan Pontiac, Inc., 372 F. Supp. 1205 (D.N.J. 1974); or a Florida soft-drink concessionaire could be summoned to Alaska to account for injuries happening there, see Uppgren v. Executive Aviation Services, Inc., 304 F. Supp. 165, 170–171 (Minn. 1969). Every seller of chattels would in effect appoint the chattel his agent for service of process. His amenability to suit would travel with the chattel.[11] * * *

---

11. Respondents' counsel, at oral argument, sought to limit the reach of the foreseeability standard by suggesting that there is something unique about automobiles. It is true that automobiles are

This is not to say, of course, that foreseeability is wholly irrelevant. But the foreseeability that is critical to due process analysis is not the mere likelihood that a product will find its way into the forum State. Rather, it is that the defendant's conduct and connection with the forum State are such that he should reasonably anticipate being haled into court there. See *Kulko v. California Superior Court.* The Due Process Clause, by ensuring the "orderly administration of the laws," *International Shoe*, gives a degree of predictability to the legal system that allows potential defendants to structure their primary conduct with some minimum assurance as to where that conduct will and will not render them liable to suit.

When a corporation "purposefully avails itself of the privilege of conducting activities within the forum State," *Hanson v. Denckla*, it has clear notice that it is subject to suit there, and can act to alleviate the risk of burdensome litigation by procuring insurance, passing the expected costs on to customers, or, if the risks are too great, severing its connection with the State. Hence if the sale of a product of a manufacturer or distributor such as Audi or Volkswagen is not simply an isolated occurrence, but arises from the efforts of the manufacturer or distributor to serve, directly or indirectly, the market for its product in other States, it is not unreasonable to subject it to suit in one of those States if its allegedly defective merchandise has there been the source of injury to its owner or to others. The forum State does not exceed its powers under the Due Process Clause if it asserts personal jurisdiction over a corporation that delivers its products into the stream of commerce with the expectation that they will be purchased by consumers in the forum State. Cf.* Gray v. American Radiator & Standard Sanitary Corp., 176 N.E.2d 761 (Ill. 1961).

But there is no such or similar basis for Oklahoma jurisdiction over World-Wide or Seaway in this case. Seaway's sales are made in Massena, N.Y. World-Wide's market, although substantially larger, is limited to dealers in New York, New Jersey, and Connecticut. There is no evidence of record that any automobiles distributed by World-Wide are sold to retail customers outside this tristate area. It is foreseeable that the purchasers of automobiles sold by World-Wide and Seaway may take them to Oklahoma. But the mere "unilateral activity of those who claim some relationship with a nonresident defendant cannot satisfy the requirement of contact with the forum State." *Hanson v. Denckla.*

---

uniquely mobile, that they did play a crucial role in the expansion of personal jurisdiction through the fiction of implied consent, e.g., *Hess v. Pawloski*, and that some of the cases have treated the automobile as a "dangerous instrumentality." But today, under the regime of *International Shoe*, we see no difference for jurisdictional purposes between an automobile and any other chattel. The "dangerous instrumentality" concept apparently was never used to support personal jurisdiction; and to the extent it has relevance today it bears not on jurisdiction but on the possible desirability of imposing substantive principles of tort law such as strict liability.

* [The Bluebook (20th ed. 2015) explains "cf." as follows: "Cited authority supports a proposition different from the main proposition but sufficiently analogous to lend support. * * * The citation's relevance will usually be clear to the reader only if it is explained. Parenthetical explanations * * * are therefore strongly recommended." — Eds.]

In a variant on the previous argument, it is contended that jurisdiction can be supported by the fact that petitioners earn substantial revenue from goods used in Oklahoma. The Oklahoma Supreme Court so found drawing the inference that because one automobile sold by petitioners had been used in Oklahoma, others might have been used there also. While this inference seems less than compelling on the facts of the instant case, we need not question the court's factual findings in order to reject its reasoning.

This argument seems to make the point that the purchase of automobiles in New York, from which the petitioners earn substantial revenue, would not occur *but for* the fact that the automobiles are capable of use in distant States like Oklahoma. Respondents observe that the very purpose of an automobile is to travel, and that travel of automobiles sold by petitioners is facilitated by an extensive chain of Volkswagen service centers throughout the country, including some in Oklahoma.[12] However, financial benefits accruing to the defendant from a collateral relation to the forum State will not support jurisdiction if they do not stem from a constitutionally cognizable contact with that State. See *Kulko v. California Superior Court.* In our view, whatever marginal revenues petitioners may receive by virtue of the fact that their products are capable of use in Oklahoma is far too attenuated a contact to justify that State's exercise of in personam jurisdiction over them.

Because we find that petitioners have no "contacts, ties, or relations" with the State of Oklahoma, *International Shoe*, the judgment of the Supreme Court of Oklahoma is

Reversed.

Justice Brennan, dissenting.

The Court's opinion[] focus[es] tightly on the existence of contacts between the forum and the defendant. In so doing, they accord too little weight to the strength of the forum State's interest in the case and fail to explore whether there would be any actual inconvenience to the defendant. * * *

Surely *International Shoe* contemplated that the significance of the contacts necessary to support jurisdiction would diminish if some other consideration helped establish that jurisdiction would be fair and reasonable. The interests of the State and other parties in proceeding with the case in a particular forum are such considerations. *McGee v. International Life Ins. Co.*, for instance, accorded great importance to a State's "manifest interest in providing effective means of redress" for its citizens.

* * *

In [this case], the interest of the forum State and its connection to the litigation is strong. The automobile accident underlying the litigation occurred in Oklahoma. The plaintiffs were hospitalized in Oklahoma when they brought suit. Essential witnesses and evidence were in Oklahoma. The State has a legitimate interest in enforcing its laws designed to keep its highway system safe, and the trial can proceed at least as efficiently in Oklahoma as anywhere else.

---

12. As we have noted, petitioners earn no direct revenues from these service centers.

The petitioners are not unconnected with the forum. Although both sell automobiles within limited sales territories, each sold the automobile which in fact was driven to Oklahoma where it was involved in an accident.[8] It may be true, as the Court suggests, that each sincerely intended to limit its commercial impact to the limited territory, and that each intended to accept the benefits and protection of the laws only of those States within the territory. But obviously these were unrealistic hopes that cannot be treated as an automatic constitutional shield.[9]

An automobile simply is not a stationary item or one designed to be used in one place. An automobile is *intended* to be moved around. Someone in the business of selling large numbers of automobiles can hardly plead ignorance of their mobility or pretend that the automobiles stay put after they are sold. It is not merely that a dealer in automobiles foresees that they will move. The dealer actually intends that the purchasers will use the automobiles to travel to distant States where the dealer does not directly "do business." The sale of an automobile does *purposefully* inject the vehicle into the stream of interstate commerce so that it can travel to distant States.

This case is similar to Ohio v. Wyandotte Chemicals Corp., 401 U.S. 493 (1971). There we indicated, in the course of denying leave to file an original-jurisdiction case, that corporations having no direct contact with Ohio could constitutionally be brought to trial in Ohio because they dumped pollutants into streams outside Ohio's limits which ultimately, through the action of the water, reached Lake Erie and affected Ohio. No corporate acts, only their consequences, occurred in Ohio. The stream of commerce is just as natural a force as a stream of water, and it was equally predictable that the cars petitioners released would reach distant States.[10]

The Court accepts that a State may exercise jurisdiction over a distributor which "serves" that State "indirectly" by "deliver[ing] its products into the stream of commerce with the expectation that they will be purchased by consumers in the forum State." It is difficult to see why the Constitution should distinguish between a case involving goods which reach a distant State through a chain of distribution and a case involving goods which reach the same State because a consumer, using them as the dealer knew the customer would, took them there.[11] In each case the seller pur-

8. On the basis of this fact the state court inferred that the petitioners derived substantial revenue from goods used in Oklahoma. The inference is not without support. Certainly, were use of goods accepted as a relevant contact, a plaintiff would not need to have an exact count of the number of petitioners' cars that are used in Oklahoma.

9. Moreover, imposing liability in this case would not so undermine certainty as to destroy an automobile dealer's ability to do business. According jurisdiction does not expand liability except in the marginal case where a plaintiff cannot afford to bring an action except in the plaintiff's own State. In addition, these petitioners are represented by insurance companies. They not only could, but did, purchase insurance to protect them should they stand trial and lose the case. The costs of the insurance no doubt are passed on to customers.

10. One might argue that it was more predictable that the pollutants would reach Ohio than that one of petitioners' cars would reach Oklahoma. The Court's analysis, however, excludes jurisdiction in a contiguous State such as Pennsylvania as surely as in more distant States such as Oklahoma.

11. For example, I cannot understand the constitutional distinction between selling an item in New Jersey and selling an item in New York expecting it to be used in New Jersey.

posefully injects the goods into the stream of commerce and those goods predictably are used in the forum State.[12]

Furthermore, an automobile seller derives substantial benefits from States other than its own. A large part of the value of automobiles is the extensive, nationwide network of highways. Significant portions of that network have been constructed by and are maintained by the individual States, including Oklahoma. The States, through their highway programs, contribute in a very direct and important way to the value of petitioners' businesses. Additionally, a network of other related dealerships with their service departments operates throughout the country under the protection of the laws of the various States, including Oklahoma, and enhances the value of petitioners' businesses by facilitating their customers' traveling.

Thus, the Court errs in its conclusion that "petitioners have no 'contacts, ties, or relations'" with Oklahoma. There obviously are contacts, and, given Oklahoma's connection to the litigation, the contacts are sufficiently significant to make it fair and reasonable for the petitioners to submit to Oklahoma's jurisdiction.

It may be that affirmance of the judgment * * * would approach the outer limits of *International Shoe*'s jurisdictional principle. But that principle, with its almost exclusive focus on the rights of defendants, may be outdated. * * *

As the Court acknowledges, both the nationalization of commerce and the ease of transportation and communication have accelerated in the generation since 1957. The model of society on which the *International Shoe* Court based its opinion is no longer accurate. Business people, no matter how local their businesses, cannot assume that goods remain in the business' locality. Customers and goods can be anywhere else in the country usually in a matter of hours and always in a matter of a very few days.

In answering the question whether or not it is fair and reasonable to allow a particular forum to hold a trial binding on a particular defendant, the interests of the forum State and other parties loom large in today's world and surely are entitled to as much weight as are the interests of the defendant. The "orderly administration of the laws" provides a firm basis for according some protection to the interests of plaintiffs and States as well as of defendants. Certainly, I cannot see how a defendant's right to due process is violated if the defendant suffers no inconvenience.

The conclusion I draw is that constitutional concepts of fairness no longer require the extreme concern for defendants that was once necessary. Rather, as I wrote in dissent from *Shaffer v. Heitner* [Note: we will see this case in Section B.6 below], minimum contacts must exist "among the *parties*, the contested transaction, and the forum State." The contacts between any two of these should not be determinative. * * *

12. The manufacturer in the case cited by the Court, Gray v. American Radiator & Standard Sanitary Corp., 176 N.E.2d 761 (Ill. 1961), had no more control over which States its goods would reach than did the petitioners in this case.

The Court's opinion * * * suggests that the defendant ought to be subject to a State's jurisdiction only if he has contacts with the State "such that he should reasonably anticipate being haled into court there."[18] There is nothing unreasonable or unfair, however, about recognizing commercial reality. Given the tremendous mobility of goods and people, and the inability of businessmen to control where goods are taken by customers (or retailers), I do not think that the defendant should be in complete control of the geographical stretch of his amenability to suit. Jurisdiction is no longer premised on the notion that nonresident defendants have somehow impliedly consented to suit. People should understand that they are held responsible for the consequences of their actions and that in our society most actions have consequences affecting many States. When an action in fact causes injury in another State, the actor should be prepared to answer for it there unless defending in that State would be unfair for some reason other than that a state boundary must be crossed.

In effect the Court is allowing defendants to assert the sovereign rights of their home States. The expressed fear is that otherwise all limits on personal jurisdiction would disappear. But the argument's premise is wrong. I would not abolish limits on jurisdiction or strip state boundaries of all significance. I would still require the plaintiff to demonstrate sufficient contacts among the parties, the forum, and the litigation to make the forum a reasonable State in which to hold the trial.

I would also, however, strip the defendant of an unjustified veto power over certain very appropriate fora — a power the defendant justifiably enjoyed long ago when communication and travel over long distances were slow and unpredictable and when notions of state sovereignty were impractical and exaggerated. But I repeat that that is not today's world. If a plaintiff can show that his chosen forum State has a sufficient interest in the litigation (or sufficient contacts with the defendant), then the defendant who cannot show some real injury to a constitutionally protected interest should have no constitutional excuse not to appear.

[The dissenting opinions of Justices Marshall and Blackmun are omitted.]

Notes and Questions

1. In *World-Wide Volkswagen*, the Court (quoting *Hanson*) stressed that the defendant must have "purposefully avail[ed] itself of the privilege of conducting activities within the forum state." The requirement of purposeful availment seems to reflect the Court's underlying belief that defendants should know in advance and be able to control where they will be subject to suit. Why should this be so? Defendants are sometimes held "strictly liable" for the injuries they cause without regard to whether they were negligent or took steps to prevent injuries. What would be wrong with "ju-

18. The Court suggests that this is the critical foreseeability rather than the likelihood that the product will go to the forum State. But the reasoning begs the question. A defendant cannot know if his action will subject him to jurisdiction in another State until we have declared what the law of jurisdiction is.

risdictional strict liability," under which manufacturers can be sued anywhere they or their products can cause injury? As one commentator has wryly observed in a different context, it is as if the Court thinks "an accused is more concerned with where he will be hanged than whether." Linda Silberman, Shaffer v. Heitner: *The End of an Era*, 53 N.Y.U. L. REV. 33, 88 (1978).

2. The majority opinion of the Court focuses on the defendants and not on the plaintiffs. However, the Robinsons were badly burned in the accident and it would likely have been difficult for them to travel to New York. Should the Court consider the burdens of distant litigation on the plaintiffs?

3. The Court states that in assessing a defendant's conduct, the foreseeability of a product's ending up in the forum is not the test. Instead, the relevant inquiry is whether in light of the defendant's conduct and connections with the state, he "should reasonably anticipate being haled into court there." Isn't this argument completely circular? Aren't reasonable expectations about where you can be haled into court a function of what the law provides? In other words, if the Supreme Court had decided in *World-Wide Volkswagen* that sellers can be sued wherever their products end up, then, from that time on, all sellers should reasonably expect to be haled into court wherever their products ended up. Aside from the role of law in shaping expectations, how can a company named "*World-Wide Volkswagen*" not expect to be sued in far away places?

One interesting question on which the Court has given no significant guidance is when defendant's contacts are to be measured. Must the defendant have contacts by the time the claim arose, or at the time the case is filed, or are post-filing contacts relevant? Professor Peterson argues that the confusion on this point in the lower federal courts traces to the Supreme Court's failure to explain why due process requires the establishment of minimum contacts. Todd David Peterson, *The Timing of Minimum Contacts*, 79 GEO. WASH. L. REV. 101 (2010). He finds that more recent Supreme Court cases have not resolved the question. Todd David Peterson, *The Timing of Minimum Contacts After* Goodyear *and* McIntyre, 80 GEO. WASH. L. REV. ARGUENDO 1, 20 (2011).

4. Consider the following variations on *World-Wide Volkswagen*. Would the seller be subject to suit in Oklahoma?

(a) When the Robinsons purchased their car, they explicitly and repeatedly told the salesman that they were planning to take the car to Oklahoma.

(b) In addition to (a) above, at the Robinsons' request, the seller arranged to have the car titled and tagged in Oklahoma.

(c) In addition to (a) and (b) above, the seller arranged to ship the car to Oklahoma for the Robinsons.

5. Review question 4(i) after *International Shoe.* Consider in particular the discussion in *World-Wide Volkswagen* about "corporation[s] that deliver [their] products into the stream of commerce." You will notice that the Court cites *Gray v. American Radiator & Standard Sanitary Corp.* That case is described supra in Section B.3.

Notice that the Court cited *Gray* with a "cf." Does this mean the Court agrees or disagrees with the result in *Gray*?

6. The Fourteenth Amendment was passed in the wake of the Civil War to secure the rights of newly freed slaves. Given this history, what do you think of the Court's assertion that the Due Process Clause of the Fourteenth Amendment is an "instrument of interstate federalism." Is this an historically accurate description of the purposes behind the Fourteenth Amendment?

7. Why would it upset the balance of interstate federalism to allow Oklahoma to hear this case? Doesn't Oklahoma have a significant territorial connection to this case? Compare this case with *Hess v. Pawloski.*

8. Two years after *World-Wide Volkswagen*, the Court retreated from its emphasis on federalism. In an opinion written by Justice White (the author of *World-Wide Volkswagen*), the Court explained:

> The personal jurisdiction requirement recognizes and protects an individual liberty interest. It represents a restriction on judicial power not as a matter of sovereignty, but as a matter of individual liberty. * * * The restriction on state sovereign power described in *World-Wide Volkswagen Corp.*, however, must be seen as ultimately a function of the individual liberty interest preserved by the Due Process Clause. That Clause is the only source of the personal jurisdiction requirement and the Clause itself makes no mention of federalism concerns. Furthermore, if the federalism concept operated as an independent restriction on the sovereign power of the court, it would not be possible to waive the personal jurisdiction requirement: Individual actions cannot change the powers of sovereignty, although the individual can subject himself to powers from which he may otherwise be protected.

Insurance Corp. v. Compagnie des Bauxites, 456 U.S. 694, 702–03 & n.10 (1982). Thus, as the Court now describes personal jurisdiction, the defendant has a constitutionally protected *liberty interest* in not being subject to the jurisdiction of a state with which that defendant has not purposefully connected herself. Do you agree that personal jurisdiction is one of the fundamental liberties protected by the Constitution?

9. Should corporations have a constitutionally protected right to "liberty"? Are corporations "persons" within the meaning of the Fourteenth Amendment? In Santa Clara County v. Southern Pacific R., 118 U.S. 394, 396 (1886), the Court held that they are. The Court offered no explanation for its holding and simply stated:

> The court does not wish to hear argument on the question whether the provision in the Fourteenth Amendment to the Constitution, which forbids a State to deny to any person within its jurisdiction the equal protection of the laws, applies to these corporations. We are of the opinion that it does.

More recently, the Court has held that corporations have freedom of speech rights protected by the First and Fourteenth Amendments. See Citizens United v. Federal

Elec. Comm'n, 558 U.S. 310 (2010). See also Burwell v. Hobby Lobby Stores, Inc., 134 S. Ct. 2751 (2014) (recognizing religious freedom rights, as a matter of statutory law, for small, closely-held corporations).

10. The Court also cites Kulko v. Superior Court, 436 U.S. 84 (1978). That case involved a suit for child support payments. Until their divorce, the Kulkos had been domiciled in New York. Following the divorce, the ex-wife moved to California, and the husband remained in New York with custody of their two children. Later the children requested that they be allowed to live with the mother. The father complied with that request and purchased a one-way plane ticket for one child (the mother sent a ticket for the other child). Upon their arrival in California, the mother filed suit in California seeking child support from the father. The Supreme Court held that California did not have jurisdiction over the father. The Court explained: "A father who agrees, in the interest of family harmony and his children's preferences, to allow them to spend more time in California than was required under a separation agreement can hardly be said to have 'purposefully availed himself' of the 'benefits and protections' of California's laws." Id. at 94. In its opinion, the Court seemed concerned that allowing jurisdiction would discourage parents from accommodating the "interests of family harmony." But doesn't this look at only half the transaction? After *Kulko*, custodial parents may be more willing to relinquish custody, but non-custodial parents may be less willing to accept custody knowing that they will not be able to get a support order without going to the other parent's home to litigate. Would the result in *Kulko* be different if Mr. Kulko had sent his ex-wife an exploding package rather than a teenager?

11. Following the Supreme Court's decision in *World-Wide Volkswagen*, the Robinsons' claim against Audi and Volkswagen was removed to federal court,* where it was tried. The Robinsons lost, but on appeal, the Court of Appeals for the Tenth Circuit ordered a retrial on their claim against Volkswagen. In the retrial, the Robinsons lost again, and this result was affirmed on appeal. The case did not end there. The Robinsons became acquainted with a University of Arizona law professor who had previously owned a Volkswagen dealership and believed Audi and Volkswagen had concealed critical information about the corporate interrelationship of those two companies. The Robinsons then filed a new lawsuit against both Volkswagen and their attorneys for fraudulently concealing information and against the Robinsons' prior lawyers for legal malpractice. This suit was filed in federal court in their new home state of Arizona. This suit generated its own personal jurisdiction battle and was transferred to the federal court in Oklahoma. In May 1995, the Robinsons lost their fraud claim. See Robinson v. Volkswagenwerk AG, 56 F.3d 1268 (10th Cir. 1995); Robinson v. Audi Aktiengesellschaft, 56 F.3d 1259 (10th Cir. 1995). See Charles Adams, World-Wide Volkswagen v. Woodson — *The Rest of the Story*, 72 Neb. L. Rev. 1122 (1993). For a further discussion

* Today the case could not have been removed because it became removable more than a year after the suit was filed. See 28 U.S.C. § 1446(b). Removal is discussed in detail in Chapter 4.

of the case, see Note 7 following *Louisville & Nashville Railroad Co. v. Mottley*, in Chapter 4.C.4.b.i, infra.

Personal Jurisdiction in Federal Court

All of the cases we have seen so far were filed originally in state court. You might be wondering whether it would be possible to avoid entirely the limits of personal jurisdiction by suing in federal court. Unfortunately, in most cases this will not work. Absent special legislation, a federal court has personal jurisdiction only if a state court in the state in which the federal court sits would have had personal jurisdiction. It is not obvious why this should be so. First, federal courts are organized by district, not by state.* Second, personal jurisdiction seems to focus on the relationship between the defendant and the sovereign government that is conducting the trial. When litigation is in federal court, the "sovereign" is the United States. One might conclude that so long as the defendant has connections with the United States, that should suffice for personal jurisdiction.

Notwithstanding the foregoing considerations, it is now clearly established that in most situations, a federal court has jurisdiction only if the state in which it sits would have jurisdiction. This understanding is embodied in Rule 4(k)(1)(A).

Rule 4 identifies several exceptions to this general rule. Rule 4(k)(1)(C) provides for jurisdiction "when authorized by a federal statute." In a few instances, Congress has passed such statutes providing for what is usually known as "nationwide service of process." These statutes permit the defendant to be served anywhere in the United States and provide personal jurisdiction regardless of whether there would have been jurisdiction in any state court. Congress has authorized nationwide service of process in areas such as antitrust, securities, bankruptcy, and interpleader.

Another exception is Rule 4(k)(2) which provides for personal jurisdiction in any federal court where: (1) the claim is based on federal law, (2) jurisdiction is constitutional, and (3) there is no state which would have personal jurisdiction. The use of Rule 4(k)(2) is illustrated by Graduate Management Admissions Council v. Raju, 241 F. Supp. 2d 589 (E.D. Va. 2003). There the plaintiff brought federal copyright, trademark, cyberpiracy and unfair competition claims against an Indian citizen who ran a web site that offered material to prepare for the Graduate Management Admission Test. Suit was brought in federal court in Virginia but the court found that the defendant had insufficient contacts with Virginia to satisfy the Fourteenth Amendment. However, the court upheld personal jurisdiction relying on Rule 4(k)(2). The court found that the defendant had "targeted the United States market" and had sufficient contacts with the United States as a whole to satisfy Rule 4(k)(2).

---

* Only one federal district includes more than one state, but many of the larger states include multiple federal districts. The District of Wyoming includes those portions of Yellowstone National Park situated in Montana and Idaho. See 28 U.S.C. § 131.

Nationwide service of process and Rule 4(k)(2) present potential due process problems, although the issue is governed by the Due Process Clause of the Fifth Amendment, rather than the Due Process Clause of the Fourteenth Amendment.* With nationwide service of process, a defendant who lived his entire life in Florida and engaged in the alleged improper activities in Florida, might nonetheless be subject to suit in federal court in California. Would this be constitutional? Although the Supreme Court has not directly addressed the issue, most lower courts have held that all the Fifth Amendment requires is contacts with the "sovereign," i.e., the United States. Under this analysis, it is constitutional for a citizen of Florida to be sued in federal court in California, since the defendant's contacts with Florida obviously are contacts with the United States. See, e.g., Federal Trade Commission v. Jim Walter Corp., 651 F.2d 251 (5th Cir. 1981). Accord Busch v. Buchman, Buchman & O'Brien, 11 F.3d 1255 (5th Cir. 1994); Go-Video, Inc. v. Akai Electric Co., 885 F.2d 1406 (9th Cir. 1989); Fitzsimmons v. Barton, 589 F.2d 330 (7th Cir. 1979); Mariash v. Morrill, 496 F.2d 1138 (2d Cir. 1974); Travis v. Anthes Imperial Ltd., 473 F.2d 515 (8th Cir. 1973). Even if there are sufficient "contacts," basic fairness may require that the forum is not unreasonably burdensome. See, e.g., Republic of Panama v. BCCI Holdings (Luxembourg), 119 F.3d 935 (11th Cir. 1997); Oxford First Corp. v. PNC Liquidating Corp., 372 F. Supp. 191 (E.D. Pa. 1974). However, some courts have concluded that this concern should not be treated as a constitutional matter and can be addressed through statutory venue or transfer provisions (which are discussed in greater detail in Chapter 5). See ESAB Group, Inc. v. Centricut, Inc., 126 F.3d 617, 627 (4th Cir. 1997).

Another unanswered question concerning Fifth Amendment limits on personal jurisdiction is whether that Amendment requires the same type of "purposeful availment" that is required under the Fourteenth Amendment. Specifically, are foreigners who lack *purposeful* contacts with the U.S. constitutionally protected from suits in U.S. federal courts, even if Congress has determined that it is in our national interest to allow such suits? For example, suppose Congress decided that foreign manufacturers of goods should be subject to suit in the U.S. whenever their products cause harm here. Most courts and commentators have assumed that the requirement of purposeful availment developed in the Fourteenth Amendment context would likewise apply under the Fifth Amendment. At least one commentator has questioned this assumption, arguing that "[t]here is no reason to assume that the scope of legitimate judicial authority of the United States as it operates in the international community is essentially parallel to the scope of authority of each of our individual states," and concluding that it is constitutional under the Fifth Amendment for U.S. courts to assert personal jurisdiction solely on the basis of effect in the U.S., without any requirement of "purposeful availment." Wendy Perdue, *Aliens, the Internet, and "Purposeful Availment"*:

* The Fifth Amendment prohibits violations of due process by the U.S. government, while the Fourteenth Amendment prohibits such violations by states.

A Reassessment of Fifth Amendment Limits on Personal Jurisidiction, 98 Nw. U. L. Rev. 455, 461, 470 (2004).

Note on Keeton, Calder, *and* Walden

In 1984, the Supreme Court addressed personal jurisdiction in two libel cases. One, Keeton v. Hustler Magazine, Inc., 465 U.S. 770 (1984), was brought against *Hustler* magazine in New Hampshire. The suit alleged defamation in one issue of *Hustler* magazine that was distributed nationwide. The plaintiff was a citizen of New York, with little connection to New Hampshire. She sued in New Hampshire because it was the only state in which her action would not have been barred by the statute of limitations. She sued for damages for the injury to her reputation suffered in New Hampshire, as well as the injury which she suffered nationwide.

The Supreme Court upheld personal jurisdiction not only as to her injury suffered in New Hampshire from the copies of the magazine that were distributed in New Hampshire, but also for her injury suffered in all other states as a result of the copies that were distributed there. The Supreme Court explained that New Hampshire has a "substantial interest in cooperating with other States * * * to provide a forum for efficiently litigating all issues and damages claims arising out of a libel in a unitary proceeding." Id. at 777. The Court upheld jurisdiction despite the plaintiff's minimal connection with New Hampshire. "[W]e have not to date required a plaintiff to have 'minimum contacts' with the forum State before permitting that State to assert personal jurisdiction over a nonresident defendant. On the contrary, we have upheld the assertion of jurisdiction where such contacts were entirely lacking." Id. at 779.

The Court did not hold that *Hustler* was subject to suit in New Hampshire on all possible causes of action. The Court held: "In the instant case, respondent's activities in the forum may not be so substantial as to support jurisdiction over a cause of action unrelated to those activities. But respondent is carrying on a 'part of its general business' in New Hampshire, and that is sufficient to support jurisdiction when the cause of action arises out of the very activity being conducted, in part, in New Hampshire." Id. at 779–80.

In the companion case of Calder v. Jones, 465 U.S. 783 (1984), the Court upheld jurisdiction in California over the editor and writer of an allegedly defamatory article about a California citizen (Academy Award–winning actress Shirley Jones). Both the writer and the editor were citizens of Florida. Neither traveled to California in connection with researching this article. The article was written and edited in Florida. The *National Enquirer*, which is widely distributed in California, published the article. In upholding jurisdiction against the writer and editor (jurisdiction over the *National Enquirer* was not disputed), the Court explained:

> The allegedly libelous story concerned the California activities of a California resident. It impugned the professionalism of an entertainer whose television career was centered in California. The article was drawn from California sources, and the brunt of the harm, in terms both of respon-

> dent's emotional distress and the injury to her professional reputation was suffered in California. In sum, California is the focal point both of the story and of the harm suffered. Jurisdiction over petitioners is therefore proper in California based on the "effects" of their Florida conduct in California.
>
> * * * [P]etitioners are not charged with mere untargeted negligence. Rather, their intentional, and allegedly tortious, actions were expressly aimed at California. Petitioner South wrote and petitioner Calder edited an article that they knew would have a potentially devastating impact upon respondent. And they knew that the brunt of that injury would be felt by respondent in the State in which she lives and works and in which the National Enquirer has its largest circulation. Under these circumstances, petitioners must "reasonably anticipate being haled into court there" to answer for the truth of the statements made in their article.

Id. at 788–89, 789–90.

Calder makes clear that the defendant need not set foot in the forum to be subject to personal jurisdiction. It can be sufficient that the defendant causes "effects" in the forum. The Court returned to the "*Calder* effects" test in Walden v. Fiore, 134 S. Ct. 1115, 1122 (2014). The plaintiffs in that case were professional gamblers who lived in Nevada. They were returning to Nevada from a gambling trip to the Caribbean. On a stopover in the Atlanta airport, a police officer working for the federal government seized a large amount of cash from their luggage. He prepared an allegedly false affidavit that connected the cash to illegal drug activity. Upon investigation, the United States Attorney's office in Atlanta determined that the money was not related to drug activity and returned it to the plaintiffs. They sued the police officer in Nevada, arguing that the officer's preparation of the allegedly false affidavit caused effects in Nevada by depriving them of their funds. The Ninth Circuit upheld jurisdiction on the ground that the officer "expressly aimed" the affidavit at Nevada because he knew it would harm people who resided there.

The Supreme Court reversed unanimously, and explained that "it is the defendant, not the plaintiff or third parties, who must create contacts with the forum State." The plaintiffs were denied use of the money in Nevada not because of anything that occurred in Nevada, but because they chose to reside there. In contrast, the defendants in *Calder* reached out by telephone to sources in California, wrote about the California activities of the plaintiff, and caused reputational harm in California by publishing alleged falsehoods about the plaintiff. In short, the Court in *Walden* concluded: "our 'minimum contacts' analysis looks to the defendant's contacts with the forum State itself, not the defendant's contacts with persons who reside there." Do *Calder* and *Walden* permit personal jurisdiction over a defendant based upon the defendant's Internet connections with the forum? Under what circumstances? The Court has yet to address a case involving personal jurisdiction based upon Internet contact. We return to that issue in Section B.8 below.

Why Litigants Care About Where Litigation Occurs

As you read the personal jurisdiction cases, one issue that may occur to you is why litigants seem to care so much about the location of the litigation. One reason might be that they want to avoid an inconvenient forum. Distant litigation could burden a party in several ways. First, it may make it more difficult to subpoena witnesses. Second, it may be more expensive to ship and store documents or other evidence. Third, the lawyer "back home," who may have counseled the party on the underlying transaction will probably not be a member of the bar in another state. Thus, the party will have to hire a new lawyer. Yet in an age of instant telecommunications and easy transportation, concern about inconvenience sometimes seems an unlikely explanation. Remember, a dismissal for lack of personal jurisdiction does not protect a defendant from litigation; it simply means that the litigation will occur in a different place. Therefore, the only expenses that a defendant would save are the incremental *additional* costs associated with litigating in one place rather than another.

Another possible reason litigants might care about the location of litigation is that they might believe that judges and juries in a particular location are more likely to be biased for or against them. As you will see in Chapter 4, the Constitution explicitly provides one solution to the problem of bias — it grants federal courts jurisdiction over cases between citizens of different states.

Probably the most common reason that litigants care about the location of jurisdiction has nothing to do with inconvenience or bias — it has to do with what law will be applied. We are a nation of 50 states, and the laws of those states vary. In *Keeton*, for example, New Hampshire was the only state with a six-year statute of limitations for libel. The statute of limitations on this claim had expired in all the other states.

In any litigation, the court must determine what law to apply to the dispute. A court does not always apply the law of its state. For example, suppose that there had been an automobile accident in Utah, but the lawsuit concerning the accident was in California. California would certainly refer to Utah's traffic and speed laws in determining the negligence of either driver. While in the foregoing example it seems clear that the court should apply Utah law, it is not always so clear which state's law should govern a dispute. Suppose that under the law of California, one spouse can sue the other, but that under the law of Utah there is inter-spousal immunity. If a California husband and wife have an auto accident in Utah, which state's rules concerning inter-spousal lawsuits should apply? States disagree about whose law to apply in this case. Some states apply the law of the place of the accident. Other states conclude that rules about inter-spousal immunity are really the concern of the state where the married couple resides and thus would apply that state's laws on this issue.

It is unconstitutional for a state with no connection to the transaction or parties to apply its law even if it has personal jurisdiction. In such a case, the forum can adjudicate the dispute, but it would be required to apply the law of a state that has the requisite connection. However, the constitutional limits imposed on choice of law are extremely modest. Consider, for example, Allstate Ins. Co. v. Hague, 449 U.S.

302 (1981). There a Wisconsin citizen was killed in a motorcycle accident in Wisconsin. The decedent's widow sued their insurance company in Minnesota. The Supreme Court allowed Minnesota to apply its pro-plaintiff insurance law on the grounds that the decedent had been employed in and commuted to Minnesota prior to his death, the insurance company did business in Minnesota, and subsequent to the accident, the widow moved to Minnesota.

Because the constitutional limits on choice of law are so modest, it is frequently the case that the law of several states can constitutionally be applied to a dispute. Who decides what law will be applied? The forum does. Therefore, where different states would apply different laws, it may matter a great deal where the litigation occurs. Personal jurisdiction imposes significant limitations on the plaintiff's choice of forum and therefore limits the plaintiff's ability to choose a forum that will apply the most advantageous law.

Despite the practical and strategic implications of the plaintiff's choice of forum, the Supreme Court has never focused on these practical implications of personal jurisdiction in delineating the scope of the doctrine. Instead, the Court has focused on personal jurisdiction as a relatively abstract liberty interest. Would it be more appropriate for the Court to delineate the contours of personal jurisdiction by reference to the pragmatic concerns that motivate actual litigants?

Burger King Corp. v. Rudzewicz

471 U.S. 462, 105 S. Ct. 2174, 85 L. Ed. 2d 528 (1985)

JUSTICE BRENNAN delivered the opinion of the Court.

The State of Florida's long-arm statute extends jurisdiction to "[a]ny person, whether or not a citizen or resident of this state," who, inter alia, "[b]reach[es] a contract in this state by failing to perform acts required by the contract to be performed in this state," so long as the cause of action arises from the alleged contractual breach. FLA. STAT. § 48.193(1)(g) (Supp. 1984). The United States District Court for the Southern District of Florida, sitting in diversity, relied on this provision in exercising personal jurisdiction over a Michigan resident who allegedly had breached a franchise agreement with a Florida corporation by failing to make required payments in Florida. The question presented is whether this exercise of long-arm jurisdiction offended "traditional conception[s] of fair play and substantial justice" embodied in the Due Process Clause of the Fourteenth Amendment.

I

A

Burger King Corporation is a Florida corporation whose principal offices are in Miami. It is one of the world's largest restaurant organizations, with over 3,000 outlets in the 50 States, the Commonwealth of Puerto Rico, and 8 foreign nations. Burger King conducts approximately 80% of its business through a franchise operation that the company styles the "Burger King System" — "a comprehensive restaurant format and operating system for the sale of uniform and quality food products." Burger King licenses its franchisees to use its trademarks and service marks for a period of 20 years and leases standardized restaurant facilities to them for the same term. In addition, franchisees acquire a variety of proprietary information concerning the "standards, specifications, procedures and methods for operating a Burger King Restaurant." They also receive market research and advertising assistance; ongoing training in restaurant management;[3] and accounting, cost-control, and inventory-control guidance. By permitting franchisees to tap into Burger King's established national reputation and to benefit from proven procedures for dispensing standardized fare, this system enables them to go into the restaurant business with significantly lowered barriers to entry.

In exchange for these benefits, franchisees pay Burger King an initial $40,000 franchise fee and commit themselves to payment of monthly royalties, advertising and sales promotion fees, and rent computed in part from monthly gross sales. Franchisees also agree to submit to the national organization's exacting regulation of virtually every conceivable aspect of their operations. Burger King imposes these standards and undertakes its rigid regulation out of conviction that "[u]niformity of service, appearance, and quality of product is essential to the preservation of the Burger King image and the benefits accruing therefrom to both Franchisee and Franchisor."

Burger King oversees its franchise system through a two-tiered administrative structure. The governing contracts provide that the franchise relationship is established in Miami and governed by Florida law, and call for payment of all required fees and forwarding of all relevant notices to the Miami headquarters. The Miami headquarters sets policy and works directly with its franchisees in attempting to resolve major problems. Day-to-day monitoring of franchisees, however, is conducted through a network of 10 district offices which in turn report to the Miami headquarters.

The instant litigation grows out of Burger King's termination of one of its franchisees, and is aptly described by the franchisee as "a divorce proceeding among commercial partners." The appellee John Rudzewicz, a Michigan citizen and resident, is the senior partner in a Detroit accounting firm. In 1978, he was approached by Brian MacShara, the son of a business acquaintance, who suggested that they jointly apply to Burger King for a franchise in the Detroit area. MacShara proposed to serve as the manager of the restaurant if Rudzewicz would put up the investment capital; in exchange, the two would evenly share the profits. Believing that MacShara's idea offered attractive investment and tax-deferral opportunities, Rudzewicz agreed to the venture.

Rudzewicz and MacShara jointly applied for a franchise to Burger King's Birmingham, Michigan, district office in the autumn of 1978. Their application was forwarded to Burger King's Miami headquarters, which entered into a preliminary agreement with them in February 1979. During the ensuing four months it was agreed that Rudzewicz and MacShara would assume operation of an existing facility in Dray-

3. Mandatory training seminars are conducted at Burger King University in Miami and at Whopper College Regional Training Centers around the country.

ton Plains, Michigan. MacShara attended the prescribed management courses in Miami during this period, and the franchisees purchased $165,000 worth of restaurant equipment from Burger King's Davmor Industries division in Miami. Even before the final agreements were signed, however, the parties began to disagree over site-development fees, building design, computation of monthly rent, and whether the franchisees would be able to assign their liabilities to a corporation they had formed. During these disputes Rudzewicz and MacShara negotiated both with the Birmingham district office and with the Miami headquarters.[7] With some misgivings, Rudzewicz and MacShara finally obtained limited concessions from the Miami headquarters, signed the final agreements, and commenced operations in June 1979. By signing the final agreements, Rudzewicz obligated himself personally to payments exceeding $1 million over the 20-year franchise relationship.

The Drayton Plains facility apparently enjoyed steady business during the summer of 1979, but patronage declined after a recession began later that year. Rudzewicz and MacShara soon fell far behind in their monthly payments to Miami. Headquarters sent notices of default, and an extended period of negotiations began among the franchisees, the Birmingham district office, and the Miami headquarters. After several Burger King officials in Miami had engaged in prolonged but ultimately unsuccessful negotiations with the franchisees by mail and by telephone, headquarters terminated the franchise and ordered Rudzewicz and MacShara to vacate the premises. They refused and continued to occupy and operate the facility as a Burger King restaurant.

B

Burger King commenced the instant action in the United States District Court for the Southern District of Florida in May 1981, invoking that court's diversity jurisdiction pursuant to 28 U.S.C. § 1332(a) and its original jurisdiction over federal trademark disputes pursuant to § 1338(a). Burger King alleged that Rudzewicz and MacShara had breached their franchise obligations "within [the jurisdiction of] this district court" by failing to make the required payments "at plaintiff's place of business in Miami, Dade County, Florida," and also charged that they were tortiously infringing its trademarks and service marks through their continued, unauthorized operation as a Burger King restaurant. Burger King sought damages, injunctive relief, and costs and attorney's fees. Rudzewicz and MacShara entered special appearances and argued, inter alia, that because they were Michigan residents and because Burger King's claim did not "arise" within the Southern District of Florida, the District Court lacked personal jurisdiction over them. The District Court denied their motions after a hearing, holding that, pursuant to Florida's long-arm statute, "a nonresident Burger King franchisee is subject to the personal jurisdiction of this

7. Although Rudzewicz and MacShara dealt with the Birmingham district office on a regular basis, they communicated directly with the Miami headquarters in forming the contracts; moreover, they learned that the district office had "very little" decision making authority and accordingly turned directly to headquarters in seeking to resolve their disputes.

Court in actions arising out of its franchise agreements." Rudzewicz and MacShara then filed an answer and a counterclaim seeking damages for alleged violations by Burger King of Michigan's Franchise Investment Law, MICH. COMP. LAWS § 445.1501 et seq. (1979).

After a 3-day bench trial, the court again concluded that it had "jurisdiction over the subject matter and the parties to this cause." Finding that Rudzewicz and MacShara had breached their franchise agreements with Burger King and had infringed Burger King's trademarks and service marks, the court entered judgment against them, jointly and severally, for $228,875 in contract damages. The court also ordered them "to immediately close Burger King Restaurant Number 775 from continued operation or to immediately give the keys and possession of said restaurant to Burger King Corporation," found that they had failed to prove any of the required elements of their counterclaim, and awarded costs and attorney's fees to Burger King.

Rudzewicz appealed to the Court of Appeals for the Eleventh Circuit.[11] A divided panel of that Circuit reversed the judgment, concluding that the District Court could not properly exercise personal jurisdiction over Rudzewicz pursuant to FLA. STAT. § 48.193(1)(g) (Supp. 1984) because "the circumstances of the Drayton Plains franchise and the negotiations which led to it left Rudzewicz bereft of reasonable notice and financially unprepared for the prospect of franchise litigation in Florida." Accordingly, the panel majority concluded that "[j]urisdiction under these circumstances would offend the fundamental fairness which is the touchstone of due process."

II

A

The Due Process Clause protects an individual's liberty interest in not being subject to the binding judgments of a forum with which he has established no meaningful "contacts, ties, or relations." *International Shoe.*[13] By requiring that individuals have "fair warning that a particular activity may subject [them] to the jurisdiction of a foreign sovereign," *Shaffer v. Heitner* (Stevens, J., concurring in judgment), the Due Process Clause "gives a degree of predictability to the legal system that allows potential defendants to structure their primary conduct with some minimum assurance as to where that conduct will and will not render them liable to suit," *World-Wide Volkswagen.*

Where a forum seeks to assert specific jurisdiction over an out-of-state defendant who has not consented to suit there, this "fair warning" requirement is satisfied if

11. MacShara did not appeal his judgment. In addition, Rudzewicz entered into a compromise with Burger King and waived his right to appeal the District Court's finding of trademark infringement and its entry of injunctive relief. Accordingly, we need not address the extent to which the tortious act provisions of Florida's long-arm statute, may constitutionally extend to out-of-state trademark infringement. Cf. *Calder v. Jones* (tortious out-of-state conduct); *Keeton v. Hustler Magazine, Inc.* (same).

13. Although this protection operates to restrict state power, it "must be seen as ultimately a function of the individual liberty interest preserved by the Due Process Clause" rather than as a function "of federalism concerns." Insurance Corp. of Ireland v. Compagnie des Bauxites de Guinee, 456 U.S. 694, 702–703, n.10 (1982).

the defendant has "purposefully directed" his activities at residents of the forum, *Keeton v. Hustler Magazine, Inc.*, and the litigation results from alleged injuries that "arise out of or relate to" those activities, Helicopteros Nacionales de Colombia, S.A. v. Hall, 466 U.S. 408, 414 (1984).[15] Thus "[t]he forum State does not exceed its powers under the Due Process Clause if it asserts personal jurisdiction over a corporation that delivers its products into the stream of commerce with the expectation that they will be purchased by consumers in the forum State" and those products subsequently injure forum consumers. *World-Wide Volkswagen.* Similarly, a publisher who distributes magazines in a distant State may fairly be held accountable in that forum for damages resulting there from an allegedly defamatory story. *Keeton v. Hustler Magazine, Inc.*; see also *Calder v. Jones* (suit against author and editor). And with respect to interstate contractual obligations, we have emphasized that parties who "reach out beyond one state and create continuing relationships and obligations with citizens of another state" are subject to regulation and sanctions in the other State for the consequences of their activities. See also *McGee v. International Life Insurance Co.*

We have noted several reasons why a forum legitimately may exercise personal jurisdiction over a nonresident who "purposefully directs" his activities toward forum residents. A State generally has a "manifest interest" in providing its residents with a convenient forum for redressing injuries inflicted by out of state actors. See also *Keeton v. Hustler Magazine, Inc.* Moreover, where individuals "purposefully derive benefit" from their interstate activities, it may well be unfair to allow them to escape having to account in other States for consequences that arise proximately from such activities; the Due Process Clause may not readily be wielded as a territorial shield to avoid interstate obligations that have been voluntarily assumed. And because "modern transportation and communications have made it much less burdensome for a party sued to defend himself in a State where he engages in economic activity," it usually will not be unfair to subject him to the burdens of litigating in another forum for disputes relating to such activity. *McGee v. International Life Insurance Co.*

Notwithstanding these considerations, the constitutional touchstone remains whether the defendant purposefully established "minimum contacts" in the forum State. *International Shoe.* Although it has been argued that foreseeability of causing injury in another State should be sufficient to establish such contacts there when policy considerations so require, the Court has consistently held that this kind of foreseeability is not a "sufficient benchmark" for exercising personal jurisdiction. *World-Wide Volkswagen.* Instead, "the foreseeability that is critical to due process analysis ... is that the defendant's conduct and connection with the forum State are such that he should reasonably anticipate being haled into court there." In defining

15. "Specific" jurisdiction contrasts with "general" jurisdiction, pursuant to which "a State exercises personal jurisdiction over a defendant in a suit not arising out of or related to the defendant's contacts with the forum." Helicopteros Nacionales de Colombia, S.A. v. Hall, 466 U.S. at 414, n.9; see also Perkins v. Benguet Consolidated Mining Co., 342 U.S. 437 (1952).

when it is that a potential defendant should "reasonably anticipate" out-of-state litigation, the Court frequently has drawn from the reasoning of *Hanson v. Denckla*:

> "The unilateral activity of those who claim some relationship with a nonresident defendant cannot satisfy the requirement of contact with the forum State. The application of that rule will vary with the quality and nature of the defendant's activity, but it is essential in each case that there be some act by which the defendant purposefully avails itself of the privilege of conducting activities within the forum State, thus invoking the benefits and protections of its laws."

This "purposeful availment" requirement ensures that a defendant will not be haled into a jurisdiction solely as a result of "random," "fortuitous," or "attenuated" contacts, or of the "unilateral activity of another party or a third person." Jurisdiction is proper, however, where the contacts proximately result from actions by the defendant *himself* that create a "substantial connection" with the forum State. Thus where the defendant "deliberately" has engaged in significant activities within a State, or has created "continuing obligations" between himself and residents of the forum, he manifestly has availed himself of the privilege of conducting business there, and because his activities are shielded by "the benefits and protections" of the forum's laws it is presumptively not unreasonable to require him to submit to the burdens of litigation in that forum as well.

Jurisdiction in these circumstances may not be avoided merely because the defendant did not *physically* enter the forum State. Although territorial presence frequently will enhance a potential defendant's affiliation with a State and reinforce the reasonable foreseeability of suit there, it is an inescapable fact of modern commercial life that a substantial amount of business is transacted solely by mail and wire communications across state lines, thus obviating the need for physical presence within a State in which business is conducted. So long as a commercial actor's efforts are "purposefully directed" toward residents of another State, we have consistently rejected the notion that an absence of physical contacts can defeat personal jurisdiction there. *Keeton v. Hustler Magazine, Inc.*; see also *Calder v. Jones*; *McGee v. International Life Insurance Co.*

Once it has been decided that a defendant purposefully established minimum contacts within the forum State, these contacts may be considered in light of other factors to determine whether the assertion of personal jurisdiction would comport with "fair play and substantial justice." *International Shoe.* Thus courts in "appropriate case[s]" may evaluate "the burden on the defendant," "the forum State's interest in adjudicating the dispute," "the plaintiff's interest in obtaining convenient and effective relief," "the interstate judicial system's interest in obtaining the most efficient resolution of controversies," and the "shared interest of the several States in furthering fundamental substantive social policies." *World-Wide Volkswagen.* These considerations sometimes serve to establish the reasonableness of jurisdiction upon a lesser showing of minimum contacts than would otherwise be required. See, e.g., *Keeton v. Hustler Magazine, Inc.*; *Calder v. Jones*; *McGee v. International Life Insurance Co.* On the other hand, where a defendant who purposefully has directed his activities at forum residents seeks to defeat jurisdiction, he must present a compelling case that the presence of some other considerations would render jurisdiction unreasonable. Most such considerations usually may be accommodated through means short of finding jurisdiction unconstitutional. For example, the potential clash of the forum's law with the "fundamental substantive social policies" of another State may be accommodated through application of the forum's choice-of-law rules. Similarly, a defendant claiming substantial inconvenience may seek a change of venue. Nevertheless, minimum requirements inherent in the concept of "fair play and substantial justice" may defeat the reasonableness of jurisdiction even if the defendant has purposefully engaged in forum activities. *World-Wide Volkswagen*; see also RESTATEMENT (SECOND) OF CONFLICT OF LAWS §§ 36–37 (1971). As we previously have noted, jurisdictional rules may not be employed in such a way as to make litigation "so gravely difficult and inconvenient" that a party unfairly is at a "severe disadvantage" in comparison to his opponent. The Bremen v. Zapata Off-Shore Co., 407 U.S. 1, 18 (1972) (re forum-selection provisions); *McGee v. International Life Insurance Co.*

B

(1)

Applying these principles to the case at hand, we believe there is substantial record evidence supporting the District Court's conclusion that the assertion of personal jurisdiction over Rudzewicz in Florida for the alleged breach of his franchise agreement did not offend due process. At the outset, we note a continued division among lower courts respecting whether and to what extent a contract can constitute a "contact" for purposes of due process analysis. If the question is whether an individual's contract with an out-of-state party alone can automatically establish sufficient minimum contacts in the other party's home forum, we believe the answer clearly is that it cannot. The Court long ago rejected the notion that personal jurisdiction might turn on "mechanical" tests, or on "conceptualistic ... theories of the place of contracting or of performance." Instead, we have emphasized the need for a "highly realistic" approach that recognizes that a "contract" is "ordinarily but an intermediate step serving to tie up prior business negotiations with future consequences which themselves are the real object of the business transaction." It is these factors—prior negotiations and contemplated future consequences, along with the terms of the contract and the parties' actual course of dealing—that must be evaluated in determining whether the defendant purposefully established minimum contacts within the forum.

In this case, no physical ties to Florida can be attributed to Rudzewicz other than MacShara's brief training course in Miami.[22] Rudzewicz did not maintain offices in

22. The Eleventh Circuit held that MacShara's presence in Florida was irrelevant to the question of Rudzewicz' minimum contacts with that forum, reasoning that "Rudzewicz and MacShara never formed a partnership" and "signed the agreements in their individual capacities." The two did jointly form a corporation through which they were seeking to conduct the franchise, however. They were required to decide which one of them would travel to Florida to satisfy the training requirements so that they could commence business, and Rudzewicz participated in the decision that MacShara would go there. We have previously noted that when commercial activities are "carried on in behalf of" an

Florida and, for all that appears from the record, has never even visited there. Yet this franchise dispute grew directly out of "a contract which had a *substantial* connection with that State." *McGee v. International Life Insurance Co.* (emphasis added). Eschewing the option of operating an independent local enterprise, Rudzewicz deliberately "reach[ed] out beyond" Michigan and negotiated with a Florida corporation for the purchase of a long-term franchise and the manifold benefits that would derive from affiliation with a nationwide organization. Upon approval, he entered into a carefully structured 20-year relationship that envisioned continuing and wide-reaching contacts with Burger King in Florida. In light of Rudzewicz' voluntary acceptance of the long-term and exacting regulation of his business from Burger King's Miami headquarters, the "quality and nature" of his relationship to the company in Florida can in no sense be viewed as "random," "fortuitous," or "attenuated." *Hanson v. Denckla; Keeton v. Hustler Magazine, Inc.; World-Wide Volkswagen v. Woodson.* Rudzewicz' refusal to make the contractually required payments in Miami, and his continued use of Burger King's trademarks and confidential business information after his termination, caused foreseeable injuries to the corporation in Florida. For these reasons it was, at the very least, presumptively reasonable for Rudzewicz to be called to account there for such injuries.

The Court of Appeals concluded, however, that in light of the supervision emanating from Burger King's district office in Birmingham, Rudzewicz reasonably believed that "the Michigan office was for all intents and purposes the embodiment of Burger King" and that he therefore had no "reason to anticipate a Burger King suit outside of Michigan." This reasoning overlooks substantial record evidence indicating that Rudzewicz most certainly knew that he was affiliating himself with an enterprise based primarily in Florida. The contract documents themselves emphasize that Burger King's operations are conducted and supervised from the Miami headquarters, that all relevant notices and payments must be sent there, and that the agreements were made in and enforced from Miami. Moreover, the parties' actual course of dealing repeatedly confirmed that decisionmaking authority was vested in the Miami headquarters and that the district office served largely as an intermediate link between the headquarters and the franchisees. When problems arose over building design, site-development fees, rent computation, and the defaulted payments, Rudzewicz and MacShara learned that the Michigan office was powerless to resolve their disputes and could only channel their communications to Miami. Throughout these disputes, the Miami headquarters and the Michigan franchisees carried on a continuous course of direct communications by mail and by telephone, and it was the Miami headquarters that made the key negotiating decisions out of which the instant litigation arose.

---

out-of-state party those activities may sometimes be ascribed to the party, *International Shoe*, at least where he is a "primary participan[t]" in the enterprise and has acted purposefully in directing those activities, *Calder v. Jones.* Because MacShara's matriculation at Burger King University is not pivotal to the disposition of this case, we need not resolve the permissible bounds of such attribution.

Moreover, we believe the Court of Appeals gave insufficient weight to provisions in the various franchise documents providing that all disputes would be governed by Florida law. The franchise agreement, for example, stated:

> "This Agreement shall become valid when executed and accepted by BKC at Miami, Florida; it shall be deemed made and entered into in the State of Florida and shall be governed and construed under and in accordance with the laws of the State of Florida. The choice of law designation does not require that all suits concerning this Agreement be filed in Florida."

The Court of Appeals reasoned that choice-of-law provisions are irrelevant to the question of personal jurisdiction, relying on *Hanson v. Denckla* for the proposition that "the center of gravity for choice-of-law purposes does not necessarily confer the sovereign prerogative to assert jurisdiction." This reasoning misperceives the import of the quoted proposition. The Court in *Hanson* and subsequent cases has emphasized that choice-of-law *analysis* — which focuses on all elements of a transaction, and not simply on the defendant's conduct — is distinct from minimum-contacts jurisdictional analysis — which focuses at the threshold solely on the defendant's purposeful connection to the forum. Nothing in our cases, however, suggests that a choice-of-law *provision* should be ignored in considering whether a defendant has "purposefully invoked the benefits and protections of a State's laws" for jurisdictional purposes. Although such a provision standing alone would be insufficient to confer jurisdiction, we believe that, when combined with the 20-year interdependent relationship Rudzewicz established with Burger King's Miami headquarters, it reinforced his deliberate affiliation with the forum State and the reasonable foreseeability of possible litigation there. As Judge Johnson argued in his dissent below, Rudzewicz "purposefully availed himself of the benefits and protections of Florida's laws" by entering into contracts expressly providing that those laws would govern franchise disputes.[24]

(2)

Nor has Rudzewicz pointed to other factors that can be said persuasively to outweigh the considerations discussed above and to establish the *unconstitutionality* of Florida's assertion of jurisdiction. We cannot conclude that Florida had no "legitimate interest in holding [Rudzewicz] answerable on a claim related to" the contacts he had established in that State. *Keeton v. Hustler Magazine, Inc.*; see also *McGee v. International Life Insurance Co.* (noting that State frequently will have a "manifest in-

---

24. In addition, the franchise agreement's disclaimer that the "choice of law designation does not *require* that all suits concerning this Agreement be filed in Florida," reasonably should have suggested to Rudzewicz that by negative implication such suits *could* be filed there.

The lease also provided for binding arbitration in Miami of certain condemnation disputes, and Rudzewicz conceded the validity of this provision at oral argument. Although it does not govern the instant dispute, this provision also should have made it apparent to the franchisees that they were dealing directly with the Miami headquarters and that the Birmingham district office was not "for all intents and purposes the embodiment of Burger King."

terest in providing effective means of redress for its residents").[25] Moreover, although Rudzewicz has argued at some length that Michigan's Franchise Investment Law governs many aspects of this franchise relationship, he has not demonstrated how Michigan's acknowledged interest might possibly render jurisdiction in Florida *unconstitutional.*[26] Finally, the Court of Appeals' assertion that the Florida litigation "severely impaired [Rudzewicz'] ability to call Michigan witnesses who might be essential to his defense and counterclaim," is wholly without support in the record. And even to the extent that it is inconvenient for a party who has minimum contacts with a forum to litigate there, such considerations most frequently can be accommodated through a change of venue. Although the Court has suggested that inconvenience may at some point become so substantial as to achieve *constitutional* magnitude, this is not such a case.

The Court of Appeals also concluded, however, that the parties' dealings involved "a characteristic disparity of bargaining power" and "elements of surprise," and that Rudzewicz "lacked fair notice" of the potential for litigation in Florida because the contractual provisions suggesting to the contrary were merely "boilerplate declarations in a lengthy printed contract." Rudzewicz presented many of these arguments to the District Court, contending that Burger King was guilty of misrepresentation, fraud, and duress; that it gave insufficient notice in its dealings with him; and that the contract was one of adhesion. After a 3-day bench trial, the District Court found that Burger King had made no misrepresentations, that Rudzewicz and MacShara "were and are experienced and sophisticated businessmen," and that "at no time" did they "ac[t] under economic duress or disadvantage imposed by" Burger King. Federal Rule of Civil Procedure 52(a) requires that "[f]indings of fact shall not be set aside unless clearly erroneous," and neither Rudzewicz nor the Court of Appeals has pointed to record evidence that would support a "definite and firm conviction" that the District Court's findings are mistaken. To the contrary, Rudzewicz was represented by counsel throughout these complex transactions and, as Judge Johnson observed in dissent below, was himself an experienced accountant "who for five months conducted negotiations with Burger King over the terms of the franchise and lease agreements, and who obligated himself personally to contracts requiring over time payments that

---

25. Complaining that "when Burger King is the plaintiff, you won't 'have it your way' because it sues all franchisees in Miami," Rudzewicz contends that Florida's interest in providing a convenient forum is negligible given the company's size and ability to conduct litigation anywhere in the country. We disagree. Absent compelling considerations, cf. *McGee v. International Life Insurance Co.*, a defendant who has purposefully derived commercial benefit from his affiliations in a forum may not defeat jurisdiction there simply because of his adversary's greater net wealth.

26. Rudzewicz has failed to show how the District Court's exercise of jurisdiction in this case might have been at all inconsistent with Michigan's interests. To the contrary, the court found that Burger King had fully complied with Michigan law, and there is nothing in Michigan's franchise Act suggesting that Michigan would attempt to assert exclusive jurisdiction to resolve franchise disputes affecting its residents. In any event, minimum-contacts analysis presupposes that two or more States may be interested in the outcome of a dispute, and the process of resolving potentially conflicting "fundamental substantive social policies," *World-Wide Volkswagen*, can usually be accommodated through choice-of-law rules rather than through outright preclusion of jurisdiction in one forum.

exceeded $1 million." Rudzewicz was able to secure a modest reduction in rent and other concessions from Miami headquarters; moreover, to the extent that Burger King's terms were inflexible, Rudzewicz presumably decided that the advantages of affiliating with a national organization provided sufficient commercial benefits to offset the detriments.

III

Notwithstanding these considerations, the Court of Appeals apparently believed that it was necessary to reject jurisdiction in this case as a prophylactic measure, reasoning that an affirmance of the District Court's judgment would result in the exercise of jurisdiction over "out-of-state consumers to collect payments due on modest personal purchases" and would "sow the seeds of default judgments against franchisees owing smaller debts." We share the Court of Appeals' broader concerns and therefore reject any talismanic jurisdictional formulas; "the facts of each case must [always] be weighed" in determining whether personal jurisdiction would comport with "fair play and substantial justice."[29] The "quality and nature" of an interstate transaction may sometimes be so "random," "fortuitous," or "attenuated" that it cannot fairly be said that the potential defendant "should reasonably anticipate being haled into court" in another jurisdiction. We also have emphasized that jurisdiction may not be grounded on a contract whose terms have been obtained through "fraud, undue influence, or overweening bargaining power" and whose application would render litigation "so gravely difficult and inconvenient that [a party] will for all practical purposes be deprived of his day in court." The Bremen v. Zapata Off-Shore Co., 407 U.S. at 12, 18. Cf. Fuentes v. Shevin, 407 U.S. 67, 94–96 (1972); National Equipment Rental, Ltd. v. Szukhent, 375 U.S. 311, 329 (1964) (Black, J., dissenting) (jurisdictional rules may not be employed against small consumers so as to "crippl[e] their defense"). Just as the Due Process Clause allows flexibility in ensuring that commercial actors are not effectively "judgment proof" for the consequences of obligations they voluntarily assume in other States, so too does it prevent rules that would unfairly enable them to obtain default judgments against unwitting customers.

For the reasons set forth above, however, these dangers are not present in the instant case. Because Rudzewicz established a substantial and continuing relationship with Burger King's Miami headquarters, received fair notice from the contract documents and the course of dealing that he might be subject to suit in Florida, and has failed to demonstrate how jurisdiction in that forum would otherwise be fundamentally unfair, we conclude that the District Court's exercise of jurisdiction pursuant to Fla. Stat. § 48.193(1)(g) (Supp. 1984) did not offend due process. The judgment of the Court of Appeals is accordingly reversed, and the case is remanded for further proceedings consistent with this opinion.

---

29. This approach does, of course, preclude clear-cut jurisdictional rules. But any inquiry into "fair play and substantial justice" necessarily requires determinations "in which few answers will be written 'in black and white. The grays are dominant and even among them the shades are innumerable.'" *Kulko.*

It is so ordered.

JUSTICE STEVENS, with whom JUSTICE WHITE joins, dissenting.

In my opinion there is a significant element of unfairness in requiring a franchisee to defend a case of this kind in the forum chosen by the franchisor. It is undisputed that appellee maintained no place of business in Florida, that he had no employees in that State, and that he was not licensed to do business there. Appellee did not prepare his French fries, shakes, and hamburgers in Michigan, and then deliver them into the stream of commerce "with the expectation that they [would] be purchased by consumers in" Florida. To the contrary, appellee did business only in Michigan, his business, property, and payroll taxes were payable in that State, and he sold all of his products there.

Throughout the business relationship, appellee's principal contacts with appellant were with its Michigan office. Notwithstanding its disclaimer, the Court seems ultimately to rely on nothing more than standard boilerplate language contained in various documents, to establish that appellee "purposefully availed himself of the benefits and protections of Florida's laws." Such superficial analysis creates a potential for unfairness not only in negotiations between franchisors and their franchisees but, more significantly, in the resolution of the disputes that inevitably arise from time to time in such relationships.

Judge Vance's opinion for the Court of Appeals for the Eleventh Circuit adequately explains why I would affirm the judgment of that court. I particularly find the following more persuasive than what this Court has written today:

> Nothing in the course of negotiations gave Rudzewicz reason to anticipate a Burger King suit outside of Michigan. The only face-to-face or even oral contact Rudzewicz had with Burger King throughout months of protracted negotiations was with representatives of the Michigan office. Burger King had the Michigan office interview Rudzewicz and MacShara, appraise their application, discuss price terms, recommend the site which the defendants finally agreed to, and attend the final closing ceremony. There is no evidence that Rudzewicz ever negotiated with anyone in Miami or even sent mail there during negotiations. He maintained no staff in the state of Florida, and as far as the record reveals, he has never even visited the state.
>
> The contracts contemplated the startup of a local Michigan restaurant whose profits would derive solely from food sales made to customers in Drayton Plains. The sale, which involved the use of an intangible trademark in Michigan and occupancy of a Burger King facility there, required no performance in the state of Florida. Under the contract, the local Michigan district office was responsible for providing all of the services due Rudzewicz, including advertising and management consultation. Supervision, moreover, emanated from that office alone. To Rudzewicz, the Michigan office was for all intents and purposes the embodiment of Burger King. He had reason to believe that his working relationship with Burger King began and ended in Michigan, not at the distant and anonymous Florida headquarters....

Given that the office in Rudzewicz' home state conducted all of the negotiations and wholly supervised the contract, we believe that he had reason to assume that the state of the supervisory office would be the same state in which Burger King would file suit. Rudzewicz lacked fair notice that the distant corporate headquarters which insulated itself from direct dealings with him would later seek to assert jurisdiction over him in the courts of its own home state....

Just as Rudzewicz lacked notice of the possibility of suit in Florida, he was financially unprepared to meet its added costs. The franchise relationship in particular is fraught with potential for financial surprise. The device of the franchise gives local retailers the access to national trademark recognition which enables them to compete with better-financed, more efficient chain stores. This national affiliation, however, does not alter the fact that the typical franchise store is a local concern serving at best a neighborhood or community. Neither the revenues of a local business nor the geographical range of its market prepares the average franchise owner for the cost of distant litigation....

The particular distribution of bargaining power in the franchise relationship further impairs the franchisee's financial preparedness. In a franchise contract, "the franchisor normally occupies [the] dominant role."

We discern a characteristic disparity of bargaining power in the facts of this case. There is no indication that Rudzewicz had any latitude to negotiate a reduced rent or franchise fee in exchange for the added risk of suit in Florida. He signed a standard form contract whose terms were non- negotiable and which appeared in some respects to vary from the more favorable terms agreed to in earlier discussions. In fact, the final contract required a minimum monthly rent computed on a base far in excess of that discussed in oral negotiations. Burger King resisted price concessions, only to sue Rudzewicz far from home. In doing so, it severely impaired his ability to call Michigan witnesses who might be essential to his defense and counterclaim.

In sum, we hold that the circumstances of the Drayton Plains franchise and the negotiations which led to it left Rudzewicz bereft of reasonable notice and financially unprepared for the prospect of franchise litigation in Florida. Jurisdiction under these circumstances would offend the fundamental fairness which is the touchstone of due process.

Accordingly, I respectfully dissent.

Notes and Questions

1. *Burger King*, like *World-Wide Volkswagen*, addresses both the need for purposeful contacts and the requirement that the forum be reasonable. Review Justice Brennan's discussion of reasonableness. Is he suggesting, contrary to *World-Wide Volkswagen*, that if a forum is very reasonable and convenient, there might be juris-

diction, even if the defendant has no "contacts" with the forum? Can you imagine a fact pattern in which jurisdiction would be convenient and reasonable in a forum with which the defendant lacked sufficient contacts?

2. The *Burger King* Court notes that states have an interest in providing their citizens with a courtroom. However, *World-Wide Volkswagen* certainly made clear that a state interest is not a substitute for purposeful contacts. While *Burger King* reaffirms that, the Court seems to reintroduce state interest as a factor in the reasonableness analysis. What does state interest mean in this context? Aren't states the best judges of their own interests and, therefore, if a state wants to assert jurisdiction doesn't that necessarily mean that it has an interest? Should the fact that the state wants to assert jurisdiction be a factor that weighs in favor of jurisdiction?

3. Consider the following hypotheticals:

(a) A West Virginia construction company orders an expensive piece of equipment from a manufacturer in Wisconsin. The contract calls for the equipment to be delivered "F.O.B. at the seller's plant in Wisconsin," meaning the buyer takes title to and assumes the risk for the equipment at the seller's plant. When a dispute arises over payment, the Wisconsin seller sues the West Virginia buyer in Wisconsin. Is there jurisdiction? Would West Virginia have jurisdiction over the seller if the buyer brought suit there? Would your answer to either question change if the seller had arranged for the transportation of the equipment to West Virginia? Would your answer change if the item in question was a $300 tool purchased by a consumer from a catalogue?

(b) A California citizen contacts an attorney in New York and retains the attorney to provide legal advice on a dispute centered in Oregon. The client frequently contacts the lawyer by phone and e-mail, and sends payment to New York. The lawyer provides advice and when the client is sued in Oregon, the lawyer assists in the Oregon litigation. Later, there is a fee dispute and the lawyer sues the client in New York. Does New York have jurisdiction over the client? If the client had been unhappy with the services, could she have sued the lawyer in California?

4. Is there a difference between buyers and sellers for purposes of jurisdiction? Consider the analysis of the Sixth Circuit in In-Flight Devices Corp. v. Van Dusen Air, Inc., 466 F.2d 220, 233 (6th Cir. 1972):

> In our economy the seller often initiates the deal, tends to set many, if not all of the terms on which it will sell, and, of course, bears the burden of producing the goods or services, in the course of which production injuries and other incidents giving rise to litigation frequently arise. The buyer, on the other hand is frequently a relatively passive party, simply placing an order, accepting the seller's price and terms as stated in his product advertising and agreeing only to pay a sum upon receipt of the goods or services. It is understandable that sellers more often seem to have acted in a manner rendering them subject to long-arm jurisdiction.

> The mere fact that a buyer is the defendant in a long-arm situation should not preclude an assertion of jurisdiction over such defendant, however. To the extent the buyer vigorously negotiates, perhaps dictates, contract terms, inspects production facilities and otherwise departs from the passive buyer role it would seem that any unfairness which would normally be associated with the exercise of long-arm jurisdiction over him disappears. Such buyer conduct is far more typical in dealings between large business organizations, of course, than in dealings involving consumers or even those involving a small shopkeeper purchaser and a large manufacturer.

5. The contract in *Burger King* included a choice of law clause. Interestingly, it did not include a choice of forum clause, although such a clause would have provided greater certainty in predicting how (and where) the contract would be interpreted. Why would the parties include a choice of law clause but not a choice of forum clause? Professor Weintraub has suggested that one reason may have been that the Michigan Franchise Investment Act, as interpreted at that time, prohibited contract provisions requiring franchisees to litigate in other states. Russell Weintraub, Commentary on the Conflict of Laws 184 (6th ed. 2010). Does Justice Brennan's reliance on the choice of law clause allow a franchisor such as Burger King to achieve indirectly the prohibited effect of a choice of forum clause?

Note on Asahi *and the "Stream of Commerce"*

The classic "stream of commerce" fact pattern is this. Company A makes components (let's say valves) in State A. It sells the valves to Company B, which operates in State B. Company B uses the Company A valves in making its finished product (let's say a widget). Company B then sells its widgets to customers in State C. So the Company A valve is shipped into State C, but Company A did not send it there. Now the Company A valve malfunctions in State C, injuring Plaintiff there. Plaintiff sues Company A in State C.* Does Company A have relevant contacts with State C for purposes of in personam jurisdiction? More specifically, did it purposefully avail itself of State C?

The Court addressed this question in Asahi Metal Indus. Co. v. Superior Court of California, 480 U.S. 102 (1987). The fact pattern was the same but in the international context and featured one procedural distinction from the above hypothetical. Asahi manufactured tire valves in Japan and sold them to Cheng Shin, which used the valves in tires it manufactured in Taiwan. Cheng Shin then marketed the tires into California. The valve in one of these tires allegedly malfunctioned, causing a

---

* Plaintiff also would sue Company B. There should be no question about personal jurisdiction over Company B in State C. Company B directly marketed and sold the product in State C, and the claim arises directly from its doing so. The difficult issue will be personal jurisdiction over Company A in State C.

motorcycle to crash. The plaintiff, Zurcher, a California citizen, was driving the motorcycle at the time and suffered serious injuries in California. He sued Cheng Shin in California. Cheng Shin "impleaded" Asahi into the case, seeking indemnification. Cheng Shin argued that if the tire was defective because of the valve, the valve manufacturer would have to indemnify it for any amounts it was required to pay to Zurcher. This indemnification claim was part of the suit in California, and Asahi moved to dismiss the claim against it on the grounds that California lacked personal jurisdiction over it. So though the plaintiff did not sue Asahi, the question was the same as if he had: did Asahi have relevant contacts with California?

The Court split badly on that issue. In fact, it failed to generate a majority opinion on the question. Four Justices, led by Justice Brennan, concluded that Asahi had purposefully availed itself of California. He explained: "The stream of commerce refers not to unpredictable currents or eddies, but to the regular and anticipated flow of products from manufacturer to distribution to retail sale. As long as a participant in this process is aware that the final product is being marketed in the forum State, the possibility of a lawsuit there cannot come as a surprise." Id. at 117. This conclusion seems to make sense, because Asahi makes money from the fact that there is a market in California for the finished product. So perhaps Asahi did avail itself of California.

But four other Justices, led by Justice O'Connor, disagreed. To them, it was not enough that Asahi placed the product into the stream of commerce and could reasonably anticipate that it would be used in California. According to Justice O'Connor, there must be some "additional conduct" by which the defendant indicates "an intent or purpose to serve the market in the forum State." Id. at 112. Examples would include designing the product for use in that state, advertising, or providing customer service in the forum. This conclusion also makes sense, because the valve got into the forum not because Asahi sent it there, but because of the unilateral act of a third party.

The ninth Justice, Justice Stevens, refused join either the Brennan or the O'Connor theory.* Id. at 122. *Asahi* left us, then, with a split decision and no definitive answer on when the stream of commerce can constitute purposeful availment. Lower courts were left to struggle with the topic, some adopting the Brennan approach and some the O'Connor approach. Finally, twenty- four years later, the Court returned to the question in the next case. As you read it, note carefully how the Justices split. Is there a majority opinion adopting either the Brennan or the O'Connor theory? Does any Justice propose a new theory? Is the state of the law any clearer after the next case than it was after *Asahi*?

---

* Though the Court was fragmented on whether there was purposeful availment, the Court was in strong agreement that the exercise of jurisdiction in California would not be reasonable. We will discuss this point in Note 7 after the *J. McIntyre* case.

J. McIntyre Machinery, Ltd. v. Nicastro

131 S. Ct. 2780, 180 L. Ed. 2d 765 (2011)

Justice Kennedy announced the judgment of the Court and delivered an opinion, in which The Chief Justice, Justice Scalia, and Justice Thomas join.

Whether a person or entity is subject to the jurisdiction of a state court despite not having been present in the State either at the time of suit or at the time of the alleged injury, and despite not having consented to the exercise of jurisdiction, is a question that arises with great frequency in the routine course of litigation. The rules and standards for determining when a State does or does not have jurisdiction over an absent party have been unclear because of decades-old questions left open in Asahi Metal Industry Co. v. Superior Court of Cal., Solano Cty., 480 U.S. 102 (1987).

Here, the Supreme Court of New Jersey, relying in part on *Asahi*, held that New Jersey's courts can exercise jurisdiction over a foreign manufacturer of a product so long as the manufacturer "knows or reasonably should know that its products are distributed through a nationwide distribution system that might lead to those products being sold in any of the fifty states." Nicastro v. McIntyre Machinery America, Ltd., 201 N.J. 48, 76, 77 (2010). Applying that test, the court concluded that a British manufacturer of scrap metal machines was subject to jurisdiction in New Jersey, even though at no time had it advertised in, sent goods to, or in any relevant sense targeted the State.

That decision cannot be sustained. Although the New Jersey Supreme Court issued an extensive opinion with careful attention to this Court's cases and to its own precedent, the "stream of commerce" metaphor carried the decision far afield. Due process protects the defendant's right not to be coerced except by lawful judicial power. As a general rule, the exercise of judicial power is not lawful unless the defendant "purposefully avails itself of the privilege of conducting activities within the forum State, thus invoking the benefits and protections of its laws." Hanson v. Denckla, 357 U.S. 235, 253 (1958). There may be exceptions, say, for instance, in cases involving an intentional tort. But the general rule is applicable in this products-liability case, and the so-called "stream-of-commerce" doctrine cannot displace it.

I

This case arises from a products-liability suit filed in New Jersey state court. Robert Nicastro seriously injured his hand while using a metal-shearing machine manufactured by J. McIntyre Machinery, Ltd. (J. McIntyre). The accident occurred in New Jersey, but the machine was manufactured in England, where J. McIntyre is incorporated and operates. The question here is whether the New Jersey courts have jurisdiction over J. McIntyre, notwithstanding the fact that the company at no time either marketed goods in the State or shipped them there. Nicastro was a plaintiff in the New Jersey trial court and is the respondent here; J. McIntyre was a defendant and is now the petitioner.

At oral argument in this Court, Nicastro's counsel stressed three primary facts in defense of New Jersey's assertion of jurisdiction over J. McIntyre.

First, an independent company agreed to sell J. McIntyre's machines in the United States. J. McIntyre itself did not sell its machines to buyers in this country beyond the U.S. distributor, and there is no allegation that the distributor was under J. McIntyre's control.

Second, J. McIntyre officials attended annual conventions for the scrap recycling industry to advertise J. McIntyre's machines alongside the distributor. The conventions took place in various States, but never in New Jersey.

Third, no more than four machines (the record suggests only one), including the machine that caused the injuries that are the basis for this suit, ended up in New Jersey.

In addition to these facts emphasized by respondent, the New Jersey Supreme Court noted that J. McIntyre held both United States and European patents on its recycling technology. It also noted that the U.S. distributor "structured [its] advertising and sales efforts in accordance with" J. McIntyre's "direction and guidance whenever possible," and that "at least some of the machines were sold on consignment to" the distributor.

In light of these facts, the New Jersey Supreme Court concluded that New Jersey courts could exercise jurisdiction over petitioner without contravention of the Due Process Clause. Jurisdiction was proper, in that court's view, because the injury occurred in New Jersey; because petitioner knew or reasonably should have known "that its products are distributed through a nationwide distribution system that might lead to those products being sold in any of the fifty states"; and because petitioner failed to "take some reasonable step to prevent the distribution of its products in this State."

Both the New Jersey Supreme Court's holding and its account of what it called "[t]he stream-of-commerce doctrine of jurisdiction," were incorrect, however. This Court's *Asahi* decision may be responsible in part for that court's error regarding the stream of commerce, and this case presents an opportunity to provide greater clarity.

II

The Due Process Clause protects an individual's right to be deprived of life, liberty, or property only by the exercise of lawful power. This is no less true with respect to the power of a sovereign to resolve disputes through judicial process than with respect to the power of a sovereign to prescribe rules of conduct for those within its sphere. As a general rule, neither statute nor judicial decree may bind strangers to the State.

A court may subject a defendant to judgment only when the defendant has sufficient contacts with the sovereign "such that the maintenance of the suit does not offend 'traditional notions of fair play and substantial justice.'" International Shoe Co. v. Washington, 326 U.S. 310, 316 (1945) (quoting Milliken v. Meyer, 311 U.S. 457, 463 (1940)). Freeform notions of fundamental fairness divorced from traditional practice cannot transform a judgment rendered in the absence of authority into law.

As a general rule, the sovereign's exercise of power requires some act by which the defendant "purposefully avails itself of the privilege of conducting activities within the forum State, thus invoking the benefits and protections of its laws," *Hanson*, though in some cases, as with an intentional tort, the defendant might well fall within the State's authority by reason of his attempt to obstruct its laws. In products-liability cases like this one, it is the defendant's purposeful availment that makes jurisdiction consistent with "traditional notions of fair play and substantial justice."

A person may submit to a State's authority in a number of ways. There is, of course, explicit consent. E.g., Insurance Corp. of Ireland v. Compagnie des Bauxites de Guinee, 456 U.S. 694, 703 (1982). Presence within a State at the time suit commences through service of process is another example. Citizenship or domicile—or, by analogy, incorporation or principal place of business for corporations—also indicates general submission to a State's powers. Each of these examples reveals circumstances, or a course of conduct, from which it is proper to infer an intention to benefit from and thus an intention to submit to the laws of the forum State. Cf. Burger King Corp. v. Rudzewicz, 471 U.S. 462, 476 (1985). These examples support exercise of the general jurisdiction of the State's courts and allow the State to resolve both matters that originate within the State and those based on activities and events elsewhere. By contrast, those who live or operate primarily outside a State have a due process right not to be subjected to judgment in its courts as a general matter.

There is also a more limited form of submission to a State's authority for disputes that "arise out of or are connected with the activities within the state." *International Shoe Co.* Where a defendant "purposefully avails itself of the privilege of conducting activities within the forum State, thus invoking the benefits and protections of its laws," it submits to the judicial power of an otherwise foreign sovereign to the extent that power is exercised in connection with the defendant's activities touching on the State. In other words, submission through contact with and activity directed at a sovereign may justify specific jurisdiction "in a suit arising out of or related to the defendant's contacts with the forum."

The imprecision arising from *Asahi*, for the most part, results from its statement of the relation between jurisdiction and the "stream of commerce." The stream of commerce, like other metaphors, has its deficiencies as well as its utility. It refers to the movement of goods from manufacturers through distributors to consumers, yet beyond that descriptive purpose its meaning is far from exact. This Court has stated that a defendant's placing goods into the stream of commerce "with the expectation that they will be purchased by consumers within the forum State" may indicate purposeful availment. World-Wide Volkswagen Corp. v. Woodson, 444 U.S. 286, 298 (1980) (finding that expectation lacking). But that statement does not amend the general rule of personal jurisdiction. It merely observes that a defendant may in an appropriate case be subject to jurisdiction without entering the forum—itself an unexceptional proposition—as where manufacturers or distributors "seek to serve" a given State's market. The principal inquiry in cases of this sort is whether the defendant's activities manifest an intention to submit to the power of a sovereign. In other words, the defendant must "purposefully avai[l] itself of the privilege of conducting activities within the forum State, thus invoking the benefits and protections of its laws." *Hanson*; *Insurance Corp. of Ireland* ("[A]ctions of the defendant may amount to a legal submission to the jurisdiction of the court"). Sometimes a defendant does so by sending its goods rather than its agents. The defendant's transmission of goods permits the exercise of jurisdiction only where the defendant can be said to have targeted the forum; as a general rule, it is not enough that the defendant might have predicted that its goods will reach the forum State.

In *Asahi*, an opinion by Justice Brennan for four Justices outlined a different approach. It discarded the central concept of sovereign authority in favor of considerations of fairness and foreseeability. As that concurrence contended, "jurisdiction premised on the placement of a product into the stream of commerce [without more] is consistent with the Due Process Clause," for "[a]s long as a participant in this process is aware that the final product is being marketed in the forum State, the possibility of a lawsuit there cannot come as a surprise." It was the premise of the concurring opinion that the defendant's ability to anticipate suit renders the assertion of jurisdiction fair. In this way, the opinion made foreseeability the touchstone of jurisdiction.

The standard set forth in Justice Brennan's concurrence was rejected in an opinion written by Justice O'Connor; but the relevant part of that opinion, too, commanded the assent of only four Justices, not a majority of the Court. That opinion stated: "The 'substantial connection' between the defendant and the forum State necessary for a finding of minimum contacts must come about by an action of the defendant purposefully directed toward the forum State. The placement of a product into the stream of commerce, without more, is not an act of the defendant purposefully directed toward the forum State."

Since *Asahi* was decided, the courts have sought to reconcile the competing opinions. But Justice Brennan's concurrence, advocating a rule based on general notions of fairness and foreseeability, is inconsistent with the premises of lawful judicial power. This Court's precedents make clear that it is the defendant's actions, not his expectations, that empower a State's courts to subject him to judgment.

The conclusion that jurisdiction is in the first instance a question of authority rather than fairness explains, for example, why the principal opinion in *Burnham v. Superior Court of California*, 495 U.S. 604 (1990), "conducted no independent inquiry into the desirability or fairness" of the rule that service of process within a State suffices to establish jurisdiction over an otherwise foreign defendant. [We will address *Burnham* in Section B.7 of this chapter.] As that opinion explained, "[t]he view developed early that each State had the power to hale before its courts any individual who could be found within its borders." Furthermore, were general fairness considerations the touchstone of jurisdiction, a lack of purposeful availment might be excused where carefully crafted judicial procedures could otherwise protect the defendant's interests, or where the plaintiff would suffer substantial hardship if forced to litigate in a foreign forum. That such considerations have not been deemed controlling is instructive. See, e.g., *World-Wide Volkswagen*.

Two principles are implicit in the foregoing. First, personal jurisdiction requires a forum-by-forum, or sovereign-by-sovereign, analysis. The question is whether a defendant has followed a course of conduct directed at the society or economy existing within the jurisdiction of a given sovereign, so that the sovereign has the power to subject the defendant to judgment concerning that conduct. Personal jurisdiction, of course, restricts "judicial power not as a matter of sovereignty, but as a matter of individual liberty," for due process protects the individual's right to be subject only to lawful power. *Insurance Corp.* But whether a judicial judgment is lawful depends on whether the sovereign has authority to render it.

The second principle is a corollary of the first. Because the United States is a distinct sovereign, a defendant may in principle be subject to the jurisdiction of the courts of the United States but not of any particular State. This is consistent with the premises and unique genius of our Constitution. Ours is "a legal system unprecedented in form and design, establishing two orders of government, each with its own direct relationship, its own privity, its own set of mutual rights and obligations to the people who sustain it and are governed by it." U.S. Term Limits, Inc. v. Thornton, 514 U.S. 779, 838 (1995) (Kennedy, J., concurring). For jurisdiction, a litigant may have the requisite relationship with the United States Government but not with the government of any individual State. That would be an exceptional case, however. If the defendant is a domestic domiciliary, the courts of its home State are available and can exercise general jurisdiction. And if another State were to assert jurisdiction in an inappropriate case, it would upset the federal balance, which posits that each State has a sovereignty that is not subject to unlawful intrusion by other States. Furthermore, foreign corporations will often target or concentrate on particular States, subjecting them to specific jurisdiction in those forums.

It must be remembered, however, that although this case and *Asahi* both involve foreign manufacturers, the undesirable consequences of Justice Brennan's approach are no less significant for domestic producers. The owner of a small Florida farm might sell crops to a large nearby distributor, for example, who might then distribute them to grocers across the country. If foreseeability were the controlling criterion, the farmer could be sued in Alaska or any number of other States' courts without ever leaving town. And the issue of foreseeability may itself be contested so that significant expenses are incurred just on the preliminary issue of jurisdiction. Jurisdictional rules should avoid these costs whenever possible.

The conclusion that the authority to subject a defendant to judgment depends on purposeful availment, consistent with Justice O'Connor's opinion in *Asahi*, does not by itself resolve many difficult questions of jurisdiction that will arise in particular cases. The defendant's conduct and the economic realities of the market the defendant seeks to serve will differ across cases, and judicial exposition will, in common-law fashion, clarify the contours of that principle.

III

In this case, petitioner directed marketing and sales efforts at the United States. It may be that, assuming it were otherwise empowered to legislate on the subject, the Congress could authorize the exercise of jurisdiction in appropriate courts. That circumstance is not presented in this case, however, and it is neither necessary nor appropriate to address here any constitutional concerns that might be attendant to that exercise of power. See *Asahi.* Nor is it necessary to determine what substantive law might apply were Congress to authorize jurisdiction in a federal court in New Jersey. A sovereign's legislative authority to regulate conduct may present considerations different from those presented by its authority to subject a defendant to judgment in its courts. Here the question concerns the authority of a New Jersey state court to exercise jurisdiction, so it is petitioner's purposeful contacts with New Jersey, not with the United States, that alone are relevant.

Respondent has not established that J. McIntyre engaged in conduct purposefully directed at New Jersey. Recall that respondent's claim of jurisdiction centers on three facts: The distributor agreed to sell J. McIntyre's machines in the United States; J. McIntyre officials attended trade shows in several States but not in New Jersey; and up to four machines ended up in New Jersey. The British manufacturer had no office in New Jersey; it neither paid taxes nor owned property there; and it neither advertised in, nor sent any employees to, the State. Indeed, after discovery the trial court found that the "defendant does not have a single contact with New Jersey short of the machine in question ending up in this state." These facts may reveal an intent to serve the U.S. market, but they do not show that J. McIntyre purposefully availed itself of the New Jersey market.

It is notable that the New Jersey Supreme Court appears to agree, for it could "not find that J. McIntyre had a presence or minimum contacts in this State — in any jurisprudential sense — that would justify a New Jersey court to exercise jurisdiction in this case." The court nonetheless held that petitioner could be sued in New Jersey based on a "stream-of-commerce theory of jurisdiction." As discussed, however, the stream-of-commerce metaphor cannot supersede either the mandate of the Due Process Clause or the limits on judicial authority that Clause ensures. The New Jersey Supreme Court also cited "significant policy reasons" to justify its holding, including the State's "strong interest in protecting its citizens from defective products." That interest is doubtless strong, but the Constitution commands restraint before discarding liberty in the name of expediency.

Due process protects petitioner's right to be subject only to lawful authority. At no time did petitioner engage in any activities in New Jersey that reveal an intent to invoke or benefit from the protection of its laws. New Jersey is without power to adjudge the rights and liabilities of J. McIntyre, and its exercise of jurisdiction would violate due process. The contrary judgment of the New Jersey Supreme Court is

Reversed.

JUSTICE BREYER, with whom JUSTICE ALITO joins, concurring in the judgment.

The Supreme Court of New Jersey adopted a broad understanding of the scope of personal jurisdiction based on its view that "[t]he increasingly fast-paced globalization of the world economy has removed national borders as a barrier to trade." I do not doubt that there have been many recent changes in commerce and communications, many of which are not anticipated by our precedents, but this case does not present any of those issues. So I think it unwise to announce a rule of broad applicability without full consideration of the modern-day consequences.

In my view, the outcome of this case is determined by our precedents. Based on the facts found by the New Jersey courts, respondent Robert Nicastro failed to meet his burden to demonstrate that it was constitutionally proper to exercise jurisdiction over petitioner J. McIntyre Machinery, Ltd. (British Manufacturer), a British firm that manufactures scrap-metal machines in Great Britain and sells them through an independent distributor in the United States (American Distributor). On that basis, I agree with the plurality that the contrary judgment of the Supreme Court of New Jersey should be reversed.

I

In asserting jurisdiction over the British Manufacturer, the Supreme Court of New Jersey relied most heavily on three primary facts as providing constitutionally sufficient "contacts" with New Jersey, thereby making it fundamentally fair to hale the British Manufacturer before its courts: (1) The American Distributor on one occasion sold and shipped one machine to a New Jersey customer, namely, Mr. Nicastro's employer, Mr. Curcio; (2) the British Manufacturer permitted, indeed wanted, its independent American Distributor to sell its machines to anyone in America willing to buy them; and (3) representatives of the British Manufacturer attended trade shows in "such cities as Chicago, Las Vegas, New Orleans, Orlando, San Diego, and San Francisco." In my view, these facts do not provide contacts between the British firm and the State of New Jersey constitutionally sufficient to support New Jersey's assertion of jurisdiction in this case.

None of our precedents finds that a single isolated sale, even if accompanied by the kind of sales effort indicated here, is sufficient. Rather, this Court's previous holdings suggest the contrary. The Court has held that a single sale to a customer who takes an accident-causing product to a different State (where the accident takes place) is not a sufficient basis for asserting jurisdiction. See *World-Wide Volkswagen Corp.* And the Court, in separate opinions, has strongly suggested that a single sale of a product in a State does not constitute an adequate basis for asserting jurisdiction over an out-of-state defendant, even if that defendant places his goods in the stream of commerce, fully aware (and hoping) that such a sale will take place. See *Asahi* (opinion of O'Connor, J.) (requiring "something more" than simply placing "a product into the stream of commerce," even if defendant is "awar[e]" that the stream "may or will sweep the product into the forum State"); (Brennan, J., concurring in part and concurring in judgment) (jurisdiction should lie where a sale in a State is part of "the regular and anticipated flow" of commerce into the State, but not where that sale is only an "edd[y]," *i.e.*, an isolated occurrence); (Stevens, J., concurring in part and concurring in judgment) (indicating that "the volume, the value, and the hazardous character" of a good may affect the jurisdictional inquiry and emphasizing Asahi's "regular course of dealing").

Here, the relevant facts found by the New Jersey Supreme Court show no "regular ... flow" or "regular course" of sales in New Jersey; and there is no "something more," such as special state-related design, advertising, advice, marketing, or anything else. Mr. Nicastro, who here bears the burden of proving jurisdiction, has shown no specific effort by the British Manufacturer to sell in New Jersey. He has introduced no list of potential New Jersey customers who might, for example, have regularly attended trade shows. And he has not otherwise shown that the British Manufacturer "purposefully avail[ed] itself of the privilege of conducting activities" within New Jersey, or that it delivered its goods in the stream of commerce "with the expectation that they will be purchased" by New Jersey users. *World-Wide Volkswagen.*

There may well have been other facts that Mr. Nicastro could have demonstrated in support of jurisdiction. And the dissent considers some of those facts. But the plaintiff bears the burden of establishing jurisdiction, and here I would take the facts precisely as the New Jersey Supreme Court stated them.

Accordingly, on the record present here, resolving this case requires no more than adhering to our precedents.

II

I would not go further. Because the incident at issue in this case does not implicate modern concerns, and because the factual record leaves many open questions, this is an unsuitable vehicle for making broad pronouncements that refashion basic jurisdictional rules.

A

The plurality seems to state strict rules that limit jurisdiction where a defendant does not "inten[d] to submit to the power of a sovereign" and cannot "be said to have targeted the forum." But what do those standards mean when a company targets the world by selling products from its Web site? And does it matter if, instead of shipping the products directly, a company consigns the products through an intermediary (say, Amazon.com) who then receives and fulfills the orders? And what if the company markets its products through popup advertisements that it knows will be viewed in a forum? Those issues have serious commercial consequences but are totally absent in this case.

B

But though I do not agree with the plurality's seemingly strict no-jurisdiction rule, I am not persuaded by the absolute approach adopted by the New Jersey Supreme Court and urged by respondent and his *amici.* Under that view, a producer is subject to jurisdiction for a products-liability action so long as it "knows or reasonably should know that its products are distributed through a nationwide distribution system that *might* lead to those products being sold in any of the fifty states." In the context of this case, I cannot agree.

For one thing, to adopt this view would abandon the heretofore accepted inquiry of whether, focusing upon the relationship between "the defendant, the *forum*, and the litigation," it is fair, in light of the defendant's contacts *with that forum*, to subject the defendant to suit there. Shaffer v. Heitner, 433 U.S. 186, 204 (1977) (emphasis added). It would ordinarily rest jurisdiction instead upon no more than the occurrence of a product-based accident in the forum State. But this Court has rejected the notion that a defendant's amenability to suit "travel[s] with the chattel." *World-Wide Volkswagen.*

For another, I cannot reconcile so automatic a rule with the constitutional demand for "minimum contacts" and "purposefu[l] avail[ment]," each of which rest upon a particular notion of defendant-focused fairness. A rule like the New Jersey Supreme Court's would permit every State to assert jurisdiction in a products-liability suit against any domestic manufacturer who sells its products (made anywhere in the United States) to a national distributor, no matter how large or small the manufacturer, no matter how distant the forum, and no matter how few the number of items that end up in the particular forum at issue. What might appear fair in the case of a large manufacturer which specifically seeks, or expects, an equal-sized distributor to sell its product in a distant State might seem unfair in the case of a small manufacturer (say, an Appalachian potter) who sells his product (cups and saucers) exclusively to a large distributor, who resells a single item (a coffee mug) to a buyer from a distant State (Hawaii). I know too little about the range of these or in-between possibilities to abandon in favor of the more absolute rule what has previously been this Court's less absolute approach.

Further, the fact that the defendant is a foreign, rather than a domestic, manufacturer makes the basic fairness of an absolute rule yet more uncertain. I am again less certain than is the New Jersey Supreme Court that the nature of international commerce has changed so significantly as to require a new approach to personal jurisdiction.

It may be that a larger firm can readily "alleviate the risk of burdensome litigation by procuring insurance, passing the expected costs on to customers, or, if the risks are too great, severing its connection with the State." *World-Wide Volkswagen.* But manufacturers come in many shapes and sizes. It may be fundamentally unfair to require a small Egyptian shirt maker, a Brazilian manufacturing cooperative, or a Kenyan coffee farmer, selling its products through international distributors, to respond to products-liability tort suits in virtually every State in the United States, even those in respect to which the foreign firm has no connection at all but the sale of a single (allegedly defective) good. And a rule like the New Jersey Supreme Court suggests would require every product manufacturer, large or small, selling to American distributors to understand not only the tort law of every State, but also the wide variance in the way courts within different States apply that law. See, e.g., Dept. of Justice, Bureau of Justice Statistics Bulletin, Tort Trials and Verdicts in Large Counties, 2001, p. 11 (reporting percentage of plaintiff winners in tort trials among 46 populous counties, ranging from 17.9% (Worcester, Mass.) to 69.1% (Milwaukee, Wis.)).

C

At a minimum, I would not work such a change to the law in the way either the plurality or the New Jersey Supreme Court suggests without a better understanding of the relevant contemporary commercial circumstances. Insofar as such considerations are relevant to any change in present law, they might be presented in a case (unlike the present one) in which the Solicitor General participates.

This case presents no such occasion, and so I again reiterate that I would adhere strictly to our precedents and the limited facts found by the New Jersey Supreme Court. And on those grounds, I do not think we can find jurisdiction in this case. Accordingly, though I agree with the plurality as to the outcome of this case, I concur only in the judgment of that opinion and not its reasoning.

Justice Ginsburg, with whom Justice Sotomayor and Justice Kagan join, dissenting.

A foreign industrialist seeks to develop a market in the United States for machines it manufactures. It hopes to derive substantial revenue from sales it makes to United States purchasers. Where in the United States buyers reside does not matter to this manufacturer. Its goal is simply to sell as much as it can, wherever it can. It excludes no region or State from the market it wishes to reach. But, all things considered, it prefers to avoid products liability litigation in the United States. To that end, it engages a U.S. distributor to ship its machines stateside. Has it succeeded in escaping personal jurisdiction in a State where one of its products is sold and causes injury or even death to a local user?

Under this Court's pathmarking precedent in *International Shoe Co.*, and subsequent decisions, one would expect the answer to be unequivocally, "No." But instead, six Justices of this Court, in divergent opinions, tell us that the manufacturer has avoided the jurisdiction of our state courts, except perhaps in States where its products are sold in sizeable quantities. Inconceivable as it may have seemed yesterday, the splintered majority today "turn[s] the clock back to the days before modern long-arm statutes when a manufacturer, to avoid being haled into court where a user is injured, need only Pilate-like wash its hands of a product by having independent distributors market it." Weintraub, *A Map Out of the Personal Jurisdiction Labyrinth*, 28 U.C. Davis L. Rev. 531, 555 (1995).

I

From at least 1995 until 2001, McIntyre UK retained an Ohio-based company, McIntyre Machinery America, Ltd. (McIntyre America), "as its exclusive distributor for the entire United States." * * * McIntyre UK never instructed its distributor to avoid certain States or regions of the country; rather, as just noted, the manufacturer engaged McIntyre America to attract customers "from anywhere in the United States."

In sum, McIntyre UK's regular attendance and exhibitions at ISRI conventions was surely a purposeful step to reach customers for its products "anywhere in the United States." At least as purposeful was McIntyre UK's engagement of McIntyre America as the conduit for sales of McIntyre UK's machines to buyers "throughout the United States." Given McIntyre UK's endeavors to reach and profit from the United States market as a whole, Nicastro's suit, I would hold, has been brought in a forum entirely appropriate for the adjudication of his claim. He alleges that McIntyre UK's shear machine was defectively designed or manufactured and, as a result, caused injury to him at his workplace. The machine arrived in Nicastro's New Jersey workplace not randomly or fortuitously, but as a result of the U.S. connections and distribution system that McIntyre UK deliberately arranged. On what sensible view of the allocation of adjudicatory authority could the place of Nicastro's injury within the United States be deemed off limits for his products liability claim against a foreign manufacturer who targeted the United States (including all the States that constitute the Nation) as the territory it sought to develop?

II

A few points on which there should be no genuine debate bear statement at the outset. First, all agree, McIntyre UK surely is not subject to general (all-purpose) jurisdiction in New Jersey courts, for that foreign-country corporation is hardly "at home" in New Jersey. The question, rather, is one of specific jurisdiction, which turns on an "affiliatio[n] between the forum and the underlying controversy."

Second, no issue of the fair and reasonable allocation of adjudicatory authority among States of the United States is present in this case. New Jersey's exercise of personal jurisdiction over a foreign manufacturer whose dangerous product caused a workplace injury in New Jersey does not tread on the domain, or diminish the sovereignty, of any sister State. Indeed, among States of the United States, the State in which the injury occurred would seem most suitable for litigation of a products liability tort claim.

Third, the constitutional limits on a state court's adjudicatory authority derive from considerations of due process, not state sovereignty. * * *

Finally, in *International Shoe* itself, and decisions thereafter, the Court has made plain that legal fictions, notably "presence" and "implied consent," should be discarded, for they conceal the actual bases on which jurisdiction rests. "[T]he relationship among the defendant, the forum, and the litigation" determines whether due process permits the exercise of personal jurisdiction over a defendant, *Shaffer*, and "fictions of implied consent" or "corporate presence" do not advance the proper inquiry.

Whatever the state of academic debate over the role of consent in modern jurisdictional doctrines, the plurality's notion that consent is the animating concept draws no support from controlling decisions of this Court. Quite the contrary, the Court has explained, a forum can exercise jurisdiction when its contacts with the controversy are sufficient; invocation of a fictitious consent, the Court has repeatedly said, is unnecessary and unhelpful. See, e.g., *Burger King Corp.* (Due Process Clause permits "forum ... to assert specific jurisdiction over an out-of-state defendant who has not consented to suit there"); McGee v. International Life Ins. Co., 355 U.S. 220, 222 (1957) ("[T]his Court [has] abandoned 'consent,' 'doing business,' and 'presence' as the standard for measuring the extent of state judicial power over [out-of-state] corporations.").[5]

III

This case is illustrative of marketing arrangements for sales in the United States common in today's commercial world. A foreign-country manufacturer engages a U.S. company to promote and distribute the manufacturer's products, not in any particular State, but anywhere and everywhere in the United States the distributor can attract purchasers. The product proves defective and injures a user in the State where the user lives or works. Often, as here, the manufacturer will have liability insurance covering personal injuries caused by its products.

When industrial accidents happen, a long-arm statute in the State where the injury occurs generally permits assertion of jurisdiction, upon giving proper notice, over the foreign manufacturer. * * *

The modern approach to jurisdiction over corporations and other legal entities, ushered in by *International Shoe*, gave prime place to reason and fairness. Is it not fair and reasonable, given the mode of trading of which this case is an example, to require the international seller to defend at the place its products cause injury? Do not litigational convenience and choice-of-law considerations point in that direction? On what measure of reason and fairness can it be considered undue to require McIntyre UK to defend in New Jersey as an incident of its efforts to develop a market for its industrial machines anywhere and everywhere in the United States?[12] Is not the burden on McIntyre UK to defend in New Jersey fair, *i.e.*, a reasonable cost of transacting business internationally, in comparison to the burden on Nicastro to go to Nottingham, England to gain recompense for an injury he sustained using McIntyre's product at his workplace in Saddle Brook, New Jersey?

McIntyre UK dealt with the United States as a single market. Like most foreign manufacturers, it was concerned not with the prospect of suit in State X as opposed to State Y, but rather with its subjection to suit anywhere in the United States. As a McIntyre UK officer wrote in an e-mail to McIntyre America: "American law — who needs it?!" If McIntyre UK is answerable in the United States at all, is it not "perfectly appropriate to permit the exercise of that jurisdiction ... at the place of injury"? See Degnan & Kane, *The Exercise of Jurisdiction Over and Enforcement of Judgments Against Alien Defendants*, 39 Hastings L.J. 799, 813–815 (1988) (noting that "[i]n the international order," the State that counts is the United States, not its component

5. The plurality's notion that jurisdiction over foreign corporations depends upon the defendant's "submission," seems scarcely different from the long-discredited fiction of implied consent. It bears emphasis that a majority of this Court's members do not share the plurality's view.

12. The plurality suggests that the Due Process Clause might permit a federal district court in New Jersey, sitting in diversity and applying New Jersey law, to adjudicate McIntyre UK's liability to Nicastro. In other words, McIntyre UK might be compelled to bear the burden of traveling to New Jersey and defending itself there under New Jersey's products liability law, but would be entitled to federal adjudication of Nicastro's state-law claim. I see no basis in the Due Process Clause for such a curious limitation.

States,[13] and that the fair place of suit within the United States is essentially a question of venue).

In sum, McIntyre UK, by engaging McIntyre America to promote and sell its machines in the United States, "purposefully availed itself" of the United States market nationwide, not a market in a single State or a discrete collection of States. McIntyre UK thereby availed itself of the market of all States in which its products were sold by its exclusive distributor. "Th[e] 'purposeful availment' requirement," this Court has explained, simply "ensures that a defendant will not be haled into a jurisdiction solely as a result of 'random,' 'fortuitous,' or 'attenuated' contacts." *Burger King.* Adjudicatory authority is appropriately exercised where "actions by the defendant *himself*" give rise to the affiliation with the forum. How could McIntyre UK not have intended, by its actions targeting a national market, to sell products in the fourth largest destination for imports among all States of the United States and the largest scrap metal market? But see plurality opinion (manufacturer's purposeful efforts to sell its products nationwide are "not ... relevant" to the personal jurisdiction inquiry).

Courts, both state and federal, confronting facts similar to those here, have rightly rejected the conclusion that a manufacturer selling its products across the USA may evade jurisdiction in any and all States, including the State where its defective product is distributed and causes injury. They have held, instead, that it would undermine principles of fundamental fairness to insulate the foreign manufacturer from accountability in court at the place within the United States where the manufacturer's products caused injury.

IV

A

While this Court has not considered in any prior case the now-prevalent pattern presented here — a foreign-country manufacturer enlisting a U.S. distributor to develop a market in the United States for the manufacturer's products — none of the Court's decisions tug against the judgment made by the New Jersey Supreme Court. McIntyre contends otherwise, citing *World-Wide Volkswagen*, and *Asahi.*

World-Wide Volkswagen concerned a New York car dealership that sold solely in the New York market, and a New York distributor who supplied retailers in three States only: New York, Connecticut, and New Jersey. * * * Rejecting the Oklahoma courts' assertion of jurisdiction over the New York dealer and distributor, this Court observed that the defendants had done nothing to serve the market for cars in Oklahoma. Jurisdiction, the Court held, could not be based on the *customer's* unilateral act of driving the vehicle to Oklahoma.

Notably, the foreign manufacturer of the Audi in *World-Wide Volkswagen* did not object to the jurisdiction of the Oklahoma courts and the U.S. importer abandoned

---

13. "For purposes of international law and foreign relations, the separate identities of individual states of the Union are generally irrelevant." Born, *Reflections on Judicial Jurisdiction in International Cases*, 17 Ga. J. Int'l & Comp. L. 1, 36 (1987).

its initially stated objection. And most relevant here, the Court's opinion indicates that an objection to jurisdiction by the manufacturer or national distributor would have been unavailing. To reiterate, the Court said in *World-Wide Volkswagen* that, when a manufacturer or distributor aims to sell its product to customers in several States, it is reasonable "to subject it to suit in [any] one of those States if its allegedly defective [product] has there been the source of injury."

Asahi arose out of a motorcycle accident in California. Plaintiff, a California resident injured in the accident, sued the Taiwanese manufacturer of the motorcycle's tire tubes, claiming that defects in its product caused the accident. The tube manufacturer cross-claimed against Asahi, the Japanese maker of the valve assembly, and Asahi contested the California courts' jurisdiction. By the time the case reached this Court, the injured plaintiff had settled his case and only the indemnity claim by the Taiwanese company against the Japanese valve-assembly manufacturer remained.

The decision was not a close call. The Court had before it a foreign plaintiff, the Taiwanese manufacturer, and a foreign defendant, the Japanese valve-assembly maker, and the indemnification dispute concerned a transaction between those parties that occurred abroad. All agreed on the bottom line: The Japanese valve-assembly manufacturer was not reasonably brought into the California courts to litigate a dispute with another foreign party over a transaction that took place outside the United States.

* * * In any event, Asahi, unlike McIntyre UK, did not itself seek out customers in the United States, it engaged no distributor to promote its wares here, it appeared at no tradeshows in the United States, and, of course, it had no Web site advertising its products to the world. Moreover, Asahi was a component-part manufacturer with "little control over the final destination of its products once they were delivered into the stream of commerce." It was important to the Court in *Asahi* that "those who use Asahi components in their final products, and sell those products in California, [would be] subject to the application of California tort law." To hold that *Asahi* controls this case would, to put it bluntly, be dead wrong.[15]

B

The Court's judgment also puts United States plaintiffs at a disadvantage in comparison to similarly situated complainants elsewhere in the world. Of particular note, within the European Union, in which the United Kingdom is a participant, the jurisdiction New Jersey would have exercised is not at all exceptional. The European Regulation on Jurisdiction and the Recognition and Enforcement of Judgments provides for the exercise of specific jurisdiction "in matters relating to tort ... in the courts for

15. The plurality notes the low volume of sales in New Jersey. A $24,900 shearing machine, however, is unlikely to sell in bulk worldwide, much less in any given State. By dollar value, the price of a single machine represents a significant sale. Had a manufacturer sold in New Jersey $24,900 worth of flannel shirts, see Nelson v. Park Industries, Inc., 717 F.2d 1120 (CA7 1983), cigarette lighters, see Oswalt v. Scripto, Inc., 616 F.2d 191 (CA5 1980), or wire-rope splices, see Hedrick v. Daiko Shoji Co., 715 F.2d 1355 (CA9 1983), the Court would presumably find the defendant amenable to suit in that State.

the place where the harmful event occurred." Council Reg. 44/2001, Art. 5, 2001 O.J. (L. 12) 4. The European Court of Justice has interpreted this prescription to authorize jurisdiction either where the harmful act occurred or at the place of injury.

V

The commentators who gave names to what we now call "general jurisdiction" and "specific jurisdiction" anticipated that when the latter achieves its full growth, considerations of litigational convenience and the respective situations of the parties would determine when it is appropriate to subject a defendant to trial in the plaintiff's community. Litigational considerations include "the convenience of witnesses and the ease of ascertaining the governing law." As to the parties, courts would differently appraise two situations: (1) cases involving a substantially local plaintiff, like Nicastro, injured by the activity of a defendant engaged in interstate or international trade; and (2) cases in which the defendant is a natural or legal person whose economic activities and legal involvements are largely home-based, *i.e.*, entities without designs to gain substantial revenue from sales in distant markets. * * * [C]ourts presented with [the] first scenario — a local plaintiff injured by the activity of a manufacturer seeking to exploit a multistate or global market — have repeatedly confirmed that jurisdiction is appropriately exercised by courts of the place where the product was sold and caused injury.

For the reasons stated, I would hold McIntyre UK answerable in New Jersey for the harm Nicastro suffered at his workplace in that State using McIntyre UK's shearing machine. While I dissent from the Court's judgment, I take heart that the plurality opinion does not speak for the Court, for that opinion would take a giant step away from the "notions of fair play and substantial justice" underlying *International Shoe*.

Notes and Questions

1. Despite the passage of twenty-four years and dramatic change in personnel (only Justice Scalia participated in both *Asahi* and *J. McIntyre*), neither case generated a majority opinion on when the stream of commerce constitutes purposeful availment. Does Justice Kennedy adopt the O'Connor theory from *Asahi*? Does Justice Ginsburg adopt the Brennan theory from *Asahi*? If not, what are their respective theories?

2. *Asahi* presented a classic stream of commerce case, with the defendant selling components that are then put into a finished product, which is marketed by a different company. *J. McIntyre* is a bit different. There, the defendant manufactured and marketed the finished product. Does either defendant — the component maker or the maker of the finished product — have more control over where its product will end up being marketed? If so, should that fact matter to the assessment of purposeful availment?

3. Justice Kennedy differentiates between "targeting" a state and "predicting" that goods will reach the state. He also observes that "foreign corporations will often target or concentrate on particular States, subjecting them to specific jurisdiction." For a manufacturer selling its product through a multi-state distributor, what would the indicia be of "targeting" or "concentrating" on a particular state? Won't manufacturers

mostly be concerned with the volume of sales (and getting paid), rather than the location of the states?

4. Justices Breyer's opinion asserts that "none of our precedents finds that a single isolated sale * * * is sufficient [for jurisdiction]." On the other hand, *International Shoe*, citing *Hess v. Pawloski*, indicated that a single act can be sufficient for jurisdiction based on a claim arising out of that act. Similarly in *McGee v. International Life Ins. Co.*, the Court upheld jurisdiction even though there was no evidence that the insurance company had done any business in the forum apart from the single policy at issue in the case. If J. McIntrye had sold this machine directly to the user in New Jersey and had shipped the machine there, would that be sufficient for a tort claim arising from the use of the machine? What about a breach of contract claim?

5. Justice Breyer's opinion stressed that in the facts of *J. McIntyre*, there was no "'regular * * * flow' or 'regular course' of sales in the forum." If there were such a regular flow, would that be sufficient for jurisdiction? Consider the facts of *Asahi*. There, the Taiwanese company Cheng Shin bought between 100,000 and 500,000 valves from Asahi for use in its tires. Cheng Shin sold its tires throughout the world but 20% of its sales in the U.S. were in California. Do you think Justice Breyer would find purposeful availment in these circumstances?

6. Justice Kennedy focuses on whether the defendant has "manifest[ed] an intention to submit to the power of a sovereign." Justice Ginsburg criticizes this focus on "consent" and argues that consent as the animating concept of personal jurisdiction "draws no support from controlling decisions of this Court." Do you agree? For further discussion of consent as the foundational principle in jurisdiction, see infra section C.1. Though Justice Ginsburg rejects consent, she does not argue that the conduct of the defendant is irrelevant. Instead she argues that the requirement of purposeful availment assures that the case has an "affiliation with the forum" and that this affiliation stems from "action by the defendant himself." To the extent that jurisdiction is about the scope of sovereign power, why should it depend at all on the actions of the defendant rather than on the impact on the people or territory of the sovereign?

7. Though the Court in *Asahi* was badly fragmented on the question of purposeful availment and therefore whether Asahi had a relevant contact with California, it was unanimous that jurisdiction was improper. Eight of the Justices so held based on the fairness or reasonableness prong of the analysis under *International Shoe*. By the time the case got to the Court, the underlying claim between the plaintiff and Cheng Shin had been settled; thus, the California plaintiff was no longer a party and the dispute was between a Taiwanese company and a Japanese company. And the dispute had nothing to do with California road safety or California law—it concerned whether the companies' commercial agreement required Asahi to indemnify Cheng Shin. Under these unique circumstances, the Court held that jurisdiction would be unreasonable. 480 U.S. at 113–116. *Asahi* remains the only case in which the Court has rejected jurisdiction on the basis of unfairness. Other decisions rejecting personal jurisdiction have done so on the basis of finding that there was no relevant contact between the defendant and the forum.

8. Justices Kennedy and Breyer raise hypothetical cases in which, they suggest, it would be problematic to find that the defendant had forged a relevant contact with the forum. Why, though, should not jurisdiction in those hypotheticals be rejected on the ground that it would not be reasonable (as in *Asahi*)?

4. General Jurisdiction

The phrase "general jurisdiction" is used when the plaintiff's claim does not arise from or relate to the defendant's activity in the forum. The paradigm case of general jurisdiction is Perkins v. Benguet Consolidated Mining Co., 342 U.S. 437 (1952). There, the defendant was a Philippine corporation that mined precious metals in the Philippines. It ceased operations during the Japanese occupation of the Philippines in World War II. The limited activities that the corporation conducted during the war were run from an office in Ohio. The Supreme Court upheld jurisdiction over the corporation in Ohio on a cause of action that had nothing to do with its Ohio activities. The Court upheld jurisdiction at the defendant's de facto corporate headquarters. Before *Perkins*, it was well established that corporations could be sued in their place of incorporation on any claim. You will recall that an analogous rule for individuals permits them to be sued in their domicile. See Milliken v. Meyer, 311 U.S. 457 (1940), which was discussed in Section B.2, supra.

In Helicopteros Nacionales de Columbia, S. A. v. Hall, 466 U.S. 408 (1984), the Court considered whether business activities that were less than a de facto headquarters were sufficient for general jurisdiction. In *Helicopteros*, the defendant's connections with the forum were that it had purchased $4 million worth of helicopters, spare parts, and accessories from a forum company and sent its pilots there for training. All of this had occurred over a period of seven years. Although this activity was in some sense "systematic and continuous," the Court held that the activities were not sufficient for general jurisdiction.

In the wake of these cases, courts concluded that corporations could be subject to general jurisdiction in states in which they did "substantial" or "continuous and systematic" business. They differed markedly, however, on how much activity within a forum constituted enough to justify general jurisdiction. In 2011, the Court decided Goodyear Dunlop Tires Operations, S.A. v. Brown, 131 S. Ct. 2846 (2011), in which it appeared to limit general jurisdiction. Instead of looking to whether the company had substantial or continuous and systematic ties with the forum, a court was to determine whether the defendant was "at home" in the forum. Three years later, in the following case, the Court returned to the issue.

Daimler AG v. Bauman

134 S. Ct. 746, 187 L.Ed. 2d 624 (2014)

JUSTICE GINSBURG delivered the opinion of the Court.

This case concerns the authority of a court in the United States to entertain a claim brought by foreign plaintiffs against a foreign defendant based on events occurring entirely outside the United States. The litigation commenced in 2004, when twenty-two Argentinian residents filed a complaint in the United States District Court for the Northern District of California against DaimlerChrysler Aktiengesellschaft (Daimler), a German public stock company, headquartered in Stuttgart, that manufactures Mercedes-Benz vehicles in Germany. The complaint alleged that during Argentina's 1976–1983 "Dirty War," Daimler's Argentinian subsidiary, Mercedes-Benz Argentina (MB Argentina) collaborated with state security forces to kidnap, detain, torture, and kill certain MB Argentina workers, among them, plaintiffs or persons closely related to plaintiffs. Damages for the alleged human-rights violations were sought from Daimler under the laws of the United States, California, and Argentina. Jurisdiction over the lawsuit was predicated on the California contacts of Mercedes-Benz USA, LLC (MBUSA), a subsidiary of Daimler incorporated in Delaware with its principal place of business in New Jersey. MBUSA distributes Daimler-manufactured vehicles to independent dealerships throughout the United States, including California.

The question presented is whether the Due Process Clause of the Fourteenth Amendment precludes the District Court from exercising jurisdiction over Daimler in this case, given the absence of any California connection to the atrocities, perpetrators, or victims described in the complaint. Plaintiffs invoked the court's general or all-purpose jurisdiction. California, they urge, is a place where Daimler may be sued on any and all claims against it, wherever in the world the claims may arise. For example, as plaintiffs' counsel affirmed, under the proffered jurisdictional theory, if a Daimler-manufactured vehicle overturned in Poland, injuring a Polish driver and passenger, the injured parties could maintain a design defect suit in California. See Tr. of Oral Arg. 28–29. Exercises of personal jurisdiction so exorbitant, we hold, are barred by due process constraints on the assertion of adjudicatory authority.

In *Goodyear Dunlop Tires Operations, S.A. v. Brown*, 131 S. Ct. 2846 (2011), we addressed the distinction between general or all-purpose jurisdiction, and specific or conduct-linked jurisdiction. As to the former, we held that a court may assert jurisdiction over a foreign corporation "to hear any and all claims against [it]" only when the corporation's affiliations with the State in which suit is brought are so constant and pervasive "as to render [it] essentially at home in the forum State." Instructed by *Goodyear*, we conclude Daimler is not "at home" in California, and cannot be sued there for injuries plaintiffs attribute to MB Argentina's conduct in Argentina.

I

In 2004, plaintiffs (respondents here) filed suit in the United States District Court for the Northern District of California, alleging that MB Argentina collaborated with Argentinian state security forces to kidnap, detain, torture, and kill plaintiffs and their relatives during the military dictatorship in place there from 1976 through 1983, a period known as Argentina's "Dirty War." Based on those allegations, plaintiffs asserted claims under the Alien Tort Statute, 28 U.S.C. § 1350, and the Torture Victim Protection Act of 1991, 106 Stat. 73, note following 28 U.S.C. § 1350, as well as claims for wrongful death and intentional infliction of emotional distress under the laws of

California and Argentina. The incidents recounted in the complaint center on MB Argentina's plant in Gonzalez Catan, Argentina; no part of MB Argentina's alleged collaboration with Argentinian authorities took place in California or anywhere else in the United States.

Plaintiffs' operative complaint names only one corporate defendant: Daimler, the petitioner here. Plaintiffs seek to hold Daimler vicariously liable for MB Argentina's alleged malfeasance. Daimler is a German *Aktiengesellschaft* (public stock company) that manufactures Mercedes-Benz vehicles in Germany and has its headquarters in Stuttgart. At times relevant to this case, MB Argentina was a subsidiary wholly owned by Daimler's predecessor in interest.

Daimler moved to dismiss the action for want of personal jurisdiction. Opposing the motion, plaintiffs submitted declarations and exhibits purporting to demonstrate the presence of Daimler itself in California. Alternatively, plaintiffs maintained that jurisdiction over Daimler could be founded on the California contacts of MBUSA, a distinct corporate entity that, according to plaintiffs, should be treated as Daimler's agent for jurisdictional purposes.

MBUSA, an indirect subsidiary of Daimler, is a Delaware limited liability corporation. MBUSA serves as Daimler's exclusive importer and distributor in the United States, purchasing Mercedes-Benz automobiles from Daimler in Germany, then importing those vehicles, and ultimately distributing them to independent dealerships located throughout the Nation. Although MBUSA's principal place of business is in New Jersey, MBUSA has multiple California-based facilities, including a regional office in Costa Mesa, a Vehicle Preparation Center in Carson, and a Classic Center in Irvine. According to the record developed below, MBUSA is the largest supplier of luxury vehicles to the California market. In particular, over 10% of all sales of new vehicles in the United States take place in California, and MBUSA's California sales account for 2.4% of Daimler's worldwide sales.

The relationship between Daimler and MBUSA is delineated in a General Distributor Agreement, which sets forth requirements for MBUSA's distribution of Mercedes-Benz vehicles in the United States. That agreement established MBUSA as an "independent contracto[r]" that "buy[s] and sell[s] [vehicles] ... as an independent business for [its] own account." The agreement "does not make [MBUSA] ... a general or special agent, partner, joint venturer or employee of DAIMLERCHRYSLER or any DaimlerChrysler Group Company"; MBUSA "ha[s] no authority to make binding obligations for or act on behalf of DAIMLERCHRYSLER or any DaimlerChrysler Group Company."

[The district court granted Daimler's motion to dismiss. The Ninth Circuit initially affirmed but subsequently granted plaintiffs' petition for rehearing, withdrew its original opinion, and reversed the district court.] * * *

We granted certiorari to decide whether, consistent with the Due Process Clause of the Fourteenth Amendment, Daimler is amenable to suit in California courts for claims involving only foreign plaintiffs and conduct occurring entirely abroad.

II

Federal courts ordinarily follow state law in determining the bounds of their jurisdiction over persons. See Fed. Rule Civ. Proc. 4(k)(1)(A) (service of process is effective to establish personal jurisdiction over a defendant "who is subject to the jurisdiction of a court of general jurisdiction in the state where the district court is located"). Under California's long-arm statute, California state courts may exercise personal jurisdiction "on any basis not inconsistent with the Constitution of this state or of the United States." Cal. Civ. Proc. Code Ann. § 410.10 (West 2004). California's long- arm statute allows the exercise of personal jurisdiction to the full extent permissible under the U.S. Constitution. We therefore inquire whether the Ninth Circuit's holding comports with the limits imposed by federal due process.

III

In *Pennoyer v. Neff*, decided shortly after the enactment of the Fourteenth Amendment, the Court held that a tribunal's jurisdiction over persons reaches no farther than the geographic bounds of the forum. In time, however, that strict territorial approach yielded to a less rigid understanding, spurred by "changes in the technology of transportation and communication, and the tremendous growth of interstate business activity." Burnham v. Superior Court of Cal., County of Marin, 495 U.S. 604, 617 (1990) (opinion of SCALIA, J.).

* * *

[The] conception [in *International Shoe Company v. Washington*] of "fair play and substantial justice" presaged the development of two categories of personal jurisdiction. The first category is represented by *International Shoe* itself, a case in which the in-state activities of the corporate defendant "ha[d] not only been continuous and systematic, but also g[a]ve rise to the liabilities sued on." *International Shoe* recognized, as well, that "the commission of some single or occasional acts of the corporate agent in a state" may sometimes be enough to subject the corporation to jurisdiction in that State's tribunals with respect to suits relating to that in-state activity. Adjudicatory authority of this order, in which the suit "aris[es] out of or relate[s] to the defendant's contacts with the forum," Helicopteros Nacionales de Colombia, S.A. v. Hall, 466 U.S. 408, 414, n. 8 (1984), is today called "specific jurisdiction." See Goodyear (citing von Mehren & Trautman, Jurisdiction to Adjudicate: A Suggested Analysis, 79 Harv. L. Rev. 1121, 1144–1163 (1966) (hereinafter von Mehren & Trautman)).

International Shoe distinguished between, on the one hand, exercises of specific jurisdiction, as just described, and on the other, situations where a foreign corporation's "continuous corporate operations within a state [are] so substantial and of such a nature as to justify suit against it on causes of action arising from dealings entirely distinct from those activities." As we have since explained, "[a] court may assert general jurisdiction over foreign (sister-state or foreign-country) corporations to hear any and all claims against them when their affiliations with the State are so 'continuous and systematic' as to render them essentially at home in the forum State." *Goodyear.*[5]

Since *International Shoe,* "specific jurisdiction has become the centerpiece of modern jurisdiction theory, while general jurisdiction [has played] a reduced role." *Goodyear. International Shoe*'s momentous departure from *Pennoyer*'s rigidly territorial focus, we have noted, unleashed a rapid expansion of tribunals' ability to hear claims against out-of-state defendants when the episode-in-suit occurred in the forum or the defendant purposefully availed itself of the forum. Our subsequent decisions have continued to bear out the prediction that "specific jurisdiction will come into sharper relief and form a considerably more significant part of the scene."

Our post-*International Shoe* opinions on general jurisdiction, by comparison, are few. "[The Court's] 1952 decision in *Perkins v. Benguet Consol. Mining Co.* remains the textbook case of general jurisdiction appropriately exercised over a foreign corporation that has not consented to suit in the forum." *Goodyear.* The defendant in *Perkins,* Benguet, was a company incorporated under the laws of the Philippines, where it operated gold and silver mines. Benguet ceased its mining operations during the Japanese occupation of the Philippines in World War II; its president moved to Ohio, where he kept an office, maintained the company's files, and oversaw the company's activities. *Perkins v. Benguet Consol. Mining Co.,* 342 U.S. 437, 448 (1952). The plaintiff, an Ohio resident, sued Benguet on a claim that neither arose in Ohio nor related to the corporation's activities in that State. We held that the Ohio courts could exercise general jurisdiction over Benguet without offending due process. That was so, we later noted, because "Ohio was the corporation's principal, if temporary, place of business."[8]

The next case on point, *Helicopteros,* arose from a helicopter crash in Peru. Four U.S. citizens perished in that accident; their survivors and representatives brought suit in Texas state court against the helicopter's owner and operator, a Colombian corporation. That company's contacts with Texas were confined to "sending its chief executive officer to Houston for a contract-negotiation session; accepting into its New York bank account checks drawn on a Houston bank; purchasing helicopters, equipment, and training services from [a Texas-based helicopter company] for substantial sums; and sending personnel to [Texas] for training." Notably, those contacts bore no apparent relationship to the accident that gave rise to the suit. We held that the company's Texas connections did not resemble the "continuous and systematic general business contacts ... found to exist in *Perkins.*" "[M]ere purchases, even if

5. Colloquy at oral argument illustrated the respective provinces of general and specific jurisdiction over persons. Two hypothetical scenarios were posed: *First,* if a California plaintiff, injured in a California accident involving a Daimler- manufactured vehicle, sued Daimler in California court alleging that the vehicle was defectively designed, that court's adjudicatory authority would be premised on specific jurisdiction. *Second,* if a similar accident took place in Poland and injured Polish plaintiffs sued Daimler in California court, the question would be one of general jurisdiction.

8. * * * All of Benguet's activities were directed by the company's president from within Ohio. * * * Given the wartime circumstances, Ohio could be considered "a surrogate for the place of incorporation or head office." * * *

occurring at regular intervals," we clarified, "are not enough to warrant a State's assertion of *in personam* jurisdiction over a nonresident corporation in a cause of action not related to those purchase transactions."

Most recently, in *Goodyear*, we answered the question: "Are foreign subsidiaries of a United States parent corporation amenable to suit in state court on claims unrelated to any activity of the subsidiaries in the forum State?" That case arose from a bus accident outside Paris that killed two boys from North Carolina. The boys' parents brought a wrongful-death suit in North Carolina state court alleging that the bus's tire was defectively manufactured. The complaint named as defendants not only The Goodyear Tire and Rubber Company (Goodyear), an Ohio corporation, but also Goodyear's Turkish, French, and Luxembourgian subsidiaries. Those foreign subsidiaries, which manufactured tires for sale in Europe and Asia, lacked any affiliation with North Carolina. A small percentage of tires manufactured by the foreign subsidiaries were distributed in North Carolina, however, and on that ground, the North Carolina Court of Appeals held the subsidiaries amenable to the general jurisdiction of North Carolina courts.

We reversed, observing that the North Carolina court's analysis "elided the essential difference between case-specific and all-purpose (general) jurisdiction." Although the placement of a product into the stream of commerce "may bolster an affiliation germane to *specific* jurisdiction," we explained, such contacts "do not warrant a determination that, based on those ties, the forum has *general* jurisdiction over a defendant." As *International Shoe* itself teaches, a corporation's "continuous activity of some sorts within a state is not enough to support the demand that the corporation be amenable to suits unrelated to that activity." Because Goodyear's foreign subsidiaries were "in no sense at home in North Carolina," we held, those subsidiaries could not be required to submit to the general jurisdiction of that State's courts. See also J. McIntyre Machinery, Ltd. v. Nicastro (GINSBURG, J., dissenting) (noting unanimous agreement that a foreign manufacturer, which engaged an independent U.S.-based distributor to sell its machines throughout the United States, could not be exposed to all-purpose jurisdiction in New Jersey courts based on those contacts).

As is evident from *Perkins*, *Helicopteros*, and *Goodyear*, general and specific jurisdiction have followed markedly different trajectories post-*International Shoe*. Specific jurisdiction has been cut loose from *Pennoyer*'s sway, but we have declined to stretch general jurisdiction beyond limits traditionally recognized. As this Court has increasingly trained on the "relationship among the defendant, the forum, and the litigation," *i.e.*, specific jurisdiction, general jurisdiction has come to occupy a less dominant place in the contemporary scheme.[11]

---

11. As the Court made plain in *Goodyear* and repeats here, general jurisdiction requires affiliations "so 'continuous and systematic' as to render [the foreign corporation] essentially at home in the forum State," i.e., comparable to a domestic enterprise in that state.

IV

* * *

A

In sustaining the exercise of general jurisdiction over Daimler, the Ninth Circuit relied on an agency theory, determining that MBUSA acted as Daimler's agent for jurisdictional purposes and then attributing MBUSA's California contacts to Daimler. The Ninth Circuit's agency analysis derived from Circuit precedent considering principally whether the subsidiary "performs services that are sufficiently important to the foreign corporation that if it did not have a representative to perform them, the corporation's own officials would undertake to perform substantially similar services."

This Court has not yet addressed whether a foreign corporation may be subjected to a court's general jurisdiction based on the contacts of its in-state subsidiary. Daimler argues, and several Courts of Appeals have held, that a subsidiary's jurisdictional contacts can be imputed to its parent only when the former is so dominated by the latter as to be its alter ego. The Ninth Circuit adopted a less rigorous test based on what it described as an "agency" relationship. Agencies, we note, come in many sizes and shapes: "One may be an agent for some business purposes and not others so that the fact that one may be an agent for one purpose does not make him or her an agent for every purpose."[13] A subsidiary, for example, might be its parent's agent for claims arising in the place where the subsidiary operates, yet not its agent regarding claims arising elsewhere. The Court of Appeals did not advert to that prospect. But we need not pass judgment on invocation of an agency theory in the context of general jurisdiction, for in no event can the appeals court's analysis be sustained.

The Ninth Circuit's agency finding rested primarily on its observation that MBUSA's services were "important" to Daimler, as gauged by Daimler's hypothetical readiness to perform those services itself if MBUSA did not exist. Formulated this way, the inquiry into importance stacks the deck, for it will always yield a pro-jurisdiction answer: "Anything a corporation does through an independent contractor, subsidiary, or distributor is presumably something that the corporation would do 'by other means' if the independent contractor, subsidiary, or distributor did not exist." The Ninth Circuit's agency theory thus appears to subject foreign corporations to general jurisdiction whenever they have an in-state subsidiary or affiliate, an outcome that would sweep beyond even the "sprawling view of general jurisdiction" we rejected in *Goodyear*.

13. Agency relationships, we have recognized, may be relevant to the existence of *specific* jurisdiction. "[T]he corporate personality," *International Shoe Co. v. Washington* observed, "is a fiction, although a fiction intended to be acted upon as though it were a fact." See generally 1 W. Fletcher, Cyclopedia of the Law of Corporations § 30, p. 30 (Supp. 2012–2013) ("A corporation is a distinct legal entity that can act only through its agents."). As such, a corporation can purposefully avail itself of a forum by directing its agents or distributors to take action there. It does not inevitably follow, however, that similar reasoning applies to *general* jurisdiction.

B

Even if we were to assume that MBUSA is at home in California, and further to assume MBUSA's contacts are imputable to Daimler, there would still be no basis to subject Daimler to general jurisdiction in California, for Daimler's slim contacts with the State hardly render it at home there.

Goodyear made clear that only a limited set of affiliations with a forum will render a defendant amenable to all-purpose jurisdiction there. "For an individual, the paradigm forum for the exercise of general jurisdiction is the individual's domicile; for a corporation, it is an equivalent place, one in which the corporation is fairly regarded as at home." With respect to a corporation, the place of incorporation and principal place of business are "paradig[m] ... bases for general jurisdiction." Those affiliations have the virtue of being unique — that is, each ordinarily indicates only one place — as well as easily ascertainable. These bases afford plaintiffs recourse to at least one clear and certain forum in which a corporate defendant may be sued on any and all claims.

Goodyear did not hold that a corporation may be subject to general jurisdiction *only* in a forum where it is incorporated or has its principal place of business; it simply typed those places paradigm all-purpose forums. Plaintiffs would have us look beyond the exemplar bases *Goodyear* identified, and approve the exercise of general jurisdiction in every State in which a corporation "engages in a substantial, continuous, and systematic course of business." That formulation, we hold, is unacceptably grasping.

As noted, the words "continuous and systematic" were used in *International Shoe* to describe instances in which the exercise of *specific* jurisdiction would be appropriate. Turning to all-purpose jurisdiction, in contrast, *International Shoe* speaks of "instances in which the continuous corporate operations within a state [are] so substantial and of such a nature as to justify suit ... *on causes of action arising from dealings entirely distinct from those activities*." Accordingly, the inquiry under *Goodyear* is not whether a foreign corporation's in-forum contacts can be said to be in some sense "continuous and systematic," it is whether that corporation's "affiliations with the State are so 'continuous and systematic' as to render [it] essentially at home in the forum State."[19]

Here, neither Daimler nor MBUSA is incorporated in California, nor does either entity have its principal place of business there. If Daimler's California activities sufficed to allow adjudication of this Argentina-rooted case in California, the same global reach would presumably be available in every other State in which MBUSA's sales are sizable.

19. We do not foreclose the possibility that in an exceptional case, see, *e.g., Perkins*, a corporation's operations in a forum other than its formal place of incorporation or principal place of business may be so substantial and of such a nature as to render the corporation at home in that State. But this case presents no occasion to explore that question, because Daimler's activities in California plainly do not approach that level. It is one thing to hold a corporation answerable for operations in the forum State, quite another to expose it to suit on claims having no connection whatever to the forum State.

Such exorbitant exercises of all-purpose jurisdiction would scarcely permit out-of-state defendants "to structure their primary conduct with some minimum assurance as to where that conduct will and will not render them liable to suit." *Burger King Corp.*

It was therefore error for the Ninth Circuit to conclude that Daimler, even with MBUSA's contacts attributed to it, was at home in California, and hence subject to suit there on claims by foreign plaintiffs having nothing to do with anything that occurred or had its principal impact in California.[20]

C

Finally, the transnational context of this dispute bears attention. * * *

The Ninth Circuit * * * paid little heed to the risks to international comity its expansive view of general jurisdiction posed. Other nations do not share the uninhibited approach to personal jurisdiction advanced by the Court of Appeals in this case. In the European Union, for example, a corporation may generally be sued in the nation in which it is "domiciled," a term defined to refer only to the location of the corporation's "statutory seat," "central administration," or "principal place of business." The Solicitor General informs us, in this regard, that "foreign governments' objections to some domestic courts' expansive views of general jurisdiction have in the past im-

20. To clarify in light of Justice Sotomayor's opinion concurring in the judgment, the general jurisdiction inquiry does not "focu[s] solely on the magnitude of the defendant's in-state contacts." General jurisdiction instead calls for an appraisal of a corporation's activities in their entirety, nationwide and worldwide. A corporation that operates in many places can scarcely be deemed at home in all of them. Otherwise, "at home" would be synonymous with "doing business" tests framed before specific jurisdiction evolved in the United States. Nothing in *International Shoe* and its progeny suggests that "a particular quantum of local activity" should give a State authority over a "far larger quantum of ... activity" having no connection to any in-state activity.

Justice Sotomayor would reach the same result, but for a different reason. Rather than concluding that Daimler is not at home in California, Justice Sotomayor would hold that the exercise of general jurisdiction over Daimler would be unreasonable "in the unique circumstances of this case." In other words, she favors a resolution fit for this day and case only. True, a multipronged reasonableness check was articulated in *Asahi*, but not as a free-floating test. Instead, the check was to be essayed when *specific* jurisdiction is at issue. See also *Burger King Corp. v. Rudzewicz*. First, a court is to determine whether the connection between the forum and the episode-in-suit could justify the exercise of specific jurisdiction. Then, in a second step, the court is to consider several additional factors to assess the reasonableness of entertaining the case. When a corporation is genuinely at home in the forum State, however, any second-step inquiry would be superfluous.

Justice Sotomayor fears that our holding will "lead to greater unpredictability by radically expanding the scope of jurisdictional discovery." But it is hard to see why much in the way of discovery would be needed to determine where a corporation is at home. Justice Sotomayor's proposal to import *Asahi*'s "reasonableness" check into the general jurisdiction determination, on the other hand, would indeed compound the jurisdictional inquiry. The reasonableness factors identified in *Asahi* include "the burden on the defendant," "the interests of the forum State," "the plaintiff's interest in obtaining relief," "the interstate judicial system's interest in obtaining the most efficient resolution of controversies," "the shared interest of the several States in furthering fundamental substantive social policies," and, in the international context, "the procedural and substantive policies of other *nations* whose interests are affected by the assertion of jurisdiction." Imposing such a checklist in cases of general jurisdiction would hardly promote the efficient disposition of an issue that should be resolved expeditiously at the outset of litigation.

peded negotiations of international agreements on the reciprocal recognition and enforcement of judgments." Considerations of international rapport thus reinforce our determination that subjecting Daimler to the general jurisdiction of courts in California would not accord with the "fair play and substantial justice" due process demands.

* * *

For the reasons stated, the judgment of the United States Court of Appeals for the Ninth Circuit is

Reversed.

[The concurrence of Justice Sotomayor is omitted.]

Notes and Questions

1. After *Daimler*, how likely is it that any corporation will be held subject to general jurisdiction in a state other than where it is incorporated or where it has its principal place of business?

2. Not all businesses are corporations. For instance, many businesses are partnerships or limited liability companies. Where are such businesses "at home"?

3. The Court says that a natural person is "at home" and therefore subject to general personal jurisdiction in the state of her domicile. Does this rule out general jurisdiction over a human anywhere else? Suppose, for example, the defendant is served with process while voluntarily present in the forum. Such transient or "tag" jurisdiction historically has supported general jurisdiction, as we will discuss in Section B.7 below.

4. In the second paragraph of footnote 20, the Court declares that there is no assessment of fairness or reasonableness in general jurisdiction cases. Once the court concludes that the defendant is "at home" in the forum, that's the end of the matter. Does the Court explain why fairness/reasonableness of jurisdiction is not relevant in general jurisdiction cases? Do you think it should be? Some courts, addressing the question before *Daimler*, had concluded that fairness/reasonableness was relevant in general jurisdiction cases. See, e.g., Metropolitan Life Ins. Co. v. Robertson-Ceco, 84 F.3d 560 (2d Cir. 1996); Amoco Egypt Oil Co. v. Leonis Navigation Co., 1 F.3d 848 (9th Cir. 1993).

5. A few courts have suggested that extensive Internet activities assessable to forum residents can be sufficient to create general jurisdiction. See Gator.com Corp. v. L.L. Bean, Inc., 341 F.3d 1072, 1079 (9th Cir. 2003) ("even if the only contacts L.L. Bean had with California were through its virtual store, a finding of general jurisdiction in the instant case would be consistent with the 'sliding scale' test that both our own and other circuits have applied to Internet-based companies"), *vacated* 366 F.3d 789 (9th Cir. 2004), *dismissed as moot,* 398 F.3d 1125 (9th Cir. 2005); Gorman v. Ameritrade Holding Corp., 293 F.3d 506, 510 (D.C. Cir. 2002). Other courts have rejected this suggestion. See Hy Cite Corp. v. Badbusinessbureau.com, 297 F. Supp. 2d 1154, 1161 (W.D. Wis. 2004). After *Daimler*, could there ever be general jurisdiction based on

Internet sales or is a "bricks and mortar" facility always necessary? The jurisdictional implications of activity on the Internet are explored further in Section B.8 infra.

6. Does the Court say *why* it limits general jurisdiction to where the defendant is "at home"? In fact, does the Court tell us why we have general jurisdiction at all? What is the purpose of the doctrine?

One justification might be that it is useful to have at least one "home base" for each defendant, that is, one place where everyone knows the defendant would be subject to suit on anything. If this is the function, however, shouldn't it be limited to the corporate headquarters? See B. Glenn George, *In Search of General Jurisdiction*, 64 TULANE L. REV. 1097 (1990) (discussing waning importance of general jurisdiction in wake of expansion of specific jurisdiction).

Another theory for general jurisdiction is based on a philosophical position about self-governance. Professor Brilmayer has argued that "[s]ystematic unrelated activities, such as domicile, incorporation, or doing business, suggests that the person or corporate entity is enough of an 'insider' that he may safely be relegated to the State's political processes." Lea Brilmayer, *How Contacts Count: Due Process Limitations on State Court Jurisdiction*, 1980 SUP. CT. REV. 77, 87. Under this approach, a defendant would be subject to general jurisdiction if its connections with the forum were sufficiently extensive that its interests are likely to be taken seriously by the political processes of the forum state. Thus, a large factory employing many workers would probably be sufficient to subject a corporation to general jurisdiction, even if the factory represented a small percentage of the corporation's total business.

Are you persuaded by either of these justifications for general jurisdiction? Does the doctrine serve other purposes or is it merely a remnant of the pre-*International Shoe* focus on "presence"? Is specific jurisdiction adequate to provide appropriate fora for litigation? See Patrick Borchers, *The Problem with General Jurisdiction*, 2001 U. CHI. LEGAL F. 119; Mary Twitchell, *Why We Keep Doing Business with Doing-Business Jurisdiction*, 2001 U. CHI. LEGAL F. 171.

7. In *Goodyear*, Justice Ginsburg criticized the lower court for "elid[ing] the essential differences between case-specific and all-purpose (general) jurisdiction." This begs the question of how connected the contacts need to be to the cause of action for the case to be considered a specific jurisdiction case. In *Helicopteros*, Justice Brennan dissented on the grounds that the defendant's contacts with the forum were sufficiently "related to" the cause of action to subject it to specific jurisdiction. The majority did not address this point because it assumed that the parties had conceded that the contacts were completely and absolutely unrelated. How closely must the contacts be related to the cause of action for a case to be deemed a specific jurisdiction case? Is it sufficient that the contacts "relate to" the cause of action, or must the cause of action "arise out of" the contacts?

Suppose, for example, that a Hawaii hotel advertises in Massachusetts. A Massachusetts citizen sees the advertising and goes to the Hawaii hotel, where she slips and falls in her Hawaii hotel room. Can she sue the hotel in Massachusetts? Some courts have held no, reasoning that the advertising was not the proximate cause of the fall. See, e.g., Wims v. Beach Terrace Motor Inn, Inc., 759 F. Supp. 264 (E.D. Pa. 1991). Other courts have reached a contrary conclusion, reasoning that "but for" the advertising, the plaintiff would never have stayed in the defendant's facilities. See Shute v. Carnival Cruise Lines, 897 F.2d 377 (9th Cir. 1990), *rev'd on other grounds*, 498 U.S. 807 (1990).

If "but for" causation is a sufficient condition for specific jurisdiction, is it also a necessary condition? Consider the situation of Audi in *World-Wide Volkswagen.* Audi presumably sold cars to Oklahoma but not the car that blew up. Is this enough of a connection for specific jurisdiction? Professor Twitchell has argued that this should be enough for specific jurisdiction:

> [T]he fact that this accident occurred within the forum, coupled with similarity between the manufacturer's conduct in the forum and the conduct underlying the plaintiff's cause of action * * * makes exercising jurisdiction over this claim particularly reasonable. Having sold and serviced identical cars in the state, the manufacturer will have foreseen such suits and insured against them. Furthermore, the forum has a very strong interest in regulating the manufacturer's conduct in this suit, not just because this particular automobile malfunctioned there, but because state residents are buying many similar cars and operating them on the forum's highways. The fact that the car was not actually sold within the state is, in this context, fortuitous. A court need not decide whether it is fair to hold the manufacturer subject to jurisdiction on all causes of action in the forum in order to decide that it is fair in this particular case. Specific jurisdiction, in which the nature of the cause of action is taken into account when considering fairness, not general jurisdiction, is the key to proper jurisdictional analysis under these circumstances.

Mary Twitchell, *The Myth of General Jurisdiction*, 101 Harv. L. Rev. 610, 661–62 (1988). See also Shoppers Food Warehouse v. Moreno, 746 A.2d 320 (D.C. 2000) (requiring only that there be a "discernable relationship" between the defendant's contacts and the cause of action). Professor Brilmayer, in contrast, has argued for a narrower approach, explaining:

> A contact is related to the controversy if it is the geographical qualification of a fact relevant to the merits. A forum occurrence which would ordinarily be alleged as part of the comparable domestic complaint is a related contact. In contrast, an occurrence in the forum State of no relevance to a totally domestic cause of action is an unrelated contact, a purely jurisdictional allegation with no substantive purpose. If a fact is irrelevant in a purely domestic dispute, it does not suddenly become related to the controversy simply because there are multistate elements.

Brilmayer, supra, 1980 Sup. Ct. Rev. at 82–83. With whom would you agree in this debate? See also George, supra, 64 Tulane L. Rev. 1097.

8. Some have suggested that the categories of general and specific jurisdiction are not really two separate categories, but are simply two ends of a continuum. See Chew v. Dietrich, 143 F.3d 24, 29 (2d Cir. 1998); Camelback Ski Corp. v. Behning, 539 A.2d 1107, 1111 (Md. 1988); William Richman, *Review Essay: Part I—Casad's Jurisdiction in Civil Actions; Part II—A Sliding Scale to Supplement the Distinction Between General and Specific Jurisdiction*, 72 CAL. L. REV. 1328 (1984). Where the cause of action is closely related to the contacts, as little as a single contact may be sufficient. At the other extreme—where the cause of action is completely unrelated to the contacts—a very high level of contacts will be required. As to the cases in between, the more closely the contacts are related to the cause of action, the fewer contacts are required.

9. Some countries consider general jurisdiction based upon a business's activities unreasonable. The Draft Hague Convention on Jurisdiction and Foreign Judgments in Civil and Commercial Matters would have prohibited jurisdiction on the basis of "the carrying on of commercial or other activities by the defendant in that State, except where the dispute is directly related to those activities." The possibility of eliminating such jurisdiction was one of the bases of U.S. concern about the Draft Convention. See Friedrich Juenger, *The American Law of General Jurisdiction*, 2001 U. CHI. LEGAL F. 141, 164–65. Nonetheless, the U.S. is not alone in allowing some type of "doing business" jurisdiction. For example, England allows general jurisdiction in its courts over a foreign business that has an "established place of business" within England, and Japan has similarly upheld jurisdiction over a foreign business with a branch office in Japan. See Linda Silberman, *Comparative Jurisdiction in the International Context: Will the Proposed Hague Judgments Convention Be Stalled?* 52 DEPAUL L. REV. 319, 340–41 (2002).

5. Explicit Consent and Forum Selection Provisions

The right to object to a court's lack of personal jurisdiction is a personal right that can be waived at any time by the defendant. It is well established that a person may consent to jurisdiction even long in advance of litigation. Consent to jurisdiction is sometimes manifested by appointing an agent for service of process within the state. The Court has upheld this type of consent. See National Equip. Rental, Ltd. v. Szukhent, 375 U.S. 311 (1964).

Parties may also consent to jurisdiction by virtue of their conduct in the litigation. In Adam v. Saenger, 303 U.S. 59 (1938), the Supreme Court held that by filing a complaint, the plaintiff consented to a counterclaim filed against the plaintiff by the defendant. Similarly, as we will see in Chapter 6, a failure to raise a timely objection to jurisdiction constitutes a waiver of the objection.

Insurance Corp. of Ireland v. Compagnie des Bauxites de Guinee, 456 U.S. 694 (1982), illustrates another type of consent. There, in response to a defendant's motion to dismiss for lack of personal jurisdiction, the plaintiff sought discovery of documents that might show that defendant had sufficient contacts with the forum. After a protracted discovery dispute, the district court ordered the defendant to produce the documents. When the defendant refused to comply with that order, the district court sanctioned the defendant under Rule 37(b)(2)(A). The sanction imposed was a finding that the court had personal jurisdiction over the defendant. The defendant appealed, arguing that it had no obligation to obey the orders of the court unless the court had personal jurisdiction. Therefore, the defendant continued, a finding of personal jurisdiction could not be imposed as a sanction, because such a finding was a prerequisite to the court's authority to impose any sanction. The Supreme Court rejected this argument explaining: "By submitting to the jurisdiction of the court for the limited purpose of challenging jurisdiction, the defendant agrees to abide by that court's determination on the issue of jurisdiction." 456 U.S. at 706.

Sometimes parties to a contract agree to litigate only in a designated forum. If, despite the agreement, one of the parties brings suit in a forum not provided for in the contract, the court must decide whether to enforce the "forum selection clause" and dismiss the suit. Historically, courts have been reluctant to enforce forum selection agreements. The traditional explanation is that private parties should not be permitted to "oust" a court of jurisdiction. "How can two individuals by private agreement limit or otherwise alter the 'jurisdiction' of the courts of state or nation!" 6A Arthur Corbin, Corbin on Contracts § 1431, at 381–82 (1962). Courts also express concern about fraud or overreaching in the formation of the contract, and about protecting local citizens' rights of access to justice. Notwithstanding the historical reluctance to enforce such agreements, courts increasingly do enforce them.

In the international arena, forum selection clauses are common, with the parties frequently selecting the courts of a neutral forum rather than the home courts of either of the parties. In The Bremen v. Zapata Off-Shore Co., 407 U.S. 1 (1972), an admiralty case, the Supreme Court held that "in the light of present-day commercial realities and expanding international trade we conclude that the forum clause should control absent a strong showing that it should be set aside." Id. at 15.

The Bremen involved a contract between international corporations, but forum selection clauses have been enforced in other contexts as well. In Carnival Cruise Lines, Inc. v. Shute, 499 U.S. 585 (1991), the Supreme Court upheld a forum selection clause printed in small type on the back of cruise ticket. In so doing, the Court highlighted the benefits of such provisions: "a clause establishing *ex ante* the forum for dispute resolution has the salutary effect of dispelling any confusion about where suits arising from the contract must be brought and defended, sparing litigants the time and expense of pretrial motions to determine the correct forum and conserving judicial resources that otherwise would be devoted to deciding those motions." Id. at 593–94. In Chapter 5, we will see that a forum selection clause may be enforced by ordering transfer from one federal court to the federal court prescribed in the clause.

6. In Rem and Quasi-in-Rem Jurisdiction

Quasi-in-rem jurisdiction allows a plaintiff to acquire jurisdiction over the defendant wherever the defendant has property in the forum simply by attaching it at the outset of the case. Quasi-in-rem jurisdiction was recognized even before *Pennoyer v. Neff*, and subsequent cases specifically upheld its constitutionality, even when the property attached was intangible. In *Harris v. Balk*, 198 U.S. 215 (1905), Harris owed Balk money, and Balk owed Epstein money. Epstein wished to sue Balk for the debt, but Epstein resided in Maryland, Balk lived in North Carolina, and Epstein did not wish to travel to North Carolina. If Balk had property in Maryland, Epstein could have attached it and thereby litigated in Maryland. Balk did not have any property there, however, until Harris, his debtor, visited Maryland. When Epstein learned of Harris' presence in Maryland, he commenced a lawsuit in Maryland and "attached" Harris, contending that since Harris owed Balk money, his debt to Balk was "property" located in Maryland. The Supreme Court upheld jurisdiction, finding that the debt was property attachable for purposes of quasi-in-rem jurisdiction, and that the debt was located wherever the debtor was.

Shaffer v. Heitner

433 U.S. 186, 97 S. Ct. 2569, 53 L. Ed. 2d 683 (1977)

JUSTICE MARSHALL delivered the opinion of the Court.

The controversy in this case concerns the constitutionality of a Delaware statute that allows a court of that State to take jurisdiction of a lawsuit by sequestering any property of the defendant that happens to be located in Delaware. Appellants contend that the sequestration statute as applied in this case violates the Due Process Clause of the Fourteenth Amendment both because it permits the state courts to exercise jurisdiction despite the absence of sufficient contacts among the defendants, the litigation, and the State of Delaware and because it authorizes the deprivation of defendants' property without providing adequate procedural safeguards. We find it necessary to consider only the first of these contentions.

I

Appellee Heitner, a nonresident of Delaware, is the owner of one share of stock in the Greyhound Corp., a business incorporated under the laws of Delaware with its principal place of business in Phoenix, Ariz. On May 22, 1974, he filed a shareholder's derivative suit* in the Court of Chancery for New Castle County, Del., in which he named as defendants Greyhound, its wholly owned subsidiary Greyhound Lines, Inc., and 28 present or former officers or directors of one or both of the cor-

* [A shareholder's derivative suit is a suit brought by one or more corporate shareholders to enforce the corporation's rights. Often, such suits are brought against the managers of the corporation, alleging that their malfeasance or misfeasance harmed the corporation by causing it to lose money. Indeed, in this case, officers and directors were accused of breaching duties to the corporation by having the company engage in activities that violated federal antitrust laws, which cost it millions of dollars. See Fed. R. Civ. P. 23.1.—Eds.]

porations. In essence, Heitner alleged that the individual defendants had violated their duties to Greyhound by causing it and its subsidiary to engage in actions that resulted in the corporations being held liable for substantial damages in a private antitrust suit and a large fine in a criminal contempt action. The activities which led to these penalties took place in Oregon.

Simultaneously with his complaint, Heitner filed a motion for an order of sequestration of the Delaware property of the individual defendants pursuant to Del. Code Ann., Tit. 10, § 366 (1975). This motion was accompanied by a supporting affidavit of counsel which stated that the individual defendants were nonresidents of Delaware. The affidavit identified the property to be sequestered as

> "common stock, Second Cumulative Preferenced Stock and stock unit credits of the Defendant Greyhound Corporation, a Delaware corporation, as well as all options and all warrants to purchase said stock issued to said individual Defendants and all contractual [sic] obligations, all rights, debts or credits due or accrued to or for the benefit of any of the said Defendants under any type of written agreement, contract or other legal instrument of any kind whatever between any of the individual Defendants and said corporation."

The requested sequestration order was signed the day the motion was filed. Pursuant to that order, the sequestrator "seized" approximately 82,000 shares of Greyhound common stock belonging to 19 of the defendants, and options belonging to another 2 defendants. These seizures were accomplished by placing "stop transfer" orders or their equivalents on the books of the Greyhound Corp. So far as the record shows, none of the certificates representing the seized property was physically present in Delaware. The stock was considered to be in Delaware, and so subject to seizure, by virtue of Del. Code Ann., Tit. 8, § 169 (1975), which makes Delaware the situs of ownership of all stock in Delaware corporations.

All 28 defendants were notified of the initiation of the suit by certified mail directed to their last known addresses and by publication in a New Castle County newspaper. The 21 defendants whose property was seized (hereafter referred to as appellants) responded by entering a special appearance for the purpose of moving to quash service of process and to vacate the sequestration order. They contended that the ex parte sequestration procedure did not accord them due process of law and that the property seized was not capable of attachment in Delaware. In addition, appellants asserted that under the rule of *International Shoe Co. v. Washington*, they did not have sufficient contacts with Delaware to sustain the jurisdiction of that State's courts.

The Court of Chancery rejected these arguments in a letter opinion which emphasized the purpose of the Delaware sequestration procedure:

> "The primary purpose of 'sequestration' as authorized by 10 Del. C. § 366 is not to secure possession of property pending a trial between resident debtors and creditors on the issue of who has the right to retain it. On the contrary, as here employed, 'sequestration' is a process used to compel the personal appearance of a nonresident defendant to answer and defend a suit brought

against him in a court of equity. It is accomplished by the appointment of a sequestrator by this Court to seize and hold property of the nonresident located in this State subject to further Court order. If the defendant enters a general appearance, the sequestered property is routinely released, unless the plaintiff makes special application to continue its seizure, in which event the plaintiff has the burden of proof and persuasion."

* * * [T]he court held that the statutory Delaware situs of the stock provided a sufficient basis for the exercise of quasi in rem jurisdiction by a Delaware court.

On appeal, the Delaware Supreme Court affirmed the judgment of the Court of Chancery. * * *

II

The Delaware courts rejected appellants' jurisdictional challenge by noting that this suit was brought as a quasi in rem proceeding. Since quasi in rem jurisdiction is traditionally based on attachment or seizure of property present in the jurisdiction, not on contacts between the defendant and the State, the courts considered appellants' claimed lack of contacts with Delaware to be unimportant. This categorical analysis assumes the continued soundness of the conceptual structure founded on the century-old case of *Pennoyer v. Neff*. * * *

[The Court reviewed the cases from *Pennoyer* to *International Shoe*. The Court concluded that "the relationship among the defendant, the forum, and the litigation, rather than the mutually exclusive sovereignty of the States on which the rules of *Pennoyer* rest, became the central concern of the inquiry in to personal jurisdiction."]

No equally dramatic change has occurred in the law governing jurisdiction in rem. There have, however, been intimations that the collapse of the in personam wing of *Pennoyer* has not left that decision unweakened as a foundation for in rem jurisdiction. Well-reasoned lower court opinions have questioned the proposition that the presence of property in a State gives that State jurisdiction to adjudicate rights to the property regardless of the relationship of the underlying dispute and the property owner to the forum. The overwhelming majority of commentators have also rejected *Pennoyer*'s premise that a proceeding "against" property is not a proceeding against the owners of that property. Accordingly, they urge that the "traditional notions of fair play and substantial justice" that govern a State's power to adjudicate in personam should also govern its power to adjudicate personal rights to property located in the State.

Although this Court has not addressed this argument directly, we have held that property cannot be subjected to a court's judgment unless reasonable and appropriate efforts have been made to give the property owners actual notice of the action. Walker v. City of Hutchinson, 352 U.S. 112 (1956); Mullane v. Central Hanover Bank & Trust Co., 339 U.S. 306 (1950). This conclusion recognizes, contrary to *Pennoyer*, that an adverse judgment in rem directly affects the property owner by divesting him of his rights in the property before the court. Moreover, in *Mullane* we held that Fourteenth Amendment rights cannot depend on the classification of an action as in rem or in personam, since that is

> "a classification for which the standards are so elusive and confused generally and which, being primarily for state courts to define, may and do vary from state to state."

It is clear, therefore, that the law of state-court jurisdiction no longer stands securely on the foundation established in *Pennoyer.* We think that the time is ripe to consider whether the standard of fairness and substantial justice set forth in *International Shoe* should be held to govern actions in rem as well as in personam.

III

The case for applying to jurisdiction in rem the same test of "fair play and substantial justice" as governs assertions of jurisdiction in personam is simple and straightforward. It is premised on recognition that "[t]he phrase, 'judicial jurisdiction over a thing,' is a customary elliptical way of referring to jurisdiction over the interests of persons in a thing." Restatement (Second) of Conflict of Laws § 56, Introductory Note (1971) (hereafter Restatement). This recognition leads to the conclusion that in order to justify an exercise of jurisdiction in rem, the basis for jurisdiction must be sufficient to justify exercising "jurisdiction over the interests of persons in a thing."[23] The standard for determining whether an exercise of jurisdiction over the interests of persons is consistent with the Due Process Clause is the minimum-contacts standard elucidated in *International Shoe.*

This argument, of course, does not ignore the fact that the presence of property in a State may bear on the existence of jurisdiction by providing contacts among the forum State, the defendant, and the litigation. For example, when claims to the property itself are the source of the underlying controversy between the plaintiff and the defendant,[24] it would be unusual for the State where the property is located not to have jurisdiction. In such cases, the defendant's claim to property located in the State would normally indicate that he expected to benefit from the State's protection of his interest. The State's strong interests in assuring the marketability of property within its borders and in providing a procedure for peaceful resolution of disputes about the possession of that property would also support jurisdiction, as would the

---

23. It is true that the potential liability of a defendant in an in rem action is limited by the value of the property, but that limitation does not affect the argument. The fairness of subjecting a defendant to state-court jurisdiction does not depend on the size of the claim being litigated. Cf. *Fuentes v. Shevin.*

24. This category includes true in rem actions and the first type of quasi in rem proceedings. [The Court then cites its prior note 17, which states:

> "A judgment in rem affects the interests of all persons in designated property. A judgment quasi in rem affects the interests of particular persons in designated property. The latter is of two types. In one the plaintiff is seeking to secure a pre-existing claim in the subject property and to extinguish or establish the nonexistence of similar interests of particular persons. In the other the plaintiff seeks to apply what he concedes to be the property of the defendant to the satisfaction of a claim against him."

Hanson v. Denckla. As did the Court in *Hanson,* we will for convenience generally use the term "in rem" in place of "in rem and quasi in rem."]

likelihood that important records and witnesses will be found in the State.[26] The presence of property may also favor jurisdiction in cases, such as suits for injury suffered on the land of an absentee owner, where the defendant's ownership of the property is conceded but the cause of action is otherwise related to rights and duties growing out of that ownership.[29]

It appears, therefore, that jurisdiction over many types of actions which now are or might be brought in rem would not be affected by a holding that any assertion of state-court jurisdiction must satisfy the *International Shoe* standard.[30] For the type of quasi in rem action typified by *Harris v. Balk* and the present case, however, accepting the proposed analysis would result in significant change. These are cases where the property which now serves as the basis for state-court jurisdiction is completely unrelated to the plaintiff's cause of action. Thus, although the presence of the defendant's property in a State might suggest the existence of other ties among the defendant, the State, and the litigation, the presence of the property alone would not support the State's jurisdiction. If those other ties did not exist, cases over which the State is now thought to have jurisdiction could not be brought in that forum.

Since acceptance of the *International Shoe* test would most affect this class of cases, we examine the arguments against adopting that standard as they relate to this category of litigation. Before doing so, however, we note that this type of case also presents the clearest illustration of the argument in favor of assessing assertions of jurisdiction by a single standard. For in cases such as *Harris* and this one, the only role played by the property is to provide the basis for bringing the defendant into court. Indeed, the express purpose of the Delaware sequestration procedure is to compel the defendant to enter a personal appearance. In such cases, if a direct assertion of personal jurisdiction over the defendant would violate the Constitution, it would seem that an indirect assertion of that jurisdiction should be equally impermissible.

The primary rationale for treating the presence of property as a sufficient basis for jurisdiction to adjudicate claims over which the State would not have jurisdiction if *International Shoe* applied is that a wrongdoer "should not be able to avoid payment of his obligations by the expedient of removing his assets to a place where he is not subject to an in personam suit." RESTATEMENT § 66, Comment a. This justification, however, does not explain why jurisdiction should be recognized without regard to whether the property is present in the State because of an effort to avoid the owner's obligations. Nor does it support jurisdiction to adjudicate the underlying claim. At most, it suggests that a State in which property is located should have jurisdiction to

---

26. We do not suggest that these illustrations include all the factors that may affect the decision, nor that the factors we mentioned are necessarily decisive.

29. Cf. Dubin v. Philadelphia, 34 Pa. D.&C. 61 (1938). If such an action were brought under the in rem jurisdiction rather than under a long-arm statute, it would be a quasi in rem action of the second type.

30. We do not suggest that jurisdictional doctrines other than those discussed in text, such as the particularized rules governing adjudications of status, are inconsistent with the standard of fairness.

attach that property, by use of proper procedures, as security for a judgment being sought in a forum where the litigation can be maintained consistently with *International Shoe.* Moreover, we know of nothing to justify the assumption that a debtor can avoid paying his obligations by removing his property to a State in which his creditor cannot obtain personal jurisdiction over him. The Full Faith and Credit Clause, after all, makes the valid in personam judgment of one State enforceable in all other States.[36] It might also be suggested that allowing in rem jurisdiction avoids the uncertainty inherent in the *International Shoe* standard and assures a plaintiff of a forum.[37] We believe, however, that the fairness standard of *International Shoe* can be easily applied in the vast majority of cases. Moreover, when the existence of jurisdiction in a particular forum under *International Shoe* is unclear, the cost of simplifying the litigation by avoiding the jurisdictional question may be the sacrifice of "fair play and substantial justice." That cost is too high.

We are left, then, to consider the significance of the long history of jurisdiction based solely on the presence of property in a State. Although the theory that territorial power is both essential to and sufficient for jurisdiction has been undermined, we have never held that the presence of property in a State does not automatically confer jurisdiction over the owner's interest in that property. This history must be considered as supporting the proposition that jurisdiction based solely on the presence of property satisfies the demands of due process, but it is not decisive. "[T]raditional notions of fair play and substantial justice" can be as readily offended by the perpetuation of ancient forms that are no longer justified as by the adoption of new procedures that are inconsistent with the basic values of our constitutional heritage. The fiction that an assertion of jurisdiction over property is anything but an assertion of jurisdiction over the owner of the property supports an ancient form without substantial modern justification. Its continued acceptance would serve only to allow state-court jurisdiction that is fundamentally unfair to the defendant.

We therefore conclude that all assertions of state-court jurisdiction must be evaluated according to the standards set forth in *International Shoe* and its progeny.[39]

IV

The Delaware courts based their assertion of jurisdiction in this case solely on the statutory presence of appellants' property in Delaware. Yet that property is not the subject matter of this litigation, nor is the underlying cause of action related to the

36. Once it has been determined by a court of competent jurisdiction that the defendant is a debtor of the plaintiff, there would seem to be no unfairness in allowing an action to realize on that debt in a State where the defendant has property, whether or not that State would have jurisdiction to determine the existence of the debt as an original matter.

37. This case does not raise, and we therefore do not consider, the question whether the presence of a defendant's property in a State is a sufficient basis for jurisdiction when no other forum is available to the plaintiff.

39. It would not be fruitful for us to re-examine the facts of cases decided on the rationales of *Pennoyer* and *Harris* to determine whether jurisdiction might have been sustained under the standard we adopt today. To the extent that prior decisions are inconsistent with this standard, they are overruled.

property. Appellants' holdings in Greyhound do not, therefore, provide contacts with Delaware sufficient to support the jurisdiction of that State's courts over appellants. If it exists, that jurisdiction must have some other foundation.

Appellee Heitner did not allege and does not now claim that appellants have ever set foot in Delaware. Nor does he identify any act related to his cause of action as having taken place in Delaware. Nevertheless, he contends that appellants' positions as directors and officers of a corporation chartered in Delaware provide sufficient "contacts, ties, or relations," *International Shoe Co. v. Washington,* with that State to give its courts jurisdiction over appellants in this stockholder's derivative action. This argument is based primarily on what Heitner asserts to be the strong interest of Delaware in supervising the management of a Delaware corporation. That interest is said to derive from the role of Delaware law in establishing the corporation and defining the obligations owed to it by its officers and directors. In order to protect this interest, appellee concludes, Delaware's courts must have jurisdiction over corporate fiduciaries such as appellants.

This argument is undercut by the failure of the Delaware Legislature to assert the state interest appellee finds so compelling. Delaware law bases jurisdiction, not on appellants' status as corporate fiduciaries, but rather on the presence of their property in the State. Although the sequestration procedure used here may be most frequently used in derivative suits against officers and directors, the authorizing statute evinces no specific concern with such actions. Sequestration can be used in any suit against a nonresident, and reaches corporate fiduciaries only if they happen to own interests in a Delaware corporation, or other property in the State. But as Heitner's failure to secure jurisdiction over seven of the defendants named in his complaint demonstrates, there is no necessary relationship between holding a position as a corporate fiduciary and owning stock or other interests in the corporation.[43] If Delaware perceived its interest in securing jurisdiction over corporate fiduciaries to be as great as Heitner suggests, we would expect it to have enacted a statute more clearly designed to protect that interest.

* * *

Appellee suggests that by accepting positions as officers or directors of a Delaware corporation, appellants performed the acts required by *Hanson v. Denckla.* He notes that Delaware law provides substantial benefits to corporate officers and directors, and that these benefits were at least in part the incentive for appellants to assume their positions. It is, he says, "only fair and just" to require appellants, in return for these benefits, to respond in the State of Delaware when they are accused of misusing their power.

* * * [T]his line of reasoning establishes only that it is appropriate for Delaware law to govern the obligations of appellants to Greyhound and its stockholders. It does not demonstrate that appellants have "purposefully avail[ed themselves] of the

43. Delaware does not require directors to own stock.

privilege of conducting activities within the forum State," *Hanson v. Denckla*, in a way that would justify bringing them before a Delaware tribunal. Appellants have simply had nothing to do with the State of Delaware. Moreover, appellants had no reason to expect to be haled before a Delaware court. Delaware, unlike some States, has not enacted a statute that treats acceptance of a directorship as consent to jurisdiction in the State. And "[i]t strains reason ... to suggest that anyone buying securities in a corporation formed in Delaware 'impliedly consents' to subject himself to Delaware's ... jurisdiction on any cause of action." Appellants, who were not required to acquire interests in Greyhound in order to hold their positions, did not by acquiring those interests surrender their right to be brought to judgment only in States with which they had had "minimum contacts."

The Due Process Clause "does not contemplate that a state may make binding a judgment ... against an individual or corporate defendant with which the state has no contacts, ties, or relations." *International Shoe Co. v. Washington*. Delaware's assertion of jurisdiction over appellants in this case is inconsistent with that constitutional limitation on state power. The judgment of the Delaware Supreme Court must, therefore, be reversed.

It is so ordered.

JUSTICE POWELL, concurring.

I agree that the principles of *International Shoe Co. v. Washington*, should be extended to govern assertions of in rem as well as in personam jurisdiction in a state court. I also agree that neither the statutory presence of appellants' stock in Delaware nor their positions as directors and officers of a Delaware corporation can provide sufficient contacts to support the Delaware courts' assertion of jurisdiction in this case.

I would explicitly reserve judgment, however, on whether the ownership of some forms of property whose situs is indisputably and permanently located within a State may, without more, provide the contacts necessary to subject a defendant to jurisdiction within the State to the extent of the value of the property. In the case of real property, in particular, preservation of the common-law concept of quasi in rem jurisdiction arguably would avoid the uncertainty of the general *International Shoe* standard without significant cost to "traditional notions of fair play and substantial justice." Subject to the foregoing reservation, I join the opinion of the Court.

JUSTICE STEVENS, concurring in the judgment.

* * * One who purchases shares of stock on the open market can hardly be expected to know that he has thereby become subject to suit in a forum remote from his residence and unrelated to the transaction. * * *

How the Court's opinion may be applied in other contexts is not entirely clear to me. I agree with Justice Powell that it should not be read to invalidate quasi in rem jurisdiction where real estate is involved. I would also not read it as invalidating other long-accepted methods of acquiring jurisdiction over persons with adequate notice of both the particular controversy and the fact that their local activities might subject them to suit. My uncertainty as to the reach of the opinion, and my fear that it purports to decide a great deal more than is necessary to dispose of this case, persuade me merely to concur in the judgment.

Justice Brennan, concurring in part and dissenting in part.

I join Parts I-III of the Court's opinion. I fully agree that the minimum-contacts analysis developed in *International Shoe Co. v. Washington* represents a far more sensible construct for the exercise of state-court jurisdiction than the patchwork of legal and factual fictions that has been generated from the decision in *Pennoyer v. Neff.* It is precisely because the inquiry into minimum contacts is now of such overriding importance, however, that I must respectfully dissent from Part IV of the Court's opinion.

I

[Justice Brennan argued that it was inappropriate for the Court to consider whether Delaware's assertion of jurisdiction met the "minimum-contacts" test. He said of the Court's discussion of this point that "a purer example of an advisory opinion is not to be found."]

My concern with the inappropriateness of the Court's action is highlighted by two other considerations. First, an inquiry into minimum contacts inevitably is highly dependent on creating a proper factual foundation detailing the contacts between the forum State and the controversy in question. Because neither the plaintiff-appellee nor the state courts viewed such an inquiry as germane in this instance, the Court today is unable to draw upon a proper factual record in reaching its conclusion; moreover, its disposition denies appellee the normal opportunity to seek discovery on the contacts issue. Second, it must be remembered that the Court's ruling is a constitutional one and necessarily will affect the reach of the jurisdictional laws of all 50 States. Ordinarily this would counsel restraint in constitutional pronouncements. Certainly it should have cautioned the Court against reaching out to decide a question that, as here, has yet to emerge from the state courts ripened for review on the federal issue.

II

Nonetheless, because the Court rules on the minimum-contacts question, I feel impelled to express my view. While evidence derived through discovery might satisfy me that minimum contacts are lacking in a given case, I am convinced that as a general rule a state forum has jurisdiction to adjudicate a shareholder derivative action centering on the conduct and policies of the directors and officers of a corporation chartered by that State. Unlike the Court, I therefore would not foreclose Delaware from asserting jurisdiction over appellants were it persuaded to do so on the basis of minimum contacts.

It is well settled that a derivative lawsuit as presented here does not inure primarily to the benefit of the named plaintiff. Rather, the primary beneficiaries are the corporation and its owners, the shareholders. "The cause of action which such a plaintiff brings before the court is not his own but the corporation's.... Such a plaintiff often may represent an important public and stockholder interest in bringing faithless managers to book."

Viewed in this light, the chartering State has an unusually powerful interest in insuring the availability of a convenient forum for litigating claims involving a possible multiplicity of defendant fiduciaries and for vindicating the State's substantive policies regarding the management of its domestic corporations. I believe that our cases fairly establish that the State's valid substantive interests are important considerations in assessing whether it constitutionally may claim jurisdiction over a given cause of action.

In this instance, Delaware can point to at least three interrelated public policies that are furthered by its assertion of jurisdiction. First, the State has a substantial interest in providing restitution for its local corporations that allegedly have been victimized by fiduciary misconduct, even if the managerial decisions occurred outside the State. The importance of this general state interest in assuring restitution for its own residents previously found expression in cases that went outside the then-prevailing due process framework to authorize state-court jurisdiction over nonresident motorists who injure others within the State. *Hess v. Pawloski.* More recently, it has led States to seek and to acquire jurisdiction over nonresident tort-feasors whose purely out-of-state activities produce domestic consequences. E.g., *Gray v. American Radiator & Standard Sanitary Corp.* Second, state courts have legitimately read their jurisdiction expansively when a cause of action centers in an area in which the forum State possesses a manifest regulatory interest. E.g., *McGee v. International Life Ins. Co.* (insurance regulation); Travelers Health Assn. v. Virginia, 339 U.S. 643 (1950) (blue sky laws). * * * Finally, a State like Delaware has a recognized interest in affording a convenient forum for supervising and overseeing the affairs of an entity that is purely the creation of that State's law. For example, even following our decision in *International Shoe*, New York courts were permitted to exercise complete judicial authority over nonresident beneficiaries of a trust created under state law, even though, unlike appellants here, the beneficiaries personally entered into no association whatsoever with New York. Mullane v. Central Hanover Bank & Trust Co., 339 U.S. 306, 313 (1950). I, of course, am not suggesting that Delaware's varied interests would justify its acceptance of jurisdiction over any transaction upon the affairs of its domestic corporations. But a derivative action which raises allegations of abuses of the basic management of an institution whose existence is created by the State and whose powers and duties are defined by state law fundamentally implicates the public policies of that forum.

* * *

This case is not one where, in my judgment, this preference for jurisdiction is adequately answered. Certainly nothing said by the Court persuades me that it would be unfair to subject appellants to suit in Delaware. The fact that the record does not reveal whether they "set foot" or committed "act[s] related to [the] cause of action" in Delaware, is not decisive, for jurisdiction can be based strictly on out-of-state acts having foreseeable effects in the forum State. E.g., *McGee v. International Life Ins. Co.*; *Gray v. American Radiator & Standard Sanitary Corp.* I have little difficulty in applying this principle to nonresident fiduciaries whose alleged breaches of trust are said to have substantial damaging effect on the financial posture of a resident corporation. Further, I cannot understand how the existence of minimum contacts in a constitutional sense is at all affected by Delaware's failure statutorily to express an interest in controlling corporate fiduciaries. To me this simply demonstrates that Delaware did not elect to assert jurisdiction to the extent the Constitution would allow.[5] Nor would I view as controlling or even especially meaningful Delaware's failure to exact from appellants their consent to be sued. Once we have rejected the jurisdictional framework created in *Pennoyer v. Neff*, I see no reason to rest jurisdiction on a fictional outgrowth of that system such as the existence of a consent statute, expressed or implied.

I, therefore, would approach the minimum-contacts analysis differently than does the Court. Crucial to me is the fact that appellants voluntarily associated themselves with the State of Delaware, "invoking the benefits and protections of its laws," by entering into a long-term and fragile relationship with one of its domestic corporations. They thereby elected to assume powers and to undertake responsibilities wholly derived from that State's rules and regulations, and to become eligible for those benefits that Delaware law makes available to its corporations' officials. E.g., Del. Code Ann., Tit. 8, § 143 (1975) (interest-free loans); § 145 (1975 ed. and Supp. 1976) (indemnification). While it is possible that countervailing issues of judicial efficiency and the like might clearly favor a different forum, they do not appear on the meager record before us; and, of course, we are concerned solely with "minimum" contacts, not the "best" contacts. I thus do not believe that it is unfair to insist that appellants make themselves available to suit in a competent forum that Delaware might create for vindication of its important public policies directly pertaining to appellants' fiduciary associations with the State.

Notes and Questions

1. *International Shoe* focused on whether jurisdiction offends "traditional notions of fair play and substantial justice." American courts have recognized quasi-in-rem jurisdiction for over a century. How could a traditionally accepted mechanism of jurisdiction violate traditional notions of fair play and substantial justice? What tradition was the Court looking to?

2. Toward the end of Part II of the majority opinion, the Court referred to "the collapse of the in personam wing of *Pennoyer*." When and where did that "collapse" occur? Have we studied any case in which the Court said it was overseeing the collapse of the in personam wing of *Pennoyer*?

3. Consider how the following hypotheticals would be analyzed after *Shaffer*:

5. In fact, it is quite plausible that the Delaware Legislature never felt the need to assert direct jurisdiction over corporate managers precisely because the sequestration statute heretofore has served as a somewhat awkward but effective basis for achieving such personal jurisdiction. E.g., Hughes Tool Co. v. Fawcett Publications, Inc., 290 A.2d 693, 695 (Del. Ch. 1972): "Sequestration is most frequently resorted to in suits by stockholders against corporate directors in which recoveries are sought for the benefit of the corporation on the ground of claimed breaches of fiduciary duty on the part of directors."

(a) Fred, a California citizen, owns real estate in Delaware. Fred doesn't make his mortgage payments. The bank which holds the mortgage wants to foreclose on the property. Is there personal jurisdiction for the bank to foreclose in Delaware?

(b) Fred owns real property in Delaware. Someone trips and falls on his property. The injured person sues Fred in Delaware. Is there personal jurisdiction?

(c) Sally (a citizen of California) has a contract with Fred (also a citizen of California). The deal goes bad, and Sally sues Fred in California and wins. Fred refuses to pay the judgment. Sally goes to Delaware and enforces the judgment by attaching Fred's Delaware real estate. Is this permitted after *Shaffer*?

(d) In *Shaffer*, the property attached was stock. Suppose that the directors had owned real estate in Delaware, and Heitner had attached that instead of the stock. Would that have changed the result? Would it have changed the result for Justices Powell or Stevens?

4. Does the Court hold that a defendant can be subject to jurisdiction by attachment only if she would be subject to in personam jurisdiction? Some commentators have interpreted *Shaffer* this way. See Gene Shreve & Peter Raven-Hansen, Understanding Civil Procedure 67–68 (4th ed. 2009). In contrast, Professor Weintraub has argued that although all assertions of jurisdiction must be evaluated under the *International Shoe* standard, that "is not the same as saying that those standards must provide the same answer no matter what the form of jurisdiction asserted. In cases that would fall close to the due process line if full personal jurisdiction were asserted, the less drastic remedy of allowing the plaintiff to reach the defendant's assets in the state may be reasonable." Russell Weintraub, Commentary on the Conflict of Laws 285 (6th ed. 2010). See Cameco Industries Inc. v. Mayatrac, S.A., 789 F. Supp. 200 (D. Md. 1992); Michael Mushkin, *The New Quasi In Rem Jurisdiction: New York's Revival of a Doctrine Whose Time Has Passed*, 55 Brook. L. Rev. 1059, 1089–99 (1990); Comment, Shaffer, Burnham, *and New York's Continuing Use of QIR-2 Jurisdiction: A Resurrection of the Power Theory*, 45 Emory L.J. 239, 258–66 (1996). Which interpretation of *Shaffer* do you think is correct?

5. Consider Part IV of the opinion. Why isn't becoming the director of a Delaware corporation a sufficient contact for those directors to be sued in personam in Delaware for breaches of their obligations as directors? Justice Marshall stresses that the directors "never set foot in Delaware" and that no act relating to the cause of action took place "in Delaware." Is physical presence in the state a prerequisite for jurisdiction? Is Part IV of *Shaffer* consistent with *Burger King*?

6. If personal jurisdiction is not proper in Delaware, where is it proper? The individual defendants resided in nine different states. The anticompetitive conduct that resulted in the antitrust verdict occurred in Oregon, although it was a Chicago court that found the company and three officers guilty of contempt. At the time of the antitrust and contempt judgments, Greyhound's headquarters was in Phoenix, though during some of the time of the alleged anticompetitive conduct, it was headquartered in Chicago. Under these circumstances, was it unreasonable to sue in the state of in-

corporation? See Wendy Perdue, *The Story of* Shaffer: *Allocating Jurisdictional Authority Among the States, in* CIVIL PROCEDURE STORIES 135, 143 (K. Clermont ed., 2d ed. 2008).

7. Shortly after the decision in *Shaffer*, Delaware passed a statute providing that every nonresident director of a Delaware corporation appointed after September 1, 1977, shall "be deemed" to have consented to the appointment of the corporation's registered agent to be his agent for service of process in any suit in Delaware alleging that the director breached his duties as a director. 10 DEL. CODE § 3114. The Delaware Supreme Court upheld this statute in Armstrong v. Pomerance, 423 A.2d 174 (Del. 1980). See also Stearn v. Malloy, 89 F.R.D. 421 (E.D. Wis. 1981) (upholding a similar Wisconsin statute). Even absent explicit consent provisions, some courts have upheld jurisdiction over corporate directors, so long as their activities fall within the scope of the state's general long arm statute. See Pittsburgh Terminal Corp. v. Mid Allegheny Corp., 831 F.2d 522 (4th Cir. 1987).

8. The Internet is bringing renewed interest to in rem jurisdiction. The 1999 Anticybersquatting Consumer Protection Act, 15 U.S.C. § 1125(d)(2)(A), provides that if an Internet domain name violates the rights of a registered trademark and the trademark owner is not able to obtain in personam jurisdiction over the offending domain name owner, the trademark owner may bring an in rem action against the domain name. For purposes of such an action, the "situs" of the domain name is deemed to include the location where the domain name "registrar, registry, or other domain name authority" is located. Is this statute consistent with *Shaffer*?

The courts that have addressed this issue have offered different approaches. Some courts have interpreted *Shaffer* narrowly and held that the requirement of minimum contacts applies only when the cause of action does not relate to the property involved. For example, in Caesars World, Inc. v. Caesars-Palace.com, 112 F. Supp. 2d 502 (E.D. Va. 2000), the court explained that "under *Shaffer*, there must be minimum contacts to support personal jurisdiction only in those in rem proceedings where the underlying cause of action is unrelated to the property which is located in the forum state. Here the property, that is, the domain name, is not only related to the cause of action but is its entire subject matter." Id. at 504. Accord Porsche Cars N. Am., Inc. v. Porsche.net, 302 F.3d 248, 259–60 (4th Cir. 2002). The court also rejected the argument that a domain name registration is not a proper kind of thing to serve as a res: "There is no prohibition on a legislative body making something property. Even if a domain name is no more than data, Congress can make data property and assign its place of registration as its situs." 112 F. Supp. 2d at 504.

Other courts have held that after *Shaffer*, courts must "apply the minimum contacts test to the * * * exercise of in rem jurisdiction over Domain names," but conclude that contacts between the property and the forum are sufficient to satisfy the requirement. Harrods Ltd. v. Sixty Internet Domain Names, 302 F.3d 214, 224 (4th Cir. 2002). Finally, some courts and commentators have questioned these interpretations of *Shaffer* and have concluded that the defendant must have minimum contacts with the forum. See FleetBoston Fin. Corp. v. FleetBostonFinancial.com, 138 F. Supp. 2d

121, 129–35 (D. Mass. 2001); Michael Allen, *In Rem Jurisdiction from* Pennoyer *to* Shaffer *to the Anticybersquatting Consumer Protection Act*, 11 GEO. MASON L. REV. 243 (2002); Catherine Struve & R. Polk Wagner, *Realspace Sovereign in Cyberspace: Problems with the Anticybersquatting Consumer Protection Act*, 17 BERKELEY TECH. L.J. 989 (2002). Other issues involving jurisdiction and the Internet are explored in Section B.8 below.

9. A number of other countries allow "assets" jurisdiction under which a court acquires in personam jurisdiction allowing judgments of any size based on the presence of property. As one commentator explained: "a Russian may leave his galoshes in a hotel in Berlin and may be sued in Berlin for a debt of 100,000 Marks because of the 'presence of assets within the jurisdiction.'" K.H. NADELMANN, JURISDICTIONALLY IMPROPER FORA, IN XXTH CENTURY COMPARATIVE AND CONFLICTS LAWS: LEGAL ESSAYS IN HONOR OF HESSEL E. YNTEMA 329 (Nadelman, von Mehren & Hazard, eds. 1961).

7. Transient Presence ("Tag" Jurisdiction)

Pennoyer established that service within the state is both necessary and sufficient to establish personal jurisdiction. Modern developments have changed the first part of that rule — in-state service is no longer necessary. In Milliken v. Meyer, 311 U.S. 457 (1940), the Court upheld personal jurisdiction over a domiciliary of the forum even though he was not served with process in the forum. But is service in the forum still sufficient to confer in personam jurisdiction? *Shaffer* held that the mere presence of property is not sufficient to establish jurisdiction. Similarly, one might argue that mere presence of the person should not be enough. Indeed, after *Shaffer*, some commentators predicted the demise of so called "transient" or "tag" jurisdiction. However, in Burnham v. Superior Court of California, 495 U.S. 604 (1990), the Supreme Court upheld personal jurisdiction based solely on the fact that the defendant was physically in the state when served with process.

The case arose out of an ugly divorce. Dennis and Francie Burnham were married and lived in New Jersey with their two children. The couple decided to separate and agreed that Mrs. Burnham would move to California and have custody of the children. They further agreed that they would file for divorce on grounds of "irreconcilable differences." Contrary to their agreement, Mr. Burnham filed for divorce in New Jersey state court on grounds of "desertion." After demanding unsuccessfully that Mr. Burnham adhere to their prior agreement, Mrs. Burnham filed for divorce in California. As part of the divorce, Mrs. Burnham sought an award of money for child support, which requires in personam jurisdiction.

Shortly after Mrs. Burnham filed for divorce, Mr. Burnham went to California on a business trip. As part of this trip, Mr. Burnham stopped by to visit the two children and took the older child to San Francisco for the weekend. When Mr. Burnham returned the child to Mrs. Burnham, he was served with a California court summons and a copy of the petition for divorce and claim for child support.

Mr. Burnham contested in personam jurisdiction. The California courts upheld jurisdiction, based upon the traditional ground that Mr. Burnham was served with process in the state.

The Supreme Court unanimously affirmed the holding of the California courts. Although nine Justices agreed that transient jurisdiction was constitutional in this case, they did not agree on the rationale. Justice Scalia, writing for himself and three other Justices, opined that transient jurisdiction is constitutional because it is a practice that has historically been permitted. "The short of the matter is that jurisdiction based on physical presence alone constitutes due process because it is one of the continuing traditions of our legal system that define the due process standard of 'traditional notions of fair play and substantial justice.'" Id. at 619. In another part of his opinion in which only two other Justices concurred, Justice Scalia attempted to distinguish the Court's prior approach in *Shaffer v. Heitner*:

> It is fair to say, however, that while our holding today does not contradict *Shaffer*, our basic approach to the due process question is different. We have conducted no independent inquiry into the desirability or fairness of the prevailing in-state service rule, leaving that judgment to the legislatures that are free to amend it; for our purposes, its validation is its pedigree, as the phrase "*traditional notions* of fair play and substantial justice" makes clear. *Shaffer* did conduct such an independent inquiry, asserting that " 'traditional notions of fair play and substantial justice' can be as readily offended by the perpetuation of ancient forms that are no longer justified as by the adoption of new procedures that are inconsistent with the basic values of our constitutional heritage." Perhaps that assertion can be sustained when the "perpetuation of ancient forms" is engaged in by only a very small minority of the States. Where, however, as in the present case, a jurisdictional principle is both firmly approved by tradition and still favored, it is impossible to imagine what standard we could appeal to for the judgment that it is "no longer justified." While in no way receding from or casting doubt upon the holding of *Shaffer* or any other case, we reaffirm today our time-honored approach. For new procedures, hitherto unknown, the Due Process Clause requires analysis to determine whether "traditional notions of fair play and substantial justice" have been offended. *International Shoe.* But a doctrine of personal jurisdiction that dates back to the adoption of the Fourteenth Amendment and is still generally observed unquestionably meets that standard.

Id. at 621–22.

Justice Brennan, writing for himself and three other Justices, agreed that transient jurisdiction was constitutional, but offered a very different explanation. He rejected Justice Scalia's historical approach, arguing that "reliance solely on historical pedigree is foreclosed by our decisions in *International Shoe Co. v. Washington* and *Shaffer v. Heitner.* * * * The critical insight of *Shaffer* is that all rules of jurisdiction, even ancient ones, must satisfy contemporary notions of due process." Id. at 629. Justice Brennan nonetheless concluded that jurisdiction was fair in this case. He explained:

> a transient defendant actually "avails" himself of significant benefits provided by the State. His health and safety are guaranteed by the State's police, fire, and emergency medical services; he is free to travel on the State's roads and waterways; he likely enjoys the fruits of the State's economy as well. * * * Without transient jurisdiction, an asymmetry would arise: A transient would have the full benefit of the power of the forum State's courts as a plaintiff while retaining immunity from their authority as a defendant.
>
> The potential burdens on a transient defendant are slight. "Modern transportation and communications have made it much less burdensome for a party sued to defend himself" in a State outside his place of residence. That the defendant has already journeyed at least once before to the forum—as evidenced by the fact that he was served with process there—is an indication that suit in the forum would likely not be prohibitively inconvenient.

Id. at 638–39.

Justice Scalia was quite pointed in his criticisms of Justice Brennan's approach. In a footnote, Justice Scalia observed: "The notion that the Constitution, through some penumbra emanating from the Privileges and Immunities Clause and the Commerce Clause, establishes this Court as a Platonic check upon the society's greedy adherence to its traditions can only be described as imperious." Id. at 627 n.5. Justice Scalia also attacked Justice Brennan's analysis of the fairness of transient jurisdiction:

> Justice Brennan lists the "benefits" Mr. Burnham derived from the State of California—the fact that, during the few days he was there, "[h]is health and safety [were] guaranteed by the State's police, fire, and emergency medical services; he [was] free to travel on the State's roads and waterways; he likely enjoy[ed] the fruits of the State's economy." Three days' worth of these benefits strike us as powerfully inadequate to establish, as an abstract matter, that it is "fair" for California to decree the ownership of all Mr. Burnham's worldly goods acquired during the 10 years of his marriage, and the custody over his children. * * * Even less persuasive are the other "fairness" factors alluded to by Justice Brennan. It would create "an asymmetry," we are told, if Burnham were permitted (as he is) to appear in California courts as a plaintiff, but were not compelled to appear in California courts as defendant; and travel being as easy as it is nowadays, and modern procedural devices being so convenient, it is no great hardship to appear in California courts. The problem with these assertions is that they justify the exercise of jurisdiction over everyone, whether or not he ever comes to California. The only "fairness" elements setting Mr. Burnham apart from the rest of the world are the three days' "benefits" referred to above—and even those do not set him apart from many other people who have enjoyed three days in the Golden State (savoring the fruits of its economy, the availability of its roads and police services) but who were fortunate enough not to be served with process while they were there and thus are not (simply by reason of that savoring) subject to the general jurisdiction of California's courts.

Id. at 623–24.

Accordingly, in personam jurisdiction generally will be upheld if the defendant is served with process in the forum, at least if she is voluntarily present there. Tag jurisdiction is a form of general jurisdiction in that the claim need not arise from or relate to the defendant's presence in the forum. Recall that *Daimler*, in Section B.4 above, held that general jurisdiction is proper only where the defendant is "at home" and indicates that a human is "at home" in the state of her domicile. Does *Daimler* render it impossible for a human to be subject to general jurisdiction in a state other than her domicile?

Suppose Mrs. Burnham had notified Mr. Burnham that one of their children was sick and had encouraged him to visit. When Mr. Burnham arrived to see his child, he was served with process. Which, if any, of the Justices would find in personam jurisdiction constitutional? Does your analysis depend on whether Mrs. Burnham had been truthful when she said the child was sick? Is it ethical for a lawyer to participate in a plan to induce a defendant into the forum? Rule 4.1 of the ABA Model Rules of Professional Conduct provides:

> In the course of representing a client a lawyer shall not knowingly:
>
> (a) make a false statement of material fact or law to a third person; or
>
> (b) fail to disclose a material fact to a third person when disclosure is necessary to avoid assisting a criminal or fraudulent act by a client * * *.

Would a lawyer's involvement in such a scheme be ethical so long as the lawyer does not literally lie or misrepresent?

A number of courts have struck down in-state service where the defendant was tricked into entering the state, although the cases are unclear as to whether this result is required under the Constitution or reflects simply a prudential common law rule of immunity designed to discourage deceitful conduct. See, e.g., Wyman v. Newhouse, 93 F.2d 313 (2d Cir. 1937); Voice Sys. Mktg. Co., L.P. v. Appropriate Technology Corp., 153 F.R.D. 117 (E.D. Mich. 1994).

In *Shaffer*, the Court invalidated a type of jurisdiction that had long been allowed. This result is in tension with Justice Scalia's historical approach. In a footnote, Justice Scalia reconciled *Shaffer* with his approach explaining that "*Shaffer* may have involved a unique state procedure in one respect: Justice Stevens noted that Delaware was the only State that treated the place of incorporation as the situs of corporate stock when both owner and custodian were elsewhere." 495 U.S. at 622 n.4. Some have argued that Scalia's opinion suggests a very narrow reading of *Shaffer* which prohibits quasi-in-rem jurisdiction only in cases involving "intangible property that has no reasonable nexus with the forum." Russell Weintraub, *An Objective Basis for Rejecting Transient Jurisdiction*, 22 Rutgers L.J. 611, 623 (1991). Subsequent to *Burnham*, Justice Scalia asserted that *Shaffer* "at least in [its] broad pronouncements if not with respect to the particular provisions at issue, [was] in my view wrongly decided." Pacific Mut. Life Ins. Co. v. Haslip, 499 U.S. 1, 36 (1991) (Scalia, J. concurring). He went on to state that he felt cases such as *Shaffer* have "no valid *stare decisis* claim upon me." Id. at 38.

Jurisdiction based solely on the transient presence of the defendant is rejected by most other countries. See Peter Hay, *Transient Jurisdiction, Especially Over International Defendants: Critical Comments on* Burnham v. Superior Court of California, 1990 U. ILL. L. REV. 593, 600. Indeed, some commentators have argued that such jurisdiction violates international law. See Russell Weintraub, *An Objective Basis for Rejecting Transient Jurisdiction*, 22 RUTGERS L.J. 611, 615–16 (1991). Interestingly, tag jurisdiction has its defenders in the international context. The Draft Hague Convention on Jurisdiction and Foreign Judgments in Civil and Commercial Matters would have eliminated tag jurisdiction, but human rights groups objected to its elimination on the grounds that this type of jurisdiction might provide a basis for suing war criminals and human rights violators in U.S. courts. Linda Silberman, *Comparative Jurisdiction in the International Context: Will the Proposed Hague Judgments Convention Be Stalled?* 52 DEPAUL L. REV. 319, 345 (2002).

Jurisdiction over Businesses

Historically, corporations were thought to exist only within the state of incorporation and could be sued only there. Today a corporation can be subject to specific jurisdiction in any state with which it has purposeful contacts. And, as we saw in *Daimler* in Section B.4 above, a corporation is subject to general jurisdiction where it is "at home," which includes the state of incorporation and the state of its principal place of business. The corporation has always been considered a legal "person," separate and distinct from the people who own and operate it, and an entity with the capacity to sue and be sued.

Not all business is transacted through the corporation. There are non-incorporated business structures, principally the partnership and the limited liability company (LLC). Historically, courts viewed the partnership as a collection of the individual partners and not as an entity. Because of this, one could not sue the partnership, but instead had to sue the partners individually, and, of course, get personal jurisdiction over each partner. Today, however, most states treat partnerships as separate legal entities that can sue and be sued. The same is generally true for the LLC. For the most part, courts have concluded that personal service over an individual partner or member of such a non-incorporated business who is present in the forum on company business will confer jurisdiction over the business. See First American Corp. v. Price Waterhouse LLP, 154 F.3d 16 (2d Cir. 1998); 1 ROBERT C. CASAD & WILLIAM M. RICHMAN, JURISDICTION IN CIVIL ACTIONS § 3-3 (3d ed. 1998).

Pennoyer recognized that a state can require a business to appoint an agent for service of process and suggested that service on such an agent would confer jurisdiction over the business itself. In *Burnham*, discussed in Section B.7 of this chapter, the Court upheld jurisdiction based on in-state service on a transient individual. This raises the question of whether "tag" jurisdiction works for businesses as it does for human defendants. In James-Dickinson Farm Mortgage Co. v. Harry, 273 U.S. 119, 122 (1927), the Court rejected the notion: "Jurisdiction over a corporation of one State cannot be acquired in another State or district in which it has no place of business and is not found, merely by serving process upon an executive officer temporarily therein, even if he is there on business of the company."

It is important to note, though, that *James-Dickenson Farm Mortgage* addressed jurisdiction based on service on a transient agent. The situation is quite different with service on a corporate agent who is not transient. All states require out-of-state businesses seeking to transact business within the state to register and to appoint an in-state agent for service of process. When a company complies with a "registration" statute and appoints an agent for service, jurisdiction based upon service on the agent is not rooted in presence or minimum contacts. Rather, it is rooted in consent. Specifically, by appointing an agent who has authority to accept service of process, the business "consents" to jurisdiction.

This raises the question of how broad such "consent" might be. In other words, does compliance with a registration statute subject the company to general jurisdiction or merely to specific jurisdiction? (If the former, the company can be sued in the forum for a claim that arose anywhere in the world. If the latter, the company can be sued in the forum only for a claim that arose from its activities in the forum.) The starting point is the statutory language. Surprisingly, though, most statutes are not clear about the scope of jurisdiction. Some statutes have been interpreted to give consent to general jurisdiction. See, e.g., King v. American Family Mut. Ins. Co., 632 F.3d 570, 576 (9th Cir. 2011); Sondergard v. Miles, Inc., 985 F.2d 1389 (8th Cir. 1993); Knowlton v. Allied Van Lines, Inc., supra; Maunula v. Westran, Inc., 845 F. Supp. 512 (M.D. Tenn. 1994); Sternberg v. O'Neil, supra. Others, however, have been read more narrowly, allowing only specific jurisdiction. See, e.g., Pittock v. Otis Elevator Co., 8 F.3d 325 (6th Cir. 1993); Siemer v. Learjet Acquisition Corp., 966 F.2d 179 (5th Cir. 1992).

The issue is of resurgent importance in the wake of *Daimler*. Some defendants have argued that *Daimler* (which permits general jurisdiction where the defendant is "at home") rules out the possibility of general jurisdiction in any other way, including consent under a registration statute. Most courts that have addressed the question disagree. In Otsuka Pharmaceutical Co. v. Mylan, Inc., 2015 U.S. Dist. LEXIS 35679 (D.N.J. Mar. 23, 2015), the court held that compliance with the Delaware registration statute rendered the defendant subject to general jurisdiction. Two judges in the District of Delaware reached the same conclusion under the Delaware statute. Acorda Therapeutics, Inc. v. Mylan Pharms, Inc., 78 F. Supp. 3d 572 (D. Del. 2015); Forest Labs, Inc. v. Anmeal Pharms., LLC, 2015 U.S. Dist. LEXIS 23215 (D. Del. Feb. 26, 2015). Interestingly, a different judge in the District of Delaware reached the opposite conclusion, and held that *Daimler* limits general jurisdiction over a corporation to states in which it is "at home." AstraZeneca AB v. Mylan Pharms, LLC, 72 F. Supp. 3d 549 (D. Del. 2014). See also Lanham v. Pilot Travel Centers, LLC, 2015 U.S. Dist. LEXIS 117497 (D. Or. Sept. 2, 2015) ("[I]t appears that the Ninth Circuit aligns itself with those circuits concluding, albeit pre-*Daimler*, that consent may be a separate basis for asserting general personal jurisdiction of a foreign defendant, independent of an *International Shoe* minimum contacts due process analysis.").

The Supreme Court has mentioned the issue only in passing. In Bendix Autolite Corp. v. Midwesco Enterprises, 486 U.S. 888, 891 (1988), the Court struck down an Ohio law that tolled the statute of limitations for corporations that failed to appoint an in-state agent for service of process. The Court's analysis was premised on the assumption that appointing "operates as consent to the general jurisdiction of the Ohio courts."

8. Personal Jurisdiction and the Internet

Although modern personal jurisdiction has advanced beyond the formalism of *Pennoyer v. Neff*, it has not abandoned its roots completely—state boundaries still matter. For purposes of personal jurisdiction, it is important where things happen and what a defendant does to connect herself to a place. The development and wide use of the Internet may pose an interesting challenge for personal jurisdiction, because boundaries and place seem largely irrelevant and meaningless on the Internet. As one court has observed, "The Internet has no territorial boundaries. To paraphrase Gertrude Stein, as far as the Internet is concerned, not only is there perhaps 'no there there,' the 'there' is *everywhere* where there is Internet access." Digital Equip. Corp. v. AltaVista Technology, Inc., 960 F. Supp. 456, 462 (D. Mass. 1997).

Some have argued that just as the rise of interstate corporate business challenged the approach of *Pennoyer* and ultimately resulted in the test set forth in *International Shoe*, so too, the rise of the Internet may require a rethinking of current doctrine. See Martin Redish, *Of New Wine and Old Bottles: Personal Jurisdiction, the Internet, and Nature of Constitutional Evolution*, 38 Jurimetrics J. 575 (1998). Others disagree, arguing the "[p]eople have been inflicting injury on each other from afar for a long time," and current doctrine can easily accommodate this new technology. Allan Stein, *Personal Jurisdiction and the Internet: Seeing Due Process Through the Lens of Regulatory Precision*, 98 Nw. U. L. Rev. 411 (2004). In his concurrence in *Nicastro*, Justice Breyer specifically raised the question of how jurisdictional doctrine should handle defendants who market through the web. Although he expressed no view as to what the right answer should be, he did observe that "there have been many recent changes in commerce and communication, many of which are not anticipated by our precedents.... So I think it unwise to announce a rule of broad applicability without full consideration of the modern-day consequences" 131 S. Ct. at 2791. The following case highlights some of the issues in this area.

Revell v. Lidov

317 F.3d 467 (5th Cir. 2002)

Higginbotham, Circuit Judge

Oliver "Buck" Revell sued Hart G.W. Lidov and Columbia University for defamation arising out of Lidov's authorship of an article that he posted on an internet bulletin board hosted by Columbia. The district court dismissed Revell's claims for lack of personal jurisdiction over both Lidov and Columbia. We affirm.

I

Hart G.W. Lidov, an Assistant Professor of Pathology and Neurology at the Harvard Medical School and Children's Hospital, wrote a lengthy article on the subject of the terrorist bombing of Pan Am Flight 103, which exploded over Lockerbie, Scotland in 1988. The article alleges that a broad politically motivated conspiracy among senior members of the Reagan Administration lay behind their wilful failure to stop the bombing despite clear advance warnings. Further, Lidov charged that the government proceeded to cover up its receipt of advance warning and repeatedly misled the public about the facts. Specifically, the article singles out Oliver "Buck" Revell, then Associate Deputy Director of the FBI, for severe criticism, accusing him of complicity in the conspiracy and cover-up. The article further charges that Revell, knowing about the imminent terrorist attack, made certain his son, previously booked on Pan Am 103, took a different flight. At the time he wrote the article, Lidov had never been to Texas, except possibly to change planes, or conducted business there, and was apparently unaware that Revell then resided in Texas.

Lidov has also never been a student or faculty member of Columbia University, but he posted his article on a website maintained by its School of Journalism. In a bulletin board section of the website, users could post their own works and read the works of others. As a result, the article could be viewed by members of the public over the internet.

Revell, a resident of Texas, sued the Board of Trustees of Columbia University, whose principal offices are in New York City, and Lidov, who is a Massachusetts resident, in the Northern District of Texas. Revell claimed damage to his professional reputation in Texas and emotional distress arising out of the alleged defamation of the defendants, and sought several million dollars in damages. Both defendants moved to dismiss for lack of personal jurisdiction under Federal Rule of Civil Procedure 12(b)(2). The district court granted the defendants' motions, and Revell now appeals.

II

B

* * * Revell first urges that the district court may assert general jurisdiction over Columbia because its website provides internet users the opportunity to subscribe to the *Columbia Journalism Review*, purchase advertising on the website or in the journal, and submit electronic applications for admission.

This circuit has drawn upon the approach of Zippo Manufacturing Co. v. Zippo Dot Com, Inc., 952 F. Supp. 1119 (W.D. Pa. 1997), in determining whether the operation of an internet site can support the minimum contacts necessary for the exercise of personal jurisdiction. *Zippo* used a "sliding scale" to measure an internet site's connections to a forum state. A "passive" website, one that merely allows the owner to post information on the internet, is at one end of the scale. It will not be sufficient to establish personal jurisdiction. At the other end are sites whose owners engage in repeated online contacts with forum residents over the internet, and in these cases personal jurisdiction may be proper. In between are those sites with some interactive elements, through which a site allows for bilateral information exchange with its visitors. Here, we find more familiar terrain, requiring that we examine the extent of the interactivity and nature of the forum contacts.

While we deployed this sliding scale in Mink v. AAAA Development LLC, 190 F.3d 333 (5th Cir. 1999), it is not well adapted to the general jurisdiction inquiry, because even repeated contacts with forum residents by a foreign defendant may not constitute the requisite substantial, continuous and systematic contacts required for a finding of general jurisdiction — in other words, while it may be doing business *with* Texas, it is not doing business *in* Texas.

Irrespective of the sliding scale, the question of general jurisdiction is not difficult here. Though the maintenance of a website is, in a sense, a continuous presence everywhere in the world, the cited contacts of Columbia with Texas are not in any way "substantial."

Columbia's contacts with Texas are in stark contrast to the facts of the Supreme Court's seminal case on general jurisdiction, *Perkins v. Benguet Consolidated Mining Co.* In *Perkins*, a Philippine corporation temporarily relocated to Ohio. The corporation's president resided in Ohio, the records of the corporation were kept in Ohio, director's meetings were held in Ohio, accounts were held in Ohio banks, and all key business decisions were made there. Columbia's internet presence in Texas quite obviously falls far short of this standard. Our conclusion also comports with the recent decision in Bird v. Parsons, 289 F.3d 865 (6th Cir. 2002), where the Sixth Circuit found Ohio courts lacked general jurisdiction over a non-resident business that registered domain names despite the fact that: (1) the defendant maintained a website open for commerce with Ohio residents and (2) over 4000 Ohio residents had in fact registered domain names with the defendant. By contrast, Columbia, since it began keeping records, never received more than twenty internet subscriptions to the *Columbia Journalism Review* from Texas residents.

C

Turning to the issue of specific jurisdiction, the question is whether Revell has made out his *prima facie* case with respect to the defendants' contacts with Texas. *Zippo's* scale does more work with specific jurisdiction — the context in which it was originally conceived.

Revell urges that, given the uniqueness of defamation claims and their inherent ability to inflict injury in far-flung jurisdictions, we should abandon the imagery of *Zippo*. It is a bold but ultimately unpersuasive argument. Defamation has its unique features, but shares relevant characteristics with various business torts. Nor is the *Zippo* scale, as has been suggested, in tension with the "effects" test of *Calder v. Jones* [which is discussed in Section B.3 above] for intentional torts, which we address in Part II.D.

For specific jurisdiction we look only to the contact out of which the cause of action arises — in this case the maintenance of the internet bulletin board. Since this defamation action does not arise out of the solicitation of subscriptions or applications by Columbia, those portions of the website need not be considered.

The district court concluded that the bulletin board was "*Zippo*-passive" and therefore could not create specific jurisdiction. The defendants insist that Columbia's bulletin board is indistinguishable from the website in *Mink*. In that case, we found the website would not support a finding of minimum contacts because it only solicited customers, provided a toll-free number to call, and an e-mail address. It did not allow visitors to place orders online. But in this case, any user of the internet can post material to the bulletin board. This means that individuals *send* information to be posted, and *receive* information that others have posted. In *Mink* and *Zippo*, a visitor was limited to expressing an interest in a commercial product. Here the visitor may participate in an open forum hosted by the website. Columbia's bulletin board is thus interactive, and we must evaluate the extent of this interactivity as well as Revell's arguments with respect to *Calder*.

D

1

In *Calder*, an editor and a writer for the *National Enquirer*, both residents of Florida, were sued in California for libel arising out of an article published in the *Enquirer* about Shirley Jones, an actress. The Supreme Court upheld the exercise of personal jurisdiction over the two defendants because they had "expressly aimed" their conduct towards California.

> The allegedly libelous story concerned the California activities of a California resident. It impugned the professionalism of an entertainer whose television career was centered in California. The article was drawn from California sources, and the brunt of the harm, in terms both of respondent's emotional distress and the injury to her professional reputation, was suffered in California. *In sum, California is the focal point both of the story and of the harm suffered.* [Calder]

The Court also relied upon the fact that the *Enquirer* had its largest circulation—over 600,000 copies—in California, indicating that the defendants knew the harm of their allegedly tortious activity would be felt there.

2

Revell urges that, measured by the "effects" test of *Calder*, he has presented his *prima facie* case for the defendants' minimum contacts with Texas. At the outset we emphasize that the "effects" test is but one facet of the ordinary minimum contacts analysis, to be considered as part of the full range of the defendant's contacts with the forum.

We find several distinctions between this case and *Calder*—insurmountable hurdles to the exercise of personal jurisdiction by Texas courts. First, the article written by Lidov about Revell contains no reference to Texas, nor does it refer to the Texas activities of Revell, and it was not directed at Texas readers as distinguished from readers in other states. Texas was not the focal point of the article or the harm suffered, unlike *Calder*, in which the article contained descriptions of the California activities of the plaintiff, drew upon California sources, and found its largest audience in California. This conclusion fits well with our decisions in other intentional tort cases where the plaintiff relied upon *Calder*. In those cases we stated that the plaintiff's residence in the forum, and suffering of harm there, will not alone support jurisdiction under *Calder*. We also find instructive the defamation decisions of the Sixth, Third, and Fourth Circuits in Reynolds v. International Amateur Athletic Federation, 23 F.3d 1110 (6th Cir. 1994), Remick v. Manfredy, 238 F.3d 248 (3d Cir. 2001), and Young v. New Haven Advocate, 315 F.3d 256 (4th Cir. 2002), respectively.

In *Reynolds* a London-based association published a press release regarding the plaintiff's disqualification from international track competition for two years following his failure of a drug test. The plaintiff, an Ohio resident, claimed that the alleged defamation had cost him endorsement contracts in Ohio and cited *Calder* in support of his argument that personal jurisdiction over the defendant in Ohio was proper. The court found *Calder* inapposite because, *inter alia*, the allegedly defamatory press release dealt with the plaintiff's activities in Monaco, not Ohio; the source of the report was a urine sample taken in Monaco and analyzed in Paris; and the "focal point" of the release was not Ohio. We agree with the *Reynolds* court that the sources relied upon and activities described in an allegedly defamatory publication should in some way connect with the forum if *Calder* is to be invoked.[48] Lidov's article, insofar as it relates to Revell, deals exclusively with his actions as Associate Deputy Director of the FBI—just as the offending press release in *Reynolds* dealt only with a failed drug test in Monaco. It signifies that there is no reference to Texas in the article or any reliance on Texas sources. These facts weigh heavily against finding the requisite minimum contacts in this case.

In *Remick* the plaintiff, a Pennsylvania lawyer, sued several individuals for defamation arising out of two letters sent to the plaintiff in Pennsylvania containing oblique charges of incompetence and accusations that the plaintiff was engaged in extortion of the defendants. The letters concerned the termination of the plaintiff's representation of one of the defendants, a professional boxer. One of the two letters was read by individuals other than the plaintiff when it was faxed to the plaintiff's Philadelphia office. The court held, however, that since there was nothing in the letter to indicate that it was targeted at Pennsylvania residents other than the plaintiff, personal juris-

48. The Tenth Circuit has suggested that this is not a requirement of *Calder*. In Burt v. Board of Regents of University of Nebraska, 757 F.2d 242 (10th Cir. 1985), *vacated as moot*, Connolly v. Burt, 475 U.S. 1063 (1986), the court upheld the application of *Calder* to support personal jurisdiction in Colorado where a University of Nebraska doctor had written unflattering and allegedly defamatory letters about the plaintiff in response to requests from Colorado hospitals, despite the fact that the content of the letters focused on the plaintiff's activities in Nebraska, not Colorado. We find more persuasive the view of Judge Seth, who remarked, in dissent, that this represented "but half a *Calder*," which requires both the harm to be felt in the forum *and* that the forum be the focal point of the publication.

diction could not be obtained under *Calder*. Furthermore, the court noted that allegations that the charges in the letter had been distributed throughout the "boxing community" were insufficient, because there was no assertion that Pennsylvania had a "unique relationship with the boxing industry, as distinguished from the relationship in *Calder* between California and the motion picture industry, with which the *Calder* plaintiff was associated."

Similarly, in *Young v. New Haven Advocate*, two newspapers in Connecticut posted on the internet articles about the housing of Connecticut prisoners in Virginia that allegedly defamed a Virginia prison warden. The Fourth Circuit held that Virginia could not exercise personal jurisdiction over the Connecticut defendants because "they did not manifest an intent to aim their websites or the posted articles at a Virginia audience." * * * [I]t reasoned that "application of *Calder* in the Internet context requires proof that the out-of-state defendant's Internet activity is expressly directed at or directed to the forum state." It observed that more than simply making the news article accessible to Virginians by defendants' posting of the article on their internet sites was needed for assertion of jurisdiction: "The newspapers must, through the Internet postings, manifest an intent to *target* and *focus* on Virginia readers."

As with *Remick* and *Young*, the post to the bulletin board here was presumably directed at the entire world, or perhaps just concerned U.S. citizens. But certainly it was not directed specifically at Texas, which has no especial relationship to the Pan Am 103 incident. Furthermore, here there is nothing to compare to the targeting of California readers represented by approximately 600,000 copies of the *Enquirer* the *Calder* defendants knew would be distributed in California, the *Enquirer*'s largest market.

3

As these cases aptly demonstrate, one cannot purposefully avail oneself of "some forum someplace"; rather, as the Supreme Court has stated, due process requires that "the defendant's conduct and connection with the forum State are such that he should reasonably anticipate being haled into court there." [*Burger King*.] Lidov's affidavit, uncontroverted by the record, states that he did not even know that Revell was a resident of Texas when he posted his article. Knowledge of the particular forum in which a potential plaintiff will bear the brunt of the harm forms an essential part of the *Calder* test.[61] The defendant must be chargeable with knowledge of the forum at which his conduct is directed in order to reasonably anticipate being haled into court in that forum, as *Calder* itself[62] and numerous cases from other circuits applying

61. Further evidence that the *Calder* defendants knew that the harm of their conduct would be felt in California came from their knowledge that the *Enquirer* enjoyed its largest circulation there.

62. *Calder*, 465 U.S. 783 at 790 ("An individual injured in California need not go to Florida to seek redress from persons who, though remaining in Florida, *knowingly cause the injury in California*." (emphasis added)).

Calder confirm. Demanding knowledge of a particular forum to which conduct is directed, in defamation cases, is not altogether distinct from the requirement that the forum be the focal point of the tortious activity because satisfaction of the latter will ofttimes provide sufficient evidence of the former. Lidov must have known that the harm of the article would hit home wherever Revell resided. But that is the case with virtually any defamation. A more direct aim is required than we have here. In short, this was not about Texas. If the article had a geographic focus it was Washington, D.C.

III

Our ultimate inquiry is rooted in the limits imposed on states by the Due Process Clause of the Fourteenth Amendment. It is fairness judged by the reasonableness of Texas exercising its power over residents of Massachusetts and New York. This inquiry into fairness captures the reasonableness of hauling a defendant from his home state before the court of a sister state; in the main a pragmatic account of reasonable expectations—if you are going to pick a fight in Texas, it is reasonable to expect that it be settled there. It is not fairness calibrated by the likelihood of success on the merits or relative fault. Rather, we look to the geographic focus of the article, not the bite of the defamation, the blackness of the calumny, or who provoked the fight. * * *

IV

In sum, Revell has failed to make out a *prima facie* case of personal jurisdiction over either defendant. General jurisdiction cannot be obtained over Columbia. Considering both the "effects" test of *Calder* and the low-level of interactivity of the internet bulletin board, we find the contacts with Texas insufficient to establish the jurisdiction of its courts, and hence the federal district court in Texas, over Columbia and Lidov. We AFFIRM the dismissal for lack of personal jurisdiction as to both defendants.

Affirmed.

Notes and Questions

1. The court relies on *Calder*, which we discussed in Section B.3 above. The reliance seems sensible, because use of the Internet can result in causing an effect in the forum. Recall that the Supreme Court revisited the *Calder* effects test in *Walden v. Fiore* in 2014 (which is discussed with *Calder* above). Would *Walden* require the court in *Revell* to come to a different conclusion today? See generally Alan M. Trammell & Derek E. Bambauer, *Personal Jurisdiction and the "Interwebs,"* 100 CORNELL L. REV. 1129 (2015).

2. The *Revell* court relies on Zippo Mfg. Co. v. Zippo Dot Com, Inc., 952 F. Supp. 1119 (W.D. Pa. 1997), one of the early and most influential Internet jurisdiction cases. The *Zippo* "sliding scale" approach focuses on the extent to which a website is interactive. How useful is interactivity as a test for personal jurisdiction? Critics of the approach raise several concerns. First, they argue, the test provides little certainty

because the majority of websites have some degree of interactivity and thus, under *Zippo*, fall within a middle zone in which criteria other than the degree of interactivity will be dispositive. Moreover, the standard for what is "active" and "passive" is shifting as technology changes. While at one point, an active email link might have been sufficient to make a site seem highly "interactive," today that is no longer true. More basically, the *Zippo* test begs the question of why the degree of interactivity should matter for jurisdictional purposes. Consider the following:

> This passive/active test represents an egregious failure of legal imagination. Lacking an adequate conceptual account of why purposeful availment matters, the courts have reverted to thinking about jurisdiction in *Pennoyer*-like physical terms: the interactive web site looks like the defendant is really operating a branch store in the forum. If the defendant is simply conveying information, he is not "really" there. * * * The interactivity of a web site has no definitive connection to the reasons why it might be reasonable to subject a defendant to jurisdiction.

Allan Stein, *Personal Jurisdiction and the Internet: Seeing Due Process through the Lens of Regulatory Precision*, 98 Nw. U. L. Rev. 411, 430–31 (2004). On the other hand, some courts have continued to rely upon *Zippo*. See, e.g., Harris v. SportBike Track Gear, 2015 U.S. Dist. LEXIS 128289 at *11 (D.N.J. September 8, 2015) (*Zippo* "is a seminal case concerning personal jurisdiction based upon the operation of Internet websites."), *recommendation adopted* 2015 U.S. Dist. LEXIS 128005 (D.N.J. September 24, 2015).

3. In *Revell*, the court does not stop with the *Zippo* test, but goes on to consider whether the defendant "targeted" Texas. The article concerned the plaintiff's activities as Associate Director of the FBI. Assuming these activities were for the most part done at the FBI headquarters in Washington, D.C., did the article "target" D.C.? Would it matter whether the plaintiff was a resident of D.C. at the time? See *Young v. New Haven Advocate* (discussed in *Revell*). Did the article "target" anyplace? Compare the result in *Revell* with System Designs, Inc. v. New CustomWare Co., 248 F. Supp. 2d 1093 (D. Utah 2003). There, the plaintiff alleged that the defendant, a California software company, used a trademark on its web site that infringed the plaintiff's Utah registered trademark. Although there was no showing that the defendant had done business with any Utah residents, the court nonetheless upheld jurisdiction in Utah, finding that the defendant's web site "demonstrates an intentional targeting of Utah" because customers in Utah could use the on-line features of the site (as could customers anywhere) and because the site listed several of NewCustomWare's large clients including Wells Fargo, Qwest, AT&T, Sprint, and Dell. According to the court, these companies had "substantial connections to Utah" and "[b]y listing them as clients, NewCustomWare was suggesting to Utah companies the desirability of doing business with it." Id. at 1102. Was there any state the site was not "targeting" by listing these companies?

4. Other nations focus on effects as a basis for jurisdiction both in the Internet context and for more traditional torts. In one case, a French court ordered U.S.-based

Yahoo! to install filters to prevent French residents from accessing sites on Yahoo! that offered Nazi memorabilia for sale. See County Court of Paris, Interim Court Order, League Against Racism & Antisemitism LICRA v. Yahoo! Inc., No. RG 00/05308 (Nov. 20, 2000). Australia has likewise upheld jurisdiction in its courts based solely on an injury to reputation suffered by an Australian plaintiff in Australia from material posted in the U.S. on a web site by a U.S. company. See Dow Jones & Co., Inc. v. Gutnick, [2002] HCA 56 (10 December 2002) (High Court of Australia).

C. A Different Perspective

1. The Purposes of Personal Jurisdiction

The constitutional doctrine of personal jurisdiction imposes a federal restriction on state adjudicative authority. But why should there be any such limits? What is the problem for which personal jurisdiction is the solution? One might argue that personal jurisdiction is simply a guaranty of immunity from the inconvenience of distant litigation. The doctrine that has developed, however, does not focus primarily on convenience. Indeed, the Court in *World-Wide Volkswagen* stated that even the most convenient forum may not have jurisdiction. Limitations on personal jurisdiction could be intended to protect a defendant from the bias of states with which she is not affiliated. Again, however, the developed doctrine is not aimed at protecting against bias. For example, there is no reason to believe that California will be less biased toward the defendants in *Calder* than Oklahoma would be toward the defendants in *World-Wide Volkswagen.*

Maybe personal jurisdiction is a concrete manifestation of a somewhat more philosophical problem. When one asks whether a court has personal jurisdiction, one in essence asks whether a sovereign has a legitimate right to exercise authority over a particular individual. If one conceives of states as wholly separate sovereigns, and one believes that legitimate authority stems only from the consent of the governed, then it may make sense to require that a defendant consent or otherwise purposefully connect herself with the sovereign. See Margaret Stewart, *A New Litany of Personal Jurisdiction*, 60 U. Colo. L. Rev. 5 (1989); Richard Epstein, *Consent, Not Power, as the Basis of Jurisdiction*, 2001 U. Chi. Legal F. 1; Charles W. "Rocky" Rhodes, *Liberty, Substantive Due Process, and Personal Jurisdiction*, 82 Tul. L. Rev. 567 (2007).

This explanation is not without its difficulties. Even if one accepts a consent theory of political legitimacy, why isn't it the case that by becoming (or remaining) a citizen of the United States, one consents to the adjudicative authority of all the states? By participating in our interdependent nation with its free interstate flow of goods and services, all citizens get many benefits. One of the costs of interstate commerce is that harms can be inflicted far from the participants to a transaction. Having accepted the benefits of our free-flowing economy, why isn't it fair to impose the burden of possible distant litigation in any of the states? Implied consent as a foundation of personal jurisdiction has its critics—most notably Justice Ginsburg who in *Nicastro* referred to the "long-discredited fiction of implied consent." 131 S. Ct. at 2799.

Professor Brilmayer has offered a related but somewhat different explanation for the purposefulness component of personal jurisdiction. She explains:

> The reason for limiting jurisdiction to cases where the defendant had some control over the eventual location of the product is to prevent the forum from always shifting the costs to persons to whom its sovereignty does not extend, namely, the out-of-state consumers who have no contact with the forum. If the defendant deliberately sent a product into the State, he has a choice to stop marketing there if the costs of doing business exceed the value to him of that market. And the State is unlikely to impose upon him jurisdictional burdens exceeding the actual cost of his activities there, because the State does not want to discourage his activities in the State unless the benefits of the activities are less than the burdens. But if jurisdiction can be asserted even where the defendant had no control, these checks cannot be assumed to be adequate. Since the defendant cannot structure his conduct in a way that makes him immune to suit there, the State is not adequately restrained by the possibility that the defendant will withdraw from its markets. And it cannot be inferred that taking advantage of activity in the forum was sufficiently profitable, even given the added jurisdictional costs, that the defendant may fairly be presumed to have agreed to take his chances.

Lea Brilmayer, *How Contacts Count: Due Process Limitations on State Court Jurisdiction*, 1980 Sup. Ct. Rev. 77, 95–96. Why can't states distribute the losses on out-of-staters? In the context of personal jurisdiction, someone, either plaintiff or defendant, will have to travel to an undesired (and undesirable?) forum. Is economic efficiency enhanced by making plaintiffs travel to defendants' states rather than the other way around?

Other commentators have suggested that personal jurisdiction should be viewed less as a protection of individual liberty and more as a device for regulating interstate federalism. Thus, Professor Stein has argued that the central issue in personal jurisdiction should be "whether the forum has any business regulating the controversy." Allan Stein, *Styles of Argument and Interstate Federalism in the Law of Personal Jurisdiction*, 65 Tex. L. Rev. 689, 751 (1987). Similarly, Professor Weinstein has argued that the rules of personal jurisdiction developed in this country as the "quid pro quo" for a strict application of the Full Faith and Credit Clause, under which all sister-state judgments (rendered with jurisdiction) must be enforced. James Weinstein, *The Early American Origins of Territoriality in Judicial Jurisdiction*, 37 St. Louis U. L.J. 1, 27 (1992). Finally, it has been argued that because plaintiffs frequently seek a forum that will apply the most advantageous law, personal jurisdiction, which limits plaintiffs' choices among fora, is an indirect way to limit plaintiffs' ability to choose the law. See Wendy Perdue, *Personal Jurisdiction and the Beetle in the Box*, 32 B.C. L. Rev. 529, 570–73 (1991).

Which, if any, of these explanations make sense? Do any of them provide adequate justifications for the federal judiciary to override state attempts to exercise jurisdiction?

2. Personal Jurisdiction in Other Countries

In *Pennoyer*, Justice Field suggested that the principles of jurisdiction which he propounds are universally accepted. They are not. For example, the German Civil Procedure Code permits in personam jurisdiction over nonresident defendants who own property in Germany. There is no requirement that the claim be related to the property, there is no need for prior attachment and jurisdiction is not limited to the value of the German assets. France goes even further. Its Civil Code permits French citizens to sue anyone in French courts without regard to the defendant's connection to France. The Code further provides that French citizens can be sued only in France. Of course, the fact that Germany and France choose to exercise jurisdiction in these circumstances does not mean that other countries will enforce these judgments. Nonetheless, some countries permit jurisdiction in circumstances that we would consider exorbitant. See generally Friedrich Juenger, *Judicial Jurisdiction in the United States and in the European Communities: A Comparison*, 82 Mich. L. Rev. 1195 (1984).

These international analogies may not seem entirely apt to the problem of interstate jurisdiction. After all, one of the purposes of the United States Constitution was to constrain the destructive chauvinistic instincts of the states. One of the most interesting international analogies to the problems we confront as a nation of states is the European Union (EU). In connection with the creation of the EU, the participating countries addressed the problems of jurisdiction by adopting Council Regulation No. 44/2001 of 22 December 2000 on Jurisdiction and the Recognition and Enforcement of Judgments in Civil and Commercial Matters. That Regulation provides for general jurisdiction in the defendant's domicile or, in the case of a business, in its principal place of business. In addition, it includes a number of specific rules, some of which are set forth below. The Regulation prohibits the use of certain types of jurisdiction, including transient jurisdiction. All of the limitations imposed by the Regulation apply only to jurisdiction asserted over domiciliaries and nationals of EU countries. The Regulation does not limit assertions of jurisdiction over other foreigners.

Chapter II, Jurisdiction

Article 5

A person domiciled in [an EU Country] may, in another [EU Country] be sued:

1. in matters relating to a contract, in the courts of the place of performance of the obligation in question; * * *

2. in matters relating to maintenance [e.g., child support and alimony], in the courts for the place where the maintenance creditor is domiciled or habitually resident; * * *

3. in matters relating to tort, delict or quasi-delict in the courts for the place where the harmful event occurred;

Article 6

A person domiciled in [an EU Country] may also be sued:

1. where he is one of a number of defendants, in the courts for the place where any one of them is domiciled, provided the claims are so closely connected that it is expedient to hear and determine them together to avoid the risk of irreconcilable judgments resulting from separate proceedings;

2. as a third party in an action on a warranty or guarantee or in any other third party proceedings, in the court seised of the original proceedings, unless these were instituted solely with the object of removing him from the jurisdiction of the court which would be competent in his case;

3. on a counter-claim arising from the same contract or facts on which the original claim was based, in the court in which the original claim is pending.

Consider *World-Wide Volkswagen, Kulko, Burger King, Asahi,* and *Burnham.* Would the results in those cases be different under the EU Regulation?

You will notice that the Regulation does not appear to impose a requirement of "purposeful availment." Indeed, with respect to torts, the European Court of Justice has held that a tort suit can be filed either in the place of the damage or in the place of the events giving rise to the damage. See Bier v. Mines de Potasse D'Alsace S.A. [1976–8] E.C.R. 1736, 1743 (European Court of Justice). Does the Regulation fail to recognize and protect the sovereignty of the signatory countries? Do you think the Regulation is unfair to the citizens of those countries? See generally Patrick Borchers, *Comparing Personal Jurisdiction in the United States and the European Community: Lessons for American Reform*, 40 AM. J. COMP. L. 121 (1992).

D. Statutory Limits on Personal Jurisdiction

Up to this point, we have been dealing with limits imposed by the Constitution on states' ability to assert personal jurisdiction. States may also impose their own limits. Obviously, states cannot assert jurisdiction beyond that which the Constitution allows. But the fact that a case may fall within those constitutional limits does not mean that a court has personal jurisdiction. Personal jurisdiction is not automatically conferred. Rather, each state must enact legislation allowing its courts to exercise personal jurisdiction. Every state has a statute permitting in personam jurisdiction over persons served with process in the state and over domiciliaries of the state. States also have nonresident motorist statutes similar to the one we saw in *Hess v. Pawloski.* Beyond that, states take different approaches as to how far (within the constitutional limits) to permit their courts to exercise personal jurisdiction.

For personal jurisdiction to be proper (1) the case must fall within the terms of a state statute, and (2) jurisdiction must be constitutional. Thus, if the statute is not met, no constitutional analysis is needed. This is consistent with the general desire of courts to avoid constitutional questions when possible. If the state has elected not to assert jurisdiction over the case at hand, the fact that it could constitutionally have done so is irrelevant.

All states have so-called "long arm statutes" that specify the scope of that state's personal jurisdiction authority. These statutes were passed in reaction to *International Shoe* and vary state to state. The Georgia statute below is typical. A few are more open-ended. For example, California law provides, "A court of this state may exercise jurisdiction on any basis not inconsistent with the Constitution of this state or of the United States." CAL. CODE OF CIV. PROC. § 410.10.

Each state is free to interpret its long arm statute however it chooses, and sometimes identical language is interpreted differently in different states. Consider the following situation. Suppose that Valve Co. manufactures valves in State A. It sells the valves to Heater Co., a heater manufacturer in State B. Heater Co. incorporates the valves into its heaters, which it sells throughout a region of several states. One of the Valve Co. valves explodes in State X, injuring the plaintiff. Plaintiff wants to sue Valve Co. in State X. Its long arm statute grants jurisdiction over one who "commits a tortious act or omission in State X." Does it apply to Valve Co?

Courts in different states have interpreted this language differently. In *Gray v. American Radiator & Std. Sanitary Corp.*, which we discussed in "Note on *McGee, Hanson* and *Gray*" in Section B.3, supra, the Illinois Supreme Court upheld jurisdiction under these facts. It reasoned that an act or omission cannot become "tortious" until someone is injured. Because plaintiff was injured in Illinois, defendant committed a tortious act or omission there.

The New York Court of Appeals interpreted an identical New York statute under similar circumstance and reached a different conclusion. It emphasized the statutory words "act or omission," and concluded that the statute could be met only if the defendant actually did (or omitted to do) something in New York. Where the negligent manufacture of the product took place in a different state, there was no tortious act or omission (and therefore no jurisdiction) in New York. Feathers v. McLucas, 209 N.E.2d 68 (N.Y. 1965).

In reaction to *Feathers*, the New York legislature amended the statute to permit jurisdiction over nonresidents who committed tortious acts or omissions out of state that caused injury in state. Jurisdiction was proper, however, only if the defendant had other contacts with the state or could reasonably expect to derive substantial revenue there.

Review the Georgia statute below. Notice that in subparts (2) and (3) the statute deals separately with cases in which the defendant acted in Georgia and those in which it acted out of state, causing injury in state. Notice also, that (3) imposes an additional requirement similar to that in the New York statute.

Official Code of Georgia Annotated

§ 9-10-91 (1992)

9-10-91. Grounds for exercise of personal jurisdiction over nonresident.

A court of this state may exercise personal jurisdiction over any nonresident or his executor or administrator, as to a cause of action arising from any of the acts, omissions, ownership, use, or possession enumerated in this Code section, in the same manner as if he were a resident of the state, if in person or through an agent, he:

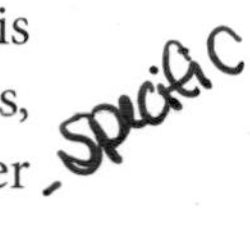

(1) Transacts any business within this state;

(2) Commits a tortious act or omission within this state, except as to a cause of action for defamation of character arising from the act;

(3) Commits a tortious injury in this state caused by an act or omission outside this state if the tortfeasor regularly does or solicits business, or engages in any other persistent course of conduct, or derives substantial revenue from goods used or consumed or services rendered in this state;

(4) Owns, uses, or possesses any real property situated within this state; or

(5) With respect to proceedings for alimony, child support, or division of property in connection with an action for divorce or with respect to an independent action for support of dependents, maintains a matrimonial domicile in this state at the time of the commencement of this action or, if the defendant resided in this state preceding the commencement of the action, whether cohabiting during that time or not. This paragraph shall not change the residency requirement for filing an action for divorce.

Notes and Questions

1. Oklahoma has a long arm statute similar to Georgia's. The Oklahoma Supreme Court has held that this statute extends jurisdiction to the full extent allowed by the Constitution. See *World-Wide Volkswagen*, supra, footnote 7. Do you think this is a plausible interpretation of the statute? Many states have strained to interpret long arm statutes broadly. See Douglas McFarland, *Dictum Run Wild: How Long-Arm Statutes Extended to the Limits of Due Process*, 84 B.U. L. Rev. 491 (2004); Michael Solimine, *The Quiet Revolution in Personal Jurisdiction*, 73 Tulane L. Rev. 1 (1998).

2. Notice that subsection (2) of the Georgia statute excludes defamation. Why do you suppose Georgia chose to treat that tort differently? It appears that the special treatment for defamation was a codification of a line of Fifth Circuit opinions that had held that because of First Amendment considerations, a greater showing of contacts was required for defamation than for other torts. See Bradlee Management Services, Inc. v. Cassells, 292 S.E.2d 717, 720 (Ga. 1982). This First Amendment argument was later rejected by the Supreme Court in Calder v. Jones, 465 U.S. 783, 790 (1984), but Georgia has not changed its statute.

3. Why would a state choose not to reach to the full constitutional limit? Professor Leflar has said of a California-type statute:

> [S]uch enactments permit the exercise of jurisdiction which reaches to the very edge of fair play and substantial justice, almost to unfair play and actual injustice. The due process clause does not require ideal or even very good procedures. It only prohibits procedures that are very bad. * * * "To say that a law does not violate the due process clause is to say the least possible good about it."

Robert Leflar, Luther McDougal & Robert Felix, American Conflicts Law 102 (4th ed. 1986), quoting Cheatham, *Conflict of Laws: Some Developments and Some Questions*, 25 Ark. L. Rev. 9, 25 (1975). If you were advising your state legislature, how far would you recommend that it extend its long arm statute? Are there any categories of cases for which jurisdiction is constitutional, but you believe the state should not assert jurisdiction?

4. In addition to long arm statutes, many states continue to authorize quasi-in-rem jurisdiction by statute. As a result, where in personam jurisdiction would be constitutional but the long arm statute does not authorize it, some courts have allowed plaintiffs to use quasi-in-rem jurisdiction as an alternative statutory basis. These statutes authorize attachment of property in the state. Of course, if a plaintiff relies on quasi-in-rem jurisdiction, the court's jurisdiction will be limited to the value of the property attached, but if the property is sufficiently valuable, this will not be a significant limitation. See, e.g., Banco Ambrosiano v. Artoc Bank & Trust Co., 464 N.E.2d 432 (N.Y. 1984); Administrators of the Tulane Educational Fund v. Cooley, 462 So. 2d 696 (Miss. 1984). See generally Michael Mushlin, *The New Quasi in Rem Jurisdiction: New York's Revival of a Doctrine Whose Time Has Passed*, 55 Brook. L. Rev. 1059 (1990); Comment, Shaffer, Burnham, *and New York's Continuing Use of QIR-2 Jurisdiction: A Resurrection of the Power Theory*, 45 Emory L.J. 239 (1996).

Chapter 3

Notice and Opportunity to Be Heard

A. Introduction and Integration

In the personal jurisdiction chapter, we explored one aspect of due process. While personal jurisdiction is a necessary condition for a court's exercise of authority, the Due Process Clauses of the Fifth and Fourteenth Amendments impose additional requirements. This chapter explores the additional due process requirements that one whose rights may be affected by litigation must be given notice and an opportunity to be heard.

B. Notice

1. The Constitutional Requirement

Mullane v. Central Hanover Bank & Trust Co.

339 U.S. 306, 70 S. Ct. 652, 94 L. Ed. 865 (1950)

Justice Jackson delivered the opinion of the Court.

This controversy questions the constitutional sufficiency of notice to beneficiaries on judicial settlement of accounts by the trustee of a common trust fund established under the New York Banking Law. The New York Court of Appeals considered and overruled objections that the statutory notice contravenes requirements of the Fourteenth Amendment and that by allowance of the account beneficiaries were deprived of property without due process of law. * * *

Common trust fund legislation is addressed to a problem appropriate for state action. Mounting overheads have made administration of small trusts undesirable to corporate trustees. In order that donors and testators of moderately sized trusts may not be denied the service of corporate fiduciaries, the District of Columbia and some thirty states other than New York have permitted pooling small trust estates into one fund for investment administration. The income, capital gains, losses and expenses of the collective trust are shared by the constituent trusts in proportion to their contribution. By this plan, diversification of risk and economy of management can be extended to those whose capital standing alone would not obtain such advantage.

* * * [New York law authorizes the pooling of small trusts into a common fund. Under New York law, each] participating trust shares ratably in the common fund, but exclusive management and control is in the trust company as trustee, and neither a fiduciary nor any beneficiary of a participating trust is deemed to have ownership in any particular asset or investment of this common fund. The trust company must keep fund assets separate from its own, and in its fiduciary capacity may not deal with itself or any affiliate. Provisions are made for accountings twelve to fifteen months after the establishment of a fund and triennially thereafter. The decree in each such judicial settlement of accounts is made binding and conclusive as to any matter set forth in the account upon everyone having any interest in the common fund or in any participating estate, trust or fund.

In January, 1946, Central Hanover Bank and Trust Company established a common trust fund in accordance with these provisions, and in March, 1947, it petitioned the Surrogate's Court for settlement of its first account as common trustee. During the accounting period a total of 113 trusts, approximately half inter vivos and half testamentary, participated in the common trust fund, the gross capital of which was nearly three million dollars. The record does not show the number or residence of the beneficiaries, but they were many and it is clear that some of them were not residents of the State of New York.

The only notice given beneficiaries of this specific application was by publication in a local newspaper in strict compliance with the minimum requirements of N.Y. Banking Laws * * *. Thus the only notice required, and the only one given, was by newspaper publication setting forth merely the name and address of the trust company, the name and the date of establishment of the common trust fund, and a list of all participating estates, trusts or funds.

At the time the first investment in the common fund was made on behalf of each participating estate, however, the trust company, pursuant to the requirements of [New York banking law], had notified by mail each person of full age and sound mind whose name and address were then known to it and who was "entitled to share in the income therefrom ... [or] ... who would be entitled to share in the principal if the event upon which such estate, trust or fund will become distributable should have occurred at the time of sending such notice." Included in the notice was a copy of those provisions of the Act relating to the sending of the notice itself and to the judicial settlement of common trust fund accounts.

Upon the filing of the petition for the settlement of accounts, appellant was, by order of the court pursuant to [the banking law], appointed special guardian and attorney for all persons known or unknown not otherwise appearing who had or might thereafter have any interest in the income of the common trust fund; and appellee Vaughan was appointed to represent those similarly interested in the principal.

There were no other appearances on behalf of any one interested in either interest or principal.

Appellant appeared specially, objecting that notice and the statutory provisions for notice to beneficiaries were inadequate to afford due process under the Fourteenth Amendment, and therefore that the court was without jurisdiction to render a final and binding decree. Appellant's objections were entertained and overruled, the Surrogate holding that the notice required and given was sufficient. A final decree accepting the accounts has been entered, affirmed by the Appellate Division of the Supreme Court, and by the Court of Appeals of the State of New York.

The effect of this decree, as held below, is to settle "all questions respecting the management of the common fund." We understand that every right which beneficiaries would otherwise have against the trust company, either as trustee of the common fund or as trustee of any individual trust, for improper management of the common trust fund during the period covered by the accounting is sealed and wholly terminated by the decree.

We are met at the outset with a challenge to the power of the State — the right of its courts to adjudicate at all as against those beneficiaries who reside without the State of New York. It is contended that the proceeding is one in personam in that the decree affects neither title to nor possession of any res, but adjudges only personal rights of the beneficiaries to surcharge their trustee for negligence or breach of trust. Accordingly, it is said, under the strict doctrine of *Pennoyer v. Neff*, the Surrogate is without jurisdiction as to nonresidents upon whom personal service of process was not made.

* * * Judicial proceedings to settle fiduciary accounts have been sometimes termed in rem, or more indefinitely quasi in rem, or more vaguely still, "in the nature of a proceeding in rem." It is not readily apparent how the courts of New York did or would classify the present proceeding, which has some characteristics and is wanting in some features of proceedings both in rem and in personam. But in any event we think that the requirements of the Fourteenth Amendment to the Federal Constitution do not depend upon a classification for which the standards are so elusive and confused generally and which, being primarily for state courts to define, may and do vary from state to state. Without disparaging the usefulness of distinctions between actions in rem and those in personam in many branches of law, or on other issues, or the reasoning which underlies them, we do not rest the power of the State to resort to constructive service in this proceeding upon how its courts or this Court may regard this historic antithesis. It is sufficient to observe that, whatever the technical definition of its chosen procedure, the interest of each state in providing means to close trusts that exist by the grace of its laws and are administered under the supervision of its courts is so insistent and rooted in custom as to establish beyond doubt the right of its courts to determine the interests of all claimants, resident or nonresident, provided its procedure accords full opportunity to appear and be heard.

Quite different from the question of a state's power to discharge trustees is that of the opportunity it must give beneficiaries to contest. Many controversies have raged about the cryptic and abstract words of the Due Process Clauses but there can be no doubt that at a minimum they require that deprivation of life, liberty or property by adjudication be preceded by notice and opportunity for hearing appropriate to the nature of the case.

In two ways this proceeding does or may deprive beneficiaries of property. It may cut off their rights to have the trustee answer for negligent or illegal impairments of their interests. Also, their interests are presumably subject to diminution in the proceeding by allowance of fees and expenses to one who, in their names but without their knowledge, may conduct a fruitless or uncompensatory contest. Certainly the proceeding is one in which they may be deprived of property rights and hence notice and hearing must measure up to the standards of due process.

Personal service of written notice within the jurisdiction is the classic form of notice always adequate in any type of proceeding. But the vital interest of the State in bringing any issues as to its fiduciaries to a final settlement can be served only if interests or claims of individuals who are outside of the State can somehow be determined. A construction of the Due Process Clauses that would place impossible or impractical obstacles in the way could not be justified.

Against this interest of the State we must balance the individual interest sought to be protected by the Fourteenth Amendment. This is defined by our holding that "The fundamental requisite of due process of law is the opportunity to be heard." This right to be heard has little reality or worth unless one is informed that the matter is pending and can choose for himself whether to appear or default, acquiesce or contest.

The Court has not committed itself to any formula achieving a balance between these interests in a particular proceeding or determining when constructive notice may be utilized or what test it must meet. Personal service has not in all circumstances been regarded as indispensable to the process due to residents, and it has more often been held unnecessary as to nonresidents. * * *

An elementary and fundamental requirement of due process in any proceeding which is to be accorded finality is notice reasonably calculated, under all the circumstances, to apprise interested parties of the pendency of the action and afford them an opportunity to present their objections. The notice must be of such nature as reasonably to convey the required information, and it must afford a reasonable time for those interested to make their appearance. But if with due regard for the practicalities and peculiarities of the case these conditions are reasonably met, the constitutional requirements are satisfied. "The criterion is not the possibility of conceivable injury but the just and reasonable character of the requirements, having reference to the subject with which the statute deals."

But when notice is a person's due, process which is a mere gesture is not due process. The means employed must be such as one desirous of actually informing the absentee might reasonably adopt to accomplish it. The reasonableness and hence the constitutional validity of any chosen method may be defended on the ground that it is in itself reasonably certain to inform those affected, or, where conditions do not reasonably permit such notice, that the form chosen is not substantially less likely to bring home notice than other of the feasible and customary substitutes.

It would be idle to pretend that publication alone, as prescribed here, is a reliable means of acquainting interested parties of the fact that their rights are before the courts. It is not an accident that the greater number of cases reaching this Court on the question of adequacy of notice have been concerned with actions founded on process constructively served through local newspapers. Chance alone brings to the attention of even a local resident an advertisement in small type inserted in the back pages of a newspaper, and if he makes his home outside the area of the newspaper's normal circulation the odds that the information will never reach him are large indeed. The chance of actual notice is further reduced when, as here, the notice required does not even name those whose attention it is supposed to attract, and does not inform acquaintances who might call it to attention. In weighing its sufficiency on the basis of equivalence with actual notice, we are unable to regard this as more than a feint.

* * * When the state within which the owner has located such property seizes it for some reason, publication or posting affords an additional measure of notification. A state may indulge the assumption that one who has left tangible property in the state either has abandoned it, in which case proceedings against it deprive him of nothing, or that he has left some caretaker under a duty to let him know that it is being jeopardized. As phrased long ago by Chief Justice Marshall in The Mary, 9 Cranch 126, 144 [1815], "It is the part of common prudence for all those who have any interest in [a thing], to guard that interest by persons who are in a situation to protect it."

In the case before us there is, of course, no abandonment. On the other hand these beneficiaries do have a resident fiduciary as caretaker of their interest in this property. But it is their caretaker who in the accounting becomes their adversary. Their trustee is released from giving notice of jeopardy, and no one else is expected to do so. Not even the special guardian is required or apparently expected to communicate with his ward and client, and, of course, if such a duty were merely transferred from the trustee to the guardian, economy would not be served and more likely the cost would be increased.

This Court has not hesitated to approve of resort to publication as a customary substitute in another class of cases where it is not reasonably possible or practicable to give more adequate warning. Thus it has been recognized that, in the case of persons missing or unknown, employment of an indirect and even a probably futile means of notification is all that the situation permits and creates no constitutional bar to a final decree foreclosing their rights.

Those beneficiaries represented by appellant whose interests or whereabouts could not with due diligence be ascertained come clearly within this category. As to them the statutory notice is sufficient. However great the odds that publication will never reach the eyes of such unknown parties, it is not in the typical case much more likely to fail than any of the choices open to legislators endeavoring to prescribe the best notice practicable.

Nor do we consider it unreasonable for the State to dispense with more certain notice to those beneficiaries whose interests are either conjectural or future or, although they could be discovered upon investigation, do not in due course of business come to knowledge of the common trustee. Whatever searches might be required in another situation under ordinary standards of diligence, in view of the character of the proceedings and the nature of the interests here involved we think them unnecessary. We recognize the practical difficulties and costs that would be attendant on frequent investigations into the status of great numbers of beneficiaries, many of whose interests in the common fund are so remote as to be ephemeral; and we have no doubt that such impracticable and extended searches are not required in the name of due process. The expense of keeping informed from day to day of substitutions among even current income beneficiaries and presumptive remaindermen, to say nothing of the far greater number of contingent beneficiaries, would impose a severe burden on the plan, and would likely dissipate its advantages. These are practical matters in which we should be reluctant to disturb the judgment of the state authorities.

Accordingly we overrule appellant's constitutional objections to published notice insofar as they are urged on behalf of any beneficiaries whose interests or addresses are unknown to the trustee.

As to known present beneficiaries of known place of residence, however, notice by publication stands on a different footing. Exceptions in the name of necessity do not sweep away the rule that within the limits of practicability notice must be such as is reasonably calculated to reach interested parties. Where the names and post-office addresses of those affected by a proceeding are at hand, the reasons disappear for resort to means less likely than the mails to apprise them of its pendency.

The trustee has on its books the names and addresses of the income beneficiaries represented by appellant, and we find no tenable ground for dispensing with a serious effort to inform them personally of the accounting, at least by ordinary mail to the record addresses. Certainly sending them a copy of the statute months and perhaps years in advance does not answer this purpose. The trustee periodically remits their income to them, and we think that they might reasonably expect that with or apart from their remittances word might come to them personally that steps were being taken affecting their interests.

We need not weigh contentions that a requirement of personal service of citation on even the large number of known resident or nonresident beneficiaries would, by reasons of delay if not of expense, seriously interfere with the proper administration of the fund. Of course personal service even without the jurisdiction of the issuing authority serves the end of actual and personal notice, whatever power of compulsion it might lack. However, no such service is required under the circumstances. This type of trust presupposes a large number of small interests. The individual interest does not stand alone but is identical with that of a class. The rights of each in the integrity of the fund and the fidelity of the trustee are shared by many other beneficiaries. Therefore notice reasonably certain to reach most of those interested in objecting is likely to safeguard the interests of all, since any objection sustained would inure to the benefit of all. We think that under such circumstances reasonable risks that notice might not actually reach every beneficiary are justifiable. "Now and then an extraordinary case may turn up, but constitutional law like other mortal contrivances has to take some chances, and in the great majority of instances no doubt justice will be done." Blinn v. Nelson, [222 U.S. 1,] 7 [1911].

The statutory notice to known beneficiaries is inadequate, not because in fact it fails to reach everyone, but because under the circumstances it is not reasonably calculated to reach those who could easily be informed by other means at hand. However it may have been in former times, the mails today are recognized as an efficient and inexpensive means of communication. Moreover, the fact that the trust company has been able to give mailed notice to known beneficiaries at the time the common trust fund was established is persuasive that postal notification at the time of accounting would not seriously burden the plan.

In some situations the law requires greater precautions in its proceedings than the business world accepts for its own purposes. In few, if any, will it be satisfied with less. Certainly it is instructive, in determining the reasonableness of the impersonal broadcast notification here used, to ask whether it would satisfy a prudent man of business, counting his pennies but finding it in his interest to convey information to many persons whose names and addresses are in his files. We are not satisfied that it would. Publication may theoretically be available for all the world to see, but it is too much in our day to suppose that each or any individual beneficiary does or could examine all that is published to see if something may be tucked away in it that affects his property interests. * * *

We hold that the notice of judicial settlement of accounts required by the New York Banking Law is incompatible with the requirements of the Fourteenth Amendment as a basis for adjudication depriving known persons whose whereabouts are also known of substantial property rights. Accordingly the judgment is reversed and the cause remanded for further proceedings not inconsistent with this opinion.

Reversed.

Notes and Questions

1. As to what group(s) of beneficiaries did the Court *reverse* the judgment of the New York Court of Appeals? Why was the notice directed toward them deficient? As to what group(s) of beneficiaries did the Court *affirm* the New York judgment? Why was the notice directed toward them sufficient?

2. The Due Process Clauses apply to takings of "life, liberty or property." What property was taken from the beneficiaries as to whom notice was held deficient in *Mullane*?

3. In-person service would be more reliable than service by mail. If the right to notice is a fundamental constitutional right, why doesn't the Court require the most reliable form of notice?

4. In *Mullane*, the Court does not require the bank to attempt to notify individually everyone whose rights might be affected. How does the Court justify allowing a judgment that affects the property of individuals whom no one tried to notify?

5. The Court in *Mullane* did not require that notice actually be received. In Dusenbery v. United States, 534 U.S. 161 (2002), the Supreme Court reaffirmed that notice need only be "reasonably calculated" to apprise the party; actual notice is not required. The case involved a forfeiture procedure against a prisoner in a federal correctional institution. Notice was sent by certified mail and was delivered to the prison, but there was no evidence as to whether the prisoner actually received the letter. The Court held that this notice was constitutionally sufficient and rejected the argument that the government was required to take special steps to assure that the prisoner actually received the notice.

What if the plaintiff is aware that notice was not received? Then, would additional follow-up steps be required? The Supreme Court answered affirmatively in Jones v. Flowers, 547 U.S. 220 (2006). In *Jones*, the state sent a certified letter to a homeowner to inform him of a tax delinquency and that failure to redeem the property would make it subject to public sale. The letter was returned as "unclaimed," after which the state took no additional steps to contact the owner. The Court held that such inactivity—in the face of knowledge that the letter was not received—violated due process. Note that while actual receipt of notice is not always constitutionally necessary, it is constitutionally sufficient. See United Student Aid Funds Inc. v. Espinosa, 559 U.S. 260, 271–272 (2010). On the other hand, as we will see in the next section, there may be statutory requirements concerning the manner and form of notice that go beyond the constitutional minimum.

6. Is service by mail always constitutionally sufficient? In Weigner v. New York City, 852 F.2d 646 (2d Cir. 1988), the court upheld a foreclosure where notice was sent by regular mail, but the owner claimed not to have received the notice. Judge Oakes in dissent worried that "[i]n our current society, when our mailboxes are usually full of quite sophisticated, and often quite personalized, 'junk mail,' it is not unlikely that the form letters sent by the City were simply thrown away by the [property owner]." Id. at 656. He argued that notice by certified or registered mail should be required. Do you agree? See also Miserandino v. Resort Properties, Inc., 691 A.2d 208 (Md. 1997) (holding service by mail of non-resident constitutionally insufficient and requiring personal service).

Is service by email constitutionally sufficient? The issue is of increasing importance in a world in which businesses do not have bricks-and-mortar presence, but operate in the ether of the Internet. Several courts have upheld email service, at least with regard to defendants who could not be served with process in the United States. See, e.g., RIO Properties, Inc. v. RIO Int'l Interlink, 284 F.3d 1007 (9th Cir. 2002) (upholding email service on foreign internet business entity); Federal Trade Commission v. PCCare 247 Inc., 2013 U.S. Dist. LEXIS 31969 (S.D.N.Y. March 7, 2013) (upholding service by email, supplemented by service on Facebook, on defendants allegedly perpetrating consumer fraud scheme from India); Fraserside IP LLC v. Letyagin, 280

F.R.D. 630, 630 (N.D. Iowa 2012) (upholding email service on "international intellectual property scofflaws"). In each of these cases, the plaintiff demonstrated that email service was reasonably calculated to give actual notice and therefore satisfied *Mullane*.

In the domestic context, some courts have rejected email service of process not because it was necessarily unconstitutional, but because there is no provision for it under the Federal Rules or applicable state law. See, e.g., Joe Hand Promotions, Inc. v. Shepard, 2013 U.S. Dist. LEXIS 113578 at *5–6 (E.D. Mo. August 12, 2013) (neither service by email nor by Facebook permitted by applicable rule).

What about service through social media? If a defendant cannot be located and served with process in the usual ways (to be discussed in the next section of this Chapter), can notice be given, for example, by Facebook, Linkedin, or Twitter? In Baidoo v. Blood-Dzraku, 48 Misc. 3d 309, 311–17 (Sup. Ct., New York County, March 27, 2015), a divorce case, a New York trial court permitted service of process by private message to the defendant's Facebook account. The court noted that the few published opinions concerning service through social media were "almost even[ly] split" between those approving and those rejecting the practice. Id. at 313. In Matter of a Support Proceeding, 2014 N.Y. Misc. LEXIS 4708 at *1–5 (Fam. Ct., Richmond County, N.Y., September 12, 2014), a New York Family Court permitted in a child support action by Facebook, followed up by mailing to the defendant's last-known address.

And, as with email, the availability of such notice may be especially important with international defendants. In *Federal Trade Commission v. PCCare, supra,* service through Facebook was permitted as a supplement to email service on defendants in India. See http://www.lawpracticetoday.org/article/facebook-notification-youve-been-served/?utm_source=November&utm_medium=email&utm_campaign=November 15LPTemail.

7. What is the purpose of notice? One possible purpose is that notice, at least when it is combined with the opportunity to be heard, may increase the likelihood of an accurate result in the ensuing litigation. The court will hear both sides and have the benefit of an adversarial presentation. If accuracy through an adversarial presentation is the goal, is notice always necessary to achieve this goal? In *Mullane* itself the court had appointed a lawyer to represent the interests of the absent beneficiaries. Why isn't that step alone sufficient? How likely is it that the small and scattered beneficiaries will get involved in the litigation? Moreover, how would individual involvement of the beneficiaries in this type of case enhance the presentation of issues? With such a homogeneous group, wouldn't the court be likely to conclude that "once you've heard one, you've heard them all."

Does notice serve some interest besides the utilitarian concern for accuracy? Professor Mashaw argues that "a lack of personal participation [in decisions affecting oneself] cause[s] alienation and a loss of that dignity and self-respect that society properly deems independently valuable." Jerry Mashaw, *The Supreme Court's Due Process Calculus for Administrative Adjudication in* Mathews v. Eldridge: *Three Factors in Search of a Theory of Value*, 44 U. Chi. L. Rev. 28, 50 (1976). Should the Due Process Clauses be interpreted to require procedures that enhance individual dignity? How might such a requirement affect the law with respect to notice?

8. What if the person to whom notice is sent cannot understand the notice for some reason? For example, in Covey v. Town of Somers, 351 U.S. 141 (1956), the Court refused to uphold notice mailed to a person known to be mentally incompetent. Suppose, however, the recipient's mental deficiencies were *not* known to the sender, would due process require that the sender make an inquiry into her mental capacity? Along similar lines, what if the defendant does not speak English? Does due process require that notice be given in a language the defendant understands?

9. *Mullane* suggested that posting notice on property could be adequate notice, though this dicta has been qualified by subsequent holdings. In Schroeder v. City of New York, 371 U.S. 208 (1962), the Court held that publication in a newspaper and posting of notices near the property was insufficient if the defendant's name and address were easily ascertainable from public records. In Greene v. Lindsey, 456 U.S. 444 (1982), the Court held that posting notice of eviction on an apartment door was not sufficient because the process servers knew that "notices posted on apartment doors in the area where these tenants lived were 'not infrequently' removed by children or other tenants before they could have their intended effect." Id. at 453. The Court required service by mail in addition to posting on the door of the premises. Despite the holding, the Court seemed to retain the possibility of notice by posting:

> It is * * * reasonable to assume that a property owner will maintain superintendence of his property, and to presume that actions physically disturbing his holdings will come to his attention. * * * Upon this understanding, a State may in turn conclude that in most cases, the secure posting of a notice on the property of a person is likely to offer that property owner sufficient warning of the pendency of proceedings possibly affecting his interests.

Id. at 451–52.

In both *Schroeder* and *Greene*, the whereabouts of the defendant were known. Providing notice by posting or publication has been upheld where the residence or location of the defendant is not known. For example, in Smith v. Islamic Emirate of Afghanistan, 2001 U.S. Dist. LEXIS 21712 (S.D.N.Y. Dec. 20, 2001), the court authorized service by publication on Osama Bin Laden in a law suit growing out of the September 11 attack on the United States. The court ordered publication in several Afghan and Pakistani newspapers, along with advertising the suit on several foreign broadcast networks, including Al Jazeera, Turkish CNN, and BBC World.

Subsequent cases have further limited the availability of posting or publication as a means of giving notice. In Mennonite Board of Missions v. Adams, 462 U.S. 791 (1983), the Court held that in a tax foreclosure case, the mortgage holder was entitled to mailed notice—posting, publishing, and mailing notice to the property owner were not sufficient to notify the mortgage holder. In Tulsa Professional Collection Services, Inc. v. Pope, 485 U.S. 478 (1988), the Court held that in a suit to settle a decedent's estate, published notice to creditors in general was insufficient when the estate knew of the claim of a particular creditor. The Court again required notice by mail. See Gaeth v. Deacon, 964 A.2d 621, 628 (Me. 2009) (noting that with increased reliance on electronic media, publication in print newspapers is even less likely to give actual notice).

10. The right to notice and a hearing are waivable personal rights. In D.H. Overmyer Co. v. Frick Co., 405 U.S. 174 (1972), the Court considered an extreme form of waiver known as a *cognovit* note, in which the debtor consents in advance to a creditor's obtaining a judgment without notice to the debtor or a hearing! The Court held that a cognovit note is not per se unconstitutional, although it stressed that under some circumstances, such as where the cognovit was part of a contract of adhesion, imposed upon a weaker party with no chance of negotiation, it might be unconstitutional.

11. We might wonder why Mullane, the special guardian appointed to represent income beneficiaries of the trust, and Vaughan, the special guardian appointed to represent principal beneficiaries, took opposing positions. Consider the following: Under New York law, the ordinary expenses associated with the accounting procedure could be billed to the common fund trust and were payable out of the principal. See In re Bank of New York, 67 N.Y.S.2d 444, 448 (1946); In re Continental Bank & Trust Co., 67 N.Y.S.2d 806, 807 (1946). Therefore, the costs of more expensive notice were paid by those Vaughan represented. Of course, a reduction of the principal also has some effect on income beneficiaries because there would be less principal upon which to earn interest.

Did Mullane act in the best interest of the income beneficiaries he represented by (1) insisting on more expensive notice, and (2) litigating the issue of notice all the way to the United States Supreme Court and thereby increasing the expenses for guardians chargeable against the trust?

2. Statutory Requirements

Due process, as interpreted in *Mullane* and other cases, sets the constitutional minimum standards for notice. In addition to the constitutional minimum, all courts have rules or statutes that spell out in detail the mechanics and form for giving notice. These provisions for service of process are frequently more demanding than the Constitution. For example, some courts may require actual in-hand personal service when the constitutional minimum would be met by mailing notice. And even if service by email or social media is constitutionally acceptable, neither is available unless an applicable statute or rule permits it. In other words, notice must comply not only with the constitutional minimum set forth in *Mullane*, but also with any additional statutory or rule requirements.

In the typical civil action, notice consists of serving upon the defendant two documents: (1) a summons from the court and (2) a copy of the complaint. Together, these two documents are called "process." "Service" of process refers to delivering them to the defendant (or, as we will see, sometimes a substitute for the defendant). See Rule 4(c)(1). Service of process is not a mere technicality. The Supreme Court has explained that service is integral to a court's acquiring jurisdiction:

> [B]efore a court may exercise personal jurisdiction over a defendant, there must be more than notice to the defendant and a constitutionally sufficient relationship between the defendant and the forum. There also must be a basis for the defendant's amenability to service of summons. Absent consent, this means there must be authorization for service of summons on the defendant.

Omni Capital International, Ltd. v. Rudolf Wolff & Co., 484 U.S. 97, 104 (1987).

In federal court, service of process is governed by Rule 4. It is clear that a copy of the complaint puts the defendant on notice of the claim against her. What, then, does the summons do? What must the summons contain? See Rule 4(a)(1).

Form summonses are available online and at the clerk's office of any federal district court. Counsel inserts the names of the parties and has the clerk sign the summons (see Rule 4(b)). Upon filing the complaint with the court (which is usually done electronically), the case is assigned a docket number, and the plaintiff arranges to have the process served on the defendant(s).

Why couldn't the function of the summons be performed by a letter from plaintiff's counsel to the defendant? Although notice is technically a separate requirement from personal jurisdiction, the two concepts are related. Service of process is the ceremonial method in which the sovereign's right to exercise personal jurisdiction is validated. As Justice Stone said in *International Shoe*, "the *capias ad respondendum* has given way to service of process." The *capias*, an order of the court, commanded that the defendant be arrested. This is still done in criminal cases. In civil cases today, we feel less strongly about the need of the sovereign to make such an overbearing demonstration of its power over the defendant. Nonetheless, we have retained a ceremonial demonstration that the government is asserting power over the defendant. Thus, the summons is a symbol of the government's power over the defendant.

We require the ceremonial show of force only once in a lawsuit for each defendant. After the summons has been served, subsequent pleadings, motions and other papers can be served by mailing a copy to the other party or her attorney. See Rule 5(b). Indeed, these subsequent documents may be served by "electronic transmission" if the party consents. See Rule 5(b)(2)(E). Whenever mail is used, any time limit for response is extended by three days. Rule 6(d). For example, suppose P serves interrogatories (a discovery device) on D by first class mail. Under Rule 33, D must respond within 30 days of service. The service of the interrogatories is complete upon mailing (Rule 5(b)(2)(C)), but D gets an additional three days to respond under Rule 6(d). Under Rule 6(d), does the same three-day extension apply if service is by email?

In earlier times, process was served by the marshal's office (which drove home the fact that the summons represented the power of the sovereign). Today, under Rule 4(c)(3), any non-party who is at least 18 years old can serve process, although the court can order service by a marshal. See Rule 4(c)(3). See also Benny v. Pipes, 799

F.2d 489 (9th Cir. 1986) (upholding service of process on several prison guards by a prisoner who was not a party). See also Constien v. United States, 628 F.3d 1207 (10th Cir. 2010) (holding that service upon the United States by mail was not properly effected when a party herself was the one who mailed it).

When the marshal's office does serve process, the plaintiff may be required to instruct the marshal on how to do so. In Mayo v. Satan & His Staff, 54 F.R.D. 282 (W.D. Pa. 1971), the court dismissed the case because the plaintiff failed to render such aid when asking the marshal to serve the devil himself.

Following service, the person effecting service is required to file with the court proof that she did so. See Rule 4(*l*)(1). If a civilian serves process, this proof must be made by affidavit, which is a statement made under penalty of perjury. The Rule explicitly provides, however, that "[f]ailure to prove service does not affect the validity of the service."

National Development Co. v. Triad Holding Corp.

930 F.2d 253 (2d Cir. 1991)

McLaughlin, Circuit Judge.

For more than a half-century, the Federal Rules of Civil Procedure have permitted service upon an individual by leaving a summons and complaint "at the individual's dwelling house or usual place of abode." For a half-century before that, Equity Rule 13 had the same provision. With approximately 1.16 billion passengers annually engaging in international airline travel, and an estimated five million people with second homes in the United States, determining a person's "dwelling house or usual place of abode" is no longer as easy as in those early days of yesteryear.

We ponder this problem upon review of an order of the United States District Court for the Southern District of New York * * * refusing, under Fed. R. Civ. P. 60(b)(4), to vacate a default judgment entered against defendant-appellant Adnan Khashoggi ("Khashoggi"). In essence, Khashoggi argues that, although he has numerous residences world-wide, his "dwelling house or usual place of abode" is in Saudi Arabia and, absent personal delivery, service of process pursuant to Rule 4(d)(1) is proper only at his compound there. [Under the current version of Rule 4, this provision appears at 4(e)(2)(B).] Therefore, he concludes that a purported service at his apartment at the Olympic Tower in New York was void and conferred no jurisdiction. We disagree and affirm the order of the district court.

Background

It is the service of the summons and complaint on Khashoggi on December 22, 1986 that forms the basis of this appeal. On that day, NDC [the plaintiff] handed a copy of the summons and complaint to Aurora DaSilva, a housekeeper at Khashoggi's Olympic Tower condominium apartment on Fifth Avenue. * * *

The district court held an evidentiary hearing on the service of process issue, at which Khashoggi and his housekeeper, Ms. DaSilva, testified. Ms. DaSilva confirmed that Khashoggi was in New York and staying at his Olympic Tower apartment from December 15 through December 23, 1986. The parties stipulated that Ms. DaSilva accepted delivery of a copy of the summons and complaint on December 22, 1986. Ms. DaSilva testified that during 1986, Khashoggi stayed at his Olympic Tower apartment for a total of 34 days. To call it an apartment is perhaps to denigrate it. Valued at approximately $20–25 million, containing more than 23,000 square feet on at least two floors, the Olympic Tower apartment contains a swimming pool, a sauna, an office and four separate furnished "apartments" to accommodate guests and Khashoggi's brother. The complex requires the attention of two full-time and three part-time staff persons.

Khashoggi testified that he is a citizen of Saudi Arabia and resides in a ten-acre, six-villa compound in its capital city, Riyadh. In 1986, Khashoggi stayed in the Riyadh compound for only three months. During the remaining nine months, Khashoggi traveled throughout the world, staying another two months at a "home" in Marabella, Spain. Khashoggi testified that he purchased the Olympic Tower apartment in 1974. Shortly thereafter, Khashoggi transferred ownership to Akorp, N.V., a company that is wholly owned by A.K. Holdings, Ltd., which, in turn, is wholly owned by Khashoggi. Before Khashoggi transferred ownership of the Olympic Tower apartment to Akorp, he personally hired contractors to complete a remodeling project costing over $1 million. The results of the remodeling project were prominently featured in the June 1984 issue of *House and Garden*.

* * * [T]he district court found that the Olympic Tower apartment was not a "dwelling house or usual place of abode" for purposes of either Fed. R. Civ. P. 4(d)(1) [now 4(e)(2)(B)] or N.Y.C.P.L.R. § 308(2), but that service was nevertheless proper because Khashoggi had actual notice. We reject the notion that "actual notice" suffices to cure a void service, but we affirm the district court because we conclude that the Olympic Tower apartment is properly characterized under Rule 4(d)(1) [now 4(e)(2)(B)] as Khashoggi's "dwelling house or usual place of abode," and service at that location was therefore valid.

Discussion

Rule 4(d)(1) [now 4(e)(2)(B)] permits service

> [u]pon an individual other than an infant or an incompetent person, by delivering a copy of the summons and of the complaint to the individual personally or by leaving copies thereof at the individual's dwelling house or usual place of abode with some person of suitable age and discretion then residing therein....

There is no dispute that Ms. DaSilva, with whom the papers were left, is a "person of suitable age and discretion then residing" at the Olympic Tower apartment. We are called upon only to determine whether the Olympic Tower apartment was Khashoggi's "dwelling house or usual place of abode," terms that thus far have eluded "any hard and fast definition." Indeed, these quaint terms are now archaic and survive only in religious hymns, romantic sonnets and, unhappily, in jurisdictional statutes.

The phrase "dwelling house or usual place of abode" to describe where service can be made has its origin in Equity Rule 13. Yet, "[d]espite the length of time the language ... has been a part of federal practice, the decisions do not make clear precisely what it means." We do not here intend to reconcile decades of conflicting authority. Instead, we decide this case on the facts presented with a recognition of the realities of life in this the winter of the twentieth century.

As leading commentators observe, "[i]n a highly mobile and affluent society, it is unrealistic to interpret Rule 4(d)(1) [now 4(e)(2)(B)] so that the person to be served has only one dwelling house or usual place of abode at which process may be left." This case presents a perfect example of how ineffectual so wooden a rule would be.

Khashoggi is a wealthy man and a frequent intercontinental traveler. Although he is a citizen of Saudi Arabia and considers the Riyadh compound his domicile, he spent only three months there in 1986. Khashoggi testified that the Olympic Tower apartment was only one of twelve locations around the world where he spends his time, including a "home" which he owns in Marabella, Spain, and "houses" in Rome, Paris and Monte Carlo. The conclusion that only *one* of these locations is Khashoggi's "usual place of abode," since he does not "usually" stay at any one of them, commends itself to neither common sense nor sound policy.

There is nothing startling in the conclusion that a person can have two or more "dwelling houses or usual places of abode," provided each contains sufficient indicia of permanence. State courts construing state statutes containing similar language have arrived at this result where the defendant maintained one residence for certain days of the week or certain months of the year and another residence for the balance of his time. Some courts have expressly required that the defendant sought to be served be actually living at the residence at the time service is effected. [S]ee also J. Moore, Moore's Federal Practice ¶ 4.11[2], at 132 ("Where a party has several residences which he permanently maintains, occupying one at one period of the year and another at another period, service is valid when made at the dwelling house in which the party is then living.") (footnote omitted).

Although federal practice under Rule 4(d)(1) [now 4(e)(2)(B)] has not produced consistent results, compare Capitol Life Ins. Co. v. Rosen, 69 F.R.D. 83 (E.D. Pa. 1975) (service at defendant's brother's house sufficient where defendant frequently journeyed but kept a room and personal belongings at brother's house and paid rent therefor), and Blackhawk Heating & Plumbing Co. v. Turner, 50 F.R.D. 144 (D. Ariz. 1970) (service at house in Arizona deemed proper where evidence suggested that defendant was living at the time in California but received actual notice), with First Nat'l Bank & Trust Co. v. Ingerton, 207 F.2d 793 (10th Cir. 1953) (usual place of abode was hotel in New Mexico notwithstanding defendant's temporary stay in Denver), and Shore v. Cornell-Dubilier Elec. Corp., 33 F.R.D. 5 (D. Mass. 1963) (service on defendant who divided his time between residences in New York and New Jersey improper where made at a house he owned in Massachusetts that was used by him only when conducting business there), we believe that application of the rule to uphold service is appropriate under these facts.

It cannot seriously be disputed that the Olympic Tower apartment has sufficient indicia of permanence. Khashoggi owned and furnished the apartment and spent a considerable amount of money remodeling it to fit his lifestyle. Indeed, in July 1989, Khashoggi listed the Olympic Tower apartment as one of his residences in a bail application submitted in connection with the criminal proceedings. Since Khashoggi was actually living in the Olympic Tower apartment on December 22, 1986, service there on that day was, if not the most likely method of ensuring that he received the summons and complaint, reasonably calculated to provide actual notice of the action. See *Mullane v. Central Hanover Bank & Trust Co.* Surely, with so itinerant a defendant as Khashoggi, plaintiff should not be expected to do more.

We conclude, therefore, that service of process on Khashoggi should be sustained under Rule 4(d)(1) [now 4(e)(2)(B)] because the Olympic Tower apartment was a "dwelling house or usual place of abode" in which he was actually living at the time service was effected. We express no opinion upon the validity of service had Khashoggi not been actually living at the Olympic Tower apartment when service was effected.

Conclusion

Since service was properly effected on Khashoggi, his motion pursuant to Rule 60(b)(4) to vacate the default judgment entered on the original complaint for want of personal jurisdiction was properly denied. Accordingly, we affirm.

Notes and Questions

1. The district court found that because Khashoggi received actual notice, compliance with Rule 4 was not required. The court of appeals rejected this argument. Why? Shouldn't actual notice always be sufficient?

2. Would the result have been different if Khashoggi had not been in New York at the time of service?

3. Would this case have come out differently if it involved Joe Smith, not Adnan Khashoggi, and service had been at Joe's summer cabin (which has never been featured in *House and Garden*)?

4. Note that Rule 4(e) permits various methods of serving process as alternatives. In contrast, practice in some states follows a "descending order rule," under which substituted service is proper only if one cannot effect personal service. See, e.g., Va. Code Ann. § 8.01-296.

5. What constitutes "the individual's dwelling or usual place of abode"? Does this phrase include a hotel room? See First Nat. Bank & Trust Co. v. Ingerton, 207 F.2d 793 (10th Cir. 1953) (yes). The parental home of a college student while the student was away at school? See Ali v. Mid-Atlantic Settlement Servs., 233 F.R. D. 32 (D.D.C. 2006) (yes). The penitentiary from which a prisoner had escaped? See United States v. Mensik, 57 F.R.D. 125 (M.D. Pa. 1972) (no). One treatise observes: "Despite the extensive factual analyses and attempts at careful statutory construction that often are undertaken by the courts, an examination of the precedents reveals that the actual receipt of the summons and complaint at the particular place where it is served may

be the real key to the disposition of many cases." 4A WRIGHT & MILLER, FEDERAL PRACTICE & PROCEDURE § 1096, at 528.

6. According to the court, there was no dispute that Ms. DaSilva was of "suitable age and discretion." How old must the person be to meet this requirement? Is a 13-year-old of "suitable age and discretion" See Holmen v. Miller, 206 N.W.2d 916 (Minn. 1973) (no). Consider also the requirement that the recipient "reside therein." Would this language apply to a house guest visiting for two weeks? Would it apply to a resident manager who lives in the same building as the defendant but not in the same apartment? See Churchill v. Barach, 863 F. Supp. 1266, 1270–71 (D. Nev. 1994) (upholding service on resident doorman); Nowell v. Nowell, 384 F.2d 951 (5th Cir. 1967) (upholding service on apartment manager who resided in a separate building in the same apartment complex).

7. Review Rule 4(h). Who is "a managing or general agent"? Should the focus be on the job title or instead on whether the position is "of sufficient responsibility so that it is reasonable to assume that the person will transmit notice of the commencement of the action to organizational superiors." 4A WRIGHT & MILLER, FEDERAL PRACTICE & PROCEDURE § 1103, at 573. Would service be proper in the following situations?

(a) Process is served on the corporation's director of sales.

(b) Process is served on the secretary to the corporation's director of sales.

(c) The process server attempts to leave the papers with the corporation's president. The president, when informed of the nature of the papers, refuses to accept them. The process server places the papers on the table next to the president just before being evicted by security guards.

8. Read Rule 4(m). What must the court do if process is not served within 90 days after the complaint is filed? Dismissing a case "without prejudice" means that the plaintiff is free to refile the case. If a plaintiff fails to show "good cause" for failing to serve process within 90 days, may the court nonetheless give the plaintiff a longer period in which to serve process?

9. Under Rule 4:

(a) If Khashoggi were not in New York, could service properly be made by mailing it or delivering it to his office in New York? By mailing it to his home in Saudi Arabia?

(b) Suppose the plaintiff had learned that Khashoggi would be visiting in Florida and wanted to serve him there. By what methods could he have Khashoggi served in Florida? (Assume that New York would have personal jurisdiction.)

(c) Could the plaintiff have asserted quasi-in-rem jurisdiction by attaching Khashoggi's New York apartment? See Rule 4(n)(2).

10. Service of process, like an objection to personal jurisdiction, is waivable. Read Rule 4(d). Suppose the plaintiff in *National Development Co.* wanted to use this provision:

(a) What must the plaintiff do to request waiver of service by Khashoggi? Could a request for waiver of service have been faxed to him at his New York apartment? His New York office? His home in Saudi Arabia?

(b) What advantage, if any, would Khashoggi get from waiving formal service? Does such waiver prejudice any defenses he may have as to personal jurisdiction?

(c) How would Khashoggi manifest his intention to waive formal service?

(d) What does the plaintiff do with the waiver form after the defendant signs and returns it?

(e) If Khashoggi does not waive service, what should the plaintiff do next? Notice the sanction available if the defendant refuses to waive formal service. How big an incentive do you think this is?

11. In serving process (as opposed to seeking a waiver), the plaintiff may follow either the procedures of the state in which the district court sits, or the procedures of the state in which service is effected, or the procedures set forth in Rule 4. Many states permit service of process by certified or registered mail.

Do not confuse actual service by mail with waiver of service under Rule 4(d). The distinction between the two can be particularly significant for purposes of statutes of limitation. In some states, the limitations period is tolled by filing a complaint, while in other states, the period runs until service on the defendant. Where the statute of limitations is of the latter type, it may be that neither the receipt of a request for waiver of service nor completion of a waiver form by the defendant will toll the statute. See Larsen v. Mayo Med. Ctr., 218 F.3d 863 (8th Cir. 2000).

12. Read Rule 4(k)(1). Suppose suit is brought in the Federal District Court in El Paso, Texas. Defendant is a citizen of New Mexico, residing in Santa Inez, New Mexico, which is 87 miles from the federal court house in El Paso. Would the federal court have personal jurisdiction over the defendant? How can service be effected?

13. Review Rule 4(k)(2). We discussed this section in connection with personal jurisdiction. See the note on Personal Jurisdiction in Federal Court in Section B.3 in Chapter 2, supra.

14. Although service was ultimately upheld in *National Development Co.*, the focus of the court of appeals was on the language of Rule 4, not on the constitutional requirement of notice. Would it have been better to provide a more open-ended standard rather than specific rules for service? For example, Rule 4 might simply provide that "service shall be effectuated using any method reasonably calculated to notify the other party." Would this be an improvement?

15. Service of process in a foreign country can present some complications. Rule 4(f) specifies several possible mechanisms for service of process abroad: compliance with the Hague Convention on Service Abroad of Judicial and Extrajudicial Documents; use of a "letter rogatory" requesting the assistance of a foreign court; compliance with the local rules for service of the foreign country; or, if permitted by the

foreign country, personal service or mail service. The last method is frequently not available because in many countries, particularly civil law countries, service of process is regarded as a "sovereign act" that can be performed in their territory "only by the state's own officials and in accordance with its own law." RESTATEMENT (THIRD) FOREIGN RELATIONS LAW OF THE UNITED STATES §471, cmt. b (1987).

3. Immunity, Evasion, and "Sewer Service"

Both state and federal courts recognize common law and statutory immunity from service under certain circumstances. See 4A WRIGHT & MILLER, FEDERAL PRACTICE & PROCEDURE § 1076. For example, witnesses, litigants or lawyers who come into the state to participate in one suit may be immune from process concerning other suits. Immunity is also sometimes granted to persons who are induced to enter the state through fraud or deceit. See, e.g., Buchanan v. Wilson, 254 F.2d 849 (6th Cir. 1958). In addition, some state statutes prohibit service on Sunday. See, e.g., FLA. STAT. § 48.20; N.Y. GEN. BUS. LAW § 11. In the 1960s, Congressman Adam Clayton Powell evaded service of a civil contempt citation for several years by returning to his New York district only on Sundays.

Some defendants without the protection of immunity will seek to evade service and thereby delay or avoid suit completely. In response to this problem, creative process servers specialize in serving the hard-to-find defendant. Such a process server may masquerade as a florist's delivery person and tuck a summons in among the roses or serve process on a groom in a wedding receiving line. One enterprising process server bought a ticket to dance on a Donny Osmond TV special, waltzed past Donny, and served him with process on live television. Martin Grayson & Bart Schwartz, *Adventures in Serving Process*, 11 LITIGATION 11, 12 (1985).

The flip side of evasive defendants is the problem of "sewer service," that is, dishonest process servers who certify that process was served when in fact it was not. This practice was shockingly common in New York during the 1960s and early 1970s and resulted in several publicized criminal prosecutions. See United States v. Wiseman, 445 F.2d 792 (2d Cir. 1971); Frank Tuerkheimer, *Service of Process in New York City: A Proposed End to Unregulated Criminality*, 72 COLUM. L. REV. 847 (1972). The practice was apparently exacerbated by New York's rigid requirement of personal service on the defendant. Because process could not ordinarily be left with someone other than the defendant, process servers falsified affidavits and threw away the summons rather than track down the defendant. A 1986 report by the New York City Department of Consumer Affairs found that at least one-third of all default judgments were based on perjured affidavits. See Margaret Taylor, *A Court Fails, an Old Woman Dies, and the Police Stand Trial*, NEW YORK TIMES, March 19, 1987, at A26. A 2008 investigation by the same state department found the same problem.

New York responded by authorizing service on a person of suitable age and discretion at the defendant's actual place of business or abode, with a second copy mailed to the defendant's last known address. N.Y. CIV. PRAC. L. & R. § 308(2) (1990). Notwithstanding this change, problems persist. New York law further requires that if service is questioned, the process server who testifies about service must also bring to the hearing all records or log books concerning the matter. N.Y. Comp. Codes R. & Regs. tit. 22, § 208.29. See Inter-Ocean Realty Assoc. v. JSA Realty Corp., 587 N.Y.S.2d 837 (N.Y. Civ. Ct. 1992).

C. Opportunity to Be Heard

In addition to notice, the Due Process Clauses of the Fifth and Fourteenth Amendments require an opportunity to be heard. This opportunity does not necessarily mandate a full-blown trial. In some circumstances, less formal procedures will suffice. For example, in Goss v. Lopez, 419 U.S. 565 (1975), the Court held that prior to suspension from a public school, a student was entitled to notice of the charges and an opportunity to offer an explanation of her version of events. In this context, however, the school was not required to hold a formal hearing with confrontation of witnesses and cross-examination. An informal discussion between the student and the school official was sufficient.

Regardless of the formality of the hearing, the defendant must ordinarily receive sufficient advance warning to allow time to prepare an adequate defense. For example, in Roller v. Holly, 176 U.S. 398 (1900), the defendant was served with process in Virginia requiring him to defend the action in Texas five days later. The Court held that in light of the distance to be traveled, "five days was not reasonable notice, or due process of law." Id. at 413. However, the amount of advance warning required depends on the nature of the proceeding. Thus, in *Goss v. Lopez*, it was sufficient for the school official to discuss with the student the alleged misconduct immediately following the incident.

The requirement of due process raises particularly difficult questions when the plaintiff seeks so-called "provisional" relief. Suppose, for example, you live near a nuclear power plant and you have just learned that the plant is about to vent radioactive steam into the air. You might wish to get a temporary restraining order (TRO), prohibiting the release of steam until a full hearing can be conducted on the lawfulness of the power plant's conduct. The power company's position may be that the steam poses no health risk and is completely lawful. Further, the power company may argue that if it is not allowed to vent the steam, it will have to shut down the plant, thereby incurring economic losses and interrupting services to the community. In this situation the court does not have the luxury of time to figure out who is correct. If it grants the TRO, it risks great harm to the defendant for what may prove to be groundless allegations. If it does not stop the venting, the plaintiff may suffer irreparable harm. What does due process require under these circumstances? Notice how Federal Rule 65 deals with this situation. You should note that notwithstanding the language of Rule 65(c) which seems to *require* the posting of security, courts have held that security is not required where there is no risk of monetary loss to the defendant or where, despite the risk of loss, the case advances an important public interest. See

Pharmaceutical Soc'y of New York, Inc. v. New York State Dep't of Soc. Servs., 50 F.3d 1168, 1174–75 (2d Cir. 1995); Cosgrove v. Board of Educ., 175 F. Supp. 2d 375, 398–99 (N.D.N.Y. 2001); Note, *Security for Interlocutory Injunctions Under Rule 65(c): Exceptions to the Rule Gone Awry*, 46 HAST. L.J. 1863 (1995).

Consider the following case involving the less dramatic but very common situation of pre-judgment attachment.

Connecticut v. Doehr

501 U.S. 1, 111 S. Ct. 2105, 115 L. Ed. 2d 1 (1991)

JUSTICE WHITE delivered an opinion, Parts I, II, and III of which are the opinion of the Court.*

This case requires us to determine whether a state statute that authorizes prejudgment attachment of real estate without prior notice or hearing, without a showing of extraordinary circumstances, and without a requirement that the person seeking the attachment post a bond, satisfies the Due Process Clause of the Fourteenth Amendment. We hold that, as applied to this case, it does not.

I

On March 15, 1988, Petitioner John F. DiGiovanni submitted an application to the Connecticut Superior Court for an attachment in the amount of $75,000 on respondent Brian K. Doehr's home in Meridan, Connecticut. DiGiovanni took this step in conjunction with a civil action for assault and battery that he was seeking to institute against Doehr in the same court. The suit did not involve Doehr's real estate nor did DiGiovanni have any pre-existing interest either in Doehr's home or any of his other property.

Connecticut law authorizes prejudgment attachment of real estate without affording prior notice or the opportunity for a prior hearing to the individual whose property is subject to the attachment. The State's prejudgment remedy statute provides, in relevant part:

> "The court or a judge of the court may allow the prejudgment remedy to be issued by an attorney without hearing as provided in sections 52-278c and 52-278d upon verification by oath of the plaintiff or of some competent affiant, that there is probable cause to sustain the validity of the plaintiff's claims and (1) that the prejudgment remedy requested is for an attachment of real property...."

CONN. GEN. STAT. § 52-278e (1991). The statute does not require the plaintiff to post a bond to insure the payment of damages that the defendant may suffer should the attachment prove wrongfully issued or the claim prove unsuccessful.

As required, DiGiovanni submitted an affidavit in support of his application. In five one-sentence paragraphs, DiGiovanni stated that the facts set forth in his pre-

* THE CHIEF JUSTICE, JUSTICE BLACKMUN, JUSTICE KENNEDY, JUSTICE SOUTER join Parts I, II, and III of this opinion, and JUSTICE SCALIA joins Parts I and III.

viously submitted complaint were true; that "I was willfully, wantonly and maliciously assaulted by the defendant, Brian K. Doehr"; that "[s]aid assault and battery broke my left wrist and further caused an ecchymosis to my right eye, as well as other injuries"; and that "I have further expended sums of money for medical care and treatment." The affidavit concluded with the statement, "In my opinion, the foregoing facts are sufficient to show that there is probable cause that judgment will be rendered for the plaintiff."

On the strength of these submissions the Superior Court judge, by an order dated March 17, found "probable cause to sustain the validity of the plaintiff's claim" and ordered the attachment on Doehr's home "to the value of $75,000." The sheriff attached the property four days later, on March 21. Only after this did Doehr receive notice of the attachment. He also had yet to be served with the complaint, which is ordinarily necessary for an action to commence in Connecticut. As the statute further required, the attachment notice informed Doehr that he had the right to a hearing: (1) to claim that no probable cause existed to sustain the claim; (2) to request that the attachment be vacated, modified, or that a bond be substituted; or (3) to claim that some portion of the property was exempt from execution.

Rather than pursue these options, Doehr filed suit against DiGiovanni in Federal District Court, claiming that § 52-278e(a)(1) was unconstitutional under the Due Process Clause of the Fourteenth Amendment. The District Court upheld the statute and granted summary judgment in favor of DiGiovanni. On appeal, a divided panel of the United States Court of Appeals for the Second Circuit reversed.

II

With this case we return to the question of what process must be afforded by a state statute enabling an individual to enlist the aid of the State to deprive another of his or her property by means of the prejudgment attachment or similar procedure. Our cases reflect the numerous variations this type of remedy can entail. In Sniadach v. Family Finance Corp. of Bay View, 395 U.S. 337 (1969), the Court struck down a Wisconsin statute that permitted a creditor to effect prejudgment garnishment of wages without notice and prior hearing to the wage earner. In Fuentes v. Shevin, 407 U.S. 67 (1972), the Court likewise found a due process violation in state replevin provisions that permitted vendors to have goods seized through an ex parte application to a court clerk and the posting of a bond. Conversely, the Court upheld a Louisiana ex parte procedure allowing a lien holder to have disputed goods sequestered in Mitchell v. W.T. Grant Co., 416 U.S. 600 (1974). *Mitchell*, however, carefully noted that *Fuentes* was decided against "a factual and legal background sufficiently different ... that it does not require the invalidation of the Louisiana sequestration statute." Those differences included Louisiana's provision of an immediate post-deprivation hearing along with the option of damages; the requirement that a judge rather than a clerk determine that there is a clear showing of entitlement to the writ; the necessity for a detailed affidavit; and an emphasis on the lien-holder's interest in preventing waste or alienation of the encumbered property. In North Georgia Finishing, Inc. v. Di-Chem, Inc., 419 U.S. 601 (1975), the Court again invalidated an ex parte garnishment statute that not only failed to provide for notice and prior hearing but that also failed to require a bond, a detailed affidavit setting out the claim, the determination of a neutral magistrate, or a prompt post-deprivation hearing.

These cases "underscore the truism that '[d]ue process, unlike some legal rules, is not a technical conception with a fixed content unrelated to time, place and circumstances.'" Mathews v. Eldridge, [424 U.S. 319, 334 (1976)] (quoting Cafeteria Workers v. McElroy, 367 U.S. 886, 895 (1961)). In *Mathews*, we drew upon our prejudgment remedy decisions to determine what process is due when the government itself seeks to effect a deprivation on its own initiative. That analysis resulted in the now familiar threefold inquiry requiring consideration of "the private interest that will be affected by the official action"; "the risk of an erroneous deprivation of such interest through the procedures used, and the probable value, if any, of additional or substitute safeguards"; and lastly "the Government's interest, including the function involved and the fiscal and administrative burdens that the additional or substitute procedural requirement would entail."

Here the inquiry is similar but the focus is different. Prejudgment remedy statutes ordinarily apply to disputes between private parties rather than between an individual and the government. Such enactments are designed to enable one of the parties to "make use of state procedures with the overt, significant assistance of state officials," and they undoubtedly involve state action "substantial enough to implicate the Due Process Clause." Nonetheless, any burden that increasing procedural safeguards entails primarily affects not the government, but the party seeking control of the other's property. For this type of case, therefore, the relevant inquiry requires, as in *Mathews*, first, consideration of the private interest that will be affected by the prejudgment measure; second, an examination of the risk of erroneous deprivation through the procedures under attack and the probable value of additional or alternative safeguards; and third, in contrast to *Mathews*, principal attention to the interest of the party seeking the prejudgment remedy, with, nonetheless, due regard for any ancillary interest the government may have in providing the procedure or forgoing the added burden of providing greater protections.

We now consider the *Mathews* factors in determining the adequacy of the procedures before us, first with regard to the safeguards of notice and a prior hearing, and then in relation to the protection of a bond.

III

We agree with the Court of Appeals that the property interests that attachment affects are significant. For a property owner like Doehr, attachment ordinarily clouds title; impairs the ability to sell or otherwise alienate the property; taints any credit rating; reduces the chance of obtaining a home equity loan or additional mortgage; and can even place an existing mortgage in technical default where there is an insecurity clause. * * *

[T]he State correctly points out that these effects do not amount to a complete, physical, or permanent deprivation of real property; their impact is less than the perhaps temporary total deprivation of household goods or wages. But the Court has never held that only such extreme deprivations trigger due process concern. To the contrary, our cases show that even the temporary or partial impairments to property rights that attachments, liens, and similar encumbrances entail are sufficient to merit due process protection. * * *

We also agree with the Court of Appeals that the risk of erroneous deprivation that the State permits here is substantial. By definition, attachment statutes premise a deprivation of property on one ultimate factual contingency — the award of damages to the plaintiff which the defendant may not be able to satisfy. For attachments before judgment, Connecticut mandates that this determination be made by means of a procedural inquiry that asks whether "there is probable cause to sustain the validity of the plaintiff's claim." The statute elsewhere defines the validity of the claim in terms of the likelihood "that judgment will be rendered in the matter in favor of the plaintiff." What probable cause means in this context, however, remains obscure. The State initially took the position, as did the dissent below, that the statute requires a plaintiff to show the objective likelihood of the suit's success. DiGiovanni, citing ambiguous state cases, reads the provision as requiring no more than that a plaintiff demonstrate a subjective good faith belief that the suit will succeed. At oral argument, the State shifted its position to argue that the statute requires something akin to the plaintiff stating a claim with sufficient facts to survive a motion to dismiss.

We need not resolve this confusion since the statute presents too great a risk of erroneous deprivation under any of these interpretations. If the statute demands inquiry into the sufficiency of the complaint, or, still less, the plaintiff's good-faith belief that the complaint is sufficient, requirement of a complaint and a factual affidavit would permit a court to make these minimal determinations. But neither inquiry adequately reduces the risk of erroneous deprivation. Permitting a court to authorize attachment merely because the plaintiff believes the defendant is liable, or because the plaintiff can make out a facially valid complaint, would permit the deprivation of the defendant's property when the claim would fail to convince a jury, when it rested on factual allegations that were sufficient to state a cause of action but which the defendant would dispute, or in the case of a mere good-faith standard, even when the complaint failed to state a claim upon which relief could be granted. The potential for unwarranted attachment in these situations is self-evident and too great to satisfy the requirements of due process absent any countervailing consideration.

Even if the provision requires the plaintiff to demonstrate, and the judge to find, probable cause to believe that judgment will be rendered in favor of the plaintiff, the risk of error was substantial in this case. As the record shows, and as the State concedes, only a skeletal affidavit need be and was filed. The State urges that the reviewing judge normally reviews the complaint as well, but concedes that the complaint may also be conclusory. It is self-evident that the judge could make no realistic assessment concerning the likelihood of an action's success based upon these one-sided, self-serving, and conclusory submissions. * * *

What safeguards the State does afford do not adequately reduce this risk. Connecticut points out that the statute also provides an "expeditiou[s]" post-attachment adversary hearing; notice for such a hearing; judicial review of an adverse decision; and a double damages action if the original suit is commenced without probable cause. Similar considerations were present in *Mitchell* where we upheld Louisiana's sequestration statute despite the lack of pre-deprivation notice and hearing. But in *Mitchell*, the plaintiff had a vendor's lien to protect, the risk of error was minimal because the likelihood of recovery involved uncomplicated matters that lent themselves to documentary proof, and plaintiff was required to put up a bond. None of these factors diminishing the need for a pre-deprivation hearing is present in this case. It is true that a later hearing might negate the presence of probable cause, but this would not cure the temporary deprivation that an earlier hearing might have prevented. "The Fourteenth Amendment draws no bright lines around three-day, 10-day or 50-day deprivations of property. Any significant taking of property by the State is within the purview of the Due Process Clause." *Fuentes.*

Finally, we conclude that the interests in favor of an ex parte attachment, particularly the interests of the plaintiff, are too minimal to supply such a consideration here. Plaintiff had no existing interest in Doehr's real estate when he sought the attachment. His only interest in attaching the property was to ensure the availability of assets to satisfy his judgment if he prevailed on the merits of his action. Yet there was no allegation that Doehr was about to transfer or encumber his real estate or take any other action during the pendency of the action that would render his real estate unavailable to satisfy a judgment. Our cases have recognized such a properly supported claim would be an exigent circumstance permitting postponing any notice or hearing until after the attachment is effected. Absent such allegations, however, the plaintiff's interest in attaching the property does not justify the burdening of Doehr's ownership rights without a hearing to determine the likelihood of recovery.

No interest the government may have affects the analysis. The State's substantive interest in protecting any rights of the plaintiff cannot be any more weighty than those rights themselves. Here the plaintiff's interest is de minimis. Moreover, the State cannot seriously plead additional financial or administrative burdens involving pre-deprivation hearings when it already claims to provide an immediate post deprivation hearing.

Historical and contemporary practices support our analysis. Prejudgment attachment is a remedy unknown at common law. * * *

Connecticut's statute appears even more suspect in light of current practice. A survey of state attachment provisions reveals that nearly every State requires either a pre-attachment hearing, a showing of some exigent circumstance, or both, before permitting an attachment to take place. Twenty-seven States, as well as the District of Columbia, permit attachments only when some extraordinary circumstance is present. In such cases, pre-attachment hearings are not required but post-attachment hearings are provided. Ten States permit attachment without the presence of such factors but require pre-writ hearings unless one of those factors is shown. Six States limit attachments to extraordinary circumstance cases but the writ will not issue prior to a hearing unless there is a showing of some even more compelling condition. Three States always require a pre-attachment hearing. Only Washington, Connecticut, and Rhode Island authorize attachments without a prior hearing in situations that do not involve any purportedly heightened threat to the plaintiff's interests. Even those States permit ex parte deprivations only in certain types of cases: Rhode Island does so only when the claim is equitable; Connecticut and Washington do so only when real estate is to be attached, and even Washington requires a bond. Conversely, the States for the most part no longer confine attachments to creditor claims. This development, however, only increases the importance of the other limitations.

We do not mean to imply that any given exigency requirement protects an attachment from constitutional attack. Nor do we suggest that the statutory measures we have surveyed are necessarily free of due process problems or other constitutional infirmities in general. We do believe, however, that the procedures of almost all the States confirm our view that the Connecticut provision before us, by failing to provide a pre-attachment hearing without at least requiring a showing of some exigent circumstance, clearly falls short of the demands of due process.

IV

A

Although a majority of the Court does not reach the issue, Justices Marshall, Stevens, O'Connor, and I deem it appropriate to consider whether due process also requires the plaintiff to post a bond or other security in addition to requiring a hearing or showing of some exigency.[7]

As noted, the impairments to property rights that attachments affect merit due process protection. Several consequences can be severe, such as the default of a homeowner's mortgage. In the present context, it need only be added that we have repeatedly recognized the utility of a bond in protecting property rights affected by the mistaken award of prejudgment remedies.

Without a bond, at the time of attachment, the danger that these property rights may be wrongfully deprived remains unacceptably high even with such safeguards as a hearing or exigency requirement. The need for a bond is especially apparent where extraordinary circumstances justify an attachment with no more than the plaintiff's ex parte assertion of a claim. * * *

---

7. Ordinarily we will not address a contention advanced by a respondent that would enlarge his or her rights under a judgment, without the respondent filing a cross-petition for certiorari. Here the Court of Appeals rejected Doehr's argument that § 52-278e(a)(1) violates due process in failing to mandate pre-attachment bond. Nonetheless, this case involves considerations that in the past have prompted us to "consider the question highlighted by respondent." First, as our cases have shown, the notice and hearing question and the bond question are intertwined and can fairly be considered facets of the same general issue. Thus "[w]ithout undue strain, the position taken by the respondent before this Court ... might be characterized as an argument in support of the judgment below" insofar as a discussion of notice and a hearing cannot be divorced from consideration of a bond. Second, this aspect of prejudgment attachment "plainly warrants our attention, and with regard to which the lower courts are in need of guidance." Third, "and perhaps most importantly, both parties have briefed and argued the question."

But the need for a bond does not end here. A defendant's property rights remain at undue risk even when there has been an adversarial hearing to determine the plaintiff's likelihood of recovery. At best, a court's initial assessment of each party's case cannot produce more than an educated prediction as to who will win. This is especially true when, as here, the nature of the claim makes any accurate prediction elusive. In consequence, even a full hearing under a proper probable-cause standard would not prevent many defendants from having title to their homes impaired during the pendency of suits that never result in the contingency that ultimately justifies such impairment, namely, an award to the plaintiff. Attachment measures currently on the books reflect this concern. All but a handful of States require a plaintiff's bond despite also affording a hearing either before, or (for the vast majority, only under extraordinary circumstances) soon after, an attachment takes place. Bonds have been a similarly common feature of other prejudgment remedy procedures that we have considered, whether or not these procedures also included a hearing.

The State stresses its double damages remedy for suits that are commenced without probable cause. CONN. GEN. STAT. § 52-568(a)(1). This remedy, however, fails to make up for the lack of a bond. As an initial matter, the meaning of "probable cause" in this provision is no more clear here than it was in the attachment provision itself. Should the term mean the plaintiff's good faith or the facial adequacy of the complaint, the remedy is clearly insufficient. A defendant who was deprived where there was little or no likelihood that the plaintiff would obtain a judgment could nonetheless recover only by proving some type of fraud or malice or by showing that the plaintiff had failed to state a claim. Problems persist even if the plaintiff's ultimate failure permits recovery. At best a defendant must await a decision on the merits of the plaintiff's complaint, even assuming that a § 52-568(a)(1) action may be brought as a counterclaim. Settlement, under Connecticut law, precludes seeking the damages remedy, a fact that encourages the use of attachments as a tactical device to pressure an opponent to capitulate. An attorney's advice that there is probable cause to commence an action constitutes a complete defense, even if the advice was unsound or erroneous. Finally, there is no guarantee that the original plaintiff will have adequate assets to satisfy an award that the defendant may win.

Nor is there any appreciable interest against a bond requirement. Section 52-278e(a)(1) does not require a plaintiff to show exigent circumstances nor any preexisting interest in the property facing attachment. A party must show more than the mere existence of a claim before subjecting an opponent to prejudgment proceedings that carry a significant risk of erroneous deprivation.

B

Our foregoing discussion compels the four of us to consider whether a bond excuses the need for a hearing or other safeguards altogether. If a bond is needed to augment the protections afforded by pre-attachment and post-attachment hearings, it arguably follows that a bond renders these safeguards unnecessary. That conclusion is unconvincing, however, for it ignores certain harms that bonds could not undo but that hearings would prevent. The law concerning attachments has rarely, if ever, required defendants to suffer an encumbered title until the case is concluded without any prior opportunity to show that the attachment was unwarranted. Our cases have repeatedly emphasized the importance of providing a prompt post-deprivation hearing at the very least. Every State but one, moreover, expressly requires a pre-attachment or post-attachment hearing to determine the propriety of an attachment.

The necessity for at least a prompt post-attachment hearing is self-evident because the right to be compensated at the end of the case, if the plaintiff loses, for all provable injuries caused by the attachment is inadequate to redress the harm inflicted, harm that could have been avoided had an early hearing been held. An individual with an immediate need or opportunity to sell a property can neither do so, nor otherwise satisfy that need or recreate the opportunity. The same applies to a parent in need of a home equity loan for a child's education, an entrepreneur seeking to start a business on the strength of an otherwise strong credit rating, or simply a homeowner who might face the disruption of having a mortgage placed in technical default. The extent of these harms, moreover, grows with the length of the suit. Here, oral argument indicated that civil suits in Connecticut commonly take up to four to seven years for completion. * * *

If a bond cannot serve to dispense with a hearing immediately after attachment, neither is it sufficient basis for not providing a pre-attachment hearing in the absence of exigent circumstances even if in any event a hearing would be provided a few days later. The reasons are the same: a wrongful attachment can inflict injury that will not fully be redressed by recovery on the bond after a prompt postattachment hearing determines that the attachment was invalid.

Once more, history and contemporary practice support our conclusion. Historically, attachments would not issue without a showing of extraordinary circumstances even though a plaintiff bond was almost invariably required in addition. Likewise, all but eight States currently require the posting of a bond. Out of this 42 State majority, all but one requires a pre-attachment hearing, a showing of some exigency, or both, and all but one expressly require a post-attachment hearing when an attachment has been issued ex parte. This testimony underscores the point that neither a hearing nor an extraordinary circumstance limitation eliminates the need for a bond, no more than a bond allows waiver of these other protections. To reconcile the interests of the defendant and the plaintiff accurately, due process generally requires all of the above.

V

Because Connecticut's prejudgment remedy provision, CONN. GEN. STAT. § 52-278e(a)(1), violates the requirements of due process by authorizing prejudgment attachment without prior notice or a hearing, the judgment of the Court of Appeals is affirmed, and the case is remanded to that court for further proceedings consistent with this opinion.

It is so ordered.

CHIEF JUSTICE REHNQUIST with whom JUSTICE BLACKMUN joins, concurring in part and concurring in the judgment.

I agree with the Court that the Connecticut attachment statute, "as applied in this case," fails to satisfy the Due Process Clause of the Fourteenth Amendment. I therefore join Parts I, II and III of its opinion. Unfortunately, the remainder of the Court's opinion does not confine itself to the facts of this case, but enters upon a lengthy disquisition as to what combination of safeguards are required to satisfy Due Process in hypothetical cases not before the Court. I therefore do not join Part IV.

As the Court's opinion points out, the Connecticut statute allows attachment not merely for a creditor's claim, but for a tort claim of assault and battery; it affords no opportunity for a pre-deprivation hearing; it contains no requirement that there be "exigent circumstances," such as an effort on the part of the defendant to conceal assets; no bond is required from the plaintiff; and the property attached is one in which the plaintiff has no pre-existing interest. The Court's opinion is, in my view, ultimately correct when it bases its holding of unconstitutionality of the Connecticut statute as applied here on our cases of *Sniadach, Fuentes, Mitchell,* and *Di-Chem.* But I do not believe that the result follows so inexorably as the Court's opinion suggests. All of the cited cases dealt with personalty—bank deposits or chattels—and each involved the physical seizure of the property itself, so that the defendant was deprived of its use. These cases, which represented something of a revolution in the jurisprudence of procedural due process, placed substantial limits on the methods by which creditors could obtain a lien on the assets of a debtor prior to judgment. But in all of them the debtor was deprived of the use and possession of the property. In the present case, on the other hand, Connecticut's pre-judgment attachment on real property statute, which secures an incipient lien for the plaintiff, does not deprive the defendant of the use or possession of the property.

The Court's opinion therefore breaks new ground, and I would point out, more emphatically than the Court does, the limits of today's holding. * * *

Justice Scalia, concurring in part and concurring in the judgment.

Since the manner of attachment here was not a recognized procedure at common law, I agree that its validity under the Due Process Clause should be determined by applying the test we set forth in *Mathews v. Eldridge*; and I agree that it fails that test. I join Parts I and III of the Court's opinion, and concur in the judgment of the Court.

Notes and Questions

1. This case grew out of an altercation in a park and a subsequent tort suit. The underlying litigation had nothing to do with the Doehrs' home. Why do you think DiGiovani attached the Doehrs' home?

2. After the attachment, Brian Doehr did not seek a post-attachment hearing, but instead filed suit in federal court challenging the constitutionality of the Connecticut statute. After the Supreme Court's decision, the case was remanded for a determination as to whether Doehr was entitled to damages for the due process violation. This phase of the litigation lasted from 1992 to 1998 and involved another trip to the Second Circuit. In the end, the court held that Doehr was not entitled to damages

because he could not prove malice or lack of probable cause and denied both sides' requests for attorney's fees.

Meanwhile, the underlying tort case proceeded in state court. The jury found for DiGiovani and awarded damages. The jury verdict was reduced based on Connecticut's comparative fault and collateral source rules. Final judgment was for $3,422.34 plus costs. For a full account of the case, see Robert Bone, *The Story of* Connecticut v. Doehr: *Balancing Costs and Benefits in Defining Procedural Rights, in* Civil Procedure Stories 159 (K. Clermont ed., 2d ed. 2008).

3. In *Mathews v. Eldridge*, discussed in *Doehr*, the issue was whether a recipient of social security disability benefits was entitled to a hearing before the government terminated his payments. In analyzing this issue, the Court articulated three factors to be considered: the interests of the party whose property would be affected, the risk of error, and the interests of the state. Applying this test, the Court held that a pre-termination hearing was not required. It noted, however, that the recipient was entitled to a post-deprivation hearing — a process that took over a year.

The three-part test of *Mathews v. Eldridge* can be read to suggest that in deciding how much process the Constitution requires, courts should do a kind of cost-benefit analysis and weigh the value of the right against the cost of the additional process. The *Mathews* Court itself invoked such terms, noting that "[a]t some point the benefit of an additional safeguard to the individual affected by the [government] action and to society in terms of increased assurance that the action is just, may be outweighed by the cost." 424 U.S. at 348. Some have applauded this approach because it seeks to ensure an "efficient" amount of procedure. As Judge Richard Posner has explained, "in general we would not want to increase the direct costs of the legal process by one dollar in order to reduce the error costs by 50 (or 99) cents." Richard Posner, *An Economic Approach to Legal Procedure and Judicial Administration*, 2 J. Legal Studies 399, 401 (1973). Do you agree that the purpose of the Due Process Clauses is to ensure an efficient level of procedure? If so, how should a court go about estimating the costs and benefits of a procedure? What should a court do when it lacks solid data about costs and benefits?

4. After *Doehr*, under what circumstances is pre-judgment attachment permissible? Consider Shaumyan v. O'Neill, 987 F.2d 122 (2d Cir. 1993), in which the Second Circuit upheld the Connecticut statute. Mr. Shaumyan had contracted for repairs, including window replacements to his home. After the work was completed, Mr. Shaumyan was dissatisfied with the work and refused to make the final payment. The contractor sued for breach of contract in Connecticut state court and attached the Shaumyan home without a hearing or bond. Shaumyan then brought suit in federal court challenging the attachment. The Second Circuit distinguished *Doehr* and upheld the attachment. The court found that the contractor, unlike the plaintiff in *Doehr*, had an interest in the property and could have filed a mechanic's lien. The court also found that there was much less risk of a wrongful deprivation because the case concerned a contract that was for a sum certain and was easily documented. How persuasive do you find these reasons? The dispute between the homeowner and

the contractor concerned the adequacy of performance. Is that something that is easily documented?

In Noatex Corp. v. King Const. of Houston, 732 F.3d 479, 485 (5th Cir. 2013), the court found unconstitutional a state statute that allowed sub-contractors to claim proceeds due from an owner to a contractor, and which provided few procedural safeguards. The court rejected the argument that the sub-contractors had an interest in the property akin to a mechanic's lien.

5. In 1993, Connecticut amended its prejudgment attachment statute. The amended statute provides:

> (a) The court or judge of the court may allow the prejudgment remedy to be issued by an attorney without hearing * * * upon the filing of an affidavit sworn to by the plaintiff or any competent affiant setting forth a statement of facts sufficient to show that there is probable cause that a judgment in the amount of the prejudgment remedy sought, or in an amount greater than the amount of the prejudgment remedy sought, taking into account any known defenses, counterclaims or set-offs, will be rendered in the matter in favor of the plaintiff and that there is reasonable likelihood that the defendant (1) has hidden himself so that process cannot be served on him or (2) is about to remove himself or his property from the state or (3) is about to fraudulently dispose of or has fraudulently disposed of any of his property with intent to hinder, delay or defraud his creditors or (4) has fraudulently hidden or withheld money, property or effects which should be liable to the satisfaction of his debts.

Conn. Gen. Stat. § 52-278e(a). The defendant may move to modify or dissolve the prejudgment remedy and the court must hold a hearing within seven days of the filing of such a motion. Id. at subsection (e). At the hearing or upon motion, the defendant may request that the court order the plaintiff to post bond. Id. at § 52-278d(d) If the court grants this request and the defendant prevails at trial or the prejudgment attachment is later dissolved, the plaintiff must pay the defendant for any damages caused by the prejudgment attachment. Is this revised statute constitutional?

6. Applying the approach set out in *Doehr* and *Mathews*, consider the following situation: The City of Parksburg is planning a program of "booting" cars that have accumulated parking tickets totaling more than $300. (A "boot" is a device that is attached to the wheel of a car and makes the car impossible to drive.) The City also plans to tow and dispose of abandoned cars. The City Attorney has asked you to describe what, if any, procedures must be in place for these programs to be constitutional. See Saukstelis v. Chicago, 932 F.2d 1171 (7th Cir. 1991).

7. Federal law permits the forfeiture of property used to commit or facilitate the commission of a federal drug offense. 21 U.S.C. § 881. In United States v. Good, 510 U.S. 43 (1993), several years after Good was convicted of drug offenses, the United States brought an ex parte procedure to seize Good's property. The property was seized without prior notice or a hearing. The Court held that there was not a sufficient government justification to support seizure without notice or a hearing. The Court

noted that although it has permitted seizure without prior notice of movable forfeitable property such as a yacht, see Calero-Toledo v. Pearson Yacht Leasing Co., 416 U.S. 663 (1974), no exigent circumstances justified a similar approach regarding the seizure of real property.

In a variation on *Good*, the Eleventh Circuit held that where the government files a lis pendens notice against real property in a civil forfeiture procedure, the owner is entitled to pre-seizure notice and a hearing, even if the government has not exercised physical control over the property. Relying in part on *Doehr*, the court noted that "the Supreme Court * * * did not intend for physical control to be of paramount importance when determining whether a constitutionally cognizable 'seizure' of real property has taken place." United States v. 408 Peyton Rd., 162 F.3d 644, 650 (11th Cir. 1998).

8. In Grupo Mexicano de Desarrollo, S.A. v. Alliance Bond Fund, Inc., 527 U.S. 308 (1999), the Supreme Court held that federal courts do not have authority to enter a preliminary injunction freezing a defendant's assets for the benefit of a non-judgment creditor. The decision was not based on any due process ground. Instead, the Court held that such injunctions go beyond traditional equitable remedies and thus were not statutorily authorized.

9. In criminal cases, arrest warrants and search warrants are routinely issued by the court on an ex parte basis. Indeed, the affidavit that DiGiovanni submitted likely would have provided sufficient probable cause for a court to issue a warrant for Doehr's arrest. On the basis of an arrest warrant, Doehr could have been jailed (subject to a later hearing on bail). Thus, the procedures which were an inadequate basis for depriving Doehr of his property would have been sufficient for depriving him of his liberty. The Court has explained this anomaly as follows:

> The historical basis of the probable cause requirement is quite different from the relatively recent application of variable procedural due process in debtor-creditor disputes and termination of government-created benefits. The Fourth Amendment was tailored explicitly for the criminal justice system, and its balance between individual and public interests always has been thought to define the "process that is due" for seizures of person or property in criminal cases, including the detention of suspects pending trial.

Gerstein v. Pugh, 420 U.S. 103, 125 n.27 (1975).

10. Even if a defendant is entitled to a hearing prior to the grant of any preliminary relief, what standards should be applied at that hearing? In Winter v. Natural Resources Defense Council, Inc., 555 U.S. 7 (2008), the Supreme Court held that "[a] plaintiff seeking a preliminary injunction must establish that he is likely to succeed on the merits, that he is likely to suffer irreparable harm in the absence of preliminary relief, that the balance of equities tips in his favor, and that an injunction is in the public interest." The Court stressed that the "possibility" of harm is not sufficient but that the plaintiff must demonstrate a "strong likelihood" of irreparable harm. In that case, the district court had granted a preliminary injunction imposing restrictions

on the Navy's use of sonar training because of concern that it would cause irreparable harm to certain marine mammals. The Supreme Court reversed, finding that the injunction was outweighed by the public interest and the Navy's interest in effective, realistic training.

11. Suppose a plaintiff attaches property to secure quasi-in-rem jurisdiction. What pre-attachment process is required? In Fuentes v. Shevin, 407 U.S. 67 (1972), the Supreme Court in enumerating several circumstances under which attachment without a prior hearing has been permitted, stated: "Another case involved attachment necessary to secure jurisdiction in state court—clearly a most basic and important public interest. *Ownbey v. Morgan*, 256 U.S. 94 (1920)." Relying on this statement, the Delaware Supreme Court upheld the ex parte sequestration procedure at issue in *Shaffer v. Heitner*, Chapter 2, despite the lack of pre-attachment procedures. Because the Supreme Court reversed for lack of jurisdiction, it did not reach the issue of pre-attachment procedures. Commentators disagree about the constitutionality of prejudgment attachment to secure quasi-in-rem jurisdiction. Compare Michael Mushlin, *The New Quasi in Rem Jurisdiction: New York's Revival of a Doctrine Whose Time Has Passed*, 55 Brook. L. Rev. 1059, 1105–11 (1990), with Comment, Shaffer, Burnham, *and New York's Continuing Use of QIR-2 Jurisdiction: A Resurrection of the Power Theory*, 45 Emory L.J. 239, 267–69 (1996).

Admiralty courts have upheld quasi-in-rem attachment without a prior hearing. See, e.g., Trans-Asiatic Oil, Ltd. v. Apex Oil Co., 743 F.2d 956 (1st Cir. 1984); Polar Shipping Ltd. v. Oriental Shipping Corp., 680 F.2d 627 (9th Cir. 1982). Outside the admiralty context, the issue appears to have arisen infrequently, and the cases are divided. Compare Cable Advertising Networks, Inc. v. DeWoody, 632 A.2d 1383 (Del. Chanc. 1993) (pre-attachment safeguards required in quasi-in-rem attachment), with Estate of Portnoy v. Cessna Aircraft Co., 603 F. Supp. 285, 294–96 (S.D. Miss. 1985) (pre-attachment safeguards not required in quasi-in-rem attachment).

Chapter 4

Subject Matter Jurisdiction

A. Introduction and Integration

"Jurisdiction" is a chameleon word; it means different things in different contexts. We have spent considerable time determining whether the forum has personal jurisdiction over the defendant, and now turn to a separate requirement: The plaintiff must file suit in a court permitted by relevant law to entertain the type of claim asserted. In other words, the court must have subject matter jurisdiction. Subject matter jurisdiction is independent of personal jurisdiction. Throughout this chapter, we assume that the plaintiff has established personal jurisdiction over the defendant in a particular state. Now the question is: What court does plaintiff go to in that state?

The principal choice will be between a state court and a federal court. In each state, there are various state trial courts, which bear a variety of names, and there is at least one federal trial court, which is always called the federal district court. The federal district court (like all federal courts) has *limited subject matter jurisdiction*; it can hear only certain kinds of cases, as prescribed by the United States Constitution and federal statutes. In contrast, the trial courts of each state collectively have *general subject matter jurisdiction*; they can, with rare exceptions, hear any cognizable claim. Many cases will satisfy subject matter jurisdiction of both the state and federal court. Such situations are examples of the two court systems' having *concurrent subject matter jurisdiction*. In cases of concurrent jurisdiction, the plaintiff decides in which court to file, usually guided by a variety of pragmatic and strategic considerations.

B. State Courts and General Subject Matter Jurisdiction

The states are free to divide subject matter jurisdiction among whatever courts they decide to establish. In some states, the matter is treated in the constitution, while in others it is addressed in statutes. There is considerable variation as to the names given the trial courts (popular names include County, District, Municipal, Circuit, and Superior Courts) and as to how to divide subject matter among them.

Many states establish specialized tribunals to handle specific cases, such as Probate Courts, Juvenile Courts, Traffic Courts, and the like. In some, subject matter is divided along monetary lines. For example, civil cases involving less than a particular monetary amount might go to one court while those involving a greater sum go to another. Many states employ a combination of these approaches, with specialized courts hearing specific substantive cases, and other courts dividing the remaining general civil cases along monetary lines.

No matter how a state chooses to allocate its trial jurisdiction, however, the key point is that within each state a plaintiff will be able to find some tribunal of that state in which to assert her claim. Thus, while not all courts in a state can hear all cases, the courts of a particular state, in the aggregate, have general subject matter jurisdiction. There is one narrow exception to the general subject matter jurisdiction of state courts. It involves those areas in which Congress has vested the federal district courts with exclusive subject matter jurisdiction. These include some admiralty proceedings (28 U.S.C. § 1333), bankruptcy matters (28 U.S.C. § 1334), patent and copyright infringement claims (28 U.S.C. § 1338(a)), and cases arising under federal antitrust and securities laws (15 U.S.C. §§ 15–26, 78aa).

Most grants of federal jurisdiction, including other specific grants, are not exclusive. For example, 28 U.S.C. § 1343 allows federal courts to hear cases involving violations of federally protected civil rights, but such cases may also be brought in state court. The same is true with the general federal question statute, 28 U.S.C. § 1331, which we will address in detail in Section C.4 below. It is a catchall provision, allowing assertion of claims that arise under federal laws but that do not have their own specialized jurisdictional grant. It does not carry exclusive federal jurisdiction.

Why would Congress establish exclusive jurisdiction in the federal courts as to *any* matters? Why wouldn't Congress establish exclusive jurisdiction over *all* matters cognizable by the federal courts?

C. Federal Courts and Limited Subject Matter Jurisdiction

1. The Constitutional Grants and Role of Congress

As discussed in Chapter 1, Section B, the Constitution creates the federal government and grants it only specified powers. Article III of the Constitution specifies the powers of the federal courts. Read Sections 1 and 2 of Article III and consider the following notes and questions.

Notes and Questions

1. Note the extraordinary protections accorded federal judges. They cannot be forced to retire. They never face an electorate. Their pay cannot be reduced. They can be removed from office only through impeachment (which has occurred only

eight times in the history of the nation). In contrast, the judges of most state courts must face an electorate at some point. Keep these protections of the federal judiciary in mind as we study the various types of cases heard by federal courts, always asking why the Founders felt it necessary to insulate federal judges from ongoing review by an electorate.

2. Compare the provisions of the first sentence of Article III, Section 1 with the second paragraph of Section 2. What federal court(s) must exist? Could Congress abolish federal district courts and federal courts of appeals? If Congress did abolish the lower federal courts, where would cases that are now filed there go?

3. The nine separate categories, or "heads," of jurisdiction provided in the first paragraph of Section 2 of Article III delineate the outer limits of jurisdiction of the federal courts. Congress cannot exceed these limits in conferring jurisdiction upon the federal courts. But *must* Congress vest the federal courts with the power to decide all of the types of disputes contained in Article III, Section 2? Although Justice Story asserted that Article III imposed that obligation on Congress, see Martin v. Hunter's Lessee, 14 U.S. 304, 327–37 (1816), Congress has never agreed. For example, Congress did not grant the lower federal courts jurisdiction over cases "arising under * * * the laws of United States" until 1875.

4. Even within a particular category of jurisdiction, Article III does not require that Congress grant jurisdiction to the full constitutional limit. Indeed, Congress has always imposed an amount in controversy requirement in diversity of citizenship cases, although no such limit exists in the Constitution. 28 U.S.C. § 1332(a)(1).

5. Should Congress vest the federal courts with judicial power over particular types of cases to the full extent of Article III? Consider Justice Chase's remarks from more than two centuries ago in Turner v. Bank of North America, 4 U.S. 8, 10 (1799): "[I]t would, perhaps, be inexpedient, to enlarge the jurisdiction of the federal courts, to every subject, in every form, which the constitution might warrant." Why would it be "inexpedient"? Should that view hold sway today?

It is rare for Congress to overreach the power given by Article III. Instead, Congress generally follows Justice Chase's advice and refuses to grant the courts jurisdiction to the full extent that the Constitution would allow. Thus, most problems regarding the proper invocation of federal jurisdiction involve interpretation of the jurisdictional statutes passed by Congress, and not the provisions of Article III.

2. Plaintiff's Burden to Establish Federal Subject Matter Jurisdiction

Several important consequences flow from the fact that federal court jurisdiction is limited to those areas granted by the Constitution and statutes. First, the parties to litigation cannot confer subject matter jurisdiction on a federal court by "consent."

Second, a federal court's lack of subject matter jurisdiction is a defense that cannot be waived. See Rule 12(h)(3). Any party or the court can raise the issue at any time in the case, even after the court has entered judgment. Surprisingly, even the plaintiff, who invoked the jurisdiction of the federal court, can seek dismissal for lack of subject matter jurisdiction. There are a surprising number of cases in which disputes bounce through different levels of the federal judiciary for years before someone notices that the case must be dismissed for lack of subject matter jurisdiction. See, e.g., Depex Reina 9 Partnership v. Texas International Petroleum Corp., 897 F.2d 461, 462–64 (10th Cir. 1990) (ordering dismissal after case had been through full trial, appeal, remand by the appellate court and subsequent treatment by the district court). Ordinarily, the plaintiff will then have to start the case over in state court. The plaintiff may be without remedy, however, if the federal jurisdictional problem is not discovered until after the statute of limitations has run for a state court action. See Clephas v. Fagelson, Shonberger, Payne & Arthur, 719 F.2d 92, 95–96 (4th Cir. 1983). We will discuss the timing and methods of jurisdictional challenges in Chapter 6.

Third, there is a presumption *against* federal jurisdiction. Thus, the plaintiff must properly plead that federal jurisdiction exists. Indeed, Rule 8(a)(1), to be discussed further in Chapter 7, requires "a short and plain statement of the grounds for the court's jurisdiction." If the defendant challenges the allegation, the plaintiff assumes the burden of proving that jurisdiction exists.

It is critical, therefore, that counsel understand not only the burden of invoking jurisdiction, but also the elements required to establish it. Detailed understanding of these elements "is not a hypertechnicality." VT Investors v. R & D Funding Corp., 733 F. Supp. 823, 826 (D.N.J. 1990). Instead, it is fundamental to the competent practice of law and critical to assure that the federal courts not decide cases beyond their power. As Judge Posner has explained: "Napoleon at his coronation took the imperial crown out of the hands of the Pope and crowned himself. Federal judges do not have a similar prerogative. A court that does not have jurisdiction cannot assume it, however worthy the cause." In re Brand Name Prescription Drugs Antitrust Litigation, 248 F.3d 668, 670 (7th Cir. 2001).

Although Article III listed nine separate categories of federal jurisdiction, we will focus on three: diversity of citizenship, alienage, and federal question jurisdiction.

3. Diversity of Citizenship and Alienage Jurisdiction

a. Introductory Note

Compare the constitutional grants of diversity of citizenship and alienage jurisdiction in Article III to the statutory grants in 28 U.S.C. § 1332(a)(1) and § 1332(a)(2). The term "original jurisdiction," in contrast to "appellate jurisdiction," refers to jurisdiction of a trial court.

The Founders provided for alienage jurisdiction principally for two related reasons. First, it gave aliens involved in litigation with American citizens a forum free from local political influence. Second, it thereby demonstrated to other countries that the United States treats litigation involving their citizens or subjects as a matter of such importance as to justify a place on the dockets of the national, as opposed to the local, courts. In JPMorgan Chase Bank v. Traffic Stream (BVI) Infrastructure Ltd., 536 U.S. 88, 94 (2002), the Supreme Court discussed the specific historical grounding for alienage jurisdiction:

> Both during and after the Revolution, state courts were notoriously frosty to British creditors trying to collect debts from American citizens, and state legislatures went so far as to hobble British debt collection by statute, despite the specific provision of the 1783 Treaty of Paris that creditors in the courts of either country would "meet with no lawful impediment" to debt collection. Ultimately, the States' refusal to honor the treaty became serious enough to prompt protests by the British Secretary of State, particularly when irked by American demands for treaty compliance on the British side. * * * This penchant of the state courts to disrupt international relations and discourage foreign investment led directly to the alienage jurisdiction provided by Article III of the Constitution.

Alienage jurisdiction accounts for a small percentage of the federal court caseload. In part because of this, and because the underlying principles for alienage remain vital, no one seriously contends that alienage jurisdiction ought to be restricted or abolished.

The same is not true of diversity of citizenship jurisdiction, which has always had opponents. The orthodox view is that diversity jurisdiction provides a neutral forum—free from local bias or influence—for resolution of cases between citizens of different states. It provides a federal forum for an out-of-state litigant who feared that she might be the victim of local bias, or be "hometowned," if forced to litigate before the locally selected state court judge. It seems clear that the Founders were most interested in relieving anxiety of commercial interests. The availability of an impartial federal forum may have made it easier for enterprises to invest in other states, and thus may have fostered economic expansion. Indeed, President and Chief Justice Taft concluded that diversity jurisdiction "was the single most important element in securing capital for the development of the southern and western United States." William Howard Taft, *Possible and Needed Reforms in Administration of Justice in Federal Courts*, 8 A.B.A. J. 601, 604 (1922).

Some critics feel that diversity jurisdiction has outlived its usefulness. They assert that local bias and the fear of local bias have largely evaporated in the modern era of mass communication and travel. Moreover, diversity jurisdiction only changes the judge who presides over the case—it does not change the law that applies, and thus cannot protect litigants from biased laws. In fact, under the landmark case of Erie Railroad Co. v. Tompkins, 304 U.S. 64 (1938), which is the focus of Chapter 10, a federal court in a diversity case must apply the same law that the state court would apply—biases and all. Thus, argue critics, diversity jurisdiction no longer provides much benefit and, given our limited resources, federal judges should be freed up to work on cases involving federal substantive law. See, e.g., Report of Federal Courts Study Committee 38–43 (1990). Moreover, diversity cases constitute a considerable portion of the federal docket. For many years, diversity cases usually accounted for about one-quarter of civil filings. More recently, however, the percentage of diversity cases has been rising. In 2014, 295,310 civil cases were commenced in the federal district courts. Of these, 100,472—over 34 percent—invoked diversity of citizenship jurisdiction. See www.uscourts.gov.

Others disagree, contending that the historic justification remains vital today. They point to cases such as Pennzoil Co. v. Texaco, Inc., 481 U.S. 1 (1987)—in which a Texas state court entered a judgment of $11 billion in favor of a Texas company against a New York entity—as evidence of local bias, or, at least, as evidence of why the fear of local bias is not irrational. See, e.g., Pappas v. Middle Earth Condominium Assoc., 963 F.2d 534, 535–36 (2d Cir. 1992) (involving lawyers' appeal to regional bias); 15 MOORE'S FEDERAL PRACTICE § 102 App. 03[2].

Consider, for example, the remarkably candid comments of Justice Neely of the West Virginia Supreme Court: "As long as I am allowed to redistribute wealth from out-of-state companies to injured in-state plaintiffs, I shall continue to do so. Not only is my sleep enhanced when I give someone else's money away, but so is my job security, because the in-state plaintiffs, their families and their friends will re-elect me." RICHARD NEELY, THE PRODUCT LIABILITY MESS: HOW BUSINESS CAN BE RESCUED FROM THE POLITICS OF STATE COURTS 4 (1988). Advocates of diversity of citizenship jurisdiction also note that federal courts generally draw their juries from wider geographic areas than state courts, which may lessen the impact of local bias.

The debate over the need for diversity of citizenship jurisdiction will continue, as it has for over two centuries. As a general rule, diversity has proved quite popular with members of the bar, in part because it affords them an option of fora. Because the bar is such a powerful lobbying force, it seems unlikely that Congress will abolish diversity of citizenship jurisdiction wholesale.

b. The Complete Diversity Rule

Strawbridge v. Curtiss

7 U.S. 267, 2 L. Ed. 435 (1806)

This was an appeal from a decree of the Circuit Court, for the District of Massachusetts, which dismissed the complainants' [complaint] * * * for want of jurisdiction.

Some of the complainants were alleged to be citizens of the State of Massachusetts. The defendants were also stated to be citizens of the same State, excepting Curtiss, who was averred to be a citizen of the State of Vermont, and upon whom the subpoena was served in that State.

MARSHALL, CHIEF JUSTICE, delivered the opinion of the Court.

The court has considered this case, and is of opinion that the jurisdiction cannot be supported.

The words of the act of congress are, "* * * the suit is between a citizen of a State where the suit is brought, and a citizen of another State."

The court understands these expressions to mean, that each distinct interest should be represented by persons, all of whom are entitled to sue, or may be sued, in the federal courts. That is, that where the interest is joint, each of the persons concerned in that interest must be competent to sue, or liable to be sued in those courts. * * *

Notes and Questions

1. *Strawbridge* establishes the complete diversity rule. Under that rule, diversity jurisdiction exists only if all plaintiffs are of diverse citizenship from all defendants. The Supreme Court explains the rationale this way:

> [We] have adhered to the complete diversity rule in light of the purpose of the diversity requirement, which is to provide a federal forum for important disputes where state courts might favor, or be perceived as favoring, home-state litigants. The presence of parties from the same State on both sides of a case dispels this concern, eliminating a principal reason for conferring § 1332 jurisdiction over any of the claims in the action.

Exxon Mobil Corp. v. Allapattah Services, 545 U.S. 546, 553 (2005).

Is the rationale plausible? Suppose a citizen of State A wants to sue you (a citizen of State Z) in state court in State A, expressly for the purpose of trying to take advantage of any local bias against you as an out-of-state citizen. She joins a second defendant, who is also a citizen of State A, thereby defeating any possibility of having the case invoke diversity of citizenship jurisdiction. How does the fact that your co-defendant is a citizen of State A reduce your fear of local bias? Indeed, does it not exacerbate that fear? After all, you are now the *only* non-local in the case.

2. Compare the wording of the statutory grant of diversity jurisdiction quoted by Chief Justice Marshall in *Strawbridge* with the current wording of that grant at 28 U.S.C. § 1332(a)(1). The older version required that at least one litigant be a citizen of the forum state. Why is that version more consistent than the current version with the historic justification for diversity of citizenship jurisdiction?

3. In 1917, Congress passed the Federal Interpleader Act, 28 U.S.C. §§ 1335, 1397, and 2361. It applies only to a very specialized type of litigation concerning ownership of property, as we will see in Chapter 13. For present purposes, it is enough to note that the statute grants federal subject matter jurisdiction based upon "minimal diversity," that is, based upon having one adverse claimant of diverse citizenship from another. In other words, if an interpleader proceeding involved adverse claims by citizens of Vermont and Maryland against a citizen of Maryland, the statute would permit jurisdiction.

The Supreme Court upheld the constitutionality of the Federal Interpleader Act in State Farm Fire & Cas. Co. v. Tashire, 386 U.S. 523, 530–31 (1967). The Court explained:

> In *Strawbridge v. Curtiss*, * * * this Court held that the diversity of citizenship statute required "complete diversity": where co-citizens appeared on both sides of a dispute, jurisdiction was lost. But Chief Justice Marshall there pur-

> ported to construe only "The words of the act of Congress," not the Constitution itself. And in a variety of contexts this Court and the lower courts have concluded that Article III poses no obstacle to the legislative extension of federal jurisdiction, founded on diversity, so long as any two adverse parties are not co-citizens. Accordingly, we conclude that the present case is properly in the federal courts.

4. *Strawbridge* governs cases brought under § 1332(a)(1) today. As made clear in *Tashire, Strawbridge* interprets merely the statutory, not the constitutional, grant of diversity of citizenship jurisdiction. But how can identical language in the Constitution ("between citizens of different states") and in the statute ("between citizens of different states") mean different things? Especially since some of the same people who drafted Article III also drafted the original statutory grant of diversity jurisdiction interpreted by Chief Justice Marshall, how likely is it that they intended to make the two mean different things?

5. It is important to remember that both the Constitution and the statute grant jurisdiction over cases involving diversity of citizenship. As we will see, citizenship is not necessarily the same as residence, and the terms should not be used interchangeably. Competent counsel will be careful to use only the term citizenship when speaking of diversity jurisdiction.

6. Until 2002, Congress had permitted jurisdiction based upon minimal diversity only once — in the Federal Interpleader Act, discussed in Note 3 above. Since 2002, it has done it twice. The Multiparty, Multiforum Trial Jurisdiction Act permits the invocation of minimal diversity in cases arising from accidents that cause at least 75 deaths. See 28 U.S.C. § 1369. And the Class Action Fairness Act expanded the availability of a federal forum for certain class actions by permitting invocation of minimal diversity, at least when the aggregate amount in controversy exceeds $5,000,000. See 28 U.S.C. § 1332(d). We will address the class action in Chapter 13.

c. Determining Citizenship of Individuals

Mas v. Perry

489 F.2d 1396 (5th Cir. 1974)

AINSWORTH, CIRCUIT JUDGE.

This case presents questions pertaining to federal diversity jurisdiction under 28 U.S.C. § 1332, which, pursuant to article III, section II of the Constitution, provides for original jurisdiction in federal district courts of all civil actions that are between, *inter alia*, citizens of different States or citizens of a State and citizens of foreign states and in which the amount in controversy is more than $10,000. [Note: The statute now requires an amount in excess of $75,000.]

Appellees Jean Paul Mas, a citizen of France, and Judy Mas were married at her home in Jackson, Mississippi. Prior to their marriage, Mr. and Mrs. Mas were graduate assistants, pursuing coursework as well as performing teaching duties, for approximately nine months and one year, respectively, at Louisiana State University in Baton

Rouge, Louisiana. Shortly after their marriage, they returned to Baton Rouge to resume their duties as graduate assistants at LSU. They remained in Baton Rouge for approximately two more years, after which they moved to Park Ridge, Illinois. At the time of the trial in this case, it was their intention to return to Baton Rouge while Mr. Mas finished his studies for the degree of Doctor of Philosophy. Mr. and Mrs. Mas were undecided as to where they would reside after that.

Upon their return to Baton Rouge after their marriage, appellees rented an apartment from appellant Oliver H. Perry, a citizen of Louisiana. This appeal arises from a final judgment entered on a jury verdict awarding $5,000 to Mr. Mas and $15,000 to Mrs. Mas for damages incurred by them as a result of the discovery that their bedroom and bathroom contained "two-way" mirrors and that they had been watched through them by the appellant during three of the first four months of their marriage.

At the close of the appellees' case at trial, appellant made an oral motion to dismiss for lack of jurisdiction. The motion was denied by the district court. Before this Court, appellant challenges the final judgment below solely on jurisdictional grounds, contending that appellees failed to prove diversity of citizenship among the parties and that the requisite jurisdictional amount is lacking with respect to Mr. Mas. Finding no merit to these contentions, we affirm. Under section 1332(a)(2), the federal judicial power extends to the claim of Mr. Mas, a citizen of France, against the appellant, a citizen of Louisiana. Since we conclude that Mrs. Mas is a citizen of Mississippi for diversity purposes, the district court also properly had jurisdiction under section 1332(a)(1) of her claim.

It has long been the general rule that complete diversity of parties is required in order that diversity jurisdiction obtain; that is, no party on one side may be a citizen of the same State as any party on the other side. *Strawbridge v. Curtiss*. This determination of one's State citizenship for diversity purposes is controlled by federal law, not by the law of any State. As is the case in other areas of federal jurisdiction, the diverse citizenship among adverse parties must be present at the time the complaint is filed. Jurisdiction is unaffected by subsequent changes in the citizenship of the parties. The burden of pleading the diverse citizenship is upon the party invoking federal jurisdiction, and if the diversity jurisdiction is properly challenged, that party also bears the burden of proof.

To be a citizen of a State within the meaning of section 1332, a natural person must be both a citizen of the United States, see Sun Printing & Publishing Association v. Edwards, 194 U.S. 377, 383 (1904); U.S. CONST. Amend. XIV, § 1, and a domiciliary of that State. For diversity purposes, citizenship means domicile; mere residence in the State is not sufficient.

A person's domicile is the place of "his true, fixed, and permanent home and principal establishment, and to which he has the intention of returning whenever he is absent therefrom...." A change of domicile may be effected only by a combination of two elements: (a) taking up residence in a different domicile with (b) the intention to remain there.

It is clear that at the time of her marriage, Mrs. Mas was a domiciliary of the State of Mississippi. While it is generally the case that the domicile of the wife—and, consequently, her State citizenship for purposes of diversity jurisdiction—is deemed to be that of her husband, we find no precedent for extending this concept to the situation here, in which the husband is a citizen of a foreign state but resides in the United States. Indeed, such a fiction would work absurd results on the facts before us. If Mr. Mas were considered a domiciliary of France—as he would be since he had lived in Louisiana as a student-teaching assistant prior to filing this suit,—then Mrs. Mas would also be deemed a domiciliary, and thus, fictionally at least, a citizen of France. She would not be a citizen of any State and could not sue in a federal court on that basis; nor could she invoke the alienage jurisdiction to bring her claim in federal court, since she is not an alien. On the other hand, if Mrs. Mas's domicile were Louisiana, she would become a Louisiana citizen for diversity purposes and could not bring suit with her husband against appellant, also a Louisiana citizen, on the basis of diversity jurisdiction. These are curious results under a rule arising from the theoretical identity of person and interest of the married couple.

An American woman is not deemed to have lost her United States citizenship solely by reason of her marriage to an alien. 8 U.S.C. § 1489. Similarly, we conclude that for diversity purposes a woman does not have her domicile or State citizenship changed solely by reason of her marriage to an alien.

Mrs. Mas's Mississippi domicile was disturbed neither by her year in Louisiana prior to her marriage nor as a result of the time she and her husband spent at LSU after their marriage, since for both periods she was a graduate assistant at LSU. Though she testified that after her marriage she had no intention of returning to her parents' home in Mississippi, Mrs. Mas did not effect a change of domicile since she and Mr. Mas were in Louisiana only as students and lacked the requisite intention to remain there. Until she acquires a new domicile, she remains a domiciliary, and thus a citizen, of Mississippi.[2]

Appellant also contends that Mr. Mas's claim should have been dismissed for failure to establish the requisite jurisdictional amount for diversity cases of more than $10,000. In their complaint Mr. and Mrs. Mas alleged that they had each been damaged in the amount of $100,000. As we have noted, Mr. Mas ultimately recovered $5,000.

It is well settled that the amount in controversy is determined by the amount claimed by the plaintiff in good faith. Federal jurisdiction is not lost because a judgment of less than the jurisdictional amount is awarded. That Mr. Mas recovered only $5,000 is, therefore, not compelling. As the Supreme Court stated in St. Paul Mercury Indemnity Co. v. Red Cab Co., 303 U.S. 283, 288–290 [1938]:

---

2. The original complaint in this case was filed within several days of Mr. and Mrs. Mas's realization that they had been watched through the mirrors, quite some time before they moved to Park Ridge, Illinois. Because the district court's jurisdiction is not affected by actions of the parties subsequent to the commencement of the suit, the testimony concerning Mr. and Mrs. Mas's moves after that time is not determinative of the issue of diverse citizenship, though it is of interest insofar as it supports their lack of intent to remain permanently in Louisiana.

> [T]he sum claimed by the plaintiff controls if the claim is apparently made in good faith. It must appear to a legal certainty that the claim is really for less than the jurisdictional amount to justify dismissal. The inability of the plaintiff to recover an amount adequate to give the court jurisdiction does not show his bad faith or oust the jurisdiction....
>
> ... His good faith in choosing the federal forum is open to challenge not only by resort to the face of his complaint, but by the facts disclosed at trial, and if from either source it is clear that his claim never could have amounted to the sum necessary to give jurisdiction there is no injustice in dismissing the suit.

Having heard the evidence presented at the trial, the district court concluded that the appellees properly met the requirements of section 1332 with respect to jurisdictional amount. Upon examination of the record in this case, we are also satisfied that the requisite amount was in controversy.

Thus the power of the federal district court to entertain the claims of appellees in this case stands on two separate legs of diversity jurisdiction: a claim by an alien against a State citizen; and an action between citizens of different States. We also note, however, the propriety of having the federal district court entertain a spouse's action against a defendant, where the district court already has jurisdiction over a claim, arising from the same transaction, by the other spouse against the same defendant. In the case before us, such a result is particularly desirable. The claims of Mr. and Mrs. Mas arise from the same operative facts, and there was almost complete interdependence between their claims with respect to the proof required and the issues raised at trial. Thus, since the district court had jurisdiction of Mr. Mas's action, sound judicial administration militates strongly in favor of federal jurisdiction of Mrs. Mas's claim.

Affirmed.

Notes and Questions

1. The anachronistic notion that a married woman takes the domicile of her husband has eroded today. Regarding the court's treatment of why the monetary amount of Mr. Mas' judgment did not affect jurisdiction, see 28 U.S.C. § 1332(b), which we will discuss in subsection g below.

2. It is clear from *Mas* that a person can have only one domicile at a time, and thus can be a citizen of only one state at a time. Everyone is ascribed a domicile at birth, which is usually based upon the domicile of her parents. She retains that domicile until she affirmatively changes it. *Mas* sets forth a standard statement of how one changes her domicile: by taking up residence in another state with the intent to make that her "true, fixed, and permanent home and principal establishment." Note, then, that there are two requirements for changing domicile: the physical requirement of moving to the new state and the mental requirement of intending to make the new state one's fixed home. While Mrs. Mas resided in Louisiana and Illinois, she

never intended to make either state her domicile. Thus, she remained a domiciliary, and therefore a citizen, of Mississippi.

The question of whether one forms the intent to establish a new domicile raises potentially difficult problems of proof. Sometimes, people move to a different state without the intent to stay. At some point, however, they may form the subjective intent to make that state their domicile. Identifying that point can be difficult, and courts look to a variety of factors in assessing this intent, including voter registration, purchase of a house, payment of taxes and of in-state college tuition. See 15 Moore's Federal Practice § 102.36[1].

Consider, for example, Galva Foundry Co. v. Heiden, 924 F.2d 729 (7th Cir. 1991). There, Heiden had been a life-long domiciliary of Illinois, although he had for many years owned a vacation home in Florida. After retiring from his job in Illinois, he spent several months a year in Florida, several months traveling, and the rest of his time at his home in Illinois. Following a sale of assets on which he would have owed substantial taxes in Illinois, Heiden registered to vote in Florida, obtained a Florida driver's license, listed his Florida address as his permanent address on his federal and Illinois tax returns, and stated in an application for a Florida tax exemption that he had become a permanent resident of Florida. (Florida does not impose income taxes on Florida citizens.) The court found that Heiden remained an Illinois domiciliary. "Heiden intended no change in the manner or style of his life, the center of gravity of which was and remains in Peoria, but only a change in his tax rate." The court further explained:

> Unfortunately, in this age of second homes and speedy transportation, picking out a single state to be an individual's domicile can be a difficult, even a rather arbitrary, undertaking. Domicile is not a thing, like a rabbit or a carrot, but a legal conclusion, though treated as a factual determination for purposes of demarcating the scope of appellate review. And in drawing legal conclusions it is always helpful to have in mind the purpose for which the conclusion is being drawn. The purpose here is to determine whether a suit can be maintained under diversity jurisdiction, a jurisdiction whose main contemporary rationale is to protect nonresidents from the possible prejudice that they might encounter in local courts. This argues for finding the defendant, Mr. Heiden, to be a domiciliary of the same state as the plaintiff, Galva—that is, Illinois. Heiden is a long-time resident of Illinois and unlikely therefore to encounter hostility in its state courts.

Id. at 730.

3. Apply these principles of domicile to the following hypotheticals.

(a) Pat, a citizen of New York, forms the intent to change her domicile to California, and sets out to drive there to establish her home. On the way, in Nevada, she is involved in an auto wreck with Dan, a citizen of California. She suffers damages of more than $75,000, and is hospitalized in Nevada. At this point, can she invoke diversity of citizenship jurisdiction in a case against Dan? Why?

(b) Paul, a citizen of Texas, properly institutes a diversity of citizenship action against Donna, a citizen of Oklahoma. After filing, but before the case proceeds to trial, Paul becomes a citizen of Oklahoma. Donna then moves to dismiss the case for lack of subject matter jurisdiction. Based upon the discussion in *Mas,* what result? If you represented Paul and knew that he planned to change his domicile from Texas to Oklahoma, would it be proper for you to recommend that he delay doing so until after filing the case?

(c) Pam, a citizen of the United States domiciled in New York, sues Doris, a citizen of the United States domiciled in New Zealand, asserting a state law claim for $100,000. Do you see why there is neither diversity nor alienage jurisdiction? Explain why an American citizen domiciled abroad cannot sue or be sued under diversity or alienage jurisdiction. Unless there is some other basis of federal jurisdiction, such as federal question, cases involving such persons must be filed in a state court.

(d) Patty, a citizen of the United States domiciled in the District of Columbia, sues Don, a citizen of the United States domiciled in California, asserting a state law claim for $100,000. Review 28 U.S.C. § 1332(e). The District of Columbia is not a state. Neither are American territories and possessions such as Puerto Rico and Guam. So how can Patty be considered a citizen of a state, as required in both § 1332(a)(1) and Article III, Section 2 of the Constitution? The notion that she can seems especially troublesome in view of a Supreme Court case, decided before enactment of § 1332(e), holding that a citizen of the District of Columbia is not a citizen of a state for diversity purposes. Hepburn & Dundas v. Ellzey, 6 U.S. 445, 453 (1805).

Nonetheless, the Supreme Court upheld the predecessor of § 1332(e) in National Mutual Insurance Co. v. Tidewater Transfer Co., 337 U.S. 582 (1949). This decision is odd, because although five Justices concluded that the statute was constitutional, they did so in two separate opinions, neither of which commanded a majority. Thus, we know that section 1332(e) is constitutional, but we have no majority rationale for the holding!

4. In 1990, Congress amended § 1332(a) to provide that an alien admitted to the United States for permanent residence (often referred to as a "green card" alien) would be deemed a citizen of the state in which she is domiciled. The provision was always problematic, because the Supreme Court had long held that one could be a citizen of a state only if she were a citizen of the United States. Sun Printing & Publishing Association v. Edwards, 194 U.S. 377, 383 (1904). Moreover, courts interpreted the provision inconsistently. Fortunately, Congress repealed the clause in 2011. In its place, Congress added the last phrase of § 1332(a)(2). It removes subject matter jurisdiction over cases between a citizen of a state, on the one hand, and a permanent resident alien who is domiciled in the same state.

Accordingly, a case between a citizen of California and a citizen of Spain admitted for permanent residence to the United States and domiciled in California will not invoke jurisdiction under § 1332. On the other hand, a case between a citizen of California and a citizen of Spain who is *not* admitted for permanent resident status in the United States will invoke alienage.

5. Congress occasionally oversteps its constitutional authority and confers jurisdiction beyond that authorized by Article III. For example, Congress originally authorized federal jurisdiction over cases in which "an alien is a party." In Hodgson v. Bowerbank, 9 U.S. 303 (1809), the Supreme Court held this statute unconstitutional as applied to a case in which alienage was the sole basis for jurisdiction and in which the plaintiff was an alien and there was no allegation concerning the citizenship of the defendants. Do you see why such a case exceeds the scope of Article III? Shortly after the decision in *Hodgson*, Congress changed the statute providing for "alienage" jurisdiction. Notice how the statutory provision reads today. See 28 U.S.C. § 1332(a)(2).

6. Suppose the court in *Mas* found that Mrs. Mas was a citizen of Louisiana. Would the court have had to dismiss the entire case, or could it simply have dismissed Mrs. Mas from the action? Federal Rule 21 gives district courts the authority to dismiss non-diverse parties from the suit (so long as they are not "indispensable"). Even though Rule 21 applies to district courts, and not to courts of appeals, the Supreme Court has held that the appellate courts also have this authority. Newman-Green, Inc. v. Alfonzo-Larrain, 490 U.S. 826, 832 (1989). Under this view, on such facts, the Fifth Circuit could have dismissed Mrs. Mas' claim, but allowed Mr. Mas' judgment to stand.

But the Supreme Court may have called this long-standing practice into question. In Exxon Mobil Corp. v. Allapattah Services, 545 U.S. 546, 554–55 (2005), the Court suggested that the case must be dismissed. It said:

> [W]e have consistently interpreted § 1332 as requiring complete diversity: In a case with multiple plaintiffs and multiple defendants, the presence in the action of a single plaintiff from the same State as a single defendant deprives the district court of original diversity jurisdiction over the entire action. * * * Incomplete diversity destroys original jurisdiction with respect to all claims * * *.

Despite this language, courts continue to use Rule 21 to drop "jurisdictional spoilers" and retain the case. They employ a "fiction that Rule 21 relates back to the date of the complaint. This way, the court may proceed as if the nondiverse parties were never part of the case. With those parties effectively scrubbed from the complaint, they are not present to contaminate the other claims." In re Lorazepam & Clorazepate Antitrust Litig., 631 F.3d 537, 542 (D.C. Cir. 2011). This can only be done, however, if the parties dropped are not "indispensable" under Rule 19. We discuss indispensable parties in Chapter 12, § F.2.

7. The plaintiff is responsible for alleging the facts establishing diversity of citizenship jurisdiction. The court retains power to "realign" the parties according to its assessment of their true interests. Of course, realignment may affect the existence of diversity jurisdiction. See, e.g., Cleveland Housing Renewal Project v. Deutsche Bank Trust Co., 621 F.3d 554, 559–60 (6th Cir. 2010) (district court properly realigned parties, resulting in diversity of citizenship jurisdiction).

8. For purposes of subject matter jurisdiction, how should the courts treat a United States citizen who has dual citizenship with another country? Although there is some split among the cases, most courts will not allow the foreign citizenship of a dual citizen to create alienage jurisdiction where diversity would not exist. See Sadat v. Mertes, 615 F.2d 1176, 1187 (7th Cir. 1980). But see Aguirre v. Nagel, 270 F. Supp. 535 (E.D. Mich. 1967). In addition, some courts interpret the complete diversity requirement to mean that if a party has dual citizenship, the other side must be diverse from both of those citizenships. Thus, in Risk v. Kingdom of Norway, 707 F. Supp. 1159, 1162–64 (N.D. Cal. 1989), the plaintiffs were citizens of California and Norway and the defendants were citizens of Norway. The court held that there was no jurisdiction. But see Soghanalian v. Soghanalian, 693 F. Supp. 1091 (S.D. Fla. 1988) (plaintiff citizen of Lebanon, defendant citizen of New York and Lebanon; court finds alienage jurisdiction).

9. Reconsider the final paragraph of the opinion in *Mas*. The court is suggesting that since it would have had jurisdiction over a claim standing alone by Mr. Mas, it may be sensible to allow Mrs. Mas' claim to ride along. As you will see in Section 5 below and in Chapter 12, there are circumstances in which the court will allow what is known as "supplemental jurisdiction" over claims for which there would not be an independent basis for jurisdiction.

d. Determining Citizenship of Entities

Not all litigants are humans (or "natural persons"). Many cases involve claims by or against entities, including states, municipalities, and (our focus here) associations formed to conduct business. For diversity of citizenship purposes, federal courts must be able to ascribe citizenships to such associations. In an upper-division course on business structures, you will study various business forms. For present purposes, we need to understand that businesses fall into two generic categories: corporate and non-corporate. Congress has defined the citizenship of corporations for diversity of citizenship purposes, but has not legislated regarding the citizenship of non-corporate entities (such as labor unions, limited liability companies, insurance associations, joint ventures, and partnerships (including many law firms)).

i. Corporations

The law has always considered the corporation to have "entity" status, meaning that the corporation is seen as a thing unto itself, separate from the people who own it and the people who run it. As a result, if a corporation commits a tort, breaches a contract, or incurs a debt, the corporation itself (not the people who made the corporate decisions) is liable. This is the principle of "limited liability"—someone investing in a corporation is (generally) not liable for what the corporation does. Other consequences also flow from entity status, including the fact that the corporation itself must pay taxes on its income. A corporation can be formed only by strict adherence to the requirements of a state's corporation law (each state has such a law). Generally, formation requires the filing of papers with the state and the recognition by a state official that the papers are complete and correct. Congress has addressed the citizenship of these entities at 28 U.S.C. § 1332(c)(1). Read that provision, focusing on the phrase before the first comma.

Randazzo v. Eagle-Picher Industries, Inc.

117 F.R.D. 557 (E.D. Pa. 1987)

Lord, Senior District Judge.

This is an asbestos case. The complaint incorporates by reference the master long form complaint filed in re Asbestos Litigation, No. 86-0457. In a written order dismissing the complaint I pointed out that the complaint failed to allege either the state of incorporation or the principal place of business of defendant Bevco Industries or the principal place of business of defendant C.E. Refractories. The complaint therefore failed to show complete diversity and was jurisdictionally deficient. Plaintiff was granted ten days to file an amended complaint.

Plaintiff's counsel, apparently laboring under the impression that I am not dealing with a full deck and that my knowledge of diversity requirements is about equal to that of a low-grade moron, chose to disregard the directional signals posted in my memorandum. Counsel brazenly, discourteously, defiantly, arrogantly, insultingly and under the circumstances rather obtusely threw back into my face the very allegations I had held insufficient by reiterating and incorporating those same crippled paragraphs. The so-called "amended complaint" itself cheekily informs me that these paragraphs allege the states of incorporation or (emphasis added) principal places of business of the defendant corporations. Of course, any law school student knows that both the state of incorporation and principal place of business must be diverse, but I suppose I can hardly expect any more from counsel whose familiarity with Title 28 U.S.C. § 1332 could be no more than a friendly wave from a distance visible only through a powerful telescope.

In view of counsel's demonstrated ignorance of diversity requirements, I think it may be profitable to set forth the rules of the game. Every plaintiff bears the burden of alleging in his pleading "a short and plain statement of the grounds upon which the court's jurisdiction depends." Fed. R. Civ. Pro. 8(a)(1). It is well established that "a plaintiff suing in a federal court must show in his pleading, affirmatively and distinctly, the existence of whatever is essential to federal jurisdiction; and if he does not do so, the court, on having the defect called to its attention or on discovering the same, *must* dismiss the case, unless the defect be corrected by amendment." For purposes of the diversity statute, "a corporation shall be deemed a citizen of any state by which it has been incorporated and of the State where it has its principal place of business." 28 U.S.C. § 1332(c) [now § 1332(c)(1)]. Courts have consistently interpreted § 1332(c)[1] to mean exactly what it says: a party must allege a corporation's state of incorporation and principal place of business. The requirements of § 1332 and Rule 8 "are straightforward and the law demands strict adherence to them."

The master complaint alleges that defendant C.E. Refractories "is a corporation organized and existing under the laws of the State of Delaware with a registered office situate [sic] at 123 S. Broad Street, Philadelphia, Pennsylvania...." The allegation that defendant has a "registered office" in Pennsylvania is not equivalent to an allegation that defendant's principal place of business is in Pennsylvania. Because the complaint fails to properly allege the principal place of business, I have no jurisdiction over this defendant and the complaint will be dismissed as to it.

Similarly, the master complaint alleges that defendant Bevco Industries "is a corporation duly organized to do business within the Commonwealth of Pennsylvania ... and is domiciled in the Commonwealth of Pennsylvania." The reference to domicile may mean that defendant is incorporated in Pennsylvania but I have no way of knowing that. Again, plaintiff has simply failed to allege the principal place of business of defendant or its state of incorporation. Section 1332 makes clear that corporations have dual citizenship, and plaintiff "does not have a choice of alleging only one of the corporation's citizenships." Therefore, the complaint will be dismissed as to this defendant.

It is important to state why I take the apparently harsh step of dismissal with prejudice. Adequately pleading the jurisdictional requirements is not an exercise in mindless formalism. "Subsection [(c)(1)] of § 1332 was adopted in 1958 by Congress as part of legislation designed to reduce the caseload of the Federal courts." It is axiomatic that "Federal courts are not courts of general jurisdiction; they have only the power that is authorized by Article III of the Constitution and the statutes enacted by Congress pursuant thereto." * * * To rebut the presumption that a Federal court lacks jurisdiction over a particular case the facts that establish jurisdiction must be affirmatively alleged. These jurisdictional principles are fundamental. That is why I have an obligation to notice want of jurisdiction *mea sponte*. See Fed. R. Civ. Pro. 12(h)(3). In the context of our federal system, to consider a case not properly within the jurisdiction of the Federal courts is not "simply wrong but indeed an unconstitutional invasion of the powers reserved to the states."

Plaintiff's counsel was given ample opportunity to amend the complaint. The language of § 1332 could not be more clear. It would have taken counsel only moments to set forth the allegations that the diversity statute so plainly requires. I fail to understand why, after having the deficiencies of the complaint explicitly identified in a written order, counsel insisted on resubmitting the exact same complaint. I understand that the asbestos bar has a heavy caseload, and applaud steps, such as the master complaint, taken to ease the administrative burden asbestos cases place upon both bench and bar. However, a heavy caseload can neither excuse faulty pleadings nor justify the retention of jurisdiction beyond that permitted by statute.

An appropriate order follows.

Notes and Questions

1. Why were allegations of a corporation's "registered office" and "domicile" inadequate?

2. The court initially dismissed the complaint in *Randazzo* with "leave" (permission) to amend. That allowed the plaintiff to file a new complaint, hopefully fixing the problems identified by the court, within a set period. Plaintiffs' lawyer filed an amended complaint, but did not fix the jurisdictional errors he had made before. In the opinion we just read, the court dismissed the case and did not grant leave to amend. This means the case is dismissed and cannot be refiled in federal court.

Courts sometimes grant a motion to dismiss "without prejudice." Then, the case is not retained on the docket; it is dismissed and judgment is entered for the defendant. Under Rule 41(b), such a dismissal does not operate as "an adjudication on the merits." This means that the plaintiff may file a new case on the same claim. In contrast, if a court dismisses a case "with prejudice," judgment is entered for the defendant and the plaintiff is not permitted to file a new case on that claim; the claim is extinguished. Though the judge in *Randazzo* indicated that he was dismissing "with prejudice," in reality the dismissal was "without leave to amend." Why? Because the plaintiff will be able to file the claim in state court; a dismissal for lack of subject matter jurisdiction in federal court would not extinguish the claim.

3. Do we know that the plaintiff could not establish diversity jurisdiction in *Randazzo*? If not, is it fair to let the errors of counsel rob the plaintiff of a federal forum? On the other hand, how many chances should counsel need to make jurisdictional allegations correctly?

4. Judges can get angry. Given the clarity of the law in this area, judges have a right to expect counsel to allege the citizenship of parties competently. Unfortunately, however, as *Randazzo* shows, some lawyers fail to rise to the task. In Guaranty National Title Co. v. J.E.G. Associates, 101 F.3d 57, 59 (7th Cir. 1996), the plaintiff failed to allege citizenship of the litigants properly, and the case was dismissed. The Seventh Circuit agreed that dismissal was warranted, and refused to remand to allow further jurisdictional allegations. The district court had given the plaintiff ample opportunity to make the appropriate allegations; plaintiff's failure to do so created the inference that there was no subject matter jurisdiction. Emphatically, the court stated that it had no "obligation to lead counsel through a jurisdictional paint-by-numbers scheme."

Congress passed § 1332(c)(1) in 1958. Before that, federal courts treated corporations as citizens of the state(s) in which they were incorporated. Covington Drawbridge Co. v. Shepherd, 61 U.S. 227, 233 (1858) (action by or against corporation is by or against its shareholders, who are presumed to be citizens of the state(s) of incorporation). But corporations can be formed in states in which they do little or no business. In fact, most of the Fortune 500 companies are incorporated in Delaware (to take advantage of what historically has been thought pro-management business law). Few of these have their primary activity in Delaware. Because diversity of citizenship jurisdiction is intended to allow access to federal court to avoid fear of local bias, the state-of-incorporation definition of citizenship is under-inclusive. A Delaware corporation that only does business in California, in theory, need not fear local bias of California state courts. It should be deemed a citizen of California.

Section 1332(c)(1) reflected that concern. It deems a corporation to be a citizen of "any" state where incorporated and *also* a citizen of "the" state in which it has its principal place of business. The word "the" implies (as the courts have concluded) that a corporation can only have one principal place of business. The problem is that the statute gives no clue what that place is. Lower federal courts wrestled with the issue for decades. Some emphasized the place where business decisions are made—the "nerve" center. Some emphasized the place where the company engaged in more activity than anywhere else—the "muscle" center. Most used a combination of the two under the "total activities" test. After 52 years of uncertainty, the Supreme Court finally addressed the statutory term in the following case.

Hertz Corporation v. Friend

130 S. Ct. 1181, 175 L. Ed. 2d 1029 (2010)

JUSTICE BREYER delivered the opinion of the Court.

The federal diversity jurisdiction statute provides that "a corporation shall be deemed to be a citizen of any State by which it has been incorporated *and of the State where it has its principal place of business.*" 28 U.S.C. § 1332(c)(1) (emphasis added). [Note: the statute has been amended since this case was decided to provide that a corporation is deemed a citizen of "every State" where incorporated and of "the State" in which it has its principal place of business. The amendment does not affect the reasoning or outcome of this case.] We seek here to resolve different interpretations that the Circuits have given this phrase. In doing so, we place primary weight upon the need for judicial administration of a jurisdictional statute to remain as simple as possible. And we conclude that the phrase "principal place of business" refers to the place where the corporation's high level officers direct, control, and coordinate the corporation's activities. Lower federal courts have often metaphorically called that place the corporation's "nerve center." We believe that the "nerve center" will typically be found at a corporation's headquarters.

I

[Two employees of the Hertz Corporation—Friend and Nhieu—sued Hertz for alleged violation of California's wage and hour laws. They sought to bring a class action on behalf of other Californians who had allegedly suffered the same harm. Friend and Nhieu were citizens of California. The issue is whether Hertz's principal place of business was in California. If it were, there would be no diversity jurisdiction.

[It may seem odd, but in this case the plaintiffs are *not* trying to invoke diversity. They wanted to sue in state court. Under the doctrine of "removal jurisdiction"—which we will address in § C.6 of this Chapter—a defendant sued in state court may "remove" the case to federal court. It may do so, though, only if the case invokes federal subject matter jurisdiction. Hertz did not want to litigate in state court and removed it to federal court. This procedural posture does not change the diversity-of-citizenship analysis. As you read the case, however, remember that it is the defendant (not the plaintiff) who is arguing in favor of diversity. Specifically, Hertz is arguing that its principal place of business is not in California.]

* * * Hertz claimed that the plaintiffs and the defendant were citizens of different States. Hence, the federal court possessed diversity-of-citizenship jurisdiction. Friend and Nhieu, however, claimed that the Hertz Corporation was a California citizen, like themselves, and that, hence, diversity jurisdiction was lacking.

To support its position, Hertz submitted a declaration by an employee relations manager that sought to show that Hertz's "principal place of business" was in New Jersey, not in California. The declaration stated, among other things, that Hertz operated facilities in 44 States; and that California—which had about 12% of the Nation's population—accounted for 273 of Hertz's 1,606 car rental locations; about 2,300 of its 11,230 full-time employees; about $811 million of its $4.371 billion in annual revenue; and about 3.8 million of its approximately 21 million annual transactions, *i.e.*, rentals. The declaration also stated that the "leadership of Hertz and its domestic subsidiaries" is located at Hertz's "corporate headquarters" in Park Ridge, New Jersey; that its "core executive and administrative functions ... are carried out" there and "to a lesser extent" in Oklahoma City, Oklahoma; and that its "major administrative operations ... are found" at those two locations.

The District Court of the Northern District of California accepted Hertz's statement of the facts as undisputed. But it concluded that, given those facts, Hertz was a citizen of California. In reaching this conclusion, the court applied Ninth Circuit precedent, which instructs courts to identify a corporation's "principal place of business" by first determining the amount of a corporation's business activity State by State. If the amount of activity is "significantly larger" or "substantially predominates" in one State, then that State is the corporation's "principal place of business." If there is no such State, then the "principal place of business" is the corporation's "'nerve center,'" *i.e.*, the place where "'the majority of its executive and administrative functions are performed.'"

Applying this test, the District Court found that the "plurality of each of the relevant business activities" was in California, and that "the differential between the amount of those activities" in California and the amount in "the next closest state" was "significant." Hence, Hertz's "principal place of business" was California, and diversity jurisdiction was thus lacking. * * *

* * * The Ninth Circuit affirmed in a brief memorandum opinion. Hertz filed a petition for certiorari. And, in light of differences among the Circuits in the application of the test for corporate citizenship, we granted the writ. Compare Tosco Corp. [v. Communities for a Better Environment, 236 F.3d 495,] 500–502 [(CA9 2001)], and Capitol Indemnity Corp. v. Russellville Steel Co., 367 F.3d 831, 836 (CA8 2004) (applying "total activity" test and looking at "all corporate activities"), with Wisconsin Knife Works [v. National Metal Crafters, 781 F.2d 1280,] 1282 [(CA7 1986)] (applying "nerve center" test).

II

[The Court here concluded that the lower court orders were appealable.]

III

* * *

Congress first authorized federal courts to exercise diversity jurisdiction in 1789 when, in the First Judiciary Act, Congress granted federal courts authority to hear suits "between a citizen of the State where the suit is brought, and a citizen of another State." § 11, 1 Stat. 78. The statute said nothing about corporations. In 1809, Chief Justice Marshall, writing for a unanimous Court, described a corporation as an "invisible, intangible, and artificial being" which was "certainly not a citizen." Bank of United States v. Deveaux, 9 U.S. 61 (1809). But the Court held that a corporation could invoke the federal courts' diversity jurisdiction based on a pleading that the corporation's shareholders were all citizens of a different State from the defendants, as "the term citizen ought to be understood as it is used in the constitution, and as it is used in other laws. That is, to describe the real persons who come into court, in this case, under their corporate name." *Id.*, at 91–92.

In Louisville, C. & C. R. Co. v. Letson, 43 U.S. 497 (1844), the Court modified this initial approach. It held that a corporation was to be deemed an artificial person of the State by which it had been created, and its citizenship for jurisdictional purposes determined accordingly. *Id.*, at 558–559. Ten years later, the Court in Marshall v. Baltimore & Ohio R. Co., 57 U.S. 314 (1854), held that the reason a corporation was a citizen of its State of incorporation was that, for the limited purpose of determining corporate citizenship, courts could conclusively (and artificially) presume that a corporation's *shareholders* were citizens of the State of incorporation. *Id.*, at 327–328. And it reaffirmed *Letson.* Whatever the rationale, the practical upshot was that, for diversity purposes, the federal courts considered a corporation to be a citizen of the State of its incorporation.

In 1928 this Court made clear that the "state of incorporation" rule was virtually absolute. * * *

At the same time as federal dockets increased in size, many judges began to believe those dockets contained too many diversity cases. A committee of the Judicial Conference of the United States studied the matter. * * *

* * * The committee recommended * * * a statutory amendment that would make a corporation a citizen both of the State of its incorporation and any State from which it received more than half of its gross income. * * *

During the spring and summer of 1951 committee members circulated their report and attended circuit conferences at which federal judges discussed the report's recommendations. Reflecting those criticisms, the committee filed a new report in September, in which it revised its corporate citizenship recommendation. It now proposed that "a corporation shall be deemed a citizen of the state of its original creation … [and] shall also be deemed a citizen of a state where it has its principal place of business." * * * The committee wrote that this new language would provide a "simpler and more practical formula" than the "gross income" test. It added that the language "ha[d] a precedent in the jurisdictional provisions of the Bankruptcy Act."

In mid-1957 the committee presented its reports to the House of Representatives Committee on the Judiciary. [During committee hearings, one witness, Judge Maris, discussed "principal place of business" as it had been interpreted in bankruptcy cases:]

> "* * * I think the courts have generally taken the view that where a corporation's interests are rather widespread, the principal place of business is an actual rather than a theoretical or legal one. It is the actual place where its business operations are coordinated, directed, and carried out, which would ordinarily be the place where its officers carry on its day-to-day business, where its accounts are kept, where its payments are made, and not necessarily a State in which it may have a plant, if it is a big corporation, or something of that sort.
>
> "But that has been pretty well worked out in the bankruptcy cases, and that law would all be available, you see, to be applied here without having to go over it again from the beginning."

* * * Subsequently, in 1958, Congress both codified the courts' traditional place of incorporation test and also enacted into law a slightly modified version of the Conference Committee's proposed "principal place of business" language. A corporation was to "be deemed a citizen of any State by which it has been incorporated and of the State where it has its principal place of business."

IV

The phrase "principal place of business" has proved more difficult to apply than its originators likely expected. Decisions under the Bankruptcy Act did not provide the firm guidance for which Judge Maris had hoped because courts interpreting bankruptcy law did not agree about how to determine a corporation's "principal place of business." * * *

After Congress' amendment, courts were similarly uncertain as to where to look to determine a corporation's "principal place of business" for diversity purposes. If a corporation's headquarters and executive offices were in the same State in which it did most of its business, the test seemed straightforward. The "principal place of business" was located in that State. See, e.g., Long v. Silver, 248 F.3d 309, 314–315 (CA4 2001); Pinnacle Consultants, Ltd. v. Leucadia Nat. Corp., 101 F.3d 900, 906–907 (CA2 1996).

But suppose those corporate headquarters, including executive offices, are in one State, while the corporation's plants or other centers of business activity are located in other States? In 1959 a distinguished federal district judge, Edward Weinfeld, relied on the Second Circuit's interpretation of the Bankruptcy Act to answer this question in part:

> "Where a corporation is engaged in far-flung and varied activities which are carried on in different states, its principal place of business is the nerve center

> from which it radiates out to its constituent parts and from which its officers direct, control and coordinate all activities without regard to locale, in the furtherance of the corporate objective. The test applied by our Court of Appeals, is that place where the corporation has an 'office from which its business was directed and controlled'—the place where 'all of its business was under the supreme direction and control of its officers.'" Scot Typewriter Co. [v. Underwood Corp., 170 F. Supp. 862,] 865 [(SDNY 1959)].

Numerous Circuits have since followed this rule, applying the "nerve center" test for corporations with "far-flung" business activities. * * *

Scot's analysis, however, did not go far enough. For it did not answer what courts should do when the operations of the corporation are not "far-flung" but rather limited to only a few States. When faced with this question, various courts have focused more heavily on where a corporation's actual business activities are located.

Perhaps because corporations come in many different forms, involve many different kinds of business activities, and locate offices and plants for different reasons in different ways in different regions, a general "business activities" approach has proved unusually difficult to apply. Courts must decide which factors are more important than others: for example, plant location, sales or servicing centers, transactions, payrolls, or revenue generation.

The number of factors grew as courts explicitly combined aspects of the "nerve center" and "business activity" tests to look to a corporation's "total activities," sometimes to try to determine what treatises have described as the corporation's "center of gravity." A major treatise confirms this growing complexity, listing Circuit by Circuit, cases that highlight different factors or emphasize similar factors differently, and reporting that the "federal courts of appeals have employed various tests"—tests which "tend to overlap" and which are sometimes described in "language" that "is imprecise." 15 Moore's § 102.54[2], at 102-112. See also id., §§ 102.54[2], [13], at 102-112 to 102-122 (describing, in 14 pages, major tests as looking to the "nerve center," "locus of operations," or "center of corporate activities"). * * *

This complexity may reflect an unmediated judicial effort to apply the statutory phrase "principal place of business" in light of the general purpose of diversity jurisdiction, *i.e.*, an effort to find the State where a corporation is least likely to suffer out-of-state prejudice when it is sued in a local court, Pease v. Peck, 59 U.S. 595 (1856). But, if so, that task seems doomed to failure. After all, the relevant purposive concern—prejudice against an out-of-state party—will often depend upon factors that courts cannot easily measure, for example, a corporation's image, its history, and its advertising, while the factors that courts can more easily measure, for example, its office or plant location, its sales, its employment, or the nature of the goods or services it supplies, will sometimes bear no more than a distant relation to the likelihood of prejudice. At the same time, this approach is at war with administrative simplicity. And it has failed to achieve a nationally uniform interpretation of federal law, an unfortunate consequence in a federal legal system.

V

A

In an effort to find a single, more uniform interpretation of the statutory phrase, we have reviewed the Courts of Appeals' divergent and increasingly complex interpretations. * * * We conclude that "principal place of business" is best read as referring to the place where a corporation's officers direct, control, and coordinate the corporation's activities. It is the place that Courts of Appeals have called the corporation's "nerve center." And in practice it should normally be the place where the corporation maintains its headquarters—provided that the headquarters is the actual center of direction, control, and coordination, *i.e.*, the "nerve center," and not simply an office where the corporation holds its board meetings (for example, attended by directors and officers who have traveled there for the occasion).

Three sets of considerations, taken together, convince us that this approach, while imperfect, is superior to other possibilities. First, the statute's language supports the approach. The statute's text deems a corporation a citizen of the "State where it has its principal place of business." 28 U.S.C. § 1332(c)(1). The word "place" is in the singular, not the plural. The word "principal" requires us to pick out the "main, prominent" or "leading" place. 12 Oxford English Dictionary 495 (2d ed. 1989) (def. (A)(I)(2)). And the fact that the word "place" follows the words "State where" means that the "place" is a place *within* a State. It is not the State itself.

A corporation's "nerve center," usually its main headquarters, is a single place. The public often (though not always) considers it the corporation's main place of business. And it is a place within a State. By contrast, the application of a more general business activities test has led some courts, as in the present case, to look, not at a particular place within a State, but incorrectly at the State itself, measuring the total amount of business activities that the corporation conducts there and determining whether they are "significantly larger" than in the next-ranking State.

This approach invites greater litigation and can lead to strange results, as the Ninth Circuit has since recognized. Namely, if a "corporation may be deemed a citizen of California on th[e] basis" of "activities [that] roughly reflect California's larger population ... nearly every national retailer—no matter how far flung its operations—will be deemed a citizen of California for diversity purposes." Davis v. HSBC Bank Nev., N.A., 557 F.3d 1026, 1029–1030 ([9th Cir.] 2009). But why award or decline diversity jurisdiction on the basis of a State's population, whether measured directly, indirectly (say proportionately), or with modifications?

Second, administrative simplicity is a major virtue in a jurisdictional statute. Complex jurisdictional tests complicate a case, eating up time and money as the parties litigate, not the merits of their claims, but which court is the right court to decide those claims. Complex tests produce appeals and reversals, encourage gamesmanship, and, again, diminish the likelihood that results and settlements will reflect a claim's legal and factual merits. Judicial resources too are at stake. * * *

Simple jurisdictional rules also promote greater predictability. Predictability is valuable to corporations making business and investment decisions. Cf. First Nat. City Bank v. Banco Para el Comercio Exterior de Cuba, 462 U.S. 611, 621 (1983) (recognizing the "need for certainty and predictability of result while generally protecting the justified expectations of parties with interests in the corporation"). Predictability also benefits plaintiffs deciding whether to file suit in a state or federal court.

A "nerve center" approach, which ordinarily equates that "center" with a corporation's headquarters, is simple to apply *comparatively speaking*. The metaphor of a corporate "brain," while not precise, suggests a single location. By contrast, a corporation's general business activities more often lack a single principal place where they take place. That is to say, the corporation may have several plants, many sales locations, and employees located in many different places. If so, it will not be as easy to determine which of these different business locales is the "principal" or most important "place."

Third, the statute's legislative history, for those who accept it, offers a simplicity-related interpretive benchmark. The Judicial Conference provided an initial version of its proposal that suggested a numerical test. A corporation would be deemed a citizen of the State that accounted for more than half of its gross income. The Conference changed its mind in light of criticism that such a test would prove too complex and impractical to apply. That history suggests that the words "principal place of business" should be interpreted to be no more complex than the initial "half of gross income" test. A "nerve center" test offers such a possibility. A general business activities test does not.

B

We recognize that there may be no perfect test that satisfies all administrative and purposive criteria. We recognize as well that, under the "nerve center" test we adopt today, there will be hard cases. For example, in this era of telecommuting, some corporations may divide their command and coordinating functions among officers who work at several different locations, perhaps communicating over the Internet. That said, our test nonetheless points courts in a single direction, towards the center of overall direction, control, and coordination. Courts do not have to try to weigh corporate functions, assets, or revenues different in kind, one from the other. Our approach provides a sensible test that is relatively easier to apply, not a test that will, in all instances, automatically generate a result.

We also recognize that the use of a "nerve center" test may in some cases produce results that seem to cut against the basic rationale for 28 U.S.C. § 1332. For example, if the bulk of a company's business activities visible to the public take place in New Jersey, while its top officers direct those activities just across the river in New York, the "principal place of business" is New York. One could argue that members of the public in New Jersey would be *less* likely to be prejudiced against the corporation than persons in New York—yet the corporation will still be entitled to remove a New Jersey state case to federal court. And note too that the same corporation would be unable to remove a New York state case to federal court, despite the New York public's presumed prejudice against the corporation.

We understand that such seeming anomalies will arise. However, in view of the necessity of having a clearer rule, we must accept them. Accepting occasionally counterintuitive results is the price the legal system must pay to avoid overly complex jurisdictional administration while producing the benefits that accompany a more uniform legal system.

The burden of persuasion for establishing diversity jurisdiction, of course, remains on the party asserting it. When challenged on allegations of jurisdictional facts, the parties must support their allegations by competent proof. And when faced with such a challenge, we reject suggestions such as, for example, the one made by petitioner that the mere filing of a form like the Securities and Exchange Commission's Form 10-K listing a corporation's "principal executive offices" would, without more, be sufficient proof to establish a corporation's "nerve center." Such possibilities would readily permit jurisdictional manipulation, thereby subverting a major reason for the insertion of the "principal place of business" language in the diversity statute. Indeed, if the record reveals attempts at manipulation—for example, that the alleged "nerve center" is nothing more than a mail drop box, a bare office with a computer, or the location of an annual executive retreat—the courts should instead take as the "nerve center" the place of actual direction, control, and coordination, in the absence of such manipulation.

VI

Petitioner's unchallenged declaration suggests that Hertz's center of direction, control, and coordination, its "nerve center," and its corporate headquarters are one and the same, and they are located in New Jersey, not in California. Because respondents should have a fair opportunity to litigate their case in light of our holding, however, we vacate the Ninth Circuit's judgment and remand the case for further proceedings consistent with this opinion.

It is so ordered.

Notes and Questions

1. Under what circumstances might using the "nerve center" not be consistent with the underlying theory of diversity of citizenship jurisdiction? Does the Court leave open the possibility that some other test might be used? If so, does the Court undermine its desire for uniform jurisdictional rules?

2. Although it is Congress's job to define the subject matter jurisdiction of the federal courts (within Article III), sometimes its efforts create uncertainty. Section 1332(c)(1) is an example. It became obvious soon after its passage in 1958 that "principal place of business" was an imprecise term. Congress essentially delegated to the judiciary the responsibility for defining the term. Is there a problem with that?

3. In *Hertz*, the Court clarified the meaning of "principal place of business" in § 1332(c)(1). As noted above, because the statute uses "the" to refer to the principal

place of business, there can only be one; no corporation can have more than one principal place of business. But remember that the statute also provides that a corporation is a citizen of "every State" in which it is incorporated. The word "every" implies that there might be more than one. It is possible to incorporate (or "charter") in more than one state. When that is done, the entity is a citizen of each such state (in addition to the state in which it has its one principal place of business).

This issue is of limited practical importance because almost no business corporations are actually incorporated in more than one state. The practice was once common, but is obviated by modern business law, which allows a corporation formed in one state to register to do business in others. Today probably the only examples of multi-state incorporation are entities formed to operate tunnels or bridges between two states. For political reasons, they incorporate in both states. It is virtually impossible to find a general business corporation that is incorporated in more than one state.*

4. In 2011, Congress amended § 1332(c)(1) to refer to the foreign country in which a corporation was incorporated or in which it has its principal place of business. So a corporation formed in France with its principal place of business in Los Angeles will be considered a citizen of both France and California. (The same would be true of a corporation formed in California with its principal place of business in Paris.)

ii. Non-Incorporated Businesses

Unlike corporations, partnerships and other non-incorporated business associations generally have not been seen as entities separate from the persons who own and run them. Rather, they have been treated for various purposes (including taxation) as aggregations of the members of the business. As we have just seen, 28 U.S.C. § 1332(c)(1) defines only the citizenship of corporations. Consequently, it does not apply to non-incorporated business associations.

The classic example of such a business is the partnership, which is an association of two or more persons to carry on as owners of a business for a profit. A partnership can be formed simply by going into business together; no formal papers are required and the partners do not need to get any approval from the state to form this association. Historically, law firms have been partnerships. Most labor unions and many

---

* When multi-state incorporation was common, the Supreme Court applied the "forum doctrine," which held that a corporation incorporated in State X and State Y would be deemed a citizen *only* of one of those states when it was involved in litigation in one such state. So if this corporation were litigating in State X, it would be deemed only a citizen of State X, and not of state Y. Chicago & N.W. Ry. Co. v. Whitten's Admin., 80 U.S. 270, 283 (1871). The doctrine was aimed at increasing access to diversity jurisdiction for railroads (which then (but not now) were incorporated in more than one state). Though a stray case or two from decades ago found that the forum doctrine survived the passage of § 1332(c)(1), see Hudak v. Port Authority Trans-Hudson Corp., 238 F. Supp. 790, 792 (S.D.N.Y. 1965), "the universal view over recent years" is that the statute's reference to citizenship in "any" state where incorporated has abrogated the forum doctrine. 15 Moore's Federal Practice § 102.53 (3d ed. 2011). See Oslick v. The Port Authority of New York and New Jersey, 83 F.R.D. 494, 495 (S.D.N.Y. 1979) (rejecting the holding of *Hudak*).

insurance associations also are not incorporated. Traditionally, because partnerships have not been seen as separate entities, each partner is jointly and severally liable for whatever liability or debt the business incurs. On the other hand, because it is not an entity, the partnership does not have to pay taxes on its income (the partners are taxed on their income from the partnership, however). Though not technically an entity, most states permit a partnership to sue or be sued. See Federal Rule 17(b)(3). How do we determine the citizenship of such a non-incorporated business?

The courts have had to answer that question, and have done so with remarkable consistency: the business is considered a citizen of all states of which its members are citizens. Thus, for instance, a law partnership with partners who are citizens of New York, Connecticut, and New Jersey is considered, for diversity jurisdiction purposes, to be a citizen of those three states. In Carden v. Arkoma Associates, 494 U.S. 185 (1990), the Supreme Court held that this rule applies even to limited partnerships and that courts must consider the citizenship of all partners—both general and limited partners. If a non-corporate association had members who were citizens of every American jurisdiction (as is probably the case for a large labor union), it could not sue or be sued under diversity of citizenship jurisdiction. (Remember what that means: it can sue or be sued in state court or in federal court if there is some other basis of federal subject matter jurisdiction, such as federal question jurisdiction.)

One of the most prevalent forms of business association today is the limited liability company, or "L.L.C." A few states pioneered this form of business in the 1970s and 1980s. Today, every state permits persons to form some type of L.L.C. The difficult issue for federal jurisdiction is determining the citizenship of the L.L.C. While it shares some of the characteristics of the corporation, the L.L.C. also has some characteristics of a partnership. Nowhere has Congress addressed the citizenship of the L.L.C., leaving the courts to determine the issue. The following case sets forth the majority conclusion on the issue, and reminds us of the importance of being precise about jurisdictional matters.

Belleville Catering Co. v. Champaign Market Place L.L.C.

350 F.3d 691 (7th Cir. 2003)

Easterbrook, Circuit Judge

Once again litigants' insouciance toward the requirements of federal jurisdiction has caused a waste of time and money. * * *

Invoking the diversity jurisdiction, see 28 U.S.C. § 1332, the complaint alleged that the corporate plaintiff is incorporated in Missouri and has its principal place of business there, and that the five individual plaintiffs (guarantors of the corporate plaintiff's obligations) are citizens of Missouri. It also alleged that the defendant is a "Delaware Limited Liability Company, with its principle [sic] place of business in the State of Illinois." Defendant agreed with these allegations and filed a counterclaim. The * * * [court] accepted these jurisdictional allegations at face value. A jury trial was held, ending in a verdict of $220,000 in defendant's favor on the counterclaim. Plaintiffs appealed; the jurisdictional statement of their appellate brief tracks the allegations of the complaint. Defendant's brief asserts that plaintiffs' jurisdictional summary is "complete and correct."

It is, however, transparently incomplete and incorrect. Counsel and the [lower court] assumed that a limited liability company is treated like a corporation and thus is a citizen of its state of organization and its principal place of business. That is not right. Unincorporated enterprises are analogized to partnerships, which take the citizenship of every general and limited partner. See Carden v. Arkoma Associates, 494 U.S. 185 (1990). In common with other courts of appeals, we have held that limited liability companies are citizens of every state of which any member is a citizen. Cosgrove v. Bartolotta, 150 F.3d 729 (7th Cir. 1998). So who are Champaign Market Place LLC's members, and of what states are they citizens? Our effort to explore jurisdiction before oral argument led to an unexpected discovery: Belleville Catering, the corporate plaintiff, appeared to be incorporated in Illinois rather than Missouri!

At oral argument we directed the parties to file supplemental memoranda addressing jurisdictional details. Plaintiffs' response concedes that Belleville Catering is (and always has been) incorporated in Illinois. Counsel tells us that, because the lease between Belleville Catering and Champaign Market Place refers to Belleville Catering as "a Missouri corporation," he assumed that it must be one. That confesses a violation of Fed. R. Civ. P. 11. [Rule 11 requires, among other things, that attorneys certify that allegations are warranted, based upon the pleader's "knowledge, information, and belief, formed after an inquiry reasonable under the circumstances."] People do not draft leases with the requirements of § 1332 in mind — perhaps the lease meant only that Belleville Catering did business in Missouri — and counsel must secure jurisdictional details from original sources before making formal allegations. That would have been easy to do; the client's files doubtless contain the certificate of incorporation. Or counsel could have done what the court did: use the Internet. Both Illinois and Missouri make databases of incorporations readily available. Counsel for the defendant should have done the same, instead of agreeing with the complaint's unfounded allegation.

Both sides also must share the blame for assuming that a limited liability company is treated like a corporation. In the memorandum filed after oral argument, counsel for Champaign Market Place relate that several of its members are citizens of Illinois. Citizens of Illinois thus are on both sides of the suit, which therefore cannot proceed under § 1332. Moreover, for all we can tell, other members are citizens of Missouri. Champaign Market Place says that one of its members is another limited liability company that "is asserting confidentiality for the members of the L.L.C." It is not possible to litigate under the diversity jurisdiction with details kept confidential from the judiciary. So federal jurisdiction has not been established. The complaint should not have been filed in federal court (for Belleville Catering had to know its own state of incorporation), the answer should have pointed out a problem (for Champaign Market Place's lawyers had to ascertain the legal status of limited liability companies), and the [trial court] should have checked all of this independently; inquiring whether the court has jurisdiction is a federal judge's first duty in every case.

Failure to perform these tasks has the potential, realized here, to waste time (including that of the put-upon jurors) and run up legal fees. Usually parties accept the inevitable and proceed to state court once the problem becomes apparent. Perhaps the most extraordinary aspect of this proceeding, however, is the following passage in defendant's post-argument memorandum:

> Defendant-Appellee, Champaign Market Place L.L.C., prays that this Court in the exercise of its appellate jurisdiction decide the case on the merits and affirm the judgment entered on the jury's verdict. Surely in the past this Court has decided a case on the merits where an examination of the issue would have shown a lack of subject matter jurisdiction in the District Court. It would be unfortunate in the extreme for Champaign Market Place L.L.C. to lose a judgment where Belleville Catering Company, Inc. misrepresented (albeit unintentionally) its State of incorporation in its Complaint.... There was no reason for Champaign Market Place L.L.C. to question diversity of citizenship, since it is not, and never has been, a citizen of Missouri.

This passage—and there is more in the same vein—leaves us agog. Just where do appellate courts acquire authority to decide on the merits a case over which there is no federal jurisdiction? The proposition that the Seventh Circuit has done so in the past—a proposition unsupported by any citation—accuses the court of dereliction combined with usurpation. "A court lacks discretion to consider the merits of a case over which it is without jurisdiction." Firestone Tire & Rubber Co v. Risjord, 449 U.S. 368 (1981). And while counsel feel free to accuse the judges of ultra vires conduct, and to invite some more of it, they exculpate themselves. Lawyers for defendants, as well as plaintiffs, must investigate rather than assume jurisdiction; to do this, they first must learn the legal rules that determine whose citizenship matters (as defendant's lawyers failed to do). And no entity that claims confidentiality for its members' identities and citizenships is well situated to assert that it could believe, in good faith, that complete diversity has been established.

One more subject before we conclude. The costs of a doomed foray into federal court should fall on the lawyers who failed to do their homework, not on the hapless clients. Although we lack jurisdiction to resolve the merits, we have ample authority to govern the practice of counsel in the litigation. * * * The best way for counsel to make the litigants whole is to perform, without additional fees, any further services that are necessary to bring this suit to a conclusion in state court, or via settlement. That way the clients will pay just once for the litigation. This is intended not as a sanction, but simply to ensure that clients need not pay for lawyers' time that has been wasted for reasons beyond the clients' control.

The judgment of the district [court] is vacated, and the proceeding is remanded with instructions to dismiss the complaint for want of subject matter jurisdiction.

Notes and Questions

1. Professor Cohen has argued, based upon an interesting functional analysis of the similarities between the L.L.C. and the corporation, that L.L.C.s should be treated,

for diversity purposes, as corporations. Debra R. Cohen, *Citizenship of Limited Liability Companies for Diversity Jurisdiction*, 6 J. Small & Emerging Bus. Law 435 (2002). Despite the force of the argument, appellate courts have agreed with the conclusion reached in the *Belleville Catering* case, and have held that the citizenship of an L.L.C. is to be determined by looking to the citizenship of all its members. See Siloam Springs Hotel, L.L.C. v. Century Sur. Co., 781 F.3d 1233, 1235–36 (10th Cir. 2015) ("[A]lthough this court had yet to address the issue, every circuit to consider the citizenship of an LLC for purposes of diversity has held that an LLC's citizenship is determined by reference to the citizenship of each and every one of its members").

Thus, courts have adopted a mechanical, bright-line test regarding business entities. If the business is designated a "corporation" by the law of the state in which it was formed, its citizenship is defined by § 1332(c)(1). If the business is not designated a "corporation," the court will look to the citizenship of all its members. See Americold Realty Trust v. Conagra Foods, Inc., 136 S. Ct. ___ (2016) (Maryland real estate investment trust deemed citizen of all states of which its shareholders are citizens).

In Kuntz v. Lamar Corp., 385 F.3d 1177, 1182–83 (9th Cir. 2004), the court applied § 1332(c)(1) to an electric power cooperative that was designated a "corporation" by California law, even though the cooperative lacked many of the characteristics of a corporation, such as stockholders and voting membership. The law of the state of formation referred to it as a corporation, and that was determinative. In Hoagland v. Sandberg, 385 F.3d 737 (7th Cir. 2004), the court reached the same conclusion regarding a professional corporation, despite its lack of various usual corporate characteristics, including perpetuity of existence and shield from individual liability. The court emphasized that a mechanical rule is preferable in matters of jurisdiction, where clarity is of utmost importance. "The more mechanical the application of a jurisdictional rule, the better," said the court. "The chief and often the only virtue of a jurisdictional rule is clarity." Id. at 740.

2. Businesses can be formed by combining various business structures. For instance, members of an L.L.C. might be corporations. Or corporations (or L.L.C.s) can serve as partners in a partnership. As with all partnerships, one looks to the citizenship of the partners. If a partner is a corporation, then that partner's citizenship is determined by applying § 1332(c)(1).

In Johnson v. SmithKline Beecham Corp., 724 F.3d 337 (3d Cir. 2013), plaintiffs (citizens of Louisiana and Pennsylvania) brought a state-court products liability case against several entities related to the pharmaceutical giant SmithKline Beecham. The defendants removed to federal court on the basis of diversity. (We saw removal jurisdiction in *Hertz* and will study it in detail later in this chapter. It permits defendants sued in state court to "remove" a case to federal court, but only if there is federal subject matter jurisdiction. So the question in *Johnson* was whether the case met the requirements for diversity of citizenship jurisdiction.) Plaintiffs moved to remand, contending that at least one of the defendants was a citizen of Pennsylvania. The district court found that none of the defendants was a citizen of Pennsylvania and refused plaintiffs' motion to remand. On interlocutory appeal, the Third Circuit affirmed.

One of the defendants, GSK LLC, was the successor to SmithKline Beecham, which was a Pennsylvania corporation. In 2009, however, before this case was filed, it re-chartered as a Delaware corporation and then converted into a Delaware LLC. The Pennsylvania entity dissolved. Operationally, the business was unaffected by the conversion. Its management remained the same and its headquarters remained in Philadelphia, where it continued to employ 1800 people. Because it was now an LLC, however, its principal place of business was irrelevant for purposes of citizenship. As we saw in *Belleville Catering,* an LLC is a citizen of the same state(s) as its member(s). GSK LLC had only one member — GSK Holdings, which was a Delaware corporation.

The issue became whether GSK Holdings had its principal place of business Delaware or Pennsylvania. If the former, there would be diversity. If the latter, there would not. The court noted that holding companies, by their nature, have limited activities. The GSK Holdings board of directors consisted of three people, one of whom lived in Philadelphia, one in England, and one in Delaware. The board met quarterly for 15 to 30 minutes in Delaware. One director usually attended, with the other two joining by conference call. Beyond this, GSK Holdings leased a 10-foot by 10-foot office in Delaware, which served chiefly to house its books and records. It paid bills from that office as well. The Third Circuit concluded that GSK Holdings' principal place of business was in Delaware, and upheld diversity jurisdiction.

3. Plaintiff, a corporation, is incorporated in Delaware. It has offices and conducts business in Delaware, Maryland, Virginia, Pennsylvania, and the District of Columbia. It sues an unincorporated insurance association that has members who are citizens of Maryland and the District of Columbia. Assuming the claim exceeds $75,000, might there be diversity of citizenship? What additional facts would you need to know?

4. In Grupo Dataflux v. Atlas Global Group, L.P., 541 U.S. 567 (2004), a limited partnership formed in Texas sued a Mexican citizen. The partners of the limited partnership were citizens of Texas and of Mexico. The presence of an alien citizen on each side of the case meant, of course, that there was no alienage jurisdiction. Neither was there diversity of citizenship, because the action was not between citizens of different states. Strangely, however, nobody noticed the lack of diversity, and the case was litigated to judgment. By the time judgment was entered, the Mexican partners of the plaintiff had left the partnership, so the requirements of alienage were satisfied. The Court held that the judgment was void because there was no subject matter jurisdiction *when the case was filed.* Subject matter jurisdiction must exist when the case is commenced; a subsequent change of a party's citizenship cannot affect jurisdiction, as we discussed in *Mas v. Perry*, supra.

e. Representative Suits and Assignments of Claims

A plaintiff who is not of diverse citizenship from the defendant but who wants to sue in federal court might try to "manufacture" diversity. She might try to do so by assigning her claim to someone who could invoke diversity of citizenship jurisdiction. As a general rule, tort claims are not assignable, but contract claims are. Suppose, then, that a citizen of Vermont has a contract claim against another citizen of Vermont, and that the claim exceeds $75,000. Obviously, she cannot invoke diversity of citizenship jurisdiction because there is no diversity. But suppose the would-be plaintiff assigns her contract claim to a citizen of New Hampshire, who then asserts the claim under diversity of citizenship jurisdiction. On the face of things, it looks as though there is diversity. What would a court do with such a case?

The court would assess whether the assignment ran afoul of 28 U.S.C. § 1359, which provides that the district court has no jurisdiction over cases "in which any party, by assignment or otherwise, has been improperly or collusively made or joined to invoke the jurisdiction of such court." The ultimate issue would be whether the New Hampshire assignee was merely a collection agent for the Vermont assignor. If, for example, the New Hampshire assignee of the claim agreed to remit to the Vermont assignee 95 percent of any recovery she won against the defendant, the court would probably conclude that there was no jurisdiction, because the assignment violated § 1359. The Supreme Court applied § 1359 to such an assignment in Kramer v. Caribbean Mills, Inc., 394 U.S. 823 (1969). The result of applying the statute is that the court ignores the citizenship of the assignee and uses that of the assignor. This means, of course, that there is no diversity of citizenship. Thus, application of § 1359 does not vitiate the assignment; the court simply ignores it for purposes of assessing diversity jurisdiction. On the other hand, an assignment for adequate consideration, in which the assignee is not a mere collection agent for the assignor, does not run afoul of § 1359.

Because § 1359 is aimed at *collusive* creation of jurisdiction, it does not apply to a single litigant's changing her domicile to create diversity. Collusion requires more than one person; one person cannot collude with herself. So long as the change of domicile comports with the rules discussed in *Mas v. Perry*, and occurs before filing, such a change can create diversity, even if motivated solely by a desire to gain access to federal court. See Morris v. Gilmer, 129 U.S. 315 (1889). In earlier times, § 1359 also came into play when litigants tried to create diversity of citizenship jurisdiction in cases involving a decedent's estate. For example, assume that Decedent was a citizen of Michigan, and that he died under circumstances that made his family want to bring a malpractice action against Hospital, which is also a citizen of Michigan. If the family members wanted to bring the case in federal court, they might agree to have Uncle Fred, who is a citizen of Montana, appointed as executor. Uncle Fred would then sue, and argue that his citizenship — not Decedent's — was relevant for jurisdiction. Hospital would then argue that the appointment of Uncle Fred violated § 1359 and should be ignored for purposes of determining diversity of citizenship.

This fact pattern no longer implicates § 1359. Why not? Read 28 U.S.C. § 1332(c)(2). This helpful provision applies to cases brought by or against representatives of decedents, "infants" (which means minors, persons who have not reached the age of majority), and incompetents. Minors and incompetents lack legal capacity to sue or be sued by themselves, so are usually represented in litigation by a fiduciary, such as a guardian. Decedents' estates are represented in litigation by executors (if the decedent left a will) or administrators (if the decedent had no will). Section 1332(c)(2) brings certainty to the area by providing that the court looks to the citizenship of the decedent, minor, or incompetent, and not to the citizenship of the representative.

f. The Domestic Relations and Probate Exceptions

Even if the requirements for diversity of citizenship jurisdiction are met, federal courts refuse to hear "domestic relations" cases. This exception dates back to Barber v. Barber, 62 U.S. 582 (1859). Although the majority opinion in that case offered little explanation for its conclusion, the dissenters discussed a rationale. They noted that the original Judiciary Act of 1791 gave jurisdiction over suits "at common law or in equity." This, according to the argument, did not include domestic relations cases because in England, such disputes were heard neither by law nor equity courts, but by ecclesiastical courts.

In Ankenbrandt v. Richards, 504 U.S. 689 (1992), the Supreme Court reaffirmed the domestic relations exception, explaining the exception on both statutory and policy grounds. The Court noted that Congress had amended the diversity statute in 1948 to replace the law/equity distinction with the phrase "all civil actions." The Court then "presume[d that] Congress did so with full cognizance of the Court's nearly century-long interpretation of the prior statutes, which had construed the statutory diversity jurisdiction to contain an exception for certain domestic relations matters." Id. at 700. The Court offered a policy explanation for the exception:

> As a matter of judicial economy, state courts are more eminently suited to work of this type than are federal courts, which lack the close association with the state and local government organizations dedicated to handling issues that arise out of conflict over divorce, alimony, and child custody decrees. Moreover, as a matter of judicial expertise, it makes far more sense to retain the rule that federal courts lack power to issue these types of decrees because of the special proficiency developed by state tribunals over the past century and a half in handling issues that arise in the granting of such decrees.

Id. at 704. What do you think of these policy justifications? Could they be used to justify a court's refusal to hear any diversity of citizenship cases?

Although the *Ankenbrandt* Court endorsed the domestic relations exception, it emphasized that the exception is narrow and applies only in cases "involving the issuance of a divorce, alimony, or child custody decree." Thus, it does not preclude jurisdiction over cases simply because they involve conflict between family members. In *Ankenbrandt* itself, for instance, a mother, suing on behalf of her minor children, sought tort damages from her ex-husband (the children's father) and his companion. She alleged that the defendants had abused the children when they were visiting their father. The lower courts invoked the domestic relations exception and refused to hear the case. The Supreme Court reversed, since the case did not involve divorce, alimony, or a child custody decree. See generally 15 Moore's Federal Practice § 102.99.

In Kahn v. Kahn, 21 F.3d 859 (8th Cir. 1994), the court refused to hear tort claims for conversion and fraud by a woman against her ex-husband. It held that the claims were "so inextricably intertwined with the property settlement incident to the divorce proceeding that subject matter jurisdiction does not lie." Id. at 861. Does this holding extend *Ankenbrandt*?

Federal courts also will not probate or administer a decedent's estate or appoint an executor. Such actions would interfere with the jurisdiction of state probate courts. Markham v. Allen, 326 U.S. 490, 494 (1946). In 2006, in a case involving the late Anna Nicole Smith, the Court emphasized that this exception is also narrow, and does not mean that federal courts will never hear cases involving the conduct of those who administer estates. In Marshall v. Marshall, 547 U.S. 293 (2006), Anna Nicole (whose married name was Marshall), widow of a wealthy decedent, asserted a claim of tortious interference against her husband's son. She alleged that the son had made it impossible for her husband to execute documents to provide a trust for her. She asserted the claim in a federal bankruptcy proceeding. That court awarded Anna Nicole $449 million in compensatory and $25 million in punitive damages against her husband's son. The son then claimed that there had been no federal subject matter jurisdiction because of the probate exception. The Supreme Court rejected the son's argument.

The Court characterized the domestic relations and probate exceptions as "judicially created doctrines stemming in large measure from misty understandings of English legal history." 547 U.S. at 299. It recognized the similarity between this case and *Ankenbrandt*. In each, the claimant asserted a well-recognized tort and sought an *in personam* judgment against an individual defendant. Because Anna Nicole's claim did not involve probate or annulment of a will, and did not seek to reach property in the custody of the Texas probate court, it did not fall within the probate exception. Five years later, the Court concluded that the bankruptcy court lacked judicial power under Article III to hear Anna Nicole's claim. Stern v. Marshall, 131 S. Ct. 2594 (2011). The opinion in *Marshall v. Marshall* remains dispositive regarding the extent of the probate exception, but because the federal bankruptcy court could not hear the claim, the state probate decision (against Anna Nicole) was determinative. So her estate recovered nothing.

g. The Amount in Controversy Requirement

Article III contains no amount in controversy limitations. Such limitations are established in jurisdictional statutes and traditionally have served two functions. First, they reflect the notion that a federal tribunal should not be a small claims court. Second, and related, they are a method of docket control. Historically, diversity of citizenship, alienage, and general federal question cases contained such requirements. Today, they remain in diversity of citizenship and alienage jurisdiction.

Congress changes the amount in controversy requirement under § 1332 from time to time. It last did so in 1997, when it set the requirement as an amount in excess of $75,000. Clearly, the requirement serves a docket control function by reducing the number of diversity of citizenship cases that may be filed. Beyond that, does the existence of an amount in controversy requirement demonstrate that alienage and diversity of citizenship cases are "less important" than federal question cases? Or is it consistent with the traditional justification of alienage and diversity jurisdiction because fear of local bias will be stronger in more substantial cases?

Notes and Questions

1. Plaintiff sues for exactly $75,000. Assuming the complete diversity rule is satisfied, is there jurisdiction? In Freeland v. Liberty Mutual Fire Ins. Co., 632 F.3d 250, 252–55 (6th Cir. 2011), neither party raised an issue concerning subject matter jurisdiction. On appeal, the court of appeals noted on its own, however, that the plaintiff had sued for relief worth exactly $75,000. The dispute was over insurance coverage. Plaintiff claimed the insurance company was liable for $100,000. The company said it was on the hook for $25,000. The amount in controversy is the difference. Because it was exactly $75,000, the case failed by one penny to invoke federal subject matter jurisdiction. The court of appeals vacated the district court's judgment. All the time and effort of litigating at the trial court was lost, because no one noticed the jurisdictional problem.

2. Again, assume the complete diversity rule is satisfied. Here, plaintiff sues for $100,000. After trial, the jury finds that plaintiff is entitled to damages of $18,000. Defendant then moves to dismiss, asserting that the amount in controversy, it turns out, was only $18,000. The motion will be denied. Why? Remember that *Mas v. Perry* addressed this issue. See also 28 U.S.C. § 1332(b). Why is it important to determine whether the case satisfies the amount in controversy early in the case, rather than to await the outcome of the litigation?

3. Ordinarily, the prevailing party is entitled to have her costs paid by the other party. See Rule 54(d). Under § 1332(b), however, a prevailing plaintiff who recovers less than $75,000 may be ordered to pay the defendant's costs. "Costs" is a term of art which includes some (but not all) expenses of litigation except attorney's fees. Included in "costs" are such things as filing and other fees assessed by the court clerk's office, some costs of discovery, witness fees, and copying costs of certain papers. Under the "American Rule," however, each party bears its own attorney's fees. In almost every case, attorney's fees are the "big ticket" item, and will far exceed costs. Note that § 1332(b) does not require the court to order a plaintiff recovering less than the jurisdictional amount to pay defendant's costs. When might the court not order such a recovery?

4. Courts dismiss very few cases for failure to satisfy the amount in controversy requirement, because the standard for satisfying the requirement is so low. In *St. Paul Mercury*, discussed in *Mas*, the Supreme Court held that the plaintiff's good faith allegation that the jurisdictional amount is satisfied will invoke jurisdiction unless it appears "to a legal certainty that the claim is really for less than the jurisdictional amount * * *." St. Paul Mercury Indem. Co. v. Red Cab Co., 303 U.S. 283, 289 (1938). Courts rarely undertake an investigation into the matter unless it is clearly raised by the defendant or by the pleadings or the evidence. In re A.H. Robins Co.,

880 F.2d 709, 724 (4th Cir. 1989) (court has no obligation to inquire absent some "apparent reason" to do so). When the issue is raised, plaintiff assumes the burden of showing that it is not clear "to a legal certainty" that the jurisdictional amount is not met. Gibbs v. Buck, 307 U.S. 66 (1939).

Some plaintiffs fail to meet even this low burden. A clear example is when one seeks recovery of damages not allowed by law. Suppose, for instance, that plaintiff sues for $60,000 damages for breach of contract and for $100,000 punitive damages for the breach. Under the traditional rule, punitive damages are not recoverable for breach of contract. Thus, it would be clear "to a legal certainty" that plaintiff's case involved only $60,000, and the case would be dismissed. See Pachinger v. MGM Grand Hotel-Las Vegas, Inc., 802 F.2d 362 (9th Cir. 1986) (holding, as matter of law, that innkeeper's liability was limited to less than jurisdictional amount); Parker v. Moitzfield, 733 F. Supp. 1023 (E.D. Va. 1990) (applicable law did not recognize damages for anticipatory breach).

Occasionally, a court will rule as a matter of law that the plaintiff could not recover the requisite amount even in the absence of a legal limitation on damages. For example, in Diefenthal v. Civil Aeronautics Board, 681 F.2d 1039 (5th Cir. 1982), the court dismissed as trivial the plaintiffs' claims that they were humiliated and embarrassed by a flight attendant's "brusque" treatment.

5. One difficult area concerns *aggregation* of claims—when may a plaintiff add separate claims to satisfy the amount in controversy requirement? The statute granting diversity of citizenship jurisdiction does not address the issue. Although the courts have established clear rules, the rules are not always logical or consistent with policy.

(a) *One plaintiff v. one defendant.* The plaintiff in such a case may aggregate all of her claims to meet the jurisdictional requirement, even if the claims are unrelated legally or transactionally. For instance, a plaintiff with a $45,000 contract claim and an unrelated $50,000 tort claim against the same defendant may aggregate them, so the amount in controversy would be $95,000. The record appears to be set in Jones Motor Co. v. Teledyne, Inc., 690 F. Supp. 310 (D. Del. 1988), in which the plaintiff aggregated 54 separate, relatively insignificant claims against the defendant to satisfy the amount in controversy requirement.

This rule is inconsistent with the premise that Congress imposes the amount in controversy requirement to prevent the federal courts from becoming tribunals for small claims. If aggregation is to be permitted, it would make more sense to allow aggregation only of transactionally related claims.

(b) *Multiple parties on either side.* If there is more than one plaintiff or more than one defendant, aggregation generally is not allowed. Thus, if (1) two plaintiffs have claims of $45,000 and $50,000, respectively, against one defendant or (2) if one plaintiff has such claims against two defendants, respectively, or (3) if two plaintiffs have such claims against two defendants, the claims cannot be aggregated, and the amount in controversy requirement is not met. This is true even if the claims are transactionally related. See, e.g., Thomson v. Gaskill, 315 U.S.

442, 447 (1942) (aggregation "cannot be made merely because the claims are derived from a single instrument * * * or because the plaintiffs have a community of interest") (citations omitted). The courts have not articulated a logical reason for this rule.

This rule against aggregation in the multiple-party context applies when the claims asserted are "separate" or "distinct," as opposed to "common, undivided, or joint." If the case involves "common, undivided, or joint" claims, courts are said to permit aggregation. One problem, of course, is that these terms are not self-defining and, to make matters worse, are encrusted with arcane historical baggage. As one scholar concludes, the use of such phrases in modern jurisdictional doctrine is akin to "attempting to drive a Model T on a superhighway." Martin Redish, *Reassessing the Allocation of Judicial Business Between State and Federal Courts: Federal Jurisdiction and "The Martian Chronicles,"* 78 Va. L. Rev. 1769, 1808 (1992).

Despite the difficulty with terminology, the results in many situations are clear. For example, personal injuries suffered by different people are separate claims, and cannot be aggregated for amount in controversy purposes. Tobie v. Don Pepe Corp., 646 F. Supp. 620 (D.P.R. 1986). Thus, suppose P-1 and P-2 are injured in a car wreck with D. P-1 suffers personal injury damages of $50,000 and P-2 suffers personal injury damages of $45,000. They may not aggregate their separate claims to meet the amount in controversy requirement.

On the other hand, suppose P suffers one injury allegedly caused by joint tortfeasors D-1 and D-2. P's personal injury damages are $76,000. Is the amount in controversy requirement satisfied? Yes. Here, because of joint liability, either defendant might be held liable for the entire amount, so a court looks to the entire amount of the claim in determining the amount in controversy. In cases such as this, discussing aggregation seems meaningless. Because of the alleged joint liability, either defendant could be held liable for the entire amount of the claim. In essence, then, there is only one claim. It exceeds $75,000, so the amount in controversy requirement is met.

6. Another difficult area concerns cases seeking equitable relief. For example, suppose that the plaintiff seeks to enjoin the defendant from polluting a stream running through plaintiff's land. How does one put a dollar value on a claim for an injunction? Courts have taken different approaches. The traditional view is to ask whether the defendant's alleged acts *harm the plaintiff* by more than $75,000. Some courts, however, look at whether complying with the injunction would cost the defendant more than $75,000.

The difference in approach may make quite a difference in result. Suppose, for example, that defendant built her house so that it encroached on plaintiff's property by six inches. While the damage to plaintiff may be minimal, it would cost defendant a considerable sum to remedy the encroachment. Most courts appear to uphold jurisdiction if the amount is met from either the plaintiff's or the defendant's viewpoint. See Bernard v. Gerber Food Prod., 938 F. Supp. 218 (S.D.N.Y. 1996) (discussing different approaches).

4. Federal Question Jurisdiction

a. *Introductory Note*

Compare the constitutional grant of federal question jurisdiction in Article III to the statutory grant in 28 U.S.C. § 1331.

Section 1331 is known as the "general" federal question statute, an omnibus provision allowing a claim arising under any federal law to be brought in federal court. While we will address only § 1331 in detail, note that there are many specialized federal question statutes allowing jurisdiction over claims arising under specific federal laws. For example, § 1337 grants jurisdiction over federal antitrust cases; § 1338 creates jurisdiction over patent and trademark cases; § 1343 relates to civil rights claims.

The historic justifications for giving federal courts jurisdiction over cases arising under federal law are clear. Federal judges can be expected to be more sympathetic to policies underlying federal legislation and to develop expertise in the interpretation of federal law. State court judges, on the other hand, might be less likely to do the former or have the time to do the latter. Moreover, federal courts would seem to be the best forum for vindicating federal rights. Nonetheless, the Founders clearly envisioned that state courts would decide cases arising under federal law. Congress did not pass a general federal question statute until 1875.* Thus, for 84 years, claims arising under federal law and not addressed by a specialized grant of jurisdiction could be heard only in the state courts. You will recall from Chapter 1 that the state courts' interpretation of federal law is ultimately subject to review by the Supreme Court, thereby ensuring, at least in theory,** that the federal judiciary remained the ultimate interpreter of federal law.

Note that § 1331 does not impose an amount in controversy requirement. It did carry the same requirement as that imposed in diversity of citizenship cases from 1875 until 1980, when Congress abolished it. In part, Congress was motivated by the fact that most of the specialized grants of federal question jurisdiction had no amount in controversy requirement. As is clear from the face of § 1331, its grant of jurisdiction is not exclusive to the federal courts. Thus, cases brought under it can be filed either in state or federal court. Indeed, this is also true under the specialized grants of federal question jurisdiction, *except* in those fairly rare situations in which the federal grant is exclusive, which we noted in Section B above.

---

* There was a brief grant of general federal question jurisdiction in the famous Midnight Judges Act of 1801. It was repealed the following year, however, and was of no particular importance.

** We say "in theory" because the Supreme Court can review only a very limited number of cases in a given year. If federal question cases were filed only in the federal courts, however, they would be assured of review by a federal district court and, if a party chose to appeal, by a federal court of appeals. The fact that general federal question jurisdiction is not exclusive to the federal courts suggests that Congress is not bothered (as the Founders were not bothered) by the fact that state courts are often the final arbiters of the meaning of federal law.

b. Narrow Interpretations of the Jurisdictional Statute

Courts have long struggled to interpret the seemingly simple language of § 1331 and its complementary constitutional grant. In particular, the term "arising under" has caused problems in two areas. First is a requirement that the federal law be set forth as a claim, not as a defense. This raises the problem of the curiously named "well-pleaded complaint" rule. Second, and more difficult to fathom, is an assessment of whether federal law is sufficiently central to the claim asserted in a well-pleaded complaint. With each of these restrictions, the federal courts have read the statutory language "arising under" more narrowly than the constitutional language. This should not surprise us. Remember that "citizens of different states" in the diversity of citizenship statute is read more narrowly than the same language in the Constitution.

i. The Well-Pleaded Complaint Rule

Louisville & Nashville Railroad Co. v. Mottley

211 U.S. 149, 29 S. Ct. 42, 53 L. Ed. 126 (1908)

Justice Moody delivered the opinion of the court.

[To settle a previous claim, the railroad gave the Mottleys lifetime passes. The railroad honored the passes for many years, until a federal statute forbade railroads from giving such passes. When the railroad then failed to honor the Mottleys' passes, the Mottleys sued.]

Two questions of law were raised by the demurrer to the bill, were brought here by appeal, and have been argued before us. They are, first, whether that part of the act of Congress of June 29, 1906 (34 Stat. 584), which forbids the giving of free passes or the collection of any different compensation for transportation of passengers than that specified in the tariff filed, makes it unlawful to perform a contract for transportation of persons, who in good faith, before the passage of the act, had accepted such contract in satisfaction of a valid cause of action against the railroad; and, second, whether the statute, if it should be construed to render such a contract unlawful, is in violation of the Fifth Amendment of the Constitution of the United States. We do not deem it necessary, however, to consider either of these questions, because, in our opinion, the court below was without jurisdiction of the cause. Neither party has questioned that jurisdiction, but it is the duty of this court to see to it that the jurisdiction of the Circuit Court [which was the federal trial court at the time], which is defined and limited by statute, is not exceeded. This duty we have frequently performed of our own motion.

There was no diversity of citizenship and it is not and cannot be suggested that there was any ground of jurisdiction, except that the case was a "suit ... arising under the Constitution and laws of the United States." It is the settled interpretation of these words, as used in this statute, conferring jurisdiction, that a suit arises under the Constitution and laws of the United States only when the plaintiff's statement of his own cause of action shows that it is based upon those laws or that Constitution.

It is not enough that the plaintiff alleges some anticipated defense to his cause of action and asserts that the defense is invalidated by some provision of the Constitution of the United States. Although such allegations show that very likely, in the course of the litigation, a question under the Constitution would arise, they do not show that the suit, that is, the plaintiff's original cause of action, arises under the Constitution. In Tennessee v. Union & Planters' Bank, 152 U.S. 454 [1894], the plaintiff, the State of Tennessee, brought suit in the Circuit Court of the United States to recover from the defendant certain taxes alleged to be due under the laws of the State. The plaintiff alleged that the defendant claimed an immunity from the taxation by virtue of its charter, and that therefore the tax was void, because in violation of the provision of the Constitution of the United States, which forbids any State from passing a law impairing the obligation of contracts. The cause was held to be beyond the jurisdiction of the Circuit Court, the court saying, by Mr. Justice Gray, "a suggestion of one party, that the other will or may set up a claim under the Constitution or laws of the United States, does not make the suit one arising under that Constitution or those laws." Again, in Boston & Montana Consolidated Copper & Silver Mining Company v. Montana Ore Purchasing Company, 188 U.S. 632 [1903], the plaintiff brought suit in the Circuit Court of the United States for the conversion of copper ore and for an injunction against its continuance. The plaintiff then alleged, for the purpose of showing jurisdiction, in substance, that the defendant would set up in defense certain laws of the United States. The cause was held to be beyond the jurisdiction of the Circuit Court, the court saying, by Mr. Justice Peckham:

"It would be wholly unnecessary and improper in order to prove complainant's cause of action to go into any matters of defence which the defendants might possibly set up and then attempt to reply to such defence, and thus, if possible, to show that a Federal question might or probably would arise in the course of the trial of the case. To allege such defence and then make an answer to it before the defendant has the opportunity to itself plead or prove its own defence is inconsistent with any known rule of pleading so far as we are aware, and is improper.

"The rule is a reasonable and just one that the complainant in the first instance shall be confined to a statement of its cause of action, leaving to the defendant to set up in his answer what his defence is and, if anything more than a denial of complainant's cause of action, imposing upon the defendant the burden of proving such defence.

"Conforming itself to that rule the complainant would not, in the assertion or proof of its cause of action, bring up a single Federal question. The presentation of its cause of action would not show that it was one arising under the Constitution or laws of the United States.

"The only way in which it might be claimed that a Federal question was presented would be in the complainant's statement of what the defence of defendants would be and complainant's answer to such defence. Under these circumstances the case is brought within the rule laid down in *Tennessee v.*

Union & Planters' Bank. That case has been cited and approved many times since...."

The interpretation of the act which we have stated was first announced in Metcalf v. Watertown, 128 U.S. 586 [1888], and has since been repeated and applied in [many cases]. The application of this rule to the case at bar is decisive against the jurisdiction of the Circuit Court.

It is ordered that the judgment be reversed and the case remitted to the Circuit Court with instructions to dismiss the suit for want of jurisdiction.

Notes and Questions

1. *Mottley* establishes the "well-pleaded complaint" rule. Despite the clear implication of the name, the doctrine has nothing to do with writing ability, grammar, spelling, sentence structure, or syntax. A well-pleaded complaint, for purposes of this rule, is one that sets forth only a claim, unadorned by anticipated defenses or other extraneous material. If the court determines that a complaint contains matter beyond the claim itself, it does not give the plaintiff a bad grade in English Composition or ask her to redraft it. Instead, it ignores the surplus language and looks only to what would have been included had the complaint been well-pleaded; that is, it looks to the essential elements of the claim itself. Why was the Mottleys' complaint not well-pleaded in this sense?

In *Mottley*, the claim was for breach of contract. To plead such a claim properly, the plaintiff must allege that there was a contract, that the defendant breached the contract, and, in some jurisdictions, that the plaintiff satisfied all conditions required by the contract and that the plaintiff has been damaged. These are the only elements to be considered in a well-pleaded complaint. The Mottleys' lawyer, like most good lawyers, considered not only the elements of their claim, but likely defenses as well. The lawyer accurately predicted that the railroad would assert that the federal statute precluded it from honoring the passes given to the Mottleys and thus that federal law required it to breach the contract. The railroad's assertion is called an "affirmative defense." With it, the defendant says, in essence, "I may have done the bad things you say, but I still win because of this statute."

There are numerous other potential affirmative defenses. For example, a defendant might assert that the statute of limitations bars plaintiff's claim, or that the contract is unenforceable under the statute of frauds because it is not in writing, or that the plaintiff's tort claim is barred by contributory negligence. For a lengthy (albeit not exclusive) list of affirmative defenses, see Rule 8(c)(1), which we will address in Chapter 7. Whether an allegation is considered part of plaintiff's claim or an affirmative defense reflects a policy decision about which side should bear the burden of raising the issue.

There is nothing wrong with a lawyer's anticipating a defense. The well-pleaded complaint rule simply provides that for purposes of determining federal question jurisdiction, the court will consider only those aspects of the complaint that are essential to the claim.

2. In Chapter 12 we will see that a defendant can file a claim — called a "counterclaim" — against the plaintiff in the pending case. Because a counterclaim is asserted by the defendant in her answer, it is not part of the plaintiff's well-pleaded complaint. So, if plaintiff's claim does not invoke federal subject matter jurisdiction, the fact that a counterclaim arises under federal law will not provide federal question jurisdiction for the case. Holmes Group v. Vornado Air Circulation, 535 U.S. 826, 831 (2002) ("[O]ur prior cases have only required us to address whether a federal defense, rather than a federal counterclaim, can establish 'arising under' jurisdiction. Nonetheless, those cases were decided on the principle that federal jurisdiction generally exists 'only when a federal question is presented on the face of the plaintiff's properly pleaded complaint.' * * * It follows that a counterclaim — which appears as part of the defendant's answer — cannot serve as a basis for 'arising under' jurisdiction.").

The *Holmes Group* case involved a claim arising under 28 U.S.C. § 1338, dealing with patent claims. In 2011, Congress amended § 1338(a) to allow federal courts to hear cases arising under federal intellectual property law even if the intellectual property law claim is asserted in a counterclaim. Although this amendment overturns the result of *Holmes Group* for cases brought under § 1338, it does not affect the well-pleaded complaint rule for "regular" federal question cases under § 1331. For those, a counterclaim cannot be the basis for original jurisdiction.

3. Do not become so carried away with the requirements of one form of jurisdiction that you overlook another possible basis for taking a case to federal court. If Mr. and Mrs. Mottley's case had met the citizenship (and amount in controversy) requirements, they could have invoked diversity of citizenship jurisdiction. (In fact, as the opinion noted, the Mottleys could not have done so.)

4. The well-pleaded complaint rule has the effect of funneling many questions of federal law out of the federal courts and into state courts. In *Mottley*, the only issues to be litigated were federal. The railroad did not dispute that it was not adhering to its contract with the Mottleys; rather, it contended that it had an excuse (the federal statute forbidding free passes). So the only matters to be determined at trial were (1) whether the federal statute required the railroad to refuse to honor the Mottleys' pass, and, (2) if so, whether it violated the Constitution. Yet, under the holding in *Mottley*, a state trial court had to decide these federal issues.

5. Proponents of the well-pleaded complaint rule argue that it serves the valuable function of allowing the court to decide at the outset whether a case arises under federal law. Specifically, if defendant's pleading could invoke federal question jurisdiction, a court would be in limbo as to whether it had jurisdiction, at least until the defendant filed her answer or otherwise raised a federal defense. Opponents of the rule (and there are many) note what we have already seen — that the rule does not funnel litigation centering on federal issues to federal court. They also argue that the question of what elements are considered part of the claim and what matters are considered defenses raises a policy issue that has no particular relation to federal jurisdiction. Further, the critics note that the rule is particularly difficult to apply in the context of a suit for declaratory judgment, as we will explore below. See generally

Donald Doernberg, *There's No Reason For It; It's Just Our Policy: Why the Well-Pleaded Complaint Rule Sabotages the Purposes of Federal Question Jurisdiction*, 38 Hast. L.J. 597 (1987).

6. The Supreme Court held that Mr. and Mrs. Mottley's claim did not "arise under" federal law and thus could not invoke the jurisdiction of a federal trial court. After the Court issued the opinion we just read, the Mottleys took their claim against the railroad to state court. After the case was appealed through the state court system, the United States Supreme Court heard it, ruling on the issues of whether the federal statute precluded the railroad from giving the pass to the Mottleys and whether the statute was unconstitutional. Louisville & Nashville Railroad v. Mottley, 219 U.S. 467 (1911). (By the way, the Court ruled for the Railroad.) Thus, just three years after the opinion you read, the Supreme Court addressed the very question it said could not fall within the federal trial court's jurisdiction!

The explanation for this anomaly lies in the mechanisms by which the two Mottley cases reached the Supreme Court. The first *Mottley* case originated in federal trial court. As a result, when the case was appealed to the Supreme Court, the Court had to determine whether the trial court had properly asserted jurisdiction under the precursor to § 1331. The second *Mottley* case originated in state court. Following the state court determination, an appeal was properly taken to the Supreme Court pursuant to 28 U.S.C. § 1257, which gives the Court appellate jurisdiction over final state court judgments in which a federal statute or constitutional provision is "drawn in question."

The fact that the Supreme Court ultimately heard the *Mottley* case highlights that the well-pleaded complaint rule is solely an interpretation of § 1331 and is not a constitutional limitation on the federal judicial power. Otherwise, there would have been no constitutional authority for the Supreme Court to review the second *Mottley* case.

7. You will recall that most of the personal jurisdiction cases we read in Chapter 2 originated in state court. Although these cases raised important federal constitutional questions concerning the scope of the Due Process Clause, this constitutional defense is not a sufficient basis to create original jurisdiction in the federal district court. If one reason for creating federal question jurisdiction is the fear that state judges may be less receptive to federal claims, shouldn't we also fear that they will be less receptive to federal defenses? In *World-Wide Volkswagen*, the Oklahoma state judge responded to the motion to dismiss by telling a defense lawyer that the Fourteenth Amendment did not "carry much water in Creek County." Of course, *World-Wide Volkswagen* was ultimately appealed to the United States Supreme Court, but that Court issues opinions in fewer than 100 cases a year.

ii. Well-Pleaded Complaint Problems Raised by Declaratory Judgments

In most cases, plaintiffs seek coercive relief—a remedy that will force the defendant to do something. For example, the plaintiff seeking damages wants the defendant to pay her money; the plaintiff seeking an injunction wants the defendant to do (or desist from doing) something. In such cases, the well-pleaded complaint rule is relatively easy to apply; if the plaintiff's claim for such relief is based upon federal law, it satisfies the well-pleaded complaint rule.

Sometimes, however, plaintiff will seek the noncoercive remedy of a declaratory judgment, in which she requests that the court declare the relative rights between the parties. For instance, an insurance company might seek a declaration that it is not required to pay under a policy because the insured breached a condition. A patent holder might seek a declaration that its patent is valid and has been infringed.

The declaratory judgment raises potentially serious questions about justiciability. Article III, Section 2 of the Constitution provides that the federal courts may be given jurisdiction only over "cases" and "controversies." Among other things, this requires that issues come to the federal bench only through contested litigation, and not through simple requests for the court's opinion on a matter. The federal courts cannot give advisory opinions. Thus, in providing for the remedy in the Federal Declaratory Judgment Act, 28 U.S.C. §§ 2201, 2202, Congress was careful to require that the request be made only "in cases of actual controversy."

In addition, the availability of declaratory relief can alter the alignment of parties one would expect in a case involving a coercive remedy. For example, just as the holder of a patent might sue for a declaration of validity, so an infringer might sue for a declaration of invalidity. And just as an insurer might seek a declaration that its policy is inoperative, so the insured might ask the court to declare that the policy is in force. In other words, the person bringing the declaratory judgment action would have been the defendant in a coercive suit.

How does this fact affect the well-pleaded complaint rule? One is tempted to say that the existence of the Federal Declaratory Judgment Act ensures that *any* declaratory judgment action will meet the well-pleaded complaint test. After all, any request for a declaratory judgment under the Act will set forth elements specified in a federal statute. But the Supreme Court rejected such a broad invocation of federal jurisdiction in Skelly Oil Co. v. Phillips Petroleum Co., 339 U.S. 667 (1950), in which it held that the Act merely creates a remedy, and does not provide a jurisdictional basis. Thus, declaratory judgment actions are proper under the Act only if supported by an independent basis of jurisdiction, such as diversity of citizenship or federal question jurisdiction.

Of course, this fact merely begs the question of how to apply the well-pleaded complaint rule to a claim for declaratory relief. The late Professor Charles Alan Wright synthesized the case law in a helpful way. He concluded that "the declaratory action may be entertained in federal court only if the coercive action that would have been necessary, absent declaratory judgment procedure, might have been so brought." WRIGHT & KANE, FEDERAL COURTS 113. For example, the patent holder who seeks a declaration that its patent is valid and is being infringed invokes federal jurisdiction because it could just as easily have sought coercive relief in the form of damages or an injunction for the same behavior.

Moreover, as Professor Wright demonstrated, it does not matter who would bring the coercive action, as long as one could be brought by one of the parties. For example, consider the flip side of the patent infringement case. Suppose the alleged infringer seeks a declaration that the manufacturer's patent is invalid or, alternatively, that its actions do not constitute infringement. It would have no right, of course, to bring a coercive action on these issues; they would be raised as defenses in a suit by the patent holder. Nonetheless, because the patent holder could have brought a coercive suit raising the same federal issues, jurisdiction is upheld. Id. at 113–14.

The Supreme Court reaffirmed this approach in Franchise Tax Board v. Construction Laborers Vacation Trust, 463 U.S. 1 (1983), the facts of which have been called (accurately) "the Exam Question from Hell masquerading as a federal lawsuit." Wright & Kane, Federal Courts 111, n.3. In that case, a labor union pooled money as a vacation trust for its members. The Franchise Tax Board, a California agency responsible for collecting state income tax, was unable to collect taxes from three union members. It sued the union vacation trust in state court, seeking tax money from the three employees' vacation fund. Among other things, the Franchise Tax Board sought a declaration that federal employee pension law did not prevent it from recovering the money from the trust.

The Supreme Court held that this claim did not create federal question jurisdiction and, thus, that the defendant could not "remove" the case to federal court. (We will discuss removal below; it permits a defendant to have a case transferred from state to federal court, but only if the case invoked federal subject matter jurisdiction. The defendant removed the case in *Franchise Tax Board*, but the Court held that there was no federal subject matter jurisdiction.) The Franchise Tax Board's claim was based upon state law. The question of whether federal law preempted the claim was raised by defense. Unless a coercive suit would arise under federal law, a declaratory judgment case cannot invoke federal question jurisdiction.

What, then, about *Mottley*? Could the Mottleys have invoked federal question jurisdiction for a declaration that federal law did not preclude the railroad from giving them their passes? Clearly not, since, as we saw, the Mottleys could not have brought a coercive action for the same claim. What about the railroad? Could it have invoked federal question jurisdiction by seeking a declaration that it was precluded from giving the passes to the Mottleys? Clearly not. Why?

iii. Centrality of the Federal Issue to the Claim

In addition to the requirement that the federal issue be injected in a well-pleaded complaint, the federal courts have imposed another statutory limitation on the words "arising under" in § 1331. Although this limitation is more difficult to describe, it basically concerns whether the federal issues set forth in the well-pleaded complaint are central enough to the dispute. In other words, to invoke federal question jurisdiction, the federal issue must be part of a well-pleaded complaint *and* must also be a sufficiently central part of the dispute to justify jurisdiction.

Does every aspect of the case have to be addressed by federal law, or can there be some state law elements? Suppose, for example, a federal statute creates a right to sue but directs the courts to determine liability by reference to state law. Does such a claim arise under federal law? These are the sorts of questions that can arise in this area. There is no doubt that the constitutional grant of federal question jurisdiction requires only that federal law be "an ingredient" of the case. Osborn v. Bank of the United States, 22 U.S. 738 (1824). Thus any case involving title to land in any part of the United States where the title is ultimately traced to a federal grant could constitutionally be heard in federal courts. But the statutory grant of federal question jurisdiction is narrower, and it is our focus here. We set the stage with a summary of four important Supreme Court opinions before reading the Court's most recent effort in the area.

The plaintiff in American Well Works Co. v. Layne & Bowler Co., 241 U.S. 257 (1916), manufactured a pump. It sued under state trade libel law, alleging that the defendant had wrongfully accused the plaintiff of infringing the defendant's patent on the pump. The complaint also alleged that the defendant had driven away customers by improperly threatening to sue anyone who bought the plaintiff's pump. Clearly, the litigation would focus solely on the federal issue of whether the plaintiff's pump actually did infringe defendant's patent. Nonetheless, the Supreme Court, in an opinion by Justice Oliver Wendell Holmes, held that the case did *not* arise under federal law. Holmes adopted a mechanical approach, concluding simply that "[a] suit arises under the law that creates the cause of action." Id. at 260. Because the claim for trade libel was based upon state law, there was no federal question jurisdiction.*

Five years later, the Court took a different tack. In Smith v. Kansas City Title & Trust Co., 255 U.S. 180 (1921), the plaintiff sued a corporation in which he held stock, seeking to enjoin the company from using corporate funds to invest in bonds issued under the Federal Farm Loan Act. He asserted that such an investment was illegal according to Missouri banking law because the Farm Loan Act was unconstitutional. Missouri law created the cause of action; thus, the case would not arise under federal law according to the *American Well Works* test. Nonetheless, the Court upheld jurisdiction, saying (over Justice Holmes' strong dissent) that "where it appears from the bill or statement of the plaintiff that the right to relief depends upon the construction or application of the Constitution or laws of the United States, and that such federal claim * * * rests upon a reasonable foundation, the District Court has

* Although the case addressed the predecessor to § 1338, concerning patent cases, and not the predecessor to § 1331, the interpretation of "arising under" applies to both.

jurisdiction." Id. at 199. Because *Smith* directly involved the construction of a federal act and the federal Constitution, jurisdiction existed.

The Court did not clarify matters when it decided Moore v. Chesapeake & Ohio Ry., 291 U.S. 205 (1934). There, the plaintiff sued under a state employers' liability act. Under that state law, contributory negligence could not bar an employee's recovery if the employer had violated a statute "enacted for the safety of employees." One such statute, incorporated into the state statute, was the Federal Safety Appliance Act. Thus, the question was whether the railroad employer had violated that federal law. The *American Well Works* case would counsel that the case did not arise under federal law because state law created the cause of action. *Smith*, however, would seem to require a finding of jurisdiction, since the case turned on the "construction or application" of federal law. The *Moore* Court found no jurisdiction, creating considerable confusion.

Thus, in *Smith* and *Moore*, plaintiffs brought state causes of action, but their cases raised significant questions of federal law. Yet one case arose under federal law for purposes of § 1331 and the other did not. The Court returned to this area and confused matters further in Merrell Dow Pharmaceuticals, Inc. v. Thompson, 478 U.S. 804 (1986). There, plaintiffs sued a manufacturer of drugs in state court on a variety of state-law claims. The claims involved birth defects allegedly caused by the ingestion of the drug Bendectin by pregnant women. One of the claims was for negligence *per se*, based upon the assertion that the drug was misbranded in violation of the Federal Food, Drug, and Cosmetic Act (FDCA). The defendant "removed" the case to federal court, and argued that the negligence *per se* claim invoked federal question jurisdiction. (We will study removal of cases from state to federal court in the last section of this chapter.) In a five-to-four decision, the Supreme Court held that the claim did not invoke federal question jurisdiction. The majority opinion, by Justice Stevens, relied in considerable measure on the fact that the FDCA did not create a private cause of action. In a footnote, Justice Stevens insisted that *Smith* remained good law, and that a state-created claim could invoke federal question jurisdiction if the federal interest were sufficiently "substantial."

In his dissent, Justice Brennan accused the majority of circular reasoning — that a state claim can invoke federal question jurisdiction only if the federal interest is substantial, while the fact that Congress had not created a private right of action showed that the claim was not substantial. Lower courts struggled mightily in the wake of *Merrell Dow*, with Courts of Appeals finally disagreeing on whether a state-created claim could ever invoke federal question jurisdiction. At bottom, the debate may mirror disagreement on the underlying reason for federal question jurisdiction. If one sees it as providing a federal forum for the vindication of federal claims, a court should reject jurisdiction over state-created claims. On the other hand, if one sees federal question jurisdiction as providing a federal forum for the interpretation of federal law, a court might accept jurisdiction over state-created claims that implicate important questions of federal law.

Observers were harshly critical of the Court's effort in *Merrell Dow.* The Court returned to the area in the following case.

Grable & Sons Metal Products, Inc. v. Darue Engineering & Manufacturing

545 U.S. 308, 125 S. Ct. 2363, 162 L. Ed. 2d 257 (2005)

Souter, J., delivered the opinion of the unanimous Court.

The question is whether want of a federal cause of action to try claims of title to land obtained at a federal tax sale precludes removal to federal court of a state action with non-diverse parties raising a disputed issue of federal title law. We answer no, and hold that the national interest in providing a federal forum for federal tax litigation is sufficiently substantial to support the exercise of federal question jurisdiction over the disputed issue on removal, which would not distort any division of labor between the state and federal courts, provided or assumed by Congress.

I

In 1994, the Internal Revenue Service seized Michigan real property belonging to petitioner Grable & Sons Metal Products, Inc., to satisfy Grable's federal tax delinquency. Title 26 U.S.C. § 6335 required the IRS to give notice of the seizure, and there is no dispute that Grable received actual notice by certified mail before the IRS sold the property to respondent Darue Engineering & Manufacturing. Although Grable also received notice of the sale itself, it did not exercise its statutory right to redeem the property within 180 days of the sale, § 6337(b)(1), and after that period had passed, the Government gave Darue a quitclaim deed. § 6339.

Five years later, Grable brought a quiet title action in state court, claiming that Darue's record title was invalid because the IRS had failed to notify Grable of its seizure of the property in the exact manner required by § 6335(a), which provides that written notice must be "given by the Secretary to the owner of the property [or] left at his usual place of abode or business." Grable said that the statute required personal service, not service by certified mail.

Darue removed the case to Federal District Court as presenting a federal question, because the claim of title depended on the interpretation of the notice statute in the federal tax law. The District Court declined to remand the case at Grable's behest after finding that the "claim does pose a significant question of federal law," and ruling that Grable's lack of a federal right of action to enforce its claim against Darue did not bar the exercise of federal jurisdiction. On the merits, the court granted summary judgment to Darue, holding that although § 6335 by its terms required personal service, substantial compliance with the statute was enough.

The Court of Appeals for the Sixth Circuit affirmed. On the jurisdictional question, the panel thought it sufficed that the title claim raised an issue of federal law that had to be resolved, and implicated a substantial federal interest (in construing federal tax law). The court went on to affirm the District Court's judgment on the merits. We granted certiorari on the jurisdictional question alone,[1] to resolve a split within

1. Accordingly, we have no occasion to pass upon the proper interpretation of the federal tax provision at issue here.

the Courts of Appeals on whether Merrell Dow Pharmaceuticals, Inc. v. Thompson, 478 U.S. 804 (1986), always requires a federal cause of action as a condition for exercising federal-question jurisdiction.[2] We now affirm.

II

Darue was entitled to remove the quiet title action if Grable could have brought it in federal district court originally, as a civil action "arising under the Constitution, laws, or treaties of the United States," § 1331. This provision for federal-question jurisdiction is invoked by and large by plaintiffs pleading a cause of action created by federal law * * *. There is, however, another longstanding, if less frequently encountered, variety of federal "arising under" jurisdiction, this Court having recognized for nearly 100 years that in certain cases federal question jurisdiction will lie over state-law claims that implicate significant federal issues. E.g., Hopkins v. Walker, 244 U.S. 486, 490–91 (1917). The doctrine captures the commonsense notion that a federal court ought to be able to hear claims recognized under state law that nonetheless turn on substantial questions of federal law, and thus justify resort to the experience, solicitude, and hope of uniformity that a federal forum offers on federal issues.

The classic example is Smith v. Kansas City Title & Trust Co., 255 U.S. 180 (1921), a suit by a shareholder claiming that the defendant corporation could not lawfully buy certain bonds of the National Government because their issuance was unconstitutional. Although Missouri law provided the cause of action, the Court recognized federal-question jurisdiction because the principal issue in the case was the federal constitutionality of the bond issue. *Smith* thus held, in a somewhat generous statement of the scope of the doctrine, that a state-law claim could give rise to federal-question jurisdiction so long as it "appears from the [complaint] that the right to relief depends upon the construction or application of [federal law]."

The *Smith* statement has been subject to some trimming to fit earlier and later cases recognizing the vitality of the basic doctrine, but shying away from the expansive view that mere need to apply federal law in a state-law claim will suffice to open the "arising under" door. As early as 1912, this Court had confined federal-question jurisdiction over state-law claims to those that "really and substantially involv[e] a dispute or controversy respecting the validity, construction or effect of [federal] law." Shulthis v. McDougal, 225 U.S. 561, 569 (1912). This limitation was the ancestor of Justice Cardozo's later explanation that a request to exercise federal-question jurisdiction over a state action calls for a "common-sense accommodation of judgment to [the] kaleidoscopic situations" that present a federal issue, in "a selective process which picks the substantial causes out of the web and lays the other ones aside." Gully v. First Bank in Meridian, 299 U.S. 109 (1936). It has in fact become a constant refrain in such cases that federal jurisdiction demands not only a contested federal

2. Compare Seinfeld v. Austen, 39 F.3d 761, 764 (7th Cir. 1994) (finding that federal-question jurisdiction over a state-law claim requires a parallel federal private right of action), with Ormet Corp. v. Ohio Power Co., 98 F.3d 799, 806 (4th Cir. 1996) (finding that a federal private action is not required).

issue, but a substantial one, indicating a serious federal interest in claiming the advantages thought to be inherent in a federal forum.

But even when the state action discloses a contested and substantial federal question, the exercise of federal jurisdiction is subject to a possible veto. For the federal issue will ultimately qualify for a federal forum only if federal jurisdiction is consistent with congressional judgment about the sound division of labor between state and federal courts governing the application of § 1331. Thus, *Franchise Tax Bd.* explained that the appropriateness of a federal forum to hear an embedded issue could be evaluated only after considering the "welter of issues regarding the interrelation of federal and state authority and the proper management of the federal judicial system." Because arising-under jurisdiction to hear a state-law claim always raises the possibility of upsetting the state-federal line drawn (or at least assumed) by Congress, the presence of a disputed federal issue and the ostensible importance of a federal forum are never necessarily dispositive; there must always be an assessment of any disruptive portent in exercising federal jurisdiction.

These considerations have kept us from stating a "single, precise, all-embracing" test for jurisdiction over federal issues embedded in state-law claims between nondiverse parties. Christianson v. Colt Industries Operating Corp., 486 U.S. 800, 821 (1988) (Stevens, J., concurring). We have not kept them out simply because they appeared in state raiment, as Justice Holmes would have done, but neither have we treated "federal issue" as a password opening federal courts to any state action embracing a point of federal law. Instead, the question is, does a state-law claim necessarily raise a stated federal issue, actually disputed and substantial, which a federal forum may entertain without disturbing any congressionally approved balance of federal and state judicial responsibilities.

III

A

This case warrants federal jurisdiction. Grable's state complaint must specify "the facts establishing the superiority of [its] claim," MICH. CT. RULE 3.411(B)(2)(c), and Grable has premised its superior title claim on a failure by the IRS to give it adequate notice, as defined by federal law. Whether Grable was given notice within the meaning of the federal statute is thus an essential element of its quiet title claim, and the meaning of the federal statute is actually in dispute; it appears to be the only legal or factual issue contested in the case. The meaning of the federal tax provision is an important issue of federal law that sensibly belongs in a federal court. The Government has a strong interest in the "prompt and certain collection of delinquent taxes," United States v. Rodgers, 461 U.S. 677, 709 (1983), and the ability of the IRS to satisfy its claims from the property of delinquents requires clear terms of notice to allow buyers like Darue to satisfy themselves that the Service has touched the bases necessary for good title. The Government thus has a direct interest in the availability of a federal forum to vindicate its own administrative action, and buyers (as well as tax delinquents) may find it valuable to come before judges used to federal tax matters. Finally, because it will be the rare state title case that raises a contested matter of federal law, federal jurisdiction to resolve genuine disagreement over federal tax title provisions will portend only a microscopic effect on the federal-state division of labor. See n. 3, infra.

This conclusion puts us in venerable company, quiet title actions having been the subject of some of the earliest exercises of federal-question jurisdiction over state-law claims. In *Hopkins*, [244 U.S. at 490–91], the question was federal jurisdiction over a quiet title action based on the plaintiffs' allegation that federal mining law gave them the superior claim. Just as in this case, "the facts showing the plaintiffs' title and the existence and invalidity of the instrument or record sought to be eliminated as a cloud upon the title are essential parts of the plaintiffs' cause of action."[3] As in this case again, "it is plain that a controversy respecting the construction and effect of the [federal] laws is involved and is sufficiently real and substantial." This Court therefore upheld federal jurisdiction in *Hopkins*, as well as in the similar quiet title matters of [other cases decided in the early twentieth century]. Consistent with those cases, the recognition of federal jurisdiction is in order here.

B

Merrell Dow Pharmaceuticals, Inc. v. Thompson, 478 U.S. 804 (1986), on which Grable rests its position, is not to the contrary. *Merrell Dow* considered a state tort claim resting in part on the allegation that the defendant drug company had violated a federal misbranding prohibition, and was thus presumptively negligent under Ohio law. The Court assumed that federal law would have to be applied to resolve the claim, but after closely examining the strength of the federal interest at stake and the implications of opening the federal forum, held federal jurisdiction unavailable. Congress had not provided a private federal cause of action for violation of the federal branding requirement, and the Court found "it would ... flout, or at least undermine, congressional intent to conclude that federal courts might nevertheless exercise federal-question jurisdiction and provide remedies for violations of that federal statute solely because the violation ... is said to be a ... 'proximate cause' under state law."

Because federal law provides for no quiet title action that could be brought against Darue,[4] Grable argues that there can be no federal jurisdiction here, stressing some broad language in *Merrell Dow* (including the passage just quoted) that on its face

3. The quiet title cases also show the limiting effect of the requirement that the federal issue in a state-law claim must actually be in dispute to justify federal-question jurisdiction. In Shulthis v. McDougal, 225 U.S. 561 (1912), this Court found that there was no federal question jurisdiction to hear a plaintiff's quiet title claim in part because the federal statutes on which title depended were not subject to "any controversy respecting their validity, construction, or effect." As the Court put it, the requirement of an actual dispute about federal law was "especially" important in "suit[s] involving rights to land acquired under a law of the United States," because otherwise "every suit to establish title to land in the central and western states would so arise [under federal law], as all titles in those States are traceable back to those laws."

4. Federal law does provide a quiet title cause of action against the Federal Government. 28 U.S.C. § 2410. That right of action is not relevant here, however, because the federal government no longer has any interest in the property, having transferred its interest to Darue through the quitclaim deed.

supports Grable's position * * *. But an opinion is to be read as a whole, and *Merrell Dow* cannot be read whole as overturning decades of precedent, as it would have done by effectively adopting the Holmes dissent in *Smith*, and converting a federal cause of action from a sufficient condition for federal-question jurisdiction[5] into a necessary one.

In the first place, *Merrell Dow* disclaimed the adoption of any bright-line rule, as when the Court reiterated that "in exploring the outer reaches of § 1331, determinations about federal jurisdiction require sensitive judgments about congressional intent, judicial power, and the federal system." The opinion included a lengthy footnote explaining that questions of jurisdiction over state-law claims require "careful judgments," about the "nature of the federal interest at stake" (emphasis deleted). And as a final indication that it did not mean to make a federal right of action mandatory, it expressly approved the exercise of jurisdiction sustained in *Smith*, despite the want of any federal cause of action available to *Smith*'s shareholder plaintiff. *Merrell Dow* then, did not toss out, but specifically retained the contextual enquiry that had been *Smith*'s hallmark for over 60 years. At the end of *Merrell Dow*, Justice Holmes was still dissenting.

Accordingly, *Merrell Dow* should be read in its entirety as treating the absence of a federal private right of action as evidence relevant to, but not dispositive of, the "sensitive judgments about congressional intent" that § 1331 requires. The absence of any federal cause of action affected *Merrell Dow*'s result two ways. The Court saw the fact as worth some consideration in the assessment of substantiality. But its primary importance emerged when the Court treated the combination of no federal cause of action and no preemption of state remedies for misbranding as an important clue to Congress's conception of the scope of jurisdiction to be exercised under § 1331. The Court saw the missing cause of action not as a missing federal door key, always required, but as a missing welcome mat, required in the circumstances, when exercising federal jurisdiction over a state misbranding action would have attracted a horde of original filings and removal cases raising other state claims with embedded federal issues. For if the federal labeling standard without a federal cause of action could get a state claim into federal court, so could any other federal standard without a federal cause of action. And that would have meant a tremendous number of cases.

One only needed to consider the treatment of federal violations generally in garden variety state tort law. "The violation of federal statutes and regulations is commonly given negligence per se effect in state tort proceedings."[6] Restatement (Third) of Torts (proposed final draft) § 14, Comment *a.* A general rule of exercising federal jurisdiction

5. For an extremely rare exception to the sufficiency of a federal right of action, see Shoshone Mining Co. v. Rutter, 177 U.S. 505, 507 (1900).

6. Other jurisdictions treat a violation of a federal statute as evidence of negligence or, like Ohio itself in *Merrell Dow*, as creating a rebuttable presumption of negligence. Restatement (Third) of Torts (proposed final draft) § 14, Comment *c.* Either approach could still implicate issues of federal law.

over state claims resting on federal mislabeling and other statutory violations would thus have heralded a potentially enormous shift of traditionally state cases into federal courts. Expressing concern over the "increased volume of federal litigation," and noting the importance of adhering to "legislative intent," *Merrell Dow* thought it improbable that the Congress, having made no provision for a federal cause of action, would have meant to welcome any state-law tort case implicating federal law "solely because the violation of the federal statute is said to [create] a rebuttable presumption [of negligence] ... under state law." 478 U.S. at 811–12. In this situation, no welcome mat meant keep out. *Merrell Dow*'s analysis thus fits within the framework of examining the importance of having a federal forum for the issue, and the consistency of such a forum with Congress's intended division of labor between state and federal courts.

As already indicated, however, a comparable analysis yields a different jurisdictional conclusion in this case. Although Congress also indicated ambivalence in this case by providing no private right of action to Grable, it is the rare state quiet title action that involves contested issues of federal law, see n. 3, *supra.* Consequently, jurisdiction over actions like Grable's would not materially affect, or threaten to affect, the normal currents of litigation. Given the absence of threatening structural consequences and the clear interest the Government, its buyers, and its delinquents have in the availability of a federal forum, there is no good reason to shirk from federal jurisdiction over the dispositive and contested federal issue at the heart of the state-law title claim.[7]

IV

The judgment of the Court of Appeals, upholding federal jurisdiction over Grable's quiet title action, is affirmed.

It is so ordered.

THOMAS, J., concurring.

The Court faithfully applies our precedents interpreting 28 U.S.C. § 1331 to authorize federal-court jurisdiction over some cases in which state law creates the cause of action but requires determination of an issue of federal law. In this case, no one has asked us to overrule those precedents and adopt the rule Justice Holmes set forth in *American Well Works Co.*, * * * limiting § 1331 jurisdiction to cases in which federal law creates the cause of action pleaded on the face of the plaintiff's complaint. In an appropriate case, and perhaps with the benefit of better evidence as to the original meaning of § 1331's text, I would be willing to consider that course.*

7. At oral argument Grable's counsel espoused the position that after *Merrell Dow*, federal-question jurisdiction over state-law claims absent a federal right of action, could be recognized only where a constitutional issue was at stake. There is, however, no reason in text or otherwise to draw such a rough line. As *Merrell Dow* itself suggested, constitutional questions may be the more likely ones to reach the level of substantiality that can justify federal jurisdiction. But a flat ban on statutory questions would mechanically exclude significant questions of federal law like the one this case presents.

* This Court has long construed the scope of the statutory grant of federal-question jurisdiction more narrowly than the scope of the constitutional grant of such jurisdiction. See *Merrell Dow*. I assume for present purposes that this distinction is proper — that is, that the language of 28 U.S.C.

Jurisdictional rules should be clear. Whatever the virtues of the *Smith* standard, it is anything but clear. ([T]he standard "calls for a 'common-sense accommodation of judgment to [the] kaleidoscopic situations' that present a federal issue, in 'a selective process which picks the substantial causes out of the web and lays the other ones aside'" (quoting Gully v. First Nat. Bank in Meridian, 299 U.S. 109, 117–18 (1936); ("[T]he question is, does a state-law claim necessarily raise a stated federal issue, actually disputed and substantial, which a federal forum may entertain without disturbing any congressionally approved balance of federal and state judicial responsibilities"); ("'[D]eterminations about federal jurisdiction require sensitive judgments about congressional intent, judicial power, and the federal system'"; "the absence of a federal private right of action [is] evidence relevant to, but not dispositive of, the 'sensitive judgments about congressional intent' that § 1331 requires" (quoting *Merrell Dow*)).

Whatever the vices of the *American Well Works* rule, it is clear. Moreover, it accounts for the "'vast majority'" of cases that come within § 1331 under our current case law—further indication that trying to sort out which cases fall within the smaller *Smith* category may not be worth the effort it entails. Accordingly, I would be willing in appropriate circumstances to reconsider our interpretation of § 1331.

Notes and Questions

1. Once the federal issue raised in *Grable* is determined definitively, will lower federal court jurisdiction continue to be necessary? In other words, once the federal courts decide whether service by certified mail suffices under the relevant tax delinquency provision, will future cases involving delinquency proceedings invoke federal question jurisdiction? Is federal question jurisdiction provided to permit access to lower federal courts for *interpretation* of federal law or *application* of federal law (or both)?

2. Does *Grable* provide meaningful guidance for future cases involving state-created claims with embedded issues of federal law? If so, is Justice Thomas's suggestion that the Court consider embracing the Holmes formula from *American Well Works* timely? Is he advocating a return to the Holmes test for the sake of certainty after the Court has provided such certainty?

3. Note what is at stake in the debate over whether a claim invokes federal question jurisdiction. If the claim "arises under" federal law under § 1331, it can be filed in a federal trial court, with an appeal to the United States Court of Appeals and possible further review by the Supreme Court—all of which are Article III courts. If the claim does not "arise under" federal law and cannot invoke jurisdiction under § 1331, it

---

§ 1331, "[t]he district courts shall have original jurisdiction of all *civil actions arising under* the Constitution, laws, or treaties of the United States" (emphasis added), is narrower than the language of Art. III, § 2, cl. 1, of the Constitution, "[t]he judicial Power shall extend to all *Cases*, in Law and Equity, *arising under* this Constitution, the Laws of the United States, and Treaties made, or which shall be made, under their Authority ..." (emphases added).

must be filed in state court (unless there is diversity of citizenship). That means a state judge will be interpreting the question of federal law, with review by the state court of appeals and supreme court— none of which is an Article III court. The only way such cases might be reviewed by an Article III court is in the extremely unlikely event that the Supreme Court grants certiorari after litigation to the highest state court.

In his dissent in *Merrell Dow*, Justice Brennan urged a broad interpretation of § 1331 because he had become convinced that the Supreme Court's certiorari jurisdiction did not permit that Court to provide sufficient supervisory authority over state-court interpretations of federal law. Consider this assessment of *Grable*:

> At the end of the day, the statutory definition of "arising under" is in better shape now than it has been in a generation, which should put to rest any latter-day calls for a return to the Holmes test for centrality. This improved state of affairs is only possible because the Court has finally unequivocally embraced the notion that federal question jurisdiction exists for more than one purpose. In addition to providing an Article III forum for the vindication of federally created rights, it also serves to open the lower federal court doors to claims requiring application or interpretation of federal law. This function reflects the reality that the Supreme Court cannot today perform that task through its appellate review of state-court decisions. And it is discharged only with a sensitive balancing approach reflecting the delicate task at hand—that of allocating judicial power between separate sovereigns.

Richard Freer, *Of Rules and Standards: Reconciling Statutory Limitations on "Arising Under" Jurisdiction*, 82 Indiana L.J. 309, 344 (2007).

4. Suppose a state enacted this statute:

> Any person who suffers injury as a result of a violation of federal drug labeling requirements shall be entitled to sue therefor, and, if successful, to recover three times her actual damages, plus attorney's fees.

After *Grable*, would a claim brought under this statute invoke federal question jurisdiction?

5. One year after deciding *Grable*, the Supreme Court rejected federal question jurisdiction over a state-created claim that raised an embedded federal issue in Empire HealthChoice Assurance, Inc. v. McVeigh, 547 U.S. 677 (2006). The Federal Health Benefits Act (FEHBA) creates a program of health insurance for federal employees. It provides that the plan administrator can seek reimbursement of medical bills for which it paid if the beneficiary recovers damages against the third-party who injured the insured. Decedent was injured in an accident, for which the plan paid $157,309. Decedent's administrator sued the alleged wrongdoer in state court and received a substantial settlement (far exceeding the amount paid by the plan). The insurer for the plan then sued the decedent's estate for reimbursement under FEHBA to recover the $157,309; it filed in federal court under § 1331.

Plaintiff (joined in an amicus curiae brief by the United States) argued that the case invoked federal question jurisdiction under *Grable*. By a five-to-four margin, the Court rejected jurisdiction. According to the majority, *Empire* and *Grable* were "poles apart." In *Grable* the dispute was triggered by an act of the IRS, while the reimbursement claim in *Empire* was triggered by the settlement of a private tort case in state court. While *Grable* involved a question of law which, when determined, would govern many tax-sale cases, the dispute in *Empire* involved a fact-bound question of whether particular services paid for by the plan were properly attributable to the accident that was the basis of the state-court suit. In sum, "an insurer's contract-derived claim to be reimbursed from the proceeds of a federal worker's state-court ... litigation" could not be "squeezed into the slim category [of cases] *Grable* exemplifies."

6. The Court applied *Grable* to reject jurisdiction in Gunn v. Minton, 133 S. Ct. 1059 (2013). Plaintiff asserted a state-law claim against his lawyers for malpractice in a patent matter. Specifically, he argued that they were negligent in not asserting the "experimental use" exception to the "on-sale" bar in underlying infringement suit. The Court held that the malpractice claim does not arise under federal law and thus did not invoke federal question jurisdiction. Decision of the malpractice claim would require resolution of a federal patent issue which was actually disputed. But the federal issue was not sufficiently substantial to the federal judicial system. Moreover, state-court jurisdiction over such malpractice claims would not upset the appropriate balance between federal and state judicial responsibilities. Chief Justice Roberts wrote for a unanimous Court:

> [E]ven where a claim finds its origins in state rather than federal law—as Minton's legal malpractice claim indisputably does—we have identified a "special and small category" of cases in which arising under jurisdiction still lies. Empire HealthChoice Assurance, Inc. v. McVeigh, 547 U.S. 677, 699 (2006). In outlining the contours of this slim category, we do not paint on a blank canvas. Unfortunately, the canvas looks like one that Jackson Pollock got to first.
>
> In an effort to bring some order to this unruly doctrine several Terms ago, we condensed our prior cases into the following inquiry: Does the "state-law claim necessarily raise a stated federal issue, actually disputed and substantial, which a federal forum may entertain without disturbing any congressionally approved balance of federal and state judicial responsibilities"? *Grable*, 545 U.S., at 314. That is, federal jurisdiction over a state law claim will lie if a federal issue is: (1) necessarily raised, (2) actually disputed, (3) substantial, and (4) capable of resolution in federal court without disrupting the federal-state balance approved by Congress. Where all four of these requirements are met, we held, jurisdiction is proper because there is a "serious federal interest in claiming the advantages thought to be inherent in a federal forum," which can be vindicated without disrupting Congress's intended division of labor between state and federal courts. *Id.*, at 313–314.

133 S. Ct. at 1064–1065.

7. Federal question jurisdiction does not require that the federal law involved be novel. Neither does it require that the federal assertion be a clear winner. Remember, the assessment here is simply whether a federal court has jurisdiction to hear the claim. The court will not know whether the plaintiff's legal and factual contentions prevail until it addresses the merits of the case. As long as federal law is part of a well-pleaded complaint and is not "plainly insubstantial," Bell v. Hood, 327 U.S. 678 (1946), the federal court can exercise jurisdiction.

8. Do you agree with the conclusion that "Justice Holmes' formula [that the claim arises under the law that created it] is more useful for inclusion than for the exclusion for which it was intended." T.B. Harms Co. v. Eliscu, 339 F.2d 823, 827 (2d Cir. 1964). Interestingly, Justice Holmes' opinion in *American Well Works* did not overrule Shoshone Mining Co. v. Rutter, 177 U.S. 505 (1900), in which a federal law empowered federal courts to hear disputes involving mining claims on federal lands. The statute provided that local customs would be applied to determine such disputes. Though federal law clearly created the claim, the Supreme Court held that there was no federal question jurisdiction, because the claim would involve merely the interpretation and application of local law. The Court has never overruled *Shoshone.*

9. Section 1331 is known as the "general" federal question statute, an omnibus provision allowing a claim arising under any federal law to be brought in federal court. While we address only § 1331 in detail, note that there are many specialized federal question statutes allowing jurisdiction over claims arising under specific federal laws. For instance, § 1337 grants jurisdiction over federal antitrust cases; § 1338 grants jurisdiction over patent and trademark cases, and § 1343 grants jurisdiction related to civil rights claims.

In American Red Cross v. S.G., 505 U.S. 247 (1992), plaintiffs sued the Red Cross, alleging that they contracted AIDS from tainted blood provided by that organization. The Red Cross is a corporation chartered by the federal government. The statute creating it authorizes it "to sue and be sued in courts of law and equity, State and Federal, within the jurisdiction of the United States." 36 U.S.C. § 2. The Supreme Court concluded that this provision not only gives the Red Cross the capacity to litigate, but also grants federal courts subject matter jurisdiction over all cases involving it. Thus, any state-law claim by or against the Red Cross invokes federal jurisdiction. Such cases are brought directly under 36 U.S.C. § 2, and not the general federal question statute (§ 1331) that we have addressed.

5. Supplemental Jurisdiction

A case that invokes federal subject matter jurisdiction — diversity of citizenship, alienage, or federal question — might include individual claims or issues that do not. For example, a plaintiff might have a federal question claim and a state law claim against a single defendant. If she cannot invoke diversity of citizenship, there is no independent basis of jurisdiction for the state law claim. Similarly, a defendant might have a state law cross-claim for indemnity against her co-defendant. Again, if she is not of diverse citizenship from her co-defendant (or if her claim does not exceed $75,000), there is no independent basis of jurisdiction for the cross-claim.

The federal courts have long recognized their power to hear such claims, as long as they are so closely related to the underlying dispute as to constitute part of the same "case or controversy" under Article III. Jurisdiction over such claims has been called "pendent" or "ancillary" jurisdiction, and has a rich, controversial history. In 1990, Congress codified the area, employing the generic rubric of "supplemental" jurisdiction.

Problems involving supplemental jurisdiction are common and often difficult. Because they arise when someone joins a claim that does not have an independent basis of subject matter jurisdiction such as diversity of citizenship, alienage, or federal question, they are best addressed in the context of the joinder rules. Thus, we will investigate this area in depth in Chapter 12.

6. Removal Jurisdiction

We encountered the concept of removal in the *Hertz* case. The removal statutes give the defendant a role in deciding whether a case will proceed in federal or state court. They permit the defendant to "remove" a case that was originally filed in state court to federal court. The case must be one over which the federal courts have subject matter jurisdiction. Removal effects a relocation of the case from the state trial court to the federal trial court. (Though removal results in a transfer of the case from the state system to the federal system, we do not use the term "transfer"; rather, we use "removal," which is a term of art applicable only to this situation.) Removal is not an appeal; as we discussed in Chapter 1, federal courts have no general power to sit in judgment of what the state courts do.*

Defendants are likely to remove cases for the same reasons that plaintiffs may select a federal forum initially — they may prefer unelected federal Article III judges or be concerned about possible local bias of the state court; they may prefer federal court procedures or believe the federal court has greater expertise; they may prefer the fact that a federal jury is drawn from a wider geographic area (the federal district) than in state court (usually the county); or the defendant's lawyer may simply have greater familiarity with federal court practice.

Read 28 U.S.C. §§ 1441 (except 1441(e), which relates to specialized litigation involving some mass accidents), 1446, and 1447. The defendant does not need the federal court's permission to remove; she simply removes the case. See § 1446(d). If removal is improper, the federal court remands the case to state court. It might do so because the defendant failed to follow the procedures for removal or because the federal court lacks subject matter jurisdiction. Because she is invoking federal subject

* In this book we discuss the general removal provisions of the Judicial Code. We do not address removal provisions that apply only in specialized cases. See, e.g., 28 U.S.C. §§ 1442 (suit or prosecution against a federal officer); 2679(d) (tort by a federal employee).

matter jurisdiction, the defendant has the burden to demonstrate that the plaintiff's claim invokes that jurisdiction.

Section 1441(a) permits removal only to the federal district "embracing the place where such action is pending." For example, a case pending in state court in St. Louis can be removed *only* to the Eastern District of Missouri, which encompasses St. Louis.* It cannot be removed to the district court in Kansas City, which is in the Western District of Missouri, or to any other federal district.

What about timing? 28 U.S.C. § 1446(b) provides 30 days in which to remove. But when does this period start to run? In Murphy Bros. v. Michetti Pipe Stringing, Inc., 526 U.S. 344 (1999), the plaintiff faxed to the defendant a "courtesy copy" of the complaint. The parties then engaged in settlement discussions for about two weeks, after which the plaintiff had process served formally. Thirty days after this formal service, but 44 days after receiving the faxed copy, the defendant removed the case to federal court. The Supreme Court held that the 30 days did not begin to run until service was effected. The "or otherwise" language is intended to address the various state approaches to the order of filing a case and serving process. For instance, in some states, the defendant is served with a summons, but not with the complaint. For such defendants, the 30-day period would start to run upon receipt of the complaint.

Section 1446(b)(2) was added by legislation in 2011. It is a very helpful provision. Under § 1446(b)(2)(A), all defendants who have been properly joined and served with process must agree to the removal. This "rule of unanimity" had been applied by courts even before the statute made it express. Suppose Plaintiff files a removable case in state court, naming four defendants. She has three of the defendants served with process immediately. If, within 30 days of being served, those three remove the case, removal is effective, even though the fourth defendant did not participate in the removal. Why? Because that fourth defendant had not been served with process; only those defendants named *and served* must participate in the removal.

In Chapter 7, on Pleadings, we will see that in federal court, the defendant generally must respond to suit against her within 21 days after service of process. In some state courts, she has a longer period in which to respond to the complaint. And, as we saw, she has 30 days from service in which to remove the case. What happens if she removes the case more than 21 days after service of process upon her? Is she then deemed to be late with her response to the complaint? The answer is no. Federal Rule 81(c)(2) contains a useful provision that allows defendants at least seven days after filing the notice of removal in which to make their defensive response in federal court. Note also that removing the case from state to federal court does not waive the defendant's potential argument that she is not subject to personal jurisdiction. Thus she can assert that defense under Federal Rule 12(b)(2) within the time permitted by Rule 81(c)(2).

In Dart Cherokee Basin Operating Co., LLC v. Owens, 135 S. Ct. 547 (2014), the Court rejected the argument that a defendant who removes a case must have *evidence*

* Thus, the venue provisions of 28 U.S.C. § 1391, which apply to cases filed by plaintiff in federal court, and which we will address in Chapter 5, do not apply to removed cases.

that the amount in controversy requirement is satisfied. All the defendant need do is have a "plausible allegation" that the amount requirement is met. The Court said: "as specified in § 1446(a), a defendant's notice of removal need include only a plausible allegation that the amount in controversy exceeds the jurisdictional threshold. Evidence establishing the amount is required by § 1446(c)(2)(B) only when the plaintiff contests, or the court questions, the defendant's allegation." 135 S.Ct. at 554.*

The Court relied upon the fact that Congress used language in § 1446(a) consistent with the general pleading requirements of Federal Rule 8(a). Each requires a "short and plain" statement. 135 S. Ct. at 553 We will study Rule 8(a) in Chapter 7.

Notes and Questions

1. Plaintiff files a removable case in state court on July 1, naming three defendants, D-1, D-2, and D-3. She has process served on D-1 and D-2 on July 1. They do not remove the case. On September 1, Plaintiff has process served on D-3.

(a) Can D-3 remove the case by herself?

(b) Can she do so if she gets D-1 and D-2 to join in her notice of removal?

2. Work through the following hypotheticals:

(a) Perry, a citizen of Missouri, sues Dale, a citizen of California, for $100,000 tort damages in a state court in St. Louis. Can Dale remove the case to federal court? When may Dale do so? What steps does Dale take to do so? What happens if, after removal, Perry seeks to add David as a defendant, and David is a citizen of Missouri?

(b) Same facts as in Question 2(a), except the case is originally filed in the appropriate state court in Los Angeles. Why can Dale not remove this case to federal court? Does this rule make sense in light of the underlying theory of diversity of citizenship jurisdiction? Articulate how the "instate defendant rule" renders removal jurisdiction narrower than original jurisdiction in this case.

(c) Here we are going to look at two fact patterns, in each of which the presence of one defendant in the case defeats removal. Then we will see if dismissal of the claim against the removal-defeating defendant will make the case removable.

Pat, a citizen of North Carolina, sues D-1, a citizen of South Carolina, and D-2, a citizen of North Carolina, in an appropriate state court in Georgia. Pat asserts that the two defendants are joint tortfeasors and asserts a state-law claim for $500,000 damages. Obviously, the case is not removable, because it does not invoke federal subject matter jurisdiction (it does not invoke diversity or federal question

---

* *Dart Cherokee* was a class action removed under the Class Action Fairness Act (CAFA), which we will study in Chapter 13. Nonetheless, because the opinion interprets the removal provision of § 1446(c), its holding will apply to the removal of diversity cases under § 1332(a). See 135 S. Ct. at 554 n.1 (assuming without deciding an issue the parties did not dispute, that § 1446(c) applies to removal of CAFA cases).

jurisdiction). But if the claim against D-2 (the non-diverse defendant) were dropped from the case, would D-1 be able to remove?

As an alternative, suppose Pat, a citizen of North Carolina, asserts a state-law claim of $500,000 against D-1, a citizen of South Carolina, and D-2, a citizen of Georgia, in a Georgia state court. Even though this case could have been filed in federal court (because it meets the requirements for a diversity of citizenship case), it cannot be removed, because of the instate defendant rule we saw in Question 2(b). But if the claim against D-2 (the instate defendant) were dropped from the case, would D-1 be able to remove?

Historically, courts stated that diversity of citizenship must exist both when the defendant removes the case and when the plaintiff files it in state court. Gibson v. Bruce, 108 U.S. 561 (1883). This rule would "prevent the defendant from acquiring a new domicile after commencement of the suit and then removing on the basis of diversity." WRIGHT & KANE, FEDERAL COURTS 232. But the reason for this limitation does not apply if the plaintiff voluntarily dismisses the claim against the nondiverse defendant or the instate defendant; the defendant has no control over whether the plaintiff voluntarily dismisses a claim. Accordingly, courts distinguish between (1) cases in which the plaintiff voluntarily dismisses the claim against the defendant who defeats removal and (2) cases in which the court dismisses the claim against that defendant. In the former, courts permit the remaining diverse defendant to remove the case. In the latter, they generally do not, because the dismissal might be reversed on appeal.

In 1949, however, Congress amended § 1446(b) to add the provision permitting removal upon "receipt by the defendant * * * of an amended pleading, motion, order, or other paper from which it may first be ascertained that the case is one which is or has become removable." Although this language appears to make no distinction as to why the claim against the nondiverse defendant is dismissed, most courts continue to make the historic distinction. See Poulos v. Naas Foods, Inc., 959 F.2d 69 (7th Cir. 1992). Thus, most courts allow D-1 to remove the case only if Pat voluntarily dismissed the claim against D-2.

(d) Why would your answer concerning the two fact patterns in Question 2(c) be different if the plaintiff voluntarily dismissed the claim against D-2 thirteen months after the case was filed in state court? Does this rule make sense in light of the underlying theory of diversity of citizenship jurisdiction? After D-2 is dismissed from the case, isn't D-1 in exactly the situation for which diversity of citizenship jurisdiction was created?

(e) Until an amendment to the removal law in 2011, the one-year limitation on removal of diversity cases was absolute. Pursuant to legislation passed in 2011, now it is not. What language makes that clear?

3. In many states, a plaintiff is not required to state a dollar figure for her damages. In most states, even when she does state a dollar figure, she may recover more than that if the case is adjudicated. A defendant might be nervous, then, about plaintiff's

failure to state a dollar figure (or setting one at $75,000 or less) to try to block removal. Section 1446(c)(2), added in 2011, addresses this issue. Assume the complete diversity rule would be satisfied and address these:

(a) When is the plaintiff's statement of a dollar amount for damages deemed to be the amount in controversy?

(b) When may the defendant state the amount in controversy in her notice of removal?

(c) When the defendant asserts the amount in controversy, the federal court will determine the actual figure. What standard does the court use in doing so?

(d) Suppose plaintiff alleged the claim was worth only $60,000, and defendant did not remove. During discovery in state court, it then becomes clear that the claim is worth substantially more than $75,000. May the defendant remove? When?

Sometimes, a plaintiff may try to thwart removal by stipulating—after the case is removed—that her claim does not exceed $75,000. The federal court must assess the situation as it existed at the time of the removal. In In re Brand Name Prescription Drugs Antitrust Litigation, 248 F.3d 668, 670–71 (7th Cir. 2001), the court explained:

> Had the plaintiffs, before the removal of the case to federal court, stipulated that they were seeking less than [$75,000], the court would have been required to remand the case to state court without further inquiry. It would have been plain that the case was not within federal jurisdiction. But the converse—that jurisdiction can be assumed without further inquiry if the plaintiffs stipulate that they are seeking more, or don't stipulate at all—does not follow. Jurisdiction cannot be conferred by stipulation or silence. For that matter, it cannot (with immaterial exceptions) be destroyed by stipulation after jurisdiction attaches. If the plaintiffs' original claim was worth more than that [$75,000], removal was proper, the case was within federal jurisdiction, and the plaintiffs could not defeat that jurisdiction by scaling back their claim.

4. There are more points to be made about removal:

(a) If Plaintiff feels that a case should not have been removed because Defendant failed to satisfy some requirement for removal *other than* subject matter jurisdiction, what should Plaintiff do? When must Plaintiff do so? If the federal court agrees with Plaintiff, what will it do?

(b) How would your answer to Question 4(a) be different if the federal court lacked subject matter jurisdiction over the case?

(c) Plaintiff, a citizen of Florida, sues Defendant, a citizen of Arizona, in a state court in Arizona, seeking $25,000 damages for Defendant's alleged violation of Plaintiff's rights under the federal civil rights laws. Defendant can remove this case. Why?

(d) The Mottleys, citizens of Kentucky, sue Railroad, also a citizen of Kentucky, in a state court, seeking breach of contract damages. The Mottleys' complaint alleges that the Railroad's reliance on a federal statute as an excuse for not giving them their lifetime passes is ill-founded. Why can this case not be removed?

(e) Plaintiff sues Defendant in a state court on a claim that could not be removed. Defendant files a counterclaim against Plaintiff. (In Chapter 12, we will see that this device permits the defendant to assert a claim against the plaintiff in the pending case.) Assume Defendant's counterclaim meets the requirements of federal subject matter jurisdiction. Can Plaintiff remove the case? The courts say no. The removal statutes allow "defendants" to remove, and the courts interpret that word narrowly—as limited to those persons sued by the plaintiff. Thus, the plaintiff, even though a defendant on the counterclaim, is not a defendant for purposes of the removal statutes. Shamrock Oil & Gas Corp. v. Sheets, 313 U.S. 100 (1941).

5. You will recall the case of *World-Wide Volkswagen* from the materials on personal jurisdiction. There, the Robinsons, citizens of New York, sued the manufacturer of their car, as well as the regional distributor and dealership from which they bought it, seeking damages for personal injuries. The Robinsons were injured when their car burst into flames after being struck by another vehicle. The Robinsons claimed that their injuries were the result of defective design and manufacture of the gas tank, as well as the manufacturer's failure to provide sufficient fire protection between the gas tank and the passenger compartment. Why, then, would they join the distributor and retailer?

The answer lies in their desire to litigate in state court. The accident occurred in Creek County, Oklahoma. Juries in that county had a reputation for being generous to plaintiffs. If a case filed there were removed to federal court, the jury would be drawn from the entire federal district, a far wider geographic area, which could dilute the largesse of the Creek County residents. The case would be removable on alienage grounds if the Robinsons sued only the manufacturer. They joined the distributor and retailer (also New York citizens) to destroy diversity of citizenship jurisdiction and thus to ensure that the case could not be removed to federal court.

The defendants knew what was at stake. The distributor and retailer were unlikely to be held liable, and therefore were unwilling to spend much money contesting jurisdiction. The manufacturer bankrolled the litigation to the Supreme Court, where the focus was on the due process rights of the distributor and retailer. See Charles W. Adams, World-Wide Volkswagen v. Woodson—*The Rest of the Story*, 72 Neb. L. Rev. 1122 (1993).

It is clear, however, that a plaintiff cannot defeat removal by joining a nondiverse defendant against whom she has no bona fide claim. Such joinder is said to be "fraudulent," although that word is a term of art and does not impugn the integrity of plaintiff or her attorney. Nobers v. Crucible, Inc., 602 F. Supp. 703, 706 (W.D. Pa. 1985). When Pete Rose sued the Commissioner of Baseball seeking to prevent the Commission from holding a hearing on gambling allegations, Rose sued in state court in Cincinnati (home town of the Reds for whom he had played and was then the manager) and included as defendants the Cincinnati Reds and Major League Baseball. Because the Reds shared Ohio citizenship with Rose, it appeared that the defendants could not remove the case. The district court upheld removal, however, finding that joinder of the team and Major League Baseball was "fraudulent." They were merely nominal defendants. Rose's real dispute was with the Commissioner, who was of diverse citizenship. Rose v. Giamatti, 721 F. Supp. 906 (S.D. Ohio 1989).

6. Suppose Plaintiff sues Defendant in state court for violating federal securities laws. Some federal securities claims invoke the exclusive jurisdiction of federal courts, which means they can only be vindicated in federal court. Can Defendant remove the case even though the state court obviously lacked subject matter jurisdiction? Historically, courts viewed removal jurisdiction as "derivative." So if the state court had no subject matter jurisdiction, as in federal securities cases, the defendant could not remove! Congress changed this silly result by adding 28 U.S.C. § 1441(f) (allowing removal even if state court did not have subject matter jurisdiction).

7. In Ruhrgas AG v. Marathon Oil Co., 526 U.S. 574 (1999), the defendant removed the case from state to federal court and then moved to dismiss for lack of personal jurisdiction. The plaintiff asserted that there was no subject matter jurisdiction. In general, a federal court must determine whether it has subject matter jurisdiction before addressing other issues. Of course, unless the court has subject matter jurisdiction, its ruling on the merits would be a nullity. See Steel Co. v. Citizens for a Better Environment, 523 U.S. 83 (1998). Some courts concluded that this rule meant that they must determine subject matter jurisdiction in a removed case before determining whether personal jurisdiction existed. In *Ruhrgas*, the Supreme Court rejected any "unyielding jurisdictional hierarchy" and upheld dismissal on personal jurisdiction grounds. The personal jurisdiction issue was straightforward and presented no difficult issue of state law, while the subject matter jurisdiction issue raised a difficult question of first impression. In such circumstances, a court would not abuse its discretion by proceeding first with the personal jurisdiction inquiry. See Joan Steinman, *After* Steel Co.: *Hypothetical Jurisdiction in the Federal Appellate Courts*, 58 WASH. & LEE L. REV. 855 (2001).

8. Section 1441(c) permits a narrow exception to the "rule of unanimity." It permits a single defendant to remove if a federal question claim has been asserted against him. He may remove the entire case to federal court, including claims that do not invoke federal question, diversity of citizenship, or supplemental jurisdiction. The federal court must then sever those claims, however, and remand them to state court, thereby keeping only the federal question claim.

9. Congress has occasionally eased requirements for removal in specialized cases. Under the Class Action Fairness Act (CAFA), for instance, a single defendant can remove certain types of complex cases from state to federal court, and may do so even if she is a citizen of the forum state. 28 U.S.C. § 1453(b). We will study CAFA in Chapter 13. For present purposes, we note one point about that legislation. Under CAFA, a class action satisfies the amount in controversy requirement if the aggregated claims of all class members exceed $5,000,000. Class action plaintiffs desiring to litigate in state court have attempted to avoid removal by stipulating that the class claims will not exceed $5,000,000. The Supreme Court rejected such an effort in Standard Fire Insurance Co. v. Knowles, 133 S. Ct. 1345 (2013). There, the representative of a class asserting a state-law claim for alleged breach of homeowners' insurance

policies sued in state court and stipulated that he would not seek damages for the class in excess of $5,000,000. Defendant removed and showed that the claims, in fact, aggregated to slightly more than that figure. Plaintiff moved to remand to state court based upon his stipulation that the class would in no event accept more than $5,000,000. The district court ordered remand and the Eighth Circuit declined to hear an interlocutory appeal.

The Supreme Court vacated the ruling and held that the case invoked federal jurisdiction under CAFA. It recognized that a plaintiff can defeat removal by stipulating that she will not accept an amount that invokes federal jurisdiction. But the stipulation must be binding on the plaintiff. In *Knowles,* the class representative had no authority to bind the class members to the stipulation, since the court had not certified a class. The Court explained:

> [A] plaintiff who files a proposed class action cannot legally bind members of the proposed class before the class is certified. * * * Because his precertification stipulation does not bind anyone but himself, Knowles has not reduced the value of the putative class members' claims. * * * The Federal District Court, therefore, wrongly concluded that Knowles' precertification stipulation could overcome its finding that the CAFA jurisdictional threshold had been met.

133 S. Ct. at 1349.

Chapter 5

Venue

A. Introduction and Integration

As you will recall from Chapters 2 and 4, a court cannot properly hear a case unless it has both personal and subject matter jurisdiction. In this chapter we address a third requirement for choosing a proper place in which to litigate — venue.

Subject matter jurisdiction determines what categories of cases a court *system* (e.g., the federal courts) has authority to decide. Likewise, personal jurisdiction, at least as applied to states, determines whether a court *system* has power over a defendant. Venue determines where *within* a court system a case can be brought. In the federal system, subject matter jurisdiction tells us that a case may be litigated in federal district court. Venue tells us exactly *which* federal district court.* The country is divided into 94 districts. Congress allocates these districts by statute. For many states, there is only one district, such as the District of South Carolina. Some states have multiple districts (anywhere from two to four), such as the "Eastern District of California" and the "Southern District of New York." Plaintiff will want to lay venue for the case in a proper district.

In civil cases, there is no federal constitutional right to venue in a particular place. Neirbo Co. v. Bethlehem Shipbuilding Corp., 308 U.S. 165 (1939). Accordingly, venue in the federal system is a matter of statutory law. And though there are scores of specialized federal venue statutes, venue in the majority of federal cases is governed by the general venue provision found in 28 U.S.C. § 1391(b).** Each state is free to prescribe its own venue rules to determine the proper place for litigation within that state's judicial system.

The goal of venue law is to ensure that the litigation proceeds in a convenient location. Accordingly, as we will see, typical (but not exclusive) provisions permit venue

---

* Thus, 28 U.S.C. § 1390(a) defines venue as "the geographic specification of the proper court or courts for the litigation of a civil action that is within the subject-matter jurisdiction of the district courts...."

** Some, such as the Federal Tort Claims Act, allow venue where the plaintiff resides, which accounts for why 28 U.S.C. § 1391(c)(2) defines the residence of entities both as defendants and as plaintiffs.

where the defendant resides and where a substantial part of the claim arose. The idea is that such places will be suitable for the defendant and for the witnesses who will testify.

The fact that subject matter jurisdiction, personal jurisdiction, and venue are all proper in a particular court gives that court authority to hear the case. But satisfying those requirements is no guarantee that a court will be the most convenient or most sensible place in which to hold the litigation. In other words, a venue, though proper under the applicable law, might not be the optimal place for the parties to engage their dispute. Accordingly, every judicial system (state and federal) permits a court to transfer to a more appropriate location within that judicial system. When the more appropriate court is not in the same judicial system, a court may invoke the doctrine of forum non conveniens and decline to hear the case. These matters are discussed later in this chapter.

B. Local and Transitory Actions

One longstanding distinction in venue law is that between "local" and "transitory" actions. Local actions include particular claims involving real property (land). Under the "local action rule," venue in such cases must be laid where the land is located. In the world of venue, every case that is not "local" is deemed "transitory," for which more flexible venue rules will apply. Though the definition of local actions varies slightly from state to state, the classic definition includes three major categories of disputes:

(1) in rem or quasi-in-rem cases, in which the real property is the basis of jurisdiction;

(2) cases in which the plaintiff seeks a remedy in or to real property, such as a claim for quiet title, ejectment, foreclosure of a mortgage, enforcement or removal of a lien; and

(3) claims for damages for injury to land, such as trespass.

The local action rule is reflected in the venue statutes of most states (we will see an example in § C of this chapter below). In the federal court system, the local action rule had a long and fascinating history, tracing back to a colorful case involving a claim for trespass to land against Thomas Jefferson. In *Livingston v. Jefferson*, 15 Fed. Cas. 660 (C.D. Va. 1811), Chief Justice John Marshall (acting as a trial judge),* adopted

* In the early days of the nation, Supreme Court Justices "rode circuit," which required them to sit as trial-court judges for the circuit to which they were assigned. (The circuit court was at the time the federal trial court; today the trial court is the federal district court.) *Livingston v. Jefferson* was rife with tension, because Chief Justice Marshall and President Jefferson were political rivals and not on friendly terms. For a fascinating account of the case, see Ronan Degnan, Livingston v. Jefferson — *A Freestanding Footnote*, 75 Cal. L. Rev. 115 (1987).

the common law local action rule as part of federal venue law. This adoption was buttressed years later by the enactment of 28 U.S.C. § 1392, which referred to local actions.

But the local action rule is now of mere historical interest in federal court, because Congress, by statute effective in 2012, repealed § 1392 and abolished the local action rule. Section 1391(a)(2) now provides that venue rules in federal court no longer depend upon whether an action is local or transitory.* It is important to note, however, that most state court venue statutes continue to recognize the local action concept.

C. State Venue Provisions

Personal jurisdiction determines whether the state as a whole has power over the defendant. Venue restrictions identify where within the state—in which county, parish, or other subdivision—cases are to be adjudicated. Most states provide a general rule for civil actions and also set out special venue rules for particular types of cases (usually including local actions). The following Maryland venue statute is typical.

Maryland Code Annotated

Courts & Judicial Procedure (1989)

§ 6-201. General rule

(a) *Civil actions.*—Subject to the provisions of §§ 6-202 and 6-203 and unless otherwise provided by law, a civil action shall be brought in a county where the defendant resides, carries on a regular business, is employed, or habitually engages in a vocation. In addition, a corporation also may be sued where it maintains its principal offices in the State.

(b) *Multiple defendants.*— If there is more than one defendant, and there is no single venue applicable to all defendants, under subsection (a), all may be sued in a county in which any one of them could be sued, or in the county where the cause of action arose.

---

* Interestingly, however, the Ninth Circuit has concluded that the local action rule did not relate to venue, but to subject matter jurisdiction. Because § 1391 relates only to venue, the court concluded, it could not affect subject matter jurisdiction of the federal courts. Eldee-K Rental Props. LLC v. DIRECTV, Inc, 748 F.3d 943, 948–949 (9th Cir. 2014). In other words, according to the court in *Eldee-K*, a case regarding trespass to real property must be brought in the federal district in which the land lies because no other district would have subject matter jurisdiction. To date, no other court appears to have interpreted the local action rule as a matter of subject matter jurisdiction. *See, e.g.*, Terra Partners v. AG Acceptance Corp., 2015 U.S. Dist. LEXIS 101492 at *11–12 (D.N.M. July 24, 2015) (finding it unnecessary to determine whether case presented a "local action," because Congress abolished the concept in federal court).

§ 6-202. Additional Venue Permitted

In addition to the venue provided in § 6-201 or § 6-203, the following actions maybe brought in the indicated county:

(1) Divorce — Where the plaintiff resides;

(2) Annulment — Where the plaintiff resides or where the marriage ceremony was performed;

(3) Action against a corporation which has no principal place of business in the State — Where the plaintiff resides;

(4) Replevin or detinue — Where the property sought to be recovered is located;

(5) Action relating to custody, guardianship, maintenance, or support of a child — Where the father, alleged father, or mother of the child resides, or where the child resides;

(6) Suit on a bond against a corporate surety — Where the bond is filed, or where the contract is to be performed;

(7) Action for possession of real property — Where a portion of the land upon which the action is based is located;

(8) Tort action based on negligence — Where the cause of action arose;

(9) Attachment on original process — Where the property is located or where the garnishee resides;

(10) Nondelivery or injury of goods against master or captain of a vessel — Where the goods are received on board the vessel or where delivery is to be made under the contract;

(11) Action for damages against a nonresident individual — Any county in the State;

(12) Action against a person who absconds from a county or leaves the State before the statute of limitations has run — Where the defendant is found;

(13) In a local action in which the defendant cannot be found in the county where the subject matter of the action is located — In any county in which the venue is proper under § 6-201.

§ 6-203. General Rule Inapplicable

(a) *In general.* — The general rule of § 6-201 does not apply to actions enumerated in this section.

(b) *Interest in land.* —

(1) The venue of the following actions is in the county where all or any portion of the subject matter of the action is located:

(i) Partition of real estate;

(ii) Enforcement of a charge or lien on land;

(iii) Eminent domain;

(iv) Trespass to land; and

(v) Waste.

(2) If the property lies in more than one county, the court in which proceedings are first brought has jurisdiction over the entire property.

(c) * * * The venue of an action to recover damages against a railroad company for injury to livestock is the county where the injury occurred.

(d) *Guardianship.* — The venue of an action for guardianship under Title 5, Subtitle 3 of the Family Law Article is in the county where the court has jurisdiction over the child in need of assistance case under Title 3, Subtitle 8 of this article.

(e) *Adoption.* —

(1) Except as provided in paragraphs (2) and (3) of this subsection, the venue for a proceeding for adoption of an individual who is physically within this State or subject to the jurisdiction of an equity court is in a county where:

(i) The petitioner is domiciled;

(ii) The petitioner has resided for at least 90 days next preceding the filing of the petition;

(iii) A licensed child placement agency having legal or physical custody of the individual is located;

(iv) The individual is domiciled, if the individual is related to the petitioner by blood or marriage or is an adult; or

(v) An equity court has continuing jurisdiction over the custody of the individual.

(2) The venue in an adoption of an individual under Title 5, Subtitle 3, Part III of the Family Law Article is in the court with jurisdiction over the individual under Title 3, Subtitle 8 of this article.

(3) The venue in an adoption of an individual under Title 5, Subtitle 3, Part IV of the Family Law Article is in the court where the individual's guardianship case is pending.

Notes and Questions

1. Note the cases in which Maryland allows venue to be laid where the *plaintiff* resides. Why might such a provision be appropriate in those types of cases?

2. Though Congress abolished the local action rule for federal venue, which provision embodies Maryland's local action rule? Note that it, like most state statutes for local actions, allows venue to be laid in the political subdivision in which "any portion" of the land lies.

3. Section 6-201(b) is a typical provision regarding multiple defendants. Suppose plaintiff sues D-1, who resides in County A and D-2, who resides in County B. She lays venue in County A. Suppose the claim against D-1 is dismissed before trial.

Should the court in County A proceed with the case, adjudicating the claim against D-2? In many jurisdictions, the case would proceed, although in some, the court would transfer to County B upon motion by D-2.

D. Venue in Federal Court

The Basic Rules

In the federal system, it is somewhat harder to conceptualize the relationship between venue and personal jurisdiction. You will recall from Chapter 2, Section B.3 that (as a general rule), a federal court has personal jurisdiction over an out-of-state defendant only if the state in which the federal court sits would have personal jurisdiction. Thus, state personal jurisdiction doctrine already limits the places for suit within the federal system. In federal court, venue and personal jurisdiction doctrines developed largely independently. The result is that both personal jurisdiction and venue restrictions exist side by side, and both must be met. (And, unlike subject matter jurisdiction, both are waivable if the defendant fails to raise a timely objection.)

While state statutes and rules lay venue in various political subdivisions of the state, federal venue provisions prescribe proper federal districts. As noted above, Congress has divided the country into 94 federal districts, including districts for Puerto Rico, and other U.S. possessions such as Guam and the Virgin Islands. With one inconsequential exception (the district of Wyoming includes parts of Yellowstone National Park that are in Idaho and Montana), no federal district crosses state lines. Not all states have the same number of federal districts. California, New York, and Texas each have four districts. Other states have three or two districts and many states comprise a single federal district each.

Sometimes Congress divides a district into separate "divisions." But "[t]here appears to be no rhyme or reason why some states are divided into any particular number of divisions, while others encompass the entire state in which they sit." 14D Wright & Miller, Federal Practice and Procedure 232. Congress has passed a statute for each state, setting out the number of districts and divisions, with detailed provisions for which counties are assigned to each division. See, e.g., 28 U.S.C. § 103 (Minnesota), § 122 (South Dakota). It is not clear why Congress continues to define divisions within districts, since there is no longer any requirement that venue be laid in a particular division. Thus, the relevant inquiry is where—meaning what *districts* (not divisions)—venue will be proper.

The general provision governing venue in federal civil practice is 28 U.S.C. § 1391(b). Note that Congress qualified the provisions of § 1391 with the phrase "except as otherwise provided by law." Just as the Maryland statute above had exceptions to its general provisions, federal law provides particular venue provisions for specialized actions. For example, 12 U.S.C. § 94 governs venue for cases against national banks; 28 U.S.C. § 1396 provides the venue choices for cases involving collection of federal taxes; and 28 U.S.C. § 1397 addresses venue under the federal interpleader act. When a specialized venue provision applies, courts must determine whether that statute is exclusive or is to apply along with the general venue choices under § 1391(b). See, e.g,. Cortez Byrd Chips, Inc. v. Bill Harbert Const. Co., 529 U.S. 193, 198–99 (2000) (venue provisions of Federal Arbitration Act not exclusive, but provide alternatives to general venue statute). We are concerned with the application of the general provisions of § 1391(b), which govern in the vast majority of cases.

That statute has a long history, dating back to the first Judiciary Act of 1789. Originally, venue was proper where the defendant was "an inhabitant" or could be "found." Over the years, this became the provision for "residential" venue, making venue proper where the defendants "resides." For over a century, Congress provided broader venue choices in diversity of citizenship cases, permitting venue where the defendant resided or where the plaintiff resided. This disparate treatment has ended, and today § 1391(b) provides unitary rules for diversity and federal question cases. Residential venue is limited under § 1391(b)(1) to where the defendant resides.

Before 1966, there was no provision allowing plaintiffs to sue multiple defendants in the district in which one of the defendants resided. A 1966 amendment attempted to fill this "gap" in the statute by making venue proper in the district "where the claim arose." This addition of "transactional" venue created its own problems when the Court interpreted "where the claim arose" to mean there was one and only one place where each claim arose. In more complex cases, there was frequently uncertainty and litigation over where that one place was. See Leroy v. Great W. United Corp.,443 U.S. 173 (1979). Today, that metaphysical inquiry is also a thing of the past. Now, transactional venue is proper under § 1391(b)(2) in any district "in which a substantial part of the events or omissions giving rise to the claim occurred."

Read §§ 1390 and 1391(a), (b), and (c) before addressing the following.

Notes and Questions

1. Section 1391(b)(1) provides for "residential" venue. Note that § 1391(c) defines the residence of various litigants.

(a) Under this provision, is the district in which the plaintiff resides relevant? Why do you suppose this is the rule?

(b) Suppose P sues two defendants in one case. D-1 resides in the District of Wyoming and D-2 resides in the District of Montana. For the case of P v. D-1 and D-2, is venue proper under § 1391(b)(1) in the District of Wyoming? In the District of Montana?

(c) Suppose P sues two defendants in one case. D-1 resides in the Southern District of California and D-2 resides in the Central District of California. For the case of P v. D-1 and D-2, is venue proper under § 1391(b)(1) in the Southern District of California? In the Central District of California? In the Northern District of California?

2. Section 1391(b)(2) provides for "transactional" venue.

(a) Can more than one district qualify as a proper venue under § 1391(b)(2)? For a tort case, what districts might qualify? For a contract case, what districts might qualify?

(b) Suppose on the facts of a case that venue would be proper under § 1391(b)(1) in the Western District of North Carolina and that venue would be proper under § 1391(b)(2) in the Eastern District of Virginia. May the plaintiff choose to lay venue in either of those districts, or does the statute require the plaintiff to use residential venue if it is available?

3. Section 1391(b)(3) provides for "fallback" venue.

(a) Read the provision very carefully. Why does it almost never apply?

(b) Assuming that a substantial part of a claim arises somewhere in the United States, will § 1391(b)(3) apply?

4. Paula is injured in an auto collision with Doug. Paula is a Massachusetts citizen. Doug is a New York citizen, with his domicile in the Eastern District of New York. The accident occurred in Maine. (The entire state of Maine comprises one federal district.) Assume that Paula's claim exceeds $75,000.

(a) Paula wants to sue Doug in federal court. In what federal districts would venue be proper?

(b) Paula sues Doug in federal court in Vermont, where Doug lives while attending college in Vermont. (There is only one federal district in Vermont.) Is venue proper in the District of Vermont?

(c) Paula sues Doug in federal court in Massachusetts. (There is only one federal district in Massachusetts.) Paula has Doug served with process while he is voluntarily present in Massachusetts doing business. Is venue proper in the District of Massachusetts?

5. Suppose the facts are the same as in Note 4 except as noted below. Where would venue be proper?

(a) Doug is a citizen of France admitted to the United States for permanent resident status and domiciled in New York.

(b) Doug is a U.S. citizen domiciled in France. Wait a minute! Regardless of venue, would there be subject matter jurisdiction in federal court over this case?

(c) Doug is a citizen of France domiciled in France.

6. Suppose Paula sues only Car Inc., the manufacturer of her car, alleging defective design and manufacture of the vehicle. Car Inc. is incorporated in Delaware with its headquarters and a factory in the Western District of Michigan. It also has factories in the Western District of Tennessee and the Northern District of Georgia. Assume that Paula's claim exceeds $75,000.

(a) In Paula v. Car Inc., where is venue proper?

(b) In addition to the facts described above, Car Inc. has a large factory in the Western District of New York. In Paula v. Car Inc., would venue be proper in the

Western District of New York? The Eastern District of New York? Would your answer be different if the car involved in the accident had been manufactured at Car Inc.'s factory in the Western District of New York?

(c) Assume that the facts are as described in 5(b). Paula sues both Doug and Car Inc. in a single case. Would venue be proper in the Western District of Michigan? The Eastern District of New York? The Western District of New York? The Western District of Tennessee? The District of Maine?

(d) Would any of your answers above be different if Car Inc. was a partnership or other unincorporated business?

7. In what circumstances could there be personal jurisdiction but no venue? Why not simply make venue proper wherever there is personal jurisdiction? Isn't that what § 1391(c)(2) now in essence provides if the defendant is a business entity?

8. As 28 U.S.C. § 1390(c) makes clear, the venue provisions of § 1391(b) do not apply in cases removed from state to federal court. Remember, cases removed from state to federal court are removed to the federal court "embracing the place where such action is pending." 28 U.S.C. § 1441(a).

9. Suppose the defendant is a U.S. corporation sued under a federal statute that provides for nationwide service of process. This means that the corporation is subject to personal jurisdiction everywhere in the United States. Does this mean that residential venue is proper in every district of the United States? After all, § 1391(c)(2) provides that businesses "reside" in every district in which they are subject to personal jurisdiction for the case at hand. There is some authority for this conclusion. See Icon Indus. Controls Corp. v. Cimetrix, Inc., 921 F. Supp. 375 (W.D. La. 1996). Commentators, however, have criticized that assertion. See, e.g., Rachel M. Janutis, *Pulling Venue Up By Its Own Bootstraps: The Relationships Among Nationwide Service of Process, Personal Jurisdiction, and Section 1391(c)*, 78 St. John's L. Rev. 37 (2004). See generally 14D Wright & Miller, Federal Practice & Procedure § 3811.1, 295–300.

Bates v. C & S Adjusters, Inc.

980 F.2d 865 (2d Cir. 1992)

Newman, Circuit Judge.

This appeal concerns venue in an action brought under the Fair Debt Collection Practices Act, 15 U.S.C. §§ 1692–1692o (1988).* Specifically, the issue is whether venue exists in a district in which the debtor resides and to which a bill collector's demand for payment was forwarded. The issue arises on an appeal by Phillip E. Bates from the May 21, 1992, judgment of the District Court for the Western District of New York (William M. Skretny, Judge), dismissing his complaint because of improper

* [Note from your casebook authors: This legislation regulates communications between debt collectors and consumers, prohibiting harassment, abuse, and false representations by debt collectors. The statute permits suits for damages against debt collectors who violate the Act.]

venue. We conclude that venue was proper under 28 U.S.C. § 1391(b)(2) (Supp. 1992) and therefore reverse and remand.

Background

Bates commenced this action in the Western District of New York upon receipt of a collection notice from C & S Adjusters, Inc. ("C & S"). Bates alleged violations of the Fair Debt Collection Practices Act, and demanded statutory damages, costs, and attorney's fees. The facts relevant to venue are not in dispute. Bates incurred the debt in question while he was a resident of the Western District of Pennsylvania. The creditor, a corporation with its principal place of business in that District, referred the account to C & S, a local collection agency which transacts no regular business in New York. Bates had meanwhile moved to the Western District of New York. When C & S mailed a collection notice to Bates at his Pennsylvania address, the Postal Service forwarded the notice to Bates' new address in New York.

In its answer, C & S asserted two affirmative defenses and also counterclaimed for costs, alleging that the action was instituted in bad faith and for purposes of harassment. C & S subsequently filed a motion to dismiss for improper venue, which the District Court granted.

Discussion

1. Venue and the 1990 amendments to 28 U.S.C. § 1391(b)

Bates concedes that the only plausible venue provision for this action is 28 U.S.C. § 1391(b)(2), which allows an action to be brought in "a judicial district in which a substantial part of the events or omissions giving rise to the claim occurred." Prior to 1990, section 1391 allowed for venue in "the judicial district ... in which the claim arose." 28 U.S.C. § 1391(b) (1988). This case represents our first opportunity to consider the significance of the 1990 amendments.

Prior to 1966, venue was proper in federal question cases, absent a special venue statue, only in the defendant's state of citizenship. If a plaintiff sought to sue multiple defendants who were citizens of different states, there might be no district where the entire action could be brought. Congress closed this "venue gap" by adding a provision allowing suit in the district "in which the claim arose." This phrase gave rise to a variety of conflicting interpretations. Some courts thought it meant that there could be only one district; others believed there could be several. Different tests developed, with courts looking for "substantial contacts," the "weight of contacts," the place of injury or performance, or even to the boundaries of personal jurisdiction under state law. District courts within the Second Circuit used at least three of these approaches.

The Supreme Court gave detailed attention to section 1391(b) in Leroy v. Great Western United Corp., 443 U.S. 173 (1979). The specific holding of *Leroy* was that Great Western, a Texas corporation, which had attempted to take over an Idaho corporation, could not bring suit in Texas against Idaho officials who sought to enforce a state anti-takeover law. Although the effect of the Idaho officials' action might be felt in Texas, the Court rejected this factor as a basis for venue, since it would allow the Idaho officials to be sued anywhere a shareholder of the target corporation could allege that he wanted to accept Great Western's tender offer. The Court made several further observations: (1) the purpose of the 1966 statute was to close venue gaps and should not be read more broadly than necessary to close those gaps, (2) the general purpose of the venue statute was to protect defendants against an unfair or inconvenient trial location, (3) location of evidence and witnesses was a relevant factor, (4) familiarity of the Idaho federal judges with the Idaho anti-takeover statute was a relevant factor, (5) plaintiff's convenience was not a relevant factor, and (6) in only rare cases should there be more than one district in which a claim can be said to arise.

Subsequent to *Leroy* and prior to the 1990 amendment to section 1391(b), most courts have applied at least a form of the "weight of contacts" test. Courts continued to have difficulty in determining whether more than one district could be proper.

Against this background, we understand Congress' 1990 amendment to be at most a marginal expansion of the venue provision. The House Report indicates that the new language was first proposed by the American Law Institute in a 1969 Study, and observes:

> The great advantage of referring to the place where things happened ... is that it avoids the litigation breeding phrase "in which the claim arose." It also avoids the problem created by the frequent cases in which substantial parts of the underlying events have occurred in several districts.

H.R. Rep. No. 734, 101st Cong., 2d Sess. 23. Thus it seems clear that *Leroy*'s strong admonition against recognizing multiple venues has been disapproved. Many of the factors in *Leroy* — for instance, the convenience of defendants and the location of evidence and witnesses — are most useful in distinguishing between two or more plausible venues. Since the new statute does not, as a general matter, require the District Court to determine the best venue, these factors will be of less significance. Apart from this point, however, *Leroy* and other precedents remain important sources of guidance.

2. Fair Debt Collection Practices Act

Under the version of the venue statute in force from 1966 to 1990, at least three District Courts held that venue was proper under the Fair Debt Collection Practices Act in the plaintiff's home district if a collection agency had mailed a collection notice to an address in that district or placed a phone call to a number in that district. None of these cases involved the unusual fact, present in this case, that the defendant did not deliberately direct a communication to the plaintiff's district.

We conclude, however, that this difference is inconsequential, at least under the current venue statute. The statutory standard for venue focuses not on whether a defendant has made a deliberate contact — a factor relevant in the analysis of personal jurisdiction[1] — but on the location where events occurred. Under the new version of

1. C & S has waived whatever claim it might have had that the District Court lacked personal jurisdiction over it. Waiver resulted from C & S's failure to allege lack of personal jurisdiction in its answer or motion to dismiss. See Fed. R. Civ. P. 12(b)(2), (h).

section 1391(b)(2), we must determine only whether a "substantial part of the events ... giving rise to the claim" occurred in the Western District of New York.

In adopting this statute, Congress was concerned about the harmful effect of abusive debt practices on consumers. See 15 U.S.C. § 1692(a) ("Abusive debt collection practices contribute to the number of personal bankruptcies, to marital instability, to the loss of jobs, and to invasions of individual privacy."). This harm does not occur until receipt of the collection notice. Indeed, if the notice were lost in the mail, it is unlikely that a violation of the Act would have occurred. Moreover, a debt collection agency sends its dunning letters so that they will be received. Forwarding such letters to the district to which a debtor has moved is an important step in the collection process. If the bill collector prefers not to be challenged for its collection practices outside the district of a debtor's original residence, the envelope can be marked "do not forward." We conclude that receipt of a collection notice is a substantial part of the events giving rise to a claim under the Fair Debt Collection Practices Act.

The relevant factors identified in *Leroy* add support to our conclusion. Although "bona fide error" can be a defense to liability under the Act, 15 U.S.C. § 1692k(c), the alleged violations of the Act turn largely not on the collection agency's intent, but on the content of the collection notice. The most relevant evidence — the collection notice — is located in the Western District of New York. Because the collection agency appears not to have marked the notice with instructions not to forward, and has not objected to the assertion of personal jurisdiction, trial in the Western District of New York would not be unfair.

Conclusion

The judgment of the District Court is reversed, and the matter is remanded for further proceedings consistent with this decision.

Notes and Questions

1. When different claims are combined in one law suit, the general rule is that venue must be established as to each separate claim. See 14D Wright & Miller, Federal Practice and Procedure § 3808 (4th ed. 2013). Often, however, this will be quite straightforward. For example, if suit is filed in a district in which significant events occurred, under § 1391(b)(2), venue will likely be proper in that district as to all claims related to those events. Likewise, if suit is filed in a district where all the defendants reside, under § 1391(b)(1), venue will likely be proper in that district for all the claims against those defendants.

2. Suppose that Mr. Bates, in a hurry to leave on a trip, had taken his unopened mail with him. He later opened the offending letter in California. Would venue be proper in California?

3. In the *Leroy* case (discussed in *Bates*), the Supreme Court rejected an economic effects test under which venue would be proper where the plaintiff's business was economically injured. In rejecting this test, the Court held that "such a reading of § 1391(b) is inconsistent with the underlying purpose of the provision, for it would

leave the venue decision entirely in the hands of plaintiffs, rather than making it primarily a matter of convenience of litigants and witnesses." 443 U.S. at 186–87. Does *Bates* revive the approach rejected in *Leroy*?

4. As noted in *Bates*, the court is not required to determine the "best venue." Nonetheless, the statute requires that "a substantial part" of the events have occurred in the district. Focusing on this language, the Second Circuit has observed: "we caution district courts to take seriously the adjective 'substantial.' We are required to construe the venue statute strictly * * *. That means for venue to be proper, *significant* events or omissions *material* to the plaintiff's claim must have occurred in the district in question, even if other material events occurred elsewhere. It would be error, for instance, to treat the venue statute's 'substantial part' test as mirroring the minimum contacts test employed in personal jurisdiction inquiries." Gulf Ins. Co. v. Glasbrenner, 417 F.3d 353, 357 (2d Cir. 2005).

5. Compare *Bates* with Magic Toyota, Inc. v. Southeast Toyota Distrib., Inc., 784 F. Supp. 306 (D.S.C. 1992). In *Magic Toyota*, the plaintiff purchased a South Carolina Toyota dealership from defendant. According to plaintiff, defendant had promised plaintiff that he would be permitted to relocate the dealership to another city in South Carolina, but defendant breached that promise. Plaintiff further alleged that when he refused to participate in various illegal activities, defendant set out to destroy plaintiff's business. Plaintiff brought suit in federal court in South Carolina, alleging violations of the Racketeering Influenced and Corrupt Organization Act (RICO), as well as state claims for breach of contract, fraud, and violation of the Automobile Dealers Day in Court Act. The district court dismissed for improper venue, finding that § 1391(b)(2) was not met because the alleged fraudulent inducement to purchase the South Carolina dealership happened during negotiations in Florida and that the other activities in support of defendants' supposed illegal scheme also occurred outside South Carolina.

Why isn't it sufficient for § 1391(b)(2) that both the alleged fraudulent inducement and the attempt to destroy plaintiff's business were directed at the South Carolina dealership? The court noted that § 1391(b)(2) focuses not on "contacts" but "events." 784 F. Supp. at 317. Does this wording in the statute justify the holding in the case?

E. Change of Venue

1. Transfer of Civil Cases in State Courts

All states have provisions permitting the transfer of civil cases from one county (or relevant political subdivision) to another. The reasons for ordering transfer differ and may depend on whether venue in the original court is proper. Most states permit a party to seek transfer if she is unlikely to get a fair trial where the case is filed. Florida has an unusual provision allowing a party to seek transfer on grounds that she "is so odious to the inhabitants of the county" that she could not receive a fair trial. FLA. STAT. § 47.101(1)(b). In some states, transfer can be ordered only on motion; in others, it can be ordered *sua sponte*.

It is important to note that such transfers are *within* the state. Because the individual states are separate political sovereigns, no state can unilaterally transfer a case from one of its courts to a court in a different state. The American Law Institute and the Commissioners on Uniform State Laws have long recommended legislation that would permit transfer among states, but no such legislation has been enacted. See American Law Institute, Complex Litigation: Statutory Recommendations and Analysis With Reporter'S Study: A Model System for State-To-State Transfer and Consolidation (1994).

A state court that concludes that the action before it ought to be litigated in another state cannot transfer the case, but it has the option to dismiss the case under the doctrine of "forum non conveniens." After the dismissal, the plaintiff can file a new action in the other state. Forum non conveniens is addressed in Section F, infra.

2. Transfer of Civil Actions in Federal Court

Federal law authorizes the transfer of civil actions from one federal district court to another. 28 U.S.C. §§ 1404(a), 1406(a). These transfers are not restricted by state lines. Recall Justice Brennan's statement in *Burger King*, in Section B.3 of Chapter 2, that the inconvenience of the Florida forum for the Michigan defendants might be ameliorated by a change of venue to Michigan. Such a transfer was conceivable in that case only because it was in federal court. Had the case been in state court in Florida, no transfer to Michigan would have been possible (unless, of course, it was first removed to federal court).

The court in which a case is originally filed, and from which it is transferred (if the motion to transfer is granted), is called the "transferor" court. The court to which the case is transferred is the "transferee" court.

Lawyers and judges routinely refer to the two transfer statutes by number, so it is common to hear them speak of a "1404 transfer" and a "1406 transfer." The most immediate difference between the two is clear from the terms of the statutes: under § 1404(a), the transferor court is a proper venue; under § 1406(a), however, the transferor court is an improper venue.

a. Where Can Cases Be Transferred?

Section 1404(a) permits transfer to any district where the suit "might have been brought." Section 1406(a) contains similar language. In Hoffman v. Blaski, 363 U.S. 335 (1960), the Supreme Court interpreted this language to mean that cases can be transferred only to a district in which venue and personal jurisdiction would be proper. Consider the following situation: A defendant requests transfer to a district in which, absent the defendant's consent, venue or personal jurisdiction would not be proper. The defendant, however, consents to venue and personal jurisdiction in that location. Couldn't one argue that since the defendant has consented to litigation in a particular location that it is now a place where the case "might have been brought"?

In *Hoffman*, the Supreme Court rejected this argument, explaining:

> We do not think the § 1404(a) phrase "where it might have been brought" can be interpreted to mean, as petitioners' theory would require, "where it may now be rebrought, with defendants' consent." * * *
>
> The thesis urged by petitioners would not only do violence to the plain words of § 1404(a), but would also inject gross discrimination. That thesis, if adopted, would empower a District Court, upon a finding of convenience, to transfer an action to any district desired by the *defendants* and in which they were willing to waive their statutory defenses as to venue and jurisdiction over their persons, regardless of the fact that such transferee district was not one in which the action "might have been brought" by the plaintiff. Conversely, that thesis would not permit the court, upon motion of the *plaintiffs* and a like showing of convenience, to transfer the action to the same district, without the consent and waiver of venue and personal jurisdiction defenses by the defendants. Nothing in § 1404(a), or in its legislative history, suggests such a unilateral objective and we should not, under the guise of interpretation, ascribe to Congress any such discriminatory purpose.

Id. at 342–44 (emphasis original). Although *Hoffman* involved a transfer under § 1404, its reasoning applies as well to transfers under § 1406. See Manley v. Engram, 755 F.2d 1463 (11th Cir. 1985). By legislation that went into effect in 2012, Congress amended § 1404(a) to reverse partially the holding of *Hoffman* by providing that a case may be transferred "to any district or division to which all parties have consented." However, even in such a case, the court must determine that transfer is appropriate under § 1404(a), and absent consent, the holding of *Hoffman* applies.

b. Goldlawr *Transfers*

Section 1406(a) permits transfer of cases filed in an improper venue. Suppose, however, that the case is filed in a district in which not only venue is improper, but which also lacks personal jurisdiction. Can this case be transferred? Some argued that if the court lacked personal jurisdiction, it also lacked the authority to transfer. In Goldlawr, Inc. v. Heiman, 369 U.S. 463 (1962), the Supreme Court held otherwise. It concluded that allowing the transfer of such cases was consistent with the objective of the statute of "removing whatever obstacles may impede an expeditious and orderly adjudication of cases and controversies on their merits." Id. at 466–67. Lower courts have applied the *Goldlawr* holding to transfers under § 1404(a) as well as § 1406(a). See, e.g., United States v. Berkowitz, 328 F.2d 358 (3d Cir. 1964).

c. Choice of Law

In connection with personal jurisdiction, we noted that in many situations a court might apply any one of several states' laws to a single transaction or occurrence. Suppose that two citizens of one state travel to another state and enter into an oral contract. Suppose further that the law of their home state would enforce this contract, but the law of the place of making would require the contract to be in writing. Which state's law should govern the validity of the contract? Each state has its own choice of law doctrine or rules to decide which state's law to apply. Choice of law doctrines vary among the states and, therefore, different courts may apply different law when confronted with the same situation.

Given that choice of law rules vary, the logical next question is whose choice of law rules apply? The answer is easy when litigation occurs in state court: the forum applies its choice of law rules. When litigation is in federal court, however, the matter becomes more complex. What law applies in federal court is a difficult question to which we devote an entire chapter. See Chapter 10. Briefly stated, on matters of substantive law (as opposed to matters of procedure), where there is no federal statute on point, a federal court ordinarily applies state law. Therefore, in a contract case in federal court, the question of whether a contract must be in writing is a matter as to which federal courts would apply state law. But suppose that some states would require that the contract be in writing, but others would not. Which state's law should the federal court apply? In Klaxon v. Stentor Elec. Mfg. Co., 313 U.S. 487 (1941), the Court held that a federal court should apply the choice of law rules of the state in which it sits. Therefore, in our contract hypothetical, a federal court would apply whichever state's law the state in which it sits would have applied.

Because choice of law rules vary from state to state, one next must determine which state's rules govern once a federal case is transferred. Should the federal court apply the law of the state of the transferee district or the law of the state of the transferor district? In Van Dusen v. Barrack, 376 U.S. 612 (1964), the Supreme Court held that when a defendant seeks a § 1404(a) transfer, that transfer is simply a change of courtroom and should not change the law that is applied. The Court was concerned that if a change of venue brought with it a change of law, then § 1404(a) would be used "by defendants to defeat the advantages accruing to plaintiffs who have chosen a forum which, although it was inconvenient, was a proper venue." Id. at 634. Therefore, the Court held that the district court to which the case is transferred should apply whatever law the transferring court would have applied.

In Ferens v. John Deere Co., 494 U.S. 516 (1990), the Supreme Court went even further and held that even where the *plaintiff* requests the § 1404(a) transfer, the transferee court (the receiving court) should apply the law that the transferor court (the original court) would have applied. The facts of *Ferens* are quite striking. The plaintiff lost his right hand when it was caught in his John Deere harvester. The accident occurred in Pennsylvania, which has a two-year statute of limitations in such cases. After that period expired, the plaintiff brought suit against John Deere in federal court in Mississippi. John Deere apparently had an agent for service of process in Mississippi or did sufficient business there to be subject to general personal jurisdiction.

The Mississippi statute of limitations was six years. If the case had been in Mississippi state court, Mississippi would have applied its statute of limitations to this case. Therefore, it was undisputed that if the case were litigated in federal court in Mississippi, the federal court would apply the six-year time limit.

The case did not, however, stay in Mississippi. Shortly after filing his complaint, the plaintiff moved for a change of venue to Pennsylvania. The motion was granted, and the Supreme Court held that the federal court in Pennsylvania should apply the law that the federal court in Mississippi would have applied, i.e., the Mississippi statute of limitations. Thus, the plaintiff got to take advantage of Mississippi law without having to litigate there.

Van Dusen and *Ferens* involved transfers under § 1404(a). Why should the holdings of these cases *not* apply to § 1406(a) transfers? See Eggleton v. Plasser & Theurer Exp. Von Bahnbaumaschinen Gesellschaft, MBH, 495 F.3d 582 (8th Cir. 2007).

d. Standard for Transfer Under §§ 1404 and 1406

Section 1404(a) expressly provides that in deciding whether to transfer, the court shall consider (1) convenience of the parties, (2) convenience of the witnesses, and (3) "the interest of justice." On the other hand, § 1406(a) prescribes no such factors, providing that if the case is filed in an improper venue, the court "shall dismiss, or if it be in the interest of justice, transfer." If there is a federal court to which the case can be transferred, won't transfer rather than dismissal always be in the interest of justice? As some commentators have noted, "In the main * * * dismissal will not usually be necessary, nor generally proper." 17 MOORE'S FEDERAL PRACTICE § 111.34[i].

In § 1404(a) transfers, the plaintiff's choice of forum is entitled to some weight. After all, by definition in § 1404(a) cases, the original court is a proper venue, so the plaintiff had a right to sue in this court. Accordingly, the party seeking transfer (almost always the defendant) bears the burden of overcoming the presumption in favor of the plaintiff's choice.

In ruling on a motion to transfer (or ordering transfer *sua sponte*) under § 1404(a), the judge considers "private interest factors" and "public interest factors," which are taken from the doctrine of forum non conveniens (addressed in § F of this Chapter). Private factors include things relating to the convenient and efficient litigation of the case. For example, maybe the bulk of the physical evidence is in the transferee court, or perhaps most of the witnesses live there. Public factors include such things as what law will be applied and what community ought to be engaged in jury service should the case go to trial. For example, perhaps several related cases are pending in the transferee district. Transfer of the present case will permit it to be consolidated with the other cases in the transferee district, which may promote efficient processing. There is no exhaustive list of relevant factors, because they vary from case to case, and the district judge has great discretion in ruling on a motion to transfer.

The breadth of discretion is shown by two cases decided by the same federal district judge. In the first case, Smith v. Colonial Penn Ins. Co., 943 F. Supp. 782 (S.D. Tex. 1996), the defendant sought a transfer from Galveston to Houston, Texas, arguing that because there was no commercial airport in Galveston, the defendant would be burdened with the inconvenience of flying to Houston and then driving the 40 miles to Galveston. The court denied the motion, and noted that the Houston airport was located about equal drive time from downtown Houston and the Galveston courthouse:

> Defendant should be assured that it is not embarking on a three-week-long trip via covered wagons when it travels to Galveston. Rather, Defendant will be pleased to discover that the highway is paved and lighted all the way to Galveston, and thanks to the efforts of this Court's predecessor, Judge Roy Bean, the trip should be free of rustlers, hooligans, or vicious varmints of unsavory kind.

Id. at 784. The court further noted that regular limousine service is available from the Houston airport, "even to the steps of this humble courthouse, which has got lights, indoor plummin', 'lectric doors, and all sorts of new stuff, almost like them big courthouses back East." Id. at 785 n.2.

In the second case, Republic of Bolivia v. Philip Morris Cos., 39 F. Supp. 2d 1008 (S.D. Tex. 1999), Bolivia had filed suit in Brazoria County, Texas (a county with a reputation as being pro-plaintiff) against a group of U.S. tobacco companies. The case was removed to federal court and the court granted the defendants' motion for a § 1404(a) transfer to the District of Columbia.

> [T]he Court can hardly imagine why the Republic of Bolivia elected to file suit in the veritable hinterlands of Brazoria County, Texas. The Court seriously doubts whether Brazoria County has ever seen a live Bolivian * * * even on the Discovery Channel. Though only here by removal, this humble Court by the sea is certainly flattered by what must be the worldwide renown of rural Texas courts for dispensing justice with unparalleled fairness and alacrity, apparently in common discussion even on the mountain peaks of Bolivia! Still the Court would be remiss in accepting an obligation for which it truly does not have the necessary resources. * * * And, while Galveston is indeed an international seaport, the capacity of this Court to address the complex and sophisticated issues of international law and foreign relations presented by this case is dwarfed by that of its esteemed colleagues in the District of Columbia who deftly address such awesome tasks as a matter of course. * * * Such a Bench, well-populated with genuinely renowned intellects, can certainly better bear and share the burden of multi-district litigation than this single judge division, where the judge moves his lips when he reads * * *.
>
> * * * Plaintiff has an embassy in Washington, D.C., and thus a physical presence and governmental representatives there, whereas there isn't even a Bolivian restaurant anywhere near here!

Id. at 1009–10.*

---

* The opinions in both *Smith* and *Republic of Bolivia* were authored by Judge Samuel B. Kent. In 2009, Judge Kent was sentenced to 33 months in prison for lying to investigators in connection with an allegation that the judge had sexually abused two female employees. Following the sentencing, the House of Representatives voted to approve articles of impeachment but the judge resigned before the Senate acted.

e. The Effect of a Forum Selection Clause

Some contracts include a "forum selection clause" that specifies where litigation concerning the contract is to occur. Historically, courts were reluctant to enforce such provisions, but that reluctance started to evaporate late in the twentieth century. Now, as a matter of federal common law and the law of most (but not all) states, such clauses are enforced if they are not the product of overreaching or unconscionable behavior. The seminal case, arising in admiralty jurisdiction, was The Bremen v. Zapata Offshore Co., 407 U.S. 1, 18 (1972).

One interesting question is whether a valid forum selection clause renders venue improper in any other district. Suppose, for example, that the parties' forum selection clause requires litigation in the Eastern District of Missouri. But suppose venue would be proper under § 1391(b) in the District of Arizona. Plaintiff files the suit in Arizona. Defendant wants that court to enforce the forum selection clause by ordering transfer under § 1404(a) to the Eastern District of Missouri. If the forum selection clause requiring suit in the Eastern District of Missouri renders venue in the District of Arizona improper, Defendant can move to dismiss under Federal Rule 12(b)(3) for improper venue or to transfer or dismiss under § 1406(a). If not — that is, if the forum selection clause does not affect what constitutes a proper venue under § 1391(b) — Defendant could only move to transfer under § 1404(a).

The Court brought certainty on this and related issues in Atlantic Marine Construction Co, Inc. v. U.S. District Court, 134 S. Ct. 568 (2013). First, the Court held that a valid forum selection clause does not render venue improper in other districts. Thus, § 1406(a) did not apply; that section applies only when plaintiff's chosen venue is contrary to the venue *statute*. Id. at 578–580.

Second, the Court held that a party to a valid forum selection clause may seek enforcement of the provision through a motion to transfer under § 1404(a). Id. at 581.

Third, in applying § 1404(a), the plaintiff's choice of forum and "private interest factors" are irrelevant, because the parties already agreed to litigate in a particular forum. The court may consider only the "public interest factors," which will rarely defeat enforcement of the forum selection clause. Id. at 581–582. "In all but the most unusual cases [of which the Court gave no examples] … 'the interest of justice' is served by holding parties to their bargain." Id. at 583.

Finally, the Court addressed the question of choice of law. As discussed above, under *Van Dusen*, usually in a § 1404(a) transfer, the transferor court applies the same law that the transferee court would have applied. Applying *Van Dusen* in the transfer of a case to enforce a forum selection clause, however, would allow the party violating that clause to "capture" favorable law of a district in another state. For this reason, the Court in *Atlantic Marine* held that *Van Dusen* does not apply in § 1404(a) transfers to enforce a forum selection clause. 134 S. Ct. at 583. Thus, the transferee will apply its own choice of law rules.

f. Multidistrict Litigation

In mass torts such as airplane crashes or toxic torts, there may be many cases pending in different federal districts, all of which raise one or more common question (e.g., why did the plane crash?). Section 1407 permits all of these federal cases to be transferred to one district and consolidated *for pretrial proceedings.* These transfers need not meet other venue requirements. The decision whether to permit such transfers is made by "the judicial panel on multidistrict litigation," a seven member panel composed of district and circuit judges appointed by the Chief Justice. Section 1407 requires that following completion of pretrial proceedings, the cases "shall be remanded" to the districts from which they came.

Not surprisingly, a court which has overseen such consolidated pretrial proceedings might conclude that it is in the best position to handle the trial phase of the litigation as well. Thus, it became common for the § 1407 transferee court to refuse to send the cases back to their original districts and, instead, to transfer the cases to itself under § 1404(a) or § 1406(a), thereby allowing that court to preside over the trial and ultimate disposition of the cases. In Lexecon, Inc. v. Milberg Weiss Bershad Hynes & Lerach, 523 U.S. 26 (1998), the Supreme Court rejected this practice and held that the language of § 1404(a) and § 1407 permits transfer and consolidation for pretrial purposes only.

Nonetheless, "pretrial proceedings" include dispositive matters such as motions to dismiss and motions for summary judgment. And they also include settlements. Increasingly, the court to which cases are transferred under MDL seeks to engineer "global settlements" of all related cases. When these succeed (or when cases are adjudicated in the pretrial stage), the cases are not remanded to their original districts. Indeed, the majority of cases transferred for consolidated MDL treatment are terminated in the MDL court and not remanded to their original court. Some MDL judges have likened the consolidation of cases under § 1407 to a class action (to be studied in Chapter 13), and have exercised the sort of supervisory power accorded judges in class actions. This is done, however, without the oversight mechanisms applicable in class action practice under Rule 23. See Linda S. Mullenix, *Aggregate Litigation and the Death of Democratic Dispute Resolution*, 107 Nw. U. L. Rev. 511 (2013); Charles Silver & Geoffrey Miller, *The Quasi-Class Action Method of Managing Multi-District Litigation: Problems and a Proposal*, 63 Vand. L. Rev. 107 (2010).

The cases consolidated for pretrial purposes under § 1407 remain separate actions; they are not merged into a single litigative unit. In Gelboim v. Bank of America Corp., 135 S. Ct. 897 (2015), about 60 cases were transferred under § 1407 for MDL treatment in the Southern District of New York. The MDL judge granted summary judgment in favor of the defendants in one of those cases. The plaintiffs attempted to appeal the final judgment in that case, but the Second Circuit dismissed the appeal because the summary judgment had not disposed of all 60 MDL cases. The Supreme Court reversed. When, as in *Gelboim*, no "master complaint" or "consolidated answer" has superseded the pleadings of the individual cases, the cases retain their individual character. Because the summary judgment completely resolved the one case, it was appealable to the Second Circuit.

F. Forum non Conveniens

Piper Aircraft Co. v. Reyno

454 U.S. 235, 102 S. Ct. 252, 70 L. Ed. 2d 419 (1981)

JUSTICE MARSHALL delivered the opinion of the Court.

These cases arise out of an air crash that took place in Scotland. Respondent, acting as representative of the estates of several Scottish citizens killed in the accident, brought wrongful-death actions against petitioners that were ultimately transferred to the United States District Court for the Middle District of Pennsylvania. Petitioners moved to dismiss on the ground of forum non conveniens. After noting that an alternative forum existed in Scotland, the District Court granted their motions. The United States Court of Appeals for the Third Circuit reversed. The Court of Appeals based its decision, at least in part, on the ground that dismissal is automatically barred where the law of the alternative forum is less favorable to the plaintiff than the law of the forum chosen by the plaintiff. Because we conclude that the possibility of an unfavorable change in law should not, by itself, bar dismissal, and because we conclude that the District Court did not otherwise abuse its discretion, we reverse.

I

A

In July 1976, a small commercial aircraft crashed in the Scottish highlands during the course of a charter flight from Blackpool to Perth. The pilot and five passengers were killed instantly. The decedents were all Scottish subjects and residents, as are their heirs and next of kin. There were no eyewitnesses to the accident. At the time of the crash the plane was subject to Scottish air traffic control.

The aircraft, a twin-engine Piper Aztec, was manufactured in Pennsylvania by petitioner Piper Aircraft Co. (Piper). The propellers were manufactured in Ohio by petitioner Hartzell Propeller, Inc. (Hartzell). At the time of the crash the aircraft was registered in Great Britain and was owned and maintained by Air Navigation and Trading Co., Ltd. (Air Navigation). It was operated by McDonald Aviation, Ltd. (McDonald), a Scottish air taxi service. Both Air Navigation and McDonald were organized in the United Kingdom. The wreckage of the plane is now in a hangar in Farnsborough, England.

In July 1977, a California probate court appointed respondent Gaynell Reyno administratrix of the estates of the five passengers. Reyno is not related to and does not know any of the decedents or their survivors; she was a legal secretary to the attorney who filed this lawsuit. Several days after her appointment, Reyno commenced separate wrongful-death actions against Piper and Hartzell in the Superior Court of California, claiming negligence and strict liability. Air Navigation, McDonald, and the estate of the pilot are not parties to this litigation. The survivors of the five passengers whose estates are represented by Reyno filed a separate action in the United Kingdom against Air Navigation, McDonald, and the pilot's estate. Reyno candidly admits that the action against Piper and Hartzell was filed in the United States because its laws regarding liability, capacity to sue, and damages are more favorable to her position than are those of Scotland. Scottish law does not recognize strict liability in tort. Moreover, it permits wrongful-death actions only when brought by a decedent's relatives. The relatives may sue only for "loss of support and society."

On petitioners' motion, the suit was removed to the United States District Court for the Central District of California. Piper then moved for transfer to the United States District Court for the Middle District of Pennsylvania, pursuant to 28 U.S.C. § 1404(a). Hartzell moved to dismiss for lack of personal jurisdiction, or in the alternative, to transfer.[5] In December 1977, the District Court quashed service on Hartzell and transferred the case to the Middle District of Pennsylvania. Respondent then properly served process on Hartzell.

B

In May 1978, after the suit had been transferred, both Hartzell and Piper moved to dismiss the action on the ground of forum non conveniens. The District Court granted these motions in October 1979. It relied on the balancing test set forth by this Court in Gulf Oil Corp. v. Gilbert, 330 U.S. 501 (1947), and its companion case, Koster v. (American) Lumbermens Mut. Cas. Co., 330 U.S. 518 (1947). In those decisions, the Court stated that a plaintiff's choice of forum should rarely be disturbed. However, when an alternative forum has jurisdiction to hear the case, and when trial in the chosen forum would "establish ... oppressiveness and vexation to a defendant ... out of all proportion to plaintiff's convenience," or when the "chosen forum [is] inappropriate because of considerations affecting the court's own administrative and legal problems," the court may, in the exercise of its sound discretion, dismiss the case. To guide trial court discretion, the Court provided a list of "private interest factors" affecting the convenience of the litigants, and a list of "public interest factors" affecting the convenience of the forum.[6]

After describing our decisions in *Gilbert* and *Koster*, the District Court analyzed the facts of these cases. It began by observing that an alternative forum existed in Scotland; Piper and Hartzell had agreed to submit to the jurisdiction of the Scottish courts and to waive any statute of limitations defense that might be available. It then stated that plaintiff's choice of forum was entitled to little weight. The court recognized

---

5. The District Court concluded that it could not assert personal jurisdiction over Hartzell consistent with due process. However, it decided not to dismiss Hartzell because the corporation would be amenable to process in Pennsylvania.

6. The factors pertaining to the private interests of the litigants included the "relative ease of access to sources of proof; availability of compulsory process for attendance of unwilling, and the cost of obtaining attendance of willing, witnesses; possibility of view of premises, if view would be appropriate to the action: and all other practical problems that make trial of a case easy, expeditious and inexpensive." *Gilbert.* The public factors bearing on the question included the administrative difficulties flowing from court congestion; the "local interest in having localized controversies decided at home"; the interest in having the trial of a diversity case in a forum that is at home with the law that must govern the action; the avoidance of unnecessary problems in conflict of laws, or in the application of foreign law; and the unfairness of burdening citizens in an unrelated forum with jury duty.

that a plaintiff's choice ordinarily deserves substantial deference. It noted, however, that Reyno "is a representative of foreign citizens and residents seeking a forum in the United States because of the more liberal rules concerning products liability law," and that "the courts have been less solicitous when the plaintiff is not an American citizen or resident, and particularly when the foreign citizens seek to benefit from the more liberal tort rules provided for the protection of citizens and residents of the United States."

The District Court next examined several factors relating to the private interests of the litigants, and determined that these factors strongly pointed towards Scotland as the appropriate forum. Although evidence concerning the design, manufacture, and testing of the plane and propeller is located in the United States, the connections with Scotland are otherwise "overwhelming." The real parties in interest are citizens of Scotland, as were all the decedents. Witnesses who could testify regarding the maintenance of the aircraft, the training of the pilot, and the investigation of the accident—all essential to the defense—are in Great Britain. Moreover, all witnesses to damages are located in Scotland. Trial would be aided by familiarity with Scottish topography, and by easy access to the wreckage.

The District Court reasoned that because crucial witnesses and evidence were beyond the reach of compulsory process, and because the defendants would not be able to implead potential Scottish third-party defendants, it would be "unfair to make Piper and Hartzell proceed to trial in this forum." The survivors had brought separate actions in Scotland against the pilot, McDonald, and Air Navigation. "[I]t would be fairer to all parties and less costly if the entire case was presented to one jury with available testimony from all relevant witnesses." Although the court recognized that if trial were held in the United States, Piper and Hartzell could file indemnity or contribution actions against the Scottish defendants, it believed that there was a significant risk of inconsistent verdicts.[7]

The District Court concluded that the relevant public interests also pointed strongly towards dismissal. The court determined that Pennsylvania law would apply to Piper and Scottish law to Hartzell if the case were tried in the Middle District of Pennsylvania.[8] As a result, "trial in this forum would be hopelessly complex and confusing for a jury." In addition, the court noted that it was unfamiliar with Scottish law and

7. The District Court explained that inconsistent verdicts might result if petitioners were held liable on the basis of strict liability here, and then required to prove negligence in an indemnity action in Scotland. Moreover, even if the same standard of liability applied, there was a danger that different juries would find different facts and produce inconsistent results.

8. Under Klaxon Co. v. Stentor Elec. Mfg. Co., 313 U.S. 487 (1941), a court ordinarily must apply the choice-of-law rules of the State in which it sits. However, where a case is transferred pursuant to 28 U.S.C. § 1404(a), it must apply the choice-of-law rules of the State from which the case was transferred. Van Dusen v. Barrack, 376 U.S. 612 (1964). Relying on these two cases, the District Court concluded that California choice-of-law rules would apply to Piper, and Pennsylvania choice-of-law rules would apply to Hartzell. It further concluded that California applied a "governmental interests" analysis in resolving choice-of-law problems, and that Pennsylvania employed a "significant contacts" analysis. The court used the "governmental interests" analysis to determine that Pennsylvania liability

thus would have to rely upon experts from that country. The court also found that the trial would be enormously costly and time-consuming; that it would be unfair to burden citizens with jury duty when the Middle District of Pennsylvania has little connection with the controversy; and that Scotland has a substantial interest in the outcome of the litigation.

In opposing the motions to dismiss, respondent contended that dismissal would be unfair because Scottish law was less favorable. The District Court explicitly rejected this claim. It reasoned that the possibility that dismissal might lead to an unfavorable change in the law did not deserve significant weight; any deficiency in the foreign law was a "matter to be dealt with in the foreign forum."

C

On appeal, the United States Court of Appeals for the Third Circuit reversed and remanded for trial. The decision to reverse appears to be based on two alternative grounds. First, the Court held that the District Court abused its discretion in conducting the *Gilbert* analysis. Second, the Court held that dismissal is never appropriate where the law of the alternative forum is less favorable to the plaintiff.

II

The Court of Appeals erred in holding that plaintiffs may defeat a motion to dismiss on the ground of forum non conveniens merely by showing that the substantive law that would be applied in the alternative forum is less favorable to the plaintiffs than that of the present forum. The possibility of a change in substantive law should ordinarily not be given conclusive or even substantial weight in the forum non conveniens inquiry.

We expressly rejected the position adopted by the Court of Appeals in our decision in Canada Malting Co. v. Paterson Steamships, Ltd., 285 U.S. 413 (1932). * * *

It is true that *Canada Malting* was decided before *Gilbert*, and that the doctrine of forum non conveniens was not fully crystallized until our decision in that case.[13] However, *Gilbert* in no way affects the validity of *Canada Malting*. Indeed, by holding that the central focus of the forum non conveniens inquiry is convenience, *Gilbert* implicitly recognized that dismissal may not be barred solely because of the possibility of an unfavorable change in law. Under *Gilbert*, dismissal will ordinarily be appropriate where trial in the plaintiff's chosen forum imposes a heavy burden on the defendant or the court, and where the plaintiff is unable to offer any specific reasons of con-

---

rules would apply to Piper, and the "significant contacts" analysis to determine that Scottish liability would apply to Hartzell.

13. * * * In previous forum non conveniens decisions, the Court has left unresolved the question whether under Erie R.R. v. Tompkins, 304 U.S. 64 (1938), state or federal law of forum non conveniens applies in a diversity case. The Court did not decide this issue because the same result would have been reached in each case under federal or state law. The lower courts in these cases reached the same conclusion: Pennsylvania and California law on forum non conveniens dismissals are virtually identical to federal law. Thus, here also, we need not resolve the *Erie* question.

venience supporting his choice.[15] If substantial weight were given to the possibility of an unfavorable change in law, however, dismissal might be barred even where trial in the chosen forum was plainly inconvenient.

The Court of Appeals' decision is inconsistent with this Court's earlier forum non conveniens decisions in another respect. Those decisions have repeatedly emphasized the need to retain flexibility. In *Gilbert*, the Court refused to identify specific circumstances "which will justify or require either grant or denial of remedy." Similarly, in *Koster*, the Court rejected the contention that where a trial would involve inquiry into the internal affairs of a foreign corporation, dismissal was always appropriate. "That is one, but only one, factor which may show convenience." And in Williams v. Green Bay & W. R. Co., 326 U.S. 549, 557 (1946), we stated that we would not lay down a rigid rule to govern discretion, and that "[e]ach case turns on its facts." If central emphasis were placed on any one factor, the forum non conveniens doctrine would lose much of the very flexibility that makes it so valuable.

In fact, if conclusive or substantial weight were given to the possibility of a change in law, the forum non conveniens doctrine would become virtually useless. Jurisdiction and venue requirements are often easily satisfied. As a result, many plaintiffs are able to choose from among several forums. Ordinarily, these plaintiffs will select that forum whose choice-of-law rules are most advantageous. Thus, if the possibility of an unfavorable change in substantive law is given substantial weight in the forum non conveniens inquiry, dismissal would rarely be proper.

The Court of Appeals' approach is not only inconsistent with the purpose of the forum non conveniens doctrine, but also poses substantial practical problems. If the possibility of a change in law were given substantial weight, deciding motions to dismiss on the ground of forum non conveniens would become quite difficult. Choice-of-law analysis would become extremely important, and the courts would frequently be required to interpret the law of foreign jurisdictions. * * *

Upholding the decision of the Court of Appeals would result in other practical problems. At least where the foreign plaintiff named an American manufacturer as defendant,[17] a court could not dismiss the case on grounds of forum non conveniens where dismissal might lead to an unfavorable change in law. The American courts, which are already extremely attractive to foreign plaintiffs,[18] would become even

15. In other words, *Gilbert* held that dismissal may be warranted where a plaintiff chooses a particular forum, not because it is convenient, but solely in order to harass the defendant or take advantage of favorable law. This is precisely the situation in which the Court of Appeals' rule would bar dismissal.

17. In fact, the defendant might not even have to be American. A foreign plaintiff seeking damages for an accident that occurred abroad might be able to obtain service of process on a foreign defendant who does business in the United States. Under the Court of Appeals' holding, dismissal would be barred if the law in the alternative forum were less favorable to the plaintiff—even though none of the parties are American, and even though there is absolutely no nexus between the subject matter of the litigation and the United States.

18. First, all but 6 of the 50 American States—Delaware, Massachusetts, Michigan, North Carolina, Virginia, and Wyoming—offer strict liability. Rules roughly equivalent to American strict liability

more attractive. The flow of litigation into the United States would increase and further congest already crowded courts.[19]

The Court of Appeals based its decision, at least in part, on an analogy between dismissals on grounds of forum non conveniens and transfers between federal courts pursuant to § 1404(a). In Van Dusen v. Barrack, 376 U.S. 612 (1964), this Court ruled that a § 1404(a) transfer should not result in a change in the applicable law. Relying on dictum in an earlier Third Circuit opinion interpreting *Van Dusen*, the court below held that that principle is also applicable to a dismissal on forum non conveniens grounds. However, § 1404(a) transfers are different than dismissals on the ground of forum non conveniens.

Congress enacted § 1404(a) to permit change of venue between federal courts. Although the statute was drafted in accordance with the doctrine of forum non conveniens, it was intended to be a revision rather than a codification of the common law. District courts were given more discretion to transfer under § 1404(a) than they had to dismiss on grounds of forum non conveniens.

The reasoning employed in *Van Dusen v. Barrack* is simply inapplicable to dismissals on grounds of forum non conveniens. That case did not discuss the common-law doctrine. Rather, it focused on "the construction and application" of § 1404(a). Emphasizing the remedial purpose of the statute, *Barrack* concluded that Congress could not have intended a transfer to be accompanied by a change in law. The statute was designed as a "federal housekeeping measure," allowing easy change of venue within a unified federal system. The Court feared that if a change in venue were accompanied by a change in law, forum-shopping parties would take unfair advantage of the relaxed standards for transfer. The rule was necessary to ensure the just and efficient operation of the statute.

---

are effective in France, Belgium, and Luxembourg. West Germany and Japan have a strict liability statute for pharmaceuticals. However, strict liability remains primarily an American innovation. Second, the tort plaintiff may choose, at least potentially, from among 50 jurisdictions if he decides to file suit in the United States. Each of these jurisdictions applies its own set of malleable choice-of-laws rules. Third, jury trials are almost always available in the United States, while they are never provided in civil law jurisdictions. Even in the United Kingdom, most civil actions are not tried before a jury. Fourth, unlike most foreign jurisdictions, American courts allow contingent attorney's fees, and do not tax losing parties with their opponents' attorney's fees. Fifth, discovery is more extensive in American than in foreign courts.

19. In holding that the possibility of a change in law favorable to the plaintiff should not be given substantial weight, we also necessarily hold that the possibility of a change in law favorable to the defendant should not be considered. Respondent suggests that Piper and Hartzell filed the motion to dismiss, not simply because trial in the United States would be inconvenient, but also because they believe the laws of Scotland are more favorable. She argues that this should be taken into account in the analysis of the private interests. We recognize, of course, that Piper and Hartzell may be engaged in reverse forum-shopping. However, this possibility ordinarily should not enter into a trial court's analysis of private interests. If the defendant is able to overcome the presumption in favor of plaintiff by showing that trial in the chosen forum would be unnecessarily burdensome, dismissal is appropriate — regardless of the fact that defendant may also be motivated by a desire to obtain a more favorable forum.

We do not hold that the possibility of an unfavorable change in law should *never* be a relevant consideration in a forum non conveniens inquiry. Of course, if the remedy provided by the alternative forum is so clearly inadequate or unsatisfactory that it is no remedy at all, the unfavorable change in law may be given substantial weight; the district court may conclude that dismissal would not be in the interests of justice.[22] In these cases, however, the remedies that would be provided by the Scottish courts do not fall within this category. Although the relatives of the decedents may not be able to rely on a strict liability theory, and although their potential damages award may be smaller, there is no danger that they will be deprived of any remedy or treated unfairly.

III

The Court of Appeals also erred in rejecting the District Court's *Gilbert* analysis. The Court of Appeals stated that more weight should have been given to the plaintiff's choice of forum, and criticized the District Court's analysis of the private and public interests. However, the District Court's decision regarding the deference due plaintiff's choice of forum was appropriate. Furthermore, we do not believe that the District Court abused its discretion in weighing the private and public interests.

A

The District Court acknowledged that there is ordinarily a strong presumption in favor of the plaintiff's choice of forum, which may be overcome only when the private and public interest factors clearly point towards trial in the alternative forum. It held, however, that the presumption applies with less force when the plaintiff or real parties in interest are foreign.

The District Court's distinction between resident or citizen plaintiffs and foreign plaintiffs is fully justified. In *Koster*, the Court indicated that a plaintiff's choice of forum is entitled to greater deference when the plaintiff has chosen the home forum.[23] When the home forum has been chosen, it is reasonable to assume that this choice is convenient. When the plaintiff is foreign, however, this assumption is much less rea-

---

22. At the outset of any forum non conveniens inquiry, the court must determine whether there exists an alternative forum. Ordinarily this requirement will be satisfied when the defendant is "amenable to process" in the other jurisdiction. In rare circumstances, however, where the remedy offered by another forum is clearly unsatisfactory, the other forum may not be an adequate alternative, and the initial requirement may not be satisfied. Thus, for example, dismissal would not be appropriate where the alternative forum does not permit litigation of the subject matter of the dispute. Cf. Phoenix Canada Oil Co. v. Texaco, Inc., 78 F.R.D. 445 (D. Del. 1978) (court refuses to dismiss, where alternative forum is Ecuador, it is unclear whether Ecuadorian tribunal will hear the case, and there is no generally codified Ecuadorian legal remedy for the unjust enrichment and tort claims asserted).

23. In *Koster*, we stated that "[i]n any balancing of conveniences, a real showing of convenience by a plaintiff who has sued in his home forum will normally outweigh the inconvenience the defendant may have shown." As the District Court correctly noted in its opinion, the lower federal courts have routinely given less weight to a foreign plaintiff's choice of forum. A citizen's forum choice should not be given dispositive weight, however. Citizens or residents deserve somewhat more deference than foreign plaintiffs, but dismissal should not be automatically barred when a plaintiff has filed suit in his home forum. As always, if the balance of conveniences suggests that trial in the chosen forum would be unnecessarily burdensome for the defendant or the court, dismissal is proper.

sonable. Because the central purpose of any forum non conveniens inquiry is to ensure that the trial is convenient, a foreign plaintiff's choice deserves less deference.[24]

B

The forum non conveniens determination is committed to the sound discretion of the trial court. It may be reversed only when there has been a clear abuse of discretion; where the court has considered all relevant public and private interest factors, and where its balancing of these factors is reasonable, its decision deserves substantial deference. * * *

(1)

In analyzing the private interest factors, the District Court stated that the connections with Scotland are "overwhelming." This characterization may be somewhat exaggerated. Particularly with respect to the question of relative ease of access to sources of proof, the private interests point in both directions. As respondent emphasizes, records concerning the design, manufacture, and testing of the propeller and plane are located in the United States. She would have greater access to sources of proof relevant to her strict liability and negligence theories if trial were held here.[25] However, the District Court did not act unreasonably in concluding that fewer evidentiary problems would be posed if the trial were held in Scotland. A large proportion of the relevant evidence is located in Great Britain.

The Court of Appeals found that the problems of proof could not be given any weight because Piper and Hartzell failed to describe with specificity the evidence they would not be able to obtain if trial were held in the United States. It suggested that defendants seeking forum non conveniens dismissal must submit affidavits identifying the witnesses they would call and the testimony these witnesses would provide if the trial were held in the alternative forum. Such detail is not necessary. Piper and Hartzell have moved for dismissal precisely because many crucial witnesses are located beyond the reach of compulsory process, and thus are difficult to identify or interview. Requiring extensive investigation would defeat the purpose of their motion. Of course, defendants must provide enough information to enable the District Court to balance the parties' interests. Our examination of the record convinces us that sufficient information was provided here. Both Piper and Hartzell submitted affidavits describing the evidentiary problems they would face if the trial were held in the United States.[27]

---

24. Respondent argues that since plaintiffs will ordinarily file suit in the jurisdiction that offers the most favorable law, establishing a strong presumption in favor of both home and foreign plaintiffs will ensure that defendants will always be held to the highest possible standard of accountability for their purported wrongdoing. However, the deference accorded to a plaintiff's choice of forum has never been intended to guarantee that the plaintiff will be able to select the law that will govern the case.

25. In the future, where similar problems are presented, district courts might dismiss subject to the condition that defendant corporations agree to provide the records relevant to the plaintiff's claims.

27. The affidavit provided to the District Court by Piper states that it would call the following witnesses: The relatives of the decedents; the owners and employees of McDonald; the persons responsible for the training and licensing of the pilot; the persons responsible for servicing and main-

The District Court correctly concluded that the problems posed by the inability to implead potential third-party defendants clearly supported holding the trial in Scotland. Joinder of the pilot's estate, Air Navigation, and McDonald is crucial to the presentation of petitioners' defense. If Piper and Hartzell can show that the accident was caused not by a design defect, but rather by the negligence of the pilot, the plane's owners, or the charter company, they will be relieved of all liability. It is true, of course, that if Hartzell and Piper were found liable after a trial in the United States, they could institute an action for indemnity or contribution against these parties in Scotland. It would be far more convenient, however, to resolve all claims in one trial. The Court of Appeals rejected this argument. Forcing petitioners to rely on actions for indemnity or contributions would be "burdensome" but not "unfair." Finding that trial in the plaintiff's chosen forum would be burdensome, however, is sufficient to support dismissal on grounds of forum non conveniens.

(2)

The District Court's review of the factors relating to the public interest was also reasonable. On the basis of its choice-of-law analysis, it concluded that if the case were tried in the Middle District of Pennsylvania, Pennsylvania law would apply to Piper and Scottish law to Hartzell. It stated that a trial involving two sets of laws would be confusing to the jury. It also noted its own lack of familiarity with Scottish law. Consideration of these problems was clearly appropriate under *Gilbert*; in that case we explicitly held that the need to apply foreign law pointed towards dismissal. The Court of Appeals found that the District Court's choice-of-law analysis was incorrect, and that American law would apply to both Hartzell and Piper. Thus, lack of familiarity with foreign law would not be a problem. Even if the Court of Appeals' conclusion is correct, however, all other public interest factors favored trial in Scotland.

Scotland has a very strong interest in this litigation. The accident occurred in its airspace. All of the decedents were Scottish. Apart from Piper and Hartzell, all potential plaintiffs and defendants are either Scottish or English. As we stated in *Gilbert*, there is "a local interest in having localized controversies decided at home." 330 U.S. at 509. Respondent argues that American citizens have an interest in ensuring that American manufacturers are deterred from producing defective products, and that additional deterrence might be obtained if Piper and Hartzell were tried in the United States, where they could be sued on the basis of both negligence and strict liability. However, the incremental deterrence that would be gained if this trial were held in an American court is likely to be insignificant. The American interest in this accident is simply not sufficient to justify the enormous commitment of judicial time and resources that would inevitably be required if the case were to be tried here.

IV

The Court of Appeals erred in holding that the possibility of an unfavorable change in law bars dismissal on the ground of forum non conveniens. It also erred in rejecting

---

taining the aircraft; and two or three of its own employees involved in the design and manufacture of the aircraft.

the District Court's *Gilbert* analysis. The District Court properly decided that the presumption in favor of the respondent's forum choice applied with less than maximum force because the real parties in interest are foreign. It did not act unreasonably in deciding that the private interests pointed towards trial in Scotland. Nor did it act unreasonably in deciding that the public interests favored trial in Scotland.

Thus, the judgment of the Court of Appeals is reversed.

Notes and Questions

1. *Piper* involves several interesting procedural wrinkles. First, the case was removed from California Superior Court in Los Angeles to the federal district court for the Central District of California. Without knowing anything about the residence of the parties or where the claim arose, why was venue proper in the Central District? Second, the case was transferred to the Middle District of Pennsylvania. (Notice what choice of law rules the court in Pennsylvania applied to Piper and Hartzell. See *Piper*, supra at n.8.) Finally, the case was dismissed under forum non conveniens. In fact, it is possible to review an impressive array of forum-selection issues by considering the procedural path of the *Piper* litigation. See Richard Freer, *Refracting Domestic and Global Choice-of-Law Doctrine Through the Lens of a Single Case*, 2007 BYU L. Rev. 959.

2. As the Court notes, the plaintiffs' primary reason for suing in the U.S. was to take advantage of U.S. liability rules that are more generous to plaintiffs than the law of Scotland would have been. The Court indicates that in ruling on a forum non conveniens motion, unfavorable changes in the law ordinarily should not be given substantial weight, though a variety of convenience factors should be considered. Does it make sense to give such weight to convenience while ignoring changes that alter the outcome of the litigation? Notice that according to the Court, in extreme cases, changes in the applicable law is a relevant factor: "if the remedy provided by the alternative forum is so clearly inadequate or unsatisfactory that it is not remedy at all, the unfavourable change in the law may be given substantial weight."

Should changes in the applicable law be treated as a "sliding scale"—the bigger the change, the more weight that change is given? After reviewing the personal papers of Justice Marshall, Professor Clermont concluded that "the Court's opinion really did mean to confine the consideration of change in law to determining the threshold question of whether an alternative forum exists. Once the lower court gets beyond that threshold question, the change in law does not go onto the balance." Kevin Clermont, *The Story of* Piper: *Fracturing the Foundation of Forum Non Conveniens, in* Civil Procedure Stories 199, 215 (K. Clermont ed., 2d ed. 2008). However, Professor Clermont concludes that, although courts frequently say that they do not consider changes in the law, "the courts' behavior does not conform to their words." Id.

3. In many cases, the grant of a forum non conveniens dismissal does not result in plaintiff's pursuing her remedy in the foreign court. Instead the claim is either abandoned or settled (frequently for a small amount). See David Robertson, *Forum Non Conveniens in America and England: "A Rather Fantastic Fiction,"* 103 Law Q. Rev. 398, 418–20 (1987) (approximately four percent of cases in study were filed in

foreign venues after forum non conveniens dismissal). Following the dismissal in *Piper*, the plaintiffs never filed a claim in Scotland. See Freer, *supra*, 2007 BYU L. REV. at 972 n.50 (e-mail from plaintiff's counsel in United States indicating case apparently was never pursued in Scotland).

4. In ruling on a forum non conveniens motion, the court is to consider the same both "the private interest factors" and "public interest factors" we saw with regard to § 1404(a) transfer. Review the list of items the Court enumerates in both of these categories in footnote 6 of *Piper*. One of the difficulties of such an open-ended test is that it reduces certainty and predictability. As the Supreme Court itself has observed, "The discretionary nature of the [forum non conveniens] doctrine, combined with the multifariousness of the factors relevant to its application * * * make uniformity and predictability of outcomes almost impossible." American Dredging Co. v. Miller, 510 U.S. 443, 455 (1994). See Martin Davies, *Time to Change the Federal Forum Non Conveniens Analysis*, 77 TUL. L. REV. 309 (2002).

In addition to the open-ended nature of the test for forum non conveniens, notice that the Supreme Court grants the district judge broad discretion in ruling on forum non conveniens motions and that such rulings will not be reversed on appeal absent abuse of discretion. As we will see in Chapter 14, abuse of discretion is the most deferential of the various standards of review.

5. In Gulf Oil Corp. v. Gilbert, 330 U.S. 501 (1947), the Court had said in passing that "the doctrine of forum non conveniens can never apply if there is absence of jurisdiction." Some lower courts had interpreted this to mean that before they could dismiss on grounds of forum non conveniens, the court was required to rule on whether there was personal jurisdiction. In Sinochem Int'l Co. Ltd. v. Malaysia Int'l Shipping Corp., 549 U.S. 422, 433 (2007), the Supreme Court rejected this approach. Noting that the quoted language from *Gulf Oil* was "perhaps less than felicitously" crafted, the Court held that a court may, "when judicial economy so warrant[s]," dispose of a suit by a forum non conveniens dismissal and bypass questions of subject matter or personal jurisdiction.

6. Would the result in *Piper* have been different if one of the decedents had been a U.S. citizen? What if all decedents were Scottish, but the beneficiary of one of their estates was a U.S. citizen? See William Reynolds, *The Proper Forum for a Suit: Transnational Forum Non Conveniens and Counter-Suit Injunctions in the Federal Courts*, 70 TEX. L. REV. 1663 (1992). Suppose the plaintiff were a U.S. citizen but was not domiciled in the American forum. In Iragorri v. United Techns. Corp., 274 F.3d 65 (2d Cir. 2001) (en banc), the decedent, a U.S. citizen and Florida domiciliary, was killed after falling down an open elevator shaft in an apartment building in Colombia, where he was temporarily residing. The decedent's widow and children brought suit against the elevator manufacturer and parent corporation in Connecticut, which was the site of the defendant's principal place of business. The district court dismissed on grounds of forum non conveniens. The Second Circuit reversed and remanded, finding that the district court had incorrectly assumed that a plaintiff's choice of forum is entitled to deference only when the plaintiff sues in the plaintiff's home district.

7. A forum non conveniens dismissal may be conditioned on the defendant's waiving the other forum defenses such as the statute of limitations or personal jurisdiction, or agreeing to discovery that may not be available in the other forum. See In re Union Carbide Corp. Gas Plant Disaster at Bhopal, India, 809 F.2d 195 (2d Cir. 1987); Russell Weintraub, *International Litigation and Forum Non Conveniens*, 29 Tex. Int'l L.J. 321, 330–32 (1994).

8. The Court in *Piper* adopts and applies principles established in *Gulf Oil v. Gilbert*. In that case, a Virginia plaintiff sued a Pennsylvania defendant in federal court in New York. The accident underlying the suit occurred in Virginia. Virtually all relevant trial witnesses and evidence were in Virginia, and it was clear that Virginia law would govern. The Court reinstated the district court's order of dismissal for forum non conveniens. At the time of *Gilbert*, the transfer provisions of § 1404(a) and § 1406(a) did not exist, so dismissal under forum non conveniens was the only option available. Indeed, Congress passed § 1404 and § 1406 in response to *Gilbert*. Now that transfer is available, forum non conveniens is used in federal courts only where the alternative forum is in a foreign country.

Forum non conveniens may also apply when a case is pending in state court and the more appropriate forum is a state court in a different state. There is no general provision allowing transfer between courts of different states, so forum non conveniens might provide an attractive option. Each state is free to develop its own doctrine of forum non conveniens. Most have done so either by common law, see, e.g., Summa Corp. v. Lancer Indus., 559 P.2d 544 (Utah 1977), or by statute, see, e.g., Ga. Code. Ann. § 9-10-31.1; La. Code Civ. Proc. Ann. Art. 123.

9. In *Piper*, the federal court had both subject matter jurisdiction and personal jurisdiction. Nonetheless, the federal court refused to adjudicate the case. Where do federal courts get the authority to do this? When Congress grants subject matter jurisdiction over a category of cases to the federal courts, is that simply a request to the courts that they adjudicate the described cases (if the court feels like it), or are such grants mandates?

There is another category of discretionary refusal to assert jurisdiction, known as "abstention." Under various abstention doctrines, federal courts will sometimes decline to decide a case where it involves a particularly sensitive or unsettled issue of state law, or where another case dealing with the same issue is pending in state court. See Wright & Kane, Federal Courts 321–38. Like forum non conveniens, the abstention doctrines are entirely court-made and are not addressed by statute. Professor Redish argues that these court-made doctrines constitute a judicial abdication of congressionally conferred jurisdiction, and thus violate the principle of separation of powers. See Martin Redish, *Abstention, Separation of Powers, and the Limits of the Judicial Function*, 94 Yale L.J. 71 (1984). Indeed, some courts have been reluctant to invoke forum non conveniens in cases based on certain federal statutory claims on the grounds that Congress intended to eliminate judicial discretion to decline jurisdiction in these cases. See Lonny Hoffman & Keith Rowley, *Forum Non Conveniens in Federal Statutory Cases*, 49 Emory L.J. 1137 (2000).

10. "As a moth is drawn to the light, so is a litigant drawn to the United States. If he can only get his case into their courts, he stands to win a fortune." Weintraub, supra, 29 Tex. Int'l L.J. at 322 (quoting Lord Denning). The attractions of U.S. courts include extensive pretrial discovery, generous tort laws, choice of law rules that make it more likely that American law will be applied, and trial by jury. See id. at 323–24. Should American courts (and these advantages) be open to foreign citizens injured abroad by American defendants? Should they be available for American citizens who travel or do business abroad and wish to sue foreign defendants here?

The lengths to which defendants will go to avoid litigation in American courts is illustrated by *In re* Air Crash off Long Island, 65 F. Supp. 2d 207 (S.D.N.Y. 1999), a case growing out of the crash of TWA Flight 800 shortly after take-off from Kennedy Airport in New York. Families of the decedents filed suits in various U.S. courts. The largest group of foreign domiciliary plaintiffs was from France, and after many of the suits were consolidated as multi-district litigation, the defendants moved to dismiss the claims of the French domiciliaries on grounds of forum non conveniens. As a condition of the dismissal, the defendants offered that if suits were refiled in France they would not contest jurisdiction and would even *concede liability*! (The defendants were apparently concerned about the possibility in a U.S. court of punitive damages and pain and suffering awards.) The district court rejected the motion explaining:

> The public interest factors weigh strongly against dismissal. At the outset, it is worth remarking that Defendants have not cited to — nor is this Court aware of — a single case, arising from a catastrophic event that happened in United States territory, that was dismissed on forum non conveniens grounds in order to be refiled in a foreign nation. The catastrophe happened not far from this Courthouse. The investigation into the cause of the catastrophe has been enormously extensive and costly, consuming the energy and resources of multiple administrative agencies of the United States Government and of the State of New York. * * * Imposition of jury duty would not be unfair, particularly as jury duty will be imposed in any event, as the non-French plaintiffs would not be subject to dismissal under this motion.

Id. at 217.

11. The doctrine of forum non conveniens is well established in England. Interestingly, in ruling on a forum non conveniens motion, English courts will consider only the interests of the litigants and have explicitly rejected consideration of public convenience. As Lord Hope has explained, "the principles on which the doctrine of forum non conveniens rest leave no room for considerations of public interest or public policy which cannot be related to the private interests of any of the parties or the ends of justice in the case which is before the court. * * * 'Obviously the Court cannot allege its own convenience, or the amount of its own business, or its distaste for trying actions which involve taking evidence in French, as a ground for refusal....'" Lubbe v. Cape PLC, [2000] 1 WLR 1545, 1566 (HL), quoting from Society du Gaz, [1926] Session Cases 13, 21 (HL).

Most civil-law systems do not permit discretionary refusals to exercise jurisdiction such as forum non conveniens. As one commentator has explained, "For civil-law systems, jurisdictional rules and principles are *designed* by the legislature and *applied* by judges. Judicial 'fine tuning' compromises, in the civilian's eyes, the predictability and administrability that all law—substantive and procedural alike—should display." ARTHUR VON MEHREN, THEORY AND PRACTICE OF ADJUDICATORY AUTHORITY IN PRIVATE INTERNATIONAL LAW: A COMPARATIVE STUDY OF THE DOCTRINE, POLICIES AND PRACTICES OF COMMON—AND CIVIL—LAW SYSTEMS 306 (2003).

Chapter 6

Raising Jurisdictional and Related Challenges

A. Introduction and Integration

To this point, we have explored doctrines governing the selection of a proper court: personal jurisdiction, subject matter jurisdiction, and venue. In this chapter, we consider how and when a defendant may object to the plaintiff's selection of forum.*

The nature of the defense affects the time in which it may be asserted. As we have seen, the rules governing personal jurisdiction and venue give the defendant personal rights, which she may waive. In addition, it is efficient to resolve questions of personal jurisdiction and venue early in the lawsuit. Consequently, courts impose strict limits as to how and when these defenses must be raised.

Subject matter jurisdiction, however, stands on a different footing. It involves not a waivable personal right of the defendant, but governmental structure. Federal courts have limited subject matter jurisdiction, reflecting the constitutional allocation of judicial power between the national and state governments.** Thus, although it would be efficient to resolve this issue at the outset of litigation, parties are not free to waive subject matter jurisdiction. By the well-established rule, this defense can be raised anytime, by any party or by the court itself (sua sponte). Although some have questioned the wisdom of this rule, it remains.

---

* In Chapter 4, Section C.6, we saw that a defendant sued in state court might remove the case to federal court, assuming the case invokes federal subject matter jurisdiction and is otherwise removable. Here, in contrast, we address ways in which a defendant might contend that the court in which she is sued is improper for some reason.

** Recall also that states are free to allocate their judicial power between various courts, prescribing the subject matter jurisdiction of each, as we studied in Chapter 4, Section B.

B. The Traditional and Modern Approaches to Challenging Personal Jurisdiction

There are two general approaches for raising a direct objection to in personam jurisdiction. The traditional method is the "special appearance," some form of which is still used in several states. The second, more modern, approach is embodied in Federal Rule 12. Of course, Rule 12 governs practice only in federal court, but many states have adopted a version of it. Both approaches address the dilemma faced by a defendant wishing to challenge in personam jurisdiction: by going to the forum and arguing that it lacks jurisdiction, does the defendant risk submitting herself to jurisdiction there through "appearance" or "consent"?

Appreciating this difficulty, courts developed the notion of the special appearance, which allows a defendant to "appear" in a forum for the *sole purpose* of contesting in personam jurisdiction. While the requirements for making the special appearance vary among the states, the important point is that the defendant generally may raise only the in personam jurisdiction issue. If the defendant does more — for example, if she asserts an additional defense — she is deemed to have made a "general appearance," which subjects her to in personam jurisdiction. See, e.g., Bumgarner v. Federal Dep. Ins. Corp., 764 P.2d 1367 (Okla. App. 1988) (moving for continuance constitutes general appearance); Pfeiffer v. Ash, 206 P.2d 438 (Cal. App. 1949) (same). Despite the rigor with which some state courts apply the special appearance doctrine, it is clear that raising an objection to personal jurisdiction along with a notice to remove the case to federal court does not constitute a general appearance. Lambert Run Coal Co. v. Baltimore & Ohio R. Co., 258 U.S. 377 (1922). Moreover, some states have relaxed the traditional special appearance rule to allow a defendant to challenge in personam jurisdiction while raising some other defenses simultaneously. See, e.g., CAL. CODE CIV. PROC. § 418.10.

The Supreme Court has held that due process does not require states to provide for a special appearance or like manner of objecting to personal jurisdiction. York v. Texas, 137 U.S. 15 (1890). Nonetheless, every state does allow defendants to contest personal jurisdiction without submitting to jurisdiction; they do so either through a version of the special appearance or of Federal Rule 12.

A defendant wishing to contest in rem or quasi-in-rem jurisdiction faces the problem of limiting her potential liability to the value of the property attached. States have taken different approaches to this problem. In some, any appearance, even simply to contest jurisdiction, may convert the action into one in personam. In others, defending on the merits of the underlying claim opens the defendant to in personam jurisdiction. For example, the Delaware sequestration statute at issue in *Shaffer v. Heitner* required that a defendant either submit to in personam jurisdiction or forfeit the property. Many states permit the defendant to make a "limited appearance," which allows her to appear and defend without facing liability beyond the value of the property attached. See, e.g., Cheshire Nat'l Bank v. Jaynes, 112 N.E. 500 (Mass. 1916).

Although Federal Rule 4(n) recognizes that federal courts may exercise in rem and quasi-in-rem jurisdiction, the Rules do not mention the concept of the limited appearance in federal court. The federal courts have reached differing conclusions on whether to recognize the limited appearance. Compare, e.g., McQuillen v. National Cash Register Co., 112 F.2d 877 (4th Cir. 1940) (yes), with Campbell v. Murdock, 90 F. Supp. 297 (N.D. Ohio 1950) (no). The dates of these cases make clear that the issue simply does not come up much anymore, undoubtedly because of the increasing availability of in personam jurisdiction and concomitant decline of in rem and quasi-in-rem jurisdiction.

Federal Rule 12 abolishes the distinction between general and special appearances in federal court by allowing the defendant to raise several defenses simultaneously with an objection to personal jurisdiction. As the last sentence of Rule 12(b) says: "No defense or objection is waived by joining it with one or more other defenses or objections in a responsive pleading or in a motion." It is a mistake to assume, however, that Rule 12 is so liberal that defendants cannot get into trouble. The lawyer who does not read Rule 12 very carefully can easily commit malpractice.

Read Rules 12(a), 12(b), 12(g), and 12(h). Note that Rule 12(b) permits the defendant to raise any of seven specific defenses either in a "responsive pleading" or "by motion." What's the difference? *Pleadings* are documents setting forth factual and legal contentions of the parties as required by Rules 8 and 9. An answer is a pleading. Read Rule 7(a). *Motions* are requests that the court order something. Read Rule 7(b)(1). Motions can be made for a nearly infinite variety of reasons. For example, a party might move* for a continuance of a trial date, for an extension of time in which to answer, for an order that certain evidence not be admitted at trial, for an order that certain witnesses be excluded from the courtroom while not testifying, for a transfer of venue, and, of course, for dismissal. A party raising Rule 12(b) defenses in a motion usually will be moving to dismiss the case for one of the specified reasons.

Notes and Questions

1. Under what circumstances might a defendant prefer to raise a Rule 12(b) defense by motion rather than in a pleading? Under what circumstances might a defendant prefer to raise a Rule 12(b) defense in a pleading rather than by motion?

2. Defendant moves to dismiss for improper service of process. The motion is denied. Now the defendant moves to dismiss for lack of personal jurisdiction. Why is the personal jurisdiction defense waived? Under what subsection(s) of Rule 12?

3. Defendant serves her answer, in which she asserts that service of process was improper. Two weeks later, Defendant moves to dismiss for lack of personal jurisdiction. Why is the personal jurisdiction defense waived? Under what subsection(s) of Rule 12? (How does this question differ from Question 2?)

---

* As noted before, a party may "move" for or can "make a motion" for something. But "motion" is never used as a verb here. Thus, a party does not "motion" the court for anything.

4. Defendant moves to dismiss for improper service of process. After the motion is denied, Defendant serves an answer, asserting the defense of lack of personal jurisdiction. Why is the personal jurisdiction defense waived? Under what subsection(s) of Rule 12? Remember, however, that some states have not adopted the Federal Rules approach here, and still follow the special appearance procedure. In Virginia, for example, a defendant must be careful to challenge personal jurisdiction through a special appearance, in which she cannot raise other defenses. Raising other defenses at the same time constitutes a general appearance and waives the personal jurisdiction defense. See, e.g., Gilpin v. Joyce, 515 S.E.2d 124, 125 (Va. 1999).

5. Which four of the Rule 12(b) defenses must be raised either in a pre-answer Rule 12 motion or (if no such motion is made) in Defendant's answer? Read Rule 12(h)(1). Why do you think the rule requires early assertion of these four "waivable defenses"?

6. Defendant moves to dismiss for lack of personal jurisdiction and improper venue. After the motion is denied, Defendant files an answer, asserting the defense of failure to state a claim under Rule 12(b)(6). Is that defense timely? The case proceeds to trial, during which Defendant moves to dismiss for failure to join a party required by Rule 19(b). Is that defense timely?

7. Suppose Defendant raises a Rule 12(b)(6) or 12(b)(7) defense for the first time on appeal. Why would that not be timely? But Defendant could raise the Rule 12(b)(1) defense for the first time on appeal. What part of Rule 12 makes this clear?

8. Defendant moves for an extension of time in which to respond to the complaint. The motion is granted, after which Defendant files a motion to dismiss for lack of personal jurisdiction. Is the personal jurisdiction defense waived? Is the motion for extension of time a "motion under this rule"? Rule 12(g)(2). Would you reach the same conclusion if the initial motion were for a stay of proceedings? How about an initial motion for transfer under 28 U.S.C. § 1404(a)? See Aetna Life Ins. Co. v. Alla Medical Serv., Inc., 855 F.2d 1470 (9th Cir. 1988) (stay; no waiver); Catalano v. BRI, Inc., 724 F. Supp. 1580 (E.D. Mich. 1989) (transfer; no waiver).

9. According to some courts, a party may waive a defense even though she originally raised it in a timely manner. In Datskow v. Teledyne, Inc., 899 F.2d 1298 (2d Cir. 1990), the defendant filed a timely answer in which it asserted insufficient service of process. The defendant failed to raise the issue in a subsequent conference between litigants and the court. Later, after the statute of limitations had expired, the defendant moved to dismiss on the service of process grounds. The court denied the motion, holding that the defendant, despite timely filing of the answer, had waited too long to revisit the question. See also Hamilton v. Atlas Turner, Inc., 197 F.3d 58 (2d Cir. 1999) (defendant raised defense of personal jurisdiction in timely answer but did not make motion to dismiss based upon it for four years; held to have waived the defense). As we will see in Chapter 8, a pretrial conference order of the court supersedes the pleadings; issues not included in such an order generally are waived.

10. As we saw in Chapter 5, a party may move to dismiss a case under the doctrine of forum non conveniens. Though some have argued that such a motion should be

brought as a motion to dismiss for improper venue under Rule 12(b)(3), most courts conclude that forum non conveniens is not raised under Rule 12(b)(3), and thus is not waived if not asserted in the first Rule 12 response. See, e.g., Abiola v. Abubakar, 267 F. Supp. 2d 907, 918 (N.D. Ill. 2003). This result seems right, because a forum non conveniens dismissal is not based upon the impropriety of venue in the original forum. Similarly, there is authority that failure to assert improper venue under Rule 12(b)(3) does not waive the right to seek transfer of venue. See, e.g., Leif Hoegh & Co. v. Alpha Motor Ways, Inc., 534 F. Supp. 624, 626 (S.D.N.Y. 1982).

C. Collateral and Direct Attacks on Personal Jurisdiction

You practice law in Virginia. Client has been served properly with summons and complaint in Richmond in a case filed in a Hawaii state court. After investigating, you conclude that it is not clear whether Hawaii has personal jurisdiction over Client. Of course, Client could make an appearance in the Hawaii case (as permitted by Hawaii law) and object to personal jurisdiction. This would be a *direct attack* on Hawaii's jurisdiction. But Client has another option.

Client could ignore the process and allow the Hawaii court to enter a default judgment against her. Then, when the plaintiff attempts to enforce the default judgment in Virginia, Client could make a *collateral attack*. In this attack, she would argue that the Hawaii judgment is not entitled to full faith and credit because Hawaii did not have personal jurisdiction. Strategically, this course has the advantage of allowing Client to litigate at home (and would also save travel expense). But it could be a risky course.

First, the plaintiff might try to enforce that judgment anywhere Client has property. If Client has property in Hawaii or, say, Montana, she will have to raise the collateral attack in a distant forum.

Second, wherever the plaintiff seeks to enforce the Hawaii judgment—even if she seeks to do so in Virginia—the collateral attack permits Client to raise *only* the issue of whether the Hawaii court had jurisdiction; she cannot contest the merits of the plaintiff's claim. Thus, if Virginia (or any other state in which the plaintiff seeks to enforce the judgment) determines that Hawaii did have jurisdiction, the default judgment against Client is enforced, without litigation concerning the merits of underlying dispute. Obviously, if the court in the collateral attack determines that Hawaii did not have jurisdiction over Client, it will refuse to enforce the judgment. At that point, the plaintiff may decide to sue in Virginia. In this litigation, the defendant will be permitted to litigate the merits of the underlying dispute.

There are also problems, however, with making a direct attack. For one, if you are not also licensed to practice law in Hawaii, Client will have to find an attorney to appear there on her behalf. That counsel will have to learn enough about the case and the jurisdictional challenge to proceed appropriately. This process can be expensive for Client and must be completed quickly because of time limits imposed for making defensive responses. The expense and tension will be forgotten, however, if Client prevails in the direct attack; in that event, of course, the Hawaii court will dismiss the case.

But what if the Hawaii court rejects Client's direct attack? The traditional rule, followed in most jurisdictions as we will see in Chapter 14, allows appellate review of right only after the trial court has entered a final judgment, which is one determining the merits of the entire underlying dispute between the parties. Some jurisdictions have an exception for personal jurisdiction, allowing review by appeal or, more commonly, by extraordinary writ, before trial on the merits. For example, the defendants in *World-Wide Volkswagen*, *Asahi*, and *Burnham*, which we studied in Chapter 2, obtained appellate review of the jurisdictional issue in this way.

Absent such an exception to the general rules of appealability, however, Client cannot appeal the jurisdictional ruling until after she litigates the entire case on the merits. Should she lose at trial, she can appeal both on jurisdiction and the merits. Thus, any defendant making a direct attack should understand that rejection of the challenge may necessitate her staying for trial. Also, as a practical matter, which court—Hawaii or Virginia—is more likely to hold that Hawaii lacks jurisdiction?

Competent counsel must be mindful of the advantages and disadvantages of the direct and collateral attacks. Most importantly, however, counsel must be careful not to mix the approaches.

Baldwin v. Iowa State Traveling Men's Association

283 U.S. 522, 51 S. Ct. 517, 75 L. Ed. 1244 (1931)

Mr. Justice Roberts delivered the opinion of the Court.

A writ of certiorari was granted herein to review the affirmance by the Circuit Court of Appeals of a judgment for respondent rendered by the District Court for Southern Iowa. The action was upon the record of a judgment rendered in favor of the petitioner against the respondent in the United States District Court for Western Missouri.

The defense was lack of jurisdiction of the person of the respondent in the court which entered the judgment. After hearing, in which a jury was waived, this defense was sustained and the action dismissed. The first suit was begun in a Missouri state court and removed to the District Court. Respondent appeared specially and moved to quash and dismiss for want of service. The court quashed the service, but refused to dismiss. An alias summons was issued and returned served, whereupon it again appeared specially, moved to set aside the service, quash the return, and dismiss the case for want of jurisdiction of its person. After a hearing on affidavits and briefs, the motion was overruled, with leave to plead within thirty days. No plea having been filed within that period, the cause proceeded and judgment was entered for the amount claimed. Respondent did not move to set aside the judgment nor sue out a writ of error.

The ground of the motion made in the first suit is the same as that relied on as a defense to this one, namely, that the respondent is an Iowa corporation, that it never was present in Missouri, and that the person served with process in the latter State was not such an agent that service on him constituted a service on the corporation. The petitioner objected to proof of these matters, asserting that the defense constituted a collateral attack and a retrial of an issue settled in the first suit. The overruling of this objection and the resulting judgment for respondent are assigned as error.

* * * The respondent * * * insists that to deprive it of the defense which it made in the court below, of lack of jurisdiction over it by the Missouri District Court, would be to deny the due process guaranteed by the Fourteenth Amendment; but there is involved in that doctrine no right to litigate the same question twice.

The substantial matter for determination is whether the judgment amounts to res judicata on the question of the jurisdiction of the court which rendered it over the person of the respondent. * * * The special appearance gives point to the fact that the respondent entered the Missouri court for the very purpose of litigating the question of the jurisdiction over its person. It had the election not to appear at all. If, in the absence of appearance, the court had proceeded to judgment and the present suit had been brought thereon, respondent could have raised and tried out the issue in the present action, because it would never have had its day in court with respect to jurisdiction. It had also the right to appeal from the decision of the Missouri District Court, as is shown by Harkness v. Hyde, 98 U.S. 476 (1879) * * *. It elected to follow neither of those courses, but, after having been defeated upon full hearing in its contention as to jurisdiction, it took no further steps, and the judgment in question resulted.

Public policy dictates that there be an end of litigation; that those who have contested an issue shall be bound by the result of the contest, and that matters once tried shall be considered forever settled as between the parties. We see no reason why this doctrine should not apply in every case where one voluntarily appears, presents his case and is fully heard, and why he should not, in the absence of fraud, be thereafter concluded by the judgment of the tribunal to which he has submitted his cause.

While this court has never been called upon to determine the specific question here raised, several federal courts have held the judgment res judicata in like circumstance. And we are in accord with this view. * * *

The judgment is reversed and the cause remanded for further proceedings in conformity with this opinion.

Reversed.

Notes and Questions

1. Do we know that the Missouri federal court was correct when it concluded that it had personal jurisdiction over the defendant? Will we ever know?

2. In *Baldwin*, the Supreme Court says that its holding is based upon the doctrine of res judicata, which is also called claim preclusion. We will study this and related doctrines in Chapter 11. For present purposes, it is enough to understand that our system generally provides a litigant one opportunity to litigate an issue. She is precluded from relitigating an issue that has already been decided. Thus, a defendant is

permitted to challenge personal jurisdiction only once—either in a direct attack or a collateral attack.

There was nothing wrong with the defendant's choice of a direct attack in *Baldwin.* The mistake was in not following through with that attack in Missouri. Having lost on the jurisdictional issue before the trial court in Missouri, the defendant (as part of its direct attack) could have appealed an adverse judgment to the appropriate court of appeals (and, ultimately, perhaps to the United States Supreme Court). As noted earlier, though, the issue probably could not have been raised on appeal until after resolution of the underlying litigation.

3. In City of New York v. Mikalis Pawn Shop, LLC, 645 F.3d 114 (2d Cir. 2011), defendants moved to dismiss for lack of personal jurisdiction. The court denied the motion, after which defendants decided to withdraw from the litigation. They were warned that the court could enter default judgment, but withdrew nonetheless. The court entered default judgment against defendants. On appeal, defendants sought to raise the personal jurisdiction defense. The Second Circuit affirmed the judgment, but not on the preclusion theory employed in *Baldwin.* Instead, it held the defendants waived the defense by withdrawing from suit. Obviously, then, a defendant who contests personal jurisdiction should decide whether to make a direct attack and, if so, should be prepared to litigate fully in that court. Changing one's mind after litigating whether that court has personal jurisdiction gives rise to preclusion or waiver of the defense.

4. Assume again that you practice law in Virginia and that Client (who lives in Virginia) has been served with process for a suit in Hawaii. The issue of whether Hawaii has jurisdiction over Client is a close one.

(a) If Client has a weak case on the merits (i.e., it is fairly clear that she will be held liable), why might you recommend a collateral, rather than a direct, attack?

(b) If Client has a strong case on the merits (e.g., has overwhelming proof that she is not liable), why (despite the expense) might you recommend a direct, rather than a collateral, attack? For example, assume that the plaintiff asserted that Client owed her on a note. Client has the canceled check showing that she paid the note on time. Suppose Client allows Hawaii to enter a default judgment and makes a collateral attack when the plaintiff seeks to enforce the judgment in Virginia. What is the only issue the Virginia court will address? If it finds that Hawaii had jurisdiction over Client, what good is the canceled check?

D. Challenging Federal Subject Matter Jurisdiction

In the usual case, the defendant will challenge subject matter jurisdiction by moving to dismiss under Rule 12(b)(1). A plaintiff may challenge subject matter jurisdiction of a removed case by moving to remand the case to state court under 28 U.S.C. § 1447(c). What happens, though, when the objecting party does not raise the issue early in the proceedings at the trial court? What does Rule 12(h) provide regarding timing of the defense?

In *Louisville & Nashville Railroad Co. v. Mottley*, which we read in Chapter 4, the Supreme Court raised lack of subject matter jurisdiction sua sponte. The case had to be dismissed, even though the jurisdictional problem was not discovered until after decision at the trial court and appeal and even though all parties wanted the federal courts to resolve the case.

The notion that lack of subject matter jurisdiction is not a waivable defense is so strong that even the party purporting to invoke federal jurisdiction can raise it after losing on the merits. In Capron v. Van Noorden, 6 U.S. 126 (1804), the plaintiff sued in federal court, apparently under diversity of citizenship jurisdiction. After losing at trial, he appealed on the grounds that the court lacked subject matter jurisdiction since there was no diversity after all! The Supreme Court held that the case must be dismissed. In American Fire & Cas. Co. v. Finn, 341 U.S. 6 (1951), a defendant who removed a case to federal court and then lost on the merits did the same thing. The federal district court had to remand the case to state court.

The nonwaivability of the subject matter jurisdiction defense can result in waste of judicial and private resources. It can also countenance outrageous gamesmanship. In some cases, plaintiffs have concealed the lack of jurisdiction until after losing on the merits. While their concealment may be punishable under various rules, such as Federal Rule 11, the judgment must be set aside. See, e.g., Rubin v. Buckman, 727 F.2d 71 (3d Cir. 1984). Similarly, defendants have successfully concealed a lack of jurisdiction until after the state court statute of limitations has run. Again, the federal case must be dismissed, perhaps leaving the plaintiff without remedy. See, e.g., Wojan v. General Motors Corp., 851 F.2d 969 (7th Cir. 1988).

Such abuse led some commentators to argue that litigants be estopped from raising lack of subject matter jurisdiction in instances of bad faith. See, e.g., Dan Dobbs, *Beyond Bootstrap: Foreclosing the Issue of Subject Matter Jurisdiction Before Final Judgment*, 51 MINN. L. REV. 491 (1967); Comment, *Second Bites at the Jurisdictional Apple: A Proposal for Preventing False Assertions of Diversity of Citizenship*, 41 HAST. L.J. 1417 (1990). Two cases seemed to indicate a move in that direction, Di Frischia v. New York Cent. R. Co., 279 F.2d 141 (3d Cir. 1960), and Klee v. Pittsburgh & W. Va. Ry. Co., 22 F.R.D. 252 (W.D. Pa. 1958), but they have had no impact on the traditional rule. Indeed, the Third Circuit later repudiated *Di Frischia* in light of Supreme Court decisions reasserting the traditional rule. Rubin v. Buckman, 727 F.2d 71 (3d Cir. 1984).

All of these cases involved direct attacks on the court's jurisdiction — that is, challenges made in the proceedings against the defendant either at the trial court or on appeal from judgment of the trial court. Does the same rule apply in collateral attacks? As we saw in *Baldwin*, a litigant usually gets only "one bite at the apple." Thus, consistent with what we have seen with personal jurisdiction, a defendant who litigates the issue of subject matter jurisdiction and loses cannot challenge it again in a separate action. Durfee v. Duke, 375 U.S. 106 (1963). This rule is subject to narrow exceptions.

For example, the Supreme Court found an exception in the policy underlying federal bankruptcy legislation. Kalb v. Feuerstein, 308 U.S. 433 (1940). See generally Karen Moore, *Collateral Attack on Subject Matter Jurisdiction: A Critique of the Restatement (Second) of Judgments*, 66 CORNELL L. REV. 534 (1981).

What if the parties litigate the merits of the case without raising the issue of subject matter jurisdiction? We know that a party can assert the lack of subject matter jurisdiction on appeal, but can she raise it in a collateral suit? The answer appears to be no. Chicot Cty. Drainage Distr. v. Baxter State Bank, 308 U.S. 371 (1940).

Chicot County involved a collateral attack of a judgment in which federal jurisdiction had been based upon a statute later held unconstitutional. Although the parties would have had no reason to suspect the lack of jurisdiction during the pendency of the prior suit and did not raise or litigate the issue, the Supreme Court refused to allow a collateral attack. According to the Court, the validity of the statute should have been raised during the first proceeding, and not after the court approved the final decree. As we will see in Chapter 11, claim preclusion can bar further litigation not only of issues actually litigated but of issues that could have been raised. See id. at 378. See also Des Moines Navigation & R.R. Co. v. Iowa Homestead Co., 123 U.S. 552 (1887).

The usual explanation for this rule is that courts have jurisdiction to decide their own jurisdiction—a concept that Professor Dobbs has called the "bootstrap principle." Dan Dobbs, *The Validation of Void Judgments: The Bootstrap Principle*, 53 VA. L. REV. 1003, 1241 (pts. 1 & 2) (1967). Subject matter derives from the legislative body or constitution that creates the court. Professor Dobbs argues that we should assume in most cases that the body creating the court intended for it to have jurisdiction to determine its own jurisdiction. He explains:

> [U]nder settled rules, if a court has jurisdiction to dismiss for want of jurisdiction, it has jurisdiction to retain the case. It may be error to dismiss or retain the case, but in either event it has jurisdiction to decide the issue. Of course, the legislature might change this rule by fiat. It might say that courts have jurisdiction to decide correctly and not other jurisdiction. But unless a legislature says this specifically, there is no reason to assume that it intended such a rule, because such a rule would not be consonant with a court's power to dismiss for want of jurisdiction.

53 VA. L. REV. at 1011–12.

And what about a collateral attack on a default judgment? There, the defendant has litigated nothing, but has suffered an adverse judgment. May she attack the default judgment for lack of subject matter jurisdiction in a collateral action? While *Chicot County* seems to indicate that she may not, remember that a defendant in a similar situation would be able to make a collateral attack based upon personal jurisdiction.*

---

* The claimants in *Chicot County* did not appear in the original proceeding. 103 F.2d 847 (8th Cir. 1939). Because many other parties were involved and did appear, the underlying case itself was litigated. The Supreme Court did not address the claimants' absence, and made no mention of a

Should the concept of jurisdiction to decide jurisdiction be applied to default judgments? Does a court in fact decide whether it has jurisdiction before entering a default judgment?

The RESTATEMENT (SECOND) OF JUDGMENTS permits a defendant to attack collaterally a default judgment based upon lack of subject matter jurisdiction, see § 65, except where "[g]ranting the relief would impair another person's substantial interest of reliance on the judgment." Id. at § 66(2). The drafters were quick to point out, however, that few modern decisions have sustained a collateral attack on a default judgment where the sole issue is lack of subject matter jurisdiction. RESTATEMENT (SECOND) OF JUDGMENTS § 12, cmt. f (1982). Often, there will be some other problems, such as lack of proper notice, which support collateral attack. Id. Professor (now Judge) Karen Moore provides a very helpful analysis of this area. Moore, supra, 66 CORNELL L. REV. at 551–53.

---

default judgment. Some commentators, however, regard *Chicot County* as a default case. See, e.g., Moore, supra, 66 CORNELL L. REV. at 553.

Chapter 7

Pleadings and Judgments Based on Pleadings

A. Introduction and Integration

In movies and on television, we often see trial scenes with surprise witnesses and unexpected revelations from the witness stand. Such things make for good theater, but rarely happen in the real world, at least not in civil cases. American civil procedure does not countenance "trial by ambush." Instead, it embraces the notion that litigants should be aware of the contentions and the evidence of their opponents before trial. Through this broad disclosure, the system seeks to find the truth, and not simply reward parties for the quick reactions of their lawyers.

In this chapter and the next, we address pleadings and discovery, which are the two major tools through which litigants gain information about each other's claims and defenses. These stages of litigation provide an education process for the parties, one that routinely consumes many months and sometimes years. The starting point is pleading. Here, the plaintiff alleges her claim against the defendant, and defendant responds to those allegations and sets forth any defenses she may have. All of this is done in writing, in documents filed with the court and served on the other parties. The pleading stage is relatively short, and gives way to the discovery process, during which parties are given broad access to information in the possession of the other parties (and sometimes nonparties).

The plaintiff initiates suit by filing what most jurisdictions call a *complaint.* You will recall from Chapter 3 that the plaintiff must arrange to give notice to the defendant through service of process, which consists of the court summons and a copy of the plaintiff's pleading. The defendant has a choice of how to respond to the complaint. One option is to file her own pleading, which most jurisdictions call an *answer*, in which she responds to the allegations in the complaint and may raise new matter called affirmative defenses.* In some jurisdictions, the plaintiff may then respond to any such new matter in another pleading, the *reply.*

* The other option will be to make a motion, which, as we see below, is not a pleading.

Rules governing pleading have a long and rich history, a glimpse of which we will see below. The history is important because it reflects the debate over the role pleadings should play in an overall system of civil procedure. The earliest system expected pleadings to perform at least four functions: (1) putting parties on notice of claims and defenses of their opponents; (2) stating facts each party believed it could prove; (3) narrowing the number and scope of issues needing trial; and (4) providing a quick method for resolving meritless claims and defenses. WRIGHT & KANE, FEDERAL COURTS 467. Modern systems expect less from pleadings, and purport to limit their function largely to giving notice. This can be done because modern practice provides other mechanisms — such as broad-ranging discovery and the motion for summary judgment (which we will see in Chapter 9) — to perform the other functions.

Though pleadings constitute a relatively short portion of most overall litigation, it is an important phase. The pleading requirements are a gatekeeper to the litigation process. If the plaintiff cannot state a claim that is both legally and factually sufficient, she will not pass through that gate. Her case will be dismissed and she will not have access to judicial machinery and other aspects of litigation, such as discovery.

There is significant debate about how difficult it should be to get through the pleading gate. Earlier systems used difficult and arcane pleading rules to erect a high barrier to entry. Modern theory, in contrast, tends to recognize that because pleadings are filed at the beginning of the case, before discovery, it is inappropriate to expect the parties to be fully familiar with the underlying facts. Modern theory thus lowers the barrier to entry by requiring less detail in pleading; it also permits ready amendment of pleadings and places the burden for factual development on the discovery process. This choice is not without cost. Discovery can be very expensive. By erecting a low barrier for entering the litigation stream, and by placing more emphasis on discovery, some argue that modern theory makes litigation too time-consuming, too difficult to settle, and too expensive.

Reflecting these concerns, the Supreme Court decided cases in 2007 and 2009 that, in the eyes of many observers, make it more difficult for plaintiffs to "get past the pleading stage" and into the litigation stream in federal court. One result of those cases has been to rekindle the debate about the role of pleadings and how much detail a plaintiff should be required to set forth at the outset of a case. We cannot understand this debate without some historical background.

B. Historical Overview of the Evolution of Pleadings

Three great theories have dominated the history of pleading: common law, "code," and the Federal Rules. So we speak of common law pleading, code pleading, and Federal Rules pleading (sometimes called "notice pleading"). The common law theory dominated English practice for centuries and American procedure for generations, but is now abandoned. Still, we need to know something about common law pleading because the other two theories evolved in reaction to its strictness. You may wish to reread the overview of English legal history in Chapter 1, Section F.

The codes and the Federal Rules may be considered generically as modern. Most of the American states adopt the Federal Rules generally, which includes, of course, their provisions on pleading. An important minority of states, however, including California, adhere to code pleading rules to this day.

Common law pleading on both sides of the Atlantic was dominated by the "writ system." The plaintiff stated her substantive cause of action by invoking the writ for her claim. Choice of the writ determined not only the pleading rules for the case, but other aspects of procedure as well. The plaintiff asked the court to issue the particular writ for her type of case, and had to plead the "form of action" appropriate to that type of case, such as trespass, trover, assumpsit, etc. The common law system included no plenary right to discovery. Thus, pleadings constituted the primary method not only for putting litigants on notice but for factual development and narrowing issues for trial as well. The parties went through round after round of pleadings, with the goal of framing a single disputed factual issue to be tried.

But the plaintiff had a serious problem if that single disputed issue did not fit the writ she had chosen at the outset of the case. If that happened, the court would dismiss the entire suit, and the plaintiff had to start again by choosing another writ. This could happen easily, for two reasons: (1) the writs were extremely narrow and (2) the parties had no way to determine the underlying facts until trial.

One example will suffice. The writ of "trespass" covered what today would be considered intentional torts. The writ of "trespass on the case," on the other hand, covered what we would consider negligence. Suppose the plaintiff was injured when her carriage hit a large rock in the roadway and that she sued the defendant in trespass, contending that the defendant had put the rock there intentionally. At trial, the evidence shows that the defendant had negligently dislodged the rock, causing it to come to rest in the roadway. Even though the plaintiff had showed a right to relief against this defendant, the court would dismiss her suit. She had pleaded trespass but proved trespass on the case. The variance was fatal. Cf. Reynolds v. Clarke, 93 Eng. Rep. 747 (K.B. 1726).

Common law pleading was part of a system not well calculated to reach a decision on the merits. Indeed, pleadings became an end in themselves, and seemed more important than any fact-finding function of the court.* The situation led to calls for reform both here and in England in the mid-nineteenth century. In the United States, the effort was spearheaded by David Dudley Field,** a lawyer from Albany, New

---

* Meanwhile, equity developed different pleading rules. Because equity courts generally did not have trial by jury the pleadings were often used as a surrogate for evidentiary presentations at trial. Accordingly, equity pleading was prolix and often argumentative.

** One of David Dudley's brothers was Stephen Field, whom we remember as the author of the Supreme Court opinion in *Pennoyer v. Neff*, which we studied in Chapter 2. Before serving on the Supreme Court, Stephen Field was a political leader and Chief Justice of the then-new state of California, and may have influenced its legislature to adopt his brother's code from New York. Another brother played an important role in establishing the trans-Atlantic telegraph cable, and another, Rev.

York, who became the perhaps most important American law reformer of the nineteenth century. His devotion to codification of reforms (including the abolition of common law pleading) led to adoption of the "Field Code" in New York in 1848.

Field's effort ushered in the second great theory of pleading. "Code pleading" (as it is still called) abolished the writ system and the forms of action. It also abolished many distinctions between procedure at law and equity. More importantly for our purposes, it stated a new role for pleadings. They were to be simplified and focused solely on giving notice to the parties and the court; they were to facilitate a decision on the merits. The role of developing the facts was shifted to discovery, which the codes liberalized considerably. Accordingly, the codes limited the number of pleadings. No longer would the parties plead back and forth to frame a single disputed issue. Instead, generally, the plaintiff would file a complaint, the defendant would serve and file an answer and the plaintiff might serve and file a reply to the answer.

The centerpiece of code pleading is its emphasis on pleading *facts*. The code complaint should contain "a statement of the facts constituting the cause of action, in ordinary and concise language, without repetition, and in such a manner as to enable a person of common understanding to know what is intended." This seemingly straightforward and pragmatic undertaking replaced the near-mystical exercise of selecting the correct writ under common law practice.

Unfortunately, however, some courts failed to interpret the code provision in the liberalizing spirit that was intended. As we will see, some judges seized on the requirement that plaintiff plead "facts" to impose stiflingly subtle distinctions. Pleading again became an end in itself, rather than a means to the end of decision-making based upon the merits.

The failure of code pleading to realize its potential led to the drive for further reform. The result came in 1938, with the promulgation of the Federal Rules, which embody the third great theory of pleading. Federal Rules pleading is not a revolutionary break from code pleading. Indeed, the Rules reaffirm David Dudley Field's central goals. Pleadings are designed to give notice and provide a mechanism for ready testing of the legal sufficiency of a claim. To avoid the major problems invented by courts in code states, the Federal Rules eschew the term "facts." Instead of pleading facts, the plaintiff makes a short and plain statement of her claim, showing that she is entitled to relief. The limited role of pleadings was buttressed by liberal discovery provisions, sanctions for abusive pleading, and retooled provisions for summary judgment.

For many years, then, there have been two basic schools of pleading in the United States: the Federal Rules (applicable in the federal courts and adopted by most states) and code pleading (adopted by a few states). The situation may be more complicated

---

Henry Field, wrote popular volumes recounting travels around the world, including a classic study on Gibraltar.

today. Supreme Court decisions in 2007 and 2009 may have created a third school ("plausibility" pleading) for the federal courts.

C. The Complaint

Both the codes and the Federal Rules limit the number of pleadings, generally to a complaint, third-party complaint, answer, and a reply. See, e.g., Rule 7(a). In most cases, there will be a complaint by the plaintiff and an answer by the defendant. (Third-party complaints are fairly rare (we see them in Chapter 12), and replies are even rarer.) Nearly all states refer to the plaintiff's initial pleading as the complaint, though some states use other terms, such as "petition" or "declaration." Regardless of the label, most of the code and Federal Rules provisions governing complaints are substantially similar.

1. Requirements

a. Elements of the Complaint

Read Rule 8(a). It requires every complaint* to contain three things. A complaint lacking any of the three must be dismissed, although the plaintiff will be permitted to amend to correct a formal deficiency.

i. A "short and plain statement of the grounds for the court's jurisdiction"

Because federal courts have limited subject matter jurisdiction, it is essential that the plaintiff allege that the case is properly within the court's jurisdiction. (The exception in Rule 8(a)(1) for cases in which the court's subject matter jurisdiction is already established will not apply to the original complaint, since it is the document that institutes the proceeding.) Some state provisions require the plaintiff to allege facts supporting *personal* jurisdiction if the defendant is a nonresident, and a statement of facts supporting venue. Rule 8 does not require allegations of personal jurisdiction or venue.

ii. A "short and plain statement of the claim showing that the pleader is entitled to relief"

This phrase, from Rule 8(a)(2), embodies the liberal Federal Rules approach to plaintiff's statement of her claim. As noted above, code states commonly require the plaintiff to allege a "statement of the facts constituting a cause of action, in ordinary

---

* Actually, Rule 8 applies to any pleading that sets forth a "claim for relief." While the complaint is the major pleading setting forth a claim for relief, it is not the only one. For example, the defendant may file a counterclaim against the plaintiff or a crossclaim against her co-defendant. All must satisfy Rule 8(a). For present purposes, though, we need only address the complaint.

and concise language, without repetition." In Section C.1.d. below, we will explore this difference between code and Federal Rules pleading. We will also see that the Supreme Court has created considerable debate concerning this requirement.

iii. A "demand for the relief sought, which may include relief in the alternative or different types of relief"

In the demand—often called the "prayer" or, if the plaintiff seeks monetary recovery, the "ad damnum" clause—the plaintiff tells the court what recovery she seeks from the defendant. Interestingly, under Federal Rule 54(c) and many state provisions, the demand does not limit plaintiff's recovery. She is entitled to recover whatever relief she proves at trial, even if that is more money than she asked for, and even if it is of a different type than she requested (e.g., equitable versus legal). (This is not true, though, in default judgment cases, as we will see in Section D.4 below.)

In federal and state practice, the prayer is a simple statement. It usually consists of something like: "Therefore, the plaintiff demands judgment against the defendant for $____, plus interest and costs." Damages generally can be pleaded as a lump sum. We will see below that parties must plead certain kinds of damages—"special damages"—with particularity.

The requirement of a demand does not mandate that the plaintiff set forth a dollar figure on damages. Instead, plaintiff can "demand damages in an amount to be shown at trial." The statement of damages in the demand differs from the allegation that the case satisfies the amount in controversy requirement for diversity of citizenship or alienage jurisdiction in federal court. The amount in controversy allegation is part of the statement of subject matter jurisdiction.There is nothing improper about alleging that the matter in controversy exceeds $75,000.00 for jurisdictional purposes and making a demand in an amount to be shown at trial.

Damages are not the only relief available. Plaintiff might seek equitable relief, such as an injunction, specific performance, or declaratory judgment. Note that Rule 8(a)(3) makes clear that the plaintiff may plead for relief "in the alternative." We will consider such pleading in Section C.1.f of this chapter.

b. Form of Pleadings

Federal Rule 10 governs the form of all pleadings in federal court. Under Rule 10(a), the caption of any pleading must state the name of the court, title of the case (by parties' names) and the identity of the document itself. It also lists the file number (sometimes called the "case number" or "docket number"), which the clerk assigns to each case when it is filed. In most districts, civil case numbers are preceded by the designation "CV." The first number following that denomination in the file number indicates the year in which the case was filed. This is followed by a number assigned sequentially to each case. Thus, the first case filed in a particular district in 2017 would have the file number "17-0001." In most districts, this indication of the year in which the case is filed is followed by the initials of the judge to whom the case is assigned. Here is a caption for a mythical case assigned to Judge Schwartz. Every pleading by each party in the case will bear the same case number.

United States District Court Southern District of California

Patti Thornton,	)	
Plaintiff	)	
	)	CV-17-0506-S
vs.	)	COMPLAINT
Louise Lambert,	)	
Defendant	)	

The body of the pleading sets forth claims or defenses in numbered paragraphs, as required by Rule 10(b). Note that the rule requires the plaintiff to state separate counts only when claims are founded on separate transactions. In practice, however, it is common for plaintiffs to set forth separate counts for different claims, even if transactionally related. Thus, a plaintiff injured in a car wreck might allege two counts, one for personal injuries and one for property damage to the car.

Rule 10(c) allows parties to adopt by reference allegations found elsewhere in the document. For example, suppose that plaintiff alleges two counts against the defendant one for personal injuries and the other for property damage sustained in an automobile wreck. In the first count, the plaintiff will allege facts common to both counts, such as the circumstances of the accident, and the defendant's breach of duty to her. Rather than reiterate this common material in the second count, the plaintiff can merely adopt those allegations by reference. In addition, Rule 10(c) allows parties to attach to their pleading a copy of a written instrument, which then becomes "a part of the pleading for all purposes." In contract cases, for example, a lawyer might attach a copy of the contract to the complaint, which can streamline the pleadings.

c. Legal Sufficiency

Plaintiff's complaint must be sufficient in two ways: legally and factually. Here we address legal sufficiency. In the next subsection, we will address factual sufficiency (an issue on which there is considerable current debate). At common law and today under code pleading, the defendant tested the legal sufficiency of a complaint by filing a *general demurrer* to the complaint.* In federal court, there is no such thing as a demurrer. See Rule 7(a). The function is served in federal court (and in those states adopting the Federal Rules) by the motion to dismiss for failure to state a claim under Rule 12(b)(6).

In ruling on legal sufficiency, a court looks only to the face of the complaint. It does not consider evidence that may support the allegations. The point is to determine whether the plaintiff has alleged a claim cognizable by the law. So the court assumes

---

* It is also proper to say that the defendant demurred to the complaint. Neither demurrer nor demur is pronounced with a long "u" sound as in "demure." Instead, the "u" sound is like that in "fur."

(for purposes of this motion) that the plaintiff's factual allegations are true and asks this: if these things are true, would the law provide a remedy for the plaintiff? If the answer to that question is no, it makes no sense to proceed in litigation—because plaintiff cannot prevail, even if she proves what she alleged. If the answer to that question is yes, then we can proceed with the litigation, including discovery. Ultimately, when the case is adjudicated, plaintiff may fail to prove what she alleged, but at least (if she gets past the Rule 12(b)(6) motion) she will have a chance to get to that stage. If the plaintiff fails to state a claim, the court will grant the Rule 12(b)(6) motion. It usually does so "with leave to amend," which gives the plaintiff another chance to state a legally sufficient claim.

For example, suppose relevant precedent establishes that a spouse of a person injured by defendant's negligence may sue to recover for loss of "consortium," which it defines as "conjugal fellowship and sexual relations between spouses." Assume now that the plaintiff sues to recover for loss of "consortium" because of injuries inflicted upon someone she names in the complaint, but whose relationship she does not allege. Because the plaintiff has not alleged that the injured person is her spouse, the law will not afford a remedy. The court will sustain defendant's general demurrer or grant defendant's Rule 12(b)(6) motion and dismiss the case. It will give the plaintiff leave to amend, however, because it is possible that she can allege that she and the injured person are married.

Courts are liberal in allowing the plaintiff to amend to try to state a claim, although at some point the judge might conclude that the plaintiff simply cannot state a claim. The record for patience may have been set in Stafford v. Russell, 255 P.2d 814 (Cal. App. 1953), in which the appellate court affirmed dismissal of a case after the plaintiff failed to state a claim in his *tenth* amended complaint!

Let's say the plaintiff files an amended complaint seeking damages for loss of "consortium" and alleges that she and the injured person cohabit. Because the relevant precedent does not permit a recovery by non-married persons, the court would sustain defendant's general demurrer or grant defendant's Rule 12(b)(6) motion, and dismiss the case. This time, it may do so without leave to amend (because there seems to be no chance that the plaintiff can state a claim satisfying the law), and will enter final judgment for the defendant. The plaintiff may now appeal and attempt to convince the appellate court to establish a right of consortium between non-married persons.

Defendants often will want to raise substantive challenges to the sufficiency of the complaint as their initial response in the suit, by asserting a general demurrer or moving to dismiss under Rule 12(b)(6). If successful, the defendant will be spared the expense of preparing an answer and otherwise litigating. Note, however, that the defendant does not lose this basis for dismissal by failing to assert it at the outset. She may not become aware of the deficiency until later in the proceedings, and can raise it then. Under Rule 12(h)(2), she may assert failure to state a claim anytime through trial. If she does so after filing her responsive pleading (her answer), her motion is brought under Rule 12(c) and is called a "motion for judgment on the pleadings." (The standard for this is identical to that used in Rule 12(b)(6).)

Defendant need not attack the entire complaint through a general demurrer or Rule 12(b)(6) motion. She can, for example, address one of several claims made by the plaintiff.

Notes and Questions

1. Plaintiff is a truck driver, who hauls goods from New Jersey to Defendant's warehouse in Chicago. When he arrived at the warehouse, Defendant's loading dock was already in use. Defendant's employees directed Plaintiff to park his rig on the public street, adjacent to the driveway leading to the warehouse, and to wait for the loading dock to clear. Plaintiff parked the truck and waited in his rig as directed. Two unidentified men then attempted to rob Plaintiff. One of the men shot Plaintiff, inflicting serious personal injuries. In each of the following variations, assume that Plaintiff sued Defendant, and alleged these facts as well as that he was an "invitee" to whom Defendant owed a duty to guard from criminal acts of third parties.

Assume that there is no question that Plaintiff was an "invitee" under the applicable law. But case law clearly establishes that property owners have a duty to guard an invitee from criminal acts of third parties *only* while the invitee is on the defendant's "premises." (This fact pattern is adapted from Mitchell v. Archibald & Kendall, Inc., 573 F.2d 429 (7th Cir. 1978).)

(a) Plaintiff alleges that he was sitting in his rig, parked on a public street when he was shot. Defendant files a general demurrer or Rule 12(b)(6) motion. What result?

(b) Plaintiff alleges that he was sitting in his rig, parked where directed by Defendant's employees when he was shot. Defendant files a general demurrer or Rule 12(b)(6) motion. What result?

(c) Plaintiff alleges that he was sitting in his rig, parked on Defendant's "premises" when he was shot. Defendant contends that Plaintiff was parked on a public street instead. Defendant cannot raise this issue through a general demurrer or Rule 12(b)(6) motion, since those devices do not address actual evidence or allow the court to determine disputed facts. Again, they assess only the sufficiency of the allegations of the complaint. In this situation, Defendant would serve and file an answer denying Plaintiff's allegation that he was parked on Defendant's "premises." At that point, the pleadings would have framed a disputed factual issue requiring resolution. It may be said that the pleadings are "joined," because they present such a dispute.

2. Rule 12(b)(6) tests whether the plaintiff has alleged enough to place the case into the litigation stream — that is, to justify its being in the court system at all. Suppose Plaintiff states a claim (as in (c) immediately above) and Defendant answers, denying the Plaintiff's allegation that he was parked on Defendant's "premises." Now suppose Defendant asserts that evidence (for example, sworn statements from witnesses) demonstrates that the rig was in fact parked on the street and not on Defendant's "premises." Defendant cannot assert this under Rule 12(b)(6); remember, that

provision tests only the sufficiency of the allegations of the complaint and does not address what actually happened as a factual matter.

Instead, Defendant could move for "summary judgment" under Rule 56. We will study summary judgment in detail in Chapter 9. For now, it is sufficient to understand that it permits the court to go beyond the allegations of the pleadings and to consider evidence. The court makes a determination as to whether, on the evidence proffered (as opposed to on the allegations in the pleadings), there is a genuine dispute of fact that requires resolution at trial.

3. Is there anything ethically improper about Plaintiff's alleging that he was on Defendant's "premises" when shot (paragraph (c) in Note 1)?

4. As noted, a court can consider evidence in ruling on a motion for summary judgment, but not in ruling on a general demurrer or Rule 12(b)(6) motion. Under modern practice, however, if a court looks to evidentiary materials in ruling on demurrer or a motion to dismiss, it simply converts the motion into one for summary judgment. See Rule 12(d).

d. Factual (or "Formal") Sufficiency: The Debate Over Specificity

In addition to legal sufficiency, the complaint must be factually sufficient. The pleadings themselves are not evidence—they are only allegations—and we do not yet know what the pleader will be able to prove. But even with respect to unproven allegations, a core policy question is how much factual detail the complaint must provide. For example, in the loss of consortium example above, should it be sufficient for the plaintiff to allege the injured person was her "husband," or should she have to plead the facts necessary to prove he was her husband? Similarly, should it be sufficient to allege that the defendant was "negligent" or should the pleader have to detail in exactly what way the other side was negligent?

Historically, the code rules required the plaintiff to allege "facts" in some detail. As we will see, courts interpreted "facts" in ways that made it difficult for the plaintiff to state her cause. In reaction to this, the Federal Rules simplified pleading by requiring less detail. This came to be called "notice" pleading—a pleading was sufficient if it put the defendant on notice of what she had been sued for. But as we will see, in 2007 and 2009, the Supreme Court interpreted the Federal Rules to impose an additional "plausibility" requirement with respect to the factual allegations. The two cases, Bell Atlantic Corp. v. Twombly, 550 U.S. 544 (2007), and Ashcroft v. Iqbal, 556 U.S. 662 (2009), are together referred to by many as "*Twiqbal.*"

Accordingly, in the United States today, there might be three pleading standards: the code requirement of "fact" pleading, the Federal Rules requirement of "notice" pleading,* and the "*Twiqbal*" standard of "plausibility" pleading. This is important because it regulates the plaintiff's access to the litigation stream. Unless the plaintiff

* This is relevant in those states that adopt the Federal Rules but do not adopt the Supreme Court's interpretations thereof in *Twombly* and *Iqbal.*

can allege her claim with appropriate specificity, the case will be dismissed, and she will not have access to discovery.

In code states, a defendant challenges the factual sufficiency of the plaintiff's pleading with a *demurrer* (in some states, a "special" demurrer; in others a "general" demurrer). In federal court and in states adopting the Federal Rules, she does so with a Rule 12(b)(6) motion to dismiss for failure to state a claim (or, if she has already answered, a Rule 12(c) motion for judgment on the pleadings).

i. Code Pleading

Code states require the plaintiff to make "a statement of facts constituting a cause of action, in ordinary and concise language, without repetition." Unfortunately, courts in some code states refined the word "facts" in ways that have created traps for the unwary. They came to require the plaintiff to state not just "facts" but the "ultimate facts" constituting her claim. Of course, "ultimate facts" is not a self-defining term.

A plaintiff who alleges facts too specifically could be guilty of "pleading the evidence," for which the court would sustain the defendant's demurrer. On the other hand, a plaintiff who alleges facts too generally could be guilty of "pleading conclusions of law," for which the court would also sustain the defendant's demurrer. Thus, counsel in some code states could find themselves stuck between the Scylla of pleading evidence (too much detail) and the Charybdis of pleading conclusions of law (too little detail). What was intended as a liberal reform of common law pleading can become an exercise in formalism, every bit as arcane and frustrating as the common law writ system.

Let's consider an example. A plaintiff suing in ejectment (to oust a defendant from possession of land) must plead and prove several issues. One of these is that her title to the property is superior to that of the defendant. Suppose the plaintiff had purchased the property from the defendant and could prove due execution of the contract, payment, and that the defendant had executed and delivered to her a deed to the property. Which, if any, of the following is a pleading of the "ultimate fact" of her superior title?

(a) Plaintiff alleges that she "has superior title to the property."

(b) Plaintiff alleges that she is "entitled to possession of the property."

(c) Plaintiff alleges that she "had paid for the property pursuant to contract and that the defendant had given her a deed to the property."

Today, courts in code states would probably accept any of these allegations. There is old authority, however, that the plaintiff in situations (a) and (b) alleged improper conclusions of law. See, e.g., Sheridan v. Jackson, 72 N.Y. 170 (1878). In (c), the California Supreme Court held that plaintiff had pleaded too specifically, and thus was setting forth evidentiary facts instead of ultimate facts. McCaughey v. Schuette, 117 Cal. 223 (1896). The result in *McCaughey* was especially absurd because it reversed a judgment for the plaintiff that had been entered after full trial. The case was to be retried! How would you formulate an allegation of "ultimate facts" that the plaintiff had superior title to property?

Many of the cases concerning pleading "ultimate facts" cannot be reconciled. Is an allegation that "defendant drove his car negligently" a statement of ultimate fact? How about "defendant became indebted to the plaintiff in the amount of $500"? You can probably find cases in code states that uphold such allegations and others that reject such allegations. We don't want to overstate the horribles. There is no doubt that courts in code states have liberalized their practice. Even today, though, there might be a problem with these allegations in some courts because they are "conclusions of law" rather than "ultimate facts." The Federal Rules were promulgated in 1938 and liberalized pleading practice, in reaction to the silly formalism of some code-state decisions.

ii. Federal Rules Pleading

The drafters of Rule 8(a)(2) consciously avoided using the word "facts" in setting the pleading standard. The following is an early classic statement of the then-new liberal approach that the Federal Rules brought to pleading.

Dioguardi v. Durning

139 F.2d 774 (2d Cir. 1944)

Clark, Circuit Judge

In his complaint, obviously home drawn, the plaintiff attempts to assert a series of grievances against the Collector of Customs at the Port of New York growing out of his endeavors to import merchandise from Italy "of great value," consisting of bottles of "tonics." We may pass certain of his claims as either inadequate or inadequately stated and consider only these two: (1) that on the auction day, October 9, 1940, when defendant sold the merchandise at "public custom," "he sold my merchandise to another bidder with my price of $110, and not of his price of $120," and (2) "that three weeks before the sale, two cases, of 19 bottles each case, disappeared." The plaintiff does not make wholly clear how these goods came into the collector's hands, since he alleges compliance with the revenue laws; but he does say he made a claim for "refund of merchandise which was two-third paid in Milano, Italy," and that the collector denied the claim. These and other circumstances alleged indicate (what, indeed, the plaintiff's brief asserts) that his original dispute was with his consignor as to whether anything more was due upon the merchandise, and that the collector, having held it for a year (presumably as unclaimed merchandise under 19 U.S.C.A. § 1491), then sold it, or such part of it as was left, at public auction. For his asserted injuries the plaintiff claimed $5,000 damages, together with interest and costs, against the defendant individually and as collector. This complaint was dismissed by the District Court, with leave, however, to the plaintiff to amend, on motion of the United States Attorney, appearing for the defendant, on the ground that it "fails to state facts sufficient to constitute a cause of action."

Thereupon the plaintiff filed an amended complaint, wherein, with an obviously heightened conviction that he was being unjustly treated, he vigorously reiterates his claims, including those quoted above and now stated as that his "medicinal extracts" were given to the Springdale Distilling Company "with my betting (bidding?) price of $110: and not their price of $120," and "It isn't so easy to do away with two cases of 37 bottles of one quart. Being protected, they can take this chance." An earlier paragraph suggests that defendant had explained the loss of the two cases by "saying that they had leaked, which could never be true in the manner they were bottled." On defendant's motion for dismissal on the same ground as before, the court made a final judgment dismissing the complaint, and the plaintiff now comes to us with increased volubility, if not clarity.

It would seem, however, that he has stated enough to withstand a mere formal motion, directed only to the face of the complaint, and that here is another instance of judicial haste which in the long run makes waste. Under the new rules of civil procedure, there is no pleading requirement of stating "facts sufficient to constitute a cause of action," but only that there be "a short and plain statement of the claim showing that the pleader is entitled to relief," Federal Rules of Civil Procedure, Rule 8(a), and the motion for dismissal under Rule 12(b) is for failure to state "a claim upon which relief can be granted." * * *

We think that, however inartistically they may be stated, the plaintiff has disclosed his claims that the collector has converted or otherwise done away with two of his cases of medicinal tonics and has sold the rest in a manner incompatible with the public auction he had announced—and, indeed, required by 19 U.S.C.A. § 1491, above cited, and the Treasury Regulations promulgated under it. As to this latter claim, it may be that the collector's only error is a failure to collect an additional ten dollars from the Springdale Distilling Company; but giving the plaintiff the benefit of reasonable intendments in his allegations (as we must on this motion), the claim appears to be in effect that he was actually the first bidder at the price for which they were sold, and hence was entitled to the merchandise. * * * [W]e do not see how the plaintiff may properly be deprived of his day in court to show what he obviously so firmly believes and what for present purposes defendant must be taken as admitting. It appears to be well settled that the collector may be held personally for a default or for negligence in the performance of his duties.

On remand, the District Court may find substance in other claims asserted by the plaintiff, which include a failure properly to catalogue the items [as the relevant Regulations provide], or to allow the plaintiff to buy at a discount from the catalogue price just before the auction sale (a claim whose basis is not apparent), and a violation of an agreement to deliver the merchandise to the plaintiff as soon as he paid for it, by stopping the payments. In view of the plaintiff's limited ability to write and speak English, it will be difficult for the District Court to arrive at justice unless he consents to receive legal assistance in the presentation of his case. The record indicates that he refused further help from a lawyer suggested by the court, and his brief (which was a recital of facts, rather than an argument of law) shows distrust of a lawyer of standing at this bar. It is the plaintiff's privilege to decline all legal help; but we fear that he will be indeed ill advised to attempt to meet a motion for summary judgment or other similar presentation of the merits without competent advice and assistance.

Judgment is reversed and the action is remanded for further proceedings not inconsistent with this opinion.*

Notes and Questions

1. Though Mr. Dioguardi represented himself (he was a "pro se" litigant — not represented by a lawyer), the Supreme Court embraced the forgiving attitude in *Dioguardi* even in cases involving lawyers. In the much-cited case of Conley v. Gibson, 355 U.S. 41 (1957), the Court cited *Dioguardi* as authority for what it called the "accepted rule that a complaint should not be dismissed for failure to state a claim unless it appears beyond doubt that the plaintiff can prove no set of facts in support of his claim which would entitle him to relief." Id. at 45. Taken literally, this statement would mean that an allegation such as "defendant is liable to me" would be factually sufficient under Rule 8(a)(2). Obviously, this simply cannot be right, and many commentators and judges said so. For instance, Judge Posner said this "no set of facts" language from *Conley* "has never been taken literally." Sutliff, Inc. v. Donovan Companies, Inc., 727 F.2d 648, 654 (7th Cir. 1984). Indeed, as we will see in the next case, the Court itself "retired" that phrase in 2007.

2. Elsewhere in *Conley*, in language that has not been "retired," the Court spoke to the question of factual sufficiency by saying that the function of the complaint is to "give the defendant fair notice of what the plaintiff's claim is and the grounds upon which it rests." 355 U.S. at 47. Based upon this language, many conclude that the Federal Rules established "notice pleading": pleadings are sufficient if they put the other litigants "on notice" of what is claimed. Some observers dislike the term. Notably, Judge Clark, who wrote the opinion in *Dioguardi*, and who was the principal

---

* Eds. — You may be interested to read the actual allegations of Mr. Dioguardi's amended complaint:

> Plaintiff, as and for his bill of amended complaint the defendant, respectfully alleges:
> FIRST: I want justice done on the basis of my medicinal extracts which have disappeared saying that they had leaked, which could never be true in the manner they were bottled.
> SECOND: Mr. E.G. Collord Clerk in Charge, promised to give me my merchandise as soon as I paid for it. Then all of a sudden payments were stopped.
> THIRD: Then, he didn't want to sell me my merchandise at catalogue price with the 5% off, which was very important to me, after I had already paid $5,000 for them, beside a few other expenses.
> FOURTH: Why was the medicinal given to the Springdale Distilling Co. with my betting price of $110; and not their price of $120.
> FIFTH: It isn't so easy to do away with two cases with 37 bottles of one quart. Being protected, they can take this chance.
> SIXTH: No one can stop my rights upon my merchandise, because of both the duty and the entry.
> WHEREFORE: Plaintiff demands judgment against the defendant, individually and as Collector of Customs at the Port of New York, in the sum of Five Thousand Dollars ($5,000) together with interest from the respective dates of payment as set forth herein, together with the costs and disbursements of this action.

JOHN COUND, JACK FRIEDENTHAL, ARTHUR MILLER & JOHN SEXTON, CIVIL PROCEDURE CASES AND MATERIALS 517–18 (8th ed. 2001). In a code pleading jurisdiction, would a court sustain a special demurrer to Mr. Dioguardi's complaint? Why?

architect of the Federal Rules of Civil Procedure, disapproved of the term "notice pleading" because "it isn't anything that we can use with any precision." Charles Clark, *Pleading Under the Federal Rules*, 12 WYO. L. REV. 177, 181 (1958).

3. It is important to remember that the factual allegations of a complaint must cover all elements of the substantive claim. Though as a matter of policy the Federal Rules seem not to require great factual specificity, "a complaint still must contain either direct or inferential allegations respecting all the material elements necessary to sustain a recovery under some viable legal theory." In re Plywood Antitrust Litigation, 655 F.2d 627, 641 (5th Cir. 1981).

The elements of a claim are established by substantive law. For example, suppose the elements for a contract claim are: (1) offer, (2) acceptance, (3) consideration, (4) performance of conditions by plaintiff, (5) breach by defendant, and (6) damages. To win, Plaintiff must prove these elements at trial. But she will not get into litigation at all if she does not plead the claim with factual sufficiency. While the plaintiff need not label the various elements as such, each must be addressed. But the vexing question still remains: in how much detail? Suppose the plaintiff alleged: "Defendant and I entered a contract, I have performed as required, Defendant has failed to perform as required, and I have been damaged by his breach." In theory, one can argue that all the elements are addressed, since the allegation that "Defendant and I entered a contract" may satisfy elements (1) through (3). Do these allegations put the defendant on notice? Should they be sufficient to permit the case to proceed to the discovery phase?

Against the forgiving background of *Dioguardi*, consider this case, which surprised many observers.

Bell Atlantic Corporation v. Twombly

550 U.S. 544, 127 S. Ct. 1955, 167 L. Ed. 2d 929 (2007)

[From your casebook co-authors: The following is our summary of the background and facts of the case. Until 1984, American Telephone & Telegraph Co. (AT&T) held a virtual monopoly on telephone service in the United States. In that year, as a result of protracted litigation, AT&T was required to give up local phone service, which was then vested in a group of regional monopolies known as "Baby Bells" or Incumbent Local Exchange Carriers (ILECs). These companies were free from competition for local phone service but were forbidden to offer long-distance phone service. In 1996, in an effort to spur competition for local telephone service, Congress passed the Telecommunications Act (1996 Act). The Act permitted ILECs to offer long-distance service, but only if they permitted competition for local telephone service. As it turns out, ILECs offered long-distance service, but generally did not attempt to provide local telephone service outside their geographic area. The result was that there was still very little competition in the provision of local phone service.

In this case, two plaintiffs brought a class action on behalf of all "subscribers of local telephone and/or high speed internet services * * * from February 8, 1996 to [the date the complaint was filed]." They alleged that ILECs had violated § 1 of the

Sherman Antitrust Act. That Act prohibits "[e]very contract, combination in the form of trust or otherwise, or conspiracy, in restraint of trade or commerce among the several States, or with foreign nations." It is aimed at ensuring that competition in various markets is vigorous and fair.

The plaintiffs' theory was that the ILECs had conspired (agreed) with one another to stay out of each other's local phone territories. Such an agreement not to compete would clearly violate the Sherman Act. The problem for plaintiffs, however, is that it is very difficult to show such an agreement. Absent evidence that the defendants met in the proverbial "smoke-filled room" and actually divided up the market for local phone service among themselves, the plaintiffs are left with trying to raise an inference that the defendants entered such an agreement.

One way to do this is to show "conscious parallelism"—that is, that the defendants were aware of each other's actions and engaged in such actions themselves. For instance, Company A might be aware that Company B was not trying to compete in Company A's territory, and might return the favor by not expanding into Company B's territory. Under antitrust law, however, such parallel behavior is actionable *only if it is the result of an agreement among them.* If the ILECs were behaving in this way because each simply concluded that it made economic sense ("if we stay out of their territory, maybe they'll stay out of ours, and we can both still have monopolies in local service"), there would be no violation of antitrust law.

Accordingly, the substantive law requires that the plaintiff show conscious parallel behavior and some "plus factor" to demonstrate that the behavior was the result of an agreement among the defendants. In this case, the question is how much the plaintiffs have to *plead* to survive a motion to dismiss for failure to state a claim. The theory of "notice pleading," as we have said, is that it should be relatively easy to get past the pleading stage of litigation and into the discovery phase, in which the plaintiffs would hope to find evidence supporting their allegations of conspiracy.

Here, the plaintiffs pleaded conscious parallelism and then asserted that such behavior was the result of an agreement. The Court holds that the plaintiffs failed to state a claim; the case is to be dismissed, and the plaintiffs will not have a chance to use discovery devices to see whether the defendants actually did enter an agreement not to compete with one another.]

Justice Souter delivered the opinion of the Court.

Liability under § 1 of the Sherman Act * * * requires a "contract, combination..., or conspiracy, in restraint of trade or commerce." The question in this putative class action is whether a § 1 complaint can survive a motion to dismiss when it alleges that major telecommunications providers engaged in certain parallel conduct unfavorable to competition, absent some factual context suggesting agreement, as distinct from identical, independent action. We hold that such a complaint should be dismissed.

I

Respondents William Twombly and Lawrence Marcus (hereinafter plaintiffs) represent a putative class consisting of all "subscribers of local telephone and/or high speed internet services . . . from February 8, 1996 to present." In this action against petitioners, a group of ILECs,[1] plaintiffs seek [remedies] for claimed violations of § 1 of the Sherman Act. * * *

The complaint alleges that the ILECs conspired to restrain trade in two ways, each supposedly inflating charges for local telephone and high-speed Internet services. Plaintiffs say, first, that the ILECs "engaged in parallel conduct" in their respective service areas to inhibit the growth of upstart [competitors]." * * *

Second, the complaint charges agreements by the ILECs to refrain from competing against one another. These [agreements] are to be inferred from the ILECs common failure "meaningfully [to] pursu[e]" "attractive business opportuni[ties]" in contiguous markets * * * and a statement of [the chief executive officer of one ILEC] that competing in the territory of another ILEC "might be a good way to turn a quick dollar but that doesn't make it right."

The complaint couches its ultimate allegations this way:

> "In the absence of any meaningful competition between the [ILECs] in one another's markets, and in light of the parallel course of conduct that each engaged in to prevent competition * * * within their respective local telephone and/or high speed internet services markets and the other facts and market circumstances alleged above, Plaintiffs allege upon information and belief that [the ILECs] have entered into a contract, combination or conspiracy to prevent competitive entry in their respective local telephone and/or high speed internet services markets and have agreed not to compete with one another and otherwise allocated customers and markets to one another."

* * * The District Court understood that allegations of parallel business conduct, taken alone, do not state a claim under § 1; plaintiffs must allege additional facts that "ten[d] to exclude independent self-interested conduct as an explanation for defendants' parallel behavior." The District Court found plaintiffs' allegations * * * inadequate because "the behavior of each ILEC [in resisting competition] is fully explained by the ILEC's own interests in defending its individual territory." As to the ILECs' supposed agreement against competing with each other, the District Court found that the complaint does not "alleg[e] facts . . . suggesting that refraining from competing in other territories * * * was contrary to [the ILECs'] apparent economic interests, and consequently [does] not rais[e] an inference that [the ILECs'] actions were the result of a conspiracy."

The Court of Appeals for the Second Circuit reversed, holding that the District Court tested the complaint by the wrong standard. It held that "plus factors" are not

1. The 1984 divestiture of AT&T's local telephone service created seven Regional Bell Operating Companies. Through a series of mergers and acquisitions, those seven companies were consolidated into the four ILECs named in this suit: BellSouth Corporation, Qwest Communications International, Inc., SBC Communications, Inc., and Verizon Communications, Inc. (successor-in-interest to Bell Atlantic Corporation). Together, these ILECs allegedly control 90 percent or more of the market for local telephone service in the 48 contiguous States.

required to be pleaded to permit an antitrust claim based on parallel conduct to survive dismissal [for failure to state a claim for relief]." * * *

We granted certiorari to address the proper standard for pleading an antitrust conspiracy through allegations of parallel conduct, and now reverse.

II

A

* * * "[T]he crucial question" is whether the challenged anticompetitive conduct "stem[s] from independent decision or from an agreement, tacit or express." While a showing of parallel "business behavior is admissible circumstantial evidence from which the fact finder may infer agreement," it falls short of "conclusively establish[ing] agreement or ... itself constitut[ing] a Sherman Act offense." Even "conscious parallelism," a common reaction of "firms in a concentrated market [that] recogniz[e] their shared economic interests and their interdependence with respect to price and output decisions" is "not in itself unlawful."

* * * [P]roof of a § 1 conspiracy must include evidence tending to exclude the possibility of independent action. * * *

B

This case presents the antecedent question of what a plaintiff must plead in order to state a claim under § 1 of the Sherman Act. Federal Rule of Civil Procedure 8(a)(2) requires only "a short and plain statement of the claim showing that the pleader is entitled to relief," in order to "give the defendant fair notice of what the ... claim is and the grounds upon which it rests," Conley v. Gibson, 355U.S. 41, 47 (1957). While a complaint attacked by a * * * motion to dismiss does not need detailed factual allegations, a plaintiff's obligation to provide the "grounds" of his "entitle[ment] to relief" requires more than labels and conclusions, and a formulaic recitation of the elements of a cause of action will not do (on a motion to dismiss, courts "are not bound to accept as true a legal conclusion couched as a factual allegation"). Factual allegations must be enough to raise a right to relief above the speculative level. ("[T]he pleading must contain something more ... than ... a statement of facts that merely creates a suspicion [of] a legally cognizable right of action"),[2] on the assumption that all the allegations in the complaint are true (even if doubtful in fact).

---

2. The dissent greatly oversimplifies matters by suggesting that the Federal Rules somehow dispensed with the pleading of facts altogether ([when opining that the] pleading standard of Federal Rules "does not require, or even invite, the pleading of facts"). While, for most types of cases, the Federal Rules eliminated the cumbersome requirement that a claimant "set out *in detail* the facts upon which he bases his claim," [per] *Conley v. Gibson* (emphasis added), Rule 8(a)(2) still requires a "showing," rather than a blanket assertion, of entitlement to relief. Without some factual allegation in the complaint, it is hard to see how a claimant could satisfy the requirement of providing not only "fair notice" of the nature of the claim, but also "grounds" on which the claim rests. (Rule 8(a) "contemplate[s] the statement of circumstances, occurrences, and events in support of the claim presented" and does not authorize a pleader's "bare averment that he wants relief and is entitled to it").

In applying these general standards to a § 1 claim, we hold that stating such a claim requires a complaint with enough factual matter (taken as true) to suggest that an agreement was made. Asking for plausible grounds to infer an agreement does not impose a probability requirement at the pleading stage; it simply calls for enough fact to raise a reasonable expectation that discovery will reveal evidence of illegal agreement. And, of course, a well-pleaded complaint may proceed even if it strikes a savvy judge that actual proof of those facts is improbable, and "that a recovery is very remote and unlikely." * * * It makes sense to say * * * that an allegation of parallel conduct and a bare assertion of conspiracy will not suffice. Without more, parallel conduct does not suggest conspiracy, and a conclusory allegation of agreement at some unidentified point does not supply facts adequate to show illegality. Hence, when allegations of parallel conduct are set out in order to make a § 1 claim, they must be placed in a context that raises a suggestion of a preceding agreement, not merely parallel conduct that could just as well be independent action.

The need at the pleading stage for allegations plausibly suggesting (not merely consistent with) agreement reflects the threshold requirement of Rule 8(a)(2) that the "plain statement" possess enough heft to "sho[w] that the pleader is entitled to relief." A statement of parallel conduct, even conduct consciously undertaken, needs some setting suggesting the agreement necessary to make out a § 1 claim; without that further circumstance pointing toward a meeting of the minds, an account of a defendant's commercial efforts stays in neutral territory. An allegation of parallel conduct is thus much like a naked assertion of conspiracy in a § 1 complaint: it gets the complaint close to stating a claim, but without some further factual enhancement it stops short of the line between possibility and plausibility of "entitle[ment] to relief."

It is no answer to say that a claim just shy of a plausible entitlement to relief can, if groundless, be weeded out early in the discovery process * * * given the common lament that the success of judicial supervision in checking discovery abuse has been on the modest side. And it is self-evident that * * * the threat of discovery expense will push cost-conscious defendants to settle even anemic cases before reaching [summary judgment or trial]. Probably, then, it is only by taking care to require allegations that reach the level suggesting conspiracy that we can hope to avoid the potentially enormous expense of discovery in cases with no "reasonably founded hope that the [discovery] process will reveal relevant evidence" to support a§ 1 claim.

* * * [In response, plaintiffs rely on] an early statement of ours construing Rule 8. Justice Black's opinion for the Court in *Conley v. Gibson* spoke not only of the need for fair notice of the grounds for entitlement to relief but of "the accepted rule that a complaint should not be dismissed for failure to state a claim unless it appears beyond doubt that the plaintiff can prove no set of facts in support of his claim which would entitle him to relief." This "no set of facts" language can be read in isolation as saying that any statement revealing the theory of the claim will suffice unless its factual impossibility may be shown from the face of the pleadings; and the Court of Appeals appears to have read *Conley* in some such way when formulating its understanding of the proper pleading standard * * *.

On such a focused and literal reading of *Conley*'s "no set of facts," a wholly conclusory statement of claim would survive a motion to dismiss whenever the pleadings left open the possibility that a plaintiff might later establish some "set of facts" to support recovery. So here, the Court of Appeals specifically found the prospect of unearthing direct evidence of conspiracy [in discovery] sufficient to preclude dismissal, even though the complaint does not set forth a single fact in a context that suggests an agreement. * * *

Seeing this, a good many judges and commentators have balked at taking the literal terms of the *Conley* passage as a pleading standard. [The Court here summarizes cases and articles echoing the sentiment expressed by Judge Posner, quoted in Note 1 preceding this case.]

We could go on, but there is no need to pile up further citations to show that *Conley*'s "no set of facts" language has been questioned, criticized, and explained away long enough. * * * [A]fter puzzling the profession for 50 years, this famous observation has earned its retirement. The phrase is best forgotten as an incomplete, negative gloss on an accepted pleading standard: once a claim has been stated adequately, it may be supported by showing any set of facts consistent with the allegations in the complaint. ([Thus,] once a claim for relief has been stated, a plaintiff "receives the benefit of imagination, so long as the hypotheses are consistent with the complaint"). *Conley*, then, described the breadth of opportunity to prove what an adequate complaint claims, not the minimum standard of adequate pleading to govern a complaint's survival.[8]

III

When we look for plausibility in this complaint, we agree with the District Court that plaintiffs' claim of conspiracy in restraint of trade comes up short. To begin with, the complaint leaves no doubt that plaintiffs rest their § 1 claim on descriptions of parallel conduct and not on any independent allegation of actual agreement among the ILECs. Although in form a few stray statements speak directly of agreement, on fair reading these are merely legal conclusions resting on the prior allegations. Thus, the complaint first takes account of the alleged "absence of any meaningful competition between [the ILECs] in one another's markets," "the parallel course of conduct that each [ILEC] engaged in to prevent competition * * * ," "and the other facts and market circumstances alleged * * * "; "in light of" these, the complaint concludes "that [the ILECs] have entered into a contract, combination or conspiracy to prevent competitive entry into their markets and have agreed not to compete with one another."

8. * * * The dissent finds relevance in Court of Appeals precedents from the 1940s, which allegedly gave rise to *Conley*'s "no set of facts" language. Even indulging this line of analysis, these cases do not challenge the understanding that before proceeding to discovery, a complaint must allege facts suggestive of illegal conduct [giving rise to civil liability]. * * * Rather, these cases stand for the unobjectionable proposition that, when a complaint adequately states a claim, it may not be dismissed based on a district court's assessment that the plaintiff will fail to find evidentiary support for his allegations or prove his claim to the satisfaction of the factfinder.

[N]othing contained in the complaint invests either the action or inaction alleged with a plausible suggestion of conspiracy. * * * We agree with the District Court's assessment that antitrust conspiracy was not suggested by the facts adduced under either theory of the complaint, which thus fails to state a valid § 1 claim.[14]

Here, * * * we do not require heightened fact pleading of specifics, but only enough facts to state a claim to relief that is plausible on its face. Because the plaintiffs here have not nudged their claims across the line from conceivable to plausible, their complaint must be dismissed.

The judgment of the Court of Appeals for the Second Circuit is reversed, and the cause is remanded for further proceedings consistent with this opinion. * * *

JUSTICE STEVENS, with whom JUSTICE GINSBURG joins except as to Part IV, dissenting.

[T]his is a case in which there is no dispute about the substantive law. If the defendants acted independently, their conduct was perfectly lawful. If, however, that conduct is the product of a horizontal agreement among potential competitors, it was unlawful. Plaintiffs have alleged such an agreement and, because the complaint was dismissed in advance of answer, the allegation has not even been denied. Why, then, does the case not proceed? Does a judicial opinion that the charge is not "plausible" provide a legally acceptable reason for dismissing the complaint? I think not.

The Court and petitioners' legal team are no doubt correct that the parallel conduct alleged is consistent with the absence of any contract, combination, or conspiracy. But that conduct is also entirely consistent with the *presence* of the illegal agreement alleged in the complaint. * * * As such, the Federal Rules of Civil Procedure, our longstanding precedent, and sound practice mandate that the District Court at least require some sort of response from petitioners before dismissing the case.

I

Rule 8(a)(2) of the Federal Rules requires that a complaint contain "a short and plain statement of the claim showing that the pleader is entitled to relief." The rule did not come about by happenstance and its language is not inadvertent. The English experience with Byzantine special pleading rules — illustrated by the hypertechnical Hilary rules of 1834 — made obvious the appeal of a pleading standard that was easy for the common litigant to understand and sufficed to put the defendant on notice as to the nature of the claim against him and the relief sought. Stateside, David Dudley Field developed the highly influential New York Code of 1848, which required "[a]

14. In reaching this conclusion, we do not apply any "heightened" pleading standard, nor do we seek to broaden the scope of Federal Rule of Civil Procedure 9, which can only be accomplished "'by the process of amending the Federal Rules, and not by judicial interpretation.'" [Note: In Section C.1.e infra we will see provisions in which claimants are required to plead in detail.] On certain subjects understood to raise a high risk of abusive litigation, a plaintiff must state factual allegations with greater particularity than Rule 8 requires. Here, our concern is not that the allegations in the complaint were insufficiently "particular[ized];" rather, the complaint warranted dismissal because it failed *in toto* to render plaintiffs' entitlement to relief plausible.

statement of the facts constituting the cause of action, in ordinary and concise language, without repetition, and in such a manner as to enable a person of common understanding to know what is intended." Substantially similar language appeared in the Federal Equity Rules adopted in 1912. See Fed. Equity Rule 25 (requiring "a short and simple statement of the ultimate facts upon which the plaintiff asks relief, omitting any mere statement of evidence").

A difficulty arose, however, in that the Field Code * * * required a plaintiff to allege "facts" rather than "conclusions," a distinction that proved far easier to say than to apply. * * *

Under the relaxed pleading standards of the Federal Rules, the idea was not to keep litigants out of court but rather to keep them in. The merits of a claim would be sorted out during a flexible pretrial process and, as appropriate, through the crucible of trial. Charles E. Clark, the "principal draftsman" of the [1938] Federal Rules, put it thus:

> "Experience has shown ... that we cannot expect the proof of the case to be made through the pleadings, and that such proof is really not their function. We can expect a general statement distinguishing the case from all others, so that the manner and form of trial and remedy expected are clear * * *."

The pleading paradigm under the new Federal Rules was well illustrated by the inclusion in the appendix of Form 9, a complaint for negligence. [Note from your casebook co-authors: until 2015, the Rules included an appendix of "Forms" to serve as examples of various assertions. Form 9, referred to by the Court, contained a model allegation of negligence. The Forms were abolished December 1, 2015.] As relevant, the Form 9 complaint states only: "On June 1, 1936, in a public highway called Boylston Street in Boston, Massachusetts, defendant negligently drove a motor vehicle against plaintiff who was then crossing said highway." The complaint then describes the plaintiff's injuries and demands judgment. The asserted ground for relief—namely, the defendant's negligent driving—would have been called a "'conclusion of law'" under the code pleading of old. But that bare allegation suffices under a system that "restrict[s] the pleadings to the task of general notice-giving and invest[s] the deposition-discovery process with a vital role in the preparation for trial."

II

Consistent with the design of the Federal Rules, *Conley*'s "no set of facts" formulation permits outright dismissal only when proceeding to discovery or beyond would be futile. Once it is clear that a plaintiff has stated a claim that, if true, would entitle him to relief, matters of proof are appropriately relegated to other stages of the trial process. Today, however, in its explanation of a decision to dismiss a complaint that it regards as a fishing expedition, the Court scraps *Conley*'s "no set of facts" language. Concluding that the phrase has been "questioned, criticized, and explained away long enough," the Court dismisses it as careless composition.

If *Conley*'s "no set of facts" language is to be interred, let it not be without a eulogy. That exact language, which the majority says has "puzzl[ed] the profession for 50 years," has been cited as authority in a dozen opinions of this Court and four separate writings. In not one of those 16 opinions was the language "questioned," "criticized," or "explained away." Indeed, today's opinion is the first by any Member of this Court to express *any* doubt as to the adequacy of the *Conley* formulation. * * *

As any civil procedure student knows, Judge Clark's opinion disquieted the defense bar and gave rise to a movement to revise Rule 8 to require a plaintiff to plead a "'cause of action [stating facts].'" The movement failed * * *. [Here Justice Stevens cites *Dioguardi v. Durning*, and commentary embracing it.]

We have consistently reaffirmed that basic understanding of the Federal Rules in the half century since *Conley*. * * *

IV

The transparent policy concern that drives the [majority's] decision is the interest in protecting antitrust defendants — who in this case are some of the wealthiest corporations in our economy — from the burdens of pretrial discovery. * * *

If the allegation of conspiracy happens to be true, today's decision obstructs the congressional policy favoring competition that undergirds both the Telecommunications Act of 1996 and the Sherman Act itself. More importantly, even if there is abundant evidence that the allegation is untrue, directing that the case be dismissed without even looking at any of that evidence marks a fundamental — and unjustified — change in the character of pretrial practice.

Accordingly, I respectfully dissent.

Notes and Questions

1. A complaint may fail because it is legally insufficient or because it is factually insufficient. As to the latter, *Conley* said the complaint must give "fair notice of what the plaintiff's claim is and the grounds upon which it rests." 355 U.S. at 47. A complaint that alleges the defendant failed to say good morning to the plaintiff and that this failure made the plaintiff feel bad gives adequate notice, but is legally insufficient; the law gives no remedy for the alleged wrong. In contrast, a complaint that merely states the conclusion that the defendant "harmed the plaintiff" fails to give fair notice (in addition to its being legally insufficient).

In *Twombly*, what was the problem: legal or factual insufficiency? The district court, which dismissed the complaint, thought it was factually insufficient because the plaintiff failed to plead the "plus factors" on which it was relying. "[T]here was simply no way to defend * * * without having some idea of how and why the defendants are alleged to have conspired. The plus factors are therefore intended to give defendants notice of the plaintiffs' legal theory, and the 'conduct which is alleged to be conspiratorial.'" Twombly v. Bell Atlantic Corp., 313 F. Supp. 2d 174, 180 (S.D.N.Y. 2003) (citation omitted). Is that what the Supreme Court concluded?

2. The Court emphasized the distinction between legal and factual sufficiency in Johnson v. City of Shelby, 135 S. Ct. 346 (2014). There, the plaintiffs, police officers, sued the City for which they worked, alleging that they had been fired for investigating possible criminal activity of city aldermen. They failed to allege that they sued under 42 U.S.C. § 1983, which creates a claim for those whose federal rights are violated by a defendant who acts under color of state law. The Fifth Circuit held that the failure to cite § 1983 was fatal, and dismissed the case under Rule 12(b)(6). The Supreme Court summarily granted certiorari and reversed without briefing or oral argument.

The Court held that *Twombly* and *Iqbal* (discussed below) did not apply. Those cases dealt with *factual* sufficiency and not *legal* sufficiency. Nothing in Rule 8(a)(2) requires the plaintiff to cite the legal authority for her claim. The Rules "do not countenance dismissal of a complaint for imperfect statement of the legal theory supporting the claim asserted." 134 S. Ct. at 346. The Court instructed that on remand, the plaintiffs should be permitted to amend their complaint to cite § 1983. 134 S. Ct. at 347. This instruction seems odd: nowhere did the Court indicate why plaintiffs should amend to state something that (the Court just said) is not necessary to stating a claim.

3. According to the Court in *Twombly*, what must be "plausible" in one's pleadings? No form of the word "plausible" appears in Rule 8. So where did the "plausibility" requirement come from?

4. How would *Dioguardi* be decided after *Twombly*? Were Mr. Dioguardi's allegations "plausible"? Depending on your answers, does *Twombly* change the pleading requirement of Rule 8(a)(2)? If so, how?

5. At the end of Part I of Justice Stevens's dissent, the Court approves an allegation that "defendant negligently drove a motor vehicle against plaintiff who was then crossing said highway." The allegation is sufficient, the Court explains, because "[a] defendant wishing to prepare an answer * * * would know what to answer." In contrast, the defendants in *Twombly* "would have little idea where to begin." The complaint "furnishes no clue as to which of the four ILECs * * * supposedly agreed, or when and where the illicit agreement took place." *Twombly*, 550 U.S. at 565 n.10.

In light of these conclusions, does Rule 8(a)(2) require one level of factual detail in negligence cases and another in antitrust? Or is the difference in detail required simply common sense? After all, if you drive your car and hit a pedestrian, you certainly will know what the plaintiff is suing you for; such events do not occur often, and leave a big impression on those involved. In contrast, large businesses interact in many ways over long periods. Without some specifics, is it reasonable to assume that an executive of a business, when reading a complaint, will know which interaction is the subject of complaint?

6. As we will see in Chapter 8, the discovery process permits each party to inspect documents, things, and electronically stored information held by other parties. The plaintiffs in *Twombly* wanted to use discovery to search the defendants' records for evidence that they had conspired to avoid competition in the local telephone markets.

Dismissal of the case at the pleading stage, however, means that the case will not continue in the litigation stream. So there will be no discovery. This saves the defendants in *Twombly* from intrusive and expensive production of materials. It also robs the plaintiffs of a chance to find evidence proving conspiracy. Do either the majority or the dissenting opinions consider the possibility of a middle ground—such as allowing discovery for limited purposes before dismissing a complaint under Rule 12(b)(6)? Would such a middle ground be a good idea? Would it countenance a mini-trial on the underlying question of conspiracy?

7. Two weeks after deciding *Twombly*, the Supreme Court cited *Conley v. Gibson* with favor in Erickson v. Pardus, 551 U.S. 89 (2007). There, a prisoner suffering from Hepatitis C sued prison officials, alleging that they had violated his constitutional rights by demonstrating deliberate indifference to his medical needs. He alleged that defendants had diagnosed his condition and placed him in appropriate treatment, but then had removed him from treatment. The trial court dismissed for failure to state a claim, in part because it read the complaint to allege that the plaintiff's harm came from the disease itself, and not from discontinuance of the treatment. The court of appeals affirmed.

The Supreme Court reversed. According to the Court, plaintiff's allegations were not too conclusory to establish that he had suffered harm from the removal of treatment. It then noted that allegation of "specific facts are not necessary; the statement need 'only give the defendant fair notice of what the * * * claim is and the grounds upon which it rests.'" Id. at 93. Can *Erickson* be reconciled with *Twombly*?

8. The Court may be shying away from a strict reading of "*Twiqbal*." In subsequent cases, it has given more favorable signals to plaintiffs. In Matrixx Initiatives, Inc. v. Siracusano, 563 U.S. 27 (2011), it found sufficient allegations of a class action claim under the securities law. In Skinner v. Switzer, 562 U.S. 521 (2011), though upholding dismissal, the Court emphasized that the question on a Rule 12(b)(6) motion is not whether the plaintiff ultimately will win, but whether she may proceed in litigation. The tone of the opinion is reminiscent of *Dioguardi*. In Fifth Third Bancorp v. Dudenhoeffer, 134 S. Ct. 2459 (2014), the Court rejected a presumption in cases involving retirement funds that the defendant had acted prudently in managing the fund. And in Johnson v. City of Shelby, 135 S. Ct. 346 (2014), discussed in Note 2 above, it emphasized that "*Twiqbal*" deals with factual sufficiency and does not require plaintiffs to cite the law under which they sue.

9. As we will see in Chapter 10, the Supreme Court is responsible for promulgating the Federal Rules. If the Court wanted to change the pleading requirements for federal court, why did it not promulgate an amended version of Rule 8(a)(2)? Try to draft a Rule embracing *Twiqbal*.

The Iqbal *Case*

The Court addressed pleading again in *Ashcroft v. Iqbal*, 556 U.S. 663 (2009). In a fractured five-to-four decision, the Court strongly reaffirmed *Twombly*'s main themes. For one thing, *Iqbal* made it clear that the plausibility standard from *Twombly* is not limited to antitrust cases. *Twombly* interpreted Rule 8(a)(2), and its interpretation applies to all civil cases in federal court. 556 U.S. at 684–685. For another, *Iqbal* interpreted *Twombly* as establishing a methodology. The Court explained:

> Two working principles underlie our decision in *Twombly*. First, the tenet that a court must accept as true all of the allegations contained in a complaint is inapplicable to legal conclusions. Threadbare recitals of the elements of a cause of action, supported by mere conclusory statements, do not suffice. * * * Rule 8 marks a notable and generous departure from the hyper-technical, code-pleading regime of a prior era, but it does not unlock the doors of discovery for a plaintiff armed with nothing more than conclusions. Second, only a complaint that states a plausible claim for relief survives a motion to dismiss. Determining whether a complaint states a plausible claim for relief will, as the Court of Appeals observed, be a context-specific task that requires the reviewing court to draw on its judicial experience and common sense. * * *

Id. at 678–679.

A court applying *Twombly*, then, must ignore *legal* conclusions. And while the court then takes *factual* allegations as true (for purposes of the motion to dismiss), the claim must be *plausible*. This, in turn, is determined on a case-by-case basis, in which the judge is to draw on her experience and common sense. So a judge who practiced as a civil-rights plaintiff's lawyer might view plausibility of a claim differently from one who practiced as general counsel for a multinational corporation. Does this mean that there are approximately 600 pleading standards in the federal courts (one for each district judge)? Now we address the facts of the case.

The plaintiff in *Iqbal* was a Muslim citizen of Pakistan. He alleged that after the terrorist attacks of September 11, 2001, federal officials arrested and detained him under restrictive conditions. Two of the defendants were John Ashcroft, the former Attorney General of the United States, and Robert Mueller, the Director of the FBI. Mr. Iqbal attempted to allege a claim for violation of federal constitutional rights by federal officials. This is called a *Bivens* claim. Bivens v. Six Unknown Federal Narcotics Agents, 403 U.S. 388 (1971). Specifically, the plaintiff alleged that Ashcroft and Mueller violated his First and Fifth Amendment rights by adopting policies that led to his designation as a person "of high interest" and by subjecting him to harsh conditions of confinement because of his race, religion, or national origin.

Ashcroft and Mueller moved to dismiss the complaint under Rule 12(b)(6). Under *Bivens*, Ashcroft and Mueller could only be liable if the rights they allegedly violated were "clearly established" at the time they acted. If they were not clearly established, the defendants would be entitled to "qualified immunity" from suit, because they were acting in good faith and did not have reason to know that their acts violated federal law. According to the Court, "to state a claim based on a violation of a clearly established right, [a plaintiff] must plead sufficient factual matter to show that [defendants] adopted and implemented the detention policies at issue not for a neutral, investigative reason but for the purpose of discriminating on account of race, religion, or national origin." Id. at 679.

The majority, in an opinion by Justice Kennedy, applied *Twombly* to conclude that the plaintiff's allegations against Ashcroft and Mueller failed to state a claim. It applied the methodology noted above—first ignoring conclusions of law and then applying the plausibility standard to allegations of fact.

> We begin our analysis by identifying the allegations in the complaint that are not entitled to the assumption of truth. Respondent pleads that petitioners "knew of, condoned, and willfully and maliciously agreed to subject [him]" to harsh conditions of confinement "as a matter of policy, solely on account of [his] religion, race, and/or national origin and for no legitimate penological interest." The complaint alleges that Ashcroft was the "principal architect" of this invidious policy, and that Mueller was "instrumental" in adopting and executing it. These bare assertions, much like the pleading of conspiracy in *Twombly*, amount to nothing more than a "formulaic recitation of the elements" of a constitutional discrimination claim, namely, that petitioners adopted a policy "'because of,' not merely 'in spite of,' its adverse effects upon an identifiable group." As such, the allegations are conclusory and not entitled to be assumed true. To be clear, we do not reject these bald allegations on the ground that they are unrealistic or nonsensical.... It is the conclusory nature of respondent's allegations, rather than their extravagantly fanciful nature, that disentitles them to the presumption of truth.
>
> We next consider the factual allegations in respondent's complaint to determine if they plausibly suggest an entitlement to relief. The complaint alleges that "the [FBI], under the direction of Defendant Mueller, arrested and detained thousands of Arab Muslim men ... as part of its investigation of the events of September 11." It further claims that "[t]he policy of holding post September-11th detainees in highly restrictive conditions of confinement until they were 'cleared' by the FBI was approved by Defendants Ashcroft and Mueller in discussions in the weeks after September 11, 2001." Taken as true, these allegations are consistent with petitioners' purposefully designating detainees "of high interest" because of their race, religion, or national origin. But given more likely explanations, they do not plausibly establish this purpose.
>
> The September 11 attacks were perpetrated by 19 Arab Muslim hijackers who counted themselves members in good standing of al Qaeda, an Islamic fundamentalist group. Al Qaeda was headed by another Arab Muslim—Osama bin Laden—and composed in large part of his Arab Muslim disciples. It should come as no surprise that a legitimate policy directing law enforcement to arrest and detain individuals because of their suspected link to the attacks would produce a disparate, incidental impact on Arab Muslims, even though the purpose of the policy was to target neither Arabs nor Muslims. On the facts [alleged] the arrests Mueller oversaw were likely lawful and justified by his nondiscriminatory intent to detain aliens who were illegally

present in the United States and who had potential connections to those who committed terrorist acts. As between that "obvious alternative explanation" for the arrests * * * and the purposeful, invidious discrimination respondent asks us to infer, discrimination is not a plausible conclusion.

But even if the complaint's well-pleaded facts give rise to a plausible inference that respondent's arrest was the result of unconstitutional discrimination, that inference alone would not entitle respondent to relief. It is important to recall that respondent's complaint challenges neither the constitutionality of his arrest nor his initial detention in the [Metropolitan Detention Center in Brooklyn]. Respondent's constitutional claims * * * rest solely on [defendants'] ostensible "policy of holding post-September-11th detainees" in the ADMAX SHU [Administrative Maximum Special Housing Unit, in which detainees are in 23-hour-a-day lockdown] once they were categorized as "of high interest." To prevail on that theory, the complaint must contain facts plausibly showing that petitioners purposefully adopted a policy of classifying post-September-11 detainees as "of high interest" because of their race, religion, or national origin.

This the complaint fails to do. Though respondent alleges that various other defendants, who are not before us, may have labeled him a person "of high interest" for impermissible reasons, his only factual allegation against [Ashcroft and Mueller] accuses them of adopting a policy approving "restrictive conditions of confinement" for post-September 11 detainees until they were "'cleared' by the FBI." Accepting the truth of that allegation, the complaint does not show, or even intimate, that petitioners purposefully housed detainees in the ADMAX SHU due to their race, religion, or national origin. All it plausibly suggests is that the Nation's top law enforcement officers, in the aftermath of a devastating terrorist attack, sought to keep suspected terrorists in the most secure conditions available until the suspects could be cleared of terrorist activity. Respondent does not argue, nor can he, that such a motive would violate petitioners' constitutional obligations. * * *

Respondent next implies that our construction of Rule 8 should be tempered where, as here, the Court of Appeals has "instructed the district court to cabin discovery in such a way as to preserve" petitioners' defense of qualified immunity "as much as possible in anticipation of a summary judgment motion." We have held, however, that the question presented by a motion to dismiss a complaint for insufficient pleadings does not turn on the controls placed upon the discovery process. *Twombly, supra*, at 559 ("It is no answer to say that a claim just shy of a plausible entitlement to relief can, if groundless, be weeded out early in the discovery process through careful case management given the common lament that the success of judicial supervision in checking discovery abuse has been on the modest side."). * * *

We decline respondent's invitation to relax the pleading requirements on the ground that the Court of Appeals promises petitioners minimally intrusive

> discovery. That promise provides especially cold comfort in this pleading context, where we are impelled to give real content to the concept of qualified immunity for high-level officials who must be neither deterred nor detracted from the vigorous performance of their duties. Because respondent's complaint is deficient under Rule 8, he is not entitled to discovery, cabined or otherwise.

Justice Souter, who wrote the majority opinion in *Twombly*, dissented, joined by Justices Stevens, Breyer, and Ginsburg. To them, *Twombly* was distinguishable because that case involved allegations of antitrust conspiracy based on parallel conduct, and such conduct was just as consistent with lawful business behavior as with conspiracy. Here in contrast, "the allegations of the complaint [in *Iqbal*] are neither confined to naked legal conclusions nor consistent with legal conduct." *Id.* at 1960.

Notes and Questions

1. Is *Iqbal* consistent with *Erickson* (discussed in Note 7 before *Iqbal*)? After all, *Erickson* also involved alleged deprivation of constitutional rights—but successfully pleaded. Why the different result in *Iqbal*?

2. It is clear that the drafters of the original Federal Rules wanted to rid federal pleading of the distinction between allegations of "conclusions" and allegations of "facts." This is one of the reasons Rule 8(a) has never required pleading of "facts." Has *Iqbal* resurrected that distinction? Please return to Section C.1.d.1. above (concerning "Code Pleading") and review the allegations of plaintiff's superior title to land. Would they be rejected under *Twombly* and *Iqbal* as conclusions of law?

3. Why was the effort of the lower court to limit discovery in *Iqbal* irrelevant to the majority?

4. Is it possible that the plaintiff's allegation—that he was designated "of high interest" because of his race, religion, or national origin—was true? How does the majority know that other explanations of the defendants' behavior were "more likely"? Does the fact that some other explanation is "more likely" make the plaintiff's allegation implausible?

5. Suppose 300 people are in a movie theater. Someone in the theater yells "Fire," after which all 300 people go to the exits and leave the building. Now suppose someone asserts that the 300 people had agreed in advance that they would stand up and leave the theater when someone yelled, "Fire." If such an assertion were legally relevant, would it pass muster? In light of your background and common sense, is the allegation that the people agreed in advance to leave the theater "plausible"? Is this hypothetical distinguishable from *Twombly* or *Iqbal*? Why?

6. Most states have adopted the Federal Rules for use in their courts. Courts in these states are free to accept or reject the Court's interpretation of Rule 8(a)(2) in *Twombly* and *Iqbal*. Most state supreme courts have not addressed the topic.

Of those that have, some have embraced the "plausibility" standard. See, e.g., Potomac Dev. Corp. v. District of Columbia, 28 A.3d 531, 550 (D.C. 2011); Doe v. Board of Regents, 788 N.W.2d 264, 278 (Mont. 2010) ("[W]e believe that the Court's decision in *Twombly* provides a balanced approach for determining whether a complaint should survive a motion to dismiss and proceed to discovery."); Iannacchino v. Ford Motor Co., 888 N.E.2d 879, 890 (Mass. 2008) ("[W]e take the opportunity to adopt the refinement of that standard that was recently articulated by the United States Supreme Court in [*Twombly*].").

At least as many, however, reject the cases. See, e.g., Walsh v. U.S. Bank, 851 N.W.2d 598, 603 (Minn. 2014) ("[W]e now decline to engraft the plausibility standard from *Twombly* and *Iqbal* onto our traditional interpretation"); Cambium Ltd. v. Trilantic Cap. Partners III L.P., Austin v. Clark, 755 S.E.2d 796, 798–799 (Ga. 2014); Webb v. Nashville Area Habitat for Humanity, Inc., 346 S.W.3d 422, 430 (Tenn. 2011) ("We decline to adopt the new plausibility standard and adhere * * * to the notice pleading standard * * *."); McCurry v. Chevy Chase Bank, FSB, 233 P.3d 861, 863 (Wash. 2010) ("The Supreme Court's plausibility standard is predicated on policy determinations specific to the federal trial courts. * * * Neither party has shown these policy determinations hold sufficiently true in the Washington trial courts to warrant such a drastic change in court procedure."); Cullen v. Auto-Owners Ins. Co, 189 P.3d 344, 345 (Ariz. 2008); Colby v. Umbrella, Inc., 955 A.2d 1082, 1087 n.1 (Vt. 2008)("We recently affirmed our minimal notice pleading standard * * * and are unpersuaded by the dissent's argument that we should now abandon it for a heightened standard."). These courts adhere to the *Dioguardi*-type approach.

Swanson v. Citibank, N.A.

614 F.3d 400 (7th Cir. 2010)

WOOD, CIRCUIT JUDGE.

Gloria Swanson sued Citibank, Andre Lanier, and Lanier's employer, PCI Appraisal Services, because she believed that all three had discriminated against her on the basis of her race (African-American) when Citibank turned down her application for a home-equity loan. * * * She was unsuccessful in the district court, which dismissed in response to the defendants' motion under Fed. R. Civ. P. 12(b)(6).

Swanson based her complaint on the following set of events, which we accept as true for purposes of this appeal. In February 2009 Citibank announced a plan to make loans using funds that it had received from [a federal program]. Encouraged by this prospect, Swanson went to a Citibank branch to apply for a home-equity loan. A representative named Skertich told Swanson that she could not apply alone, because she owned her home jointly with her husband; he had to be present as well. Swanson was skeptical, suspecting that Skertich's demand was a ploy to discourage loan applications from African-Americans. She therefore asked to speak to a manager. When the manager joined the group, Swanson disclosed to both Skertich and the manager that Washington Mutual Bank previously had denied her a home-equity loan. The manager warned Swanson that, although she did not want to discourage Swanson from applying for the loan, Citibank's loan criteria were more stringent than those of other banks.

Still interested, Swanson took a loan application home and returned the next day with the necessary information. She was again assisted by Skertich, who entered the information that Swanson had furnished into the computer. When he reached a question regarding race, Skertich told Swanson that she was not required to respond. At some point during this exchange, Skertich pointed to a photograph on his desk and commented that his wife and son were part African-American.

A few days later Citibank conditionally approved Swanson for a home-equity loan of $50,000. It hired Andre Lanier, who worked for PCI Appraisal Services, to visit Swanson's home for an onsite appraisal. Although Swanson had estimated in her loan application that her house was worth $270,000, Lanier appraised it at only $170,000. The difference was critical: Citibank turned down the loan and explained that its conditional approval had been based on the higher valuation. Two months later Swanson paid for and obtained an appraisal from Midwest Valuations, which thought her home was worth $240,000.

Swanson saw coordinated action in this chain of events, and so she filed a complaint * * * charging that Citibank, Lanier, and PCI disfavor providing home-equity loans to African-Americans, and so they deliberately lowered the appraised value of her home far below its actual market value, so that they would have an excuse to deny her the loan. She charges that in so doing, they violated the Fair Housing Act, 42 U.S.C. § 3605 * * *. The district court granted the defendants' motions to dismiss * * *. This appeal followed.

* * * It is by now well established that a plaintiff must do better than putting a few words on paper that, in the hands of an imaginative reader, might suggest that something has happened to her that might be redressed by the law. Cf. Conley v. Gibson, 355 U.S. 41, 45–46 (1957), disapproved by Bell Atlantic Corp. v. Twombly, 550 U.S. 544, 563 (2007) ("after puzzling the profession for 50 years, this famous observation [the 'no set of facts' language] has earned its retirement"). The question with which courts are still struggling is how much higher the Supreme Court meant to set the bar, when it decided not only *Twombly*, but also Erickson v. Pardus, 551 U.S. 89 (2007), and Ashcroft v. Iqbal, 129 S. Ct. 1937 (2009). This is not an easy question to answer, as the thoughtful dissent from this opinion demonstrates. On the one hand, the Supreme Court has adopted a "plausibility" standard, but on the other hand, it has insisted that it is not requiring fact pleading * * *.

As one respected treatise put it in 2004,

> "[A]ll that is necessary is that the claim for relief be stated with brevity, conciseness, and clarity.... [T]his portion of Rule 8 indicates that a basic objective of the rules is to avoid civil cases turning on technicalities and to require that the pleading discharge the function of giving the opposing party fair notice of the nature and basis or grounds of the pleader's claim and a general indication of the type of litigation that is involved...." 5 Charles Alan Wright & Arthur R. Miller, Federal Practice and Procedure § 1215 at 165–173 (3d ed. 2004).

Nothing in the recent trio of cases has undermined these broad principles. As *Erickson* underscored, "[s]pecific facts are not necessary." The Court was not engaged in a *sub rosa* campaign to reinstate the old fact-pleading system called for by the Field Code or even more modern codes. We know that because it said so in *Erickson*: "the statement need only give the defendant fair notice of what the ... claim is and the grounds upon which it rests." *Id.* Instead, the Court has called for more careful attention to be given to several key questions: what, exactly, does it take to give the opposing party "fair notice"; how much detail realistically can be given, and should be given, about the nature and basis or grounds of the claim; and in what way is the pleader expected to signal the type of litigation that is being put before the court?

This is the light in which the Court's references in *Twombly*, repeated in *Iqbal*, to the pleader's responsibility to "state a claim to relief that is plausible on its face" must be understood. "Plausibility" in this context does not imply that the district court should decide whose version to believe, or which version is more likely than not. Indeed, the Court expressly distanced itself from the latter approach in *Iqbal*, "the plausibility standard is not akin to a probability requirement." As we understand it, the Court is saying instead that the plaintiff must give enough details about the subject-matter of the case to present a story that holds together. In other words, the court will ask itself *could* these things have happened, not *did* they happen. * * * [I]t is not necessary to stack up inferences side by side and allow the case to go forward only if the plaintiff's inferences seem more compelling than the opposing inferences.

The Supreme Court's explicit decision to reaffirm the validity of Swierkiewicz v. Sorema N.A., 534 U.S. 506 (2002) [discussed in Note 1 after the *Leatherman* case in the next subsection of this chapter], which was cited with approval in *Twombly*, 550 U.S. at 556, indicates that in many straightforward cases, it will not be any more difficult today for a plaintiff to meet that burden than it was before the Court's recent decisions. A plaintiff who believes that she has been passed over for a promotion because of her sex will be able to plead that she was employed by Company X, that a promotion was offered, that she applied and was qualified for it, and that the job went to someone else. That is an entirely plausible scenario, whether or not it describes what "really" went on in this plaintiff's case. A more complex case involving financial derivatives, or tax fraud that the parties tried hard to conceal, or antitrust violations, will require more detail, both to give the opposing party notice of what the case is all about and to show how, in the plaintiff's mind at least, the dots should be connected. * * *

We realize that one powerful reason that lies behind the Supreme Court's concern about pleading standards is the cost of the discovery that will follow in any case that survives a motion to dismiss on the pleadings. The costs of discovery are often asymmetric, as the dissent points out, and one way to rein them in would be to make it more difficult to earn the right to engage in discovery. That is just what the Court did, by interring the rule that a complaint could go forward if any set of facts at all could be imagined, consistent with the statements in the complaint, that would permit the pleader to obtain relief. Too much chaff was moving ahead with the wheat. * * *

Returning to Swanson's case, we must analyze her allegations defendant-by-defendant. We begin with Citibank. * * * The Fair Housing Act prohibits businesses engaged in residential real estate transactions, including "[t]he making ... of loans or providing other financial assistance ... secured by residential real estate," from discriminating against any person on account of race. 42 U.S.C. § 3605(a), (b)(1)(B). Swanson's complaint identifies the type of discrimination that she thinks occurs (racial), by whom (Citibank, through Skertich, the manager, and the outside appraisers it used), and when (in connection with her effort in early 2009 to obtain a home-equity loan). This is all that she needed to put in the complaint. * * *

The fact that Swanson included other, largely extraneous facts in her complaint does not undermine the soundness of her pleading. She points to Citibank's announced plan to use federal money to make more loans, its refusal to follow through in her case, and Skertich's comment that he has a mixed-race family. She has not pleaded herself out of court by mentioning these facts; whether they are particularly helpful for proving her case or not is another matter that can safely be put off for another day. It was therefore error for the district court to dismiss Swanson's Fair Housing Act claim against Citibank.

We now turn to Swanson's claims against Lanier and PCI. * * *

Swanson accuses the appraisal defendants of skewing their assessment of her home because of her race. It is unclear whether she believes that they did so as part of a conspiracy with Citibank, or if she thinks that they deliberately undervalued her property on their own initiative. Once again, we find that she has pleaded enough to survive a motion under Rule 12(b)(6). The appraisal defendants knew her race, and she accuses them of discriminating against her in the specific business transaction that they had with her. When it comes to proving her case, she will need to come up with more evidence than the mere fact that PCI (through Lanier) placed a far lower value on her house than Midwest Valuations did. * * * All we hold now is that she is entitled to take the next step in this litigation.

[The court affirmed dismissal of fraud claims against all three defendants.]

We therefore reverse the judgment of the district court insofar as it dismissed Swanson's Fair Housing Act claims against all three defendants * * *. Each side will bear its own costs on appeal.

Posner, Circuit Judge, dissenting [as to the Fair Housing claims].

* * * I have difficulty squaring [the majority opinion] with *Ashcroft v. Iqbal* * * *.

There is language in my colleagues' opinion to suggest that discrimination cases are outside the scope of *Iqbal*, itself a discrimination case. The opinion says that "a plaintiff who believes that she has been passed over for a promotion because of her sex will be able to plead that she was employed by Company X, that a promotion was offered, that she applied and was qualified for it, and that the job went to someone else." Though this is not a promotion case, the opinion goes on to say that "Swanson's complaint identifies the type of discrimination that she thinks occurs (racial), by whom (Citibank, through Skertich, the manager, and the outside appraisers it used), and when (in connection with her effort in early 2009 to obtain a home equity loan). This is all that she needed to put in the complaint." * * *

Suppose this *were* a promotion case, and several people were vying for a promotion, all were qualified, several were men and one was a woman, and one of the men received the promotion. * * * [T]he district court would "draw on its judicial experience and common sense," *Iqbal*, 129 S. Ct. at 1950, to conclude that discrimination would not be a plausible explanation of the hiring decision, without additional allegations.

This case is even stronger for dismissal because it lacks the competitive situation—man and woman, or white and black, vying for the same job and the man, or the white, getting it. We had emphasized this distinction, long before *Twombly* and *Iqbal*, in Latimore v. Citibank Federal Savings Bank, 151 F.3d 712 (7th Cir. 1998), like this a case of credit discrimination rather than promotion. "Latimore was not competing with a white person for a $51,000 loan. A bank does not announce, 'We are making a $51,000 real estate loan today; please submit your applications, and we'll choose the application that we like best and give that applicant the loan.'" We held that there was no basis for an inference of discrimination. Noland v. Commerce Mortgage Corp., 122 F.3d 551, 553 (8th Cir. 1997) * * *.

There is no allegation that the plaintiff in this case was competing with a white person for a loan. It was the low appraisal of her home that killed her chances for the $50,000 loan that she was seeking. The appraiser thought her home worth only $170,000, and she already owed $146,000 on it (a first mortgage of $121,000 and a home-equity loan of $25,000). A further loan of $50,000 would thus have been undersecured. We must assume that the appraisal was a mistake, and the house worth considerably more, as she alleges. But errors in appraising a house are common because "real estate appraisal is not an exact science," *Latimore v. Citibank Federal Savings Bank, supra*, 151 F.3d at 715—common enough to have created a market for "Real Estate Appraisers Errors & Omissions" insurance policies. * * * The Supreme Court would consider error the plausible inference in this case, rather than discrimination, for it said in *Iqbal* that "as between that 'obvious alternative explanation' for the [injury of which the plaintiff is complaining] and the purposeful, invidious discrimination [the plaintiff] asks us to infer, discrimination is not a plausible conclusion."

Even before *Twombly* and *Iqbal*, complaints were dismissed when they alleged facts that refuted the plaintiffs' claims. Under the new regime, it should be enough that the allegations render a claim implausible. The complaint alleges that Citibank was the second bank to turn down the plaintiff's application for a home-equity loan. This reinforces the inference that she was not qualified. We further learn that, subject to the appraisal, which had not yet been conducted, Citibank had approved the $50,000 home-equity loan that the plaintiff was seeking on the basis of her representation that her house was worth $270,000. But she didn't think it was worth that much when she applied for the loan. The house had been appraised at $260,000 in 2004, and the complaint alleges that home values had fallen by "only" 16 to 20 percent since. This implies that when she applied for the home-equity loan her house was worth between $208,000 and $218,400—much less than what she told Citibank it was worth.

If the house was worth $208,000, she would have owed a total of $196,000 had she gotten the loan, or just a shade under the market value of the house. If the bank had insisted that she have a 20 percent equity in the house, which would be $41,600, it would have lent her only $20,400 ($166,400—80 percent of $208,000—minus the $146,000 that she already owed on the house). The loan figure rises to $28,720 if the house was worth $218,400 rather than $208,000. In either case a $50,000 loan would have been out of the question, especially in the wake of the financial crash of September 2008, when credit, including home-equity credit, became extremely tight. For it was a home-equity loan that the plaintiff was seeking in early February of 2009, at the nadir of the economic collapse—and seeking it from troubled Citibank, one of the banks that required a federal bailout in the wake of the crash. Financial reports in the weeks surrounding the plaintiff's application make clear the difficulty of obtaining credit from Citibank during that period.

In Erickson v. Pardus, 551 U.S. 89 (2007) (per curiam), decided two weeks after *Twombly*, the Supreme Court, without citing *Twombly*, reinstated a prisoner's civil rights suit that had been dismissed on the ground that the allegations of the complaint were "conclusory." The suit had charged deliberate indifference to the plaintiff's need for medical treatment. In the key passage in the Court's opinion, we learn that "the complaint stated that Dr. Bloor's decision to remove the petitioner [that is, the plaintiff] from his prescribed hepatitis C medication was 'endangering [his] life.' It alleged this medication was withheld 'shortly after' petitioner had commenced a treatment program that would take one year, that he was 'still in need of treatment for this disease,' and that the prison officials were in the meantime refusing to provide treatment. *This alone was enough to satisfy Rule 8(a)(2).* * * *" It was reasonable to infer from these allegations, assuming their truth, that the defendants (who included Dr. Bloor, a prison doctor) had acted with deliberate indifference to the petitioner's serious medical need by refusing to provide him with any medical treatment after taking away his medication. Indeed it's difficult (again assuming the truth of the allegations) to imagine an alternative interpretation. Hepatitis C is a serious disease and the prisoner had been put in a treatment program expected to last a year. To refuse him any treatment whatsoever seemed (as the other allegations to which the Court referred confirmed) to be punitive. I think *Erickson* is good law even after *Iqbal*, but I also think it's miles away from a case in which all that's alleged (besides pure speculation about the defendants' motive) is that someone was denied a loan because her house is mistakenly appraised for less than its market value.

[The Supreme Court established the plausibility standard in *Iqbal*] in opaque language: "The plausibility standard is not akin to a 'probability requirement,' but it asks for more than a sheer possibility that a defendant has acted unlawfully." * * * It seems (no stronger word is possible) that what the Court was driving at was that even if the district judge doesn't think a plaintiff's case is more likely than not to be a winner * * * , as long as it is substantially justified that's enough to avert dismissal.

But when a bank turns down a loan applicant because the appraisal of the security for the loan indicates that the loan would not be adequately secured, the alternative hypothesis of racial discrimination does not have substantial merit; it is implausible.

Behind both *Twombly* and *Iqbal* lurks a concern with asymmetric discovery burdens and the potential for extortionate litigation * * * that such an asymmetry creates. * * * In most suits against corporations or other institutions, and in both *Twombly* and *Iqbal*—but also in the present case—the plaintiff wants or needs more discovery of the defendant than the defendant wants or needs of the plaintiff, because the plaintiff has to search the defendant's records (and, through depositions, the minds of the defendant's employees) to obtain evidence of wrongdoing. With the electronic archives of large corporations or other large organizations holding millions of emails and other electronic communications, the cost of discovery to a defendant has become in many cases astronomical. And the cost is not only monetary; it can include, as well, the disruption of the defendant's operations. [T]he costs to the defendant may induce it to agree early in the litigation to a settlement favorable to the plaintiff.

* * * This structural flaw helps to explain and justify the Supreme Court's new approach. It requires the plaintiff to conduct a more extensive precomplaint investigation than used to be required and so creates greater symmetry between the plaintiff's and the defendant's litigation costs, and by doing so reduces the scope for extortionate discovery. If the plaintiff shows that he can't conduct an even minimally adequate investigation without limited discovery, the judge presumably can allow that discovery, meanwhile deferring ruling on the defendant's motion to dismiss. * * * No one has suggested such a resolution for this case.

The plaintiff has an implausible case of discrimination, but she will now be permitted to serve discovery demands that will compel elaborate document review by Citibank and require its executives to sit for many hours of depositions. * * * The threat of such an imposition will induce Citibank to consider settlement even if the suit has no merit at all. That is the pattern that the Supreme Court's recent decisions are aimed at disrupting.

We should affirm the dismissal of the suit in its entirety.

Notes and Questions

1. Does the majority opinion consider "*Twiqbal*" to have brought substantial change to federal pleading standards? Does the dissent?

2. It may seem counter-intuitive, but a plaintiff can plead *too much* detail. This happens if she alleges so many facts that she refutes her own claim. It is called "pleading herself out of court." In his dissent, Judge Posner suggests that under "*Twiqbal*," a plaintiff's over-pleading of facts may render her claim implausible and therefore subject to dismissal. He points out that the plaintiff alleged that she had been turned down for a loan before, thereby "reinforce[ing] the inference that she was not qualified." In addition, she alleged that her house was appraised at $260,000 in 2004 and that home values had fallen between 16 and 20 percent between then and the time

of her application to Citibank. These facts imply that when she applied to the defendant bank, the house was worth "much less than what she told Citibank it was worth." What did the majority opinion say regarding these allegations?

3. Is this a case in which the burdens imposed by the discovery phase of litigation would be "asymmetrical"? Why? Should the answer to that question affect the assessment of plausibility?

iii. The Common Counts

Historically, courts have allowed plaintiffs to state certain claims in a shorthand form called "common counts." Common counts were permitted under the writ system of the common law and basically allow a one-sentence allegation for money had and received, quantum meruit (value of labor done), quantum valebant (value of goods delivered), and for indebitatus assumpsit (for money owed). The common counts for such claims seem to violate the code requirement for a statement of the facts underlying a cause of action. Nonetheless, code states permit them, and they will suffice in federal court.

e. Heightened Specificity Requirements in Certain Cases

Read Rule 9, concentrating on subsections (a), (b), (c), and (g). Rules 9(b) and 9(g) impose heightened pleading requirements, meaning that the claimant must allege these matters in more detail than is required under Rule 8(a)(2). As courts became more crowded, and litigation became more expensive, some courts in the 1980s and 1990s required detailed pleadings even in cases not listed in Rule 9; some developed categories of cases for which they routinely required heightened specificity in pleading. These included claims involving conspiracy, see, e.g., Fullman v. Graddick, 739 F.2d 553, 557 (11th Cir. 1984), and civil rights claims filed under 42 U.S.C. § 1983, which prohibits deprivation of civil rights "under color of state law," see, e.g., Palmer v. San Antonio, 810 F.2d 514 (5th Cir. 1987) (suit against municipality); Elliott v. Perez, 751 F.2d 1472 (5th Cir. 1985) (suit against officer). In the following case, the Supreme Court reacts to such efforts.

Leatherman v. Tarrant County

507 U.S. 163, 113 S. Ct. 1160, 122 L. Ed. 2d 517 (1993)

Chief Justice Rehnquist delivered the opinion of the Court.

We granted certiorari to decide whether a federal court may apply a "heightened pleading standard" — more stringent than the usual pleading requirements of Rule 8(a) of the Federal Rules of Civil Procedure — in civil rights cases alleging municipal liability under 42 U.S.C. § 1983. We hold it may not.

We review here a decision granting a motion to dismiss, and therefore must accept as true all the factual allegations in the complaint. This action arose out of two separate incidents involving the execution of search warrants by local law enforcement officers. Each involved the forcible entry into a home based on the detection of odors associated with the manufacture of narcotics. One homeowner claimed that he was assaulted by the officers after they had entered; another claimed that the police had entered her home in her absence and killed her two dogs. The plaintiffs sued several local officials in their official capacity and the county and two municipal corporations that employed the police officers involved in the incidents, asserting that the police conduct had violated the Fourth Amendment to the United States Constitution. The stated basis for municipal liability under Monell v. New York City Dept. of Social Services, 436 U.S. 658 (1978), was the failure of these bodies adequately to train the police officers involved.

The United States District Court for the Northern District of Texas ordered the complaints dismissed, because they failed to meet the "heightened pleading standard" required by the decisional law of the Court of Appeals for the Fifth Circuit. 755 F. Supp. 726 (1991). The Fifth Circuit, in turn, affirmed the judgment of dismissal, 954 F.2d 1054 (1992), and we granted certiorari to resolve a conflict among the Courts of Appeals concerning the applicability of a heightened pleading standard to § 1983 actions alleging municipal liability. Cf., Karim-Panahi v. Los Angeles Police Dept., 839 F.2d 621, 624 (9th Cir. 1988) ("a claim of municipal liability under section 1983 is sufficient to withstand a motion to dismiss even if the claim is based on nothing more than a bare allegation that the individual officers' conduct conformed to official policy, custom, or practice") (internal quotation marks omitted). We now reverse.

Respondents seek to defend the Fifth Circuit's application of a more rigorous pleading standard on two grounds. First, respondents claim that municipalities' freedom from respondeat superior liability necessarily includes immunity from suit. In this sense, respondents assert, municipalities are not different from state or local officials sued in their individual capacity. Respondents reason that a more relaxed pleading requirement would subject municipalities to expensive and time consuming discovery in every § 1983 case, eviscerating their immunity from suit and disrupting municipal functions.

This argument wrongly equates freedom from liability with immunity from suit. To be sure, we reaffirmed in *Monell* that "a municipality cannot be held liable under § 1983 on a respondeat superior theory." But, contrary to respondents' assertions, this protection against liability does not encompass immunity from suit. Indeed, this argument is flatly contradicted by *Monell* and our later decisions involving municipal liability under § 1983. In *Monell*, we overruled Monroe v. Pape, 365 U.S. 167 (1961), insofar as it held that local governments were wholly immune from suit under § 1983, though we did reserve decision on whether municipalities are entitled to some form of limited immunity. Yet, when we took that issue up again in Owen v. City of Independence, 445 U.S. 622, 650 (1980), we rejected a claim that municipalities should be afforded qualified immunity, much like that afforded individual officials, based on the good faith of their agents. These decisions make it quite clear that, unlike various government officials, municipalities do not enjoy immunity from suit — either absolute or qualified — under § 1983. In short, a municipality can be sued under § 1983, but it cannot be held liable unless a municipal policy or custom caused the constitutional injury. We thus have no occasion to consider whether our qualified immunity jurisprudence would require a heightened pleading in cases involving individual government officials.

Second, respondents contend that the Fifth Circuit's heightened pleading standard is not really that at all. See Brief for Respondents Tarrant County Narcotics Intelligence and Coordination Unit et al. 9–10 ("[T]he Fifth Circuit's so-called 'heightened' pleading requirement is a misnomer"). According to respondents, the degree of factual specificity required of a complaint by the Federal Rules of Civil Procedure varies according to the complexity of the underlying substantive law. To establish municipal liability under § 1983, respondents argue, a plaintiff must do more than plead a single instance of misconduct. This requirement, respondents insist, is consistent with a plaintiff's Rule 11 obligation to make a reasonable pre-filing inquiry into the facts.

But examination of the Fifth Circuit's decision in this case makes it quite evident that the "heightened pleading standard" is just what it purports to be: a more demanding rule for pleading a complaint under § 1983 than for pleading other kinds of claims for relief. This rule was adopted by the Fifth Circuit in Elliott v. Perez, 751 F.2d 1472 (1985), and described in this language:

> "In cases against government officials involving the likely defense of immunity we require of trial judges that they demand that the plaintiff's complaints state with factual detail and particularity the basis for the claim which necessarily includes why the defendant-official cannot successfully maintain the defense of immunity." Id. at 1473.

In later cases, the Fifth Circuit extended this rule to complaints against municipal corporations asserting liability under § 1983.

We think that it is impossible to square the "heightened pleading standard" applied by the Fifth Circuit in this case with the liberal system of "notice pleading" set up by the Federal Rules. Rule 8(a)(2) requires that a complaint include only "a short and plain statement of the claim showing that the pleader is entitled to relief." In Conley v. Gibson, 355 U.S. 41 (1957), we said in effect that the Rule meant what it said:

> "[T]he Federal Rules of Civil Procedure do not require a claimant to set out in detail the facts upon which he bases his claim. To the contrary, all the Rules require is 'a short and plain statement of the claim' that will give the defendant fair notice of what the plaintiff's claim is and the grounds upon which it rests." Id. at 47 (footnote omitted).

Rule 9(b) does impose a particularity requirement in two specific instances. It provides that "[i]n all averments of fraud or mistake, the circumstances constituting fraud or mistake shall be stated with particularity." [Note: Rule 9(b) was amended in 2007, but retains the requirement of "particularity" for the allegations noted.] Thus, the Federal Rules do address in Rule 9(b) the question of the need for greater particularity in pleading certain actions, but do not include among the enumerated actions any reference to complaints alleging municipal liability under § 1983. *Expressio unius est exclusio alterius.*

The phenomenon of litigation against municipal corporations based on claimed constitutional violations by their employees dates from our decision in *Monell*, where we for the first time construed § 1983 to allow such municipal liability. Perhaps if Rules 8 and 9 were rewritten today, claims against municipalities under § 1983 might be subjected to the added specificity requirement of Rule 9(b). But that is a result which must be obtained by the process of amending the Federal Rules, and not by judicial interpretation. In the absence of such an amendment, federal courts and litigants must rely on summary judgment and control of discovery to weed out unmeritorious claims sooner rather than later.

The judgment of the Court of Appeals is reversed, and the case remanded for further proceedings consistent with this opinion.

It is so ordered.

Notes and Questions

1. Less than a decade after *Leatherman*, the Supreme Court again had to tell lower courts that, absent a statute or Rule to the contrary, it is inappropriate to require a claimant to allege her claim in greater detail than that required by Rule 8(a)(2). In Swierkiewicz v. Sorema N.A., 534 U.S. 506 (2002), the plaintiff alleged that he had been fired on the bases of his national origin and age, in violation of federal law. Applicable precedent requires such a plaintiff in such cases to prove (1) that she is a member of a group protected by federal law; (2) that she is qualified for the job in question; (3) that she was discharged; and (4) circumstances that support an inference of discrimination. The lower courts required the plaintiff to allege each of these four elements of a prima facie case. The Supreme Court reversed, and distinguished what plaintiff must *prove* from what plaintiff must *plead.* Because no federal statute or Rule requires a plaintiff in such discrimination cases specifically to allege each of the four elements, Rule 8(a)(2) governed the case. Plaintiff's allegations that he was terminated on the bases of national origin and age, of the relevant events, persons involved, and dates satisfied Rule 8(a)(2). Would these allegations suffice under the plausibility standard of "*Twiqbal*"?

The Court continues to reject efforts to impose heightened pleading requirements in civil rights cases. In Jones v. Bock, 549 U.S. 199, 211–17 (2007), it disapproved of the Sixth Circuit's requirement that prisoners suing to challenge conditions of their confinement specifically allege that they had first attempted to resolve their dispute by using administrative remedies in the prison system. Though the Prison Litigation Reform Act requires that prisoners so "exhaust" administrative remedies before suing, nothing in that Act or Rule 8(a)(2) requires a prisoner to *allege* exhaustion as part of her claim. Rather, the Court held, the issue should be injected into the case, if at all, by the defendant, as an affirmative defense. Prisoner cases such as *Jones* account for nearly ten percent of all civil filings in the federal court system. And "[m]ost of these cases have no merit; many are frivolous." 549 U.S. at 203. Why is the Court so forgiving of plaintiffs' efforts in such cases and seemingly so demanding in "*Twiqbal*"?

2. Why should there ever be a heightened specificity requirement? Why should there be such a requirement in the situations listed in Rule 9(b) and 9(g)? Is it to help the plaintiff by making her think more carefully about bringing claims that may be more difficult to prove? Or is it to help the defendant, by providing some protection from glib assertions of claims, such as fraud, that may be especially damaging to her reputation? Heightened pleading requirements make it more difficult for a plaintiff to gain access to the judicial system. Therefore, although requiring detailed pleading "looks" procedural, it clearly has a substantive impact.

3. Rule 9(b) requires particularity with regard to "circumstances constituting fraud or mistake." It thus does not require detailed allegations of every element, for example, of a fraud claim. Obviously, the plaintiff must do more than make the blanket statement "the defendant defrauded me." The courts have not been wholly uniform in assessing "particularity." See 2 MOORE'S FEDERAL PRACTICE § 9.03[1]. One court held that the plaintiff "must adequately specify the statements [she] claims were false or misleading, give particulars as to the respect in which the plaintiff contends the statements were fraudulent, state when and where the statements were made, and identify those responsible for the statements." Cosmas v. Hassett, 886 F.2d 8, 11 (2d Cir. 1989).

4. What policy supports the rule that state of mind, including malice, may be "alleged generally" under Rule 9(b)? After all, an allegation that the defendant acted with malice may hold the defendant up to ridicule and defamation. The theory seems to be that conditions of the defendant's mind are within the defendant's knowledge, and thus impossible for the plaintiff to state with particularity. Caliber Partners, Ltd. v. Affeld, 583 F. Supp. 1308, 1311 (N.D. Ill. 1984). Does this reasoning apply, however, when the issue is malice?

5. Note also that under Rule 9(c) satisfaction of conditions precedent may be pleaded generally, but a denial that a condition precedent has occurred must be made "with particularity." Can you articulate a reason for this different treatment?

6. Special damages are "those which, although resulting from the commission of the wrong, are neither such a necessary result that they will be implied by law nor be deemed within the contemplation of the parties." Cotton Bros. Baking Co. v. Industrial Risk Insurers, 102 F.R.D. 964, 966 (W.D. La. 1984). They are to be contrasted with "general damages," which are said to "flow naturally" from the commission of the wrong. Based upon your studies in other law school courses, can you think of any claims that would constitute special damages?

Consider Rule 9(g) in light of this statement from a medical malpractice case, in which health care providers allegedly failed to diagnose a cancerous tumor, leading to a claim for general damages (including medical expenses already incurred) and to a special damages claim for future medical treatment:

> Decisions on what needs to be pleaded by way of special damages are sparse. The tendency is liberalization. We believe the purpose is to give notice. We are satisfied with "Karen will incur * * * extensive major medical costs and

> expenses and will require costly health care services until her death." The subject had been opened; defendants could seek details by inquiry.

Matos v. Ashford Presbyterian Community Hospital, Inc., 4 F.3d 47, 51–52 (1st Cir. 1993).

The court's statement that "defendants could seek details by inquiry" presumably refers to discovery devices. Because these are available in all civil cases, why should we ever require more specificity than is provided by notice pleading?

7. If the defendant feels that allegations in the plaintiff's complaint do not satisfy Rule 9(b) or 9(g), what motion(s) should she make? When may she make such motions? See Rules 12(g) and 12(h).

8. Although it has done so rarely, Congress may impose heightened pleading requirements for the assertion of federal claims. A good example is the Private Securities Litigation Reform Act, which relates to claims alleging federal securities fraud. Under this statute, the plaintiffs must specify the misleading statements on which their claims are based and must identify "with particularity facts giving rise to a strong inference that the defendant acted with the required state of mind." 15 U.S.C. § 78u-4(b)(3)(A). Lower courts disagreed on what this direction for particularized pleadings means. In Tellabs, Inc. v. Makor Issues & Rights, Ltd., 551 U.S. 308, 314 (2007), the Supreme Court resolved the split of authority by holding that "[t]o qualify as 'strong' within the intendment of [the PSLRA], * * * an inference of scienter must be more than merely plausible or reasonable — it must be cogent and at least as compelling as any opposing inference of nonfraudulent intent."

But such detailed information about the defendant's intent to deceive the plaintiff would likely be in the defendant's possession. So is it fair to require the plaintiff to allege such details? How can she possibly do so without discovery?

f. Pleading Inconsistent Facts and Alternative Theories

Pleadings are not evidence, but they do set forth the pleader's theory of what happened. Is it permissible to plead alternative versions of what happened? Rule 8(d)(2) permits alternative statements of a claim or defense. Rule 8(d)(3) permits a pleader to "state as many separate claims or defenses as it has, regardless of consistency." Though these provisions seem to give some leeway, Rule 11(b)(3) requires that factual contentions "have evidentiary support."

Consider McCormick v. Kopmann, 161 N.E.2d 720 (Ill. Ct. App. 1959), which applied Illinois provisions that are similar to the Federal Rules. There, McCormick was killed when the car he drove was hit by a truck driven by Kopmann. Before driving, McCormick had been in a tavern owned by Huls. McCormick's wife sued for wrongful death, and in one case joined both Kopmann and Huls. As to Kopmann, she alleged that Kopmann drove negligently and that her husband was not negligent. As to Huls, the plaintiff alleged dram shop liability because Huls served her husband alcohol when he was intoxicated. So, in one case, the plaintiff alleged both that her husband was free from negligence and that he was intoxicated.

Clearly, both allegations cannot be true. Is there anything ethically improper about pleading two theories when only one can be true? Is this pleading permissible under Rules 8 and 11? The court in *McCormick* permitted the inconsistent pleading, noting that the plaintiff, who was not with her husband on the evening of the accident, had no way of knowing which theory was true. Suppose, however, that the plaintiff uncovers evidence during discovery which leads her to believe that one of her alternative theories is more likely based upon fact than the other. Should she still be able to pursue the alternative theories?

What if Mr. McCormick had survived the wreck and sued for personal injuries. Would he be allowed to plead inconsistently against Kopmann and Huls?

Mrs. McCormick could have sued the two defendants in separate cases. One problem with doing that would be that pleadings from one case generally can be used against a party in the other case. See Dugan v. EMS Helicopters, Inc., 915 F.2d 1428 (10th Cir. 1990). Beside this consideration, can you think of other reasons for Mrs. McCormick to want to sue both the driver of the truck and the owner of the bar in a single proceeding?

Rule 8(d) applies to defendants as well as to plaintiffs. Suppose the defendant in a breach of contract case asserts as a defense that there was no contract and also asserts a counterclaim suing the plaintiff for breach of that same contract! Is this permissible? In Olympia Hotels Corp. v. Johnson Wax Development Corp., 908 F.2d 1363 (7th Cir. 1990), the court held that it was.

2. Voluntary Dismissal

A plaintiff institutes suit by filing her complaint. Does she have the power to withdraw that complaint? Why would she want to? Read Rule 41(a)(1). A dismissal "without prejudice" means that the plaintiff can reinstitute the case. A dismissal "with prejudice" or "on the merits" bars the plaintiff from bringing the claim again. Rule 41(a)(1) permits the plaintiff to dismiss unilaterally in some situations and by stipulation (agreement of the parties) in others. Rule 41(a)(2) permits voluntary dismissal only with a court order in other circumstances.

Are there limits on a court's power to order dismissal without prejudice under Rule 41(a)(2)? Consider Grover v. Eli Lilly & Co., 33 F.3d 716 (6th Cir. 1994), which is one of hundreds of cases concerning birth defects allegedly caused by diethylstilbestrol (DES), a female hormone manufactured by Eli Lilly and other pharmaceutical companies, and prescribed to countless pregnant women from the 1940s through the 1960s. It was used to prevent miscarriages, but apparently injured female children in utero. The injuries to the female offspring did not become discernible, however, until those children were of childbearing age. In *Grover*, the alleged injury was a generation further removed. The plaintiff was a boy who had suffered serious birth defects. Those suing on his behalf claimed that the boy was injured because his maternal grandmother had taken DES when she was pregnant with the boy's mother. They claimed that the drug affected the boy's mother in such a way as to cause his birth defects.

The plaintiffs sued in state court in 1983 and the defendant removed the case to federal court under diversity of citizenship jurisdiction. Defendant asserted that Ohio law (which governed the dispute) did not recognize a claim in such circumstances. In 1988, the plaintiffs sought certification of the legal question to the Ohio Supreme Court. Over the defendant's objection, the district judge certified the question, noting that the answer would be dispositive of the suit. After the Ohio court held, in a four-to-three decision, that the boy could not sue because he had not ingested the drug directly or in utero, the district judge dismissed the case *without prejudice.* He did so because he felt that the Ohio court might change its mind or the legislature might provide a remedy for persons such as the boy involved in *Grover.*

The Sixth Circuit reversed and remanded with instructions to dismiss the case with prejudice. According to the court, "[t]he primary purpose of the rule [41(a)(2)] in interposing the requirement of court approval is to protect the nonmovant from unfair treatment." Id. at 718. Such unfair treatment consisted not of the possibility of being sued a second time, but of "plain legal prejudice," which was shown by the delay and expense of certification and the court's order of dismissal without prejudice in the face of the Ohio court's rejection of the claim. The court concluded: "At the point when the law clearly dictates a result for the defendant, it is unfair to subject him to continued exposure to potential liability by dismissing the case without prejudice." Id. at 719.

Why should the plaintiff in *Grover* be denied the opportunity to take advantage of any subsequent change in Ohio substantive law?

Notes and Questions

1. Under what circumstances may a plaintiff dismiss unilaterally without prejudice?

2. Under what circumstances may a plaintiff dismiss with the agreement of the other parties who have appeared? Under what circumstances may she do so without prejudice?

3. Under what circumstances may a plaintiff dismiss with the permission of the court? Under what circumstances may she do so without prejudice?

4. Based upon your study of Rule 41(a), work through these hypotheticals:

(a) The plaintiff files and serves her complaint in federal court. Before the defendant takes any action, the plaintiff files a notice of dismissal. Now the plaintiff brings the case in federal court a second time, but voluntarily dismisses by stipulation of all parties who have appeared. Why is this dismissal without prejudice? See Sutton Place Dev. Co. v. Abacus Mortgage Inv. Co., 826 F.2d 637 (7th Cir. 1987) (reaching that conclusion based upon language of Rule 41(a)).

(b) Same facts as in Question 4(a), except the second case is dismissed by notice of dismissal. Why is this dismissal with prejudice?

(c) Assume the plaintiff's second case (asserting the same claim) is in federal court and that she dismisses it through notice of dismissal. Assume also that she had dismissed her first case voluntarily. In determining whether the second dismissal is with prejudice, does it matter whether the first case was filed in federal or state court? Should it matter that the state court system does not have a similar rule?

(d) If the second action to be dismissed voluntarily was brought in state court, Rule 41 would not apply. Why?

(e) The plaintiff files and serves her complaint in federal court. The defendant moves to dismiss for failure to state a claim on which relief can be granted. Can the plaintiff dismiss without prejudice by filing a notice of voluntary dismissal?

5. Is a plaintiff's right to dismiss under Rule 41(a)(1)(A)(i) absolute? In American Soccer Co. v. Score First Enterprises, 187 F.3d 1108 (9th Cir. 1999), the court said yes. In that case, the court had invested a good bit of time over two months, during which the parties litigated the question of whether defendant was entitled to a preliminary injunction. Despite this investment of judicial resources, the plaintiff was entitled to a dismissal, because the defendant had served neither an answer nor a motion for summary judgment.

6. Why should procedural rules limit the number of times a plaintiff can dismiss unilaterally without prejudice? Why should this right be available only relatively early in the case?

3. Involuntary Dismissal

Any litigant can find herself in trouble for failing to play by the rules. In addition to sanctions under Rule 11 or other provisions, or the court's inherent powers, see Section G below, the court may dismiss the plaintiff's case. Read Rule 41(b).

The rule appears to preclude the court from ordering involuntary dismissal on its own motion, since it provides that "a defendant may move for dismissal" for any of the reasons listed. Despite this language, the Supreme Court has held that the district court may order involuntary dismissal sua sponte. Link v. Wabash RR., 370 U.S. 626 (1962). *Link* is the leading case on involuntary dismissal. There, the plaintiff filed his personal injury suit in August 1954; the case lingered on the district court docket until dismissed in October 1960. The plaintiff had consistently sought extensions (including extensions of two trial dates) to perform various tasks, such as respond to discovery requests. The straw that broke the camel's back was the plaintiff's counsel's failure to attend the pretrial conference in October 1960. Counsel called the judge's chambers the day of the conference and left a message for His Honor that counsel was busy working on papers in a state court case and could not make it to the conference. He would be available the two following days, however. The district court dismissed "for failure of the plaintiff's counsel to appear at the pretrial, for failure to prosecute this action." Id. at 629 (quoting opinion of trial court).

The Supreme Court affirmed, with Justice Harlan writing for the majority of four (two Justices did not participate in the decision, so only seven took part). Although the delay was not attributable entirely to the plaintiff (indeed, sixteen months were lost while the plaintiff secured a reversal of the district judge's earlier wrongful dismissal of the case), the majority concluded that the district judge had not abused his discretion in ordering the dismissal. Id. at 633.

Justice Black wrote a vigorous dissent, arguing, inter alia, that "it seems * * * contrary to the most fundamental ideas of fairness and justice to impose the punishment for the lawyer's failure to prosecute upon the plaintiff who, as far as this record shows, was simply trusting his lawyer to take care of his case as clients generally do." Id. at 643 (Black, J., dissenting). The majority said that "[p]laintiff voluntarily chose this attorney * * * and he cannot now avoid the consequences of the acts or omissions of this freely selected agent." Id. at 633–34.

Aren't there problems with both approaches? Does Justice Black's view lead to the possibility that no dismissal could be entered, no matter how dilatory the lawyer? Shouldn't a reasonable client begin to think that something was amiss when, six years after filing, the case had not gone to trial? On the other hand, isn't the majority shortsighted in saying that the involuntary dismissal will alleviate court congestion? After all, won't Mr. Link now be able to file a malpractice action against his lawyer?

The district court in *Link* did not specifically warn the plaintiff's counsel that the case might be dismissed if he failed to attend the pretrial conference. Neither did it set up a proceeding to elicit explanations from the plaintiff's counsel. On the record, however, the majority of the Supreme Court felt that Mr. Link's lawyer understood the gravity of the situation. Still, providing warning and an opportunity to be heard is the preferred course. See generally 8 Moore's Federal Practice § 41.50. Indeed, as we will see below, Rule 11 now requires notice and an opportunity to be heard before sanctions can be imposed.

Notes and Questions

1. For what reasons may the court dismiss under Rule 41(b)? Must the court do so? May it dismiss less than the entire case?

2. Rule 83 allows district courts to adopt local rules providing for involuntary dismissal if no action is shown of record within a stated time. Such local rules are quite common. If the plaintiff has taken no action within the given period—say, for example, one year—the court issues an Order to Show Cause (universally referred to as an OSC) to the plaintiff. The OSC requires the plaintiff to show the court why it should not dismiss for lack of prosecution. Many states have similar provisions, granting the trial judge discretion to determine whether the plaintiff has been so dilatory as to justify an order of involuntary dismissal.

California has such a provision for cases that have not gone to trial within three years of filing. Cal. Code Civ. Proc. § 583.410(a). Another statute goes further, and automatically deprives the trial court of jurisdiction over any case in which trial has not commenced within five years of filing. Cal. Code Civ. Proc. § 583.360.

3. Notice how Rule 60(b) might make involuntary dismissal less harsh. Rule 60(b) is discussed at Section D.4 below.

4. Note the provision in Rule 41(b) that certain types of dismissals operate as an adjudication on the merits. How can it be said that dismissal for failure to prosecute is in any way related to the merits? We will see why this provision is important in Chapter 11, where we will see that only judgments on the merits are entitled to preclusive (claim or issue preclusion) effect.

D. Defendant's Options in Response

The defendant has two choices in responding to a complaint: she can bring a motion or she can "answer." A motion, as we have seen elsewhere, is a request that the court order something, such as dismissal of the case; it is not a "pleading." The answer, on the other hand, is a pleading that responds to allegations of the complaint and may add new matter as well. In a given case, the defendant might use one or the other. For example, she may eschew bringing a motion and simply file an answer. Or she might bring a motion to dismiss, which, if granted, obviates the need for an answer. In some cases, the defendant may use both, as when her motion to dismiss is denied, and she must thereafter file an answer.

1. Motions

Read Rules 12(a) and 12(b). Earlier in this chapter, we discussed how a defendant may challenge the legal or factual sufficiency of the complaint with a motion to dismiss for failure to state a claim, under Rule 12(b)(6). The same motion, if made after the defendant had answered, is the Rule 12(c) motion for judgment on the pleadings. In Chapter 6, we addressed the timing of motions to dismiss on other grounds under Rule 12(b), paying particular attention to lack of personal jurisdiction, subject matter jurisdiction, and venue.*

In addition, the defendant may bring motions for relief other than dismissal. Specifically, she may seek a more definite statement under Rule 12(e) or move to strike under Rule 12(f). Read those two subparts. The 1938 version of Rule 12(e) permitted a motion for more definite statement or for a bill of particulars to allow a party to prepare a responsive pleading "or to prepare for trial." The rule was amended in 1946 to strike the reference to trial preparation, in express recognition that the discovery rules were the appropriate avenue for fleshing out details in trial preparation. A motion under Rule 12(e) is not aimed at pleadings that fail to state a claim. Instead, it "is plainly designed to strike at unintelligibility rather than lack of detail." 2 MOORE'S FEDERAL PRACTICE § 12.36 at p. 12–87.

---

* In Section B of Chapter 6, we saw that the defendant must raise four Rule 12(b) defenses — lack of personal jurisdiction, improper venue, insufficient process and insufficient service of process — in her first Rule 12 response. Failure to do so waives the defense. In this chapter, we see that Rule 12 gives the defendant a choice: she may respond by motion or by answer. Whichever she does first, under Rule 12(g) and 12(h), must include defenses under Rule 12(b)(2), (3), (4), and (5), or else they will be waived.

Despite the provision that the defendant should make a motion to strike before responding to a pleading, courts have inherent power to entertain such motion (or to strike sua sponte) at any time. Hoppe v. G.D. Searle & Co., 779 F. Supp. 1413, 1421 (S.D.N.Y. 1991). Note the categories of allegations that may be stricken. A scandalous allegation has been defined as one that "reflect[s] cruelly" on the defendant's moral character, which uses "repulsive language," or which detracts from the "dignity of the court." Khalid Bin Talal Bin Abdul Azaiz Seoud v. E.F. Hutton & Co., 720 F. Supp. 671, 686 (N.D. Ill. 1989).

The motion to strike can serve a similar substantive function to the Rule 12(b)(6) motion. For example, a claim for relief not available as a matter of law can be stricken under Rule 12(f). Brokke v. Stauffer Chem. Co., 703 F. Supp. 215 (D. Conn. 1988) (striking claim for punitive damages).

If the facts are undisputed, and a party is entitled to judgment as a matter of law, she may bring a motion for summary judgment under Rule 56. Thus, for example, if the statute of limitations has run, or if the claim is barred by claim or issue preclusion (res judicata or collateral estoppel), summary judgment may provide the defendant with a vehicle for early adjudication of the case.

Questions

1. Defendant files and serves an answer which the plaintiff finds unintelligible. Why can the plaintiff not file a motion for more definite statement?

2. Why is the plaintiff not able to file a 12(b)(6) motion regarding an *answer* that is insufficient as a matter of law? What is the appropriate motion?

3. Defendant responds by filing and serving a motion to dismiss for lack of personal jurisdiction. The motion is timely. The court denies the motion. How long does Defendant have in which to serve her answer? See Rule 12(a)(4).

2. The Answer

Read Rule 8(b), 8(c), and 8(d). These provisions set forth the modern philosophy of defensive pleading. The defendant can do two things in her answer: respond to the allegations of the complaint and raise new matter through an affirmative defense. In all cases, she will do the former; in most cases, she will probably do the latter as well.

a. Responses to the Plaintiff's Allegations

Under Rule 8(b), there are three possible responses to the various allegations of the plaintiff's complaint. The defendant can admit, deny, or claim that she lacks sufficient information to admit or deny. These choices must be read against the backdrop of Rule 8(b)(6), which provides that allegations not denied are deemed admitted (except allegations regarding the amount of damage). Those allegations that are properly denied are said to be "joined," which means that they are in dispute and may proceed to adjudication.

i. Admissions

There will usually be some allegations in the complaint which the defendant will admit. For example, the defendant may admit that the parties entered into a contract (and deny that she breached it or have some affirmative defense against the claim of breach). It is incumbent on the defendant to admit such allegations. Thus, the pleadings serve to establish undisputed facts on which there need be no trial.

ii.. Denials

The *general denial*, noted in Rule 8(b)(3), is a very short pleading, the operative language of which can be as simple as "Defendant denies each and every allegation of the complaint." See Stringfellow v. Perry, 869 F.2d 1140 (8th Cir. 1989). It is acceptable under the Federal Rules and in code pleading, but only if the defendant can in good faith deny all allegations of the complaint. Because there will almost always be at least one material allegation the defendant cannot contest, general denials should be used with caution.

Almost always, the defendant will use *specific denials* in combination with admissions. The Rules do not prescribe a particular form for denials, though Rules 8(b)(3) and (4) provide some good practical advice. Responding to each paragraph of the complaint individually is a common practice. For example, an answer could say: "Defendant admits the allegations of Paragraph One of the Complaint. Defendant denies the allegations of Paragraph Two of the Complaint," and so forth.

But the defendant need not match the complaint paragraph for paragraph, so long as she denies those allegations she needs to deny. For instance, if appropriate on the facts, the answer could provide: "Defendant admits the allegations of Paragraph Five of the Complaint, and denies each and every other allegation of the Complaint." This form is often called a *qualified general denial.*

What if a single paragraph of the complaint contains both material the defendant wishes to admit and material she wishes to deny? Here, the defendant needs to be careful to separate the former from the latter. Suppose, for example, you represent a corporate defendant in a diversity of citizenship case. Your client is incorporated in Nebraska with its principal place of business in Iowa. Paragraph Four of the complaint alleges "defendant is a Nebraska corporation with its principal place of business in Nebraska." Your associate suggests that you file an answer responding to that paragraph by saying: "In response to Paragraph Four of the Complaint, Defendant admits that it is a Nebraska corporation and denies the remainder of the Paragraph."

What do you think of the associate's suggestion? Shouldn't the plaintiff's counsel, reading this response, be tipped off to the possibility that the principal place of business is not in Nebraska? Or do you have an ethical obligation to tell the plaintiff that your client's principal place of business is in Iowa?

Rule 8(b)(2) requires that "[a] denial must fairly respond to the substance of the allegation." Thus, counsel should resist temptation to plead contrary facts. For example, suppose the complaint alleged that on a certain date, "the defendant negligently drove her car on Main Street in Apalachicola, Florida, and ran over the plaintiff." Instead of simply denying the allegations, defendant alleges that on the date mentioned, "defendant was on vacation in Brazil." This is an "argumentative denial," and runs the risk, at least in code states, of being deemed an admission of the facts alleged by the plaintiff. In federal court, it will likely be effective as a denial, but it may create problems if it is not clear what allegations are being put in issue. See generally 2 Moore's Federal Practice § 8.06[1].

Another potential problem is the "negative pregnant," which can result from a denial that is too literal. Suppose the plaintiff alleges that defendant "made, executed, and delivered" a contract. Defendant's response is: "Defendant denies that he made, executed, and delivered" the contract. Is this response an admission that defendant made and executed the contract? Or that she executed and delivered the contract? Or that she made and delivered the contract? Why? How should she have responded to avoid this problem?

Thus, in Freedom National Bank v. Northern Illinois Corp., 202 F.2d 601 (7th Cir. 1953), the plaintiff alleged that the value of a trailer exceeded $4,718.25. Defendant denied that the value exceeded $4,718.25. The court treated this as an admission that the trailer was worth exactly $4,718.25 or any lesser amount. How should defendant have phrased the denial to avoid the negative pregnant?

Problems with literal denials and negative pregnants are hypertechnical, and most federal courts today will construe such allegations as denials. Some state courts, however, may be less forgiving.

iii. Denials for Lack of Knowledge or Information

Rule 8(b)(5) provides that "[a] party that lacks knowledge or information sufficient to form a belief about the truth of an allegation must so state." Doing so "has the effect of a denial." Because of the requirements of good faith and veracity under Rule 11, however, this defense cannot be used if the defendant has reasonable access to the information or if it is a matter of public record or general knowledge. See 2 Moore's Federal Practice § 8.06[5].

As noted above, when the defendant denies an allegation of the plaintiff's complaint, the allegation is "joined." This simply means that the issue is contested and is thus one on which an evidentiary determination is required. When the defendant admits an allegation of the plaintiff's complaint (either expressly or by failing to deny), the allegation can be taken as true; no proof is required of such issues at trial.

b. Affirmative Defenses

Rule 8(c)(1) requires the defendant to raise affirmative defenses. The rule's list of 18 such defenses is not exhaustive, because the rule requires that "a party must affirmatively state any avoidance or affirmative defense." Use of the term "avoidance" is a vestige of common law pleading. At common law, a defendant could use a plea in confession and avoidance, which would admit the plaintiff's allegations but raise new matter that would "avoid" liability for those allegations. For example, a defendant might admit that she had breached a contract, but assert that the contract was unenforceable because it violated the rule that it must be in writing under the Statute of Frauds.

Affirmative defenses inject new matter into the dispute. Suppose, for example, that the plaintiff sues for battery, alleging that the defendant struck her. If the defendant did not strike the plaintiff, she will simply deny the plaintiff's allegation. On the other hand, if the defendant struck the plaintiff, but did so in self-defense, she will admit the plaintiff's allegation and plead the affirmative defense of self-defense. In the first case, the defendant is merely denying the plaintiff's version of the story. In the second, she is injecting a new set of facts upon which her defense is premised. In light of *McCormick*, could the defendant deny the allegation that she struck the plaintiff and raise the affirmative defense of self-defense?

Why is self-defense an affirmative defense to be pleaded by the defendant, rather than as a part of the plaintiff's claim? In other words, why didn't the plaintiff have to allege that the defendant did not act in self-defense? In an influential article, Professor Cleary shed light on this subject in his discussion of the elements of a claim and affirmative defenses as "conditional imperatives." Edward Cleary, *Presuming and Pleading: An Essay on Juristic Immaturity*, 12 Stan. L. Rev. 5 (1959).

Under this analysis, for example, a contract claimant might prevail if she showed offer, acceptance, consideration, and breach *unless* the contract should have been in writing under the statute of frauds, or the contract was illegal, or a party lacked capacity to contract, etc. Roughly stated, the "ifs" in this equation are elements of the plaintiff's claim, and the "unlesses" are affirmative defenses. The substantive law of each jurisdiction allocates each of the items to the "if" or "unless" category. Thus, in the battery hypothetical above, the substantive law requires the defendant to allege self-defense.

As Professor Cleary discussed, however, the fact that precedent clearly establishes the burden of pleading "does nothing for the inquiring mind." How does each jurisdiction determine the matter of allocation? The answer is largely one of policy, influenced by the fact that a litigant usually has the burden of producing evidence at trial on the elements she must plead. For instance, it would be an intolerable burden if the contract plaintiff had to plead not only offer, acceptance, consideration, and breach, but also that there had been no accord and satisfaction, that there was no capacity problem, that the statute of limitations had not run, etc. The better approach has the plaintiff assert the prima facie case and allows the defendant to inject whichever of the potential "unlesses" might negate recovery.

While this explanation counsels toward limiting the number of things the plaintiff has to plead and prove, it does not tell us why the line is drawn at a particular point. In part, as Cleary examined, the line is drawn because of an assessment of the fairness of requiring one party or the other to bear the burden of proof at trial. Suppose the plaintiff sues to recover on a note. Defendant claims that she repaid the note. Who should have the burden of pleading and proving the issue of whether payment was made? Think about the case from the plaintiff's viewpoint. How can you prove that the defendant failed to pay? How can one ever prove a negative?*

On the other hand, can't the defendant more readily prove that she made payment (as, for example, by producing a canceled check)? In such a case, doesn't it make sense to prescribe, as Rule 8(c) does, that the issue of payment be raised as an affirmative defense? Such cases represent one of the exceptions to the rule that the burden of proving an issue at trial follows the burden of pleading the issue. In many jurisdictions, both the plaintiff and defendant are required to plead regarding the issue of repayment (plaintiff that it has not been made, defendant that it has). Only the defendant, however, bears the burden of proof at trial. See, e.g., West Coast Credit Corp. v. Pedersen, 390 P.2d 551 (Wash. 1964).

Notes and Questions

1. In her answer in a contract case in federal court, the defendant asserts that the contract is not enforceable because it was not in writing, as required by the Statute of Frauds.

(a) Why is this an affirmative defense?

(b) If the plaintiff thinks that the Statute of Frauds does not apply to this contract, what response does she make? Why?

2. Rule 8(c) provides that the defendant "must" plead her affirmative defenses. A defendant who fails to do so risks waiving the defense. As we will see in Section E of this chapter, however, the defendant might be able to amend her answer to assert the affirmative defense.

3. The assertion that the plaintiff's claim is barred by the statute of limitations is an affirmative defense which, like the others, "must" be pleaded in the defendant's answer. Rule 8(c). Nonetheless, some courts have permitted defendants to assert the defense in a motion for summary judgment, notwithstanding the defendants' failure to plead the affirmative defense, as long as no prejudice is shown. See, e.g., Brinkley v. Harbour Rec. Club, 180 F.3d 598, 612 (4th Cir. 1999); Blaney v. United States, 34 F.3d 509, 512 (7th Cir. 1994). As we will see in Chapter 9, courts can grant summary judgment if there is no dispute as to a material issue of fact and the moving party is entitled to judgment as a matter of law. So if the facts are clear, and the statute of limitations barred the claim, the defendant may win on summary judgment.

Other courts disagree and hold that the Federal Rules require assertion of the affirmative defense in the answer, to give the plaintiff notice and an opportunity to investigate the defense before a dispositive motion is on the docket. See, e.g., Harris v. Dep't of Veterans Affairs, 126 F.3d 339, 345 (D.C. Cir. 1997); Lucas v. United States, 807 F.2d 414, 417–18 (5th Cir. 1986). See also Arizona v. California, 530 U.S. 392

* The same problem arises in cases involving defamation, which is the publication of a false statement about the plaintiff, tending to hold her up to ridicule. Suppose defendant publicly called plaintiff a prostitute, or a murderer, or a traitor. How can plaintiff prove that she is none of these?

(2000) (refusing to allow the defendant to raise claim preclusion years after failing to assert it as an affirmative defense).

4. Under the practice in some states, the plaintiff must file a pleading (usually called a reply) responding to the affirmative defenses. This is not required in federal court. Rule 8(b)(6) provides that allegations of an answer are automatically considered denied or avoided by the plaintiff. Under Federal Rule 7(a), a reply to an answer is not required but may be ordered.

3. Claims by the Defendant

Thus far, we have considered how a defending party may avoid the imposition of liability on herself. A defending party can also assert claims against other parties and, in some circumstances, force the joinder of additional parties. The principal claims by a defending party are the counterclaim (against an opposing party) and the crossclaim (against a co-party). The plaintiff must file an answer to a "counterclaim designated as a counterclaim." We will discuss counterclaims, crossclaims, and other possible assertions of liability by the defendant in Chapter 12.

4. Failure to Respond: Default and Default Judgment

If a defending party fails to respond in an appropriate and timely way, she may find herself in default. Default must be distinguished from default judgment. The former is a notation on the court's docket sheet that the defendant has failed to plead or otherwise respond in time. The plaintiff cannot obtain money or other relief on the basis of a default. Instead, she must get a default judgment, which is enforced like any other judgment. Entry of default judgment presents a clash of important policies: while we do not want to subject a worthy plaintiff to untoward delay, we also prefer to decide cases on the merits rather than on technicalities.

Read Rules 6(b), 54(c), and 55 before addressing the following.

Notes and Questions

1. You are Plaintiff's counsel. You file suit on behalf of Plaintiff seeking liquidated damages of $95,000, plus costs and whatever other relief the court may find appropriate. You have process served upon Defendant properly. Defendant fails to respond in any way within the appropriate period.

(a) What documents do you prepare, and to whom do you give them, to get the entry of default? Do you serve these documents on the defendant?

(b) If you prepare and file the proper documents, must the person to whom you go to file them (the clerk of the court) enter the default, or does she have discretion to refuse?

(c) To whom do you go for entry of the default judgment? What document(s) do you prepare for that step?

(d) Can the default judgment be for damages of $100,000? Can it be for damages of $20,000?

2. Same facts, except that the claim is for unspecified damages.

(a) Is there any difference in acquiring the default from the fact pattern in Question 1?

(b) To whom do you go for entry of the default judgment? What document(s) do you prepare for this step?

(c) What proceedings follow? Why does the defendant not get notice of these proceedings on these facts? Under what facts would she get notice?

3. Under Rule 55(a), the defendant's failure to respond within the prescribed time does not *automatically* result in entry of default. Rather, the plaintiff must ask the clerk to enter the default on the docket sheet. Once the default is entered, defendant may not respond by motion or answer. See Cohen v. Rosenthal, 2015 U.S. Dist. LEXIS 159990 at *5–6 n.2 (D. Conn. 2015).

4. The hearing addressed in Rule 55(b)(2) does not necessarily result in default judgment. In other words, the plaintiff has no right to a default judgment. See Ganther v. Ingle, 75 F.3d 207, 209 (5th Cir. 1996). The issue is vested in the court's discretion, and the judge may look at a wide variety of factors in determining whether to enter the judgment. For example, one court refused to enter default judgment, despite the defendant's technical failure to respond within the appropriate time, when the sum at stake was large and the merits clearly in dispute. Pinaud v. County of Suffolk, 52 F.3d 1139 (2d Cir. 1995). See also Sony Corp. v. Elm State Elec., Inc., 800 F.2d 317 (2d Cir. 1986) (default judgment not favored in cases involving large claims).

5. It may seem perplexing that a party can be in default even though she has "appeared personally or by a representative." Consider this possibility. The defendant may make a timely motion to dismiss under Rule 12(b). After it is denied, the defendant must serve her answer within 14 days. Rule 12(a)(4)(A). If she fails to do so, she can be in default even though she has appeared in the case.

6. A plaintiff whose claim proceeds to trial may recover whatever relief the evidence supports, even if it exceeds the amount she demanded in the complaint. See Rule 54(c). As you have seen, this is not true in default judgment cases. Can you articulate a reason for this different rule in default judgment cases?

7. Client comes to your office and tells you that she was sued and has defaulted, although no default judgment has yet been entered. She wants to avoid liability. What should you do on her behalf? How do you do so? Where do you do so? What do you have to show? When do you have to do so?

If the judgment has already been entered, what do you do? How, where, and when do you do it? Rule 60(b) allows a motion to set aside a judgment, among other reasons, for "excusable neglect." The decision of whether to set aside a judgment for this (or any other) reason is committed to the discretion of the district judge. The defaulting defendant must convince the court that she was not guilty of culpable conduct, that she has a meritorious defense, and that reopening the case would not prejudice the plaintiff. Because of the preference for determinations on the merits, courts often conclude that the defendant was not culpable if she acted without deviousness or deliberate willfulness or bad faith. See, e.g., TCI Group Life Ins. Plan v. Knoebber, 244 F.3d 691, 698–99 (9th Cir. 2001).

Will a court set aside a default judgment based upon lawyer's failure to respond appropriately on behalf of the defendant? A party may move to set aside a judgment under Rule 60(b)(6) only if no other provision of Rule 60(b) applies and if the circumstances are "extraordinary." Lowe v. McGraw-Hill Cos., 361 F.3d 335, 342 (7th Cir. 2004). Most courts conclude that the lawyer's negligence is not "extraordinary," and refuse to set aside a judgment on that basis. See, e.g., Dickerson v. Board of Educ., 32 F.3d 1114, 1118 (7th Cir. 1994).

8. As we saw in Chapter 6, a defendant may knowingly take a default judgment if she believes that the court lacks personal jurisdiction. Are there other circumstances in which a default judgment would be a sensible strategy? Allowing entry of default judgment obviates the need to answer and avoids discovery. (Of course, it results in liability too.) Some argued that after the Supreme Court rejected his immunity claim in a case against him by Paula Jones, President Clinton should have refused to participate in discovery and simply allowed entry of a default judgment. See NAN D. HUNTER, THE POWER OF PROCEDURE. THE LITIGATION OF *JONES V. CLINTON* 172–73 (2002).

E. Amended Pleadings

1. Basic Principles Under Rule 15(a)

Read Rule 15(a) before addressing the following.

Notes and Questions

1. Based upon Rule 15(a), work through these hypotheticals:

(a) Plaintiff files her complaint and has process properly served on Defendant on May 1. On May 10, before Defendant answers, Plaintiff files an amended complaint adding new claims and seeking an additional $6 million in damages. Did Plaintiff have a right to do this? Why?

(b) Plaintiff files her complaint and has process properly served on Defendant on May 1. Defendant serves and files a motion to dismiss under Rule 12(b)(6) on May 10. Reading Defendant's motion, Plaintiff realizes that Defendant is correct, since Plaintiff left out material allegations of her claim. On May 25 (before the hearing on Defendant's motion), Plaintiff files an amended complaint fixing the problem raised by Defendant's motion (and thereby mooting the motion). Did Plaintiff have a right to do this. Why? Suppose instead that Defendant served an answer, which demonstrated that Plaintiff's claim had omitted material allegations. Would Plaintiff have a right to file an amended complaint fixing that problem?

(c) Plaintiff files her complaint and has process properly served on Defendant on May 1. Defendant serves and files her answer on May 10. On May 22, Defendant files and serves an amended answer, correcting some errors in the original answer. Did Defendant have a right to do this? Why?

(d) If Plaintiff or Defendant had waited too long to take advantage of amendment as a matter of course, what showing would they have to make to be allowed to amend? Notice that Rule 15(a)(2) instructs that the court "should freely give leave when justice so requires."

(e) Return to Question 1(a). After Plaintiff serves and files his amended complaint on May 10, how long does Defendant have in which to respond?

2. Because the Federal Rules embody a preference for deciding controversies on their merits rather than on technicalities, courts have allowed amendment liberally. For instance, amendment generally will not be denied solely because it will substantially change the character of the action. The court has to find a weightier reason not to allow amendment. In the words of the Supreme Court:

> If the underlying facts or circumstances relied upon by a plaintiff may be a proper subject of relief, he ought to be afforded an opportunity to test his claim on the merits. In the absence of any apparent or declared reason—such as undue delay, bad faith or dilatory motive on the part of the movant, repeated failure to cure deficiencies by amendments previously allowed, undue prejudice to the opposing party by virtue of allowance of the amendment, futility of amendment, etc.—the leave sought should, as the rules require, be "freely given." Of course, the grant or denial of an opportunity to amend is within the discretion of the District Court.

Foman v. Davis, 371 U.S. 178, 182 (1962).

Review the list of examples in detail. The moving party may jeopardize her privilege of amendment by undue delay, bad faith, dilatory motive, or failure to cure problems with previous amendments. The court may also refuse amendment if it would result in undue prejudice to the opposing party or if the amendment would be futile. Can you give specific examples of the latter two? When would prejudice become "undue"? Couldn't prejudice always be abated by allowing the party opposing amendment more time to prepare for trial?

3. Although many cases involve amendment by the plaintiff, the rule applies equally to defendants. Suppose Plaintiff sued Manufacturer for injuries sustained while using a water slide. The complaint was filed October 15, 2012. Manufacturer's answer, served and filed within 21 days of service of process, admitted that it had manufactured the slide on which Plaintiff was injured, but denied liability. A year and a half later, Manufacturer's president inspected the slide and determined that Manufacturer had not built it. Manufacturer sought leave to amend its answer to deny manufacture of the slide. What result? What other factors would you determine relevant? See Beeck v. Aquaslide 'N' Dive Corp., 562 F.2d 537 (8th Cir. 1977) (affirming district court's grant of leave to amend).

4. Rule 15(a)(2) does not limit the time in which one can seek leave to amend. As a practical matter, however, the longer one waits to ask for leave to amend, the more likely it is that the other side can claim prejudice. See Nilsen v. City of Moss Point, 621 F.2d 117 (5th Cir. 1980).

5. There are due process limitations on a court's power to amend and enter judgment. In Nelson v. Adams USA, Inc., 529 U.S. 460 (2000), the trial court ordered a corporation to pay the attorney's fees of the other party to the litigation. When it became apparent that the corporation lacked sufficient funds to pay the fees, the other party moved to amend to add an individual (the owner and sole officer of the corporation) as a party. The trial court granted that motion and simultaneously entered an order against the individual, holding him liable for the attorney's fees. The Supreme Court held that this procedure violated the due process limitations reflected in Rules 12 and 15. The Rules envision that a party will have an opportunity to respond to a pleading that seeks affirmative recovery, and do not permit such "swift passage from pleading to judgment in the pleader's favor." What portions of Rules 12 and 15 reflect this due process concern?

6. Note how the policy of liberal amendment under the Federal Rules is facilitated by Rule 42(b).

2. The Problem of Variance Under Rule 15(b)

Suppose plaintiff's complaint alleges breach of contract, and at trial she introduces evidence that defendant breached a different contract, or committed a tort. The presentation of evidence on a point not covered in pleading is called *variance*. Some older opinions decided under code pleading rules were extremely harsh, holding that a plaintiff's failure to prove exactly what she pleaded was fatal, at least if the defendant raised the objection of variance.

For example, in Wabash Western Ry. Co. v. Friedman, 30 N.E. 353 (Ill. 1892), the plaintiff was injured when a train derailed. The wreck occurred between Kirksville and Glenwood Junction, Missouri, which was one leg of a longer trip that the plaintiff was taking from Moberly to Ottumwa. The plaintiff boarded the train at Moberly, bound for Ottumwa, but alleged in his complaint that he became a passenger at Kirksville, bound for Glenwood Junction. The Illinois Supreme Court reversed a $30,000 judgment in the plaintiff's favor, holding that the variance between what was pleaded and what was proved was fatal.

Wabash Western is an example of elevating form over substance. On the other hand, it is not ridiculous to require plaintiffs to be accurate in what they allege, at least as to things about which they have knowledge. Most likely, all code states today would be more forgiving on this point. The federal provision regarding variance is Rule 15(b), which you should read before answering the following questions. It concerns amendment during and after trial in reaction to evidence presented at trial. Rule 15(b)(1) addresses variance to which a party objects at trial; Rule 15(b)(2) concerns variance to which no objection is made.

Notes and Questions

1. Plaintiff sues for breach of Contract 1 and introduces evidence regarding Defendant's breach of Contract 1 and breach of Contract 2. Defendant does not object to introduction of the evidence regarding Contract 2. Does this constitute "implied consent" to trial regarding breach of Contract 2? Some courts say yes, at least if the evidence on Contract 2 did not also relate to Contract 1. If it did, then it seems unfair to conclude that the defendant knowingly consented to trial of Contract 2. See, e.g., Corsica Livestock Sales, Inc. v. Sumitomo Bank of Cal., 726 F.2d 374 (8th Cir. 1983) (finding consent); Southwestern Stationery & Bank Supply, Inc. v. Harris Corp., 624 F.2d 168 (10th Cir. 1980) (no consent where evidence was also relevant to pleaded issues).

The evidence beyond the scope of the pleadings need not relate to a different claim. It might, for example, simply support a different theoretical basis for the claim already asserted. Thus, in D. Federico Co. v. New Bedford Redevelopment Authority, 723 F.2d 122 (1st Cir. 1983), the court upheld amendment by implied consent to introduce an unpleaded equitable theory of recovery in a contract case.

Amendment to conform to the evidence can benefit defendants as well as the plaintiffs. For example, in Prinz v. Greate Bay Casino Corp., 705 F.2d 692 (3d Cir. 1983), the court held that the jury should have been allowed to consider a defense of claim preclusion (res judicata) which, while not pleaded, was tried by implied consent. Rule 15(b) permits a defendant to overcome the general rule that affirmative defenses not pleaded are waived. Fejta v. GAF Co., 800 F.2d 1395 (5th Cir. 1986). See generally 3 Moore's Federal Practice § 15.18. Of course, express consent, either by the plaintiff or defendant, will be more obvious, usually being embodied in a stipulation or pretrial conference order.

2. Again, assume Plaintiff sues for breach of Contract 1 and also introduces evidence of breach of Contract 2. Assuming the court finds implied consent to try the second contract claim, *must* it grant plaintiff leave to amend to conform to the evidence? Why? What effect would there be on the proceedings if Plaintiff did not seek leave to amend?

3. Plaintiff sues for patent infringement and then introduces evidence of a claim for unfair competition. Defendant objects to introduction of evidence on the latter claim.

(a) The court will sustain the objection and bar admission of the evidence. Why?

(b) After the court sustains the objection, what motion might Plaintiff want to make? What is the standard for granting that motion? How does this standard differ from the standard applied when seeking leave to amend under Rule 15(a)(2)?

4. In Brandon v. Holt, 469 U.S. 464 (1985), the plaintiffs brought a civil rights action against a police officer and a city's director of police. At the time the plaintiffs sued, cities could not be held liable for such violations, but that rule was changed shortly thereafter. The district court held for the plaintiffs, but the court of appeals reversed, holding that the director was immune from suit under relevant law. Id. at

471–72. The Supreme Court reinstated the judgment for the plaintiffs. It treated the complaint as amended to conform to the evidence and as stating a claim against the city itself, under the recent change in the law. The claim against the director was essentially a claim for damages against the city. *Brandon* is unusual in permitting amendment even on appeal. Almost all motions for amendment to conform to the evidence will be made in the trial court.

3. Amendment and the Statute of Limitations Under Rule 15(c)

a. Amendment to Claims or Defenses

The liberal policy of the Federal Rules' amendment provisions may clash with policies underlying other rules, notably statutes of limitations. These statutes impose temporal limits on asserting a claim. Thus, for example, such a statute might require a plaintiff asserting a claim for personal injuries to sue within two years after the accrual of the claim. Statutes of limitations vary from state to state. As a general rule, they give tort claimants a shorter period in which to sue than contract claimants. Such statutes are said to embody a policy of "repose"—meaning that after passage of a certain period, a defendant should be assured that she will not be sued for an act or omission. In addition, limitations rules may ensure that cases proceed while events are relatively fresh in the minds of witnesses.

These goals may be undermined if a plaintiff is permitted to amend her complaint to add a new claim after the relevant statute of limitations would have run. For example, suppose Plaintiff files suit before the statute of limitations runs. Then, after the statute would have run, she seeks leave to amend to state a new claim. Is the new claim barred by the statute of limitations? In other words, which policy—that supporting liberal amendment or that underlying the limitation of actions—should prevail? Read Rule 15(c)(1).

Marsh v. Coleman Company

774 F. Supp. 608 (D. Kan. 1991)

Crow, District Judge.

[Marsh started working for Coleman Company in 1960 as an industrial engineer in the Outing Products Group, which manufactured outdoor equipment and various thermal and marine products. After three years, he moved from the manufacturing side of the Outing Products Group to the design side of the same group. He worked in other capacities, as detailed in the opinion below. Coleman terminated Marsh's employment on January 20, 1988.

[Marsh filed suit on January 19, 1990, alleging that the termination was in breach of contract and violated the federal Age Discrimination in Employment Act, 29 U.S.C. § 621, et seq. On November 5, 1990, Marsh sought leave to amend his complaint to add a claim for fraud, based on alleged representations made by his superiors in 1985.

Coleman opposed the motion for leave to amend, and argued that the fraud claim was barred by the applicable two-year Kansas statute of limitations. Marsh argued that the fraud claim could take advantage of relation back under what is now Rule 15(c)(1)(B).]

During his years at the Coleman Company the plaintiff enjoyed several promotions and advancements. One of his highest achievements occurred in 1969, when the plaintiff was made Director of Design Engineering for the Outing Products Group. He held that position until 1985 when he became Director of Manufacturing for the Manufactured Housing (Mobile Home) Division of the Heating and Air Conditioning Group.

The plaintiff's move in 1985 was due to several events. In 1984, Sheldon C. Coleman ("Sheldon Junior") became the General Manager for the Outing Products Group. Around the same time, the Outing Products Group was broken down into several divisions causing the question whether the employees of the Design Department would still have jobs. After the divisionalization occurred, discussions between Sheldon Junior and the plaintiff concluded that no positions remained for the plaintiff in the new organization of the group. Sheldon Junior told the plaintiff that a divisionalization was also occurring in the Heating and Air Conditioning Group and that he should contact Bob Hoffman, Manager of the Manufactured Housing Division of the Heating and Air Conditioning Group, about a position as Director of Manufacturing in the Mobile Home Division. Around this same time, the plaintiff met with Sheldon Senior about the concerns of employees in the Design Department over the reorganization. Sheldon Senior told the plaintiff to assure his employees that there would be jobs for everyone in his department after the divisionalization.

The plaintiff was interviewed and hired by Bob Hoffman for the position of Director of Manufacturing for the Mobile Home Division, effective January, 1985. Hoffman was Marsh's immediate supervisor. Don Berchtold headed up the entire Heating and Air Conditioning Group. In 1985, this group was divided into three divisions: Manufactured Housing (Mobile Homes), Residential, and Recreational Vehicles.

In February of 1985, the Outing Products Group held a party to honor the plaintiff. Sheldon Junior spoke to the Group praising Marsh's accomplishments in design. Marsh recalls that Sheldon Junior said, among other things, that "there will always be a place for Bill Marsh at the Coleman Company."

In May of 1987, Hoffman and Marsh transferred from the Manufactured Housing Division to the Residential Division of the Group. On January 2, 1988, Marsh received a memorandum sent to all weekly and monthly salaried employees from Berchtold dated December 31, 1987, stating that the Manufactured Housing Division and the Residential Division would be merged, explaining the business reasons for that decision, and naming the heads for the various combined departments. Joe Nold was designated to head up the manufacturing operation.

After January 2, 1988, the plaintiff recalled having several conversations with Joe Nold. Nold told Marsh: "Don't worry, you're working for the world's nicest guy now;

everything's going to be all right. And what I want you to do is just continue what you're doing and just sit back, relax, don't worry." Marsh also remembered Nold calling on another occasion and saying everything was fine and not to worry.

Nold's responsibility was to decide who was to remain in the combined division and to select a staff who would report directly to him. Nold decided to streamline the manufacturing operation and reduce the number of employees by twenty-nine. Nold and his staff considered each of existing manufacturing employees in both divisions for the remaining positions. The plaintiff was not selected by Nold for any of the positions. Nold's reason was that other employees had skills and abilities better suited for the particular positions required in the streamlined operation. * * *

On January 20, 1988, Nold met with Marsh and told him that he was one of thirty people being let go as a result of the divisions combining. At that time, Nold also went over Marsh's separation package which included regular pay through January 31, 1988, unused vacation pay, and then ten months severance pay at his current base salary. * * * Following the ten months of severance pay, Marsh took early retirement with Coleman Company.

[In his motion for leave to amend, Marsh] alleges he was defrauded in one or more of the following particulars:

(1) by falsely representing through its agent, Sheldon C. Coleman (Sheldon Junior):

(a) there would be jobs available for everyone in the Design Group, including the plaintiff;

(b) that employees in the Design Group need not be concerned about their jobs;

(c) that the plaintiff would have permanent employment with defendant as long as there was a Coleman Company.

(2) by enticing the plaintiff not to look for other employment as a result of the representations of Sheldon C. Coleman, which representations were relied upon by the plaintiff and which representations caused the plaintiff to forego seeking other job opportunities during the period 1984 until the date of his termination.

(3) by falsely representing through its agent Sheldon Coleman (Sheldon Senior), that there would be jobs for everyone in the plaintiff's group.

(4) by expressly or impliedly approving the false statements of Sheldon C. Coleman, through its then president Sheldon Coleman (Senior).

(5) by falsely representing to the plaintiff through its agent, Joe Nold, on numerous occasions, not to worry about his position in the company and that everything would be fine.

(6) by enticing the plaintiff over a period of years to believe that his position was permanently secure when, in fact, defendant had no intention of providing the plaintiff job security.

The plaintiff did not allege a fraud claim in his original complaint filed January 19, 1990. On November 5, 1990, the plaintiff moved for leave to amend his complaint to include [the claim for fraud]. * * *

Defendant contends the fraud claim is barred by the statute of limitations and does not relate back to the filing of the original complaint. In the alternative, defendant argues the the plaintiff is unable to prove the elements to his claims of fraudulent promises. The plaintiff responds that the fraud claims come within the terms of Fed. R. Civ. P. 15(c) [now 15(c)(1)(B)] and properly relate back to the original complaint * * *.

* * * Rule 15(c)[(1)(B)] is built upon the premise that once notified of pending litigation over particular conduct or a certain transaction or occurrence, the defendant has been given all the notice required for purposes of the statute of limitations. Baldwin County Welcome Center v. Brown, 466 U.S. 147, 149 n.3 (1984). The linchpin to Rule 15(c)[(1)(B)] is notice before the limitations period expires. Relation back does not offend the notice policies underlying a statute of limitations if the original complaint fairly discloses the general fact situation out of which the new claims arise. 3 James W. Moore & Richard D. Freer, Moore's Federal Practice ¶ 15.15[2] at 15-144, 145 (1985). Amendments will relate back if they only flesh out the factual details, change the legal theory, or add another claim arising out of the same transaction, occurrence or conduct. Relation back is denied those amendments which are based on entirely different facts, transactions, and occurrences. Holmes v. Greyhound Lines, Inc., 757 F.2d 1563, 1566 (5th Cir. 1985).

Looking back at the plaintiff's original complaint, he limited his factual allegations to his termination on January 20, 1988, to the reasons given for his termination, to his replacement being younger, and to the defendant's actions being in breach of his employment contract. All alleged events occurred on January 20, 1988, or after. The complaint made no reference to any transactions or event occurring in 1984 or 1985. None of the claims were based on promises by defendant that the plaintiff would always have employment with it. Not until his amended complaint did the plaintiff ever allege that defendant's agents made fraudulent statements to him prior to his discharge. For that matter, the plaintiff never sought damages for lost employment opportunities until he added his new claim for fraud. The only factual overlap between the plaintiff's fraud claim and his original claims is that his employment with defendant ended on January 20, 1988. Other than this, the claims are based on events and transactions that are distinct in time and not closely related. A reasonably prudent person would not have expected from reading the plaintiff's original complaint that promises made to the plaintiff before termination, in particular those made more than three years earlier, might be called into question through subsequent pleadings. * * *

The plaintiff's promissory fraud claims are based on conduct substantially different in kind and time from that alleged in the plaintiff's original complaint. The crux of a promissory fraud claim is not that the promisor breached his promise to perform, rather it is that the promisor fraudulently represented his present intent to perform. Defendant had no reason to anticipate from reading the plaintiff's original complaint that it should prepare to defend a case based on acts more than three years earlier. For these reasons, the court finds the plaintiff's fraud claim does not relate back to the filing of the original complaint and, therefore, is barred by the two-year statute of limitations.

Notes and Questions

1. Explain how relation back, if applicable in *Marsh*, would have saved the plaintiff's fraud claim. Explain the justification for allowing relation back.

2. It is not clear that all courts would have reached the same result as the court in *Marsh*. Indeed, the court's interpretation of the relation-back provision of Rule 15(c)(1)(B) seems narrow. Can you make an argument that the events underlying the fraud claim were part of the same "conduct, transaction, or occurrence" as the termination of Mr. Marsh's employment in 1988? After all, it certainly seems that Mr. Marsh's firing violated the reassurances given to him through the years, including on January 1, 1988. The court in *Marsh* does a good job of explaining why and when relation back is appropriate, but appears stingy in applying the principle to the facts of the case.

3. Suppose Mr. Marsh had not sought leave to amend and that his case proceeded to trial. Suppose he then proffered evidence on the fraud claim. If the defendant objected to that evidence on the basis of variance, how would the court rule? If the defendant failed to object to that evidence, would the court amend to conform to the evidence after trial? Would such amendment relate back?

4. Should relation back be permitted if the new claim would add considerably more exposure for the defendant? For example, suppose that the amended claim, although meeting the "conduct, transaction, or occurrence" standard, allowed the plaintiff to seek punitive and other damages far exceeding the original claim. Does Rule 15 speak to this possibility?

b. Amendment Changing a Party

Marsh involved amendment to add a claim after the statute of limitations had run. A more difficult (but less common) problem deals with relation back when an amendment adds a new party after the statute of limitations has run. The issue is now addressed in Rule 15(c)(1)(C). That rule contemplates a very narrow class of cases, in which the "wrong" party is joined before the statute of limitations runs, but in which the "right" party somehow knows about the case and that it should have been involved.

For example, suppose Plaintiff attempted to sue Fortune magazine for defamation. In her complaint, Plaintiff named "Fortune" as defendant and described it as a New York corporation with its principal place of business in the Time and Life Building in New York. In fact, however, there is no such entity. "Fortune" is a trademark and division of Time, Incorporated, which should have been named as the defendant. Plaintiff filed her complaint before the statute of limitations ran, and had process served on Time's registered agent.

Because of service on Time's registered agent, two requirements of the rule were met: (1) Time, Incorporated, was charged with notice of the suit (Rule 15(c)(1)(C)(i)), and (2) it was obvious to Time that "but for a mistake concerning the proper party's identity" the action would have been brought against it (Rule 15(c)(1)(C)(ii)). Relation back would depend upon whether these requirements were met within the time prescribed by the Rule, or "within the period provided by Rule 4(m) for serving the summons and complaint." Thus, if the service on Time, Incorporated were effected within that period — even though that may be after the statute of limitations would have run in the interim — the court will allow relation back.

In Krupski v. Costa Crociere S.p.A., 560 U.S. 538 (2010), the Court held that relation back depends upon the knowledge of the party to be joined, and not the plaintiff. Thus, it is the party to be joined that must know, within the period under Rule 4(m) that it should have been named but for a mistake. The plaintiff's knowledge or lack thereof is not the test.

F. Supplemental Pleadings

Read Rule 15(d).

A supplemental pleading sets forth events occurring after a pleading is filed. This does not include facts that occurred before the original filing but which were discovered after filing. As to such facts, amendment is the proper course. Supplemental pleadings update the dispute by bringing such new facts to the attention of the court, even if they change the relief sought or add additional parties.

A supplemental pleading is allowed only with court permission; there is no such thing as supplementation as of right. Nonetheless, the same policies we saw with amendment counsel the liberal reading of Rule 15(d). Thus, courts freely grant leave to supplement, unless there is undue delay, prejudice, or bad faith. For example, in Twin Disc, Inc. v. Big Bud Tractor, Inc., 772 F.2d 1329 (7th Cir. 1985), the plaintiff sought leave to supplement one week before trial to add additional alleged failures to pay for goods delivered to the defendant. The defendant lacked notice of the additional amounts claimed and would require discovery to prepare adequately to meet the allegations. The court denied the plaintiff's motion to file the supplemental pleading, concluding that the trial should not be delayed. The Seventh Circuit affirmed, holding that the district judge had not abused his discretion in so ruling.

G. Veracity in Pleading: Rule 11 and Other Devices

1. Rule 11

The original version of Rule 11, included in the 1938 Rules, required that attorneys have "good grounds to support" their pleading. The Rule permitted, but did not require, the imposition of sanctions for violations. Courts found violations only if the attorney was guilty of subjective bad faith. In the first forty years of its existence, Rule 11 was invoked in fewer than a dozen reported cases.

This all changed in 1983. In reaction to a perceived need to curb frivolous litigation, the Supreme Court amended the rule in that year to require counsel to certify various specifics about the paper they signed, all aimed at ensuring the assertions were grounded in law and fact, after reasonable investigation. Interestingly, the amended rule *required* courts to impose sanctions for violations.*

This 1983 version of Rule 11 unleashed a torrent of litigation. Critics noted major problems with the provision. First, it had a "chilling" effect on plaintiffs, urging them not to be zealous in asserting new theories. Second, it created a great deal of wasteful "satellite litigation" over whether a party had run afoul of its provisions. Third, the required sanctions struck many as draconian. And finally, observers concluded that Rule 11 deteriorated lawyer professionalism and civility in litigation. See Interim Report of the Committee on Civility of the Seventh Circuit, 143 F.R.D. 371, 389 (1991).

In the face of such criticism, the Supreme Court amended Rule 11 again in 1993. This version has its critics as well, including Justices Scalia and Thomas, who opposed promulgation of the new Rule, arguing that it "gutted" Rule 11. 146 F.R.D. at 507–10. Professor Stempel offered this insightful explanation for the divergent views of the Rule:

> [T]he sanctions debate is a distributional political battle that has some unavoidable aspects of a zero-sum game. If Rule 11 is written or interpreted stringently, some claims are sacrificed in the name of efficiency, deterring the unfounded or abusive, and thinning court dockets. If Rule 11's text or application is made more forgiving, some of these values are sacrificed in favor of zealous advocacy, innovative lawyering, and claimants' rights. Because some lawyers tend to favor the access/advocacy/innovation goals while others prefer the efficiency/expense/ deterrence goals, no theory of Rule 11 can hope to satisfy all sides of the sanctions debate completely.

Jeffrey Stempel, *Sanction, Symmetry, and Safe Harbors: Limiting Misapplications of Rule 11 By Harmonizing It with Pre-Verdict Dismissal Devices*, 60 FORDHAM L. REV. 257, 260–61 (1991).

Before we address the current version of Rule 11, we note two Supreme Court decisions which, though interpreting the older version of Rule 11, undoubtedly remain good law. They concern a federal court's authority to impose Rule 11 sanctions even when it might lack jurisdiction. In Cooter & Gell v. Hartmarx Corp., 496 U.S. 384 (1990), the Court held that a district court can impose Rule 11 sanctions on the plaintiff and its attorney for inadequate pre-filing inquiry, even after the plaintiff had voluntarily dismissed the suit; the voluntary dismissal neither cured the defect nor deprived the court of jurisdiction to impose sanctions.

And in Willy v. Coastal Corp., 503 U.S. 131 (1992), the Court held that a district court may impose Rule 11 sanctions in a case in which the court is later determined

* Recall the prevailing party in any case will recover "costs" from the losing party under Federal Rule 54(d). "Costs" are limited, however, to various litigation expenses such as filing fees and other charges by the clerk of the court, witness and discovery fees. They do not include attorney's fees, which will always be the most significant amount of expense. One of the reasons Rule 11 has generated such intense debate is that it permits the recovery of attorney's fees.

to be without subject matter jurisdiction. The case was originally filed in state court and the defendant removed it to federal court. The plaintiff objected to the removal on the grounds of lack of subject matter jurisdiction, but the district court rejected the argument. Then the plaintiff moved for partial summary judgment and the defendant moved to dismiss for failure to state a claim. While these motions were pending, the plaintiff twice more moved unsuccessfully for remand. The district court granted the defendant's motion to dismiss and imposed Rule 11 sanctions on the plaintiff for bringing a baseless motion for summary judgment which confused the proceedings. The court of appeals held that the district court lacked subject matter jurisdiction, but nonetheless affirmed the imposition of sanctions. The Supreme Court unanimously affirmed. Plaintiff's lawyer was sanctioned nearly $23,000 because the district court found that the summary judgment motion "create[d] a blur of absolute confusion." Although it ultimately lacked subject matter jurisdiction, the district court had power to impose sanctions.

Rule 11 is not the only source of standards for proper conduct in litigation. The Rules of Professional Responsibility also address this issue. Although each state bar has its own rules governing professional responsibility, and there are some important variations among these, we have reproduced below some of the relevant rules from the American Bar Association's MODEL RULES OF PROFESSIONAL CONDUCT. Read these rules, then read Rule 11 and the 1993 Advisory Committee Notes to Rule 11.

Model Rules of Professional Conduct

Rule 3.1: A lawyer shall not bring or defend a proceeding, or assert or controvert an issue therein, unless there is a basis in law and fact for doing so that is not frivolous, which includes a good faith argument for an extension, modification or reversal of existing law. A lawyer for the defendant in a criminal proceeding, or the respondent in a proceeding that could result in incarceration, may nonetheless so defend the proceeding as to require that every element of the case be established.

Rule 3.2: A lawyer shall make reasonable efforts to expedite litigation consistent with the interests of the client.

Rule 3.3: (a) A lawyer shall not knowingly:

(1) make a false statement of material fact or law to a tribunal or fail to correct a false statement of material fact or law previously made to the tribunal by the lawyer;

(2) fail to disclose to the tribunal legal authority in the controlling jurisdiction known to the lawyer to be directly adverse to the position of the client and not disclosed by opposing counsel; or

(3) offer evidence that the lawyer knows to be false. If a lawyer has offered material evidence and comes to know of its falsity, the lawyer shall take reasonable remedial measures.

(b) A lawyer who represents a client in an adjudicative proceeding and who knows that a person intends to engage, is engaging or has engaged in criminal or fraudulent conduct related to the proceeding shall take reasonable remedial measures, including, if necessary, disclosure to the tribunal.

(c) The duties stated in paragraphs (a) and (b) continue to the conclusion of the proceeding, and apply even if compliance requires disclosure of information otherwise protected by [the duty of confidentiality].

(d) In an ex parte proceeding, a lawyer shall inform the tribunal of all material facts known to the lawyer which will enable the tribunal to make an informed decision, whether or not the facts are adverse.

Rule 3.4: A lawyer shall not:

(a) unlawfully obstruct another party's access to evidence or unlawfully alter, destroy or conceal a document or other material having potential evidentiary value. A lawyer shall not counsel or assist another person to do any such act;

(b) falsify evidence, counsel or assist a witness to testify falsely, or offer an inducement to a witness that is prohibited by law;

(c) knowingly disobey an obligation under the rules of a tribunal, except for an open refusal based on an assertion that no valid obligation exists;

(d) in pretrial procedure, make a frivolous discovery request or fail to make reasonably diligent effort to comply with a legally proper discovery request by an opposing party;

(e) in trial, allude to any matter that the lawyer does not reasonably believe is relevant or that will not be supported by admissible evidence, assert personal knowledge of facts in issue except when testifying as a witness, or state a personal opinion as to the justness of a cause, the credibility of a witness, the culpability of a civil litigant or the guilt or innocence of an accused; or

(f) request a person other than a client to refrain from voluntarily giving relevant information to another party unless:

(1) the person is a relative or an employee or other agent of a client; and

(2) the lawyer reasonably believes that the person's interest will not be adversely affected by refraining from giving such information.

Rule 4.1 Truthfulness in Statements to Others

In the course of representing a client a lawyer shall not knowingly:

(a) make a false statement of material fact or law to a third person; or

(b) fail to disclose a material fact when disclosure is necessary to avoid assisting a criminal or fraudulent act by a client, unless disclosure is prohibited by Rule 1.6.

Notes and Questions

Read Rule 11, then consider the following:

1. Who makes the Rule 11 certification? How does she do so? When does she do so? Note that the certification attaches to every "presenting" of any "pleading, written

motion, or other paper." Rule 11(b). When does such presenting occur? Explain how this puts counsel under an ongoing duty to assess whether a position continues to be tenable under Rule 11.

2. What is the certification made under Rule 11(b)? Consider the following:

(a) What is "an inquiry reasonable under the circumstances"? Suppose Client comes to your office at 5:50 p.m. on the day before the statute of limitations would run. If her complaint is not filed by 5:00 p.m. the following day, her claim will be barred forever. Her story, if true, would entitle her to recovery. What inquiry must you undertake before drafting and filing the complaint? How would your answer differ if she came to your office ten days earlier?

(b) What is a "nonfrivolous" argument for change in the law under Rule 11(b)(2)? One court, in an opinion before adoption of the present version of Rule 11, said "[s]ometimes there are reasons to sue even when one cannot win. Bad court decisions must be challenged if they are to be overruled, but the early challenges are certainly hopeless." Eastway Construction Corp. v. City of New York, 637 F. Supp. 558, 575 (E.D.N.Y. 1986). If the "bad court decision" you wished to challenge was established by a Supreme Court opinion last year, in which one Justice dissented, would your advocating the dissent's position be "nonfrivolous"? What if the case were decided ten years ago? What if four Justices dissented?

(c) When may a plaintiff allege that she is likely to find evidentiary support later? When may a defendant deny allegations based solely upon her information and belief?

3. Rule 11 does not *require* the imposition of sanctions for violation. What language of the rule makes this clear? Why shouldn't sanctions for violating Rule 11 be mandatory?

(a) On whom can sanctions be imposed under Rule 11(c)? Under what circumstance can a monetary sanction be imposed only on counsel, and not on the party? Why does this limitation make sense? When can a law firm be sanctioned for the errors of its employee?

(b) What is the goal of sanctions? What are appropriate sanctions? What non-monetary sanctions are possible?

(c) Note that no sanctions of any kind can be imposed without notice and an opportunity to be heard.

(d) When can a party recover attorney's fees under Rule 11?

(e) Can you think of any "nonmonetary directives" under Rule 11(c)(4)?

4. Rule 11 violations may be raised by the court sua sponte. What is the procedure for this?

5. Consider *McCormick*, which we discussed in Section C.1.f of this chapter. There, a man was killed in an auto collision. It was unclear whether the decedent was intoxicated at the time of the wreck. His widow sued for wrongful death, and joined

both the driver of the other vehicle and the owner of a bar that had served alcohol to the decedent before the wreck. To prevail against the other driver, the plaintiff had to show that the decedent was not negligent. To prevail against the bar owner on a dram shop theory, she had to show that the decedent was visibly intoxicated when served with alcohol. Clearly, only one of those theories can be right. Alleging the two claims was proper under Rule 8(d). But did alleging these alternative theories violate Rule 11?

6. The most controversial provision in Rule 11 is probably the 21-day "safe harbor" in Rule 11(c)(2). The following case addresses this and other aspects of the Rule.

Rector v. Approved Federal Savings Bank

265 F.3d 248 (4th Cir. 2001)

Gregory, Circuit Judge.

In this case of first impression, we must decide whether the 21-day "safe harbor" provision of Fed. R. Civ. P. 11 is a non-waivable rule of jurisdiction. We hold that it is not a jurisdictional rule and affirm the district court's assessment of sanctions.

I.

On April 9, 1999, Virginia attorney Edwin Rector ("Rector"), personally and as trustee for the Edwin Rector 1995 Charitable Remainder Trust ("the Trust"), filed suit against Approved Financial Corporation, Approved Financial Federal Savings Bank, Coopers and Lybrand, PriceWaterhouse Coopers, Allen D. Wykle, Stephen R. Kinner, Peter Coode, Patrick M. Barberich, and Gray Lambe (collectively "Approved"), seeking "at least 60 billion dollars" in compensatory damages and an additional 20 billion dollars in punitive damages. The suit arose from a 1995 agreement in which Rector and the Trust agreed to sell to Approved all of Rector's majority interest in First Security Federal Savings Bank. Closing occurred on September 11, 1996. Rector and the Trust claimed that the contract required Approved to pay "at least 20 billion dollars" more than the $3,157,743 purchase price.

On July 3, 1999, the district court dismissed Rector and the Trust's conspiracy, RICO [a federal statute creating a claim for racketeering-type activity], and fraud claims, finding that they failed to state fraud and RICO with particularity [as required by applicable law] and that no private right of action existed for bank fraud under [federal law]. The order allowed Rector and the Trust to file an amended complaint, which they did on August 10, 1999. Among other things, Rector and the Trust amended the complaint by changing the ad damnum clause from 60 billion dollars to "an infinite amount of money." On September 17, 1999, the district court granted Approved's motion to dismiss all claims.

On September 27, 1999, Approved filed a motion for sanctions under Fed. R. Civ. P. 11. The motion states that Approved served it on Rector and the Trust on June 11, 1999. In this appeal, though, Rector and the Trust contend that they did not receive the motion until September 27, 1999, in contravention of the 21-day "safe harbor" provision of Rule 11. Approved concedes that it "cannot now confirm the notice was [served] as intended." * * * Rather, Approved states that on June 11, 1999, [Approved] served [Rector and the Trust] with [its] Objections to Plaintiffs' First Request for Production of Documents, [its] initial Motion to Dismiss * * * and [its] Memorandum in Support of such motion. [It] also believed that the Federal Express package containing these three items also included a Notice of Motion and Motion for the Award of Litigation Expenses and so certified that pleading. * * * [Approved] cannot confirm that the notice and motion were included in the June 11, 1999 Federal Express packet as intended and as believed and it is possible that a clerical error resulted in their inadvertent omission.

* * * Additionally, counsel for another party submitted an affidavit stating that he was not served with the motion until September 27, 1999.

Importantly, though, Rector and the Trust's opposition to the motion for sanctions argued only that they conducted an appropriate pre-filing investigation. They did not argue that the motion failed to comply with the 21-day "safe harbor" provision of Rule 11.

On January 14, 2000, the district court entered a Memorandum Order granting Approved's motion for sanctions and attorney's fees and ordering Rector and the Trust to pay Approved $33,503.82. On appeal, though, this Court vacated and remanded the suit, explaining that the district court applied an incorrect standard. [This] Court vacated the district court's judgment and remanded the matter "so that the district court may apply the proper standard in assessing the Rule 11 sanctions." Notably, on appeal, Rector and the Trust did not argue that the sanctions motion failed to comply with the Rule's "safe harbor" provision.

During Rector's deposition following remand, he testified that the Trust contained assets of "something over" $1,000,000, that he is the Trust's sole income beneficiary, and that the Trust pays him two distributions annually in an amount equaling twelve percent of the Trust's assets. Rector testified that he received approximately $230,000 in income distributions from the Trust in 1999, received approximately $100,000 on June 30, 2000, and would receive the same amount on December 31, 2000. Rector testified that he also has several checking and savings accounts in a combined amount of approximately $163,000, and that he owns his home and a condominium in Florida. He pays approximately $2,000/month on the home mortgage and approximately $450/month on the condominium mortgage, which represent his only liabilities. Rector further testified that he is not married and has no financial dependents, and that the Trust similarly has no significant liabilities.

On this record, and without any argument by Rector or the Trust about Approved's service of the Rule 11 motion, the district court once again imposed a sanction of $33,503.82. In its January 4, 2001 Memorandum Opinion, the district court explained that

> the dismissal of the Complaints in their entirety, the finding of Rule 11 liability for frivolous claims and the finding that the attorney's fees and costs sought were reasonable, supports this award of sanctions under Rule 11. In view of

> Rector's deposition concerning his and the Trust's ability to pay and the continuing litigation in state court after imposition of the sanction, it is clear that all of the elements of the [In re] Kunstler[, 914 F.2d 505 (4th Cir. 1990),] analysis have been met and the amount of the sanction is appropriate.

II.

The only meritorious argument raised in this appeal is whether the 21-day "safe harbor" provision of Rule 11[(c)(2)] is a non-waivable jurisdictional rule. Under [that provision], a Rule 11 motion for sanctions "shall be served [on the opposing party] but shall not be filed with or presented to the court unless, within 21 days after service of the motion ..., the challenged paper, claim, defense, contention, allegation, or denial is not withdrawn or appropriately corrected." The Rule further provides that the motion "shall be made separately from other motions or requests and shall describe the specific conduct alleged to violate" the Rule. [Note: the rule has since been restyled to change this language slightly, but retains the safe harbor provision.]

Congress amended Rule 11 in 1993 by adding the 21-day "safe harbor" provision. The primary purpose for this amendment was to provide immunity from sanctions to those litigants who self-regulate by withdrawing potentially offending filings or contentions within the 21-day period. The Advisory Committee Notes to Rule 11's 1993 Amendments explain that the

> provisions are intended to provide a type of "safe harbor" against motions under Rule 11 in that a party will not be subject to sanctions on the basis of another party's motion unless, after receiving the motion, it refuses to withdraw that position or to acknowledge candidly that it does not currently have evidence to support a specified allegation. Under the former rule, parties were sometimes reluctant to abandon a questionable contention lest that be viewed as evidence of a violation of Rule 11; under the revision, the timely withdrawal of a contention will protect a party against a motion for sanctions.

Through this self-regulation, the amendment also worked "to reduce the number of motions for sanctions presented to the court." Fed. R. Civ. P. 11 Advisory Committee Notes (1993 Amendments).

Several courts have termed the "safe harbor" provision "mandatory" or an "absolute requirement." See Ridder [v. City of Springfield], 109 F.3d [288] at 294 [(6th Cir. 1997)] (safe harbor provision is "absolute requirement"); Aerotech, Inc. v. Estes, 110 F.3d 1523, 1529 (10th Cir. 1997) (safe harbor provision is "mandatory"); Elliott v. Tilton, 64 F.3d 213, 216 (5th Cir. 1995) (same); Hadges v. Yonkers Racing Corp., 48 F.3d 1320, 1328 (2d Cir. 1995) (reversing sanctions award in part because no evidence indicated compliance with safe harbor period); Thomas v. Treasury Management Ass'n, 158 F.R.D. 364, 369 (D. Md. 1994) (finding that failure to comply with the "absolute[] prerequisite" of the safe harbor provision precludes imposition of sanctions).

While these cases may stand for the proposition that the safe harbor provision is mandatory, they do not stand for the proposition that it is jurisdictional. Not only do the cases fail to define the requirement as a rule of jurisdiction, but nothing in the language of the Rule supports such a conclusion. While Rule 11 does, indeed, state that a sanctions motion "shall be served" [Note: it now says "must be served"] at least 21 days before it is filed, the Rule also states that the motion "shall be made separately from other motions" and "shall describe the specific conduct" violating Rule 11. [Note: again, the precise language was amended in 2007, but not to change the meaning.] Neither Rector nor the Trust contends that federal courts lack jurisdiction over Rule 11 motions that are not "made separately from other motions" or those that do not "describe the specific conduct" purportedly violating Rule 11. The use of the word "shall" is not determinative to this analysis.

Further evidence that the safe harbor provision is not jurisdictional is found in the Advisory Committee Notes accompanying Rule 11. The Notes explain that the safe harbor provision was added to Rule 11, in part, to help reduce the number of sanctions motions filed in the courts. The number would be reduced not by narrowing the courts' jurisdiction, but by giving litigants a specific amount of time in which to withdraw an offending filing or allegation before a motion is filed. As the Notes explain, "under the former rule, parties were sometimes reluctant to abandon a questionable contention lest that be viewed as evidence of a violation of Rule 11; under the revision, the timely withdrawal of a contention will protect a party against a motion for sanctions." This, in turn, would "reduce the number of motions for sanctions presented to the courts." Nothing in the Advisory Committee Notes suggests that the number of motions filed would be reduced by narrowing the power of the federal courts to address such motions. The Notes simply do not address the courts' authority to entertain Rule 11 motions, regardless of whether the motions were filed in compliance with or in violation of the safe harbor provision.

An analogy can be drawn to the statutes of limitation context. A statute of limitation requires a litigant to file a claim within a specified period * * *. If the litigant files the claim after the time period expires, the defendant may assert the statute of limitation as an affirmative defense. Importantly, the litigant's untimely filing does not preclude the court from addressing the claim; the court does not lack jurisdiction simply because the litigant filed an untimely claim. Rather, the court may address the claim, limited only by the defendant's assertion of a statute of limitation defense. Moreover, the defendant may waive the defense by failing to raise it.

Similarly, a movant filing under Rule 11 must serve the motion at least 21 days before filing it with the court. If the movant files the motion less than 21 days after giving notice, the party against whom the motion is filed may assert the 21-day safe harbor provision as a defense. Should the litigant fail to do so, the defense is waived.

A distinction, on the other hand, can be made with Fed. R. App. P. 4, which states that, "in a civil case ... the notice of appeal ... must be filed with the district court clerk within 30 days after the judgment or order appealed from is entered." Courts clearly consider the Rule's 30-day limitation "mandatory and jurisdictional." Browder v. Director, Dep't. of Corrections, 434 U.S. 257, 264 (1978). No court, though, has used such language to describe Rule 11's safe harbor provision, instead calling it merely "mandatory" or an "absolute prerequisite."

Moreover, a significant difference exists between Fed. R. App. P. 4 and Fed. R. Civ. P. 11. Rule 4 "sets a definite point of time when litigation shall be at an end, unless within that time the prescribed application has been made; and if it has not, to advise prospective appellees that they are freed of the appellant's demands." *Browder*, 434 U.S. at 264 (quoting Matton Steamboat Co. v. Murphy, 319 U.S. 412, 415 (1943)). Rule 4 allows for finality by requiring the filing of a document with the court within a specific period of time. Rule 11, on the other hand, does no such thing, merely instructing litigants about the time periods involved in the service and filing of a motion for sanctions.

Accordingly, we hold that the 21-day safe harbor provision of Rule 11 is not jurisdictional and may be waived.[5] Here, it is undisputed that neither Rector nor the Trust objected to Approved's service of the Rule 11 motion until the case reached this Court on its second appeal, after remand.[6] Neither Rector nor the Trust raised the argument to the district court in the first instance nor raised it to this Court in their first appeal. When presented with that appeal, we vacated the district court's opinion and remanded solely "so that the district court may apply the proper standard in assessing the Rule 11 sanctions." Our remand order did not allow the district court to consider any issue other than the proper assessment of the sanction amount.[7] Rector and the Trust's failure to raise Approved's failure to comply with the 21-day

---

5. Even if we were to find the safe harbor provision a jurisdictional rule, we nonetheless would find it waivable. While subject matter jurisdiction "delimits federal-court power" and serves institutional interests by "keeping the federal courts within the bounds" prescribed by the Constitution and Congress, it "must be policed by the courts" at all times and, thus, is not waivable. Ruhrgas, AG v. Marathon Oil Co., 526 U.S. 574, 583 (1999). On the other hand, personal jurisdiction restricts a court's jurisdiction over the person, "protecting individual rights." Id. Personal jurisdiction "represents a restriction on judicial power ... as a matter of individual liberty." Id. at 584. Thus, "a party must insist that the limitation be observed, or he may forgo that right, effectively consenting to the court's exercise of adjudicatory authority." Id. (quoting Insurance Corp. of Ireland v. Compagnie des Bauxites de Guinee, 456 U.S. 694, 702 (1982)). Accordingly, personal jurisdiction is waivable.

Here, the safe harbor provision was added to Rule 11 primarily to provide litigants the opportunity of avoiding sanctions by withdrawing offending filings or contentions within the 21-day period and, thereby, reducing the number of sanctions motions brought before the courts. See, e.g., *Ridder*, 109 F.3d at 294. Thus, the provision protects litigants; it does not establish a structural limitation on the power of the courts. Accordingly, it was incumbent upon Rector and the Trust to "insist that the limitation be observed, or ... forgo that right."

6. The dissent refers to Rector and the Trust as "hapless" victims, without any fault for any of the judicial events occurring after June 11, 1999, the date on which Approved purportedly served its Rule 11 motion. In fact, Rector and the Trust are primarily at fault for virtually every event that occurred after that date. Had they merely notified the district court on or after September 27, 1999, when Approved filed its Rule 11 motion, that Approved failed to comply with the safe harbor provision, every event that occurred thereafter (including this appeal) could have been avoided.

7. Curiously, the dissent fails even to mention our previous opinion in this case, which reviewed the merits of the sanctions award and remanded and vacated the decision on the sole issue of the amount of the sanctions award. Following remand, the only issue before the district court, and before this Court on appeal, is the calculation of the sanction amount, not the propriety of the sanction award.

safe harbor provision in the district court in the first instance constituted a waiver of this argument.

III.

For the foregoing reasons, the judgment of the district court is affirmed. *Affirmed.*

KING, CIRCUIT JUDGE, dissenting:

Stripped to its essence, the question before us is not whether a party may defeat a motion for Rule 11 sanctions by complaining it has received insufficient notice of the proceeding against it, and therefore no meaningful opportunity to cure the alleged defect in its submission to the court. The language of the Rule is plain, and the majority does not contend otherwise: "A motion for sanctions under this rule ... shall not be filed with or presented to the court unless, within 21 days after service of the motion ... the challenged paper, claim, defense, contention, allegation, or denial is not withdrawn or appropriately corrected." Fed. R. Civ. P. 11(c)(1)(A).

Rather, the question is whether any action (or inaction) on the part of the party against whom sanctions are sought can somehow justify disregarding Rule 11's mandatory "safe harbor" provision, thereby vitiating the institutional protections it affords. In this case, the majority penalizes a hapless plaintiff for invoking the Rule only belatedly. As a result, the defendants' counsel—who was at least as much responsible for protracting the unfortunate proceedings below—not only escapes sanction for his lack of diligence, but delivers his clients a windfall. Because I cannot subscribe to the "ignore it and hope it goes away" approach advocated by the defendants and adopted by the majority, I am constrained to dissent.

Notes and Questions

1. According to the majority, why is the safe harbor provision of Rule 11 "mandatory" but not at the same time "jurisdictional"?

2. The Supreme Court has been remarkably active in recent years in addressing whether various time limits are jurisdictional. Again, jurisdictional limits cannot be waived or forfeited. When a jurisdictional time limit runs, the court is divested over power in the case. Such jurisdictional rules are to be distinguished from "claim-processing rules," which set time limits but which do not extinguish the court's power in the case; claim-processing time limits can be extended. In Kontrick v. Ryan, 540 U.S. 443, 454–55 (2004), the Supreme Court held that the time for objecting to a discharge in bankruptcy, set in the Federal Rules of Bankruptcy Procedure, is merely a processing rule, and is not jurisdictional. Similarly, in Eberhart v. United States, 546 U.S. 12, 20 (2005), the Court held that the seven-day limit for requesting a new trial under the Federal Rules of Criminal Procedure is not jurisdictional.

On the other hand, in Bowles v. Russell, 551 U.S. 205, 208–13 (2007), the Court held that the time for filing an appeal from a judgment in district court is jurisdictional. The Court noted that the time in which to appeal, though reflected in a Federal Rule of Appellate Procedure, is based upon a federal statute. Because Congress has the authority to set the jurisdiction of the federal courts, the Court concluded that Congress intended to remove jurisdiction to hear an untimely appeal. Claim-processing rules such as those in *Kontrick* and *Eberhart*, in contrast, were promulgated pursuant to authority Congress delegated to other bodies.

There is an emerging body of scholarship in this area of "jurisdictionality." Professors Dodson and Wasserman have contributed meaningfully to the analysis. *See, e.g.*, Scott Dodson, *In Search of Removal Jurisdiction*, 102 Nw. U. L. Rev. 55 (2008); Scott Dodson, *Mandatory Rules*, 61 Stan. L. Rev. 1 (2008); Scott Dodson, *The Complexity of Jurisdictional Clarity*, 97 Va. L. Rev. 1 (2011); Howard M. Wasserman, *Jurisdiction, Merits, and Procedure: Thoughts on Dodson's Trichotomy*, 102 Nw. U. L. Rev. Colloquy 215, 220 (2008); Howard M. Wasserman, *Jurisdiction, Merits, and Non-Extant Rights*, 56 U. Kan. L. Rev. 227 (2008); Howard M. Wasserman, *Jurisdiction and Merits*, 80 Wash. L. Rev. 643 (2005). E. King Poor, a distinguished lawyer who argued the *Kontrick* case at the Supreme Court, has also written insightfully in this area. *See* E. King Poor, *Jurisdictional Deadlines in the Wake of* Kontrick *and* Eberhart: *Harmoninzing 160 Years of Precedent*, 40 Creighton L. Rev. 181 (2007); E. King Poor, *The Jurisdictional Time Limit for an Appeal: The Worst Kind of Deadline—Except for All the Others*, 102 Nw. U. L. Rev. Colloquy 151 (2007).

3. Does the "safe harbor" provision provide too much protection for lawyers who fail to cite contrary authority? Suppose Defendant's lawyer knows there is a case that is largely contrary to her asserted position. Could the lawyer omit reference to the case and wait to see if Plaintiff's lawyer finds it? If Plaintiff's lawyer does find the case and serves a motion for sanctions, Defendant's lawyer can then amend her papers to explain why that case is distinguishable or should be overruled. If Plaintiff's lawyer never finds the case, Defendant does not have to address it.

4. Note that Rule 11(b)(3) requires only that factual contentions have "evidentiary support" or that they be likely to have such support upon further investigation. In light of this language, must a lawyer ever go beyond what her client tells her? Consider the following:

(a) Client tells Lawyer about auto accident. Client says that she was hit by another car and that the other car ran a red light. Must lawyer review the police accident report or any other evidence before filing suit to determine if Client's story is consistent with this other evidence?

(b) Lawyer does do some additional investigating and discovers that the police report and all witnesses to the accident (other than Client) state that it was Client who ran the red light and hit the other car. Is it a Rule 11 violation for the lawyer to file suit based on Client's story?

5. The 1993 amendments to Rule 11 did not change everything about the rule. There is no question, for example, that the rule requires an objective assessment of the signer's inquiry, rather than an assessment of the signer's state of mind. See Business Guides, Inc. v. Chromatic Communications Ent., Inc., 498 U.S. 533 (1991). See 2 Moore's Federal Practice § 11.11[3]. Further, district court decisions under Rule 11 are reviewed on appeal by the "abuse of discretion" standard, which we will see

in Chapter 14. Cooter & Gell v. Hartmarx Corp., 496 U.S. 384 (1990) (cited with approval in 1993 Note of Advisory Committee).

6. Rule 11 does not apply to discovery documents. For these, Rule 26(g) provides for certification and sanctions. We will consider Rule 26(g) with the discovery materials in Chapter 8.

7. "Verified pleadings" are signed under oath (and, therefore, under penalty of perjury) and once were quite common. Indeed, the Field Code originally required verification of many pleadings, later changing to give the plaintiff an option to file a verified complaint, to which the defendant was required to respond with a verified answer.

Today, the federal courts and many states have abolished verified pleadings except in limited circumstances. Thus, except in a few instances, the plaintiff's complaint and the defendant's answer will not be signed under oath. (Examples of verified pleadings may be found in Rules 23.1, 27(a), and 65(b).) What purpose is served by requiring verification in such situations? Verified pleadings are still used widely in a few states.

Verified pleadings may be of especial importance with summary judgment, a procedure which, as we will see in Chapter 9, usually involves the consideration of evidence that would be admissible at trial. Because verified pleadings are executed under penalty of perjury, they can constitute such evidence. Unverified pleadings cannot.

2. Other Sanctions

In addition to Rule 11, 28 U.S.C. § 1927 provides that any lawyer in federal court who "multiplies the proceeding in any case unreasonably and vexatiously may be required by the court to satisfy personally the excess costs, expenses, and attorneys' fees reasonably incurred because of such conduct." Although the statute has been in existence since 1813, it, like the original Rule 11, was almost never invoked. In the latter years of the twentieth century, courts and lawyers seemed to discover § 1927.

Section 1927 applies to all proceedings in any federal court. It can be applied to misconduct that is entirely oral. It also applies only to attorneys, not to parties or pro se litigants. Indeed, the Sixth Circuit has held that it applies only to individual lawyers, and does not permit imposition of fees on a law firm. BDT Prods., Inc. v. Lexmark Intern., Inc., 602 F.3d 742, 751 (6th Cir. 2010). There is a split among the circuits as to whether a showing of bad faith must be made in addition to a showing of objective unreasonableness. Compare Oliveri v. Thompson, 803 F.2d 1265 (2d Cir. 1986); Ford v. Temple Hospital, 790 F.2d 342 (3d Cir. 1986) (bad faith required), with Coleman v. Comm'r, 791 F.2d 68 (7th Cir. 1986) (objective unreasonableness sufficient).

Section 1927 can be used to sanction frivolous appeals, but there are two other provisions addressed specifically to appeals — Rule 38 of the Federal Rules of Appellate Procedure and 28 U.S.C. § 1912. Although the language of the statute is not identical to the Rule, courts generally treat the two provisions as if they were redundant and rely primarily on the Rule. Rule 38 provides: "If a court of appeals shall determine that an appeal is frivolous, it may award just damages and single and double costs to the appellee." The damages awarded may include attorney's fees.

In the absence of a statute or rule, courts have the "inherent power" to sanction bad faith conduct by litigants or counsel. This fact was reasserted forcefully in Chambers v. NASCO, Inc., 501 U.S. 32 (1991), discussed in Chapter 10, in Note 7 of Section B.3.b. In that case, the Court affirmed a district court's order that the losing party in a breach of contract case pay nearly $1,000,000 in attorney's fees to the prevailing party. Even though some of the conduct sanctioned was not covered by either Rule 11 or § 1927, the Court upheld the full award, explaining that courts have "inherent power" to police and punish those before it. Notwithstanding *Chambers*, courts are unlikely to rely on inherent power if a rule or statute applies to the conduct in question. In addition, a court must provide procedural safeguards (such as notice and an opportunity to be heard) to the sanctioned party or lawyer.

Rule 11, Federal Rule of Appellate Procedure 38, §§ 1927 and 1912, and "inherent power" are all bases on which a court can impose sanctions intended to punish improper conduct. Other Rules permit the prevailing party to recover "costs" from the losing side. See Rule 54(d); Fed. R. App. P. 39. These are not intended as punishment but simply as reimbursement for the winning party. As noted before, "costs" include various litigation expenses, but do not include attorney's fees. The "American Rule" is that each side bears its own attorney's fees, though there are some important statutory exceptions to this rule. See, e.g., 15 U.S.C. § 26 (antitrust); 42 U.S.C. § 2000e-5(k) (civil rights).

Chapter 8

Discovery

A. Introduction and Integration

In Chapter 7 we saw that the Federal Rules of Civil Procedure historically embraced "notice pleading," under which pleadings did not require the inclusion of much factual detail. Even under the regime of *Twombly* and *Iqbal*, parties will not be required to plead every detail of their claim or defense. Frequently they are not in a position to know all the facts when they plead. Accordingly, modern procedure leaves the detailed disclosure of facts for the discovery phase of litigation. This chapter focuses on the discovery* provisions of the Federal Rules. Although those provisions apply only in federal court, most states have adopted discovery rules that largely mirror the Federal Rules.

The discovery rules were one of the most significant innovations introduced by the Federal Rules. The Rules vastly expanded the availability of discovery over earlier provisions and make the process litigant-driven. In general, the quantity and timing of the information sought is left to the parties, with judicial intervention only when there is a problem. This is an example of the American adversarial system of justice, under which each party fends for itself and advocates its interest, with the judge playing a reactive role. In contrast, civil law countries follow an inquisitorial model, under which the court runs the process of information-gathering. As we will see in Section E of this chapter, the American system has taken on some aspects of inquisitorial systems; specifically, the Federal Rules now require that the judge take charge of the pretrial phase of litigation and oversee it actively. Still, most of the discovery phase is based upon each party's initiative.

* There is an enormous range of informal, non-compulsory mechanisms by which lawyers acquire information about a case. Lawyers interview their clients, talk to witnesses, inspect the scene, and hire private detectives. In addition to these mechanisms, the rules of procedure give lawyers tools by which they can *compel* others to disclose, in advance of trial, information relevant to a case. Thus, although there are many ways by which lawyers can discover information, the word "discovery" usually refers to those compulsory processes permitted by the rules of procedure.

The discovery rules serve three basic purposes. First, they permit preservation of evidence that might otherwise be lost before trial. Second, by allowing parties to find out during the pretrial phase what "really" happened, discovery may narrow the issues in dispute and permit the parties to settle their dispute or the court to adjudicate through summary judgment. Third, discovery permits the parties to acquire greater factual detail about their own and the other side's case. The last purpose is the most controversial and deserves specific attention.

Through discovery, each party can gain access to the relevant evidence the other side has. This is beneficial for several reasons. By eliminating the element of surprise, the trial may be less of a sporting event that rewards quick wits and be more likely to produce a just result. After all, "the purpose of litigation is not to conduct a contest or to oversee a game of skill, but to do justice as between the parties and to decide controversies on their merits." Alexander Holtzoff, *The Elimination of Surprise in Federal Practice*, 7 Vand. L. Rev. 576, 577 (1954). The discovery rules were intended to "make a trial less a game of blind man's bluff and more a fair contest with the basic issues and facts disclosed to the fullest practicable extent." United States v. Procter & Gamble Co., 356 U.S. 677, 683 (1958).

Better knowledge of the other side's evidence may also lead to quicker and fairer settlements of disputes. In theory, each party should be willing to settle for the expected value of a claim. The expected value of a claim equals the possible value, discounted by the probability of receiving that judgment, minus the costs. Thus, a plaintiff who believes that she has a 50 percent likelihood of receiving a $1 million verdict should be willing to settle for $500,000, minus the costs necessary to achieve that verdict. If the defendant agrees that the plaintiff has a 50 percent likelihood of $1 million verdict, the defendant should be willing to offer $500,000, plus expected costs. By exchanging information, the parties are more likely to reach agreement on both the size of the possible verdict and its likelihood, and, thus, they are more likely to settle without incurring the expense of trial.* See Steven Shavell, *Suit, Settlement, and Trial: A Theoretical Analysis Under Alternative Methods for the Allocation of Legal Costs*, 11 J. Leg. Stud. 55, 57–58 (1982).

The elimination of surprise is not without costs. The possibility of surprise may have the salutary effect of discouraging perjury or other manipulation of evidence. As one judge has written:

> A certain amount of surprise is often the catalyst which precipitates the truth. Alternatively it may serve as a medium by which the court or jury may gauge the accuracy of the account.
>
> If every witness consistently told the truth, and none cut his cloth to the wind, little possible harm and much good might come from maximum pretrial disclosure. Experience indicates, however, that there are facile witnesses

---

* Of course, even where parties know a great deal about the other side's proof, cases don't always settle. One side may persist in an unrealistic assessment, or parties may be motivated by a non-economic desire for justice, revenge, or to establish a principle.

> whose interest in "knowing the truth before trial" is prompted primarily by a desire to find the most plausible way to defeat the truth.

Margeson v. Boston & M. R.R., 16 F.R.D. 200, 201 (D. Mass. 1954). In criminal cases, discovery is far more limited than in civil cases. A primary justification for this is the fear of witness intimidation and perjury.

Beyond this, though, the discovery rules permit parties to acquire information for the purpose of strengthening their own cases. In many suits, there will be "information asymmetry" — meaning that the other party will be in possession of the most meaningful information. In *Twombly*, for example, any evidence of a conspiracy to violate the antitrust laws would be in the possession of the defendant, not the plaintiff. Of course, in that case, the Supreme Court held that the plaintiffs failed to state a claim, so the case did not proceed to the discovery phase. In many cases that do proceed past the pleading stage, however, one side will be hoping to find in an opponent's possession evidence that helps it prove its claim or defense.

Using discovery for this purpose has always had its critics. Many view it as wrong and unfair to require a party to produce evidence that may ultimately be used against that party. It is important to remember that litigation is government activity. Though the discovery rules are used by the parties, they are backed up by the power of the state. As we will see below, a party who does not play by the rules is subject to sanction — including, in extreme cases, an order of contempt (which may result in imposition of a fine or even incarceration).

This fact may implicate the Fifth Amendment, which protects criminal defendants from self-incrimination. Concern about fairness also partially explains the limited discovery permitted in civil law countries. The German Supreme Court, in describing its discovery rules, has explained:

> A request for evidence is designed to enable the requesting party to prove contested facts that it already knows, not to find out facts that it does not know. For it is fundamental that no party is obligated to help its adversary to victory by furnishing him with information that he does not already have.*

Decision of Supreme Court (Bundesgerichtshof) of May 4, 1964, 17 Neue Juristische Wochenschrift 1414 (1964).

Today, the principal concerns about discovery focus less on the underlying theory and more on how it should be conducted. In addition to being intrusive, discovery can be expensive and time-consuming. In *Twombly*, as you will recall, the Court justified raising the pleading requirement in part to avoid the "potentially enormous expense of discovery." For decades, many lawyers and judges have believed that discovery is used "as a weapon rather than an information gathering mechanism." Interim Report of the Committee on Civility of the Seventh Federal Judicial Circuit,

---

* A number of countries have laws, including criminal sanctions, "designed to thwart efforts by United States courts to secure production of documents situated abroad." Russell Weintraub, *International Litigation and Forum Non Conveniens*, 29 Tex. Int'l L.J. 321, 337 (1994). See Section C.7, infra.

143 F.R.D. 371, 387 (1991). One report concluded that "[d]iscovery has become a battlefield on which verbal hostility, overly aggressive tactics and often automatic and unreasoned denials of cooperation are the principal weapons." Id. at 383.When the discovery provisions were promulgated, discovery consisted of hard-copy documents and physical things. Technology has brought tremendous change in the format of discoverable information and methods of searching it. A great deal of discovery today concerns electronically stored information (ESI). The world of ESI has increased exponentially the amount of material that may be subject to discovery and, concomitantly, the potential expense of complying with discovery requests. The expense is compounded if ESI has been deleted from online servers.

Although concerns about the expense of discovery are real, it is important to keep them in context. Empirical studies have shown for a generation that abuse is a problem in a relatively low percentage of cases. See, e.g., Linda S. Mullenix, *Discovery in Disarray: The Pervasive Myth of Pervasive Discovery Abuse and the Consequences for Unfounded Rulemaking*, 46 STAN. L. REV. 1393 (1994). In a 2008 survey of attorneys with cases in federal court, the majority indicated that the discovery expenses in their cases were proportionate to the amounts at stake in the litigation. Emery Lee & Thomas Willging, *Defining the Problem of Costs in Federal Civil Litigation*, 60 DUKE L.J. 765, 773–74 (2010).

Rule 26(b)(1) was amended December 1, 2015 to make this latter factor—proportionality—more of a focus than it had been. We start this chapter with the means available to parties to discovery information from other parties and, sometimes, from non-parties. These include required disclosures (discussed in Section B) and the five traditional discovery tools (discussed in Section C). Then, in Section D, we discuss the scope of discovery—that is, the type of material one can access through the means of discovery. It is here that we will address the increased importance of proportionality. In Section E, we put discovery in context as one phase of litigation, and discuss the increasing role of the judge in managing the case. Finally, Section F looks in detail at sanctions for failure to comply with discovery requirements.

B. Required Disclosures

Federal Rule 26(a) requires each party to disclose information to other parties even though no one asks her to do so. These mandatory disclosures therefore differ from the traditional discovery tools, discussed in Section C, with which parties must take the initiative of requesting information from others. Required disclosures, which were introduced in the Federal Rules in 1993, were controversial because they were antithetical to the adversary system. Indeed, three Justices of the Supreme Court dissented from promulgation of Rule 26(a) in 1993 on this basis. 507 U.S. 1099, 1100 (1993) (dissenting statement of Justice Scalia, joined by Justices Thomas and Souter). Despite the initial controversy, practice under Rule 26(a) has been smooth, and mandatory disclosures are now a routine part of federal litigation. Interestingly, though, very few states have adopted such requirements.

Rule 26(a) mandates production of information at three times during the case: initial disclosures under Rule 26(a)(1), disclosures about experts under Rule 26(a)(2), and pretrial disclosures under Rule 26(a)(3).

1. Required Initial Disclosures (Rule 26(a)(1))

Subject to a few exceptions,* Rule 26(a)(1) requires each party to disclose certain information (including electronically stored information (ESI)) without any request by another party. Notice that under subparts (a)(1)(A) and (B), a party is required to disclose only that information "that the disclosing party may use to support its claims or defenses." In contrast, in criminal cases, the prosecution has an obligation to disclose exculpatory material to the defense, regardless of whether the material is specifically requested by the defense. See Kyles v. Whitley, 514 U.S. 419 (1995).

Rule 26(a)(1)(C) requires the parties to produce information under Rule 26(a)(1) no later than 14 days after the Rule 26(f) conference. That conference, as discussed in Section E below, will generally be held between two and three months after the defendant is served with process.

Questions

(a) Who must make initial disclosures?

(b) To whom must the disclosures be made?

(c) What categories of information must be disclosed?

(d) Which party will have an obligation to make disclosures concerning damages? What must be disclosed?

(e) The fact that a party is insured will ordinarily be inadmissible at trial. Why do you think the Rule requires automatic disclosure of insurance policies?

(f) Plaintiff sues Company, alleging that Plaintiff was fired because of her age, in violation of federal law. On its server, Company has an email from a supervisor indicating that age was indeed a factor in firing Plaintiff. Why is Company *not* required to produce this email under Rule 26(a)(1)? Does that mean that Company can suppress the information? No. It will be discoverable using the discovery tools we discuss in Section C, but Plaintiff will have to make a proper request for it.

2. Required Disclosures Concerning Expert Witnesses (Rule 26(a)(2))

The second set of required disclosures becomes relevant later in the case—generally no later than 90 days before the trial date. See Rule 26(a)(2)(C)(i). This disclosure is relevant only in cases that will feature testimony by an expert. An expert is one who is someone "qualified ... by knowledge, skill, experience, training, or education" to

* Rule 26(a)(1)(B) exempts certain very specialized types of cases from these required disclosures. Most of the civil cases with which this course deals, however, will involved required disclosures.

express opinions. (Most witnesses are "lay" witnesses, who are permitted to testify at trial only about matters they observed; they may not offer their opinions.) For example, a psychiatrist, qualified as an expert witness, may testify that in her opinion the defendant was acting under delusions at the time of the accident.

To avoid surprise, and to permit discovery of expert testimony to be presented at trial, Rule 26(a)(2) requires detailed disclosure of information about the expert and a report of her findings, conclusions, and opinions.

3. Required Pretrial Disclosures (Rule 26(a)(3))

Even later in the case—generally no more than 30 days before trial—each party must disclose information under Rule 26(a)(3). At this point, the parties will have been litigating for months if not years—through the pleading stage, motions, and discovery. Now, as they approach trial, they must set forth detailed information about witnesses and evidence they intend to present at trial. At this point, the parties will have honed the issues remaining to be adjudicated. The pretrial disclosures ensure that there will be no surprises at trial. Remember that very few cases actually progress to trial—in the federal system fewer than two percent of cases filed will go to trial. The vast majority will have been settled or resolved at an earlier stage, perhaps by motion to dismiss or summary judgment.

C. Discovery Tools

After the Rule 26(f) conference, the parties may use the five discovery tools that have always been recognized under the federal discovery provisions. With these, parties make requests for information from other parties (and, sometimes, non-parties). The party to whom these discovery requests are made must respond. Failure to do so (or failure to respond completely to proper requests) may result in sanctions, as we are about to see. As we review the discovery tools, consider whether any may be available to get information from non-parties as well as from parties. (Parties are litigants in the present case.)

Rule 26(g) requires that disclosures, discovery requests, and discovery responses be signed by counsel, which is a certification that the document is basically correct and not interposed for an improper purpose (such as delay or harassment). In addition, under Rule 26(e)(1)(a), a party must supplement discovery responses "if the party learns that in some material respect the disclosure or response is incomplete or incorrect, and if the additional or corrective information has not otherwise been made known to the other parties." Such supplemental responses are required even though no party asks for them. Thus, each party must police itself to ensure that responses previously made have not become inaccurate as the case unfolds.

After being served with requests for discovery, the party from whom discovery is sought is required to respond. In that response, the party may assert objections to the discovery. For example, perhaps the requests seek material that is beyond the scope of discoverability under Rule 26(b)(1). Sometimes, a party from whom discovery is sought will seek a "protective order" under Rule 26(c), asking the court to prohibit or limit discovery.

1. Depositions (Rules 30, 31)

In a deposition, a witness (the "deponent") is placed under oath and responds to questions, in much the same way that a witness testifies at trial. Unlike a trial, at a deposition there is no judge present—only the witness, the lawyers, and a court officer designated to administer oaths. See Rule 28. The deponent responds orally under oath to questions asked by the lawyers for the various parties. She testifies based upon her present recollection, and thus need not study files or records or otherwise do any "homework" to prepare for the deposition.

Anyone (party or non-party) with discoverable information can be deposed. When a party seeks information from a corporation or other organization, but does not know who within the organization would have the relevant information, the party can name the organization as the deponent and describe the matters on which information is sought. The organization must then identify the appropriate person to be deposed. See Rule 30(b)(6). When deposing a non-party, the party seeking discovery should subpoena the non-party. The subpoena is an order from the court commanding the non-party to sit for the deposition. Without a subpoena, a non-party cannot be compelled to attend her deposition. If the requesting party wants the non-party to testify at deposition and to produce documents or things at the deposition, she will serve the non-party with a subpoena "duces tecum." (By the way, parties need not be subpoenaed to attend their depositions. Why?)

Traditionally, depositions have been stenographically recorded by a court reporter and transcribed. The Rules also permit depositions to be recorded electronically, see Rule 30(b)(3)(A), with a transcript required only if the deposition is later offered into evidence. See Rule 32(c).

Depositions can be a very effective way to learn what an individual knows about a particular matter. Depositions are time-intensive and can be quite expensive. The cost of a court reporter to record and transcribe a day-long deposition can be hundreds of dollars. In addition, each party must bear the expense of the time her attorney spends preparing for and attending the deposition.

The Rules impose a presumptive limit of ten depositions per side, see Rule 30(a)(2)(A)(i), with each deposition limited to one day of seven hours, see Rule 30(d)(1). These limits may be altered by stipulation of the parties or by court order.

Rule 31 permits a variation of the traditional oral deposition. Under this rule, a party may serve on the other parties a set of questions that will be asked a witness. The court officer then swears in the witness and asks the questions to the witness. The advantage is that the lawyer need not attend the deposition. The disadvantages are that the witness is likely to know in advance exactly the questions that will be asked and there is no opportunity for follow up questions based on the responses received.

Questions

(a) Who can be deposed?

(b) If you want to take someone's deposition, what do you have to do?

(c) Where can the deposition of a party be taken?

(d) Suppose you have served a notice of deposition to the other party and she doesn't show up, what sanctions are available? See Rule 37(d).

(e) Suppose instead that the deponent shows up and answers some questions but refuses to answer other questions. What sanctions are available? See Rule 37(a) & (b).

(f) Where can the deposition of a non-party witness be taken? See Rule 45(c)(1)(A).

(g) Suppose you serve a notice of deposition to a non-party witness who doesn't show up. What sanctions are available against *you*? See Rule 30(g). What can you do to avoid being subject to sanctions for a no-show non-party deponent? See Rule 45(b)(2).

2. Interrogatories (Rule 33)

Under Rule 33, any party may send to any other party written questions that require a written response under oath. These can be a far less expensive and more effective device than depositions for acquiring detailed, objective information. In a deposition, a witness is required to answer based on the knowledge and information she has at the time of the deposition. In contrast, in responding to interrogatories, parties are required to provide facts that are reasonably available to them, even if this requires reviewing files of documents, though parties are not required to supply information that they do not already have. Thus, a party would not be required to conduct new tests to answer interrogatories.

Interrogatories also have limitations. Because answers to interrogatories are typically drafted by the party's lawyer, interrogatories are not an effective device for ascertaining the testimony or credibility of particular witnesses. They are, however, a useful way to get objective information including names, dates, and lists of documents. They can also pave the way for other discovery by, for example, identifying people with information whom it may be appropriate to depose. Interrogatories can also be used to clarify the allegations set forth in the pleadings. For example, in a tort case in which the plaintiff generally alleged negligence, the defendant could include an interrogatory asking in what respect defendant's conduct was negligent. See Rule 33(a)(2).

There is a presumptive limit of 25 interrogatories (including subparts) per party. See Rule 33(a)(1). As with the limit on the number of depositions, this presumptive limit can be modified by stipulation or court order.

When the answer to an interrogatory can be found in business records, including electronically stored information, Rule 33(d) permits the responding party to specify the records in which the answer can be found. This option is permitted only if the relative burden of uncovering the answer from the records is substantially equal for the two parties.

Questions

(a) To whom may interrogatories be directed? It is common to serve interrogatories by mail under Rule 5(b)(2)(C). In such cases, the responding party gets an extra three days in which to respond. See Rule 6(d).

(b) How long does the recipient of the interrogatories have to respond?

(c) Suppose that the recipient of interrogatories considers some of the questions burdensome or irrelevant. What can she do?

(d) Suppose that the recipient of the interrogatories does not respond at all within the allowed time. What sanctions are available? See Rule 37(d).

(e) Suppose instead that the responding party responds in time, answering some interrogatories but refusing to answer others. What sanctions are available? See Rule 37(a) & (b).

3. Production of Documents and Things (Rule 34)

There are many situations in which ESI or hard-copy documentary or even physical evidence may be critical to proving what happened and why. Rule 34 permits a party to require another party to produce for inspection, copying, or testing all relevant documents or other tangible things. In most cases, Rule 34 is used to compel the production of documents and ESI. Note, however, how much more information is available through this device. For example, in a patent infringement case, a party can use Rule 34 to gain access to the allegedly offending widget. In a property dispute, a party can gain access to land to run geologic tests or surveys. The party to whom the request is directed must respond within 30 days after service of the request, Rule 34(b)(2)(A), either stating objections or agreeing to the request, Rule 34(b)(2)(B).*

Lawyers are careful to sequence their discovery requests. Often, for example, they use interrogatories and requests for production to get learn identities of people with discoverable information, obtain ESI and documents relevant to claims and defenses. They use this background information to plan for depositions.

Questions

(a) To whom may requests for production be directed?

(b) How can a party secure ESI, documents, or tangible things from a non-party? See Rules 34(c), 45(c)(2)(A).

---

* As a general rule, a party may not serve discovery requests on other parties until after the Rule 26(f) conference. By a change made in 2015, however, Rule 34(d)(2) permits "early" use of requests to produce. More than 21 days after service of process, a party may serve a request to produce, and it is deemed served at the Rule 26(f) conference.

(c) What sanctions are available if a party fails to respond at all to a request for production within the prescribed time? See Rule 37(d).

(d) What sanctions are available if a party responds in time and indicates that it will produce some of the requested information but refuses to produce other requested information? See Rule 37(a) & (b).

4. Medical Examination (Rule 35)

When the health, physical, or mental condition of a party is in controversy, the court may order the party to submit to a physical or mental examination by a "suitably licensed or certified examiner." The party requesting the examination chooses the medical professional who will make the examination and write a report concerning the condition of the person examined.

Unlike the other discovery devices, for which the intervention of the court is not ordinarily required, Rule 35 requires a court order. The order is appropriate only where the movant shows "good cause" and the mental or physical condition is "in controversy." The Supreme Court has said of these requirements:

> They are not met by mere conclusory allegations of the pleadings—nor by mere relevance to the case—but require an affirmative showing by the movant that each condition as to which the examination is sought is really and genuinely in controversy and that good cause exists for ordering each particular examination. Obviously, what may be good cause for one type of examination may not be so for another. The ability of the movant to obtain the desired information by other means is also relevant.

Schlagenhauf v. Holder, 379 U.S. 104, 118 (1964).

Under Rule 35, a party may be ordered to undergo a medical exam, and so may a non-party who is in the "custody" or "legal control" of a party. This is a very narrow standard. For example, consider a tort case alleging physical injury to a minor. The minor cannot sue in her own name, because she lacks legal capacity. Her parent or guardian will sue on her behalf. Though the child is not a "party" she is in the "custody" or "legal control" of a party, and thus the court may order that the child be examined.

Questions

(a) If the court orders a party to submit to a medical exam, and the party refuses to do so, what sanctions are available? See Rule 37(b)(2)(A).

(b) Under Rule 35(b)(1), the person being examined is entitled to request a copy of the examiner's report. Are there reasons why the person being examined might not request the report? See Rule 35(b)(3) & (4).

(c) Under Rule 35, could the court order a party to submit to an examination by a physical therapist (who is not a physician)? A chiropractor?

(d) Suppose that one party believes that a non-party eyewitness has very poor eyesight. Upon motion, can the court order the witness to submit to an eye exam under Rule 35? If the answer is no, what course(s) do you suggest to discover information about the non-parties vision?

5. Requests for Admission (Rule 36)

Requests for admission are used to determine what issues are and are not in dispute. By identifying contested issues early, both sides can conserve resources. Rule 36 is a valuable tool both for acquiring a more detailed knowledge of the evidence and for narrowing the issues.

Questions

(a) To whom may requests for admission be directed?

(b) What happens if the recipient simply ignores the requests for admission and does not respond? See Rule 36(a)(3).

(c) Suppose that the recipient of a request for admission denies a fact that is later established at trial, what sanctions are available? See Rule 37(c).

6. Practice Problem

Kay Robinson and two of her children were badly burned when the Audi in which they were driving was hit by another car, and the Robinsons' car exploded. The Robinsons have filed suit against Audi in federal court alleging defective design and manufacture of the car. The plaintiffs believe that the location of the gas tank made it more susceptible to puncture in a rear-end collision and that there was insufficient fire protection between the gas tank and the passenger compartment. They have the name and address of one eyewitness to the crash. Prepare a discovery plan for the Robinsons. What types of information would you like to acquire? Which discovery devices should you use for which kinds of information? Which discovery requests would you serve first?

D. Scope of Discovery

Now that we know what discovery tools can be used, the next question is what can sorts of information can be discovered.

1. General Scope

Rule 26(b)(1) sets forth the basic standard for what information may be discovered. Two of the requirements — that the request be for "relevant" information and that it be for "nonprivileged" information — have been in the Rule for decades. A significant amendment effective December 1, 2015 added the requirement that discovery requests be "proportional" to the case.

a. *"Relevant to a claim or defense."*

Rule 26(b)(1) requires that a discovery request ask for information that is "relevant to a claim or defense."

United Oil Co. v. Parts Associates, Inc.

227 F.R.D. 404 (D. Md. 2005)

Background

United Oil Company, Inc. ("United Oil"), a distributor of hydraulic oils and industrial chemicals has brought an action in indemnity and contribution to recover the $820,098.89, which it paid to Mr. and Mrs. Jerry Tiede in settlement of their product liability claims against United Oil. Plaintiff sued Rohm & Haas ("R&H") as the manufacturer of dyes to which Mr. Tiede was allegedly exposed and sued Parts Associates ("Parts") as the distributor of the Fleet-Fill brake cleaner to which Mr. Tiede was allegedly exposed. United Oil's expert, Dr. Kenneth Brown, has opined that certain chemicals in the dyes, specifically xylene and ethyl benzene, and in the brake cleaning fluid, specifically perchloroethylene (a.k.a tetrachloroethylene) caused Mr. Tiede's liver disease. * * *

Plaintiff United Oil Company's Motion to Compel R&H to Answer Interrogatories & Requests

The theory of the lawsuit against R&H and Parts Associates is a failure to properly warn about the dangers of liver damage, specifically hepatitis, from exposure to R&H's red and blue dyes and Parts' brake cleaner. United Oil asserts that "R&H and Parts Associates' knowledge about these dangers is ... relevant [to the failure to warn]. In addition, information concerning any other claims or lawsuits, whether before or after Mr. Tiede's injuries, is relevant on the issue of causation."

R&H challenges the discoverability of this information based on lack of relevance. To evaluate R&H's challenge, the Court must determine the standard of relevance at the discovery stage and which party carries the burden on the issue of relevance at the discovery stage — the propounding or resisting party. For the reasons set forth below, the Court has determined that United Oil had the obligation to demonstrate threshold relevance of discovery requests to its failure to warn claim under applicable rules and case law, that United Oil successfully made such a showing, and that R&H, as the resisting party, did not demonstrate and support the irrelevance of the discovery requests under governing law.

Rule 26 governs discovery entitlement and provides that "parties may obtain discovery regarding any matter, not privileged, that is relevant to the claim or defense of any party...."[3] Fed. R. Civ. P. 26(b)(1). While the Federal Rules of Civil Procedure

---

3. The rule further provides that "for good cause, the court may order discovery of any matter relevant to the subject matter involved in the action." Fed. R. Civ. P. 26(b)(1). The 2000 amendments to Rule 26 created these two categories of discoverable information, one as a matter of right and one conditional on proof of good cause. Commentators have noted that "it is [only] at this point where a *new* claim or defense is the focus of discovery not relevant to the current ones that calls for a de-

do not define relevance, the Federal Rules of Evidence do, as "evidence having any tendency to make the existence of any fact that is of consequence to the determination of the action more probable or less probable than it would be without the evidence." Fed. R. Evid. 401. Or, as rephrased in the commentary, "does the item of evidence tend to prove the matter sought to be proved?"

* * * Moreover, relevance for discovery purposes is viewed more liberally than relevance for evidentiary purposes. * * *

The commentary * * * admonishes courts to "focus on the actual claims and defenses involved in the action" in determining relevance. United Oil has brought a failure to warn claim against the defendants. To prove a failure to warn claim, plaintiff must prove, *inter alia*, that the supplier or manufacturer "knows or has reason to know that the chattel is or is likely to be dangerous for the use for which it is supplied [or manufactured]." Restatement (Second) of Torts §§ 388, 394. And, of course, as in any tort case, plaintiff must prove that the exposure was a proximate cause of Mr. Tiede's injury.

Courts have allowed plaintiffs to introduce evidence of substantially similar occurrences or lawsuits on the issue of notice and causation. Accordingly, there appears to be little dispute that R&H's notice of claims, complaints or lawsuits regarding the dyes, or products "substantially similar" to the dyes would be admissible on the notice and causation elements of the failure to warn claim.

The question thus becomes whether United Oil is entitled to the discovery it seeks: information on claims, complaints and lawsuits involving R&H products (other than the dyes) containing xylene and ethyl benzene as substantially similar products.

R&H acknowledges that "some courts have permitted discovery of other litigation where it involves (1) the same or similar claims arising from (2) the same or similar products at issue." Indeed, that is the widely-accepted view. "Discovery of similar, if not identical, models is routinely permitted in product liability cases." Culligan v. Yamaha Motor Corp., 110 F.R.D. 122, 126 (S.D.N.Y. 1986). "[Discovery] of other

---

termination whether to allow discovery that goes to the subject matter limit." See, e.g., 8 Wright, Miller & Marcus, Federal Practice & Procedure: Civil 2D § 2008 (Supp. 2004). (emphasis added). * * *

The commentary rejects the bright line urged by the parties here, to allow only discovery as to the specific incident and specific product as a matter of right, with all other discovery requiring demonstration of good cause.

Rather the commentary states:

> A variety of types of information not directly pertinent to the incident in suit could be relevant to the claims or defenses raised in a given action. For example, other incidents of the same type, or involving the same product, could be properly discoverable under the revised standard.

Id. Accordingly, the commentary strongly indicates that "same" and, by extension, similar incidents, products, etc. are related to the claim, not the subject matter; and therefore discovery is not dependent on demonstration of good cause.

accidents involving similar products is relevant in products liability cases to show notice to defendants of the danger and cause of the accident." In re Aircrash Disaster near Roselawn, 172 F.R.D. 295, 306 (N.D. Ill. 1997). Moreover, courts have allowed discovery of information regarding the same component part in a different product in a number of product defect cases. However, R&H makes two arguments in resisting the scope of discovery United Oil seeks here.

First, R&H argues that "the same or similar claims" should be limited to failure to warn claims both involving exposure to the identified dyes and alleging liver damage. The Court agrees in part. The claim here against R&H is for the failure to sufficiently warn as to the dangers of exposure to the dyes as to liver damage. Claims, complaints, and litigation about other dangers and the sufficiency of the product warning as to those dangers are plainly not relevant, as that evidence would not "tend to make the existence of any fact that is of consequence to the determination of the action more probable or less probable than it would be without the evidence." Fed. R. Evid. 401. Obviously, claims involving alleged heart disease as a result of exposure to the dyes would not assist the trier of fact to determine what the manufacturer knew or reasonably should have known about the effect of exposure to the liver. However, other strict liability or negligence claims against the manufacturer alleging liver damage as a result of exposure to the dyes or their identified liver toxic chemical constituents could constitute a "similar claim" as they could demonstrate defendant R&H's knowledge of risks posed by xylene and ethyl benzene.

Second, as to the "same or similar products" prong, R&H argues that the mere fact that other R&H products contain xylene or ethyl benzene—in any amount—does not make those products the "same or similar" to the subject dyes for purposes of relevancy and discoverability in this case.

Neither R&H's nor the Court's research has revealed any case directly on point. However, review of Rule 26 and the core principles of relevancy and discovery and existing case law suggest that discovery of R&H's knowledge of the dangers of exposure to xylene and ethyl benzene to the liver through claims, complaints, and lawsuits regarding *other* products containing these chemical compounds is probative of what R&H knew or should have known about the liver toxicity of the dyes at issue here and may also provide admissible evidence on causation.

Plaintiff's position is that claims, complaints, and lawsuits regarding liver damage from exposure to other products containing xylene and ethyl benzene would demonstrate R&H's notice of the liver toxicity of the dyes at issue here. In theory, that seems correct. Of course, it may well be that the claims, complaints, and lawsuits, if any, will concern products so different in formulation, so different in the quantity of the liver toxic chemical constituents or method of exposure, that the trial judge would exclude the evidence of these claims. Essentially, R&H posits that at this point in the litigation United Oil must prove the substantial similarity of other R&H products, containing, as they logically do, different amounts of the chemical constituents, different formulations, and possibly a different method of exposure. The Court disagrees.

Generally, the burden is on the party resisting discovery to clarify and explain precisely why its objections are proper given the broad and liberal construction of the federal discovery rules. This includes, of course, where the resisting party asserts that the discovery is irrelevant.

By contrast at the trial, it is the offering party that bears the burden of demonstration of relevance. It is at that juncture that courts require the plaintiff to demonstrate the "substantial similarity" of other accidents, complaints, claims or lawsuits. * * *

The Court is not insensitive to R&H's arguments that the manner of application, quantity of the particular chemical component, and indeed the different formula of the product might affect the level of toxicity of the constituent chemical and thus the duty to warn. * * *

If discovery reveals that R&H received claims, complaints, and lawsuits complaining of liver damage involving other products containing the subject chemical compounds, it will be the plaintiff's responsibility to show that notice as to the dangerous properties of those products — with different amounts of xylene and/ or ethyl benzene and in different formulation — should have put R&H on notice of the dangerous properties of the red and blue dyes and of the insufficiency of the existing warning. To decide that issue now — without knowledge of how similar the amounts, formulation, etc. of the other products and without scientific input and context — would be premature and possibly deprive plaintiff of discovery which might demonstrate notice and causation in similar exposure situations.

Of course, there are other grounds, such as burdensomeness, upon which a party can resist even relevant discovery. While R&H has complained generally about the burdensomeness of such a discovery request R&H has not demonstrated that burden with the requisite specificity and formal affidavit.

Accordingly, the Court grants the motion to compel answers to interrogatory nos. 15 (as modified in the June 2, 2004, meet and confer conference) * * * and requests for production nos. 20 (limited to the last 10 years) and 27 (limited to the last 10 years).[6] Unless the parties have agreed otherwise, the ten years shall be measured backwards from the date of the discovery request.

---

6. Interrogatory No. 15: "State whether you have ever been a party in any administrative, civil, or criminal proceeding or lawsuit arising out of or resulting from personal injury of Permatex or Fleet-Fill Brake Cleaner, perchloroethylene, tetrachloroethylene, trichloroethane, or methylene chloride exposure related to your business, indicating in your answer the case name, case number, name of the complaining party, state, county, and tribunal before whom the proceeding took place." * * *

Request for production No. 20: "All deposition and trial transcripts related to any other claims or lawsuits based in whole or in part on alleged hazards of Permatex or Fleet-Fill Brake Cleaner, perchloroethylene, tetrachloroethylene, trichloroethane, or methylene chloride."

Request for production No. 27: "Produce copies of all workers compensation claims filed by defendant employees related to exposure to Permatex or Fleet-Fill Brake Cleaner, perchloroethylene, tetrachloroethylene, trichloroethane, or methylene chloride." * * *

Information about claims, complaints, and lawsuits about other substantially similar products post-incident may be relevant as to causation and would be admissible for causation only. * * * Accordingly, United Oil is entitled to postincident discovery, which the definition of the 10-year period permits.

As to request for production no. 22,[7] it is too broad as drafted, and the request should be limited to defined categories of documents and to a 10 year period. However, within 10 business days of this Memorandum and Order, United Oil may pose a request for defined categories of documents.

As to request no. 23,[8] it is too broad as drafted, and the request should be limited to the chemicals at issue and to defined categories of documents and for a 10 year period. Again, within 10 business days of this Memorandum and Order, United Oil may pose a request for defined categories of documents. * * *

The Court also grants the motion to compel as to the listed "contention" interrogatories 5, 6, 7, and 8[13] * * *.

The Court denies the motion to compel as to request for production no. 3 as too broad.[14] * * *

The Court denies the motion to compel as to interrogatory 17 and request for production no. 24 as too broad and non-specific.[16] * * *

---

7. Request for production No. 22: "All documents that relate or refer to every claim that has ever been filed against you (whether or not the claim resulted in the filing of a lawsuit) for alleged personal injuries related to Permatex or Fleet-Fill Brake Cleaner, perchloroethylene, tetrachloroethylene, trichloroethane, or methylene chloride."

8. Request for production No. 23: "All documents that relate or refer to any administrative, civil, or criminal proceeding or lawsuit arising out of or resulting from the sale of products, including, but certainly not limited to all pleadings, discovery responses, and deposition transcripts in every claim that has ever been filed against you (that resulting [sic] in the filing of a lawsuit) for personal injuries."

13. Interrogatory No. 5: "Is Automate Blue 8, Anthraquinone dye, C.I. Solvent Blue 98, Xylene, and Ethyl benzene safe for unprotected human exposure under all circumstances? If not, why?"

Interrogatory No. 6: "Is Automate Red B, Disazo dye, C.I. Solvent Red 164, Xylene, and Ethyl benzene safe for unprotected human exposure under all circumstances? If not, why?"

Interrogatory No. 7: "If you contend that you did not cause or contribute to the injuries and damages that are alleged in the Complaint, state in detail the entire basis for such contention."

Interrogatory No. 8: "If you contend that any person(s) other than you caused or contributed to any of the alleged occurrences described in the Complaint, identify the other person(s) and state each and every fact upon which you rely in support of your contention."

14. Request for production No. 3: "All documents that relate or refer to the allegations in this case."

16. Interrogatory No. 17: "Identify each and every license, or certificate that you have obtained in the past 10 years, and if such license or certificate has ever been suspended or revoked, or your renewal has ever been refused or delayed, set forth all the facts surrounding such suspension, revocation, refusal, or delay including, but not limited to, the date of such suspension, revocation, refusal or delay, the name of the authority which directed such suspension, revocation, refusal or delay, and reason(s) thereof."

Request for production No. 24: "All licenses or certificates to sell products for the past five years."

Defendant Parts Associates, Inc.'s Motion to Compel

The Court grants in part and denies in part the defendant's motion, as set forth below. As a general matter, the Court agrees with Parts that the plaintiff's answers to interrogatories through reference to certain boxes of files of documents is inadequate under Rule 33. Production of documents under Rule 33(d) is inappropriate where, as here, the burden of ascertaining the answer is not the same for defendant as for plaintiff. Rule 33 production is suited to those discovery requests requiring compilation or analysis, accomplished as easily by one party as another, or where neither side has clear superiority of knowledge or familiarity with the documents. Accordingly, Rule 33 is well-suited to reply to inquiries of an intensely objective nature.

Here, however, the interrogatories pose questions of fact or mixed questions of law and fact which require the exercise of particular knowledge and judgment on the part of the responding party. Moreover, United Oil as a defendant in the *Tiede* suit obviously has superior familiarity with the documents at issue.

Here defendant Parts has said that even after review of the referenced documents, it still cannot derive the answer to its specific questions. Accordingly, even if the Court accepted the burden of ascertainment as the same between the parties (which the Court does not), or determined that Parts' law firm had the resources to do the necessary review (which the Court does not), the documents do not provide any certain or clear answers to the interrogatories. This Court agrees that "defendants are entitled to know the factual content of plaintiff's claims with a reasonable degree of precision." Martin v. Easton Publishing Co., 85 F.R.D. 312, 315 (E.D. Pa. 1980). Thus, as to interrogatory nos. 8, * * * [and] 15 * * *,[29] plaintiff should answer completely and specifically rather than by reference to documents. * * *

Questions

1. The court in *United Oil* found that requests nos. 22 and 23 were too broad. How would you redraft these interrogatories to respond to the court's concerns?

2. In *United Oil*, the court was prepared to allow discovery concerning other products and defer until later the question whether those products were sufficiently similar to the product at issue in the litigation. In some other cases, courts have made a more detailed inquiry into similarity before deciding about discoverability. See Piacenti v. General Motors Corp., 173 F.R.D. 221 (N.D. Ill. 1997). Of course, sometimes it can

29. Interrogatory No. 8: "State each fact on which United Oil bases the allegation in paragraph 10 of the Complaint that Fleet-Fill Brake Cleaner contains the chemicals Trichloroethane and Perchloroethylene; identify all documents you rely on in support of your answer to this interrogatory and each and every person who has knowledge of the facts set forth in your answer to this interrogatory. For each such person identified, state the nature or substance of his or her knowledge, and the basis of his or her knowledge." * * *

Interrogatory No. 15: "Identify all individuals not otherwise identified above who have knowledge of any and all facts that form the basis for any and all allegations set forth in the Complaint; and for each such person identified, state the nature or substance of his or her knowledge, and the basis for his or her knowledge." * * *

be difficult for the requesting party to know whether products are sufficiently similar without first getting some discovery.

3. Suppose that Plaintiff was fired from her job and sues Employer alleging racial discrimination. Can Plaintiff discover evidence concerning Employer's firing practices and patterns with respect to other employees? What about hiring practices or data that might show pay disparities based on race, or information concerning discrimination against other groups (e.g., women or older people)? See Jeffrey Stempel & David Herr, *Applying Amended Rule 26(B)(1) in Litigation: The New Scope of Discovery*, 199 F.R.D. 396, 405 (2001). Stempel and Herr offer the following test for determining relevance for purposes of discovery: "An item of information sought is relevant to a claim or defense if the requesting party can articulate a logical relationship between the information sought and possible proof or refutation of the claim or defense at trial." Id. at 408–09. How much constraint on discovery would this test impose?

4. What is "relevant" under Rule 26(b)(1) should not be confused with what evidence will be *admissible* at trial. In federal court, admissibility of evidence is governed by the Federal Rules of Evidence, which you will study in detail in an Evidence course. Until 2015, Rule 26(b)(1) specifically provided that "[r]elevant information need not be admissible at the trial if the discovery appears reasonably calculated to lead to the discovery of admissible evidence." That language was deleted from the Rule effective December 1, 2015. The Advisory Committee notes to the Rule insist, however, that no change in practice was intended. The last sentence of Rule 26(b)(1) provides that "[i]nformation within this scope of discovery need not be admissible in evidence to be discoverable."

For example, "hearsay" is evidence that comes not from the knowledge of the witness but from mere repetition of what the witness has heard others say. Hearsay is generally inadmissible at trial (though there are several exceptions to that rule). See Fed. R. Evid. 801–805. Suppose in an automobile crash case that a third-party witness to the wreck says that she heard brakes screech immediately before impact. She may testify to that at trial, because her testimony reflects her actual perception. But she would (probably) not be allowed to testify at trial that her husband told her that he heard brakes screech, because that is hearsay.

Suppose this person is being deposed. Would it be permissible to ask her whether anyone told her that he or she had heard brakes screech? Yes — because even though the testimony elicited is hearsay (and therefore inadmissible), it is reasonably calculated to lead to admissible evidence. Why? Because it will lead to the identification of the witness's husband, who has relevant first-hand knowledge of the case.

5. Plaintiff sues Company, alleging that Plaintiff was fired because of her age, in violation of federal law. On its server, Company has an email from a supervisor indicating that age was indeed a factor in firing Plaintiff. In Section B of this chapter, we saw that Company is *not* required to produce this email under the required disclosure provision of Rule 26(a)(1). Suppose Plaintiff serves a request to produce on

Company asking for all ESI and documents containing information relevant to Plaintiff's claim. Would this email be discoverable?

6. Suppose Paul sues Dave for damages suffered in a car wreck between the two. Paul claims that he has suffered physical injuries that render him sedentary and largely unable to engage in vigorous physical activity. Dave serves a request to produce for all ESI and documents related to Paul's physical activity after the accident. Must Paul produce his FitBit information?

b. "Nonprivileged."

Rule 26(b)(1) permits discovery only of "nonprivileged" material. "Privileged," as used in Rule 26, is a term of art. It does not refer to everything that one person intends to keep secret or confidential when she tells another person. Rather, "privileged" refers to a narrow category of material delineated by the rules of evidence. The law protects confidential communications that are made between specific types of people. The classic privileged communications, recognized by the laws of many states, are between lawyer and client, doctor and patient, priest and parishioner, and spouses.

In each of these cases it is only the *communication* itself that is protected, and not the underlying facts. Thus, in the Robinsons' case against Audi in *World-Wide Volkswagen*, it would be improper for Audi to ask Mrs. Robinson the following question either in discovery or at trial: "What did you tell your lawyer about how much gas was in the tank at the time of the accident?" On the other hand, it would be permissible to ask: "How much gas was in the tank at the time of the accident?" In addition to protecting only confidential communications, the attorney-client privilege is further limited in that the communication must have been in connection with the rendering of legal services (as opposed to, for example, business advice).

The protective veil of privilege conceals information that may be important to fact finding and truth seeking. The recognition of some information as privileged reflects a policy judgment that certain interests are more important than fact finding and truth seeking. Thus, the attorney-client privilege encourages complete and honest disclosure between client and lawyer, which, in turn, facilitates better legal representation. As one treatise explains: "The consequent loss to justice of the power to bring all pertinent facts before the court is, according to the theory, outweighed by the benefit to justice (not to the individual client) of a franker disclosure in the lawyer's office." 1 McCormick On Evidence § 87 (7th ed. 2013). Because recognition of a privilege conceals relevant information, the privileges are narrowly construed and can be waived by disclosure to third parties.

One issue with which the Supreme Court has struggled is the scope of the attorney-client privilege when the client is a corporation. Should the privilege protect all communications between all employees of the corporation and the corporation's lawyer or only between managers and the lawyer? In Upjohn Co. v. United States, 449 U.S. 383, 394–395 (1981), the Court rejected as too narrow the position that the privilege extends only to communications with the "control group," i.e., top managers, of the corporation. The Court declined to articulate a specific alternative test, though it suggested that the privilege would apply only where the communication was needed to supply a basis for legal advice, concerned matters within the scope of the employees' duties, and was treated as confidential within the corporation.

Privileged communications are protected from discovery. However, the party from whom the information is sought cannot simply withhold the allegedly privileged information. Rule 26(b)(5)(A) requires a party to claim the privilege "expressly" and to describe in sufficient detail the documents, communications, or things not produced so as to enable "other parties to assess the claim." A party claiming a privilege will usually submit a "privilege log" to the court "identifying the documents or other communications by date and by the names of the author(s) and recipient(s), and describing their general subject matter (without revealing the privileged or protected material)." Fed. Judicial Ctr., Manual for Complex Litigation 63 (4th ed. 2004).

What happens if the claimant does not properly claim the privilege or protection? This issue may arise because privileged material is overlooked in the large volume of material produced or because there is "embedded data" in electronic material that is not immediately visible but which reveals privileged drafts or comments. Federal Rule of Evidence 502(b) provides that in any federal proceeding, inadvertent disclosure of privileged information does not waive the privilege provided the holder of the privilege took reasonable steps to prevent disclosure and also took reasonable steps to rectify the error. See Rule 26(b)(5)(B).

As noted, the fact that litigants might consider information "secret" or "confidential" does not make it privileged. Any relevant, nonprivileged information is subject to discovery, regardless of how private and embarrassing the information might be. Some courts have held, however, that where confidential information is sought, the burden is on the party seeking discovery to establish that the information sought is not only relevant but necessary to the case. See Hartley Pen Co. v. United States Dist. Court, 287 F.2d 324, 331 (9th Cir. 1961). A court has authority under Rule 26(c) to issue a "protective order" placing conditions on the disclosure or protecting against disclosure altogether. If the information is relevant, it ordinarily must be disclosed subject to appropriate protective conditions.

The potential reach of discovery is illustrated by litigation between the Coca-Cola Company and several of its bottlers. The secret formula for Coca-Cola has been described as "one of the best-kept trade secrets in the world." It is known by only two people and the only written record of the formula is kept in a bank vault that can be opened only upon resolution of the company's Board of Directors. The formula was never patented because patents are of finite duration, and Coke wanted to maintain the secret indefinitely. Despite the extraordinarily secret nature of the formula, a court ordered it disclosed in connection with discovery in a civil suit. The circumstances were this. In 1921, Coca-Cola had entered into a consent decree settling a suit by several of its bottlers. The consent decree set the price the bottlers would pay for syrup from Coca-Cola. When Coca-Cola introduced Diet Coke, the company took the position that this was a new product that was not covered by the consent decree. Several bottlers disagreed and filed suit against Coca-Cola alleging that Diet

Coke was "simply a version of a product which has undergone evolutionary change but which retains its identity as Coke." Because the major issue in the case was whether Diet Coke and Coke were the same product, the plaintiffs sought discovery of the secret formula for Diet Coke and Coca-Cola. The court agreed with the plaintiffs and ordered production of the formula though it granted a protective order that limited disclosure to plaintiffs' trial counsel and independent experts.

Not surprisingly, Coca-Cola refused to comply with the order to produce. Although the court did not enter a default judgment, as the plaintiffs had requested, it did enter an order that the bottlers were entitled to a non-rebuttable factual finding that the two formulae were within the range of formulae for syrups that had previously been sold as Coca-Cola syrup. Coca-Cola Bottling Co. v. Coca-Cola Co., 110 F.R.D. 363, 371–72 (D. Del. 1986). Notwithstanding this order, Coca-Cola ultimately prevailed, although the litigation lasted 10 years and generated at least eight published opinions. See Coca-Cola Bottling Co. v. Coca-Cola Co. (*Coke VIII*), 988 F.2d 386 (3d Cir. 1993). Do you think the plaintiffs in the *Coke* case really needed the formula for their suit, or were they trying to use the threat of discovery to pressure Coke into settlement?

The potential invasiveness of discovery is not limited to commercial cases. Consider the following description of the A.H. Robins Company's litigation strategy in Dalkon Shield litigation:

> Robins took the position that multiple sex partners, with the accompanying increased risk of contracting sexually transmitted diseases, were a more likely cause of uterine infections than was the Dalkon Shield. Attorneys for the company would ask the plaintiff to identify her sex partners so that these men could be subpoenaed and asked about their medical histories. Women were also asked to describe their sexual practices and the details of their personal hygiene, on the theory that these might relate to the risk of pelvic infection. The courts divided on whether to require answers to these questions, but the mere fact that questions suggesting uncleanliness, promiscuity, or sexual aberration were asked dissuaded many women from pressing forward with their claims (or from making claims at all) and induced others to accept cheap settlements offered by Robins.

Richard Sobol, Bending The Law 13 (1991).

As these cases illustrate, discovery can be a potent weapon. One of the potential costs of liberal discovery rules is that litigants with meritorious claims or defenses may be discouraged from pursuing their rights out of fear that private or confidential information will be disclosed. The benefits of liberal discovery may be worth this cost, but its cost should be taken into account.

c. *"Proportional."*

For many years, Rule 26(b)(1) permitted discovery of "nonprivileged" material that is "relevant to a claim or defense." This raised the question of whether a party was entitled to *all* relevant, nonprivileged matter. In 1983, Rule 26 was amended to introduce the principle of proportionality. Under Rule 26(b)(2)(C), as it existed until December 1, 2015, a court was able to limit discovery requests because they were not "proportional" to the case. In other words, lack of proportionality was a "filter" that allowed the court to restrict discovery. The issue was raised by the party responding to discovery, either in an objection to discovery or in a request for a protective order. The court could then limit discovery, for example, if the request was unreasonably cumulative or burdensome.

Effective December 1, 2015, Rule 26(b)(1) was amended to make proportionality part of the definition of discoverability. Today, under Rule 26(b)(1), one may discover nonprivileged matter that is relevant to a claim or defense

> and [is] proportional to the needs of the case, considering the importance of the issues at stake in the action, the amount in controversy, the parties' relative access to relevant information, the parties' resources, the importance of discovery in resolving the issues, and whether the burden or expense of the proposed discovery outweighs its likely benefit. Information within this scope of discovery need not be admissible in evidence to be discoverable.

Now, proportionality is a factor to be taken into account by the party seeking discovery. That party should not serve discovery requests that are not proportional to the needs of the case. The Advisory Committee received an unprecedented number of comments about this change, almost all of them negative. The major fear expressed, in short, was that parties responding to discovery (especially defendants) may object that the requests are not proportional, which will lead to satellite litigation and, some predict, a restriction of the scope of discovery. The burden evidently has shifted from the responding party (which used to be required to object and show that discovery was not proportional) to the party seeking discovery (which now, apparently, must show that the discovery sought is proportional). See, e.g., Patricia W. Hatamyar Moore, *The Anti-Plaintiff Pending Amendments to the Federal Rules of Civil Procedure and the Pro-Defendant Composition of the Federal Rulemaking Committees*, 83 U. Cinn. L. Rev. 1083 (2015).

One especially significant area of concern regarding proportionality is discovery of ESI, to which we now turn.

2. Issues Concerning Discovery of ESI

The following is one of several published opinions in an employment discrimination case brought by an equities trader against her former employer. Ordinarily, the party from whom discovery is sought must bear the expense of producing the information. As seen in this case, the court has discretion to "shift" these costs. As amended in 2015, Rule 26(c)(1)(B) expressly permits cost-shifting as part of the court's issuance of a protective order. Consider how cost-shifting complements the goal of ensuring proportional discovery.

Zubulake v. UBS Warburg LLC

216 F.R.D. 280 (S.D.N.Y. 2003)

Scheindlin, District Judge.

On May 13, 2003, I ordered defendants UBS Warburg LLC, UBS Warburg, and UBS AG (collectively "UBS") to restore and produce certain e-mails from a small group of backup tapes. Having reviewed the results of this sample restoration, Laura Zubulake now moves for an order compelling UBS to produce all remaining backup e-mails at its expense. UBS argues that based on the sampling, the costs should be shifted to Zubulake.

For the reasons fully explained below, Zubulake must share in the costs of restoration, although UBS must bear the bulk of that expense. In addition, UBS must pay for any costs incurred in reviewing the restored documents for privilege.

I. BACKGROUND

* * * In brief, Zubulake, an equities trader who earned approximately $650,000 a year with UBS, is now suing UBS for gender discrimination, failure to promote, and retaliation under federal, state, and city law. To support her claim, Zubulake seeks evidence stored on UBS's backup tapes that is only accessible through costly and time-consuming data retrieval. In particular, Zubulake seeks e-mails relating to her that were sent to or from five UBS employees. Matthew Chapin (Zubulake's immediate supervisor and the alleged primary discriminator), Jeremy Hardisty (Chapin's supervisor and the individual to whom Zubulake originally complained about Chapin), Rose Tong (a human relations representative who was assigned to handle issues concerning Zubulake), Vinay Datta (a co-worker), and Andrew Clarke (another co-worker). The question presented in this dispute is which party should pay for the costs incurred in restoring and producing these backup tapes.

* * * I ordered UBS to restore and produce e-mails from five of the ninety-four backup tapes that UBS had then identified as containing responsive documents; Zubulake was permitted to select the five tapes to be restored. UBS now reports, however, that there are only seventy-seven backup tapes that contain responsive data, including the five already restored. I further ordered UBS to "prepare an affidavit detailing the results of its search, as well as the time and money spent." UBS has complied by submitting counsel's declaration.

According to the declaration, Zubulake selected the backup tapes corresponding to Matthew Chapin's e-mails from May, June, July, August, and September 2001. * * * UBS hired an outside vendor, Pinkerton Consulting & Investigations, to perform the restoration.

Pinkerton was able to restore each of the backup tapes, yielding a total of 8,344 e-mails. That number is somewhat inflated, however, because it does not account for duplicates. Because each month's backup tape was a snapshot of Chapin's server for that month — and not an incremental backup reflecting only new material — an e-mail that was on the server for more than one month would appear on more than one backup tape. For example, an e-mail received in January 2001 and deleted in November 2001 would have been restored from all five backup tapes. With duplicates eliminated, the total number of *unique* e-mails restored was 6,203.

Pinkerton then performed a search for e-mails containing (in either the e-mail's text or its header information, such as the "subject" line) the terms "Laura", "Zubulake", or "LZ". The searches yielded 1,541 e-mails, or 1,075 if duplicates are eliminated. Of these 1,541 e-mails, UBS deemed approximately 600 to be responsive to Zubulake's document request and they were produced. UBS also produced, under the terms of the May 13 Order, fewer than twenty e-mails extracted from UBS's optical disk storage system.

Pinkerton billed UBS 31.5 hours for its restoration services at an hourly rate of $245, six hours for the development, refinement and execution of a search script at $245 an hour, and 101.5 hours of "CPU Bench Utilization" time for use of Pinkerton's computer systems at a rate of $18.50 per hour. Pinkerton also included a five percent "administrative overhead fee" of $459.38. Thus, the total cost of restoration and search was $11,524.63. In addition, UBS incurred the following costs: $4,633 in attorney time for the document review (11.3 hours at $410 per hour) and $2,845.80 in paralegal time for tasks related to document production (16.74 hours at $170 per hour). UBS also paid $432.60 in photocopying costs, which, of course, will be paid by Zubulake and is not part of this cost-shifting analysis. The total cost of restoration and production from the five backup tapes was $19,003.43.

UBS now asks that the cost of any further production—estimated to be $273,649.39, based on the cost incurred in restoring five tapes and producing responsive documents from those tapes—be shifted to Zubulake. The total figure includes $165,954.67 to restore and search the tapes and $107,694.72 in attorney and paralegal review costs. These costs will be addressed separately below.

II. LEGAL STANDARD

* * *

Although "the presumption is that the responding party must bear the expense of complying with discovery requests," requests that run afoul of the Rule 26(b)(2) [Note from your casebook co-authors: this refers to the proportionality filter that was deleted by amendment in 2015; now, proportionality is part of the definition of discoverability in Rule 26(b)(1)] proportionality test may subject the requesting party to protective orders under Rule 26(c), "including orders conditioning discovery on the requesting party's payment of the costs of discovery." A court will order such a cost-shifting protective order only upon motion of the responding party to a discovery request, and "for good cause shown." Thus, the responding party has the burden of proof on a motion for cost-shifting.

III. DISCUSSION

A. Cost-shifting Generally

In [an earlier opinion in the case], I considered plaintiff's request for information contained only on backup tapes and determined that cost-shifting *might* be appropriate. It is worth emphasizing again that cost-shifting is potentially appropriate only when *inaccessible* data is sought. When a discovery request seeks accessible data—for example, active on-line or near-line data—it is typically inappropriate to consider cost-shifting. * * * [The court now applied a seven-factor test it had set out in the earlier opinion.]

B. Application of the Seven Factor Test

1. Factors One and Two

These two factors should be weighted the most heavily in the cost-shifting analysis. * * *

a. The Extent to Which the Request Is Specifically Tailored to Discover Relevant Information

The document request at issue asks for "[a]ll documents concerning any communication by or between UBS employees concerning Plaintiff," and was subsequently narrowed to pertain to only five employees (Chapin, Hardisty, Tong, Datta, and Clarke) and to the period from August 1999 to December 2001. This is a relatively limited and targeted request, a fact borne out by the e-mails UBS actually produced, both initially and as a result of the sample restoration.

At oral argument, Zubulake presented the court with sixty-eight e-mails (of the 600 she received) that she claims are "highly relevant to the issues in this case" and thus require, in her view, that UBS bear the cost of production. And indeed, a review of these e-mails reveals that they are relevant. Taken together, they tell a compelling story of the dysfunctional atmosphere surrounding UBS's U.S. Asian Equities Sales Desk (the "Desk"). Presumably, these sixty-eight e-mails are reasonably representative of the seventy-seven backup tapes.

* * *

While all of these e-mails are likely to have some "tendency to make the existence of any fact that is of consequence to the determination of the action more probable or less probable than it would be without the evidence," *none* of them provide any direct evidence of discrimination. To be sure, the e-mails reveal a hostile relationship between Chapin and Zubulake—UBS does not contest this. But nowhere (in the sixty-eight e-mails produced to the Court) is there evidence that Chapin's dislike of Zubulake related to her gender.

b. The Availability of Such Information from Other Sources

The other half of the marginal utility test is the availability of the relevant data from other sources. Neither party seemed to know how many of the 600 e-mails produced in response to the May 13 Order had been previously produced. UBS argues that "nearly all of the restored e-mails that relate to plaintiff's allegations in this matter or to the merits of her case were already produced." This statement is perhaps too careful, because UBS goes on to observe that "the vast majority of the restored e-mails that were produced do *not* relate at all to plaintiff's allegations in this matter or to the merits of her case." But this determination is not for UBS to make; as the saying goes, "one man's trash is another man's treasure."

It is axiomatic that a requesting party may obtain "any matter, not privileged, that is relevant to the claim or defense of any party." The simple fact is that UBS previously produced only 100 pages of e-mails, but has now produced 853 pages (comprising the 600 responsive e-mails) from the five selected backup tapes alone. UBS itself decided that it was obliged to provide these 853 pages of e-mail pursuant to the requirements of Rule 26. Having done so, these numbers lead to the unavoidable conclusion that there are a significant number of responsive e-mails that now exist only on backup tapes.

* * *

c. Weighing Factors One and Two

The sample restoration, which resulted in the production of relevant e-mail, has demonstrated that Zubulake's discovery request was narrowly tailored to discover relevant information. And while the subject matter of some of those e-mails was addressed in other documents, these particular e-mails are only available from the backup tapes. Thus, direct evidence of discrimination may only be available through restoration. As a result, the marginal utility of this additional discovery may be quite high.

While restoration may be the only means for obtaining direct evidence of discrimination, the existence of that evidence is still speculative. The best that can be said is that Zubulake has demonstrated that the marginal utility is *potentially* high. All-in-all, because UBS bears the burden of proving that cost-shifting is warranted, the marginal utility test tips slightly against cost-shifting.

2. Factors Three, Four and Five

"The second group of factors addresses cost issues: 'How expensive will this production be?' and, 'Who can handle that expense?'"

a. The Total Cost of Production Compared to the Amount in Controversy

UBS spent $11,524.63, or $2,304.93 per tape, to restore the five back-up tapes. Thus, the total cost of restoring the remaining seventy-two tapes extrapolates to $165,954.67.

* * * I posed the following question to the parties: Assuming that a jury returns a verdict in favor of plaintiff, what economic damages can the plaintiff reasonably expect to recover? Plaintiff answered that reasonable damages are between $15,271,361 and $19,227,361, depending upon how front pay is calculated. UBS answered that damages could be as high as $1,265,000.

Obviously, this is a significant disparity. At this early stage, I cannot assess the accuracy of either estimate. Plaintiff had every incentive to high-ball the figure and UBS had every incentive to low-ball it. It is clear, however, that this case has the potential for a multi-million dollar recovery. Whatever else might be said, this is not a nuisance value case, a small case or a frivolous case. Most people do not earn $650,000 a year. If Zubulake prevails, her damages award undoubtedly will be higher than that of the vast majority of Title VII plaintiffs.

In an ordinary case, a responding party should not be required to pay for the restoration of inaccessible data if the cost of that restoration is significantly disproportionate to the value of the case. Assuming this to be a multi-million dollar case, the cost of restoration is surely not "significantly disproportionate" to the projected value of this case. This factor weighs against cost-shifting.

b. The Total Cost of Production Compared to the Resources Available to Each Party

There is no question that UBS has exponentially more resources available to it than Zubulake. While Zubulake is an accomplished equities trader, she has now been unemployed for close to two years. Given the difficulties in the equities market and the fact that she is suing her former employer, she may not be particularly marketable. On the other hand, she asserts that she has a $19 million claim against UBS. So while UBS's resources clearly dwarf Zubulake's, she may have the financial wherewithal to cover at least some of the cost of restoration. In addition, it is not unheard of for plaintiff's firms to front huge expenses when multi-million dollar recoveries are in sight. Thus, while this factor weighs against cost shifting, it does not rule it out.

c. The Relative Ability of Each Party to Control Costs and Its Incentive to Do So

Restoration of backup tapes must generally be done by an outside vendor. Here, UBS had complete control over the selection of the vendor. It is entirely possible that a less-expensive vendor could have been found. However, once that vendor is selected, costs are not within the control of either party. In addition, because these backup tapes are relatively well-organized — meaning that UBS knows what e-mails can be found on each tape — there is nothing more that Zubulake can do to focus her discovery request or reduce its cost. Zubulake has already made a targeted discovery request and the restoration of the sample tapes has not enabled her to cut back on that request. Thus, this factor is neutral.

3. Factor Six: The Importance of the Issues at Stake in the Litigation

As noted in [an earlier decision], this factor "will only rarely come into play." Although this case revolves around a weighty issue — discrimination in the workplace — it is hardly unique. Claims of discrimination are common, and while discrimination is an important problem, this litigation does not present a particularly novel issue. If I were to consider the issues in this discrimination case sufficiently important to weigh in the cost-shifting analysis, then this factor would be virtually meaningless. Accordingly, this factor is neutral.

4. Factor Seven: The Relative Benefits to the Parties of Obtaining the Information

Although Zubulake argues that there are potential benefits to UBS in undertaking the restoration of these backup tapes — in particular, the opportunity to obtain evidence that may be useful at summary judgment or trial — there can be no question that Zubulake stands to gain far more than does UBS, as will typically be the case. Certainly, absent an order, UBS would not restore any of this data of its own volition. Accordingly, this factor weighs in favor of cost-shifting.

5. Summary and Conclusion

Factors one through four tip against cost-shifting (although factor two only slightly so). Factors five and six are neutral, and factor seven favors cost-shifting. * * * [A] list of factors is not merely a matter of counting and adding; it is only a guide. Because some of the factors cut against cost shifting, but only *slightly so*—in particular, the possibility that the continued production will produce valuable new information—some cost-shifting is appropriate in this case, although UBS should pay the majority of the costs. There is plainly relevant evidence that is only available on UBS's backup tapes. At the same time, Zubulake has not been able to show that there is indispensable evidence on those backup tapes (although the fact that Chapin apparently deleted certain e-mails indicates that such evidence may exist).

The next question is how much of the cost should be shifted. * * * Because the seven factor test requires that UBS pay the lion's share, the percentage assigned to Zubulake must be less than fifty percent. A share that is too costly may chill the rights of litigants to pursue meritorious claims. However, because the success of this search is somewhat speculative, any cost that fairly can be assigned to Zubulake is appropriate and ensures that UBS's expenses will not be unduly burdensome. A twenty-five percent assignment to Zubulake meets these goals.

C. Other Costs

[The court concluded that only the cost of restoring the backup tapes would be shared. Beyond this, the cost of reviewing the materials to see whether any are protected from discovery (e.g., subject to attorney-client privilege) is borne by the responding party.]

Documents stored on backup tapes can be likened to paper records locked inside a sophisticated safe to which no one has the key or combination. The cost of accessing those documents may be onerous, and in some cases the parties should split the cost of breaking into the safe. But once the safe is opened, the production of the documents found inside is the sole responsibility of the responding party. The point is simple: technology may increasingly permit litigants to reconstruct lost or inaccessible information, but once restored to an accessible form, the usual rules of discovery apply.

IV. CONCLUSION

For the reasons set forth above, the costs of restoring any backup tapes are allocated between UBS and Zubulake seventy-five percent and twenty-five percent, respectively. * * *

Notes and Questions

1. *Zubulake* was decided before the 2015 amendments to Rule 26(b)(1) made proportionality part of the definition of discoverability. How, if at all, would the current version of Rule 26(b)(1) affect the outcome of the case?

2. Are the seven factors assessed by the court in *Zubulake* consistent with the considerations set forth in Rule 26(b)(1) for analyzing proportionality?

3. If UBS had sued Zubulake, would the cost-shifting analysis have been different?

4. The volume of ESI can be staggering. Indeed, in the ordinary course of business, companies generate large quantities of electronic and hard copy materials. Because they cannot reasonably retain all of them, businesses adopt so-called "document retention" policies (though they really address document destruction or deletion). These establish guidelines for how long different categories of materials will be retained. Such policies not only allow companies to save storage space, they allow them to destroy potentially incriminating documents. If the policy was well established and consistently followed, the destruction or deletion might not raise an inference that the destruction was improper. See Christopher R. Chase, *To Shred or Not to Shred: Document Retention Policies and Federal Obstruction of Justice Statutes*, 8 FORDHAM J. CORP. & FIN. L. 721 (2003).

On the other hand, once litigation is reasonably anticipated, parties must put a "litigation hold" on all relevant materials. Destruction of documents or ESI in violation of a litigation may raise the potential of an "adverse inference" instruction — that is, an instruction to the jury that it should assume that such materials were harmful to the party on the merits.

5. Until December 1, 2015, Rule 37(e) addressed failure to "produce" ESI. As amended effective that date, the provision addresses failure to "preserve" ESI. The amended Rule applies only when (1) ESI should have been preserved under a litigation hold but (2) was lost because of failure to take reasonable preservation steps, and (3) cannot be restored or recovered. If these things are shown, and the party seeking discovery was prejudiced by the loss of information, the court may order "measures" (not "sanctions") to cure the prejudice. The Advisory Committee notes do not specify what such orders might be. Only if the party from whom discovery is sought is found to have "acted with intent to deprive another party of the information's use in the litigation" may the court (1) presume that the lost information was unfavorable to the propounding party, (2) instruct the jury that it may/must presume it was unfavorable, or (3) dismiss or enter default judgment. Accordingly, a court has no authority to enter an "adverse inference" instruction based upon anything less than intentional deprivation of the material.

6. As part of the required Rule 26(f) discovery planning conference, parties must address ESI, including what material must be preserved and the form in which ESI will be produced, e.g., "native format" (the format in which the files were originally created and stored), TIFF, or PDF files. Rule 26(b)(2)(B) provides that a party need not provide discovery of ESI "from sources that the party identifies as not reasonably accessible because of undue burden or cost." Such data might include backup tapes, or erased, fragmented or damaged data.

3. Work Product

What lawyers call "work product" must not be confused with the attorney-client privilege, which we discussed in Section B.1.b above. Privilege protects confidential communications between lawyer and client. Work product protects from discovery material one party has generated in anticipation of litigation. The following is the classic case discussing the doctrine. It was decided long before Rule 26(b)(3) was promulgated in its present form. That Rule sets forth federal doctrine for work product (and calls it "trial preparation materials").

Hickman v. Taylor

329 U.S. 495, 67 S. Ct. 385, 91 L. Ed. 451 (1947)

Justice Murphy delivered the opinion of the Court.

* * *

On February 7, 1943, the tug "J. M. Taylor" sank while engaged in helping to tow a car float of the Baltimore & Ohio Railroad across the Delaware River at Philadelphia. The accident was apparently unusual in nature, the cause of it still being unknown. Five of the nine crew members were drowned. Three days later the tug owners and the underwriters employed a law firm, of which respondent Fortenbaugh is a member, to defend them against potential suits by representatives of the deceased crew members and to sue the railroad for damages to the tug.

A public hearing was held on March 4, 1943, before the United States Steamboat Inspectors, at which the four survivors were examined. This testimony was recorded and made available to all interested parties. Shortly thereafter, Fortenbaugh privately interviewed the survivors and took statements from them with an eye toward the anticipated litigation; the survivors signed these statements on March 29. Fortenbaugh also interviewed other persons believed to have some information relating to the accident and in some cases he made memoranda of what they told him. At the time when Fortenbaugh secured the statements of the survivors, representatives of two of the deceased crew members had been in communication with him. Ultimately claims were presented by representatives of all five of the deceased; four of the claims, however, were settled without litigation. The fifth claimant, petitioner herein, brought suit in a federal court under the Jones Act on November 26, 1943, naming as defendants the two tug owners, individually and as partners, and the railroad.

One year later, petitioner filed 39 interrogatories directed to the tug owners. The 38th interrogatory read: "State whether any statements of the members of the crews of the Tugs 'J. M. Taylor' and 'Philadelphia' or of any other vessel were taken in connection with the towing of the car float and the sinking of the Tug 'John M. Taylor.' Attach hereto exact copies of all such statements if in writing, and if oral, set forth in detail the exact provisions of any such oral statements or reports."

Supplemental interrogatories asked whether any oral or written statements, records, reports or other memoranda had been made concerning any matter relative to the towing operation, the sinking of the tug, the salvaging and repair of the tug, and the death of the deceased. If the answer was in the affirmative, the tug owners were then requested to set forth the nature of all such records, reports, statements or other memoranda.

The tug owners, through Fortenbaugh, answered all of the interrogatories except No. 38 and the supplemental ones just described. While admitting that statements of the survivors had been taken, they declined to summarize or set forth the contents. They did so on the ground that such requests called "for privileged matter obtained in preparation for litigation" and constituted "an attempt to obtain indirectly counsel's private files." It was claimed that answering these requests "would involve practically turning over not only the complete files, but also the telephone records and, almost, the thoughts of counsel."

* * * The District Court for the Eastern District of Pennsylvania, sitting en banc, held that the requested matters were not privileged. The court then decreed that the tug owners and Fortenbaugh, as counsel and agent for the tug owners, forthwith "answer Plaintiff's 38th interrogatory and supplementary interrogatories; produce all written statements of witnesses obtained by Mr. Fortenbaugh, as counsel and agent for Defendants; state in substance any fact concerning this case which Defendants learned through oral statements made by witnesses to Mr. Fortenbaugh whether or not included in his private memoranda and produce Mr. Fortenbaugh's memoranda containing statements of fact by witnesses or to submit these memoranda to the Court for determination of those portions which should be revealed to Plaintiff." Upon their refusal, the court adjudged them in contempt and ordered them imprisoned until they complied.

The Third Circuit Court of Appeals, also sitting en banc, reversed the judgment of the District Court. It held that the information here sought was part of the "work product of the lawyer" and hence privileged from discovery under the Federal Rules of Civil Procedure. The importance of the problem, which has engendered a great divergence of views among district courts, led us to grant certiorari.

The pre-trial deposition discovery mechanism established by Rules 26 to 37 is one of the most significant innovations of the Federal Rules of Civil Procedure. Under the prior federal practice, the pre-trial functions of notice-giving, issue-formulation and fact-revelation were performed primarily and inadequately by the pleadings. Inquiry into the issues and the facts before trial was narrowly confined and was often cumbersome in method. The new rules, however, restrict the pleadings to the task of general notice-giving and invest the deposition-discovery process with a vital role in the preparation for trial. The various instruments of discovery now serve (1) as a device, along with the pre-trial hearing under Rule 16, to narrow and clarify the basic issues between the parties, and (2) as a device for ascertaining the facts, or information as to the existence or whereabouts of facts, relative to those issues. Thus civil trials in the federal courts no longer need be carried on in the dark. The way is now clear, consistent with recognized privileges, for the parties to obtain the fullest possible knowledge of the issues and facts before trial.

* * *

[The Court here concluded that the district judge erred in considering the matter to raise a problem of interrogatories as opposed to one regarding a request for production.]

* * * It matters little at this late stage whether Fortenbaugh fails to answer interrogatories filed under Rule 26 [Note — the Rules no longer require that discovery re-

quests and responses be filed with the court.] or under Rule 33 or whether he refuses to produce the memoranda and statements pursuant to a subpoena under Rule 45 or a court order under Rule 34. The deposition-discovery rules create integrated procedural devices. And the basic question at stake is whether any of those devices may be used to inquire into materials collected by an adverse party's counsel in the course of preparation for possible litigation. The fact that the petitioner may have used the wrong method does not destroy the main thrust of his attempt. Nor does it relieve us of the responsibility of dealing with the problem raised by that attempt. * * *

In urging that he has a right to inquire into the materials secured and prepared by Fortenbaugh, petitioner emphasizes that the deposition-discovery portions of the Federal Rules of Civil Procedure are designed to enable the parties to discover the true facts and to compel their disclosure wherever they may be found. It is said that inquiry may be made under these rules, epitomized by Rule 26, as to any relevant matter which is not privileged; and since the discovery provisions are to be applied as broadly and liberally as possible, the privilege limitation must be restricted to its narrowest bounds. * * * As additional support for this result, petitioner claims that to prohibit discovery under these circumstances would give a corporate defendant a tremendous advantage in a suit by an individual plaintiff. Thus in a suit by an injured employee against a railroad or in a suit by an insured person against an insurance company the corporate defendant could pull a dark veil of secrecy over all the pertinent facts it can collect after the claim arises merely on the assertion that such facts were gathered by its large staff of attorneys and claim agents. * * *

We agree, of course, that the deposition-discovery rules are to be accorded a broad and liberal treatment. No longer can the time-honored cry of "fishing expedition" serve to preclude a party from inquiring into the facts underlying his opponent's case. Mutual knowledge of all the relevant facts gathered by both parties is essential to proper litigation. To that end, either party may compel the other to disgorge whatever facts he has in his possession. The deposition-discovery procedure simply advances the stage at which the disclosure can be compelled from the time of trial to the period preceding it, thus reducing the possibility of surprise. But discovery, like all matters of procedure, has ultimate and necessary boundaries. * * *

We also agree that the memoranda, statements and mental impressions in issue in this case fall outside the scope of the attorney-client privilege and hence are not protected from discovery on that basis. It is unnecessary here to delineate the content and scope of that privilege as recognized in the federal courts. For present purposes, it suffices to note that the protective cloak of this privilege does not extend to information which an attorney secures from a witness while acting for his client in anticipation of litigation. Nor does this privilege concern the memoranda, briefs, communications and other writings prepared by counsel for his own use in prosecuting his client's case; and it is equally unrelated to writings which reflect an attorney's mental impressions, conclusions, opinions or legal theories.

But the impropriety of invoking that privilege does not provide an answer to the problem before us. Petitioner has made more than an ordinary request for relevant, nonprivileged facts in the possession of his adversaries or their counsel. He has sought discovery as of right of oral and written statements of witnesses whose identity is well known and whose availability to petitioner appears unimpaired. He has sought production of these matters after making the most searching inquiries of his opponents as to the circumstances surrounding the fatal accident, which inquiries were sworn to have been answered to the best of their information and belief. Interrogatories were directed toward all the events prior to, during and subsequent to the sinking of the tug. Full and honest answers to such broad inquiries would necessarily have included all pertinent information gleaned by Fortenbaugh through his interviews with the witnesses. Petitioner makes no suggestion, and we cannot assume, that the tug owners or Fortenbaugh were incomplete or dishonest in the framing of their answers. In addition, petitioner was free to examine the public testimony of the witnesses taken before the United States Steamboat Inspectors. We are thus dealing with an attempt to secure the production of written statements and mental impressions contained in the files and the mind of the attorney Fortenbaugh without any showing of necessity or any indication or claim that denial of such production would unduly prejudice the preparation of petitioner's case or cause him any hardship or injustice. For aught that appears, the essence of what petitioner seeks either has been revealed to him already through the interrogatories or is readily available to him direct from the witnesses for the asking.

The District Court, after hearing objections to petitioner's request, commanded Fortenbaugh to produce all written statements of witnesses and to state in substance any facts learned through oral statements of witnesses to him. Fortenbaugh was to submit any memoranda he had made of the oral statements so that the court might determine what portions should be revealed to petitioner. All of this was ordered without any showing by petitioner, or any requirement that he make a proper showing, of the necessity for the production of any of this material or any demonstration that denial of production would cause hardship or injustice. The court simply ordered production on the theory that the facts sought were material and were not privileged as constituting attorney-client communications.

In our opinion, neither Rule 26 nor any other rule dealing with discovery contemplates production under such circumstances. That is not because the subject matter is privileged or irrelevant, as those concepts are used in these rules. Here is simply an attempt, without purported necessity or justification, to secure written statements, private memoranda and personal recollections prepared or formed by an adverse party's counsel in the course of his legal duties. As such, it falls outside the arena of discovery and contravenes the public policy underlying the orderly prosecution and defense of legal claims. Not even the most liberal of discovery theories can justify unwarranted inquiries into the files and the mental impressions of an attorney.

Historically, a lawyer is an officer of the court and is bound to work for the advancement of justice while faithfully protecting the rightful interests of his clients. In performing his various duties, however, it is essential that a lawyer work with a certain degree of privacy, free from unnecessary intrusion by opposing parties and their counsel. Proper preparation of a client's case demands that he assemble information, sift what he considers to be the relevant from the irrelevant facts, prepare his legal theories and plan his strategy without undue and needless interference. That is the historical and the necessary way in which lawyers act within the framework of our system of jurisprudence to promote justice and to protect their clients' interests. This work is reflected, of course, in interviews, statements, memoranda, correspondence, briefs, mental impressions, personal beliefs, and countless other tangible and intangible ways—aptly though roughly termed by the Circuit Court of Appeals in this case as the "work product of the lawyer." Were such materials open to opposing counsel on mere demand, much of what is now put down in writing would remain unwritten. An attorney's thoughts, heretofore inviolate, would not be his own. Inefficiency, unfairness and sharp practices would inevitably develop in the giving of legal advice and in the preparation of cases for trial. The effect on the legal profession would be demoralizing. And the interests of the clients and the cause of justice would be poorly served.

We do not mean to say that all written materials obtained or prepared by an adversary's counsel with an eye toward litigation are necessarily free from discovery in all cases. Where relevant and non-privileged facts remain hidden in an attorney's file and where production of those facts is essential to the preparation of one's case, discovery may properly be had. Such written statements and documents might, under certain circumstances, be admissible in evidence or give clues as to the existence or location of relevant facts. Or they might be useful for purposes of impeachment or corroboration. And production might be justified where the witnesses are no longer available or can be reached only with difficulty. Were production of written statements and documents to be precluded under such circumstances, the liberal ideals of the deposition-discovery portions of the Federal Rules of Civil Procedure would be stripped of much of their meaning. But the general policy against invading the privacy of an attorney's course of preparation is so well recognized and so essential to an orderly working of our system of legal procedure that a burden rests on the one who would invade that privacy to establish adequate reasons to justify production through a subpoena or court order. * * *

But as to oral statements made by witnesses to Fortenbaugh, whether presently in the form of his mental impressions or memoranda, we do not believe that any showing of necessity can be made under the circumstances of this case so as to justify production. Under ordinary conditions, forcing an attorney to repeat or write out all that witnesses have told him and to deliver the account to his adversary gives rise to grave dangers of inaccuracy and untrustworthiness. No legitimate purpose is served by such production. The practice forces the attorney to testify as to what he remembers or what he saw fit to write down regarding witnesses' remarks. Such testimony could not qualify as evidence; and to use it for impeachment or corroborative purposes would make the attorney much less an officer of the court and much more an ordinary witness. The standards of the profession would thereby suffer.

Denial of production of this nature does not mean that any material, non-privileged facts can be hidden from the petitioner in this case. He need not be unduly hindered in the preparation of his case, in the discovery of facts or in his anticipation of his opponents' position. Searching interrogatories directed to Fortenbaugh and the tug owners, production of written documents and statements upon a proper showing and direct interviews with the witnesses themselves all serve to reveal the facts in Fortenbaugh's possession to the fullest possible extent consistent with public policy. Petitioner's counsel frankly admits that he wants the oral statements only to help prepare himself to examine witnesses and to make sure that he has overlooked nothing. That is insufficient under the circumstances to permit him an exception to the policy underlying the privacy of Fortenbaugh's professional activities. If there should be a rare situation justifying production of these matters, petitioner's case is not of that type.

We fully appreciate the wide-spread controversy among the members of the legal profession over the problem raised by this case. It is a problem that rests on what has been one of the most hazy frontiers of the discovery process. But until some rule or statute definitely prescribes otherwise, we are not justified in permitting discovery in a situation of this nature as a matter of unqualified right. When Rule 26 and the other discovery rules were adopted, this Court and the members of the bar in general certainly did not believe or contemplate that all the files and mental processes of lawyers were thereby opened to the free scrutiny of their adversaries. And we refuse to interpret the rules at this time so as to reach so harsh and unwarranted a result.

We therefore affirm the judgment of the Circuit Court of Appeals.

Affirmed.

Justice Jackson, concurring.

The primary effect of the practice advocated here would be on the legal profession itself. But it too often is overlooked that the lawyer and the law office are indispensable parts of our administration of justice. Law-abiding people can go nowhere else to learn the ever changing and constantly multiplying rules by which they must behave and to obtain redress for their wrongs. The welfare and tone of the legal profession is therefore of prime consequence to society, which would feel the consequences of such a practice as petitioner urges secondarily but certainly.

"Discovery" is one of the working tools of the legal profession. It traces back to the equity bill of discovery in English Chancery practice and seems to have had a forerunner in Continental practice. Since 1848 when the draftsmen of New York's Code of Procedure recognized the importance of a better system of discovery, the impetus to extend and expand discovery, as well as the opposition to it, has come from within the Bar itself. It happens in this case that it is the plaintiff's attorney who demands such unprecedented latitude of discovery and, strangely enough, *amicus* briefs in his support have been filed by several labor unions representing plaintiffs as a class. It is the history of the movement for broader discovery, however, that in actual experience the chief opposition to its extension has come from lawyers who specialize in representing plaintiffs, because defendants have made liberal use of it to force plaintiffs to disclose their cases in advance. Discovery is a two-edged sword and we cannot decide this problem on any doctrine of extending help to one class of litigants.

Counsel for the petitioner candidly said on argument that he wanted this information to help prepare himself to examine witnesses, to make sure he overlooked nothing. He bases his claim to it in his brief on the view that the Rules were to do away with the old situation where a law suit developed into "a battle of wits between counsel." But a common law trial is and always should be an adversary proceeding. Discovery was hardly intended to enable a learned profession to perform its functions either without wits or on wits borrowed from the adversary.

The real purpose and the probable effect of the practice ordered by the district court would be to put trials on a level even lower than a "battle of wits." I can conceive of no practice more demoralizing to the Bar than to require a lawyer to write out and deliver to his adversary an account of what witnesses have told him. Even if his recollection were perfect, the statement would be his language, permeated with his inferences. Every one who has tried it knows that it is almost impossible so fairly to record the expressions and emphasis of a witness that when he testifies in the environment of the court and under the influence of the leading question there will not be departures in some respects. Whenever the testimony of the witness would differ from the "exact" statement the lawyer had delivered, the lawyer's statement would be whipped out to impeach the witness. Counsel producing his adversary's "inexact" statement could lose nothing by saying, "Here is a contradiction, gentlemen of the jury. I do not know whether it is my adversary or his witness who is not telling the truth, but one is not." Of course, if this practice were adopted, that scene would be repeated over and over again. The lawyer who delivers such statements often would find himself branded a deceiver afraid to take the stand to support his own version of the witness's conversation with him, or else he will have to go on the stand to defend his own credibility—perhaps against that of his chief witness, or possibly even his client.

Every lawyer dislikes to take the witness stand and will do so only for grave reasons. This is partly because it is not his role; he is almost invariably a poor witness. But he steps out of professional character to do it. He regrets it; the profession discourages it. But the practice advocated here is one which would force him to be a witness, not as to what he has seen or done but as to other witnesses' stories, and not because he wants to do so but in self-defense.

And what is the lawyer to do who has interviewed one whom he believes to be a biased, lying or hostile witness to get his unfavorable statements and know what to meet? He must record and deliver such statements even though he would not vouch for the credibility of the witness by calling him. Perhaps the other side would not want to call him either, but the attorney is open to the charge of suppressing evidence at the trial if he fails to call such a hostile witness even though he never regarded him as reliable or truthful.

Having been supplied the names of the witnesses, petitioner's lawyer gives no reason why he cannot interview them himself. If an employee-witness refuses to tell his story, he, too, may be examined under the Rules. He may be compelled on discovery, as fully as on the trial, to disclose his version of the facts. But that is his own disclosure—it can be used to impeach him if he contradicts it and such a deposition is not useful to promote an unseemly disagreement between the witness and the counsel in the case.

I agree to the affirmance of the judgment of the Circuit Court of Appeals which reversed the district court.

Notes and Questions

1. Why were the witness statements not protected by the attorney-client privilege?

2. Why did the plaintiff's attorney want the witness statements? The Court suggests that the plaintiff can learn all the facts contained in these statements through other means. Is that true? Suppose that a witness has told the defense lawyer one story and then, at deposition, tells a somewhat different story. How can the plaintiff's lawyer learn of the inconsistency without getting the witness' prior statement?

3. Consider the justifications offered by Justices Murphy and Jackson for protecting work product:

(a) "Sharp practices." What "sharp practices" might develop without work product protection? Is the risk of sharp practices any greater with respect to work product than with respect to any other type of discoverable information?

(b) "[M]uch of what is now put down in writing would remain unwritten." Do you agree that the elimination of work product would cause lawyers to stop writing things down? Couldn't a similar argument be made with respect to other types of discovery? For example, if manufacturers know that written reports of safety tests can be discovered, they might stop recording such tests. As a result, information that might improve the safety of a product could be lost. If this argument is not sufficiently compelling to limit discovery from parties, why is it so compelling with respect to discovery from lawyers?

(c) Relying on "wits borrowed from the adversary." Without work product protection, would lawyers stop preparing cases and instead gain a free ride on the work of their opponents?

(d) Lawyers would become witnesses at trial. Doesn't this argument confuse the question of discoverability with the question of admissibility? Couldn't work product be discoverable without its being admissible at trial?

(e) What "demoralizing" effect would the elimination of work product have on the profession?

4. Even if work product protection does encourage greater investigation and preparation, is this greater preparation something we should encourage? Judge Frank Easterbrook has asserted that most litigation simply concerns how to divide up the stakes among the parties and that the resources "spent bickering over the distribution of a pile of money" are largely a waste to society. He argues that the attorney-client privilege and work product protection should be restricted because these protections

encourage overinvestment in information creation that is useful principally to divide the stakes. "To say, as the Court did, that a restriction of the scope of the attorney-client and work product privileges would reduce the investment in information in litigation may be to praise that result, not to condemn it." Frank Easterbrook, *Insider Trading, Secret Agents, Evidentiary Privileges, and the Production of Information*, 1981 Sup. Ct. Rev. 309, 361.

Regardless of whether greater trial preparation is socially useful, work product protection, like the evidentiary privileges, has the potential cost of concealing relevant information. Professor Elizabeth Thornburg has argued that this cost is not worth the benefits. Do you agree? See Elizabeth Thornburg, *Rethinking Work Product*, 77 Va. L. Rev. 1515 (1991).

5. Rule 26(b)(3), which governs work product practice in federal courts, was promulgated 23 years after the decision in *Hickman*. Read Rule 26(b)(3) carefully. Notice that Rule 26(b)(3) only applies to "documents and tangible things." Are answers to interrogatories or responses to deposition questions protected as work product? Courts generally hold that while these are not covered by Rule 26(b)(3), the principle articulated by *Hickman v. Taylor* continues to apply to protect information in an intangible form. See 8 Wright & Miller, Federal Practice & Procedure § 2024 at 490–492; Richard Marcus, *The Story of* Hickman: *Preserving Adversarial Incentives While Embracing Broad Discovery, in* Civil Procedure Stories 323, 347–349 (K. Clermont, ed., 2d ed. 2008). How would the materials in *Hickman* be treated under Rule 26(b)(3)?

6. As *Hickman* makes clear, work product (like attorney-client privilege) does not protect the underlying facts from discovery. Thus, in the Robinsons' suit against Audi, if Audi sent an interrogatory to the Robinsons asking whether there were skid marks at the scene of the accident, the Robinsons could not decline to answer on the grounds that their lawyer learned the answer to that question while preparing for litigation. Suppose that one side, through great expense and ingenuity, locates a previously unknown witness to an accident. Is the name of that witness protected under Rule 26? For many years, Rule 26(b)(1) expressly permitted discovery of "the existence ... and location of any documents or other tangible things and the identity and location of persons who know of any discoverable matter." Effective December 1, 2015, that language was removed from the Rule. Nonetheless, the Advisory Committee notes state that such matters will still be discoverable. Can you fashion an argument to the contrary?

7. Rule 26(b)(3) protects only material prepared "in anticipation of litigation." Courts generally agree that this language does not require that litigation actually have commenced — it is sufficient that it is anticipated. One treatise explains the test as follows:

> Prudent parties anticipate litigation, and begin preparation prior to the time suit is formally commenced. Thus the test should be whether, in light of the nature of the document and the factual situation in the particular case, the

document can fairly be said to have been prepared or obtained because of the prospect of litigation.

8 Wright & Miller, Federal Practice & Procedure § 2024 at 500–502. Some courts have suggested that because of the word "litigation," the protection extends only where adversarial proceedings are contemplated. In one case, a commercial customer had complained to a product manufacturer that a product was defective. In response to the complaint, employees of the manufacturer prepared several internal memoranda discussing the defect in the product and possible solutions. Ultimately, the customer sued the manufacturer and in the course of that litigation, the manufacturer refused to produce the memoranda on grounds of work product. The court held that the documents were not protected because when the documents were prepared, the manufacturer was primarily concerned about maintaining good relations with its customer and with finding a commercial settlement that avoided litigation. Scott Paper Co. v. Ceilcote Co., 103 F.R.D. 591 (D. Me. 1984). See Binks Mfg. Co. v. National Presto Indus., Inc., 709 F.2d 1109 (7th Cir. 1983). Doesn't this create disincentives for parties to seek non-adversarial solutions to disputes?

Assuming litigation is anticipated, how closely connected to the litigation must the material be to be protected? Some courts have held that the material must have been prepared *to assist* in the litigation. See Evans v. Atwood, 177 F.R.D. 1, 6–7 (D.D.C. 1997). Others are a little less demanding and require only that the material was prepared *because of* the litigation. See United States v. Adlman, 134 F.3d 1194, 1203 (2d Cir. 1998). Even under the "because of" approach, some courts require that the prospect of litigation be "the driving force behind the preparation" of the document. National Union Fire Ins. Co. v. Murray Sheet Metal Co., 967 F.2d 980, 984 (4th Cir. 1992).

8. The Advisory Committee Notes state that "materials assembled in the ordinary course of business, or pursuant to public requirements unrelated to litigation, or for other nonlitigation purposes are not under the qualified immunity provided by this subdivision." Relying on this language, courts regularly deny work product protection to accident reports and insurance claim assessments. See, e.g., Heath v. F/V Zolotoi, 221 F.R.D. 545 (W.D. Wash. 2004); Kidwiler v. Progressive Paloverde Ins. Co., 192 F.R.D. 536 (N.D. W. Va. 2000).

9. Is material that was produced in anticipation of litigation in one suit protected from discovery in future litigation? In FTC v. Grolier Inc., 462 U.S. 19, 25 (1983), the Court observed in dicta, "the literal language of [Rule 26(b)(3)] protects materials prepared for *any* litigation or trial as long as they were prepared by or for a party to the subsequent litigation." Some courts have held that the protection continues only if the subsequent litigation is related to the case for which the material was originally prepared. See, e.g., Leonen v. Johns-Manville, 135 F.R.D. 94, 97 (D.N.J. 1990). Moreover, where the entity for which the material was prepared is not a party to the subsequent litigation, some courts have held that the material is not protected. See, e.g., Hawkins v. South Plains Int'l Trucks, Inc., 139 F.R.D. 682 (D. Colo. 1991). See Note, *The Work Product Doctrine in Subsequent Litigation*, 83 Colum. L. Rev. 412 (1983).

10. What must a party show to overcome the work product protection? Suppose that one side cannot now obtain the substantial equivalent, but could have obtained it if she had acted earlier? One court allowed discovery of the work product material under these circumstances, explaining, "Our role in administering the discovery rules * * * is not to reward diligence or to penalize laziness." Southern Ry. v. Lanham, 403 F.2d 119, 130 (5th Cir. 1968). Other courts have denied discovery where the other party could through diligence have obtained the equivalent. See, e.g., Hoffman v. Owens-Illinois Glass Co., 107 F.R.D. 793 (D. Mass. 1985).

11. Though *Hickman* concerned work product generated by a lawyer, does Rule 26(b)(3) apply to materials generated by someone other than an attorney? Some state rules do not, and require that work product be generated by an attorney or her agent. Pennsylvania limits work product protection much more significantly. Rule 4003.3 of the Pennsylvania Rules of Civil Procedure provides:

> a party may obtain discovery of any matter discoverable * * * even though prepared in anticipation of litigation or trial by or for another party or by or for that other party's representative, including his attorney, consultant, surety, indemnitor, insurer or agent. The discovery shall not include disclosure of the mental impressions of a party's attorney or his conclusions, opinions, memoranda, notes or summaries, legal research or legal theories. With respect to the representative of a party other than the party's attorney, discovery shall not include disclosure of his mental impressions, conclusions or opinions respecting the value or merit of a claim or defense or respecting strategy or tactics.

12. Ordinarily, discovery orders cannot be appealed immediately and instead are reviewable only after there is a final judgment in the case. See Chapter 14.B.7, infra. However, a contempt judgment is immediately appealable. This is what happened in *Hickman* — the district court found Fortenbaugh and the tug boat's owners in contempt for failing to produce the witnesses' statements, and ordered them imprisoned until they complied with the order. The appeal was filed immediately and neither Fortenbaugh nor the tug owners actually went to jail. See Marcus, supra, at 320.

13. Rule 26(b)(3) provides that the court "shall protect against disclosure of the mental impressions, conclusions, opinions, or legal theories of an attorney." Is this provision inconsistent with Rule 33(c) which permits interrogatories that call for "an opinion or contention that relates to fact or the application of law to fact"? The Advisory Committee Notes to Rule 26(b)(3) state:

> Under those rules [33 and 36], a party and his attorney or other representative may be required to disclose, to some extent, mental impressions, opinions, or conclusions. But documents or parts of documents containing these matters are protected against discovery by this subdivision. Even though a party may ultimately have to disclose in response to interrogatories or requests to admit, he is entitled to keep confidential documents containing such matters prepared for internal use.

One commentator has explained this comment as follows:

> The distinction between discoverable and nondiscoverable creative trial preparation material more logically can be expressed if it is described as not merely a distinction between the oral and the written but as primarily one between the general and specific. The general shape of a party's assertions must be known in order to determine what is and what is not in issue. It is not, however, necessary in order to determine the genuine issues in the cases to have detailed knowledge of the other side's contentions. Obtaining detailed knowledge could improperly serve as a substitute for the discovering party's own trial preparation work.

James Underwood, A Guide to Federal Discovery Rules 40 (2d ed. 1985).

For examples of contention interrogatories, see footnote 13 in *United Oil Co*, supra.

4. Experts

Experts can be extremely valuable, both as consultants who assist in preparation, but do not testify, and as expert witnesses at trial. They are widely used in civil litigation. A survey of California state civil jury cases showed that expert witnesses testified in 86 percent of these cases with an average of 3.3 experts per trial. Samuel Gross, *Expert Evidence*, 1991 Wis. L. Rev. 1113, 1119. Although ordinary witnesses are not permitted to testify as to their opinions, see Fed. R. Evid. 701, qualified experts may offer opinions where "scientific, technical, or other specialized knowledge will assist the trier of fact to understand the evidence or to determine a fact in issue." Fed. R. Evid. 702.

As discussed in Section B.2 above, Rule 26(a)(2) requires parties to disclose detailed information about experts who will testify at trial, in addition to a report created by the expert. Under Rule 26(a)(2)(B)(ii), the report must include "the facts or data considered by the witness." Some courts had interpreted a prior version of Rule 26 to require disclosure of all communications between counsel and a testifying expert witness and all draft reports. As a result, it had become common for lawyers to employ two sets of experts — one who would not testify with whom counsel could freely communicate and a second testifying expert. In 2010, Rule 26(b)(4) was amended to provide explicit work product protection for "drafts of any reports or disclosures required under Rule 26(b)(2)."

What about discovery concerning an expert who has been retained but will not testify at trial? Rule 26(b)(4)(B) addresses discovery concerning such "consulting" experts. Study that rule, then consider the following case:

Ager v. Jane C. Stormont Hospital & Training School for Nurses

622 F.2d 496 (10th Cir. 1980)

Barrett, Circuit Judge.

Lynn R. Johnson, counsel for plaintiff Emily Ager, appeals from an order of the District Court adjudging him guilty of civil contempt. Jurisdiction vests by reason of 28 U.S.C. § 1826(b).

Emily was born April 4, 1955, at Stormont-Vail Hospital in Topeka, Kansas. During the second stage of labor, Emily's mother suffered a massive rupture of the uterine wall. The ensuing loss of blood led to Mrs. Ager's death. Premature separation of the placenta from the uterine wall also occurred, resulting in fetal asphyxia. Following Emily's delivery, it was discovered that she evidenced signs of severe neurological dysfunction. Today, she is mentally impaired and a permanently disabled quadriplegic with essentially no control over her body functions.

In March, 1977, Emily's father filed, on her behalf, a complaint for the damages sustained at her birth. The complaint alleges, in essence, that "the hemorrhaging and resultant death of her mother and the brain damage and other injuries which she sustained ... while still in her mother's womb and/or during her delivery, were directly and proximately caused by the negligence and carelessness of the defendants (Stormont-Vail Hospital and Dr. Dan L. Tappen, the attending physician) which joined and concurred in causing plaintiff's mother's death and plaintiff's bodily injuries and damages and resultant disability." After joining the issues, Dr. Tappen propounded a series of interrogatories to the plaintiff. The specific interrogatories at issue here are:

> 1. Have you contacted any person or persons, whether they are going to testify or not, in regard to the care and treatment rendered by Dr. Dan Tappen involved herein?
>
> 2. If the answer to the question immediately above is in the affirmative, please set forth the name of said person or persons and their present residential and/or business address.
>
> 3. If the answer to question #1 is in the affirmative, do you have any statements or written reports from said person or persons?

In response, plaintiff filed written objections, accompanied by a lengthy brief. Dr. Tappen answered the plaintiff's objections. The answer brief was treated by the United States Magistrate as a motion for an order compelling discovery pursuant to the Federal Rules of Civil Procedure, Rule 37(a). Following his review, the Magistrate ordered the plaintiff to answer the interrogatories:

> Interrogatories No. 1, 2 and 3 should be answered with the single exception, if the plaintiff has contacted an expert who was informally consulted in preparation for trial, but who was never retained or specifically employed and will not be called as a witness, it will not be necessary for the plaintiff to supply the name and address of such person or persons or to set forth any statement or report which such person or persons may have made.

Plaintiff's counsel answered the interrogatories in part, but failed to provide any information concerning consultative experts not expected to testify at trial. Plaintiff apparently based the refusal to answer on her contention that an expert who advises a party that his opinion will not aid the party in the trial of the case falls within the definition of experts informally consulted but not retained or specially employed. At defendant's suggestion, the Magistrate ordered plaintiff to provide further answers to the interrogatories, specifically defining the terms retained or specially employed:

> In the generally accepted meaning of the term in everyday usage, "retained" or "specially employed" ordinarily implies some consideration, a payment or reward of some kind, as consideration for being "retained" or "specially employed." It follows, therefore, that if a medical expert is consulted for the purpose of rendering advice or opinion on a hospital chart, or a physician's medical records pertaining to a case, and is paid or makes a charge for such service, he has been "retained" or "specially employed" within the meaning of the Rule. If [such an] expert is not to be called as a witness, he would be subject to the provisions of Rule 26(b)(4)(B) and, * * * there would be routine access to the names and addresses of such experts; but if they are not to be called as witnesses, facts known or opinions held by such experts would be subject to the requirements of Rule 26(b)(1)(B). However, if the consultation with the medical expert was strictly on an informal basis and such expert was not "retained" or "specially employed," the identity of such expert need not be disclosed.

Rather than complying with the Magistrate's order, Ager sought review by the District Court pursuant to 28 U.S.C. § 636(b)(1)(A). The District Court denied plaintiff's motion for review as untimely. On reconsideration, the Court affirmed the Magistrate's order:

> In the context of this malpractice case the question is whether plaintiff must identify each and every doctor, physician or medical expert plaintiff's counsel retained or specially employed during pretrial investigation and preparation. The courts have been divided on the issue. The Magistrate * * * held the identities of persons retained or specially employed for an opinion (i.e. to whom some consideration had been paid) to be discoverable. We have again read the Magistrate's Order and the suggestions of counsel. We find plaintiff's argument based upon the Advisory Committee Notes to be unpersuasive. After reviewing the cases and the suggestions of counsel we cannot find the Magistrate's Order to be "contrary to law."

Plaintiff's counsel filed a formal response to the Court's order and refused to comply. The Court thereafter entered a civil contempt order against Johnson. Johnson was committed to the custody of the United States Marshal until his compliance with the Court's order. Execution of the custody order was stayed pending appeal, after Johnson posted a recognizance bond. The Court specifically found that the appeal was not frivolous or taken for purposes of delay.

The issues on appeal are whether: (1) the District Court erred in adjudging Johnson guilty of civil contempt; and (2) a party may routinely discover the names of retained or specially employed consultative non-witness experts, pursuant to the Federal Rules of Civil Procedure, rule 26(b)(4)(B), absent a showing of exceptional circumstances justifying disclosure.

The Contempt Power

When a recalcitrant witness fails to obey the duly issued orders of a court, he may be cited for contempt, either criminal, civil, or both. Whether the adjudication of contempt "survives the avoidance of [the] underlying order depends on the nature of the contempt decree. If the contempt is criminal it stands; if it is civil it fails."

The primary purpose of a criminal contempt is to punish defiance of a court's judicial authority. Accordingly, the normal beneficiaries of such an order are the courts and the public interest. On the other hand, civil contempt is characterized by the court's desire "to *compel* obedience of the court order or to compensate the litigant for injuries sustained from the disobedience." The remedial aspects outweigh the punitive considerations. Thus, the primary beneficiaries of such an order are the individual litigants. The judicial system benefits to a lesser extent.

Our review of the order, and the proceedings held in connection therewith, convinces us that the citation was framed in the nature of a coercive civil contempt. * * *

Validity of the Underlying Order

Having held that the viability of the contempt citation depends upon the validity of the underlying order, we now turn to the issue of whether a party may routinely discover the identities of non-witness expert consultants absent a showing of exceptional circumstances justifying disclosure.

[Rule 26 of the] Federal Rules of Civil Procedure governs the scope of discovery concerning experts or consultants. Subdivision (b)(4) separates these experts into four categories, applying different discovery limitations to each:

> (1) Experts a party expects to use at trial. * * *
>
> (2) Experts retained or specially employed in anticipation of litigation or preparation for trial but not expected to be used at trial. Except as provided in rule 35 for an examining physician, the facts and opinions of experts in this category can be discovered only on a showing of exceptional circumstances.
>
> (3) Experts informally consulted in preparation for trial but not retained. No discovery may be had of the names or views of experts in this category.
>
> (4) Experts whose information was not acquired in preparation for trial. This class, which includes both regular employees of a party not specially employed on the case and also experts who were actors or viewers of the occurrences that gave rise to suit, is not included within Rule 26(b)(4) at all and facts and opinions they have are freely discoverable as with any ordinary witness.

Wright & Miller, Federal Practice and Procedure: Civil § 2029. We are here concerned *only* with the second and third category of experts.

A. Discovery of Experts Informally Consulted, But Not Retained or Specially Employed

No provision in Fed. Rules of Civ. Proc. Rule 26(b)(4) expressly deals with non-witness experts who are informally consulted by a party in preparation for trial, but not retained or specially employed in anticipation of litigation. The advisory committee notes to the rule indicated, however, that subdivision (b)(4)(B) "precludes discovery against experts who [are] informally consulted in preparation for trial, but not retained or specially employed." We agree with the District Court that this preclusion not only encompasses information and opinions developed in anticipation of litigation, but also insulates discovery of the identity and other collateral information concerning experts consulted informally. Graham, *Discovery of Experts Under Rule 26(b)(4) of the Federal Rules of Civil Procedure: Part One, an Analytical Study*, 1976 U. Ill. L.F. 895, 938–939.

Relying on Professor Graham's article, Ager urges that "an expert 'would be considered informally consulted if, for any reason, the consulting party did not consider the expert of any assistance,' and that '[a] consulting party may consider the expert of no assistance because of his insufficient credentials, his unattractive demeanor, or his excessive fees.'" This view is, of course, at odds with the Trial Court's ruling that:

> The commonly accepted meaning of the term "informally consulted" necessarily implies a consultation without formality. If one makes an appointment with a medical expert to discuss a case or examine records and give advice or opinion for which a charge is made and the charge is paid or promised what is informal about such consultation? On the other hand, an attorney meets a doctor friend at a social occasion or on the golf course and a discussion occurs concerning the case no charge is made or contemplated no written report rendered such could clearly be an "informal consultation."

We decline to embrace either approach in its entirety. In our view, the status of each expert must be determined on an ad hoc basis. Several factors should be considered: (1) the manner in which the consultation was initiated; (2) the nature, type and extent of information or material provided to, or determined by, the expert in connection with his review; (3) the duration and intensity of the consultative relationship; and, (4) the terms of the consultation, if any (e.g. payment, confidentiality of test data or opinions, etc.). Of course, additional factors bearing on this determination may be examined if relevant.

Thus, while we recognize that an expert witness' lack of qualifications, unattractive demeanor, excessive fees, or adverse opinions may result in a party's decision not to use the expert at trial, nonetheless, there are situations where a witness is retained or specifically employed in anticipation of litigation prior to the discovery of such undesirable information or characteristics. On the other hand, a telephonic inquiry to an expert's office in which only general information is provided may result in informal consultation, even if a fee is charged, provided there is no follow-up consultation.

The determination of the status of the expert rests, in the first instance, with the party resisting discovery. Should the expert be considered informally consulted, that categorization should be provided in response. The propounding party should then be provided the opportunity of requesting a determination of the expert's status based on an in camera review by the court. Inasmuch as the District Court failed to express its views on this question, we deem it appropriate to remand rather than attempt to deal with the merits of this issue on appeal. If the expert is considered to have been only informally consulted in anticipation of litigation, discovery is barred.

B. Discovery of the Identities of Experts Retained or Specially Employed

Subdivision (b)(4)(B) of rule 26 specifically deals with non-witness experts who have been retained or specially employed by a party in anticipation of litigation. The text of that subdivision provides that "facts or opinions" of non-witness experts retained or specially employed may only be discovered upon a showing of "exceptional circumstances under which it is impracticable for the party seeking discovery to obtain facts or opinions on the same subject by other means." Inasmuch as discovery of the identities of these experts, absent a showing of exceptional circumstances, was not expressly precluded by the text of subdivision (b)(4)(B), the District Court found the general provisions of rule 26(b)(1) controlling. * * *

The District Court's ruling on this issue follows [several cases]. Several [other] decisions, however, have held that rule 26(b)(4)(B) requires a showing of exceptional circumstances before names of retained or specially employed consultants may be discovered.

The advisory committee notes indicate that the structure of rule 26 was largely developed around the doctrine of unfairness designed to prevent a party from building his own case by means of his opponent's financial resources, superior diligence and more aggressive preparation. Dr. Tappen contends that "[d]iscoverability of the identity of an expert retained or specially employed by the other party but who is not to be called to testify hardly gives the discovering party a material advantage or benefit at the expense of the opposing party's preparation. Once those identities are disclosed, the discovering party is left to his own diligence and resourcefulness in contacting such experts and seeking to enlist whatever assistance they may be both able and willing to offer." The drafters of rule 26 did not contemplate such a result:

> Subdivision (b)(4)(B) is concerned only with experts retained or specially consulted in relation to trial preparation. Thus the subdivision precludes discovery against experts who were informally consulted in preparation for trial, but not retained or specially employed. As an ancillary procedure, a party may *on a proper showing* require the other party to *name* experts retained or specially employed, but not those informally consulted. (Emphasis supplied).

We hold that the "proper showing" required to compel discovery of a non-witness expert retained or specially employed in anticipation of litigation[5] corresponds to a

5. The distinction between experts who are retained or specially employed in anticipation of litigation is somewhat unclear.

showing of "exceptional circumstances under which it is impracticable for the party seeking discovery to obtain facts or opinions on the same subject by other means." Federal Rules of Civil Procedure, rule 26(b)(4)(B).

There are several policy considerations supporting our view. Contrary to Dr. Tappen's view, once the identities of retained or specially employed experts are disclosed, the protective provisions of the rule concerning facts known or opinions held by such experts are subverted. The expert may be contacted or his records obtained and information normally non-discoverable, under rule 26(b)(4)(B), revealed. Similarly, although perhaps rarer, the opponent may attempt to compel an expert retained or specially employed by an adverse party in anticipation of trial, but whom the adverse party does not intend to call, to testify at trial.[6] The possibility also exists, although we do not suggest it would occur in this case, or that it would be proper, that a party may call his opponent to the stand and ask if certain experts were retained in anticipation of trial, but not called as a witness, thereby leaving with the jury an inference that the retaining party is attempting to suppress adverse facts or opinions. Finally, we agree with Ager's view that "[d]isclosure of the identities of [medical] consultative experts would inevitably lessen the number of candid opinions available as well as the number of consultants willing to even discuss a potential medical malpractice claim with counsel.... [I]n medical malpractice actions [perhaps] more than any other type of litigation, the limited availability of consultative experts and the widespread aversion of many health care providers to assist plaintiff's counsel require that, absent special circumstances, discovery of the identity of evaluative consultants be denied. If one assumes that access to informed opinions is desirable in both prosecuting valid claims and eliminating groundless ones, a discovery practice that would do harm to these objectives should not be condoned."

In sum, we hold that the identity, and other collateral information concerning an expert who is retained or specially employed in anticipation of litigation, but not expected to be called as a witness at trial, is not discoverable except as "provided in Rule 35(b) or upon a showing of exceptional circumstances under which it is impracticable for the party seeking discovery to obtain facts or opinions on the same subject by other means."[8] Fed. Rules Civ. Proc., rule 26(b)(4)(B). The party "seeking

---

6. We do not here decide the propriety of this action.

8. Professor Albert Sacks, reporter to the advisory committee, listed two examples of exceptional circumstances:

> (a) Circumstances in which an expert employed by the party seeking discovery could not conduct important experiments and test[s] because an item of equipment, etc., needed for the test[s] has been destroyed or is otherwise no longer available. If the party from whom discovery is sought had been able to have its experts test the item before its destruction or nonavailability, then information obtained from those tests might be discoverable.
>
> (b) Circumstances in which it might be impossible for a party to obtain its own expert. Such circumstances would occur when the number of experts in a field is small and their time is already fully retained by others.

See: ALI-ABA, Civil Trial Manual p. 189.

disclosure under Rule 26(b)(4)(B) carries a heavy burden" in demonstrating the existence of exceptional circumstances.

Disposition

The order of the District Court adjudging Lynn R. Johnson guilty of civil contempt is vacated. The cause is remanded. On remand, the status of the non-witness experts against whom discovery is sought should be undertaken as a two-step process. First, was the expert informally consulted in anticipation of litigation but not retained or specially employed? If so, no discovery may be had as to the identity or opinions of the expert. Second, if the expert was not informally consulted, but rather retained or specially employed in anticipation of litigation, but not expected to testify at trial, do exceptional circumstances exist justifying disclosure of the expert's identity, opinions or other collateral information?

Vacated and remanded.

Notes and Questions

1. If you represented the plaintiff in *Ager*, why would you want the names of defendant's *non*-testifying experts?

2. In *Ager*, suppose that the court refuses to permit plaintiff to discover the identity of the defendant's non-testifying experts. Nonetheless, in preparing for trial, plaintiff contacts an expert who happens to be one defendant had consulted. Would Rule 26(b)(4) prohibit the plaintiff from consulting that expert or calling her to testify? The cases are in conflict on this issue. See Note, *Must the Show Go On? Defining When One Party May Call or Compel an Opposing Party's Consultative Expert to Testify*, 78 MINN. L. REV. 1191 (1994).

3. Prior to the 1993 amendments, discovery of even testifying experts was more limited. These past limitations were justified by the Advisory Committee of the prior rule because they "reflect[ed] the fear that one side will benefit unduly from the other's better preparation." The 1993 amendments, which allow relatively unfettered discovery from testifying experts, apparently reject this fairness argument, at least as it is applied to testifying experts. Should the argument also be rejected with respect to non-testifying experts? Are there other reasons to protect non-testifying experts from discovery?

4. Why should information from informally consulted experts be absolutely protected?

5. As *Ager* suggests, there is a split of authority on the question whether the names of non-testifying experts are protected under Rule 26(b)(4)(B). See, e.g., Eisai Co. v. Teva Pharms. USA, Inc., 247 F.R.D. 440 (D.N.J. 2007). What are the arguments for and against routine disclosure of such experts' identities? Which argument do you think is stronger? See Note, *Discovery of Retained Nontestifying Experts' Identities Under the Federal Rules of Civil Procedure*, 80 MICH. L. REV. 513 (1982).

6. Consider the following case: Goldman Paper Company hires a consultant to test land owned by the corporation for contamination. Later the corporation is sold

to another entity. When the buyer learns that the land is contaminated, it sues to rescind the purchase and seeks to depose the consultant. Goldman objects to the deposition on the grounds that the consultant is an non-testifying expert whom Goldman has retained to assist in the preparation of litigation. Should the buyer be permitted to depose the consultant? See Bunzl Pulp & Paper Sales, Inc. v. Golder, 1990 U.S. Dist. LEXIS 16355 (E.D. Pa. Dec. 4, 1990).

7. As *Ager* explains, experts whose information was not acquired in anticipation of litigation are considered ordinary fact witnesses and information is freely discoverable from them. But notice that the disclosure requirement of Rule 26(a)(2) mandating that a testifying expert provide a report to the other side applies only to testifying experts who were "retained or specially employed." Does this mean that a party whose trial expert is a regular employee (and who was therefore not "retained or specially employed") can ignore the mandatory disclosure requirement of Rule 26(a)(2)? Although a few courts have so held, see Navajo Nation v. Norris, 189 F.R.D. 610 (E.D. Wash. 1999), others have not, concluding that this would create an unintended loophole. See Prieto v. Malgor, 361 F.3d 1313, 1319 (11th Cir. 2004); Day v. Consolidated Rail Corp., 1996 U.S. Dist. LEXIS 6596 (S.D.N.Y. May 14, 1996).

8. Can independent experts, such as research scientists, who have not been hired by any party, be forced to testify? In general, such experts can be forced to testify, but Rule 45(c)(3)(C)(ii) gives the court authority to order appropriate compensation. As the Advisory Committee Notes explain: "Experts are not exempt from the duty to give evidence, * * * but compulsion to give evidence may threaten the intellectual property of experts denied the opportunity to bargain for the value of their services."

9. In both *Ager* and *Hickman*, counsel for one of the parties disobeyed a discovery order, was held in contempt of court, and sent to jail. You may wonder why a lawyer would behave so defiantly. The reason is that the contempt citation is necessary to ensure immediate appellate review of the discovery ruling. As we will see in Chapter 14, in federal court, litigants ordinarily cannot appeal until there is a final judgment which ends the whole case. Because discovery rulings come long before the end of the case, those rulings are not immediately appealable. However, a contempt citation is immediately appealable because it is considered a separate proceeding.

10. The discovery dispute in *Ager* was decided in the first instance by a magistrate judge. Magistrate judges are not appointed pursuant to Article III of the Constitution. They are not appointed by the President and do not enjoy life tenure. Instead they are appointed to eight-year terms by the district judges of each district court. 28 U.S.C. § 631. On referral from a district judge, magistrate judges are authorized to decide matters that are not dispositive of a claim or defense. See 28 U.S.C. § 636(b)(1); Rule 72. Most discovery falls into this category, and magistrate judges are widely used in scheduling and planning conferences under Rule 16 and in resolving discovery disputes. Decisions of a magistrate judge are reviewable by the district court, and only a district court can enter a contempt citation. With consent of the parties, magistrate judges can also adjudicate cases. See 28 U.S.C. § 636(c); Rule 73; Roell v. Withrow, 538 U.S. 580 (2003).

5. Discovery in the International Context

The availability of broad discovery is unique to the U.S. system. In civil law countries, lawyer-conducted discovery is very limited — the court rather than the lawyers has primary responsibility for developing the evidence. See Stephen Subrin, *Discovery in Global Perspective: Are We Nuts?*, 52 DEPAUL L. REV. 299, 301–02 (2002). Other common law countries permit some discovery, but it is significantly more limited than in the U.S. — constrained by time limitations, pleading rules, and a strong aversion to using discovery for "fishing expeditions." Id. at 303–08; Geoffrey Hazard, *From Whom No Secrets Are Hid*, 76 TEX. L. REV. 1665, 1677–82 (1998). What happens when information or witnesses that would otherwise be discoverable are located abroad? First, you should notice that as to discovery from another party, the Rules do not have geographic limits. Rules 34 requires production of documents or other materials within "the custody or control" of a party. The fact that the documents are located abroad does not obviate the obligation to produce them. Similarly, the fact that the relevant persons are located abroad, does not relieve a party of its obligation to comply with a deposition notice under Rule 30(b)(6). Sometimes the deponent will be required to come to the U.S. In other cases, the deposition will take place abroad. Rule 28(b) addresses the mechanics of taking depositions abroad.

The United States and 58 other nations are signatories to the Hague Convention on the Taking of Evidence Abroad in Civil or Commercial Matters (known as the Hague Evidence Convention) which provides mechanisms for one court to request the judicial assistance of the country in which evidence abroad is located. The basic mechanism is a Letter of Request which is sent from the requesting court to a designated Central Authority in the receiving country and from there to the appropriate court to conduct an evidentiary proceeding and return the completed Letter of Request to the requesting court. The Convention can be particularly useful in situations where the U.S. courts lack the power to compel cooperation such as in the case of a nonparty witness who is not subject to jurisdiction in the U.S. However, the Convention can also be cumbersome — evidence collected abroad pursuant to the Convention is overseen by a local judge at a formal hearing, rather than by lawyers as would be the case at a U.S. deposition The Supreme Court has held that the Hague Evidence Convention supplements but does not displace the discovery tools that are otherwise available, and there is no requirement that courts always use the Convention as the preferred approach. Societe Nationale Industrielle Aerospatiale v. United States Dist. Court, 482 U.S. 522 (1987). Thus, a litigant may use a Rule 34 request to seek documents within the control of a party that are located abroad. Although the Court did not require use of the Convention in all cases, it did admonish:

> American courts, in supervising pretrial proceedings, should exercise special vigilance to protect foreign litigants from the danger that unnecessary, or unduly burdensome, discovery may place them in a disadvantageous position. Judicial supervision of discovery should always seek to minimize its costs and inconvenience and to prevent improper uses of discovery requests. * * *

> In addition, we have long recognized the demands of comity in suits involving foreign states, either as parties or as sovereigns with a coordinate interest in the litigation. American courts should therefore take care to demonstrate due respect for any special problem confronted by the foreign litigant on account of its nationality or the location of its operations, and for any sovereign interest expressed by a foreign state.

Id. at 546.

Some other countries have responded to the U.S. discovery system by enacting "blocking statutes" which prohibit disclosure of certain information even in response to discovery requests. Although these statutes may impose civil or criminal penalties, "such statutes do not deprive an American court of the power to order a party subject to its jurisdiction to produce evidence even though the act of production may violate that statute." Id. at 544 n.29. See, e.g., Bodner v. Banque Paribas, 202 F.R.D. 370 (E.D.N.Y. 2000). Nonetheless, following the Court's admonition in *Aerospatiale*, courts tend to examine cases individually, taking into account the competing interests of the nations whose laws are in conflict, the hardship of compliance on the party from whom discovery is sought, the importance of the information requested, and the good faith of the party resisting discovery. See James Nafziger, *Another Look at the Hague Evidence Convention After Aerospatiale*, 38 Tex. Int'l L.J. 103 (2003).

Sometimes the shoe is on the other foot, and U.S. courts are called upon to assist foreign tribunals in the production of evidence located in the U.S. Federal law specifically authorizes such assistance:

> The district court of the district in which a person resides or is found may order him to give his testimony or statement or to produce a document or other thing for use in a proceeding in a foreign or international tribunal, including criminal investigations conducted before formal accusation. The order may be made pursuant to a letter rogatory issued, or request made, by a foreign or international tribunal or upon the application of any interested person * * *.

28 U.S.C. § 1782(a). The leading case interpreting this statute is Intel Corp. v. Advanced Micro Devices, Inc., 542 U.S. 241 (2004). There, Advanced Micro Devices (AMD) had filed a complaint with the Directorate-General for Competition of the Commission of the European Communities, asking that that body to investigate Intel for alleged antitrust violations. After the Directorate-General declined to seek documents that Intel had previously produced in litigation in the U.S., AMD asked a U.S. district court to order Intel to produce the documents. The Supreme Court held that the district court did have authority under § 1782 to order production of the documents. Specifically, the Court held that (1) AMD was "an interested person" within the meaning of the statute and therefore had standing to request assistance; (2) the Commission was a "tribunal" within the meaning of the statute and that it was not necessary for a suit to be pending before that tribunal—the investigation was sufficient; and (3) the statute does not require a showing that the material would

be discoverable under the law of the foreign tribunal, nor a showing that it would be discoverable in comparable litigation in the U.S.

Finally, the Court held that although the statute allowed discovery assistance, it did not require such assistance. The Court laid out several factors for courts to take into account. First, the court should consider whether the person from whom discovery is sought is a participant in the foreign proceeding since "[a] foreign tribunal has jurisdiction over those appearing before it, and can itself order them to produce evidence." Id. at 264. Second, the court "may take into account the nature of the foreign tribunal, the character of the proceedings underway abroad, and the receptivity of the foreign government or the court or agency abroad to U.S. federal-court judicial assistance." Id.

6. Review Problem

A tanker owned by Gasson Oil Co. runs aground causing a massive oil spill off the coast of Alaska. Immediately following the spill, Gasson sends a team of investigators to learn all they can about the incident. The investigative team is lead by Gasson's General Counsel and includes lawyers, engineers, environmental specialists, as well as other experts. The team is instructed to inspect the site, interview people and write a report for the Gasson Board of Directors on the causes and effects of the spill.

1. A group of fishermen sue Gasson to recover damages caused to their business by the oil spill. In the course of discovery, plaintiffs make a request for production of documents seeking:

(a) a copy of the report to the Board;

(b) all photos or videos of the accident site taken by the investigative team;

(c) all photos or videos of the accident site taken by witnesses or other non-parties and given or sold to Gasson;

(d) all signed statements given by witnesses;

(e) all audio- or videotapes of interviews with witnesses;

(f) all notes and memos concerning the investigation;

(g) the results of all tests conducted by the Gasson investigative team.

The plaintiffs also serve interrogatories which ask for:

(h) names of everyone interviewed as part of the investigation;

(i) a summary of what was said by each person who was interviewed.

Which, if any, of these items are discoverable?

2. Would any of the items listed in Question 1 have to be disclosed if Gasson decided to call as an expert witness at trial one of the experts who participated in the investigation?

3. Assume that plaintiffs' interrogatories also request detailed information concerning how the accident occurred. Can Gasson refuse to answer on the grounds

that the information was acquired as part of a work product protected investigation? Can it refuse to answer on the grounds that its attorney has that information?

4. Suppose that in the course of the investigation, the captain of the ship admitted to one of the lawyers that the evening before the ship sailed, he spent time in a bar and had 8 to 10 drinks. In addition, he gave the lawyer the names of the crew who were with him at the bar. In discovery the plaintiffs' interrogatories ask:

(a) For the 24-hour period immediately prior to the departure of the tanker, state whether the captain consumed any alcohol.

(b) If the captain did consume any alcohol during the 24 hours prior to the departure of the tanker, state when and where the alcohol was consumed and the quantity consumed. Also state the names and addresses of any people who were present with the captain when he consumed the alcohol.

Does Gasson have to answer these interrogatories?

5. Suppose that during the course of the investigation, a witness who was with the captain shortly before the ship ran aground noted that the captain was not wearing his eyeglasses. In his deposition, the captain say he does not remember whether he was wearing his glasses at the time of the accident, but asserted "I don't need them anyway—my vision is fine without glasses." Can plaintiffs' counsel have the captain subjected to ophthalmological testing? How?

6. Suppose that the plaintiffs alleged that Gasson acted with recklessness. Gasson sends the following interrogatory:

Specify each act or omission by Gasson that you contend was reckless.

Must the plaintiffs answer this interrogatory?

E. Timing and Pretrial Disclosures, Conferences, and Orders

1. Timing

Rule 26(f)(1) requires that all parties or their counsel confer "as soon as practicable—and in any event at least 21 days before a scheduling conference is to be held or a scheduling order is due under Rule 16(b)." The purpose of the conference is to "consider the nature and basis of their claims and defenses and the possibilities for promptly settling or resolving the case; make or arrange for the disclosures required by Rule 26(a)(1); discuss any issues about preserving discoverable information; and develop a proposed discovery plan." Rule 26(f)(2). Absent court order or agreement of the parties, no formal discovery can commence until after this conference has occurred. Rule 26(d)(1).

Under Rule 16(b)(2), as amended December 1, 2015, the judge "must issue the scheduling order as soon as practicable," which in general will be 60 days after the appearance of the defendant or 90 days after service of the complaint. Thus, where the court complies with the outer limits of Rule 16(b), the Rule 26(f) conference between the parties could be as late as 69 days after service, with no formal discovery permitted during that period. The initial disclosures required by Rule 26(a)(1) must be produced within 14 days after the Rule 26(f) conference.

Within 14 days after the Rule 26(f) conference, the parties must submit a written report of this conference.

2. Pretrial Conferences and Orders

As we saw above, Rule 26(f) requires an early conference between the parties to discuss settlement and to agree on a discovery plan and schedule. In this Section, we address conferences under Rule 16. Action taken at a conference will be reflected in a court order that "controls the course of the action unless the court modifies it." See Rule 16(d).

Rule 16 generally reflects the increasing involvement of the federal judge in the management of cases in her court. As we discussed in Chapter 1, the traditional adversary model of litigation envisions a reactive, umpireal judge, largely removed from the day-to-day management of the litigation. Increasingly, modern litigation is marked by more hands-on involvement of the court in keeping the parties' feet to the fire, narrowing the scope of the dispute, and fostering settlement. As Rule 16(a)(2) provides, the court may hold a conference to "establish[] early and continuing control so that the case will not be protracted because of lack of management." This and similar provisions reflect the embrace of case management through conferences and court oversight. The panoply of sanctions available under Rule 16(f) underscores the importance of these conferences.

Rule 16(a) sets out a broad range of proper goals for conferences. Rule 16(c) specifies the subjects that might be considered in achieving the objectives of Rule 16(a). Since 1983, an express objective has been "facilitating settlement." Rule 16(a)(5). Prior to inclusion of this provision, there was considerable debate over whether facilitating settlement is an appropriate goal of pretrial conferences. The inclusion of this objective in Rule 16 reflects concern, voiced in many quarters, that court dockets are too crowded and must be pared through negotiation if possible.

Some commentators feel that the judge's involvement in settlement efforts raises serious problems if the parties do not reach an agreement. Specifically, the judge might be exposed to something in settlement discussions that would not be admissible at trial. Professor Resnik concludes that this responsibility was imposed upon judges without proper consideration of whether it should affect the standards governing when a judge should recuse herself (step aside and let another judge preside over the case). Judith Resnik, *Managerial Judges*, 96 Harv. L. Rev. 374 (1982). See generally Carrie Menkel-Meadow, *For and Against Settlement: Uses and Abuses of the Mandatory Settlement Conference*, 33 UCLA L. Rev. 485 (1985).

One way to insulate the judge from compromising her objectivity is to shield her from the settlement process. Federal judges can do this by referring Rule 16 matters to a magistrate judge who may perform a variety of pretrial tasks to facilitate the case and often take part in efforts to settle cases.* See Rule 16(b)(1). (Magistrate judges are discussed in Note 10 following *Ager*, supra Section C.6.)

If the case does not settle, Rule 16 arms the court with considerable authority to streamline the trial. To understand Rule 16, it is important to remember that the course of pretrial litigation — from plaintiff's filing the complaint until the start of trial — usually takes months or even years to complete. During that time, the parties are busy with pleadings, motions, discovery, and other facets of litigation.

Rule 16(b) requires a *scheduling order* in all cases except those falling into categories exempted by court rule.** It permits, but does not require, the court to hold a *scheduling conference* with the parties or their lawyers to assist in her preparation of the scheduling order. The scheduling order is entered early in the lawsuit and *must* establish time limits for joinder of additional claims or parties, amendment of pleadings, motions (including motions challenging jurisdiction or venue or sufficiency of pleadings), and discovery. Rule 16(b)(3)(A). (The Rule 26(f) plan filed by the parties obviously will assist the judge in determining deadlines for the discovery phase.) The scheduling order is a *blueprint for the pretrial litigation as a whole*, determining when various tasks must be completed and at least suggesting when the case might be ready for trial.

As the case progresses, the court may hold as many *pretrial conferences* as it sees fit. In the federal courts, the same judge usually presides over a case from inception to completion.*** This gives the judge an opportunity to learn about the case and the evidence along with the parties. As discovery progresses, for example, parties may stipulate as to certain facts or recognize the need for amended pleadings or perhaps the court will be able to grant summary judgment on some or all issues. Through ongoing monitoring, the court may be able to narrow the number and scope of issues still needing resolution at trial. See Rule 16(c).

Very late in the pretrial stage, "as close to the start of trial as is reasonable," the court may hold the *final pretrial conference*. Rule 16(e). At this point, the parties have completed discovery and should be in a position to know what issues remain in contention and their respective evidence and witnesses on those issues. The purpose of the final pretrial conference is to "formulate a trial plan, including a plan to facilitate the admission of evidence." Id. As she does with all pretrial conferences, the judge enters an order (the "final pretrial conference order") "reciting the action taken" at

---

* In discussing settlement, litigants must be aware of the "offer of judgment" provision of Rule 68. Under that rule, the defendant can offer to settle the claim against her on terms she specifies. The plaintiff is not required to accept that offer, of course. If she does not, however, and does not thereafter obtain a judgment more favorable than the offer, she must pay the defendant's costs (not including attorney's fees) incurred after making the offer.

** For example, parties can seek federal court review of findings of the Social Security Administration concerning disability benefits. Courts routinely exempt such cases from the requirement of a scheduling order.

*** This is not true in many state court systems, in which a different judge may preside over issues arising in each phase of the litigation, such as pleadings, motions, discovery, pretrial conferences, and trial.

the conference. Rule 16(d). Just as the scheduling order was a blueprint for the litigation as a whole, the final pretrial conference order is a blueprint for the trial itself.

Preparing for the pretrial conference is a major task, one that is facilitated by the required pretrial disclosures under Rule 26(a)(3). Even before mandatory disclosure, however, local rules almost invariably required counsel to submit similar information. The order will generally contain each party's assertion of every factual and legal contention to be raised at trial, every witness she will call, and every piece of evidence she will seek to introduce. It is especially important because it governs the conduct of the trial. Thus, stipulations made in the final pretrial conference order are binding.

In addition, the statement of issues to be tried and the witness list embodied in the order will govern at trial. Thus, "[a]n order entered after a final pretrial conference supersedes the parties' pleadings and controls the subsequent course of action." 3 Moore's Federal Practice § 16.78[3] at p. 16-210. Issues framed in the pleadings but not included in the final pretrial conference order may not be tried. Conversely, issues not raised in the pleadings but included in the final pretrial conference order may be tried. Moreover, the standard for amending the final pretrial conference order is quite stringent: The order "shall be modified only to prevent manifest injustice." Rule 16(e). The reason for the strict standard is that "allowing modification of that order without restriction would defeat the function of the final pretrial order to structure and control the course of trial." Teply & Whitten, Civil Procedure 886. See generally 3 Moore's Federal Practice § 16.78[4][a].

The strict approach is illustrated by Walker v. Anderson Elec. Connectors, 944 F.2d 841 (11th Cir. 1991). There, the plaintiff sued her employer, Anderson, and others for sexual harassment. In her complaint, Walker sought damages as well as injunctive and declaratory relief. At the final pretrial conference, however, she abandoned her claims for equitable relief and went to trial seeking damages as her sole remedy. The jury found that Anderson had committed sexual harassment in violation of federal law and invaded plaintiff's privacy. Nonetheless, the jury also found that plaintiff had suffered no monetary damage. Thus, although plaintiff showed a violation, she was entitled to no remedy. The district court entered judgment for the defendant.

Plaintiff then sought to amend the pretrial order to reinstate the claims for injunctive and declaratory relief. She argued that her showing of a violation of federal law not only entitled her to this relief, but made her a "prevailing party" entitled to recover attorney's fees under federal employment statutes. The district court refused to amend the final pretrial order and denied her request for attorney's fees. The Eleventh Circuit affirmed.

> The district court's decision to follow the pre-trial order can be reversed on appeal only where the district court has abused its discretion. "[W]e realize that for pretrial procedures to continue as viable mechanisms of court efficiency, appellate courts must exercise minimal interference with trial court discretion in matters such as the modification of its orders." Hodges [v. United States, 597 F.2d 1014, 1018 (5th Cir. 1979)].

> While Rule 16(e) requires that the pretrial order be modified to "prevent manifest injustice," in this case the modification requested by Walker would only serve to work an injustice against the defendant [employer]. As the district court pointed out in its Memorandum Opinion of July 9, 1990, "Walker chose her strategy, forcing [defendant] to choose its strategy. It would be disingenuous of any court to find at this late date that this pretrial order can be modified post-trial in order to 'prevent manifest injustice.'"
>
> We agree with this reasoning and find that the district court did not abuse its discretion in following the pre-trial order. Walker pursued a damages trial and got just that. It would be unfair to [defendant] to give Walker relief which she did not request; relief for which [defendant] was never permitted to establish a defense.
>
> Walker's central argument on this matter is that the district court has not complied with Fed. R. Civ. P. 54(c). Rule 54(c) states, in pertinent part, that "every final judgment shall grant the relief to which the party in whose favor it is rendered is entitled, even if the party has not demanded such relief in the party's pleadings." Applying Rule 54(c) to the facts of her case, Walker contends that she is "entitled" to equitable relief based on the jury's finding of sexual harassment even though she abandoned this claim for relief in the pretrial conference and actively pursued a monetary award. Walker further contends that Rule 54(c) and Rule 16(e) conflict under these facts and that Rule 54(c) prevails * * *.
>
> We see no conflict and find that Rule 54(c) does not apply to this case. Rule 54(c) requires that the district court grant Walker only the relief to which she is "entitled," even when that relief is not requested in the pleadings. But Walker *did* request a declaratory judgment and an injunction in her pleadings and then abandoned this form of relief at the pretrial conference in favor of something else, namely a money award. Rule 54(c) simply does not sanction this type of maneuvering. We hold that Walker is not entitled to the relief abandoned in the pretrial order * * *.

Walker, 944 F.2d at 844.

Should a final pretrial conference order be amended to conform to evidence presented at trial? Recall from Chapter 7 that Rule 15(b) permits the court to amend pleadings to conform to evidence presented at trial by express or implied consent of the parties. Suppose that plaintiff presents evidence at trial of a claim clearly not envisioned in the final pretrial conference order, and that defendant does not object. Should the court permit amendment of the order without requiring the plaintiff to satisfy the more stringent standard of Rule 16(e)? See Wright & Kane, Federal Courts 647; 3 Moore's Federal Practice § 16.78[4][c].

At the beginning of Chapter 7, we noted that early procedure systems used pleadings to perform several tasks beyond giving notice to parties and the court. Specifically, they were thought to be a vehicle for narrowing the issues and winnowing out insubstantial claims and defenses. Modern theory asks less of pleadings and provides other mechanisms better suited to these tasks. Broad ranging discovery may put the parties and the court in position to redefine the scope of the dispute, perhaps by permitting summary judgment or by suggesting the need for amended pleadings. Pretrial conferences focus attention on those matters for which resolution is required, and the final pretrial conference order further clarifies the issues that need to be tried. Thus, the process begun by pleadings is completed largely by other tools.

F. Sanctions

We have already seen that some actions permit a party to seek an order compelling discovery while others justify the imposition of sanctions. We turn now to a detailed consideration of this latter issue.

Washington State Physicians Insurance Exchange & Association v. Fisons Corp.

858 P.2d 1054 (Wash. 1993)

Andersen, Chief Justice.

Facts of Case

We are asked in this case to decide whether a physician has a cause of action against a drug company for personal and professional injuries which he suffered when his patient had an adverse reaction to a drug he had prescribed. The physician claimed the drug company failed to warn him of the risks associated with the drug. If such action is legally cognizable, we are then asked to determine whether damages awarded by the jury were excessive and whether attorneys' fees were properly awarded by the trial court. We are also asked to rule that the trial court erred in denying sanctions against the drug company for certain abuses in the discovery process.

The physician's action began as part of a malpractice and product liability suit brought on behalf of a child who was the physician's patient. On January 18, 1986, 2-year-old Jennifer Pollock suffered seizures which resulted in severe and permanent brain damage. It was determined that the seizures were caused by an excessive amount of theophylline in her system. The Pollocks sued Dr. James Klicpera (Jennifer's pediatrician), who had prescribed the drug, as well as Fisons Corporation (the drug manufacturer and hereafter drug company) which produced Somophyllin Oral Liquid, the theophylline-based medication prescribed for Jennifer.

Dr. Klicpera cross-claimed against the drug company both for contribution and for damages and attorneys' fees under the Consumer Protection Act as well as for damages for emotional distress.

In January 1989, after nearly 3 years of discovery, Dr. Klicpera, his partner and the Everett Clinic settled with the Pollocks. The settlement agreement essentially provided that the doctors' insurer, Washington State Physicians Insurance Exchange & Association (WSPIE), would loan $500,000 to the Pollocks which would be contributed in the event of a settlement between the Pollocks and the drug company. The Pollocks were guaranteed a minimum total recovery of $1 million, and in the event of trial Dr. Klicpera agreed to remain as a party and to pay a maximum of $1 million. The settlement between the Pollocks and Dr. Klicpera was determined by the trial court to be reasonable pursuant to RCW 4.22.060.

More than 1 year after this settlement, an attorney for the Pollocks provided Dr. Klicpera's attorney a copy of a letter received from an anonymous source. The letter, dated June 30, 1981, indicated that the drug company was aware in 1981 of "life-threatening theophylline toxicity" in children who received the drug while suffering from viral infections. The letter was sent from the drug company to only a small number of what the company considered influential physicians. The letter stated that physicians needed to understand that theophylline can be a "capricious drug."

The Pollocks and Dr. Klicpera contended that their discovery requests should have produced the June 1981 letter and they moved for sanctions against the drug company. The request for sanctions was initially heard by a special discovery master, who denied sanctions, but who required the drug company to deliver all documents requested which related to theophylline. Documents that the drug company and its counsel had immediately available were to be produced by the day following the hearing before the special master. The remainder of the documents were to be produced within 2 weeks. The trial court subsequently denied Dr. Klicpera's request to reverse the discovery master's denial of sanctions and at the close of trial denied a renewed motion for sanctions.

The day after the hearing on sanctions, the drug company delivered approximately 10,000 documents to Dr. Klicpera's and Pollocks' attorneys. Among the documents provided was a July 10, 1985 memorandum from Cedric Grigg, director of medical communications for the drug company, to Bruce Simpson, vice president of sales and marketing for the company.

This 1985 memorandum referred to a dramatic increase in reports of serious toxicity to theophylline in early 1985 and also referred to the current recommended dosage as a significant "mistake" or "poor clinical judgment." The memo alluded to the "sinister aspect" that the physician who was the "pope" of theophylline dosage recommendation was a consultant to the pharmaceutical company that was the leading manufacturer of the drug and that this consultant was "heavily into [that company's] stocks." The memo also noted that the toxicity reports were not reported in the journal read by those who most often prescribed the drug and concluded that those physicians may not be aware of the "alarming increase in adverse reactions such as seizures, permanent brain damage and death." The memo concluded that the "epidemic of theophylline toxicity provides strong justification for our corporate decision to cease promotional activities with our theophylline line of products." The record at trial showed that the drug company continued to promote and sell theophylline after the date of this memo.

On April 27, 1990, shortly after the 1985 memo was revealed, the drug company settled with the Pollocks for $6.9 million. The trial court determined that settlement to be reasonable, dismissed the Pollocks' claims, extinguished Dr. Klicpera's contribution/indemnity claims against Fisons pursuant to RCW 4.22.060 and reserved determination of what claims remained for trial. The trial court then ordered the lawsuit recaptioned, essentially as Dr. James Klicpera, plaintiff v. Fisons Corporation, defendant.

* * *

On a special verdict form, the jury concluded that Dr. Klicpera was entitled to recover against the drug company under his Consumer Protection Act claim and under his product liability claim, but not under the fraud claim. The jury awarded Dr. Klicpera $150,000 for loss of professional consultations, $1,085,000 for injury to professional reputation, and $2,137,500 for physical and mental pain and suffering. The jury further found Dr. Klicpera to be 3.3 percent contributorily negligent. The jury found that WSPIE was not entitled to recover under its fraud claim against the drug company the $500,000 settlement paid to the Pollocks.

The trial court denied the drug company's motion for judgment n.o.v. and for a new trial. On a motion for reduction of the jury award, the trial court reduced the amount awarded for loss of professional consultations from $150,000 to $2,250 but refused to reduce the awards for loss of reputation and for pain and suffering. The trial court also denied WSPIE's motion for judgment n.o.v. or a new trial based on the dismissal of WSPIE's Consumer Protection Act claim.

* * *

ISSUE NINE

Conclusion. The trial court applied an erroneous legal standard when ruling on the motion for sanctions for discovery abuse and erred when it refused to sanction the drug company and/or its attorneys for violation of CR 26(g).

The doctor and his insurer, Washington State Physicians Insurance & Exchange Association (hereinafter referred to collectively as "the doctor"), asked the trial court to sanction the drug company and its lawyers for discovery abuse. This request was based on the fact that at least two documents crucial to the doctor's defense as well as to the injured child's case were not discovered until March of 1990—more than 1 year after the doctor had settled with the child, nearly 4 years after the complaint was filed and approximately 1 month before the scheduled trial date. The two documents, dubbed the "smoking guns" by the doctor, show that the drug company knew about, and in fact had warned selected physicians about, the dangers of theophylline toxicity in children with viral infections at least as early as June 1981, 4 years before Jennifer Pollock was injured.

Although interrogatories and requests for production should have led to the discovery of the "smoking gun" documents, their existence was not revealed to the doctor until one of them was anonymously delivered to his attorneys.

A motion for sanctions based on discovery abuse was heard first by a special discovery master on March 28, 1990, before the child's case was settled. The special master ruled that he could not find "on the basis of this record that there was an intentional withholding of this document." The special master then turned to what he determined was the more relevant issue, additional and full discovery of other theophylline-related documents in the drug company's possession. The special master ordered the drug company's attorneys to turn over any immediately available documents concerning theophylline to attorneys for the child and the doctor by noon the next day and to review the remainder of the drug company's files and produce other relevant documents at the end of 2 weeks. The next day, the second "smoking gun," a 1985 internal memorandum describing theophylline toxicity in children, was delivered along with about 10,000 other documents.

Although other documents were relevant to the case, the two smoking gun documents were the most important. The first, a letter, dated June 30, 1981, discussed an article that contained a study confirming reports "of life threatening theophylline toxicity when pediatric asthmatics ... contract viral infections." The second, an interoffice memorandum, dated July 10, 1985, talks of an "epidemic" of theophylline toxicity and of "a dramatic increase in reports of serious toxicity to theophylline."

Both documents contradicted the position taken by the drug company in the litigation, namely, that it did not know that theophylline-based medications were potentially dangerous when given to children with viral infections.

After the 1985 memorandum was discovered and still prior to trial, the special master's denial of the sanctions motion was appealed and affirmed, without specific findings, by a judge of the Superior Court (Judge Knight), who essentially deferred to the special master.

The motion for sanctions was renewed and heard by another judge of the Superior Court, the trial judge (Judge French), at the close of trial. The trial court declined to impose sanctions, deferring to the earlier decisions of the special master and Judge Knight. The doctor then appealed the denial of his sanctions motion directly to this court.

The standard of review to be applied to sanctions decisions under CR 11 and CR 26(g) has not yet been specifically articulated by this court.

The doctor urges us to review the sanctions decision de novo. However, decisions either denying or granting sanctions, under CR 11 or for discovery abuse, are generally reviewed for abuse of discretion. We hold that the proper standard to apply in reviewing sanctions decisions is the abuse of discretion standard.

The abuse of discretion standard again recognizes that deference is owed to the judicial actor who is "better positioned than another to decide the issue in question." Cooter & Gell v. Hartmarx Corp., 496 U.S. 384 (1990) (quoting Miller v. Fenton, 474 U.S. 104 (1985)). Further, the sanction rules are "designed to confer wide latitude and discretion upon the trial judge to determine what sanctions are proper in a given case and to 'reduce the reluctance of courts to impose sanctions.' ... If a review de novo was the proper standard of review, it could thwart these purposes; it could also have a chilling effect on the trial court's willingness to impose ... sanctions." Cooper

v. Viking Ventures, 53 Wash. App. 739, 742–43, 770 P.2d 659 (1989) (quoting Fed. R. Civ. P. 11 advisory committee note).

A trial court abuses its discretion when its order is manifestly unreasonable or based on untenable grounds. A trial court would necessarily abuse its discretion if it based its ruling on an erroneous view of the law.

The doctor asked that sanctions be awarded pursuant to CR 11, CR 26(g), CR 37(d), or the inherent power of the court. CR 11 sanctions are not appropriate where, as here, other court rules more properly apply. Similarly, the sanctions provisions of CR 37 do not apply where, as here, the more specific sanction rule better fits the situation. Furthermore, the inherent power of the court should not be resorted to where rules adequately address the problem. Because CR 26(g), the discovery sanctions rule, was adopted to specifically address the type of conduct involved here, it, rather than CR 11, CR 37 or the inherent power of the court, is applicable in the present case.

CR 26(g) has not yet been interpreted by this court. The rule parallels Federal Rule of Civil Procedure 26(g) (Rule 26(g)) and, like its federal counterpart and like CR 11, CR 26(g) is aimed at reducing delaying tactics, procedural harassment and mounting legal costs. Such practices "tend to impose unjustified burdens on other parties, frustrate those who seek to vindicate their rights in the courts, obstruct the judicial process, and bring the civil justice system into disrepute." Schwarzer, *Sanctions Under the New Federal Rule 11 — A Closer Look*, 104 F.R.D. 181, 182 (1985).

Because it is essentially identical to Rule 26(g), this court may look to federal court decisions interpreting that rule for guidance in construing CR 26(g). In turn, federal courts analyzing the Rule 26 sanctions provision look to interpretations of [Rule] 11. The federal advisory committee notes describe the discovery process and problems that led to the enactment of Rule 26(g) as follows:

> Excessive discovery and evasion or resistance to reasonable discovery requests pose significant problems....
>
> The purpose of discovery is to provide a mechanism for making relevant information available to the litigants. "Mutual knowledge of all the relevant facts gathered by both parties is essential to proper litigation." Hickman v. Taylor, 329 U.S. 495 (1947). Thus the spirit of the rules is violated when advocates attempt to use discovery tools as tactical weapons rather than to expose the facts and illuminate the issues by overuse of discovery or unnecessary use of defensive weapons or evasive responses. All of this results in excessively costly and time-consuming activities that are disproportionate to the nature of the case, the amount involved, or the issues or values at stake....
>
> ... Rule 26(g) imposes an affirmative duty to engage in pretrial discovery in a responsible manner that is consistent with the spirit and purposes of Rules 26 through 37. In addition, *Rule 26(g) is designed to curb discovery abuse by explicitly encouraging the imposition of sanctions....* The term "response" includes answers to interrogatories and to requests to admit as well as responses to production requests....

Concern about discovery abuse has led to widespread recognition that there is a need for more aggressive judicial control and supervision. Sanctions to deter discovery abuse would be more effective if they were diligently applied "not merely to penalize those whose conduct may be deemed to warrant such a sanction, but to deter those who might be tempted to such conduct in the absence of such a deterrent." ... *Thus the premise of Rule 26(g) is that imposing sanctions on attorneys who fail to meet the rule's standards will significantly reduce abuse by imposing disadvantages therefor.* The concept that a spirit of cooperation and forthrightness during the discovery process is necessary for the proper functioning of modern trials is reflected in decisions of our Court of Appeals. In Gammon v. Clark Equip. Co., 38 Wash. App. 274, 686 P.2d 1102 (1984), *aff'd*, 104 Wash. 2d 613, 707 P.2d 685 (1985), the Court of Appeals held that a new trial should have been ordered because of discovery abuse by the defendant. Then Court of Appeals Judge Barbara Durham wrote for the court:

> The Supreme Court has noted that the aim of the liberal federal discovery rules is to "make a trial less a game of blindman's b[l]uff and more a fair contest with the basic issues and facts disclosed to the fullest practicable extent." The availability of liberal discovery means that civil trials no longer need be carried on in the dark. The way is now clear ... for the parties to obtain the fullest possible knowledge of the issues and facts before trial.
>
> This system obviously cannot succeed without the full cooperation of the parties. Accordingly, the drafters wisely included a provision authorizing the trial court to impose sanctions for unjustified or unexplained resistance to discovery.

It was after *Gammon* that this court adopted CR 26(g) in order to provide a deterrent to discovery abuses as well as an impetus for candor and reason in the discovery phase of litigation.

It is with these purposes in mind, that we now articulate the standard to be applied by trial courts which are asked to impose sanctions for discovery abuse.

On its face, Rule 26(g) requires an attorney signing a discovery response to certify that the attorney has read the response and that after a reasonable inquiry believes it is (1) consistent with the discovery rules and is warranted by existing law or a good faith argument for the extension, modification or reversal of existing law; (2) not interposed for any improper purpose such as to harass or cause unnecessary delay or needless increase in the cost of litigation; and (3) not unreasonable or unduly burdensome or expensive, given the needs of the case, the discovery already had, the amount in controversy, and the importance of the issues at stake in the litigation.

Whether an attorney has made a reasonable inquiry is to be judged by an objective standard. Subjective belief or good faith alone no longer shields an attorney from sanctions under the rules.

In determining whether an attorney has complied with the rule, the court should consider all of the surrounding circumstances, the importance of the evidence to its proponent, and the ability of the opposing party to formulate a response or to comply with the request.

The responses must be consistent with the letter, spirit and purpose of the rules. To be consistent with CR 33, an interrogatory must be "answered separately and fully in writing under oath, unless it is objected to, in which event the reasons for objection shall be stated in lieu of an answer." CR 33(a). A response to a request for production "shall state, with respect to each item or category, that inspection and related activities will be permitted as requested, unless the request is objected to, in which event the reasons for objection shall be stated. If objection is made to part of an item or category, the part shall be specified." CR 34(b).

In applying the rules to the facts of the present case, the trial court should have asked whether the attorneys' certifications to the responses to the interrogatories and requests for production were made after reasonable inquiry and (1) were consistent with the rules, (2) were not interposed for any improper purpose and (3) were not unreasonable or unduly burdensome or expensive. The trial court did not have the benefit of our decision to guide it and it did not apply this standard in this case.

Instead, the trial court considered the opinions of attorneys and others as to whether sanctions should be imposed. This was error. Legal opinions on the ultimate *legal* issue before the court are not properly considered under the guise of expert testimony. It is the responsibility of the court deciding a sanction motion to interpret and apply the law.

The trial court then denied sanctions, in part because: (1) The evidence did not support a finding that the drug company *intentionally* misfiled documents to avoid discovery; (2) neither the doctor nor the child had formally moved for a definition of "product" and neither had moved to compel production of documents or answers before requesting sanctions; (3) the conduct of the drug company and its counsel was consistent with the customary and accepted litigation practices of the bar of Snohomish County and of this state; and (4) the doctor failed to meet his burden of proving that the "evidence of discovery abuse is so clear that reasonable minds could not differ on the appropriateness of sanctions."

The trial court erred in concluding as it did. As stated above, intent need not be shown before sanctions are mandated. A motion to compel compliance with the rules is not a prerequisite to a sanctions motion. Conduct is to be measured against the spirit and purpose of the rules, not against the standard of practice of the local bar. Furthermore, the burden placed on the doctor by the trial court in this regard was greater than that mandated under the rule.

Additionally, we agree with the doctor's claim that many of the findings of fact entered by the trial court are, instead, erroneous conclusions of law or are not supported by the evidence. For example, the trial court implicitly found in finding of fact 7, and then again in finding of fact 14b, that the "product scope" had been defined by the plaintiffs early in the litigation. The record does not support this finding. In finding of fact 14c the trial court stated that the doctor had been put on notice by the drug company's discovery responses that production of documents "would be limited to responsive documents from Somophyllin Oral Liquid *files*." (Italics ours.) There is no evidence in the record to support this finding and while findings of fact which are supported by substantial evidence will not be disturbed on appeal, unsupported findings cannot stand.

A remand for a determination as to whether sanctions are warranted would be appropriate but is not necessary. Where, as here, the trial judge has applied the wrong legal standard to evidence consisting entirely of written documents and argument of counsel, an appellate court may independently review the evidence to determine whether a violation of the certification rule occurred. If a violation is found, as it is here, then sanctions are mandated, but in fairness to the attorneys and parties, a remand is required for a hearing on the appropriate sanctions required and against whom they should be imposed.

We now measure the conduct of the drug company and its attorneys against the standard set forth in the rule.

The drug company was persistent in its resistance to discovery requests. Fair and reasoned resistance to discovery is not sanctionable. Rather it is the misleading nature of the drug company's responses that is contrary to the purposes of discovery and which is most damaging to the fairness of the litigation process.

The specific instances alleged to be sanctionable in this case involve misleading or "non" responses to a number of requests which the doctor claims should have produced the smoking gun documents themselves or a way to discover the information they contained. The two smoking gun documents reportedly were contained in files which related to Intal, a cromolyn sodium product, which was manufactured by Fisons and which competed with Somophyllin. The manager of medical communications had a thorough collection of articles, materials and other documents relating to the dangers of theophylline and used the information from those materials to market Intal, as an alternative to Somophyllin Oral Liquid. The drug company avoided production of these theophylline-related materials, and avoided identifying the manager of medical communications as a person with information about the dangers of theophylline, by giving evasive or misleading responses to interrogatories and requests for production.

The following is but a sampling of the discovery between the parties.

The first discovery documents directed to the drug company were prepared by the child's attorney and were dated September 26, 1986. The interrogatories contained a short definition section stating in part:

> The term "the product" as used hereinafter in these interrogatories shall mean the product which is claimed to have caused injury or damage to Jennifer Marie Pollock as alleged in pleadings filed on her behalf, namely, to wit: "Somophyllin" oral liquid.

These first interrogatories requested information about "the product" which is manufactured by the drug company, Fisons, as well as about theophylline, a drug entity which is the primary ingredient of the drug company's product Somophyllin Oral Liquid. The interrogatory regarding theophylline was answered by the drug company, as were the interrogatories about "the product."

Somophyllin and its primary ingredient, theophylline, were not distinguished in discussions between the attorneys or in drug company literature. The printed package insert for Somophyllin Oral Liquid and marketing brochures refer to the names Somophyllin and theophylline interchangeably. * * *

The drug company's responses to discovery requests contained the following general objection:

> *Requests Regarding Fisons Products Other Than Somophyllin Oral Liquid.* Fisons objects to all discovery requests regarding Fisons products other than Somophyllin Oral Liquid as overly broad, unduly burdensome, harassing, and not reasonably calculated to lead to the discovery of admissible evidence.
>
> Theophylline is not a Fisons "product." Furthermore, because theophylline is the primary ingredient in Somophyllin Oral Liquid, any document focusing on theophylline would, necessarily, be one *regarding* Somophyllin Oral Liquid.

In November 1986 the doctor served his first requests for production on the drug company. Four requests were made. Three asked for documents concerning Somophyllin. Request 3 stated:

> 3. Produce genuine copies of any letters sent by your company to physicians concerning theophylline toxicity in children.

The drug company's response was:

> Such letters, *if any*, regarding Somophyllin Oral Liquid will be produced at a reasonable time and place convenient to Fisons and its counsel of record.

Had the request, as written, been complied with, the first smoking gun letter (exhibit 3) would have been disclosed early in the litigation. That June 30, 1981 letter concerned theophylline toxicity in children; it was sent by the drug company to physicians.

The child's first requests for production, and the responses thereto, included the following:

> Request for Production No. 12: All documents pertaining to any warning letters including "Dear Doctor letters" or warning correspondence to the medical professions regarding the use of the drug Somophyllin Oral Liquid.
>
> Response: Fisons objects to this request as overbroad in time and scope for the reasons identified in response to request number 2, hereby incorporated by reference. *Without waiver of these objections and subject to these limitations, Fisons will produce documents responsive to this request* at plaintiffs' expense at a mutually agreeable time at Fisons' headquarters.

> Request for Production No. 13: All documents of any clinical investigators who at any time stated or recommended to the defendant that the use of the drug Somophyllin Oral Liquid might prove dangerous.
>
> Response: Fisons objects to this request as overbroad in time and scope for the reasons identified in response to request number 2 hereby incorporated by reference. Fisons further objects to this request as calling for materials not within Fisons' possession, custody or control. Fisons further objects to this request to the extent it calls for expert disclosures beyond the scope of CR 26(b)(4) or which may be protected by the work-product and/or attorney-client privilege. *Without waiver of these objections and subject to these limitations, Fisons will produce documents responsive to this interrogatory* at plaintiffs' expense at a mutually agreeable time at Fisons' headquarters.

(Italics ours.)

The doctor further requested:

> Request for Production No. 4: Please produce copies of any and all seminar materials, regardless of their source, in Fisons' possession on or before January 16, 1986 regarding asthma, bronchopulmonary dysplasia, theophylline and/or allergy.
>
> Response: Fisons objects to this discovery request as overbroad, burdensome, and not reasonably calculated to lead to the discovery of admissible evidence *to the extent it seeks seminar materials regarding subjects other than theophylline.* Without waiving these objections, Fisons answers as follows:
>
> *Fisons has no documents regarding theophylline* and otherwise responsive to this discovery request.

(Some italics ours.)

These requests, and others of a similar tenor, should have led to the production of the smoking gun documents.

When the child or the doctor attempted to see information from the files of other products, the drug company objected. For example:

> Request for Production No. 1: All documents contained in all files from the regulating department, marketing department, drug surveillance department, pharmaceutical development department, product manager department and the medical departments regarding all cromolyn [Intal] products of Fisons Corporation. Regarding this request for production all documents should include from inception of file to the present.
>
> Answer: Defendant Fisons objects to this discovery request as not reasonably calculated to lead to the discovery of admissible evidence, as overbroad in time, and as incredibly burdensome and harassing. This discovery request encompasses approximately *eighty-five* percent of all documents in the subject files and departments — millions of pages of documents. *Neither cromolyn (which should be referred to as cromolyn sodium), nor any cromolyn product,*

> *nor the properties or efficacy of cromolyn is at issue in this litigation.* Furthermore, Fisons objects to this discovery request as calling for the production of extremely sensitive trade secret and proprietary material.

(Some italics ours.)

To requests asking for correspondence, memoranda, articles and other documents "concerning," "regarding" or "covering" Somophyllin Oral Liquid, the drug company generally objected to the requests and then stated:

> Without waiver of these objects and subject to these limitations, Fisons will produce documents responsive to this request at plaintiffs' expense at a mutually agreeable time at Fisons' headquarters.

In support of the drug company's motion for a protective order, the drug company's in-house counsel and its Seattle lawyer filed similar affidavits. Seattle counsel's affidavit declares:

> Plaintiffs allege that Fisons failed to provide adequate warnings of possible dangers associated with the use of Somophyllin Oral Liquid, a theophylline-based prescription medication distributed by Fisons ... [Plaintiffs'] discovery requests are extremely broad in scope. Many of these discovery requests are not reasonably related to plaintiffs' failure-to-warn allegations against Fisons.
>
> Following receipt of plaintiffs' First Request for Production, I traveled to Fisons in Bedford, Massachusetts in order to ascertain firsthand the scope and extent of documents responsive to plaintiffs' request for production. At that time I confirmed that to produce all of the documents responsive to plaintiffs' catch-all requests would be extremely burdensome and oppressive to Fisons. Between one and two million pages of documents, most of which have no colorable relevance to the issues in this action, would have to be located, assembled, and made available for review or copying. The time, expense, and intrusion upon the day-to-day business activities of Fisons would be immense.
>
> While at Fisons I identified those documents reasonably related to the claims asserted by plaintiffs in this litigation and arranged to have them copied and forwarded to Seattle for production to plaintiffs.

The affidavit goes on to say that the drug company had "agreed to make available those documents reasonably related to plaintiffs' allegations against Fisons."

In its memorandum to the court in support of the motion for a protective order, the attorney for the drug company outlined the documents contained in the regulatory file on Somophyllin Oral Liquid. That file purportedly contained complete information regarding the drug including: Summaries of adverse reactions associated with the use of the medication that had been reported to Fisons; all promotional or advertising material disseminated by Fisons *with regard to the medication*; the complete product file for Somophyllin Oral Liquid, which contained records of communications with the Food and Drug Administration, internal memoranda, and miscellaneous medical literature regarding theophylline. The memorandum goes on to tell the court

> In short, Fisons' Regulatory File for Somophyllin Oral Liquid contains all or nearly all documents in Fisons' possession that are reasonably related to plaintiffs' failure-to-warn allegations.

A footnote to this comment states "Fisons has also agreed to make available to plaintiffs an index of periodicals maintained in Fisons' internal library as well as certain other documents."

The drug company's responses and answers to discovery requests are misleading. The answers state that all information *regarding* Somophyllin Oral Liquid which had been requested would be provided. They further imply that all documents which are relevant to the plaintiffs' claims were being produced. They do not specifically object to the production of documents that discuss the dangers of theophylline, but which are not within the Somophyllin Oral Liquid files. They state that there is no relevant information within the cromolyn sodium product files.

It appears clear that no conceivable discovery request could have been made by the doctor that would have uncovered the relevant documents, given the above and other responses of the drug company. The objections did not specify that certain documents were not being produced. Instead the general objections were followed by a promise to produce requested documents. These responses did not comply with either the spirit or letter of the discovery rules and thus were signed in violation of the certification requirement.

The drug company does not claim that its inquiry into the records did not uncover the smoking gun documents. Instead, the drug company attempts to justify its responses by arguing as follows: (1) The plaintiffs themselves limited the scope of discovery to documents contained in Somophyllin Oral Liquid *files*. (2) The smoking gun documents were not intended to relate to Somophyllin Oral Liquid, but rather were intended to promote another product of the drug company. (3) The drug company produced all of the documents it agreed to produce or was ordered to produce. (4) The drug company's failure to produce the smoking gun documents resulted from the plaintiffs' failure to specifically ask for those documents or from their failure to move to compel production of those documents. (5) Discovery is an adversarial process and good lawyering required the responses made in this case.

If the discovery rules are to be effective, then the drug company's arguments must be rejected.

First, neither the child nor the doctor limited the scope of discovery in this case. Attorneys for the child, the doctor and the drug company repeatedly referred to both theophylline and Somophyllin Oral Liquid. There was no clear indication from the drug company that it was limiting all discovery *regarding* Somophyllin Oral Liquid to material from that product's file. Nor was there any indication from the drug company that it had information about theophylline, which is not a Fisons "product," or information *regarding* Somophyllin Oral Liquid that it was not producing because the information was in another product's file. The doctor was justified in relying on the statements made by the drug company's attorneys that all relevant documents had been produced and he cannot be determined to have impliedly, albeit unknowingly, acquiesced in limiting the scope of discoverable information.

Second, the drug company argues that the smoking gun documents and other documents relating to theophylline were not documents *regarding* Somophyllin Oral Liquid because they were intended to market another product. No matter what its initial purpose, and regardless of where it had been filed, under the facts of this case, a document that warned of the serious dangers of the primary ingredient of Somophyllin Oral Liquid is a document *regarding* Somophyllin Oral Liquid.

Third, the discovery rules do not require the drug company to produce only what it agreed to produce or what it was ordered to produce. The rules are clear that a party must *fully* answer all interrogatories and all requests for production, unless a specific and clear objection is made. If the drug company did not agree with the scope of production or did not want to respond, then it was required to move for a protective order. In this case, the documents requested were relevant. The drug company did not have the option of determining what it would produce or answer, once discovery requests were made.

Fourth, the drug company further attempts to justify its failure to produce the smoking guns by saying that the request were not specific enough. Having read the record herein, we cannot perceive of any request that could have been made to this drug company that would have produced the smoking gun documents. Unless the doctor had been somehow specifically able to request the June 30, 1981, "dear doctor" letter, it is unlikely that the letter would have been discovered. Indeed the drug company claims the letter was not an official "dear doctor" letter and therefore was not required to be produced.

Fifth, the drug company's attorneys claim they were just doing their job, that is, they were vigorously representing their client. The conflict here is between the attorney's duty to represent the client's interest and the attorney's duty as an officer of the court to use, but not abuse the judicial process.

> [V]igorous advocacy is not contingent on lawyers being free to pursue litigation tactics that they cannot justify as legitimate. The lawyer's duty to place his client's interests ahead of all others presupposes that the lawyer will live with the rules that govern the system. Unlike the polemicist haranguing the public from his soapbox in the park, the lawyer enjoys the privilege of a professional license that entitles him to entry into the justice system to represent his client, and in doing so, to pursue his profession and earn his living. He is subject to the correlative obligation to comply with the rules and to conduct himself in a manner consistent with the proper functioning of that system.

Schwarzer, *Sanctions Under the New Federal Rule 11—A Closer Look*, 104 F.R.D. 181,184 (1985).

Like CR 11, CR 26(g) makes the imposition of sanctions mandatory, if a violation of the rule is found. Sanctions are warranted in this case. What the sanctions should be and against whom they should be imposed is a question that cannot be fairly answered without further factual inquiry, and that is the trial court's function. While we recognize that the issue of imposition of sanctions upon attorneys is a difficult and disagreeable task for a trial judge, it is a necessary one if our system is to remain accessible and responsible.

> Misconduct, once tolerated, will breed more misconduct and those who might seek relief against abuse will instead resort to it in self-defense.

Schwarzer, 104 F.R.D. at 205.

In making its determination, the trial court should use its discretion to fashion "appropriate" sanctions. The rule provides that sanctions may be imposed upon the signing attorney, the party on whose behalf the response is made, or both.

In determining what sanctions are appropriate, the trial court is given wide latitude. However certain principles guide the trial court's consideration of sanctions. First, the least severe sanction that will be adequate to serve the purpose of the particular sanction should be imposed. The sanction must not be so minimal, however, that it undermines the purpose of discovery. The sanction should insure that the wrongdoer does not profit from the wrong. The wrongdoer's lack of intent to violate the rules and the other party's failure to mitigate may be considered by the trial court in fashioning sanctions.

The purposes of sanctions orders are to deter, to punish, to compensate and to educate. Where compensation to litigants is appropriate, then sanctions should include a compensation award. However, we caution that the sanctions rules are not "fee shifting" rules. Furthermore, requests for sanctions should not turn into satellite litigation or become a "cottage industry" for lawyers. To avoid the appeal of sanctions motions as a profession or profitable specialty of law, we encourage trial courts to consider requiring that monetary sanctions awards be paid to a particular court fund or to court-related funds. In the present case, sanctions need to be severe enough to deter these attorneys and others from participating in this kind of conduct in the future.

The trial court's denial of sanctions is reversed and the case is remanded for a determination of appropriate sanctions.

Notes and Questions

1. On the remand of *Fisons*, Dr. Klicpera's counsel sought a public evidentiary hearing at which Fisons' officials and their lawyers could be cross-examined about their conduct. The hearing never took place. Instead, Fisons and its lawyers settled, agreeing to pay $350,000 for the discovery abuse and to admit publicly that they violated the rules. See Stuart Taylor, Jr., *Sleazy in Seattle*, The American Lawyer, Apr. 1, 1994, at 5.

2. The *Fisons* court states that Rules 11 and 37(d) were not applicable in that case. Why?

3. What sanctions were available against Fisons? Could the court have imposed any of the sanctions enumerated in Rule 37(b)(2)?

4. Suppose that in *Fisons* the "smoking gun" documents did not become known until after all the claims had settled or judgments had been entered. Could the court have imposed sanctions after the case was over? In Cooter & Gell v. Hartmarx Corp., 496 U.S. 384 (1990), the Court held that federal courts could impose Rule 11 sanctions after a case had been voluntarily dismissed. "It is well established that a federal court may consider collateral issues after an action is no longer pending." Id. at 395. The Court explained that "whether the attorney has abused the judicial process" is collateral to the merits of the underlying suit and hence "[s]uch a determination may be made after the principal suit has been terminated." Id. at 396. After the 1993 amendments to Rule 11, monetary sanctions cannot be awarded unless a show cause order is issued prior to a voluntary dismissal or settlement of the suit, see Rule 11(c)(4), but there is no such limitation in 26(g)(3).

5. Can a defendant be sanctioned under Rule 37(c) for failing to admit an ultimate issue (such as negligence) in response to a Rule 36 request? Consider Marchand v. Mercy Medical Center, 22 F.3d 933 (9th Cir. 1994). In connection with a medical malpractice suit, the plaintiff served on the defendant the following request to admit:

> [a]dmit that the care and treatment provided to [plaintiff by defendant] * * * failed to comply with the applicable standard of care which existed for that person on that date.

The defendant responded, "denied." Following trial, the court imposed Rule 37(c) sanctions of over $205,000 on defendant for failing to admit this statement and the court of appeals upheld the award. The court of appeals explained that although defendant presented an expert witness who testified that the defendant satisfied the standard of care, "[t]he district court had ample evidence to discredit the expert testimony." Id. at 937. The court concluded that the defendant "could not under the circumstances have reasonably denied his negligence." Id.

6. Recall that in *Zubulake*, supra, the court imposed sanctions for destruction of electronic data. That case was decided before the enactment of Rule 37(e) which provides that "a court may not impose sanctions under these rules on a party for failing to provide electronically stored information lost as a result of the routine, good faith operation of an electronic information system." Would this provision have protected the defendant in *Zubulake*? The Advisory Committee Notes to this section explains:

> Rule 37[e] applies to information lost due to the routine operation of an information system only if the operation was in good faith. Good faith in the routine operation of an information system may involve a party's intervention to modify or suspend certain features of that routine operation to prevent the loss of information. A preservation obligation may arise from many sources, including common law, statutes, regulations, or a court order in the case. The good faith requirement of Rule 37[e] means that a party is not permitted to exploit the routine operation of an information system to thwart

> discovery obligations by allowing that operation to continue in order to destroy specific stored information that it is required to preserve. When a party is under a duty to preserve information because of pending or reasonably anticipated litigation, intervention in the routine operation of an information system is one aspect of what is often called a "litigation hold."

7. The sanctions in *Zubulake* included an adverse jury instruction and payment of the costs of the motion. In addition to these sanctions, courts have sometimes imposed substantial monetary penalties for destruction of evidence. See United States v. Philip Morris USA, Inc., 327 F. Supp. 2d 21 (D.D.C. 2004) (imposing penalty of $2,750,000). In the most extreme situations, courts have on occasion entered judgment against the party that destroyed the evidence, see Metropolitan Opera Assoc. v. Local 100, 212 F.R.D. 178 (S.D.N.Y. 2003), although courts are generally reluctant to invoke this sanction in response to attorney misconduct. One court has observed that the harsh sanction of dismissal is "usually inappropriate where the neglect is solely the fault of the attorney." Carter v. Memphis, Tennessee, 636 F.2d 159, 161 (6th Cir. 1980). Should dismissal be reserved for cases in which the client was actually involved in the misconduct? Doesn't this remove from the court one of its most powerful sanctions? Clients pay the price for other attorney mistakes such as failing to file within the statute of limitations. If clients paid the price for attorney discovery abuse, would this make overly aggressive or abusive lawyers less attractive in the market place?

8. What is a lawyer's obligation if she discovers that her client has not undertaken an appropriately thorough document search or lied at a deposition or presented false evidence? See Model Rules of Professional Conduct, Rule 3.3(a)(3), reproduced in Section G.1 of Chapter 7, supra. Several states have held that the obligation to disclose applies even at the pretrial stage. See, e.g., Kath v. Western Media Inc., 684 P.2d 98 (Wyo. 1984) (attorney had a letter that was inconsistent with deposition testimony; attorney required to disclose letter prior to settlement negotiations). See also Fire Insurance Exchange v. Bell, 643 N.E.2d 310 (Ind. 1994) (permitting claim of fraudulent misrepresentation against lawyer who misrepresented insurance policy limits in settlement negotiations).

9. In Jones v. Clinton, 36 F. Supp. 2d 1118 (E.D. Ark. 1999), the court found then-President Clinton in civil contempt for lying under oath at a deposition in the judge's presence. Civil contempt is more commonly used to coerce compliance with a court order. See, e.g., *Hickman v. Taylor*, supra. The criminal law can also be used in extreme cases as a way of policing discovery abuse. False statements made under oath at a deposition may be prosecuted as perjury under 18 U.S.C. § 1623. In addition, destruction of documents during civil discovery can constitute obstruction of justice under 18 U.S.C. § 1503. See United States v. Lundwall, 1 F. Supp. 2d 249 (S.D.N.Y. 1998).

One famous prosecution for obstruction of justice based on destruction of documents is Arthur Andersen v. United States, 544 U.S. 696 (2005). There, as the Enron scandal began to unravel, senior managers of Arthur Andersen, Enron's accounting firm, urged all employees to pay close attention to the firm's "document retention policy." At one training meeting, a manager added, "[I]f it's destroyed in the course of [the] normal policy and litigation is filed the next day, that's great ... [W]e've followed our own policy, and whatever there was that might have been of interest to somebody is gone and irretrievable." Id. at 700. Significant document destruction occurred for several weeks until Arthur Andersen was formally served with a subpoena for records. Arthur Andersen was indicted and convicted of obstruction of justice. The Supreme Court ultimately reversed the conviction on the ground that the jury instructions had failed to convey that it needed to find a consciousness of wrongdoing. The reversal did little good for the firm which by that point had dissolved.

Chapter 9

Adjudication With and Without a Trial or a Jury

A. Introduction and Integration

In prior chapters, we saw that courts may resolve cases early in the course of litigation for a variety of reasons, including lack of personal or subject matter jurisdiction, failure to state a claim, default, or improper venue. However, most cases survive such preliminary hurdles. How are cases that survive adjudicated? This chapter focuses on two critical aspects of the adjudication process — whether the adjudication process will include an actual trial with witnesses and evidence presented under oath in open court and second, if there is a trial, whether the finder of fact will be a jury or a judge. As you will see, these two questions are interrelated.

B. The Right to a Jury

1. Scope of the Constitutional Right

The jury with which we are concerned is the "petit" (pronounced "petty") jury, as opposed to the "grand" jury. Both types consist of members of the public, drawn at random. The grand jury sits for a given period and determines, based upon evidence presented by the prosecutor's office, whether criminal indictments ought to be filed. The petit jury sits as fact-finder for a particular case, civil or criminal. The right to a petit jury was very important to this country's founders. Breach of the right was one of the British abuses listed in the Declaration of Independence and the failure of the original Constitution to guarantee the right in civil cases was one of the strong arguments of the anti-federalists against the adoption of the Constitution.

Professor Madison has detailed the constitutional evolution of the jury, recounting federalist and anti-federalist writings. He concludes that "[i]n the Anglo-American tradition * * * persons of all political stripes have agreed on one thing: the jury system serves justice by allowing average citizens to serve as a check within the broader scheme of governmental checks and balances." Benjamin V. Madison, III, *Trial by*

Jury or by Military Tribunal for Accused Terrorist Detainees Facing the Death Penalty? An Examination of the Principles That Transcend the U.S. Constitution, 17 U. Fla. J.L.& Pub. Pol. 347, 391 (2006).

The right to a jury appears in three places in the Constitution. Article III, Section 2, and the Sixth Amendment address juries in criminal cases, and the Seventh Amendment addresses juries in civil cases. Although we will focus on the Seventh Amendment, the Sixth Amendment provides a useful comparison.

Notice that although the Sixth Amendment refers to "all criminal prosecutions," the Seventh Amendment does not provide for juries in all civil cases. Instead, it provides for juries "[i]n suits at common law." As discussed in Chapter 1, Section F, the British had two separate court systems—courts of law and courts of equity. Juries were available in the former, but generally not the latter. The American Colonies followed this British model and likewise had separate law and equity courts. Thus, the phrase "suits at common law" refers to suits in the courts of law as opposed to the courts of equity. In 1938, federal courts of law and equity were merged into one court system. As we will see, this merger creates some interpretative complications with respect to the Seventh Amendment.

A second important difference in the language of the Sixth and Seventh Amendments is that while the Sixth Amendment explicitly grants a right to a jury, the Seventh Amendment provides that the right shall be "preserved." As we will see, the word "preserved" has been interpreted to impose an historical test, under which the court determines whether there was a right to a jury at the time of the Seventh Amendment's ratification in 1791. In other words, one has a right to a jury trial today if she would have had such a right for her claim in 1791.

One potential difficulty of focusing on whether one would have had a right to a jury in 1791 is that there were some differences among state jury practices at that time. Thus, one might ask, "A right to a jury *where*?" Justice Story answered this question decisively in a case that has never subsequently been doubted:

> Beyond all question, the common law here alluded to is not the common law of any individual state, (for it probably differs in all), but it is the common law of England, the grand reservoir of all our jurisprudence. It cannot be necessary for me to expound the grounds of this opinion, because they must be obvious to every person acquainted with the history of the law.

United States v. Wonson, 28 F. Cas. 745, 750 (No. 16,750) (C.C.D. Mass. 1812). Of course England, that grand reservoir of our jurisprudence, largely abolished the civil jury in 1920, but that doesn't change the historical practices in the United States as of 1791. As we will see, using an historical test to analyze modern claims under modern procedures presents complications.

A final difference between the Sixth and Seventh Amendments is not apparent from the language. At the time of their ratification, the first ten amendments applied only to the federal government and not to the states. After the adoption of the Fourteenth Amendment, the Court began a process of selective incorporation, finding that some of the protections of the first ten amendments were part of the liberty interest protected by the Fourteenth Amendment and thus required of the states. The Court has held that the Sixth Amendment is applicable to the states, see Duncan v. Louisiana, 391 U.S. 145 (1968), but it has never so held with respect to the Seventh Amendment. Thus, in a civil case in state court there is no *federal* constitutional right to a jury, though a state constitutional or statutory provision may ensure the right.

a. "Actions at Common Law" and the Historical Test

Chauffeurs Local 391 v. Terry

494 U.S. 558, 110 S. Ct. 1339, 108 L. Ed. 2d 519 (1990)

JUSTICE MARSHALL delivered the opinion of the Court, except as to Part III-A.

This case presents the question whether an employee who seeks relief in the form of backpay for a union's alleged breach of its duty of fair representation has a right to trial by jury. We hold that the Seventh Amendment entitles such a plaintiff to a jury trial.

I

McLean Trucking Company and the Chauffeurs, Teamsters and Helpers Local No. 391 (Union) were parties to a collective-bargaining agreement that governed the terms and conditions of employment at McLean's terminals. The 27 respondents were employed by McLean as truck drivers in bargaining units covered by the agreement, and all were members of the Union. In 1982 McLean implemented a change in operations that resulted in the elimination of some of its terminals and the reorganization of others.

[In connection with reorganization, respondents were laid off and lost seniority rights. Respondents filed two grievances against McLean and were represented by the Union. When respondents filed a third grievance, the union declined to refer the charges to the grievance committee on the grounds that the relevant issue had been determined in prior proceedings.]

In July 1983, respondents filed an action in District Court, alleging that McLean had breached the collective-bargaining agreement in violation of § 301 of the Labor Management Relations Act, 1947, 61 Stat. 156, 29 U.S.C. § 185 (1982 ed.), and that the Union had violated its duty of fair representation. Respondents requested a permanent injunction requiring the defendants to cease their illegal acts and to reinstate them to their proper seniority status; in addition, they sought, inter alia, compensatory damages for lost wages and health benefits. In 1986 McLean filed for bankruptcy; subsequently, the action against it was voluntarily dismissed, along with all claims for injunctive relief.

Respondents had requested a jury trial in their pleadings. The Union moved to strike the jury demand on the ground that no right to a jury trial exists in a duty of fair representation suit. * * * We granted the petition for certiorari to resolve a Circuit conflict on this issue, and now affirm the judgment of the Fourth Circuit.

II

The duty of fair representation is inferred from unions' exclusive authority under the National Labor Relations Act to represent all employees in a bargaining unit. The duty requires a union "to serve the interests of all members without hostility or discrimination toward any, to exercise its discretion with complete good faith and honesty, and to avoid arbitrary conduct." A union must discharge its duty both in bargaining with the employer and in its enforcement of the resulting collective-bargaining agreement. Thus, the Union here was required to pursue respondents' grievances in a manner consistent with the principles of fair representation.

Because most collective-bargaining agreements accord finality to grievance or arbitration procedures established by the collective-bargaining agreement, an employee normally cannot bring a § 301 action against an employer unless he can show that the union breached its duty of fair representation in its handling of his grievance. Whether the employee sues both the labor union and the employer or only one of those entities, he must prove the same two facts to recover money damages: that the employer's action violated the terms of the collective-bargaining agreement and that the union breached its duty of fair representation.

III

We turn now to the constitutional issue presented in this case — whether respondents are entitled to a jury trial.[3] The Seventh Amendment provides that "[i]n Suits at common law, where the value in controversy shall exceed twenty dollars, the right of trial by jury shall be preserved." The right to a jury trial includes more than the common-law forms of action recognized in 1791; the phrase "Suits at common law" refers to "suits in which *legal* rights [are] to be ascertained and determined, in contradistinction to those where equitable rights alone [are] recognized, and equitable remedies [are] administered." The right extends to causes of action created by Congress. Tull v. United States, 481 U.S. 412, 417 (1987). Since the merger of the systems of law and equity, see Fed. Rule Civ. Proc. 2, this Court has carefully preserved the right to trial by jury where legal rights are at stake. As the Court noted in Beacon Theatres, Inc. v. Westover, 359 U.S. 500, 501 (1959), "Maintenance of the jury as a fact-finding body is of such importance and occupies so firm a place in our history and jurisprudence that any seeming curtailment of the right to a jury trial should be scrutinized with the utmost care."

To determine whether a particular action will resolve legal rights, we examine both the nature of the issues involved and the remedy sought. "First, we compare the statutory action to 18th-century actions brought in the courts of England prior to the merger of the courts of law and equity. Second, we examine the remedy sought

3. Because the NLRA does not expressly create the duty of fair representation, resort to the statute to determine whether Congress provided for a jury trial in an action for breach of that duty is unavailing. Cf. Curtis v. Loether, 415 U.S. 189, 192, n.6 (1974) (recognizing the "cardinal principle that this Court will first ascertain whether a construction of the statute is fairly possible by which the [constitutional] question may be avoided" * * *).

and determine whether it is legal or equitable in nature." *Tull*, supra. The second inquiry is the more important in our analysis. Granfinanciera, S.A. v. Nordberg, 492 U.S. 33, 42 (1989).

A

An action for breach of a union's duty of fair representation was unknown in 18th-century England; in fact, collective bargaining was unlawful. We must therefore look for an analogous cause of action that existed in the 18th century to determine whether the nature of this duty of fair representation suit is legal or equitable.

The Union contends that this duty of fair representation action resembles a suit brought to vacate an arbitration award because respondents seek to set aside the result of the grievance process. In the 18th century, an action to set aside an arbitration award was considered equitable. 2 J. STORY, COMMENTARIES ON EQUITY JURISPRUDENCE § 1452, pp. 789–90 (13th ed. 1886) (equity courts had jurisdiction over claims that an award should be set aside on the ground of "mistake of the arbitrators"); see, e.g., Burchell v. Marsh, 17 How. 344 (1855) (reviewing bill in equity to vacate an arbitration award). * * *

The arbitration analogy is inapposite, however, to the Seventh Amendment question posed in this case. No grievance committee has considered respondents' claim that the Union violated its duty of fair representation; the grievance process was concerned only with the employer's alleged breach of the collective-bargaining agreement. Thus, respondents' claim against the Union cannot be characterized as an action to vacate an arbitration award because "[t]he arbitration proceeding did not, and indeed, could not, resolve the employee's claim against the union.... Because no arbitrator has decided the primary issue presented by this claim, no arbitration award need be undone, even if the employee ultimately prevails."

The Union next argues that respondents' duty of fair representation action is comparable to an action by a trust beneficiary against a trustee for breach of fiduciary duty. Such actions were within the exclusive jurisdiction of courts of equity. 2 STORY, *supra* , § 960, p. 266; RESTATEMENT (SECOND) OF TRUSTS § 199(c) (1959). * * *

Respondents contend that their duty of fair representation suit is less like a trust action than an attorney malpractice action, which was historically an action at law, see, e.g., Russell v. Palmer, 2 Wils. K.B. 325, 95 Eng. Rep. 837 (1767). In determining the appropriate statute of limitations for a hybrid § 301/duty of fair representation action, this Court in *DelCostello* [*v. Teamsters*] noted in dictum that an attorney malpractice action is "the closest state-law analogy for the claim against the union." 462 U.S. 151, 167. The Court in *DelCostello* did not consider the trust analogy, however. Presented with a more complete range of alternatives, we find that, in the context of the Seventh Amendment inquiry, the attorney malpractice analogy does not capture the relationship between the union and the represented employees as fully as the trust analogy does.

The attorney malpractice analogy is inadequate in several respects. Although an attorney malpractice suit is in some ways similar to a suit alleging a union's breach of its fiduciary duty, the two actions are fundamentally different. The nature of an action is in large part controlled by the nature of the underlying relationship between the parties. Unlike employees represented by a union, a client controls the significant decisions concerning his representation. Moreover, a client can fire his attorney if he is dissatisfied with his attorney's performance. This option is not available to an individual employee who is unhappy with a union's representation, unless a majority of the members of the bargaining unit share his dissatisfaction. Thus, we find the malpractice analogy less convincing than the trust analogy.

Nevertheless, the trust analogy does not persuade us to characterize respondents' claim as wholly equitable. The Union's argument mischaracterizes the nature of our comparison of the action before us to 18th-century forms of action. As we observed in Ross v. Bernhard, 396 U.S. 531 (1970), "The Seventh Amendment question depends on the nature of the *issue* to be tried rather than the character of the overall action." Id. at 538. As discussed above, to recover from the Union here, respondents must prove both that McLean violated § 301 by breaching the collective-bargaining agreement and that the Union breached its duty of fair representation. When viewed in isolation, the duty of fair representation issue is analogous to a claim against a trustee for breach of fiduciary duty. The § 301 issue, however, is comparable to a breach of contract claim — a legal issue.

Respondents' action against the Union thus encompasses both equitable and legal issues. The first part of our Seventh Amendment inquiry, then, leaves us in equipoise as to whether respondents are entitled to a jury trial.

B

Our determination under the first part of the Seventh Amendment analysis is only preliminary. In this case, the only remedy sought is a request for compensatory damages representing backpay and benefits. Generally, an action for money damages was "the traditional form of relief offered in the courts of law." Curtis v. Loether, 415 U.S. 189, 196 (1974). This Court has not, however, held that "any award of monetary relief must *necessarily* be 'legal' relief." Ibid. (emphasis added). Nonetheless, because we conclude that the remedy respondents seek has none of the attributes that must be present before we will find an exception to the general rule and characterize damages as equitable, we find that the remedy sought by respondents is legal.

First, we have characterized damages as equitable where they are restitutionary, such as in "action[s] for disgorgement of improper profits." The backpay sought by respondents is not money wrongfully held by the Union, but wages and benefits they would have received from McLean had the Union processed the employees' grievances properly. Such relief is not restitutionary.

Second, a monetary award "incidental to or intertwined with injunctive relief" may be equitable. Because respondents seek only money damages, this characteristic is clearly absent from the case.[8]

8. Both the Union and the dissent argue that the backpay award sought here is equitable because it is closely analogous to damages awarded to beneficiaries for a trustee's breach of trust. Such damages

The Union argues that the backpay relief sought here must nonetheless be considered equitable because this Court has labeled backpay awarded under Title VII of the Civil Rights Act of 1964 as equitable. See Albemarle Paper Co. v. Moody, 422 U.S. 405, 415–18 (1975) (characterizing backpay awarded against employer under Title VII as equitable in context of assessing whether judge erred in refusing to award such relief). It contends that the Title VII analogy is compelling in the context of the duty of fair representation because the Title VII backpay provision was based on the NLRA provision governing backpay awards for unfair labor practices. We are not convinced.

The Court has never held that a plaintiff seeking backpay under Title VII has a right to a jury trial. Assuming, without deciding, that such a Title VII plaintiff has no right to a jury trial, the Union's argument does not persuade us that respondents are not entitled to a jury trial here. Congress specifically characterized backpay under Title VII as a form of "equitable relief." 42 U.S.C. § 2000e-5(g) (1982 ed.). * * * Congress made no similar pronouncement regarding the duty of fair representation. Furthermore, the Court has noted that backpay sought from an employer under Title VII would generally be restitutionary in nature, in contrast to the damages sought here from the Union. Thus, the remedy sought in this duty of fair representation case is clearly different from backpay sought for violations of Title VII.

Moreover, the fact that Title VII's backpay provision may have been modeled on a provision in the NLRA concerning remedies for unfair labor practices does not require that the backpay remedy available here be considered equitable. The Union apparently reasons that if Title VII is comparable to one labor law remedy it is comparable to all remedies available in the NLRA context. Although both the duty of fair representation and the unfair labor practice provisions of the NLRA are components of national labor policy, their purposes are not identical. Unlike the unfair labor practice provisions of the NLRA, which are concerned primarily with the public interest in effecting federal labor policy, the duty of fair representation targets "the wrong done the individual employee." Thus, the remedies appropriate for unfair labor practices may differ from the remedies for a breach of the duty of fair representation, given the need to vindicate different goals. Certainly, the connection between backpay under Title VII and damages under the unfair

---

were available only in courts of equity because those courts had exclusive jurisdiction over actions involving a trustee's breach of his fiduciary duties.

The Union's argument, however, conflates the two parts of our Seventh Amendment inquiry. Under the dissent's approach, if the action at issue were analogous to an 18th-century action within the exclusive jurisdiction of the courts of equity, we would necessarily conclude that the remedy sought was also equitable because it would have been unavailable in a court of law. This view would, in effect, make the first part of our inquiry dispositive. We have clearly held, however, that the second part of the inquiry — the nature of the relief — is more important to the Seventh Amendment determination. The second part of the analysis, therefore, should not replicate the "abstruse historical" inquiry of the first part, but requires consideration of the general types of relief provided by courts of law and equity.

labor practice provision of the NLRA does not require us to find a parallel connection between Title VII backpay and money damages for breach of the duty of fair representation.

We hold, then, that the remedy of backpay sought in this duty of fair representation action is legal in nature. Considering both parts of the Seventh Amendment inquiry, we find that respondents are entitled to a jury trial on all issues presented in their suit.

IV

On balance, our analysis of the nature of respondents' duty of fair representation action and the remedy they seek convinces us that this action is a legal one. Although the search for an adequate 18th-century analog revealed that the claim includes both legal and equitable issues, the money damages respondents seek are the type of relief traditionally awarded by courts of law. Thus, the Seventh Amendment entitles respondents to a jury trial, and we therefore affirm the judgment of the Court of Appeals.

It is so ordered.

JUSTICE BRENNAN, concurring in part and concurring in the judgment.

I agree with the Court that respondents seek a remedy that is legal in nature and that the Seventh Amendment entitles respondents to a jury trial on their duty of fair representation claims. I therefore join Parts I, II, III-B, and IV of the Court's opinion. I do not join that part of the opinion which reprises the particular historical analysis this Court has employed to determine whether a claim is a "Sui[t] at common law" under the Seventh Amendment, because I believe the historical test can and should be simplified.

The current test, first expounded in *Curtis v. Loether*, requires a court to compare the right at issue to 18th-century English forms of action to determine whether the historically analogous right was vindicated in an action at law or in equity, and to examine whether the remedy sought is legal or equitable in nature. However, this Court, in expounding the test, has repeatedly discounted the significance of the analogous form of action for deciding where the Seventh Amendment applies. I think it is time we dispense with it altogether. I would decide Seventh Amendment questions on the basis of the relief sought. If the relief is legal in nature, i.e., if it is the kind of relief that historically was available from courts of law, I would hold that the parties have a constitutional right to a trial by jury — unless Congress has permissibly delegated the particular dispute to a non-Article III decision maker and jury trials would frustrate Congress' purposes in enacting a particular statutory scheme.

I believe that our insistence that the jury trial right hinges in part on a comparison of the substantive right at issue to forms of action used in English courts 200 years ago needlessly convolutes our Seventh Amendment jurisprudence. For the past decade and a half, this Court has explained that the two parts of the historical test are not equal in weight, that the nature of the remedy is more important than the nature of the right. Since the existence of a right to jury trial therefore turns on the nature of the remedy, absent congressional delegation to a specialized decision maker, there remains little purpose to our rattling through dusty attics of ancient writs. The time has come to borrow William of Occam's razor and sever this portion of our analysis.

We have long acknowledged that, of the factors relevant to the jury trial right, comparison of the claim to ancient forms of action, "requiring extensive and possibly abstruse historical inquiry, is obviously the most difficult to apply." Requiring judges, with neither the training nor time necessary for reputable historical scholarship, to root through the tangle of primary and secondary sources to determine which of a hundred or so writs is analogous to the right at issue has embroiled courts in recondite controversies better left to legal historians. * * *

To be sure, it is neither unusual nor embarrassing for members of a court to disagree and disagree vehemently. But it better behooves judges to disagree within the province of judicial expertise. Furthermore, inquiries into the appropriate historical analogs for the rights at issue are not necessarily susceptible of sound resolution under the best of circumstances. As one scholar observes: "[T]he line between law and equity (and therefore between jury and non-jury trial) was not a fixed and static one. There was a continual process of borrowing by one jurisdiction from the other; there were less frequent instances of a sloughing off of older functions.... The borrowing by each jurisdiction from the other was not accompanied by an equivalent sloughing off of functions. This led to a very large overlap between law and equity." James, *Right to a Jury Trial in Civil Actions*, 72 YALE L.J. 655, 658–59 (1963).

In addition, modern statutory rights did not exist in the 18th century, and even the most exacting historical research may not elicit a clear historical analog. The right at issue here, for example, is a creature of modern labor law quite foreign to Georgian England. Justice Stewart recognized the perplexities involved in this task in his dissent in *Ross v. Bernhard*, albeit drawing a different conclusion. "The fact is," he said, "that there are, for the most part, no such things as inherently 'legal issues' or inherently 'equitable issues.' There are only factual issues, and, 'like chameleons [they] take their color from surrounding circumstances.' Thus, the Court's 'nature of the issue' approach is hardly meaningful." I have grappled with this kind of inquiry for three decades on this Court and have come to the realization that engaging in such inquiries is impracticable and unilluminating.

To rest the historical test required by the Seventh Amendment solely on the nature of the relief sought would not, of course, offer the federal courts a rule that is in all cases self-executing. Courts will still be required to ask which remedies were traditionally available at law and which only in equity. But this inquiry involves fewer variables and simpler choices, on the whole, and is far more manageable than the scholastic debates in which we have been engaged. Moreover, the rule I propose would remain true to the Seventh Amendment, as it is undisputed that, historically, "[j]urisdictional lines [between law and equity] were primarily a matter of remedy." McCoid, *Procedural Reform and the Right to Jury Trial: A Study of* Beacon Theatres, Inc. v. Westover, 116 U. PA. L. REV. 1 (1967). See also Redish, *Seventh Amendment Right to Jury Trial: A Study in the Irrationality of Rational Decision Making*, 70 NW. U. L. REV. 486, 490 (1975) ("In the majority of cases at common law, the equitable or legal nature of a suit was determined not by the substantive nature of the cause of action but by the remedy sought").[7]

This is not to say that the resulting division between claims entitled to jury trials and claims not so entitled would exactly mirror the division between law and equity in England in 1791. But it is too late in the day for this Court to profess that the Seventh Amendment preserves the right to jury trial only in cases that would have been heard in the British law courts of the 18th century. See, e.g., *Curtis v. Loether*, 415 U.S. at 193 ("Although the thrust of the Amendment was to preserve the right to jury trial as it existed in 1791, it has long been settled that the right extends beyond the common-law forms of action recognized at that time"); Beacon Theatres, Inc. v. Westover, 359 U.S. 500 (1959) (rejecting the relevance of the chancellor's historic ability to decide legal claims incidental to a case brought in equity and holding that, in mixed cases, the parties are not only entitled to a jury trial on the legal claims but that this jury trial must precede a decision on the equitable claims—with the attendant collateral-estoppel effects); Ross v. Bernhard, 396 U.S. 531 (1970) (requiring a jury trial on the legal issues in a shareholders' derivative suit even though the procedurally equivalent suit in the 18th century would have been heard only in equity).

Indeed, given this Court's repeated insistence that the nature of the remedy is always to be given more weight than the nature of the historically analogous right, it is unlikely that the simplified Seventh Amendment analysis I propose will result in different decisions than the analysis in current use. In the unusual circumstance that the nature of the remedy could be characterized equally as legal or equitable, I submit that the comparison of a contemporary statutory action unheard of in the 18th century to some ill-fitting ancient writ is too shaky a basis for the resolution of an issue as

---

7. There are, to be sure, some who advocate abolishing the historical test altogether. See, e.g., Wolfram, *The Constitutional History of the Seventh Amendment*, 57 Minn. L. Rev. 639, 742–47 (1973). Contrary to the intimations in Justice Kennedy's dissent, I am not among them. I believe that it is imperative to retain a historical test for determining when parties have a right to jury trial for precisely the same reasons Justice Kennedy does. It is mandated by the language of the Seventh Amendment and it is a bulwark against those who would restrict a right our forefathers held indispensable. Like Justice Kennedy, I have no doubt that courts can and do look to legal history for the answers to constitutional questions, and therefore the Seventh Amendment test I propose today obliges courts to do exactly that.

Where Justice Kennedy and I differ is in our evaluations of which historical test provides the more reliable results. That three learned Justices of the Supreme Court cannot arrive at the same conclusion in this very case, on what is essentially a question of fact, does not speak well for the judicial solvency of the current test. My concern is not merely the competence of courts to delve into this peculiarly recalcitrant aspect of legal history and certainly not, as Justice Kennedy summarizes it, the "competence of the Court to understand legal history" in general. My concern is that all too often the first prong of the current test requires courts to measure modern statutory actions against 18th-century English actions so remote in form and concept that there is no firm basis for comparison. In such cases, the result is less the discovery of a historical analog than the manufacture of a historical fiction. By contrast, the nature of relief available today corresponds more directly to the nature of relief available in Georgian England. Thus the historical test I propose, focusing on the nature of the relief sought, is not only more manageable than the current test, it is more reliably grounded in history.

significant as the availability of a trial by jury. If, in the rare case, a tie breaker is needed, let us break the tie in favor of jury trial.

We can guard this right and save our courts from needless and intractable excursions into increasingly unfamiliar territory simply by retiring that prong of our Seventh Amendment test which we have already cast into a certain doubt. If we are not prepared to accord the nature of the historical analog sufficient weight for this factor to affect the outcome of our inquiry, except in the rarest of hypothetical cases, what reason do we have for insisting that federal judges proceed with this arduous inquiry? It is time we read the writing on the wall, especially as we ourselves put it there.

JUSTICE KENNEDY, with whom JUSTICE O'CONNOR and JUSTICE SCALIA join, dissenting.

This case asks whether the Seventh Amendment guarantees the respondent union members a jury trial in a duty of fair representation action against their labor union. The Court is quite correct, in my view, in its formulation of the initial premises that must govern the case. Under *Curtis v. Loether*, the right to a jury trial in a statutory action depends on the presence of "legal rights and remedies." To determine whether rights and remedies in a duty of fair representation action are legal in character, we must compare the action to the 18th-century cases permitted in the law courts of England, and we must examine the nature of the relief sought. I agree also with those Members of the Court who find that the duty of fair representation action resembles an equitable trust action more than a suit for malpractice.

I disagree with the analytic innovation of the Court that identification of the trust action as a model for modern duty of fair representation actions is insufficient to decide the case. The Seventh Amendment requires us to determine whether the duty of fair representation action "is more similar to cases that were tried in courts of law than to suits tried in courts of equity." Tull v. United States, 481 U.S. 412, 417 (1987). Having made this decision in favor of an equitable action, our inquiry should end. Because the Court disagrees with this proposition, I dissent.

* * *

The Court must adhere to the historical test in determining the right to a jury because the language of the Constitution requires it. The Seventh Amendment "preserves" the right to jury trial in civil cases. We cannot preserve a right existing in 1791 unless we look to history to identify it. Our precedents are in full agreement with this reasoning and insist on adherence to the historical test. No alternatives short of rewriting the Constitution exist. If we abandon the plain language of the Constitution to expand the jury right, we may expect Courts with opposing views to curtail it in the future.

It is true that a historical inquiry into the distinction between law and equity may require us to enter into a domain becoming less familiar with time. Two centuries have passed since the Seventh Amendment's ratification, and the incompleteness of our historical records makes it difficult to know the nature of certain actions in 1791. The historical test, nonetheless, has received more criticism than it deserves. Although our application of the analysis in some cases may seem biased in favor of jury trials, the test has not become a nullity. We do not require juries in all statutory actions. The historical test, in fact, resolves most cases without difficulty.

I would hesitate to abandon or curtail the historical test out of concern for the competence of the Court to understand legal history. We do look to history for the answers to constitutional questions. Although opinions will differ on what this history shows, the approach has no less validity in the Seventh Amendment context than elsewhere.

If Congress has not provided for a jury trial, we are confined to the Seventh Amendment to determine whether one is required. Our own views respecting the wisdom of using a jury should be put aside. Like Justice Brennan, I admire the jury process. Other judges have taken the opposite view. See, e.g., J. Frank, Law and The Modern Mind 170–85 (1931). But the judgment of our own times is not always preferable to the lessons of history. Our whole constitutional experience teaches that history must inform the judicial inquiry. Our obligation to the Constitution and its Bill of Rights, no less than the compact we have with the generation that wrote them for us, do not permit us to disregard provisions that some may think to be mere matters of historical form.

Notes and Questions

1. In which, if any, of the following situations is there a Seventh Amendment right to a jury:

(a) Patty and David sign a contract. A dispute arises and Patty files suit for breach of contract seeking money damages.

(b) Same as (a), except that Patty seeks only specific performance.

(c) Patty seeks an injunction preventing Construction Company from dumping construction scraps on her property.

2. In Question 1(a) above, suppose that the plaintiff requested a judge and the defendant a jury. Whose request prevails?

3. Under Rule 38, a party must demand a jury "no later than 14 days after the last pleading directed to the issue is served." Rule 38(b)(1). Failure to request a jury constitutes a waiver, see Rule 38(d), and if neither party demands a jury, the case is then tried to the judge. See Rule 39(b). (When the judge is the fact-finder, the proceeding is called a "bench trial.") Although the Rule allows the jury demand to be included in a separate document, most parties include the demand in their pleadings. The federal requirement of a demand is in contrast to the practice in some states. In Georgia, for example, a jury is presumed unless explicitly waived by all parties. See Ga. Code Ann. § 9-11-39; Whitaker & Rambo Interior Designs, Inc. v. Prudential Property Cas. Ins. Co., 510 F. Supp. 97 (N.D. Ga. 1981) (under Rule 81(c) no demand required if case is removed from a state court in which right to a jury is presumed).

4. All of the hypotheticals in Question 1 involve common law claims that existed in 1791. In contrast, *Terry* involved a claim that did not exist in 1791. Notwithstanding

that the claim didn't exist in 1791, the Court uses what it calls a historical test. Thus, as noted above, to determine whether a party has a constitutional right to a jury in America today, one asks: "In 1791, in England, to what court would this claim (which didn't exist then) have been assigned?" Isn't this a little like asking in what room of Monticello Thomas Jefferson would have put his television set? Consider the following complications:

A. In Part III-A, of his opinion in *Terry*, Justice Marshall concluded that the "duty of fair representation issue" is equitable while the "§ 301 issue" is legal. However, in 1791, courts would not have focused on whether an issue in a claim was legal or equitable. Instead, the *entire* claim would have gone either to the law court or to the equity court.

In explaining his analysis, Justice Marshall relied on Ross v. Bernhard, 396 U.S. 531 (1970). *Ross* was a shareholder's derivative suit in which shareholders of a corporation alleged that the defendant breached its contract with the corporation. Although historically shareholder derivative suits could only be brought in courts of equity, the Court held there was nonetheless a right to a jury. It explained that a derivative suit "has dual aspects: first, the stockholder's right to sue on behalf of the corporation, historically an equitable matter; second, the claim of the corporation against directors or third parties on which, if the corporation had sued and the claim presented legal issues, the company could demand a jury trial." Id. at 538. The Court concluded:

> The historical rule preventing a court of law from entertaining a shareholder's suit on behalf of the corporation is obsolete; it is no longer tenable for a district court, administering both law and equity in the same action, to deny legal remedies to a corporation, merely because the corporation's spokesmen are its shareholders rather than its directors. Under the rules, law and equity are procedurally combined; nothing turns now upon the form of the action or the procedural devices by which the parties happen to come before the court.

Id. at 540.

Justice Brennan responded to Justice Marshall's analysis in *Terry* by quoting from Justice Stewart's dissent in *Ross* that "there are, for the most part, no such things as inherently 'legal issues' or inherently 'equitable issues.' There are only factual issues, and 'like chameleons [they] take their color from surrounding circumstances.'" Do you agree? How far can a court go in splitting a claim into its equitable and legal components? Consider, for example, a breach of contract claim seeking specific performance. Could it be said that such a claim has two components: the remedy, which is equitable, and the question of whether the contract was breached, which is legal?

B. In *Terry*, the Court focuses on whether the *remedy* sought is legal or equitable. The historical inquiry even as to remedy can be complex. For example, as the Court notes in *Terry*, although money damages was a traditional form of relief given by courts of law, occasionally money awards were given as part of equitable relief. The Court goes on to suggest that money awards in the form of "restitution" or "back pay" are equitable. Professor Murphy has argued that this suggestion is contradicted by history, and that most claims for monetary restitution would have been tried in the law courts. Colleen Murphy, *Misclassifying Monetary Restitution*, 55 SMU L. Rev. 1577, 1598–1607, 1626–28 (2002). According to her, the only exception to this was the relatively rare case "in which the plaintiff needed to trace its money or property." Id. at 1637. She similarly argues that for right to jury trial purposes, backpay should be considered a legal remedy. Id. at 1628–34.

C. A further complication of a historical inquiry is the relationship between law and equity. Traditionally, a precondition for equity was that legal remedies were inadequate. Because the scope of equitable remedies is thus tied to the scope of legal remedies, the Court has held that "procedural changes which remove the inadequacy of a remedy at law may sharply diminish the scope of traditional equitable remedies by making them unnecessary in many cases." Dairy Queen v. Wood, 369 U.S. 469, 478 n.19 (1962). This principle is well illustrated by *Dairy Queen.* There, the plaintiff sought an "accounting," an historically equitable remedy. Nonetheless, the Court held that there was a right to a jury, explaining:

> The respondents' contention that this money claim is "purely equitable" is based primarily upon the fact that their complaint is cast in terms of an "accounting," rather than in terms of an action for "debt" or "damages." But the constitutional right to trial by jury cannot be made to depend upon the choice of words used in the pleadings. The necessary prerequisite to the right to maintain a suit for an equitable accounting, like all other equitable remedies, is, as we pointed out in *Beacon Theatres*, the absence of an adequate remedy at law. Consequently, in order to maintain such a suit on a cause of action cognizable at law, as this one is, the plaintiff must be able to show that the "accounts between the parties" are of such a "complicated nature" that only a court of equity can satisfactorily unravel them. In view of the powers given to District Courts by Federal Rule of Civil Procedure 53(b) to appoint masters to assist the jury in those exceptional cases where the legal issues are too complicated for the jury adequately to handle alone, the burden of such a showing is considerably increased and it will indeed be a rare case in which it can be met. But be that as it may, this is certainly not such a case. A jury under proper instructions from the court, could readily determine the recovery, if any, to be had here, where the theory finally settled upon is that of breach of contract, that of trademark infringement, or any combination of the two. The legal remedy cannot be characterized as inadequate merely because the measure of damages may necessitate a look into petitioner's business records.

Id. at 477–79.

5. In light of these complications, what do you think of Justice Brennan's suggestion that the Court should abandon its search for historical analogies and instead confine its inquiry to the historical character of the *remedy* sought? Do you agree with Justice Kennedy that a historical test is mandated by the plain language of the

Seventh Amendment? Are there any other plausible ways to interpret that Amendment? See Charles Wofram, *The Constitutional History of the Seventh Amendment*, 57 MINN. L. REV. 639, 745 (1973) (arguing that the founders intended a "dynamic" interpretation of the Seventh Amendment, not a fixed historical meaning). With respect to the use of history, consider the following observation by Judge Posner:

> [J]udges do not have either the leisure or the training to conduct responsible historical research or completely umpire historical controversies. The term "law office history" is properly derisory and the derision embraces the efforts of judges and law professors, as well as of legal advocates, to play historian. * * * Judges don't try to decide contested issues of science without the aid of expert testimony, and we fool ourselves if we think we can unaided resolve issues of historical truth.

Velasquez v. Frapwell, 160 F.3d 389, 393 (7th Cir. 1998), *vac. in part*, 165 F.3d 593 (7th Cir. 1999).

6. As Justice Brennan notes in his footnote 7, some commentators have urged abandoning an historical approach in favor of a "functional approach" focusing "on whether the judge is in a better position than the jury to decide a particular case in a fashion comporting with notions of fair and efficient justice." Mary Kay Kane, *Civil Jury Trial: The Case for Reasoned Iconoclasm*, 28 HAST. L.J. 1, 2 (1976). Advocates of this approach have drawn some support from a footnote in Ross v. Bernhard, 396 U.S. 531, 538 n.10 (1970), in which the Court observed:

> As our cases indicate, the "legal" nature of an issue is determined by considering, first, the pre-merger custom with reference to such questions. Second, the remedy sought; and third, the practical abilities and limitations of juries. Of the factors, the first, requiring extensive and possible abstruse historical inquiry, is obviously the most difficult to apply.

In *Terry*, the Court does not mention the third factor listed above. Should the Court consider "the practical abilities and limitations of juries" in deciding whether there is a right to a jury? If so, what are the abilities and limitations of juries? Suppose, for example, the case will be extremely long or complex, is a jury appropriate? See, e.g., In re Japanese Electronic Prods. Antitrust Litigation, 631 F.2d 1069 (3d Cir. 1980). At least one historian has concluded that a "complexity exception" would be consistent with the historical test. See James Oldham, *In the Question of a Complexity Exception to the Seventh Amendment Guarantee of Trial by Jury*, 71 OHIO ST. L. REV. 1031 (2010).

7. In Markman v. Westview Instruments, Inc., 517 U.S. 370 (1996), the Court relied on functional considerations in holding that the judge, rather than a jury, should determine the scope of a patent. Though there is generally a constitutional right to a jury in patent infringement cases, the judge is better suited to make the decision on scope of the patent. The Court said: "The construction of written instruments is one of those things that judges often do and are likely to do better than jurors unburdened by training in exegesis." Though the decision raised some eyebrows

initially, it has been limited to the patent context and has not supported a broad functional analysis or "complexity" exception to the Seventh Amendment.

8. In Tull v. United States, 481 U.S. 412 (1987), the Court held that there is a right to a jury in cases seeking civil penalties under the Clean Water Act. The government contended that the defendant had dumped fill material on wetlands in violation of the Act. The Act authorized civil penalties of up to $10,000 per day during the period of the violation, and the government sought the maximum penalty of over $22 million. The defendant argued that the suit was analogous to an action in debt, which was a legal claim. The government responded that the suit was more analogous to an action to abate a public nuisance, which was equitable. The Court declined to rest its holding on an "'abstruse historical' search for the nearest 18th-century analog." Id. at 421. Instead the Court focused on the remedy. The Court observed that the penalties were not intended simply to restore the status quo—a traditional equitable function, but were designed to deter and punish. It concluded that "the nature of the relief authorized by [the Act] was traditionally available only in a court of law" and therefore the defendant was entitled to a jury on the question of liability under the Act. Id. at 423.

Although the Court found a right to a jury on the question of liability, it also held that there was no right to have a jury determine the amount of the civil penalty. The Court observed that "[n]othing in the [Seventh] Amendment's language suggested that the right to a jury extends to the remedy phase of a civil trial." Id. at 426 n.9. The Court concluded that "[t]he assessment of civil penalties * * * cannot be said to involve the 'substance of a common-law right to a trial by jury,' nor a 'fundamental element of a jury trial.'" Id. at 426. Thus, although the reason the defendant got a jury on liability was because of the remedy, he wasn't allowed a jury to determine the amount of the remedy. Does this make any sense?

In probing whether the assessment of civil penalties is an essential function of the jury trial, *Tull* leaves unanswered whether the Seventh Amendment requires that the jury determine other types of remedies, such as compensatory or punitive damages. Professor Murphy concludes that the Seventh Amendment does not compel a jury assessment of punitive damages. She argues that the assessment of punitive damages, like that of civil penalties, is unconstrained by meaningful standards and that this sort of discretionary decision making is better performed by judges, who have legal training and experience in the civil justice system. Colleen Murphy, *Integrating the Constitutional Authority of Civil and Criminal Juries*, 61 GEO. WASH. L. REV. 723, 739–82 (1993). In contrast, Professor Murphy concludes that the Seventh Amendment does require that juries determine compensatory damages because that assessment is rooted in factfinding and subjective evaluation of the facts, which are decisions that are at the heart of the jury's constitutional province. Colleen Murphy, *Determining Compensation: The Tension Between Legislative Power and Jury Authority*, 74 TEX. L. REV. 345 (1995). See also Colleen Murphy, *Judicial Assessment of Legal Remedies*, 94 NW. L. REV. 153 (1999).

9. Distinguishing *Tull*, the Court in Feltner v. Columbia Pictures Television, Inc., 523 U.S. 340 (1998), held that there is a right to have a jury decide the amount

of statutory damages under the Copyright Act. Under that Act, a plaintiff may elect statutory damages in lieu of actual damages. The amount of the statutory damages is "a sum of not less than $500 or more than $20,000 as the court considers just." The Court acknowledged that the statute clearly contemplated damages would be set by the judge, but held that the Seventh Amendment grants a right to a jury. The opinion focused on the "overwhelming evidence that the consistent practice at common law was for juries to award damages." Id. at 353. The Court distinguished *Tull*, noting that "we were presented with no evidence that juries had historically determined the amount of civil penalties to be paid to the Government." Id. at 355.

b. *The Complications of Merger and the Federal Rules*

The Federal Rules not only merge the courts of law and equity, they permit parties to join legal and equitable claims in a single suit. Thus today, in federal and most state courts, parties can raise legal and equitable claims in one suit. Suppose, for example, the plaintiff files suit seeking injunctive relief and the defendant counterclaims with a legal claim. Is there a right to jury?

In Beacon Theatres v. Westover, 359 U.S. 500 (1959), the Supreme Court held that there is a right to a jury on the legal claim and that, therefore, the legal claim should ordinarily be tried first. The reason for trying the legal claim first is tied to the concept of preclusion, which we will study in Chapter 11. Under preclusion doctrine, once a claim or issue has been determined, that decision will generally be binding on future adjudications involving that claim or issue. Therefore, if the equitable claim were decided first, the facts decided in connection with that claim would then be treated as having been established for purposes of the legal claim. This would mean that the only issues left for the jury would be any that were not addressed in connection with the equitable claim. Thus, the Court in *Beacon Theatres* concluded:

> If there should be cases [joining equitable and legal claims] * * * the trial court will necessarily have to use its discretion in deciding whether the legal or equitable cause should be tried first. Since the right to jury trial is a constitutional one, however, while no similar requirement protects trials by the court, that discretion is very narrowly limited and must, wherever possible, be exercised to preserve jury trial. As this Court said in Scott v. Neely, 140 U.S. 106, 109–10 (1891): "In the Federal courts this [jury] right cannot be dispensed with, except by the assent of the parties entitled to it, nor can it be impaired by any blending with a claim, properly cognizable at law, of a demand for equitable relief in aid of the legal action or during its pendency." This long-standing principle of equity dictates that only under the most imperative circumstances, circumstances which in view of the flexible procedures of the Federal Rules we cannot now anticipate, can the right to a jury trial of legal issues be lost through prior determination of equitable claims.

Id. at 510–11.

The Court reaffirmed this holding of *Beacon Theatres* in Dairy Queen v. Wood, 369 U.S. 469 (1962). In *Dairy Queen*, the Court stressed that there is a right to a jury on legal issues even if the equitable claims predominate or the legal issues are "incidental" to the equitable ones. Id. at 473.

Another modern innovation is the declaratory judgment, a remedy unknown in 1791, and which we encountered in Chapter 4, section C.4.b.ii. Is there a right to a jury in a declaratory judgment action? In answering this, courts determine in what kind of an action the suit would have been brought absent the availability of the declaratory judgment. See, e.g., Northgate Homes v. City of Dayton, 126 F.3d 1095, 1099 (8th Cir. 1997); 9 WRIGHT & MILLER, FEDERAL PRACTICE & PROCEDURE § 2313. For example, if a party to a contract is unable to perform because of some unforeseen circumstance, that party might seek a declaratory judgment that the failure to perform is not a breach of contract. Since the other way the issue of the breach could have arisen would have been in a suit for damages, which would carry a jury right, there is a jury right in the declaratory judgment action. Given that many issues could be litigated in either an equitable or legal action, this test can be difficult. Suppose that a plaintiff brings a school desegregation claim seeking an injunction. Can the school board get a jury if it counterclaims for a declaratory judgment that it is not liable for damages? See Robinson v. Brown, 320 F.2d 503 (6th Cir. 1963).

One modern innovation that has been permitted to diminish in some respects the right to a jury is non-mutual issue preclusion, which we will examine in detail in Chapter 11. In that chapter, we will read Parklane Hosiery Co. v. Shore, 439 U.S. 322 (1979). There, the Securities and Exchange Commission sought a declaratory judgment against a corporation and some of its directors and officers that they had issued false proxy statements in violation of federal laws. After the SEC won that case, private litigants, suing the same defendants for the same proxy statements, asserted that the defendants were estopped to deny that the proxy statements were false. The Court agreed, even though the SEC proceeding had not involved a jury and the assertion of preclusion meant that defendants would never be able to litigate the question before a jury.

c. *Juries in Non-Article III Courts*

Article III of the Constitution describes the judicial power of the United States and provides, among other things, for judges with life tenure. However, not all adjudication of federal claims occurs in courts with Article III judges. First, and most obviously, state courts are not covered by Article III. Because of concurrent jurisdiction, many federal claims are adjudicated in state court. Indeed prior to the establishment of general federal question jurisdiction in 1875, most federal claims were litigated in state court. In addition, Congress has established numerous federal agencies which, among other powers, have authority to adjudicate disputes within their jurisdiction. These administrative courts are staffed with administrative law judges who are appointed for fixed terms and are not covered by Article III. In addition to administrative agencies, Congress, pursuant to its powers in Article. I, has created other so called "Article I courts," including the local courts of the District of Columbia and the Bankruptcy Courts.

Is there a Seventh Amendment right to a jury in litigation outside of Article III courts? The Supreme Court has held that in non-Article III courts, a jury is required for the adjudication of "private rights," but not for "new statutory 'public rights.'" Atlas Roofing Co. v. OSHRC, 430 U.S. 442, 455 (1977). Applying this distinction between public and private rights, the Court has held that juries are not required in adjudications of civil penalties before the Occupational Safety and Health Review Commission, see id., but are required in bankruptcy court in a suit brought by a trustee in bankruptcy seeking to void an allegedly fraudulent conveyance. Granfinanciera, S.A. v. Nordberg, 492 U.S. 33 (1989). See Mark Greenberg, *The Right to Jury Trial in Non-Article III Courts and Administrative Agencies After* Granfinanciera v. Nordberg, 1990 U. CHI. LEGAL F. 479.

d. Juries in State Courts

As noted earlier, the Seventh Amendment does not apply to litigation in state court. Nonetheless, most state constitutions provide a right to a jury in civil cases comparable to the Seventh Amendment. A few, such as Georgia, North Carolina, Tennessee, and Texas grant a right to jury in equity cases. However, among states that limit juries to actions at law, there are significant variations in interpretation. Some, for example, do not follow *Beacon Theatres*, and instead hold that there is no right to a jury on a legal counterclaim filed in response to an equitable claim. See, e.g., Vanier v. Ponsoldt, 833 P.2d 949 (Ka. 1992). Similarly, a state may grant a right to a jury when the federal courts would not. See Byrd v. Blue Ridge Rural Electric Cooperative, Inc., 356 U.S. 525 (1958), infra Chapter 10, Section B.2.

Although the Seventh Amendment does not require juries in state court, some federal statutes explicitly provide for a right to a jury trial, see, e.g., The Jones Act, 46 U.S.C. § 30104, and others, though not explicit, have been interpreted to require a jury. Where the right to a jury is "part and parcel of the remedy afforded" by the federal statute, the Court has held that state courts must provide a jury when claims under that federal statute are litigated in state court. See Dice v. Akron, Canton & Youngstown R., 342 U.S. 359 (1952).

State court systems are generally organized by governmental subunits such as counties, and jurors are typically drawn from those geographic areas. The federal courts are organized by federal districts, and these are generally larger than counties. As a result, jurors in a federal case are likely to be drawn from a broader geographic region than jurors in a state case. This can result in significant demographic differences among jury pools and these differences can be important to lawyers considering their forum choices. For example, in *World-Wide Volkswagen*, supra Chapter 2, the plaintiffs' lawyer concluded that because of differences in the jury pools, a case in Creek County, Oklahoma was worth substantially more than the same case litigated in federal court in Oklahoma. Charles Adams, World-Wide Volkswagen v. Woodson —

The Rest of the Story, 72 Neb. L. Rev. 1122, 1128 (1993). As a result, the plaintiff wanted very much to stay in state court and the defendants wanted equally much to have the non-diverse defendant dismissed from the case so that they could remove the case to federal court. The battle over personal jurisdiction was really a battle over which jury pool would hear the case.

2. Selection and Size of the Jury

a. The Venire and Voir Dire

Jurors are summoned from a master roll of prospective jurors. For much of our history, these master lists systematically excluded certain groups such as minorities and women. Beginning in the 1940s, the Supreme Court began to strike down this exclusion of groups from jury rolls, and in 1975, it held that the lists from which juries are summoned must reflect a reasonable cross-section of the population. Taylor v. Louisiana, 419 U.S. 522 (1975). Today, courts rely on a variety of sources for the names on their jury rolls. Voter registration lists are a common source, but increasingly courts rely in addition on lists of licensed drivers, taxpayers, or welfare recipients.

The jurors summoned for duty are called the venire. The jury is selected from the venire through the process of voir dire.* The purpose of voir dire is to gather information about prospective jurors' possible knowledge, bias, or opinions about the case or the parties. Based on the information gleaned during voir dire, there are two paths for "striking" (removing) a potential juror. The judge may strike a juror "for cause" if the voir dire shows that she cannot be expected to be unbiased. Thus, jurors can be struck for cause when they have a close connection with any of the parties or witnesses or "when they have such fixed opinions that they could not judge impartially the guilt of the defendant." Patton v. Yount, 467 U.S. 1025, 1035 (1984). There is no limit to the number of strikes "for cause."

The second path for striking a juror is through the parties' "peremptory challenges." Peremptory challenges, which are discussed in detail below, allow lawyers to strike potential jurors, historically without a need to state a reason. Parties have a limited number of peremptory challenges, which, historically, have allowed lawyers to remove jurors based upon their intuition — their "lawyer's sense" — that the juror would be unfavorable.

Courts may conduct voir dire in different ways. Prospective jurors may be questioned in groups or individually, and the questioning may be done entirely by the lawyers, entirely by the judge, or by both the lawyers and the judge. See Rule 47(a). The judge has wide discretion both as to the conduct of voir dire and the scope of

* "Voir dire" is traditionally translated either "to speak the truth" or "to see what is said."

the questions. Sometimes, particularly in cases involving substantial pre-trial publicity, the court may give prospective jurors a written questionnaire to expedite voir dire and more easily screen out those with obvious biases.

b. Peremptory Challenges

In England, peremptory challenges, at least in criminal cases, date back to the 13th century. Originally, the crown had unlimited peremptory strikes. However, in 1305, to correct what was perceived as an unfairness, Parliament eliminated the prosecution's (but not the defendant's) right to exercise peremptories. Despite this change, the crown retained the power to ask jurors to "stand aside." Under this procedure, no reason for the request was required unless there was an insufficient number of jurors remaining to compose a jury. Peremptory challenges remained entrenched in the British system until the practice was abolished by Parliament in 1988.

In the United States, the practice of allowing defendants peremptory challenges dates back to colonial times. After independence, Congress codified the practice, granting defendants twenty peremptories in felonies punishable by death and thirty-five peremptories in trials for treason. In contrast, it was not until the early twentieth century that the prosecutor's right to exercise peremptories was fully established. For a history of peremptory challenges, see Richard Friedman, *An Asymmetrical Approach to the Problem of Peremptories*, 28 Crim. L. Bull. 507 (Nov.–Dec. 1992); Deborah Zalesne & Kinney Zalesne, *Saving the Peremptory Challenge: The Case for a Narrow Interpretation of* McCollum, 70 Denv. U. L. Rev. 313, 315–19 (1993).

Proponents of peremptory challenges offer several justifications for them. First, particularly in earlier times, the government was perceived as having an inherent advantage in controlling the selection of the venire. Thus, the defendant's peremptories helped equalize the defendant's position. Second, by giving participants some power in the selection of the jury, peremptories helped legitimize verdicts. As Blackstone explained, "a prisoner (when put to defend his life) should have a good opinion of his jury, the want of which might totally disconcert him, the law wills not that he should be tried by any one man against whom he has conceived a prejudice, even without being able to assign a reason for such his dislike." 4 William Blackstone, Commentaries *353 (1859). Finally, peremptory challenges supplement the challenges for cause, allowing lawyers to strike jurors whom they believe to be biased, without having to ask the potentially time-consuming and intrusive voir dire questions that would be necessary to establish a challenge for cause.

Today, the number of peremptories is usually fixed by statute. In federal civil cases, each side is entitled to three peremptories. 28 U.S.C. § 1870. In non-capital federal felony prosecutions, the defendant is entitled to ten peremptories, the prosecution six. Fed. R. Crim. P. 24(b). In capital cases, each side is entitled to twenty peremptory strikes. Id.

Traditionally, lawyers could exercise peremptory challenges for any reason or no reason without explanation. As the following case highlights, that tradition is now subject to some important qualifications.

J.E.B. v. Alabama

511 U.S. 127, 114 S. Ct. 1419, 128 L. Ed. 2d 89 (1994)

Justice Blackmun delivered the opinion of the Court.

In Batson v. Kentucky, 476 U.S. 79 (1986), this Court held that the Equal Protection Clause of the Fourteenth Amendment governs the exercise of peremptory challenges by a prosecutor in a criminal trial. The Court explained that although a defendant has "no right to a 'petit jury composed in whole or in part of persons of his own race,'" id. at 85, quoting Strauder v. West Virginia, 100 U.S. 303, 305 (1880), the "defendant does have the right to be tried by a jury whose members are selected pursuant to nondiscriminatory criteria." Since *Batson*, we have reaffirmed repeatedly our commitment to jury selection procedures that are fair and nondiscriminatory. We have recognized that whether the trial is criminal or civil, potential jurors, as well as litigants, have an equal protection right to jury selection procedures that are free from state-sponsored group stereotypes rooted in, and reflective of, historical prejudice. See Powers v. Ohio, 499 U.S. 400 (1991); Edmonson v. Leesville Concrete Co., 500 U.S. 614 (1991); Georgia v. McCollum, 505 U.S. 42 (1992).

Although premised on equal protection principles that apply equally to gender discrimination, all our recent cases defining the scope of *Batson* involved alleged racial discrimination in the exercise of peremptory challenges. Today we are faced with the question whether the Equal Protection Clause forbids intentional discrimination on the basis of gender, just as it prohibits discrimination on the basis of race. We hold that gender, like race, is an unconstitutional proxy for juror competence and impartiality.

I

On behalf of relator T.B., the mother of a minor child, respondent State of Alabama filed a complaint for paternity and child support against petitioner J.E.B. in the District Court of Jackson County, Alabama. On October 21, 1991, the matter was called for trial and jury selection began. The trial court assembled a panel of 36 potential jurors, 12 males and 24 females. After the court excused three jurors for cause, only 10 of the remaining 33 jurors were male. The State then used 9 of its 10 peremptory strikes to remove male jurors; petitioner used all but one of his strikes to remove female jurors. As a result, all the selected jurors were female.

Before the jury was empaneled, petitioner objected to the State's peremptory challenges on the ground that they were exercised against male jurors solely on the basis of gender, in violation of the Equal Protection Clause of the Fourteenth Amendment. Petitioner argued that the logic and reasoning of *Batson v. Kentucky*, which prohibits peremptory strikes solely on the basis of race, similarly forbids intentional discrimination on the basis of gender. The court rejected petitioner's claim and empaneled the all-female jury. The jury found petitioner to be the father of the child and the court entered an order directing him to pay child support. On post-judgment motion, the court reaffirmed its ruling that *Batson* does not extend to gender-based peremptory challenges. The Alabama Court of Civil Appeals affirmed, relying on Alabama precedent. The Supreme Court of Alabama denied certiorari.

We granted certiorari to resolve a question that has created a conflict of authority—whether the Equal Protection Clause forbids peremptory challenges on the basis of gender as well as on the basis of race. Today we reaffirm what, by now, should be axiomatic: Intentional discrimination on the basis of gender by state actors violates the Equal Protection Clause, particularly where, as here, the discrimination serves to ratify and perpetuate invidious, archaic, and overbroad stereotypes about the relative abilities of men and women.

II

Discrimination on the basis of gender in the exercise of peremptory challenges is a relatively recent phenomenon. Gender-based peremptory strikes were hardly practicable for most of our country's existence, since, until the 19th century, women were completely excluded from jury service.[2] So well-entrenched was this exclusion of women that in 1880 this Court, while finding that the exclusion of African-American men from juries violated the Fourteenth Amendment, expressed no doubt that a State "may confine the selection [of jurors] to males." Strauder v. West Virginia, 100 U.S. 303, 310 [1880].

Many States continued to exclude women from jury service well into the present century, despite the fact that women attained suffrage upon ratification of the Nineteenth Amendment in 1920.[3] States that did permit women to serve on juries often erected other barriers, such as registration requirements and automatic exemptions, designed to deter women from exercising their right to jury service.

The prohibition of women on juries was derived from the English common law which, according to Blackstone, rightfully excluded women from juries under "the doctrine of *propter defectum sexus*, literally, the 'defect of sex.'" United States v. De Gross, 960 F.2d 1433, 1438 (9th Cir. 1992) (*en banc*), quoting 2 W. Blackstone, Commentaries *362.[4] In this country, supporters of the exclusion of women from juries tended to couch their objections in terms of the ostensible need to protect women from the ugliness and depravity of trials. Women were thought to be too

---

2. There was one brief exception. Between 1870 and 1871, women were permitted to serve on juries in Wyoming Territory. They were no longer allowed on juries after a new chief justice who disfavored the practice was appointed in 1871.

3. In 1947, women still had not been granted the right to serve on juries in 16 States. As late as 1961, three States, Alabama, Mississippi, and South Carolina, continued to exclude women from jury service. Indeed, Alabama did not recognize women as a "cognizable group" for jury-service purposes until after the 1966 decision in White v. Crook, 251 F. Supp. 401 (M.D. Ala.) (three-judge court).

4. In England there was at least one deviation from the general rule that only males could serve as jurors. If a woman was subject to capital punishment, or if a widow sought postponement of the disposition of her husband's estate until birth of a child, a writ *de ventre inspiciendo* permitted the use of a jury of matrons to examine the woman to determine whether she was pregnant. But even when a jury of matrons was used, the examination took place in the presence of 12 men, who also composed part of the jury in such cases. The jury of matrons was used in the United States during the Colonial period, but apparently fell into disuse when the medical profession began to perform that function.

fragile and virginal to withstand the polluted courtroom atmosphere. See Bailey v. State, 215 Ark. 53, 61, 219 S.W.2d 424, 428 (1949) ("Criminal court trials often involve testimony of the foulest kind, and they sometimes require consideration of indecent conduct, the use of filthy and loathsome words, references to intimate sex relationships, and other elements that would prove humiliating, embarrassing and degrading to a lady") * * * .; In re Goodell, 39 Wis. 232, 245–46 (1875) (endorsing statutory ineligibility of women for admission to the bar because "[r]everence for all womanhood would suffer in the public spectacle of women ... so engaged"); Bradwell v. State, 16 Wall. 130, 141 (1873) (concurring opinion) ("[T]he civil law, as well as nature herself, has always recognized a wide difference in the respective spheres and destinies of man and woman. Man is, or should be, woman's protector and defender. The natural and proper timidity and delicacy which belongs to the female sex evidently unfits it for many of the occupations of civil life.... The paramount destiny and mission of woman are to fulfil the noble and benign offices of wife and mother. This is the law of the Creator"). Cf. Frontiero v. Richardson, 411 U.S. 677, 684 (1973) (plurality opinion) (This "attitude of 'romanticpaternalism'... put women, not on a pedestal, but in a cage").

This Court in Ballard v. United States, 329 U.S. 187 (1946), first questioned the fundamental fairness of denying women the right to serve on juries. Relying on its supervisory powers over the federal courts, it held that women may not be excluded from the venire in federal trials in States where women were eligible for jury service under local law. * * *

Fifteen years later, however, the Court still was unwilling to translate its appreciation for the value of women's contribution to civic life into an enforceable right to equal treatment under state laws governing jury service. In *Hoyt v. Florida*, 368 U.S. 57, 61 (1961), the Court found it reasonable, "despite the enlightened emancipation of women," to exempt women from mandatory jury service by statute, allowing women to serve on juries only if they volunteered to serve. The Court justified the differential exemption policy on the ground that women, unlike men, occupied a unique position "as the center of home and family life."

In 1975, the Court finally repudiated the reasoning of *Hoyt* and struck down, under the Sixth Amendment, an affirmative registration statute nearly identical to the one at issue in *Hoyt*. See Taylor v. Louisiana, 419 U.S. 522 (1975). We explained: "Restricting jury service to only special groups or excluding identifiable segments playing major roles in the community cannot be squared with the constitutional concept of jury trial." The diverse and representative character of the jury must be maintained "partly as assurance of a diffused impartiality and partly because sharing in the administration of justice is a phase of civic responsibility."

III

Taylor relied on Sixth Amendment principles, but the opinion's approach is consistent with the heightened equal protection scrutiny afforded gender-based classifications. Since Reed v. Reed, 404 U.S. 71 (1971), this Court consistently has subjected gender-based classifications to heightened scrutiny in recognition of the real danger that government policies that professedly are based on reasonable considerations in fact may be reflective of "archaic and overbroad" generalizations about gender, or based on "outdated misconceptions concerning the role of females in the home rather than in the 'marketplace and world of ideas.'" Craig v. Boren, 429 U.S. 190, 198–99 (1976).

Despite the heightened scrutiny afforded distinctions based on gender, respondent argues that gender discrimination in the selection of the petit jury should be permitted, though discrimination on the basis of race is not. Respondent suggests that "gender discrimination in this country ... has never reached the level of discrimination" against African-Americans, and therefore gender discrimination, unlike racial discrimination, is tolerable in the courtroom.

While the prejudicial attitudes toward women in this country have not been identical to those held toward racial minorities, the similarities between the experiences of racial minorities and women, in some contexts, "overpower those differences." As a plurality of this Court observed in Frontiero v. Richardson, 411 U.S. 677, 685 (1973):

> "[T]hroughout much of the 19th century the position of women in our society was, in many respects, comparable to that of blacks under the pre-Civil War slave codes. Neither slaves nor women could hold office, serve on juries, or bring suit in their own names, and married women traditionally were denied the legal capacity to hold or convey property or to serve as legal guardians of their own children.... And although blacks were guaranteed the right to vote in 1870, women were denied even that right—which is itself 'preservative of other basic civil and political rights'—until adoption of the Nineteenth Amendment half a century later." (Footnotes omitted.)

Certainly, with respect to jury service, African-Americans and women share a history of total exclusion, a history which came to an end for women many years after the embarrassing chapter in our history came to an end for African-Americans.

We need not determine, however, whether women or racial minorities have suffered more at the hands of discriminatory state actors during the decades of our Nation's history. It is necessary only to acknowledge that "our Nation has had a long and unfortunate history of sex discrimination," a history which warrants the heightened scrutiny we afford all gender-based classifications today. Under our equal protection jurisprudence, gender-based classifications require "an exceedingly persuasive justification" in order to survive constitutional scrutiny. Thus, the only question is whether discrimination on the basis of gender in jury selection substantially furthers the State's legitimate interest in achieving a fair and impartial trial.[6] In making this assessment, we do not weigh the value of peremptory challenges as an institution against our as-

6. Because we conclude that gender-based peremptory challenges are not substantially related to an important government objective, we once again need not decide whether classifications based on gender are inherently suspect.

serted commitment to eradicate invidious discrimination from the courtroom.[7] Instead, we consider whether peremptory challenges based on gender stereotypes provide substantial aid to a litigant's effort to secure a fair and impartial jury.[8]

Far from proffering an exceptionally persuasive justification for its gender-based peremptory challenges, respondent maintains that its decision to strike virtually all the males from the jury in this case "may reasonably have been based upon the perception, supported by history, that men otherwise totally qualified to serve upon a jury might be more sympathetic and receptive to the arguments of a man alleged in a paternity action to be the father of an out-of-wedlock child, while women equally qualified to serve upon a jury might be more sympathetic and receptive to the arguments of the complaining witness who bore the child."[9]

We shall not accept as a defense to gender-based peremptory challenges "the very stereotype the law condemns." Respondent's rationale, not unlike those regularly expressed for gender-based strikes, is reminiscent of the arguments advanced to justify the total exclusion of women from juries.[10] Respondent offers virtually no support

---

7. Although peremptory challenges are valuable tools in jury trials, they "are not constitutionally protected fundamental rights; rather they are but one state-created means to the constitutional end of an impartial jury and a fair trial." Georgia v. McCollum, 505 U.S. 42, 57 (1992).

8. Respondent argues that we should recognize a special state interest in this case: the State's interest in establishing the paternity of a child born out of wedlock. Respondent contends that this interest justifies the use of gender-based peremptory challenges, since illegitimate children are themselves victims of historical discrimination and entitled to heightened scrutiny under the Equal Protection Clause.

What respondent fails to recognize is that the only legitimate interest it could possibly have in the exercise of its peremptory challenges is securing a fair and impartial jury. See Edmonson v. Leesville Concrete Co., 500 U.S. 614, 620 (1991) ("[T]he sole purpose [of the peremptory challenge] is to permit litigants to assist the government in the selection of an impartial trier of fact"). This interest does not change with the parties or the causes. The State's interest in *every* trial is to see that the proceedings are carried out in a fair, impartial, and nondiscriminatory manner.

9. Respondent cites one study in support of its quasi-empirical claim that women and men may have different attitudes about certain issues justifying the use of gender as a proxy for bias. See R. Hastie, S. Penrod & N. Pennington, Inside The Jury 140 (1983). The authors conclude: "Neither student nor citizen judgments for typical criminal case material have revealed differences between male and female verdict preferences. * * * The picture differs [only] for rape cases, where female jurors appear to be somewhat more conviction-prone than male jurors." The majority of studies suggest that gender plays no identifiable role in jurors' attitudes. See, e.g., V. Hans & N. Vidmar, Judging The Jury 76 (1986) ("[I]n the majority of studies there are no significant differences in the way men and women perceive and react to trials; yet a few studies find women more defense-oriented, while still others show women more favorable to the prosecutor"). Even in 1956, before women had a constitutional right to serve on juries, some commentators warned against using gender as a proxy for bias. See 1 F. Busch, Law and Tactics in Jury Trials § 143, p. 207 (1949) ("In this age of general and specialized education, availed of generally by both men and women, it would appear unsound to base a peremptory challenge in any case upon the sole ground of sex....").

10. A manual formerly used to instruct prosecutors in Dallas, Texas, provided the following advice: "I don't like women jurors because I can't trust them. They do, however, make the best jurors in cases involving crimes against children. It is possible that their 'women's intuition' can help you if you can't win your case with the facts." Another widely circulated trial manual speculated:

"If counsel is depending upon a clearly applicable rule of law and if he wants to avoid

for the conclusion that gender alone is an accurate predictor of juror's attitudes; yet it urges this Court to condone the same stereotypes that justified the wholesale exclusion of women from juries and the ballot box.[11] Respondent seems to assume that gross generalizations that would be deemed impermissible if made on the basis of race are somehow permissible when made on the basis of gender.

Discrimination in jury selection, whether based on race or on gender, causes harm to the litigants, the community, and the individual jurors who are wrongfully excluded from participation in the judicial process. The litigants are harmed by the risk that the prejudice which motivated the discriminatory selection of the jury will infect the entire proceedings. See *Edmonson* (discrimination in the courtroom "raises serious questions as to the fairness of the proceedings conducted there"). The community is harmed by the State's participation in the perpetuation of invidious group stereotypes and the inevitable loss of confidence in our judicial system that state-sanctioned discrimination in the courtroom engenders.

When state actors exercise peremptory challenges in reliance on gender stereotypes, they ratify and reinforce prejudicial views of the relative abilities of men and women. Because these stereotypes have wreaked injustice in so many other spheres of our country's public life, active discrimination by litigants on the basis of gender during jury selection "invites cynicism respecting the jury's neutrality and its obligation to adhere to the law." *Powers v. Ohio*, 499 U.S. at 412. The potential for cynicism is particularly acute in cases where gender-related issues are prominent, such as cases involving rape, sexual harassment, or paternity. Discriminatory use of peremptory challenges may create the impression that the judicial system has acquiesced in suppressing full participation by one gender or that the "deck has been stacked" in favor of one side. See id. at 413 ("The verdict will not be accepted or understood [as fair] if the jury is chosen by unlawful means at the outset").

---

a verdict of 'intuition' or 'sympathy,' if his verdict in amount is to be proved by clearly demonstrated blackboard figures for example, generally he would want a male juror....

"[But women] are desired jurors when the plaintiff is a man. A woman juror may see a man impeached from the beginning of the case to the end, but there is at least the chance with the woman juror (particularly if the man happens to be handsome or appealing) [that] the plaintiff's derelictions in and out of court will be overlooked. A woman is inclined to forgive sin in the opposite sex; but definitely not her own...." 3 M. Belli, Modern Trials §§ 51.67 and 51.68, pp. 446–47 (2d ed. 1982).

11. Even if a measure of truth can be found in some of the gender stereotypes used to justify gender-based peremptory challenges, that fact alone cannot support discrimination on the basis of gender in jury selection. We have made abundantly clear in past cases that gender classifications that rest on impermissible stereotypes violate the Equal Protection Clause, even when some statistical support can be conjured up for the generalization. The generalization advanced by Alabama in support of its asserted right to discriminate on the basis of gender is, at the least, overbroad, and serves only to perpetuate the same "outmoded notions of the relative capabilities of men and women," that we have invalidated in other contexts. The Equal Protection Clause, as interpreted by decisions of this Court, acknowledges that a shred of truth may be contained in some stereotypes, but requires that state actors look beyond the surface before making judgments about people that are likely to stigmatize as well as to perpetuate historical patterns of discrimination.

In recent cases we have emphasized that individual jurors themselves have a right to nondiscriminatory jury selection procedures. Contrary to respondent's suggestion, this right extends to both men and women. See *Mississippi University for Women v. Hogan*, 458 U.S. at 723 (that a state practice "discriminates against males rather than against females does not exempt it from scrutiny or reduce the standard of review"). All persons, when granted the opportunity to serve on a jury, have the right not to be excluded summarily because of discriminatory and stereotypical presumptions that reflect and reinforce patterns of historical discrimination.[13] Striking individual jurors on the assumption that they hold particular views simply because of their gender is "practically a brand upon them, affixed by law, an assertion of their inferiority." Strauder v. West Virginia, 100 U.S. 303, 308 (1880). It denigrates the dignity of the excluded juror, and, for a woman, reinvokes a history of exclusion from political participation.[14] The message it sends to all those in the courtroom, and all those who may later learn of the discriminatory act, is that certain individuals, for no reason other than gender, are presumed unqualified by state actors to decide important questions upon which reasonable persons could disagree.[15]

IV

Our conclusion that litigants may not strike potential jurors solely on the basis of gender does not imply the elimination of all peremptory challenges. Neither does it conflict with a State's legitimate interest in using such challenges in its effort to secure a fair and impartial jury. Parties still may remove jurors whom they feel might be less acceptable than others on the panel; gender simply may not serve as a proxy for bias. Parties may also exercise their peremptory challenges to remove from the venire any group or class of individuals normally subject to "rational basis" review. Even

---

13. It is irrelevant that women, unlike African-Americans, are not a numerical minority and therefore are likely to remain on the jury if each side uses its peremptory challenges in an equally discriminatory fashion. Because the right to nondiscriminatory jury selection procedures belongs to the potential jurors, as well as to the litigants, the possibility that members of both genders will get on the jury despite the intentional discrimination is beside the point. The exclusion of even one juror for impermissible reasons harms that juror and undermines public confidence in the fairness of the system.

14. The popular refrain is that all peremptory challenges are based on stereotypes of some kind, expressing various intuitive and frequently erroneous biases. But where peremptory challenges are made on the basis of group characteristics other than race or gender (like occupation, for example), they do not reinforce the same stereotypes about the group's competence or predispositions that have been used to prevent them from voting, participating on juries, pursuing their chosen professions, or otherwise contributing to civic life. See B. Babcock, *A Place in the Palladium, Women's Rights and Jury Service*, 61 U. Cin. L. Rev. 1139, 1173 (1993).

15. Justice Scalia argues that there is no "discrimination and dishonor" in being subject to a race- or gender-based peremptory strike. Justice Scalia's argument has been rejected many times, and we reject it once again. The only support Justice Scalia offers for his conclusion is the fact that race- and gender-based peremptory challenges have a long history in this country. We do not dispute that this Court long has tolerated the discriminatory use of peremptory challenges, but this is not a reason to continue to do so. Many of "our people's traditions," such as de jure segregation and the total exclusion of women from juries, are now unconstitutional even though they once co-existed with the Equal Protection Clause.

strikes based on characteristics that are disproportionately associated with one gender could be appropriate, absent a showing of pretext.[16]

If conducted properly, voir dire can inform litigants about potential jurors, making reliance upon stereotypical and pejorative notions about a particular gender or race both unnecessary and unwise. Voir dire provides a means of discovering actual or implied bias and a firmer basis upon which the parties may exercise their peremptory challenges intelligently.

The experience in the many jurisdictions that have barred gender-based challenges belies the claim that litigants and trial courts are incapable of complying with a rule barring strikes based on gender.[17] As with race-based *Batson* claims, a party alleging gender discrimination must make a prima facie showing of intentional discrimination before the party exercising the challenge is required to explain the basis for the strike. *Batson.* When an explanation is required, it need not rise to the level of a "for cause" challenge; rather, it merely *must* be based on a juror characteristic other than gender, and the proffered explanation may not be pretextual.

Failing to provide jurors the same protection against gender discrimination as race discrimination could frustrate the purpose of *Batson* itself. Because gender and race are overlapping categories, gender can be used as a pretext for racial discrimination.[18] Allowing parties to remove racial minorities from the jury not because of their race, but because of their gender, contravenes well-established equal protection principles and could insulate effectively racial discrimination from judicial scrutiny.

---

16. For example, challenging all persons who have had military experience would disproportionately affect men at this time, while challenging all persons employed as nurses would disproportionately affect women. Without a showing of pretext, however, these challenges may well not be unconstitutional, since they are not gender- or race-based.

17. Respondent argues that Alabama's method of jury selection would make the extension of *Batson* to gender particularly burdensome. In Alabama, the "struck-jury" system is employed, a system which requires litigants to strike alternately until 12 persons remain, who then constitute the jury. Respondent suggests that, in some cases at least, it is necessary under this system to continue striking persons from the venire after the litigants no longer have an articulable reason for doing so. As a result, respondent contends, some litigants may be unable to come up with gender-neutral explanations for their strikes.

We find it worthy of note that Alabama has managed to maintain its struck-jury system even after the ruling in *Batson*, despite the fact that there are counties in Alabama that are predominately African-American. In those counties, it presumably would be as difficult to come up with race-neutral explanations for peremptory strikes as it would be to advance gender-neutral explanations. No doubt the voir dire process aids litigants in their ability to articulate race-neutral explanations for their peremptory challenges. The same should be true for gender. Regardless, a State's choice of jury-selection methods cannot insulate it from the strictures of the Equal Protection Clause. Alabama is free to adopt whatever jury-selection procedures it chooses so long as they do not violate the Constitution.

18. The temptation to use gender as a pretext for racial discrimination may explain why the majority of the lower court decisions extending *Batson* to gender involve the use of peremptory challenges to remove minority women. All four of the gender-based peremptory cases to reach the federal courts of appeals * * * involved the striking of minority women.

V

Equal opportunity to participate in the fair administration of justice is fundamental to our democratic system.[19] It not only furthers the goals of the jury system. It reaffirms the promise of equality under the law — that all citizens, regardless of race, ethnicity, or gender, have the chance to take part directly in our democracy. *Powers v. Ohio*, 499 U.S. at 407 ("Indeed, with the exception of voting, for most citizens the honor and privilege of jury duty is their most significant opportunity to participate in the democratic process."). When persons are excluded from participation in our democratic processes solely because of race or gender, this promise of equality dims, and the integrity of our judicial system is jeopardized.

In view of these concerns, the Equal Protection Clause prohibits discrimination in jury selection on the basis of gender, or on the assumption that an individual will be biased in a particular case for no reason other than the fact that the person happens to be a woman or happens to be a man. As with race, the "core guarantee of equal protection, ensuring citizens that their State will not discriminate..., would be meaningless were we to approve the exclusion of jurors on the basis of such assumptions, which arise solely from the jurors' [gender]." *Batson.*

The judgment of the Court of Civil Appeals of Alabama is reversed and the case is remanded to that court for further proceedings not inconsistent with this opinion.

It is so ordered.

Justice O'Connor, concurring.

I agree with the Court that the Equal Protection Clause prohibits the government from excluding a person from jury service on account of that person's gender. The State's proffered justifications for its gender-based peremptory challenges are far from the "'exceedingly persuasive'" showing required to sustain a gender-based classification. I therefore join the Court's opinion in this case. But today's important blow against gender discrimination is not costless. I write separately to discuss some of these costs, and to express my belief that today's holding should be limited to the government's use of gender-based peremptory strikes.

---

19. This Court almost a half century ago stated:

"The American tradition of trial by jury, considered in connection with either criminal or civil proceedings, necessarily contemplates an impartial jury drawn from a cross-section of the community.... This does not mean, of course, that every jury must contain representatives of all the economic, social, religious, racial, political and geographical groups of the community; frequently such complete representation would be impossible. But it does mean that prospective jurors shall be selected by court officials without systematic and intentional exclusion of any of these groups. Recognition must be given to the fact that those eligible for jury service are to be found in every stratum of society. Jury competence is an individual rather than a group or class matter. That fact lies at the very heart of the jury system. To disregard it is to open the door to class distinctions and discriminations which are abhorrent to the democratic ideals of trial by jury."

Thiel v. Southern Pacific Co., 328 U.S. 217, 220 (1946).

Batson v. Kentucky itself was a significant intrusion into the jury selection process. *Batson* mini-hearings are now routine in state and federal trial courts, and *Batson* appeals have proliferated as well. Demographics indicate that today's holding may have an even greater impact than did *Batson* itself. In further constitutionalizing jury selection procedures, the Court increases the number of cases in which jury selection—once a sideshow—will become part of the main event.

For this same reason, today's decision further erodes the role of the peremptory challenge. The peremptory challenge is "a practice of ancient origin" and is "part of our common law heritage." The principal value of the peremptory is that it helps produce fair and impartial juries. "Peremptory challenges, by enabling each side to exclude those jurors it believes will be most partial toward the other side, are a means of eliminat[ing] extremes of partiality on both sides, thereby assuring the selection of a qualified and unbiased jury." The peremptory's importance is confirmed by its persistence: it was well established at the time of Blackstone and continues to endure in all the States.

Moreover, "[t]he essential nature of the peremptory challenge is that it is one exercised without a reason stated, without inquiry and without being subject to the court's control." Indeed, often a reason for it cannot be stated, for a trial lawyer's judgments about a juror's sympathies are sometimes based on experienced hunches and educated guesses, derived from a juror's responses at voir dire or a juror's "bare looks and gestures." That a trial lawyer's instinctive assessment of a juror's predisposition cannot meet the high standards of a challenge for cause does not mean that the lawyer's instinct is erroneous. Cf. V. Starr & M. Mccormick, Jury Selection 522 (1993) (nonverbal cues can be better than verbal responses at revealing a juror's disposition). Our belief that experienced lawyers will often correctly intuit which jurors are likely to be the least sympathetic, and our understanding that the lawyer will often be unable to explain the intuition, are the very reason we cherish the peremptory challenge. But, as we add, layer by layer, additional constitutional restraints on the use of the peremptory, we force lawyers to articulate what we know is often inarticulable.

In so doing we make the peremptory challenge less discretionary and more like a challenge for cause. We also increase the possibility that biased jurors will be allowed onto the jury, because sometimes a lawyer will be unable to provide an acceptable gender-neutral explanation even though the lawyer is in fact correct that the juror is unsympathetic. Similarly, in jurisdictions where lawyers exercise their strikes in open court, lawyers may be deterred from using their peremptories, out of the fear that if they are unable to justify the strike the court will seat a juror who knows that the striking party thought him unfit. Because I believe the peremptory remains an important litigator's tool and a fundamental part of the process of selecting impartial juries, our increasing limitation of it gives me pause.

Nor is the value of the peremptory challenge to the litigant diminished when the peremptory is exercised in a gender-based manner. We know that like race, gender matters. A plethora of studies make clear that in rape cases, for example, female jurors are somewhat more likely to vote to convict than male jurors. See R. Hastie, S. Penrod, & N. Pennington, Inside The Jury 140–41 (1983) (collecting and summarizing empirical studies). Moreover, though there have been no similarly definitive studies regarding, for example, sexual harassment, child custody, or spousal or child abuse, one need not be a sexist to share the intuition that in certain cases a person's gender and resulting life experience will be relevant to his or her view of the case. "Jurors are not expected to come into the jury box and leave behind all that their human experience has taught them." Individuals are not expected to ignore as jurors what they know as men—or women.

Today's decision severely limits a litigant's ability to act on this intuition, for the import of our holding is that any correlation between a juror's gender and attitudes is irrelevant as a matter of constitutional law. But to say that gender makes no difference as a matter of law is not to say that gender makes no difference as a matter of fact. I previously have said with regard to *Batson*: "That the Court will not tolerate prosecutors' racially discriminatory use of the peremptory challenge, in effect, is a special rule of relevance, a statement about what this Nation stands for, rather than a statement of fact." Today's decision is a statement that, in an effort to eliminate the potential discriminatory use of the peremptory, gender is now governed by the special rule of relevance formerly reserved for race. Though we gain much from this statement, we cannot ignore what we lose. In extending *Batson* to gender we have added an additional burden to the state and federal trial process, taken a step closer to eliminating the peremptory challenge, and diminished the ability of litigants to act on sometimes accurate gender-based assumptions about juror attitudes.

These concerns reinforce my conviction that today's decision should be limited to a prohibition on the government's use of gender-based peremptory challenges. The Equal Protection Clause prohibits only discrimination by state actors. In *Edmonson*, we made the mistake of concluding that private civil litigants were state actors when they exercised peremptory challenges; in *Georgia v. McCollum*, we compounded the mistake by holding that criminal defendants were also state actors. Our commitment to eliminating discrimination from the legal process should not allow us to forget that not all that occurs in the courtroom is state action. Private civil litigants are just that—private litigants. "The government erects the platform; it does not thereby become responsible for all that occurs upon it." *Edmonson* (O'Connor, J., dissenting).

Clearly, criminal defendants are not state actors. "From arrest, to trial, to possible sentencing and punishment, the antagonistic relationship between government and the accused is clear for all to see … [T]he unique relationship between criminal defendants and the State precludes attributing defendants' actions to the State.…" *McCollum* (O'Connor, J., dissenting). The peremptory challenge is "'one of the most important of the rights secured to the *accused*.'" Limiting the accused's use of the peremptory is "a serious misordering of our priorities," for it means "we have exalted the right of citizens to sit on juries over the rights of the criminal defendant, even though it is the defendant, not the jurors, who faces imprisonment or even death." *McCollum* (Thomas, J., concurring in judgment).

Accordingly, I adhere to my position that the Equal Protection Clause does not limit the exercise of peremptory challenges by private civil litigants and criminal defendants. This case itself presents no state action dilemma, for here the State of Alabama itself filed the paternity suit on behalf of petitioner. But what of the next case? Will we, in the name of fighting gender discrimination, hold that the battered wife—on trial for wounding her abusive husband—is a state actor? Will we preclude her from using her peremptory challenges to ensure that the jury of her peers contains as many women members as possible? I assume we will, but I hope we will not.

Chief Justice Rehnquist, dissenting.

I agree with the dissent of Justice Scalia, which I have joined. I add these words in support of its conclusion. Accepting Batson v. Kentucky, 476 U.S. 79 (1986), as correctly decided, there are sufficient differences between race and gender discrimination such that the principle of *Batson* should not be extended to peremptory challenges to potential jurors based on sex.

That race and sex discrimination are different is acknowledged by our equal protection jurisprudence, which accords different levels of protection to the two groups. Classifications based on race are inherently suspect, triggering "strict scrutiny," while gender-based classifications are judged under a heightened, but less searching standard of review. Racial groups comprise numerical minorities in our society, warranting in some situations a greater need for protection, whereas the population is divided almost equally between men and women. Furthermore, while substantial discrimination against both groups still lingers in our society, racial equality has proved a more challenging goal to achieve on many fronts than gender equality. See, e.g., D. Kirp, M. Yudof, M. Franks, Gender Justice 137 (1986).

Under the Equal Protection Clause, these differences mean that the balance should tilt in favor of peremptory challenges when sex, not race, is the issue. Unlike the Court, I think the State has shown that jury strikes on the basis of gender "substantially further" the State's legitimate interest in achieving a fair and impartial trial through the venerable practice of peremptory challenges. The two sexes differ, both biologically and, to a diminishing extent, in experience. It is not merely "stereotyping" to say that these differences may produce a difference in outlook which is brought to the jury room. Accordingly, use of peremptory challenges on the basis of sex is generally not the sort of derogatory and invidious act which peremptory challenges directed at black jurors may be.

Justice Scalia, with whom The Chief Justice and Justice Thomas join, dissenting.

Today's opinion is an inspiring demonstration of how thoroughly up-to-date and right-thinking we Justices are in matters pertaining to the sexes (or as the Court would have it, the genders), and how sternly we disapprove the male chauvinist attitudes of our predecessors. The price to be paid for this display—a modest price, surely—is that most of the opinion is quite irrelevant to the case at hand. The hasty reader will be surprised to learn, for example, that this lawsuit involves a complaint about the use of peremptory challenges to exclude *men* from a petit jury. To be sure, petitioner, a man, used all but one of *his* peremptory strikes to remove *women* from the jury (he used his last challenge to strike the sole remaining male from the pool), but the validity of *his* strikes is not before us. Nonetheless, the Court treats itself to an extended discussion of the historic exclusion of women not only from jury service, but also from service at the bar (which is rather like jury service, in that it involves going to the courthouse a lot). All this, as I say, is irrelevant, since the case involves state action that allegedly discriminates against men. The parties do not contest that discrimination on the basis of sex[1] is subject to what our cases call "heightened scrutiny," and the citation of one of those cases (preferably one involving men rather than women) is all that was needed.

The Court also spends time establishing that the use of sex as a proxy for particular views or sympathies is unwise and perhaps irrational. The opinion stresses the lack of statistical evidence to support the widely held belief that, at least in certain types of cases, a juror's sex has some statistically significant predictive value as to how the juror will behave. This assertion seems to place the Court in opposition to its earlier Sixth Amendment "fair cross-section" cases. See, e.g., Taylor v. Louisiana, 419 U.S. 522, 532, n.12 (1975) ("Controlled studies ... have concluded that women bring to juries their own perspectives and values that influence both jury deliberation and result"). But times and trends do change, and unisex is unquestionably in fashion. Personally, I am less inclined to demand statistics, and more inclined to credit the perceptions of experienced litigators who have had money on the line. But it does not matter. The Court's fervent defense of the proposition *il n'y a pas de difference entre les hommes et les femmes* (it stereotypes the opposite view as hateful "stereotyping") turns out to be, like its recounting of the history of sex discrimination against women, utterly irrelevant. Even if sex was a remarkably good predictor in certain cases, the Court would find its use in peremptories unconstitutional.

Of course the relationship of sex to partiality *would have been* relevant if the Court had demanded in this case what it ordinarily demands: that the complaining party have suffered some injury. Leaving aside for the moment the reality that the defendant himself had the opportunity to strike women from the jury, the defendant would have some cause to complain about the prosecutor's striking male jurors if male jurors tend to be more favorable towards defendants in paternity suits. But if men and women jurors are (as the Court thinks) fungible, then the only arguable injury from the prosecutor's "impermissible" use of male sex as the basis for his peremptories is injury to the stricken juror, not to the defendant. Indeed, far from having suffered

1. Throughout this opinion, I shall refer to the issue as sex discrimination rather than (as the Court does) gender discrimination. The word "gender" has acquired the new and useful connotation of cultural or attitudinal characteristics (as opposed to physical characteristics) distinctive to the sexes. That is to say, gender is to sex as feminine is to female and masculine to male. The present case does not involve peremptory strikes exercised on the basis of femininity or masculinity (as far as it appears, effeminate men did not survive the prosecution's peremptories). The case involves, therefore, sex discrimination plain and simple.

harm, petitioner, a state actor under our precedents, has himself actually *inflicted* harm on female jurors. The Court today presumably supplies petitioner with a cause of action by applying the uniquely expansive third-party standing analysis of Powers v. Ohio, 499 U.S. 400, 415 (1991), according petitioner a remedy because of the wrong done to male jurors. This case illustrates why making restitution to Paul when it is Peter who has been robbed is such a bad idea. Not only has petitioner, by implication of the Court's own reasoning, suffered no harm, but the scientific evidence presented at trial established petitioner's paternity with 99.92% accuracy. Insofar as petitioner is concerned, this is a case of harmless error if there ever was one; a retrial will do nothing but divert the State's judicial and prosecutorial resources, allowing either petitioner or some other malefactor to go free.

The core of the Court's reasoning is that peremptory challenges on the basis of any group characteristic subject to heightened scrutiny are inconsistent with the guarantee of the Equal Protection Clause. That conclusion can be reached only by focusing unrealistically upon individual exercises of the peremptory challenge, and ignoring the totality of the practice. Since all groups are subject to the peremptory challenge (and will be made the object of it, depending upon the nature of the particular case) it is hard to see how any group is denied equal protection. That explains why peremptory challenges coexisted with the Equal Protection Clause for 120 years. This case is a perfect example of how the system as a whole is even-handed. While the only claim before the Court is petitioner's complaint that the prosecutor struck male jurors, for every man struck by the government petitioner's own lawyer struck a woman. To say that men were singled out for discriminatory treatment in this process is preposterous. The situation would be different if both sides systematically struck individuals of one group, so that the strikes evinced group-based animus and served as a proxy for segregated venire lists. See Swain v. Alabama, 380 U.S. 202, 223–24 (1965). The pattern here, however, displays not a systemic sex-based animus but each side's desire to get a jury favorably disposed to its case. That is why the Court's characterization of respondent's argument as "reminiscent of the arguments advanced to justify the total exclusion of women from juries," is patently false. Women were categorically excluded from juries because of doubt that they were competent; women are stricken from juries by peremptory challenge because of doubt that they are well disposed to the striking party's case. There is discrimination and dishonor in the former, and not in the latter—which explains the 106-year interlude between our holding that exclusion from juries on the basis of race was unconstitutional, and our holding that peremptory challenges on the basis of race were unconstitutional, *Batson v. Kentucky*, supra.

Although the Court's legal reasoning in this case is largely obscured by anti-male-chauvinist oratory, to the extent such reasoning is discernible it invalidates much more than sex-based strikes. After identifying unequal treatment (by separating individual exercises of peremptory challenge from the process as a whole), the Court applies the "heightened scrutiny" mode of equal-protection analysis used for sex-based discrimination, and concludes that the strikes fail heightened scrutiny because they do not substantially further an important government interest. The Court says that the only important government interest that could be served by peremptory strikes is "securing a fair and impartial jury."[3] It refuses to accept respondent's argument that these strikes further that interest by eliminating a group (men) which may be partial to male defendants, because it will not accept any argument based on "'the very stereotype the law condemns.'" This analysis, entirely eliminating the only allowable argument, implies that sex-based strikes do not even rationally further a legitimate government interest, let alone pass heightened scrutiny. That places *all* peremptory strikes based on *any* group characteristic at risk, since they can all be denominated "stereotypes." Perhaps, however (though I do not see why it should be so), only the stereotyping of groups entitled to heightened or strict scrutiny constitutes "the very stereotype the law condemns"—so that other stereotyping (e.g., wide-eyed blondes and football players are dumb) remains OK. Or perhaps when the Court refers to "impermissible stereotypes," it means the adjective to be limiting rather than descriptive—so that we can expect to learn from the Court's peremptory/stereotyping jurisprudence in the future which stereotypes the Constitution frowns upon and which it does not.

Even if the line of our later cases guaranteed by today's decision limits the theoretically boundless *Batson* principle to race, sex, and perhaps other classifications subject to heightened scrutiny (which presumably would include religious belief), much damage has been done. It has been done, first and foremost, to the peremptory challenge system, which loses its whole character when (in order to defend against "impermissible stereotyping" claims) "reasons" for strikes must be given. The right of peremptory challenge "is, as Blackstone says, an arbitrary and capricious right; and it must be exercised with full freedom, or it fails of its full purpose." The loss of the real peremptory will be felt most keenly by the criminal defendant, whom we have until recently thought "should not be held to accept a juror, apparently indifferent, whom he distrusted for any reason or for no reason." And make no mistake about it: there really is no substitute for the peremptory. Voir dire (though it can be expected to expand as a consequence of today's decision) cannot fill the gap. The biases that go along with group characteristics tend to be biases that the juror himself does not perceive, so that it is no use asking about them. It is fruitless to inquire of a male juror whether he harbors any subliminal prejudice in favor of unwed fathers.

And damage has been done, secondarily, to the entire justice system, which will bear the burden of the expanded quest for "reasoned peremptories" that the Court demands. The extension of *Batson* to sex, and almost certainly beyond, will provide the basis for extensive collateral litigation, which especially the criminal defendant (who litigates full-time and cost-free) can be expected to pursue. While demographic

---

3. It does not seem to me that even this premise is correct. Wise observers have long understood that the appearance of justice is as important as its reality. If the system of peremptory strikes affects the actual impartiality of the jury not a bit, but gives litigants a greater belief in that impartiality, it serves a most important function. See, e.g., 4 W. Blackstone, Commentaries *353. In point of fact, that may well be its greater value.

reality places some limit on the number of cases in which race-based challenges will be an issue, every case contains a potential sex-based claim. Another consequence, as I have mentioned, is a lengthening of the voir dire process that already burdens trial courts.

The irrationality of today's strike-by-strike approach to equal protection is evident from the consequences of extending it to its logical conclusion. If a fair and impartial trial is a prosecutor's only legitimate goal; if adversarial trial stratagems must be tested against that goal in abstraction from their role within the system as a whole; and if, so tested, sex-based stratagems do not survive heightened scrutiny — then the prosecutor presumably violates the Constitution when he selects a male or female police officer to testify because he believes one or the other sex might be more convincing in the context of the particular case, or because he believes one or the other might be more appealing to a predominantly male or female jury. A decision to stress one line of argument or present certain witnesses before a mostly female jury — for example, to stress that the defendant victimized women — becomes, under the Court's reasoning, intentional discrimination by a state actor on the basis of gender.

In order, it seems to me, not to eliminate any real denial of equal protection, but simply to pay conspicuous obeisance to the equality of the sexes, the Court imperils a practice that has been considered an essential part of fair jury trial since the dawn of the common law. The Constitution of the United States neither requires nor permits this vandalizing of our people's traditions.

For these reasons, I dissent.

Notes and Questions

1. Does the Court's holding in *Batson* and its progeny elevate concerns for the dignity of excluded jurors over concerns for the fairness of trials? If litigants and the public believe that jurors' attitudes are affected by race and gender, does it increase or decrease the perception of fairness to allow parties to strike those whom they believe (rightly or wrongly) are likely to be more inclined to find for the other side?

2. In Grutter v. Bollinger, 539 U.S. 306, 332–33 (2003), the University of Michigan affirmative action case, Justice O'Connor observed: "Just as growing up in a particular region or having particular professional experiences is likely to affect an individual's views, so too is one's own, unique experience of being a racial minority in a society, like our own, in which race unfortunately still matters." Would people with different life experiences evaluate evidence differently? Is the possibility of different perspectives an argument for or against constraining the use of peremptory strikes?

3. In Georgia v. McCollum, 505 U.S. 42 (1992), the Court held that a white defendant's use of peremptories to strike black jurors on the basis of race violates the Equal Protection Clause of the Fourteenth Amendment. Justice Thomas, writing separately, agreed that the holding was consistent with the Court's precedents, but he questioned the wisdom of those precedents. He explained:

> The public, in general, continues to believe that the makeup of juries can matter in certain instances. Consider, for example, how the press reports criminal trials. Major newspapers regularly note the number of whites and blacks that sit on juries in important cases. Their editors and readers apparently recognize that conscious and unconscious prejudice persists in our society and that it may influence some juries. Common experience and common sense confirm this understanding.

Id. at 61. He concluded, "I am certain that black criminal defendants will rue the day that this court ventured down this road that inexorably will lead to the elimination of peremptory strikes." Id. at 60. Justice O'Connor suggests a similar concern with respect to women litigants in sexual harassment, child custody, or abuse cases. Do you think *Batson* and *McCollum* will harm the interests of women and minority litigants?

4. Are there other cognizable groups to which *Batson* applies? Groups that have been held to be covered by *Batson* include: American Indians, United States v. Chalan, 812 F.2d 1302 (10th Cir. 1987); Italian-Americans, United States v. Biaggi, 673 F. Supp. 96 (E.D.N.Y. 1987), *aff'd*, 853 F.2d 89 (2d Cir. 1988); and Hispanics, United States v. Ruiz, 894 F.2d 501 (2d Cir. 1990). On the other hand, courts have refused to extend *Batson* to cover exclusions based on age, United States v. Cresta, 825 F.2d 538 (1st Cir. 1987); socioeconomic status, United States v. Pofahl, 990 F.2d 1456, 1465–66 (5th Cir. 1993); and disability or obesity, United States v. Santiago-Martinez, 58 F.3d 422, 423 n.1 (9th Cir. 1995). The courts have split with respect to religion, though some courts have differentiated between religious *affiliation* as an impermissible basis, and religious *belief* or *activity* as an allowable basis. See United States v. DeJesus, 347 F.3d 500 (3d Cir. 2003); United States v. Brown, 352 F.3d 654, 666 (2d Cir. 2003); State v. Davis, 504 N.W.2d 767 (Minn. 1993); State v. Hodge, 726 A.2d 531, 552 (Conn. 1999); A.C. Johnstone, *Peremptory Pragmatism: Religion and the Administration of the* Batson *Rule*, 1998 U. Chi. Legal F. 441.

The Ninth Circuit has held that equal protection prohibits the exercise of peremptory challenges on the basis of sexual orientation. See SmithKline Beecham Corp. v. Abbott Labs., 740 F.3d 471 (9th Cir. 2014). A California state appellate court had earlier concluded that exclusion from jury service on the basis of sexual orientation violates the state constitution. People v. Garcia, 92 Cal. Rptr. 2d 339 (Cal. Ct. App. 2000). This ruling was later codified by the California legislature. See Cal. Code Civ. Proc. § 231.5.

5. Identifying discriminatory motive is easier said than done. As the Supreme Court noted in Miller-El v. Dretke, 545 U.S. 231, 238 (2005): "The rub has been the practical difficulty of ferreting out discrimination in selections discretionary by nature, and choices subject to myriad legitimate influences, whatever the race of the individuals on the panel from which jurors are selected." To address the mechanics of proof, the Court has identified a three step process for determining whether a peremptory challenge was improper: first, the opponent must establish a prima facie case of discrimination; second, the burden shifts to the proponent of the strike to come forward with a constitutionally permissible explanation; and third, the court must determine whether impermissible discrimination has been established.

In determining whether a prima facie case is established, the court should look to "the totality of the relevant facts," including the overall numbers with respect to the use of peremptory challenges. For example, in one case "[t]he prosecutors used their peremptory strikes to exclude 91% of the eligible African-American venire members." The Court observed that "[h]appenstance is unlikely to produce this disparity." Miller-El v. Cockrell, 537 U.S. 322, 342 (2003). Where a prima facie case of discrimination has been established, the challenged party must offer an explanation for its use of its peremptory challenges — stating why it struck the jurors that it did. In assessing the plausibility of the explanation, the court should consider whether jurors were asked similar questions and whether the proffered explanation for striking particular jurors would have applied equally to other jurors who were not struck. See also Felkner v. Jackson, 131 S. Ct. 1305 (2011), holding that in an appeal of a *Batson* motion, great deference should be given to the trial court's ability to distinguish the legitimate use of a peremptory strike from pretextual ones.

6. Suppose that one side objects to the other side's use of a peremptory challenge and the trial court agrees that there has been a *Batson* violation. Should the trial court dismiss the entire venire and select a new jury, or should it seat the improperly dismissed juror? In *Batson*, the Supreme Court explicitly declined to answer this question, 476 U.S. at 99 n.24, and the lower courts are split. See Jones v. Maryland, 659 A.2d 361, 367–70 (Md. Ct. Spec. App. 1995), *aff'd*, 683 A.2d 520 (Md. 1996), and cases collected therein.

7. In United States v. Martinez-Salazar, 528 U.S. 304 (2000), a criminal case, the trial judge refused to dismiss a prospective juror for cause. The juror had responded to a questionnaire that he would "probably tend to favor the prosecution." Even after the judge explained the burden of proof, the juror stated that he would "probably be more favorable to the prosecution. * * * You assume that people are on trial because they did something wrong." The judge declined to dismiss the juror for cause, noting that the juror said he could follow the court's instructions, and the defendant used a peremptory challenge to strike the juror. Following his conviction, the defendant appealed on the ground that he should not have had to use one of his peremptory challenges to remove the juror. The Supreme Court affirmed the conviction. The government did not dispute that the juror should have been dismissed for cause. However, the Supreme Court held that because the juror was removed, there was no constitutional violation, And the fact that the defendant had to use one of his peremptory challenges was not a basis for reversing the conviction.

8. You are on the staff of the House Judiciary Committee. The Committee has asked you to consider whether it should revise 28 U.S.C. § 1870 or Crim. R. 24, dealing with peremptory challenges in civil and criminal cases. Some changes that have been suggested are:

(a) expand the number of peremptories;

(b) eliminate peremptories;

(c) in criminal cases, allow only defendants to exercise peremptories;

(d) prohibit the use of peremptories to strike jurors based on:

- ethnic origin
- religion
- age
- wealth

Would you favor these or any other changes? Should the rules concerning peremptory challenges be different in civil and criminal cases?

9. The underlying issue in *J.E.B.* was paternity. A blood test done prior to trial established a 99.92% likelihood that the defendant was the father. Following the remand by the Supreme Court, and on the day before the new trial was to begin, the case settled.

c. *Two Views of Voir Dire and Peremptory Strikes*

The first of these two excerpts was written by two experienced trial lawyers, the second by a trial judge. They obviously have quite different views about the purposes and value of voir dire.

The Mapplethorpe Obscenity Trial

by Marc Mezibov and H. Louis Sirkin
18 Litigation 12 (Summer 1992)

Only the most prescient of lawyers (or perhaps the most cynical) could have anticipated that legal history would be made on a Saturday morning at an art museum. At approximately 10:30 a.m. on Saturday, April 7, 1990, grand jurors were summoned to the Hamilton County Courthouse in Cincinnati, Ohio, and from there marched approximately six blocks south to join several hundred people already waiting in line at the Contemporary Art Center (CAC), one of Cincinnati's premier museums. On public display for the first time that day was *The Perfect Moment*, a retrospective of the works of the late photographer Robert Mapplethorpe, who died of AIDS in 1989.

The Perfect Moment comprised approximately 175 of Mapplethorpe's photographs and surveyed the photographer's view of, among other things, flora, portraiture, and homoerotic, all of which were presented in the "formalist" or "classical" mode of visual art. Not surprisingly, only the homoerotic category engaged the attention of the grand jurors. They were sufficiently offended by several of the images — form, lighting, and composition notwithstanding — that shortly after noon that same day they returned a two-count indictment against the CAC and its director, Dennis Barrie. Barrie and the CAC were each charged by the grand jurors with pandering obscenity and displaying photographs of minors in a state of nudity. The former charge, a misdemeanor carrying a maximum jail term of six months and a fine of $1,000, related specifically to five images contained in Mapplethorpe's *X* portfolio, which has as its thematic core sexual acts and practices prevalent in the homosexual subculture of Greenwich Village during the 1970s. The other charge, also a misdemeanor, involved two pictures of children: "Jessie," a boy approximately five years old, and "Rosie," a three-year-old girl. Both photographs are similar to those in most family albums.

In this new frontier of obscenity prosecution, the challenge to the defense was twofold: first, to pick a jury from an array of potential jurors whose lives revealed an amazing dearth of experience with museums, to say nothing of art museums, much less contemporary art museums displaying photographs of sado-masochistic acts; and second, to creatively adapt a body of case law developed over several decades that dealt primarily with the sort of sexually explicit forms of expression typically available in adult bookstores and cinema.

Our emphasis in voir dire, * * * was primarily on * * * the artistic value of *The Perfect Moment* exhibition and the individual images in it. Rather than attempt to sell the jurors on the beauty of the photographs, we offered them the notion that to be valued, art need not — indeed sometimes should not — please the eye. Early in the jury selection process, to underscore our argument that art need not be beautiful and to desensitize the jurors to what they would be shown once the trial began, we described in graphic detail the photographs listed in the indictment. * * *

Jury selection took four complete days and involved not only desensitization but a penetrating inquiry into the potential jurors' attitudes toward a variety of topics not necessarily associated with artistic themes. For example, we were especially interested in the jurors' views on choice and privacy issues, clearly subthemes in our defense. To elicit what we hoped would be meaningful responses, we asked open-ended questions about such subjects as abortion rights and legal rights for homosexuals. We also asked each juror's opinion about whether adults should be restricted in what they may see, read, or hear. Most interesting was the uniformity of the jurors' liberalism, or seeming libertarianism, in their response to such general questions as, Do you think adults should be prevented or restricted from seeing movies of their choice? Curiously, the very jurors who answered no invariably responded yes to the more pointed question of whether adults should be restricted from viewing films involving acts of oral sex or group sex. Our exchanges with jurors on those points demonstrated the wisdom of an in-depth inquiry, especially when a case involves the fundamental values to which most Americans give all-too-easy lip service.

Our Model Juror

Although expert witnesses played a central role in our defense strategy, we did not use jury selection experts, despite the many who offered assistance. Our decision did not result entirely from a professional bias against expert-assisted jury selection. In part, we were skeptical about whether we could take advantage of expert assistance. Because we would not receive the panel lists until immediately before the trial, we would not be able to analyze and factor into our selection process the sparse background information about the jurors. And the trial judge refused to use questionnaires prepared by counsel. Moreover, in the weeks before trial, while the propriety of the Mapplethorpe exhibition was a topic of unprecedented public debate in Cincinnati, the CAC commissioned a survey to assess community attitudes on this issue. Going into trial, we felt that that survey would give us a useful frame of reference in choosing a jury. As it turned out, the results of the survey were more interesting than practical. On the basis of the survey, our model juror was a single black male living within the boundaries of the city of Cincinnati. Out of a jury array of approximately 60 persons, only one fit the model profile. In the end we were forced to rely on our experience, our instincts, and the considerable knowledge we acquired through intensive questioning of prospective jurors.

In voir dire another major theme that we emphasized was the "human factor." We frequently referred to the men and women who, either as paid staff or as volunteers, operate the CAC along with Barrie. We sought not only to humanize our corporate client but to divert the jurors' attention from the controversial photographs toward the people who, as we viewed it, were being held accountable for their principled fidelity to the CAC's cultural and educational mission. To accomplish these twin goals, we asked many of the potential jurors about their familiarity with the CAC, its purpose, and the various community-based programs for implementing that purpose. We wanted to disabuse the jurors of any notion planted by the prosecution that our clients were "panderers" in the worst sense of the word. During the defense's case in chief, we presented, in addition to Barrie, both the CAC's assistant director and member of its governing board who also serves as the museum's legal counsel. Through the attorney we explained to the jury the nature, purpose, and significance of the CAC's not-for-profit status. That was simply another way of establishing that when it came to the Mapplethorpe exhibition, the case was motivated not by money but by "art for art's sake."

The manner in which prospective jurors are selected in Hamilton County gave us considerable cause for concern. The names of prospective jurors are taken from the lists of registered voters on file with the county elections board. Historically, Hamilton County, which is in the southwest corner of Ohio, is a bastion of conservatism. Traditional values for the most part go unquestioned. Free speech battles are rare. In the last 20 years a community-wide understanding has developed of acceptable forms and means of expression, largely the result of rigorous law enforcement. X-rated movies are not acceptable, nor are adult bookstores. Neither type of establishment exists any longer in Hamilton County.

In Search of Diversity

The Hamilton county voters retain in office political leaders who perpetuate a climate hostile to a diversity of opinion and alternative lifestyles. We were concerned about selecting a jury from among those voters. In Ohio, as in many other states, the law authorizes driver's license registration lists as a source for jury enpanelment. Therefore, we moved that the court strike the entire array of jurors in favor of a panel chosen from driver's license registration lists. We believed that jurors selected from that pool would be more urban and diverse, reflecting a wider spectrum of opinion on social issues in general and on free speech and choice issues in particular. To our disappointment, but not our surprise, the court overruled our motion on the ground that there was no evidence of irregularity in the way this particular group of prospective jurors had been assembled.

In a case as emotionally and politically charged as ours, it was not surprising to find individuals with their own agendas in this politically conservative community. They gave our painstakingly planned and exhaustive jury selection process some peak moments. Perhaps the most memorable occurred during the questioning of a Mrs. Murphy. Her jury questionnaire said she was employed as an administrative secretary to a well-known local clergyman who also happened to be a leader not only locally but nationally in a crusade against pornography. We were confident that because of her professional and personal affiliations, Mrs. Murphy would be excused for cause. That would obviate the need for additional questions of this woman, who we feared would want to educate the jurors about her cause in much the same way we were seeking to educate them about ours. The judge disagreed. Further questioning revealed that Mrs. Murphy's personal involvement and interest in the antiporn movement was such that when *The Perfect Moment* was first announced in the press, she had gone out of her way to be shown photocopies of the two images of the children listed in the indictment. She also acknowledged that she had already formed an opinion about those photographs. In Mrs. Murphy's view, the photographs of the two children were "not morally decent" and should not have been shown in a museum. The following exchange between Mrs. Murphy and defense counsel ensued:

Q: Is it your opinion that the pictures should not be shown for any purpose?

A: Yes.

Q: Anywhere?

A: Yes.

Q: Anytime?

A: Yes.

Q: To anyone?

A: Yes.

We asked again that Mrs. Murphy be excused for cause. Rather than rule immediately on our request, the judge proceeded to serve up a softball, underhanded. He asked Mrs. Murphy whether she could set aside her convictions and be fair to both sides. In dutiful response to whatever cause greater than the truth that Mrs. Murphy served, she hit the judge's pitch a mile. Mrs. Murphy's impartiality having been assured to his satisfaction, the judge ruled that although she might be opinionated, she had given him the impression she could follow the law. When the groans of disbelief from the gallery subsided, we exercised our final peremptory challenge to keep Mrs. Murphy off the jury.

Our jury consisted of eight persons, four men and four women, all from rather conventional Cincinnati backgrounds. All were employed. Two had some college education, and one had a college degree. Not one of the jurors had attended the Mapplethorpe exhibition; nor, for that matter, had any ever visited the CAC.

Because the long, involved jury selection process addressed virtually all the legal issues and themes in the case, the evidentiary portion of the trial provided little that was new to the jurors. By design, the testimony of our witnesses dovetailed in all important respects with the voir dire. And imagine our professional satisfaction when we learned that in explaining the verdict to the media after the trial, more than one of the jurors hearkened back to our presentation during voir dire. Biases notwithstanding, it became clear by the case's end that those jurors finally selected were willing to hold themselves open to a broad range of human experiences, as well as the appropriateness of those experiences, as subjects for artistic inquiry. Despite the graphic nature of the photographs, which some jurors described as gross and disgusting, the jury concluded that the prosecution had not made its case because, like a poorly baked apple pie, "it was missing an ingredient. [The exhibition] had artistic value, and that's what kept it from being obscene."

A Critical Role

The jury's verdict did show how critical the lawyer's role is in jury selection. In many jurisdictions, especially in federal courts, lawyers are losing the opportunity to participate meaningfully in jury selection. We have little doubt that if our role in voir dire had been less than it was, we would now be before an appellate court.

10 Trial Mistakes

by Morris Hoffman

19 The Docket 17 (Spring 1994)

Most prospective jurors report for jury duty angry and skeptical. The first thing most lawyers do is to make them more angry and more skeptical by engaging in a process whose fundamental assumption is that there are prospective jurors who must be hunted down like dogs and removed for their "biases." These "biases" are discovered by a series of tricky Rorschach questions designed to open hidden psychiatric vistas in mere minutes.

My trial observations have confirmed my instincts that this entire approach to voir dire is baloney. All any of us can realistically hope for in voir dire is to find out if any jurors have a direct financial interest in the litigation, are related to any of the parties or the lawyers, or for any other gross reason cannot be fair or impartial. In my opinion, all the other energy lawyers waste on pop psychology in voir dire is not just a waste, it is waste which insults the jurors, and does irreparable damage to the legendary "rapport" which is supposed to be created at this stage of the trial.

The most effective voir dire I've ever seen was by a well-known Denver trial lawyer who stood up, asked about five minutes' worth of questions aimed simply at whether the prospective jurors thought they could be fair, and sat down. That exchange did more to build rapport than a hundred questions about the jurors' children, reading habits and toilet training.

d. Jury Size

At common law, both criminal and civil juries were composed of twelve people. In Williams v. Florida, 399 U.S. 78 (1970), the Supreme Court held that the use in criminal cases of juries of fewer than twelve did not violate the Sixth Amendment right to a jury. Similarly, in Colgrove v. Battin, 413 U.S. 149 (1973), the Court upheld the use of six person juries in civil cases. The Court explained that "by referring to the 'common law,' the Framers of the Seventh Amendment were concerned with preserving the *right* of trial by jury in civil cases where it existed at common law, rather than the various incidents of trial by jury." Id. at 155–56. The size of the jury was an incident of trial by jury, not part of the right.

Rule 48 allows federal courts in civil cases to empanel juries of "not fewer than six and not more than twelve members." Driven by economics, the result is that federal juries are usually six persons. Some commentators have expressed concern about the use of small juries, noting that smaller panels are less reflective of the community. See Peter Sperlich, *... And Then There Were Six: The Decline of the American Jury*, 63 JUDICATURE 262 (1980); Hans Zeisel & Shari Diamond, *"Convincing Empirical Evidence" on the Six Member Jury*, 41 U. CHI. L. REV. 281 (1974).

The 1991 amendments to Rule 47 abolished alternate jurors in federal civil cases. All jurors must participate in the verdict unless excused for good cause. Moreover, a verdict cannot be taken from fewer than six jurors. So if a lengthy trial is anticipated, the court may empanel seven or eight jurors to ensure (if any are excused for good cause) that there will be at least six jurors. Regardless of the number of jurors, Rule 48 requires a unanimous verdict unless the parties otherwise stipulate.

3. Jury Nullification and Its Limits

In the criminal arena, the defendant's right to a jury is absolute. Even when the evidence of guilt is overwhelming and the defendant has no defense, the defendant can still demand that the case be sent to a jury. Moreover, if in such a case, the jury returns a verdict of not guilty, that verdict will be allowed to stand even though it is contrary to all the evidence.* The criminal jury's absolute authority to acquit reflects, in large part, the long accepted principle of jury nullification. Jury nullification occurs "when a jury—based on its own sense of justice or fairness—refuses to follow this law and convict in a particular case even though the facts seem to allow no other conclusion but guilt." Jack Weinstein, *Considering Jury "Nullification:" When May and Should a Jury Reject the Law to Do Justice*, 30 AM. CR. L. REV. 239 (1993). Judge Weinstein has explained the role of jury nullification as follows:

> When jurors return with a "nullification" verdict, then, they have not in reality "nullified" anything: they have done their job. "[N]ullification is in-

* The jury's discretion in criminal cases is one-sided. The jury may acquit in the face of overwhelming evidence and the judge cannot disturb the verdict. However, where the judge finds there is too little evidence of guilt, the judge may refuse to send the case to the jury and can enter judgment of acquittal herself or enter judgment of acquittal despite a contrary jury verdict. See Fed. R. Crim. P. 29.

> herent in the jury's role as the conscience of the democratic community and a cushion between the citizens and overly harsh or arbitrary government criminal prosecution." Juries are charged not with the task of blindly and mechanically applying the law, but of doing justice in light of the law, the evidence presented at trial, and their own knowledge of society and the world. To decide that some outcomes are just and some are not is not possible without drawing upon personal views.

Id. at 244–45. See James Duane, *Jury Nullification: The Top Secret Constitutional Right*, 22 LITIGATION 6 (Summer 1996).

We could extend the concept of jury nullification to civil cases and give the parties to a civil suit an absolute right to have their case decided by a jury. A justice system, for example, could allow plaintiffs to argue in essence, "I have no proof to support my claim, but I should win anyway." Do you think this would be a good idea? Are there differences between civil and criminal adjudication that make jury nullification appropriate for one, but not the other? See Murphy, supra, 61 GEO. WASH. L. REV. at 736–54, 762–70.

While one could imagine a system in which the right to a jury is absolute in civil cases, that is not our system. Indeed, in some circumstances, the Court has held that the failure to provide judicial review of jury verdicts violates the Due Process Clause. See Honda Motor Co., Ltd. v. Oberg, 512 U.S. 415 (1994) (state must provide judicial review of jury award of punitive damages). As we will see in the following sections, in cases in which the judge concludes that there is insufficient evidence, several procedural devices permit her to decide the case without a jury or to enter judgment contrary to a jury's verdict.

C. Summary Judgment — Adjudication Without Trial

Rule 56 authorizes the court to enter judgment whenever it appears that "there is no genuine issue as to any material fact and that the movant is entitled to a judgment as a matter of law." Rule 56(a). The purpose of summary judgment is not to permit the court to decide issues of fact but to determine whether there is an issue of fact to be tried. Motions for summary judgment are filed before trial and if the motion is granted, judgment is entered without benefit of a trial (or a jury). The court may hold a hearing on the motion, but such a hearing is not a trial — there is no presentation of witnesses. The hearing is simply an opportunity for the lawyers to amplify their motion papers and for the court to ask questions. A court may enter partial summary judgment disposing of some, but not all, issues in the case. See Rule 56(g). For example, a court could grant summary judgment on the issue of liability, but not on the issue of damages, or as to one claim, but not another.

There are two basic situations in which summary judgment is appropriate. First, the parties may agree on the facts and have a dispute about the law — for example, whether liability attaches under the particular facts. Indeed, sometimes the parties will stipulate to the facts and then file competing motions for summary judgment, with each side arguing that under these undisputed facts, it is entitled to a judgment. When the parties agree on the facts and the dispute is entirely one of law, there is no need for a trial or a jury. Matters of law are for the judge to decide. The judge may hold oral argument to assist her in understanding the law, but there is no need to have a trial with witnesses testifying about the facts.

Summary judgment also is used when the parties disagree about the facts, but there is no "genuine" dispute, that is, one side has so little evidence that no reasonable jury could find for that side. For example, in Dyer v. MacDougall, 201 F.2d 265 (2d Cir. 1952), the plaintiff alleged that the defendant slandered him in the presence of two other people. The defendant filed a motion for summary judgment attaching his own affidavit plus the affidavits of the two supposed witnesses and all three affidavits denied that the statements attributed to the defendant were uttered. The plaintiff offered no admissible evidence that the statement was made, and the court granted summary judgment.

Sometimes the party opposing summary judgment lacks direct evidence to support her claim, but has indirect or circumstantial evidence. Circumstantial evidence is not inherently unreliable and can create a genuine issue of fact. The court should draw from the evidence all reasonable inferences on behalf of the non-moving party, but the court must make a threshold determination that the inferences are reasonable. The court should "not slip into 'sheer speculation.'" Gibson v. Old Town Trolley Tours, 160 F.3d 177, 181 (4th Cir. 1998). For example, the Court has held that evidence that the plaintiff was mentally stable prior to World War I and that twelve years after the war he was unstable is insufficient from which to infer that trauma suffered during the war caused the mental breakdown. See Galloway v. United States, 319 U.S. 372 (1943).

Summary judgment should be granted when there is no genuine issue of material *fact*. But what constitutes a fact? Suppose the parties agree on the historical facts, but the issue turns on which of several reasonable conclusions should be drawn from those facts—for example, whether certain conduct (which everyone agrees occurred) was negligent. These questions are sometimes called "mixed" questions of law and fact, because they require the application of a legal standard, such as the definition of negligence, to a set of facts. Are these mixed questions to be decided through trial by jury or through summary judgment by the court? There is no categorical answer. Issues such as proximate cause, reasonableness of notice, and whether a person exercised due care are usually treated as factual questions to be left to the jury. The Supreme Court has written that in the case of negligence

> it is a matter of judgment and discretion, of sound inference, what is the deduction to be drawn from the undisputed facts. Certain facts we may suppose to be clearly established from which one sensible, impartial man would infer that proper care had not been used, and that negligence existed; another man equally sensible and equally impartial would infer that proper care had been used, and that there was no negligence. It is this class of cases and those

> akin to it that the law commits to the decision of a jury. * * * It is assumed that twelve men know more of the common affairs of life than does one man, that they can draw wiser and safer conclusions from admitted facts thus occurring than can a single judge.

Railroad Co. v. Stout, 84 U.S. 657, 663–64 (1874).

On the other hand, issues such as whether plaintiff is a "public figure" for purposes of libel law, see Rosenblatt v. Baer, 383 U.S. 75, 88 (1966), or the interpretation of a corporate resolution, see Fox v. Johnson & Wimsatt, Inc., 127 F.2d 729, 736–37 (D.C. Cir. 1942), have been treated as matters of law to be decided by the court. In characterizing an issue as one of law or fact for these purposes, the fundamental determination is a policy choice as to whether the conclusions to be drawn from the evidence are ones better left to juries or more appropriately decided by the court.

Summary judgment should be distinguished from a motion to dismiss under Rule 12(b)(6) or a motion for judgment on the pleadings under Rule 12(c). In ruling on the Rule 12 motions, the court relies solely on the pleadings to determine whether the case belongs in the litigation stream at all—has the plaintiff stated a claim that justifies going forward through discovery and the other phases of litigation? In making this assessment, we saw in Chapter 7 that all facts alleged in the complaint (at least all "plausible" facts) are assumed to be true. The question is one of law: do the alleged facts state a claim that the law recognizes?

With summary judgment, in contrast, the case is in the litigation stream; the plaintiff has stated a plausible claim. Now the question becomes whether we need to go to trial. The only reason to go to trial is to resolve genuine disputes of material fact. If there is no such dispute, there is no need for trial, and the judge can enter summary judgment. In ruling on summary judgment, the court looks beyond the pleadings and considers material such as affidavits or other sworn statements such as depositions or interrogatory answers. All such evidence is in written form. The court does not take oral evidence from witnesses in open court as it would at a trial (the whole point of summary judgment is to avoid trial).

In addition, in ruling on a motion for summary judgment, the court does not assess credibility. Instead, the court views the evidence in the light most favorable to the non-moving party. This is true even if the court believes the moving party's witness is more credible than the non-moving party's witness. The question of which witness is more credible is left to the trier of fact, and if the resolution of the case turns on which witness is believed, the court will deny summary judgment.

As we will see, summary judgment is not the only procedure in which the court enters judgment without a jury verdict. In the next section, we will study directed verdicts (now called judgments as a matter of law). Under this procedure, if the court, having heard the evidence at trial, concludes that no reasonable jury could find for one side, the court may enter judgment without submitting the case to the jury. The directed verdict is a close cousin of summary judgment. The standard for granting the two motions is essentially the same. The difference is that in summary judgment, the court makes its ruling on the basis of affidavits, while a directed verdict is granted on the basis of the evidence presented at trial.

To test the basic principles of summary judgment, consider the following hypothetical. Suppose there is an automobile accident at an intersection. The plaintiff's theory is that the defendant ran the red light. Would summary judgment be appropriate in the following cases:

(a) Defendant moves for summary judgment and submits the affidavit of a witness who says the light was green.

(i) Plaintiff responds by relying on the allegation in her complaint that the light was red.

(ii) Plaintiff responds with an affidavit of a witness who says the light was red.

(b) Defendant moves for summary judgment and submits affidavits of 10 witnesses who say the light was green.

(i) Plaintiff responds with an affidavit of one witness who says the light was red.

(ii) Plaintiff responds with her own affidavit stating that she saw the light and it was red.

(c) Defendant moves for summary judgment and submits the affidavit of one witness who says the light was green. Plaintiff responds with the affidavit of a witness who says that she did not see the light, but she saw that cars in the other lane of traffic that were going in the same direction as defendant's car (and were controlled by the same traffic light) had stopped.

Anderson v. Liberty Lobby, Inc.

477 U.S. 242, 106 S. Ct. 2505, 91 L. Ed. 2d 202 (1986)

Justice White delivered the opinion of the Court.

In New York Times Co. v. Sullivan, 376 U.S. 254, 279–80 (1964), we held that, in a libel suit brought by a public official, the First Amendment requires the plaintiff to show that in publishing the defamatory statement the defendant acted with actual malice—"with knowledge that it was false or with reckless disregard of whether it was false or not." We held further that such actual malice must be shown with "convincing clarity." * * *

This case presents the question whether the clear-and-convincing-evidence requirement must be considered by a court ruling on a motion for summary judgment under Rule 56 of the Federal Rules of Civil Procedure in a case to which *New York Times* applies. The United States Court of Appeals for the District of Columbia Circuit held that that requirement need not be considered at the summary judgment stage. * * * We now reverse.

I

Respondent Liberty Lobby, Inc., is a not-for-profit corporation and self-described "citizens' lobby." Respondent Willis Carto is its founder and treasurer. In October 1981, The Investigator magazine published two articles: "The Private World of Willis Carto" and "Yockey: Profile of an American Hitler." These articles were introduced by a third, shorter article entitled "America's Neo-Nazi Underground: Did *Mein Kampf* Spawn Yockey's *Imperium*, a Book Revived by Carto's Liberty Lobby?" These articles portrayed respondents as neo-Nazi, anti- Semitic, racist, and Fascist.

Respondents filed this diversity libel action in the United States District Court for the District of Columbia, alleging that some 28 statements and 2 illustrations in the 3 articles were false and derogatory. * * * Following discovery, petitioners moved for summary judgment pursuant to Rule 56. In their motion, petitioners asserted that because respondents are public figures they were required to prove their case under the standards set forth in *New York Times*. Petitioners also asserted that summary judgment was proper because actual malice was absent as a matter of law. In support of this latter assertion, petitioners submitted the affidavit of Charles Bermant, an employee of petitioners and the author of the two longer articles. In this affidavit, Bermant stated that he had spent a substantial amount of time researching and writing the articles and that his facts were obtained from a wide variety of sources. He also stated that he had at all times believed and still believed that the facts contained in the articles were truthful and accurate. Attached to this affidavit was an appendix in which Bermant detailed the sources for each of the statements alleged by respondents to be libelous.

Respondents opposed the motion for summary judgment, asserting that there were numerous inaccuracies in the articles and claiming that an issue of actual malice was presented by virtue of the fact that in preparing the articles Bermant had relied on several sources that respondents asserted were patently unreliable. Generally, respondents charged that petitioners had failed adequately to verify their information before publishing. Respondents also presented evidence that William McGaw, an editor of The Investigator, had told petitioner Adkins before publication that the articles were "terrible" and "ridiculous."

[The district court granted summary judgment and entered judgment in favor of the petitioners. The court of appeals affirmed summary judgment as to some of the allegedly defamatory statements, but reversed as to others.]

II

A

Our inquiry is whether the Court of Appeals erred in holding that the heightened evidentiary requirements that apply to proof of actual malice in this *New York Times* case need not be considered for the purposes of a motion for summary judgment. Rule 56(c) of the Federal Rules of Civil Procedure provides that summary judgment "shall be rendered forthwith if the pleadings, depositions, answers to interrogatories, and admissions on file, together with the affidavits, if any, show that there is no genuine issue as to any material fact and that the moving party is entitled to a judgment as a matter of law." By its very terms, this standard provides that the mere existence of *some* alleged factual dispute between the parties will not defeat an otherwise properly supported motion for summary judgment; the requirement is that there be no *genuine* issue of *material* fact.

As to materiality, the substantive law will identify which facts are material. Only disputes over facts that might affect the outcome of the suit under the governing law will properly preclude the entry of summary judgment. Factual disputes that are irrelevant or unnecessary will not be counted. This materiality inquiry is independent of and separate from the question of the incorporation of the evidentiary standard into the summary judgment determination. That is, while the materiality determination rests on the substantive law, it is the substantive law's identification of which facts are critical and which facts are irrelevant that governs. Any proof or evidentiary requirements imposed by the substantive law are not germane to this inquiry, since materiality is only a criterion for categorizing factual disputes in their relation to the legal elements of the claim and not a criterion for evaluating the evidentiary underpinnings of those disputes.

More important for present purposes, summary judgment will not lie if the dispute about a material fact is "genuine," that is, if the evidence is such that a reasonable jury could return a verdict for the nonmoving party. * * *

Our prior decisions may not have uniformly recited the same language in describing genuine factual issues under Rule 56, but it is clear enough from our recent cases that at the summary judgment stage the judge's function is not himself to weigh the evidence and determine the truth of the matter but to determine whether there is a genuine issue for trial. * * * [T]here is no issue for trial unless there is sufficient evidence favoring the nonmoving party for a jury to return a verdict for that party. If the evidence is merely colorable, or is not significantly probative, summary judgment may be granted.

That this is the proper focus of the inquiry is strongly suggested by the Rule itself. Rule 56(e) provides that, when a properly supported motion for summary judgment is made, the adverse party "must set forth specific facts showing that there is a genuine issue for trial."[5] And, as we noted above, Rule 56(c) provides that the trial judge shall then grant summary judgment if there is no genuine issue as to any material fact and if the moving party is entitled to judgment as a matter of law. There is no requirement that the trial judge make findings of fact. The inquiry performed is the threshold inquiry of determining whether there is the need for a trial—whether, in other words, there are any genuine factual issues that properly can be resolved only by a finder of fact because they may reasonably be resolved in favor of either party.

---

5. This requirement in turn is qualified by Rule 56(f)'s provision that summary judgment be refused where the nonmoving party has not had the opportunity to discover information that is essential to his opposition. In our analysis here, we assume that both parties have had ample opportunity for discovery.

Petitioners suggest, and we agree, that this standard mirrors the standard for a directed verdict [now called a "motion for judgment as a matter of law"] under Federal Rule of Civil Procedure 50(a), which is that the trial judge must direct a verdict if, under the governing law, there can be but one reasonable conclusion as to the verdict. If reasonable minds could differ as to the import of the evidence, however, a verdict should not be directed. As the Court long ago said, and has several times repeated:

> "Nor are judges any longer required to submit a question to a jury merely because some evidence has been introduced by the party having the burden of proof, unless the evidence be of such a character that it would warrant the jury in finding a verdict in favor of that party. Formerly it was held that if there was what is called a *scintilla* of evidence in support of a case the judge was bound to leave it to the jury, but recent decisions of high authority have established a more reasonable rule, that in every case, before the evidence is left to the jury, there is a preliminary question for the judge, not whether there is literally no evidence, but whether there is any upon which a jury could properly proceed to find a verdict for the party producing it, upon whom the onus of proof is imposed."

The Court has said that summary judgment should be granted where the evidence is such that it "would require a directed verdict for the moving party." And we have noted that the "genuine issue" summary judgment standard is "very close" to the "reasonable jury" directed verdict standard: "The primary difference between the two motions is procedural; summary judgment motions are usually made before trial and decided on documentary evidence, while directed verdict motions are made at trial and decided on the evidence that has been admitted." In essence, though, the inquiry under each is the same: whether the evidence presents a sufficient disagreement to require submission to a jury or whether it is so one-sided that one party must prevail as a matter of law.

B

Progressing to the specific issue in this case, we are convinced that the inquiry involved in a ruling on a motion for summary judgment or for a directed verdict necessarily implicates the substantive evidentiary standard of proof that would apply at the trial on the merits. If the defendant in a run-of-the-mill civil case moves for summary judgment or for a directed verdict based on the lack of proof of a material fact, the judge must ask himself not whether he thinks the evidence unmistakably favors one side or the other but whether a fair-minded jury could return a verdict for the plaintiff on the evidence presented. The mere existence of a scintilla of evidence in support of the plaintiff's position will be insufficient; there must be evidence on which the jury could reasonably find for the plaintiff. The judge's inquiry, therefore, unavoidably asks whether reasonable jurors could find by a preponderance of the evidence that the plaintiff is entitled to a verdict — "whether there is [evidence] upon which a jury can properly proceed to find a verdict for the party producing it, upon whom the *onus* of proof is imposed."

Thus, in ruling on a motion for summary judgment, the judge must view the evidence presented through the prism of the substantive evidentiary burden. This conclusion is mandated by the nature of this determination. The question here is whether a jury could reasonably find *either* that the plaintiff proved his case by the quality and quantity of evidence required by the governing law *or* that he did not. Whether a jury could reasonably find for either party, however, cannot be defined except by the criteria governing what evidence would enable the jury to find for either the plaintiff or the defendant: It makes no sense to say that a jury could reasonably find for either party without some benchmark as to what standards govern its deliberations and within what boundaries its ultimate decision must fall, and these standards and boundaries are in fact provided by the applicable evidentiary standards.

Our holding that the clear-and-convincing standard of proof should be taken into account in ruling on summary judgment motions does not denigrate the role of the jury. It by no means authorizes trial on affidavits. Credibility determinations, the weighing of the evidence, and the drawing of legitimate inferences from the facts are jury functions, not those of a judge, whether he is ruling on a motion for summary judgment or for a directed verdict. The evidence of the nonmovant is to be believed, and all justifiable inferences are to be drawn in his favor. Neither do we suggest that the trial courts should act other than with caution in granting summary judgment or that the trial court may not deny summary judgment in a case where there is reason to believe that the better course would be to proceed to a full trial.

In sum, we conclude that the determination of whether a given factual dispute requires submission to a jury must be guided by the substantive evidentiary standards that apply to the case. This is true at both the directed verdict and summary judgment stages. Consequently, where the *New York Times* "clear and convincing" evidence requirement applies, the trial judge's summary judgment inquiry as to whether a genuine issue exists will be whether the evidence presented is such that a jury applying that evidentiary standard could reasonably find for either the plaintiff or the defendant. Thus, where the factual dispute concerns actual malice, clearly a material issue in a *New York Times* case, the appropriate summary judgment question will be whether the evidence in the record could support a reasonable jury finding either that the plaintiff has shown actual malice by clear and convincing evidence or that the plaintiff has not.

III

Respondents argue, however, that whatever may be true of the applicability of the "clear and convincing" standard at the summary judgment or directed verdict stage, the defendant should seldom if ever be granted summary judgment where his state of mind is at issue and the jury might disbelieve him or his witnesses as to this issue. They rely on Poller v. Columbia Broadcasting Co., 368 U.S. 464 (1962), for this proposition. We do not understand *Poller*, however, to hold that a plaintiff may defeat a defendant's properly supported motion for summary judgment in a conspiracy or libel case, for example, without offering any concrete evidence from which a reasonable juror could return a verdict in his favor and by merely asserting that the jury might, and legally could, disbelieve the defendant's denial of a conspiracy or of legal malice. The movant has the burden of showing that there is no genuine issue of fact, but the plaintiff is not thereby relieved of his own burden of producing in turn evidence that would support a jury verdict. Rule 56(e) itself provides that a party opposing a properly supported motion for summary judgment may not rest upon mere allegation or denials of his pleading, but must set forth specific facts showing that there is a genuine issue for trial. * * * As we have recently said, "discredited testimony is not [normally] considered a sufficient basis for drawing a contrary conclusion." Instead, the plaintiff must present affirmative evidence in order to defeat a properly supported motion for summary judgment. This is true even where the evidence is likely to be within the possession of the defendant, as long as the plaintiff has had a full opportunity to conduct discovery. We repeat, however, that the plaintiff, to survive the defendant's motion, need only present evidence from which a jury might return a verdict in his favor. If he does so, there is a genuine issue of fact that requires a trial.

IV

In sum, a court ruling on a motion for summary judgment must be guided by the *New York Times* "clear and convincing" evidentiary standard in determining whether a genuine issue of actual malice exists — that is, whether the evidence presented is such that a reasonable jury might find that actual malice had been shown with convincing clarity. Because the Court of Appeals did not apply the correct standard in reviewing the District Court's grant of summary judgment, we vacate its decision and remand the case for further proceedings consistent with this opinion.

It is so ordered.

JUSTICE BRENNAN, dissenting.

* * * This case is about a trial court's responsibility when considering a motion for summary judgment, but in my view, the Court, while instructing the trial judge to "consider" heightened evidentiary standards, fails to explain what that means. In other words, how does a judge assess how one-sided evidence is, or what a "fairminded" jury could "reasonably" decide? The Court provides conflicting clues to these mysteries, which I fear can lead only to increased confusion in the district and appellate courts.

The Court's opinion is replete with boiler plate language to the effect that trial courts are not to weigh evidence when deciding summary judgment motions. * * *

But the Court's opinion is also full of language which could surely be understood as an invitation — if not an instruction — to trial courts to assess and weigh evidence much as a juror would. * * *

I simply cannot square the direction that the judge "is not himself to weigh the evidence" with the direction that the judge also bear in mind the "quantum" of proof required and consider whether the evidence is of sufficient "caliber or quantity" to meet that "quantum." I would have thought that a determination of the "caliber and quantity," i.e., the importance and value, of the evidence in light of the "quantum," i.e., amount "required," could *only* be performed by weighing the evidence.

If in fact, this is what the Court would, under today's decision, require of district courts, then I am fearful that this new rule — for this surely would be a brand new procedure — will transform what is meant to provide an expedited "summary" procedure into a full-blown paper trial on the merits. It is hard for me to imagine that a responsible counsel, aware that the judge will be assessing the "quantum" of the evidence he is presenting, will risk either moving for or responding to a summary judgment motion without coming forth with *all* of the evidence he can muster in support of his client's case. Moreover, if the judge on motion for summary judgment really is to weigh the evidence, then in my view grave concerns are raised concerning the constitutional right of civil litigants to a jury trial.

It may well be, as Justice Rehnquist suggests, that the Court's decision today will be of little practical effect. I, for one, cannot imagine a case in which a judge might plausibly hold that the evidence on motion for summary judgment was sufficient to enable a plaintiff bearing a mere preponderance burden to get to the jury — i.e., that a prima facie case had been made out — but insufficient for a plaintiff bearing a clear-and-convincing burden to withstand a defendant's summary judgment motion. Imagine a suit for breach of contract. If, for example, the defendant moves for summary judgment and produces one purported eyewitness who states that he was present at the time the parties discussed the possibility of an agreement, and unequivocally denies that the parties ever agreed to enter into a contract, while the plaintiff produces one purported eyewitness who asserts that the parties did in fact come to terms, presumably that case would go to the jury. But if the defendant produced not one, but 100 eyewitnesses, while the plaintiff stuck with his single witness, would that case, under the Court's holding, still go to the jury? After all, although the plaintiff's burden in this hypothetical contract action is to prove his case by a mere preponderance of the evidence, the judge, so the Court tells us, is to "ask himself ... whether a fair-minded jury could return a verdict for the plaintiff on the evidence presented." Is there, in this hypothetical example, "a sufficient disagreement to require submission to a jury," or is the evidence "so one-sided that one party must prevail as a matter of law?" Would the result change if the plaintiff's one witness were now shown to be a convicted perjurer? Would the result change if, instead of a garden-variety contract claim, the plaintiff sued on a fraud theory, thus requiring him to prove his case by clear and convincing evidence?

It seems to me that the Court's decision today unpersuasively answers the question presented, and in doing so raises a host of difficult and troubling questions for which there may well be no adequate solutions. What is particularly unfair is that the mess we make is not, at least in the first instance, our own to deal with; it is the district courts and courts of appeals that must struggle to clean up after us.

In my view, if a plaintiff presents evidence which either directly or by permissible inference (and these inferences are a product of the substantive law of the underlying claim) supports all of the elements he needs to prove in order to prevail on his legal claim, the plaintiff has made out a prima facie case and a defendant's motion for summary judgment must fail regardless of the burden of proof that the plaintiff must meet. In other words, whether evidence is "clear and convincing," or proves a point by a mere preponderance, is for the factfinder to determine. As I read the case law, this is how it has been, and because of my concern that today's decision may erode the constitutionally enshrined role of the jury, and also undermine the usefulness of summary judgment procedure, this is how I believe it should remain.

JUSTICE REHNQUIST, with whom THE CHIEF JUSTICE joins, dissenting.

There is a large class of cases in which the higher standard imposed by the Court today would seem to have no effect at all. Suppose, for example, on motion for summary judgment in a hypothetical libel case, the plaintiff concedes that his only proof of malice is the testimony of witness A. Witness A testifies at his deposition that the reporter who wrote the story in question told him that she, the reporter, had done absolutely no checking on the story and had real doubts about whether or not it was correct as to the plaintiff. The defendant's examination of witness A brings out that he has a prior conviction for perjury.

May the Court grant the defendant's motion for summary judgment on the ground that the plaintiff has failed to produce sufficient proof of malice? Surely not, if the Court means what it says, when it states: "Credibility determinations ... are jury functions, not those of a judge, whether he is ruling on a motion for summary judgment or for a directed verdict. The evidence of the nonmovant is to be believed, and all justifiable inferences are to be drawn in his favor."

The case proceeds to trial, and at the close of the plaintiff's evidence the defendant moves for a directed verdict on the ground that the plaintiff has failed to produce sufficient evidence of malice. The only evidence of malice produced by the plaintiff is the same testimony of witness A, who is duly impeached by the defendant for the prior perjury conviction. In addition, the trial judge has now had an opportunity to observe the demeanor of witness A, and has noticed that he fidgets when answering critical questions, his eyes shift from the floor to the ceiling, and he manifests all other indicia traditionally attributed to perjurers.

May the trial court at this stage grant a directed verdict? Again, surely not; we are still dealing with "credibility determinations."

The defendant now puts on its testimony, and produces three witnesses who were present at the time when witness A alleges that the reporter said she had not checked the story and had grave doubts about its accuracy as to plaintiff. Witness A concedes that these three people were present at the meeting, and that the statement of the reporter took place in the presence of all these witnesses. Each witness categorically denies that the reporter made the claimed statement to witness A.

May the trial court now grant a directed verdict at the close of all the evidence? Certainly the plaintiff's case is appreciably weakened by the testimony of three disinterested witnesses, and one would hope that a properly charged jury would quickly return a verdict for the defendant. But as long as credibility is exclusively for the jury, it seems the Court's analysis would still require this case to be decided by that body.

Thus, in the case that I have posed, it would seem to make no difference whether the standard of proof which the plaintiff had to meet in order to prevail was the preponderance of the evidence, clear and convincing evidence, or proof beyond a reasonable doubt. But if the application of the standards makes no difference in the case that I hypothesize, one may fairly ask in what sort of case *does* the difference in standards make a difference in outcome? Cases may be posed dealing with evidence that is essentially documentary, rather than testimonial; but the Court has held in a related context involving Federal Rule of Civil Procedure 52(a) that inferences from documentary evidence are as much the prerogative of the finder of fact as inferences as to the credibility of witnesses. The Court affords the lower courts no guidance whatsoever as to what, if any, difference the abstract standards that it propounds would make in a particular case.

The three differentiated burdens of proof in civil and criminal cases, vague and impressionistic though they necessarily are, probably do make some difference when considered by the finder of fact, whether it be a jury or a judge in a bench trial. Yet it is not a logical or analytical message that the terms convey, but instead almost a state of mind; we have previously said:

> "Candor suggests that, to a degree, efforts to analyze what lay jurors understand concerning the differences among these three tests ... may well be largely an academic exercise.... Indeed, the ultimate truth as to how the standards of proof affect decision making may well be *unknowable*, given that factfinding is a process shared by countless thousands of individuals throughout the country. We probably can assume no more than that the difference between a preponderance of the evidence and proof beyond a reasonable doubt probably is better understood than either of them in relation to the intermediate standard of clear and convincing evidence."

The Court's decision to engraft the standard of proof applicable to a factfinder onto the law governing the procedural motion for a summary judgment (a motion that has always been regarded as raising a question of law rather than a question of fact), will do great mischief with little corresponding benefit. The primary effect of the Court's opinion today will likely be to cause the decisions of trial judges on summary judgment motions in libel cases to be more erratic and inconsistent than before. This is largely because the Court has created a standard that is different from the standard traditionally applied in summary judgment motions without even hinting as to how its new standard will be applied to particular cases.

Notes and Questions

1. In analyzing summary judgment, you should distinguish between burden of production and burden of persuasion (sometimes called burden of proof). Burden of production refers to the obligation of one side to come forward with evidence to support its claim. The burdens of production and persuasion usually follow the burden of pleading. Thus, as to elements of a claim, the plaintiff shoulders these burdens, but as to affirmative defenses such as those listed in Rule 8(c)(1), the defendant

must produce evidence and prove the defense. For example, if contributory negligence is a defense and no evidence is introduced on the question of plaintiff's negligence, the defense fails — plaintiff does not have to produce evidence of her freedom from negligence. Burden of persuasion refers to the degree of certainty the fact finder must have before it can find for one side. There are different standards for the degree of certainty the fact finder must have to find in favor of the party with the burden of persuasion. In most civil cases, the standard is "preponderance of the evidence." The standard means that the fact finder must believe that the claimant's version of events is more probable than not. As a result, if the fact finder concludes that the evidence is evenly balanced, the party with the burden of persuasion must lose. In criminal cases, the government has the burden of proof and must meet the much higher standard of "beyond a reasonable doubt." In a few civil cases, the standard is "clear and convincing evidence," which is generally understood to be somewhere between the preponderance and beyond a reasonable doubt standards.

These concepts can be illustrated as follows:

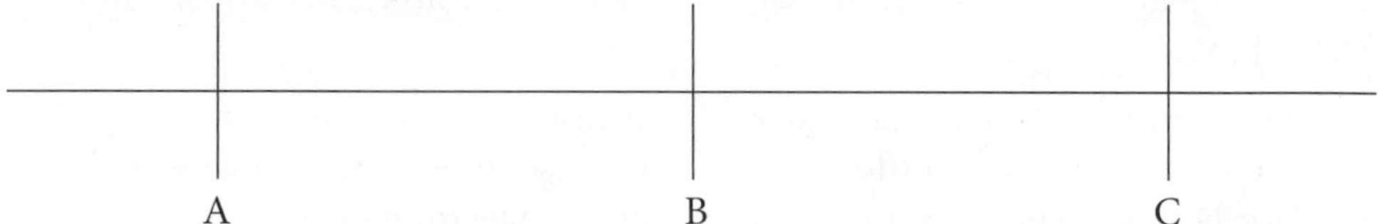

The line at A marks the burden of production. The plaintiff must introduce enough evidence to get past line A or the court will grant summary judgment for the defendant. If the evidence is to the right of line C, then the court will enter summary judgment for the plaintiff. If the evidence falls between A and C, then the issue is one for the jury. Line B marks the burden of persuasion. It is up to the fact finder to determine whether the evidence falls to the right or left of that line. In addition, if the factfinder concludes that the evidence falls on the line, the burden acts as the tiebreaker — the person with the burden on that issue loses. For example, in a slander case, suppose that the jury concludes that it is just as likely as it is not that the injurious statement was true. If the plaintiff had the burden of showing falsity, she loses. If, on the other hand, defendant had the burden of showing truth, then she loses.

The majority opinion in *Anderson* suggests that where the burden of persuasion line (B) moves to a higher standard, the burden of production line should also move. Thus if B moves to B', then A should move to A'.

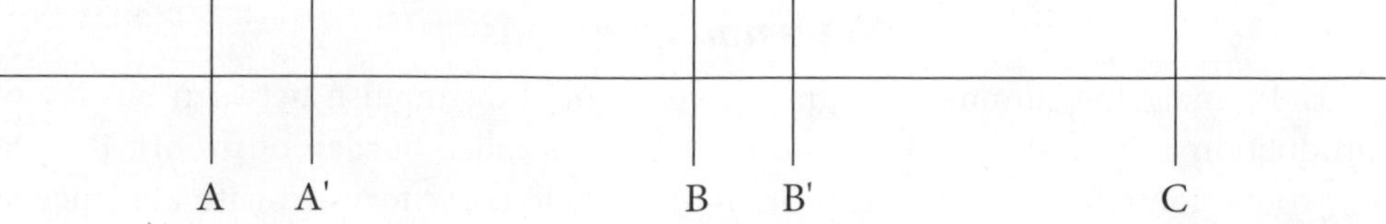

2. Although, according to Justice White, the trial judge is not to "weigh" the evidence, the judge is to assess the sufficiency of evidence. In other words, the judge is

to "assess[] the evidence to insure that it is at least plausible and capable of being accepted by a rational factfinder." James Duane, *The Four Greatest Myths About Summary Judgment*, 52 WASH. & LEE L. REV. 1523, 1561 (1996). In *Anderson*, Justice Brennan expresses skepticism that the judge can evaluate the evidence without engaging in impermissible weighing.

Dean Friedenthal has argued that summary judgment "rests on the often unarticulated determination that decisions concerning the sufficiency of evidence to get to a trier of fact, even when based on human judgment, are of a different quality than decisions by the trier of fact on evidence that it receives, and that the former falls outside the scope of the right to trial by jury." Jack Friedenthal, *Cases on Summary Judgment: Has There Been a Material Change in Standards?*, 63 NOTRE DAME L. REV. 770, 783 (1988). Do you agree? Do you think there is a fundamental difference between assessing the sufficiency of evidence and weighing the evidence?

3. In *Anderson*, the Court says that the test for summary judgment is whether a reasonable jury could find for the non-moving party. However, at the summary judgment stage, the court does not have before it all the evidence that would be available at trial. Instead it has only a few selected pieces offered by counsel. Does it make sense to frame a test for summary judgment in terms of what a reasonable jury would do where the court does not yet have before it all the evidence a jury would have? Professor Miller has noted that at the pretrial stage, "without the safeguards and environment of a trial setting, courts may be tempted to treat the evidence in a piecemeal rather than cumulative fashion, drawing inferences against the non-moving party, or discount the non-moving party's evidence by weighing it against contradictory evidence." Arthur Miller, *The Pretrial Rush to Judgment: Are the "Litigation Explosion," "Liability Crisis," and Efficiency Cliches Eroding Our Day in Court and Jury Trial Commitments?*, 78 N.Y.U. L. REV. 982, 1071 (2003).

4. Although unusual, it is possible for a court to enter summary judgment for the party with the burden of proof. (Do you see why it is unusual?) In American Airlines v. Ulen, 186 F.2d 529, 532 (D.C. Cir. 1949), the plaintiff sued for injuries sustained when the airplane in which he was a passenger crashed into a mountain. Federal Aviation Administration regulations require air carriers to fly at 1,000 feet above "the highest obstacle located with a horizontal distance of 5 miles from the center of the course." The filed flight plan called for the plane to fly at 4,000 feet on a course that took it within 1.5 miles of a mountain 4,080 feet high. The court granted the plaintiff's motion for judgment on the question of defendant's negligence.

5. Suppose that in *Anderson*, the district court had denied summary judgment and that the plaintiff had won at trial. Could the defendant appeal the trial verdict on the ground that the court erred in denying summary judgment? In Ortiz v. Jordan, 562 U.S. 180 (2011), the Supreme Court held that in federal court, a party may not appeal a denial of summary judgment after a full trial on the merits.

6. In *Anderson*, as in *Dyer*, the moving party came forward with affirmative evidence that contradicted the plaintiff's allegation. Suppose, however, that instead of

offering affirmative evidence, the defendant simply asserts that the plaintiff lacks sufficient evidence to prove her claim. In essence, the defendant simply challenges the plaintiff to "put up or shut up." Under these circumstances, must the plaintiff produce some evidence to avoid summary judgment?

In Celotex Corp. v. Catrett, 477 U.S. 317 (1986), the Supreme Court addressed this question. There the plaintiff alleged that her husband's death was the result of his exposure to the defendants' asbestos products. The defendants moved for summary judgment on the grounds that the plaintiff had no proof of her husband's exposure to the defendant's products. The Supreme Court held that the defendant was not required to offer affirmative evidence of the husband's non-exposure and explained:

> Of course, a party seeking summary judgment always bears the initial responsibility of informing the district court of the basis for its motion, and identifying those portions of "the pleadings, depositions, answers to interrogatories, and admissions on file, together with the affidavits, if any," which it believes demonstrate the absence of a genuine issue of material fact. But unlike the Court of Appeals, we find no express or implied requirement in Rule 56 that the moving party support its motion with affidavits or other similar materials *negating* the opponent's claim.

Thus, if a discovery answer demonstrates that a party has no proof with respect to a critical issue, it would be appropriate to point to that answer as a basis for summary judgment. Notice that under Rule 56(d), if the non-moving party shows "for specified reasons" why it cannot present essential facts, the court can delay ruling on the motion or allow discovery.

7. In Matsushita Elec. Indus. Co. v. Zenith Radio, 475 U.S. 574 (1986), the Court upheld a grant of summary judgment in an antitrust case. American television manufacturers alleged that Japanese manufacturers conspired to maintain low prices for Japanese televisions sold in the United States. The Court concluded that the scheme alleged by plaintiffs would have been economically irrational. It then observed, "if the factual context renders respondents' claim implausible—if the claim is one that simply makes no economic sense—respondents must come forward with more persuasive evidence to support their claim than would otherwise be necessary." Id. at 587. Notice the similarity of concern about factual plausibility in *Matsushita* and the pleading cases Bell Atlantic Corp. v. Twombly, 550 U.S. 544 (2007), and Ashcroft v. Iqbal, 556 U.S. 662 (2009) (covered in Chapter 7). Is factual plausibility best addressed at the pleading stage, at summary judgment or both? See Richard Marcus, *The Revival of Fact Pleading Under the Federal Rules of Civil Procedure*, 86 Colum. L. Rev. 433, 484–85 (1986).

8. *Anderson, Matsushita*, and *Celotex* were all decided the same term and collectively seem to signal a new receptiveness to such motions. See Stephen Calkins, *Summary Judgment, Motions to Dismiss, and Other Examples of Equilibrating Tendencies in the Antitrust System*, 74 Geo. L.J. 1065, 1114–15 (1986). Data, though limited, suggest that between 1960 and 2000, there was a significant increase in the use of summary judgment, though the increase appears to have begun before these cases

were decided. See Stephen Burbank, *Vanishing Trials and Summary Judgment in Federal Civil Cases: Drifting Toward Bethlehem or Gomorrah?* 1 J. EMPIRICAL LEGAL STUD. 591 (2004). Thus, the trilogy of cases may not have caused a change so much as reflect a trend that began in the 1970s.

9. The motion for summary judgment in *Celotex* was filed in December 1981. Following the Supreme Court decision in 1986, the case was remanded. The court of appeals again held that summary judgment was not appropriate, and in 1988, the Supreme Court denied certiorari. Some time later, the case settled. See David Shapiro, *The Story of* Celotex: *The Role of Summary Judgment in the Administration of Civil Justice, in* CIVIL PROCEDURE STORIES 359, 376 (K. Clermont ed., 2d ed. 2008). Thus, the litigation concerning summary judgment lasted nearly seven years. Wouldn't it have been quicker just to have tried the case rather than to litigate about summary judgment? Indeed, some judges have expressed concern that summary judgment motions may increase delay and costs. One Magistrate Judge has offered the following advice:

> Summary judgment has become an expensive procedural device that is unnecessary for the majority of cases filed in federal court. It is often used by defendants to obtain a complete look at the plaintiff's case and to discourage the plaintiff from going forward. By increasing the cost of going forward, the defendant is able to pressure the plaintiff into accepting a lower settlement. In cases that would take a week or less to try, the parties and the court would be better served by focusing on settlement or an early trial date accompanied by a simple final pretrial order. This will ultimately improve the quality of justice and result in the resolution of more cases on the merits, with the full participation of the parties.

Morton Denlow, *Summary Judgment: Boon or Burden*, THE JUDGE'S JOURNAL 26,30 (Summer 1998).

Coble v. City of White House

634 F.3d 865 (6th Cir. 2011)

BELL, DISTRICT JUDGE.

Plaintiff Jerry T. Coble ("Coble") appeals the district court's entry of summary judgment in favor of Officer Curtis Carney, Jr. on Coble's claim under 42 U.S.C. § 1983 that Officer Carney used excessive force against him during his arrest for drunk driving. [Section 1983 creates a claim for violation of one's federal rights by state officers.] The issue on appeal is whether the district court erred in finding that there was no question of fact for trial because Coble's testimony regarding the force used was contradicted by a contemporaneous audio recording. For the reasons that follow, we reverse the district court's judgment.

I.

On April 6, 2007, at approximately 10:40 p.m., Officer Curtis Carney, Jr., was on patrol for the City of White House Police Department, when a truck driven by Coble exited the parking lot of Bob & Rhonda's Sports Grill and pulled onto the highway in front of Officer Carney's patrol car. After seeing the truck cross the fog line three times, Officer Carney activated his in-car video camera and flashing lights. Coble did not stop. He continued driving until he turned into the driveway of his home and reached the end of his driveway.

Officer Carney pulled up behind him and exited his patrol car. Coble did not obey Officer Carney's preliminary commands or answer his questions. Instead, he argued with Officer Carney, told him to get off his property, and began walking toward his house. When he failed to obey Officer Carney's command to stop, Officer Carney removed his chemical agent from its holster, sprayed Coble, and performed a takedown maneuver, during which Coble sustained an open fracture of his right ankle. After a struggle on the ground, Officer Carney, with the assistance of Officer Scott Bilbrey, who had arrived on the scene, succeeded in bringing Coble's arms behind his back and handcuffing him. Once Coble was handcuffed, he did not offer any further resistance.

The dispute that is at the heart of this appeal concerns what happened after Coble was handcuffed. None of these events were captured on videotape because they did not occur in front of the patrol car. However, even after Officer Carney and Coble were out of camera range, sounds transmitted by the microphone worn by Officer Carney continued to be recorded. Coble testified that Officer Carney pulled him up by the handcuffs, and, pushing him from behind, walked him 7 or 8 steps on his broken ankle, leaving a 34-foot trail of blood. Coble testified that Officer Carney would have known that his leg was broken because bones were sticking out of Coble's leg, his tennis shoe was laid over sideways, one of his legs was shorter than the other, and he was screaming and calling Officer Carney names. Coble testified that when Officer Carney finally stopped, he let go of the handcuffs and dropped Coble face-first on the concrete.

Officer Carney's testimony differs markedly from Coble's testimony. Officer Carney testified that, after handcuffing Coble, he and Officer Bilbrey helped Coble to a standing position and began walking with him toward the patrol car. After three or four steps, Coble said his leg was broken. Officer Carney testified that he looked down, saw that Coble's leg was broken, and immediately sat him down on the driveway.

Coble was transported by helicopter to a hospital. A blood sample collected from him at 2:10 a.m. on April 7, 2007, indicated a blood alcohol level of 0.16. Coble pled guilty to charges of driving under the influence and resisting arrest.

Coble filed this action against Officer Carney, Officer Bilbrey, and the City of White House, alleging claims of excessive force, false arrest, and failure to implement appropriate policies under 42 U.S.C. § 1983, as well as state law claims of negligence, negligent infliction of emotional distress, negligent training and supervision, reckless infliction of emotional distress, and assault and battery. * * * With respect to Coble's claim that Officer Carney used excessive force after he was handcuffed by walking him on a broken ankle and dropping him face-first onto the ground, the district court cited Scott v. Harris, 550 U.S. 372 (2007), in support of its determination that, in light of the audio recording, it was not required to accept Coble's version of the events:

> Listening to the audiotape, no reasonable jury could find by a preponderance of the evidence that Coble screamed during the first few steps while he was being escorted, that he called Officer Carney names to get him to stop walking, or that Coble "splattered" on the pavement. To the contrary, the audiotape reveals only the sound of shuffling bodies as if the three men were walking, and Coble was silent. After a few moments, Coble cried out that his leg was broken, and the shuffling stopped. An officer said, "Sit down!" There is no audible noise that one could associate with a body dropping or "splattering" to the pavement." ... The testimony of Officers Carney and Bilbrey square with the audiotape, while Coble's testimony does not. Therefore, under *Scott*, the Court need not adopt Coble's version in ruling on the motions for summary judgment.

The district court concluded that because Coble failed to generate a genuine issue of material fact for trial on his constitutional claim, Officer Carney was entitled to summary judgment. * * *

II.

Coble's sole challenge on appeal is to the district court's determination that Officer Carney did not use excessive force after Coble was restrained in handcuffs.

We review a district court order granting summary judgment de novo. "Summary judgment is proper if the evidence, taken in the light most favorable to the nonmoving party, shows that there are no genuine issues of material fact and that the moving party is entitled to a judgment as a matter of law."

A constitutional excessive force claim is analyzed under an "objective-reasonableness standard, which depends on the facts and circumstance of each case viewed from the perspective of a reasonable officer on the scene." "The first step in assessing the constitutionality of [an officer's] actions is to determine the relevant facts." To the extent there is disagreement about the facts, we must review the evidence in the light most favorable to the plaintiff, and draw all inferences in his favor.

Construing the facts on summary judgment in the light most favorable to the non-moving party usually means adopting the plaintiff's version of the facts. However, the Supreme Court clarified in *Scott* that facts must be viewed in the light most favorable to the non-moving party "only if there is a 'genuine' dispute as to those facts." In *Scott*, the Supreme Court held that a police officer was entitled to summary judgment on a motorist's claim that the officer used excessive force in ramming his car after a high-speed chase, notwithstanding the fact that the motorist and the officer gave conflicting testimony regarding the events in question. In *Scott*, the conflicting testimony did not create an issue of fact for trial because the record included a videotape capturing the police chase which clearly contradicted the motorist's contention that he was driving carefully. As noted by the Supreme Court:

> When opposing parties tell two different stories, one of which is blatantly contradicted by the record, so that no reasonable jury could believe it, a court

should not adopt that version of the facts for purposes of ruling on a motion for summary judgment.

In the summary judgment context, "appeals courts should not accept 'visible fiction' that is 'so utterly discredited by the record that no reasonable jury could have believed' it."

Coble contends that *Scott* and its progeny in the Sixth Circuit have limited *Scott* to cases where the events were recorded on a videotape,[3] and that it was improper for the district court to extend *Scott* to a case involving an audio recording. There is nothing in the *Scott* analysis that suggests that it should be restricted to cases involving videotapes. The *Scott* opinion does not focus on the characteristics of a videotape, but on "the record." ("When opposing parties tell two different stories, one of which is *blatantly contradicted by the record....*"; "Respondent's version of events is so *utterly discredited by the record....*"; "At the summary judgment stage ... once we have determined the relevant set of facts and drawn all inferences in favor of the nonmoving party to the extent *supportable by the record* ... the reasonableness of [the respondent's] actions ... is a pure question of law." (emphasis added)). Although we have not had occasion to apply the *Scott* analysis to audio recordings, courts routinely look to *Scott* for guidance in determining whether the non-moving party's version of the events is so blatantly contradicted by objective evidence in the record that it fails to create a genuine issue of material fact for trial, even in the absence of a videotape. See, e.g., White v. Georgia, 380 F. App'x 796, 798 (11th Cir. 2010) (refusing to credit the plaintiff's testimony that she was shot where the medical records conclusively established that her injuries where not caused by a gunshot); Carter v. City of Wyoming, 294 F. App'x 990, 992 (6th Cir. 2008) (holding that MRI evidence did not "blatantly contradict" the plaintiff's claim); Cooper v. City of Rockford, 2010 U.S. Dist. Lexis 79539, at *2 n.3 (N.D. Ill. Aug. 17, 2010) (refusing to credit a witness statement that the victim was running away when he was shot because the autopsy report was clear that the bullet entered the victim from the front); see also Shreve v. Jessamine Cnty. Fiscal Ct., 453 F.3d 681, 688 (6th Cir. 2006) (suggesting, before *Scott* was decided, that it would be proper to discount the plaintiff's evidence where the defendants' evidence was "so objectively compelling" that no reasonable juror could believe the plaintiff).

Accordingly, our decision does not turn on whether it was proper for the district court to consider the audio recording—it was—but on whether the district court

3. See, e.g., Dunn v. Matatall, 549 F.3d 348, 350 (6th Cir. 2008) (finding officer's use of force objectively reasonable based on undisputed facts recorded on police video); Williams v. City of Grosse Pointe Park, 496 F.3d 482, 486 (6th Cir. 2007) (finding officer's use of force objectively reasonable based almost exclusively on the police video); Marvin v. City of Taylor, 509 F.3d 234, 239 (6th Cir. 2007) ("[T]his Court will view the events as they unfolded in the light most favorable to Marvin, but never in such a manner that is wholly unsupportable—in the view of any reasonable jury—by the video recording."); see also Griffin v. Hardrick, 604 F.3d 949, 954 (6th Cir. 2010) ("[A] court may properly consider videotape evidence at the summary-judgment stage.").

properly found that Coble's testimony was "blatantly contradicted" by the audio recording in this case. We think not.

The district court found that the audio recording blatantly contradicted Coble's deposition testimony that he screamed during the first few steps while he was being escorted, and called Officer Carney names to get him to stop walking. This finding was based upon the lack of any audible screams or name-calling on the recording. The district court also found that no reasonable jury could find that Coble "splattered" on the pavement because there was "no audible noise that one could associate with a body dropping or 'splattering' to the pavement." The lack of sound on an audio recording cannot be reliably used to discount Coble's testimony. Many factors could affect what sounds are recorded, including the volume of the sound, the nature of the activity at issue, the location of the microphone, whether the microphone was on or off, and whether the microphone was covered. This case differs from *Scott*, where there were no allegations or indications that the recording was doctored or altered in any way, or any contention that what it depicted differed from what actually happened. Here, in contrast to the plaintiff in *Scott*, Coble does not merely characterize the recording differently. Rather, Coble insists that the facts differed from what was recorded. Coble testified that he screamed, that he called Officer Carney names, that he was forced to walk on his broken ankle, and that he was dropped face-first on the ground. His testimony is not "blatantly contradicted" by the lack of corroborating sound on the audio recording. A reasonable jury could believe Coble's version of the events.[4]

In addition, the recording does not indicate when Officer Carney became aware of Coble's broken ankle, or how far he made Coble walk after he became aware of the injury. Facts that are not blatantly contradicted by the audio recording remain entitled to an interpretation most favorable to the non-moving party. Coble's testimony that Officer Carney would have known that his ankle was broken is not "so utterly discredited" by the audio recording, and must be construed in the light most favorable to Coble. Cf. *Carter*, 294 F. App'x at 992 (denying summary judgment where the videotape did not "blatantly contradict" the plaintiff's description of what happened inside the store, and did not purport to cover, much less contradict, the excessive-force allegations regarding activities outside of the store).

Even if part of Coble's testimony is blatantly contradicted by the audio recording, that does not permit the district court to discredit his entire version of the events. We allow cases to proceed to trial even though a party's evidence is inconsistent, be-

4. We do not suggest that discounting a non-movant's testimony at the summary judgment stage on the basis of an audio recording would never be appropriate. An audio recording may very well provide objectively compelling evidence, particularly when it is presented to show what sounds or statements were made. See, e.g., Marksmeier v. Davie, 622 F.3d 896, 900 (8th Cir. 2010) (finding no genuine issue of fact for trial where the plaintiff's admissions, captured on audiotape, blatantly contradicted his version of the events). However, an audio recording is less reliable when it is presented to support findings based on the lack of recorded sound.

cause "[i]n reviewing a summary judgment motion, credibility judgments and weighing of the evidence are prohibited." "[W]hen the non-moving party presents direct evidence refuting the moving party's motion for summary judgment, the court must accept that evidence as true." "This is the case even when the nonmovant's account is contradictory." See also *Shreve*, 453 F.3d at 688 (crediting, for summary judgment purposes, the plaintiff's testimony as to excessive force, despite contradictions in her deposition); Jones v. Garcia, 345 F. App'x 987, 990 (6th Cir. 2009) ("But Jones' account does not require such a suspension of reality that no reasonable juror could accept it, and that is enough to allow a jury to hear the claim. That Jones may have a difficult time winning his case does not disable him from trying, at least so far as Rule 56 is concerned.").

We cannot say that Coble's version of the events was so utterly discredited by the record that no reasonable jury could believe it. Accordingly, there is a genuine question of material fact as to whether Officer Carney used excessive force, and the district court erred by granting summary judgment for Office Carney.

VI. CONCLUSION

Because there is a genuine issue of material fact as to whether Officer Carney used excessive force after Coble was handcuffed, we reverse the order of the district court granting summary judgment to Officer Carney and remand for further proceedings consistent with this opinion.

Notes and Questions

1. The court in *Coble* refers to the Supreme Court's decision in Scott v. Harris, 550 U.S. 372 (2007). The case involved a suit against a police department by a motorist who had been injured in connection with a high speed chase. The motorist had been clocked going 73 miles per hour in a 55 mile per hour zone, and the police gave chase. When the motorist failed to stop, the police attempted to cause the fleeing vehicle to go into a spin but instead the driver to lost control of his vehicle, ran down an embankment and was rendered a quadriplegic. A critical issue was whether the fleeing motorist had been driving in a manner to endanger human life (and hence the police action was warranted). The police moved for summary judgment on this issue and argued that a video from the police car dashboard camera established that there was no genuine issue of material fact. The trial court denied summary judgment, the court of appeals affirmed, but the Supreme Court reversed and granted summary judgment. The majority concluded that there was only one reasonable understanding of the facts in light of the videotape: "[w]hen opposing parties tell two different stories, one of which is blatantly contradicted by the record, so that no reasonable jury could believe it, a court should not adopt that version of the facts for purposes of ruling on a motion for summary judgment." Justice Stevens, who viewed the same video, drew a completely different conclusion from the majority about whether the vehicle was driving so as to endanger human life. The video can be viewed at: http://www.supremecourt.gov/media/media.aspx.

2. Does recorded evidence "speak for itself"? One research team showed the *Scott* video to a wide cross section of Americans and found not only that people varied in their perceptions, but that these people were "not idiosyncratic statistical outliers; they are members of groups who share a distinctive understanding of social reality that informs their view of the facts." Dan Kahan, David Hoffman & Donald Braman, *Whose Eyes Are You Going to Believe?* Scott v. Harris *and the Perils of Cognitive Illiberalism*, 122 HARV. L. REV. 837 (2009).

> Our empirical study found that when we "allow the videotape to speak for itself," what it says depends on to whom it is speaking. To be sure, a substantial majority of American society is inclined to see in Harris's flight from the police the sort of lethal threat to public safety that in turn warrants a potentially deadly response on the part of the police. But this view is not uniform across subcommunities. Whites and African Americans, high-wage earners and low-wage earners, Northeasterners and Southerners and Westerners, liberals and conservatives, Republicans and Democrats — all varied significantly in their perceptions of the risk that Harris posed, of the risk the police created by deciding to pursue him, and of the need to use deadly force against Harris in the interest of reducing public risk.

Id. at 903.

3. In *J.E.B. v. Alabama*, which we studied earlier in this chapter, the plaintiff had scientific evidence establishing with 99.92 percent certainty that the defendant was the father. The defendant contended that he was not with the child's mother at the time of conception and, in addition, was sterile. If the plaintiff had moved for summary judgment, should it have been granted?

Suppose that the facts were reversed: The scientific evidence established with 99.92 percent certainty that the defendant was *not* the father. The mother's affidavit stated that she had sexual relations with the defendant at the time of conception. Should summary judgment be granted for the defendant? Does your answer depend on whether the mother states that the defendant was the only man with whom she had relations? In Simblest v. Maynard, 427 F.2d 1, 6 (2d Cir. 1970), the court held that "[p]laintiff's testimony * * * in the teeth of the proven physical facts * * * is tantamount to no proof at all on that issue." Could the same be said of the *J.E.B.* hypothetical?

4. In Tolan v. Cotton, 134 S. Ct. 1861 (2014) (per curiam), the Court repeated that "in ruling on a motion for summary judgment '[t]he evidence of the non-moving party is to be believed, and all justifiable inferences are to be drawn in his favor.'" In *Tolan*, the unarmed plaintiff was shot by police and sued for damages, alleging that the officer used excessive force. The district court granted summary judgment for the officer and the Fifth Circuit affirmed. The Supreme Court vacated and remanded the case. The Court's discussion of the disputed evidence is instructive:

> In holding that Cotton's actions did not violate clearly established law, the Fifth Circuit failed to view the evidence at summary judgment in the light most favorable to Tolan with respect to the central facts of this case.

By failing to credit evidence that contradicted some of its key factual conclusions, the court improperly "weigh[ed] the evidence" and resolved disputed issues in favor of the moving party [citing *Anderson*].

First, the court relied on its view that at the time of the shooting, the Tolans' front porch was "dimly-lit." The court appears to have drawn this assessment from Cotton's statements in a deposition that when he fired at Tolan, the porch was "fairly dark," and lit by a gas lamp that was "decorative." In his own deposition, however, Tolan's father was asked whether the gas lamp was in fact "more decorative than illuminating." He said that it was not. Moreover, Tolan stated in his deposition that two floodlights shone on the driveway during the incident, and Cotton acknowledged that there were two motion-activated lights in front of the house. And Tolan confirmed that at the time of the shooting, he was "not in darkness."

Second, the Fifth Circuit stated that Tolan's mother "refus[ed] orders to remain quiet and calm," thereby "compound[ing]" Cotton's belief that Tolan "presented an immediate threat to the safety of the officers." But here, too, the court did not credit directly contradictory evidence. Although the parties agree that Tolan's mother repeatedly informed officers that Tolan was her son, that she lived in the home in front of which he had parked, and that the vehicle he had been driving belonged to her and her husband, there is a dispute as to how calmly she provided this information. Cotton stated during his deposition that Tolan's mother was "very agitated" when she spoke to the officers. By contrast, Tolan's mother testified at Cotton's criminal trial that she was neither "aggravated" nor "agitated."

Third, the Court concluded that Tolan was "shouting," and "verbally threatening" the officer, in the moments before the shooting. The court noted, and the parties agree, that while Cotton was grabbing the arm of his mother, Tolan told Cotton, "[G]et your fucking hands off my mom." But Tolan testified that he "was not screaming." And a jury could reasonably infer that his words, in context, did not amount to a statement of intent to inflict harm. Tolan's mother testified in Cotton's criminal trial that he slammed her against a garage door with enough force to cause bruising that lasted for days. A jury could well have concluded that a reasonable officer would have heard Tolan's words not as a threat, but as a son's plea not to continue any assault of his mother.

Fourth, the Fifth Circuit inferred that at the time of the shooting, Tolan was "moving to intervene in Sergeant Cotton's" interaction with his mother. The court appears to have credited Edwards' account that at the time of the shooting, Tolan was on both feet "[i]n a crouch" or a "charging position" looking as if he was going to move forward. Tolan testified at trial, however, that he was on his knees when Cotton shot him, a fact corroborated by his mother. Tolan also testified in his deposition that he "wasn't going anywhere," and emphasized that he did not "jump up."

> Considered together, these facts lead to the inescapable conclusion that the court below credited the evidence of the party seeking summary judgment and failed properly to acknowledge key evidence offered by the party opposing that motion. And while "this Court is not equipped to correct every perceived error coming from the lower federal courts," we intervene here because the opinion below reflects a clear misapprehension of summary judgment standards in light of our precedents.

5. Most discussions of summary judgment assume that the finder of fact would be a jury (if the case were to go to trial). However, Rule 56 does not differentiate between cases that would go to trial before a jury and those that would be tried before a judge. Judge Schwarzer has suggested that the test for determining whether summary judgment is proper should be somewhat different when the court would be the trier of fact. He argues that in this context, the proper question is "What does a trial add to the judge's ability to decide the issue submitted on motion?" *Summary Judgment Under the Federal Rules: Defining Genuine Issues of Material Fact*, 99 F.R.D. 465, 471 (1984). He explains:

> The point here is not that the provisions of Rule 56 should be ignored in nonjury cases. Rather it is that in the absence of a genuine need to assess testimonial credibility or demeanor, the decision of issues which would otherwise go to the jury may be made on motion for summary judgment when trial is to the court. In such cases it is not enough to classify an issue as one of "law" or "fact" or "ultimate fact" as those terms are conventionally understood; the court must determine whether a trial of the issue would serve any purpose, if it would not, then the issue is one of law *for purposes of Rule 56*, even if it is a fact issue for other purposes, including Rule 56 purposes in *jury* cases.

Id. at 479–80 (emphasis in original). Does it make sense to apply a different test for summary judgment depending on whether the trier of fact is a judge or a jury?

6. Charles E. Clark, the senior reporter for the committee that drafted the Federal Rules, along with other legal realists, disliked juries. "Jurists of experience find little to say in support of the delays, the expense, and the aleatory results of trial by jury," said Clark. Laura Kalman, Legal Realism At Yale 21 (1986). Indeed, it has been argued that one of the attractions of summary judgment to the drafters of the Rules was that it was a device for taking cases away from juries. See id. On the other hand, the fact that summary judgment deprives litigants of a right to a jury trial is the reason some commentators have argued that the courts should be cautious in granting summary judgment, and in particular should distinguish "between allowing a judge to dispose of a case by applying a determinative legal principle to undisputed facts and allowing a judge to decide a factual issue because he or she believes the evidence allows only one conclusion." Arthur Miller, *The Pretrial Rush to Judgment: Are the "Litigation Explosion," "Liability Crisis," and Efficiency Cliches Eroding Our Day in Court and Jury Trial Commitments?*, 78 N.Y.U. L. Rev. 982, 1091–92 (2003).

D. Controlling and Second-Guessing Juries

1. Judgment as a Matter of Law (Directed Verdict and JNOV)

When a case goes to trial before a jury, the court continues to have authority to determine whether there is sufficient evidence to support a jury verdict. If the court determines that there is insufficient evidence, it may decline to submit the case to the jury and instead enter judgment (historically called a directed verdict). In the alternative, the court can submit the case to the jury and if the jury returns a verdict for which there is insufficient evidentiary support, the court may enter judgment notwithstanding the verdict (historically referred to as a JNOV*). The standard for directed verdict and JNOV is the same as the standard for summary judgment—"whether a fair-minded jury could return a verdict for the plaintiff on the evidence presented." *Anderson v. Liberty Lobby, Inc.*, 477 U.S. at 252.

Rule 50 was amended in 1991 and changed the terminology. Directed verdict is now a "motion for judgment as a matter of law" (JMOL) and the JNOV is now a renewed motion for judgment as a matter of law. Despite the name change in the Rule, "directed verdict" and "JNOV" are still sometimes used in federal practice and are widely used in most state practice.

Summary judgment and a JMOL entered prior to submission to the jury have the effect of taking some cases away from juries. Why don't these procedures violate the Seventh Amendment? In Galloway v. United States, 319 U.S. 372 (1943), the Court upheld the constitutionality of these procedures explaining that at common law there were equivalent (though not identical) mechanisms for withdrawing cases from juries. But see Suja A. Thomas, *Why Summary Judgment is Unconstitutional*, 93 Va. L. Rev. 139 (2007); John Bronsteen, *Against Summary Judgment*, 75 Geo. Wash. L. Rev. 522 (2007).

A JNOV (JMOL granted after a jury verdict) presents a somewhat trickier problem. The Seventh Amendment provides "no fact tried by a jury, shall be otherwise reexamined in any Court of the United States, than according to the rules of the common law." At common law, there was no procedure equivalent to JNOV. After first holding that JNOV was unconstitutional, see Slocum v. New York Life Insurance Co., 228 U.S. 364 (1913), the Court found a way to uphold the procedure. In Baltimore & Carolina Line, Inc. v. Redman, 295 U.S. 654 (1935), the Court upheld JNOV where the defendant had moved for a directed verdict and the trial court submitted the case to the jury, but expressly reserved its ruling on the motion. The theory was that JNOV was simply a delayed ruling on a directed verdict.

Notice how this principle is now incorporated into Rule 50(b). The Rule provides that if a motion for JMOL is denied, "the court is considered to have submitted the action to the jury subject to the court's later deciding the legal questions raised by the motion." The Rule also allows a party to file a "renewed" motion for JMOL, but

---

* The letters JNOV stand for "judgment non obstante veredicto."

a motion can be renewed only if there was a prior motion. An earlier version of Rule 50 required not only that there have been a preverdict motion, but that the motion had been made "at the close of all the evidence." This requirement had proved to be a trap for the unwary and was eliminated in 2006. You should note, however, that not all timing traps have been eliminated—a renewed motion for JMOL must be filed within 28 days after the entry of a judgment and this time limit cannot be enlarged by the court. See 9B Wright & Miller, Federal Practice & Procedure § 2537, at 628–31.

Suppose a party moves for JMOL before the case is submitted to the jury and then does not renew the motion after the verdict. May the trial court grant a renewed JMOL on its own motion? The Supreme Court has stated that in the absence of such a timely motion, the trial court lacks authority to enter a JMOL. Johnson v. New York, New Haven & Hartford R.R., 344 U.S. 48, 50 (1952). Though a few courts have dismissed this as dicta, the widely accepted rule is that a motion by a party is required. See 9 Moore's Federal Practice § 50.05[5][b].

Is JMOL proper in any of the following situations?

(a) Plaintiff presents overwhelming evidence in her favor. At the close of the presentation of her evidence, Plaintiff moves for JMOL.

(b) Plaintiff and Defendant both present their evidence. Neither side moves for JMOL. After the case has been submitted to the jury, but before a verdict has been returned, Defendant moves for JMOL.

(c) At the close of all the evidence, Defendant moves for JMOL, stating, "Your Honor, plaintiff just hasn't proved her case." The motion is denied. Following a verdict and judgment for Plaintiff, Defendant again moves for JMOL.

(d) Both sides present their evidence and neither moves for JMOL. Following a jury verdict for Plaintiff, the judge on her own concludes that there was insufficient evidence. Can the judge enter JMOL?

(e) Defendant moves for JMOL at the close of all the evidence. The court denies the motion. After the jury returns a verdict for Plaintiff, the court, without motion from Defendant, grants JMOL.

(f) Defendant moves for JMOL at the close of all the evidence. After verdict for Plaintiff, the court enters judgment, and Defendant immediately makes an oral motion for JMOL. Defendant doesn't get around to filing a written motion for JMOL until thirty days after entry of judgment.

We turn now to the standard for granting JMOL.

Lavender v. Kurn

327 U.S. 645, 66 S. Ct. 740, 90 L. Ed. 916 (1946)

Justice Murphy delivered the opinion of the Court.

The Federal Employers' Liability Act permits recovery for personal injuries to an employee of a railroad engaged in interstate commerce if such injuries result "in whole or in part from the negligence of any of the officers, agents, or employees of such carrier, or by reason of any defect or insufficiency, due to its negligence, in its cars, engines, appliances, machinery, track, roadbed, works, boats, wharves, or other equipment."

Petitioner, the administrator of the estate of L.E. Haney, brought this suit under the Act against the respondent trustees of the St. Louis-San Francisco Railway Company (Frisco) and the respondent Illinois Central Railroad Company. It was charged that Haney, while employed as a switch-tender by the respondents in the switch yard of the Grand Central Station in Memphis, Tennessee, was killed as a result of respondents' negligence. Following a trial in the Circuit Court of the City of St. Louis, Missouri, the jury returned a verdict in favor of petitioner and awarded damages in the amount of $30,000. Judgment was entered accordingly. On appeal, however, the Supreme Court of Missouri reversed the judgment, holding that there was no substantial evidence of negligence to support the submission of the case to the jury. We granted certiorari to review the propriety of the Supreme Court's action under the circumstances of this case.

It was admitted that Haney was employed by the Illinois Central, or a subsidiary corporation thereof, as a switch-tender in the railroad yards near the Grand Central Station, which was owned by the Illinois Central. His duties included the throwing of switches for the Illinois Central as well as for the Frisco and other railroads using that station. For these services, the trustees of Frisco paid the Illinois Central two-twelfths of Haney's wages; they also paid two-twelfths of the wages of two other switch-tenders who worked at the same switches. In addition, the trustees paid Illinois Central $1.87 1/2 for each passenger car switched into Grand Central Station, which included all the cars in the Frisco train being switched into the station at the time Haney was killed.

The Illinois Central tracks run north and south directly past and into the Grand Central Station. About 2,700 feet south of the station the Frisco tracks cross at right angles to the Illinois Central tracks. A west-bound Frisco train wishing to use the station must stop some 250 feet or more west of this crossing and back into the station over a switch line curving east and north. The events in issue center about the switch several feet north of the main Frisco tracks at the point where the switch line branches off. This switch controls the tracks at this point.

It was very dark on the evening of December 21, 1939. At about 7:30 p.m. a west-bound interstate Frisco passenger train stopped on the Frisco main line, its rear some 20 or 30 feet west of the switch. Haney, in the performance of his duties, threw or opened the switch to permit the train to back into the station. The respondents claimed that Haney was then required to cross to the south side of the track before the train passed the switch; and the conductor of the train testified that he saw Haney so cross. But there was also evidence that Haney's duties required him to wait at the switch north of the track until the train had cleared, close the switch, return to his shanty near the crossing and change the signals from red to green to permit trains on the Illinois Central tracks to use the crossing. The Frisco train cleared the switch, backing at the rate of 8 or 10 miles per hour. But the switch remained open and the signals still were red. Upon investigation Haney was found north of the track near the switch lying face down on the ground, unconscious. An ambulance was called, but he was dead upon arrival at the hospital.

Haney had been struck in the back of the head, causing a fractured skull from which he died. There were no known eyewitnesses to the fatal blow. Although it is not clear, there is evidence that his body was extended north and south, the head to the south. Apparently he had fallen forward to the south; his face was bruised on the left side from hitting the ground and there were marks indicating that his toes had dragged a few inches southward as he fell. His head was about 5 1/2 feet north of the Frisco tracks. Estimates ranged from 2 feet to 14 feet as to how far west of the switch he lay.

The injury to Haney's head was evidenced by a gash about two inches long from which blood flowed. The back of Haney's white cap had a corresponding black mark about an inch and a half long and an inch wide, running at an angle downward to the right of the center of the back of the head. A spot of blood was later found at a point 3 or 4 feet north of the tracks. The conclusion following an autopsy was that Haney's skull was fractured by "some fast moving small round object." One of the examining doctors testified that such an object might have been attached to a train backing at the rate of 8 or 10 miles per hour. But he also admitted that the fracture might have resulted from a blow from a pipe or club or some similar round object in the hands of an individual.

Petitioner's theory is that Haney was struck by the curled end or tip of a mail hook hanging down loosely on the outside of the mail car of the backing train. This curled end was 73 inches above the top of the rail, which was 7 inches high. The overhang of the mail car in relation to the rails was about 2 to 2 1/2 feet. The evidence indicated that when the mail car swayed or moved around a curve the mail hook might pivot, its curled end swinging out as much as 12 to 14 inches. The curled end could thus be swung out to a point 3 to 3 1/2 feet from the rail and about 73 inches above the top of the rail. Both east and west of the switch, however, was an uneven mound of cinders and dirt rising at its highest points 18 to 24 inches above the top of the rails. Witnesses differed as to how close the mound approached the rails, the estimates varying from 3 to 15 feet. But taking the figures most favorable to the petitioner, the mound extended to a point 6 to 12 inches north of the overhanging side of the mail car. If the mail hook end swung out 12 to 14 inches it would be 49 to 55 inches above the highest parts of the mound. Haney was 67 1/2 inches tall. If he had been standing on the mound about a foot from the side of the mail car he could have been hit by the end of the mail hook, the exact point of contact depending upon the height of the mound at the particular point. His wound was about 4 inches below the top of his head, or 63 1/2 inches above the point where he stood on the mound—well within the possible range of the mail hook end.

Respondents' theory is that Haney was murdered. They point to the estimates that the mound was 10 to 15 feet north of the rail, making it impossible for the mail hook end to reach a point of contact with Haney's head. Photographs were placed in the record to support the claim that the ground was level north of the rail for at least 10 feet. Moreover, it appears that the area immediately surrounding the switch was quite dark. Witnesses stated that it was so dark that it was impossible to see a 3-inch pipe 25 feet away. It also appears that many hoboes and tramps frequented the area at night in order to get rides on freight trains. Haney carried a pistol to protect himself. This pistol was found loose under his body by those who came to his rescue. It was testified, however, that the pistol had apparently slipped out of his pocket or scabbard as he fell. Haney's clothes were not disarranged and there was no evidence of a struggle or fight. No rods, pipes or weapons of any kind, except Haney's own pistol, were found near the scene. Moreover, his gold watch and diamond ring were still on him after he was struck. Six days later his unsoiled billfold was found on a high board fence about a block from the place where Haney was struck and near the point where he had been placed in an ambulance. It contained his social security card and other effects, but no money. His wife testified that he "never carried very much money, not very much more than $10." Such were the facts in relation to respondents' theory of murder.

Finally, one of the Frisco foremen testified that he arrived at the scene shortly after Haney was found injured. He later examined the fireman's side of the train very carefully and found nothing sticking out or in disorder. In explaining why he examined this side of the train so carefully he stated that while he was at the scene of the accident "someone said they thought that train No. 106 backing into Grand Central Station is what struck this man" and that Haney "was supposed to have been struck by something protruding on the side of this train." The foreman testified that these statements were made by an unknown Illinois Central switchman standing near the fallen body of Haney. The foreman admitted that the switchman "didn't see the accident...." This testimony was admitted by the trial court over the strenuous objections of respondents' counsel that it was mere hearsay falling outside the *res gestae* rule.

The jury was instructed that Frisco's trustees were liable if it was found that they negligently permitted a rod or other object to extend out from the side of the train as it backed past Haney and that Haney was killed as the direct result of such negligence, if any. The jury was further told that Illinois Central was liable if it was found that the company negligently maintained an unsafe and dangerous place for Haney to work, in that the ground was high and uneven and the light insufficient and inadequate, and that Haney was injured and killed as a direct result of the said place being unsafe and dangerous. This latter instruction as to Illinois Central did not require the jury to find that Haney was killed by something protruding from the train.

The Supreme Court, in upsetting the jury's verdict against both the Frisco trustees and the Illinois Central, admitted that "It could be inferred from the facts that Haney could have been struck by the mail hook knob if he were standing on the south side of the mound and the mail hook extended out as far as 12 or 14 inches." But it held that "all reasonable minds would agree that it would be mere speculation and conjecture to say that Haney was struck by the mail hook" and that "plaintiff failed to make a submissible case on that question." It also ruled that there "was no substantial evidence that the uneven ground and insufficient light were causes or contributing causes of the death of Haney." Finally, the Supreme Court held that the testimony of the foreman as to the statement made to him by the unknown switchman was inadmissible under the *res gestae* rule since the switchman spoke from what he had heard rather than from his own knowledge.

We hold, however, that there was sufficient evidence of negligence on the part of both the Frisco trustees and the Illinois Central to justify the submission of the case to the jury and to require appellate courts to abide by the verdict rendered by the jury.

The evidence we have already detailed demonstrates that there was evidence from which it might be inferred that the end of the mail hook struck Haney in the back of the head, an inference that the Supreme Court admitted could be drawn. That inference is not rendered unreasonable by the fact that Haney apparently fell forward toward the main Frisco track so that his head was 5 1/2 feet north of the rail. He may well have been struck and then wandered in a daze to the point where he fell forward. The testimony as to blood marks some distance away from his head lends credence to that possibility, indicating that he did not fall immediately upon being hit. When that is added to the evidence most favorable to the petitioner as to the height and swing-out of the hook, the height and location of the mound and the nature of Haney's duties, the inference that Haney was killed by the hook cannot be said to be unsupported by probative facts or to be so unreasonable as to warrant taking the case from the jury.

It is true that there is evidence tending to show that it was physically and mathematically impossible for the hook to strike Haney. And there are facts from which it might reasonably be inferred that Haney was murdered. But such evidence has become irrelevant upon appeal, there being a reasonable basis in the record for inferring that the hook struck Haney. The jury having made that inference, the respondents were not free to relitigate the factual dispute in a reviewing court. Under these circumstances it would be an undue invasion of the jury's historic function for an appellate court to weigh the conflicting evidence, judge the credibility of witnesses and arrive at a conclusion opposite from the one reached by the jury.

It is no answer to say that the jury's verdict involved speculation and conjecture. Whenever facts are in dispute or the evidence is such that fair-minded men may draw different inferences, a measure of speculation and conjecture is required on the part of those whose duty it is to settle the dispute by choosing what seems to them to be the most reasonable inference.

Only when there is a complete absence of probative facts to support the conclusion reached does a reversible error appear. But where, as here, there is an evidentiary basis for the jury's verdict, the jury is free to discard or disbelieve whatever facts are inconsistent with its conclusion. And the appellate court's function is exhausted when that evidentiary basis becomes apparent, it being immaterial that the court might draw a contrary inference or feel that another conclusion is more reasonable.

We are unable, therefore, to sanction a reversal of the jury's verdict against Frisco's trustees. Nor can we approve any disturbance in the verdict as to Illinois Central.

The evidence was uncontradicted that it was very dark at the place where Haney was working and the surrounding ground was high and uneven. The evidence also showed that this area was entirely within the domination and control of Illinois Central despite the fact that the area was technically located in a public street of the City of Memphis. It was not unreasonable to conclude that these conditions constituted an unsafe and dangerous working place and that such conditions contributed in part to Haney's death, assuming that it resulted primarily from the mail hook striking his head.

In view of the foregoing disposition of the case, it is unnecessary to decide whether the allegedly hearsay testimony was admissible under the *res gestae* rule. Rulings on the admissibility of evidence must normally be left to the sound discretion of the trial judge in actions under the Federal Employers' Liability Act. But inasmuch as there is adequate support in the record for the jury's verdict apart from the hearsay testimony, we need not determine whether that discretion was abused in this instance.

The judgment of the Supreme Court of Missouri is reversed and the case is remanded for whatever further proceedings may be necessary not inconsistent with this opinion.

Reversed.

Notes and Questions

1. In *Lavender*, what reasonable rationale could the jury have used to find Illinois Central liable? To find Frisco liable?

2. If you had been on the *Lavender* jury, how would you have voted in the case? Why? Would it have been proper for the jury to decide for the plaintiff on the theory that of the two theories (the mail hook vs. the hobo), the mail hook theory was the more likely? Consider Reeves v. Sanderson Plumbing Prods., 530 U.S. 133 (2000), an age discrimination case. Under federal discrimination law, once the plaintiff establishes a prima facie case of discrimination, the employer must proffer a nondiscriminatory explanation for the challenged conduct. The burden then shifts to the employee to show that the proffered explanation was pretext. In *Reeves*, the plaintiff presented sufficient evidence to meet the requirements for a prima facie case. He also introduced evidence that his employer's proffered nondiscriminatory explanation for the firing was pretextual. The jury returned a verdict for the plaintiff, and the trial court entered judgment in his favor, refusing to enter JMOL. The Fifth Circuit reversed, holding that although plaintiff had stated a prima facie case and also had sufficient evidence from which a jury could conclude that the employer's explanation was pretextual, these were not sufficient to meet the plaintiff's burden of proving that he was fired because of his age. The Supreme Court reversed. It held that proof that the defendant's explanation is not credible is "one form of circumstantial evidence that is probative of intentional discrimination."

3. Compare *Lavender* with Reid v. San Pedro, Los Angeles & Salt Lake R.R., 118 P. 1009 (Utah 1911). In *Reid*, a cow got onto a railroad right-of-way and was killed

by a train. The right-of-way was protected by a fence for which the railroad was responsible. If the cow got onto the right-of-way through an open gate, the railroad was not liable but if the cow came through a break in the fence, it was liable. The jury returned a verdict for the cow's owner. In holding that the judge should have entered JNOV for the railroad, the Utah Supreme Court explained:

> There is no direct evidence as to where the cow got on to the right of way. It is conceded, however, that she was killed in the immediate vicinity of the gate mentioned, and, as shown by the evidence, about one mile from the point where the fence inclosing the right of way was down and out of repair. The inference, therefore, is just as strong, if not stronger, that she entered upon the right of way through the open gate as it is that she entered through the fence at the point where it was out of repair. The plaintiff held the affirmative and the burden was on her to establish the liability of the defendant by a preponderance of the evidence. It is a familiar rule that where the undisputed evidence of the plaintiff, from which the existence of an essential fact is sought to be inferred, points with equal force to two things, one of which renders the defendant liable and the other not, the plaintiff must fail. So in this case, in order to entitle respondent to recover it was essential for her to show by a preponderance of the evidence that the cow entered upon the right of way through the broken down fence. This the respondent failed to do.

Id. at 1010. In *Lavender*, as in *Reid*, did the evidence point with equal force to the two possible theories?

4. Consider the facts of Wratchford v. S.J. Groves & Sons Co., 405 F.2d 1061 (4th Cir. 1969). Late at night, the plaintiff parked his car on the eastbound shoulder of a country road. He apparently intended to walk across the east and westbound lanes of the road to a market, where he could purchase groceries on his way home from work. The next morning, he was found at the bottom of an open highway drainage hole which was in the median of the road, between the east and westbound lanes. He had a fractured skull and was totally incapacitated. He had retrograde amnesia, meaning that he could recall nothing about the event. His car keys were found in the bottom of the hole, and there were blood stains on the side of the hole near where his head was.

His representative sued the construction company doing work on the median, alleging that it had negligently failed to put a grate over the hole and to erect a barricade or warning light around the hole. The defendant contended that the injured person had slipped on ice several feet from the open hole, and sustained his head injuries in that slip, after which he slid or crawled into the hole. In the defendant's view, then, the fall into the hole was not the proximate cause of the injuries. On these facts, the district judge concluded that the evidence showed that the injury could have been caused with equal probability in either way, and he entered judgment as a matter of law for the defendant. The Fourth Circuit reversed and remanded the case, noting:

> Permissible inferences must still be within the range of reasonable probability * * * and it is the duty of the court to withdraw the case from the jury when the necessary inference is so tenuous that it rests merely upon speculation and conjecture. * * * Had Wratchford's body and car keys not been found in the hole, had there been no stains on the side of the hole near where his head was, stains believed to have been blood, the probability that he received his injury as a result of a step into the hole may have been so slight as to require the direction of a verdict for the defendants. The probability that he received his injury as a result of a step into the hole is here, at least, equally as great as the probability that he was injured before entering the hole, and the situation is not complicated by a multitude of other competing inferences, the existence of which would diminish the probability of the injury's having been sustained in the manner the plaintiffs' theory suggests.

Id. at 1066. The court concluded that the case should have been submitted to a jury "instructed that * * * plaintiffs must persuade them by the preponderance of the evidence that the injury was sustained as a result of a step into the hole rather than in an earlier fall on the ice." Id. How could the plaintiff discharge that burden on this evidence without encouraging the jury to engage in speculation?

5. In ruling on a motion for JMOL, what evidence should the court consider? In *Lavender*, for example, suppose the defendant had produced a witness who testified that she saw a "hobo" attack Haney, or suppose that it had produced a video tape showing a "hobo" attacking Haney. Should this additional evidence affect the court's ruling on JMOL? Some courts have held that in ruling on JMOL, the court should consider only the evidence produced by the non-moving party. In Reeves v. Sanderson Plumbing Prods., 530 U.S. 133 (2000), the Supreme Court rejected this approach and held that the court should review "all of the evidence in the record," not just the evidence favorable to the non-moving party. Thus, in federal court, in ruling on a motion for JMOL, the court "may consider all of the evidence favorable to the position of the party opposing the motion for judgment as a matter of law as well as any unfavorable evidence that the jury is required to believe." 9B Wright & Miller, Federal Practice & Procedure § 2529 at 470. Therefore, the court "may take into account evidence supporting the moving party that is uncontradicted and unimpeached, at least to the extent that evidence comes from disinterested witnesses." Id. at 473–74. However, where evidence is conflicting, the court should not make credibility assessments — that is the role of the jury.

6. As discussed earlier, a party moving for judgment as a matter of law must so move before submission of the case to the jury. If the judge grants the motion, the jury is dismissed and judgment entered. If the judge denies the motion, and there is an adverse jury verdict, that party may renew her motion (provided that she moved for JMOL at a proper time at trial). Given that the test for JMOL before submission to a jury and after a verdict is the same, why would a judge ever deny the motion before submission, but then grant the motion after the verdict? One court of appeals has explained:

> We have in the past cautioned trial judges that it is preferable, "in the best interests of efficient judicial administration," to refrain from granting a motion for a directed verdict and instead to allow the case to be decided—at least in the first instance—by the jury. Pursuant to the recommended practice, if the jury reaches what the judge considers to be an irrational verdict, the judge may grant a motion for judgment notwithstanding the verdict. If this ruling is reversed on appeal, the jury's verdict may simply be reinstated. If, however, a verdict has been directed and that ruling is reversed on appeal, an entire new trial must be held.

Konik v. Champlain Valley Physicians Hosp., 733 F.2d 1007, 1013 n.4 (2d Cir. 1984).

7. Some read *Lavender* as adopting a "scintilla of evidence" test—that is, holding that all the plaintiff need have is some scintilla of evidence to support his theory. You will recall that in *Anderson*, the Court rejected the scintilla test for summary judgment and, as we have noted, said that the test for summary judgment is the same as the test for directed verdict and JNOV. The plaintiff's claim in *Lavender* was based on the Federal Employers' Liability Act (FELA). Thus, if *Lavender* does adopt a scintilla test, its application may be confined to FELA and other related statutory negligence cases. See Edward Cooper, *Directions for Directed Verdicts: A Compass for Federal Court*, 55 MINN. L. REV. 903, 926–27 (1971).

8. The original suit in *Lavender* was brought in state court. Although the plaintiff's claim was based on federal law (the Federal Employers' Liability Act (FELA)), the defendant could not have removed the case to federal court because 28 U.S.C. § 1445 specifically prohibits removal of claims arising under FELA. (The federal court has jurisdiction if the plaintiff chooses to file there originally; § 1445 simply prohibits removal where the plaintiff has chosen state court.) In addition, because railroads are likely to be subject to personal jurisdiction in many states, a plaintiff suing a railroad under FELA is likely to have a choice of forum. Notice that in *Lavender*, the accident occurred in Tennessee, but suit was filed in St. Louis, Missouri.

2. New Trials

Judgment as a matter of law gives the court one tool to control juries. But JMOL is available only where the evidence is so weak for one side that no reasonable jury could find for that side. It thus permits court intervention only in limited and extreme circumstances. Suppose, however, that there is sufficient evidence that JMOL is inappropriate. Nonetheless, the court strongly disagrees with the jury's verdict and thinks it was against the heavy weight of the evidence. Under these circumstances, should we give the court any power to override the jury's verdict? If we had complete confidence in juries, the answer to this question would likely be no. Nonetheless, Rule 59 provides a mechanism for some court intervention under these circumstances by allowing the court to order a new trial. Notice that in ordering a new trial, the judge is not directly substituting her view of the evidence. The determination of who wins and loses will be left to a jury—but, to a new jury.

Rule 59 gives courts authority to grant new trials "for any reason for which a new trial has heretofore been granted in an action at law in federal court." Rule 59(a)(1)(A). We consider now the circumstances under which courts may order new trials.

Dadurian v. Underwriters at Lloyd's of London

787 F.2d 756 (1st Cir. 1986)

CAMPBELL, CHIEF JUDGE.

This diversity case arose out of the refusal of defendant-appellant Lloyd's, London ("Lloyd's") to indemnify plaintiff-appellee Paul Dadurian after he claimed the loss of certain jewelry that he allegedly owned and that had been insured under a Lloyd's insurance policy. As affirmative defenses to the suit for nonpayment, Lloyd's asserted that Dadurian's claim was fraudulent and that Dadurian had knowingly made false statements about facts material to his claim. The jury entered special verdicts favorable to Dadurian, resulting in his recovering $267,000 plus interest. Lloyd's moved for judgment notwithstanding the verdict, or alternatively, for a new trial. The United States District Court for the District of Rhode Island denied the motion, and Lloyd's now appeals. As we find the jury's verdict was against the great weight of the evidence, we vacate and remand for a new trial.

I

Dadurian claimed that he purchased 12 pieces of "specialty" jewelry for investment purposes over a period of 30 months, from August 1977 to January 1980. The pieces allegedly ranged in price from $12,000 to $35,000, costing him $233,000 in total. Dadurian testified that he purchased all the jewelry from James Howe, a jeweler in Providence, Rhode Island, and paid for each item in cash. Dadurian did not present any sales slips, receipts or other documents of transfer reflecting any of his alleged purchases; and Howe not only presented no records of his sale of the jewelry to Dadurian, but he could not remember from whom he had originally obtained the jewelry and had no records showing that the jewelry had ever actually been in his possession.

On or about March 2, 1980, Dadurian purchased a "Jewelry Floater" policy from Lloyd's, which insured him against loss of the 12 items of jewelry. The jewelry pieces were described on an attached schedule, which also set forth the maximum amount recoverable for each piece. The maximum recoverable under the policy was $267,000. Dadurian obtained the insurance coverage on the strength of eight appraisal certificates for the jewelry, which were prepared by Howe at Dadurian's request. Some certificates were dated on the same day as certain of the alleged purchases, while the others were dated months later.

Dadurian claimed that on or about April 12, 1980, armed robbers entered his home and forced him to open his safe, where the jewelry was kept. He was shot in the right shoulder, allegedly by one of the robbers, and was taken to the hospital. It is Dadurian's contention that the insured pieces of jewelry were stolen during the robbery. After preliminary investigation by an adjuster representing Lloyd's, Dadurian was asked to appear for a formal examination under oath by counsel for Lloyd's. The examination took place on September 10, 1980, and again on May 28, 1981. Because of alleged false and fraudulent statements made under oath by Dadurian at this examination, Lloyd's refused to indemnify Dadurian for the claimed losses.

On March 31, 1982, Dadurian brought this action in the district court seeking compensation for his losses under the jewelry insurance policy issued by Lloyd's. The action was tried before a jury from October 29 through November 5, 1984. The jury rendered four special verdicts, all favorable to Dadurian: that Dadurian had been robbed on April 12, 1980; that he had not given false answers or information on any material subject when he was examined under oath before the commencement of this suit; that he had not made any false statement or fraudulent claims as to any of the 12 jewelry items for which he claimed a loss; and that the total fair market value of all the jewelry on April 12, 1980, was $267,000. Judgment was entered for plaintiff in the amount of $267,000 with interest.

Pursuant to Fed. R. Civ. P. 50, Lloyd's moved for judgment n.o.v. or, in the alternative, for a new trial. The district court denied defendant's motion, and this appeal followed.

II

Lloyd's argues on appeal that Dadurian swore falsely, and necessarily knowingly, with respect to at least two key issues, and that either instance of false swearing was sufficient to void the insurance policy. First, Dadurian is said to have clearly lied in asserting that he purchased and owned the 12 pieces of jewelry for which he later obtained the insurance; and second, he is said to have knowingly lied in telling Lloyd's, at the formal examination under oath conducted before this action was begun, that the cash he used to purchase the jewelry came from certain bank loans. Lloyd's contends that evidence presented at trial was so overwhelmingly against Dadurian on both these issues that no reasonable jury could have rendered a verdict in his favor.

A. The Purchase of the Jewelry

Pointing to the suspicious absence of documentation for any of the jewelry purchases, Lloyd's asserts that the record shows that Dadurian had sworn falsely when he testified to having purchased the jewelry at all. Dadurian procured the Lloyd's insurance on the basis of written appraisals executed by Howe, the man from whom he allegedly purchased all 12 pieces. But he obtained no receipts nor did Howe have any records of the alleged sales to Dadurian. Moreover, although Dadurian testified to specific dates and prices paid for each of his jewelry purchases, in support of his story of ownership, his testimony that he had obtained that information from Howe's records was contradicted by testimony that Howe kept no such records.

But whatever may be thought of Dadurian's story, we cannot say, as a matter of law, that no jury could have properly found that Dadurian had purchased the jewelry as he claimed. Nor can we say the verdict on this issue was so far contrary to the clear weight of the evidence as, by itself, to provide grounds for our ordering the district court to grant a new trial. Not only did Howe testify at trial that he sold each one of the jewelry pieces to Dadurian at the prices Dadurian claimed, but Howe's employees, Cheryl Cousineau and Edward Proulx, gave testimony which, in material respects, tended to support the story that Dadurian purchased at least some jewelry items from Howe with cash. And Howe and Cousineau testified that they did not usually give receipts for cash purchases of "investment jewelry" or of jewelry sold "on consignment," thus tending to explain why Dadurian had no receipts. Despite extensive cross-examination by counsel for Lloyd's, the jury apparently chose to credit the testimony of Dadurian and his witnesses, and the jury was entitled to overlook the lack of any documentation for the purchases.

B. The Source of the Funds

Lloyd's also argues that Dadurian knowingly lied under oath at the formal examination when he swore that certain specific bank loans were the source of the cash he used to buy the jewelry. If Dadurian swore falsely and knowingly on this issue, he is not entitled to recover under the insurance contract. This is so because under the Lloyd's policy Dadurian was required to give "such information and evidence as to the property lost and the circumstances of the Loss as the Underwriters may reasonably require and as may be in the Assured's power" — and it is undisputed that under the policy, as well as under established case law, knowingly false testimony by Dadurian as to any fact considered "material" to his claim voids the policy.

The district court instructed the jury, and Dadurian does not dispute, that the issue of where he obtained the cash used for his jewelry purchases was "material" to his claim. To be considered material, a statement need not "relate[] to a matter or subject which ultimately proves to be decisive or significant in the ultimate disposition of the claim"; rather, it is sufficient if the statement was reasonably relevant to the insurance company's investigation of a claim. We agree that where Dadurian got the cash was material to his insurance claim, since Dadurian insisted that he paid Howe a total of $223,000 in cash over a 30-month period for the jewelry, and the credibility of this story, and hence of Dadurian's ownership of the insured items, turned in part on his ability to explain plausibly where he obtained such large sums of cash.[5]

The details of Dadurian's testimony about the bank loans are as follows: Soon after the alleged robbery of the jewelry items in April 1980, Dadurian was interviewed by an adjuster for Lloyd's. At this initial interview Dadurian, to explain the sources of his cash, stated that he "may have borrowed from the bank for the purchase of certain of the personal items of jewelry and [would] check [his] records in this regard." He later submitted to Lloyd's certain promissory notes which he contended represented the bank loans used to finance many of his purchases. Apparently still dissatisfied with the information provided by Dadurian, Lloyd's notified Dadurian in a letter dated August 18, 1980, that he would be required to appear at a formal exam-

5. Lloyd's was understandably interested in hearing Dadurian's explanation of the source of his cash, particularly when it discovered that in 1978, the year Dadurian allegedly bought four of the twelve jewelry items for a total of $90,000 in cash, his income as reported in his federal tax return was only about $3,000.

ination under oath for further questioning at which time he "should be prepared to produce all documents in any way relating to the occurrence of the loss...."

At the first examination session on September 10, 1980, and again at the second session on May 28, 1981, when he was examined under oath by counsel for Lloyd's, Dadurian testified to the effect that most of his cash had come from loans from the Rhode Island Hospital Trust National Bank ("Hospital Trust").[7] During the two sessions, Dadurian was specifically questioned in turn about the sources of the cash used to purchase each one of the jewelry pieces. For 11 of the 12 items, Dadurian identified the individual promissory notes of his—by date and by loan amount—that purportedly represented the bank loans he said was used to finance his purchases. In total, he identified 13 specific bank loans as the source of $166,000 of the $233,000 which he claimed to have paid to Howe.

At trial, however, Richard Niedzwiadek, an employee of the bank, testified that the loans associated with four of the jewelry pieces, totaling $49,500, were simply renewals of earlier loans which could not have generated any cash for Dadurian. He also produced bank statements for Dadurian's accounts at Hospital Trust showing that the proceeds from several other loans which Dadurian had identified as having financed a number of the jewelry pieces had been deposited in those accounts and then withdrawn in too small amounts over a period of time to have been used for purchasing the jewelry as Dadurian claimed. Niedzwiadek further testified that the proceeds of yet another loan supposedly associated with a jewelry item had been deposited in the corporate account of a company named U.S. Enterprises, Inc., and that Dadurian had stated the purpose of the loan as "real estate investment."[9] Confronted with this cumulative evidence, Dadurian essentially conceded that some, if not most, of the promissory notes he had selected had been the wrong ones, and that his testimony as to the sources of the funds was therefore in part false. He insisted, however, that he had selected the notes "to the best of [his] recollection" and that he had been honestly mistaken.

Since it is thus uncontroverted that a substantial number of Dadurian's representations under oath about the sources of his cash were untrue, the only remaining

---

7. Dadurian testified during his September 1980 examination as follows:

> If you want to know how I wound up with the cash, how all this jewelry was paid up in cash, how I got all the cash for the jewelry, the insurance company has copies of these. (indicating) These are all bank notes. When a good piece of jewelry came along for the right price, which I had to pay for in cash, I went to the bank. I borrowed from the bank, borrowed the money on notes, and the [insurance] company has these copies which you may take them if you like, and you may make copies of them. That's how I purchased the jewelry.

I have a quarter of a million dollars loss, and the money came from here from bank notes. I still owe this bank. I borrowed this money, and it's as simple as that.

9. According to the bank records presented at trial, Dadurian did not state the purchase of jewelry as the purpose for obtaining any of the bank loans; and for four of the nine non-renewal loans, Dadurian specifically stated that he would use the loans for real estate investment, working capital, or his used car business.

question is whether Dadurian made these false statements *knowingly* or whether he was simply mistaken in good faith as he claims. False swearing is "swearing knowingly and intentionally false and not through mere mistake." Black's Law Dictionary 725 (rev. 5th ed. 1979). Lloyd's forcefully contends that where Dadurian testified with such certainty, yet incorrectly, about so many of his own promissory notes and bank loans, the inference of intentional falsehood is so compelling as to render the jury's finding contrary, at very least, to the great weight of the evidence.

After carefully considering the entire record, we find that the great weight of the evidence indicates overwhelmingly that Dadurian knew he was giving false testimony. At the formal examination under oath Dadurian specifically identified 13 promissory notes, apparently from those he had given Lloyd's sometime before the examination, and explicitly linked each note to a particular jewelry purchase. He did not qualify his identifications, but rather couched his testimony in terms of misleading certainty. Only when confronted at trial with the patent falsity of his earlier testimony did Dadurian testify, by way of explanation, that he had made his selections only to the "best of his recollection" in order to satisfy the insurance company's inquiries. It was only then that he explained that because he had "files and files" of such notes in his possession,[10] he must have simply selected the wrong ones under pressure of time and circumstances.

This explanation strains credulity. This was not a case where Dadurian was confronted for the first time at the examination with "files and files" of his promissory notes and asked to come up with correct ones "on the spot." Rather it was Dadurian himself who originated and put forward the story that most of his cash had come from bank loans, and it was Dadurian who apparently first tendered the supposedly relevant promissory notes to Lloyd's at some time before the formal examination. Dadurian admitted at trial that he had known before the first examination session that he would be questioned further about the bank loans. He apparently marked each of the notes before the examination sessions with the number of the jewelry piece with which it was supposedly associated. By the first session in September 1980, and certainly by the May 1981 session, Dadurian had had ample notice as well as opportunity to discover the correct promissory notes or, if he found he was wrong or in doubt, to say so. The uncontested facts simply belie Dadurian's excuse that he was pressured into making identifications prematurely.

Dadurian had much to gain by providing a plausible explanation for the sources of his cash. By piecing together notes executed on dates close to the times of the alleged purchases, he could hope to create an impression of credibility. That he linked the notes to the jewelry purchases so positively — without bothering to ascertain readily available information showing that they were not so related — indicates, at the least, a wilful misrepresentation as to the state of his own knowledge concerning the matters to which he was testifying. We think the only fair inference from this

10. At one point in his testimony at trial, Dadurian stated that he had "maybe ... 50, 60, 70 notes" in his possession.

kind of total indifference to the truth or falsity of his assertions was that Dadurian knew that he was not telling the truth.

It follows, we believe, that the jury's verdict was against the clear weight of the evidence insofar as it found that Dadurian did not knowingly give false answers or information on any material subject when he was examined under oath before commencement of this suit.[11] We emphasize that Dadurian himself conceded that some of his answers were incorrect, and it is clear the district court properly found them "material." This leaves open only the question of their possible innocence, which, to be sure, Dadurian attested to—but with implausible explanations as to why he put forward these patently unfounded and incorrect assertions. We conclude that the jury's finding that Dadurian did not give knowingly false answers was contrary to the great weight of the evidence. For that aspect of the verdict to stand would, in our view, amount to a manifest miscarriage of justice. We hold, therefore, that the district court abused its discretion in denying defendant's motion for a new trial, and remand the case for retrial by a new jury.

We are mindful of the alternative plea by Lloyd's that we should reverse the court's refusal to grant a judgment n.o.v. and, in effect, direct a finding for Lloyd's rather than order a new trial. Whether to do so is a very close question. A factor weighing against this alternative is that Lloyd's had the burden of proving that Dadurian was lying, and this circuit, like most courts, is reluctant to direct a verdict for the party having the burden of proof. The issue, moreover, involves a determination of credibility. Hence, even though we find it hard to see how a reasonable jury could reach any result other than that Dadurian was knowingly lying, we believe that the more appropriate relief is a new trial.

A remaining question is whether the new trial should encompass both the issue of Dadurian's ownership of the jewelry and the issue of his knowingly false testimony as to the sources of his funds. We hold that it should, even though it was on the latter issue that the district court erred. Dadurian's credibility is cast into serious doubt by our finding that the clear weight of the evidence shows that he must have knowingly lied about a material issue. It follows that this loss of credibility necessarily affects the jury finding in Dadurian's favor on the issue of his jewelry purchases, since Dadurian was his own main witness for all aspects of his story. A new trial as to both issues also makes sense since the issue of where Dadurian obtained the cash to make his purchases is so interrelated with the question of whether Dadurian bought the

11. It strikes us that the jury may not have paid sufficient attention to determining whether Dadurian had knowingly lied as to the sources of his cash. There were many issues raised at trial. Once the jury concluded that Dadurian had indeed purchased the jewelry as he alleged, it could have thought that the issue of Dadurian's false swearing as to the bank loans was a mere technicality. But, as we discussed, a finding that Dadurian had knowingly given false testimony as to any material fact voids the policy just as a finding that Dadurian had not owned the jewelry would have voided it. It is possible that the jury, despite instructions in the jury charge to the contrary, decided on its own that since Lloyd's had insured the jewelry it should pay for its loss, regardless of whether Dadurian lied as to the source of his funds.

jewelry he claimed as to make it difficult to hold a meaningful trial on the first without the second.

Vacated and remanded for a new trial.

Notes and Questions

1. *Dadurian* raises two issues. First, what is the standard by which a district court decides whether to grant a new trial? Second, what is the standard of review by which an appellate court reviews the decision of the district court? These two issues are discussed separately below.

2. A district court may order a new trial on grounds that the verdict is against the clear weight of the evidence. As *Dadurian* illustrates, a new trial may be granted even though there is sufficient evidence to preclude JMOL. In ruling on a new trial, the judge is permitted to weigh the evidence and is not required to view the evidence in the light most favorable to the non-moving party. Nonetheless, courts have been admonished not to substitute their

> judgment of the facts and credibility of the witnesses for that of the jury. Such an action effects a denigration of the jury system and to the extent that new trials are granted the judge takes over, if he does not usurp, the prime function of the jury as the trier of fact.

Lind v. Schenley Indus., Inc., 278 F.2d 79, 90 (3d Cir. 1960). Professors Wright and Miller have explained the test as follows: "If, having given full respect to the jury's findings, the judge on the entire evidence is left with the definite and firm conviction that a mistake has been committed, it is to be expected that he will grant a new trial." 11 Wright & Miller, Federal Practice & Procedure § 2806 at 75.

An illustration of a case in which the trial judge impermissibly substituted his judgment for that of the jury is Latino v. Kaizer, 58 F.3d 310, 316 (7th Cir. 1995). There the district court judge had granted the new trial because he found inherently unbelievable the defendants' story that they had observed the plaintiffs trying to sell four tickets to a Chicago Bulls playoff game. In ruling that the grant of a new trial was improper, the court of appeals explained: "Preferring to sell all of one's tickets for a steep profit rather than to actually attend a Bulls-Lakers game might seem inherently incredible to a diehard fan, but legally it is not so."

3. In *Dadurian*, the court of appeals reversed the trial court's denial of a new trial. This is extremely rare, and some courts have held that the denial of a motion for new trial on grounds of sufficiency of the evidence was not reviewable. See, e.g., Stonewall Ins. Co. v. Asbestos Claims Mgmt. Corp., 73 F.3d 1178, 1199 (2d Cir. 1995); Portman v. American Home Products Corp., 201 F.2d 847, 848 (2d Cir. 1953). In Gasperini v. Center for Humanities, Inc., 518 U.S. 415 (1996), infra Chapter 10, Section B.3.c, the Supreme Court upheld such review provided that the appellate court applies an "abuse of discretion" standard of review.

4. Suppose that following a second trial in *Dadurian*, the jury finds for the plaintiff. Should the trial court grant another new trial?

5. Suppose that the trial in *Lavender* had occurred in federal court:

(a) Upon a proper motion, would it have been reversible error for the trial court to grant a new trial?

(b) Upon a proper motion, would it have been reversible error for the trial court not to grant a new trial?

(c) Could the trial court have granted a new trial on its own, without a motion by a party?

(d) Suppose the defendants had never moved for JMOL. Could they properly move for a new trial?

6. The judge may grant a new trial on grounds of misconduct by counsel or other unfairness at trial or because of newly discovered evidence. As with all motions for a new trial, even a motion on grounds of new evidence must be made within 28 days of the judgment. However, if a party discovers new evidence more than 28 days after the judgment, she may move for relief under Rule 60(b)(2), provided the motion is filed no later than one year after entry of the judgment.

7. The court may grant a new trial on grounds that the size of the verdict is contrary to the weight of the evidence. Federal courts frequently assert that the test is whether the size of the verdict "shock[s] the conscience of the Court," Nye v. Fenton, 496 F. Supp. 136, 139 (D. Kan. 1980), or is "so grossly excessive that it is not rationally related to any evidence adduced at trial." Warner v. Lawrence, 754 F. Supp. 449, 456 (D.V.I. 1991). In contrast, state law may require or permit greater scrutiny by courts of the size of the verdict. In *Gasperini*, the Supreme Court held that in a diversity action in federal court, the federal district court should apply the state standard in reviewing the size of the verdict. For an interesting discussion of problems relating to assessment of punitive damages, see Colleen P. Murphy, *Judgment as a Matter of Law on Punitive Damages*, 75 TUL. L. REV. 459 (2000).

8. When the amount of the verdict is excessive, the district court may use "remittitur" as an alternative to ordering a new trial. For example, if the jury returned a verdict of $6 million for the plaintiff, the court might offer the plaintiff the option of accepting a verdict of $1 million as an alternative to a new trial. The plaintiff is not required to accept the amount, but if she rejects it, the court will order a new trial. The converse of remittitur is "additur," in which the court finds that the verdict is unreasonably low and gives the defendant the choice of a specified higher verdict or a new trial. The Supreme Court has held that remittitur is permitted under the Seventh Amendment, provided the court offers the plaintiff the option of a new trial. See Hetzel v. Prince William County, 523 U.S. 208 (1998) (per curiam). See generally Suja Thomas, *Re-Examining the Constitutionality of Remittitur Under the Seventh Amendment*, 64 OHIO ST. L. REV. 731 (2003). On the other hand, the Supreme Court concluded long ago, in a much-criticized opinion, that additur violates the Seventh Amendment. Dimick v. Schiedt, 293 U.S. 474 (1935). Thus, additur is unconstitutional in federal court. Because the Seventh Amendment does not apply in state court, however, many state courts permit additur.

9. A party disappointed with a jury verdict may renew her motion for judgment as a matter of law (assuming that she preserved the right to do so) and, in the alternative, request a new trial. If the court grants the JMOL, its ruling on the new trial motion would seem to be unnecessary. However, the court must "conditionally" rule on the new trial motion, essentially stating what its ruling on the new trial request would be in the event the JMOL is reversed. See Rule 50(c)(1).

A party wanting to protect the option of a new trial should be sure to press the trial court to rule on the conditional new trial motion. Consider Arenson v. Southern University Law Center, 43 F.3d 194 (5th Cir. 1995). After a jury returned a verdict in the plaintiff's favor, the defendant renewed his motion for judgment as a matter of law and moved, in the alternative, for a new trial. The district court granted the JMOL and did not rule on the new trial. After the JMOL was reversed on appeal, the defendant sought a ruling from the district court on the new trial. The district court granted the new trial, and the defendant won at the second trial. The plaintiff appealed and won on the ground that the grant of the new trial was improper.

Acknowledging that "no matter how it comes out, our decision will not be entirely just," the court of appeals reversed, explaining that Rule 50(c) is a "use-it-or-lose-it" provision. Id. at 196. Defendant failed to "use" its right to seek a new trial by failing to obtain a ruling after the grant of the JMOL and by failing to note on appeal its new trial motion. Thus, defendant lost the right to seek a new trial after the JMOL was reversed and the district court erred in granting a new trial on remand. Consequently, the defendant's victory in the second trial was reversed. Is this pushing "use-it-or-lose-it" too far?

10. Remittitur and new trials are techniques that are used after the jury verdict to respond to an excessive award. The litigants can also enter into a private agreement in advance of the submission to the jury which guarantees some minimum recovery but also caps liability. These so-called "high-low agreements" are a type of partial settlement whereby the case goes to the jury, but the parties agree that regardless of what the jury decides, the damages will be within some set range. See Samuel Gross & Kent Syverud, *Don't Try: Civil Jury Verdicts in a System Geared to Settlement*, 62 UCLA L. Rev. 1, 62 (1996). High-low agreements are common in tort cases with uncertain liability but large potential damages. These agreements are considered legal and enforceable. See Hoops v. Watermelon City Trucking, Inc., 846 F.2d 637 (10th Cir. 1988).

3. Other Techniques for Controlling Juries

a. Admissibility of Evidence

Not everything that a litigant may want the fact finder to consider will necessarily be admissible under the rules of evidence. For example, under the Federal Rules of Evidence, a litigant's criminal record will usually be inadmissible, as will privileged material and hearsay (subject to a number of hearsay exceptions). The rules also allow the judge to exclude evidence where "its probative value is substantially outweighed by the danger of unfair prejudice, confusion of the issues, or misleading the jury." Fed. R. Evid. 403.

One area of evidence that has generated significant discussion and concern is expert witnesses. Many observers have expressed concern that jurors may be unduly swayed by expert testimony and may be unable to differentiate "junk science" from reliable scientific opinion. On the other hand, expert testimony may be essential for the plaintiff to establish an element of her claim. Litigation may turn on issues such as whether a drug causes birth defects, a chemical causes cancer or a medical implant causes particular side effects. Proof of such claims will necessarily turn on expert evidence. But who should be considered an expert and how much testing or investigating must the expert have done before we will permit her to testify about her conclusions?

In Daubert v. Merrell Dow Pharmaceuticals, 509 U.S. 579 (1993), the Supreme Court held that trial judges must act as the gatekeepers for expert evidence and assure that an expert's testimony rests on a reliable foundation. The Court enumerated a number of factors that the trial court should consider, including whether the expert's conclusions have been subjected to peer review and publication, and the degree to which the expert's approach and conclusions have been accepted within the scientific community. Id. at 593–94. See Fed. R. Evid. 702. Subsequently, the Court has held that the "gatekeeping" function described in *Daubert* applies to the testimony of all experts, not only scientific experts. Kumho Tire Co. v. Carmichael, 526 U.S. 137 (1999).

The facts of *Daubert* highlight the significance of the judge's gatekeeping function. The plaintiffs in *Daubert* alleged that they had suffered birth defects as a result of their mothers' prenatal ingestion of the drug Bendectin. The defendant's expert reviewed the literature on Bendectin and concluded that none of the studies found that Bendectin caused birth defects. In contrast, the plaintiffs' experts re-analyzed a number of previously published studies and concluded that Bendectin can cause birth defects. The plaintiffs' experts' analysis had been prepared specifically for the litigation and had never been published or peer reviewed. The trial court found that the plaintiffs' experts' technique of re-analysis had not been accepted as reliable within the scientific community. The court therefore excluded the plaintiffs' experts and granted the defendant's motion for summary judgment on grounds that the plaintiffs could not prove causation. Note that the critical determinations concerning the reliability of scientific evidence were made by the judge, not the jury.

Even if a plaintiff is successful in getting expert testimony admitted, there are further risks associated with relying too heavily on such evidence. Consider Weisgram v. Marley Co., 528 U.S. 440 (2000). There, the trial court admitted certain expert testimony, and the jury returned a verdict for the plaintiff. The defendant moved for a JMOL and in the alternative for a new trial, arguing that the testimony of the plaintiff's expert was unreliable and inadmissible. The trial court rejected these motions and entered judgment for the plaintiff. On appeal, the court of appeals held that that expert's testimony should have been excluded and, without it, there was insufficient evidence to support the jury's verdict. The court of appeals entered judgment for the defendant and did not order a new trial. Thus, the plaintiff had no opportunity to present his case with alternative evidence that might have filled the hole created by the excluded expert testimony. The Supreme Court held that Rule 50 permits appellate courts to enter JMOL without a remand or new trial. In addition, the Court found that there was no unfairness to this approach noting that "[s]ince *Daubert*, * * * parties relying on expert evidence have had notice of the exacting standards of reliability such evidence must meet." See Rule 50 (e).

b. Jury Instructions

Earlier we saw that a court may grant summary judgment where there is no genuine issue of material fact. That standard distinguishes between disputes of fact and of law, and is premised on the understanding that matters of law are properly decided by the court, not the jury. This division of responsibility is also reflected in jury instructions. The judge determines what the law is and then instructs the jury about it. The jury's job is to resolve disputes of fact and then apply the law to the facts.

Jury instructions provide another mechanism for controlling juries. They identify and define the elements of each claim or defense, explain which party has the burden of proof and what the burden of persuasion is. Although there is no guarantee that juries will in fact follow instructions, the instructions can focus the jury's attention on particular matters and provide a structure for the deliberations.

It is the judge's job to instruct the jury orally on the relevant law. Even in simple cases, the judge's oral instructions can last 30 minutes to an hour. Traditionally, juries were not permitted to take notes on the instructions, nor were they given a written copy. This rule stemmed from a concern that jurors would improperly focus on a single phrase in the instructions rather than taking them as a whole. Faced with increasingly complex law and instructions, resourceful juries have found ways around this. In one libel case, for example, the jury asked that a copy of the instructions be sent into the jury room. The judge refused but told the jurors he would read the instructions again. The jury foreman later explained what the jury did:

> [W]e agreed before we went back in to have the judge read the instructions again that since the judge said we could not take notes, that we would divide up what was being said, and we would all come back and remember the part we were each assigned, and we would write it down when we got back into the jury room.

David Branson & Andrea Johnson, *Aids Needed for Jury to Understand Instructions*, Legal Times Of Washington, March 5, 1984 at A9. Increasingly today, judges give jurors written copies of the instructions or a tape recording of the oral instructions.

Errors in jury instructions are a common basis for appeal and reversal. As a result, courts tend to rely on jury instructions that have been previously challenged and upheld. Unfortunately, such instructions, while legally accurate, are not always easy for lay juries to understand. Consider this standard jury instruction on proximate cause:

> The proximate cause is that which, in the natural and continuous sequence, unbroken by other causes, produces an event, and without which the event would not have occurred. Proximate cause is that which is nearest in the order of responsible causes, as distinguished from remote, that which stands last in causation, not necessarily in time or place, but in causal relation. It is sometimes called the dominant cause.

1 SUGGESTED PATTERN JURY INSTRUCTIONS 231 (3d ed. 1991) (for Georgia).

Some states have begun to rewrite jury instructions into "plain English." For example, an instruction such as: "Failure of recollection is common. Innocent misrecollection is not uncommon," may be replaced with: "People often forget things or make mistakes in what they remember." Leonard Post, *Spelling it out in plain English: Calif. simplifies its jury instructions*, NAT'L L.J., Nov. 8, 2004 at 1.

c. *Form of the Verdict*

In most civil cases, the jury renders a general verdict, that is, it announces who wins and how much, but does not indicate its rationale or how it resolved particular issues. Rule 49 offers alternatives to the general verdict.

Rule 49(a) authorizes use of the special verdict by which the court asks the jury to decide one or more specific factual questions but is not asked to decide the bottom-line issue of who wins or loses. Proponents of the special verdict claim, because the questions focus the jury's attention on the critical disputed facts, and the jury never actually decides who wins and who loses, its decision will be more scientific and less subject to prejudices. This argument assumes that juries will be unable to determine, or at least guess, which side benefits from a particular factual conclusion. Moreover, some question the desirability of making jury verdicts more scientific. Dissenting from the adoption of the 1963 amendments to the Federal Rules of Civil Procedure, Justices Black and Douglas wrote of Rule 49:

> Such devices are used to impair or wholly take away the power of a jury to render a general verdict. One of the ancient, fundamental reasons for having general jury verdicts was to preserve the right of trial by jury as an indispensable part of a free government. Many of the most famous constitutional controversies in England revolved around litigants' insistence, particularly in seditious libel cases, that a jury had the right to render a general verdict without being compelled to return a number of subsidiary findings to support its general verdict. Some English jurors had to go to jail because they insisted upon their right to render general verdicts over the repeated commands of tyrannical judges not to do so. Rule 49 is but another means utilized by courts to weaken the constitutional power of juries and to vest judges with more power to decide cases according to their own judgments. A scrutiny of the special verdict and written interrogatory cases in appellate courts will show the confusion that necessarily results from the employment of these devices and the ease with which judges can use them to take away the right to trial by jury. We believe that Rule 49 should be repealed, not amplified.

374 U.S. 861, 867–68 (1963).

At a practical level, it is not always easy to write a set of unambiguous questions. Courts that use special verdicts must often deal with apparently inconsistent answers. See, e.g., Gallick v. Baltimore & Ohio R.R., 372 U.S. 108 (1963) (no fatal inconsistency where jury answered foreseeability interrogatories in negative, but still found negligence).

Rule 49(b) allows the use of a general verdict supplemented with one or more specific questions. As with the special verdict, this can be used to focus the jury's attention on particular issues, although, here too, ambiguity and inconsistent answers sometimes result.

d. Judicial Comment

In federal court, the judge is not limited merely to instructing the jury on the law. The judge is also permitted to comment on the evidence and express her opinion on factual issues. As the Supreme Court has explained:

> In a trial by jury in a federal court, the judge is not a mere moderator, but is the governor of the trial for the purpose of assuring its proper conduct and of determining questions of law. In charging the jury, the trial judge is not limited to instructions of an abstract sort. It is within his province, whenever he thinks it necessary, to assist the jury in arriving at a just conclusion by explaining and commenting upon the evidence, by drawing their attention to the parts of it which he thinks important; and he may express his opinion upon the facts, provided he makes it clear to the jury that all matters of fact are submitted to their determination.

Quercia v. United States, 289 U.S. 466, 469 (1933). Despite this apparently broad range for judicial comment, the Court held that the following comment by the trial judge went too far in invading the province of the jury:

> And now I am going to tell you what I think of the defendant's testimony. You may have noticed, Mr. Foreman and gentlemen, that he wiped his hands during his testimony. It is rather a curious thing, but that is almost always an indication of lying. Why it should be so we don't know, but that is the fact. I think that every single word that man said, except when he agreed with the Government's testimony, was a lie.

Id. at 468.

e. Juror Misconduct

Suppose that following a jury verdict, interviews with jurors revealed that they misunderstood the instructions, flipped a coin to decide the case, were intoxicated during deliberations or were bribed. Would this information be a basis to overturn the verdict?

The common law rule was that the affidavits of jurors could not be used to impeach their verdict. Although this rule was framed as a rule of evidence, which made jurors' testimony inadmissible, its effect was to insulate from review most types of juror misconduct, because frequently the jurors themselves will be the only source of evidence.

What are the costs and benefits of insulating jury conduct from scrutiny? The justifications for the traditional rule are:

> (1) the need for stability of verdicts; (2) the need to protect jurors from fraud and harassment by disappointed litigants; (3) the desire to prevent prolonged litigation; (4) the need to prevent verdicts from being set aside because of subsequent doubts or change of attitude by a juror; (5) the concept of the sanctity of the jury room.

Sopp v. Smith, 377 P.2d 649, 653 (Cal. 1963) (Peters, J., dissenting). To what extent does the traditional rule meet these goals? Are these goals of sufficient importance to justify the rule? Are there some kinds of jury conduct (or misconduct) that should be subject to scrutiny?

Some jurisdictions have modified the traditional approach and adopted instead what has come to be called "the Iowa rule." This approach is based upon the distinction between extrinsic and intrinsic influences. Extrinsic influences involve overt acts which may be objectively corroborated or disproved. Extrinsic influences include a juror conducting an independent investigation of the facts outside the courtroom, or the jury using an illegal method of reaching a verdict (such as flipping a coin). Evidence concerning extrinsic influences is admissible. Intrinsic influences are matters known only to the individual juror, such as a juror's thought processes, motives, misunderstandings, or prejudices. Intrinsic influences are not readily capable of being either corroborated or disproved and are, therefore, excluded. Intrinsic influences are sometimes said to "inhere in the verdict."

Rule 606(b) of the Federal Rules of Evidence provides:

> Upon an inquiry into the validity of a verdict or indictment, a juror may not testify as to any matter or statement occurring during the course of the jury's deliberations or to the effect of anything upon that or any other juror's mind or emotions as influencing the juror to assent to or dissent from the verdict or indictment or concerning the juror's mental processes in connection therewith. But a juror may testify about (1) whether extraneous prejudicial information was improperly brought to the jury's attention, (2) whether any outside influence was improperly brought to bear upon any juror, or (3) whether there was a mistake in entering the verdict on the verdict form. A juror's affidavit or evidence may not be received on a matter about which he would be precluded from testifying.

Under this rule, could a juror testify that members of the jury were under the influence of drugs or alcohol during the trial or deliberations? Would this constitute an "outside influence" that was improperly brought to bear? In Tanner v. United States, 483 U.S. 107 (1987), the Supreme Court held that such evidence was *not* admissible to impeach a verdict. According to the juror whose testimony was not admissible, several of the jurors regularly had several alcoholic drinks during lunch and regularly smoked marijuana during the trial. Two other jurors ingested cocaine on multiple occasions. Justice O'Connor explained that "[h]owever severe their effect and improper their use, drugs or alcohol voluntarily ingested by a juror seems no more an 'outside influence' than a virus, poorly prepared food, or a lack of sleep." Id. at 122. Is taking cocaine really equivalent to having indigestion? Mr. Tanner's felony conviction was upheld despite the alleged outrageous conduct of the jury. Was this just?

Suppose that some jurors made racially derogatory remarks to other jurors concerning one of the parties. Would this be a basis to grant a new trial? The Florida Supreme Court, applying Florida law, held that a new trial was proper under these circumstances. Powell v. Allstate Ins. Co., 652 So. 2d 354 (Fla. 1995). The court concluded that because the racially biased remarks were spoken, not merely thought privately, they constituted "sufficient 'overt acts' to permit trial court inquiry." The court further reasoned that "the conduct alleged herein, if established, [would] be violative of the guarantees of both the federal and state constitutions which ensures all litigants a fair and impartial jury and equal protection of the law." Would the verdict in *Powell* be subject to impeachment under Federal Evidence Rule 606? See Carson v. Polley, 689 F.2d 562, 581 (5th Cir. 1982) (racially biased remark by juror not admissible to impeach verdict). Does it make sense for the federal courts to prohibit race-based use of peremptory challenges, but to allow blatant racism within the jury once it is selected?

Suppose that after the verdict, you learn that one of the jurors gave an incorrect answer during voir dire. Is that a basis for a new trial? In McDonough Power Equipment, Inc. v. Greenwood, 464 U.S. 548, 555–56 (1984), the Supreme Court held that incorrect voir dire answers provide a basis for a new trial in only limited circumstances:

> To invalidate the result of a 3-week trial because of a juror's mistaken, though honest, response to a question, is to insist on something closer to perfection than our judicial system can be expected to give. A trial represents an important investment of private and social resources, and it ill serves the important end of finality to wipe the slate clean simply to recreate the peremptory challenge process because counsel lacked an item of information which objectively he should have obtained from a juror on voir dire examination. * * * We hold that to obtain a new trial in such a situation, a party must first demonstrate that a juror failed to answer honestly a material question on voir dire, and then further show that a correct response would have provided a valid basis for a challenge for cause. The motives for concealing information may vary, but only those reasons that affect a juror's impartiality can truly be said to affect the fairness of a trial.

The Court returned to the area in Warger v. Shauers, 135 S. Ct. 521 (2014). There, the plaintiff in a vehicle crash case moved for new trial based upon the affidavit of one juror that another juror concealed at voir dire that her daughter had been involved in a crash and that her life would have been ruined had she been sued. If the juror had admitted this view in voir dire, she would have been stricken for cause as lacking impartiality. The Court unanimously held that the evidence was inadmissible under Federal Rule of Evidence 606(b). The evidence concerned an "internal" matter concerning the juror and did not constitute extrinsic evidence concerning the case.

An increasingly common problem is jurors using the Internet to do independent research on a case. In one case, an eight-week criminal trial ended in a mistrial when the judge learned that nine of twelve jurors had done Internet research on the case. See *As Jurors Turn to Google and Twitter, Mistrials Are Popping Up*, N.Y. Times, March 1, 2009, at A1. Some courts are beginning to limit jurors' use of cell phones in the courthouse, but unless the jury is sequestered, there is nothing other than the judge's instructions to prevent jurors from doing research at home. See also Russo v. Takata Corp., 774 N.W.2d 441 (S.D. 2009) (granting a new trial in a civil case because a juror did Internet research on the defendant and shared the results with rest of the jury).

Chapter 10

What Law Applies in Federal Court

A. Introduction and Integration

As mentioned in earlier chapters, when an issue is controlled by state law, a court frequently faces the question of which state's law applies. Each state has its own choice of law rules to answer this question. You may study the various choice of law rules in a different course, usually entitled "Choice of Law" or "Conflict of Laws." The problem of which of several states' laws apply is sometimes referred to as a "horizontal" choice of law problem. For purposes of this course we need to understand that there are choice of law rules, that these rules vary among the states, and that, as a result, different states may apply different laws to the same incident or transaction.

This chapter focuses on a "vertical" choice of law problem, that is, whether federal or state law governs a decision. Students sometimes assume that federal courts only apply federal law, but that is not the case. As we already saw in personal jurisdiction, absent a federal provision, a federal court has personal jurisdiction only if the state court in which it sits has personal jurisdiction. As you will see in this chapter, federal courts apply state law on other matters as well.

Our starting point for analyzing when federal courts apply state law is the Rules of Decision Act, the original version of which was contained in Section 34 of the Judiciary Act of 1789. The current version, codified at 28 U.S.C. § 1652, provides:

> The laws of the several states, except where the Constitution or treaties of the United States or Acts of Congress otherwise require or provide, shall be regarded as rules of decision in civil actions in the courts of the United States, in cases where they apply.

Notice that the statute requires the use of state law only if there is no federal statute, treaty, or constitutional provision on point. The Supremacy Clause in Article VI of the Constitution makes federal law "the supreme law of the land." Because of the Supremacy Clause, Congress may, if it wishes, completely preempt state law in a particular area so long as Congress has authority to legislate in that area. For example, Congress could pass a statute requiring that all interstate railroads provide at least an eight-foot right-of-way on either side of the track. Such a statute would preempt or override a conflicting state statute requiring only a one-foot right of way.

Whether a federal statute preempts state law depends entirely on the meaning of that federal statute. Thus, in the right of way example, suppose that the federal statute requires a two-foot right-of-way but one state requires three feet. Whether the federal statute preempts the state law turns on whether Congress intended the federal statute merely to provide a minimum standard or instead to provide a nationwide uniform standard. In answering this question, a court would ascertain the intent of Congress from the statutory language and, when appropriate, from the legislative history. If the court determined that the federal statute was on point and preemptive, then that federal statute would apply, not only in federal court, but also in state court.

If no preemptive federal law is on point, then the Rules of Decision Act provides that "the laws of the several states * * * shall be regarded as rules of decision." Close examination of the statute raises several questions.

First, does this language mean that if there is no preemptive federal law, that state law controls as to every issue? If a state passes a statute that requires that no trial can start before 10 a.m. and there is no federal statute addressing this issue, would federal courts be required to abide by the state law? Notice that the Rules of Decision Act provides that state law shall be the "rules of decision." This phrase might mean that state law is required only as to those issues that concern the decision on the merits. In other words, it might refer only to laws relating to the substance of the claims and not to matters of procedure.

History provides some support for this view. Shortly after the First Congress passed the Judiciary Act, it passed another statute, the Process Act (later revised and called the Conformity Act), which required that federal courts apply state law concerning "the forms of writs and execution, except their style, and modes of process and rates of fees." Although this statute is no longer in effect, the fact that the First Congress thought it necessary might suggest that Congress believed that at least some matters of procedure were not covered by § 34 of the Judiciary Act. There is, however, little legislative history available on the Rules of Decision Act, so this argument is largely speculative.

It is now accepted that the Rules of Decision Act does not require the use of state law on all matters. As a rough generalization, one can say that where there is no preemptive federal law, state law applies on all substantive matters, but not on procedural matters. As we will see, however, the line between these two categories is uncertain and the labels of "substance" and "procedure" are not helpful as analytical tools.

Second, the Rules of Decision Act refers to the "laws of the several states." It does not specify which state law a federal court should apply. It is now established that a federal court is to apply the law that the state in which it sits would apply, but this result is not obvious from the language of the Rules of Decision Act.

Third, what is included within the phrase "laws of the several states"—does "laws" include common law doctrine as well as statutes? In Swift v. Tyson, 41 U.S. 1 (1842), the Supreme Court held that the "laws of the several states" included only statutory laws, plus court-made doctrine on matters of "local" law. However, according to the Court, that phrase did not include court-made doctrine on matters of "general" law. The Court explained:

> In the ordinary use of language, it will hardly be contended, that the decisions of courts constitute laws. They are, at most, only evidence of what the laws are; and are not, of themselves, laws. They are often re-examined, reversed, and qualified by the courts themselves, whenever they are found to be either defective, or ill-founded, or otherwise incorrect. The laws of a state are more usually understood to mean the rules and enactments promulgated by the legislative authority thereof, as long-established customs having the force of laws. * * * It never has been supposed by us, that the section did apply, or was designed to apply, to questions of a more general nature * * * as, for example, * * * questions of general commercial law * * *.

41 U.S. at 18–19.

The distinction between matters of general and local law proved elusive and produced great uncertainty. The legal realists of the twentieth century ridiculed the idea that judges' decisions are only "evidence of the law" and not law themselves. Judges make law every bit as much as legislatures do, the legal realists declared. It was against this backdrop that the Supreme Court decided Erie Railroad Co. v. Tompkins, 304 U.S. 64 (1938), a case later described by Justice Black as "one of the most important cases at law in American history." Hugo Black, *Address*, 13 MO. B.J. 173, 174 (1942).

B. Determining What Law Applies

1. The *Erie* Doctrine

Erie Railroad Co. v. Tompkins

304 U.S. 64, 58 S. Ct. 817, 82 L. Ed. 1188 (1938)

JUSTICE BRANDEIS delivered the opinion of the Court.

The question for decision is whether the oft-challenged doctrine of *Swift v. Tyson* shall now be disapproved.

Tompkins, a citizen of Pennsylvania, was injured on a dark night by a passing freight train of the Erie Railroad Company while walking along its right of way at Hughestown in that State. He claimed that the accident occurred through negligence in the operation, or maintenance, of the train; that he was rightfully on the premises as licensee because on a commonly used beaten footpath which ran for a short distance alongside the tracks; and that he was struck by something which looked like a door projecting from one of the moving cars. To enforce that claim he brought an action in the federal court for southern New York, which had jurisdiction because the company is a corporation of that State. It denied liability; and the case was tried by a jury.

The Erie insisted that its duty to Tompkins was no greater than that owed to a trespasser. It contended, among other things, that its duty to Tompkins, and hence its liability, should be determined in accordance with the Pennsylvania law; that under the law of Pennsylvania, as declared by its highest court, persons who use pathways along the railroad right of way—that is a longitudinal pathway as distinguished from a crossing—are to be deemed trespassers; and that the railroad is not liable for injuries to undiscovered trespassers resulting from its negligence, unless it be wanton or wilful. Tompkins denied that any such rule had been established by the decisions of the Pennsylvania courts; and contended that, since there was no statute of the State on the subject, the railroad's duty and liability is to be determined in federal courts as a matter of general law.

The trial judge refused to rule that the applicable law precluded recovery. The jury brought in a verdict of $30,000; and the judgment entered thereon was affirmed by the Circuit Court of Appeals, which held that it was unnecessary to consider whether the law of Pennsylvania was as contended, because the question was one not of local, but of general, law and that "upon questions of general law the federal courts are free, in the absence of a local statute, to exercise their independent judgment as to what the law is; and it is well settled that the question of the responsibility of a railroad for injuries caused by its servants is one of general law.... Where the public has made open and notorious use of a railroad right of way for a long period of time and without objection, the company owes to persons on such permissive pathway a duty of care in the operation of its trains.... It is likewise generally recognized law that a jury may find that negligence exists toward a pedestrian using a permissive path on the railroad right of way if he is hit by some object projecting from the side of the train."

The Erie had contended that application of the Pennsylvania rule was required, among other things, by §34 of the Federal Judiciary Act of September 24, 1789, [the Rules of Decision Act, now codified at 28 U.S.C. §1652] which provides:

> "The laws of the several States, except where the Constitution, treaties, or statutes of the United States otherwise require or provide, shall be regarded as rules of decision in trials at common law, in the courts of the United States, in cases where they apply."

Because of the importance of the question whether the federal court was free to disregard the alleged rule of the Pennsylvania common law, we granted certiorari.

First. Swift v. Tyson held that federal courts exercising jurisdiction on the ground of diversity of citizenship need not, in matters of general jurisprudence, apply the unwritten law of the State as declared by its highest court; that they are free to exercise an independent judgment as to what the common law of the State is—or should be; and that, as there stated by Justice Story:

> "the true interpretation of the thirty-fourth section limited its application to state laws strictly local, that is to say, to the positive statutes of the state, and the construction thereof adopted by the local tribunals, and to rights and titles to things having a permanent locality, such as the rights and titles to

> real estate, and other matters immovable and intraterritorial in their nature and character. It never has been supposed by us, that the section did apply, or was intended to apply, to questions of a more general nature, not at all dependent upon local statutes or local usages of a fixed and permanent operation, as, for example, to the construction of ordinary contracts or other written instruments, and especially to questions of general commercial law, where the state tribunals are called upon to perform the like functions as ourselves, that is, to ascertain upon general reasoning and legal analogies, what is the true exposition of the contract or instrument, or what is the just rule furnished by the principles of commercial law to govern the case."

The Court in applying the rule of § 34 to equity cases * * * said: "The statute, however, is merely declarative of the rule which would exist in the absence of the statute." The federal courts assumed, in the broad field of "general law," the power to declare rules of decision which Congress was confessedly without power to enact as statutes. Doubt was repeatedly expressed as to the correctness of the construction given § 34, and as to the soundness of the rule which it introduced. But it was the more recent research of a competent scholar, who examined the original document, which established that the construction given to it by the Court was erroneous; and that the purpose of the section was merely to make certain that, in all matters except those in which some federal law is controlling, the federal courts exercising jurisdiction in diversity of citizenship cases would apply as their rules of decision the law of the State, unwritten as well as written.[1]

Criticism of the doctrine became widespread after the decision of Black & White Taxicab Co. v. Brown & Yellow Taxicab Co., 276 U.S. 518 (1928). There, Brown and Yellow, a Kentucky corporation owned by Kentuckians, and the Louisville and Nashville Railroad, also a Kentucky corporation, wished that the former should have the exclusive privilege of soliciting passenger and baggage transportation at the Bowling Green, Kentucky, railroad station; and that the Black and White, a competing Kentucky corporation, should be prevented from interfering with that privilege. Knowing that such a contract would be void under the common law of Kentucky, it was arranged that the Brown and Yellow reincorporate under the law of Tennessee, and that the contract with the railroad should be executed there. The suit was then brought by the Tennessee corporation in the federal court for western Kentucky to enjoin competition by the Black and White; an injunction issued by the District Court was sustained by the Court of Appeals; and this Court, citing many decisions in which the doctrine of *Swift v. Tyson* had been applied, affirmed the decree.

Second. Experience in applying the doctrine of *Swift v. Tyson* had revealed its defects, political and social; and the benefits expected to flow from the rule did not accrue. Persistence of state courts in their own opinions on questions of common law prevented uniformity; and the impossibility of discovering a satisfactory line of de-

1. Charles Warren, *New Light on the History of the Federal Judiciary Act of 1789* (1923) 37 Harv. L. Rev. 49, 51–52, 81–88, 108.

marcation between the province of general law and that of local law developed a new well of uncertainties.[8]

On the other hand, the mischievous results of the doctrine had become apparent. Diversity of citizenship jurisdiction was conferred in order to prevent apprehended discrimination in state courts against those not citizens of the State. *Swift v. Tyson* introduced grave discrimination by non-citizens against citizens. It made rights enjoyed under the unwritten "general law" vary according to whether enforcement was sought in the state or in the federal court; and the privilege of selecting the court in which the right should be determined was conferred upon the non-citizen. Thus, the doctrine rendered impossible equal protection of the law. In attempting to promote uniformity of law throughout the United States, the doctrine had prevented uniformity in the administration of the law of the State.

The discrimination resulting became in practice far-reaching. This resulted in part from the broad province accorded to the so-called "general law" as to which federal courts exercised an independent judgment. In addition to questions of purely commercial law, "general law" was held to include the obligations under contracts entered into and to be performed within the State, the extent to which a carrier operating within a State may stipulate for exemption from liability for his own negligence or that of his employee; the liability for torts committed within the State upon persons resident or property located there, even where the question of liability depended upon the scope of a property right conferred by the State; and the right to exemplary or punitive damages. Furthermore, state decisions construing local deeds, mineral conveyances, and even devises of real estate were disregarded.

In part the discrimination resulted from the wide range of persons held entitled to avail themselves of the federal rule by resort to the diversity of citizenship jurisdiction. Through this jurisdiction individual citizens willing to remove from their own State and become citizens of another might avail themselves of the federal rule. And, without even change of residence, a corporate citizen of the State could avail itself of the federal rule by re-incorporating under the laws of another State, as was done in the *Taxicab* case.

The injustice and confusion incident to the doctrine of *Swift v. Tyson* have been repeatedly urged as reasons for abolishing or limiting diversity of citizenship jurisdiction. Other legislative relief has been proposed. If only a question of statutory construction were involved, we should not be prepared to abandon a doctrine so widely applied throughout nearly a century. But the unconstitutionality of the course pursued has now been made clear and compels us to do so.

---

8. Compare 2 Warren, The Supreme Court In United States History (rev. ed. 1935) 89: "Probably no decision of the Court has ever given rise to more uncertainty as to legal rights; and though doubtless intended to promote uniformity in the operation of business transactions, its chief effect has been to render it difficult for businessmen to know in advance to what particular topic the Court would apply the doctrine...." The Federal Digest, through the 1937 volume, lists nearly 1000 decisions involving the distinction between questions of general and of local law.

Third. Except in matters governed by the Federal Constitution or by Acts of Congress, the law to be applied in any case is the law of the State. And whether the law of the State shall be declared by its Legislature in a statute or by its highest court in a decision is not a matter of federal concern. There is no federal general common law. Congress has no power to declare substantive rules of common law applicable in a State whether they be local in their nature or "general," be they commercial law or a part of the law of torts. And no clause in the Constitution purports to confer such a power upon the federal courts. As stated by Justice Field when protesting in Baltimore & Ohio R. Co. v. Baugh, 149 U.S. 368, 401 (1893), against ignoring the Ohio common law of fellow servant liability:

> "I am aware that what has been termed the general law of the country—which is often little less than what the judge advancing the doctrine thinks at the time should be the general law on a particular subject—has been often advanced in judicial opinions of this court to control a conflicting law of a State. I admit that learned judges have fallen into the habit of repeating this doctrine as a convenient mode of brushing aside the law of a State in conflict with their views. And I confess that, moved and governed by the authority of the great names of those judges, I have, myself, in many instances, unhesitatingly and confidently, but I think now erroneously, repeated the same doctrine. But, notwithstanding the great names which may be cited in favor of the doctrine, and notwithstanding the frequency with which the doctrine has been reiterated, there stands, as a perpetual protest against its repetition, the Constitution of the United States, which recognizes and preserves the autonomy and independence of the States—independence in their legislative and independence in their judicial departments. Supervision over either the legislative or the judicial action of the States is in no case permissible except as to matters by the Constitution specifically authorized or delegated to the United States. Any interference with either, except as thus permitted, is an invasion of the authority of the State and, to that extent, a denial of its independence."

The fallacy underlying the rule declared in *Swift v. Tyson* is made clear by Justice Holmes. The doctrine rests upon the assumption that there is "a transcendental body of law outside of any particular State but obligatory within it unless and until changed by statute," that federal courts have the power to use their judgment as to what the rules of common law are; and that in the federal courts "the parties are entitled to an independent judgment on matters of general law":

> "but law in the sense in which courts speak of it today does not exist without some definite authority behind it. The common law so far as it is enforced in a State, whether called common law or not, is not the common law generally but the law of that State existing by the authority of that State without regard to what it may have been in England or anywhere else....
>
> "the authority and only authority is the State, and if that be so, the voice adopted by the State as its own [whether it be of its Legislature or of its Supreme Court] should utter the last word."

Thus the doctrine of *Swift v. Tyson* is, as Justice Holmes said, "an unconstitutional assumption of powers by courts of the United States which no lapse of time or respectable array of opinion should make us hesitate to correct." In disapproving that doctrine we do not hold unconstitutional § 34 of the Federal Judiciary Act of 1789 or any other Act of Congress. We merely declare that in applying the doctrine this Court and the lower courts have invaded rights which in our opinion are reserved by the Constitution to the several States.

Fourth. The defendant contended that by the common law of Pennsylvania as declared by its highest court * * * the only duty owed to the plaintiff was to refrain from wilful or wanton injury. The plaintiff denied that such is the Pennsylvania law. In support of their respective contentions the parties discussed and cited many decisions of the Supreme Court of the State. The Circuit Court of Appeals ruled that the question of liability is one of general law; and on that ground declined to decide the issue of state law. As we hold this was error, the judgment is reversed and the case remanded to it for further proceedings in conformity with our opinion.

Reversed.

Justice Cardozo took no part in the consideration or decision of this case.

Justice Reed.

I concur in the conclusion reached in this case, in the disapproval of the doctrine of *Swift v. Tyson*, and in the reasoning of the majority opinion except in so far as it relies upon the unconstitutionality of the "course pursued" by the federal courts.

To decide the case now before us and to "disapprove" the doctrine of *Swift v. Tyson* requires only that we say that the words "the laws" include in their meaning the decisions of the local tribunals. As the majority opinion shows, by its reference to Mr. Warren's researches and the first quotation from Justice Holmes, that this Court is now of the view that "laws" includes "decisions," it is unnecessary to go further and declare that the "course pursued" was "unconstitutional," instead of merely erroneous.

The "unconstitutional" course referred to in the majority opinion is apparently the ruling in *Swift v. Tyson* that the supposed omission of Congress to legislate as to the effect of decisions leaves federal courts free to interpret general law for themselves. I am not at all sure whether, in the absence of federal statutory direction, federal courts would be compelled to follow state decisions. There was sufficient doubt about the matter in 1789 to induce the first Congress to legislate. No former opinions of this Court have passed upon it. * * * If the opinion commits this Court to the position that the Congress is without power to declare what rules of substantive law shall govern the federal courts, that conclusion also seems questionable. The line between procedural and substantive law is hazy but no one doubts federal power over procedure. The Judiciary Article and the "necessary and proper" clause of Article One may fully authorize legislation, such as this section of the Judiciary Act.

In this Court, stare decisis, in statutory construction, is a useful rule, not an inexorable command. It seems preferable to overturn an established construction of an Act of Congress, rather than, in the circumstances of this case, to interpret the Constitution.

There is no occasion to discuss further the range or soundness of these few phrases of the opinion. It is sufficient now to call attention to them and express my own non-acquiescence.

Notes and Questions

1. In the Supreme Court, as in the lower courts, the parties in *Erie* framed their arguments in terms of *Swift v. Tyson*, with Tompkins arguing that the issue (the standard of care owed by the railroad to trespassers) was one of "general law" as to which federal courts could apply federal law, and the railroad arguing that the issue was one of "local law" controlled by state law. Neither party argued that *Swift v. Tyson* should be overruled. If you had represented Tompkins and the railroad had argued for overruling *Swift*, what arguments could you have made in support of *Swift*?

2. In his opinion in *Swift*, Justice Story supported his call for a general common law with Cicero's statement that the law cannot be one thing in Rome and another in Athens. 41 U.S. at 19. How would Justice Brandeis respond to this argument? Consider Justice Brandeis' arguments for overruling *Swift*. Which arguments do you find most persuasive?

3. As noted above, the railroad never directly attacked *Swift v. Tyson*. Indeed, at oral argument, when counsel for the railroad was asked whether *Swift* should be overruled, he replied that the doctrine was too well established to be overturned. The railroad's failure to attack *Swift* directly was not an oversight. On the contrary, as Professor Purcell has explained, the railroad's lawyer "did not attack *Swift* for a simple and compelling reason: he did not want it overturned." Edward Purcell, *The Story of* Erie: *How Litigants, Lawyers, Judges, Politics, and Social Change Reshape the Law*, *in* Civil Procedure Stories 21, 48 (K. Clermont ed., 2d ed. 2008). Diversity jurisdiction and the "general federal common law" applied by federal courts were highly valued by national companies such as railroads, because federal courts were perceived to be pro-business and the law applied by federal courts was generally more favorable to corporate interests than state law. See id. at 31–32. In fact, progressives had begun to view removal and the *Swift* doctrine as oppressive tools of big corporations. See Edward Purcell, Jr., Brandeis And The Progressive Constitution: *Erie*, The Judicial Power, And The Politics Of The Federal Courts In Twentieth-Century America 66–67 (2000). Thus, *Erie* may be seen as an anti-corporate decision. Of course, it is doubtful that Mr. Tompkins viewed the decision as anti-corporate.

4. Suppose a federal statute provided that railroads are not liable to trespassers injured on a railroad right-of-way. An injured trespasser files suit in federal court in a state in which property owners are liable for negligence toward trespassers. After *Erie*, must the federal court apply state law or the federal statute?

5. Justice Brandeis uses *Black & White Taxicab* as an illustration of the mischief caused by *Swift*. At the time of *Erie*, corporations were considered citizens only of

their state of incorporation for diversity purposes. Thus, as in *Black & White Taxicab*, a corporation could change its citizenship relatively easily by reincorporating in a different state. In 1958, Congress amended § 1332 to add subpart (c) which makes corporations also citizens of their principal place of business. See Chapter 4, Section C.3.d. Was *Erie* an overreaction to a problem with a simple statutory solution?

6. The Court refers to a draft of § 34 of the Judiciary Act discovered by Professor Charles Warren. That draft provided: "the Statute law of the several States in force for the time being and their unwritten or common law now in use, whether by adoption from the common law of England, the ancient statutes of the same or otherwise" shall be the rules of decision in federal court. The final version of the statute substituted the phrase "laws of the several states" in place of the longer draft version. Professor Warren concluded that the final version was intended to mean the same thing as the earlier version, and the change was simply stylistic. Charles Warren, *New Light on the History of the Federal Judiciary Act of 1789*, 37 HARV. L. REV. 49, 86 (1923). Is this the only possible explanation for the change?

Another historian, Wilfred Ritz, draws a different conclusion from this earlier draft. While he agrees that the change in language was probably stylistic, he argues that the draft demonstrates that "the laws of the several states" meant American law as opposed to English law. He concludes that § 34 of the Judiciary Act of 1789:

> is a direction to the national courts to apply American law, as distinguished from English law. American law is to be found in the "laws of the several states" viewed as a group of eleven states in 1789, and not viewed separately and individually. It is not a direction to apply the law of a particular state, for if it had been so intended, the section would have referred to the "laws of the respective states."

WILFRED J. RITZ, REWRITING THE HISTORY OF THE JUDICIARY ACT OF 1789, 148 (1990). See Patrick Borchers, *The Origins of Diversity Jurisdiction, The Rise of Legal Positivism, and a Brave New World for* Erie *and* Klaxon, 72 TEX. L. REV. 79 (1993).

7. Notice that although the Court decides that the state "laws" referred to in the Rules of Decision Act include all common law as well as statutory laws, the majority does not discuss whether reference to these state laws is required on absolutely every issue. Indeed, Justice Reed states in concurrence, that "no one doubts federal power over procedure." It is Justice Reed's concurrence that may have given birth to the jurisprudence of labels about "substance" and "procedure." See Gregory Gelfand & Howard Abrams, *Putting* Erie *on the Right Track*, 49 U. PITT. L. REV. 937, 958–64 (1988).

8. The accident in *Erie* occurred in Pennsylvania, but Tompkins filed suit in federal court in New York. Although the Court decided that the issue of standard of care was to be governed by state law, it did not discuss *which* state law controlled, though it assumed that the relevant law was that of Pennsylvania. A few years later, in Klaxon Co. v. Stentor Electric Mfg. Co., 313 U.S. 487 (1941), the Supreme Court held that in a diversity case, federal courts must follow the choice of law rules of the state in

which it sits. Thus, in *Erie*, the federal court in New York should apply whatever state's law a New York state court would apply. Because New York would have almost certainly applied Pennsylvania law (because that was the site of the accident), the Court's assumption in *Erie* that Pennsylvania law applied is not inconsistent with *Klaxon*. The *Klaxon* rule led Judge Friendly to observe in a diversity case, "Our principal task * * * is to determine what New York Courts would think California Courts would think on an issue about which neither has thought." Nolan v. Transocean Air Lines, 276 F.2d 280, 281 (2d Cir. 1960). Although some commentators have criticized *Klaxon*, see, e.g., William Baxter, *Choice of Law and the Federal System*, 16 STAN. L. REV. 1, 41–42 (1963), the Supreme Court reaffirmed its holding in Day & Zimmerman, Inc. v. Challoner, 423 U.S. 3, 4 (1975).

9. *Erie* has come to be understood as a cornerstone of our federalism. But the opinion was issued without much fanfare or immediate recognition of the opinion's significance. Then-Professor Frankfurter wrote to President Roosevelt: "I certainly didn't expect to live to see the day when the Court would announce, as they did on Monday, that it itself has usurped power for nearly a hundred years. And think of not a single New York paper — at least none that I saw — having a nose for the significance of such a decision. How fluid it all makes the Constitution." ROOSEVELT AND FRANKFURTER: THEIR CORRESPONDENCE 1928–45, at 456 (Max Freedman ed., 1967).

10. The year *Erie* was decided, 1938, marked dramatic change in federal court practice. With *Erie*, the federal courts began looking to state law on matters of substantive law that had previously been governed by federal common law. However, the year brought another dramatic change. In 1934, Congress had enacted the Rules Enabling Act authorizing the Supreme Court to promulgate a uniform set of procedural rules to be applied in the federal courts. An advisory committee worked for several years on these rules and in 1938 these rules went into effect. Thus, prior to 1938, federal courts, pursuant to the Conformity Act, applied state procedural rules but federal common law on matters of general law; whereas after 1938, federal courts applied federal procedural rules but state substantive law on matters covered by *Erie*. See Mary Kay Kane, *The Golden Wedding Year:* Erie Railroad Company v. Tompkins *and the Federal Rules*, 63 NOTRE DAME L. REV. 671 (1988). See also Jack Weinstein, *The Ghost of Process: The Fiftieth Anniversary of the Federal Rules of Civil Procedure and* Erie, 54 BROOK. L. REV. 1 (1988).

11. *Erie* can be understood as reflecting two jurisprudential trends of its era — realism and positivism. The realists argued that law is not a set of abstract rules but rather is the reality of what courts in fact do. As Justice Holmes famously explained, "The prophecies of what the courts will do in fact, and nothing more pretentious, are what I mean by the law." Oliver Wendell Holmes, Jr., *The Path of the Law*, 10 HARV. L. REV. 457, 461 (1897). Thus, it is not surprising that realists such as Justice Brandeis would conclude that "laws" include judge-made law. Positivists reject the existence of transcendent natural law and believe that all law is simply the command of a sovereign. Thus, for a positivist, all law is either state law or federal law — there can be no "general" law. As Justice Holmes argued in dissent in *Black & White Taxi-*

cab, there is "no transcendental body of law outside of any particular State but obligatory within it unless and until changed by statute." Justice Frankfurter explained the significance of *Erie* as follows:

> In overruling *Swift v. Tyson, Erie R. Co. v. Tompkins* did not merely overrule a venerable case. It overruled a particular way of looking at law which dominated the judicial process long after its inadequacies had been laid bare. Law was conceived as a "brooding omnipresence" of Reason, of which decisions were merely evidence and not themselves the controlling formulations. Accordingly, federal courts deemed themselves free to ascertain what Reason, and therefore Law, required wholly independent of authoritatively declared State law, even in cases where a legal right as the basis for relief was created by State authority and could not be created by federal authority and the case got into a federal court merely [on the basis of diversity jurisdiction].

Guaranty Trust Co. v. York, 326 U.S. 99, 101–02 (1945).

12. At trial, Tompkins won a verdict of $30,000. Shortly thereafter, the railroad offered to settle with Tompkins for $7,500. To Tompkins, who was unemployed and had a wife and child to support, the sum was substantial and accepting it would have avoided the delay and uncertainty associated with appeals. Although Tompkins was inclined to accept, his lawyer advised him strongly against it. Reportedly, his lawyer was so concerned that Tompkins might settle precipitously that he invited Tompkins to visit him at his home in New York where Tompkins stayed for two weeks until the appeal was well underway and the settlement offer withdrawn. On remand, the court held that under Pennsylvania law, the railroad was liable to Tompkins only if it acted with "wanton negligence." Because Tompkins had neither pleaded nor proved that degree of culpability, the court entered judgment for the railroad and Tompkins recovered nothing. See Irving Younger, *What Happened in* Erie, 56 TEX. L. REV. 1011, 1021–22 (1978).

Note: Constitutional Bases of Erie

Although the Court in *Erie* did not strike down the Rules of Decision Act, it referred to the "unconstitutionality of the course pursued" under the regime of *Swift v. Tyson.* The Court cites no provision of the Constitution that was violated. One treatise observed that "it is unusual to have a constitutional decision that avoids making specific reference to the constitutional provision involved." WRIGHT & KANE, FEDERAL COURTS 381. It is especially perplexing because Justice Brandeis was known for avoiding constitutional issues if possible. In a letter, Justice Stone called the language "unfortunate dicta." Id. Others also criticized the idea of a constitutional underpinning. See Charles Clark, *State Law in the Federal Courts: The Brooding Omnipresence of* Erie v. Tompkins, 55 YALE L.J. 267, 273, 278 (1946). Judge Friendly's rejoinder is the best: If the Court says it's making a constitutional ruling, we should take it at its word until it says otherwise. Henry Friendly, *In Praise* of Erie — *And of the New Federal Common Law*, 39 N.Y.U. L. REV. 383, 386 n.15 (1964). Of course, this still begs the question of what provision was violated.

Under *Swift*, federal courts were required to apply state law only where there was an applicable state statute or the issue was one of "local law." Where there was no statute and the issue was one of "general law," the Rules of Decision Act was thought to be silent. This created a gap, and the federal courts assumed that they had the authority to fill the gap by creating general federal common law. It was this judicially assumed power to create general federal common law that *Erie* held to be unconstitutional.

While it is relatively clear what the Court held unconstitutional, it is less clear *why* it did so. The generally accepted argument about why the federal courts were acting unconstitutionally under *Swift* focuses on the fact that the federal government is limited to those powers enumerated in the Constitution. As Dean John Hart Ely has explained, "[t]he Constitution is * * * a sort of checklist, enumerating in a general way those things the central government may do and by implication denying it power to do anything else." John Ely, *The Irrepressible Myth of* Erie, 87 HARV. L. REV. 693, 701 (1974) (quoting McCulloch v. Maryland, 17 U.S. 316, 404 (1819)). Under the Tenth Amendment, those powers not granted to the federal government "are reserved to the States, respectively, or to the people." Thus, the constitutional problem is that "nothing in the Constitution provided the central government with a general lawmaking authority of the sort the Court had been exercising under *Swift*." Ely, supra, at 703. *Erie*, explains one treatise, "returns to the states a power that had for nearly a century been exercised by the federal government." WRIGHT & KANE, FEDERAL COURTS 376.

One difficulty with this argument is that the enumerated powers of Congress, particularly its power under the Commerce Clause, have been broadly construed. Although the Commerce Clause has some limits, see United States v. Lopez, 514 U.S. 549 (1995), there is no doubt that it extends to the regulation of interstate railroads, as was at issue in *Erie*. If Congress could have legislated in this area, why can't the courts act in the area to create common law?

The answer may be that while *Congress* has *legislative* authority, the federal courts' judicial authority is not as broad. The more limited authority of the courts reflects separation of powers concerns about the appropriate role for courts. It may also reflect federalism concerns because, although the interests of states are represented in Congress through Senators and Representatives, those interests are less likely to be represented in the federal judiciary. See Thomas Merrill, *The Common Law Powers of Federal Courts*, 52 U. CHI. L. REV. 1, 13–24 (1985).

The argument that federal courts exceeded their constitutional authority in creating general federal common law assumes that nothing in the Constitution confers such authority on the courts. However, one might argue that the grant of diversity jurisdiction in Article III, section 2 of the Constitution carried with it authority to make general federal common law to be applied in diversity cases. After all, the whole purpose of diversity jurisdiction was to prevent bias against citizens of another state, and the laws themselves might be biased. Indeed, the Supreme Court has long held that the grant of jurisdiction over cases in admiralty carried with it just such a common law authority. Why couldn't the same be true of diversity jurisdiction?

Consider, for example, the reported remarks of John Wilson, arguing in favor of ratification of the Constitution before the Pennsylvania convention. He praised diversity jurisdiction, explaining:

> [I]s it not necessary, if we mean to restore either public or private credit, that foreigners, as well as ourselves, have a just and impartial tribunal to which they may resort? I would ask how a merchant must feel to have his property be at the mercy of the laws of Rhode Island. * * * [S]ecurity [for contracts] cannot be obtained, unless we give the power of deciding upon those contracts to the general government.

2 The Debates in the Several State Conventions on the Adoption of the Federal Constitution 491–92 (J. Elliot ed., 2d ed. 1836). Does Wilson's concern about "the laws of Rhode Island" suggest that he assumed federal diversity courts would not be bound by the law of that state?

Concerning the argument that diversity jurisdiction carries with it a grant of law making authority, Dean Ely responded:

> It would not be irrational to fight bias against out-of-staters by giving them access to a body of law, developed by persons beholden to no particular state, unavailable in suits between co-citizens. Not irrational, but the founders of our Republic—by not including any such power in the Constitution, and even more clearly by enacting the Rules of Decision Act—refused to do it. Bias against out-of-staters was to be resisted, but only by providing an unbiased tribunal. To provide more, or so it was felt, would create an unfairness in the other direction.

Ely, supra, 87 Harv. L. Rev. at 713.

Regardless of whether you are persuaded by this argument, *Erie* unequivocally rejected the notion that federal courts have authority to make general common law.

2. Early Efforts to Describe When State Law Applies

The Court in *Erie* decided that the state "laws" referred to in § 34 of the Judiciary Act include all common law as well as statutory law. The majority opinion did not discuss whether federal courts were required to apply these state laws on absolutely every issue that might arise in a case. Subsequent opinions established that federal courts are not required to apply state law on absolutely every issue, but as you will see, the Court has struggled to articulate a test for determining the issues as to which state law must be applied. The first effort to delineate a test can be found in Justice Reed's concurrence in *Erie.* He observed that "no one doubts federal power over procedure." This language might suggest that the proper test is one that attempts to label issues as either "procedural" or "substantive." A few years after *Erie*, in Guaranty Trust Co. v. York, 326 U.S. 99 (1945), the Court squarely rejected a labeling test and offered instead a more functional analysis that focused on the effect of the rule in question on the outcome of the case. The issue in *York* was whether in a diversity case in federal court, the federal court was required to apply the state statute of limitations. The Court held that state law must be applied. It explained:

> Matters of "substance" and matters of "procedure" are much talked about in the books as though they defined a great divide cutting across the whole domain of law. But, of course, "substance" and "procedure" are the same keywords to very different problems. Neither "substance" nor "procedure" represents the same invariants. Each implies different variables depending upon the particular problem for which it is used. * * *
>
> Here we are dealing with a right to recover derived not from the United States but from one of the States. When, because the plaintiff happens to be a non-resident, such a right is enforceable in a federal as well as in a State court, the forms and mode of enforcing the right may at times, naturally enough, vary because the two judicial systems are not identic. But since a federal court adjudicating a State-created right solely because of the diversity of citizenship of the parties is for that purpose, in effect, only another court of the State, it cannot afford recovery if the right to recover is made unavailable by the State nor can it substantially affect the enforcement of the right as given by the State.
>
> And so the question is not whether a statute of limitations is deemed a matter of "procedure" in some sense. The question is whether such a statute concerns merely the manner and the means by which a right to recover, as recognized by the State, is enforced, or whether such statutory limitation is a matter of substance in the aspect that alone is relevant to our problem, namely, does it significantly affect the result of a litigation for a federal court to disregard a law of a State that would be controlling in an action upon the same claim by the same parties in a State court?
>
> It is therefore immaterial whether statutes of limitation are characterized either as "substantive" or "procedural" in State court opinions in any use of those terms unrelated to the specific issue before us. *Erie R. Co. v. Tompkins* was not an endeavor to formulate scientific legal terminology. It expressed a policy that touches vitally the proper distribution of judicial power between State and federal courts. In essence, the intent of that decision was to insure that, in all cases where a federal court is exercising jurisdiction solely because of the diversity of citizenship of the parties, the outcome of the litigation in the federal court should be substantially the same, so far as legal rules determine the outcome of a litigation, as it would be if tried in a State court. The nub of the policy that underlies *Erie R. Co. v. Tompkins* is that for the same transaction the accident of a suit by a non-resident litigant in a federal court instead of in a State court a block away should not lead to a substantially different result. And so, putting to one side abstractions regarding "substance" and "procedure," we have held that in diversity cases the federal courts must follow the law of the State as to burden of proof, as to conflict of laws, as to contributory negligence. *Erie R. Co. v.*

> *Tompkins* has been applied with an eye alert to essentials in avoiding disregard of State law in diversity cases in the federal courts. A policy so important to our federalism must be kept free from entanglements with analytical or terminological niceties.
>
> Plainly enough, a statute that would completely bar recovery in a suit if brought in a State court bears on a State-created right vitally and not merely formally or negligibly. As to consequences that so intimately affect recovery or non-recovery a federal court in a diversity case should follow State law.

Id. at 108–10. The approach of *York* was applied a few years later in a trilogy of cases all handed down the same day:

(a) Ragan v. Merchants Transfer & Warehouse Co., 337 U.S. 530 (1949). Rule 3 of the Federal Rules provides that "[a] civil action is commenced by filing a complaint." Nonetheless, relying on *York*, the Court held that state law controls when an action is "commenced" for purposes of the statute of limitations.

(b) Woods v. Interstate Realty Co., 337 U.S. 535 (1949). A Mississippi "door closing statute" provided that out-of-state corporations that had failed to register properly in Mississippi were barred from suing in state court. The Supreme Court held that a Mississippi federal court should apply the state statute and bar such corporations from suing in federal court.

(c) Cohen v. Beneficial Industrial Loan Corp., 337 U.S. 541 (1949). To discourage so-called strike suits, state law required plaintiffs in shareholder derivative actions to post a substantial bond. Although Rule 23.1 enumerates the criteria for shareholder derivative actions and does not require a bond, the Court held that the state bond requirement applied in a shareholder derivative action in federal court.

Although the outcome test of *York* avoided the problems of formalistic labeling, it had its own difficulties. While *Erie* had expressed some concern that litigants be treated equally in federal and state court, nothing in that case seemed to require that the *outcome* of cases be the same in both courts. Any procedural rule that included a sanction of potential dismissal could be said to affect outcome. For example, suppose that on the last day before the expiration of the statute of limitations, the federal clerk refuses to accept your filing because it is printed on the wrong size paper. If the state would have accepted the filing and the federal court will not, one might argue that a rule about paper size affects the outcome. This in turn might suggest that federal courts are required to follow state law on such trivial matters. Arguments such as this, combined with *Ragan, Woods*, and *Cohen* led to concern that federal law would never be found to prevail and that the Federal Rules were in trouble. Judge Clark said that few of the rules "[could] be considered safe from attack" after *Ragan*. Charles Clark, *Book Review*, 36 CORNELL L.Q. 181, 183 (1950). Some commentators urged repeal of the Federal Rules in diversity cases. See Bernard Gavit, *States' Rights and Federal Procedure*, 25 IND. L.J. 1, 26 (1949); Edward Merrigan, *Erie* to *York* to *Ragan — A Triple Play on the Federal Rules*, 3 VAND. L. REV. 711 (1950). As we will see, concern about the validity of the Federal Rules of Civil Procedure proved unfounded.

Byrd v. Blue Ridge Rural Electrical Cooperative, Inc.

356 U.S. 525, 78 S. Ct. 893, 2 L. Ed. 2d 953 (1958)

JUSTICE BRENNAN delivered the opinion of the Court.

This case was brought in the District Court for the Western District of South Carolina. Jurisdiction was based on diversity of citizenship. The petitioner, a resident of North Carolina, sued respondent, a South Carolina corporation, for damages for injuries allegedly caused by the respondent's negligence. He had judgment on a jury verdict. The Court of Appeals for the Fourth Circuit reversed and directed the entry of judgment for the respondent. We granted certiorari, and subsequently ordered reargument.

The respondent is in the business of selling electric power to subscribers in rural sections of South Carolina. The petitioner was employed as a lineman in the construction crew of a construction contractor. * * *

One of respondent's affirmative defenses was that, under the South Carolina Workmen's Compensation Act, the petitioner—because the work contracted to be done by his employer was work of the kind also done by the respondent's own construction and maintenance crews—had the status of a statutory employee of the respondent and was therefore barred from suing the respondent at law because obliged to accept statutory compensation benefits as the exclusive remedy for his injuries. Two questions concerning this defense are before us: (1) whether the Court of Appeals erred in directing judgment for respondent without a remand to give petitioner an opportunity to introduce further evidence; and (2) whether petitioner, state practice notwithstanding, is entitled to a jury determination of the factual issues raised by this defense.

I

[As to the first issue, the Court held that the court of appeals erred in directing judgment for respondent. The Court ordered the case remanded to permit petitioner an opportunity to present evidence on the question of whether respondent was a statutory employee within the meaning of the South Carolina Workers Compensation statute.]

II

A question is also presented as to whether on remand the factual issue is to be decided by the judge or by the jury. The respondent argues on the basis of the decision of the Supreme Court of South Carolina in Adams v. Davison-Paxon Co., 230 S.C. 532, 96 S.E.2d 566 (1957), that the issue of immunity should be decided by the judge and not by the jury. * * *

The respondent argues that this state-court decision governs the present diversity case and "divests the jury of its normal function" to decide the disputed fact question of the respondent's immunity under § 72-111. This is to contend that the federal court is bound under *Erie R. Co. v. Tompkins* to follow the state court's holding to secure uniform enforcement of the immunity created by the State.

First. It was decided in *Erie R. Co. v. Tompkins* that the federal courts in diversity cases must respect the definition of state-created rights and obligations by the state courts. We must, therefore, first examine the rule in *Adams v. DavisonPaxon Co.* to determine whether it is bound up with these rights and obligations in such a way that its application in the federal court is required.

The Workmen's Compensation Act is administered in South Carolina by its Industrial Commission. The South Carolina courts hold that, on judicial review of actions of the Commission under § 72-111, the question whether the claim of an injured workman is within the Commission's jurisdiction is a matter of law for decision by the court, which makes its own findings of fact relating to that jurisdiction. The South Carolina Supreme Court states no reasons in *Adams v. Davison-Paxon Co.* why, although the jury decides all other factual issues raised by the cause of action and defenses, the jury is displaced as to the factual issue raised by the affirmative defense under § 72-111. * * * A State may, of course, distribute the functions of its judicial machinery as it sees fit. The decisions relied upon, however, furnish no reason for selecting the judge rather than the jury to decide this single affirmative defense in the negligence action. They simply reflect a policy, that administrative determination of "jurisdictional facts" should not be final but subject to judicial review. The conclusion is inescapable that the *Adams* holding is grounded in the practical consideration that the question had theretofore come before the South Carolina courts from the Industrial Commission and the courts had become accustomed to deciding the factual issue of immunity without the aid of juries. We find nothing to suggest that this rule was announced as an integral part of the special relationship created by the statute. Thus the requirement appears to be merely a form and mode of enforcing the immunity, Guaranty Trust Co. v. York, 326 U.S. 99 (1945), and not a rule intended to be bound up with the definition of the rights and obligations of the parties. The situation is therefore not analogous to that in Dice v. Akron, C. & Y. R. Co., 342 U.S. 359 (1952), where this Court held that the right to trial by jury is so substantial a part of the cause of action created by the Federal Employers' Liability Act that the Ohio courts could not apply, in an action under that statute, the Ohio rule that the question of fraudulent release was for determination by a judge rather than by a jury.

Second. But cases following *Erie* have evinced a broader policy to the effect that the federal courts should conform as near as may be — in the absence of other considerations — to state rules even of form and mode where the state rules may bear substantially on the question whether the litigation would come out one way in the federal court and another way in the state court if the federal court failed to apply a particular local rule. E.g., *Guaranty Trust Co. v. York.* Concededly the nature of the tribunal which tries issues may be important in the enforcement of the parcel of rights making up a cause of action or defense, and bear significantly upon achievement of uniform enforcement of the right. It may well be that in the instant personal-injury case the outcome would be substantially affected by whether the issue of immunity is decided by a judge or a jury. Therefore, were "outcome" the only consideration, a strong case might appear for saying that the federal court should follow the state practice.

But there are affirmative countervailing considerations at work here. The federal system is an independent system for administering justice to litigants who properly invoke its jurisdiction. An essential characteristic of that system is the manner in which, in civil common-law actions, it distributes trial functions between judge and jury and, under the influence—if not the command[10]—of the Seventh Amendment, assigns the decisions of disputed questions of fact to the jury. The policy of uniform enforcement of state-created rights and obligations, see, e.g., *Guaranty Trust Co. v. York*, cannot in every case exact compliance with a state rule—not bound up with rights and obligations—which disrupts the federal system of allocating functions between judge and jury. Herron v. Southern Pacific Co., 283 U.S. 91 (1931). Thus the inquiry here is whether the federal policy favoring jury decisions of disputed fact questions should yield to the state rule in the interest of furthering the objective that the litigation should not come out one way in the federal court and another way in the state court.

We think that in the circumstances of this case the federal court should not follow the state rule. It cannot be gainsaid that there is a strong federal policy against allowing state rules to disrupt the judge-jury relationship in the federal courts. In *Herron v. Southern Pacific Co.*, the trial judge in a personal-injury negligence action brought in the District Court for Arizona on diversity grounds directed a verdict for the defendant when it appeared as a matter of law that the plaintiff was guilty of contributory negligence. The federal judge refused to be bound by a provision of the Arizona Constitution which made the jury the sole arbiter of the question of contributory negligence. This Court sustained the action of the trial judge, holding that "state laws cannot alter the essential character or function of a federal court" because that function "is not in any sense a local matter, and state statutes which would interfere with the appropriate performance of that function are not binding upon the federal court under either the Conformity Act or the 'rules of decision' Act." Perhaps even more clearly in light of the influence of the Seventh Amendment, the function assigned to the jury "is an essential factor in the process for which the Federal Constitution provides." Concededly the *Herron* case was decided before *Erie R. Co. v. Tompkins*, but even when *Swift v. Tyson* was governing law and allowed federal courts sitting in diversity cases to disregard state decisional law, it was never thought that state statutes or constitutions were similarly to be disregarded. Yet *Herron* held that state statutes and constitutional provisions could not disrupt or alter the essential character or function of a federal court.

Third. We have discussed the problem upon the assumption that the outcome of the litigation may be substantially affected by whether the issue of immunity is decided by a judge or a jury. But clearly there is not present here the certainty that a different result would follow, cf. *Guaranty Trust Co. v. York*, or even the strong possibility that this would be the case, cf. Bernhardt v. Polygraphic Co., [350 U.S. 198 (1956)]. There are factors present here which might reduce that possibility. The trial judge

10. Our conclusion makes unnecessary the consideration of—and we intimate no view upon—the constitutional question whether the right of jury trial protected in federal courts by the Seventh Amendment embraces the factual issue of statutory immunity when asserted, as here, as an affirmative defense in a common-law negligence action.

in the federal system has powers denied the judges of many States to comment on the weight of evidence and credibility of witnesses, and discretion to grant a new trial if the verdict appears to him to be against the weight of the evidence. We do not think the likelihood of a different result is so strong as to require the federal practice of jury determination of disputed factual issues to yield to the state rule in the interest of uniformity of outcome.

The Court of Appeals did not consider other grounds of appeal raised by the respondent because the ground taken disposed of the case. We accordingly remand the case to the Court of Appeals for the decision of the other questions, with instructions that, if not made unnecessary by the decision of such questions, the Court of Appeals shall remand the case to the District Court for a new trial of such issues as the Court of Appeals may direct.

Reversed and remanded.

Notes and Questions

1. Suppose that the South Carolina Workers' Compensation statute had explicitly required that determinations about who is an employee be made by judges not juries. Suppose further that it is clear from the statute and its legislative history that the reason for this requirement was the perception that juries tended to be moved by sympathy for the injured worker and to find workers were or were not employees depending on what would ensure the largest recovery. Would this have changed the result in *Byrd*?

2. *Byrd* requires that federal courts analyze the state and federal interests in having their respective rules applied. However, the Court does not elaborate on how those interests are to be assessed. Professor Redish and Mr. Phillips have offered a framework for analyzing these interests. See Martin Redish & Carter Phillips, Erie *and the Rules of Decision Act: In Search of the Appropriate Dilemma*, 91 Harv. L. Rev. 356 (1977). As to the state interest, they have argued that the state rules which need to be respected are those that affect "primary conduct," that is, what people do outside of litigation. Obviously, basic rules of liability or standard of care meet this criteria. They note that in addition to these obviously "substantive" state rules, there are some state rules that regulate procedure but which nonetheless affect primary conduct, and should therefore be regulated. Two categories of these substantive procedural rules are (1) rules designed to provide behavioral guides such as evidentiary privilege, and (2) rules for conducting trials that tend to benefit one party more than the other such as burdens of proof.

As to the federal interest, Redish and Phillips have argued that as an "independent system for administering justice," the federal court system has an interest in conducting its business in "what it deems the fairest and most efficient manner." They caution that courts should not put too much weight on the federal interest in using what the federal courts deem the fairest procedure. Id. at 391. They explain that "[i]n the face of a relatively significant countervailing state interest, the 'doing justice' factor should be outbalanced. But where the competing state interest is of relatively slight significance, the interest of a federal court in determining for itself what procedures are 'just' should prevail." Id. Redish and Phillips argue that the one federal interest that should always prevail over state interests is the federal interest in avoiding costs or inconvenience to the federal court.

3. Professor Stein has argued for a somewhat different approach in assessing the state and federal interests. See Allan Stein, Erie *and Court Access*, 100 YALE L.J. 1935 (1991). Stein argues that the first step in a *Byrd* analysis is to determine whether the policy underlying the state rule would be hampered by application of a different rule in federal court. One asks, in essence, whether the state would care if the federal court applied a different rule. Thus, for example, where a state rule is designed simply to cut the costs of operating the state judicial system, the rule can be disregarded in federal court. Of course, in some situations the state policy may be undermined by the application of a different rule in federal court, creating a "true conflict" between the state and federal interests. Where a true conflict exists, Stein argues that the federal practice must be justified by a "paramount federal interest." Id. at 2000. Stein disagrees with Redish and Phillips' willingness to allow federal courts to ignore state rules that impose costs on federal courts. "Most state laws enforced in federal courts implicate the expenditure of federal resources," he argues. Id. at 2001. Stein would allow federal courts to apply federal rules where the purposes underlying federal jurisdiction are implicated, as for example, where a state rule discriminates against out-of-staters.

4. What law should apply when the court concludes that the state and federal interests are equal? For example, in Taylor v. Titan Midwest Construction Corp., 474 F. Supp. 145, 147 (N.D. Tex. 1979), the court found the relative state and federal interests "equally strong," and applied federal law. Is the presence of an equally strong interest sufficient to justify the vertical non-uniformity that results from application of federal law?

5. The Court in *Byrd* refers to "the influence — if not the command" of the Seventh Amendment. What does this mean? If the Seventh Amendment commands a jury trial, could the Rules of Decision Act or state law ever override that command? If the Seventh Amendment does not require a jury trial, how can that Amendment have "influence"?

6. Under South Carolina law, the South Carolina state courts have no jurisdiction over cases brought by an out-of-state plaintiff against an out-of-state corporation for a cause of action that arises out-of-state. Under *Byrd*, would a federal court in South Carolina be required to apply this state door-closing statute? See Szantay v. Beech Aircraft Corp., 349 F.2d 60 (4th Cir. 1965).

7. Professor Ely has described the *Byrd* opinion as one that "exhibits a confusion that exceeds even that normally surrounding a balancing test." Ely, supra, 87 HARV. L. REV. at 709. In a similar vein, Professors Wright and Kane described *Byrd* as "the most Delphic of the Supreme Court's major *Erie*-doctrine decisions." WRIGHT & KANE, FEDERAL COURTS 402.

8. Despite its weaknesses, several commentators praised *Byrd* for restoring some equilibrium to vertical choice of law. See Henry Friendly, *In Praise* of Erie — *And of*

the New Federal Common Law, 39 N.Y.U. L. Rev. 383, 403 n.95 (1964); Allen Smith, Blue Ridge *and Beyond: A* Byrd's *Eye View of Federalism in Diversity Litigation*, 36 Tulane L. Rev. 443 (1962), and for breathing life back into the Federal Rules. Although *Byrd* did not involve a Federal Rule of Civil Procedure, some saw it as providing "a formula by which the rules might coexist with the Erie doctrine." Wright & Kane, Federal Courts 402.

3. The Federal Rules of Civil Procedure

Hanna v. Plumer

380 U.S. 460, 85 S. Ct. 1136, 14 L. Ed. 2d 8 (1965)

Chief Justice Warren delivered the opinion of the Court.

The question to be decided is whether, in a civil action where the jurisdiction of the United States district court is based upon diversity of citizenship between the parties, service of process shall be made in the manner prescribed by state law or that set forth in Rule 4(d)(1) [now Rule 4(e)(2)] of the Federal Rules of Civil Procedure.

On February 6, 1963, petitioner, a citizen of Ohio, filed her complaint in the District Court for the District of Massachusetts, claiming damages in excess of $10,000 [now $75,000] for personal injuries resulting from an automobile accident in South Carolina, allegedly caused by the negligence of one Louise Plumer Osgood, a Massachusetts citizen deceased at the time of the filing of the complaint. Respondent, Mrs. Osgood's executor and also a Massachusetts citizen, was named as defendant. On February 8, service was made by leaving copies of the summons and the complaint with respondent's wife at his residence, concededly in compliance with Rule 4(d)(1), which provides:

> "The summons and complaint shall be served together. The plaintiff shall furnish the person making service with such copies as are necessary. Service shall be made as follows:
>
> "(1) Upon an individual other than an infant or an incompetent person, by delivering a copy of the summons and of the complaint to him personally or by leaving copies thereof at his dwelling house or usual place of abode with some person of suitable age and discretion then residing therein...."

Respondent filed his answer on February 26, alleging, inter alia, that the action could not be maintained because it had been brought "contrary to and in violation of the provisions of Massachusetts General Laws Chapter 197, Section 9." That section provides:

> "Except as provided in this chapter, an executor or administrator shall not be held to answer to an action by a creditor of the deceased which is not commenced within one year from the time of his giving bond for the performance of his trust, or to such an action which is commenced within

said year unless before the expiration thereof the writ in such action has been served by delivery in hand upon such executor or administrator or service thereof accepted by him or a notice stating the name of the estate, the name and address of the creditor, the amount of the claim and the court in which the action has been brought has been filed in the proper registry of probate...."

On October 17, 1963, the District Court granted respondent's motion for summary judgment, citing *Ragan v. Merchants Transfer Co.* and *Guaranty Trust Co. v. York* in support of its conclusion that the adequacy of the service was to be measured by § 9, with which, the court held, petitioner had not complied. On appeal, petitioner admitted noncompliance with § 9, but argued that Rule 4(d)(1) defines the method by which service of process is to be effected in diversity actions. The Court of Appeals for the First Circuit, finding that "[r]elatively recent amendments [to § 9] evince a clear legislative purpose to require personal notification within the year,"[1] concluded that the conflict of state and federal rules was over "a substantive rather than a procedural matter," and unanimously affirmed. Because of the threat to the goal of uniformity of federal procedure posed by the decision below, we granted certiorari.

We conclude that the adoption of Rule 4(d)(1), designed to control service of process in diversity actions, neither exceeded the congressional mandate embodied in the Rules Enabling Act nor transgressed constitutional bounds, and that the Rule is therefore the standard against which the District Court should have measured the adequacy of the service. Accordingly, we reverse the decision of the Court of Appeals.

The Rules Enabling Act, 28 U.S.C. § 2072, provides, in pertinent part:

"The Supreme Court shall have the power to prescribe, by general rules, the forms of process, writs, pleadings, and motions, and the practice and procedure of the district courts of the United States in civil actions.

"Such rules shall not abridge, enlarge or modify any substantive right and shall preserve the right of trial by jury...."

1. Section 9 is in part a statute of limitations, providing that an executor need not "answer to an action ... which is not commenced within one year from the time of his giving bond...." This part of the statute, the purpose of which is to speed the settlement of estates, is not involved in this since the action clearly was timely commenced. * * *

Section 9 also provides for the manner of service. Generally, service of process must be made by "delivery by hand," although there are two alternatives: acceptance of service by the executor, or filing of a notice of claim, the components of which are set out in the statute, which *is* involved here, is, as the court below noted, to insure that executors will receive actual notice of claims. Actual notice is of course also the goal of Rule 4(d)(1); however, the Federal Rule reflects a determination that this goal can be achieved by a method less cumbersome than that prescribed in § 9. In this case the goal seems to have been achieved; although the affidavit filed by respondent in the District Court asserts that he had not been served in hand nor had he accepted service, it does not allege lack of actual notice.

Under the cases construing the scope of the Enabling Act, Rule 4(d)(1) clearly passes muster. Prescribing the manner in which a defendant is to be notified that a suit has been instituted against him, it relates to the "practice and procedure of the district courts."

> "The test must be whether a rule really regulates procedure,—the judicial process for enforcing rights and duties recognized by substantive law and for justly administering remedy and redress for disregard or infraction of them." Sibbach v. Wilson & Co., 312 U.S. 1, 14 (1941).

In Mississippi Pub. Corp. v. Murphree, 326 U.S. 438 (1946), this Court upheld Rule 4(f) [now 4(k)(1)], which permits service of a summons anywhere within the State (and not merely the district) in which a district court sits:

> "We think that Rule 4(f) is in harmony with the Enabling Act ... Undoubtedly most alterations of the rules of practice and procedure may and often do affect the rights of litigants. Congress' prohibition of any alteration of substantive rights of litigants was obviously not addressed to such incidental effects as necessarily attend the adoption of the prescribed new rules of procedure upon the rights of litigants who, agreeably to rules of practice and procedure, have been brought before a court authorized to determine their rights. *Sibbach v. Wilson & Co.* The fact that the application of Rule 4(f) will operate to subject petitioner's rights to adjudication by the district court for northern Mississippi will undoubtedly affect those rights. But it does not operate to abridge, enlarge or modify the rules of decision by which that court will adjudicate its rights."

Thus were there no conflicting state procedure, Rule 4(d)(1) would clearly control. However, respondent, focusing on the contrary Massachusetts rule, calls to the Court's attention another line of cases, a line which—like the Federal Rules—had its birth in 1938. *Erie R. Co. v. Tompkins*, overruling *Swift v. Tyson*, held that federal courts sitting in diversity cases, when deciding questions of "substantive" law, are bound by state court decisions as well as state statutes. The broad command of *Erie* was therefore identical to that of the Enabling Act: federal courts are to apply state substantive law and federal procedural law. However, as subsequent cases sharpened the distinction between substance and procedure, the line of cases following *Erie* diverged markedly from the line construing the Enabling Act. *Guaranty Trust Co. v. York* made it clear that *Erie*-type problems were not to be solved by reference to any traditional or common-sense substance-procedure distinction:

> "And so the question is not whether a statute of limitations is deemed a matter of 'procedure' in some sense. The question is ... does it significantly affect the result of a litigation for a federal court to disregard a law of a State that would be controlling in an action upon the same claim by the same parties in a State court?"

Respondent, by placing primary reliance on *York* and *Ragan*, suggests that the *Erie* doctrine acts as a check on the Federal Rules of Civil Procedure, that despite the clear command of Rule 4(d)(1), *Erie* and its progeny demand the application of the Massachusetts rule. Reduced to essentials, the argument is: (1) *Erie*, as refined in *York*, demands that federal courts apply state law whenever application of federal law in its stead will alter the outcome of the case. (2) In this case, a determination that the Massachusetts service requirements obtain will result in immediate victory for respondent. If, on the other hand, it should be held that Rule 4(d)(1) is applicable, the litigation will continue, with possible victory for petitioner. (3) Therefore, *Erie* demands application of the Massachusetts rule. The syllogism possesses an appealing simplicity, but is for several reasons invalid.

In the first place, it is doubtful that, even if there were no Federal Rule making it clear that in-hand service is not required in diversity actions, the *Erie* rule would have obligated the District Court to follow the Massachusetts procedure. "Outcome-determination" analysis was never intended to serve as a talisman. *Byrd v. Blue Ridge Cooperative.* Indeed, the message of *York* itself is that choices between state and federal law are to be made not by application of any automatic, "litmus paper" criterion, but rather by reference to the policies underlying the *Erie* rule. *Guaranty Trust Co. v. York.*

The *Erie* rule is rooted in part in a realization that it would be unfair for the character or result of a litigation materially to differ because the suit had been brought in a federal court. * * * The decision was also in part a reaction to the practice of "forum-shopping" which had grown up in response to the rule of *Swift v. Tyson.* That the *York* test was an attempt to effectuate these policies is demonstrated by the fact that the opinion framed the inquiry in terms of "substantial" variations between state and federal litigation. Not only are nonsubstantial, or trivial, variations not likely to raise the sort of equal protection problems which troubled the Court in *Erie*; they are also unlikely to influence the choice of a forum. The "outcome-determination" test therefore cannot be read without reference to the twin aims of the *Erie* rule: discouragement of forum shopping and avoidance of inequitable administration of the laws.[9]

9. The Court of Appeals seemed to frame the inquiry in terms of how "important" § 9 is to the State. In support of its suggestion that § 9 serves some interest the State regards as vital to its citizens, the court noted that something like § 9 has been on the books in Massachusetts a long time, that § 9 has been amended a number of times, and that § 9 is designed to make sure that executors receive actual notice. See note 1, supra. The apparent lack of relation among these three observations is not surprising, because it is not clear to what sort of question the Court of Appeals is addressing itself. One cannot meaningfully ask how important something is without first asking "important for what purpose?" *Erie* and its progeny make clear that when a federal court sitting in a diversity case is faced with a question of whether or not to apply state law, the importance of a state rule is indeed relevant, but only in the context of asking whether application of the rule would make so important a difference to the character or result of the litigation that failure to enforce it would unfairly discriminate against citizens of the forum state, or whether application of the rule would have so important an effect upon the fortunes of one or both of the litigants that failure to enforce it would be likely to cause a plaintiff to choose the federal court.

The difference between the conclusion that the Massachusetts rule is applicable, and the conclusion that it is not, is of course at this point "outcome-determinative" in the sense that if we hold the state rule to apply, respondent prevails, whereas if we hold that Rule 4(d)(1) governs, the litigation will continue. But in this sense *every* procedural variation is "outcome-determinative." For example, having brought suit in a federal court, a plaintiff cannot then insist on the right to file subsequent pleadings in accord with the time limits applicable in the state courts, even though enforcement of the federal timetable will, if he continues to insist that he must meet only the state time limit, result in determination of the controversy against him. So it is here. Though choice of the federal or state rule will at this point have a marked effect upon the outcome of the litigation, the difference between the two rules would be of scant, if any, relevance to the choice of a forum. Petitioner, in choosing her forum, was not presented with a situation where application of the state rule would wholly bar recovery; rather, adherence to the state rule would have resulted only in altering the way in which process was served.[11] Moreover, it is difficult to argue that permitting service of defendant's wife to take the place of in-hand service of defendant himself alters the mode of enforcement of state-created rights in a fashion sufficiently "substantial" to raise the sort of equal protection problems to which the *Erie* opinion alluded.

There is, however, a more fundamental flaw in respondent's syllogism: the incorrect assumption that the rule of *Erie R. Co. v. Tompkins* constitutes the appropriate test of the validity and therefore the applicability of a Federal Rule of Civil Procedure. The *Erie* rule has never been invoked to void a Federal Rule. It is true that there have been cases where this Court has held applicable a state rule in the face of an argument that the situation was governed by one of the Federal Rules. But the holding of each such case was not that *Erie* commanded displacement of a Federal Rule by an inconsistent state rule, but rather that the scope of the Federal Rule was not as broad as the losing party urged, and therefore, there being no Federal Rule which covered the point in dispute, *Erie* commanded the enforcement of state law.

> "Respondent contends, in the first place, that the charge was correct because of the fact that Rule 8(c) of the Rules of Civil Procedure makes contributory negligence an affirmative defense. We do not agree. Rule 8(c) covers only the manner of pleading. The question of the burden of establishing contributory negligence is a question of local law which federal courts in diversity of citizenship cases must apply." Palmer v. Hoffman, 318 U.S. 109, 117 (1943).

(Here, of course, the clash is unavoidable; Rule 4(d)(1) says—implicitly, but with unmistakable clarity—that in-hand service is not required in federal courts.) At the same time, in cases adjudicating the validity of Federal Rules, we have not applied

11. We cannot seriously entertain the thought that one suing an estate would be led to choose the federal court because of a belief that adherence to Rule 4(d)(1) is less likely to give the executor actual notice than § 9, and therefore more likely to produce a default judgment. Rule 4(d)(1) is well designed to give actual notice, as it did in this case. See note 1, supra.

the *York* rule or other refinements of *Erie*, but have to this day continued to decide questions concerning the scope of the Enabling Act and the constitutionality of specific Federal Rules in light of the distinction set forth in *Sibbach*.

Nor has the development of two separate lines of cases been inadvertent. The line between "substance" and "procedure" shifts as the legal context changes. "Each implies different variables depending upon the particular problem for which it is used." *Guaranty Trust Co. v. York*; COOK, THE LOGICAL AND LEGAL BASES OF THE CONFLICTS OF LAWS 154–83 (1942). It is true that both the Enabling Act and the *Erie* rule say, roughly, that federal courts are to apply state "substantive" law and federal "procedural" law, but from that it need not follow that the tests are identical. For they were designed to control very different sorts of decisions. When a situation is covered by one of the Federal Rules, the question facing the court is a far cry from the typical, relatively unguided *Erie* choice: the court has been instructed to apply the Federal Rule, and can refuse to do so only if the Advisory Committee, this Court, and Congress erred in their prima facie judgment that the Rule in question transgresses neither the terms of the Enabling Act nor constitutional restrictions.

We are reminded by the *Erie* opinion that neither Congress nor the federal courts can, under the guise of formulating rules of decision for federal courts, fashion rules which are not supported by a grant of federal authority contained in Article I or some other section of the Constitution; in such areas state law must govern because there can be no other law. But the opinion in *Erie*, which involved no Federal Rule and dealt with a question which was "substantive" in every traditional sense (whether the railroad owed a duty of care to Tompkins as a trespasser or a licensee), surely neither said nor implied that measures like Rule 4(d)(1) are unconstitutional. For the constitutional provision for a federal court system (augmented by the Necessary and Proper Clause) carries with it congressional power to make rules governing the practice and pleading in those courts, which in turn includes a power to regulate matters which, though falling within the uncertain area between substance and procedure, are rationally capable of classification as either. Neither *York* nor the cases following it ever suggested that the rule there laid down for coping with situations where no Federal Rule applies is coextensive with the limitation on Congress to which *Erie* had adverted. Although this Court has never before been confronted with a case where the applicable Federal Rule is in direct collision with the law of the relevant State, courts of appeals faced with such clashes have rightly discerned the implications of our decisions.

> "One of the shaping purposes of the Federal Rules is to bring about uniformity in the federal courts by getting away from local rules. This is especially true of matters which relate to the administration of legal proceedings, an area in which federal courts have traditionally exerted strong inherent power, completely aside from the powers Congress expressly conferred in the Rules. The purpose of the *Erie* doctrine even as extended in *York* and *Ragan*, was never to bottle up federal courts with 'outcome-determinative' and 'integral-relations' stoppers — when there are 'affirmative countervailing [federal] con-

siderations' and when there is a Congressional mandate (the Rules) supported by constitutional authority."

Erie and its offspring cast no doubt on the long-recognized power of Congress to prescribe housekeeping rules for federal courts even though some of those rules will inevitably differ from comparable state rules. "When, because the plaintiff happens to be a non-resident, such a right is enforceable in a federal as well as in a State court, the forms and mode of enforcing the right may at times, naturally enough, vary because the two judicial systems are not identic." *Guaranty Trust Co. v. York*; *Cohen v. Beneficial Loan Corp.* Thus, though a court, in measuring a Federal Rule against the standards contained in the Enabling Act and the Constitution, need not wholly blind itself to the degree to which the Rule makes the character and result of the federal litigation stray from the course it would follow in state courts, it cannot be forgotten that the *Erie* rule, and the guidelines suggested in *York*, were created to serve another purpose altogether. To hold that a Federal Rule of Civil Procedure must cease to function whenever it alters the mode of enforcing state-created rights would be to disembowel either the Constitution's grant of power over federal procedure or Congress' attempt to exercise that power in the Enabling Act. Rule 4 (d)(1) is valid and controls the instant case.

Reversed.

Justice Harlan, concurring.

It is unquestionably true that up to now *Erie* and the cases following it have not succeeded in articulating a workable doctrine governing choice of law in diversity actions. I respect the Court's effort to clarify the situation in today's opinion. However, in doing so I think it has misconceived the constitutional premises of *Erie* and has failed to deal adequately with those past decisions upon which the courts below relied.

Erie was something more than an opinion which worried about "forum-shopping and avoidance of inequitable administration of the laws," although to be sure these were important elements of the decision. I have always regarded that decision as one of the modern cornerstones of our federalism, expressing policies that profoundly touch the allocation of judicial power between the state and federal systems. *Erie* recognized that there should not be two conflicting systems of law controlling the primary activity of citizens, for such alternative governing authority must necessarily give rise to a debilitating uncertainty in the planning of everyday affairs. And it recognized that the scheme of our Constitution envisions an allocation of law-making functions between state and federal legislative processes which is undercut if the federal judiciary can make substantive law affecting state affairs beyond the bounds of congressional legislative powers in this regard. Thus, in diversity cases *Erie* commands that it be the state law governing primary private activity which prevails.

The shorthand formulations which have appeared in some past decisions are prone to carry untoward results that frequently arise from oversimplification. The Court is quite right in stating that the "outcome-determinative" test of *Guaranty Trust Co. v. York*, if taken literally, proves too much, for any rule, no matter how clearly "procedural," can affect the outcome of litigation if it is not obeyed. In turning from the "outcome" test of *York* back to the unadorned forum-shopping rationale of *Erie*, however, the Court falls prey to like oversimplification, for a simple forum-shopping rule also proves too much; litigants often choose a federal forum merely to obtain what they consider the advantages of the Federal Rules of Civil Procedure or to try their cases before a supposedly more favorable judge. To my mind the proper line of approach in determining whether to apply a state or a federal rule, whether "substantive" or "procedural," is to stay close to basic principles by inquiring if the choice of rule would substantially affect those primary decisions respecting human conduct which our constitutional system leaves to state regulation.[2] If so, *Erie* and the Constitution require that the state rule prevail, even in the face of a conflicting federal rule.

The Court weakens, if indeed it does not submerge, this basic principle by finding, in effect, a grant of substantive legislative power in the constitutional provision for a federal court system and through it, setting up the Federal Rules as a body of law inviolate. * * * So long as a reasonable man could characterize any duly adopted federal rule as "procedural," the Court, unless I misapprehend what is said, would have it apply no matter how seriously it frustrated a State's substantive regulation of the primary conduct and affairs of its citizens. Since the members of the Advisory Committee, the Judicial Conference, and this Court who formulated the Federal Rules are presumably reasonable men, it follows that the integrity of the Federal Rules is absolute. Whereas the unadulterated outcome and forum-shopping tests may err too far toward honoring state rules, I submit that the Court's "arguably procedural, ergo constitutional" test moves too fast and far in the other direction.

The courts below relied upon this Court's decisions in *Ragan v. Merchants Transfer Co.* and *Cohen v. Beneficial Loan Corp.* Those cases deserve more attention than this Court has given them, particularly *Ragan* which, if still good law, would in my opinion call for affirmance of the result reached by the Court of Appeals. Further, a discussion of these two cases will serve to illuminate the "diversity" thesis I am advocating.

In *Ragan* a Kansas statute of limitations provided that an action was deemed commenced when service was made on the defendant. Despite Federal Rule 3 which provides that an action commences with the filing of the complaint, the Court held that for purposes of the Kansas statute of limitations a diversity tort action commenced only when service was made upon the defendant. The effect of this holding was that although the plaintiff had filed his federal complaint within the state period of limitations, his action was barred because the federal marshal did not serve a summons on the defendant until after the limitations period had run. I think that the decision was wrong. At most, application of the Federal Rule would have meant that potential

2. *Byrd v. Blue Ridge Coop., Inc.* indicated that state procedures would apply if the State had manifested a particularly strong interest in their employment. However, this approach may not be of constitutional proportions.

Kansas tort defendants would have to defer for a few days the satisfaction of knowing that they had not been sued within the limitations period. The choice of the Federal Rule would have had no effect on the primary stages of private activity from which torts arise, and only the most minimal effect on behavior following the commission of the tort. In such circumstances the interest of the federal system in proceeding under its own rules should have prevailed.

Cohen v. Beneficial Loan Corp. held that a federal diversity court must apply a state statute requiring a small stockholder in a stockholder derivative suit to post a bond securing payment of defense costs as a condition to prosecuting an action. Such a statute is not "outcome determinative"; the plaintiff can win with or without it. The Court now rationalizes the case on the ground that the statute might affect the plaintiff's choice of forum, but as has been pointed out, a simple forum-shopping test proves too much. The proper view of *Cohen* is, in my opinion, that the statute was meant to inhibit small stockholders from instituting "strike suits," and thus it was designed and could be expected to have a substantial impact on private primary activity. Anyone who was at the trial bar during the period when *Cohen* arose can appreciate the strong state policy reflected in the statute. I think it wholly legitimate to view Federal Rule 23 [now Fed. R. Civ. P. 23.1] as not purporting to deal with the problem. But even had the Federal Rules purported to do so, and in so doing provided a substantially less effective deterrent to strike suits, I think the state rule should still have prevailed. That is where I believe the Court's view differs from mine; for the Court attributes such overriding force to the Federal Rules that it is hard to think of a case where a conflicting state rule would be allowed to operate, even though the state rule reflected policy considerations which, under *Erie*, would lie within the realm of state legislative authority.

It remains to apply what has been said to the present case. The Massachusetts rule provides that an executor need not answer suits unless in-hand service was made upon him or notice of the action was filed in the proper registry of probate within one year of his giving bond. The evident intent of this statute is to permit an executor to distribute the estate which he is administering without fear that further liabilities may be outstanding for which he could be held personally liable. If the Federal District Court in Massachusetts applies Rule 4(d)(1) of the Federal Rules of Civil Procedure instead of the Massachusetts service rule, what effect would that have on the speed and assurance with which estates are distributed? As I see it, the effect would not be substantial. It would mean simply that an executor would have to check at his own house or the federal courthouse as well as the registry of probate before he could distribute the estate with impunity. As this does not seem enough to give rise to any real impingement on the vitality of the state policy which the Massachusetts rule is intended to serve, I concur in the judgment of the Court.

Note on Understanding Hanna

Notice that *Hanna* identified two distinct prongs of analysis for *Erie* cases. Where there is a Federal Rule on point, the proper analysis is the Rules Enabling Act prong (described in the second half of the opinion). In contrast, the Rules of Decision Act prong (discussed in the first part of the opinion) applies only if there is no Federal Rule on point. The Court stressed that it is a "fundamental flaw" to apply Rules of Decision Act analysis to a Federal Rule. Notwithstanding the Court's explicit bifurcation of the analysis, courts as well as commentators sometimes loosely refer to "the *Erie* doctrine" as if it were a unitary principle. For an excellent analysis of the two prongs of analysis, see Ely, supra, 87 HARV. L. REV. 693. Dean Ely was a law clerk to Chief Justice Warren the term *Hanna* was decided. In the sections below, we analyze the two prongs separately.

a. *What Happens When There Is a Federal Rule of Civil Procedure on Point — The Rules Enabling Act Prong*

The Federal Rules were made possible by the Rules Enabling Act, which directed the Supreme Court to promulgate a set of rules of procedure for the federal courts. The Rules Enabling Act is preemptive federal legislation that requires that the Federal Rules of Civil Procedure apply in federal court. Indeed, the Rules Enabling Act explicitly provides that "[a]ll laws in conflict with such rules shall be of no further force or effect after such rules have taken effect." 28 U.S.C. § 2072(b). Where a Federal Rule is involved, if the rule is valid and on point, then the Supremacy Clause dictates that the rule governs.

The Court in *Hanna* endorsed this approach to the Federal Rules, but a few courts have resisted applying it. For example, in Marshall v. Mulrenin, 508 F.2d 39 (1st Cir. 1974), the plaintiff was injured while on business premises and sued the defendant whom she believed owned the property. The suit was filed in federal court in Massachusetts. While the suit was pending but after the statute of limitations had expired, the plaintiff learned that the defendant she sued had owned the property but had sold it before the accident occurred. The plaintiff then attempted to amend her complaint to name the current owner. Massachusetts law permitted any amendments that would "sustain the action for the cause for which it was intended to be brought." On the other hand, Rule 15(c) of the Federal Rules is more restrictive. The First Circuit refused to apply Rule 15(c), explaining

> We do not accept the "singularly hard-hearted" view that *Hanna* commands that the Federal Rules be woodenly applied irrespective of a discoverable substantive, as distinguished from a merely procedural, state purpose. * * * Such a construction does not, of course, render Federal Rules inoperative in their procedural aspects. It merely means that a rule is not to be applied to the extent, if any, that it would defeat rights arising from state substantive law as distinguished from state procedure.

Id. at 44.

Notwithstanding *Marshall*, the Rules Enabling Act prong of *Hanna* is clear — if there's a valid Federal Rule of Civil Procedure on point, it must be applied. *Hanna*'s holding is surely correct under the Supremacy Clause. The escape from its "hard-hearted" effects is to find, where appropriate, that a Rule does not cover the particular point at issue. See Section b, infra.

i. Determining Whether a Federal Directive Is on Point

Although the Court has never struck down a Federal Rule of Civil Procedure, it has on some occasions concluded that a Rule which might appear to control is not in fact applicable.

In Walker v. Armco Steel Corp., 446 U.S. 740 (1980), state law provided that an action has not "commenced" for purposes of the statute of limitations until the defendant is actually served. In contrast, Rule 3 of the Federal Rules provides that "[a] civil action is commenced by filing a complaint." Despite Rule 3, the Supreme Court reaffirmed its ruling in *Ragan*, Section B.2, supra, and held that state law controlled. The Court explained that Rule 3 was not intended to toll a state statute of limitations.

A similar explanation can be offered for *Cohen*, which is discussed in Section B.2. supra. There, the Court held that federal courts must apply a state law requirement that plaintiffs in shareholder derivative actions post bond. Rule 23.1 of the Federal Rules specifically addresses shareholder derivative actions and specifies the requirements for such actions. The Rule includes nothing about a bond requirement. One can reconcile Rule 23.1 and *Cohen* by concluding that the Rule simply does not address the question of whether the plaintiff must post a bond. It does not require a bond, but it also does not prohibit it. Thus, the federal directive and the state bond requirement may co-exist.

Should Federal Rules generally be read narrowly to avoiding infringing on the rights of states? On at least some occasions, the Court has urged the importance of "interpret[ing] the Federal Rules * * * with sensitivity to important state interests." Gasperini v. Center for Humanities, Inc., 518 U.S. 415, 427 n.7 (1996), infra in Section B.3.c. However, the Court does not always give the narrowest possible interpretation to a Federal Rule. In Burlington Northern Railroad Co. v. Woods, 480 U.S. 1 (1987), the Court dealt with Rule 38 of the Federal Rules of Appellate Procedure. That Rule then provided: "If a court of appeals shall determine that an appeal is frivolous, it may award just damages and single or double costs to the appellee." A state law imposed a mandatory fixed penalty of ten percent of the judgment on appellants who obtain stays of judgment and then lose their appeals. The Court held that Rule 38 controls, and the state rule does not. It concluded that Rule 38, by permitting, but not requiring, sanctions, prohibits mandatory sanctions and that the only sanctions available were those that fell within Rule 38.

Consider the following situations:

(1) Rule 41(b) of the Federal Rules permits dismissal for failure to prosecute a claim. The Nevada rules of procedure mandate dismissal for failure to prosecute after five years. Should a federal court in Nevada apply the Nevada rule? See Harvey's Wagon Wheel, Inc. v. Van Blitter, 959 F.2d 153 (9th Cir. 1992).

(2) Illinois law provides that in tort cases "no complaint shall be filed containing a prayer for relief for punitive damages. However, a plaintiff may, pursuant to pretrial motion and after a hearing before the Court, amend the complaint to include a prayer for relief seeking punitive damages." Federal Rule 8 provides that the complaint "must contain * * * a demand for the relief sought." Rule 9 sets forth special pleading rules for certain specified situations but says nothing about punitive damages. Should a federal court in Illinois apply the Illinois rule? Compare Cohen v. Office Depot, Inc., 184 F.3d 1292 (11th Cir. 1999); Pruett v. Erickson Air-Crane Co., 183 F.R.D. 248 (D. Or. 1998) (refusing to apply state law), with Al-Site Corp. v. VSI Intern, Inc., 842 F. Supp. 507, 511–14 (S.D. Fla. 1993); Nelson v. Zurich Insurance Co., 1992 U.S. Dist. LEXIS 12955 (D.N.D. 1992) (applying state law).

(3) Forum selection clauses are contractual terms providing where litigation arising from the contract must be filed. The modern view, adopted by the federal courts in cases in which state law does not govern, upholds such clauses as long as they are not the product of overreaching. Although most states adopt this modern approach, about a dozen do not. To them, such clauses violate a public policy by "ousting" a court of jurisdiction.

Suppose P, a citizen of Alabama, and D, a citizen of New York, enter a contract which contains a clause mandating that any dispute arising from the contract be filed in New York. After a dispute arises, P sues in state court in Alabama. D moves to dismiss, based on the forum selection clause. Because Alabama law does not allow enforcement of such provisions, the court will deny the motion. Suppose, however, D removes the case to federal court based upon diversity of citizenship. Should the federal court follow Alabama law?

The Supreme Court held that the transfer of venue statute, 28 U.S.C. § 1404(a), applies in this situation, noting that "when the federal law sought to be applied is a congressional statute, the first and chief question * * * is whether the statute is 'sufficiently broad to control the issue before the court.'" Stewart Organization Inc. v. Ricoh Corp., 487 U.S. 22 (1988). As we saw in Chapter 5, the Court reiterated the conclusion in Atlantic Marine Construction Co, Inc. v. U.S. District Court, 134 S. Ct. 568 (2013). In the Court's view, Congress intended courts to consider the existence of a forum selection clause as one of the factors in determining whether to transfer under § 1404(a). It is not apparent that Congress ever considered the issue when it passed § 1404(a); indeed, at the time § 1404(a) was enacted, courts generally did not enforce forum selection clauses. *Atlantic Marine* and *Stewart* address only change of venue in federal court pursuant to § 1404(a) and do not alter the law in Alabama concerning enforceability of forum selection clauses. Thus, a forum selection clause may be enforceable in federal court in Alabama and not in state court there. How does this situation differ from *Swift v. Tyson*?

Although § 1404 is obviously not a Federal Rule of Civil Procedure, the Court followed fundamentally the same approach it uses with the Federal Rules — first interpret the Rule or statute and if it is on point and covers the matter at issue, then to assess whether it is valid. If it is, the Rule or statute applies. Thus, regardless of whether you agree with the Court's interpretation of § 1404, the Court's approach in the case is instructive.

ii. Determining Whether a Federal Directive Is Valid

As with a statute, a Federal Rule is valid only if it is constitutional, and a statute beyond the scope of Congress' authority would, of course, be unconstitutional. In *Hanna*, the Court delineated the scope of Congress' authority with respect to rules of procedure for the federal courts. The Court explained that Congress' authority to create a federal court system carries with it authority to mandate the procedural rules for those courts. The Court concluded that although the line between substance and procedure is fuzzy, Congress' constitutional power over federal procedure extends to anything "rationally capable of classification" as procedure. Thus, so long as any Federal Rule is arguably procedural, it is constitutional.

Finding that a Federal Rule is constitutional is only one step in determining the Rule's validity. Congress did not itself enact the Rules, but instead delegated authority to the Supreme Court to promulgate them. Therefore, for a Rule to be valid, it must not only be constitutional, it must also be within the delegated authority. It is the Rules Enabling Act, 28 U.S.C. § 2072, that delegates this authority to the Supreme Court. That statute provides:

> (a) The Supreme Court shall have the power to prescribe general rules of practice and procedure and rules of evidence for cases in the United States district courts (including proceedings before magistrates thereof) and courts of appeals.
>
> (b) Such rules shall not abridge, enlarge or modify any substantive right. All law in conflict with such rules shall be of no further force or effect after such rules have taken effect.

Although subpart (a) appears to delegate broad authority, subpart (b) seems to restrict that authority. In essence the statute says that the Supreme Court may promulgate procedural rules, but not procedural rules that alter or amend substantive rights.

The first challenge to the Rules came three years after their promulgation, in Sibbach v. Wilson & Co., 312 U.S. 1 (1941). There, pursuant to Rule 35, the court ordered the plaintiff to submit to physical examination. State law did not permit a court to order such examinations, and the plaintiff argued that Rule 35 was invalid because it abridged a substantive right to be free from the indignity and intrusion of court-ordered physical exams. The Supreme Court rejected this argument, concluding that subsection (b) of the statute simply restated, but did not modify, subsection (a). According to the Court, the categories of substance and procedure are mutually exclusive. The test for the validity of a federal rule, the Court explained, is whether that Rule "really regulates procedure." If the Rule does concern procedure, then, by definition, it cannot be one that alters or amends substantive rights. In Burlington N. R. Co. v. Woods, 480 U.S. 1 (1987), the Court again considered the impact of subsection (b). The Court explained that "Rules which incidentally affect litigants' substantive rights do not violate this provision if reasonably necessary to maintain the integrity of that system of rules." Id. at 5.

Would the following Rules be within the scope of the Rules Enabling Act?

(a) a Rule providing that where a judgment is rendered, the loser shall pay the costs, including attorney's fees, of the winner;

(b) a Rule providing for a three-year statute of limitations in all cases in federal court;

(c) a Rule providing for nationwide service of process in all cases in federal court.

Notwithstanding *Sibbach* and *Woods*, subsection (b) may have some constraining effect on what Rules are promulgated and how courts interpret them. For example, in *Wal-Mart Stores, Inc. v. Dukes*, 131 S. Ct. 2541, 2551 (2011), the Court refused to interpret Federal Rule 23, concerning class actions, in a particular way because doing so would affect the substantive rights of a party and thus violate the Rules Enabling Act.

The Supreme Court has never struck down a Federal Rule of Civil Procedure. This is not surprising given the way the Rules are promulgated. Proposed Rules are drafted by an advisory committee composed of lawyers and judges and transmitted to the Judicial Conference, a group composed entirely of federal judges. The Conference then transmits any proposed Rules to the Supreme Court for its review and approval. The Rules are then sent to Congress which has seven months to review them. Thus, as the Supreme Court observed in *Hanna*, a challenge to a Rule can succeed "only if the Advisory Committee, this Court, and Congress erred in their prima facie judgment that the Rule in question transgresses neither the terms of the Enabling Act nor constitutional restrictions." This promulgation process gives the Rules "presumptive validity under both the constitutional and statutory constraints." *Burlington N. R. Co.*, 480 U.S. at 6.

b. What Happens When There Is No Federal Rule of Civil Procedure on Point — The Rules of Decision Act Prong

Although *Hanna* found that there was a valid Federal Rule of Civil Procedure on point in that case, the Court nonetheless explained how to analyze cases where there is no such Rule. A few commentators have pointed out that this portion of the opinion is dicta. (Do you see why?) See REDISH, FEDERAL JURISDICTION 220 n.71. According to the Court, this analysis should focus on the "twin aims of *Erie*" — discouraging forum shopping and avoiding inequitable administration of the laws.

Notes and Questions

1. Are the "twin aims of *Erie*" really only one aim? Several commentators have argued that "the 'twin aims' collapse into a single concern for equality: forum shopping results from and contributes to different treatment of litigants on the basis of their citizenship." Stein, supra, 100 YALE L.J. at 1947. See REDISH, FEDERAL JURISDICTION at 225. In a similar vein, the test articulated by the Court in *Hanna* has been called a "modified outcome test." As Professor Freer has explained, "Instead of assessing

outcome determination at the point at which it is raised in litigation—when it will always make a difference in outcome—it should be assessed ex ante, as of the outset of litigation." Freer, supra, 63 TULANE L REV. at 1106. See Ely, supra, 87 HARV. L. REV. at 717–18.

2. What's so bad about "forum shopping"? Isn't the whole point of diversity jurisdiction to provide out-of-state litigants with an alternative forum?

3. Reconsider Note 6 after *Byrd.* Would this situation be analyzed differently under the *Hanna* test?

4. The *Hanna* Court suggests that the difference between the state and federal service rules was not sufficient to affect a litigant's choice of forum. But is this really true? In *Hanna*, the plaintiff filed suit a little more than three weeks before the statute of limitations expired. Isn't it possible that a litigant who had only three weeks within which to effectuate service might choose federal court because federal court does not require in-hand personal service? Would such circumstances of an individual case matter under *Hanna*?

5. How is *Hanna* different from *York*? What is left of *York* after *Hanna*?

6. Does *Hanna* overrule *Byrd*?

7. Consider Chambers v. NASCO, Inc., 501 U.S. 32 (1991), a post-*Hanna* decision. There, a federal district court in Louisiana ordered the defendant to pay the plaintiff's attorney's fees and expenses of nearly $1,000,000 as a sanction for the defendant's bad faith conduct in litigation. In imposing this sanction, the court relied not on Rule 11 or 28 U.S.C. § 1927, but on its "inherent power." The defendant argued that under Louisiana law, such sanctions were not available and that the federal court was required to apply state law. Applying the "twin aims" test of *Hanna*, the Supreme Court rejected this argument. The Court concluded that different sanctions for bad faith conduct would not result in forum shopping. The Court also reasoned that because parties control their own conduct, application of the federal rule would not result in an inequitable administration of the laws. The Court did not cite or purport to apply *Byrd*, although it did observe that no state substantive policy was implicated in the case. The Court's analysis ended with a curious quotation from the Court of Appeals: "'[W]e do not see how the district court's inherent power to tax fees for that conduct can be made subservient to any state policy without transgressing the boundaries set out in *Erie, Guaranty Trust Co.*, and *Hanna*,' for '[f]ee-shifting here is not a matter of substantive remedy, but of vindicatory judicial authority.'" Id. at 55. How would *Erie* be transgressed if federal interests were made "subservient" to state policy?

8. Notwithstanding the possible rejection of *Byrd* by *Hanna*, many lower courts have continued to rely on *Byrd*. Some courts ignore *Hanna* entirely, other courts acknowledge *Hanna* but conclude that *Byrd* is the proper test in at least some situations, and still others attempt to use both *Byrd* and *Hanna*. See REDISH, FEDERAL JURISDICTION at 221–25. Professor Redish explains this state of affairs:

> The lower federal courts' widespread refusal to apply *Hanna* as the exclusive Rules of Decision test * * * may well represent more than failure to grasp

> the subtleties of the *Hanna* Court's analysis. Instead, it may reflect the view that *Hanna*'s modified outcome determination test inadequately accommodates all of the significant social interests to be served by both *Erie* and the Rules of Decision Act.

Redish, Federal Jurisdiction at 225. Do you agree? Do you think *Byrd* or *Hanna* better captures the underlying purposes of *Erie* and the Rules of Decision Act?

c. *Applying the* Hanna *Structure*

Cases frequently present both prongs of *Hanna.* The court must first decide the scope and applicability of a Federal Rule of Civil Procedure that arguably applies and, if it concludes the Rule does not apply to the case at hand, goes on to do a Rules of Decision Act analysis. This is true in both of the following cases. You will notice that for at least some of the Justices, the analysis of the first issue seems to be influenced by their assessment of the second.

Gasperini v. Center for Humanities, Inc.

518 U.S. 415, 116 S. Ct. 2211, 135 L. Ed. 2d 659 (1996)

Justice Ginsburg delivered the opinion of the Court.

Under the law of New York, appellate courts are empowered to review the size of jury verdicts and to order new trials when the jury's award "deviates materially from what would be reasonable compensation." N.Y. Civ. Prac. Law and Rules (CPLR) § 5501(c) (McKinney 1995). Under the Seventh Amendment, which governs proceedings in federal court, but not in state court, "the right of trial by jury shall be preserved, and no fact tried by a jury, shall be otherwise re-examined in any Court of the United States, than according to the rules of the common law." U.S. Const., Amdt. 7. The compatibility of these provisions, in an action based on New York law but tried in federal court by reason of the parties' diverse citizenship, is the issue we confront in this case. We hold that New York's law controlling compensation awards for excessiveness or inadequacy can be given effect, without detriment to the Seventh Amendment, if the review standard set out in CPLR § 5501(c) is applied by the federal trial court judge, with appellate control of the trial court's ruling limited to review for "abuse of discretion."

I

Petitioner William Gasperini, a journalist for CBS News and the Christian Science Monitor, began reporting on events in Central America in 1984. He earned his living primarily in radio and print media and only occasionally sold his photographic work. During the course of his seven-year stint in Central America, Gasperini took over 5,000 slide transparencies, depicting active war zones, political leaders, and scenes from daily life. In 1990, Gasperini agreed to supply his original color transparencies to The Center for Humanities, Inc. (Center) for use in an educational videotape, Conflict in Central America. Gasperini selected 300 of his slides for the Center; its videotape included 110 of them. The Center agreed to return the original transparencies, but upon the completion of the project, it could not find them.

Gasperini commenced suit in the United States District Court for the Southern District of New York, invoking the court's diversity jurisdiction pursuant to 28 U.S.C. § 1332. He alleged several state-law claims for relief, including breach of contract, conversion, and negligence. The Center conceded liability for the lost transparencies and the issue of damages was tried before a jury.

At trial, Gasperini's expert witness testified that the "industry standard" within the photographic publishing community valued a lost transparency at $1,500. This industry standard, the expert explained, represented the average license fee a commercial photograph could earn over the full course of the photographer's copyright, i.e., in Gasperini's case, his lifetime plus 50 years. Gasperini estimated that his earnings from photography totaled just over $10,000 for the period from 1984 through 1993. He also testified that he intended to produce a book containing his best photographs from Central America.

After a three-day trial, the jury awarded Gasperini $450,000 in compensatory damages. This sum, the jury foreperson announced, "is [$]1500 each, for 300 slides." Moving for a new trial under Federal Rule of Civil Procedure 59, the Center attacked the verdict on various grounds, including excessiveness. Without comment, the District Court denied the motion.

The Court of Appeals for the Second Circuit vacated the judgment entered on the jury's verdict. 66 F.3d 427 (1995). Mindful that New York law governed the controversy, the Court of Appeals endeavored to apply CPLR § 5501(c), which instructs that, when a jury returns an itemized verdict, as the jury did in this case, the New York Appellate Division "shall determine that an award is excessive or inadequate if it deviates materially from what would be reasonable compensation." * * * Surveying Appellate Division decisions that reviewed damage awards for lost transparencies, the Second Circuit concluded that testimony on industry standard alone was insufficient to justify a verdict; prime among other factors warranting consideration were the uniqueness of the slides' subject matter and the photographer's earning level.

Guided by Appellate Division rulings, the Second Circuit held that the $450,000 verdict "materially deviates from what is reasonable compensation." Some of Gasperini's transparencies, the Second Circuit recognized, were unique, notably those capturing combat situations in which Gasperini was the only photographer present. But others "depicted either generic scenes or events at which other professional photojournalists were present." No more than 50 slides merited a $1,500 award, the court concluded, after "giving Gasperini every benefit of the doubt." Absent evidence showing significant earnings from photographic endeavors or concrete plans to publish a book, the court further determined, any damage award above $100 each for the remaining slides would be excessive. Remittiturs "present difficult problems for appellate courts," the Second Circuit acknowledged, for court of appeals judges review the evidence from "a cold paper record."

Nevertheless, the Second Circuit set aside the $450,000 verdict and ordered a new trial, unless Gasperini agreed to an award of $100,000.

This case presents an important question regarding the standard a federal court uses to measure the alleged excessiveness of a jury's verdict in an action for damages based on state law. We therefore granted certiorari.

II

Before 1986, state and federal courts in New York generally invoked the same judge-made formulation in responding to excessiveness attacks on jury verdicts: courts would not disturb an award unless the amount was so exorbitant that it "shocked the conscience of the court." * * *

In both state and federal courts, trial judges made the excessiveness assessment in the first instance, and appellate judges ordinarily deferred to the trial court's judgment.

In 1986, as part of a series of tort reform measures, New York codified a standard for judicial review of the size of jury awards. Placed in CPLR § 5501(c), the prescription reads:

> "In reviewing a money judgment ... in which it is contended that the award is excessive or inadequate and that a new trial should have been granted unless a stipulation is entered to a different award, the appellate division shall determine that an award is excessive or inadequate if it deviates materially from what would be reasonable compensation."

As stated in Legislative Findings and Declarations accompanying New York's adoption of the "deviates materially" formulation, the lawmakers found the "shock the conscience" test an insufficient check on damage awards; the legislature therefore installed a standard "inviting more careful appellate scrutiny." At the same time, the legislature instructed the Appellate Division, in amended § 5522, to state the reasons for the court's rulings on the size of verdicts, and the factors the court considered in complying with § 5501(c). In his signing statement, then-Governor Mario Cuomo emphasized that the CPLR amendments were meant to rachet up the review standard: "This will assure greater scrutiny of the amount of verdicts and promote greater stability in the tort system and greater fairness for similarly situated defendants throughout the State."

New York state-court opinions confirm that § 5501(c)'s "deviates materially" standard calls for closer surveillance than "shock the conscience" oversight.

Although phrased as a direction to New York's intermediate appellate courts, § 5501(c)'s "deviates materially" standard, as construed by New York's courts, instructs state trial judges as well. Application of § 5501(c) at the trial level is key to this case.

To determine whether an award "deviates materially from what would be reasonable compensation," New York state courts look to awards approved in similar cases. Under New York's former "shock the conscience" test, courts also referred to analogous cases. The "deviates materially" standard, however, in design and operation, influences outcomes by tightening the range of tolerable awards.

III

In cases like Gasperini's, in which New York law governs the claims for relief, does New York law also supply the test for federal court review of the size of the verdict? The Center answers yes. The "deviates materially" standard, it argues, is a substantive standard that must be applied by federal appellate courts in diversity cases. The Second Circuit agreed. Gasperini, emphasizing that § 5501(c) trains on the New York Appellate Division, characterizes the provision as procedural, an allocation of decisionmaking authority regarding damages, not a hard cap on the amount recoverable. Correctly comprehended, Gasperini urges, § 5501(c)'s direction to the Appellate Division cannot be given effect by federal appellate courts without violating the Seventh Amendment's re-examination clause.

As the parties' arguments suggest, CPLR § 5501(c), appraised under *Erie R. Co. v. Tompkins*, and decisions in *Erie's* path, is both "substantive" and "procedural": "substantive" in that § 5501(c)'s "deviates materially" standard controls how much a plaintiff can be awarded; "procedural" in that § 5501(c) assigns decisionmaking authority to New York's Appellate Division. Parallel application of § 5501(c) at the federal appellate level would be out of sync with the federal system's division of trial and appellate court functions, an allocation weighted by the Seventh Amendment. The dispositive question, therefore, is whether federal courts can give effect to the substantive thrust of § 5501(c) without untoward alteration of the federal scheme for the trial and decision of civil cases.

A

Federal diversity jurisdiction provides an alternative forum for the adjudication of state-created rights, but it does not carry with it generation of rules of substantive law. As *Erie* read the Rules of Decision Act: "Except in matters governed by the Federal Constitution or by Acts of Congress, the law to be applied in any case is the law of the State." Under the *Erie* doctrine, federal courts sitting in diversity apply state substantive law and federal procedural law.

Classification of a law as "substantive" or "procedural" for *Erie* purposes is sometimes a challenging endeavor.[7] *Guaranty Trust Co. v. York*, an early interpretation of *Erie*, propounded an "outcome-determination" test: "Does it significantly affect the result of a litigation for a federal court to disregard a law of a State that would be controlling in an action upon the same claim by the same parties in a State court?" Ordering application of a state statute of limitations to an equity proceeding in federal court, the Court said in *Guaranty Trust*: "Where a federal court is exercising juris-

---

7. Concerning matters covered by the Federal Rules of Civil Procedure, the characterization question is usually unproblematic: It is settled that if the Rule in point is consonant with the Rules Enabling Act, 28 U.S.C. § 2072, and the Constitution, the Federal Rule applies regardless of contrary state law. See *Hanna v. Plumer*; *Burlington Northern R. Co. v. Woods*. Federal courts have interpreted the Federal Rules, however, with sensitivity to important state interests and regulatory policies. See, e.g., Walker v. Armco Steel Corp., 446 U.S. 740, 750–752 (1980) (reaffirming decision in *Ragan v. Merchants Transfer & Warehouse Co.*), that state law rather than Rule 3 determines when a diversity action commences for the purposes of tolling the state statute of limitations; Rule 3 makes no reference to the tolling of state limitations, the Court observed, and accordingly found no "direct conflict"); S.A. Healy Co. v. Milwaukee Metropolitan Sewerage Dist., 60 F.3d 305, 310–312 (7th Cir. 1995) (state provision for offers of settlement by plaintiffs is compatible with Federal Rule 68, which is limited to offers by defendants).

diction solely because of the diversity of citizenship of the parties, the outcome of the litigation in the federal court should be substantially the same, so far as legal rules determine the outcome of a litigation, as it would be if tried in a State court." A later pathmarking case, qualifying *Guaranty Trust*, explained that the "outcome-determination" test must not be applied mechanically to sweep in all manner of variations; instead, its application must be guided by "the twin aims of the *Erie* rule: discouragement of forum-shopping and avoidance of inequitable administration of the laws." *Hanna v. Plumer.*

Informed by these decisions, we address the question whether New York's "deviates materially" standard, codified in CPLR § 5501(c), is outcome-affective in this sense: Would "application of the [standard] ... have so important an effect upon the fortunes of one or both of the litigants that failure to [apply] it would [unfairly discriminate against citizens of the forum State, or] be likely to cause a plaintiff to choose the federal court"? *Hanna* at n.9.

We start from a point the parties do not debate. Gasperini acknowledges that a statutory cap on damages would supply substantive law for *Erie* purposes.[9] Although CPLR § 5501(c) is less readily classified, it was designed to provide an analogous control.

New York's Legislature codified in § 5501(c) a new standard, one that requires closer court review than the common law "shock the conscience" test. More rigorous comparative evaluations attend application of § 5501(c)'s "deviates materially" standard. To foster predictability, the legislature required the reviewing court, when overturning a verdict under § 5501(c), to state its reasons, including the factors it considered relevant. We think it a fair conclusion that CPLR § 5501(c) differs from a statutory cap principally "in that the maximum amount recoverable is not set by statute, but rather is determined by case law." Brief for City of New York as Amicus Curiae 11. In sum, § 5501(c) contains a procedural instruction, but the State's objective is manifestly substantive.

It thus appears that if federal courts ignore the change in the New York standard and persist in applying the "shock the conscience" test to damage awards on claims governed by New York law,[10] "'substantial' variations between state and federal [money judgments]" may be expected. See *Hanna.*[11] We therefore agree with the Sec-

---

9. While we have not specifically addressed the issue, courts of appeals have held that district court application of state statutory caps in diversity cases, post verdict, does not violate the Seventh Amendment.

10. JUSTICE SCALIA questions whether federal district courts in New York "actually apply" or "*ought*" to apply the "shock the conscience" test in assessing a jury's award for excessiveness. If there is a federal district court standard, it must come from the Court of Appeals, not from the over 40 district court judges in the Southern District of New York, each of whom sits alone and renders decisions not binding on the others.

11. JUSTICE SCALIA questions whether application of CPLR § 5501(c), in lieu of the standard generally used by federal courts within the Second Circuit, will in fact yield consistent outcome differentials. The numbers, as the Second Circuit believed, are revealing. Is the difference between an award of $450,000 and $100,000, or between $1,500 per transparency and $500, fairly described as insubstantial? We do not see how that can be so.

ond Circuit that New York's check on excessive damages implicates what we have called *Erie*'s "twin aims."[12] Just as the *Erie* principle precludes a federal court from giving a state-created claim "longer life ... than [the claim] would have had in the state court," *Ragan*, so *Erie* precludes a recovery in federal court significantly larger than the recovery that would have been tolerated in state court.

B

CPLR § 5501(c), as earlier noted, is phrased as a direction to the New York Appellate Division. Acting essentially as a surrogate for a New York appellate forum, the Court of Appeals reviewed Gasperini's award to determine if it "deviated materially" from damage awards the Appellate Division permitted in similar circumstances. The Court of Appeals performed this task without benefit of an opinion from the District Court, which had denied "without comment" the Center's Rule 59 motion. Concentrating on the authority § 5501(c) gives to the Appellate Division, Gasperini urges that the provision shifts fact-finding responsibility from the jury and the trial judge to the appellate court. Assigning such responsibility to an appellate court, he maintains, is incompatible with the Seventh Amendment's re-examination clause, and therefore, Gasperini concludes, § 5501(c) cannot be given effect in federal court. Although we reach a different conclusion than Gasperini, we agree that the Second Circuit did not attend to "an essential characteristic of [the federal-court] system," *Byrd v. Blue Ridge Rural Elec. Cooperative*, when it used § 5501(c) as "the standard for [federal] appellate review."

That "essential characteristic" was described in *Byrd*, a diversity suit for negligence in which a pivotal issue of fact would have been tried by a judge were the case in state court. The *Byrd* Court held that, despite the state practice, the plaintiff was entitled to a jury trial in federal court. In so ruling, the Court said that the *Guaranty Trust* "outcome-determination" test was an insufficient guide in cases presenting countervailing federal interests. See *Byrd*. The Court described the countervailing federal interests present in *Byrd* this way:

> "The federal system is an independent system for administering justice to litigants who properly invoke its jurisdiction. An essential characteristic of that system is the manner in which, in civil common-law actions, it distributes trial functions between judge and jury and, under the influence—if not the command—of the Seventh Amendment, assigns the decisions of disputed questions of fact to the jury." (footnote omitted).

The Seventh Amendment, which governs proceedings in federal court, but not in state court, bears not only on the allocation of trial functions between judge and jury, the issue in *Byrd*; it also controls the allocation of authority to review verdicts, the issue of concern here. The Amendment reads:

---

12. For rights that are state-created, state law governs the amount properly awarded as punitive damages, subject to an ultimate federal constitutional check for exorbitancy. An evenhanded approach would require federal court deference to endeavors like New York's to control compensatory damages for excessiveness. See infra, at n.18.

"In Suits at common law, where the value in controversy shall exceed twenty dollars, the right of trial by jury shall be preserved, and no fact tried by a jury, shall be otherwise re-examined in any Court of the United States, than according to the rules of the common law."

Byrd involved the first clause of the Amendment, the "trial by jury" clause. This case involves the second, the "re-examination" clause. In keeping with the historic understanding, the re-examination clause does not inhibit the authority of trial judges to grant new trials "for any of the reasons for which new trials have heretofore been granted in actions at law in the courts of the United States." Fed. Rule Civ. Proc. 59(a). That authority is large. This discretion includes overturning verdicts for excessiveness and ordering a new trial without qualification, or conditioned on the verdict winner's refusal to agree to a reduction (remittitur). See Dimick v. Schiedt, 293 U.S. 474, 486–487 (1935) (recognizing that remittitur withstands Seventh Amendment attack, but rejecting additur as unconstitutional).

In contrast, appellate review of a federal trial court's denial of a motion to set aside a jury's verdict as excessive is a relatively late, and less secure, development. Such review was once deemed inconsonant with the Seventh Amendment's re-examination clause. See, e.g., Lincoln v. Power, 151 U.S. 436, 437–438 (1894); Williamson v. Osenton, 220 F. 653, 655 (4th Cir. 1915); see also 6A MOORE'S FEDERAL PRACTICE § 59.08[6], at 59–167 (collecting cases). We subsequently recognized that, even in cases in which the *Erie* doctrine was not in play—cases arising wholly under federal law—the question was not settled; we twice granted certiorari to decide the unsettled issue, but ultimately resolved the cases on other grounds. See Grunenthal v. Long Island R. Co., 393 U.S. 156, 158 (1968); Neese v. Southern R. Co., 350 U.S. 77, 77 (1955).

Before today, we have not "expressly [held] that the Seventh Amendment allows appellate review of a district court's denial of a motion to set aside an award as excessive." Browning-Ferris Industries of Vt., Inc. v. Kelco Disposal, Inc., 492 U.S. 257, 279, n. 25 (1989). But in successive reminders that the question was worthy of this Court's attention, we noted, without disapproval, that courts of appeals engage in review of district court excessiveness determinations, applying "abuse of discretion" as their standard. See *Grunenthal*, 393 U.S. at 159.[18] * * *

As the Second Circuit explained, appellate review for abuse of discretion is reconcilable with the Seventh Amendment as a control necessary and proper to the fair administration of justice: "We must give the benefit of every doubt to the judgment of the trial judge; but surely there must be an upper limit, and whether that has been surpassed is not a question of fact with respect to which reasonable men may differ, but a question of law." We now * * * make explicit what Justice Stewart thought implicit in our *Grunenthal* disposition: "Nothing in the Seventh Amendment ... pre-

18. *Browning-Ferris* concerned punitive damages. We agree with the Second Circuit, however, that "for purposes of deciding whether state or federal law is applicable, the question whether an award of compensatory damages exceeds what is permitted by law is not materially different from the question whether an award of punitive damages exceeds what is permitted by law."

cludes appellate review of the trial judge's denial of a motion to set aside [a jury verdict] as excessive." 393 U.S. at 164 (Stewart, J., dissenting) (internal quotation marks and footnote omitted).

C

In *Byrd*, the Court faced a one-or-the-other choice: trial by judge as in state court, or trial by jury according to the federal practice.[21] In the case before us, a choice of that order is not required, for the principal state and federal interests can be accommodated. The Second Circuit correctly recognized that when New York substantive law governs a claim for relief, New York law and decisions guide the allowable damages. But that court did not take into account the characteristic of the federal-court system that caused us to reaffirm: "The proper role of the trial and appellate courts in the federal system in reviewing the size of jury verdicts is ... a matter of federal law." Donovan v. Penn Shipping Co., 429 U.S. 648, 649 (1977) (per curiam).

New York's dominant interest can be respected, without disrupting the federal system, once it is recognized that the federal district court is capable of performing the checking function, i.e., that court can apply the State's "deviates materially" standard in line with New York case law evolving under CPLR § 5501(c).[22] We recall, in this regard, that the "deviates materially" standard serves as the guide to be applied in trial as well as appellate courts in New York.

Within the federal system, practical reasons combine with Seventh Amendment constraints to lodge in the district court, not the court of appeals, primary responsibility for application of § 5501(c)'s "deviates materially" check. Trial judges have the "unique opportunity to consider the evidence in the living courtroom context," while appellate judges see only the "cold paper record."

District court applications of the "deviates materially" standard would be subject to appellate review under the standard the Circuits now employ when inadequacy or excessiveness is asserted on appeal: abuse of discretion. In light of *Erie*'s doctrine, the federal appeals court must be guided by the damage-control standard state law

21. The two-trial rule posited by Justice Scalia, surely would be incompatible with the existence of "the federal system [as] an independent system for administering justice," *Byrd v. Blue Ridge Rural Elec. Cooperative, Inc.* We discern no disagreement on such examples among the many federal judges who have considered this case.

22. Justice Scalia finds in Federal Rule of Civil Procedure 59 a "federal standard" for new trial motions in "direct collision" with, and "leaving no room for the operation of," a state law like CPLR § 5501 (c). The relevant prescription, Rule 59(a), has remained unchanged since the adoption of the Federal Rules by this Court in 1937. Rule 59(a) is as encompassing as it is uncontroversial. It is indeed "Hornbook" law that a most usual ground for a Rule 59 motion is that "the damages are excessive." See C. Wright, Law Of Federal Courts 676–677 (5th ed. 1994). Whether damages are excessive for the claim-in-suit must be governed by some law. And there is no candidate for that governance other than the law that gives rise to the claim for relief—here, the law of New York. See 28 U.S.C. § 2072(a) and (b) ("Supreme Court shall have the power to prescribe general rules of ... procedure"; "such rules shall not abridge, enlarge or modify any substantive right").

supplies,[23] but as the Second Circuit itself has said: "If we reverse, it must be because of an abuse of discretion.... The very nature of the problem counsels restraint.... We must give the benefit of every doubt to the judgment of the trial judge."

IV

It does not appear that the District Court checked the jury's verdict against the relevant New York decisions demanding more than "industry standard" testimony to support an award of the size the jury returned in this case. As the Court of Appeals recognized, the uniqueness of the photographs and the plaintiff's earnings as photographer—past and reasonably projected—are factors relevant to appraisal of the award. Accordingly, we vacate the judgment of the Court of Appeals and instruct that court to remand the case to the District Court so that the trial judge, revisiting his ruling on the new trial motion, may test the jury's verdict against CLPR § 5501(c)'s "deviates materially" standard.

It is so ordered.

[Dissent of Justice Stevens omitted.]

JUSTICE SCALIA, with whom the CHIEF JUSTICE and JUSTICE THOMAS join, dissenting.

The Court * * * holds today that a state practice that relates to the division of duties between state judges and juries must be followed by federal courts in diversity cases. On this issue, too, our prior cases are directly to the contrary. * * *

II

* * * The Court also directs that the case be remanded to the District Court, so that it may "test the jury's verdict against CPLR § 5501(c)'s 'deviates materially' standard." This disposition contradicts the principle that "the proper role of the trial and appellate courts in the federal system in reviewing the size of jury verdicts is ... a matter of federal law." Donovan v. Penn Shipping Co., 429 U.S. 648, 649 (1977) (per curiam).

The Court acknowledges that state procedural rules cannot, as a general matter, be permitted to interfere with the allocation of functions in the federal court system. Indeed, it is at least partly for this reason that the Court rejects direct application of § 5501(c) at the appellate level as inconsistent with an "essential characteristic" of the federal court system—by which the Court presumably means abuse-of-discretion review of denials of motions for new trials. But the scope of the Court's concern is oddly circumscribed. The "essential characteristic" of the federal jury, and, more specifically, the role of the federal trial court in reviewing jury judgments, apparently counts for little. The Court approves the "accommodation" achieved by having district courts review jury verdicts under the "deviates materially" standard, because it regards that as a means of giving effect to the State's purposes "without disrupting the federal sys-

---

23. If liability and damage-control rules are split apart here, as JUSTICE SCALIA says they must be to save the Seventh Amendment, then Gasperini's claim and others like it would be governed by a most curious "law." The sphinx-like, damage-determining law he would apply to this controversy has a state forepart, but a federal hindquarter. The beast may not be brutish, but there is little judgment in its creation.

tem." But changing the standard by which trial judges review jury verdicts does disrupt the federal system, and is plainly inconsistent with "the strong federal policy against allowing state rules to disrupt the judge-jury relationship in federal court." *Byrd.* The Court's opinion does not even acknowledge, let alone address, this dislocation.

We discussed precisely the point at issue here in *Browning-Ferris*, and gave an answer altogether contrary to the one provided today. *Browning-Ferris* rejected a request to fashion a federal common-law rule limiting the size of punitive-damages awards in federal courts, reaffirming the principle of *Erie*, that "in a diversity action, or in any other lawsuit where state law provides the basis of decision, the propriety of an award of punitive damages ... and the factors the jury may consider in determining their amount, are questions of state law." But the opinion expressly stated that "federal law ... will control on those issues involving the proper review of the jury award by a federal district court and court of appeals." "In reviewing an award of punitive damages," it said, "the role of the district court is to determine whether the jury's verdict is within the confines of state law, and to determine, by reference to federal standards developed under Rule 59, whether a new trial or remittitur should be ordered." The same distinction necessarily applies where the judgment under review is for compensatory damages: State substantive law controls what injuries are compensable and in what amount; but federal standards determine whether the award exceeds what is lawful to such degree that it may be set aside by order for new trial or remittitur.[10]

The Court does not disavow those statements in *Browning-Ferris* (indeed, it does not even discuss them), but it presumably overrules them, at least where the state rule that governs "whether a new trial or remittitur should be ordered" is characterized as "substantive" in nature. That, at any rate, is the reason the Court asserts for giving § 5501(c) dispositive effect. The objective of that provision, the Court states, "is manifestly substantive," since it operates to "control how much a plaintiff can be awarded" by "tightening the range of tolerable awards." Although "less readily classified" as substantive than "a statutory cap on damages," it nonetheless "was designed to provide an analogous control," by making a new trial mandatory when the award "deviates materially" from what is reasonable.

I do not see how this can be so. It seems to me quite wrong to regard this provision as a "substantive" rule for *Erie* purposes. The "analogy" to "a statutory cap on damages," fails utterly. There is an absolutely fundamental distinction between a rule of law such as that, which would ordinarily be imposed upon the jury in the trial court's instructions, and a rule of review, which simply determines how closely the jury

10. Justice Stevens thinks that if an award "exceeds what is lawful," the result is "legal error" that "may be corrected" by the appellate court. But the sort of "legal error" involved here is the imposition of legal consequences (in this case, damages) in light of facts that, under the law, may not warrant them. To suggest that every fact may be reviewed, because what may ensue from an erroneous factual determination is a "legal error," is to destroy the notion that there is a factfinding function reserved to the jury.

verdict will be scrutinized for compliance with the instructions. A tighter standard for reviewing jury determinations can no more plausibly be called a "substantive" disposition than can a tighter appellate standard for reviewing trial-court determinations. The one, like the other, provides additional assurance that the law has been complied with; but the other, like the one, leaves the law unchanged.

The Court commits the classic *Erie* mistake of regarding whatever changes the outcome as substantive. That is not the only factor to be considered. See *Byrd* ("Were 'outcome' the only consideration, a strong case might appear for saying that the federal court should follow the state practice. But there are affirmative countervailing considerations at work here"). Outcome-determination "was never intended to serve as a talisman," *Hanna v. Plumer*, and does not have the power to convert the most classic elements of the process of assuring that the law is observed into the substantive law itself. The right to have a jury make the findings of fact, for example, is generally thought to favor plaintiffs, and that advantage is often thought significant enough to be the basis for forum selection. But no one would argue that *Erie* confers a right to a jury in federal court wherever state courts would provide it; or that, were it not for the Seventh Amendment, *Erie* would require federal courts to dispense with the jury whenever state courts do so.

In any event, the Court exaggerates the difference that the state standard will make. It concludes that different outcomes are likely to ensue depending on whether the law being applied is the state "deviates materially" standard of § 5501 (c) or the "shocks the conscience" standard. Of course it is not the federal appellate standard but the federal district-court standard for granting new trials that must be compared with the New York standard to determine whether substantially different results will obtain—and it is far from clear that the district-court standard ought to be "shocks the conscience." Indeed, it is not even clear (as the Court asserts) that "shocks the conscience" is the standard (erroneous or not) actually applied by the district courts of the Second Circuit. The Second Circuit's test for reversing a grant of a new trial for an excessive verdict is whether the award was "clearly within the maximum limit of a reasonable range," so any district court that uses that standard will be affirmed. And while many district-court decisions express the "shocks the conscience" criterion, some have used a standard of "indisputably egregious," or have adopted the inverse of the Second Circuit's test for reversing a grant of new trial, namely, "clearly outside the maximum limit of a reasonable range." Moreover, some decisions that say "shocks the conscience" in fact apply a rule much less stringent. One case, for example, says that any award that would not be sustained under the New York "deviates materially" rule "shocks the conscience." In sum, it is at least highly questionable whether the consistent outcome differential claimed by the Court even exists. What seems to me far more likely to produce forum-shopping is the consistent difference between the state and federal appellate standards, which the Court leaves untouched. Under the Court's disposition, the Second Circuit reviews only for abuse of discretion, whereas New York's appellate courts engage in a de novo review for material deviation, giving the defendant a double shot at getting the damages award set aside. The only result that would produce the conformity the Court erroneously believes *Erie* requires is the one adopted by the Second Circuit and rejected by the Court: de novo federal appellate review under the § 5501(c) standard.

To say that application of § 5501(c) in place of the federal standard will not consistently produce disparate results is not to suggest that the decision the Court has made today is not a momentous one. The principle that the state standard governs is of great importance, since it bears the potential to destroy the uniformity of federal practice and the integrity of the federal court system. Under the Court's view, a state rule that directed courts "to determine that an award is excessive or inadequate if it deviates in any degree from the proper measure of compensation" would have to be applied in federal courts, effectively requiring federal judges to determine the amount of damages de novo, and effectively taking the matter away from the jury entirely. Cf. *Byrd*. Or consider a state rule that allowed the defendant a second trial on damages, with judgment ultimately in the amount of the lesser of two jury awards. Under the reasoning of the Court's opinion, even such a rule as that would have to be applied in the federal courts.

The foregoing describes why I think the Court's *Erie* analysis is flawed. But in my view, one does not even reach the *Erie* question in this case. The standard to be applied by a district court in ruling on a motion for a new trial is set forth in Rule 59 of the Federal Rules of Civil Procedure, which provides that "[a] new trial may be granted ... for any of the reasons for which new trials have heretofore been granted in actions at law *in the courts of the United States*" (emphasis added). That is undeniably a federal standard.[12] Federal district courts in the Second Circuit have interpreted that standard to permit the granting of new trials where "it is quite clear that the jury has reached a seriously erroneous result" and letting the verdict stand would result in a "miscarriage of justice." Assuming (as we have no reason to question) that this is a correct interpretation of what Rule 59 requires, it is undeniable that the federal rule is "'sufficiently broad' to cause a 'direct collision' with the state law or, implicitly, to 'control the issue' before the court, thereby leaving no room for the operation of that law." *Burlington Northern R. Co. v. Woods*. It is simply not possible to give controlling effect both to the federal standard and the state standard in reviewing the jury's award. That being so, the court has no choice but to apply the Federal Rule, which is an exercise of what we have called Congress's "power to regulate matters which, though falling within the uncertain area between substance and procedure, are rationally capable of classification as either," *Hanna*.

---

12. I agree with the Court's entire progression of reasoning in its footnote 22, leading to the conclusion that state law must determine "whether damages are excessive." But the question of whether damages are excessive is quite separate from the question of when a jury award may be set aside for excessiveness. It is the latter that is governed by Rule 59; as *Browning-Ferris* said, district courts are "to determine, by reference to federal standards developed under Rule 59, whether a new trial or remittitur should be ordered."

Notes and Questions

1. *Gasperini* addresses two separate issues: first, the proper standard for the district court to apply in ruling on a motion for new trial, and second, the proper standard of appellate review of the district court's ruling. As to the first issue — the standard that a federal court should apply in ruling on a motion for new trial — Justice Scalia argues that Rule 59 mandates a federal standard. Justice Ginsburg disagrees. (see n.22 of the majority opinion). Which argument do you find more persuasive? Given the majority's conclusion that Rule 59 does not include a standard for the trial court to apply, what standard should a federal court apply in the absence of a state statute such as New York had?

2. The Court concludes that if federal courts applied the "shock the conscience" test rather than New York law, there would be substantial variations between state and federal money judgments. Does the Court consider whether there are any countervailing federal interests that point in favor of applying a federal standard? Consider the following argument:

> Decisions such as ... *Gasperini* ... can be seen as the product of impulses that lead the Supreme Court to deemphasize the goals of uniformity and integrity of the operation of federal courts in an effort to promote compatibility with state law. While this concern is legitimate and deserving of consideration, it compromises the entire federal court system when the Court over-reacts and distorts the Federal Rules to accommodate state law. The efficient, fair, and uniform operation of the federal courts is a matter of ever-greater concern in a time of the increasing nationalization of law practice.

Earl C. Dudley & George Rutherglen, *Deforming the Federal Rules: An Essay on What's Wrong the Recent* Erie *Decision* s, 92 Va. L. Rev. 707, 747–48 (2006).

3. The majority held that appellate courts must apply an abuse of discretion standard of review. Why? Is this required by the Seventh Amendment? Will the standard of review affect outcome or choice of forum?

4. After *Gasperini*, how are lower courts supposed to use *Hanna* and *Byrd*? Notice that the Supreme Court relies on both but says nothing about the relationship between the two.

5. Justice Scalia accuses the majority of committing the "classic *Erie* mistake of regarding whatever changes the outcome as substantive." Did the majority do what Scalia alleges? Is this a mistake?

6. Justice Scalia argues that Rule 59 mandates a federal standard for granting a new trial. Do you agree?

7. *Gasperini* involved the standard for evaluating whether a damage award is excessive. Should state law also provide the standard for determining whether to grant a new trial on the issue of liability? The standard for granting summary judgment? See Snead v. Metropolitan Prop. & Cas. Ins. Co., 237 F.3d 1080, 1090–91 (9th Cir. 2001); Sturdivant v. Target Corp., 464 F. Supp. 2d 596 (N.D. Tex. 2006) (applying a

federal standard); Jeffrey O. Cooper, *Symposium: The Future of Summary Judgement in the Shadow of* Erie, 43 AKRON L. REV. 1245 (2010). The standard for granting JMOL? Compare Deimer v. Cincinnati Sub-Zero Prod., Inc., 58 F.3d 341 (7th Cir. 1995) (federal standard), with K & T Enterprises, Inc. v. Zurich Ins. Co., 97 F.3d 171 (6th Cir. 1996) (state standard).

8. The scholarly reviews of *Gasperini* have been generally negative, see C. Douglas Floyd, Erie *Awry: A Comment on* Gasperini v. Center for Humanities, Inc., 1997 B.Y.U. L. REV. 267; Richard Freer, *Reflections on the State of* Erie *after* Gasperini, 76 TEX. L. REV. 1637 (1998); Wendy Collins Perdue, *The Sources and Scope of Federal Procedural Common Law: Some Reflections on* Erie *and* Gasperini, 46 U. KAN. L. REV. 751 (1998), with the exception of Thomas Rowe, *Not Bad for Government Work: Does Anyone Else Think the Supreme Court is Doing a Halfway Decent Job in its* Erie-Hanna *Jurisprudence?*, 73 NOTRE DAME L. REV. 963 (1998).

9. Following the remand of *Gasperini*, the district court concluded that 240 of the photos were worth $1,500 each and another 70 photos were worth $200 each. The court ordered a new trial unless the plaintiff accepted a remittitur of $75,000 (reducing the jury's original award of from $450,000 to $375,000), plus pre-judgment interest. The plaintiff accepted the remittitur but the defendant appealed. The Court of Appeals largely affirmed the district court, finding that the district court acted within its discretion. The court did find that the district court erred in including ten disputed pictures in its calculation. Unfortunately, the district court did not specify whether it had valued those ten pictures at $1,500 or $200. Therefore, the Court of Appeals held that the plaintiff could either stipulate that the ten slides had been valued at $1,500 and accept an award of $359,000 or the case would be remanded to the district court to recalculate damages excluding the ten slides. Gasperini v. The Center for Humanities, Inc., 149 F.3d 137 (2d Cir. 1998).

Note on "SLAPP" Suits

California, Virginia, and some other states have special rules regarding "SLAPP" suits, which are "strategic lawsuits against public participation." The rules are based on the idea that one should not be subject to suit (typically for defamation) for statements made in exercise of her rights of free speech or petition of the government. They permit the defendant in such cases to make an "anti-SLAPP" motion to dismiss the suit (or to strike the suit). The defendant must demonstrate that she is being sued for her exercise of protected activity. If she does, the burden then shifts to the plaintiff to show that the defendant acted with malice in making the statements. If the plaintiff cannot make that showing (which is usually difficult to do), the case is dismissed or stricken.

Must a district court in a diversity case apply such a SLAPP provision, or may the case simply proceed pursuant to the Federal Rules? In Makaeff v. Trump University, 715 F.3d 254 (9th Cir. 2013) (applying California law), the plaintiff made an anti-SLAPP motion to strike a defamation counterclaim against her. The district court denied the motion, but the Ninth Circuit here reversed. Judge Kozinsky wrote a concurring opinion, in which Judge Paez joined, raising the *Erie* question. Judge Kozinsky joined the opinion for the court, because previous Ninth Circuit law ("*Newsham*") required application of state law. He then argued that the precedent was wrong and should be reconsidered. He reasoned:

> In most cases, it's easy enough to tell whether a rule is substantive or procedural. Whether a defendant is liable in tort for a slip-and-fall, or has a Statute of Frauds defense to a contract claim, is controlled by state law. Just as clearly, the time to answer a complaint, the manner in which process is served, the methods and time limits for discovery, and whether the jury must be unanimous are controlled by the Federal Rules of Civil Procedure. The latter is true, even though such procedural rules can affect outcomes and, hence, substantive rights. *See Hanna*, 380 U.S. at 471.
>
> But the distinction between substance and procedure is not always clear-cut. While many rules are easily recognized as falling on one side or the other of the substance/procedure line, there are some close cases that call for a more nuanced analysis. * * *
>
> Most of *Newsham*'s analysis was devoted to showing that there's no "conflict" between California's anti-SLAPP statute and the Federal Rules of Civil Procedure and, therefore, the two regimes can operate side-by-side in the same lawsuit. But the question of a conflict only arises if the state rule is substantive; state procedural rules have no application in federal court, no matter how little they interfere with the Federal Rules. *Newsham*'s mistake was that it engaged in conflict analysis without first determining whether the state rule is, in fact, substantive.
>
> It's not. The anti-SLAPP statute creates no substantive rights; it merely provides a procedural mechanism for vindicating existing rights. The language of the statute is procedural: Its mainspring is a "special motion to strike"; it contains provisions limiting discovery; it provides for sanctions for parties who bring a non-meritorious suit or motion; the court's ruling on the potential success of plaintiff's claim is not "admissible in evidence at any later stage of the case"; and an order granting or denying the special motion is immediately appealable. * * * The statute deals only with the conduct of the lawsuit; it creates no rights independent of existing litigation; and its only purpose is the swift termination of certain lawsuits the legislators believed to be unduly burdensome. It is codified in the state code of civil procedure and the California Supreme Court has characterized it as a "procedural device to screen out meritless claims."
>
> Federal courts must ignore state rules of procedure because it is Congress that has plenary authority over the procedures employed in federal court, and this power cannot be trenched upon by the states. *Erie*, 304 U.S. at 78 ("[T]he law to be applied in any [diversity] case is the law of the State" except for "matters governed by the Federal Constitution or *acts of Congress*. ..."

> (emphasis added)). To me, this is the beginning and the end of the analysis. Having determined that the state rule is quintessentially procedural, I would conclude it has no application in federal court.

715 F.3d at 272–275 (citations and footnote omitted). How would you analyze the issue?

Shady Grove Orthopedic Association v. Allstate Insurance Co.

559 U.S. 393, 130 S. Ct. 1431, 176 L. Ed. 2d 311 (2010)

Justice Scalia announced the judgment of the Court and delivered the opinion of the Court with respect to Parts I and II-A, an opinion with respect to Parts II-B and II-D, in which The Chief Justice, Justice Thomas, and Justice Sotomayor join, and an opinion with respect to Part II-C, in which The Chief Justice and Justice Thomas join.

New York law prohibits class actions in suits seeking penalties or statutory minimum damages.[1] We consider whether this precludes a federal district court sitting in diversity from entertaining a class action under Federal Rule of Civil Procedure 23.[2]

I

The petitioner's complaint alleged the following: Shady Grove Orthopedic Associates, P.A., provided medical care to Sonia E. Galvez for injuries she suffered in an automobile accident. As partial payment for that care, Galvez assigned to Shady

---

1. N.Y. Civ. Prac. Law Ann. § 901 (2006) provides:
"(a) One or more members of a class may sue or be sued as representative parties on behalf of all if:
"1. the class is so numerous that joinder of all members, whether otherwise required or permitted, is impracticable;
"2. there are questions of law or fact common to the class which predominate over any questions affecting only individual members;
"3. the claims or defenses of the representative parties are typical of the claims or defenses of the class;
"4. the representative parties will fairly and adequately protect the interests of the class; and
"5. a class action is superior to other available methods for the fair and efficient adjudication of the controversy.
"(b) Unless a statute creating or imposing a penalty, or a minimum measure of recovery specifically authorizes the recovery thereof in a class action, an action to recover a penalty, or minimum measure of recovery created or imposed by statute may not be maintained as a class action."

2. Rule 23(a) provides:
"(a) Prerequisites. One or more members of a class may sue or be sued as representative parties on behalf of all members only if:
"(1) the class is so numerous that joinder of all members is impracticable;
"(2) there are questions of law or fact common to the class;
"(3) the claims or defenses of the representative parties are typical of the claims or defenses of the class; and
"(4) the representative parties will fairly and adequately protect the interests of the class."

Subsection (b) says that "[a] class action may be maintained if Rule 23 (a) is satisfied and if" the suit falls into one of three described categories (irrelevant for present purposes).

Grove her rights to insurance benefits under a policy issued in New York by Allstate Insurance Co. Shady Grove tendered a claim for the assigned benefits to Allstate, which under New York law had 30 days to pay the claim or deny it. See N.Y. Ins. Law Ann. § 5106(a) (2009). Allstate apparently paid, but not on time, and it refused to pay the statutory interest that accrued on the overdue benefits (at two percent per month).

Shady Grove filed this diversity suit in the Eastern District of New York to recover the unpaid statutory interest. Alleging that Allstate routinely refuses to pay interest on overdue benefits, Shady Grove sought relief on behalf of itself and a class of all others to whom Allstate owes interest. The District Court dismissed the suit for lack of jurisdiction. It reasoned that N.Y. Civ. Prac. Law Ann. § 901(b), which precludes a suit to recover a "penalty" from proceeding as a class action, applies in diversity suits in federal court, despite Federal Rule of Civil Procedure 23. Concluding that statutory interest is a "penalty" under New York law, it held that § 901(b) prohibited the proposed class action. And, since Shady Grove conceded that its individual claim (worth roughly $500) fell far short of the amount-in-controversy requirement for individual suits under 28 U.S.C. § 1332(a), the suit did not belong in federal court.[3]

The Second Circuit affirmed. * * *

II

The framework for our decision is familiar. We must first determine whether Rule 23 answers the question in dispute. Burlington Northern R. Co. v. Woods, 480 U.S. 1, 4–5 (1987). If it does, it governs—New York's law notwithstanding—unless it exceeds statutory authorization or Congress's rulemaking power. Id., at 5; see Hanna v. Plumer, 380 U.S. 460, 463–464 (1965). We do not wade into *Erie*'s murky waters unless the federal rule is inapplicable or invalid.

A

The question in dispute is whether Shady Grove's suit may proceed as a class action. Rule 23 provides an answer. It states that "[a] class action may be maintained" if two conditions are met: The suit must satisfy the criteria set forth in subdivision (a) (*i.e.*, numerosity, commonality, typicality, and adequacy of representation), and it also must fit into one of the three categories described in subdivision (b). Fed. Rule Civ. Proc. 23(b). By its terms this creates a categorical rule entitling a plaintiff whose suit meets the specified criteria to pursue his claim as a class action. (The Federal Rules regularly use "may" to confer categorical permission, see, *e.g.*, Fed. Rules Civ. Proc. 8(d)(2)–(3), 14(a)(1), 18(a)–(b), 20(a)(1)–(2), 27(a)(1), 30(a)(1), as do federal statutes that establish procedural entitlements.) Thus, Rule 23 provides a one-size-fits-all formula for deciding the class-action question. Because § 901(b) attempts to answer the same question—*i.e.*, it states that Shady Grove's suit "may *not* be main-

3. Shady Grove had asserted jurisdiction under 28 U.S.C. § 1332(d)(2), which relaxes, for class actions seeking at least $5 million, the rule against aggregating separate claims for calculation of the amount in controversy.

tained as a class action" (emphasis added) because of the relief it seeks—it cannot apply in diversity suits unless Rule 23 is ultra vires.

The Second Circuit believed that § 901(b) and Rule 23 do not conflict because they address different issues. Rule 23, it said, concerns only the criteria for determining whether a given class can and should be certified; section 901(b), on the other hand, addresses an antecedent question: whether the particular type of claim is eligible for class treatment in the first place—a question on which Rule 23 is silent. Allstate embraces this analysis.

We disagree. To begin with, the line between eligibility and certifiability is entirely artificial. Both are preconditions for maintaining a class action. Allstate suggests that eligibility must depend on the "particular cause of action" asserted, instead of some other attribute of the suit. But that is not so. Congress could, for example, provide that only claims involving more than a certain number of plaintiffs are "eligible" for class treatment in federal court. In other words, relabeling Rule 23(a)'s prerequisites "eligibility criteria" would obviate Allstate's objection—a sure sign that its eligibility-certifiability distinction is made-to-order.

There is no reason, in any event, to read Rule 23 as addressing only whether claims made eligible for class treatment by some *other* law should be certified as class actions. Allstate asserts that Rule 23 neither explicitly nor implicitly empowers a federal court "to certify a class in each and every case" where the Rule's criteria are met. But that is *exactly* what Rule 23 does: It says that if the prescribed preconditions are satisfied "[a] class action *may be maintained*" (emphasis added)—not "*a class action may be permitted.*" Courts do not maintain actions; litigants do. The discretion suggested by Rule 23's "may" is discretion residing in the plaintiff: He may bring his claim in a class action if he wishes. And like the rest of the Federal Rules of Civil Procedure, Rule 23 *automatically* applies "in all civil actions and proceedings in the United States district courts," Fed. Rule Civ. Proc. 1.

Allstate points out that Congress has carved out some federal claims from Rule 23's reach, see, e.g., 8 U.S.C. § 1252(e)(1)(B)—which shows, Allstate contends, that Rule 23 does not authorize class actions for all claims, but rather leaves room for laws like § 901(b). But Congress, unlike New York, has ultimate authority over the Federal Rules of Civil Procedure; it can create exceptions to an individual rule as it sees fit—either by directly amending the rule or by enacting a separate statute overriding it in certain instances. The fact that Congress has created specific exceptions to Rule 23 hardly proves that the Rule does not apply generally. In fact, it proves the opposite. If Rule 23 did *not* authorize class actions across the board, the statutory exceptions would be unnecessary.

Allstate next suggests that the structure of § 901 shows that Rule 23 addresses only certifiability. Section 901(*a*), it notes, establishes class-certification criteria roughly analogous to those in Rule 23 (wherefore it agrees *that* subsection is pre-empted). But § 901(b)'s rule barring class actions for certain claims is set off as its own subsection, and where it applies § 901(a) does not. This shows, according to Allstate, that § 901(b) concerns a separate subject. Perhaps it does concern a subject separate from the subject of § 901(a). But the question before us is whether it concerns a subject separate from the subject of Rule 23—and for purposes of answering *that* question the way New York has structured its statute is immaterial. Rule 23 permits all class actions that meet its requirements, and a State cannot limit that permission by structuring one part of its statute to track Rule 23 and enacting another part that imposes additional requirements. Both of § 901's subsections undeniably answer the same question as Rule 23: whether a class action may proceed for a given suit. Cf. *Burlington*, 480 U.S., at 7–8.

The dissent argues that § 901(b) has nothing to do with whether Shady Grove may maintain its suit as a class action, but affects only the *remedy* it may obtain if it wins. Whereas "Rule 23 governs procedural aspects of class litigation" by "prescrib[ing] the considerations relevant to class certification and postcertification proceedings," § 901(b) addresses only "the size of a monetary award a class plaintiff may pursue." Accordingly, the dissent says, Rule 23 and New York's law may coexist in peace.

We need not decide whether a state law that limits the remedies available in an existing class action would conflict with Rule 23; that is not what § 901(b) does. By its terms, the provision precludes a plaintiff from "maintain[ing]" a class action seeking statutory penalties. Unlike a law that sets a ceiling on damages (or puts other remedies out of reach) in properly filed class actions, § 901(b) says nothing about what remedies a court may award; it prevents the class actions it covers from coming into existence at all. Consequently, a court bound by § 901(b) could not certify a class action seeking both statutory penalties and other remedies even if it announces in advance that it will refuse to award the penalties in the event the plaintiffs prevail; to do so would violate the statute's clear prohibition on "maintain[ing]" such suits as class actions.

The dissent asserts that a plaintiff can avoid § 901(b)'s barrier by omitting from his complaint (or removing) a request for statutory penalties. Even assuming all statutory penalties are waivable, the fact that a complaint omitting them could be brought as a class action would not at all prove that § 901(b) is addressed only to remedies. If the state law instead banned class actions for fraud claims, a would-be class-action plaintiff could drop the fraud counts from his complaint and proceed with the remainder in a class action. Yet that would not mean the law provides no remedy for fraud; the ban would affect only the procedural means by which the remedy may be pursued. In short, although the dissent correctly abandons Allstate's eligibility-certifiability distinction, the alternative it offers fares no better.

The dissent all but admits that the literal terms of § 901(b) address the same subject as Rule 23—*i.e.*, whether a class action may be maintained—but insists the provision's *purpose* is to restrict only remedies. Unlike Rule 23, designed to further procedural fairness and efficiency, § 901(b) (we are told) "responds to an entirely different concern": the fear that allowing statutory damages to be awarded on a class-wide basis would "produce overkill." * * *

This evidence of the New York Legislature's purpose is pretty sparse. But even accepting the dissent's account of the Legislature's objective at face value, it cannot override the statute's clear text. Even if its aim is to restrict the remedy a plaintiff can obtain, § 901(b) achieves that end by limiting a plaintiff's power to maintain a class action. The manner in which the law "could have been written," has no bearing; what matters is the law the Legislature *did* enact. We cannot rewrite that to reflect our perception of legislative purpose. The dissent's concern for state prerogatives is frustrated rather than furthered by revising state laws when a potential conflict with a Federal Rule arises; the state-friendly approach would be to accept the law as written and test the validity of the Federal Rule.

The dissent's approach of determining whether state and federal rules conflict based on the subjective intentions of the state legislature is an enterprise destined to produce "confusion worse confounded," Sibbach v. Wilson & Co., 312 U.S. 1, 14 (1941). It would mean, to begin with, that one State's statute could survive pre-emption (and accordingly affect the procedures in federal court) while another State's identical law would not, merely because its authors had different aspirations. It would also mean that district courts would have to discern, in every diversity case, the purpose behind any putatively pre-empted state procedural rule, even if its text squarely conflicts with federal law. That task will often prove arduous. Many laws further more than one aim, and the aim of others may be impossible to discern. Moreover, to the extent the dissent's purpose-driven approach depends on its characterization of § 901(b)'s aims as substantive, it would apply to many state rules ostensibly addressed to procedure. Pleading standards, for example, often embody policy preferences about the types of claims that should succeed — as do rules governing summary judgment, pretrial discovery, and the admissibility of certain evidence. Hard cases will abound. * * *

But while the dissent does indeed artificially narrow the scope of § 901(b) by finding that it pursues only substantive policies, that is not the central difficulty of the dissent's position. The central difficulty is that even artificial narrowing cannot render § 901(b) compatible with Rule 23. *Whatever* the policies they pursue, they flatly contradict each other. Allstate asserts (and the dissent implies) that we can (and must) *interpret* Rule 23 in a manner that avoids overstepping its authorizing statute. If the Rule were susceptible of two meanings — one that would violate § 2072(b) and another that would not — we would agree. See Ortiz v. Fibreboard Corp., 527 U.S. 815, 842, 845 (1999); cf. Semtek Int'l Inc. v. Lockheed Martin Corp., 531 U.S. 497, 503–504 (2001). But it is not. Rule 23 unambiguously authorizes *any* plaintiff, in *any* federal civil proceeding, to maintain a class action if the Rule's prerequisites are met. We cannot contort its text, even to avert a collision with state law that might render it invalid. See Walker v. Armco Steel Corp., 446 U.S. 740, 750, n. 9 (1980). What the dissent's approach achieves is not the avoiding of a "conflict between Rule 23 and § 901(b)," but rather the invalidation of Rule 23 (pursuant to § 2072(b) of the Rules Enabling Act) to the extent that it conflicts with the substantive policies of § 901. There is no other way to reach the dissent's destination. We must therefore confront head-on whether Rule 23 falls within the statutory authorization.

B

Erie involved the constitutional power of federal courts to supplant state law with judge-made rules. In that context, it made no difference whether the rule was technically one of substance or procedure; the touchstone was whether it "significantly affect[s] the result of a litigation." Guaranty Trust Co. v. York, 326 U.S. 99, 109 (1945). That is not the test for either the constitutionality or the statutory validity of a Federal Rule of Procedure. Congress has undoubted power to supplant state law, and undoubted power to prescribe rules for the courts it has created, so long as those rules regulate matters "rationally capable of classification" as procedure. *Hanna.* In the Rules Enabling Act, Congress authorized this Court to promulgate rules of procedure subject to its review, 28 U.S.C. § 2072(a), but with the limitation that those rules "shall not abridge, enlarge or modify any substantive right," § 2072(b).

We have long held that this limitation means that the Rule must "really regulat[e] procedure — the judicial process for enforcing rights and duties recognized by substantive law and for justly administering remedy and redress for disregard or infraction of them," *Sibbach*; see *Hanna*; *Burlington*. The test is not whether the rule affects a litigant's substantive rights; most procedural rules do. Mississippi Publishing Corp. v. Murphree, 326 U.S. 438, 445 (1946). What matters is what the rule itself *regulates:* If it governs only "the manner and the means" by which the litigants' rights are "enforced," it is valid; if it alters "the rules of decision by which [the] court will adjudicate [those] rights," it is not. Id., at 446.

Applying that test, we have rejected every statutory challenge to a Federal Rule that has come before us. We have found to be in compliance with § 2072(b) rules prescribing methods for serving process, see id., at 445–446 (Fed. Rule Civ. Proc. 4(f)); *Hanna* (Fed. Rule Civ. Proc. 4(d)(1)), and requiring litigants whose mental or physical condition is in dispute to submit to examinations, see *Sibbach* (Fed. Rule Civ. Proc. 35); Schlagenhauf v. Holder, 379 U.S. 104, 113–114 (1964) (same). Likewise, we have upheld rules authorizing imposition of sanctions upon those who file frivolous appeals, see *Burlington* (Fed. Rule App. Proc. 38), or who sign court papers without a reasonable inquiry into the facts asserted, see Business Guides, Inc. v. Chromatic Communications Enterprises, Inc., 498 U.S. 533, 551–554 (1991) (Fed. Rule Civ. Proc. 11). Each of these rules had some practical effect on the parties' rights, but each undeniably regulated only the process for enforcing those rights; none altered the rights themselves, the available remedies, or the rules of decision by which the court adjudicated either.

Applying that criterion, we think it obvious that rules allowing multiple claims (and claims by or against multiple parties) to be litigated together are also valid. See, *e.g.*, Fed. Rules Civ. Proc. 18 (joinder of claims), 20 (joinder of parties), 42(a) (consolidation of actions). Such rules neither change plaintiffs' separate entitlements to relief nor abridge defendants' rights; they alter only how the claims are processed.

For the same reason, Rule 23—at least insofar as it allows willing plaintiffs to join their separate claims against the same defendants in a class action—falls within § 2072(b)'s authorization. A class action, no less than traditional joinder (of which it is a species), merely enables a federal court to adjudicate claims of multiple parties at once, instead of in separate suits. And like traditional joinder, it leaves the parties' legal rights and duties intact and the rules of decision unchanged.

Allstate contends that the authorization of class actions is not substantively neutral: Allowing Shady Grove to sue on behalf of a class "transform[s] [the] dispute over a five *hundred* dollar penalty into a dispute over a five *million* dollar penalty." Allstate's aggregate liability, however, does not depend on whether the suit proceeds as a class action. Each of the 1,000-plus members of the putative class could (as Allstate acknowledges) bring a freestanding suit asserting his individual claim. It is undoubtedly true that some plaintiffs who would not bring individual suits for the relatively small sums involved will choose to join a class action. That has no bearing, however, on Allstate's or the plaintiffs' legal rights. The likelihood that some (even many) plaintiffs will be induced to sue by the availability of a class action is just the sort of "incidental effec[t]" we have long held does not violate § 2072(b), *Mississippi Publishing.*

Allstate argues that Rule 23 violates § 2072(b) because the state law it displaces, § 901(b), creates a right that the Federal Rule abridges—namely, a "substantive right ... not to be subjected to aggregated class-action liability" in a single suit. To begin with, we doubt that that is so. Nothing in the text of § 901(b) (which is to be found in New York's procedural code) confines it to claims under New York law; and of course New York has no power to alter substantive rights and duties created by other sovereigns. As we have said, the *consequence* of excluding certain class actions may be to cap the damages a defendant can face in a single suit, but the law itself alters only procedure. In that respect, § 901(b) is no different from a state law forbidding simple joinder. As a fallback argument, Allstate argues that even if § 901(b) is a procedural provision, it was enacted "for *substantive reasons.*" Its end was not to improve "the conduct of the litigation process itself" but to alter "the outcome of that process."

The fundamental difficulty with both these arguments is that the substantive nature of New York's law, or its substantive purpose, *makes no difference.* A Federal Rule of Procedure is not valid in some jurisdictions and invalid in others—or valid in some cases and invalid in others—depending upon whether its effect is to frustrate a state substantive law (or a state procedural law enacted for substantive purposes). That could not be clearer in *Sibbach:*

> "The petitioner says the phrase ['substantive rights' in the Rules Enabling Act] connotes more; that by its use Congress intended that in regulating procedure this Court should not deal with important and substantial rights theretofore recognized. Recognized where and by whom? The state courts are divided as to the power in the absence of statute to order a physical examination. In a number such an order is authorized by statute or rule....

> "The asserted right, moreover, is no more important than many others enjoyed by litigants in District Courts sitting in the several states before the Federal Rules of Civil Procedure altered and abolished old rights or privileges and created new ones in connection with the conduct of litigation.... If we were to adopt the suggested criterion of the importance of the alleged right we should invite endless litigation and confusion worse confounded. The test must be whether a rule really regulates procedure...." 312 U.S., at 13–14 (footnotes omitted).

Hanna unmistakably expressed the same understanding that compliance of a Federal Rule with the Enabling Act is to be assessed by consulting the Rule itself, and not its effects in individual applications:

> "[T]he court has been instructed to apply the Federal Rule, and can refuse to do so only if the Advisory Committee, this Court, and Congress erred in their prima facie judgment that the Rule in question transgresses neither the terms of the Enabling Act nor constitutional restrictions." 380 U.S., at 471.

In sum, it is not the substantive or procedural nature or purpose of the affected state law that matters, but the substantive or procedural nature of the Federal Rule. We have held since *Sibbach*, and reaffirmed repeatedly, that the validity of a Federal Rule depends entirely upon whether it regulates procedure. See *Sibbach*; *Hanna*; *Burlington*. If it does, it is authorized by § 2072 and is valid in all jurisdictions, with respect to all claims, regardless of its incidental effect upon state-created rights.

C

A few words in response to the concurrence. We understand it to accept the framework we apply—which requires first, determining whether the federal and state rules can be reconciled (because they answer different questions), and second, if they cannot, determining whether the Federal Rule runs afoul of § 2072(b). * * *

The concurrence would decide this case on the basis, not that Rule 23 is procedural, but that the state law it displaces is procedural, in the sense that it does not "function as a part of the State's definition of substantive rights and remedies." A state procedural rule is not preempted, according to the concurrence, so long as it is "so bound up with," or "sufficiently intertwined with," a substantive state-law right or remedy "that it defines the scope of that substantive right or remedy."

This analysis squarely conflicts with *Sibbach*, which established the rule we apply. The concurrence contends that *Sibbach* did not rule out its approach, but that is not so. Recognizing the impracticability of a test that turns on the idiosyncrasies of state law, *Sibbach* adopted and applied a rule with a single criterion: whether the Federal Rule "really regulates procedure." That the concurrence's approach would have yielded the same result in *Sibbach* proves nothing; what matters is the rule we *did* apply, and that rule leaves no room for special exemptions based on the function or purpose of a particular state rule. * * *

In reality, the concurrence seeks not to apply *Sibbach*, but to overrule it (or, what is the same, to rewrite it). Its approach, the concurrence insists, gives short shrift to the statutory text forbidding the Federal Rules from "abridg[ing], enlarg[ing], or modify[ing] any substantive right," § 2072(b). There is something to that. It is possible to understand how it can be determined whether a Federal Rule "enlarges" substantive rights without consulting State law: If the Rule creates a substantive right, even one that duplicates some state-created rights, it establishes a new *federal* right. But it is hard to understand how it can be determined whether a Federal Rule "abridges" or "modifies" substantive rights without knowing what state-created rights would obtain if the Federal Rule did not exist. *Sibbach*'s exclusive focus on the challenged Federal Rule — driven by the very real concern that Federal Rules which vary from State to State would be chaos — is hard to square with § 2072(b)'s terms.

Sibbach has been settled law, however, for nearly seven decades. Setting aside any precedent requires a "special justification" beyond a bare belief that it was wrong. And a party seeking to overturn a *statutory* precedent bears an even greater burden, since Congress remains free to correct us, and adhering to our precedent enables it do so. We do Congress no service by presenting it a moving target. In all events, Allstate has not even asked us to overrule *Sibbach*, let alone carried its burden of persuading us to do so. Why we should cast aside our decades-old decision escapes us, especially since (as the concurrence explains) that would not affect the result.

The concurrence also contends that applying *Sibbach* and assessing whether a Federal Rule regulates substance or procedure is not always easy. Undoubtedly some hard cases will arise (though we have managed to muddle through well enough in the 69 years since *Sibbach* was decided). But as the concurrence acknowledges, the basic difficulty is unavoidable: The statute itself refers to "substantive right[s]," § 2072(b), so there is no escaping the substance-procedure distinction. What is more, the concurrence's approach does nothing to diminish the difficulty, but rather magnifies it many times over. Instead of a single hard question of whether a Federal Rule regulates substance or procedure, that approach will present hundreds of hard questions, forcing federal courts to assess the substantive or procedural character of countless state rules that may conflict with a single Federal Rule. And it still does not sidestep the problem it seeks to avoid. At the end of the day, one must come face to face with the decision whether or not the state policy (with which a putatively procedural state rule may be "bound up") pertains to a "substantive right or remedy" — that is, whether it is substance or procedure. The more one explores the alternatives to *Sibbach*'s rule, the more its wisdom becomes apparent.

D

We must acknowledge the reality that keeping the federal-court door open to class actions that cannot proceed in state court will produce forum shopping. That is unacceptable when it comes as the consequence of judge-made rules created to fill supposed "gaps" in positive federal law. See *Hanna*. For where neither the Constitution, a treaty, nor a statute provides the rule of decision or authorizes a federal court to supply one, "state law must govern because there can be no other law." Ibid.; see Clark, Erie's *Constitutional Source*, 95 Cal. L. Rev. 1289, 1302, 1311 (2007). But divergence from state law, with the attendant consequence of forum shopping, is the inevitable (indeed, one might say the intended) result of a uniform system of federal procedure. Congress itself has created the possibility that the same case may follow a different course if filed in federal instead of state court. Cf. *Hanna.* The short of the matter is that a Federal Rule governing procedure is valid whether or not it alters the outcome of the case in a way that induces forum shopping. To hold otherwise would be to "disembowel either the Constitution's grant of power over federal procedure" or Congress's exercise of it. Id.

The judgment of the Court of Appeals is reversed, and the case is remanded for further proceedings.

It is so ordered.

JUSTICE STEVENS, concurring in part and concurring in the judgment.

The New York law at issue, N.Y. Civ. Prac. Law Ann. (CPLR) § 901(b) (2006), is a procedural rule that is not part of New York's substantive law. Accordingly, I agree with Justice Scalia that Federal Rule of Civil Procedure 23 must apply in this case and join Parts I and II-A of the Court's opinion. But I also agree with Justice Ginsburg that there are some state procedural rules that federal courts must apply in diversity cases because they function as a part of the State's definition of substantive rights and remedies.

I

* * * Congress has provided for a system of uniform federal rules, under which federal courts sitting in diversity operate as "an independent system for administering justice to litigants who properly invoke its jurisdiction," Byrd v. Blue Ridge Rural Elec. Cooperative, Inc., 356 U.S. 525, 537 (1958), and not as state-court clones that assume all aspects of state tribunals but are managed by Article III judges. See *Hanna.* But while Congress may have the constitutional power to prescribe procedural rules that interfere with state substantive law in any number of respects, that is not what Congress has done. Instead, it has provided in the Enabling Act that although "[t]he Supreme Court" may "prescribe general rules of practice and procedure," § 2072(a), those rules "shall not abridge, enlarge or modify any substantive right," § 2072(b). Therefore, "[w]hen a situation is covered by one of the Federal Rules, ... the court has been instructed to apply the Federal Rule" unless doing so would violate the Act or the Constitution. *Hanna.*

Congress has thus struck a balance: "[H]ousekeeping rules for federal courts" will generally apply in diversity cases, notwithstanding that some federal rules "will inevitably differ" from state rules. *Hanna.* But not every federal "rul[e] of practice or procedure," § 2072(a), will displace state law. To the contrary, federal rules must be interpreted with some degree of "sensitivity to important state interests and regulatory policies," Gasperini v. Center for Humanities, Inc., 518 U.S. 415, 427, n. 7 (1996), and applied to diversity cases against the background of Congress' command that such rules not alter substantive rights and with consideration of "the degree to which the Rule makes the character and result of the federal litigation stray from the course it would follow in state courts," *Hanna.* This can be a tricky balance to implement.

It is important to observe that the balance Congress has struck turns, in part, on the nature of the state law that is being displaced by a federal rule. And in my view, the application of that balance does not necessarily turn on whether the state law at issue takes the *form* of what is traditionally described as substantive or procedural. Rather, it turns on whether the state law actually is part of a State's framework of substantive rights or remedies. See § 2072(b); cf. *Hanna* ("The line between 'substance' and 'procedure' shifts as the legal context changes"); *Guaranty Trust Co. v. York* (noting that the words "'substance'" and "'procedure'" "[e]ach impl[y] different variables depending upon the particular problem for which [they] are used").

Applying this balance, therefore, requires careful interpretation of the state and federal provisions at issue. "The line between procedural and substantive law is hazy," *Erie R. Co. v. Tompkins* (Reed, J., concurring), and matters of procedure and matters of substance are not "mutually exclusive categories with easily ascertainable contents," *Sibbach*, (Frankfurter, J., dissenting). Rather, "[r]ules which lawyers call procedural do not always exhaust their effect by regulating procedure," Cohen v. Beneficial Industrial Loan Corp., 337 U.S. 541, 555 (1949), and in some situations, "procedure and substance are so interwoven that rational separation becomes well-nigh impossible," id., at 559 (Rutledge, J., dissenting). A "state procedural rule, though undeniably 'procedural' in the ordinary sense of the term," may exist "to influence substantive outcomes," S.A. Healy Co. v. Milwaukee Metropolitan Sewerage Dist., 60 F.3d 305, 310 (CA7 1995) (Posner, J.), and may in some instances become so bound up with the state-created right or remedy that it defines the scope of that substantive right or remedy. Such laws, for example, may be seemingly procedural rules that make it significantly more difficult to bring or to prove a claim, thus serving to limit the scope of that claim. See, e.g., *Cohen* (state "procedure" that required plaintiffs to post bond before suing); *Guaranty Trust Co.* (state statute of limitations). Such "procedural rules" may also define the amount of recovery. See, e.g., *Gasperini* (state procedure for examining jury verdicts as means of capping the available remedy); MOORE § 124.07[3][a] (listing examples of federal courts' applying state laws that affect the amount of a judgment).

In our federalist system, Congress has not mandated that federal courts dictate to state legislatures the form that their substantive law must take. And were federal courts to ignore those portions of substantive state law that operate as procedural devices, it could in many instances limit the ways that sovereign States may define their rights and remedies. When a State chooses to use a traditionally procedural vehicle as a means of defining the scope of substantive rights or remedies, federal courts must recognize and respect that choice. Cf. *Ragan v. Merchants Transfer & Warehouse Co.* ("Since th[e] cause of action is created by local law, the measure of it is to be found only in local law.... Where local law qualifies or abridges it, the federal court must follow suit").

II

When both a federal rule and a state law appear to govern a question before a federal court sitting in diversity, our precedents have set out a two-step framework for federal courts to negotiate this thorny area. At both steps of the inquiry, there is a critical question about what the state law and the federal rule mean.

The court must first determine whether the scope of the federal rule is "'sufficiently broad'" to "'control the issue'" before the court, "thereby leaving no room for the operation" of seemingly conflicting state law. See Burlington Northern R. Co. v. Woods, 480 U.S. 1, 4–5 (1987); Walker v. Armco Steel Corp., 446 U.S. 740, 749–750, and n. 9 (1980). If the federal rule does not apply or can operate alongside the state rule, then there is no "Ac[t] of Congress" governing that particular question, 28 U.S.C. § 1652, and the court must engage in the traditional Rules of Decision Act inquiry under *Erie* and its progeny. In some instances, the "plain meaning" of a federal rule will not come into "'direct collision'" with the state law, and both can operate. *Walker*. In other instances, the rule "when fairly construed," *Burlington Northern R. Co.*, with "sensitivity to important state interests and regulatory policies," *Gasperini*, 518 U.S., at 427, n. 7, will not collide with the state law.

If, on the other hand, the federal rule is "sufficiently broad to control the issue before the Court," such that there is a "direct collision," *Walker*, the court must decide whether application of the federal rule "represents a valid exercise" of the "rulemaking authority ... bestowed on this Court by the Rules Enabling Act." *Burlington Northern R. Co.* That Act requires, *inter alia*, that federal rules "not abridge, enlarge or modify *any* substantive right." 28 U.S.C. § 2072(b) (emphasis added). Unlike Justice Scalia, I believe that an application of a federal rule that effectively abridges, enlarges, or modifies a state-created right or remedy violates this command. Congress may have the constitutional power "to supplant state law" with rules that are "rationally capable of classification as procedure," but we should generally presume that it has not done so. Indeed, the mandate that federal rules "shall not abridge, enlarge or modify any substantive right" evinces the opposite intent, as does Congress' decision to delegate the creation of rules to this Court rather than to a political branch.

Thus, the second step of the inquiry may well bleed back into the first. When a federal rule appears to abridge, enlarge, or modify a substantive right, federal courts must consider whether the rule can reasonably be interpreted to avoid that impermissible result. See, e.g., Semtek Int'l Inc. v. Lockheed Martin Corp., 531 U.S. 497, 503 (2001) (avoiding an interpretation of Federal Rule of Civil Procedure 41(b) that "would arguably violate the jurisdictional limitation of the Rules Enabling Act" contained in § 2072(b)). And when such a "saving" construction is not possible and the rule would violate the Enabling Act, federal courts cannot apply the rule. See 28 U.S.C. § 2072(b) (mandating that federal rules "shall not" alter "*any* substantive right" (emphasis added)); *Hanna* ("[A] court, in measuring a Federal Rule against the standards contained in the Enabling Act ... need not wholly blind itself to the degree to which the Rule makes the character and result of the federal litigation stray from the course it would follow in state courts"); see also *Semtek Int'l Inc.* (noting that if state law granted a particular right, "the federal court's extinguishment of that right ... would seem to violate [§ 2072(b)]"); cf. Statement of Justices Black and Douglas, 372 U.S. 865, 870 (1963) (observing that federal rules "as applied in given situations might have to be declared invalid"). A federal rule, therefore, cannot govern a particular case in which the rule would displace a state law that is procedural in the ordinary use of the term but is so intertwined with a state right or remedy that it functions to define the scope of the state-created right. And absent a governing federal rule, a federal court must engage in the traditional Rules of Decision Act inquiry, under the *Erie* line of cases. This application of the Enabling Act shows "sensitivity to important state interests," and "regulatory policies," but it does so as Congress authorized, by ensuring that federal rules that ordinarily "prescribe general rules of practice and procedure," § 2072(a), do "not abridge, enlarge or modify any substantive right," § 2072(b).

Justice Scalia believes that the sole Enabling Act question is whether the federal rule "really regulates procedure," which means, apparently, whether it regulates "the manner and the means by which the litigants' rights are enforced." I respectfully disagree. This interpretation of the Enabling Act is consonant with the Act's first limitation to "general rules of practice and procedure," § 2072(a). But it ignores the second limitation that such rules also "not abridge, enlarge or modify *any* substantive right," § 2072(b) (emphasis added), and in so doing ignores the balance that Congress struck between uniform rules of federal procedure and respect for a State's construction of its own rights and remedies. It also ignores the separation-of-powers presumption, and federalism presumption, that counsel against judicially created rules displacing state substantive law.

Although the plurality appears to agree with much of my interpretation of § 2072, it nonetheless rejects that approach for two reasons, both of which are mistaken. First, Justice Scalia worries that if federal courts inquire into the effect of federal rules on state law, it will enmesh federal courts in difficult determinations about whether application of a given rule would displace a state determination about substantive rights. I do not see why an Enabling Act inquiry that looks to state law necessarily is more taxing than Justice Scalia's. But in any event, that inquiry is what the Enabling Act requires: While it may not be easy to decide what is actually a "substantive right," "the designations substantive and procedural become important, for the Enabling Act has made them so." Ely, *The Irrepressible Myth of* Erie, 87 HARV. L. REV. 693, 723 (1974). The question, therefore, is not what rule *we* think would be easiest on federal courts. The question is what rule Congress established. Although, Justice Scalia may generally prefer easily administrable, bright-line rules, his preference does not give us license to adopt a second-best interpretation of the Rules Enabling Act. Courts cannot ignore text and context in the service of simplicity.

Second, the plurality argues that its interpretation of the Enabling Act is dictated by this Court's decision in *Sibbach*, which applied a Federal Rule about when parties must submit to medical examinations. But the plurality misreads that opinion. As Justice Harlan observed in *Hanna*, "shorthand formulations which have appeared in earlier opinions are prone to carry untoward results that frequently arise from oversimplification." (concurring opinion). To understand *Sibbach*, it is first necessary to understand the issue that was before the Court. The petitioner raised only the facial question whether "Rules 35 and 37 [of the Federal Rules of Civil Procedure] are ... within the mandate of Congress to this court" and not the specific question of "the obligation of federal courts to apply the substantive law of a state." The Court, therefore, had no occasion to consider whether the particular application of the Federal Rules in question would offend the Enabling Act.

Nor, in *Sibbach*, was any further analysis necessary to the resolution of the case because the matter at issue, requiring medical exams for litigants, did not pertain to "substantive rights" under the Enabling Act. Although most state rules bearing on the litigation process are adopted for some policy reason, few seemingly "procedural" rules define the scope of a substantive right or remedy. The matter at issue in *Sibbach* reflected competing federal and state judgments about privacy interests. Those privacy concerns may have been weighty and in some sense substantive; but they did not pertain to the scope of any state right or remedy at issue in the litigation. * * *

III

Justice Ginsburg views the basic issue in this case as whether and how to apply a federal rule that dictates an answer to a traditionally procedural question (whether to join plaintiffs together as a class), when a state law that "defines the dimensions" of a state-created claim dictates the opposite answer. As explained above, I readily acknowledge that if a federal rule displaces a state rule that is "'procedural' in the ordinary sense of the term," *S.A. Healy Co.*, 60 F.3d, at 310, but sufficiently interwoven with the scope of a substantive right or remedy, there would be an Enabling Act problem, and the federal rule would have to give way. In my view, however, this is not such a case.

At bottom, the dissent's interpretation of Rule 23 seems to be that Rule 23 covers only those cases in which its application would create no *Erie* problem. The dissent would apply the Rules of Decision Act inquiry under *Erie* even to cases in which there is a governing federal rule, and thus the Act, by its own terms, does not apply. But "[w]hen a situation is covered by one of the Federal Rules, the question facing the court is a far cry from the typical, relatively unguided *Erie* choice." *Hanna*. The question is only whether the Enabling Act is satisfied. Although it reflects a laudable concern to protect "state regulatory policies," Justice Ginsburg's approach would, in my view, work an end run around Congress' system of uniform federal rules, see 28 U.S.C. § 2072, and our decision in *Hanna*. Federal courts can and should interpret federal rules with sensitivity to "state prerogatives," but even when "state interests ... warrant our respectful consideration," federal courts cannot rewrite the rules. If my dissenting colleagues feel strongly that § 901(b) is substantive and that class certification should be denied, then they should argue within the Enabling Act's framework. Otherwise, "the Federal Rule applies regardless of contrary state law." *Gasperini*, 518 U.S., at 427, n. 7.

In my view, * * * the bar for finding an Enabling Act problem is a high one. The mere fact that a state law is designed as a procedural rule suggests it reflects a judgment about how state courts ought to operate and not a judgment about the scope of state-created rights and remedies. And for the purposes of operating a federal court system, there are costs involved in attempting to discover the true nature of a state procedural rule and allowing such a rule to operate alongside a federal rule that appears to govern the same question. The mere possibility that a federal rule would alter a state-created right is not sufficient. There must be little doubt.

The legislative history of § 901 * * * reveals a classically procedural calibration of making it easier to litigate claims in New York courts (under any source of law) only when it is necessary to do so, and not making it *too* easy when the class tool is not required. This is the same sort of calculation that might go into setting filing fees or deadlines for briefs. There is of course a difference of degree between those examples and class certification, but not a difference of kind; the class vehicle may have a greater practical effect on who brings lawsuits than do low filing fees, but that does not transform it into a damages "proscription" or "limitation."

The difference of degree is relevant to the forum shopping considerations that are part of the Rules of Decision Act or *Erie* inquiry. If the applicable federal rule did not govern the particular question at issue (or could be fairly read not to do so), then those considerations would matter, for precisely the reasons given by the dissent. But that is not *this* case. As the Court explained in *Hanna*, it is an "incorrect assumption that the rule of *Erie R. Co. v. Tompkins* constitutes the appropriate test of ... the applicability of a Federal Rule of Civil Procedure." "It is true that both the Enabling Act and the *Erie* rule say, roughly, that federal courts are to apply state 'substantive' law and federal 'procedural' law," but the tests are different and reflect the fact that "they were designed to control very different sorts of decisions."

Because Rule 23 governs class certification, the only decision is whether certifying a class in this diversity case would "abridge, enlarge or modify" New York's substantive rights or remedies. § 2072(b). Although one can argue that class certification would enlarge New York's "limited" damages remedy, such arguments rest on extensive speculation about what the New York Legislature had in mind when it created § 901(b). But given that there are two plausible competing narratives, it seems obvious to me that we should respect the plain textual reading of § 901(b), a rule in New York's procedural code about when to certify class actions brought under any source of law, and respect Congress' decision that Rule 23 governs class certification in federal courts. In order to displace a federal rule, there must be more than just a possibility that the state rule is different than it appears.

Accordingly, I concur in part and concur in the judgment.

JUSTICE GINSBURG, with whom JUSTICE KENNEDY, JUSTICE BREYER, and JUSTICE ALITO join, dissenting.

The Court today approves Shady Grove's attempt to transform a $500 case into a $5,000,000 award, although the State creating the right to recover has proscribed this alchemy. If Shady Grove had filed suit in New York state court, the 2% interest payment authorized by New York Ins. Law Ann. § 5106(a) (2009) as a penalty for overdue benefits would, by Shady Grove's own measure, amount to no more than $500. By instead filing in federal court based on the parties' diverse citizenship and requesting class certification, Shady Grove hopes to recover, for the class, statutory damages of more than $5,000,000. The New York Legislature has barred this remedy, instructing that, unless specifically permitted, "an action to recover a penalty, or minimum measure of recovery created or imposed by statute may not be maintained as a class action." N.Y. Civ. Prac. Law Ann. (CPLR) § 901(b) (2006). The Court nevertheless holds that Federal Rule of Civil Procedure 23, which prescribes procedures for the conduct of class actions in federal courts, preempts the application of § 901(b) in diversity suits.

The Court reads Rule 23 relentlessly to override New York's restriction on the availability of statutory damages. Our decisions, however, caution us to ask, before undermining state legislation: Is this conflict really necessary? Cf. Traynor, *Is This Conflict Really Necessary?* 37 Tex. L. Rev. 657 (1959). Had the Court engaged in that inquiry, it would not have read Rule 23 to collide with New York's legitimate interest in keeping certain monetary awards reasonably bounded. I would continue to interpret Federal Rules with awareness of, and sensitivity to, important state regulatory policies. Because today's judgment radically departs from that course, I dissent.

I

A

"Under the *Erie* doctrine," it is long settled, "federal courts sitting in diversity apply state substantive law and federal procedural law." *Gasperini*; see *Erie*. Justice Harlan aptly conveyed the importance of the doctrine; he described *Erie* as "one of the modern cornerstones of our federalism, expressing policies that profoundly touch the allocation of judicial power between the state and federal systems." *Hanna* (concurring opinion). Although we have found *Erie*'s application "sometimes [to be] a challenging endeavor," *Gasperini*, two federal statutes mark our way.

The first, the Rules of Decision Act, prohibits federal courts from generating substantive law in diversity actions. See *Erie*. Originally enacted as part of the Judiciary Act of 1789, this restraint serves a policy of prime importance to our federal system. We have therefore applied the Act "with an eye alert to ... avoiding disregard of State law." *Guaranty Trust Co. v. York*.

The second, the Rules Enabling Act, enacted in 1934, authorizes us to "prescribe general rules of practice and procedure" for the federal courts, but with a crucial restriction: "Such rules shall not abridge, enlarge or modify any substantive right." Pursuant to this statute, we have adopted the Federal Rules of Civil Procedure. In interpreting the scope of the Rules, including, in particular, Rule 23, we have been mindful of the limits on our authority. See, e.g., *Ortiz v. Fibreboard Corp.*, 527 U.S. 815, 845 (1999) (The Rules Enabling Act counsels against "adventurous application" of Rule 23; any tension with the Act "is best kept within tolerable limits."); *Amchem Products, Inc. v. Windsor*, 521 U.S. 591, 612–613 (1997). See also *Semtek Int'l Inc. v. Lockheed Martin Corp.*, 531 U.S. 497, 503–504 (2001).

If a Federal Rule controls an issue and directly conflicts with state law, the Rule, so long as it is consonant with the Rules Enabling Act, applies in diversity suits. See

Hanna. If, however, no Federal Rule or statute governs the issue, the Rules of Decision Act, as interpreted in *Erie*, controls. That Act directs federal courts, in diversity cases, to apply state law when failure to do so would invite forum-shopping and yield markedly disparate litigation outcomes. See *Gasperini; Hanna.* Recognizing that the Rules of Decision Act and the Rules Enabling Act simultaneously frame and inform the *Erie* analysis, we have endeavored in diversity suits to remain safely within the bounds of both congressional directives.

B

In our prior decisions in point, many of them not mentioned in the Court's opinion, we have avoided immoderate interpretations of the Federal Rules that would trench on state prerogatives without serving any countervailing federal interest. "Application of the *Hanna* analysis," we have said, "is premised on a 'direct collision' between the Federal Rule and the state law." *Walker v. Armco Steel Corp.* (quoting *Hanna*). To displace state law, a Federal Rule, "when fairly construed," must be "'sufficiently broad'" so as "to 'control the issue' before the court, thereby leaving *no room* for the operation of that law." *Burlington Northern R. Co. v. Woods* (quoting *Walker*); cf. Stewart Organization, Inc. v. Ricoh Corp., 487 U.S. 22, 37–38 (1988) (Scalia, J., dissenting) ("[I]n deciding whether a federal ... Rule of Procedure encompasses a particular issue, a broad reading that would create significant disuniformity between state and federal courts should be avoided if the text permits.").

In pre-*Hanna* decisions, the Court vigilantly read the Federal Rules to avoid conflict with state laws. * * *

In all of these cases, the Court stated in *Hanna*, "the scope of the Federal Rule was not as broad as the losing party urged, and therefore, there being no Federal Rule which covered the point in dispute, *Erie* commanded the enforcement of state law." In *Hanna* itself, the Court found the clash "unavoidable," the petitioner had effected service of process as prescribed by Federal Rule 4(d)(1), but that "how-to" method did not satisfy the special Massachusetts law applicable to service on an executor or administrator. Even as it rejected the Massachusetts prescription in favor of the federal procedure, however, "[t]he majority in *Hanna* recognized ... that federal rules ... must be interpreted by the courts applying them, and that the process of interpretation can and should reflect an awareness of legitimate state interests." R. Fallon, J. Manning, D. Meltzer & D. Shapiro, Hart and Wechsler's The Federal Courts and The Federal System 593 (6th ed. 2009) (hereinafter Hart & Wechsler).

Following *Hanna*, we continued to "interpre[t] the federal rules to avoid conflict with important state regulatory policies." Hart & Wechsler 593. * * *

In sum, both before and after *Hanna*, the above-described decisions show, federal courts have been cautioned by this Court to "interpre[t] the Federal Rules ... with sensitivity to important state interests," *Gasperini*, 518 U.S., at 427, n. 7, and a will "to avoid conflict with important state regulatory policies," *id.*, at 438, n. 2.[2] The

2. Justice Stevens stakes out common ground on this point: "[F]ederal rules," he observes, "must be interpreted with some degree of 'sensitivity to important state interests and regulatory policies,'..."

Court veers away from that approach—and conspicuously, its most recent reiteration in *Gasperini*,—in favor of a mechanical reading of Federal Rules, insensitive to state interests and productive of discord.

C

* * * Section 901(a) allows courts leeway in deciding whether to certify a class, but § 901(b) rejects the use of the class mechanism to pursue the particular remedy of statutory damages. The limitation was not designed with the fair conduct or efficiency of litigation in mind. Indeed, suits seeking statutory damages are arguably *best* suited to the class device because individual proof of actual damages is unnecessary. New York's decision instead to block class-action proceedings for statutory damages therefore makes scant sense, except as a means to a manifestly substantive end: Limiting a defendant's liability in a single lawsuit in order to prevent the exorbitant inflation of penalties—remedies the New York Legislature created with individual suits in mind.

D

The Court, I am convinced, finds conflict where none is necessary. Mindful of the history behind § 901(b)'s enactment, the thrust of our precedent, and the substantive-rights limitation in the Rules Enabling Act, I conclude, as did the Second Circuit and every District Court to have considered the question in any detail, that Rule 23 does not collide with § 901(b). As the Second Circuit well understood, Rule 23 prescribes the considerations relevant to class certification and postcertification proceedings—but it does not command that a particular remedy be available when a party sues in a representative capacity. Section 901(b), in contrast, trains on that latter issue. Sensibly read, Rule 23 governs procedural aspects of class litigation, but allows state law to control the size of a monetary award a class plaintiff may pursue.

In other words, Rule 23 describes a method of enforcing a claim for relief, while § 901(b) defines the dimensions of the claim itself. In this regard, it is immaterial that § 901(b) bars statutory penalties in wholesale, rather than retail, fashion. The New York Legislature could have embedded the limitation in every provision creating a cause of action for which a penalty is authorized; § 901(b) operates as shorthand to the same effect. It is as much a part of the delineation of the claim for relief as it would be were it included claim by claim in the New York Code.

The Court single-mindedly focuses on whether a suit "may" or "may not" be maintained as a class action. Putting the question that way, the Court does not home in on the reason *why*. Rule 23 authorizes class treatment for suits satisfying its prerequisites because the class mechanism generally affords a fair and efficient way to ag-

---

and applied to diversity cases against the background of Congress' command that such rules not alter substantive rights and with consideration of 'the degree to which the Rule makes the character and result of the federal litigation stray from the course it would follow in state courts,'" Nevertheless, Justice Stevens sees no reason to read Rule 23 with restraint in this particular case; the Federal Rule preempts New York's damages limitation, in his view, because § 901(b) is "a procedural rule that is not part of New York's substantive law." This characterization of § 901(b) does not mirror reality, as I later explain. But a majority of this Court, it bears emphasis, agrees that Federal Rules should be read with moderation in diversity suits to accommodate important state concerns.

gregate claims for adjudication. Section 901(b) responds to an entirely different concern; it does not allow class members to recover statutory damages because the New York Legislature considered the result of adjudicating such claims en masse to be exorbitant. The fair and efficient *conduct* of class litigation is the legitimate concern of Rule 23; the *remedy* for an infraction of state law, however, is the legitimate concern of the State's lawmakers and not of the federal rulemakers. Cf. Ely, *The Irrepressible Myth of* Erie, 87 HARV. L. REV. 693, 722 (1974) (It is relevant "whether the state provision embodies a substantive policy or represents only a procedural disagreement with the federal rulemakers respecting the fairest and most efficient way of conducting litigation.").

Suppose, for example, that a State, wishing to cap damages in class actions at $1,000,000, enacted a statute providing that "a suit to recover more than $1,000,000 may not be maintained as a class action." Under the Court's reasoning—which attributes dispositive significance to the words "may not be maintained"—Rule 23 would preempt this provision, nevermind that Congress, by authorizing the promulgation of rules of procedure for federal courts, surely did not intend to displace state-created ceilings on damages. The Court suggests that the analysis might differ if the statute "limit[ed] the remedies available in an existing class action," such that Rule 23 might not conflict with a state statute prescribing that "no more than $1,000,000 may be recovered in a class action." There is no real difference in the purpose and intended effect of these two hypothetical statutes. The notion that one directly impinges on Rule 23's domain, while the other does not, fundamentally misperceives the office of Rule 23.

The absence of an inevitable collision between Rule 23 and § 901(b) becomes evident once it is comprehended that a federal court sitting in diversity can accord due respect to both state and federal prescriptions. Plaintiffs seeking to vindicate claims for which the State has provided a statutory penalty may pursue relief through a class action if they forgo statutory damages and instead seek actual damages or injunctive or declaratory relief; any putative class member who objects can opt out and pursue actual damages, if available, and the statutory penalty in an individual action. In this manner, the Second Circuit explained, "Rule 23's procedural requirements for class actions can be applied along with the substantive requirement of CPLR 901(b)." In sum, while phrased as responsive to the question whether certain class actions may begin, § 901(b) is unmistakably aimed at controlling how those actions must end. On that remedial issue, Rule 23 is silent.

Any doubt whether Rule 23 leaves § 901(b) in control of the remedial issue at the core of this case should be dispelled by our *Erie* jurisprudence, including *Hanna*, which counsels us to read Federal Rules moderately and cautions against stretching a rule to cover every situation it could conceivably reach. The Court states that "[t]here is no reason ... to read Rule 23 as addressing only whether claims made eligible for class treatment by some *other* law should be certified as class actions." To the contrary, *Palmer, Ragan, Cohen, Walker, Gasperini*, and *Semtek* provide good reason to look to the law that creates the right to recover. That is plainly so on a more accurate statement of what is at stake: Is there any reason to read Rule 23 as authorizing a claim for relief when the State that created the remedy disallows its pursuit on behalf of a class? None at all is the answer our federal system should give.

By finding a conflict without considering whether Rule 23 rationally should be read to avoid any collision, the Court unwisely and unnecessarily retreats from the federalism principles undergirding *Erie*. Had the Court reflected on the respect for state regulatory interests endorsed in our decisions, it would have found no cause to interpret Rule 23 so woodenly—and every reason not to do so. Cf. Traynor, 37 TEX. L. REV., at 669 ("It is bad enough for courts to prattle unintelligibly about choice of law, but unforgiveable when inquiry might have revealed that there was no real conflict.").

II

Because I perceive no unavoidable conflict between Rule 23 and § 901(b), I would decide this case by inquiring "whether application of the [state] rule would have so important an effect upon the fortunes of one or both of the litigants that failure to [apply] it would be likely to cause a plaintiff to choose the federal court." *Hanna*. See *Gasperini*.

* * * When no federal law or rule is dispositive of an issue, and a state statute is outcome affective in the sense our cases on *Erie* (pre- and post-*Hanna*) develop, the Rules of Decision Act commands application of the State's law in diversity suits. *Gasperini*; *Hanna*; *York*. As this case starkly demonstrates, if federal courts exercising diversity jurisdiction are compelled by Rule 23 to award statutory penalties in class actions while New York courts are bound by § 901(b)'s proscription, "substantial variations between state and federal [money judgments] may be expected." *Gasperini*. The "variation" here is indeed "substantial." Shady Grove seeks class relief that is *ten thousand times* greater than the individual remedy available to it in state court. As the plurality acknowledges, forum shopping will undoubtedly result if a plaintiff need only file in federal instead of state court to seek a massive monetary award explicitly barred by state law. See *Gasperini* ("*Erie* precludes a recovery in federal court significantly larger than the recovery that would have been tolerated in state court."). The "accident of diversity of citizenship," Klaxon Co. v. Stentor Elec. Mfg. Co., 313 U.S. 487, 496 (1941), should not subject a defendant to such augmented liability. See *Hanna* ("The *Erie* rule is rooted in part in a realization that it would be unfair for the character or result of a litigation materially to differ because the suit had been brought in a federal court.").

It is beyond debate that "a statutory cap on damages would supply substantive law for *Erie* purposes." *Gasperini*. See also id. (Stevens, J., dissenting) ("A state-law ceiling on allowable damages ... is a substantive rule of decision that federal courts must apply in diversity cases governed by New York law."); id. (Scalia, J., dissenting) ("State substantive law controls what injuries are compensable and in what amount."). In *Gasperini*, we determined that New York's standard for measuring the alleged excessiveness of a jury verdict was designed to provide a control analogous to a damages cap. The statute was framed as "a procedural instruction," we noted, "but the State's objective [wa]s manifestly substantive."

Gasperini's observations apply with full force in this case. By barring the recovery of statutory damages in a class action, § 901(b) controls a defendant's maximum liability in a suit seeking such a remedy. The remedial provision could have been written as an explicit cap: "In any class action seeking statutory damages, relief is limited to the amount the named plaintiff would have recovered in an individual suit." That New York's Legislature used other words to express the very same meaning should be inconsequential.

We have long recognized the impropriety of displacing, in a diversity action, state-law limitations on state-created remedies. See *Woods* (in a diversity case, a plaintiff "barred from recovery in the state court ... should likewise be barred in the federal court"); *York* (federal court sitting in diversity "cannot afford recovery if the right to recover is made unavailable by the State nor can it substantively affect the enforcement of the right as given by the State"). Just as *Erie* precludes a federal court from entering a deficiency judgment when a State has "authoritatively announced that [such] judgments cannot be secured within its borders," Angel v. Bullington, 330 U.S. 183, 191 (1947), so too *Erie* should prevent a federal court from awarding statutory penalties aggregated through a class action when New York prohibits this recovery. See also *Ragan* ("Where local law qualifies or abridges [a claim], the federal court must follow suit. Otherwise there is a different measure of the cause of action in one court than in the other, and the principle of *Erie* ... is transgressed."). In sum, because "New York substantive law governs [this] claim for relief, New York law ... guide[s] the allowable damages." *Gasperini.*

III

The Court's erosion of *Erie*'s federalism grounding impels me to point out the large irony in today's judgment. Shady Grove is able to pursue its claim in federal court only by virtue of the recent enactment of the Class Action Fairness Act of 2005 (CAFA), 28 U.S.C. § 1332(d). In CAFA, Congress opened federal-court doors to state-law-based class actions so long as there is minimal diversity, at least 100 class members, and at least $5,000,000 in controversy. By providing a federal forum, Congress sought to check what it considered to be the overreadiness of some state courts to certify class actions. See, e.g., S. Rep. No. 109-14, p. 4 (2005) (CAFA prevents lawyers from "gam[ing] the procedural rules [to] keep nationwide or multi-state class actions in state courts whose judges have reputations for readily certifying classes." (internal quotation marks omitted)); id., at 22 (disapproving "the 'I never met a class action I didn't like' approach to class certification" that "is prevalent in state courts in some localities"). In other words, Congress envisioned fewer—not more—class actions overall. Congress surely never anticipated that CAFA would make federal courts a mecca for suits of the kind Shady Grove has launched: class actions seeking state-created penalties for claims arising under state law—claims that would be barred from class treatment in the State's own courts. Cf. *Woods* ("[T]he policy of *Erie* ... preclude[s] maintenance in ... federal court ... of suits to which the State ha[s] closed its courts.").

I would continue to approach *Erie* questions in a manner mindful of the purposes underlying the Rules of Decision Act and the Rules Enabling Act, faithful to precedent, and respectful of important state interests. I would therefore hold that the New York

Legislature's limitation on the recovery of statutory damages applies in this case, and would affirm the Second Circuit's judgment.

Notes and Questions

1. This case presents two interrelated issues—the meaning of Rule 23 and, if it is interpreted to preempt § 901, whether it is valid under the Rules Enabling Act. Consider the approaches of each of the opinions on these questions. Which do you find more persuasive?

2. Justices Scalia and Stevens spar over the meaning of the substance/procedure proviso in the Rules Enabling Act. What is Justice Ginsburg's position on the proper interpretation of the Rules Enabling Act proviso?

3. Justices Ginsburg and Stevens agree that the Federal Rules of Civil Procedure should be construed to take state substantive interests into account, at least in some cases, although they seem to do this as different stages of the analysis. Justice Ginsburg does this as part of determining whether the Federal Rule is on point. In contrast, Justice Stevens reaches this only after having first determined that the rule is on point. As some commentators have observed, both Justices seem to have imported into the Rules Enabling Act inquiry, the Rules of Decision Act inquiry of *Byrd* as to whether the state rule is bound up with substantive rights and obligations. See Richard Freer & Thomas Arthur, *The Irrepressible Influence of* Byrd, 44 CREIGHTON L. REV. 61, 76 (2010).

4. Justice Ginsburg argues that "our *Erie* jurisprudence ... counsels us to read Federal Rules moderately." What in the *Erie* jurisprudence offers counsel with respect to interpretations of the Federal Rules of Civil Procedure? The Rules Enabling Act pursuant to which the Rules were promulgated was passed four years before *Erie* was decided. Professor Burbank has argued that the substance/procedure limitation in the Rules Enabling Act was directed at separation of powers (limiting the scope of the Court's power vis-à-vis Congress) rather than federalism concerns. See Stephen B. Burbank, *The Rules Enabling Act of 1934*, 130 U. PA. L. REV. 1015 (1982).

5. With the multiple opinions in *Shady Grove*, lower courts confront the problem of which approach to use. In Garman v. Campbell County School District No. 1, 630 F.3d 977 (10th Cir. 2010), the Tenth Circuit explicitly relied on Justice Stevens' concurrence. There, in a suit against a county school district, the federal court applied a state law that required any plaintiff suing a state or local government entity to provide to the government entity within a specified time written notice that meets certain signature and certification requirements. Although these requirementa were different from the pleading requirements of Rule 8, the court, relying on the Stevens opinion, concluded that this state law was "part of the State's framework of substantive rights or remedies."

C. Determining the Content of State Law

Once the federal court has determined that it should apply state law (and, under *Klaxon*, has determined which state's law applies), it next must ascertain the content of that state law. This can, at times, be a difficult task. In *Erie*, Justice Brandeis stated that federal courts had to follow the state law as decided by the "highest court" of the state. 304 U.S. at 78. But what if there were no supreme court decisions? Courts went through a fairly comical period in which they focused on whatever authority there was—no matter how low. In Gustin v. Sun Life Assurance Co., 154 F.2d 961 (6th Cir. 1946), the court felt absolutely bound by an unpublished Ohio intermediate court of appeals opinion even though state law provided that it was of no precedential value. This sort of thing led Judge Jerome Frank to utter his wonderful line: Federal judges were now "to play the role of the ventriloquist's dummy to the courts of some particular state." Richardson v. Commissioner, 126 F.2d 562, 567 (2d Cir. 1942).

Later, federal courts came to accept that in addressing issues of state law, a federal court should do what it believed the state supreme court would have done. As one treatise explained:

> Thus, the federal judge need no longer be a ventriloquist's dummy. Instead he or she is free, just as state judges are, to consider all the data the highest court of the state would use in an effort to determine how the highest court of the state would decide. This is as it should be. Unless this much freedom is allowed the federal judge, the Erie doctrine would simply have substituted one kind of forum-shopping for another. The lawyer whose case was dependent on an old or shaky state-court decision that might no longer be followed within the state would have a strong incentive to maneuver the case into federal court, where, on the mechanical jurisprudence that the Erie doctrine was once thought to require, the state decision could not have been impeached.

Wright & Kane, Federal Courts 394. See also Geri Yonover, *Ascertaining State Law: The Continuing* Erie *Dilemma*, 38 DePaul L. Rev. 1 (1989).

Thus, the federal court is to look to all available data to make its best guess as to the content of state law. Particularly where the law is in flux or the relevant state precedents are old, the federal courts may have difficulty accurately predicting state law. It is hard to generalize whether a federal court will be more or less conservative than its state counterparts in declaring state law to have changed. For example, a federal court may be reluctant to predict that the state supreme court will overrule itself. See Orkin v. Taylor, 487 F.3d 734 (9th Cir. 2007) ("we take state law as it exists without speculating as to future changes in the law"). On the other hand, the federal court can get ahead of state law, predicting change before the state court is willing to make it. What happens when a federal judgment is based on an incorrect interpretation of state law? Consider the following case:

Deweerth v. Baldinger

38 F.3d 1266 (2d Cir. 1994)

Walker, Circuit Judge.

This appeal is the latest episode in a decade-long dispute over the ownership of an oil painting entitled "Champs de Blé à Vétheuil" by Claude Monet. The work by the celebrated French Impressionist was previously owned by plaintiff Gerda Dorothea DeWeerth, a German citizen. It was discovered missing from DeWeerth's family castle after World War II, and was subsequently purchased by defendant Edith Marks Baldinger, a New York resident, from * * * Wildenstein & Co., a New York art gallery. * * *

In 1982, DeWeerth discovered that Baldinger was in possession of the Monet and demanded its return. When Baldinger refused, DeWeerth promptly commenced a diversity action to recover it. * * *

[Although the district court found for DeWeerth, the Second Circuit] reversed the district court's judgment on the ground that New York limitations law required a showing of reasonable diligence in locating stolen property and that DeWeerth had failed to make such a showing. * * *

[Several years later, in an entirely separate action, the New York Court of Appeals held that the relevant New York statute of limitations applicable to this action did not require a showing of reasonable diligence in locating stolen property. The New York Court of Appeals specifically discussed the Second Circuit's earlier opinion and stated that it was contrary to New York's long-standing policy of favoring owners over bona fide purchasers.

[DeWeerth then returned to the district court and asked that her case be reopened under Rule 60 and judgment entered in her favor.]

Based on the New York Court of Appeals' opinion, the district court determined that DeWeerth would have prevailed in this case had she originally brought her suit in the New York state courts. It then held that *Erie Railroad Co. v. Tompkins* and its progeny entitled plaintiff to a modification of the final judgment in this case to avoid this inconsistency. It determined that the countervailing interest of both the parties and the courts in the finality of litigation was outweighed by the need "to prevent the working of an extreme and undue hardship upon plaintiff, to accomplish substantial justice and to act with appropriate regard for the principles of federalism which underlie our dual judicial system."

* * * In our view, *Erie* simply does not stand for the proposition that a plaintiff is entitled to reopen a federal court case that has been closed for several years in order to gain the benefit of a newly-announced decision of a state court, a forum in which she specifically declined to litigate her claim. The limited holding of *Erie* is that federal courts sitting in diversity are bound to follow state law on any matter of substantive law not "governed by the Federal Constitution or by Acts of Congress." 304 U.S. at 78. However, the fact that federal courts must follow state law when deciding a di-

versity case does not mean that a subsequent change in the law of the state will provide grounds for relief under Rule 60(b)(6). See Brown v. Clark Equip. Co., 96 F.R.D. 166, 173 (D. Me. 1982) ("mere change in decisional law does not constitute an 'extraordinary circumstance'" under Rule 60(b)(6), especially where "[p]laintiffs elected to proceed in the federal forum, thereby voluntarily depriving themselves of the opportunity to attempt to persuade the [state court]"); Atwell v. Equifax, Inc., 86 F.R.D. 686, 688 (D. Md. 1980) (change in the state decisional law upon which appellate court based decision held "insufficient to warrant reopening a final judgment"). This principle also applies in federal cases where the Supreme Court has changed the applicable rule of law.

When confronted with an unsettled issue of state law, a federal court sitting in diversity must make its best effort to predict how the state courts would decide the issue. The comprehensive opinion by now Chief Judge Jon O. Newman in *DeWeerth* accordingly surveyed New York case law and determined that a New York court called upon to decide the issue would be likely to impose a requirement of due diligence. The decision was based in part on the fact that plaintiff's argument would create an incongruity in the treatment of bona fide purchasers and thieves. In New York, the three-year statute of limitations starts running against thieves once the owner discovers that the art object has been stolen, while under plaintiff's theory, it would not start running against a good faith purchaser until he refused the owner's request to return the art object. The court determined in *DeWeerth* that this rule conflicted with a policy inherent in certain New York cases of protecting bona fide purchasers of stolen objects from stale claims by alleged owners. Based on this incongruity, New York's policy of discouraging stale claims in other settings, and the fact that in most other states the limitations period begins to run when a good faith purchaser acquires stolen property thereby prompting due diligence on the part of the previous owner, we determined that New York courts would adopt a due diligence requirement for owners attempting to locate stolen property.

It turned out that the *DeWeerth* panel's prediction was wrong. However, by filing her state law claim in a federal forum, *DeWeerth* assumed the risk that her adversaries would argue for a change in the applicable rules of law and that any open question of state law would be decided by a federal as opposed to a New York state court. * * *

We conclude that the prior *DeWeerth* panel conscientiously satisfied its duty to predict how New York courts would decide the due diligence question, and that *Erie* and its progeny require no more than this. The fact that the New York Court of Appeals subsequently reached a contrary conclusion * * * does not constitute an "extraordinary circumstance" that would justify reopening this case in order to achieve a similar result. There is nothing in *Erie* that suggests that consistency must be achieved at the expense of finality, or that federal cases finally disposed of must be revisited anytime an unrelated state case clarifies the applicable rules of law. Attempting to obtain such a result through Rule 60(b)(6) is simply an improvident course that would encourage countless attacks on federal judgments long since closed. While our conclusion relies in part on our belief that the prior *DeWeerth* decision fully comported with *Erie* and did not, as plaintiffs suggest, mistakenly apply settled state law and reach a clearly wrong result, we note that even if those were the circumstances, the doctrine of finality would still pose a considerable hurdle to reopening the final judgment in this case. Whether, in such circumstances, the result would be different if the issue were raised within one year pursuant to Rule 60(b)(1) is an issue we need not decide.

For the foregoing reasons, we reverse the judgment of the district court.

Owen, District Judge. I respectfully dissent.

The clear applicability of Rule 60(b)(6) to this case was well-stated by Judge Broderick below, 804 F. Supp. at 547:

> The range of fundamental policy and constitutional considerations which have informed the *Erie* doctrine are fully evident in the present case. Failure to act on the present Rule 60 motion would deny Mrs. DeWeerth the right to recover her property solely because she initially brought this action in federal rather than state court. Had Mrs. DeWeerth brought suit in state court, her claim would have been deemed timely commenced under the applicable statute of limitations.
>
> Such inconsistency is exactly the type of result that *Erie* was enacted to avoid. As Justice Frankfurter noted, "[t]he nub of the policy that underlies *Erie R. Co. v. Tompkins* is that for the same transaction the accident of a suit by a non-resident litigant in a federal court instead of in a State Court a block away should not lead to a substantially different result." *Guaranty Trust Company of New York v. York.*

I am, of course, unhesitatingly one with the majority as to the "integrity of the [prior] *DeWeerth* decision [and] ... the fairness of the process that was accorded *De Weerth.*" However, given the majority's acknowledgment "that the [prior] *DeWeerth* panel's prediction was wrong[,]" I cannot accept the result here * * *. Should not the impact of [the New York Court of Appeals decision] * * * be shouldered by us, notwithstanding the integrity of our error? While the doctrine of finality of judgments does address an important interest, it should not deter us from using Rule 60 today to do justice because we may have to deal hereafter with the Rule's invocation in unworthy cases.

Accordingly, contrary to the majority, I * * * would affirm on the scholarly and thorough opinion of Judge Broderick below.

Notes and Questions

1. Read Rule 60(b). Notice the grounds upon which a judgment can be reopened and that the first three grounds are subject to a one-year time limit. The motion in *DeWeerth* was based on Rule 60(b)(6). Although there is not a specific time limit applicable to that provision, the Supreme Court has held that relief under Rule 60 (b)(6) requires a showing of "extraordinary circumstances," Gonzalez v. Crosby, 545 U.S. 524, 535 (2005), and courts have generally held that neither a mistake of law nor

even a change in the law is an extraordinary circumstance. See id.; United States ex rel. Garibaldi v. Orleans Parish Sch. Bd., 397 F.3d 334 (5th Cir. 2005); Cincinnati Ins. Co. v. Flanders Elec. Motor Serv., 131 F.3d 625 (7th Cir. 1997). But see Adams v. Merrill Lynch Pierce Fenner & Smith, 888 F.2d 696 (10th Cir. 1989) (change in law by U.S. Supreme Court warrants relief under Rule 60(b)(6)).

2. In *DeWeerth*, it was the plaintiff who was disadvantaged by the incorrect interpretation of state law by the federal court. The majority concludes that by choosing the federal forum, the plaintiff "assumed the risk" that this might happen. Suppose that it was the defendant who lost because of an incorrect interpretation. Does a defendant (who does not choose the forum, unless she removed the case from state court) "assume" the same risk?

3. Some commentators have argued that "a federal court, whose decisions are not reviewable by the state's highest court, may feel less constrained than a state court in interpreting past state law precedents, and a party might well prefer federal court for this reason." Dudley & Rutherglen, 92 VA. L. REV. at 746. Does this suggest that the majority in *DeWeerth* put too much weight on concerns of finality and gave too little weight to the underlying concerns of *Erie*?

4. In ruling on the motion to reopen, should the federal court have considered whether a New York state court would have allowed a New York judgment to be reopened under similar circumstances?

5. A federal district judge is likely to be a member of the bar of the state in which she sits, and to have practiced law in the courts of the state. A federal appeals court panel of three judges may be drawn from judges covering the various states in the circuit. Thus, it is possible that the appellate panel will have no judge who is a member of the bar of the state whose law applies. To the appellate court, it might seem reasonable to defer to the judgment of the local district judge on a question of state law. Indeed, some appellate courts announced that they would defer to such judgments unless they appeared clearly erroneous. The Supreme Court rejected this practice in Salve Regina College v. Russell, 499 U.S. 225 (1991), in which it held that the courts must review determinations of state law just as they would any question of law. Thus, they are to review the questions de novo, and without deference to the local judge. See Dan Coenen, *To Defer or Not to Defer: A Study of Federal Circuit Court Deference to District Court Rulings on State Law*, 73 MINN. L. REV. 899 (1989). See also Leavitt v. Jane L., 518 U.S. 137, 145 (1996) (Supreme Court does not owe deference to court of appeals' interpretations of state law).

6. If there is absolutely no state law on point, can the federal court refuse to hear the case? No. The court's "duty is tolerably clear. It is to decide, not avoid, the question." Daily v. Parker, 152 F.2d 174, 177 (7th Cir. 1945). See also Meredith v. Winter Haven, 320 U.S. 228 (1943) (federal court may not abstain because of difficulty in determining state law).

7. One mechanism for eliminating uncertainty about the content of state law is "certification." Under this procedure, when a federal court is confronted with an un-

certainty in state law, it can certify the state law issue to that state's highest court and request the opinion of that court on the issue. See Arizonans for Official English v. Arizona, 520 U.S. 43, 77 (1997) ("Through certification of novel or unsettled questions of state law for authoritative answers by a State's highest court, a federal court may save 'time, energy, and resources and hel[p] build a cooperative judicial federalism'"). Certification is not always a solution because it is not available in every state; some states will not decide certified questions that depend on issues of fact, see Exxon Co. v. Banque de Paris Et Des Pays-bas, 889 F.2d 674 (5th Cir. 1989), and sometimes the federal court simply doesn't understand the answer it receives, see Sun Ins. Office v. Clay, 319 F.2d 505, 509–10 (5th Cir. 1963), *rev'd*, 377 U.S. 179 (1964). See generally Ira Robbins, *Interstate Certification of Questions of Law: A Valuable Process in Need of Reform*, 76 JUDICATURE 125 (1992). See also Jonathan Nash, *Examining the Power of Federal Courts to Certify Questions of State Law*, 88 CORNELL L. REV. 1672 (2003) (arguing that there may be constitutional problems with the practice of certification).

D. Federal Common Law

Although *Erie* held that there is no *general* federal common law, in a few limited areas of unique federal interest, there is federal common law that survives *Erie*. Indeed, on the very day the Court decided *Erie*, it also held that issues of interstate water allocation are governed by federal common law. See Hinderlider v. La Plata River & Cherry Creek Ditch Co., 304 U.S. 92 (1938). The explanation is that although "*Erie* 'le[ft] to the states what ought be left to them,'" it did not disable federal courts from creating common law rules in "'areas of national concern'" that are the "subjects of national legislative power." American Elec. Power Co., Inc. v. Connecticut, 564 U.S. 410 (2011) (quoting Friendly, *In Praise of* Erie—*And of the New Federal Common Law*, 39 N.Y.U. L. REV. 383 (1964)). Thus, for example, in Boyle v. United Techs. Corp., 487 U.S. 500 (1988), the Court created a common law "military contractors defense" that would apply in tort suit against military equipment manufacturers. The Court justified this creation of federal common law on the grounds that the imposition of liability on government contractors would "directly affect the terms of Government contracts: either the contractor will decline to manufacture the design specified by the Government, or it will raise its price." Id. at 507.

Even as to areas of national concern that might be appropriate for federal common law, the courts will create a federal common law rule only if there is a need for a single, uniform federal standard. "Absent a demonstrated need for a federal rule of decision, the Court has taken 'the prudent course' of 'adopt[ing] the readymade body of state law as the federal rule of decision until Congress strikes a different accommodation.'" *American Elec. Power Co.*, 131 S. Ct. at 2536. As Professor Field has explained, "federal rules will be made when there is a need for national uniformity that outweighs the need for uniformity within a state; or when the national interests require. But state law should apply whenever that result is not inconsistent with the federal purpose." Martha Field, *Sources of Law: The Scope of Federal Common Law*, 99 HARV. L. REV.

883, 962 (1986). This point is well illustrated by United States v. Kimbell Foods, Inc., 440 U.S. 715 (1979). There the Court held that federal law governs the priority of liens stemming from federal lending programs, but the Court also held that a uniform national rule was unnecessary to protect the federal interests and the Court instead applied state law concerning the relative priority of liens. The areas in which the Court has created uniform federal common law are relative few and include admiralty, interstate border disputes, suits brought by one state to abate pollution emanating from another state, certain issues affected by international relations, and issues affecting the proprietary interests of the U.S. government. See id.; United States v. Kimbell Foods, Inc., 440 U.S. 715, 726–29 (1979); Banco Nacional de Cuba v. Sabbatino, 376 U.S. 398, 426–27 (1964); Clearfield Trust Co. v. United States, 318 U.S. 363 (1943). See generally Wright & Kane, Federal Courts 412–22.

Although federal common law is judicially created, it is in many respects treated as if it were statutory law. It can be changed by Congress through legislation (a constitutional amendment is not required). It is preemptive of state law and binding on state courts. It has even been held that "laws" as used in § 1331, includes federal common law. See Illinois v. City of Milwaukee, 406 U.S. 91, 98–101 (1972).

E. Federal Law in State Court

As discussed in Chapter 4, states have concurrent jurisdiction over most federal causes of action. The only exception is where Congress has granted the federal courts exclusive jurisdiction. Thus, for example, a railroad employee injured on the job can bring suit against her employer based on the Federal Employees' Liability Act (FELA) and can file that suit in either state or federal court. Under the Supremacy Clause, a state court adjudicating that claim is required to apply federal law. But how far does this obligation extend? Must the state court apply all the same procedures that would be applied in federal court?

State courts must follow federal procedures "essential to effectuate" the purposes behind the federal law. Dice v. Akron, Canton & Youngstown R., 342 U.S. 359, 361 (1952). Thus, in *Dice*, an FELA case, the Court held that the right to a jury is "part and parcel of the remedy afforded" by that statute and, therefore, federal law governs the availability of juries in FELA cases in state court. Id. at 363. Compare this holding with *Byrd.* In other FELA cases, the Court has held that states must also follow federal law concerning burden of proof on contributory negligence, Central Vermont Ry. v. White, 238 U.S. 507 (1915), and sufficiency of evidence to sustain a verdict, see Brady v. Southern Ry., 320 U.S. 476 (1943). See generally Anthony Bellia, *Federal Regulation of State Court Procedures*, 110 Yale L.J. 947 (2001).

Chapter 11

The Preclusion Doctrines

A. Introduction and Integration

In this chapter, we study the circumstances under which a judgment precludes subsequent litigation. The assessment of such a preclusive effect requires consideration of at least two suits, one of which has gone to judgment. The question then becomes whether the judgment in the first case precludes the parties from litigating anything in the second case. By "first case," we refer to the first case in which a court enters judgment; the order in which they are filed is irrelevant.

A judgment can preclude subsequent litigation in two basic ways, traditionally referred to as *res judicata* ("the thing is adjudicated") and *collateral estoppel.* In recent years, influenced by the RESTATEMENT (SECOND) OF JUDGMENTS, courts have begun to use the more descriptive terms *claim preclusion* and *issue preclusion.* The confusion over labels is compounded by the fact that some courts refer to the generic effect of preclusion as res judicata and to collateral estoppel as a sub-species of res judicata. For our purposes, what we refer to generically as preclusion is divided into two doctrines, claim preclusion (which many courts still call res judicata or the rule against splitting a cause of action) and issue preclusion (which many courts still call collateral estoppel or, less frequently, estoppel by judgment).

Claim preclusion stands for the proposition that a claimant may only sue on a single claim or "cause of action" once. Obviously, then, a claimant must appreciate the scope of her claim before filing suit. As we will see, one claim can encompass more than one right to relief. For instance, a single act by the defendant may cause personal injuries as well as property damage. If the claim is defined to include all harms caused by the defendant's act, it will encompass both personal injuries and property damage. In such a situation, a claimant who sues only for property damage in the first case will be precluded from bringing a second suit for personal injuries. She has one chance to vindicate *all rights to relief encompassed in a single claim*; failure to do so means that she has lost the right to pursue other aspects of relief encompassed in that claim.

Issue preclusion is narrower, and prevents relitigation of particular issues that were actually litigated and determined in the first case. For example, assume that in the first case the claimant litigated and established issues A, B, C, and D; assume further that in her second case, to recover on a different claim against the same defendant, the claimant must establish issues A, X, Y, and Z. Issue preclusion, if applicable, would operate to deem issue A established in the second case. The defendant could not relitigate that issue, and the plaintiff would establish her right to relief by proving issues X, Y, and Z. Of course, issue preclusion will apply only if the second case is permitted to proceed. If claim preclusion bars the second suit, there is no occasion to consider issue preclusion. One obvious policy justification for preclusion is efficiency. Claim preclusion counsels claimants to seek all rights to relief from a single cause of action in one case. Issue preclusion teaches that one may not relitigate an issue on which she has litigated and lost. There are other policy justifications, as we will see. On the other hand, overzealous application of preclusion might jeopardize a party's opportunity to litigate, and thus might undermine important due process protection. Accordingly, throughout the chapter, consider the relative costs that would be imposed on the parties and the judicial system if the courts did not follow the preclusion doctrines, on the one hand, and the litigant's right to present evidence, on the other.

At the outset, it is useful to contrast claim and issue preclusion with several similar concepts. *Double jeopardy* is the criminal law analog to claim preclusion. While the requirements of the two are not the same, each ensures that no one is made to answer twice for the same wrong. Once a criminal defendant has been tried and acquitted or otherwise put in "jeopardy" of conviction (a point for which there is no particularly easy definition), the prosecution cannot bring the same charge against that defendant in a subsequent proceeding.

Stare decisis, or the doctrine of precedent, requires that courts of a particular jurisdiction follow the legal pronouncements of appellate courts in that jurisdiction. For example, if a state supreme court determines that comparative negligence should supplant the common law rule of contributory negligence, all courts of that state are required to apply comparative negligence. Stare decisis differs from issue preclusion in three important ways. First, it is concerned with appellate pronouncements on questions of law, while preclusion addresses trial court determinations of issues of law or fact.* Second, an opinion's stare decisis effect binds all litigants in all cases in the jurisdiction, while issue preclusion binds only litigants to the particular case (and persons in "privity" with them). Third, the court that issued the precedent has the discretion to overrule or alter it, whereas there is less discretion with the preclusion rules.

The doctrine of *law of the case* provides that issues decided in a suit will not be relitigated later in that same suit. For example, if a court decides an issue during pretrial motions, that determination will bind the parties whenever that issue reappears in the course of the litigation. It differs from issue preclusion in two ways. First, law of the case concerns the same issue being raised multiple times in the same action,

* Although issue preclusion can apply both to matters of fact and law, it is most commonly used regarding questions of fact. Issue preclusion on matters of law can raise special problems, as we will see in Section C below.

while issue preclusion is concerned with raising the same issue in different actions. Second, law of the case is less formal than issue preclusion; a judge is free to depart from an earlier ruling on an issue when appropriate.

Finally, the principle of *judicial estoppel* prevents a party from taking a different position from one taken in previous litigation. It is a doctrine of equity, for which there are no hard-and-fast rules. Courts invoke it to preclude a party from "playing fast and loose" with judicial process by adopting a position that favors it at the moment. An interesting example is New Hampshire v. Maine, 532 U.S. 742, 753–55 (2001), in which New Hampshire contended that the boundary between it and Maine was to be determined by reference to a particular point of a river. New Hampshire had taken a contrary position regarding the boundary point in other litigation in 1970. The Supreme Court invoked judicial estoppel to reject New Hampshire's position in the more recent litigation.

B. Claim Preclusion

Although the language employed by various courts differs, the standard statement of claim preclusion contains three requirements: (1) the two cases must involve the same claim (or, as some jurisdictions refer to it, "cause of action"); (2) the parties to the two suits must be identical or in "privity"; and (3) the first case must have ended in a valid final judgment "on the merits." See, e.g., Kale v. Combined Ins. Co., 924 F.2d 1161, 1164–65 (1st Cir. 1991).

1. Scope of a Claim

a. In General

Courts and commentators agree that defining the scope of a claim is sometimes difficult. For example, the Pennsylvania Supreme Court admits that it "has never adopted a comprehensive definition of what constitutes a cause of action, for the excellent reason that no such definition exists." Kuisis v. Baldwin-Lima-Hamilton Corp., 319 A.2d 914, 918 n.7 (Pa. 1974). Because of different contending definitions, one commentator over half a century ago said "on a given set of facts there seems to be at least one rule to buttress any result, and the same tests often can sustain opposite positions." *Developments in the Law—Res Judicata*, 65 Harv. L. Rev. 818, 825 (1952). One can say much the same thing today. The continuing uncertainty reflects important policy choices on which jurisdictions may disagree.

Carter v. Hinkle

52 S.E.2d 135 (Va. 1949)

Gregory, J., delivered the opinion of the Court.

A taxicab owned and driven by Hinkle was involved in a head-on collision with an automobile owned by the defendant, Smith, and operated by his agent, the defendant, Carter. The collision occurred in Alleghany county, on U.S. Route 60, near the town of Covington, on December 20, 1946, and it is conceded that it was the proximate result of the negligence of the defendant, Carter. The taxi was damaged and an action was instituted by the plaintiff, Hinkle, against the defendant, Smith, for $1,000, $750 of which represented damage to the taxi and $250 damages for the loss of the use of it. Judgment was recovered, the full amount paid thereon and it was marked satisfied.

Later, Hinkle instituted another action against the two named defendants seeking to recover for personal injuries received by him by reason of the collision. The defendants pleaded that the judgment and its satisfaction in the first action was a bar to Hinkle's right to bring the second action for the personal injuries. The court overruled that contention and permitted the case to go to the jury. A verdict was returned in favor of the plaintiff for the sum of $1,000, and judgment was entered, from which this writ of error was obtained.

The question involved is one of law: May one who has suffered both damage to his property and injury to his person as the result of a single wrongful act maintain two separate actions therefor, or is a judgment obtained in the first action a bar to the second? We have no Virginia decision upon the point.

The question has been presented to the courts many times and there is a direct conflict of American authority on the subject. The majority of the American courts of last resort are of the view that but one single cause of action exists and that but one action may be brought therefor.

On the other hand a respectable * * * minority of the courts are of the view that a single tort, resulting in damage to both person and property, gives rise to two distinct causes of action, and that, therefore, recovery in one is no bar to an action subsequently commenced for the other. The minority view is based upon the English case of Brunsden v. Humphrey (1884), L.R. 14 Q.B.D. 141.

Typical of the minority rule are the cases of Vasu v. Kohlers, Inc. (1945), 145 Ohio St. 321, and Reilly v. Sicilian Asphalt Paving Co. (1902), 170 N.Y. 40. In the latter case, which is a leading one, the court had this to say: "The question now before us has been the subject of conflicting decisions in different jurisdictions. In England it has been held by the court of appeals (Lord Coleridge, C.J., dissenting) that damages to the person and to property, though occasioned by the same wrongful act, give rise to different causes of action (*Brunsden v. Humphrey*), while in Massachusetts, Minnesota, and Missouri the contrary doctrine has been declared. The argument of those courts which maintain that an injury to person and property creates but a single cause of action is that, as the defendant's wrongful act was single, the cause of action must be single, and that the different injuries occasioned by it are merely items of damage proceeding from the same wrong, while that of the English court is that the negligent act of the defendant in itself constitutes no cause of action, and becomes an actionable wrong only out of the damage which it causes. 'One wrong was done as soon as the plaintiff's enjoyment of his property was substantially interfered with.

A further wrong arose as soon as the driving also caused injury to the plaintiff's person.' *Brunsden v. Humphrey*."

The court, in that case (*Reilly v. Sicilian Asphalt Paving Co.*), concluded that injury to person and injury to property were essentially different and gave rise to two causes of action; that to hold that only one cause of action exists would be impractical or at least very inconvenient in the administration of justice, and that they should not be blended. The court noted that different periods of limitation applied; that the plaintiff cannot assign his right of action for the injury to his person, while he could assign that for injury to his property; that action for injury to his person would abate or be lost by his death before a recovery; and that injury to property would be an action that would survive and might be seized by creditors or pass to an assignee in bankruptcy. * * *

The right of personal security and the right of property which are invaded by a single wrong give rise to two remedial rights, said the court, and further, in giving the reason for the rule, it said that consideration must be given to the fact that where a property right is invaded the title to the property must be shown to be in the plaintiff, whereas there is no such requirement as to personal injuries. * * *

The court further called attention to the fact that nearly all of the cases which support the single-cause-of action rule involve situations where the plaintiff brought the action in his own right to recover both his property and personal injury damages, and that the rule against splitting demands which would limit the plaintiff to a single action is based on the idea of unreasonable vexation of the defendant rather than upon a discriminating conception of a cause of action. However, when a tort-feasor has committed a tort resulting in damage to both person and property there is nothing vexatious or unreasonable in prosecuting separate actions against him. * * *

It will be observed that an argument to support the majority view is that the single-cause-of-action rule will prevent the crowding of courts with unnecessary litigation, prevent vexatious litigation, eliminate added court costs and delay, and expeditiously end litigation.

That argument is answered in *Vasu v. Kohlers, Inc.*, where the court said: "* * * Short cuts and improvisations may be appealing, but if certainty and predictability, qualities so necessary in the law, are to be maintained, the logical and symmetrical distinctions of the substantive common law, carefully developed through the necessities of experience, should be preserved and not destroyed. In the complexity of life the combinations of fact which give rise to legal liability are infinite, and as a consequence a heavy burden is necessarily imposed upon procedural processes. Nevertheless, rights are too important and liability is too oppressive to be determined and administered in wholesale fashion. * * *"

The minority view follows a less practical but a more logical path. Each jurisdiction concerned has chosen a measuring stick regarded by it as the most important. When it is remembered that the plaintiff usually institutes an action in order to obtain compensation for damages done to his rights rather than to punish the defendant for the wrong, it would seem that the question of the number of rights invaded would be the more important one. * * *

In the English case of *Brunsden v. Humphrey*, the plaintiff brought an action to recover for damages done to his cab in a collision caused by the negligence of the defendant's servant, and after having recovered the amount claimed he brought another action against the defendant claiming damages for personal injury sustained through the same negligent act. After he obtained a verdict the court ruled in favor of the defendant on the ground that the action was not for a new wrong but for a consequence of the same wrongful act which was the subject of the former suit. On appeal the judgment was reversed and the judgment on the verdict for the plaintiff was restored. The Master of the Rolls said that the causes of action were distinct and therefore the court was not called upon to apply the doctrine of res judicata. It was suggested that different evidence would be required to support the respective claims for injury to property and to the person of the plaintiff, and on this point Lord Justice Bowen said, "In the one case the identity of the man injured and the character of his injuries would be in issue, and justifications might conceivably be pleaded as to the assault, which would have nothing to do with the damage done to the goods and chattels."

In speaking of the gist of the action, Lord Justice Bowen said, "[I]t is sufficient to say that the gist of an action for negligence seems to me to be the harm to person or property negligently perpetrated. * * * Both causes of action, in one sense, may be said to be founded upon one act of the defendant's servant, but they are not on that account identical causes of action. The wrong consists in the damage done without lawful excuse, not the act of driving, which (if no damage had ensued) would have been legally unimportant."

Lord Chief Justice Coleridge dissented, taking the other view. He said: "It appears to me that whether the negligence of the servant or the impact of the vehicle which the servant drove, be the technical cause of action, equally the cause of action is one and the same; that the injury done to the plaintiff is injury done to him at one and the same moment by one and the same act in respect to different rights, i.e., his person and his goods, I do not in the least deny; but it seems to me a subtlety not warranted by law to hold that a man cannot bring two actions, if he is injured in his arm and in his leg, but can bring two, if besides his arm and leg being injured, his trousers which contain his leg, and his coat sleeve which contains his arm, have been torn."

This case does not hold that it would have been improper to join the two causes of action in one, subject to certain exceptions not important here. The English rule permits a plaintiff to unite in the same action several causes of action, but he is not compelled to do so.

The weight of American authority, as we have previously stated, disagrees with the decision in *Brunsden v. Humphrey*, but we believe that the principles announced in that case, upon which the minority rule is founded, are more logical and better suited to our practice in Virginia.

Notes and Questions

1. Do you agree that the "primary rights" test, adopted in *Carter*, is "less practical but * * * more logical" than the "single wrongful act" test? How is it less practical? How is it more logical? Between these two—pragmatism and logic—which should prevail?

2. Can you articulate how the single wrongful act definition of claim is broader than the primary rights definition?

3. The court supported its conclusion in *Carter* by noting several differences between claims for property damages and for personal injuries. The former are assignable and do not abate at the plaintiff's death. The latter are not assignable and do abate. The two have different statutes of limitations. Should these factors be relevant in defining a claim for preclusion purposes? What role should pleading rules have? Suppose, for example, Virginia's joinder rules restricted a plaintiff's ability to seek recovery for property and personal damage in a single case. Would that rule affect the definition of claim? If so, why shouldn't these other rules?

4. In *Carter*, the plaintiff sued in the first case both for damage to the taxi and loss of its use. Suppose instead that he had sought only recovery for damage to the taxi. Would Virginia law permit a second case for loss of use?

5. The tests discussed in *Carter* are not the only formulations for determining the scope of a claim. Some courts have used a "sameness of the evidence" test (which the court mentioned in *Carter*). Under this test, courts assess whether the same evidentiary showing would justify recovery for the claimant in both suits. If so, the cases involve the same claim. It is not always clear, however, how much evidentiary overlap is required for the assertions to be considered a single claim.

For example, consider the facts of *Carter*. If the plaintiff sued only for property damage in the first case, would the sameness of the evidence test lead to dismissal of a second suit for personal injuries? To be sure, the evidence in the two cases will not be exactly the same, since the damages are different in the two cases. Indeed, recall the discussion of this point by Lord Justice Bowen in *Brunsden*, quoted in *Carter*. On the other hand, the evidence showing the defendant's liability will be identical. Is that enough to justify the conclusion that both cases involve the same cause of action? Most courts seem to think so. See, e.g., Sure-Snap Corp. v. State Street Bank & Trust Co., 948 F.2d 869, 874 (2d Cir. 1991) ("the test for deciding sameness of the claims requires that the same transaction, evidence, and factual issues be involved"); Buck Creek Indus. v. Alcon Constr., Inc., 631 F.2d 75, 78 (5th Cir. 1980) ("if the evidence needed to sustain the second action would have also sustained the first"); Kent County Bd. of Educ. v. Bilbrough, 525 A.2d 232, 235 (Md. 1987); Morris v. Union Oil Co., 421 N.E.2d 278, 284–85 (Ill. App. 1981).

If that is true, does the sameness of the evidence test differ from the transactional test in any meaningful way? After all, the same evidence will establish liability both for personal injuries and for property damage. On the other hand, what was Lord Justice Bowen's conclusion regarding sameness of the evidence in *Brunsden*, as discussed in *Carter*?

Some older cases adopted a "legal theory" test for claim. Under this, a plaintiff could sue twice regarding the same act if the theory of recovery in the second case were different. For example, a plaintiff who sued for breach of contract and lost could sue the same defendant for restitution, claiming that the defendant was unjustly enriched by his failure to perform under the contract. This view was the product of common law pleading, which, as we saw in Chapter 7, narrowly circumscribed the plaintiff's ability to join claims against the defendant. Under the writ system, the plaintiff could pursue only a single legal theory in one case. With the fall of common law pleading, the narrow "legal theory" definition of claim has waned.

6. The clear trend is to force claimants to package claims into a single case along transactional lines. This trend is typified by § 24(1) of the RESTATEMENT (SECOND) OF JUDGMENTS, which may be considered a fourth test for claim. The RESTATEMENT (SECOND) considers a claim to encompass all rights to relief "with respect to all or any part of the transaction, or series of connected transactions, out of which the action arose." The drafters of this definition state that a transaction is "a natural grouping or common nucleus of operative facts." RESTATEMENT (SECOND) OF JUDGMENTS § 24 cmt. b (1982). They stress a pragmatic approach, focusing on factors such as whether the facts are closely connected in "time, space, origin, or motivation, * * * whether, taken together, they form a convenient unit for trial purposes," and whether treating them as a single transaction comports with the expectations of the parties and of business practice. Id.

The RESTATEMENT (SECOND) view comports with modern joinder rules and the rules for supplemental jurisdiction, all of which emphasize the transactional test as the appropriate definition of the litigative unit. Consistent with this modern trend, the Ohio Supreme Court overruled *Vasu v. Kohlers, Inc.* (discussed in *Carter*) and adopted a transactional test for claim in Rush v. City of Maple Heights, 147 N.E.2d 599, 607–08 (Ohio 1958).

7. How many claims would arise from the following fact patterns under (a) the primary rights definition, (b) the single wrongful act definition, and (c) the RESTATEMENT (SECOND) definition?

(i) D places foreign substances in P's rum jug, thereby ruining the rum and damaging the jug. A week later, P drinks from the jug and becomes ill because of the adulteration. See Boerum v. Taylor, 19 Conn. 122 (1848).

(ii) P and D, each driving her own car, collide. P suffers personal injuries and her car is damaged. In addition, two items of personal property in P's car are destroyed by the collision — a video camera with which P pursues her livelihood of recording weddings and other special events, and an heirloom hand-beveled mirror, which her grandmother had just given to her.

(iii) Same facts as in (ii), but assume that immediately after the collision, D jumps from her car and screams obscenities at P, causing P emotional distress, and defames P by shouting libelous falsehoods about P to the crowd of onlookers.

8. Although most courts today employ relatively broad, transactional definitions of claim, not all jurisdictions have abandoned the primary rights approach. The New York Court of Appeals has never overruled *Reilly v. Sicilian Asphalt Paving Co.*, upon which the court relied in *Carter*. California continues to use the primary rights test. See Graham v. Philip Morris U.S.A., Inc., 40 Cal. 4th 623, 643 (2007).

Similarly, do not assume that jurisdictions choose one test for all types of cases. A Virginia Rule of Court expressly adopts the "same transaction or occurrence" test as the scope of a cause of action. Va. Rule of Court 1:6(a). Interestingly, however, the Rule contains an exception, which adopts the primary rights test for cases in which a claimant suffers personal injury and property damage from a single transaction. So the result in *Carter* would be the same under the new Rule. Similarly, a Georgia statute provides that motor vehicle crash cases create two causes of action—one for property damage and one for personal injury. GA. CODE ANN. § 51-1-32.

9. The primary rights approach seems to promote duplicative litigation. In *Carter*, for example, the court's definition of claim permits the claimant to bring separate suits for property damage and for personal injuries. The taxpayers of Virginia therefore may be required to provide judicial machinery—judges, jurors, clerks, etc.—twice for adjudications concerning one set of underlying facts. Indeed, the court in *Carter* admitted that the single wrongful act definition would "expeditiously end litigation." What policy can justify the seeming inefficiency of adopting the primary rights definition?

Proponents of the primary rights theory argue that the rule avoids hardship in cases involving insurance coverage. Suppose that Insured is injured and suffers property damage in an automobile crash with Bad Driver. Pursuant to Insured's policy, Insco, her insurer, pays her for the property damage. Upon doing so, the insurer is "subrogated" to Insured's right to sue for that property damage; that is, it "stands in the shoes" of the insured for that claim. Before Insurer sues, however, Insured recovers a judgment against Bad Driver for personal injuries. A strict reading of the transaction test could preclude Insurer from suing. The primary rights rule avoids this result by holding that there are two claims. Thus, several jurisdictions adopting a transaction test definition for claim simply make an exception for this subrogation situation. See, e.g., Smith v. Hutchins, 566 P.2d 1136 (Nev. 1977); *Rush v. City of Maple Heights*, supra (noting that jurisdictions adopting transaction test "almost universally recognize[ ]" an exception to protect insurers).

10. It may be that the primary rights definition is not as inefficient as one might surmise. Consider the facts of *Carter* again. After prevailing in her first case, for property damage, the plaintiff brings a second action to recover for personal injuries. Under the primary rights approach, although the second case is not precluded by claim preclusion, the defendant may be barred by issue preclusion from relitigating the question of her negligence. As we will see in Section C below, issue preclusion bars the relitigation of particular issues that were litigated and determined in a prior case between the same parties. Thus, the plaintiff in the second case will not be required to prove the defendant's negligence. In Andrews v. Christenson, 692 P.2d 687,

690 n.1 (Ore. App. 1984), overruled on other grounds in Peterson v. Temple, 881 P.2d 833 (Ore. App. 1994), the court noted:

> The total judicial time consumed, even if both parts are actually tried, may not be significantly greater than trying them together. In fact, it is likely that both will not be tried. If the decision in the property damage case is against the plaintiff, there can be no second trial. If it is in favor of the plaintiff, the parties may well settle the damages claim.

11. Whatever definition is used for determining the scope of claim, that claim is personal to each individual harmed. Suppose Pam and Pat are passengers in a car and each is injured. However we define their claims — by primary rights or by transaction, etc. — Pam's is separate from Pat's. The fact that they were hurt in a single transaction may affect the scope of their individual claims, but it does not merge their separate claims into one.

12. The different approaches to claim preclusion reflect differences in styles of legal argument. The "primary rights" test is more consistent with a formalistic approach to law. Under this approach, one reasons about law and its consequences by beginning with abstract, a priori concepts. In personal jurisdiction, *Pennoyer v. Neff* reflected a formalistic approach, deriving the rules of personal jurisdiction from the nature of sovereignty. In contrast to formalism, legal realism focuses on the purposes and consequence of the legal principles at stake. The RESTATEMENT (SECOND) approach to preclusion, with its pragmatic focus on litigation efficiency, reflects a legal realist approach.

b. Contract Cases

Do the various tests we have seen help us define the scope of a claim in contract and similar suits? Suppose P and D enter an installment sales contract, under which D is to pay P $5,000 per month for twelve months. D makes the first two payments, but misses the third; then D makes the fourth and fifth payments, but fails to make the sixth. Can P bring separate suits against D for the two missed payments, or do they constitute a single claim?

Generally, courts conclude that the claim includes all amounts owed at the time the claimant files suit. Thus, in this hypothetical, P's claim would include both the breach in the third month and the breach in the sixth month. If P sued for only one of these, claim preclusion would prohibit her seeking damages for the other. If P had sued in the fourth month, however, at which time D had failed to pay only one installment, her claim would have consisted of only that single breach. She could then maintain a separate action for the breach in the sixth month (or could add the later claim in the pending case through a supplemental pleading under Rule 15(d)). The same rule applies to cases involving interest payments on a bond or other security.

This discussion assumes that the payments were due under a single instrument. Generally, each contract or bond gives rise to a separate claim or series of claims. Assume that both Contract-1 and Contract-2 require D to make periodic payments to P. One month, D fails to make the required payments under both contracts. Generally, P may maintain separate actions for the breach of Contract-1 and for the breach of Contract-2.

2. Parties or Persons in Privity

a. Who Can Be Bound?

Even if a second case involves the same claim as one that has gone to judgment, claim preclusion requires that the parties to the two suits be the same or in "privity" with a litigant in the prior case. This requirement reflects an abiding theme in our civil justice system: everyone is entitled to her "day in court." Put more accurately, the Due Process Clause generally requires that one cannot be bound by a judgment unless she had an opportunity to appear and litigate. Martin v. Wilks, 490 U.S. 755, 761–62 (1989). (We discussed the importance of adequate notice in ensuring this opportunity in Chapter 3.)

This constitutional precept dictates that the principle of "privity" not be overly broad. After all, binding someone who was not a formal party to the first case will rob her of her "day in court." Accordingly, while there are situations in which "nonparty preclusion" is appropriate, courts are careful to ensure that it applies only when the relationship between a party and a nonparty is such that the nonparty can fairly be bound by the judgment. Historically, such a relationship has been referred to as "privity." That ancient word, in its technical sense, is very formalistic and narrow. The modern approach, then, as exemplified by the Restatement (Second) of Judgments, is to eschew the term "privity" altogether. Still, "privity" can be a useful shorthand for those circumstances in which nonparty preclusion is acceptable.

For years, some courts attempted to extend "privity" to include "virtual representation." There was no single definition of "virtual representation," but the idea was that parties in Case 1 and Case 2 were raising the same arguments (often through the same lawyers) and that the court system should not be burdened with adjudicating these arguments a second time. The Supreme Court rejected "virtual representation" in the following case, and set forth six examples of when nonparty preclusion may be used.

Taylor v. Sturgell

553 U.S. 880 (2008)

[Herrick, an antique aviation enthusiast, used the Freedom of Information Act (FOIA) to seek the release of technical documents from the Federal Aviation Administration (FAA). He wanted the documents to help him restore an antique airplane, a Fairchild F-45, to its original condition. After the FAA denied the request on the basis that they constituted trade secrets, Herrick sued the FAA. The district court entered summary judgment in favor of the FAA.

Less than a month later, Taylor, who was a friend of Herrick and also an aircraft enthusiast, sought the same documents from the FAA. The FAA refused, and Taylor sued the agency. The corporation that succeeded to the interests of the airplane's manufacturer intervened and sought to block release of the documents. The lower courts held that Taylor's suit was barred by claim preclusion. They reasoned that although Taylor was not a party in Herrick's suit, the Herrick had "virtually representated" Taylor in that case. Thus, they concluded, Taylor was bound by the judgment in Herrick's case. Here, the Supreme Court reverses.]

GINSBURG, J., for a unanimous Court.

* * *

The Eighth Circuit's seven-factor test for virtual representation, adopted by the District Court in Taylor's case, requires an "identity of interests" between the person to be bound and a party to the judgment. Six additional factors counsel in favor of virtual representation under the Eighth Circuit's test, but are not prerequisites: (1) a "close relationship" between the present party and a party to the judgment alleged to be preclusive; (2) "participation in the prior litigation" by the present party; (3) the present party's "apparent acquiescence" to the preclusive effect of the judgment; (4) "deliberat[e] maneuver[ing]" to avoid the effect of the judgment; (5) adequate representation of the present party by a party to the prior adjudication; and (6) a suit raising a "public law" rather than a "private law" issue. These factors, the D.C. District Court observed, "constitute a fluid test with imprecise boundaries" and call for "a broad, case-by-case inquiry."

The record before the District Court in Taylor's suit revealed the following facts about the relationship between Taylor and Herrick: Taylor is the president of the Antique Aircraft Association, an organization to which Herrick belongs; the two men are "close associate[s]"; Herrick asked Taylor to help restore Herrick's F-45, though they had no contract or agreement for Taylor's participation in the restoration; Taylor was represented by the lawyer who represented Herrick in the earlier litigation; and Herrick apparently gave Taylor documents that Herrick had obtained from the FAA during discovery in his suit.

Fairchild and the FAA conceded that Taylor had not participated in Herrick's suit. The D.C. District Court determined, however, that Herrick ranked as Taylor's virtual representative because the facts fit each of the other six indicators on the Eighth Circuit's list. Accordingly, the District Court held Taylor's suit, seeking the same documents Herrick had requested, barred by the judgment against Herrick.

The D.C. Circuit * * * observed, first, that other Circuits "vary widely" in their approaches to virtual representation. Taylor v. Blakey, 490 F.3d 965, 971 (2007). In this regard, the D.C. Circuit contrasted the multifactor balancing test applied by the Eighth Circuit and the D.C. District Court with the Fourth Circuit's narrower approach, which "treats a party as a virtual representative only if the party is 'accountable to the nonparties who file a subsequent suit' and has 'the tacit approval of the court' to act on the nonpart[ies'] behalf." Ibid. (quoting Klugh v. United States, 818 F.2d 294, 300 (CA4 1987)).

Rejecting both of these approaches, the D.C. Circuit announced its own five-factor test. The first two factors — "identity of interests" and "adequate representation" —

are necessary but not sufficient for virtual representation. In addition, at least one of three other factors must be established: "a close relationship between the present party and his putative representative," "substantial participation by the present party in the first case," or "tactical maneuvering on the part of the present party to avoid preclusion by the prior judgment."

Applying this test to the record in Taylor's case, the D.C. Circuit found both of the necessary conditions for virtual representation well met. As to identity of interests, the court emphasized that Taylor and Herrick sought the same result—release of the F-45 documents. Moreover, the D.C. Circuit observed, Herrick owned an F-45 airplane, and therefore had "if anything, a stronger incentive to litigate" than Taylor, who had only a "general interest in public disclosure and the preservation of antique aircraft heritage." Id., at 973.

Turning to adequacy of representation, the D.C. Circuit acknowledged that some other Circuits regard notice of a prior suit as essential to a determination that a non-party was adequately represented in that suit. See id., at 973–974 (citing Perez v. Volvo Car Corp., 247 F.3d 303, 312 (CA1 2001), and Tice v. American Airlines, Inc., 162 F.3d 966, 973 (CA7 1998)). Disagreeing with these courts, the D.C. Circuit deemed notice an "important" but not an indispensable element in the adequacy inquiry. The court then concluded that Herrick had adequately represented Taylor even though Taylor had received no notice of Herrick's suit. For this conclusion, the appeals court relied on Herrick's "strong incentive to litigate" and Taylor's later engagement of the same attorney, which indicated to the court Taylor's satisfaction with that attorney's performance in Herrick's case. See 490 F.3d at 974–975.

The D.C. Circuit also found its "close relationship" criterion met, for Herrick had "asked Taylor to assist him in restoring his F-45" and "provided information to Taylor that Herrick had obtained through discovery"; furthermore, Taylor "did not oppose Fairchild's characterization of Herrick as his 'close associate.'" Id., at 975. Because the three above-described factors sufficed to establish virtual representation under the D.C. Circuit's five-factor test, the appeals court left open the question whether Taylor had engaged in "tactical maneuvering." See id., at 976 (calling the facts bearing on tactical maneuvering "ambigu[ous]").

We granted certiorari to resolve the disagreement among the Circuits over the permissibility and scope of preclusion based on "virtual representation."[3]

* * *

3. The Ninth Circuit applies a five-factor test similar to the D.C. Circuit's. See Kourtis v. Cameron, 419 F.3d 989, 996 (2005). The Fifth, Sixth, and Eleventh Circuits, like the Fourth Circuit, have constrained the reach of virtual representation by requiring, *inter alia*, the existence of a legal relationship between the nonparty to be bound and the putative representative. See Pollard v. Cockrell, 578 F.2d 1002, 1008 (CA5 1978); Becherer v. Merrill Lynch, Pierce, Fenner, & Smith, Inc., 193 F.3d 415, 424 (CA6 1999); EEOC v. Pemco Aeroplex, Inc., 383 F.3d 1280, 1289 (CA11 2004). The Seventh Circuit, in contrast, has rejected the doctrine of virtual representation altogether. See Perry v. Globe Auto Recycling, Inc., 227 F.3d 950, 953 (2000).

Though hardly in doubt, the rule against nonparty preclusion is subject to exceptions. For present purposes, the recognized exceptions can be grouped into six categories.

First, "[a] person who agrees to be bound by the determination of issues in an action between others is bound in accordance with the terms of his agreement." 1 RESTATEMENT (SECOND) OF JUDGMENTS § 40 (1980) (hereinafter RESTATEMENT). For example, "if separate actions involving the same transaction are brought by different plaintiffs against the same defendant, all the parties to all the actions may agree that the question of the defendant's liability will be definitely determined, one way or the other, in a 'test case.'" D. SHAPIRO, CIVIL PROCEDURE: PRECLUSION IN CIVIL ACTIONS 77–78 (2001) (hereinafter SHAPIRO). See also California v. Texas, 459 U.S. 1096, 1097 (1983) (dismissing certain defendants from a suit based on a stipulation "that each of said defendants ... will be bound by a final judgment of this Court" on a specified issue).

Second, nonparty preclusion may be justified based on a variety of pre-existing "substantive legal relationship[s]" between the person to be bound and a party to the judgment. SHAPIRO 78. See also Richards [v. Jefferson], 517 U.S. [793], 798 [(1996)]. Qualifying relationships include, but are not limited to, preceding and succeeding owners of property, bailee and bailor, and assignee and assignor. See 2 RESTATEMENT §§ 43-44, 52, 55. These exceptions originated "as much from the needs of property law as from the values of preclusion by judgment." 18A C. WRIGHT, A. MILLER, & E. COOPER, FEDERAL PRACTICE AND PROCEDURE § 4448, p 329 (2d ed. 2002).[8]

Third, we have confirmed that, "in certain limited circumstances," a nonparty may be bound by a judgment because she was "adequately represented by someone with the same interests who [wa]s a party" to the suit. *Richards*, 517 U.S., at 798. Representative suits with preclusive effect on nonparties include properly conducted class actions, see *Martin*, 490 U.S., at 762, n. 2 (citing Fed. Rule Civ. Proc. 23), and suits brought by trustees, guardians, and other fiduciaries, see Sea-Land Services, Inc. v. Gaudet, 414 U.S. 573, 593.

Fourth, a nonparty is bound by a judgment if she "assume[d] control" over the litigation in which that judgment was rendered. Montana [v. United States], 440 U.S. 147], 154 [(1979)]. Because such a person has had "the opportunity to present proofs and argument," he has already "had his day in court" even though he was not a formal party to the litigation.

Fifth, a party bound by a judgment may not avoid its preclusive force by relitigating through a proxy. Preclusion is thus in order when a person who did not participate

---

8. The substantive legal relationships justifying preclusion are sometimes collectively referred to as "privity." See, e.g., Richards v. Jefferson County, 517 U.S. 793, 798 (1996); 2 RESTATEMENT § 62, Comment *a*. The term "privity," however, has also come to be used more broadly, as a way to express the conclusion that nonparty preclusion is appropriate on any ground. To ward off confusion, we avoid using the term "privity" in this opinion.

in a litigation later brings suit as the designated representative of a person who was a party to the prior adjudication. See Chicago, R. I. & P. R. Co. v. Schendel, 270 U.S. 611, 620, 623. And although our decisions have not addressed the issue directly, it also seems clear that preclusion is appropriate when a nonparty later brings suit as an agent for a party who is bound by a judgment.

Sixth, in certain circumstances a special statutory scheme may "expressly foreclos[e] successive litigation by nonlitigants ... if the scheme is otherwise consistent with due process." *Martin*, 490 U.S., at 762, n. 2. Examples of such schemes include bankruptcy and probate proceedings, and *quo warranto* actions or other suits that, "under [the governing] law, [may] be brought only on behalf of the public at large," *Richards*, 517 U.S., at 804.

* * *

[W]e disapprove the theory of virtual representation on which the decision below rested.

* * * Although references to "virtual representation" have proliferated in the lower courts, our decision is unlikely to occasion any great shift in actual practice. Many opinions use the term "virtual representation" in reaching results at least arguably defensible on established grounds. In these cases, dropping the "virtual representation" label would lead to clearer analysis with little, if any, change in outcomes.

[The Court then noted that five of the six grounds for nonparty preclusion discussed above were clearly inapplicable.] That leaves only the fifth category: preclusion because a nonparty to an earlier litigation has brought suit as a representative or agent of a party who is bound by the prior adjudication. Taylor is not Herrick's legal representative and he has not purported to sue in a representative capacity. He concedes, however, that preclusion would be appropriate if respondents could demonstrate that he is acting as Herrick's "undisclosed agen[t]."

Respondents argue here, as they did below, that Taylor's suit is a collusive attempt to relitigate Herrick's action. The D.C. Circuit considered a similar question in addressing the "tactical maneuvering" prong of its virtual representation test. The Court of Appeals did not, however, treat the issue as one of agency, and it expressly declined to reach any definitive conclusions due to "the ambiguity of the facts." We therefore remand to give the courts below an opportunity to determine whether Taylor, in pursuing the instant FOIA suit, is acting as Herrick's agent.

We have never defined the showing required to establish that a nonparty to a prior adjudication has become a litigating agent for a party to the earlier case. Because the issue has not been briefed in any detail, we do not discuss the matter elaboratively here. We note, however, that courts should be cautious about finding preclusion on this basis. A mere whiff of "tactical maneuvering" will not suffice; instead, principles of agency law are suggestive. They indicate that preclusion is appropriate only if the putative agent's conduct of the suit is subject to the control of the party who is bound by the prior adjudication. See 1 Restatement (Second) of Agency § 14, p. 60 (1957)

("A principal has the right to control the conduct of the agent with respect to matters entrusted to him.").

[Because claim and issue preclusion are affirmative defenses, the Court held that the defendant had the burden to prove on remand that Herrick acted as Taylor's agent when he litigated the first case.]

Notes and Questions

1. Realistically, what is to be gained by allowing Taylor to sue the FAA? Exactly the same claim concerning exactly the same airplane has already been adjudicated. Why should the taxpayers pay to have two cases litigate the same thing? Why should the defendant have to defend two cases asserting the same thing? If Taylor is allowed to proceed with his case, don't we also open the door to the possibility of inconsistent outcomes? If Herrick lost Case 1 and Taylor wins Case 2—raising exactly the same arguments—what is the public to think about the rule of law and consistency? What important interest outweighs all these considerations?

2. If the opportunity to appear and litigate is a requirement of due process, how can nonparties ever be bound by a judgment? What policy supports binding nonparties in the circumstances discussed in *Taylor v. Sturgell*? Consider such questions in light of the following.

(a) P-1, the owner of Greenacre, sues D, the adjoining landowner, to establish that she has a right-of-way to travel across D's property. After trial, the court enters judgment for D. P-1 sells Greenacre to P-2, who then sues, asserting the same right-of-way rejected in the prior suit. Should the fact that P-2 was not a party to the first case permit her to maintain this new action? What are the costs to D and to the community if we permit the second action to proceed? What are the costs to P-2 if we do not permit the second action to proceed?

(b) Same facts as in (a), but assume that the judgment in the first case was erroneous as a matter of law. To correct that, P-1 could have appealed the judgment. Assume, however, that she did not. Is P-2 bound by the judgment? If not, can you articulate the circumstances under which P-2 should be allowed to proceed? What if it was "possible" that the judgment in the first case was wrong?

3. Can a nonparty be bound by a judgment simply because she is represented by a litigant, or does she have to be notified of the proceedings? Section 41(2) of the Restatement (Second) Of Judgments expressly provides that a nonparty represented by a litigant "is bound by the judgment even though [she] does not have notice of the action, is not served with process, or is not subject to service of process." How can this statement be justified, however, in light of other materials we have studied? For most of this course, we have considered the due process ideal to be that no one is bound by a judgment unless she is joined as a party and given notice and an opportunity to participate. That is why due process restrictions on personal jurisdiction sought to ensure that the defendant not litigate in an unduly burdensome forum. Similarly, the notice we discussed in Chapter 3 was intended to make meaningful a

party's opportunity to appear and litigate. But if the person to be bound is not going to be joined as a party, why should personal jurisdiction and notice be required?

b. Configuration of the Parties

Even assuming that the parties to the first and second actions are the same (or closely related enough to justify preclusion), claim preclusion generally requires that they have the same litigation posture in both cases. Claim preclusion bars repeat assertions of a claim by the same person. Therefore, it is not enough simply to say that both cases involve the same parties. Instead, in most jurisdictions, both the first and second cases must be brought by the same claimant against the same defendant. Put another way, the second suit must involve the same parties *in the same configuration.*

For instance, suppose that in the first case Adams sues Baker for injuries sustained in an auto collision between the two. After a final judgment in that case, Baker sues Adams to recover for injuries sustained in the same wreck. Can Adams assert claim preclusion against Baker? The general principles of claim preclusion would suggest not. Even though the two cases involved the same parties, Baker has not asserted a claim before and thus cannot be guilty of trying to get two bites of the same apple. Another way to look at it is that the first case involved a different claim, since it was for the vindication of Adams' rights, while the second case was for vindication of Baker's rights.

This result emphasizes another aspect of the ingrained sense that a claimant has a right to her "day in court." In general, a potential claimant can sue when and where she pleases, subject, of course, to jurisdictional principles and the statute of limitations. In this scenario, the fact that Adams decided to sue Baker may not preclude Baker from deciding to pursue her own claim in a separate proceeding. Obviously, absolute litigant autonomy in this regard is inefficient. Here, it would require the judicial system to process two pieces of litigation over a single factual occurrence. This may create a risk of inconsistent results, which can erode public confidence in the administration of justice.

Because of concerns about efficiency and consistency, most jurisdictions modify the result suggested by the general principles of claim preclusion by adopting a *compulsory counterclaim rule.* See, e.g., Rule 13(a)(1). Such a rule, which we will study in detail in Chapter 12, requires a defendant to assert all transactionally related claims against the plaintiff in the pending case. Thus, when Adams sues Baker, the compulsory counterclaim rule would require Baker to assert her claim arising from the same accident in that case. If she failed to do so, the same rule would require the court in which Baker brings suit against Adams to dismiss.

This explains why we are careful to use the term "claimant" (instead of "plaintiff") in discussing claim preclusion; parties other than the plaintiff can assert claims. For example, suppose again that Adams sues Baker for injuries sustained in an auto collision between them. Here, however, assume that Baker files a compulsory counterclaim against Adams, seeking to recover for her personal injuries from the same collision. After a valid final judgment is entered in that case, suppose that Baker sues

Adams again regarding the same claim. Here, claim preclusion may bar the second case. Even though Baker was not the plaintiff in the first action, she was a "claimant."

Notes and Questions

1. The compulsory counterclaim rule requires a party to assert transactionally related claims against an opposing party. It overrides only the defendant's perceived "right" to choose the forum for her claim. The notion of binding a nonparty to the case, obviously, is a far more serious matter, because it precludes the nonparty from pursuing a claim at all.

2. The compulsory counterclaim rule certainly seems to promote efficiency and avoid inconsistent results. But aren't these policies vindicated by issue preclusion as well? Suppose Adams sues Baker for damages arising from their auto collision. The court finds that Baker was negligent, and enters judgment for Adams. Now, because there is no compulsory counterclaim rule, Baker sues Adams for injuries sustained in the same wreck. Won't issue preclusion prevent Baker from relitigating the issue of his negligence? Will this result foster efficiency and consistency to the same degree as the compulsory counterclaim rule?

3. The permissive counterclaim allows the defendant to assert transactionally unrelated claims against the plaintiff. See Rule 13(b). As the name implies, the defendant is not required to assert such a claim. Thus, assume that Adams sues Baker for injuries suffered in their auto crash. If Baker has an unrelated contract claim against Adams, she may choose to file it as a permissive counterclaim in the pending case, or she may assert it in a separate action. If she does assert it, however, she is a "claimant" on that contract claim; claim preclusion will prevent her from suing again on the contract claim.

3. Valid, Final Judgment on the Merits

a. Validity

Courts accord claim or issue preclusion only to valid judgments. Validity as used here refers to the competence of the court, and requires basically that it have had subject matter and personal jurisdiction. A judgment by a court having both forms of jurisdiction is valid, even though it may have been wrong on the merits. If a party feels that the judgment was erroneous, the proper course is to appeal it in the original jurisdiction. As the Supreme Court has explained, "the res judicata consequences of a final, unappealed judgment on the merits [are not] altered by the fact that the judgment may have been wrong or rested on a legal principle subsequently overruled in another case." Federated Dept. Stores, Inc. v. Moitie, 452 U.S. 394, 398 (1981).

b. Finality

Preclusion attaches only to final judgments. Thus individual rulings during the course of a litigation are not entitled to preclusive effect, since they may be revisited by the judge before decision on the case as a final matter. At best, such nonfinal, or interlocutory, orders are entitled to such deference as dictated by the law of the case doctrine, noted in Section A of this chapter.

Suppose a court enters a valid final judgment on the merits, and the losing party appeals. It will take months, likely more than a year, for the appellate court to decide the case. In the interim, is the trial court's judgment entitled to claim preclusion effect? The federal courts conclude that it is. See, e.g., Wagner v. Taylor, 836 F.2d 596 (D.C. Cir. 1987). The state courts, on the other hand, disagree on the issue.

What arguments support recognition of a preclusive effect during appeal? What arguments counsel the opposite result? Suppose the court in the second case affords preclusive effect to a judgment that is later reversed. What can the court that decided the second case do to remedy the problem? See Rule 60(b).

c. *On the Merits*

Traditionally, courts have accorded preclusive effect only to judgments "on the merits," meaning judgments based "on the underlying dispute, the question of who did what." FREER, CIVIL PROCEDURE 538. Clearly, a judgment entered after plenary trial would be on the merits. But a trial is not required. For example, summary judgments and directed verdicts constitute decisions on the merits. Indeed, it is virtually impossible for a claimant to win without establishing her right to recover. Thus virtually any judgment in *favor* of the claimant is considered on the merits. Even a judgment by default is on the merits, because it establishes the substantive validity of the claim. Morris v. Jones, 329 U.S. 545 (1947).

The more difficult situations arise when the claimant loses. Again, she may lose after trial, or on summary judgment or pursuant to directed verdict, any of which is on the merits. But she may also lose for a variety of other reasons. For example, the court may dismiss for claimant's failure to prosecute, or as a discovery sanction, or for lack of jurisdiction or venue. Judgments on these bases would appear to have nothing to do with the merits of the underlying dispute. On the other hand, given liberal modern provisions for pleading, amendment, joinder, and discovery, is there any reason to permit a claimant to bring the same claim again after such a dismissal?

In view of such modern provisions, and because of historic difficulty defining "on the merits," the current approach avoids the phrase. The RESTATEMENT (SECOND) OF JUDGMENTS simply eschews the phrase. Section 20(1)(a) of the RESTATEMENT (SECOND) thus provides a blanket rule that any judgment against the claimant, *except* one "for lack of jurisdiction, for improper venue, or for nonjoinder or misjoinder of parties" is accorded claim preclusive effect.

Federal Rule 41(b) adopts this approach, dictating that any judgment against the claimant, with exceptions similar to those in the RESTATEMENT (SECOND), "operates as an adjudication upon the merits." In Semtek International, Inc. v. Lockheed Martin Corp., 531 U.S. 497, 506–07 (2001), the Supreme Court held that this language means that a second case cannot be brought in the same federal court as the original case. Whether the dismissal has claim preclusion effects that prohibit the claimant from asserting the claim in any court is determined by federal common law. If the case had been brought in federal court under diversity of citizenship jurisdiction, the federal common law will usually incorporate state law. Thus, an involuntary dismissal of a diversity case by a federal court in California would bar subsequent assertion of the same claim in a state court in Maryland only if California law so provides.

Under both Rule 41(b) and the RESTATEMENT (SECOND) the court in the first case is free to provide that its judgment will not operate on the merits. Usually, courts do this by providing that the dismissal is entered "without prejudice." This means that the plaintiff is free to assert the claim again in a new action.

Read Rule 41(b).

Notes and Questions

1. Why should dismissals for lack of jurisdiction, improper venue, and failure to join a party under Rule 19 not preclude a second suit?

2. By "lack of jurisdiction," should Rule 41(b) be construed to refer to personal jurisdiction, subject matter jurisdiction, or both? Why?

3. P sues D for personal injuries suffered in an auto crash with D. Before trial, the court enters judgment for the plaintiff because the defendant committed abuses under the discovery rules. Now P sues D for property damage suffered in the same crash. Assume that the jurisdiction adopts a transactional test for claim. Can D successfully assert claim preclusion against P? Note that Rule 41(b) does not apply. Why?

4. Suppose the court dismisses P's case against D under Rule 12(b)(6), because P failed to state a claim under which relief can be granted. (In some state courts, the functional equivalent would be dismissal based upon D's demurrer.) The court's order says nothing about whether the dismissal is with prejudice. Now P brings a separate case, correcting the allegations of the first complaint in a way that states a claim. Can D successfully assert claim preclusion? Most federal courts say yes. See, e.g., Hall v. Tower Land & Investment Co., 512 F.2d 481, 483 (5th Cir. 1975). State courts adopting the Federal Rules generally agree. See, e.g., Velasquez v. Franz, 589 A.2d 143, 147–48 (N.J. Super. 1991).

Most courts avoid a debate over whether dismissals under Rule 12(b)(6) or state equivalents are on the merits by expressly making them with or without prejudice. The latter seems appropriate, at least if the court is convinced that the error can be remedied by improved pleading. Indeed, it is not unusual for a plaintiff to be allowed several chances to state a claim on which relief can be granted. At some point, however, even a patient judge may conclude that a claimant simply has no claim to state, and may grant a motion under Rule 12(b)(6) or sustain a demurrer with prejudice.

5. Suppose P sues D for medical malpractice, but fails, as required by relevant state law, to proffer an "affidavit of good cause," which is a sworn statement supporting her claim. The court dismisses P's case because of this failure, and does not indicate whether the dismissal is with prejudice. P then files a second case against D, this time including the affidavit of good cause. Assuming that Rule 41(b) applies, can D suc-

cessfully assert claim preclusion? On similar facts, the Supreme Court permitted the plaintiff to proceed with the second action, holding that the failure to satisfy the condition precedent of filing the affidavit constituted a lack of jurisdiction under Rule 41(b). Costello v. United States, 365 U.S. 265, 285 (1961).

Could the same argument be used for other dismissals? For example, suppose the court dismisses the first case because it is brought by the wrong person (for example, someone lacking "standing")? What if the case is brought prematurely? For example, suppose P sues D to recover on a contract. At trial, it is established that D was not required to perform under the contract for six more months. Will the dismissal preclude P from filing a second suit? See Watkins v. Resorts International Hotel & Casino, Inc., 591 A.2d 592, 601 (N.J. 1991) (first case dismissed for plaintiffs' lack of standing deemed a dismissal on jurisdictional grounds; second case not precluded).

6. Some cases use the terms "merger" and "bar" in discussing claim preclusion. The difference focuses on whether the claimant won or lost the first case. If the court entered final judgment in favor of the claimant in the first case, claim preclusion is said to operate as "merger." That is, upon entry of such a judgment, the claim is extinguished and merged into the claimant's judgment. Thus, while claim preclusion precludes her from reasserting the *claim*, she can recover by suing on the *judgment*.

On the other hand, courts refer to the claim preclusion effect of a final judgment for the defendant as "bar." Thus, a claimant who lost the first case is barred from reasserting the claim. As our discussion above shows, it is these "bar" situations that raise the most serious problems concerning whether the judgment is "on the merits," or, under modern principles, to be treated as an adjudication supporting preclusion.

4. Exceptions to the Operation of Claim Preclusion

All courts recognize that claim preclusion is inappropriate in certain circumstances. Section 26(1) of the Restatement (Second) of Judgments provides a helpful list of such circumstances, providing that the doctrine will not apply if:

> (a) The parties have agreed in terms or in effect that the plaintiff may split his claim, or the defendant has acquiesced therein; or
>
> (b) The court in the first action has expressly reserved the plaintiff's right to maintain the second action; or
>
> (c) The plaintiff was unable to rely on a certain theory of the case or to seek a certain remedy or form of relief in the first action because of the limitations on the subject matter jurisdiction of the courts or restrictions on their authority to entertain multiple theories or demands for multiple remedies or forms of relief in a single action, and the plaintiff desires in the second action to rely on that theory or to seek that remedy or form of relief; or

(d) The judgment in the first action was plainly inconsistent with the fair and equitable implementation of a statutory or constitutional scheme, or it is the sense of the scheme that the plaintiff should be permitted to split his claim; or

(e) For reasons of substantive policy in a case involving a continuing or recurrent wrong, the plaintiff is given an option to sue once for the total harm, both past and prospective, or to sue from time to time for the damages incurred to the date of suit, and chooses the latter course; or

(f) It is clearly and convincingly shown that the policies favoring preclusion of a second action are overcome for an extraordinary reason, such as the apparent invalidity of a continuing restraint or condition having a vital relation to personal liberty or the failure of the prior litigation to yield a coherent disposition of the controversy.

Notes and Questions

1. D's vessel rams P's motorboat. Although the motorboat was damaged, P did not seem to be hurt. P sued D in small claims court to recover the $500 damage to her boat. After winning a judgment in that case, P experienced neck problems, which, her doctor concluded, resulted from the boat collision. Now P sues D to recover $250,000 for personal injuries. Assume the jurisdiction adopts a transactional test for claim preclusion. Can D successfully assert claim preclusion?

2. P was involved in a motorcycle accident and suffered both personal injuries and property damage. He filed suit for the property damage in the Justice of the Peace Court (which, under state law, can hear property cases involving no more than $5,000 but cannot hear claims for personal injuries), and won a judgment of $1000. Now he sues for personal injuries in Superior Court. D asserts claim preclusion, because the jurisdiction adopts the RESTATEMENT (SECOND) definition of cause of action. P attempts to invoke exception (c) from § 26(1) of the RESTATEMENT (SECOND) OF JUDGMENTS. What result? See Mells v. Billops, 482 A.2d 759, 761 (Del. Super. 1984) (plaintiff "voluntarily chose a court of limited jurisdiction when he could have presented all his claims * * * had he brought the original action in this Court."). Accord City of Los Angeles v. Superior Court, 149 Cal. Rptr. 320 (Cal. Ct. App. 1978); McKibben v. Zamora, 358 So. 2d 866 (Fla. App. 1978).

3. D injures P and destroys P's car in a collision. P files two suits against D in the same court, one seeking damages for personal injury and the other seeking damages for loss of the car. D does not object, and does not seek consolidation of the two cases. After one of the cases goes to judgment for P, D moves to dismiss the other case under claim preclusion. Will the motion be successful? In other words, is claim preclusion a waivable defense? Does Federal Rule 8(c)(1) help you answer? Compare Lake v. Jones, 598 A.2d 858 (Md. 1991) (claim preclusion waived), with Buchanan v. Dain Bosworth, Inc., 469 N.W.2d 508 (Minn. App. 1991) (only waived if defendant gives affirmative indication of waiver). Should a court raise claim preclusion sua sponte? When would it do so?

In Scherer v. Equitable Life Assur. Soc. of America, 347 F.3d 394, 398 (2d Cir. 2003), plaintiff brought her first case in state court in November 2001, seeking to recover disability benefits from April 1998 to the date of filing. The court ruled for the defendant. In 2003, while the judgment in that case was on appeal, plaintiff brought a second case, this time in federal court, seeking recovery of disability benefits from April 1998 to the date of filing. The federal trial court applied preclusion and held that plaintiff could seek only benefits accruing after the date of the state court judgment. The resulting claim did not exceed $75,000 and thus did not meet the amount-in-controversy requirement for diversity of citizenship jurisdiction. The Second Circuit reversed, holding that preclusion is an affirmative defense which was waived because the defendant did not assert it.

4. P sues D for divorce, based upon irreconcilable differences. After the court enters final judgment granting the divorce, P sues D for emotional distress caused by D's alleged physical abuse of P during their marriage. Because physical abuse is also a basis for divorce, D argues that P's tort claim is barred by claim preclusion because it was not included in P's divorce suit. In Henriksen v. Cameron, 622 A.2d 1135 (Me. 1993), the court rejected D's argument. Formulate two arguments: (1) that the two suits involved different claims; and (2) even if they involved the same claim, an exception applies.

5. Consider Federated Department Stores, Inc. v. Moitie, 452 U.S. 394 (1981), in which retail purchasers brought several cases against owners of department stores, alleging that the defendants had illegally agreed to fix retail prices in violation of federal antitrust law. The district court dismissed all of the cases, holding that retail purchasers could not show the kind of injury required by the antitrust provisions. Some of the plaintiffs ("Set 1") appealed to the Ninth Circuit. Others ("Set 2") did not, and instead filed new suits in state court, which the defendants removed to federal court. The district court dismissed the claims by the Set 2 plaintiffs under claim preclusion. The Set 2 plaintiffs then appealed to the Ninth Circuit.

While the cases of both Set 1 and Set 2 plaintiffs were on appeal, the Supreme Court decided a different case, and held that retail purchasers can show injury as required by the antitrust laws. The Ninth Circuit reversed and remanded the Set 1 cases for reconsideration in light of this new precedent. As to the Set 2 cases, the Ninth Circuit recognized an exception to claim preclusion, to the effect that "non-appealing parties may benefit from a reversal when their position is closely interwoven with that of appealing parties." That court thus held that the Set 2 plaintiffs could take advantage of the new precedent because claim preclusion should give way to "public policy" and "simple justice."

The Supreme Court reversed, holding that claim preclusion barred the Set 2 plaintiffs from proceeding under the new precedent. The Court rejected the Ninth Circuit's exception, saying:

> [W]e do not see the grave injustice which would be done by the application of accepted principles of res judicata. "Simple justice" is achieved when a

> complex body of law developed over a period of years is evenhandedly applied. The doctrine of res judicata serves vital public interests beyond any individual judge's ad hoc determination of the equities in a particular case. There is simply "no principle of law or equity which sanctions the rejection by a federal court of the salutary principle of res judicata." The Court of Appeals' reliance on "public policy" is similarly misplaced. This Court has long recognized that "[p]ublic policy dictates that there be an end of litigation; that those who have contested an issue shall be bound by the result of the contest, and that matters once tried shall be considered forever settled as between the parties." We have stressed that "[the] doctrine of res judicata is not a mere matter of practice or procedure inherited from a more technical time than ours. It is a rule of fundamental and substantial justice * * *."

452 U.S. at 400.

Does *Moitie* counsel unsuccessful litigants to pursue appeals for which they have no precedent, in the hope that the Supreme Court will take their case or decide another case in favor of their position? Is taking such an appeal consistent with principles underlying Rule 11? Is *Moitie* consistent with *Chicot County*, in Chapter 6, Section D?

6. Note that the provision of § 26(1)(e) of the Restatement (Second) Of Judgments embodies the principles we discussed at Section B.1 of this chapter regarding breach of contract and similar claims.

C. Issue Preclusion

Application of issue preclusion requires assessment of five questions: (1) was the same issue litigated and determined in the first case? (2) was the issue essential to the judgment in the first case? (3) was the holding on that issue embodied in a valid, final judgment on the merits? (4) *against whom* may preclusion be asserted? and (5) *by whom* may preclusion be asserted? Because we addressed the third requirement in discussing claim preclusion, we proceed now to the other four.

1. Same Issue Litigated and Determined

Whether the same issue was involved in both cases often will be obvious. Occasionally, however, the second court will be required to review the record from the first case in considerable detail to determine whether the same issue was litigated and determined. In O'Connor v. G & R Packing Co., 423 N.E.2d 397 (N.Y. 1981), a teenager was injured while trespassing in a railroad yard. In the boy's first case, the defendants prevailed when the judge ruled in their favor at the close of the plaintiff's evidence (by granting what in federal court would be called a motion for judgment as a matter of law). Among other things, the judge noted that the boy "not only disobeyed * * * statutes which were enacted for the benefit of the public but also deliberately and needlessly exposed himself to a known danger * * *." Id. at 398 (quoting oral opinion of trial court).

The plaintiff brought a second case against a different defendant, who sought preclusion on the issue of the plaintiff's contributory negligence. After a thorough review of the transcript of the trial judge's ruling in the first case, the New York Court of Appeals refused preclusion. Although the quoted language seemed to address contributory negligence, it was also consistent with the finding that the defendant breached no duty to the boy (because it owed minimal duty to a trespasser). The court continued, id. at 399:

> The ambivalence of the words used, and of the holding in relation to that issue, arises from a number of factors: the words "contributory negligence" were not used; the Trial Judge could not have had in mind the effect of his holding on the present action, which was not begun until several months after his dismissal of the action against the railroads; none of the cases cited concerned contributory negligence, nor does the language used indicate that consideration had been given to Anthony's age, experience, intelligence, and degree of development * * *. Litigation of the contributory negligence issue is not precluded by such a nonspecific nonfactual determination.

Cromwell v. County of Sac

94 U.S. 351, 24 L. Ed. 195 (1877)

Mr. Justice Field delivered the opinion of the Court.

This was an action on four bonds of the county of Sac, in the State of Iowa, each for $1,000, and four coupons for interest, attached to them, each for $100. The bonds were issued in 1860, and were made payable to bearer, in the city of New York, in the years 1868, 1869, 1870, and 1871, respectively, with annual interest at the rate of ten per cent a year. To defeat this action, the defendant relied upon the estoppel of a judgment rendered in favor of the county in a prior action brought by one Samuel C. Smith upon certain earlier maturing coupons on the same bonds, accompanied with proof that the plaintiff Cromwell was at the time the owner of the coupons in that action, and that the action was prosecuted for his sole use and benefit.

The questions presented for our determination relate to the operation of this judgment as an estoppel against the prosecution of the present action, and the admissibility of the evidence to connect the present plaintiff with the former action as a real party in interest.

In considering the operation of this judgment, it should be borne in mind, as stated by counsel, that there is a difference between the effect of a judgment as a bar or estoppel against the prosecution of a second action upon the same claim or demand, and its effect as an estoppel in another action between the same parties upon a different claim or cause of action. In the former case, the judgment, if rendered upon the merits, constitutes an absolute bar to a subsequent action. It is a finality as to the claim or demand in controversy, concluding parties and those in privity with them, not only as to every matter which was offered and received to sustain or defeat the claim or demand, but as to any other admissible matter which might have been offered for that purpose. Thus, for example, a judgment rendered upon a promissory note is conclusive as to the validity of the instrument and the amount due upon it, although it be subsequently alleged that perfect defences actually existed, of which no proof was offered, such as forgery, want of consideration, or payment. If such defences were not presented in the action, and established by competent evidence, the subsequent allegation of their existence is of no legal consequence. The judgment is as conclusive, so far as future proceedings at law are concerned, as though the defences never existed. The language, therefore, which is so often used, that a judgment estops not only as to every ground of recovery or defence actually presented in the action, but also as to every ground which might have been presented, is strictly accurate, when applied to the demand or claim in controversy. Such demand or claim, having passed into judgment, cannot again be brought into litigation between the parties in proceedings at law upon any ground whatever.

But where the second action between the same parties is upon a different claim or demand, the judgment in the prior action operates as an estoppel only as to those matters in issue or points controverted, upon the determination of which the finding or verdict was rendered. In all cases, therefore, where it is sought to apply the estoppel of a judgment rendered upon one cause of action to matters arising in a suit upon a different cause of action, the inquiry must always be as to the point or question actually litigated and determined in the original action, not what might have been thus litigated and determined. Only upon such matters is the judgment conclusive in another action.

The difference in the operation of a judgment in the two classes of cases mentioned is seen through all the leading adjudications upon the doctrine of estoppel. Thus, in the case of Outram v. Morewood, 3 East, 346 [England 1803], the defendants were held estopped from averring title to a mine, in an action of trespass for digging out coal from it, because, in a previous action for a similar trespass, they had set up the same title, and it had been determined against them. In commenting upon a decision cited in that case, Lord Ellenborough, in his elaborate opinion, said: "It is not the recovery, but the matter alleged by the party, and upon which the recovery proceeds, which creates the estoppel. The recovery of itself in an action of trespass is only a bar to the future recovery of damages for the same injury; but the estoppel precludes parties and privies from contending to the contrary of that point or matter of fact, which, having been once distinctly put in issue by them, or by those to whom they are privy in estate or law, has been, on such issue joined, solemnly found against them." * * *

* * * [Such] cases, usually cited in support of the doctrine that the determination of a question directly involved in one action is conclusive as to that question in a second suit between the same parties upon a different cause of action, negative the proposition that the estoppel can extend beyond the point actually litigated and determined. * * *

Various considerations, other than the actual merits, may govern a party in bringing forward grounds of recovery or defence in one action, which may not exist in another action upon a different demand, such as the smallness of the amount or the value of the property in controversy, the difficulty of obtaining the necessary evidence, the expense of the litigation, and his own situation at the time. A party acting upon considerations like these ought not to be precluded from contesting in a subsequent action other demands arising out of the same transaction. * * *

If, now, we consider the main question presented for our determination by the light of the views thus expressed and the authorities cited, its solution will not be difficult. It appears from the findings in the original action of Smith, that the county of Sac, by a vote of its people, authorized the issue of bonds to the amount of $10,000, for the erection of a court-house; that bonds to that amount were issued by the county judge, and delivered to one Meserey, with whom he had made a contract for the erection of the court-house; that immediately upon receipt of the bonds the contractor gave one of them as a gratuity to the county judge; and that the court-house was never constructed by the contractor, or by any other person pursuant to the contract. It also appears that the plaintiff had become, before their maturity, the holder of twenty-five coupons, which had been attached to the bonds, but there was no finding that he had ever given any value for them. The court below held, upon these findings, that the bonds were void as against the county, and gave judgment accordingly. The case coming here on writ of error, this court held that the facts disclosed by the findings were sufficient evidence of fraud and illegality in the inception of the bonds to call upon the holder to show that he had given value for the coupons; and, not having done so, the judgment was affirmed. Reading the record of the lower court by the opinion and judgment of this court, it must be considered that the matters adjudged in that case were these: that the bonds were void as against the county in the hands of parties who did not acquire them before maturity and give value for them, and that the plaintiff, not having proved that he gave such value, was not entitled to recover upon the coupons. Whatever illegality or fraud there was in the issue and delivery to the contractor of the bonds affected equally the coupons for interest attached to them. The finding and judgment upon the invalidity of the bonds, as against the county, must be held to estop the plaintiff here from averring to the contrary. But as the bonds were negotiable instruments, and their issue was authorized by a vote of the county, and they recite on their face a compliance with the law providing for their issue, they would be held as valid obligations against the county in the hands of a bona fide holder taking them for value before maturity, according to repeated decisions of this court upon the character of such obligations. If, therefore, the plaintiff received the bond and coupons in suit before maturity for value, as he offered to prove, he should have been permitted to show that fact. There was nothing adjudged in the former action in the finding that the plaintiff had not made such proof in that case which can preclude the present plaintiff from making such proof here. The fact that a party may not have shown that he gave value for one bond or coupon is not even presumptive, much less conclusive, evidence that he may not have given value for another and different bond or coupon. The exclusion of the evidence offered by the plaintiff was erroneous, and for the ruling of the court in that respect the judgment must be reversed and a new trial had.

Upon the second question presented, we think the court below ruled correctly. Evidence showing that the action of Smith was brought for the sole use and benefit of the present plaintiff was, in our judgment, admissible. The finding that Smith was the holder and owner of the coupons in suit went only to this extent, that he held the legal title to them, which was sufficient for the purpose of the action, and was not inconsistent with an equitable and beneficial interest in another. Judgment reversed, and cause remanded for a new trial.

Notes and Questions

1. The first case was brought by Smith and the second by Cromwell. Nonetheless, why would that fact not negate claim preclusion? Why, then, did claim preclusion not apply in *Cromwell*? In other words, why were the case by Smith and the case by Cromwell not brought to vindicate the same claim?

2. Why can there be no issue preclusion as to the question of whether Cromwell held the bonds as a bona fide purchaser? After all, Smith (as Cromwell's agent) could have raised that issue in the first case. Recall that claim preclusion generally stops a claimant from litigating something that she has never presented to a court. The reason is that she had an opportunity to present those issues in the previous case on the same claim. Issue preclusion, on the other hand, stops someone from relitigating issues which she actually litigated before. Why the difference? What policy is served by the requirement of actual litigation and determination of an issue?

3. In the case brought by Cromwell, could the county have asserted issue preclusion as to whether the bond issuance was fraudulent?

4. As we saw in Section B.3.c of this chapter, a default judgment and dismissal for failure to prosecute carry claim preclusion effect. As a general matter, why should default judgments and dismissals for failure to prosecute not carry issue preclusion consequences? See, e.g., Schuldiner v. K Mart Corp., 284 Fed. Appx. 918, 921 (3d Cir. 2008) ("It has long been determined that a default judgment is a final judgment with res judicata effect."). Should stipulations among litigants or judgments pursuant to settlement carry issue preclusion consequences? See Rule 36(b).

On the other hand, some courts treat a default judgment as a confession of the truth of all material allegations in the complaint and thus give it issue preclusion effect. See, e.g., In re Calvert, 105 F.3d 315 (6th Cir. 1997). And, as we discussed when we covered defaults in Chapter 7, Section D.4, a court may hold an evidentiary hearing before entering default judgment. Such a hearing could, of course, constitute litigation of various issues, which would (when embodied in a valid final judgment) be the subject of issue preclusion.

5. Recall *Baldwin v. Iowa Men's Traveling Association*, in Chapter 6, Section C. There, the defendant made a direct attack on the personal jurisdiction of the court in which the plaintiff filed the first case. That court held that it had personal jurisdiction. The defendant failed to seek appellate review and refused to litigate further. The court entered default judgment. When the plaintiff sought to enforce the judg-

ment in another state, the defendant made a collateral attack on the personal jurisdiction of the first court. Although the Supreme Court stated that a collateral attack was precluded on grounds of "res judicata," it used that term in a generic sense. In fact, the case was based upon issue preclusion. In *Baldwin*, the issue of jurisdiction was fully litigated in the first proceeding and could not be relitigated in the second.

6. Courts may view the scope of "the issue" differently depending upon which party raised it. Suppose P sues D for injuries sustained in an auto crash, alleging that D was negligent because she failed to keep a proper lookout. Suppose D wins, with the court finding that D was not negligent. Now D files a separate action against P to recover for her injuries from the same accident. Assuming that there is no compulsory counterclaim rule, the action will proceed. Can P defend this case by asserting that D was negligent because she drove too fast for road conditions? The drafters of the RESTATEMENT (SECOND) OF JUDGMENTS conclude that P cannot raise the issue, since P reasonably could be expected to have raised the speeding issue in support of her claim in the first action. See RESTATEMENT (SECOND), § 27, cmt. c, illus. 4. In other words, they treat "the issue" as the relatively broad question of whether D was negligent.

In contrast, suppose P sues D to recover an installment payment under an oral contract. D raises a single defense: that the contract is unenforceable under the statute of frauds because it is not in writing. The court rejects the defense and enters judgment for P. Then P sues to recover a different installment (coming due after the judgment in the first case) under the same contract. Clearly, D cannot raise the statute of frauds defense. But can she raise the defense that the contract is unenforceable because it violates some fundamental public policy? The drafters of the RESTATEMENT (SECOND) OF JUDGMENTS conclude that she may. Id. at illus. 6. Here, they treat "the issue" as the narrower question of statute of frauds, rather than enforceability of the contract.

What policy justifies this divergent treatment? As a practical matter, what does the RESTATEMENT (SECOND) approach counsel plaintiffs to do?

The Sally and Joe Hypotheticals. Here we undertake a series of hypotheticals involving a single fact pattern. Assume that two cars collide and that their respective drivers — Sally and Joe — suffer personal injuries and property damage. Assume further that the jurisdiction recognizes contributory negligence, so a negligent claimant cannot recover, and that the issues of defendant's negligence and plaintiff's contributory negligence are litigated in each case. Also assume that the jurisdiction does not have a compulsory counterclaim rule.

(a) Sally sues Joe for negligence. Joe raises the defense of contributory negligence. The jury returns a general verdict in favor of Sally, and the court enters judgment for Sally on the basis of that verdict.

Now Joe sues Sally to recover his damages arising from the same accident. Can Sally assert issue preclusion against Joe as to (1) Joe's negligence or (2) her freedom from negligence? Can we deduce from the general verdict in the first case what issues must have been determined in the first case? If the only issues proffered were the negligence of the two parties, what two findings must have been made for the jury to find in Sally's favor in the first case?

(b) Sally sues Joe for negligence. Joe raises the defense of contributory negligence. The jury returns a general verdict in favor of Joe, and the court enters judgment for Joe on the basis of that verdict.

Now Joe sues Sally to recover his damages arising from the same accident. Can Joe assert issue preclusion against Sally as to (1) his own freedom from negligence or (2) Sally's negligence? Can we know what issues were litigated and determined in the first case?

(c) Sally sues Joe for negligence. Joe raises the defense of contributory negligence. The jury returns a special verdict finding that Sally was negligent, and the court enters judgment for Joe on the basis of that verdict.

Now Joe sues Sally to recover his damages arising from the same accident. Can Joe assert issue preclusion against Sally as to (1) his own freedom from negligence or (2) Sally's negligence? Based upon your conclusion, what, if anything, remains to be litigated in Joe v. Sally?

(d) Sally sues Joe for negligence. Joe raises the defense of contributory negligence. The jury returns a special verdict finding that Sally was not negligent, and that Joe was negligent. The court enters judgment for Sally on the basis of that verdict.

Now Joe sues Sally to recover his damages arising from the same accident. Can Sally assert issue preclusion against Joe as to (1) her own freedom from negligence or (2) Joe's negligence? Legally, which of the prior hypotheticals ((a) through (c)) is the same as this one?

2. Issue Determined Was Essential to the Judgment

Issue preclusion is proper only if the issue litigated and decided was essential to the judgment. This requirement is demonstrated by another twist to our Sally and Joe hypotheticals.

(e) Sally sues Joe for negligence. Joe raises the defense of contributory negligence. The jury returns a special verdict finding that both Sally and Joe were negligent, and the court enters judgment for Joe on the basis of that verdict.

Now Joe sues Sally to recover his damages arising from the same accident. Can Sally assert issue preclusion against Joe as to his negligence? Can Joe assert issue preclusion against Sally as to her negligence? Before concluding, consider the following case.

Rios v. Davis

373 S.W.2d 386 (Tex. Ct. Civ. App. 1963)

Collings, J.

Juan C. Rios brought this suit against Jessie Hubert Davis in the District Court to recover damages in the sum of $17,500.00, alleged to have been sustained as a result of personal injuries received on December 24, 1960, in an automobile collision. Plaintiff alleged that his injuries were proximately caused by negligence on the part of the defendant. The defendant answered alleging that Rios was guilty of contributory negligence. Also, among other defenses, the defendant urged a plea of res judicata and collateral estoppel based upon the findings and the judgment entered on December 17, 1962, in a suit between the same parties in the County Court at Law of El Paso County. The plea of res judicata was sustained and judgment was entered in favor of the defendant Jessie Hubert Davis. Juan C. Rios has appealed.

It is shown by the record that on April 11, 1961, Popular Dry Goods Company brought suit against appellee Davis in the El Paso County Court at Law, seeking to recover for damages to its truck in the sum of $443.97, alleged to have been sustained in the same collision here involved. Davis answered alleging contributory negligence on the part of Popular and joined appellant Juan C. Rios as a third party defendant and sought to recover from Rios $248.50, the alleged amount of damages to his automobile. The jury in the County Court at Law found that Popular Dry Goods Company and Rios were guilty of negligence proximately causing the collision. However, the jury also found that Davis was guilty of negligence proximately causing the collision, and judgment was entered in the County Court at Law denying Popular Dry Goods any recovery against Davis and denying Davis any recovery against Rios.

Appellant Rios in his third point contends that the District Court erred in sustaining appellee's plea of res judicata based upon the judgment of the County Court at Law because the findings on the issues regarding appellant's negligence and liability in the County Court at Law case were immaterial because the judgment entered in that case was in favor of appellant. We sustain this point. We are unable to agree with appellee's contention that the findings in the County Court at Law case that Rios was guilty of negligence in failing to keep a proper lookout and in driving on the left side of the roadway, and that such negligent acts were proximate causes of the accident were essential to the judgment entered therein. The sole basis for the judgment in the County Court at Law as between Rios and Davis was the findings concerning the negligence of Davis. The finding that Rios was negligent was not essential or material to the judgment and the judgment was not based thereon. On the contrary, the finding in the County Court at Law case that Rios was negligent proximately causing the accident would, if it had been controlling, have led to a different result. Since the judgment was in favor of Rios he had no right or opportunity to complain of or to appeal from the finding that he was guilty of such negligence even if such finding had been without any support whatever in the evidence. The right of appeal is from a judgment and not from a finding. The principles controlling the fact situation here involved are, in our opinion, stated in the following quoted authorities and cases. The annotation in 133 A.L.R. 840, page 850 states:

> "According to the weight of authority, a finding of a particular fact is not res judicata in a subsequent action, where the finding not only was not essential to support the judgment, but was found in favor of the party against

> whom the judgment was rendered, and, if allowed to control, would have led to a result different from that actually reached."

In the case of Word v. Colley, Tex. Civ. App., 173 S.W. 629, at page 634 of its opinion (Error Ref.), the court stated as follows:

> "It is the judgment, and not the verdict or the conclusions of fact, filed by a trial court which constitutes the estoppel, and a finding of fact by a jury or a court which does not become the basis or one of the grounds of the judgment rendered is not conclusive against either party to the suit."

For the reasons stated the court erred in entering judgment for Jessie Hubert Davis based upon his plea of res judicata and collateral estoppel. The judgment is, therefore, reversed and the cause is remanded.

Notes and Questions

1. In light of *Rios*, how should hypothetical (e), set out before the case, be decided? Why?

2. What policy supports an essentiality requirement? After all, it is clear that the factfinder in the first case determined that Rios was negligent. We can assume that Rios' self-interest motivated him to litigate the issue seriously. He had his "day in court" and lost on the issue. Why should Rios be able to relitigate that issue?

3. Exactly why was the finding of Rios's negligence in the first case not essential to the judgment? Would a finding that Rios was not negligent have changed the judgment in the first case? Once the plaintiff was found negligent in the first case, was Rios's negligence relevant? Is that why the finding on Rios was not essential?

4. The court notes that Rios could not have appealed the finding that he was negligent in the first case, since he won the judgment. Is that why the finding on his negligence was not essential? Again, even though he could not appeal, Rios had an opportunity and incentive to litigate the question, and lost. Is the possibility of an appeal part of one's "day in court"? See Mower v. Boyer, 811 S.W.2d 560, 562–63 (Tex. 1991) (inability to appeal finding one reason not to accord issue preclusion effect).

5. Are we more confident that the factfinder assessed an issue more carefully if it was essential to the judgment? If so, is that a sign of faith, or lack of faith, in factfinders?

6. It is not sufficient that the facts determined in the prior case "support" the judgment of that case. They must be essential to the judgment in the way we have discussed here. See, e.g., Kloth v. Microsoft Corp., 355 F.3d 322, 328 (4th Cir. 2004) (remanding for determination of what findings were "critical and necessary" to the judgment in the first case); National Satellite Sports, Inc. v. Eliadis, Inc., 253 F.3d 900, 910 (6th Cir. 2001) (where "one ground for the decision is clearly primary and the other only secondary, the secondary ground is not 'necessary to the outcome' for purposes of preclusion").

7. Another aspect of essentiality is raised by our final hypothetical involving Sally and Joe.

> (f) Sally sues Joe for negligence. Joe raises the defense of contributory negligence. The jury returns a special verdict finding that Sally was negligent and that Joe was not negligent. The court enters judgment for Joe.
>
> Now Joe sues Sally to recover his damages arising from the same accident. Can Joe assert issue preclusion against Sally as to (1) his own freedom from negligence or (2) Sally's negligence? Why?

The two findings in the first case are "alternative determinations." Do you see why? If only one of the two were made in the first case, would the judgment have been the same? The original RESTATEMENT OF JUDGMENTS § 68, cmt. n, accords preclusive effect to both alternative determinations. The RESTATEMENT (SECOND) OF JUDGMENTS § 27, denies preclusive effect to both determinations, unless one or both are later affirmed on appeal. See cmt. o. See, e.g., Winters v. Diamond Shamrock Chem. Co., supra, 149 F.3d at 394 (refusing "collateral estoppel effect to an alternative ground left unaddressed by the appellate court").

Does the RESTATEMENT (SECOND) punish a litigant for doing too well? After all, if Joe had won on only one of the two questions, issue preclusion would apply in the second action. Why should he be denied issue preclusion when he wins on both questions? The drafters of the RESTATEMENT (SECOND) explain their reasoning as follows:

> * * * First, a determination in the alternative may not have been as carefully or rigorously considered as it would have if it had been necessary to the result, and in that sense it has some of the characteristics of dicta. Second, and of critical importance, the losing party, although entitled to appeal from both determinations, might be dissuaded from doing so because of the likelihood that at least one of them would be upheld and the others not even reached. If he were to appeal solely for the purpose of avoiding the application of the rule of issue preclusion, then the rule might be responsible for increasing the burdens of litigation on the parties and the courts rather than lightening those burdens. * * *

RESTATEMENT (SECOND) OF JUDGMENTS § 27 cmt. i (1982). Are you persuaded?

Not surprisingly, courts disagree on how the question should be resolved. Some courts take a flexible approach in this area, looking at the facts to determine whether it would be proper to permit issue preclusion on alternative findings. For example, in Malloy v. Trombley, 405 N.E.2d 213, 216 (N.Y. 1980), the judge in the first case found that the defendant was not negligent and further found, "[although] unnecessary to a decision herein," that the plaintiff was barred by contributory negligence. The court of appeals upheld issue preclusion on contributory negligence in a second action. After reviewing the record, the court was impressed that the "thorough and careful deliberation" by the trial judge showed that the alternative holding was not a casual finding.

3. Valid, Final Judgment on the Merits

This requirement is the same as the third requirement for claim preclusion. Preclusion of either type — claim or issue — flows only from a valid, final judgment on the merits.

4. Against Whom Can Issue Preclusion Be Asserted?

You will recall that claim preclusion could only be asserted against parties to the prior litigation or nonparties so closely related to them as to be considered in "privity" with a litigant. In *Taylor v. Sturgell*, which we read in the section on claim preclusion, the Court listed six examples of proper "nonparty preclusion." Recall that this rule — that only parties or persons in "privity" with a party may be bound by a judgment — is rooted in due process. A contrary rule (allowing preclusion against one who was a complete stranger to the earlier case) would bind the stranger to a judgment even though she had never had her day in court.

Notes and Questions

1. Asbestos is a fireproof, incombustible fibrous building material. It was used for decades in countless structures and appliances such as hand-held hair dryers. Breathing asbestos fibers, however, can cause asbestosis, mesothelioma and other potentially deadly lung diseases. This risk became widely apparent in the 1960s and 1970s, and led to thousands of lawsuits for personal injuries and wrongful death. The federal government ordered that asbestos be removed from buildings, which resulted in litigation concerning liability for the cost of such abatement. In addition, there was widespread litigation concerning insurance coverage for the manufacturers of asbestos. Asbestos-related suits constitute the largest series of related litigation in history.

In one personal injury case, plaintiffs won a judgment against six manufacturers of asbestos. Borel v. Fibreboard Paper Prod. Corp., 493 F.2d 1076 (5th Cir. 1974). In a later case, Hardy v. Johns-Manville Sales Corp., 681 F.2d 334 (5th Cir. 1983), different plaintiffs sued six of the same manufacturers and thirteen additional manufacturers who had not been parties to *Borel*. The trial court in *Hardy* held that the judgment in *Borel* was entitled to issue preclusion as to various matters concerning liability, including defendants' breach of a duty to warn workers of the potential dangers of asbestos. The trial court concluded that the plaintiffs could assert issue preclusion against all defendants before it in *Hardy*. There is no question that issue preclusion was proper against the six manufacturers who were defendants in *Borel* (after all, they had had their day in court and lost). The question was whether preclusion could be asserted against those manufacturers who were not parties to *Borel*. Review the six categories of nonparty preclusion recognized in *Taylor v. Sturgell* and assess whether preclusion could be used against the thirteen manufacturers who were not parties to *Borel*. (The answer is no. How would you explain that answer?)

2. What would be wrong with imposing a binding effect on those raising identical issues in subsequent litigation? Suppose the defendants in *Borel* litigated intensely and competently, raised the relevant issues, and were represented by competent counsel. Why should different defendants be allowed to force the courts (a public resource) to relitigate the same issues in a second case? The answer is summed up in the court's conclusion in *Hardy* and other cases that no one can be bound without her "day in court." But, as we have seen, the "day in court" can be constructive, since nonparties can be bound if the litigant is a proper "representative" as that term is used in RESTATEMENT (SECOND) § 41(1). The issue is where to draw the line — when is a constructive "day in court" acceptable? This issue spurred significant debate for decades before the Supreme Court spoke definitively.

5. By Whom Can Issue Preclusion Be Asserted?

a. Mutuality and Exceptions

We have just seen that due process requires that issue preclusion be asserted only *against* one who was a party (or in "privity" with a party) to the first case. Now we address a completely different issue: *by whom* can issue preclusion be asserted? Traditionally, courts answered this question by invoking the principle of *mutuality of estoppel*, which dictates that issue preclusion can be used only by someone who was a party (or in "privity" with a party) to the first case. Mutuality is based upon a basic fairness rationale: that someone who cannot be hurt by a prior judgment should not be entitled to take advantage of it.

Although it implicates notions of fairness, mutuality is not rooted in due process. It is, instead, a product of history that courts are free to reject. Commentators have urged courts to do so for generations. One of the most strident critics, Jeremy Bentham, felt that mutuality brought to legal actions the "aura of the gaming table." 3 JEREMY BENTHAM, RATIONALE OF JUDICIAL EVIDENCE 579 (1827), *reprinted in* 7 WORKS OF JEREMY BENTHAM 171 (J. Bowring ed. 1843). Slowly, in response to such criticism and to illogical results from the application of mutuality, courts have moved away from the doctrine. Indeed, the most important development in recent decades has been the widespread jettisoning of the traditional rule to permit *nonmutual* issue preclusion — that is, assertion of issue preclusion by someone who was not a party to the first case.

The mutuality doctrine started to erode when courts recognized two "exceptions" to its operation in vicarious liability cases. For example, consider the employer-employee relationship. The employer is vicariously liable for the acts of the employee. Suppose the employee allegedly committed a tort within the scope of her employment (say, spilling hot soup on a restaurant patron whom she was serving). Assume that Patron sues Employee; the court enters judgment for Employee because it found her not negligent. Now Patron sues Employer, seeking to impose vicarious liability on her.

Under vicarious liability, Employer is liable only if Employee committed a tort. Because the court in the first case found that Employee had not committed a tort,

Employer would like to use issue preclusion. All of the requirements for issue preclusion are met except that it is being asserted by one who was not a party to the first case. A strict view of the mutuality rule would prohibit Employer from asserting preclusion.

But let's consider what could happen in this situation. Suppose that the second case (Patron v. Employer) goes forward and Patron wins. Employer then must pay the judgment to Patron. Under vicarious liability, however, Employer is entitled to indemnification from Employee. Obviously, then, she will sue Employee to recover for the judgment she has had to pay to Patron. In this suit by Employer against Employee, a judgment for either party will be anomalous. If Employer wins, what good was Employee's original victory? If Employee wins, what good is Employer's "right" to indemnification?

To avoid these anomalies, courts recognized an exception to mutuality and permitted Employer to assert issue preclusion on the finding from the first case that Employee was not negligent.* This is known generally as the "narrow exception" to mutuality.

Now suppose that the first case was Patron v. Employer, and Employer won. When Patron sues Employee in a second case, could Employee use issue preclusion? Again, the mutuality doctrine would say no, because Employee was not a party to the first case. Does the logic of the narrow exception compel an exception here? No. If Employee loses this case, she has no right to indemnification from Employer. Thus, there will be no second suit for indemnity, and no possibility of the anomalous results we saw above. Despite this lack of logical compulsion, some courts permit the employee to assert nonmutual issue preclusion here. This is known generally as the "broad exception" to mutuality.

Not all jurisdictions in the United States have rejected the mutuality doctrine expressly. Among those still adhering to it, however, all seem to recognize at least the narrow exception; many embrace the broad exception.

b. Rejection of Mutuality for Defensive Use

The exceptions just considered apply only in vicarious liability cases. Eventually, some courts took the further step of rejecting mutuality outright, rather than looking for an exception to its operation. The most influential case was Bernhard v. Bank of America, 122 P.2d 892 (Cal. 1942). In *Bernhard*, an elderly woman in failing health made her home with the Cooks, a married couple, and permitted Mr. Cook to write checks on her behalf against one of her accounts. Mr. Cook withdrew a large sum of money from the account and deposited it in his own. After the woman died, Mr.

* Some people have argued that the Employer and Employee are in privity. Thus, they argue, Employer should have the case against it dismissed under claim preclusion. This conclusion is suspect. If the assertion were true, the law would never have had to find exceptions to mutuality in vicarious liability cases. The better approach is that Employer and Employee are not in privity. Thus, there is no claim preclusion. But issue preclusion should be permitted, for reasons explored in the text.

Cook became executor of her estate. The decedent's relatives sued to challenge Mr. Cook's accounting, arguing that he should return the money to the estate. The court found that the decedent authorized Mr. Cook to withdraw the money as a gift to him and his wife. It entered judgment in his favor.

Mr. Cook then resigned as executor, and one of the decedent's daughters was appointed executrix. She sued the bank that had handled the accounts, arguing that her mother had never authorized the withdrawal. The bank asserted preclusion on the finding in the first case that the decedent had indeed given the money to Mr. Cook. The mutuality doctrine would not permit the assertion of preclusion; neither would the exceptions for vicarious liability cases. Nonetheless, the California Supreme Court permitted the bank to assert nonmutual issue preclusion. Justice Traynor criticized the mutuality rule:

> No satisfactory rationalization has been advanced for the requirement of mutuality. Just why a party who was not bound by a previous action should be precluded from asserting it as res judicata against a party who was bound by it is difficult to comprehend. Many courts have abandoned the requirement of mutuality and confined the requirement of privity to the party against whom the plea of res judicata is asserted. The commentators are almost unanimously in accord. The courts of most jurisdictions have in effect accomplished the same result by recognizing a broad exception to the requirements of mutuality and privity, namely, that they are not necessary where the liability of the defendant asserting the plea of res judicata is dependent upon or derived from the liability of one who was exonerated in an earlier suit brought by the same plaintiff upon the same facts. Typical examples of such derivative liability are master and servant, principal and agent, and indemnitor and indemnitee.
>
> In determining the validity of a plea of res judicata three questions are pertinent: Was the issue decided in the prior adjudication identical with the one presented in the action in question? Was there a final judgment on the merits? Was the party against whom the plea is asserted a party or in privity with a party to the prior adjudication?

122 P.2d at 895.

Again, the revolutionary aspect of *Bernhard* is that it does not struggle to find an exception to mutuality; it simply *rejects* the concept. Thus, it expands the availability of nonmutual issue preclusion beyond the vicarious liability area. Many courts have followed the lead. Indeed, Professor Wright considered *Bernhard* one of those rare situations in which "a major change in established legal doctrine can be identified with a single decision and judge." Wright & Kane, Federal Courts 730. In addition to numerous state courts, the United States Supreme Court has embraced *Bernhard.*

In Blonder-Tongue Laboratories, Inc. v. University of Illinois Foundation, 402 U.S. 313 (1971), a patent holder sued Defendant-1, alleging patent infringement. The court held plaintiff's patent invalid and entered judgment for the defendant. Then plaintiff sued Defendant-2, asserting that it was infringing the same patent. Adhering to the mutuality principle, the lower courts refused to let Defendant-2 use issue preclusion as to the finding that the patent was invalid. The Supreme Court reversed, and discussed policy reasons for rejecting mutuality.

> The cases and authorities discussed above [principally *Bernhard*] connect erosion of the mutuality requirement to the goal of limiting relitigation of issues where that can be achieved without compromising fairness in particular cases. The courts have often discarded the rule while commenting on crowded dockets and long delays preceding trial. Authorities differ on whether the public interest in efficient judicial administration is a sufficient ground in and of itself for abandoning mutuality, but it is clear that more than crowded dockets is involved. The broader question is whether it is any longer tenable to afford a litigant more than one full and fair opportunity for judicial resolution of the same issue. * * * In any lawsuit where a defendant, because of the mutuality principle, is forced to present a complete defense on the merits to a claim which the plaintiff has fully litigated and lost in a prior action, there is an arguable misallocation of resources. To the extent the defendant in the second suit may not win by asserting, without contradiction, that the plaintiff had fully and fairly, but unsuccessfully, litigated the same claim in the prior suit, the defendant's time and money are diverted from alternative uses—productive or otherwise—to relitigation of a decided issue. And, still assuming that the issue was resolved correctly in the first suit, there is reason to be concerned about the plaintiff's allocation of resources. Permitting repeated litigation of the same issue as long as the supply of unrelated defendants holds out reflects either the aura of the gaming table or "a lack of discipline and of disinterestedness on the part of the lower courts, hardly a worthy or wise basis for fashioning rules of procedure." Although neither judges, the parties, nor the adversary system performs perfectly in all cases, the requirement of determining whether the party against whom an estoppel is asserted had a full and fair opportunity to litigate is a most significant safeguard.

402 U.S. at 328–29.

Notes and Questions

1. What justifies the Supreme Court's concern in *Blonder-Tongue* with "plaintiff's allocation of resources"? If the plaintiff wants to spend money on repeated litigation, what business is that of the judiciary's?

2. In *Blonder-Tongue*, the Court abandoned mutuality so long as the party against whom issue preclusion is used had a "full and fair opportunity to litigate" the relevant issue in the first case. Does this add anything to requirements we have already seen for issue preclusion? Can you think of any situations (short of the court's binding and gagging the party's lawyers) in which a party would not have had a "full and fair opportunity to litigate" in the first case?

3. Each state is free to determine its own rules concerning preclusion, including mutuality. As noted, *Bernhard* has been influential among the states. *Blonder-Tongue* represents federal law on the subject, to be applied in cases in which state law does not govern. As we will see in Section D of this chapter, state law will govern if the judgment in the first case was entered in a state court, and the second action was filed in federal court.

Still, as noted, outright rejection of mutuality is not universal. Some jurisdictions adhere to mutuality as the standard, while recognizing exceptions in vicarious liability situations. See, e.g., Gilmer v. Porterfield, 212 S.E.2d 842 (Ga. 1975); Kyreacos v. Smith, 572 P.2d 723 (Wash. 1977).

4. It is important to note that in both *Blonder-Tongue* and *Bernhard*, the person asserting nonmutual issue preclusion was the defendant in the second case. In other words, both cases involved "nonmutual defensive issue preclusion." Yet, neither opinion seems to make much of that fact, leaving open the possibility that nonmutual issue preclusion might be available to a *plaintiff* in the second case. Professor Brainerd Currie foresaw the possibility of such "nonmutual *offensive* issue preclusion" even before *Blonder-Tongue*, and was worried by it. In a justly famous article, he argued against expansion of *Bernhard* to the offensive situation. Brainerd Currie, *Mutuality of Estoppel: Limits of the* Bernhard *Doctrine*, 9 STAN. L. REV. 281 (1957).

Let us consider a variation of a hypothetical posed by Professor Currie. Suppose a train crashes, and 100 passengers (P) are injured.

(a) In the first case, P-1 sues Train. The court finds that Train was not negligent and enters judgment for Train. In the second case, P-2 sues Train concerning the same crash. It is clear that Train cannot assert issue preclusion on the finding that it was not negligent. Why?

(b) Same facts, but P-1 wins the first case, the court finding Train negligent. Now P-2 sues Train concerning the same crash. Unless *Bernhard* and *Blonder-Tongue* are limited to their facts, P-2 can assert issue preclusion against Train on the finding that it was negligent (assuming, of course, that Train had a "full and fair opportunity to litigate" the issue in the first case). Why? Indeed, wouldn't P-2 through P-100 all be able to "ride" the victory of P-1?

Train would have to win all one hundred cases individually to escape liability. It could never use issue preclusion against a successive plaintiff. The passengers, however, would simply be able to wait until a single passenger won, and then assert nonmutual offensive issue preclusion based upon that case. Professor Ratliff calls this the "option effect," which he criticizes as an unfair one-way street. Jack Ratliff, *Offensive Collateral Estoppel and the Option Effect*, 67 TEX. L. REV. 63 (1988).

Another fact pattern makes the unfairness clearer. Suppose Train wins each of the first 55 cases brought against it concerning the crash, defeating P-1 through P-55 by proving that it was not negligent. Then P-56 prevails, with a finding that Train was negligent. Allowing P-57 through P-100 to "ride" this victory seems especially unpalatable because the victory seems clearly to be an aberration. Can the legal system really give such weight to one victory out of 56? This type of scenario especially bothered Professor Currie, who counseled great caution when it came to nonmutual offensive issue preclusion. Currie, supra, 9 STAN. L. REV. at 304–21. Do these concerns militate toward a flat rejection of nonmutual offensive issue preclusion, or toward its use with appropriate limitations? If the latter, what sorts of limitations would be appropriate? Consider the Supreme Court's reactions to such questions in the following case.

c. Rejection of Mutuality for Offensive Use

Parklane Hosiery Co. v. Shore

439 U.S. 322, 99 S. Ct. 645, 58 L. Ed. 2d 552 (1979)

MR. JUSTICE STEWART delivered the opinion of the Court.

This case presents the question whether a party who has had issues of fact adjudicated adversely to it in an equitable action may be collaterally estopped from relitigating the same issues before a jury in a subsequent legal action brought against it by a new party.

The respondent brought this stockholder's class action against the petitioners in a Federal District Court. The complaint alleged that the petitioners, Parklane Hosiery Co., Inc. (Parklane), and 13 of its officers, directors, and stockholders, had issued a materially false and misleading proxy statement in connection with a merger. The proxy statement, according to the complaint, had violated §§ 14(a), 10(b), and 20(a) of the Securities Exchange Act of 1934, as well as various rules and regulations promulgated by the Securities and Exchange Commission (SEC). The complaint sought damages, rescission of the merger, and recovery of costs.

Before this action came to trial, the SEC filed suit against the same defendants in the Federal District Court, alleging that the proxy statement that had been issued by Parklane was materially false and misleading in essentially the same respects as those that had been alleged in the respondent's complaint. Injunctive relief was requested. After a 4-day trial, the District Court found that the proxy statement was materially false and misleading in the respects alleged, and entered a declaratory judgment to that effect. The Court of Appeals for the Second Circuit affirmed this judgment.

The respondent in the present case then moved for partial summary judgment against the petitioners, asserting that the petitioners were collaterally estopped from relitigating the issues that had been resolved against them in the action brought by the SEC.[2] The District Court denied the motion on the ground that such an application of collateral estoppel would deny the petitioners their Seventh Amendment right to

2. A private plaintiff in an action under the proxy rules is not entitled to relief simply by demonstrating that the proxy solicitation was materially false and misleading. The plaintiff must also show that he was injured and prove damages. Since the SEC action was limited to a determination of whether the proxy statement contained materially false and misleading information, the respondent conceded that he would still have to prove these other elements of his prima facie case in the private action. The petitioners' right to a jury trial on those remaining issues is not contested.

a jury trial. The Court of Appeals for the Second Circuit reversed, holding that a party who has had issues of fact determined against him after a full and fair opportunity to litigate in a nonjury trial is collaterally estopped from obtaining a subsequent jury trial of these same issues of fact. The appellate court concluded that "the Seventh Amendment preserves the right to jury trial only with respect to issues of fact, [and] once those issues have been fully and fairly adjudicated in a prior proceeding, nothing remains for trial, either with or without a jury." Because of an intercircuit conflict, we granted certiorari.

I

The threshold question to be considered is whether, quite apart from the right to a jury trial under the Seventh Amendment, the petitioners can be precluded from relitigating facts resolved adversely to them in a prior equitable proceeding with another party under the general law of collateral estoppel. Specifically, we must determine whether a litigant who was not a party to a prior judgment may nevertheless use that judgment "offensively" to prevent a defendant from relitigating issues resolved in the earlier proceeding.

A

Collateral estoppel, like the related doctrine of res judicata, has the dual purpose of protecting litigants from the burden of relitigating an identical issue with the same party or his privy and of promoting judicial economy by preventing needless litigation. Until relatively recently, however, the scope of collateral estoppel was limited by the doctrine of mutuality of parties. Under this mutuality doctrine, neither party could use a prior judgment as an estoppel against the other unless both parties were bound by the judgment. Based on the premise that it is somehow unfair to allow a party to use a prior judgment when he himself would not be so bound, the mutuality requirement provided a party who had litigated and lost in a previous action an opportunity to relitigate identical issues with new parties.

By failing to recognize the obvious difference in position between a party who has never litigated an issue and one who has fully litigated and lost, the mutuality requirement was criticized almost from its inception. Recognizing the validity of this criticism, the Court in *Blonder-Tongue Laboratories, Inc. v. University of Illinois Foundation*, abandoned the mutuality requirement, at least in cases where a patentee seeks to relitigate the validity of a patent after a federal court in a previous lawsuit has already declared it invalid. The "broader question" before the Court, however, was "whether it is any longer tenable to afford a litigant more than one full and fair opportunity for judicial resolution of the same issue." 402 U.S. at 328. The Court strongly suggested a negative answer to that question.

B

The *Blonder-Tongue* case involved defensive use of collateral estoppel — a plaintiff was estopped from asserting a claim that the plaintiff had previously litigated and lost against another defendant. The present case, by contrast, involves offensive use of collateral estoppel — a plaintiff is seeking to estop a defendant from relitigating the issues which the defendant previously litigated and lost against another plaintiff. In both the offensive and defensive use situations, the party against whom estoppel is asserted has litigated and lost in an earlier action. Nevertheless, several reasons have been advanced why the two situations should be treated differently.

First, offensive use of collateral estoppel does not promote judicial economy in the same manner as defensive use does. Defensive use of collateral estoppel precludes a plaintiff from relitigating identical issues by merely "switching adversaries." Thus defensive collateral estoppel gives a plaintiff a strong incentive to join all potential defendants in the first action if possible. Offensive use of collateral estoppel, on the other hand, creates precisely the opposite incentive. Since a plaintiff will be able to rely on a previous judgment against a defendant but will not be bound by that judgment if the defendant wins, the plaintiff has every incentive to adopt a "wait and see" attitude, in the hope that the first action by another plaintiff will result in a favorable judgment. Thus offensive use of collateral estoppel will likely increase rather than decrease the total amount of litigation, since potential plaintiffs will have everything to gain and nothing to lose by not intervening in the first action.

A second argument against offensive use of collateral estoppel is that it may be unfair to a defendant. If a defendant in the first action is sued for small or nominal damages, he may have little incentive to defend vigorously, particularly if future suits are not foreseeable. Allowing offensive collateral estoppel may also be unfair to a defendant if the judgment relied upon as a basis for the estoppel is itself inconsistent with one or more previous judgments in favor of the defendant. Still another situation where it might be unfair to apply offensive estoppel is where the second action affords the defendant procedural opportunities unavailable in the first action that could readily cause a different result.[15]

C

We have concluded that the preferable approach for dealing with these problems in the federal courts is not to preclude the use of offensive collateral estoppel, but to grant trial courts broad discretion to determine when it should be applied. The general rule should be that in cases where a plaintiff could easily have joined in the earlier action or where, either for the reasons discussed above or for other reasons, the application of offensive estoppel would be unfair to a defendant, a trial judge should not allow the use of offensive collateral estoppel.

In the present case, however, none of the circumstances that might justify reluctance to allow the offensive use of collateral estoppel is present. The application of offensive collateral estoppel will not here reward a private plaintiff who could have joined in

15. If, for example, the defendant in the first action was forced to defend in an inconvenient forum and therefore was unable to engage in full scale discovery or call witnesses, application of offensive collateral estoppel may be unwarranted. Indeed, differences in available procedures may sometimes justify not allowing a prior judgment to have estoppel effect in a subsequent action even between the same parties * * *. The problem of unfairness is particularly acute in cases of offensive estoppel, however, because the defendant against whom estoppel is asserted typically will not have chosen the forum in the first action.

the previous action, since the respondent probably could not have joined in the injunctive action brought by the SEC even had he so desired. Similarly, there is no unfairness to the petitioners in applying offensive collateral estoppel in this case. First, in light of the serious allegations made in the SEC's complaint against the petitioners, as well as the foreseeability of subsequent private suits that typically follow a successful Government judgment, the petitioners had every incentive to litigate the SEC lawsuit fully and vigorously.

Second, the judgment in the SEC action was not inconsistent with any previous decision. Finally, there will in the respondent's action be no procedural opportunities available to the petitioners that were unavailable in the first action of a kind that might be likely to cause a different result.

We conclude, therefore, that none of the considerations that would justify a refusal to allow the use of offensive collateral estoppel is present in this case. Since the petitioners received a "full and fair" opportunity to litigate their claims in the SEC action, the contemporary law of collateral estoppel leads inescapably to the conclusion that the petitioners are collaterally estopped from relitigating the question of whether the proxy statement was materially false and misleading.

II

[The Court then concluded that application of issue preclusion did not violate the Seventh Amendment right to jury trial, which we considered in Chapter 9.]

Notes and Questions

1. In *Parklane*, the Court abandoned mutuality in the offensive context, but only after arming the district courts with discretion to determine whether the use of preclusion would be fair under the circumstances. Consider them individually.

(a) *Easy joinder in the first case.* Is the Court correct in its opinion that nonmutual defensive issue preclusion promotes efficiency while nonmutual offensive issue preclusion does not? In an interesting article, Professor Hay demonstrates the Court's point through economic analysis, noting that by suing separately, a "free rider" gets two "bites at the apple." If the first litigant loses, the judgment does not bind her. If the first litigant wins, nonmutual offensive issue preclusion will permit her to take advantage of the victory. Bruce Hay, *Some Settlement Effects of Preclusion*, 1993 U. Ill. L. Rev. 21, 49.

To reduce the incentives to sue separately, the Court will not let "a plaintiff who could easily have joined in the earlier action" use offensive preclusion. Is this a meaningful limitation? After all, the "penalty" for waiting in the wings is simply that the second plaintiff must present her entire case. See Ratliff, supra, 67 Tex. L. Rev. at 83.

In Chapter 12, we will see that certain nonparties are able to intervene in a pending case. The ability to intervene depends, of course, on knowledge of the pending case. But assuming knowledge and an ability to intervene, what does "easily" mean? If a case is pending in Philadelphia and the would-be intervenor lives across the river in Camden, New Jersey, could she join "easily"? What if the case were in federal court and she wanted to sue in state court?

(b) *Foreseeability of litigation/incentive to litigate.* How can this be shown? Will it not be obvious in mass tort cases? Won't the defendant's incentive to litigate in the first case be especially high if the jurisdiction adopts nonmutual offensive issue preclusion?

(c) *Inconsistent judgments.* The Court would not permit nonmutual offensive issue preclusion if there were inconsistent judgments in litigation already completed. Is there any limit to this notion? Suppose that 30 successive plaintiffs proved that the defendant was negligent and that defendant had only won one case — the first one, at that. In a well-known pre-*Parklane* decision, the Oregon Supreme Court said, "[w]e do not mean to say that one favorable determination can never be overcome and estoppel never applied despite the number of subsequent determinations to the contrary." State Farm Fire & Cas. Co. v. Century Home Components, Inc., 550 P.2d 1185, 1192 n.5 (Ore. 1976). In Hoppe v. G.D. Searle & Co., 779 F. Supp. 1425 (S.D.N.Y. 1991), the court rejected nonmutual offensive issue preclusion because the defendant had won sixteen of twenty prior jury adjudications.

(d) *Different procedures.* What examples did the Court give for this factor? Can you think of any others?

2. Would you expect plaintiffs to use nonmutual offensive issue preclusion whenever it is available? It may be that some plaintiffs do not try to take advantage of the doctrine because it may "eliminate [their] opportunity to present the 'horribles' of defendant's conduct to the jury in each subsequent case." Spencer Williams, *Mass Tort Class Actions: Going, Going, Gone?*, 98 F.R.D. 323, 328–29 (1983). Should plaintiffs be allowed to burden courts with such unnecessary presentation of evidence?

3. Does the *Parklane* opinion address sufficiently Professor Currie's concerns (discussed supra, in Section C.4.b)? Recall the mass disaster hypothetical, in which 100 passengers are injured in a single accident. Train wins the first 55 cases, proving that it was not negligent. Then P-56 wins a judgment, based upon a finding that Train was negligent. Professor Currie was wary of allowing P-57 through P-100 to use preclusion because it seems that P-56's judgment is an aberration.

Suppose instead P-1 wins the first case to go to judgment. Because it is first, there are obviously no inconsistent judgments. Thus, *Parklane* would appear to permit P-2 through P-100 to use issue preclusion (assuming, of course, that no other fairness factor is violated). But how do we know (especially given the possibility of "plaintiff shopping," discussed in Note 4 immediately below) that the judgment for P-1 is not an aberration? That is, if we litigated all 100 cases separately, is it not possible that Train would win 99? Even if Train would win just one, why should it be "railroaded" for 99 judgments just because it lost the first one? Currie, supra, 9 Stan. L. Rev. at 308-21. Is there an alternative, such as trying ten test cases to see which way the wind is blowing?

Does *Parklane* tell us why we should repose such confidence in the first judgment?

4. Would you expect acceptance of nonmutual offensive issue preclusion to give rise to "plaintiff shopping"—that is, to cooperation among counsel for numerous plaintiffs to ensure that the most compelling case (the one with the best chance to show that the defendant was liable) go to judgment first? If that plaintiff wins, the others may then use preclusion to ride that victory. Is there anything wrong with that? A good example of this type of litigation strategy is found in the asbestos cases. Interestingly, for a variety of reasons, the courts have not readily employed nonmutual offensive issue preclusion there. See Note, *Exposing the Extortion Gap: An Economic Analysis of the Rules of Collateral Estoppel*, 105 HARV. L. REV. 1940 (1992).

5. Rejection of the mutuality doctrine was driven in part by concerns about "the litigation crisis" and the growing costs of litigation. Interestingly, there is very little empirical evidence concerning the actual efficiency gains from abandoning mutuality. See Lewis Grossman, *The Story of* Parklane: *The "Litigation Crisis" and the Efficiency Imperative, in* CIVIL PROCEDURE STORIES 387 (K. Clermont ed., 2004).

5. Exceptions to the Operation of Issue Preclusion

As with claim preclusion, the courts recognize exceptions to the operation of issue preclusion. These are cataloged in § 28 of the RESTATEMENT (SECOND) OF JUDGMENTS, which provides that issue preclusion will not apply if:

> (1) The party against whom preclusion is sought could not, as a matter of law, have obtained review of the judgment in the initial action; or
>
> (2) The issue is one of law and (a) the two actions involve claims that are substantially unrelated, or (b) a new determination is warranted in order to take account of an intervening change in the applicable legal context or otherwise to avoid inequitable administration of the laws; or
>
> (3) A new determination of the issue is warranted by differences in the quality or extensiveness of the procedures followed in the two courts or by factors relating to the allocation of jurisdiction between them; or
>
> (4) The party against whom preclusion is sought had a significantly heavier burden of persuasion with respect to the issue in the initial action than in the subsequent action; the burden has shifted to his adversary; or the adversary has a significantly heavier burden than he had in the first action; or
>
> (5) There is a clear and convincing need for a new determination of the issue (a) because of the potential adverse impact of the determination on the public interest or the interests of persons not themselves parties in the initial action, (b) because it was not sufficiently foreseeable at the time of the initial action that the issue would arise in the context of a subsequent action, or (c) because the party sought to be precluded, as a result of the conduct of his adversary or other special circumstances, did not have an adequate opportunity or incentive to obtain a full and fair adjudication in the initial action.

Notes and Questions

1. At least three of the *Parklane* "fairness" factors seem to be addressed by this list. Which ones? Does this suggest that *Parklane* is not particularly revolutionary?

2. While riding her bicycle, P crashes because of faulty paving on a city street. She is injured, and her bike is damaged. First, she sues the city in small claims court for $80.00 in property damage. She proves that the city was negligent and wins. Second, she sues the city in a state court of general subject matter jurisdiction for $1,000,000 in personal injuries. Assuming that the applicable law adopts the primary rights definition of claim (so the case is not dismissed for claim preclusion), can she use issue preclusion to establish the city's negligence?

3. Criminal defendants must be convicted by evidence that proves guilt beyond a reasonable doubt. In civil cases, the claimant must prevail by a lesser standard—a preponderance of the evidence.

Suppose the state prosecutes D for theft, and gains a conviction. Then, the person from whom D stole institutes a civil action against D to recover damages. Can the plaintiff in the civil case use issue preclusion on the question of whether D stole the item? Why? See Crowall v. Heritage Mutual Ins. Co., 346 N.W.2d 327 (Wis. 1984) (criminal conviction for driving under influence given issue preclusive effect in later civil case).

Suppose instead the state prosecutes D for theft, but the jury returns a verdict of not guilty. Now the person from whom D allegedly stole institutes a civil action against D to recover damages. Aside from the fact that the civil plaintiff was not a party to the criminal case, why can D not assert issue preclusion to the effect that he did not steal the item?

4. Consider the fact pattern we just saw, but assume now that D entered a guilty plea in the criminal case. Now the victim of the theft sues D in a civil action to recover damages for the theft. Assuming the jurisdiction would allow nonmutual assertion of issue preclusion by the civil plaintiff, would it be proper in this case? The problem, of course, is that the guilty plea means that nothing was actually litigated and determined in the first case. So issue preclusion should not be available. But it "appears unseemly to allow a defendant who has pleaded guilty to deny guilt of the elements of the offense in later civil litigation." 18B Wright & Miller 450. Accordingly, some courts will allow preclusion on these facts. Technically, careful courts will base preclusion on the doctrine of "judicial estoppel," which we saw in Section A of this chapter. It is a doctrine of equity that will not permit a litigant to profit from taking inconsistent positions. See id. § 4474.1.

5. Inventor patented an invention and entered into Contract-1 with Manufacturer. Under the agreement, Manufacturer made and marketed the invention and paid a royalty to Inventor's spouse. The Internal Revenue Service sued, claiming that the income from Contract-1 ought to be taxed to Inventor and not to Spouse. The court disagreed, holding that the income was taxable to Spouse. (Inventor liked this result because Spouse had a lower income tax rate.)

Because the product continued to sell well, at the expiration of Contract-1, Inventor entered Contract-2 with Manufacturer; it was identical to Contract-1 in every detail except dates. The IRS sued concerning tax liabilities for a different year, again claiming that the income — this time from Contract-2 — should be taxable to Inventor. Should issue preclusion prevent the IRS from arguing that issue? See Commissioner of Internal Revenue v. Sunnen, 333 U.S. 591, 602 (1948) (no issue preclusion; "For income tax purposes, what is decided as to one contract is not conclusive as to any other contract which is not then in issue, however similar or identical it may be."). In *Sunnen*, the Court was influenced by the fact that relevant case law intervened and made it clear that the income should be taxed to the inventor. Where is the holding in *Sunnen* reflected in § 28 of the RESTATEMENT (SECOND) OF JUDGMENTS?

Sunnen may be a good example of why issue preclusion should be applied with especial care to issues of law. Although it was once widely stated that there could be no issue preclusion on matters of law, the opposite view now prevails. See Colin Buckley, *Issue Preclusion and Issues of Law: A Doctrinal Framework Based on Rules of Recognition, Jurisdiction and Legal History*, 24 HOUS. L. REV. 875 (1987); Geoffrey Hazard, *Preclusion as to Issues of Law: The Legal System's Interest*, 70 IOWA L. REV. 81 (1984). Still, as *Sunnen* shows, issues of law raise special problems, since allowing a party to use issue preclusion on a matter of law might allow her to avoid the consequences of subsequent changes in the law. This could give one person a preferred position vis a vis other citizens.

6. Nonmutual offensive issue preclusion is not available in litigation against the United States. United States v. Mendoza, 464 U.S. 154, 162–63 (1984). This rule is dictated by policy. The government is involved in litigation around the country, and may litigate the same issue in numerous cases. It would be required to appeal every adverse ruling in an effort to avoid preclusion. This result "might disserve the economy interest in whose name estoppel is advanced by requiring the government to abandon virtually any exercise of discretion in seeking to review judgments unfavorable to it." Id. at 163. Does this exception find support in § 28 of the RESTATEMENT (SECOND) OF JUDGMENTS?

D. Problems of Federalism

What preclusion rules apply if judgment is entered in one jurisdiction and the second case is filed in another? In answering this, we need to consider separately the four possible fact patterns: (1) "state-to-state," in which the first judgment is rendered in State A and the second case is filed in State B; (2) "state-to-federal," in which the first judgment is rendered in state court and the second case is filed in federal court; (3) "federal-to-state," in which the first judgment is rendered in federal court and the second case is filed in state court; and (4) "federal-to-federal," in which the first judgment is rendered in one federal district court and the second case is filed in another.

The analysis of what rules apply starts with the Full Faith and Credit Clause of the Constitution, Article IV, § 1, and the full faith and credit statute, 28 U.S.C. § 1738.

Read both provisions carefully. Two things are noteworthy at this point. First, the constitutional provision is narrower; it covers only the fact pattern (1) above, and requires every state court to give full faith and credit to the judicial proceedings of every other state. The statutory provision covers this situation as well as fact pattern (2) above, and requires every state court *and federal court* to give "the same full faith and credit" to a judgment as it would receive in the judgment-rendering state. Second, neither the Constitution nor the statute covers situations (3) or (4), in which the judgment is rendered in a federal court. See David Engdahl, *The Classic Rule of Faith and Credit*, 118 YALE L.J. 1584 (2009); Stephen Sachs, *Full Faith and Credit in the Early Congress*, 95 VA. L. REV. 1201 (2009).

1. State-to-State

In Chapter 2 on personal jurisdiction, we saw that the courts of all states must give full faith and credit to a valid judgment of a court of another state. In determining whether a judgment of State A was valid, the court in State B could inquire only as to whether the court in State A had personal jurisdiction. If it did not, the judgment of State A was void and unenforceable. But if the court in State A had jurisdiction, its judgment was entitled to full faith and credit in State B, even if the judgment was wrong on the merits of the dispute. See Fauntleroy v. Lum, 210 U.S. 230 (1908). If the losing party felt that the State A judgment was erroneous, she should have appealed it in State A. We also discussed this topic in Chapter 6, where we saw these distinctions between direct and collateral attacks on personal jurisdiction.

2. State-to-Federal

Here, § 1738 requires a federal court in State B to give full faith and credit to a valid judgment of State A. Thus, this situation is functionally equivalent to the "state-to-state" fact pattern. Allen v. McCurry, 449 U.S. 90, 96 (1980) ("Congress has specifically required all federal courts to give preclusive effect to state court judgments whenever the courts of the State from which the judgments emerged would do so."). See generally William Luneberg, *The Opportunity to be Heard and the Doctrines of Preclusion: Federal Limits on State Law*, 31 VILL. L. REV. 81 (1986); Gene Shreve, *Preclusion and Federal Choice of Law*, 64 TEX. L. REV. 1209 (1986).

In each of these two situations, however, does the statutory requirement that the second court give the "same full faith and credit" as the judgment-rendering court mean "same" in every detail? The drafters of the RESTATEMENT (SECOND) OF JUDGMENTS conclude that it does. To them, § 1738 requires the second court "to give to the state judgment the same effect—*no more and no less*—than the [judgment-rendering] court would give it." Id. § 86 cmt. g (1982). Although this summarizes the majority view, some commentators argue, and a few courts conclude, that the second court is free to diverge somewhat from the preclusion rules of the judgmentrendering state. There are two possibilities.

First, one can argue that full faith and credit encompasses only the "central doctrines of claim and issue preclusion" and not "every minute detail." WRIGHT & KANE, FEDERAL COURTS 733. Under this approach, full faith and credit would be "limited to the rules that support the core values of finality, repose, and reliance, as well as some of the rules that facilitate control by the first court over its own procedure." It would not, however, "demand obeisance to other aspects of preclusion doctrine that are incidental to the central role of preclusion and that may intrude on substantial interests of later courts." Id. Can you think of any such "other aspects of preclusion doctrine"? Perhaps reflecting the difficulty in drawing this line, courts have not accepted this argument.

Second, there is some support for the conclusion that § 1738 does not preclude the second court from giving a judgment a *greater* preclusive effect than it would receive in the first court. According to this view, the main purpose of the statute is to ensure respect for the original court's judgment; giving it greater effect than it would receive in that court does not violate that policy. A few opinions have embraced this proposition. See In re TransOcean Tender Offer Securities Litigation, 455 F. Supp. 999 (N.D. Ill. 1978); Hart v. American Airlines, Inc., 304 N.Y.S.2d 810 (Sup. Ct. 1969). For example, suppose the judgment-rendering state does not allow nonmutual assertion of issue preclusion, but the second court would. In *TransOcean*, the second court, a federal district court, extended the effect of the first judgment by enforcing it through nonmutual preclusion. Such holdings are rare, and are criticized. See WRIGHT & KANE, FEDERAL COURTS 733–734. What policy counsels against providing greater preclusive effect than the original court would give?

The more widely held view is that when § 1738 instructs the second court to give the "same full faith and credit" as the original court, "same" means "same." This requirement can create odd situations in the second fact pattern, where a federal court must apply the preclusion law of the judgment rendering state. In Marrese v. American Academy of Orthopaedic Surgeons, 470 U.S. 373 (1985), doctors sued a professional association in state court, asserting that they were denied membership in violation of various state laws. After losing there, the doctors sued in federal court, asserting a violation of federal antitrust laws. Because the federal antitrust claims invoked exclusive federal jurisdiction, the doctors could not have asserted them in the first proceeding. Nonetheless, the lower courts dismissed the second case under claim preclusion, noting that the plaintiffs could have sued on both the federal and state claims in federal court.

The Supreme Court reversed and remanded for consideration of what the law of the judgment-rendering state would provide in this situation. But what sort of assessment will that be? How can a state have rules of preclusion for claims that cannot be asserted in its courts? Recall that one exception to claim preclusion is that the claim could not have been asserted before because of jurisdictional limitations. See supra Section B.4. Does this exception ensure that the state rules cannot prescribe preclusion on these facts? Indeed, on remand in *Marrese*, the district court denied claim preclusion precisely because the federal claim could not have been joined in the state proceeding. Marrese v. American Academy of Orthopaedic Surgeons, 628 F. Supp. 918 (N.D. Ill.

1986) (court's "task is an exercise in extrapolation because, of course, the Illinois courts never address issues pertaining to exclusively federal lawsuits").

3. Federal-to-State

As noted, neither the Constitution nor the statute addresses this fact pattern. Nonetheless, courts and commentators agree that the state courts must respect federal judgments. Professor Degnan concluded that this result is compelled by the Supremacy Clause of Article VI of the Constitution. Ronan Degnan, *Federalized Res Judicata*, 85 YALE L.J. 741, 742–49, 768–69 (1976). See also Stephen Burbank, *Federal Judgments Law: Sources of Authority and Sources of Rules*, 70 TEX. L. REV. 1551 (1992).

Thus, a state court would ascribe to the judgment of a federal court the same preclusive effect that the federal court would. Does this mean that federal law on preclusion would apply? Certainly, the answer is yes if the case had invoked federal question jurisdiction. But what if the case had been in federal court under diversity jurisdiction? In Semtek International Inc. v. Lockheed Martin Corp., 531 U.S. 497, 508–09 (2001), the Supreme Court held that the preclusive effect of a federal diversity judgment should be governed by federal common law. The Court further held, however, that in most instances, there was no need for a uniform federal common law rule and instead federal common law would "borrow" the preclusion law of the state in which the federal court sits. So the judgment of a California federal court would be preclusive in a subsequent Maryland case only if California law would dictate that result.

4. Federal-to-Federal

It is not surprising that this fact pattern is not mentioned in either the Constitution or § 1738, since here the litigants do not deal with intersystem enforcement of a judgment; all of the litigation is in a single court system. That does not mean there are not problems, however. If the first case was in federal court based upon federal question jurisdiction, the courts assume that federal common law governs the preclusion question. The Supreme Court did this in *Blonder-Tongue* and *Parklane.* (Is this result consistent with the Rules of Decision Act?)

But what if the federal court's jurisdiction in the first case was based upon diversity of citizenship jurisdiction? Clearly, the *Erie* doctrine, discussed in Chapter 10, requires the federal court to apply state substantive law in diversity cases. Does that mean that the federal court in the second action must look to the preclusion law of the state in which the federal court sat in the first case? Suppose, for example, that the first federal judgment is entered in a district court in Iowa in a diversity of citizenship case, and that the second action is filed in federal district court in Hawaii. Should the Hawaii federal judge use Iowa law of preclusion to determine the preclusive effect of the first judgment? Or is she free to apply a federal law of preclusion?

The RESTATEMENT (SECOND) OF JUDGMENTS § 87 takes the position that federal law should govern. That section bears the influence of Professor Ronan Degnan, who reached the conclusion that federal law should govern in *Federalized Res Judicata*, supra, 85 YALE L.J. 741. Other commentators disagree. See, e.g., Stephen Burbank, *Interjurisdictional Preclusion, Full Faith and Credit and Federal Common Law: A General Approach*, 71 CORNELL L. REV. 733 (1986). Not surprisingly, the courts have disagreed. Compare Adkins v. Allstate Ins. Co., 729 F.2d 974 (4th Cir. 1984) (federal law applies), with Bates v. Union Oil Co., 944 F.2d 647 (9th Cir. 1991) (state law applies).

As noted in the preceding subsection, the Supreme Court has held that federal common law of preclusion governs in these situations, but that in most instances the federal common law will incorporate the law of the state in which the federal court was situated. Semtek International Inc. v. Lockheed Martin Corp., 531 U.S. at 508–09.

Chapter 12

Scope of Litigation — Joinder and Supplemental Jurisdiction

A. Introduction and Integration

In this chapter we address the scope of litigation. In other words, what parties can be joined and what claims can they assert in a civil action? At common law, joinder rules were restrictive, resulting in multiple suits for what could easily be seen as a single overall dispute. Equity practice relaxed the joinder rules considerably, with the express goal of determining disputes by the whole, rather than piecemeal. Modern joinder practice, as embodied in the Federal Rules, adopts this theme from equity, and permits (indeed, sometimes compels) the joinder of parties and claims along transactional lines. This trend is supported by the evolution of preclusion doctrines that also focus on "transaction or occurrence" in defining a claim.

This inclination toward "packaging" of disputes brings various benefits.

Principally, it avoids duplicative litigation by putting all transactionally related claims and parties into a single case. This not only avoids unnecessary expense for the litigants, but reduces backlog in burdened court systems. Remember, litigation is publicly funded dispute resolution. The public has some right to insist on efficiency in the process. Packaging also may contribute to public confidence in the judicial system by avoiding inconsistent results that may flow from duplicative litigation. The classic discussion of the benefits of packaging is John McCoid, *A Single Package for Multiparty Disputes*, 27 Stan. L. Rev. 707 (1976). See also Martin Redish, *Intersystemic Redundancy and Federal Court Power: Proposing a Zero Tolerance Solution to the Duplicative Litigation Problem*, 75 Notre Dame L. Rev. 1347 (2000).

But packaging is not a panacea. It makes litigation more complex and therefore may not reduce queuing time significantly. Clearly, the court must be equipped with mechanisms to ensure that multiple claims and parties do not confuse the jury at trial. Moreover, mandatory packaging may override the plaintiff's ability to choose her forum and the scope of the litigation she wishes to pursue. Historically, courts have given great deference to plaintiff autonomy. Today, with growing concerns for efficiency, many argue that the plaintiff must share the decision-making authority regarding scope of the litigation.* One of the significant debates in procedure concerns the balance between plaintiff autonomy and efficiency.

It is important to remember, however, that joinder rules merely provide *procedural* mechanisms by which to assert a variety of claims. They do not—indeed, they cannot—alter the requirements of personal jurisdiction, subject matter jurisdiction, and venue. See Rule 82. As we will see, some joinder rules countenance the addition of new parties; when such parties are added in a defensive capacity, they must be subject to personal jurisdiction of the court. (If the added party is joined in an offensive capacity—that is, to assert a claim—she will have waived any personal jurisdiction objection to the court.) As a general rule, throughout our discussion in this chapter, we will assume that the joinder of claims and parties present no problems of personal jurisdiction or venue.**

Every claim joined in federal court must have a basis of federal subject matter jurisdiction. Sometimes the basis will be clear because the claim asserted under the joinder rules will be supported by federal question, alienage, or diversity of citizenship jurisdiction. But sometimes, the claim will not be supported by one of the bases of jurisdiction we studied in Chapter 4. In these situations, the court may nonetheless permit assertion of a claim under *supplemental jurisdiction*. This doctrine allows a federal court to hear claims that are so closely related to an underlying dispute that properly invoked federal jurisdiction as to be considered part of the same "case or controversy" as that dispute. As we will see, the courts generally define this close relationship along transactional lines. This has created a confluence between the procedural test for joinder and the supplemental jurisdictional test and has greatly facilitated packaging.

In this chapter, we integrate the discussion of supplemental jurisdiction with the discussion of the joinder rules. Thus, throughout this chapter, there are always two questions. First, is there a joinder Rule that permits the assertion of this claim? If so, second, is the claim supported by subject matter jurisdiction? An affirmative answer to the second question can be based upon any of the bases of subject matter jurisdiction discussed in Chapter 4 or upon supplemental jurisdiction. Accordingly, as to the joinder devices throughout the chapter, we will have separate subparts on "procedural aspects" and "jurisdictional aspects."

---

* We have already discussed how the plaintiff's choice of forum may be overridden by removal and by transfer of venue. See Chapter 4, Section C.6 and Chapter 5, Section E.

** Occasionally a plaintiff will combine one claim for which personal jurisdiction or venue is proper with another for which one or both of these would not be proper if the claim were sued on alone. Such a situation could arise where one claim based on a federal statute that includes nationwide service of process or a specialized venue provision is joined with a state claim. Where claims arise out of the same core of facts, courts have sometimes recognized "pendent personal jurisdiction" or "pendent venue" and heard the claims as to which personal jurisdiction or venue is otherwise lacking. See 4A Wright & Miller, Federal Practice And Procedure § 1069.7 (pendent personal jurisdiction); 15 Wright & Miller, Federal Practice And Procedure § 3808 (pendent venue).

B. Real Party in Interest, Capacity, and Standing

Our system does not allow everyone who is irked about something to bring a suit. The plaintiff, generally speaking, must have been harmed by the defendant and must be the appropriate recipient of any remedy the court may award.

The first sentence of Rule 17(a)(1) requires that "[a]n action must be prosecuted in the name of the real party in interest." The second sentence makes it clear that the real party in interest (RPI) will not necessarily be the person who receives the benefit of a favorable judgment. For example, a trustee suing on behalf of beneficiaries to the trust will not be enriched by a judgment. She is acting merely as a representative of the beneficiaries.

Most of the difficult RPI cases involve assignment or subrogation of the plaintiff's claim. Suppose P has a claim against D, but assigns the right to sue to Z. Common law did not recognize the assignment, and required the case to be brought by P, even though she obviously had no interest in the outcome of the case. Equity, on the other hand, recognized the assignment, and allowed Z to bring suit as the RPI. Rule 17(a) follows this historic equity practice.*

Subrogation is an assignment by operation of law and arises commonly in cases involving insurance coverage. For example, suppose Corporation purchases fire insurance from Insurer to cover fire damage to its manufacturing plant. The plant is destroyed by a fire caused by the negligence of D. Obviously, Corporation has a claim against D. Pursuing litigation, however, will take a long time; Corporation wants money now so it can rebuild the plant and get back in business. That is why it bought insurance. Under the policy, Insurer will write a check to Corporation immediately *and will, in return, be subrogated to Corporation's right to sue D.* In other words, Insurer pays Corporation for the loss and receives, by operation of law, an assignment of Corporation's right to sue D. In the case against D, Insurer would be the RPI. If Corporation brought the case, D would move to substitute Insurer as RPI.

RPI inquiries are to be contrasted with the notion of *capacity.* Capacity refers to a person's or an entity's ability to sue and be sued. For example, minors and incompetent persons lack the capacity to represent their own interests in litigation; a case by or against them should be brought by or against such a person's representative. Similarly, some entities, such as labor unions and partnerships, may lack capacity to sue in their common name; litigation by or against them will be brought by or against individual members of the group instead. (It may be possible to pursue the litigation as a class action, as we will see in Chapter 13. Rule 17(b) addresses these and other capacity issues.

---

* We have already discussed problems that can arise under 28 U.S.C. § 1359 when a claim is assigned for the purpose of creating diversity of citizenship jurisdiction. See supra Chapter 4, Section C.3.c.

Both RPI and capacity must be distinguished from *standing*, a doctrine of considerable difficulty requiring that the plaintiff have suffered some "injury in fact" before she can sue. Standing is often an issue in cases challenging governmental action. For example, can a private group interested in environmental issues sue to enjoin the government's building of a dam that may endanger certain animals? Can persons opposed to capital punishment sue to enjoin the execution of a convicted murderer? The answers to such questions are not easy, and are addressed in detail in courses on constitutional law and federal courts.

Notes and Questions

Read Rule 17(a) and (b) and answer the following.

1. If someone other than an RPI sues a defendant, what can the defendant do?

2. Paula, a citizen of North Carolina, sues Dana, a citizen of Washington, on a claim arising under state law in federal court, seeking damages of $150,000. Assume that the RPI is not Paula, but Pamela, who is a citizen of Washington. Notwithstanding Rule 17(a)(3), why must this action be dismissed? What *two* motions should Dana make?

3. Harvey has a homeowner's insurance policy insuring his house from damage. His house is severely damaged when a small airplane crashes into it. Although the damage is $100,000, his insurance company pays him $99,500 under the policy, because the policy has a $500 deductible. In a suit against the pilot of the airplane, why are both Harvey and the insurance company RPIs? See, e.g, Ocean Ships, Inc. v. Stiles, 315 F.3d 111, 116–17 (2d Cir. 2002) (insured is RPI to extent of deductible).

4. Same facts as in Note 3. Assume that Harvey is a citizen of Missouri, the pilot is a citizen of Kansas, and the insurance company is a citizen of Connecticut. Clearly, the insurance company could sue the pilot under diversity of citizenship jurisdiction, because the parties are of diverse citizenship and the insurance company has a claim exceeding $75,000.

(a) Could Harvey invoke diversity of citizenship jurisdiction against the pilot? Isn't he an RPI only for a claim of $500? See Travelers Ins. Co. v. Riggs, 671 F.2d 810 (4th Cir. 1982) (similar fact pattern; court allows both insured and insurer to proceed as RPIs without discussing this problem).

(b) Instead of making an outright payment to Harvey, suppose the insurance company "lent" Harvey $99,500, with the stipulation that he would return any judgment recovered to the insurance company. Who is the RPI? Would your answer differ if the agreement stated that Harvey need never return the money if he recovers no judgment against the pilot?

5. The scenario described in Note 4(b) is fairly common, because insurance companies generally prefer to have the litigation filed and prosecuted in the name of the insured individual rather than in their names. They fear that a jury will be less sympathetic to an insurance company than to an aggrieved individual. Why? Probably, it is because many potential jurors see an insurance company as a "deep pocket" for a judgment. In addition, many jurors may have had their own disagreements with

insurance companies. Courts have not been consistent in addressing this "loan receipt" situation. Some see the insured as the RPI, some say it is the insurer. See generally June Entman, *More Reasons for Abolishing Federal Rule of Civil Procedure 17(a): The Problem of the Proper Plaintiff and Insurance Subrogation*, 68 N.C. L. Rev. 893 (1990).

6. Does the RPI rule add any protection not already accorded by the substantive law? That is, if the "wrong" person sues the defendant, won't the substantive law preclude her from recovering? Noting this and other arguments, critics have argued for decades that the RPI rule is more trouble than it is worth, and ought to be jettisoned. See, e.g., Thomas Atkinson, *The Real Party in Interest Rule: A Plea for its Abolition*, 32 N.Y.U. L. Rev. 926 (1957).

7. Assume a state law precludes a partnership from suing in its own name. If the partnership is involved in a case in federal court that invokes federal question jurisdiction, why would a federal court allow it to sue by the common name? See Rule 17(b)(3)(A).

C. Claim Joinder by Plaintiffs

1. Procedural Aspects

Assuming the plaintiff is an RPI and that she has capacity and standing, what claims can she assert against a defendant? Read Rule 18(a). Note its breadth; it allows a claimant to assert every claim she has against the opposing party. This rule applies even if the claims are not transactionally related, are based upon different theories, and even if the claimant is seeking different remedies. It declares "open season" on the defendant. It says "anything goes." Such open-ended joinder may facilitate settlement by allowing parties to put their entire dispute in one litigation. There are other points to consider.

First, Rule 18(a) is permissive; the plaintiff is not required to assert all claims she has against the defendant. Remember, however, that the joinder rules are not the only things that animate a plaintiff's choices. The plaintiff must also consider the preclusion rules. Thus, although Rule 18(a) is permissive, the preclusion rules may, as a practical matter, force the plaintiff to join several assertions of liability in a single case. Rule 18(a) is the carrot and claim preclusion is the stick.

Second, if the plaintiff's claims are *not* transactionally related, and claim preclusion does not act as a stick (why not?), why would the plaintiff ever want to "load up" a case by asserting them together? Can you imagine a less than noble motive? Can you imagine a sensible motive? Read Rule 42(b). Does this allow the court to avoid problems created by overzealous claim joinder by the plaintiff?

Third, note that Rule 18(a) does not empower the "plaintiff," but speaks instead of "[a] party asserting a claim, counterclaim, crossclaim, or third-party claim." This inclusive drafting recognizes that plaintiffs are not the only litigants who can assert claims. But it is important to understand that Rule 18(a) does not automatically grant all litigants the right to assert all claims against all other litigants. Rather, it declares "open season" only for those litigants who assert one of the claims listed in the rule. For example, as we will see, a crossclaim is a transactionally related claim that one has against a co-party. If a defendant asserts a crossclaim against her co-defendant, *then* Rule 18(a) permits her to declare open season on the co-defendant by joining all other claims. If she does not assert the crossclaim, however, she cannot invoke Rule 18(a).

Fourth, joinder rules such as Rule 18(a) are procedural only, and cannot affect subject matter jurisdiction. Thus, once the procedural propriety of a claim is established, we then must assess whether the claim is supported by federal subject matter jurisdiction.

2. Jurisdictional Aspects

In some cases, multiple claims will have independent bases of subject matter jurisdiction. Suppose, for example, that Paul, a citizen of Georgia, sues Don, a citizen of Arizona, asserting a violation of federal antitrust laws and a completely unrelated $80,000 claim for breach of contract. The antitrust claim invokes federal question jurisdiction, and the contract claim invokes diversity of citizenship jurisdiction.

What happens, however, when a party uses Rule 18(a) to join a claim over which there is no federal question or diversity of citizenship jurisdiction?

United Mine Workers v. Gibbs

383 U.S. 715, 86 S. Ct. 1130, 16 L. Ed. 2d 218 (1966)

MR. JUSTICE BRENNAN delivered the opinion of the Court.

Respondent Paul Gibbs was awarded compensatory and punitive damages in this action against petitioner United Mine Workers of America (UMW) for alleged violations of § 303 of the Labor Management Relations Act, 1947, as amended, and of the common law of Tennessee. The case grew out of the rivalry between the United Mine Workers and the Southern Labor Union over representation of workers in the southern Appalachian coal fields. Tennessee Consolidated Coal Company, not a party here, laid off 100 miners of the UMW's Local 5881 when it closed one of its mines in southern Tennessee during the spring of 1960. Late that summer, Grundy Company, a wholly owned subsidiary of Consolidated, hired respondent as mine superintendent to attempt to open a new mine on Consolidated's property at nearby Gray's Creek through use of members of the Southern Labor Union. As part of the arrangement, Grundy also gave respondent a contract to haul the mine's coal to the nearest railroad loading point.

On August 15 and 16, 1960, armed members of Local 5881 forcibly prevented the opening of the mine, threatening respondent and beating an organizer for the rival union. The members of the local believed Consolidated had promised them the jobs at the new mine; they insisted that if anyone would do the work, they would. * * *

Respondent lost his job as superintendent, and never entered into performance of his haulage contract. He testified that he soon began to lose other trucking contracts and mine leases he held in nearby areas. Claiming these effects to be the result of a concerted union plan against him, he sought recovery not against Local 5881 or its members, but only against petitioner, the international union. The suit was brought in the United States District Court for the Eastern District of Tennessee, and jurisdiction was premised on allegations of secondary boycotts under § 303. The state law claim, for which jurisdiction was based upon the doctrine of pendent jurisdiction, asserted "an unlawful conspiracy and an unlawful boycott aimed at him and [Grundy] to maliciously, wantonly and willfully interfere with his contract of employment and with his contract of haulage."

The trial judge refused to submit to the jury the claims of pressure intended to cause mining firms other than Grundy to cease doing business with Gibbs; he found those claims unsupported by the evidence. [Today, we would say the court granted defendant's motion for judgment as a matter of law on those claims.] The jury's verdict was that the UMW had violated both § 303 and state law. Gibbs was awarded $60,000 as damages under the employment contract and $14,500 under the haulage contract; he was also awarded $100,000 punitive damages. On motion, the trial court set aside the award of damages with respect to the haulage contract on the ground that damage was unproved. It also held that union pressure on Grundy to discharge respondent as supervisor would constitute only a primary dispute with Grundy, as respondent's employer, and hence was not cognizable as a claim under § 303. Interference with the employment relationship was cognizable as a state claim, however, and a remitted award was sustained on the state law claim. The Court of Appeals for the Sixth Circuit affirmed. We granted certiorari. We reverse.

A threshold question is whether the District Court properly entertained jurisdiction of the claim based on Tennessee law. * * *

* * * The Court held in Hurn v. Oursler, 289 U.S. 238 [1933], that state law claims are appropriate for federal court determination if they form a separate but parallel ground for relief also sought in a substantial claim based on federal law. * * *

Hurn was decided in 1933, before the unification of law and equity by the Federal Rules of Civil Procedure. At the time, the meaning of "cause of action" was a subject of serious dispute; the phrase might "mean one thing for one purpose and something different for another." United States v. Memphis Cotton Oil Co., 288 U.S. 62, 67–68 [1933]. The Court in *Hurn* identified what it meant by the term by citation of Baltimore S.S. Co. v. Phillips, 274 U.S. 316 [1927], a case in which "cause of action" had been used to identify the operative scope of the doctrine of res judicata. In that case the Court had noted that "the whole tendency of our decisions is to require a plaintiff to try his whole cause of action and his whole case at one time." It stated its holding in the following language, quoted in part in the *Hurn* opinion:

> "Upon principle, it is perfectly plain that the respondent [a seaman suing for an injury sustained while working aboard ship] suffered but one actionable wrong and was entitled to but one recovery, whether his injury was due to one or the other of several distinct acts of alleged negligence or to a combination of some or all of them. In either view, there would be but a single

> wrongful invasion of a single primary right of the plaintiff, namely, the right of bodily safety, whether the acts constituting such invasion were one or many, simple or complex.
>
> "A cause of action does not consist of facts, but of the unlawful violation of a right which the facts show. The number and variety of the facts alleged do not establish more than one cause of action so long as their result, whether they be considered severally or in combination, is the violation of but one right by a single legal wrong. The mere multiplication of grounds of negligence alleged as causing the same injury does not result in multiplying the causes of action. 'The facts are merely the means, and not the end. They do not constitute the cause of action, but they show its existence by making the wrong appear.'"

With the adoption of the Federal Rules of Civil Procedure and the unified form of action, Fed. Rule Civ. Proc. 2, much of the controversy over "cause of action" abated. The phrase remained as the keystone of the *Hurn* test, however, and, as commentators have noted, has been the source of considerable confusion. Under the Rules, the impulse is toward entertaining the broadest possible scope of action consistent with fairness to the parties; joinder of claims, parties and remedies is strongly encouraged. Yet because the *Hurn* question involves issues of jurisdiction as well as convenience, there has been some tendency to limit its application to cases in which the state and federal claims are, as in *Hurn*, "little more than the equivalent of different epithets to characterize the same group of circumstances."

This limited approach is unnecessarily grudging. Pendent jurisdiction, in the sense of judicial *power*, exists whenever there is a claim "arising under [the] Constitution, the Laws of the United States, and Treaties made, or which shall be made, under their Authority...," U.S. Const., Art. III, § 2, and the relationship between that claim and the state claim permits the conclusion that the entire action before the court comprises but one constitutional "case." The federal claim must have substance sufficient to confer subject matter jurisdiction on the court. The state and federal claims must derive from a common nucleus of operative fact. But if, considered without regard to their federal or state character, a plaintiff's claims are such that he would ordinarily be expected to try them all in one judicial proceeding, then, assuming substantiality of the federal issues, there is *power* in federal courts to hear the whole.[13]

That power need not be exercised in every case in which it is found to exist. It has consistently been recognized that pendent jurisdiction is a doctrine of discretion, not of plaintiff's right. Its justification lies in considerations of judicial economy, convenience and fairness to litigants; if these are not present a federal court should hesitate to exercise jurisdiction over state claims, even though bound to apply state law to them, Erie R. Co. v Tompkins, 304 U.S. 64 [1938]. Needless decisions of state law should be avoided both as a matter of comity and to promote justice between

13. While it is commonplace that the Federal Rules of Civil Procedure do not expand the jurisdiction of federal courts, they do embody "the whole tendency of our decisions ... to require a plaintiff to try his ... whole case at one time," and to that extent emphasize the basis of pendent jurisdiction.

the parties, by procuring for them a surer-footed reading of applicable law.[15] Certainly, if the federal claims are dismissed before trial, even though not insubstantial in a jurisdictional sense, the state claims should be dismissed as well. Similarly, if it appears that the state issues substantially predominate, whether in terms of proof, of the scope of the issues raised, or of the comprehensiveness of the remedy sought, the state claims may be dismissed without prejudice and left for resolution to state tribunals. There may, on the other hand, be situations in which the state claim is so closely tied to questions of federal policy that the argument for exercise of pendent jurisdiction is particularly strong. In the present case, for example, the allowable scope of the state claim implicates the federal doctrine of pre-emption; while this interrelationship does not create statutory federal question jurisdiction, Louisville & N. R. Co. v. Mottley, 211 U.S. 149 [1908], its existence is relevant to the exercise of discretion. Finally, there may be reasons independent of jurisdictional considerations, such as the likelihood of jury confusion in treating divergent legal theories of relief, that would justify separating state and federal claims for trial, Fed. Rule Civ. Proc. 42 (b). If so, jurisdiction should ordinarily be refused.

The question of power will ordinarily be resolved on the pleadings. But the issue whether pendent jurisdiction has been properly assumed is one which remains open throughout the litigation. Pretrial procedures or even the trial itself may reveal a substantial hegemony of state law claims, or likelihood of jury confusion, which could not have been anticipated at the pleading stage. Although it will of course be appropriate to take account in this circumstance of the already completed course of the litigation, dismissal of the state claim might even then be merited. For example, it may appear that the plaintiff was well aware of the nature of his proofs and the relative importance of his claims; recognition of a federal court's wide latitude to decide ancillary questions of state law does not imply that it must tolerate a litigant's effort to impose upon it what is in effect only a state law case. Once it appears that a state claim constitutes the real body of a case, to which the federal claim is only an appendage, the state claim may fairly be dismissed.

We are not prepared to say that in the present case the District Court exceeded its discretion in proceeding to judgment on the state claim. We may assume for purposes of decision that the District Court was correct in its holding that the claim of pressure on Grundy to terminate the employment contract was outside the purview of § 303. Even so, the § 303 claims based on secondary pressures on Grundy relative to the haulage contract and on other coal operators generally were substantial. Al-

---

15. Some have seen this consideration as the principal argument against exercise of pendent jurisdiction. Thus, before *Erie*, it was remarked that "the limitations [on pendent jurisdiction] are in the wise discretion of the courts to be fixed in individual cases by the exercise of that statesmanship which is required of any arbiter of the relations of states to nation in a federal system." Shulman & Jaegerman, [45 Yale L.J.] at 408. In his oft-cited concurrence in Strachman v. Palmer, 177 F.2d 427, 431 (C.A. 1st Cir. 1949), Judge Magruder counseled that "federal courts should not be overeager to hold on to the determination of issues that might be more appropriately left to settlement in state court litigation," at 433.

though § 303 limited recovery to compensatory damages based on secondary pressures, and state law allowed both compensatory and punitive damages, and allowed such damages as to both secondary and primary activity, the state and federal claims arose from the same nucleus of operative fact and reflected alternative remedies. Indeed, the verdict sheet sent in to the jury authorized only one award of damages, so that recovery could not be given separately on the federal and state claims.

It is true that the § 303 claims ultimately failed and that the only recovery allowed respondent was on the state claim. We cannot confidently say, however, that the federal issues were so remote or played such a minor role at the trial that in effect the state claim only was tried. Although the District Court dismissed as unproved the § 303 claims that petitioner's secondary activities included attempts to induce coal operators other than Grundy to cease doing business with respondent, the court submitted the § 303 claims relating to Grundy to the jury. The jury returned verdicts against petitioner on these § 303 claims, and it was only on petitioner's motion for a directed verdict and a judgment *n.o.v.* that the verdicts on those claims were set aside. The District Judge considered the claim as to the haulage contract proved as to liability, and held it failed only for lack of proof of damages. Although there was some risk of confusing the jury in joining the state and federal claims—especially since, as will be developed, differing standards of proof of UMW involvement applied—the possibility of confusion could be lessened by employing a special verdict form, as the District Court did. Moreover, the question whether the permissible scope of the state claim was limited by the doctrine of pre-emption afforded a special reason for the exercise of pendent jurisdiction; the federal courts are particularly appropriate bodies for the application of pre-emption principles. We thus conclude that although it may be that the District Court might, in its sound discretion, have dismissed the state claim, the circumstances show no error in refusing to do so.

[The Court then reviewed the trial record and concluded that respondent had failed to prove the necessary elements for a claim.]

Notes and Questions

1. *Gibbs* allows a federal court to entertain a claim over which there is no diversity of citizenship or federal question jurisdiction. It does so through what the Court calls "pendent jurisdiction." The federal courts have used different terminology through the years to refer to their power to decide such nonfederal, nondiversity claims. Traditionally, courts exercised "pendent jurisdiction" over claims asserted by the plaintiff in a federal question case, and have exercised "ancillary jurisdiction" over claims asserted by some party other than the plaintiff in any case—federal question, diversity of citizenship, or alienage. Commentators long asserted that there was no functional difference between the two concepts and that a generic rubric, "supplemental jurisdiction," ought to be employed. See, e.g., Richard Matasar, *A Pendent and Ancillary Jurisdiction Primer: The Scope and Limits of Supplemental Jurisdiction*, 17 U.C. Davis L. Rev. 103, 150–57 (1983).

Congress followed this suggestion. Its 1990 statute codifying this area uses the term "supplemental jurisdiction." 28 U.S.C. § 1367(a). Throughout this book, we will use this generic terminology. It is important to remember, though, that the terms pendent and ancillary are employed not only in the older cases, but by many judges and practitioners today. See, e.g., Ameritox, Ltd. v. Millennium Labs., Inc., 803 F.3d 518, 530 (11th Cir. 2015) (discussing supplemental jurisdiction, "sometimes referred to as 'pendent jurisdiction'").

The terminology is less important than understanding what such jurisdiction does. Whether we call it pendent, ancillary, or supplemental, this form of jurisdiction allows a federal court to hear *claims* which are not supported by any of the independent bases of subject matter jurisdiction we studied in Chapter 4. Note, then, that supplemental jurisdiction does not give jurisdiction over a *case*. The case must already be in federal court (because it invoked diversity of citizenship or federal question jurisdiction). Now, in that case, a separate claim is asserted (maybe by the plaintiff, maybe by another party). And that separate claim does not invoke diversity of citizenship or federal question jurisdiction. The federal court might nonetheless be able to hear that claim under supplemental jurisdiction.

2. How can the result in *Gibbs* be constitutional? After all, as we saw in Chapter 4, the federal courts are of limited subject matter jurisdiction. Nothing in Article III speaks of "pendent" or "ancillary" or "supplemental" jurisdiction—at least not expressly. According to the Court in *Gibbs*, what part of Article III permits supplemental jurisdiction?

3. *Gibbs* defines the *constitutional* power of the federal courts to hear claims that have no independent statutory basis of federal jurisdiction. According to the Court, the following are elements of the definition.

(a) The federal and nonfederal claims must share a "common nucleus of operative fact." Why did the claims in *Gibbs* meet this test? Note the similarity between this test and the modern view of the definition of claim for claim preclusion purposes.

(b) The Court seems to require that the federal and nonfederal claims be so related that a plaintiff "would ordinarily be expected to try them all in one judicial proceeding." Note, however, that the Court preceded discussion of this factor with "But if" instead of "And if." Despite the language, courts tended to treat this as a separate requirement. See Ferguson v. Mobil Oil Corp., 443 F. Supp. 1334, 1340 (S.D.N.Y. 1978), *aff'd*, 607 F.2d 995 (2d Cir. 1979). Realistically, this factor does not seem to add anything meaningful to the equation.

(c) The federal question must "have substance sufficient to confer subject matter jurisdiction." Did the dismissal of the federal question on directed verdict in *Gibbs* mean that the federal question failed this test?

(d) The *Gibbs* requirement that the federal question be substantial is not revolutionary. For any case to invoke federal question jurisdiction, the federal issue must not be "wholly insubstantial or frivolous." Bell v. Hood, 327 U.S. 678, 682 (1946). We discussed this point in considering federal question jurisdiction in Chapter 4, Section C.4.b. The timing of when the federal question is dismissed may affect whether it was substantial. For example, if the federal claim in *Gibbs* were dismissed on a Rule 12(b)(6) motion three weeks after filing, could it be considered substantial? On the facts of *Gibbs*, the federal claim survived until after trial. Is that what made it substantial? What if the claim were dismissed on a Rule 12(b)(6) motion six months after filing?

4. Today, the doctrine discussed in *Gibbs* is codified in § 1367. Study § 1367(a) and (b) carefully. How would *Gibbs* be decided under § 1367? The legislative history states that "subsection (a) codifies the scope of supplemental jurisdiction first articulated by the Supreme Court in *United Mine Workers v. Gibbs.*" H.R. Rep. No. 734, 101st Cong., 2d Sess. (1990), reprinted in 1990 U.S.C.C.A.N. 6873, 6875 n.15. Would it have been preferable for the statute to use the phrase "common nucleus of operative fact" from *Gibbs*?

5. *Gibbs* established that federal courts can exercise supplemental jurisdiction. But why should they? What purposes are served by it? Let us consider these questions in the context of *Gibbs* itself. If the Supreme Court had rejected supplemental jurisdiction, Mr. Gibbs would have had two options. First, he could have filed the LMRA claim in federal court and the state law claim in state court. Obviously, this course would force Mr. Gibbs, the defendant, and the taxpayers to pay for two suits and endure the inconvenience caused by them.

As his second option, Mr. Gibbs could bring both of his claims in state court. Wouldn't this serve any efficiency rationale as readily as supplemental jurisdiction? As one court explained, "the efficiency plaintiff seeks so avidly is available without question in the state courts." Kenrose Mfg. Co. v. Fred Whitaker Co., 512 F.2d 890, 894 (4th Cir. 1972). What, if any, disadvantage is there to having Mr. Gibbs file his federal claim in state court? Would Mr. Gibbs have any opportunity for federal court review of his federal claim? Does this weigh in favor of supplemental jurisdiction in federal question cases and against it in diversity cases?

By the way, would the case for supplemental jurisdiction be stronger if the federal question claim were within the exclusive jurisdiction of the federal court? (Keep this in mind when considering the *Finley* case, discussed in Section D.2, infra.)

6. In *Gibbs*, the Court distinguished between a federal court's *power* to exercise supplemental jurisdiction and its *discretion* to refuse to do so. Study § 1367(c) and compare it to the discretionary factors discussed in *Gibbs*. Although the legislative history of § 1367(c) indicates that Congress intended to codify the discretionary factors from case law, including *Gibbs*, the statute permits discretionary dismissal in two circumstances (codified at § 1367(c)(1) and (c)(4)) that were never addressed in *Gibbs*. And at least one factor in *Gibbs* (avoidance of jury confusion) is not reflected in the statute.

In *Gibbs*, the Court said that the justification for supplemental jurisdiction "lies in considerations of judicial economy, convenience and fairness to litigants," as well as comity. One question is whether § 1367(c) replaces these considerations. Courts have taken different approaches. The majority approach seems to be that the *Gibbs* considerations become relevant only after one of the four express factors in § 1367(c) is satisfied. See, e.g., Ameritox, Ltd. v. Millennium Labs., Inc., 803 F.3d 518, 532 (11th

Cir. 2015). At least one court appears to conclude that § 1367 did not affect the discretion granted by *Gibbs.* Araya v. JPMorgan Chase Bank, N.A., 775 F.3d 409, 416–417 (D.C. Cir. 2014). And the Fifth Circuit has held that courts must balance the *Gibbs* factors with the statutory provisions of § 1367(b). Enochs v. Lampasas County, 641 F.3d 155, 159 (5th Cir. 2011). A spirited dissent in that case noted that "[o]n its face, § 1367(c) is a list of situations in which it may be permissible for a district court to remand pendent state-law claims, and not a set of factors to be balanced." Id. at 163–66.

An order declining supplemental jurisdiction under § 1367(c) is not an order that the court lacks subject matter jurisdiction. Rather, jurisdiction was invoked over a claim under § 1367(a), and a subsequent decision to decline supplemental jurisdiction is a discretionary (not a jurisdictional) decision. Carlsbad Tech., Inc. v. HIF Bio, Inc., 556 U.S. 635, 638–641 (2009).

7. *Gibbs* had important ancestors. In Osborn v. Bank of the United States, 22 U.S. 738, 820 (1824), Chief Justice John Marshall recognized that "[t]here is scarcely any case, every part of which depends on the constitution, laws, or treaties of the United States." But, he continued, because the federal court takes jurisdiction over an entire "case or controversy," it can determine incidental questions over which there would be no independent basis of subject matter jurisdiction. In Hurn v. Oursler, 289 U.S. 238 (1933), the plaintiff asserted a federal copyright claim and a state unfair competition claim against a nondiverse defendant. The Court upheld jurisdiction over both, calling them "different grounds asserted in support of the same cause of action." Id. at 246. Is *Gibbs* broader than *Hurn*?

8. Sometimes a litigant will argue that a substantive requirement of liability is "jurisdictional" and thus that the plaintiff's failure to prove the substantive element compels the conclusion that there is no subject matter jurisdiction. If there is no subject matter jurisdiction, then there is no claim to which a supplemental claim can attach. In Arbaugh v. Y&H Corp., 546 U.S. 500, 514–16 (2006), the Supreme Court held that a substantive provision—that Title VII (a federal antidiscrimination law) applies only to employers with at least 15 employees—is not "jurisdictional." Thus a showing that the employer had fewer than 15 employees did not deprive the court of jurisdiction; it simply meant the Title VII claim failed on the merits. The fact that it invoked subject matter jurisdiction enabled the court to exercise supplemental jurisdiction over a closely related state-law claim.

D. Permissive Party Joinder by Plaintiffs

1. Procedural Aspects

We have seen that (procedurally, at least), the plaintiff may assert any *claims* she has against a defendant. Now we turn to *party* joinder options for the plaintiff; specifically, how many plaintiffs and defendants may she join? Rule 20 defines what are often called "proper" parties—that is, those who *may* (as opposed to *must*) be joined in a single case.* Rule 20(a)(1) defines proper plaintiffs and Rule 20(a)(2) defines proper defendants. Because Rule 20 is permissive, the plaintiff is not required to join all potential parties who satisfy Rule 20. Instead, she can use it to structure the suit as best serves her purposes. Various considerations (e.g., personal and subject matter jurisdiction, litigation strategy) may affect her choices. Later in this chapter, we will address the tools available for overriding the plaintiff's choices for party structure.

Schwartz v. Swan

211 N.E.2d 122 (Ill. App. 1965)

Goldenhersh, J.

Plaintiffs, Dorothy Schwartz, Clarence Schwartz and Adelia Schwartz appeal from judgments entered on jury verdicts finding the issues in favor of defendants, on plaintiffs' claims for personal injuries and loss of consortium. Proper presentation of the issues raised by the appeal requires a review of the pleadings, and of certain procedural questions which arose prior to trial.

Plaintiffs, Dorothy Schwartz and Clarence Schwartz, are husband and wife. Plaintiff, Adelia Schwartz, is the widow of the deceased brother of plaintiff, Clarence Schwartz.

On July 2, 1962, plaintiffs, Dorothy and Clarence Schwartz, filed a four count complaint in the Circuit Court of St. Clair County. In Count I, plaintiff, Dorothy Schwartz, alleges that on August 13, 1960, she was a passenger in an automobile operated by plaintiff, Adelia Schwartz, that while the car in which she was riding was stopped at a stop sign, automobiles driven by the defendants, Vada Abernathy [whose name is now Swan], and Lawrence Allen Bray, collided, causing Vada Abernathy's automobile to strike the automobile in which plaintiff was riding. This count contains the usual allegation of plaintiff's freedom from contributory negligence, and charges the defendants with various acts of negligence.

Count II alleges that on August 23, 1960, plaintiff, Dorothy Schwartz was riding in an automobile being driven by plaintiff, Clarence Schwartz; that the automobile was struck by a car driven by defendant, Mary J. Polivick; that plaintiff was free of contributory negligence and defendant, Mary J. Polivick was negligent.

Count I alleges that in the occurrence on August 13, 1960, plaintiff, Dorothy Schwartz, suffered injuries to her head, neck and shoulders, that on August 23, 1960, her head, neck, shoulders, arms and back were injured, and that she is unable to allege to what extent the occurrence of August 13, 1960, caused or contributed to her condition of ill being.

Count II alleges that the occurrence on August 23, 1960, in addition to the injuries caused thereby, aggravated the injuries suffered on August 13, 1960, and that she is unable to allege to what extent the injuries of which she complains resulted from either of the two occurrences.

* The question of who *must* be joined in a case is addressed by Rule 19, governing necessary and indispensable parties. See below at Section F.2.

In Count III, plaintiff, Clarence Schwartz, sues for loss of consortium resulting from the occurrence of August 13, 1960, and in Count IV seeks to recover damages for loss of consortium suffered by reason of the occurrence of August 23, 1960.

On July 3, 1962, plaintiff, Adelia Schwartz, filed suit seeking to recover damages from defendants Abernathy and Bray for injuries allegedly suffered in the occurrence of August 13, 1960.

Defendants, Bray and Polivick, answered the complaints. The three defendants, Bray, Polivick, and Abernathy, filed separate motions for severance of Counts I and II of the complaint in the case of Dorothy Schwartz and Clarence Schwartz. Defendant Bray, in his motion, stated that he had no part in the occurrence of August 23,1960, cannot be held responsible for any injury caused plaintiffs on that date, and the trial of issues involving two separate accidents would prejudice a substantial right to a fair and just trial, of the defendant, Bray. Defendant, Polivick, represented by the same counsel, in identical language, moved for severance for the same reasons. Defendant, Abernathy, in her motion, states that Counts I and II constitute entirely separate causes of action, involve claims against different defendants, allege different facts, and the evidence and instructions would be so complicated and cause such confusion as to make it impossible for the jury to comprehend the proceedings, making it impossible for defendant to receive a fair trial.

After hearing arguments of counsel, the court ordered a severance of the cases, directing that the counts pertinent to the occurrence of August 13, 1960, be severed from those pertinent to the occurrence of August 23, 1960, and further directing that they be thereafter treated as two separate cases, with different docket numbers.

[Subsequently], the court, over the objection of plaintiffs, allowed the motion of defendant, Abernathy, to consolidate the case of Adelia Schwartz with the case of Dorothy Schwartz and Clarence Schwartz, each case seeking to recover from defendants, Bray and Abernathy, for injuries suffered on August 13, 1960.

The consolidated cases involving the collision on August 13, 1960, came on for trial, the jury found for all defendants as to the claims of all three plaintiffs, judgments were entered on the verdicts, and this appeal followed.

Plaintiffs contend that the Circuit Court erred in ordering a severance in the case of plaintiff, Dorothy Schwartz, and a consolidation of the case of Adelia Schwartz, with that of Dorothy Schwartz. Numerous errors are charged during the course of the trial, and to the extent material to this decision will be hereinafter enumerated and discussed. Since the case of Clarence Schwartz is predicated solely on alleged loss of consortium, the disposition thereof is governed by the result reached in the case of Dorothy Schwartz.

We shall first consider plaintiffs' contention that the court erred in ordering the severance. Section 44 of the Civil Practice Act provides:

> "(1) Subject to rules any plaintiff or plaintiffs may join any causes of action, whether legal or equitable or both, against any defendant or defendants;...."

Section 24 of the Civil Practice Act provides:

> "Joinder of defendants. (1) Any person may be made a defendant who, either jointly, severally or in the alternative, is alleged to have or claim an interest in the controversy, or in any part thereof, or in the transaction or series of transactions out of which the controversy arose, or whom it is necessary to make a party for the complete determination or settlement of any question involved therein, or against whom a liability is asserted either jointly, severally or in the alternative arising out of the same transaction or series of transactions, regardless of the number of causes of action joined.
>
> "(2) It is not necessary that each defendant be interested as to all the relief prayed for, or as to every cause of action included in any proceeding against him; but the court may make any order that may be just to prevent any defendant from being embarrassed or put to expense by being required to attend any proceedings in which he may have no interest.
>
> "(3) If the plaintiff is in doubt as to the person from whom he is entitled to redress, he may join two or more defendants, and state his claim against them in the alternative in the same count or plead separate counts in the alternative against different defendants, to the intent that the question which, if any, of the defendants is liable, and to what extent, may be determined as between the parties."

Section 51 of the Civil Practice Act provides:

> "Consolidation and severance of actions. An action may be severed, and actions pending in the same court may be consolidated, as an aid to convenience, whenever it can be done without prejudice to a substantial right."

In Johnson v. Moon, 121 N.E.2d 774 [1954], the [Illinois] Supreme Court stated that joinder of multiple plaintiffs and defendants depends broadly upon the assertion of a right to relief, or a liability, arising out of the same transaction or series of transactions, and the existence of a common question of law or fact.

In our opinion the provisions of the Civil Practice Act, as interpreted in *Johnson v. Moon*, authorize the joinder of these defendants, since the complaint clearly asserts a liability arising out of the series of transactions alleged. Unless it can be determined with reasonable certainty to which occurrence plaintiff's alleged injuries are attributable, the nature and severity of plaintiff's injuries, and the extent to which each collision contributed thereto is a common question of fact.

Having determined this issue, we must consider whether the order of severance is an abuse of the discretion vested in the trial court. Our Supreme and Appellate Courts have consistently held that the disposition of many procedural issues rests within the sound discretion of the trial court. The exercise of sound discretion requires the availability of information sufficient to support the conclusion reached. In this case the order of severance was entered on September 28, 1962 without presenting to the court evidence readily available through appropriate discovery procedures. If after deposition and interrogatory, the defendants were to move for severance on the ground that medical testimony could establish to a reasonable degree of medical certainty which injuries, if any, were attributable to a particular occurrence, severance would not be improper. If, on the other hand, it appears that the cumulative effect of the acts of which plaintiff complains is a single indivisible injury, or that it is unlikely that it can be ascertained to a reasonable degree of medical certainty which occurrence caused the injuries, then severance is prejudicial to the plaintiff. The fact that it might be difficult, under these circumstances to establish the exact proportion of injury caused by each occurrence, is not sufficient reason to deprive plaintiff of the substantial right of a proper evaluation of her damages. To hold otherwise would require plaintiff to prosecute her claim in separate trials, in each of which the defense would be the uncertainty of the injuries resulting from each occurrence. In view of plaintiff, Dorothy Schwartz's status as a passenger in a standing automobile, it is difficult to attribute the verdict in this case to any reason except that here suggested.

We are not impressed with the contention that the trial of the negligence issues in two comparatively simple fact situations would be beyond the comprehension of a jury. Juries try and determine fact issues in extremely complicated cases involving third party complaints, cross claims, counterclaims, multiple plaintiffs and defendants, with a high degree of perception. One of hundreds of examples is the case of Nelson v. Union Wire Rope Corporation, 187 N.E.2d 425 [1963], in which the jury assessed damages in 18 separate verdicts, some involving injuries and some wrongful deaths, and distinguished between the defendants in a complicated case to the extent that one was exonerated. Properly instructed, there is no reason to anticipate confusion of the jury, or prejudice to the rights of any of the parties.

Appellants suggest to the court that the evidence might warrant separate verdicts, apportioning the damages between the defendants in the first occurrence, and the defendant in the second. Section 50 of the Civil Practice Act provides:

> "More than one judgment or decree may be rendered in the same cause."

In the light of the holding in *Johnson v. Moon* that the effect of the Civil Practice Act is to make applicable to actions at law, the practices which theretofore prevailed in equity, we agree. After proper instruction, if the evidence warrants, such apportionment by the jury would not be objectionable.

We have carefully examined the medical testimony and conclude that justice requires that plaintiff, Dorothy Schwartz, be permitted to prosecute her claims against these defendants in a single trial. As to the consolidation of the case of Adelia Schwartz, that is a matter for the discretion of the trial court, to be determined in the light of the views here expressed.

Judgment reversed and cause remanded.

Notes and Questions

1. *Schwartz* was decided under Illinois state procedural rules. Read Federal Rules 20, 21, and 42.

(a) What is the federal counterpart to state § 44? How do they differ? How are they similar?

(b) What is the federal counterpart to state § 24(1) and § 24(2)? How do they differ? How are they similar?

(c) What is the federal counterpart to state § 51? How do they differ? How are they similar?

(d) How would *Schwartz* have been decided under the Federal Rules?

2. Under Federal Rule 20(a)(2), why would Abernathy and Bray have been proper co-defendants in a suit concerning the August 13 crash? Under Rule 20(a)(1), why would Mr. and Mrs. Schwartz have been proper co-plaintiffs in a suit concerning either the August 13 or August 23 crash? Note that the two requirements for joining co-plaintiffs in Rule 20(a)(1) and those for joining co-defendants under Rule 20(a)(2) are the same. With each, there must be claims sharing transactional relatedness and that raise at least one common question of law or fact.

The requirement contained in Rule 20(a)(1)(B) and (a)(2)(B)—that the claims by or against the proper parties involve a common question of law or fact—usually does not present difficulty.*

Usually, the more vexing issue is whether the claims by or against the parties have the transactional relatedness required by Rule 20(a)(1)(A) and (a)(2)(A). We have addressed this transactional issue before. Recall that the Restatement (Second) of Judgments definition of "cause of action" for claim preclusion purposes is "transaction or occurrence or series of related transactions or occurrences." As we discovered in studying preclusion, and as *Schwartz* and other cases confirm, the definition of a transaction or occurrence, or even a series thereof, is not always easy. Courts are flexible in considering the issue, looking at a variety of other factors, such as legal and factual similarity, logical relatedness, and overlap of evidence, in making the case-by-case analysis of whether the requirement is met. Ultimately, the court must make the common-sense assessment of whether joinder of parties in a single case is fair and consistent with the liberal joinder policy of the Federal Rules.**

* In Chapter 13, we will see that a case can proceed as a class action under Rule 23 only if, inter alia, there are common questions of law or fact. That requirement, like the one we address here in Rule 20, has generally been thought easy to satisfy. In 2011, however, the Supreme Court rejected class action status in an employment discrimination case for lack of such commonality. Wal-Mart Stores, Inc. v. Dukes, 131 S. Ct. 2541, 2550–57 (2011). Plaintiffs' expert in that case testified that some employment decisions by the defendant were based upon stereotypical thinking about gender roles. He admitted, however, that he could not tell what percentage of the decisions was so affected. Thus, the Court concluded, the claims by class plaintiffs did not raise common questions of law or fact. The decision may have implications for the commonality requirement of Rule 20(a) as well. See, e.g., Bozek v. Wal-Mart Stores, 2015 U.S. Dist. LEXIS 78774 *6–9 (N.D. Ill. June 17, 2015) (rejecting joinder under Rule 20(a)(1) of plaintiffs who had been members of nationwide class decertified by Supreme Court).

** In fact, we will see more of this problem below. The basic test for compulsory counterclaims under Rule 13(a) and for crossclaims under Rule 13(g) is whether the claim arises from the same "transaction or occurrence" as the underlying dispute. At first glance, the Rule 20 seems broader than Rule 13(a) and 13(g) because it allows for a "series" of transactions or occurrences. In practice, however, most courts construe Rules 13(a) and 13(g) broadly. See generally 3 Moore's Federal Practice § 13.10.

3. The most difficult issue in *Schwartz* is why the defendants from the two separate crashes could be joined. According to the court in *Schwartz*, why were the two accidents sufficiently related to meet the transactional component of the joinder rule? How important was it that Mrs. Schwartz alleged that the second accident aggravated the condition caused in the first?

In Poster v. Central Gulf Steamship Corp., 25 F.R.D. 18 (E.D. Pa. 1960), a seaman contracted amebiasis, a painful gastric illness, while sailing through the Suez Canal for Company 1. Several months later, while working for Company 2, he again sailed through the Suez Canal, and again contracted amebiasis. Plaintiff alleged that the condition was caused by unsanitary practices of local workers employed to help the ships' cooks, and further asserted that the second episode exacerbated the condition caused by the first. The court recognized that the two bouts were separate "occurrences," but upheld joinder because "the second of which might result in concurrent liability of both companies." In other words, the court was influenced by the fact that the alleged negligence of both defendants contributed to the plaintiff's plight.

How does invocation of a tort theory of concurrent liability affect whether injuries arise from the same transaction or occurrence?

Some courts have shown remarkable ability to expand the notion of transactional relatedness under Rule 20 through tort theories. In Hall v. E.I. DuPont De Nemours Co., 345 F. Supp. 353 (E.D.N.Y. 1972), thirteen plaintiffs attempted to join together in a suit against six manufacturers of blasting caps and their trade association. The plaintiffs were representatives of children injured while playing with blasting caps. Their basic theory of liability was that the defendants, who together constituted the entire blasting cap industry in the United States, had failed to warn users that something called blasting caps might explode and hurt people.

Although the children were injured in twelve different explosions in ten states over a four-year period, and although no child was certain which of the defendants had made the cap that injured him, the court allowed joinder of all plaintiffs and defendants. Among other things, the court relied on the "enterprise liability" theory, noting that the plaintiffs in essence were suing an entire industry, members of which had joint awareness of the risk and joint capacity to reduce the risk. The court noted "[t]he allegations in this case suggest that the entire blasting cap industry and its trade association provide the logical locus at which precautions should be taken and liability imposed." Id. at 378. What does this rationale have to do with whether the plaintiffs' claims arose from the same transaction or occurrence?

What if it turned out at trial that Mr. Poster's two bouts of amebiasis were completely unrelated? Or that the blasting cap manufacturers did not make an industry-wide decision to eschew labels? Or that Mrs. Schwartz's injuries were divisible?

4. Note that under Rule 21, the penalty for misjoinder of parties is not dismissal of the case. Rather, the court may add or drop a party or "may also sever any claim against a party." See, e.g., Letherer v. Alger Group, LLC, 328 F.3d 262, 267–68 (6th Cir. 2003). "Sever" is a term of art and should not be confused with the court's power

to order separate trials under Rule 42(b). Severance results in two (or more) separate suits, each with its own docket number and judgment. See United States v. O'Neil, 709 F.2d 361 (5th Cir. 1983). In *Schwartz*, severance by the trial court resulted in separate cases, one by Mr. and Mrs. Schwartz against Abernathy and Bray, and one by Mr. and Mrs. Schwartz against Polivick.

In contrast, Rule 42(b) allows a court in the context of a single case to order separate trials on various issues or claims. It might do so, for instance, to avoid confusing the jury in a case involving numerous claims. Rule 20(b) contains a similar provision.

5. Why would a plaintiff not join all possible plaintiffs and defendants whose joinder would satisfy Rule 20? There may be jurisdictional problems; perhaps she cannot get personal jurisdiction over all defendants or perhaps joinder of a particular person would destroy diversity of citizenship jurisdiction. Another reason for underinclusive joinder by the plaintiff may be litigation strategy. Consider this discussion of litigation incentives:

> As a general rule, underinclusive joinder of defendants would seem less likely than underinclusive joinder of plaintiffs. The typical plaintiff wants to sue once; serial litigation against successive defendants is expensive and time-consuming. Moreover, whatever incentive there may be to sue serially is sapped, to a degree at least, by the adoption of nonmutual defensive issue preclusion. * * *
>
> Further, inclusive joinder of defendants robs the individual defendants of the ability to "whipsaw" the plaintiff by convincing the jury that some absentee is really to blame. A whipsawed plaintiff may well convince two juries that he is entitled to recovery, but end up with nothing, since each jury believed that the defendant before it was not the responsible party. Thus plaintiffs often prefer to join all possible defendants, and may gain from the defendants' efforts to lay the blame on each other. * * *
>
> More commonly, the underinclusive joinder will be on the plaintiff's side. * * * [H]ere there are strong strategic reasons for the plaintiff to eschew joining co-plaintiffs. A single plaintiff may try to strike first, recovering against a defendant of limited resources or an insurance fund before others can do so. She may decide that she is the most attractive of the potential plaintiffs, and that she does not want to go before a jury allied with less sympathetic characters. Most likely, * * * she will be influenced by the widely held view that she can recover more if she is the only plaintiff, since the jury will focus solely on her claim.

Richard Freer, *Avoiding Duplicative Litigation: Rethinking Plaintiff Autonomy and the Court's Role in Defining the Litigative Unit*, 50 U. Pitt. L. Rev. 809, 824–25 (1989).

(a) Why do you suppose Mr. and Mrs. Schwartz wanted to have both sets of defendants (Abernathy and Bray for the first collision and Polivick for the second) joined in a single case? What litigation advantages might there be to joining all possible defendants under Rule 20 (or the Illinois equivalent of Rule 20)? Was Mrs. Schwartz whipsawed by the trial court?

(b) Why do you suppose Mr. and Mrs. Schwartz, on the one hand, and Adelia Schwartz, on the other, did not want to litigate as co-plaintiffs? Could the three Schwartzes have joined as co-plaintiffs in a single case under Rule 20?

(c) Given the nature of Mr. Schwartz's claim, why do you suppose that the husband and wife decided to sue together?

(d) Why would the emergence of nonmutual defensive collateral estoppel encourage a plaintiff to sue all potential defendants in a single proceeding?

6. Litigation strategy is often driven by what the plaintiff, as initial architect of the suit, thinks will impress the jury at trial. If the appearance at trial is most important, consider the possible utility of Rule 42(a)(2), which permits consolidation. That rule addresses the situation where more than one action is pending in a single district,* and allows the separate cases to be treated together for any of various purposes.** A court may order consolidation for specific purposes, such as discovery, or for all purposes. Consolidation — even for all purposes — does not result in merging the two cases; they retain their separate docket numbers and will result in separate judgments. Johnson v. Manhattan Ry. Co., 289 U.S. 479 (1933).

What is the standard for consolidation under Rule 42(a)(2)? How does it differ from the standard for joinder under Rule 20(a)? Because Rule 42(a)(2) is "easier" to meet than Rule 20(a), it might be a valuable safety valve for a plaintiff who is denied joinder.

An instructive case is Stanford v. Tennessee Valley Authority, 18 F.R.D. 152 (M.D. Tenn. 1955), in which the plaintiff sued two chemical companies, each of which spewed pollutants into the air near his home. In a parsimonious reading of Rule 20(a), the court denied joinder, holding that the claims against the two companies did not meet the transactional test of that rule. Thus, the cases against the two companies were severed. Then, in the same opinion, the court ordered consolidation for the purpose of trial. Would you agree that the plaintiff lost the battle and won the war? Why?

7. For an example of a plaintiff with even tougher luck than Mrs. Schwartz, see Watts v. Smith, 134 N.W.2d 194 (Mich. 1965), in which the plaintiff was injured in

* If two cases are pending in different districts, but would benefit from consolidated treatment, what tool might be available to put the cases in a single district, thereby allowing invocation of Rule 42(a)? Remember the possibility of changing venue, which we studied in Chapter 5.

** In federal district courts, cases are assigned to judges of the district at random. Cases are assigned docket numbers according to when they are filed. The lower the docket number, the earlier the case was filed. All districts have local rules allowing related cases to be placed before the judge assigned to the original case. For example, if a series of asbestos cases was filed in a district, the first one being assigned to Judge A, the clerk's office would thereafter assign all related asbestos cases to Judge A, rather than assigning them at random to other judges. This practice is usually called "low numbering." Low numbering does not cause consolidation; it simply puts related cases before a single judge, who is then in a good position to determine whether consolidation is appropriate.

separate auto collisions on the same day! (Yes, he was allowed to join the drivers from both of the collisions.)

2. Jurisdictional Aspects

Rule 20(a) permits joinder of multiple plaintiffs and defendants. What if a claim by or against one of them is not supported by an independent basis of subject matter jurisdiction? Suppose, for example, the plaintiff has a claim against one defendant which invokes federal question jurisdiction and a claim against a second defendant that does not have an independent basis of jurisdiction. In other words, suppose in *Gibbs* that the federal claim was against D-1 and the state claim was against D-2, as to whom there was no diversity of citizenship.

This raises what traditionally has been called *pendent parties jurisdiction.* It differs from the situation in *Gibbs* in that the nonfederal, nondiversity claim is against a second defendant against whom no claim invoking federal jurisdiction has been asserted. As long as the state claim shares a nucleus of operative fact with the jurisdiction-invoking claim, assertion of supplemental jurisdiction would appear to be constitutional. Recognizing this, the Second Circuit upheld pendent parties jurisdiction. Leather's Best, Inc. v. S.S. Mormaclynx, 451 F.2d 800 (2d Cir. 1971). Other courts, however, rejected it. See, e.g., Moor v. Madigan, 458 F.2d 1217 (9th Cir. 1972).

The Supreme Court resolved the split, at least as to some cases, in Aldinger v. Howard, 427 U.S. 1 (1976). Although admitting that pendent parties jurisdiction would be constitutional, the Court rejected its use in that case on statutory grounds. In *Aldinger*, the plaintiff asserted a federal civil rights claim under 42 U.S.C. § 1983 against a county official who had fired her for living with her boyfriend. She joined a state law claim against the county itself.* Because she was a co-citizen with the county, the plaintiff's claim against that entity was not supported by federal question or diversity jurisdiction. The Court rejected supplemental jurisdiction over the claim against the county, citing what it called "clear congressional intent" that the civil rights statute not allow a case against the county.

Thus, in *Aldinger*, the Court recognized that supplemental jurisdiction must be supported by a statutory grant. It presumed, however, that such a statutory grant existed so long as Congress had not *precluded* supplemental jurisdiction, as it theoretically had in the civil rights statute. In other words, as it had in *Gibbs* and as it did two years later in another case, Owen Equipment & Erection Co. v. Kroger, 437 U.S.

---

* Section 1983 allows suits for violation of federal constitutional rights "under color of state law." At the time, a municipality could not be sued under § 1983. Monroe v. Pape, 365 U.S. 167 (1961). The Supreme Court changed its position on this point after *Aldinger* was decided, and permitted such cases against municipalities, at least in some circumstances. Monell v. Department of Social Servs. of New York, 436 U.S. 658 (1978).

365 (1978), the Court was willing to *presume that supplemental jurisdiction was proper unless the legislature said otherwise.* The default position (in case of congressional silence), then, was that supplemental jurisdiction would be upheld so long as the constitutional requirements of *Gibbs* were met.

In *Aldinger*, the Court expressly left open the possibility of pendent parties jurisdiction if the plaintiff's federal claim invoked the *exclusive* jurisdiction of the federal courts. The case of Finley v. United States, 490 U.S. 545 (1989), presented that situation. There, the plaintiff's husband and two children were killed when the airplane in which they were traveling struck electric transmission lines during its approach to a San Diego airfield. Mrs. Finley brought a Federal Tort Claims Act (FTCA) suit in federal court against the United States for the alleged negligence of the Federal Aviation Administration (FAA) in maintaining runway lights and performing air traffic control duties. She later sought to amend her complaint to add state law tort claims against the city and the utility company that maintained the lines. Because Mrs. Finley and the added defendants were co-citizens, there was no independent basis for jurisdiction over these state law claims, and the issue was whether the court could hear them through supplemental jurisdiction.

Finley presented an especially strong case for supplemental jurisdiction. The federal courts have exclusive jurisdiction over FTCA cases. Thus, the only court that could hear the entire case was a federal court. Moreover, allowing supplemental jurisdiction was not inconsistent with any purpose underlying the FTCA. There was no evidence that Congress had "negated" jurisdiction over claims against the added parties.

In an opinion by Justice Scalia, the Supreme Court rejected supplemental jurisdiction. The Court stressed that no matter how sensible or convenient supplemental jurisdiction might be, the FTCA did not explicitly authorize jurisdiction over additional parties. According to the Court, supplemental jurisdiction required such statutory authorization. The Court acknowledged that *Gibbs* allowed jurisdiction over pendent *claims*, but characterized pendent *parties* jurisdiction as a "departure from prior practice." Although the Court explicitly declined to overrule *Gibbs*, it also declined to expand *Gibbs* to apply in situations involving additional parties. Four Justices dissented and criticized the majority opinion as inconsistent with the Court's approach in earlier cases.

Notes and Questions

1. Because Mrs. Finley's FTCA claim was within the exclusive jurisdiction of the federal courts, the result of the *Finley* decision was to *require* Mrs. Finley to pursue two separate cases—one against the federal government in federal court and one against the city and utility company in state court. In addition to the expense imposed on Mrs. Finley by this result, what strategic difficulties does this result impose?

2. Suppose Mrs. Finley did file two separate actions, and that the first one to go to judgment resulted in favorable findings and a substantial recovery for her. Why

could she not employ either claim preclusion or issue preclusion against the defendant in the remaining case?

3. While the result in *Finley* can be lamented, at least it is clear on the facts: There can be no pendent parties jurisdiction without an express statutory allowance. The real problem with *Finley* was language—broader than necessary to decide the issue before the Court—that seemed to require express statutory provision for all forms of supplemental jurisdiction.

Commentators criticized *Finley* and voiced concern that it threatened all of supplemental jurisdiction by requiring congressional action. One urged that supplemental jurisdiction was endangered unless courts could read *Finley* narrowly, which, she felt, would be difficult to do in a principled way. Wendy Perdue, Finley v. United States: *Unstringing Pendent Jurisdiction*, 76 VA. L. REV. 539 (1990). One concluded that *Finley* presaged the end of all supplemental jurisdiction as we knew it. Thomas Mengler, *The Demise of Pendent and Ancillary Jurisdiction*, 1990 BYU L. REV. 247. And one urged a cautious approach, emphasizing some language of the opinion and suggesting that a five-to-four decision might be read narrowly. Richard Freer, *Compounding Confusion and Hampering Diversity: Life After Finley and the Supplemental Jurisdiction Statute*, 40 EMORY L.J. 445, 464–69 (1991). The debate over the reach of *Finley* was never resolved conclusively because Congress intervened.

4. The unfortunate result in *Finley* deserved to be corrected legislatively. Congress did this with 28 U.S.C. § 1367. Because of uncertainty over the reach of *Finley*, Congress felt the need to address all of supplemental jurisdiction. Although the legislature purported to codify "pre-*Finley* practice," we will see that it did not do so in some areas.

Note the structure of the statute. Section (a) gives supplemental jurisdiction to the full extent of the Constitution. Section (b) precludes supplemental jurisdiction in several situations in diversity cases thought by the drafters to have been precluded by precedent. Section (c) gives courts discretion to refuse supplemental jurisdiction, ostensibly along the lines established by *Gibbs*. Section (d) tolls the statute of limitations on supplemental claims that are later dismissed.

Exactly how does § 1367(a) overrule the result in *Finley*? Does it overrule *Aldinger* as well? In answering, note that the limitations of § 1367(b) would not apply in *Finley* or *Aldinger*. Why? Because those cases invoked federal question jurisdiction. Section 1367(b) imposes limitations on the exercise of supplemental jurisdiction only in diversity of citizenship cases; by its express terms, it does not apply in federal question cases.

5. Suppose Alice, Betty, and Carol, each driving her own car, are involved in a three-way collision. Alice's damages are $90,000. Betty's damages are $25,000. Suppose the two of them join as co-plaintiffs in a case against Carol and their citizenships present no impediment to invoking diversity of citizenship jurisdiction. What about the amount in controversy? Clearly, Alice's claim meets the requirement of 28 U.S.C.

§ 1332, while Betty's does not. Under the rules of aggregation, which we studied in Chapter 4, Section C.3.g, the claims could not be added together, because they are not joint claims and because they are asserted by multiple plaintiffs. Moreover, the Supreme Court long ago held that each plaintiff's claim independently must satisfy the amount-in-controversy requirement. Clark v. Paul Gray, Inc., 306 U.S. 583 (1939).

Is this result altered by § 1367? Specifically, does the supplemental jurisdiction statute overrule the result of *Clark* by allowing supplemental jurisdiction over Betty's claim of $25,000? Under the literal language of the statute, the answer seems to be yes. For starters, of course, Betty's claim falls within the grant of supplemental jurisdiction under § 1367(a). (Review: Why?) The issue then becomes whether anything in § 1367(b) precludes the exercise of supplemental jurisdiction in a diversity of citizenship case. Nothing does on these facts. While that subsection prohibits supplemental jurisdiction over claims by plaintiffs *against defendants joined under Rule 20*, this is not such a case. Here, the claims are *by plaintiffs joined under Rule 20* against a single defendant. Section 1367(b) simply does not remove supplemental jurisdiction here.

The Supreme Court adopted this literal approach in Exxon Mobil Corp. v. Allapattah Services, Inc., 545 U.S. 546 (2005). So Alice's claim for $90,000 invoked diversity of citizenship jurisdiction and Betty's $25,000 claim can be heard under supplemental jurisdiction. It satisfies § 1367(a) because it shares a common nucleus of operative fact with Alice's claim, and nothing in § 1367(b) removes that grant of supplemental jurisdiction.

6. But if supplemental jurisdiction can be used to overcome a lack of amount in controversy for a claim in a diversity case (as we just saw in Note 5), can it be used to overcome the complete diversity rule? Returning to the facts in Note 5, suppose now the claims by Alice and Betty each meet the amount in controversy requirement for a diversity of citizenship case. Alice is a citizen of Utah. Betty is a citizen of California. Carol is a citizen of California. Alice and Betty sue Carol. The suit clearly violates the complete diversity rule of *Strawbridge v. Curtiss*, which we studied in Chapter 4, Section C.3.b. But does § 1367 authorize supplemental jurisdiction over Betty's claim against Carol? The literal approach discussed above would lead us to say yes—the claim by Alice against Carol invokes diversity and Betty's claim against Carol seems to invoke supplemental jurisdiction. It satisfies § 1367(a) and § 1367(b) seems not to remove jurisdiction, because this is not a claim by plaintiffs against defendants joined under Rule 20.

The Court in the *Allapattah* case, discussed in Note 5, rejected supplemental jurisdiction in this context. According to the Court, the complete diversity rule must be treated differently from the amount-in-controversy requirement. The Court had to do some gymnastics on this score, because both the complete diversity rule and the amount-in-controversy requirement are imposed by statute, not by the Constitution (so one would think the two requirements would be treated the same way). We will read *Allapattah* for its treatment of these issues in the class action context in Chapter 13, Section C.5.

E. Claim Joinder by Defendants

In Chapter 7, we addressed options available to the defendant to avoid the imposition of liability. As you will recall, the defendant could make a Rule 12 motion or serve and file an answer denying liability and raising affirmative defenses. Here, we consider a defending party's ability to go on the offensive and assert *claims* against others, that is, to impose liability on someone else in the course of the pending litigation.

1. Counterclaims

Read Federal Rules 13(a), 13(b), and 13(c). The modern counterclaim, as reflected in these rules (and in similar state provisions), grew out of the more restrictive early devices of recoupment and set-off. At common law, a defendant could use recoupment to file a claim against the plaintiff if it arose from the same transaction as the plaintiff's claim. The defendant's claim could not exceed the plaintiff's claim, however, and thus was available only to diminish or defeat the plaintiff's assertion. Set-off permitted a defendant to assert a very limited set of claims (basically for contract or on a judgment), again to diminish or defeat the plaintiff's claim. Neither permitted the joinder of new parties.

Modern practice, as reflected in the Federal Rules, is far more liberal. Note the provisions for two types of counterclaims.

a. Compulsory Counterclaims

i. Procedural Aspects

Dindo v. Whitney

451 F.2d 1 (1st Cir. 1971)

Aldrich, Chief Judge.

Briefly, plaintiff Dindo alleges that defendant Whitney was a passenger in a car belonging to Whitney, but driven by Dindo; that the car went off the road, severely injuring Dindo, and that the cause of the accident was Whitney's putting his hand through the steering wheel in reaching for a flashlight on the steering shaft. Suit was brought in the district court of New Hampshire on October 29, 1968, within the New Hampshire period for suit, the accident having occurred on October 30, 1965. Dindo and Whitney had long been friends, Dindo living in Vermont and Whitney in New Hampshire. In June, 1966 Whitney sued Dindo in the district court of Vermont. Dindo gave the papers to his insurance agent, who forwarded them to Whitney's insurer which, by virtue of a clause in the policy, insured Dindo as a driver of Whitney's car with Whitney's permission. The insurer retained counsel, but informed Dindo that he should retain his own counsel as well, as the *ad damnum* [demand for judgment] exceeded the coverage. Dindo did not do so. In March, 1967 the insurer paid Whitney a sum within the policy limit in settlement, and an entry was made on the court docket, "Settled and discontinued." The present action is defended by the same insurer, Whitney, as the car's owner, being covered by the policy that had included coverage of Dindo.

It is clear on the record that before insurance company counsel settled the case they conferred with Dindo on a number of occasions, and apparently saw no defense to the suit. * * * Dindo did not request counsel to file a counterclaim against Whitney. * * * [H]e did not realize, until he spoke with new counsel in September 1968, that he had a basis for so doing, namely, Whitney's conduct in reaching for the flashlight. Dindo, assertedly, had thought that because he was driving the car he could have no claim.

Dindo claims * * * that the compulsory [counterclaim] rule is inapplicable to him since the original case was settled, rather than pursued to final judgment on the merits. Alternatively, he says that it is inequitable to assert the rule against him when he had not realized he had a counterclaim until afterwards.

The bar arising out of Rule 13(a) has been characterized variously. Some courts have said that a judgment is res judicata of whatever could have been pleaded in a compulsory counterclaim. Other courts have viewed the rule not in terms of res judicata, but as creating an estoppel or waiver. The latter approach seems more appropriate, at least when the case is settled rather than tried. The purposes of the rule are "to prevent multiplicity of actions and to achieve resolution in a single lawsuit of all disputes arising out of common matter." Southern Constr. Co. v. Pickard, 1962, 371 U.S. 57, 60. If a case has been tried, protection both of the court and of the parties dictates that there should be no further directly related litigation. But if the case is settled, normally the court has not been greatly burdened, and the parties can protect themselves by demanding cross-releases. In such circumstances, absent a release, better-tailored justice seems obtainable by applying principles of equitable estoppel.

If, in the case at bar, Dindo, clearly having opportunity to assert it, knew of the existence of a right to counterclaim, the fact that there was no final judgment on the merits should be immaterial, and a Rule 13(a) bar would be appropriate. His conscious inaction not only created the very additional litigation the rule was designed to prevent it exposed the insurer to double liability. We are not persuaded that a final judgment is a *sine qua non* to invocation of the bar; there is nothing in the rule limning the term "judgment."

* * * We are not prepared to say at this time what lesser facts would compel a conclusion of estoppel as a matter of law. There should be a hearing on the merits, the facts to be found by the jury. In this connection the court may consider the effect of the cooperation clause in the policy, if there were such, since Dindo, as the insured, would be bound by such a provision. Regardless of whether he thought he had no cross-claim [sic; the court should have said "counterclaim"], Dindo's failure, presently asserted by the insurer, to give it a full and true account of the accident, might well be found by the jury to be a breach of a cooperation clause, which, in turn, might form a basis for estoppel. Or, a matter on which we do not presently express views, without such a clause estoppel might be based upon misrepresentation.

The judgment of the district court is vacated and the action remanded for further proceedings consistent herewith.

Carteret Savings & Loan Assn. v. Jackson

812 F.2d 36 (1st Cir. 1987)

Aldrich, Senior Circuit Judge.

Defendants-appellants Dr. Jackson and his wife were led into an allegedly painless get-rich enterprise by one Garfinkel, now absent. Simply by signing a few papers they expected to achieve gains in the form of substantial deductions on their income tax returns. However, as a result of our present affirmance of the district court, they will realize some unexpected, and very tangible, losses.

Without ever leaving [Massachusetts], defendants authorized the purchase of a yacht in Florida that was to be taken to the Virgin Islands and chartered, the charter fees, allegedly, to meet all expenses. The purchase was to be financed by defendants' note to plaintiff, Carteret Savings & Loan Association. From defendants' understanding, the only backing for the note—defendants, allegedly, having been told it was without recourse—was the prospective yacht. Nothing on the note, however, indicated it was without recourse. Following suit, and a default judgment on the note in the Florida District Court, the yacht, still in Florida, was sold by the U.S. Marshal in partial satisfaction of the judgment. The present suit on the judgment in the Massachusetts District Court is to recover the balance. * * * Following summary judgment for plaintiff, defendants appeal.

* * * [Defendants challenge the Massachusetts District Court's] holding that defendants' present claims against plaintiff, for negligence, fraud, abuse of process, and unfair and deceptive business practices, should have been asserted as compulsory counterclaims in the Florida action pursuant to Fed. R. Civ. P. 13(a), and hence are barred. * * *

Defendants' basic position is a legal one: that since they served no pleading [in the first case, in Florida], the rule did not become applicable.

We could agree that if a pleading had never been required, as, for example, if "the time of serving" had never been reached, * * * the rule would not apply. We hold, however, that when a defendant is defaulted for failure to file a pleading, the default applies to whatever the party should have pleaded.

The purpose of Rule 13(a) is "to prevent multiplicity of actions and to achieve resolution in a single lawsuit of all disputes arising out of common matters." Southern Constr. Co. v. Pickard, 371 U.S. 57, 60 (1962). This has a number of beneficial consequences. The most obvious may be to save judicial effort. On this basis one court has found the rule inapposite when the judgment on the initial cause was by consent. Martino v. McDonald's System, Inc., 598 F.2d 1079, 1082 (7th Cir. 1979) * * *. While we agree with defendants that relatively little judicial effort, also, is involved in entering a default judgment on a note, we can see grounds for considering consent judgments differently. More to the point, there is a purpose in the rule quite apart from concern for the courts—the interest of the plaintiff in obtaining a complete and final resolution of the essential matters of the litigation. If we accepted defendants' position, a default judgment would be of uncertain value, and represent simply one step toward resolving the dispute between the parties. Instead of having a truly final judgment, the judgment creditor would remain faced with a prospect of litigating other aspects of the same transaction or occurrence at some later time, and in a forum of the defendant's choosing.

As against these considerations, defendants offer a mere wooden interpretation of the rule. We are aided in rejecting it by Fed. R. Civ. P. 1's general principle, that the rules are to "be construed to secure the just, speedy, and inexpensive determination of every action." As we have said earlier, "The policy of the federal rules favors resolving all disputes between the parties in a single litigation." Gutor International AG v. Raymond Packer Co., 493 F.2d 938, 946 (1st Cir. 1974). We hold that this policy applies here, and that all of defendants' present claims that would have been compulsory counterclaims are, accordingly, barred. * * *

Affirmed.

Notes and Questions

1. In *Dindo*, the court was willing to forgive a failure to file a compulsory counterclaim, permitting further litigation as to whether Mr. Dindo was guilty of "conscious inaction" in failing to assert the claim. Among other things, the court noted that the first case had ended in settlement, with little expenditure of court or litigant effort. In *Carteret Savings*, however, the court was unwilling to consider whether the Jacksons were guilty of "conscious inaction," despite the fact that the first case ended in default, which obviously required very little expenditure of effort by the court or the bank.

We sometimes see different approaches to issues by different courts. Interestingly, however, not only were *Dindo* and *Carteret Savings* decided by the same court, the opinions were written by the same judge! Can you articulate differences in the facts of the cases that might explain the different approaches?

2. Consider Rule 13(a)(1) in detail. Note that it requires assertion of a transactionally related counterclaim only if the defending party is asserting "[a] pleading." A motion is not a pleading, so if the defendant moves to dismiss, for example, she is not required to assert a transactionally related counterclaim with it. See United States v. Snider, 779 F.2d 1151 (6th Cir. 1985). In the first case involved in *Carteret Savings*, it is clear that the defendant did not answer (it is not clear whether the defendant failed to answer in the first case in *Dindo*). How does the *Carteret Savings* court justify its result in view of this fact?

3. In *Dindo*, Judge Aldrich noted that some courts characterize a dismissal for failure to plead a compulsory counterclaim as "res judicata." Based on our study of preclusion, however, why could an omitted compulsory counterclaim not carry claim

preclusion effects? Judge Aldrich also noted that some courts consider the compulsory counterclaim rule to operate on the basis of waiver or estoppel. Another approach, typified by *Carteret Savings*, simply holds that the defendant is precluded from asserting the claim by "rule preclusion"—because Rule 13(a)(1) says that such claims "must" be asserted in the pending case. The word "must" is distinguished from "may," which signifies that a party has discretion to choose whether to do something. The practical result of applying rule preclusion, of course, is the same as claim preclusion: The party is denied the opportunity to assert the claim.

Because estoppel and waiver are equitable doctrines, courts may find an exception if operation of the compulsory counterclaim rule would be unfair or unduly harsh. *Dindo* is an example of this flexible approach. Courts that view the rule as mandating preclusion are less likely to find an exception to it. *Carteret Savings* may be an example of this approach, which may be called "rule preclusion"—a second case is precluded by operation of the compulsory counterclaim rule.

The Restatement (Second) of Judgments § 22(2), provides that failure to assert a counterclaim does not preclude subsequent litigation, unless (a) "the counterclaim is required to be interposed by a compulsory counterclaim statute or rule of court," or (b) "[t]he relationship between the counterclaim and the plaintiff's claim is such that successful prosecution of the second action would nullify the initial judgment or would impair rights established in the initial action." Does (b) explain the result in *Carteret Savings*?

4. In the first case involved in *Carteret Savings*, the plaintiff sued the Jacksons in federal court in Florida. In the second case, the plaintiff sued the Jacksons in federal court in Massachusetts. Why was the second case not subject to dismissal under claim preclusion?

5. In *Carteret Savings*, why was the Jacksons' fraud claim against Carteret a compulsory counterclaim in the first case? A classic case discussing the scope of compulsory counterclaims is Moore v. New York Cotton Exchange, 270 U.S. 593 (1926), decided under the old Federal Equity Rule 30, a precursor of today's Federal Rule 13(a). (Before the merger of law and equity in federal court in 1938, there were separate Equity Rules.) In *Moore*, the Cotton Exchange entered a contract with Western Union allowing that telegraph company to furnish quotes throughout the country to persons approved by the Exchange. Upon orders from the Cotton Exchange, Western Union refused to furnish the quotes to a different exchange ("Odd-Lot"). Odd-Lot then sued the Cotton Exchange and Western Union under federal antitrust laws. The defendants filed a counterclaim alleging that Odd-Lot had been stealing Cotton Exchange quotations.

The Court held that the counterclaim was compulsory because it arose from the same "transaction" as the plaintiff's claim. It explained:

> "Transaction" is a word of flexible meaning. It may comprehend a series of many occurrences, depending not so much upon the immediateness of their connection as upon their logical relationship. The refusal to furnish the quo-

> tations is one of the links in the chain which constitutes the transaction upon which [Odd-Lot] here bases its cause of action. * * * It is the one circumstance without which neither party would have found it necessary to seek relief. Essential facts alleged by [Odd-Lot] enter into and constitute in part the cause of action set forth in the counterclaim. That they are not precisely identical, or that the counterclaim embraces additional allegations, as, for example, that [Odd-Lot] is unlawfully getting the quotations, does not matter. To hold otherwise would be to rob [the compulsory counterclaim rule] of all serviceable meaning, since the facts relied upon by the plaintiff rarely, if ever, are, in all particulars, the same as those constituting the defendant's counterclaim.

270 U.S. at 610.

Rule 13(a)(1)(A) uses the term "transaction or occurrence," which may be broader than "transaction." At any rate, courts today still cite *Moore* for the proposition that a claim is a compulsory counterclaim if it is "logically related" to the underlying suit. See, e.g., Sparks Constructors, Inc. v. Hartzell Hardwoods, 2015 U.S. Dist. LEXIS 153682 * 10 (relying on *Moore*, "all 'logically related' events entitling a person to institute a legal action against another generally are regarded as comprising a transaction or occurrence").

6. What if the defendant failed to file a compulsory counterclaim because counsel did not tell her she could? One fact pattern routinely gives rise to this possibility. Suppose the plaintiff is injured in an accident with Employee. Assume Employee is also hurt. Plaintiff sues both Employee and Employer, alleging that the act took place in Employee's normal course of employment activities. Employee turns the process over to Employer's attorney, who undertakes to represent both Employer and Employee. Now suppose the case goes to trial and the defendants win. Employee then sues the former plaintiff in a second suit for injuries sustained in the same accident. In response to the argument that the claim should have been asserted in the first case, Employee argues that counsel never told her she could do so.

(a) Should the case by Employee be dismissed? Would your answer be different if the first case had not gone to trial, but had been decided on an early Rule 12 motion? (What does *Carteret Savings* say about saving judicial resources?)

(b) If the case by Employee is not dismissed, how do you respond to the argument that you have created duplicative litigation and burdened the original plaintiff unduly?

(c) If the case by Employee is dismissed, is judicial economy really served? Might a new case appear on a judicial docket anyway (one which will cause the lawyer to check anxiously whether she has paid the premium on her malpractice insurance)?

7. The court notes in *Carteret Savings* that some courts treat judgments by consent (settlement) as exceptions to the compulsory counterclaim rule. Is there any support for such an exception in the text of Rule 13(a)? Would courts use an exception if the first case were settled on the eve of trial, after two years of litigation?

ii. Jurisdictional Aspects

It is axiomatic that neither Rule 13(a) nor any of the Federal Rules affects the subject matter jurisdiction of the federal courts. Many compulsory counterclaims will be supported by an independent basis of subject matter jurisdiction, such as diversity of citizenship or federal question jurisdiction. For example, assume P, a citizen of Florida, sues D, a citizen of Massachusetts, asserting a state-law claim of $100,000. The case is brought in federal court under diversity of citizenship jurisdiction. Now assume that D asserts a compulsory counterclaim against P for $125,000. The compulsory counterclaim also invokes diversity of citizenship jurisdiction. After all, it is asserted by a citizen of Massachusetts against a citizen of Florida, and the amount in controversy exceeds $75,000.

Take the same case and say that P's original claim against D arose under federal law, and thus invoked federal question jurisdiction. D's counterclaim for $125,000, however, arises under state law. Again, just as in the first version, the counterclaim invokes diversity of citizenship jurisdiction and may be asserted in the pending case. If D's counterclaim against P had arisen under federal law, it would invoke federal question jurisdiction and could be asserted in federal court on that basis.

Now let's take a rather unusual fact pattern. P and D are citizens of the same state, so no claim between them can invoke diversity of citizenship jurisdiction. P purports to assert a federal question claim against D, but the claim does not arise under federal law. Before the court can dismiss the case, however, D asserts a compulsory counterclaim against P that does meet the requirements for federal question jurisdiction. Does the federal court have federal question jurisdiction over this case (or at least over the counterclaim)? For many years, the answer would have been yes. The counterclaim by D against P would be seen as invoking federal question jurisdiction. P could assert her original claim against D *as a compulsory counterclaim* and then attempt to invoke supplemental jurisdiction. This is what happened in Great Lakes Rubber Corp. v. Herbert Cooper Co., 286 F.2d 631 (3d Cir. 1961).

The Supreme Court rejected this practice, however, in Holmes Group v. Vornado Air Circulation, 535 U.S. 826 (2002), which we discussed in Chapter 4, Section C.4.b.i. In that case, the Court held that the "well-pleaded complaint rule"—a requisite for invoking federal question jurisdiction—prohibited the court from looking at the counterclaim for a jurisdictional basis. That rule requires a court to assess federal question jurisdiction on the face of the *complaint* alone. Because a counterclaim appears in the defendant's answer, it cannot be a source of federal question jurisdiction. Thus, in such a fact pattern today, the court would dismiss the entire case for lack of subject matter jurisdiction. Clearly, however, D could file a new case in federal court, asserting her federal claim and invoking federal question jurisdiction. (By the way, Congress amended the statute, granting jurisdiction over certain intellectual property claims to allow jurisdiction to be based upon a counterclaim. 28 U.S.C. § 1338. That change applies only in specialized intellectual property cases, however, and not to "regular" federal question cases under § 1331.)

Now let's return to the normal case, in which the plaintiff's claim does invoke a basis of federal subject matter jurisdiction—say, either diversity of citizenship or federal question. Now the defendant asserts a compulsory counterclaim. But let's say the compulsory counterclaim does *not* meet the requirements for diversity of citizenship or federal question jurisdiction (or any other independent basis of federal subject matter jurisdiction). In this circumstance, the only way the compulsory counterclaim can be heard in the pending case in federal court is if it invokes supplemental jurisdiction.

Notes and Questions

Study § 1367(a) and (b) and try these hypotheticals.

1. P, a citizen of Louisiana, sues D, a citizen of North Dakota, for $85,000 in damages from an auto collision between the two.

(a) Suppose D's counterclaim arising from the same accident is for $45,000. Why is supplemental jurisdiction required here? Why is it clearly available under § 1367(a)? Why is it not withdrawn by § 1367(b)?

(b) Suppose D wants to assert a counterclaim for her damages arising from the same accident and that the damages are $100,000. Why is supplemental jurisdiction irrelevant?

2. P, a citizen of Oklahoma, sues D, also a citizen of Oklahoma, on a claim that arises under federal law. D's compulsory counterclaim against P, which arises under state law, is for $500,000. Why does the counterclaim require supplemental jurisdiction? Why is it available under § 1367(a)? Why is § 1367(b) completely irrelevant to this hypothetical? (Be careful with this. In Question 1, § 1367(b) had to be consulted, but did not preclude the exercise of supplemental jurisdiction. In this Question, § 1367(b) does not apply at all. Why?)

3. Notice that the requirement for a compulsory counterclaim ("same transaction or occurrence") is very similar but not identical to the *Gibbs* test ("common nucleus of operative fact"). Will a compulsory counterclaim always satisfy § 1367(a)?

b. Permissive Counterclaims

i. Procedural Aspects

Rule 13(b) permits a defending party to assert any claim she has against an opposing party. This provision is as broad as the "open season" or "anything goes" rule we saw for plaintiffs under Rule 18(a). If there is some question as to whether a counterclaim arises from the same transaction or occurrence as the underlying dispute (and thus as to whether it is a compulsory counterclaim), the existence of Rule 13(b) allows the defendant to err on the side of asserting any claim against the plaintiff in the pending case.

Notes and Questions

1. Suppose Manuel quits his job with Unique Concepts and opens his own design business. Unique claims that Manuel's new business is infringing some of its patents, and sues him for that reason. Unique then sends a letter to Manuel's customers, saying that Manuel's products are unsafe and mentioning its pending patent suit. Manuel wants to sue Unique, alleging that its letter defamed him and violated state consumer protection laws. In Unique Concepts, Inc. v. Manuel, 930 F.2d 573 (7th Cir. 1991), the court concluded that Manuel's claims were not compulsory counterclaims. Can you fashion an argument that the court was correct? Can you fashion an argument that the court was incorrect?

Assume that Manuel asserts the claims in the pending action under Rule 13(b). What can the judge do if she is concerned that hearing all of the claims in a single trial will be confusing or that evidence of defamation will prejudice the factfinder?

2. Suppose P and D have entered a business contract that is not faring well. In a completely unrelated event, each is driving her own car, and they collide. P sues D to recover damages for the auto collision. D wants to counterclaim for (1) her injuries from the collision and (2) P's alleged breach of contract in the business deal.

(a) May she assert these two in the pending case? Why? Does Rule 13(b) add anything to Rule 18(a)?

(b) Must she assert either of these two in the pending case or risk losing the claim? Why?

(c) Assume that D asserts both claims in the pending case and that P had a claim against D arising from the contract dispute. Why is that claim a compulsory counterclaim?

3. After the defendant asserts a counterclaim against the plaintiff, how must the plaintiff respond? See Rule 7(a) and Rule 12(a). Why does Rule 12 eschew the labels "plaintiff" and "defendant"?

ii. Jurisdictional Aspects

Again, a procedural rule cannot affect jurisdiction, so each claim must be assessed separately as to whether it can be asserted in federal court. After concluding that any claim is procedurally proper, always assess whether the claim invokes an independent basis of federal subject matter jurisdiction. In other words, assess whether it invokes federal question or diversity of citizenship (or alienage) jurisdiction. If it does, the claim can be asserted in federal court.

But if the claim does not satisfy an independent basis of federal subject matter jurisdiction, the only way it can be heard in federal court is by invoking supplemental jurisdiction. Under § 1367(a), supplemental jurisdiction attaches only to claims that satisfy the *Gibbs* test, i.e., they arise from a "common nucleus of operative fact." For many years, courts came to equate the *Gibbs* test with "transaction or occurrence," as used in various Federal Rules, including Rule 13(a). These courts easily concluded that compulsory counterclaims always satisfy *Gibbs* (and therefore § 1367(a)). But many courts also concluded that permissive counterclaims—which do *not* arise from the same transaction or occurrence as the underlying dispute—could not satisfy *Gibbs* and thus cannot invoke supplemental jurisdiction under § 1367(a). In other words, they equated "transaction or occurrence" with "common nucleus of operative fact." See, e.g., Iglesias v. Mutual Life Ins. Co., 156 F.3d 237, 241 (1st Cir. 1998) ("Only compulsory counterclaims can rely upon supplemental jurisdiction; permissive counterclaims require their own jurisdictional basis").

Increasingly, though, courts hold that the *Gibbs* test (codified in § 1367(a)) is broader than "transaction or occurrence." Accordingly, some permissive counterclaims can invoke supplemental jurisdiction. Global Naps, Inc. v. Verizon New England, Inc., 603 F.3d 71, 76 (1st Cir. 2010) (§ 1367(a) "gives federal courts supplemental jurisdiction over both compulsory and at least some permissive counterclaims. This alters this circuit's former rule, adopted before the enactment of § 1367, that required permissive counterclaims to have an independent basis for jurisdiction.").

- Plaintiff buys a car and gets a loan to pay for part of the purchase price. After making several payments on the loan, Plaintiff becomes convinced that the loan was made on unfavorable terms because of Plaintiff's race. Plaintiff sues Loan Co. for racial discrimination in violation of the Federal Equal Credit Opportunity Act. The case is properly in federal court under federal question jurisdiction. Loan Co. asserts a counterclaim in that case, seeking recovery of the unpaid balance on the auto loan. The counterclaim does not invoke federal question or diversity of citizenship jurisdiction. Does it invoke supplemental jurisdiction?

Several courts have concluded that the counterclaim in such a case is permissive because it does not arise from the same transaction or occurrence which underlies the plaintiff's claim. Nonetheless, they have upheld supplemental jurisdiction under § 1367(a) because the counterclaim shares a common nucleus of operative fact with plaintiff's claim and thus constitutes part of the same case or controversy as that claim. These courts hold that § 1367(a) requires only some "loose factual connection" between the supplemental claim and the jurisdiction-invoking claims. The test was met because both claims were connected to the purchase of the automobile. See, e.g., Jones v. Ford Motor Credit Co., 358 F.3d 205, 210–215 (2d Cir. 2004); Channell v. Citcorp Nat'l Servs., Inc., 89 F.3d 379, 385–386 (7th Cir. 1996). See also Elements Spirits, Inc. v. Iconic Brands, Inc., 2015 U.S. Dist. LEXIS 124645 *11 (C.D. Cal. Sept. 17, 2015); Graf v. Pinnacle Asset Gp., LLC, 2015 U.S. Dist. LEXIS 18069 *15 (D. Minn. Jan. 27, 2015).

Not all courts agree. In Ramirez v. Amazing Home Contractors, Inc., 2014 U.S. Dist. LEXIS 164739 *11–12 (D. Md. Nov. 25, 2014), the court relied upon pre-§ 1367 Fourth Circuit precedent holding that permissive counterclaims cannot invoke supplemental jurisdiction. See Painter v. Harvey, 863 F.2d 329, 331 (4th Cir 1988). See generally Douglas D. McFarland, *Supplemental Jurisdiction over Permissive Counterclaims and Set Offs: A Misconception*, 64 Mercer L. Rev. 437 (2013).

2. Crossclaims

a. Procedural Aspects

Rule 13(g) allows a party to assert an offensive claim against a *co-party* (not, as with counterclaims, against an opposing party) if it arises from the same transaction or occurrence as the underlying action. Study the rule carefully and answer the following.

Notes and Questions

1. The operative test for the crossclaim is the same as that for the compulsory counterclaim; both arise from the "transaction or occurrence" that is the subject matter of the original action or of a counterclaim. But the crossclaim is not compulsory. A litigant may choose to assert it in the pending case or to sue on it in a separate proceeding. What one word in Rule 13(g) makes it clear that crossclaims are permissive?

The fact that crossclaims are permissive can be wasteful. In Davis & Cox v. Summa Corp., 751 F.2d 1507 (9th Cir. 1985), P could have asserted its claim against D as a crossclaim in a prior case in which both were joined as defendants. It did not do so, opting instead to burden the court system (and the taxpayers) with a separate proceeding. The district court dismissed the second case, but the Ninth Circuit reversed. Because Rule 13(g) did not require P to assert the crossclaim in the prior case, it was free to proceed.

To avoid the possibility of such wasted effort, some state statutes make crossclaims compulsory, at least under certain circumstances. See, e.g., KAN. CIV. PROC. CODE ANN. § 60-213(g) (compulsory if asserting comparative negligence). Although Georgia adopts Federal Rule 13(g)'s permissive language, the existence of a general preclusion statute leads courts in that state to conclude that crossclaims are compulsory. See Citizens Exchange Bank of Pearson v. Kirkland, 344 S.E.2d 409 (Ga. 1986) (GA. CODE. ANN. § 9-12-40 provides that a judgment is conclusive as to all matters that could have been raised in the case).

2. Perry is injured when the car he operates is involved in a collision with a car owned by Olive and driven by Donna. Perry sues both Olive and Donna. (By way of review, why is the joinder of Olive and Donna as co-defendants proper?) In addition to filing an appropriate defensive response to the complaint, Olive wants to assert offensive claims (1) to recover for the damage to her car and, (2) if Donna was at fault in the collision, to receive indemnification from Donna for the judgment in Perry's favor. Note that the first of these two claims can be asserted against both Perry and Donna; the second is against Donna only.

(a) What claim may Olive assert against Perry? What, if anything, might happen to her claim if she failed to assert it?

(b) What claim may Olive file against Donna? Must she do so? Note the last sentence of Rule 13(g). It clearly allows the indemnity claim against Donna. What part of the rule allows her to sue Donna for damage to the car?

(c) Suppose Olive asserted a claim against Donna for indemnity but not for damage to the car. The entire case, including this claim against Donna, goes to trial, and the court concludes that Donna was solely responsible for the accident. Now Olive files a separate action against Donna to recover for damages to her car. Why would this case be dismissed in most jurisdictions? (Hint: The answer is not based upon Rule 13(g) or Rule 13(a).)

(d) Suppose Olive asserted against Donna both the claim for indemnification and the claim for property damage to her car in the original proceeding. If Olive had a completely unrelated claim against Donna—say, for trespass on her farm—how could Olive assert that claim in the pending case? Must she do so?

(e) Suppose Olive asserted a crossclaim against Donna seeking both indemnification and damages for wrecking her car. Now assume that Donna wants to assert a claim against Olive, alleging that the car Olive lent her had defective brakes, which caused the collision with Perry. What argument can you fashion for the proposition that Donna *must* assert this claim in the pending case? (Hint: The argument has nothing to do with claim preclusion.) Once Olive asserted the crossclaim against Donna, did they cease to be co-parties (at least for purposes of their relationship with each other) and become something else? See 3 Moore's Federal Practice § 13.71.

(f) Suppose Olive had a claim against Donna that was not transactionally related to the pending case, for which there would be subject matter jurisdiction. Why can she not assert that claim alone in the pending case? If she had a claim against Donna that was transactionally related to the pending case, how would she assert it *and* the unrelated claim in the pending suit?

3. Most crossclaims are asserted by a defendant against a co-defendant. Can a plaintiff assert a crossclaim against a co-plaintiff? Some courts have concluded that a plaintiff may do so only if a defendant has asserted a counterclaim against the plaintiffs. See Danner v. Anskis, 256 F.2d 123 (3d Cir. 1958). Does this interpretation find any support in Rule 13(g)? In policy? In a different joinder device, as we will see, the drafters of the rules expressly allow a plaintiff to file only after being sued with a counterclaim. See Rule 14(b).

b. Jurisdictional Aspects

The fact that the crossclaim must arise from the same transaction or occurrence as the underlying dispute is helpful because it opens the door for the use of supplemental jurisdiction. Never jump to supplemental jurisdiction, however, without first assessing whether a claim is supported by some independent basis of subject matter jurisdiction.

Notes and Questions

1. P, a citizen of Vermont, D-1, a citizen of Kentucky, and D-2, also a citizen of Kentucky, all were injured when they collided while skiing. Each will seek damages

in excess of $75,000. P sues D-1 and D-2, properly invoking diversity of citizenship jurisdiction.

(a) Why is D-1's claim against P a compulsory counterclaim? Why does it not need supplemental jurisdiction?

(b) Why is D-1's claim against D-2 a crossclaim? Why does it need supplemental jurisdiction? Review § 1367(a) and (b), and explain why the crossclaim will be supported by supplemental jurisdiction.

2. P-1 drives a car in which P-2 is a passenger. Each is a citizen of Nevada. They collide with a car driven by D, who is a citizen of Colorado. Each of the three suffers damages in excess of $75,000. P-1 and P-2 join as plaintiffs in a suit against D, properly invoking diversity of citizenship jurisdiction. (What rule allows their joinder?) Suppose D files a compulsory counterclaim against P-1 only, alleging that her negligence caused the collision and seeking recovery of damages for her injuries.

(a) P-1 now wants to assert a claim against P-2, alleging (1) that P-2 should indemnify her if D's counterclaim is successful and (2) that P-2 may be liable for P-1's injuries. She argues that P-2 is at fault because she distracted P-1 while P-1 was trying to drive. What would she file in the pending case to assert these two claims?

(b) Why would the claim by P-1 need supplemental jurisdiction?

(c) Although historically no one would have objected to having P-1's claim invoke supplemental jurisdiction, would a literal reading of § 1367(b) preclude such jurisdiction?

F. Overriding Plaintiff's Party Structure

To this point, we have seen that Rule 20(a) allows the plaintiff to make the initial choice of who the parties to a lawsuit will be, and we have seen the various claims those original parties can make against each other. Note that the defendant has equal freedom in naming parties to her claims. Rule 13(h) allows the defendant to join additional parties to her counterclaim or crossclaim so long as the joinder meets the requirements of either Rule 19 or Rule 20. Rule 13(h) thus puts the defendant on the same procedural footing as the plaintiff in selecting parties to her claims.

For example, in Federal Deposit Ins. Corp. v. Bathgate, 27 F.3d 850 (3d Cir. 1994), the FDIC sued to recover on a note (which is a loan). The defendant asserted a compulsory counterclaim against the FDIC, to which it joined bank officers as additional counterclaim defendants. Of course, defending parties so joined must be subject to personal jurisdiction, and there must be subject matter jurisdiction over the claim against added parties. If needed, supplemental jurisdiction should readily be available under § 1367(a) for all claims sharing a common nucleus of operative fact with the jurisdiction-invoking claim. In diversity of citizenship cases, § 1367(b) appears not to block supplemental jurisdiction. Why? For two reasons. First, § 1367(b) purports to preclude supplemental jurisdiction only over claims "by plaintiffs." So long as the defendant is asserting the counterclaim, § 1367(b) should not thwart it. And second, § 1367(b) does not include Rule 13(h) in its list of claims over which supplemental jurisdiction is precluded.

A Fifth Circuit case illustrates the point. In State National Ins. Co. v. Yates, 391 F.3d 577 (5th Cir. 2004), P sued D, invoking diversity of citizenship jurisdiction. D asserted a compulsory counterclaim against P, which also invoked diversity of citizenship jurisdiction. Using Rule 13(h), D asserted his counterclaim (arising under state law) against P and against an additional party. That additional party was a co-citizen of D, so the counterclaim did not invoke diversity of citizenship or federal question. The Fifth Circuit upheld supplemental jurisdiction over the counterclaim under Rule 13(h), based upon the two points made in the preceding paragraph.

Through the remainder of this chapter, we will focus on whether the plaintiff's choice of parties can be overridden other than by use of Rule 13(h). It is important to remember that the plaintiff need not join all Rule 20(a) parties. For a variety of tactical or jurisdictional reasons, the plaintiff may have been underinclusive in joining parties. Such underinclusiveness may lead to wasteful duplicative litigation, may subject a defending party to risk of multiple liability, or may render it difficult for a nonparty (or "absentee") to protect her interest from practical impairment. Moreover, duplicative litigation may lead to inconsistent results, which can undermine society's confidence in the judicial process.

The Federal Rules address such problems by allowing others to override the plaintiff's party structure with various devices, including impleader, compulsory joinder, and intervention. In each, the most important question will be *why* we would allow someone to override the plaintiff's choices. We will see the same themes played out over and over. In addition, pay attention to *who* may invoke these rules.

1. Impleader (Third-Party Practice)

a. *Procedural Aspects*

The first tool available to override the plaintiff's party structure of a suit is impleader, or third-party practice, which is governed by Rule 14. It allows a "defending party" (that is, one against whom a claim has been asserted) to join an absentee in limited situations. The defending party who invokes impleader is called the "third-party plaintiff," while the absentee brought in becomes the "third-party defendant." Study Rule 14(a).

Under what circumstances can a party implead an absentee? Note how narrow the rule is in this regard, permitting only joinder of one "who is or may be liable to [the defending party] for all or part of the claim against it." Almost always, this provision is used to join one who owes either indemnity or contribution to the third-party plaintiff. Impleader promotes efficiency by litigating the underlying claim and any "claim over" for indemnity or contribution in a single proceeding. Concomitantly, it avoids the possibility of inconsistent results.

Suppose, for example, that P sues D for damages and that D has a right to indemnity for this claim from T. D can implead T. Then, any judgment for P against D can be deflected to T. If D could not implead T, consider the problems she might face. After losing to P, she would have to sue T in a separate proceeding. Thus, she (and the taxpayers) would pay for two suits, delaying the ultimate resolution of the dispute.

Moreover, in that separate action, D could not use issue preclusion against T. (By way of review, why not?) She therefore runs the risk of losing that case to T, thereby absorbing the entire loss herself. Allowing her to implead here, then, may be seen as a way of avoiding imposition on her of multiple liability or inconsistent obligations.

Markvicka v. Brodhead-Garrett Co.

76 F.R.D. 205 (D. Neb. 1977)

Denny, District Judge.

This matter is before the Court upon the motion of third-party defendant, the School District of Ralston, to dismiss the third-party complaint against it filed by defendant and third-party plaintiff, Brodhead-Garrett Company.

This action was brought on behalf of a minor child who suffered severe injuries while using a jointer machine manufactured by the defendant. Plaintiff attributes his injuries to the defective design and condition of the jointer machine.

The defendant's third-party complaint against the School District of Ralston alleges that the accident occurred in the course of a woodworking class held by the third-party defendant and charges that the School District's improper maintenance of the machine and inadequate supervision of the students caused plaintiff's injuries.

The third-party complaint alleges a right to indemnity from the School District. However, the Court finds that the third-party complaint more accurately states a claim for contribution. The distinctions between contribution and indemnity, often difficult to apply, are well stated by D. Busick, *Contribution and Indemnity between Tortfeasors in Nebraska*, 7 Creighton L. Rev. 182 (1974) and cases cited therein.

> Contribution and indemnity are two separate remedies which may be available to a tortfeasor who seeks to place all or part of the burden of a judgment upon his fellow tortfeasor. Contribution is based upon the common, though not necessarily identical, liability of two or more actors for the same injury. It equalizes the burden on the wrongdoers by requiring each to pay his own proportionate share of damages. Indemnity, on the other hand, enables one tortfeasor to shift the entire burden of the judgment to another. It tempers the harshness of the doctrines of respondeat superior and vicarious liability since it allows one who has been compelled to pay solely because of a certain legal relationship to shift the ultimate burden of the judgment to the actual culprit.
>
> In sum, Nebraska law seems to permit indemnity when it has been provided for in a specifically drawn contract or when liability has been imposed

> upon a party simply because of his legal relationship to the negligent party. It appears, however, that indemnity will not be allowed when both parties have been negligent to a certain degree.

In Royal Indem. Co. v. Aetna Cas. & Sur. Co., 229 N.W.2d 183 (1975), the Nebraska Supreme Court clarified the law of contribution among negligent joint tortfeasors in Nebraska.

> We, therefore, hold that in this jurisdiction there is no absolute bar to contribution among negligent joint tort-feasors; and also, as in this case, that a right to equitable contribution exists among judgment debtors jointly liable in tort for damages negligently caused, which right becomes enforceable on behalf of any party when he discharges more than his proportionate share of the judgment. * * *

Thus it is now clear that as between defendants against whom a joint judgment in tort has been rendered, contribution is allowed. The court did not directly rule as to contribution between negligent joint tortfeasors against whom judgments have not yet been rendered. However, the statement that "there is no absolute bar to contribution among negligent joint tortfeasors" would seem to envision contribution not only among those against whom a plaintiff has successfully obtained judgments but also among those whose liability remains to be fixed either in a third-party claim in the original plaintiff's suit or in an independent action for contribution by the original defendant.

The third party complaint alleges a factual basis for contribution from the School District of Ralston should Brodhead-Garrett be found liable to the plaintiff. If the defendant's allegations are true, the School District's negligence was a concurrent cause of the plaintiff's injury.

Fed. R. Civ. P. 14(a) permits the joinder of a party who "is or may be liable" to the defending party for all or part of the plaintiff's claim. Where state law creates a right to contribution or indemnity among tortfeasors, the wrongdoer who has been sued by an injured party may implead his co-wrongdoers before the plaintiff successfully obtains a judgment. "The fact that contribution may not actually be obtained until the original defendant has been cast in judgment and has paid does not prevent impleader; the impleader judgment may be so fashioned as to protect the rights of the other tortfeasors, so that defendant's judgment over against them may not be enforced until the defendant has paid plaintiff's judgment or more than his proportionate share, whichever the law may require." 3 MOORE'S FED. PRACTICE § 14.11 at 14-322 (1976) et seq.

The defendant has alleged that if it was at fault in the design or construction of the jointer machine, so was the School District in its maintenance of the machine and supervision of the students. Both owed the plaintiff a duty of care.

Therefore, as the School District "may be liable" for contribution, it may be joined as third-party defendant in this action in order to determine its accountability. The fact that the defendant erroneously defined its claim as "indemnity" does not alter this conclusion. A claim should not be dismissed for insufficiency "unless it appears to a certainty that plaintiff is entitled to no relief under any state of facts which could be proved in support of the claim." Morton Bldgs. of Neb., Inc. v. Morton Bldgs., 333 F. Supp. 187, 191 (D. Neb. 1971). At this stage of the proceedings, the Court will grant the defendant leave to amend the third-party complaint to state the correct theory for its cause of action. Accordingly,

It is ordered that the motion of third-party defendant, the School District of Ralston, to dismiss the third-party complaint will be denied if, within ten (10) days hereof, the defendant, Brodhead-Garrett Company, amends its third-party complaint against the School District to allege a claim for contribution.

Notes and Questions

1. In *Markvicka*, state law apparently would not allow the defendant to recover against the third-party defendant until it had paid the entire judgment to the plaintiff. Nonetheless, after *Hanna v. Plumer*, which we discussed in Chapter 10, Rule 14(a) clearly governs practice in federal court. If the underlying claim by the plaintiff fails, the claim against the third-party defendant obviously fails as well. If the plaintiff wins in the underlying suit, then the court can address the impleader claim. Rule 14, then, merely accelerates assertion of the claim against the third-party defendant. See Hiatt v. Mazda Motor Corp., 75 F.3d 1252, 1255 (8th Cir. 1996) (Federal Rule 14(a) governs procedural issues such as acceleration of claim). Thus, even if state law would not allow assertion of the claim until after judgment against the defendant, Rule 14(a) permits the defendant to assert it.

On the other hand, if state law does not recognize a substantive claim at all, there would be nothing for Rule 14(a) to accelerate. See Connors v. Suburban Propane Co., 916 F. Supp. 73, 76 (D.N.H. 1996) ("Rule 14 does not operate to create causes of action; it merely prescribes a method for bringing causes of action already recognized under applicable statutory or common law."). The rule provides a procedural method for asserting claims recognized by the governing substantive law.

2. Suppose P is injured when struck by a car operated by T, but owned by D. T was using the car with D's permission. D is vicariously liable for T's acts and D has a substantive right of indemnity from T. P sues D for damages.

(a) D can implead T, seeking indemnification should P prevail in the underlying suit. When may she do so? Does she need court permission to do so? *Must* she do so? Why should she run no claim preclusion risk if she does not implead T?

(b) If D impleads T, can T raise an affirmative defense (say, statute of limitations) that D forgot to raise in the underlying case?

(c) Will D want to assert more than the indemnity claim against T? If the accident is the fault of T, liability for the judgment against D will be deflected to T. But what about D's property damage claim against T for ruining her car? How can she join that claim in the pending case? Note that D needs to use one joinder rule to assert the indemnity claim against T and a separate rule to join the property damage claim.

On the other hand, if D and T were co-defendants (that is, if P had joined them both originally under Rule 20), D could assert both the indemnity claim and the property damage claim against T through a single device—Rule 13(g). The crossclaim under Rule 13(g) permits assertion of all claims arising from the same transaction or occurrence as the underlying dispute. Impleader is narrower, and allows only the indemnity or contribution claim. Additional claims (even if transactionally related, as here) must be joined through Rule 18(a).

(d) In (c), suppose D impleads T, claiming indemnity, but does not join the claim for property damage. If D later tries to sue T for property damage, can T assert claim preclusion?

(e) In addition to impleading T and joining the property damage claim against T, what will D assert against P?

(f) If D impleads T and T has a claim against D for lending her a faulty car, how can she assert it in the pending case? Indeed, *must* she assert it here? (Hint: When D impleaded T, did they become opposing parties?)

(g) Suppose applicable law gave D no right of indemnity or contribution against T, but that she still has her claim against T for damage to the car. Even though it is transactionally related to the underlying dispute, why can she not use Rule 14 to assert that claim in the pending case? Why does Rule 18(a) do her no good?

3. Rule 14(b) permits a plaintiff to implead an absentee who is or may be liable to her for a counterclaim asserted against her by the defendant. In view of Rule 14(a)'s provision that any "defending party" may implead, Rule 14(b) appears unnecessary.

4. Rules 14(a)(2)(D) and 14(a)(3) permit two other claims, neither of which has a widely adopted name. Under what circumstances can the plaintiff assert a claim against the third-party defendant (TPD)? Under what circumstances can a TPD assert a claim against the plaintiff? Some commentators, diagramming the three claims as follows, refer to these latter two as, respectively, "upsloping 14(a) claims" and "downsloping 14(a) claims." These are not impleader claims. That term applies only to the initial joinder of the absentee for indemnity or contribution. These are merely additional claims permitted by Rule 14(a) to flesh out the suit.

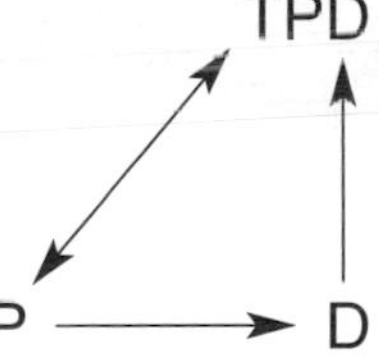

Could both upsloping and downsloping 14(a) claims be asserted in the same case? Once P asserted an upsloping 14(a) claim against TPD, wouldn't any claim by TPD against P be a counterclaim?

b. Jurisdictional Aspects

Obviously, any of the three claims permitted under Rule 14(a)—impleader, upsloping 14(a), and downsloping 14(a)—might be supported by an independent basis of subject matter jurisdiction. It is important to remember that jurisdiction must be assessed for each claim. Thus, suppose that P, a citizen of Florida, sues D, a citizen of Wisconsin, invoking diversity of citizenship. D then impleads T, a citizen of Florida, for an indemnity claim exceeding $75,000. The fact that T and P are co-citizens is irrelevant, since there is (as yet) no claim between them. The claim being asserted (the impleader claim) is by a citizen of Wisconsin against a citizen of Florida and exceeds $75,000. Therefore, it has an independent basis of subject matter jurisdiction.

What if one of the three claims does not have an independent basis of subject matter jurisdiction? Can supplemental jurisdiction attach? As always, the first question under § 1367(a) is whether the claim satisfies the *Gibbs* test, sharing a common nucleus of operative fact with the underlying action. The impleader claim seems to, since it requires that the third-party defendant be liable to the defendant for all or part of the plaintiff's claim, that is, the underlying dispute. Similarly, both the upsloping and downsloping 14(a) claims seem to meet the test, since by definition they can be asserted only if they arise from the same transaction or occurrence as the underlying dispute.

For decades, there has been no significant doubt that the impleader claim and the downsloping 14(a) claim invoke supplemental jurisdiction. See, e.g., Agrashell, Inc. v. Bernard Sirotta Co., 344 F.2d 583 (2d Cir. 1965) (impleader); Revere Copper & Brass, Inc. v. Aetna Cas. & Sur. Co., 426 F.2d 709 (5th Cir. 1970) (downsloping 14(a) claim). Upsloping 14(a) claims, however, raise different concerns, as shown in the next case. Note that this case was decided before passage of § 1367.

Owen Equipment & Erection Co. v. Kroger

437 U.S. 365, 98 S. Ct. 2396, 57 L. Ed. 2d 274 (1978)

Mr. Justice Stewart delivered the opinion of the Court.

In an action in which federal jurisdiction is based on diversity of citizenship, may the plaintiff assert a claim against a third-party defendant when there is no independent basis for federal jurisdiction over that claim? The Court of Appeals for the Eighth Circuit held in this case that such a claim is within the ancillary jurisdiction [now, of course, called "supplemental jurisdiction" under § 1367] of the federal courts. We granted certiorari, because this decision conflicts with several recent decisions of other Courts of Appeals.

I

On January 18, 1972, James Kroger was electrocuted when the boom of a steel crane next to which he was walking came too close to a high-tension electric power line. The respondent (his widow, who is the administratrix of his estate) filed a wrongful-death action in the United States District Court for the District of Nebraska against the Omaha Public Power District (OPPD). Her complaint alleged that OPPD's negligent construction, maintenance, and operation of the power line had caused Kroger's death. Federal jurisdiction was based on diversity of citizenship, since the respondent was a citizen of Iowa and OPPD was a Nebraska corporation.

OPPD then filed a third-party complaint pursuant to Fed. Rule Civ. Proc. 14(a) against the petitioner, Owen Equipment and Erection Co. (Owen), alleging that the crane was owned and operated by Owen, and that Owen's negligence had been the proximate cause of Kroger's death.[3] OPPD later moved for summary judgment on the respondent's complaint against it. While this motion was pending, the respondent was granted leave to file an amended complaint naming Owen as an additional defendant. Thereafter, the District Court granted OPPD's motion for summary judgment in an unreported opinion. The case thus went to trial between the respondent and the petitioner alone.

The respondent's amended complaint alleged that Owen was "a Nebraska corporation with its principal place of business in Nebraska." Owen's answer admitted that it was "a corporation organized and existing under the laws of the State of Nebraska," and denied every other allegation of the complaint. On the third day of trial, however, it was disclosed that the petitioner's principal place of business was in Iowa, not Nebraska[5] and that the petitioner and the respondent were thus both citizens of Iowa.[6] The petitioner then moved to dismiss the complaint for lack of jurisdiction. The District Court reserved decision on the motion, and the jury thereafter returned a verdict in favor of the respondent. In an unreported opinion issued after the trial, the District Court denied the petitioner's motion to dismiss the complaint.

The judgment was affirmed on appeal. The Court of Appeals held that under this Court's decision in *Mine Workers v. Gibbs*, the District Court had jurisdictional power, in its discretion, to adjudicate the respondent's claim against the petitioner because that claim arose from the "core of 'operative facts' giving rise to both [respondent's] claim against OPPD and OPPD's claim against Owen." It further held that the District Court had properly exercised its discretion in proceeding to decide the case even after summary judgment had been granted to OPPD, because the petitioner had concealed its Iowa citizenship from the respondent. Rehearing en banc was denied by an equally divided court.

II

It is undisputed that there was no independent basis of federal jurisdiction over the respondent's state-law tort action against the petitioner, since both are citizens of Iowa. And although Fed. Rule Civ. Proc. 14(a) permits a plaintiff to assert a claim

---

3. Under Rule 14(a), a third-party defendant may not be impleaded merely because he may be liable to the *plaintiff*. While the third-party complaint in this case alleged merely that Owen's negligence caused Kroger's death, and the basis of Owen's alleged liability *to OPPD* is nowhere spelled out, OPPD evidently relied upon the state common-law right of contribution among joint tortfeasors. The petitioner has never challenged the propriety of the third-party complaint as such.

5. The problem apparently was one of geography. Although the Missouri River generally marks the boundary between Iowa and Nebraska, Carter Lake, Iowa, where the accident occurred and where Owen had its main office, lies west of the river, adjacent to Omaha, Neb. Apparently the river once avulsed at one of its bends, cutting Carter Lake off from the rest of Iowa.

6. Title 28 U.S.C. § 1332(c) provides that "[for] the purposes of [diversity jurisdiction] . . . , a corporation shall be deemed a citizen of any State by which it has been incorporated and of the State where it has its principal place of business."

against a third-party defendant, it does not purport to say whether or not such a claim requires an independent basis of federal jurisdiction. Indeed, it could not determine that question, since it is axiomatic that the Federal Rules of Civil Procedure do not create or withdraw federal jurisdiction.

In affirming the District Court's judgment, the Court of Appeals relied upon the doctrine of ancillary jurisdiction, whose contours it believed were defined by this Court's holding in *Mine Workers v. Gibbs*. The *Gibbs* case differed from this one in that it involved pendent jurisdiction, which concerns the resolution of a plaintiff's federal- and state-law claims against a single defendant in one action. By contrast, in this case there was no claim based upon substantive federal law, but rather state-law tort claims against two different defendants. Nonetheless, the Court of Appeals was correct in perceiving that *Gibbs* and this case are two species of the same generic problem: Under what circumstances may a federal court hear and decide a state-law claim arising between citizens of the same State?[8] But we believe that the Court of Appeals failed to understand the scope of the doctrine of the *Gibbs* case.

The plaintiff in *Gibbs* alleged that the defendant union had violated the common law of Tennessee as well as the federal prohibition of secondary boycotts. This Court held that, although the parties were not of diverse citizenship, the District Court properly entertained the state-law claim as pendent to the federal claim. The crucial holding was stated as follows:

> "Pendent jurisdiction, in the sense of judicial *power*, exists whenever there is a claim 'arising under [the] Constitution, the Laws of the United States, and Treaties made, or which shall be made, under their Authority...,' U.S. Const., Art. III, § 2, and the relationship between that claim and the state claim permits the conclusion that the entire action before the court comprises but one constitutional 'case.'... The state and federal claims must derive from a common nucleus of operative fact. But if, considered without regard to their federal or state character, a plaintiff's claims are such that he would ordinarily be expected to try them all in one judicial proceeding, then, assuming substantiality of the federal issues, there is *power* in federal courts to hear the whole."[9]

It is apparent that *Gibbs* delineated the constitutional limits of federal judicial power. But even if it be assumed that the District Court in the present case had constitutional power to decide the respondent's lawsuit against the petitioner, it does not follow that the decision of the Court of Appeals was correct. Constitutional power is merely the first hurdle that must be overcome in determining that a federal court

---

8. No more than in Aldinger v. Howard, 427 U.S. 1 (1976), is it necessary to determine here "whether there are any 'principled' differences between pendent and ancillary jurisdiction; or, if there are, what effect *Gibbs* had on such differences."

9. The Court further noted that even when such power exists, its exercise remains a matter of discretion based upon "considerations of judicial economy, convenience and fairness to litigants," and held that the District Court had not abused its discretion in retaining jurisdiction of the state-law claim.

has jurisdiction over a particular controversy. For the jurisdiction of the federal courts is limited not only by the provisions of Art. III of the Constitution, but also by Acts of Congress.

That statutory law as well as the Constitution may limit a federal court's jurisdiction over nonfederal claims[11] is well illustrated by two recent decisions of this Court, Aldinger v. Howard, 427 U.S. 1 [1976], and Zahn v. International Paper Co., 414 U.S. 291 [1973]. In *Aldinger* the Court held that a Federal District Court lacked jurisdiction over a state-law claim against a county, even if that claim was alleged to be pendent to one against county officials under 42 U.S.C. § 1983. In *Zahn* the Court held that in a diversity class action under Fed. Rule Civ. Proc. 23(b)(3), the claim of each member of the plaintiff class must independently satisfy the minimum jurisdictional amount set by 28 U.S.C. § 1332(a), and rejected the argument that jurisdiction existed over those claims that involved $10,000 or less as ancillary to those that involved more. [At the time, diversity of citizenship cases required an amount in controversy in excess of $10,000.] In each case, despite the fact that federal and nonfederal claims arose from a "common nucleus of operative fact," the Court held that the statute conferring jurisdiction over the federal claim did not allow the exercise of jurisdiction over the nonfederal claims.

The *Aldinger* and *Zahn* cases thus make clear that a finding that federal and nonfederal claims arise from a "common nucleus of operative fact," the test of *Gibbs*, does not end the inquiry into whether a federal court has power to hear the nonfederal claims along with the federal ones. Beyond this constitutional minimum, there must be an examination of the posture in which the nonfederal claim is asserted and of the specific statute that confers jurisdiction over the federal claim, in order to determine whether "Congress in [that statute] has ... expressly or by implication negated" the exercise of jurisdiction over the particular nonfederal claim.

III

The relevant statute in this case, 28 U.S.C. § 1332(a)(1), confers upon federal courts jurisdiction over "civil actions where the matter in controversy exceeds the sum or value of $10,000 [now $75,000] ... and is between ... citizens of different States." This statute and its predecessors have consistently been held to require complete diversity of citizenship. That is, diversity jurisdiction does not exist unless *each* defendant is a citizen of a different State from *each* plaintiff. Over the years Congress has repeatedly re-enacted or amended the statute conferring diversity jurisdiction, leaving intact this rule of complete diversity. Whatever may have been the original purposes of diversity-of-citizenship jurisdiction, this subsequent history clearly demonstrates a congressional mandate that diversity jurisdiction is not to be available when any plaintiff is a citizen of the same State as any defendant.

Thus it is clear that the respondent could not originally have brought suit in federal court naming Owen and OPPD as codefendants, since citizens of Iowa would have

11. As used in this opinion, the term "nonfederal claim" means one as to which there is no independent basis for federal jurisdiction. Conversely, a "federal claim" means one as to which an independent basis for federal jurisdiction exists.

been on both sides of the litigation. Yet the identical lawsuit resulted when she amended her complaint. Complete diversity was destroyed just as surely as if she had sued Owen initially. In either situation, in the plain language of the statute, the "matter in controversy" could not be "between ... citizens of different States."

It is a fundamental precept that federal courts are courts of limited jurisdiction. The limits upon federal jurisdiction, whether imposed by the Constitution or by Congress, must be neither disregarded nor evaded. Yet under the reasoning of the Court of Appeals in this case, a plaintiff could defeat the statutory requirement of complete diversity by the simple expedient of suing only those defendants who were of diverse citizenship and waiting for them to implead nondiverse defendants.[17] If, as the Court of Appeals thought, a "common nucleus of operative fact" were the only requirement for ancillary jurisdiction in a diversity case, there would be no principled reason why the respondent in this case could not have joined her cause of action against Owen in her original complaint as ancillary to her claim against OPPD. Congress' requirement of complete diversity would thus have been evaded completely.

It is true, as the Court of Appeals noted, that the exercise of ancillary jurisdiction over nonfederal claims has often been upheld in situations involving impleader, cross-claims or counterclaims. But in determining whether jurisdiction over a nonfederal claim exists, the context in which the nonfederal claim is asserted is crucial. See *Aldinger v. Howard*, 427 U.S. at 14. And the claim here arises in a setting quite different from the kinds of nonfederal claims that have been viewed in other cases as falling within the ancillary jurisdiction of the federal courts.

First, the nonfederal claim in this case was simply not ancillary to the federal one in the same sense that, for example, the impleader by a defendant of a third-party defendant always is. A third-party complaint depends at least in part upon the resolution of the primary lawsuit. See n.3, supra. Its relation to the original complaint is thus not mere factual similarity but logical dependence. Cf. Moore v. New York Cotton Exchange, 270 U.S. 593, 610 [1926]. The respondent's claim against the petitioner, however, was entirely separate from her original claim against OPPD, since the petitioner's liability to her depended not at all upon whether or not OPPD was also liable. Far from being an ancillary and dependent claim, it was a new and independent one.

Second, the nonfederal claim here was asserted by the plaintiff, who voluntarily chose to bring suit upon a state-law claim in a federal court. By contrast, ancillary jurisdiction typically involves claims by a defending party haled into court against

17. This is not an unlikely hypothesis, since a defendant in a tort suit such as this one would surely try to limit his liability by impleading any joint tortfeasors for indemnity or contribution. Some commentators have suggested that the possible abuse of third-party practice could be dealt with under 28 U.S.C. § 1359, which forbids collusive attempts to create federal jurisdiction. * * * The dissenting opinion today also expresses this view. But there is nothing necessarily collusive about a plaintiff's selectively suing only those tortfeasors of diverse citizenship, or about the named defendants' desire to implead joint tortfeasors. Nonetheless, the requirement of complete diversity would be eviscerated by such a course of events.

his will, or by another person whose rights might be irretrievably lost unless he could assert them in an ongoing action in a federal court. A plaintiff cannot complain if ancillary jurisdiction does not encompass all of his possible claims in a case such as this one, since it is he who has chosen the federal rather than the state forum and must thus accept its limitations. "[The] efficiency plaintiff seeks so avidly is available without question in the state courts." Kenrose Mfg. Co. v. Fred Whitaker Co., 512 F.2d 890, 894 [4th Cir. 1972].[20]

It is not unreasonable to assume that, in generally requiring complete diversity, Congress did not intend to confine the jurisdiction of federal courts so inflexibly that they are unable to protect legal rights or effectively to resolve an entire, logically entwined lawsuit. Those practical needs are the basis of the doctrine of ancillary jurisdiction. But neither the convenience of litigants nor considerations of judicial economy can suffice to justify extension of the doctrine of ancillary jurisdiction to a plaintiff's cause of action against a citizen of the same State in a diversity case. Congress has established the basic rule that diversity jurisdiction exists under 28 U.S.C. § 1332 only when there is complete diversity of citizenship. "The policy of the statute calls for its strict construction." To allow the requirement of complete diversity to be circumvented as it was in this case would simply flout the congressional command.[21]

Accordingly, the judgment of the Court of Appeals is reversed.

It is so ordered.

Mr. Justice White, with whom Mr. Justice Brennan joins, dissenting.

The Court today states that "[It] is not unreasonable to assume that, in generally requiring complete diversity, Congress did not intend to confine the jurisdiction of federal courts so inflexibly that they are unable ... effectively to resolve an entire, logically entwined lawsuit." In spite of this recognition, the majority goes on to hold that in diversity suits federal courts do not have the jurisdictional power to entertain a claim asserted by a plaintiff against a third-party defendant, no matter how entwined it is with the matter already before the court, unless there is an independent basis for jurisdiction over that claim. Because I find no support for such a requirement in either Art. III of the Constitution or in any statutory law, I dissent from the Court's "unnecessarily grudging" approach. * * *

The majority correctly points out, however, that the analysis cannot stop [with constitutional assessment]. As Aldinger v. Howard, 427 U.S. 1 (1976), teaches, the jurisdictional power of the federal courts may be limited by Congress, as well as by the Constitution. * * *

---

20. Whether Iowa's statute of limitations would now bar an action by the respondent in an Iowa court is, of course, entirely a matter of state law.

21. Our holding is that the District Court lacked power to entertain the respondent's lawsuit against the petitioner. Thus, the asserted inequity in the respondent's alleged concealment of its citizenship is irrelevant. Federal judicial power does not depend upon "prior action or consent of the parties."

In the present case, the only indication of congressional intent that the Court can find is that contained in the diversity jurisdictional statute, 28 U.S.C. § 1332(a), which states that "district courts shall have original jurisdiction of all civil actions where the matter in controversy exceeds the sum or value of $10,000 ... and is between ... citizens of different States." Because this statute has been interpreted as requiring complete diversity of citizenship between each plaintiff and each defendant, Strawbridge v. Curtiss, 3 Cranch 267 (1806), the Court holds that the District Court did not have ancillary jurisdiction over Mrs. Kroger's claim against Owen. In so holding, the Court unnecessarily expands the scope of the complete-diversity requirement while substantially limiting the doctrine of ancillary jurisdiction.

The complete-diversity requirement, of course, could be viewed as meaning that in a diversity case, a federal district court may adjudicate only those claims that are between parties of different States. Thus, in order for a defendant to implead a third-party defendant, there would have to be diversity of citizenship; the same would also be true for cross-claims between defendants and for a third-party defendant's claim against a plaintiff. Even the majority, however, refuses to read the complete-diversity requirement so broadly; it recognizes with seeming approval the exercise of ancillary jurisdiction over nonfederal claims in situations involving impleader, cross-claims, and counterclaims. Given the Court's willingness to recognize ancillary jurisdiction in these contexts, despite the requirements of § 1332(a), I see no justification for the Court's refusal to approve the District Court's exercise of ancillary jurisdiction in the present case.

It is significant that a plaintiff who asserts a claim against a third-party defendant is not seeking to add a new party to the lawsuit. In the present case, for example, Owen had already been brought into the suit by OPPD, and, that having been done, Mrs. Kroger merely sought to assert against Owen a claim arising out of the same transaction that was already before the court. Thus the situation presented here is unlike that in *Aldinger.*

Because in the instant case Mrs. Kroger merely sought to assert a claim against someone already a party to the suit, considerations of judicial economy, convenience, and fairness to the litigants—the factors relied upon in *Gibbs*—support the recognition of ancillary jurisdiction here. Already before the court was the whole question of the cause of Mr. Kroger's death. Mrs. Kroger initially contended that OPPD was responsible; OPPD in turn contended that Owen's negligence had been the proximate cause of Mr. Kroger's death. In spite of the fact that the question of Owen's negligence was already before the District Court, the majority requires Mrs. Kroger to bring a separate action in state court in order to assert that very claim. Even if the Iowa statute of limitations will still permit such a suit, see ante, n.20, considerations of judicial economy are certainly not served by requiring such duplicative litigation.

The majority, however, brushes aside such considerations of convenience, judicial economy, and fairness because it concludes that recognizing ancillary jurisdiction over a plaintiff's claim against a third-party defendant would permit the plaintiff to circumvent the complete-diversity requirement and thereby "flout the congressional command." Since the plaintiff in such a case does not bring the third-party defendant into the suit, however, there is no occasion for deliberate circumvention of the diversity requirement, absent collusion with the defendant. In the case of such collusion, of which there is absolutely no indication here, the court can dismiss the action under the authority of 28 U.S.C. § 1359. In the absence of such collusion, there is no reason to adopt an absolute rule prohibiting the plaintiff from asserting those claims that he may properly assert against the third-party defendant pursuant to Fed. Rule Civ. Proc. 14(a). The plaintiff in such a situation brings suit against the defendant only, with absolutely no assurance that the defendant will decide or be able to implead a particular third-party defendant. Since the plaintiff has no control over the defendant's decision to implead a third party, the fact that he could not have originally sued that party in federal court should be irrelevant. Moreover, the fact that a plaintiff in some cases may be able to foresee the subsequent chain of events leading to the impleader does not seem to me to be a sufficient reason to declare that a district court does not have the *power* to exercise ancillary jurisdiction over the plaintiff's claims against the third-party defendant.

Notes and Questions

1. Consider when *Kroger* was decided—after *Gibbs* and *Aldinger*, but before *Finley*. It seems consistent with *Gibbs* and *Aldinger* in indulging the presumption that supplemental jurisdiction applies (if *Gibbs* is met) unless Congress has taken it away. As in *Aldinger*, the Court hunts for legislative action denying supplemental jurisdiction. According to *Kroger*, what statute denies supplemental jurisdiction over upsloping 14(a) claims?

2. Note the Court's statutory analysis in *Kroger*. It seems to stress three factors.

(a) *Logical dependence. Kroger* was the first case to identify "logical dependence" as a factor in supplemental jurisdiction. Of all the claims asserted under the federal rules, only one—the impleader claim—is always logically dependent on the underlying case. If the plaintiff wins, the impleader claim goes to trial; if she loses, it does not. Yet, in *Kroger* the Court recognized that it had long accepted supplemental jurisdiction over other claims not satisfying logical dependence, so long as the *Gibbs* test was met.

(b) *Defensive initiation.* The Court also said that supplemental jurisdiction is usually employed to support claims by a party in a defensive posture. But what about *Gibbs*? There, it upheld supplemental jurisdiction over a claim by a plaintiff. What is the key distinction between *Gibbs* and *Kroger* on this score? Why do you suppose the Court is more willing to allow supplemental jurisdiction in federal question cases than in diversity cases?

(c) *The clever plaintiff.* The majority felt that a clever plaintiff could foresee that a defendant would join a third-party defendant and could use an upsloping 14(a) claim as an end-run around the complete diversity rule of *Strawbridge*. Does it strike you as realistic to fear that the plaintiff and defendant will collude in this way? If there were such collusion, wouldn't 28 U.S.C. § 1359 handle the situation?

At any rate, there was no evidence of such behavior in *Kroger*. Indeed, until the third day of trial, everyone apparently thought that there was diversity between Mrs. Kroger and Owen. Or did everyone? Look very carefully at the allegations of citizenship made by Mrs. Kroger and the response thereto by Owen. Should the response by Owen have caused anyone to look into the issue further?

3. Suppose Mr. Kroger had not been killed, and that he sued OPPD to recover for his personal injuries. Suppose also that after OPPD impleaded Owen, Owen filed a downsloping 14(a) claim against Kroger, alleging that he damaged its equipment. If Kroger then counterclaimed against Owen, would the court have supplemental jurisdiction over the counterclaim? Some courts have upheld supplemental jurisdiction in this context. See, e.g., Finkle v. Gulf & W. Mfg. Co., 744 F.2d 1015 (3d Cir. 1984). How does this situation differ from *Kroger*?

4. Although Mrs. Kroger amended her complaint to include the third-party defendant, the Court chose to treat the assertion as an upsloping 14(a) claim. If treated as an amended complaint, there is no doubt that the case would be dismissed as violating the complete diversity rule. Should the result be different just because of timing—just because she added the claim against Owen later?

5. As a practical matter, what happens to plaintiffs in Mrs. Kroger's situation? The litigation with the defendant and between the defendant and the third-party defendant go forward in federal court, while the transactionally related upsloping 14(a) claim must be asserted in state court. What problems does this scenario raise?

6. What is the effect of the supplemental jurisdiction statute on *Kroger* and related situations? Assume that the case is in federal court because the plaintiff's claim against the defendant invoked diversity of citizenship jurisdiction. Consider the following under § 1367.

(a) Why is there supplemental jurisdiction over an impleader claim filed by a defendant?

(b) Why is there supplemental jurisdiction over a downsloping 14(a) claim?

(c) Why is there *not* supplemental jurisdiction over an upsloping 14(a) claim?

(d) What about an impleader claim filed by the plaintiff? Suppose P, a citizen of New York, sues D, a citizen of Missouri, invoking diversity of citizenship jurisdiction. Now D files a counterclaim against P. P has a claim for indemnity against T, and would like to implead T. T, however, is a citizen of New York, so there is no diversity of citizenship on that claim. Before § 1367, there appears to have been no question that supplemental jurisdiction would attach. By the terms of § 1367(b), however, why is there no supplemental jurisdiction? See Guaranteed Systems, Inc. v. American National Can Co., 842 F. Supp. 855, 857 (M.D.N.C. 1994) (rejecting supplemental jurisdiction in this context).

7. One potential problem for Mrs. Kroger, after the federal courts dismissed her claim, was whether the statute of limitations had run. If so, it would bar her from asserting the claim in state court. To address this situation, Congress passed § 1367(d).

The Court upheld the constitutionality of § 1367(d) in Jinks v. Richland County, S.C., 538 U.S. 456 (2003). In that case, the plaintiff sued a county in federal court, asserting that it had violated his federal civil rights. The case invoked federal question jurisdiction. The plaintiff also asserted state law claims that invoked supplemental jurisdiction under § 1367(a). The district court granted defendant's motion for summary judgment on the federal question claim and then exercised its discretion to dismiss the supplemental state law claims under § 1367(c)(3). The plaintiff asserted in state court the state law claims that, absent § 1367(d), would have been barred under the statute of limitations. The South Carolina Supreme Court held that § 1367(d) was unconstitutional because it interfered with state "sovereign authority to establish the extent to which its political subdivisions are subject to suit." The United States Supreme Court unanimously reversed and upheld the tolling provision as "necessary and proper for carrying into execution Congress's power" to establish the lower federal courts and assure that they fairly exercise the judicial power of the United States.

2. Compulsory Joinder (Necessary and Indispensable Parties)

a. Procedural Aspects

Haas v. Jefferson National Bank

442 F.2d 394 (5th Cir. 1971)

Aldisert, Circuit Judge.

Invoking jurisdiction on the basis of diversity of citizenship, 28 U.S.C. § 1332, Haas, a citizen of Ohio, sought a mandatory injunction from the district court directing the Jefferson National Bank, a citizen of Florida, to issue to him 169 1/2 shares of its common stock. Alternatively, he asked for damages reflecting the stock's value. He alleged a 1963 agreement with Glueck, also an Ohio citizen, under which they were to jointly purchase 250 shares of the bank's stock; the certificates were to issue in the name of Glueck but Haas was to have a one-half ownership of the shares. He also pleaded a similar 1966 agreement with Glueck to purchase 34 additional shares. According to Haas, he paid Glueck amounts representing one-half ownership, the bank had knowledge of his ownership interest, and the certificates and subsequent dividends were issued to Glueck.

Haas contends, however, that in 1967 he requested Glueck to order the bank to issue certificates in Haas' name, reflecting his ownership of 169 1/2 shares, and that pursuant to this request Glueck presented to the bank properly endorsed certificates for 250 shares with instructions to reissue 170 shares to Haas and the balance to Glueck.

In its answer, the Bank explained that it had refused to make the assignment because at the time of the transfer request Glueck was indebted to it under the terms of a promissory note which required that Glueck pledge, assign, and transfer to the bank property of any kind owned by Glueck and coming into the possession of the

Bank. The Bank averred that Glueck withdrew the transfer request and instead pledged the stock certificates with a second bank as collateral for a loan there.

Following the pre-trial conference * * * , the district court entered an order directing Haas to amend his complaint to join Glueck as a party. The court then denied his motion to dismiss Glueck as a party, and granted the Bank's motion to dismiss the amended complaint on the jurisdictional ground of incomplete diversity.

* * * [I]f the district court did not err in ordering the joinder of Glueck, it was obviously correct in finding a jurisdictional defect. It is clear beyond any doubt that the diversity statute requires complete diversity of citizenship. "The policy of the statute calls for its strict construction." It is of course immaterial that the nondiverse party has been required to be joined as an indispensable party. It is settled that failure of the district court to acquire jurisdiction over indispensable parties to an action deprives "the court of jurisdiction to proceed in the matter and render a judgment."

In approaching the dispositive question whether Rule 19 required the joinder of Glueck, we begin with the formulation of Shields v. Barrow, 58 U.S. 130, 139 (1854). Indispensable parties were defined as "persons who not only have an interest in the controversy, but an interest of such a nature that a final decree cannot be made without either affecting that interest, or leaving the controversy in such a condition that its final termination may be wholly inconsistent with equity and good conscience."

As Mr. Justice Harlan declared in Provident Tradesmens Bank & Trust Co. v. Patterson, 390 U.S. 102, 124 [1968], the generalizations of *Shields* "are still valid today, and they are consistent with the requirements of Rule 19. * * * Indeed, the * * * *Shields* definition states, in rather different fashion, the criteria for decision announced in Rule 19(b)." It is essential, however, to bear in mind that the broad statements in *Shields* "are not a substitute for the analysis required by that Rule."

The Rule * * * commands that we address ourselves to two broad questions: (1) Was Glueck a party "to be joined if feasible" under section (a)? If so, (2) was the court correct, under section (b), in dismissing the action or should it have proceeded without the additional party?

It is readily apparent that Glueck "falls within the category of persons who, under § (a), should be 'joined if feasible,'" *Provident Tradesmens Bank & Trust Co. v. Patterson*, for his presence is critical to the disposition of the important issues in the litigation. His evidence will either support the complaint or bolster the defense: it will affirm or refute Haas' claim to half ownership of the stock; it will substantiate or undercut Haas' contention that the Bank had knowledge of his alleged ownership interest; it will corroborate or compromise the Bank's contention that Glueck rescinded the transfer order; and it will be crucial to the determination of Glueck's obligation to the Bank under the promissory note. The essence of Haas' action against the Bank is that it "unlawfully and recklessly seized, detained, [and] exercised improper dominion" over his shares in transferring and delivering them to the second bank as collateral for Glueck's loan. Thus, Glueck becomes more than a key witness whose testimony would be of inestimable value. Instead he emerges as an active participant in the alleged conversion of Haas' stock.

Applying the criterion of Rule 19(a)(2)(ii) [Note: this provision, slightly amended, is now found at Rule 19(a)(1)(B)(ii)], we believe that Glueck's absence would expose the defendant Bank "to a substantial risk of incurring double, multiple, or otherwise inconsistent obligations by reason of his claimed interest." If Haas prevailed in this litigation in the absence of Glueck and were adjudicated owner of half of the stock, Glueck, not being bound by res adjudicata, could theoretically succeed in later litigation against the Bank in asserting ownership of the whole. In addition, a favorable resolution of Haas' claim against the Bank could, under (a)(2)(i) [Note: this provision, slightly amended, is now found at Rule 19(a)(1)(B)(i)], "as a practical matter impair or impede [the absent party's] ability to protect [his] interest" in all of the shares — an interest that is at least apparent since all of the stock was issued in Glueck's name.

Because Glueck cannot be made a party without destroying diversity, however, it remains to be decided whether, under Rule 19(b), his presence is so vital that "in equity and good conscience the action * * * should be dismissed, the absent person being thus regarded as indispensable." This decision is always a matter of judgment and must be exercised with sufficient knowledge of the facts in order to evaluate the exact role of the absentees. As the Supreme Court has said:

> "The decision whether to dismiss (i.e., the decision whether the person missing is 'indispensable') must be based on factors varying with the different cases, some such factors being substantive, some procedural, some compelling by themselves, and some subject to balancing against opposing interests. Rule 19 does not prevent the assertion of compelling substantive interests; it merely commands the courts to examine each controversy to make certain that the interests really exist."

Provident Tradesmens Bank, supra. The spirit of the Rule is to depart from the tyranny of the old labels of "necessary" and "indispensable," and to solve each problem "in the context of particular litigation."

We turn now to the specific factors enumerated in Rule 19(b), as applied to the facts before us. In our view the first factor tracks the considerations of 19(a)(2)(ii) [now 19(a)(1)(B)] discussed above: "to what extent a judgment rendered in the person's absence might be prejudicial to him or those already parties." And based on the reasoning previously set forth, we believe this factor supplies weighty reason for a finding of indispensability.[6]

---

6. "The defendant may properly wish to avoid multiple litigation, or inconsistent relief, or sole responsibility for a liability he shares with another. * * * There is [also] the interest of the outsider * * *. Of course, since the outsider is not before the court, he cannot be bound by the judgment rendered. This means, however, only that a judgment is not res judicata as to, or legally enforceable against, a nonparty * * *. Instead, as Rule 19(a) expresses it, the court must consider the extent to which the judgment may 'as a practical matter impair or impede his ability to protect' his interest in the subject matter. * * *"

The second factor directs the court to consider the extent to which the shaping of relief might avoid or lessen the prejudice to existing or absent parties.[7] Because the title to the stock certificates, although not the immediate issue in this litigation, assumes such commanding importance, it is difficult to conceptualize a form of relief or protective provisions which would not require as a preliminary matter the determination of the question of title with all the resulting potential for prejudice.

In analyzing the third factor, "whether a judgment rendered in the person's absence will be adequate," Mr. Justice Harlan cautioned:

> "[T]here remains the interest of the courts and the public in complete, consistent, and efficient settlement of controversies. We read the Rule's third criterion, whether the judgment issued in the absence of the nonjoined person will be 'adequate,' to refer to this public stake in settling disputes by wholes, whenever possible, for clearly the plaintiff, who himself chose both the forum and the parties defendant, will not be heard to complain about the sufficiency of the relief obtainable against them. * * *"

Provident Tradesmens Bank, supra. It seems evident to us that the absence of Glueck in this litigation would, of necessity, result in less than a complete settlement of this controversy. For reasons already discussed, there is no semblance of a guarantee that a judgment on Haas' terms would settle the whole dispute generated by the facts here.

Finally Rule 19(b) requires us to consider whether the plaintiff will have an avenue for relief if the district court's dismissal for nonjoinder is affirmed.[8] Clearly, the state courts of Ohio afford plaintiff Haas an opportunity to adjudicate his rights against Glueck.[9] They provide a ready forum to settle the question of title to the stock. Moreover, assuming the disposition of the preliminary question of title in the Ohio courts, it is not difficult to conceptualize circumstances permitting the possibility of a second action against the Bank in which the problem of nonjoinder will not be so acute.

Accordingly, applying Rule 19(b)'s "equity and good conscience test," we hold that the district court did not abuse its discretion in concluding that Glueck was an indispensable party and in dismissing this action.

Affirmed.

---

7. Rule 19(b) also directs a district court to consider the possibility of shaping relief to accommodate these four interests. Commentators had argued that greater attention should be paid to this potential solution to a joinder stymie, and the Rule now makes it explicit that a court should consider modification of a judgment as an alternative to dismissal.

8. "[T]he plaintiff has an interest in having a forum. Before the trial, the strength of this interest obviously depends upon whether a satisfactory alternative forum exists. * * *" See James, Civil Procedure, § 9.20 at 432 (1965):

"[T]he availability of the state court is a factor properly to be considered by the federal court in weighing the relative interests which will be affected by a ruling of indispensability. Even if the plaintiff's preference for the federal forum deserves the court's enthusiastic protection, the disappointment of that choice is not so great a hardship on the plaintiff as the foreclosing of all courts to him."

9. In response to the court's inquiry at oral argument, Haas' counsel reported that a state action between Haas and Glueck is now pending.

Temple v. Synthes Corp.

498 U.S. 5, 111 S. Ct. 315, 112 L. Ed. 2d 263 (1990)

Per Curiam.

Petitioner Temple, a Mississippi resident [sic; the Court means "citizen"], underwent surgery in October 1986 in which a "plate and screw device" was implanted in his lower spine. The device was manufactured by respondent Synthes, Ltd. (U.S.A.) (Synthes), a Pennsylvania corporation. Dr. S. Henry LaRocca performed the surgery at St. Charles General Hospital in New Orleans, Louisiana. Following surgery, the device's screws broke off inside Temple's back.

Temple filed suit against Synthes in the United States District Court for the Eastern District of Louisiana. The suit, which rested on diversity jurisdiction, alleged defective design and manufacture of the device. At the same time, Temple filed a state administrative proceeding against Dr. LaRocca and the hospital for malpractice and negligence. At the conclusion of the administrative proceeding, Temple filed suit against the doctor and the hospital in Louisiana state court.

Synthes did not attempt to bring the doctor and the hospital into the federal action by means of a third-party complaint, as provided in Federal Rule of Civil Procedure 14(a). Instead, Synthes filed a motion to dismiss Temple's federal suit for failure to join necessary parties pursuant to Federal Rule of Civil Procedure 19. Following a hearing, the District Court ordered Temple to join the doctor and the hospital as defendants within 20 days or risk dismissal of the lawsuit. According to the court, the most significant reason for requiring joinder was the interest of judicial economy. The court relied on this Court's decision in Provident Tradesmens Bank & Trust Co. v. Patterson, 390 U.S. 102 (1968), wherein we recognized that one focus of Rule 19 is "the interest of the courts and the public in complete, consistent, and efficient settlement of controversies." When Temple failed to join the doctor and the hospital, the court dismissed the suit with prejudice.

Temple appealed, and the United States Court of Appeals for the Fifth Circuit affirmed. The court deemed it "obviously prejudicial to the defendants to have the separate litigations being carried on," because Synthes' defense might be that the plate was not defective but that the doctor and the hospital were negligent, while the doctor and the hospital, on the other hand, might claim that they were not negligent but that the plate was defective. The Court of Appeals found that the claims overlapped and that the District Court therefore had not abused its discretion in ordering joinder under Rule 19. * * *

In his petition for certiorari to this Court, Temple contends that it was error to label joint tortfeasors as indispensable parties under Rule 19(b) and to dismiss the lawsuit with prejudice for failure to join those parties. We agree. Synthes does not deny that it, the doctor, and the hospital are potential joint tortfeasors. It has long been the rule that it is not necessary for all joint tortfeasors to be named as defendants in a single lawsuit. Nothing in the 1966 revision of Rule 19 changed that principle. The Advisory Committee Notes to Rule 19(a) explicitly state that "a tortfeasor with the usual 'joint-and-several' liability is merely a permissive party to an action against another with like liability." There is nothing in Louisiana tort law to the contrary.

The opinion in *Provident Bank* does speak of the public interest in limiting multiple litigation, but that case is not controlling here. There, the estate of a tort victim brought a declaratory judgment action against an insurance company. We assumed that the policyholder was a person "who, under § (a), should be 'joined if feasible,'" and went on to discuss the appropriate analysis under Rule 19(b), because the policyholder could not be joined without destroying diversity. After examining the factors set forth in Rule 19(b), we determined that the action could proceed without the policyholder; he therefore was not an indispensable party whose absence required dismissal of the suit.

Here, no inquiry under Rule 19(b) is necessary, because the threshold requirements of Rule 19(a) have not been satisfied. As potential joint tortfeasors with Synthes, Dr. LaRocca and the hospital were merely permissive parties. The Court of Appeals erred by failing to hold that the District Court abused its discretion in ordering them joined as defendants and in dismissing the action when Temple failed to comply with the court's order. For these reasons, we grant the petition for certiorari, reverse the judgment of the Court of Appeals for the Fifth Circuit, and remand for further proceedings consistent with this opinion.

It is so ordered.

Notes and Questions

1. Rule 19 analysis proceeds in three steps, "although this fact is obscured by its language." Western Maryland R. Co. v. Harbor Ins. Co., 910 F.2d 960, 963 n.5 (D.C. Cir. 1990). First, the court must assess whether the absentee is a "required party" under Rule 19(a)(1)(A) or 19(a)(1)(B). Traditionally, such absentees have been called necessary parties—persons who should be joined in the pending case. Although Rule 19 has not employed the term "necessary" since 1966, it is commonly used in practice.

Second, if the absentee is a "required party," the court must assess whether her joinder is "feasible." The factors relevant here are whether the absentee is subject to personal jurisdiction, whether venue would be proper, and, most significantly, whether the claim asserted by or against the absentee would invoke federal question or diversity of citizenship jurisdiction. For example, suppose the absentee is a citizen of New York and would be joined as a plaintiff to assert a state-law claim against the defendant, who is also a citizen of New York. Joinder of the absentee is not possible, since her claim does not invoke either federal question or diversity jurisdiction. Accordingly, joinder of the absentee is not feasible.

Third, if joinder is not feasible, the court must assess whether it should "in equity and good conscience" proceed with the litigation without the absentee or dismiss the pending case. This assessment is guided by the four factors in Rule 19(b). If the court decides that it should dismiss, the absentee traditionally has been referred to as "indispensable." The 2007 restyling of the Rules removed the word "indispensable," but the bench and bar will undoubtedly continue to use it. (After all, as noted, Rule 19 dropped the word "necessary" over four decades ago and it is still part of common parlance.) Thus, an indispensable party is one (1) who is a "required party," (2) whose joinder cannot be effectuated (because, for example, there is no subject matter jurisdiction over the claim asserted by or against her) and (3) as to whose absence the court has determined that it should dismiss the pending case rather than run the risk of proceeding without her. See generally Richard Freer, *Rethinking Compulsory Joinder: A Proposal to Restructure Federal Rule 19*, 60 N.Y.U. L. Rev. 1061, 1075–80 (1985).

Rule 19 prescribes a pragmatic *process* and not an exercise in formalistic labeling. The operative language of Rule 19 was part of a major amendment of related joinder rules in 1966, spearheaded by trenchant scholarly criticism of the prior practice. Geoffrey Hazard, *Indispensable Party: The Historical Origin of a Procedural Phantom*, 61 Colum. L. Rev. 1254 (1961); John Reed, *Compulsory Joinder of Parties in Civil Actions*, 55 Mich. L. Rev. 327 (pt.1) & 483 (pt.2) (1957). In response to this criticism, the amendments introduced reasoning for what had become a sometimes mindless exercise of slapping labels on absentees. Professor Wright aptly explained the reasoning behind the current version of the rule:

> Labels are not bad things in the law if they are understood for what they are, a shorthand way of expressing the result of a more complicated reasoning process. Labels become treacherous and misleading if they are applied as a substitute for reasoning. It is perfectly appropriate to say: "this absentee has such a strong interest in this case that it would be unjust to let it go to decision in his absence. Therefore we will refer to him as 'indispensable.'" It is not appropriate to say, as many courts seemed to do, that "this person is 'indispensable.' Therefore we will not let the case go to decision in his absence." The latter reasoning—or nonreasoning—suggests that absent parties wear labels indicating their relation to a controversy and obscures the pragmatic examination of all the circumstances that is required in the light of the very particular facts of a particular case.

Wright & Kane, Federal Courts 495.

2. Let us return to the first step of the Rule 19 analysis. Rule 19(a)(1) gives three alternative reasons for compelling the joinder of an absentee, set out in Rule 19(a)(1)(A), 19(a)(1)(B)(i), and 19(a)(1)(B)(ii). What are the three reasons? What interests are protected by each of the three?

(a) *Rule 19(a)(1)(A)*. In *Haas*, did Glueck satisfy Rule 19(a)(1)(A)? Could the court "accord complete relief among existing parties" if Glueck were not joined? This phrase seems to have two possible readings. First, it might mean that without Glueck, the court could not wrap up things between Haas and the bank. If that is the correct interpretation, will it ever be met? After all, the court is always in a position to determine the respective rights of those before it.

Second, the phrase might mean that without Glueck, the court could not wrap up things in some overall sense between all interested persons. If that is the correct interpretation, won't it always be met? Doesn't such a reading require joinder anytime there is an absentee who threatens multiple litigation? Some courts seem to suggest that the rule means exactly this, although even these courts do not rely exclusively upon Rule 19(a)(1)(A) in ordering joinder. See, e.g., Prestenback v. Employers' Ins. Co., 47 F.R.D. 163 (E.D. La. 1969); Davila Mendez v. Vatican Shrimp Co., 43 F.R.D. 294 (S.D. Tex. 1966).

Because these two possible interpretations seem, respectively, either never or always met, Rule 19(a)(1)(A) has had little, if any, independent impact in compelling joinder of absentees. The more important bases for joinder lie in Rule 19(a)(1)(B). See Freer, supra, 60 N.Y.U. L. Rev. at 1080–82.

(b) *Rule 19(a)(1)(B)(i).* In *Haas*, what was Glueck's interest in the pending case? How would his ability to protect that interest have been impaired or impeded had the case gone to judgment without his joinder? Remember, as a nonparty, Glueck could not have been bound by claim or issue preclusion. Why not? That is why the rule speaks of "practical" (as opposed to "legal") impairment of the absentee's interest. Because Glueck thus would be free to sue the bank in a second proceeding, how can his interest be harmed?

Why would it be easier to conclude that Rule 19(a)(1)(B)(i) was met if Haas had sought to have the bank cancel Glueck's shares?

The fear of practical harm to the absentee underlies not only this rule, but intervention of right under Rule 24(a)(2) as well. It is also relevant in class actions.

(c) *Rule 19(a)(1)(B)(ii).* In *Haas*, how did Glueck's absence threaten the bank with "a substantial risk of incurring double, multiple, or otherwise inconsistent obligations"? Remember that the bank could not use the judgment from the case by Haas as a defense to a second case by Glueck. Why not?

The rule defines harm to a party as subjecting her to multiple "obligations," not to multiple "litigation." For instance, suppose Plaintiff sues Airline for injuries sustained in a crash. Fifteen other injured passengers are not joined. Their nonjoinder certainly threatens Airline with multiple suits, some of which the plaintiff might win, others of which the plaintiff might lose. Does this possibility subject Airline to "double, multiple, or otherwise inconsistent obligations"? Apparently not. Most courts seem to feel that the rule does not refer to inconsistent monetary damages awards by successive plaintiffs. How did the potential harm to the bank in *Haas* differ from this?

The fear of subjecting someone to multiple or inconsistent obligations underlies not only this rule, but impleader and interpleader as well. It is also relevant in class actions.

3. Analyze these cases under Rule 19.

(a) Black firefighters sue City, alleging racial discrimination in granting promotions in the fire department. Among other things, they seek an order placing them ahead of some white firefighters on the promotion list. The white firefighters who would be displaced by this order are not joined. Are they "required"? See Martin v. Wilks, 490 U.S. 755 (1989).

(b) Why are joint tortfeasors, such as the doctor and hospital in *Temple*, not necessary parties under Rule 19(a)?

(c) Plaintiff, representative of persons killed in the crash of a private airplane, sues the manufacturer of the aircraft for wrongful death. The crash may have been caused by the company that owned the plane or by the company that serviced it, but neither of these alleged joint tortfeasors is joined. Are they "required"? In Whyham v. Piper Aircraft Corp., 96 F.R.D. 557 (M.D. Pa. 1982), the district court concluded that joinder was required under Rule 19(a)(1)(A), 19(a)(1)(B)(i), and 19(a)(1)(B)(ii). Although the court did not have the guidance of *Temple*, can you argue that it was wrong on all three bases?

(d) Owen contracts to sell his house to Paul. When Nina offers Owen more money, Owen breaches his contract with Paul and contracts with Nina. Paul sues Owen for specific performance. Is Nina a necessary (or "required") party? If so, and she cannot be joined, must the case be dismissed? If Paul sought damages instead of specific performance, could the suit proceed without joinder of Nina?

4. The availability of other joinder devices may obviate the need to do a full Rule 19 analysis. For example, suppose the defendant complains that nonjoinder of her fellow tortfeasor subjects her to Rule 19(a)(1)(B)(ii) harm because she might be subjected to full liability and later lose a contribution case against the fellow tortfeasor. Rather than address the question under Rule 19, it seems appropriate for the court to point out to the defendant that she can avoid the perceived harm by impleading the fellow tortfeasor under Rule 14(a).

5. The holding in *Temple* that joint tortfeasors are not necessary parties gives the plaintiff significant control over the structuring of such cases. Should the rules require a plaintiff to join all joint tortfeasors? What advantages and disadvantages would such a provision have?

b. Jurisdictional Aspects

Rule 19(a) purports to allow joinder only if, inter alia, "joinder will not deprive the court of subject-matter jurisdiction." If the claim asserted by or against the necessary party would not invoke federal question or diversity of citizenship jurisdiction, the court must consider whether to proceed or dismiss under Rule 19(b). Professor Fink long ago objected that the lack of supplemental jurisdiction put the court to this "cruel choice." Howard Fink, *Indispensable Parties and the Proposed Amendment to Federal Rule 19*, 74 YALE L.J. 403, 448 (1965).

One critical factor in assessing subject matter jurisdiction under diversity jurisdiction is *alignment*. The party proposing to join an absentee under Rule 19 will suggest whether she is to join as a plaintiff or a defendant. This suggestion is not binding, and the court always has the authority to realign the absentee on that side of the dispute with which her interests are most compatible. This realignment may affect subject matter jurisdiction. Suppose the plaintiff is a citizen of New Hampshire, and that the defendant is a citizen of Vermont, and that the absentee to be joined is also a citizen of Vermont. If the absentee is aligned as a defendant, jurisdiction is unaffected. If she is aligned as a plaintiff, however, there will be no diversity of citizenship over her claim against the defendant. This power to realign is consistent with the court's power to realign parties at the outset of a diversity of citizenship case.

The absence of supplemental jurisdiction in compulsory joinder seems to be a historical accident. The Supreme Court decided a seminal compulsory joinder case—Shields v. Barrow, 58 U.S. 130 (1854)—just six years before its first major recognition of supplemental jurisdiction in Freeman v. Howe, 65 U.S. 450 (1861). In *Shields*, the Court upheld dismissal of a case in which the necessary absentee's joinder would have destroyed diversity of citizenship. The holding was consistent with the complete diversity rule, but never considered the possibility that that rule could be overcome. As we have seen, supplemental jurisdiction can overcome the complete diversity rule. At the time *Shields* was decided, though, the Court simply had not recognized supplemental jurisdiction. The two doctrines—compulsory party joinder and supplemental jurisdiction—never intersected as they grew.

Did the supplemental jurisdiction statute change this historic limitation? Remember that § 1367(a) grants supplemental jurisdiction to the full extent of the Constitution and that § 1367(b) cuts it back in certain situations in diversity of citizenship cases. Virtually everyone agrees that claims by or against a party "needed for a just adjudication" would fall within the *Gibbs* test for same case or controversy; thus, the only question is whether § 1367(b) removes that jurisdiction.

Notes and Questions

1. How would § 1367 operate on the facts of *Haas*? Glueck would be joined as a defendant, but has the same citizenship as the plaintiff. Clearly, § 1367(b) denies supplemental jurisdiction over claims asserted by an absentee who is joined as a plaintiff under Rule 19. Because that statute says nothing about claims by a Rule 19 defendant, however, some commentators conclude that § 1367 expands the use of supplemental jurisdiction by permitting it in cases such as *Haas*, where the absentee is joined as a defendant. Stephen Burbank, Thomas Rowe & Thomas Mengler, *Compounding or Creating Confusion About Supplemental Jurisdiction? A Reply to Professor Freer*, 40 Emory L.J. 943, 957 (1991). Thus, they assert, a Rule 19 defendant who is a citizen of the same state as the plaintiff can be joined under § 1367.

Others have criticized this interpretation, noting that § 1367(b) would deny supplemental jurisdiction over any claim by the plaintiff against a Rule 19 defendant. In other words, because supplemental jurisdiction is exercised over claims (not over parties), it can't be used to join a Rule 19 defendant against whom no claim is asserted. Thomas Arthur & Richard Freer, *Grasping at Burnt Straws: The Disaster of the Supplemental Jurisdiction Statute*, 40 Emory L.J. 963, 966–72 (1991). In Picciotto v. Continental Cas. Co., 512 F.3d 9, 22–23 (1st Cir. 2008), the court agreed with these critics of the statute.

2. If the absentee is needed for a just adjudication but her joinder is not feasible, the court must then decide whether to proceed or dismiss under Rule 19(b). The four factors listed in Rule 19(b) seem redundant of the Rule 19(a)(1)(A) and Rule 19(a)(1)(B) factors, but is there a difference in their thrust?

The Rule 19(b) factors are neither exclusive nor arranged hierarchically. In practice, however, courts often treat factor number 4 as especially important. It is concerned with whether the plaintiff would have a remedy if the case were dismissed. In other words, is there an alternative forum to which the plaintiff can go and effect joinder of all interested parties, including the absentee? Note the discussion of this factor in *Haas*. Because state courts do not need to worry about diversity of citizenship, that alternative forum will almost invariably be a state court. Does dismissal by the federal court in these circumstances constitute an abdication of their responsibility to decide cases properly invoking diversity of citizenship jurisdiction?

3. The court can raise Rule 19 problems sua sponte. Read Rule 19(c), which is intended to put the court in a position to do so. Unfortunately, it has not worked, because lawyers rarely comply with Rule 19(c). Does counsel's failure to list absentees under Rule 19(c) violate Rule 11?

Thus, the most likely user of Rule 19 will be the defendant. Why is it more likely that she will do so in Rule 19(a)(1)(B)(ii) cases rather than in Rule 19(a)(1)(B)(i) cases? If the potential harm is to the absentee, why (besides altruism) would the defendant raise the issue to the court? She is more likely to do so if joinder of the absentee is not feasible, because then she might possibly get the case dismissed under Rule 19(b). A defendant wanting to join an absentee would make a motion to join her under Rule 19. A defendant wanting to have the case dismissed for nonjoinder of the absentee would move for dismissal under Rule 12(b)(7). See Scott Paper Co. v. National Cas. Co., 151 F.R.D. 577, 579 (E.D. Pa. 1993) (discussing incentives for defendant to raise issue of nonjoinder of absentee).

4. What if the defendant does not raise the nonjoinder issue in a Rule 19(a)(1)(B)(i) case? As we see below, the absentee can protect herself by intervening.

5. Do you agree with the court in *Haas* that Glueck should have been aligned as a defendant? Can you articulate an argument for aligning him as a plaintiff? If he had been aligned as a plaintiff, could the court have joined him?

6. Some federal courts recognize an exception to Rule 19(b), refusing to dismiss "public rights" cases for nonjoinder of what would be seen as indispensable parties. Such cases frequently involve citizens' challenge to governmental action. Courts often conclude that such cases ought to proceed even though a judgment might affect absentees. Professor Carl Tobias criticizes this exception in *Rule 19 and the Public Rights Exception to Party Joinder*, 65 N.C. L. Rev. 745 (1987).

7. In Republic of Philippines v. Pimentel, 553 U.S. 851 (2008), the Supreme Court applied Rule 19(b) to compel dismissal in an interesting context. The case was an interpleader action. As we will study in Chapter 13, interpleader allows one in possession of money or other property to join all potential claimants to the property in

a single case. *Pimentel* involved billions of dollars in assets stolen by the late ruler of the Philippines, Ferdinand Marcos. A corporation founded by Marcos held the assets and instituted interpleader in federal court in California, to return them to their rightful owners.

Thousands of claimants were joined. Two claimants — the Republic of the Philippines and a commission created by it — could not be joined, however, because of sovereign immunity. The Court concluded that the interpleader proceeding could not proceed without these two claimants, and that it had to be dismissed under Rule 12(b)(7). First, the Philippines and its commission were necessary under Rule 19(a)(1)(B)(i). If they did not participate, the assets to which they were entitled would be distributed to others. Second, the Court confirmed that judges applying Rule 19(b) routinely must consider the merits of claims and defenses. Rule 19(b), after all, requires a court to assess whether it is likely that a party or absentee will be harmed by nonjoinder. The lower courts had done so and had concluded that the claims by the Philippines and its commission were frivolous. The Court disagreed. In equity and good conscience, the interpleader case had to be dismissed, at least in part to allow a sovereign nation to determine in its own courts who owns the assets absconded with by its former leader.

3. Intervention

a. Procedural Aspects

Read Rule 24. It defines the circumstances in which an absentee can attempt to join a pending case. Thus, it permits an absentee to override the plaintiff's party structure of the suit.

Note that there are two types of intervention: of right and permissive. As you see from the Rule, either type may be granted by statute. The most important of these statutes allow the United States to intervene to protect a government interest. For instance, 28 U.S.C. § 2403 requires notification of the Attorney General and intervention by the United States in any case "wherein the constitutionality of any Act of Congress affecting the public interest is drawn in question."*

Rule 24 also allows intervention — of right and permissive — in circumstances not addressed by statute. Note the breadth of the provision for permissive intervention under Rule 24(b)(1)(B). By definition, such intervenors have no "right" to be in the action. Indeed, they might not even be joined as proper parties under Rule 20. (By way of review, why is this so?) How does this test for intervention compare with the test for consolidation of separate actions? Does permissive intervention serve the same purpose as consolidation? Obviously, the court addressing a motion for permissive intervention must weigh the benefits of allowing participation against the disruption and delay caused by the intervention. Such motions are vested in the

* Interestingly, the statute was not followed when the Supreme Court questioned the constitutionality of the Rules of Decision Act in *Erie R.R. v. Tompkins*. Perhaps this fact should have required the Court to order reargument.

sound discretion of the district judge. In ruling on a motion to intervene under Rule 24(b), the judge is instructed to "consider whether the intervention will unduly delay or prejudice the adjudication of the original parties' rights." Fed. R. Civ. P. 24(b)(3).

Intervention of right under Rule 24(a)(2) is more interesting. It has roots in Roman law, which allowed one to enter a case if he "consider[ed] that his interest will be affected [by judgment in that case]." Dalrymple v. Dalrymple, 2 Hagg. Con. Rep. 137 (1811), quoted at 6 Moore's Federal Practice § 24 App.101. Rather than invoking the discretion of the district judge, intervention of right thus serves to avoid harm to the absentee. Rule 24(a)(2) addresses this notion of prejudice to the absentee. It is functionally identical to one of the bases for joining an absentee under Rule 19. Specifically, Rule 24(a)(2) is aimed at avoiding the same kind of harm to the absentee that motivated the drafters to promulgate Rule 19(a)(1)(B)(i). Thus, the kind of practical impairment of an absentee's interest that would justify joinder under Rule 19(a)(1)(B)(i) will be relevant under intervention of right under Rule 24(a)(2).

Why should the Rules contain two provisions doing essentially the same thing? The answer lies in who uses the respective Rules. Rule 19 will be invoked (almost always) by the defendant. Rule 24, on the other hand, will be invoked by the absentee herself. Thus, it protects the absentee in cases in which the defendant might not raise the issue of the absentee's nonjoinder.

In United States v. Alisal Water Corp., 370 F.3d 915 (9th Cir. 2004), the United States sued a provider of drinking water for alleged violations of the Safe Drinking Water Act. A non-party sought to intervene. It held a judgment of $1.7 million against the defendant (from an unrelated dispute). It claimed that the case by the United States threatened to impose such substantial fines on the defendant that the defendant would be unable to pay it the $1.7 million. The Ninth Circuit recognized that financial impact of the pending case can constitute an "interest" under Rule 24(a)(2), but held that the intervenor must also have an interest related to the underlying litigation. Because the non-party's interest had nothing to do with the purpose of the underlying case—to enforce environmental laws—it lacked a relevant interest and could not invoke Rule 24(a)(2).

Notes and Questions

1. In the *Haas* case, supra Section F.2.a, would Glueck have had a right to intervene into the underlying proceeding?

2. Should the absentee's ability to intervene under Rule 24(a)(2) lead a court to deny Rule 12(b)(7) dismissal? Suppose P sues D and that A, a nonparty, satisfies both Rule 19(a)(1)(B)(i) and 24(a)(2). Suppose further that A cannot be joined because the court lacks personal jurisdiction over her. Should the court deny D's Rule 12(b)(7) motion because A could protect herself by intervening?

3. What three things must be established to grant intervention of right under Rule 24(a)(2)? Of those three, which two are also required for compulsory joinder under Rule 19(a)(1)(B)(i)? How significant is the one difference between Rule 24(a)(2) and

Rule 19(a)(1)(B)(i)? Should intervention of right require a greater showing than joinder under Rule 19(a)(1)(B)(i)? Although there was some early confusion, it now seems clear that the intervenor assumes the burden of showing that the extant parties do not adequately represent her interests. According to the Supreme Court, however, this burden is "minimal." Trbovich v. United Mine Workers, 404 U.S. 528, 538 n.10 (1972). It seems to be met simply by showing that the parties have different interests from the intervenor. 6 Moore's Federal Practice § 24.03[4][a].

4. On its face, Rule 24 does not require someone who could intervene to do so. But refusal to intervene can create duplicative litigation. Noting this, Justice Harlan once suggested (as to an absentee who was a witness at trial in a case but who refused to exercise his right to intervene) that the absentee might be estopped from suing separately. Provident Tradesmens Bank & Trust Co. v. Patterson, 390 U.S. 102, 114 (1968). The Supreme Court subsequently rejected this notion in Martin v. Wilks, 490 U.S. 755 (1989).

In *Martin*, black firefighters sued a city, alleging racial discrimination in hiring and promotion. The action resulted in a consent decree ordering promotion of some blacks over some white firefighters. The white firefighters knew of the pendency of the action, but eschewed their clear right to intervene under Rule 24(a)(2). Instead, they sued separately to challenge the consent decree, and the Court held that they could not be bound by the judgment in the prior case. The Court emphasized the interrelation between Rules 19 and 24, noting that the parties to the first case should have joined the white firefighters under Rule 19.

> Joinder as a party, rather than knowledge of a lawsuit and an opportunity to intervene, is the method by which potential parties are subject to the jurisdiction of the court and bound by a judgment. * * * The parties to a lawsuit presumably know better than anyone else the nature and scope of relief sought in the action, and at whose expense such relief might be granted. It makes sense, therefore, to place on them a burden of bringing in additional parties where such a step is indicated, rather than placing on potential additional parties a duty to intervene when they acquire knowledge of the lawsuit.

Martin, 490 U.S. at 765 (footnote omitted).

5. Obviously, an absentee's ability to intervene is worthless if she does not know of the pendency of the case. If she does not, how can she protect her interest? Read Rule 19(c). The Advisory Committee Report to the 1966 Amendments to that rule suggested that the court contact such absentees identified under Rule 19(c) and notify them of their right to intervene.

Does such notification from the court to a nonparty accord with your view of the court's role? Under what circumstances does Rule 19(c) envision the court's giving notice to a nonparty? Should the parties play a role in notifying the absentee? Should they be prohibited from notifying the absentee?

6. Note that any petition for intervention—of right or permissive—must be "timely." The Rule provides no set time frame for determining timeliness. A repre-

sentative, albeit nonexclusive, catalogue of relevant factors includes: (1) how long the intervenor knew of her interest before moving to intervene, (2) whether the intervenor's delay will prejudice an extant party, (3) whether denial of intervention will prejudice the absentee, and (4) any unusual circumstances affecting a finding of timeliness. Farmland Dairies v. Commissioner of the New York State Dept. of Agric. & Mkts., 847 F.2d 1038, 1044 (2d Cir. 1988).

Courts generally agree that the timeliness standard should be applied less strictly in intervention of right than in permissive intervention. See, e.g., Fiandaca v. Cunningham, 827 F.2d 825, 832 (1st Cir. 1987). Why should this be so?

7. Rule 24(c) addresses the procedure for intervening. The absentee must make a motion—even under Rule 24(a)(2)—and file the appropriate pleading. For a plaintiff-intervenor, the appropriate pleading would be a complaint. If the court grants intervention, the intervenor becomes a party to the litigation and will assert her claim against the defendant. Similarly, a defendant-intervenor will make the motion, supported by an answer in intervention. If the court grants the motion, the intervenor becomes a party and asserts her answer to the plaintiff's complaint. (Remember, the court can "realign" an intervenor if it thinks she is seeking to intervene on the "wrong" side of the litigation; such realignment, obviously, may affect whether the claim by or against the intervenor invokes diversity of citizenship jurisdiction.) Once the absentee intervenes, she has all the rights and responsibilities of any party

In contrast to intervention, nonparties sometimes ask for permission to file "amicus curiae" ("friend of the court") briefs setting forth their analysis of an issue before the court. One who files an amicus brief is not a party to the litigation.

8. As we will see in Chapter 14, litigants usually cannot appeal until the trial court has entered a final judgment disposing of the entire case. Nonetheless, federal courts traditionally have allowed immediate appeal of a denial of an absentee's motion to intervene of right. See Wright & Kane, Federal Courts 547 ("the traditional doctrine is that if the applicant has contended it may intervene as of right, denial of leave to intervene is appealable"). Such immediate appeal can delay resolution of the underlying case.

b. *Jurisdictional Aspects*

As always, the court must assess whether a claim joined under the federal rules is supported by subject matter jurisdiction. If a plaintiff-intervenor asserts a federal question claim or a defendant-intervenor defends a federal question claim by the plaintiff, there is, obviously, subject matter jurisdiction. The same is true in a nonfederal claim if the plaintiff-intervenor is of diverse citizenship from all defendants and has a claim in excess of $75,000 or if the defendant-intervenor is of diverse citizenship from all plaintiffs and defends a claim in excess of $75,000.*

* As we saw in Note 7 in the preceding Section, the intervenor chooses which side of the dispute to enter on. As with Rule 19, the court is free to realign her if it feels that her interests more closely approximate those of the other side.

But what if there is no such independent basis of subject matter jurisdiction? Traditionally, supplemental jurisdiction supported claims by or against intervenors of right. The reasoning is that if an absentee is so closely related to the fray that her interest may be impeded, her claim (or the claim against her) will share a common nucleus of operative fact with the underlying suit. Thus, under *Gibbs*, the claim by or against the intervenor of right would form part of the same constitutional case or controversy already before the court. See, e.g., Curtis v. Sears, Roebuck & Co., 754 F.2d 781 (8th Cir. 1985).

As to claims by or against permissive intervenors, the tendency has been to reject supplemental jurisdiction. After all, the test of "common question" does not require the same degree of closeness with the underlying case as *Gibbs* required. Some claims involving permissive intervenors, however, would satisfy *Gibbs*. Consider, for example, an intervenor who would satisfy Rule 24(a)(2) except that her interest is adequately represented by existing parties.

The availability of supplemental jurisdiction under Rule 24(a)(2) led to an anomalous situation. Recall that joinder is precluded under Rule 19 if the claim by or against the absentee does not invoke diversity of citizenship or federal question jurisdiction; in such an event the court must proceed or dismiss the entire case under Rule 19(b). Recall also that the operative language of Rule 19(a)(1)(B)(i) and Rule 24(a)(2) is identical. Suppose that an absentee will face harm of the type contemplated by these rules, but that the claim asserted by or against the intervenor of right does not invoke diversity of citizenship or federal question jurisdiction. Rule 19 would not facilitate joinder, because it has never carried supplemental jurisdiction, but Rule 24 would facilitate joinder, because it historically did invoke supplemental jurisdiction. Thus, the same absentee in the same situation can be joined under one rule but not the other. Ultimately, joinder depends upon who raises the issue.

Every commentator addressing this issue before Congress acted recommended that supplemental jurisdiction be expanded to the Rule 19 context. See, e.g., George Fraser, *Ancillary Jurisdiction of Federal Courts of Persons Whose Interest May Be Impaired if Not Joined*, 62 F.R.D. 483, 485–87 (1974); Freer, supra, 60 N.Y.U. L. Rev. at 1101–09; Kennedy, *Let's All Join In: Intervention under Federal Rule 24*, 57 KY. L.J. 329, 362–63 (1969). Congress resolved the anomaly the other way, however, when it codified supplemental jurisdiction in 28 U.S.C. § 1367. See Joan Steinman, *Postremoval Changes in the Party Structure of Diversity Cases: The Old Law, the New Law, and Rule 19*, 38 U. Kan. L. Rev. 864, 950 (1990).

Notes and Questions

1. Apply § 1367(b) to the following. In each, P, a citizen of California, has asserted a $500,000 state-law claim against D, a citizen of Florida, in federal court; obviously, the case invokes diversity of citizenship jurisdiction. A is the absentee who seeks to intervene. Let us assume that she, as the absentee in *Haas*, would satisfy Rule 24(a)(2).

(a) Suppose A is a citizen of Florida and would intervene as a plaintiff. What part of § 1367(b) precludes supplemental jurisdiction over her claim?

(b) Suppose A is a citizen of California and would intervene as a defendant. Nothing in § 1367(b) seems to prohibit her joinder.

(i) But can the plaintiff assert a claim against her?

(ii) After intervening, can A assert a claim against P? What would that claim be called? If A can assert a claim against P, can P respond with a compulsory counterclaim? Wouldn't such a claim be prohibited because it is a claim by a plaintiff against one joined under Rule 24?

(c) Suppose A is a citizen of Florida and would properly be aligned as a plaintiff. Nonetheless, she intervenes as a defendant. May she thus avoid the bar in § 1367(b) over claims by absentees who "seek to intervene as plaintiffs"? In Colonial Penn Ins. Co. v. American Centennial Ins. Co., 1992 U.S. Dist. Lexis 17552 (S.D.N.Y. Nov. 16, 1992), the court, sua sponte, realigned the plaintiff-intervenor as a defendant and thus avoided the stricture of the statute. Is this decision sound?

2. After wrestling with questions such as these, most scholars have criticized the supplemental jurisdiction statute's removing of supplemental jurisdiction in intervention of right.

Chapter 13

Special Multiparty Litigation: Interpleader and the Class Action

A. Introduction and Integration

Starting a new chapter does not mean abandoning a theme. The materials in this chapter build upon the preceding chapter on joinder and supplemental jurisdiction. Here we consider two specialized types of group litigation. Each presents some of the same policy issues underlying those joinder rules that permit parties or the court to override the plaintiff's choice of party joinder. In addition, each presents significant issues relating to litigation management and some interesting jurisdictional problems.

B. Interpleader

1. Background

Interpleader is a procedure for resolving conflicting claims to a tangible res or a fund of money. It is instituted by the *stakeholder*, who, as the name implies, is in possession of the res (sometimes called the "stake"). In "true," or "pure" interpleader, the stakeholder is "disinterested," which means she does not claim to own the res. In a proceeding "in the nature of interpleader," however, the stakeholder does claim to own the disputed property. In either event, the stakeholder is aware that others claim ownership of the stake. Rather than engage in successive litigation with each potential claimant, interpleader allows the stakeholder to force all *claimants* into a single proceeding. So interpleader serves the same policies—efficiency and avoidance of inconsistent results—as impleader under Federal Rule 14(a) and joinder of a necessary party under Federal Rule 19(a)(1)(B)(ii).

> Interpleader flourished as an equitable remedy to protect a stakeholder from having to defend against multiple suits and from the risk of multiple liability or inconsistent obligations when several claimants assert rights to a single stake. Thus, a many-sided dispute can be resolved economically and expeditiously in a single proceeding, and the stakeholder can be relieved from

> the obligation of determining who has the rightful claim to the money or property. In addition, the stakeholder avoids possible multiple liability resulting from inconsistent judgments for different claimants in different suits. Even if multiple liability is unlikely, both the stakeholder and the judicial system avoid the expense and delay of multiple litigation. Conflicting claimants to the stake also may benefit from interpleader, since all conflicting claims are resolved in a single action.

4 Moore's Federal Practice § 22.02[1].

Interpleader litigation proceeds in two stages. First, the stakeholder files the action and joins the claimants. The only issue facing the court at this point is whether interpleader is proper. If so, the stakeholder usually deposits the res with the court and the case then proceeds to the second stage, in which the claimants litigate the ownership of the res. If the case is one of "true" interpleader, the stakeholder does not participate in the second stage. If it is "in the nature of interpleader," the stakeholder does participate as a claimant.

Although most courts regard interpleader as an equitable proceeding, it was first used in the common law courts and "crossed over" into equity centuries ago in England. See generally Geoffrey Hazard & Myron Moskovitz, *An Historical and Critical Analysis of Interpleader*, 52 Cal. L. Rev. 706 (1964). The characterization remains important because it affects the availability of a jury trial. As we saw in Chapter 9, the Seventh Amendment guarantees a jury in actions at law, but not in suits at equity. What do we do in interpleader, which has a history of both? The answer depends upon the stage of the interpleader proceeding. It is clear that there is no right to a jury trial in the first stage. See, e.g., Odum v. Penn Mutual Life Ins. Co., 288 F.2d 744 (5th Cir. 1961). In the second stage however, most courts recognize a right to jury trial under a typical Seventh Amendment analysis.

Because interpleader involves claims to the ownership of a res, courts could have treated it as quasi-in-rem for purposes of personal jurisdiction. Under that view, as we saw in Chapter 2, a court's jurisdiction over the stake would give it authority to determine the relative claimants' interests to the res. In New York Life Ins. Co. v. Dunlevy, 241 U.S. 518 (1916), however, the Supreme Court did not adopt such an approach. Instead, it held that an interpleader court must have in personam jurisdiction over the claimants. *Dunlevy* thus imposed a substantial limitation on the usefulness of interpleader.

In *Dunlevy*, New York Life held an insurance policy having a surrender value of approximately $2,500. The insured, Joseph Gould, claimed that it was his. His daughter, Effie Dunlevy, claimed that it was hers because Joseph had assigned the proceeds to her. In addition, a Pittsburgh department store claimed it (or at least a portion thereof) to satisfy a judgment it had recovered against Effie. New York Life instituted interpleader in a state court in Pittsburgh. Although that court lacked in personam jurisdiction over Effie (who had moved to California), it held that the fund belonged to Joseph. Effie then sued New York Life in California, asserting that it had wrongfully paid the proceeds to Joseph and seeking $2,500. The lower courts held in Effie's favor.

The Supreme Court affirmed, holding that the Pittsburgh interpleader proceeding did not bind Effie, because that court lacked in personam jurisdiction over her. "The result, of course, was that the insurance company had to pay the policy amount twice. In other words, it suffered exactly the kind of harm—double liability—that interpleader is intended to avoid." FREER, CIVIL PROCEDURE 712.

In reaction to *Dunlevy*, Congress passed the Federal Interpleader Act in 1917. In its present form, the Act is codified at 28 U.S.C. §§ 1335, 1397, and 2361. Of these provisions, § 1335 is an express grant of federal subject matter jurisdiction. A proceeding under the Federal Interpleader Act is usually called *statutory interpleader*.

In addition to (or in lieu of) statutory interpleader, a stakeholder can rely on any of the regular bases of federal subject matter jurisdiction discussed in Chapter 4 and join conflicting claimants under Federal Rule 22. Commonly, the stakeholder using Rule 22 will proceed under diversity of citizenship jurisdiction via 28 U.S.C. § 1332(a)(1), establishing that she is of diverse citizenship from all claimants and that the amount in controversy exceeds $75,000. A proceeding under Rule 22 is usually called *rule interpleader*.

2. The Two Types of Interpleader in Federal Court

Thus, in federal court, there are two mechanisms for invoking interpleader. Review and compare the provisions for "statutory interpleader" (28 U.S.C. §§ 1335, 1397, and 2361) and "rule interpleader" (Rule 22) before considering this case.

Interpleader is a strange kind of claim. The stakeholder as plaintiff sues claimants to force them to assert their claims *against* the stakeholder. In other words, the stakeholder sues to force others to sue her! Why should she do this? Again, to realize the benefits of efficiency and to avoid the threat of inconsistent rulings.

For example, recall the *Haas* case, which we saw at Chapter 12, Section F.2.a. There, Haas sued the Bank to force it to issue stock to him. Glueck, a nonparty to the case, also claimed the stock. The Bank moved to dismiss for failure to join an indispensable party, because Glueck's interest subjected the Bank to the possibility of inconsistent obligations—one if Haas won, another if Glueck sued the Bank and won. Instead, the Bank might have used interpleader to force the two claimants (Haas and Glueck) into a single proceeding to determine ownership of the stock.

Pan American Fire & Casualty Co. v. Revere

188 F. Supp. 474 (E.D. La. 1960)

WRIGHT, DISTRICT JUDGE.

On February 3, 1960, a tragic highway accident occurred near Covington, Louisiana. A large tractor and trailer collided head-on with a bus carrying school children. The bus driver and three of the children were killed and 23 others were injured, some very seriously. A few moments later, compounding the disaster, another collision occurred between two cars following the bus. Having stopped in time to avoid ramming the disabled bus obstructing the highway, the first of the following vehicles was struck from the rear by the other, and John Wells, a passenger in the lead car, was injured.

Alleging that three suits against it have already been filed and that numerous other claims have been made, the tractor's liability insurer has instituted this interpleader action, citing all potential claimants. It asks that they be enjoined from initiating legal proceedings elsewhere or further prosecuting the actions already filed and that they be directed to assert their claims in the present suit. Plaintiff has deposited a bond in the full amount of its policy limits, $100,000, and avers that "it has no interest" in these insurance proceeds, being merely "a disinterested stakeholder." On the other hand, the Company denies liability toward any and all claimants. This apparently contradictory position is explained by the statement of its counsel, incorporated in the record as an amendment to the complaint, that plaintiff "has no further claim" on the sum deposited with the court, but cannot technically admit "liability" since that would amount to a concession that its assured was negligent and expose him to a deficiency judgment. [This refers to the possibility that the insured would be personally liable for claims that exceed the amount of his insurance.]

The only question presented at this stage of the proceeding is whether, under the circumstances outlined, the remedy of interpleader is available to the insurer. * * *

1. *Jurisdiction.* * * * Plaintiff here invokes both the Interpleader Act and Rule 22 of the Federal Rules of Civil Procedure and alleges diversity of citizenship as a basis for federal jurisdiction.

Considering that four deaths and many serious injuries are involved and that the fund to be distributed is $100,000, the usual jurisdictional amount requirement for diversity suits applicable to an action under the Rule is clearly satisfied. A fortiori, the $500 amount stipulated in the Act is present.

* * * [S]ufficient diversity exists in this instance for an action under either provision. Plaintiff is a citizen of Texas with its principal place of business in that state, while one defendant, Wells, is a citizen of Wisconsin and all the others are Louisiana residents [sic — the court means "citizens"]. Thus, the normal requirement of complete diversity between plaintiff on the one hand and defendants on the other is satisfied. This is viewed as sufficient to support jurisdiction for interpleader under Rule 22. As for the Act, the only requirement, at least for true interpleader, is diversity between some of the defendant claimants, the citizenship of the plaintiff stakeholder being immaterial. The joinder of the Wisconsin resident [sic] together with the Louisiana claimants satisfies this condition. And even if [this] rule * * * does not apply here on the ground that this is not a strict interpleader but rather an action "in the nature of interpleader" in which the plaintiff's citizenship is relevant, sufficient diversity exists since there is both "normal" diversity between the plaintiff and all defendants under § 1332 and "interpleader diversity" between at least two co-claimants.

4. *Exposure to Multiple Liability.* Though the Interpleader Act makes no such requirement, Rule 22 apparently permits interpleader only if the claims "are such that

the plaintiff is or may be exposed to double or multiple liability." In theory at least, this is not necessarily the same thing as exposure to double or multiple vexation on a single obligation. There may be situations in which the debtor, though harassed by many suits on account of one transaction, is never in danger of being compelled to pay the same debt twice. Indeed, here, the argument is advanced that because it has fixed the limits of its liability in its policy, the insurer is not exposed to multiple liability no matter how many claims are filed, and, therefore, is not entitled to maintain interpleader, at least under the Rule.

* * * The key to the clause requiring exposure to "double or multiple liability" is in the words "may be." The danger need not be immediate; any possibility of having to pay more than is justly due, no matter how improbable or remote, will suffice. At least, it is settled that an insurer with limited contractual liability who faces claims in excess of his policy limits is "exposed" within the intendment of Rule 22, and we need go no further to find the requirement satisfied here.

7. *Unliquidated Tort Claims as Justifying Interpleader.* Over and above the technical obligations already disposed of, the argument is advanced that interpleader is not an appropriate method of adjudicating unliquidated tort claims. Such a bald proposition might be rejected summarily were it not for the startling fact that there appears to be no precedent in the federal courts for granting interpleader in the present situation. The matter must be examined closely.

At the outset, it seems clear that interpleader will lie when there are several tort claimants who have obtained judgments which aggregate more than the amount of the policy. Indeed, in that case it can make no difference whether the claims originated in tort or contract. Moreover, it is settled that interpleader is available to an insurer whose policy is insufficient to satisfy contract claims, though they have not been reduced to judgment. Why, then, should the remedy be denied to a blameless insurer faced with excessive tort claims? Three reasons have been suggested: (1) As to quantum, at least, tort claims are more conjectural than contract claims; (2) since it is not directly liable to the claimants, the insurer's exposure as to tort claims is "remote" until they have been reduced to judgment; and (3) tort claims "are peculiarly appropriate for jury trial," which would have to be denied under the equitable practice of interpleader.

The effect of the first objection is only this: that it is more difficult in the case of tort claims to determine whether the aggregate will exceed the policy limits so as to render the claimants "adverse" and expose the insurer to "multiple liability." It may be that there are few cases in which this result can be reasonably anticipated, but, clearly, this is one of them.

The second objection * * * is no better. Indeed, under the "may be exposed" clause of Rule 22 and the "may claim" clause of the Interpleader Act, it would not seem to matter how remote the danger might be. But, in any event, prematurity is no defense under the peculiar Louisiana law which allows a direct action against the automobile liability insurer.

9. *Enjoining of Other Proceedings.* Usually interpleader will not be really effective unless all claimants are brought before the same court in one proceeding and restricted to that single forum in the assertion of their claims. To accomplish that end, absent voluntary self-restraint on the part of all interested parties, it is of course essential that the interpleader court enjoin the institution or prosecution of other suits on the same subject matter elsewhere. Immediately, the question arises whether Section 2283 of Title 28 of the Code presents an obstacle to enjoining state court proceedings.

* * * [T]hat section prohibits a federal court from interfering with a pending state court action except in three situations: (1) Where such a course is "expressly authorized by Act of Congress"; (2) where the issuance of an injunction by the federal court is "necessary in aid of its jurisdiction"; and (3) where the court's action is required "to protect or effectuate its judgments." Clearly, the first exception is applicable to a suit brought under the Interpleader Act since that statute expressly empowers the court to enjoin the claimants "from instituting or prosecuting any proceeding in any State or United States court affecting the property, instrument or obligation involved in the interpleader action * * *." But the exception does not apply to an action under Rule 22, for the quoted provision authorizing stay orders is restricted to statutory interpleader. If state court proceedings can be enjoined when interpleader is brought under the Rule it must be by virtue of the second exception in Section 2283.

The question whether the court entertaining a non-statutory interpleader suit may enjoin state court proceedings on the same issues on the theory that it is "necessary in aid of its jurisdiction" is not free from doubt. * * * [E]very indication is that, regardless of the Interpleader Act, the power of a federal court to enjoin pending state court proceedings in a case like this one will be sustained. Certainly the result is desirable, if not indispensable. If the court had no power to enjoin concurrent state court proceedings, the grant of interpleader would often create more problems than it solved.

10. *Venue and Service of Process.* It has been demonstrated thus far that, except as to strictly jurisdictional matters, the requirements for interpleader under Rule 22 and under the Interpleader Act are identical, and that the present action could be maintained under either provision. But there are two procedural limitations on actions under the Rule which become important whenever the claimants are not all within the territorial jurisdiction of the district court. The first is that the only proper venue for the suit when the defendants do not all reside in the same state is the residence of the plaintiff [this was true at the time this case was decided; the current version of § 1391 does not permit venue to be laid where the plaintiff resides]; the second, that process cannot run beyond the boundaries of the state in which the court sits. These restrictions are of course waivable, but if objection is raised by the affected defendant, they usually form an absolute bar to the action. Thus, here, if Rule 22 alone were applicable, absent a waiver of venue by Wells, the suit would have to be instituted at the plaintiff's domicile in Texas, and none of the defendants could be validly served unless they were found in that state.

But the situation is different when jurisdiction exists under the statute, for the Interpleader Act specially provides that the action may be commenced in any district where one defendant resides and that process will run throughout the United States. Unfortunately, these exceptional rules apply only to statutory interpleader. The present suit, then, is maintainable only under the Interpleader Act unless the Wisconsin defendant waives venue and voluntarily appears or is found in Louisiana.

11. *Conclusion.* Although, because of the venue and service problems just recited, Rule 22 is not available, the court clearly has jurisdiction of the action under the Interpleader Act. Accordingly, the prayer for interpleader will be granted, without, however, discharging the plaintiff who is contractually bound to resist the demands. Injunctions will issue restraining all parties from further prosecuting any pending suits against plaintiff or its assured on account of the accident described, or from instituting like proceedings before this or any other court. All defendants will be required to enter their claims by way of answer in this action within thirty days from notice of this judgment. Thereafter, upon timely demand by any one of the parties, the court will order a joint jury trial of all the claims upon the issues of liability and damages. In the event the aggregate of the verdicts should exceed the amount of plaintiff's liability, the court reserves unto itself the task of apportioning the insurance proceeds in such manner as it deems just.

The motion to dismiss will be denied.

Notes and Questions

1. Note the two important differences for invoking federal jurisdiction under statutory interpleader and under rule interpleader:

(a) Because rule interpleader generally invokes federal jurisdiction through diversity of citizenship under 28 U.S.C. § 1332(a)(1), it must comport with the complete diversity requirement of *Strawbridge v. Curtiss*, 7 U.S. 267 (1806), in Chapter 4, supra. Statutory interpleader, on the other hand, invokes federal jurisdiction under § 1335, which repeals *Strawbridge* in such cases, allowing jurisdiction based upon "minimal" diversity. Exactly what language of § 1335 does so?

(b) In addition, rule and statutory interpleader focus on different litigants for determining whether there is diversity of citizenship. Under Rule 22, who has to be of diverse citizenship from whom? Under the statute, who has to be of diverse citizenship from whom?

2. Is the provision for statutory interpleader jurisdiction based upon "minimal" diversity constitutional? The answer depends upon whether the complete diversity rule of *Strawbridge* was based upon the diversity statute or Article III. Most observers felt that Chief Justice John Marshall engaged only in statutory, not constitutional, interpretation in *Strawbridge.* In 1967, the Supreme Court made this clear, holding that the Constitution permits jurisdiction based upon minimal diversity of citizenship, and therefore statutory interpleader is constitutional. That case, State Farm Fire &

Cas. Co. v. Tashire, 386 U.S. 523 (1967), is important for other points as well, as we will see below.

3. Based upon the differences in subject matter jurisdiction, assess which kind of interpleader, if either, could be invoked in the following:

(a) Stakeholder is an insurance company incorporated in Delaware with its principal place of business in Connecticut. It issued a $1,000,000 life insurance policy insuring Anna, a citizen of New York. After Anna died, claimants to the policy fund are Anna's estate, Betty (a citizen of Delaware), and Claudia (a citizen of Arizona). (Remember, as we saw in Chapter 4, under § 1332(c)(2), the citizenship of the representative of Anna's estate will be deemed to be the same as Anna's; so her estate, as a claimant, is treated as a citizen of New York.)

(b) Would the supplemental jurisdiction statute, 28 U.S.C. § 1367, permit the case in (a) to proceed under rule interpleader?

(c) Same facts as in (a) except that Anna was a citizen of Nevada at the time she died, and Betty and Claudia are citizens of Nevada.

(d) Same facts as in (c), except Stakeholder contended that it was entitled to keep the funds because Anna breached the insurance contract. Can you fashion an argument that statutory interpleader should be available?

(e) Same facts as in (c) except the insurance policy is for $50,000. Why can neither rule nor statutory interpleader be used here?

4. As *Pan American* also makes clear, service of process rules differ between rule and statutory interpleader. Again, because rule interpleader is simply a diversity of citizenship case, the standard rules we addressed in Chapter 3 apply, including the territorial limitations imposed by Federal Rule 4. Under statutory interpleader, though, a district court may issue process for service in "the respective districts where the claimants reside or may be found." 28 U.S.C. § 2361. Thus, the court can exercise nationwide service of process in statutory interpleader.

Suppose, for example, that Stakeholder institutes a statutory interpleader proceeding in federal district court in Maine. One of the claimants to be joined is a citizen of Hawaii, who has never left that state. Because statutory interpleader allows nationwide service of process, the district court in Maine can exercise personal jurisdiction over the Hawaiian. This is so even though that claimant has no contacts with Maine (let alone minimum contacts under *International Shoe*). How, then, can the provision for nationwide service of process be constitutional? (Notice what the "sovereign" is in litigation in federal court. Would the Hawaiian claimant have purposeful contacts with that sovereign?) See Chapter 2, Section B.3 ("Personal Jurisdiction in Federal Court").

5. Compare the two types of interpleader in these additional ways:

(a) *Amount in controversy.* Under either Rule 22 or the interpleader statute, "[t]he total amount to be distributed is the amount in controversy, and supports jurisdiction though individual claims may be for less than this amount." Wright & Kane, Federal Courts 536.

(b) *Venue.* Suppose Stakeholder wants to interplead two claimants, one of whom resides in the Southern District of Florida and the other in the Northern District of Georgia. The venue provision for statutory interpleader, § 1397, permits venue in a district in which "any claimant resides." Thus, Stakeholder could proceed against both in either the Southern District of Florida or the Northern District of Georgia. In contrast, a general venue provision, § 1391(b)(1), which we studied in Chapter 5, permits venue only in a district in which all defendants reside (unless all defendants reside in the same state). On the facts of our hypothetical here, that provision cannot be met, because the defendants reside in different states. By its terms, § 1397 does not apply to rule interpleader cases. What about the converse situation — does § 1391 apply in statutory interpleader cases? Court have concluded that it does not, because that section provides for venue "except as otherwise provided by law." Because § 1397 has "otherwise provided" for statutory interpleader, § 1391 does not apply. See, e.g., Carolina Cas. Ins. Co. v. Mares, 826 F. Supp. 149, 152 (E.D. Va. 1993). In view of the liberality of § 1397, though, it seems unlikely that most stakeholders in statutory interpleader would care about trying to invoke § 1391(b)(1).

On the other hand, § 1391(b)(2) provides a stakeholder with an especially liberal venue choice, at least in rule interpleader. That section, as we saw in Chapter 5, permits venue where a "substantial part" of the claim arose. Unfortunately, there is little meaningful guidance on the question of where an interpleader claim arises. But note the rest of § 1391(b)(2): It permits venue in any district where "a substantial part of property that is the subject of the action is situated." This provision "potentially allows the stakeholder [in rule interpleader] to control venue by moving the stake to the forum in which it wishes to litigate." 7 Wright & Miller, Federal Practice And Procedure § 1712 at 612. In view of the requirement that claimants be subject to personal jurisdiction, does the manipulability of venue under this provision create a serious concern?

(c) *Deposit of the res.* Is it required? If not, does the court have discretion to order it? Why might a stakeholder prefer not to deposit the res?

6. Consider how much less useful interpleader would be if the interpleader court could not enjoin claimants and potential claimants from litigating their claims in other proceedings. Statutory interpleader, of course, expressly provides for such injunctions against parties to state or federal court proceedings. 28 U.S.C. § 2361. Rule interpleader has no similar provision. Nonetheless, most courts agree with the court's assessment in *Pan American*, and conclude that such an injunction is "necessary in aid of [the] jurisdiction" of the interpleader court. Thus, it satisfies an exception to the anti-injunction statute, 28 U.S.C. § 2283. See, e.g., General Railway Signal Co. v. Corcoran, 921 F.2d 700 (7th Cir. 1991). In addition, after conclusion of the federal action, a permanent injunction would be proper "to protect or effectuate [the] judgments" of the interpleader court, thereby satisfying another exception to § 2283.

7. What if Stakeholder does not sue first? For example, assume Stakeholder is in possession of a diamond watch that she found in her house and claims it under a

finder's statute. Claimant-1 is the previous owner of the house, and argues that the watch is hers because she bought it and inadvertently left it in the house when she moved. Claimant-2 is a former houseguest of Stakeholder, who claims that she left the watch in the house. Claimant-3 is an insurance company, which claims that it has reimbursed Claimant-1 for the loss of the watch, and thus that it is entitled to it.

Instead of Stakeholder's acting first, however, suppose Claimant-1 sues Stakeholder, naming no other parties, and seeking return of the watch. Can Stakeholder force the joinder of Claimants 2 and 3 through interpleader in the pending case? In other words, can a defendant invoke interpleader? See Rule 22(a)(2).

Rule 22 expressly provides that she can. The statute is silent on the point. Nonetheless, Federal Rule 13(h), which applies in statutory interpleader as well as any other case in federal court, allows the addition of parties to a counterclaim if, inter alia, the persons being joined would satisfy Rule 19. See, e.g., Bauer v. Uniroyal Tire Co., 630 F.2d 1287 (8th Cir. 1980); Dove v. Massachusetts Mut. Life Ins. Co., 509 F. Supp. 248 (S.D. Ga. 1981). Why, by definition, do absentee claimants in the interpleader situation satisfy Rule 19? More specifically, why are they always going to satisfy Rule 19(a)(1)(B)(ii)? See generally 4 MOORE'S FEDERAL PRACTICE § 22.02[4].

Thus, in either statutory or rule interpleader, the defendant-stakeholder could use Rule 13(h) to join the claimants to an interpleader proceeding. But she may have another option as well. Because the nonjoinder of the claimants threatens her with multiple or inconsistent obligations, she could seek compulsory joinder under Rule 19(a)(1)(B)(ii). This overlap of joinder rules is not surprising; again, Rule 19(a)(1)(B)(ii) and interpleader are different devices for raising the same concerns. That does not mean, of course, that they are always available in all cases. With its provision for jurisdiction based upon minimal diversity among claimants, statutory interpleader may be available in cases in which Rule 19 would not work because joinder would destroy diversity.

Suppose, for example, that Plaintiff is a citizen of New York and Defendant (the Stakeholder) is a citizen of Maryland. Absentee claimants are citizens of New York, Maryland, and California. Defendant could interplead the absentees under statutory interpleader, because at least one claimant is of diverse citizenship from one other. She could not join the absentees under Rule 19, however, because the Maryland claimant's joinder would put Maryland citizens on both sides of the case, thereby preventing diversity of citizenship jurisdiction. This possibility raises an interesting litigation tactic for Defendant in these cases. If she likes the forum in which she is sued, she can use interpleader to have all claims resolved in a single proceeding there. If she does not like the forum, however, she might seek dismissal under Rule 12(b)(7) by claiming that the absentee-claimants are indispensable.

8. Historically, equity courts imposed four significant limitations on interpleader. First, they required that the claimants vie for the same debt. Second, the claims had to share a common origin. Third, the stakeholder could not be interested, that is, she could not claim ownership of the stake. And fourth, the stakeholder could owe no independent liability to any of the claimants. See 4 MOORE'S FEDERAL PRACTICE § 22.07.

Rule 22 and statutory interpleader expressly abolish the first three of these equitable requirements, albeit with language of varying clarity. For example, regarding the third requirement, Rule 22 clearly provides that there is no problem if the stakeholder avers that she is not liable to any claimant. The statute does the same thing by providing for proceedings "in the nature of interpleader." 28 U.S.C. § 1335(a). On the other hand, neither the rule nor the statute expressly addresses the fourth requirement. Although some earlier opinions disagree, most courts conclude that this equity limitation has been abolished as well. See, e.g., Companion Life Ins. Co. v. Schaffer, 442 F. Supp. 826 (S.D.N.Y. 1977). Thus, interpleader can proceed even if the stakeholder is independently liable to one of the claimants.

Of course, the states are free to determine their own rules for interpleader, or whether to permit the procedure at all. Thus, the traditional equitable limitations on interpleader may still exist in some states. See, e.g., Midland National Life Ins. Co. v. Emerson, 174 S.E.2d 211 (Ga. App. 1970) (interested stakeholder cannot proceed with equitable interpleader; legislation permits "interpleader at law" rejecting this rule).

3. The Limits of Interpleader to Avoid Duplicative Litigation

State Farm Fire & Casualty Co. v. Tashire

386 U.S. 523, 87 S. Ct. 1199, 18 L. Ed. 2d 270 (1967)

Mr. Justice Fortas delivered the opinion of the Court.

Early one September morning in 1964, a Greyhound bus proceeding northward through Shasta County, California, collided with a southbound pickup truck. Two of the passengers aboard the bus were killed. Thirty-three others were injured, as were the bus driver, the driver of the truck and its lone passenger. One of the dead and 10 of the injured passengers were Canadians; the rest of the individuals involved were citizens of five American States. The ensuing litigation led to the present case, which raises important questions concerning administration of the interpleader remedy in the federal courts.

The litigation began when four of the injured passengers filed suit in California state courts, seeking damages in excess of $1,000,000. Named as defendants were Greyhound Lines, Inc., a California corporation; Theron Nauta, the bus driver; Ellis Clark, who drove the truck; and Kenneth Glasgow, the passenger in the truck who was apparently its owner as well. Each of the individual defendants was a citizen and resident of Oregon. Before these cases could come to trial and before other suits were filed in California or elsewhere, petitioner State Farm Fire & Casualty Company, an Illinois corporation, brought this action in the nature of interpleader in the United States District Court for the District of Oregon.

In its complaint State Farm asserted that at the time of the Shasta County collision it had in force an insurance policy with respect to Ellis Clark, driver of the truck, providing for bodily injury liability up to $10,000 per person and $20,000 per occurrence and for legal representation of Clark in actions covered by the policy. It asserted that actions already filed in California and others which it anticipated would be filed far exceeded in aggregate damages sought the amount of its maximum liability under the policy. Accordingly, it paid into court the sum of $20,000 and asked the court (1) to require all claimants to establish their claims against Clark and his insurer in this single proceeding and in no other, and (2) to discharge State Farm from all further obligations under its policy—including its duty to defend Clark in lawsuits arising from the accident. Alternatively, State Farm expressed its conviction that the policy issued to Clark excluded from coverage accidents resulting from his operation of a truck which belonged to another and was being used in the business of another. The complaint, therefore, requested that the court decree that the insurer owed no duty to Clark and was not liable on the policy, and it asked the court to refund the $20,000 deposit.

Joined as defendants were Clark, Glasgow, Nauta, Greyhound Lines, and each of the prospective claimants. Jurisdiction was predicated upon 28 U.S.C. § 1335, the federal interpleader statute, and upon general diversity of citizenship, there being diversity between two or more of the claimants to the fund and between State Farm and all of the named defendants. [At the time, the diversity of citizenship statute required an amount in controversy in excess of only $10,000, which was met by deposit of the $20,000 fund.]

An order issued, requiring the defendants to show cause why they should not be restrained from filing or prosecuting "any proceeding in any state or United States Court affecting the property or obligation involved in this interpleader action, and specifically against the plaintiff and the defendant Ellis D. Clark." Personal service was effected on each of the American defendants, and registered mail was employed to reach the 11 Canadian claimants. Defendants Nauta, Greyhound, and several of the injured passengers responded, contending that the policy did cover this accident and advancing various arguments for the position that interpleader was either impermissible or inappropriate in the present circumstances. Greyhound, however, soon switched sides and moved that the court broaden any injunction to include Nauta and Greyhound among those who could not be sued except within the confines of the interpleader proceeding.

When a temporary injunction along the lines sought by State Farm was issued by the United States District Court for the District of Oregon, the present respondents moved to dismiss the action * * *. After a hearing, the court declined to dissolve the temporary injunction * * *. The injunction was later broadened to include the protection sought by Greyhound, but modified to permit the filing—although not the prosecution—of suits. The injunction, therefore, provided that all suits against Clark, State Farm, Greyhound, and Nauta be prosecuted in the interpleader proceeding.

On * * * appeal, the Court of Appeals for the Ninth Circuit reversed. The court found it unnecessary to reach respondents' contentions relating to service of process and the scope of the injunction, for it concluded that interpleader was not available in the circumstances of this case. It held that in States like Oregon, which do not permit "direct action" suits against insurance companies until judgments are obtained against the insured, the insurance companies may not invoke federal interpleader until the claims against the insured, the alleged tortfeasor, have been reduced to judgment. Until that is done, said the court, claimants with unliquidated tort claims are not "claimants" within the meaning of § 1335, nor are they "persons having claims against the plaintiff" within the meaning of Rule 22 of the Federal Rules of Civil Procedure.[3] In accord with that view, it directed dissolution of the temporary injunction and dismissal of the action. Because the Court of Appeals' decision on this point conflicts with those of other federal courts, and concerns a matter of significance to the administration of federal interpleader, we granted certiorari. Although we reverse the decision of the Court of Appeals upon the jurisdictional question, we direct a substantial modification of the District Court's injunction for reasons which will appear.

I

[Here the Court upheld the constitutionality of the provision of § 1335 for jurisdiction based upon minimal diversity among claimants. We discussed this point in Chapter 4, Section C.3.b, when we noted that the complete diversity rule is not constitutionally mandated.]

II

We do not agree with the Court of Appeals that, in the absence of a state law or contractual provision for "direct action" suits against the insurance company, the company must wait until persons asserting claims against its insured have reduced those claims to judgment before seeking to invoke the benefits of federal interpleader. That may have been a tenable position under the 1926 and 1936 interpleader statutes. These statutes did not carry forward the language in the 1917 Act authorizing interpleader where adverse claimants "may claim" benefits as well as where they "are claiming" them. In 1948, however, in the revision of the Judicial Code, the "may claim" language was restored. Until the decision below, every court confronted by the question has concluded that the 1948 revision removed whatever requirement there might previously have been that the insurance company wait until at least two claimants reduced their claims to judgments. The commentators are in accord.

Considerations of judicial administration demonstrate the soundness of this view which, in any event, seems compelled by the language of the present statute, which is remedial and to be liberally construed. Were an insurance company required to await reduction of claims to judgment, the first claimant to obtain such a judgment

3. We need not pass upon the Court of Appeals' conclusions with respect to the interpretation of interpleader under Rule 22, which provides that "(1) Persons having claims against the plaintiff may be joined as defendants and required to interplead when their claims are such that the plaintiff is or may be exposed to double or multiple liability...." First, as we indicate today, this action was properly brought under § 1335. Second, State Farm did not purport to invoke Rule 22. Third, State Farm could not have invoked it in light of venue and service of process limitations. * * *

or to negotiate a settlement might appropriate all or a disproportionate slice of the fund before his fellow claimants were able to establish their claims. The difficulties such a race to judgment pose for the insurer, and the unfairness which may result to some claimants, were among the principal evils the interpleader device was intended to remedy.

III

The fact that State Farm had properly invoked the interpleader jurisdiction under § 1335 did not, however, entitle it to an order both enjoining prosecution of suits against it outside the confines of the interpleader proceeding and also extending such protection to its insured, the alleged tortfeasor. Still less was Greyhound Lines entitled to have that order expanded so as to protect itself and its driver, also alleged to be tortfeasors, from suits brought by its passengers in various state or federal courts. Here, the scope of the litigation, in terms of parties and claims, was vastly more extensive than the confines of the "fund," the deposited proceeds of the insurance policy. In these circumstances, the mere existence of such a fund cannot, by use of interpleader, be employed to accomplish purposes that exceed the needs of orderly contest with respect to the fund.

There are situations, of a type not present here, where the effect of interpleader is to confine the total litigation to a single forum and proceeding. One such case is where a stakeholder, faced with rival claims to the fund itself, acknowledges — or denies — his liability to one or the other of the claimants. In this situation, the fund itself is the target of the claimants. It marks the outer limits of the controversy. It is, therefore, reasonable and sensible that interpleader, in discharge of its office to protect the fund, should also protect the stakeholder from vexatious and multiple litigation. In this context, the suits sought to be enjoined are squarely within the language of 28 U.S.C. § 2361 * * *.

But the present case is another matter. Here, an accident has happened. Thirty-five passengers or their representatives have claims which they wish to press against a variety of defendants: the bus company, its driver, the owner of the truck, and the truck driver. The circumstance that one of the prospective defendants happens to have an insurance policy is a fortuitous event which should not of itself shape the nature of the ensuing litigation. For example, a resident of California, injured in California aboard a bus owned by a California corporation should not be forced to sue the corporation anywhere but in California simply because another prospective defendant carried an insurance policy. And an insurance company whose maximum interest in the case cannot exceed $20,000 and who in fact asserts that it has no interest at all, should not be allowed to determine that dozens of tort plaintiffs must be compelled to press their claims — even those claims which are not against the insured and which in no event could be satisfied out of the meager insurance fund — in a single forum of the insurance company's choosing. There is nothing in the statutory scheme, and very little in the judicial and academic commentary upon that scheme, which requires that the tail be allowed to wag the dog in this fashion.

State Farm's interest in this case, which is the fulcrum of the interpleader procedure, is confined to its $20,000 fund. That interest receives full vindication when the court restrains claimants from seeking to enforce against the insurance company any judgment obtained against its insured, except in the interpleader proceeding itself. To the extent that the District Court sought to control claimants' lawsuits against the insured and other alleged tortfeasors, it exceeded the powers granted to it by the statutory scheme.

We recognize, of course, that our view of interpleader means that it cannot be used to solve all the vexing problems of multiparty litigation arising out of a mass tort. But interpleader was never intended to perform such a function, to be an all-purpose "bill of peace." Had it been so intended, careful provision would necessarily have been made to insure that a party with little or no interest in the outcome of a complex controversy should not strip truly interested parties of substantial rights — such as the right to choose the forum in which to establish their claims, subject to generally applicable rules of jurisdiction, venue, service of process, removal, and change of venue. None of the legislative and academic sponsors of a modern federal interpleader device viewed their accomplishment as a "bill of peace," capable of sweeping dozens of lawsuits out of the various state and federal courts in which they were brought and into a single interpleader proceeding. And only in two reported instances has a federal interpleader court sought to control the underlying litigation against alleged tortfeasors as opposed to the allocation of a fund among successful tort plaintiffs. See Commercial Union Insurance Co. of New York v. Adams, 231 F. Supp. 860 (S.D. Ind. 1964) (where there was virtually no objection and where all of the basic tort suits would in any event have been prosecuted in the forum state), and Pan American Fire & Casualty Co. v. Revere, 188 F. Supp. 474 (E.D. La. 1960). Another district court, on the other hand, has recently held that it lacked statutory authority to enjoin suits against the alleged tortfeasor as opposed to proceedings against the fund itself. Travelers Indemnity Co. v. Greyhound Lines, Inc., 260 F. Supp. 530 (W.D. La. 1966).

In light of the evidence that federal interpleader was not intended to serve the function of a "bill of peace" in the context of multiparty litigation arising out of a mass tort, of the anomalous power which such a construction of the statute would give the stakeholder, and of the thrust of the statute and the purpose it was intended to serve, we hold that the interpleader statute did not authorize the injunction entered in the present case. Upon remand, the injunction is to be modified consistently with this opinion.

IV

The judgment of the Court of Appeals is reversed, and the case is remanded to the United States District Court for proceedings consistent with this opinion.

It is so ordered.

Notes and Questions

1. In *Pan American*, the court thought it "startling" that there "appears to be no precedent in the federal courts for granting interpleader" for unliquidated tort claims.

In Part III of *Tashire*, Justice Fortas mentions *Pan American* critically. Is there a distinction between the two cases that would support the results in each? Or does *Tashire* mean that *Pan American* was wrongly decided?

2. The Court in *Tashire* certainly would not quarrel with Judge Wright's decision in *Pan American* that claims need not be reduced to judgment before interpleader is appropriate. Indeed, *Tashire* makes this clear, even in the absence of a direct action suit, at least in statutory interpleader. Should the same be true under rule interpleader? Why did Judge Wright think so?

3. Justice Fortas explained that interpleader was not intended to be a "'bill of peace,' capable of sweeping dozens of lawsuits out of the various state and federal courts in which they were brought and into a single interpleader proceeding." If interpleader will not force all related claims into a single litigation, what device(s) will? If none comes to mind, should there be any? What policies would favor such a device? What policies would be harmed by such a device?

As to the latter question, consider Justice Fortas' statement that had interpleader "been so intended, careful provision would necessarily have been made to insure that a party with little or no interest in the outcome of a complex controversy should not strip truly interested parties of substantial rights—such as the right to choose the forum in which to establish their claims, subject to generally applicable rules of jurisdiction, venue, service of process, removal, and change of venue." Why is there a "right" to sue in a particular forum? Is the "right" violated by removal of a case from state to federal court? By transfer under 28 U.S.C. § 1404?

4. The Indianapolis Colts franchise of the National Football League was for many years based in Baltimore. The owner of the Colts moved the team to Indianapolis in 1984, and entered a stadium lease with the appropriate authorities in that city. Baltimore, meanwhile, tried to keep the team by having the state legislature pass a statute seizing the team through the power of eminent domain. The Colts brought a statutory interpleader proceeding in federal court in Indiana, joining Indianapolis and Baltimore as claimants. The Seventh Circuit rejected the use of interpleader, holding that the two cities were not claiming the same stake. While Baltimore claimed ownership of the franchise, Indianapolis did not; it merely wanted to enforce its lease with the franchise. The court reasoned:

> A successful eminent domain action obviously will defeat [Indianapolis'] interests in keeping the Colts in Indianapolis. Nevertheless, interpleader is not designed to aid every plaintiff confronted by one claim which, if successful, would defeat a second claim because the plaintiff has lost the ability to pay damages. Such an interpretation would twist interpleader into protection for defendants from losing the opportunity to recover damages because the plaintiff's resources already have been depleted. Interpleader is warranted only to protect the plaintiff-stakeholder from conflicting liability to the stake.

Indianapolis Colts v. Baltimore, 741 F.2d 954, 956 (7th Cir. 1984).

C. The Class Action

1. Background

In class action litigation, one or more class representatives (or "named representatives") are formally joined as parties in the case. The members of the group they represent are not joined, and thus are not technically considered parties, but are bound by the outcome of the litigation. Although most class action litigation involves claims asserted by a plaintiff class, the procedural rules generally permit defendant classes as well.

Like so many other procedural devices, the modern class action finds its roots in English equity practice. The law courts of England permitted multiparty litigation based only upon the legal relationship between the parties, such as joint obligors or obligees. Equity developed a broader practice, based not upon legal relationships, but upon the efficiency of deciding transactionally related issues, even when they involved multiple parties. In *Tashire*, recall that Justice Fortas referred to the bill of peace. This was a device developed at equity to permit resolution of disputes between all interested parties. It was limited, however, by the insistence that all interested persons be joined as parties. Knight v. Knight, 24 Eng. Rep. 1088 (Ch. 1734). See generally Zecchariah Chafee, Jr., *Bills of Peace with Multiple Parties*, 45 Harv. L. Rev. 1297 (1932).

But what if some interested person could not be joined? Or what if there were so many interested persons that joinder in any traditional sense would not be workable? In such situations, equity developed the notion that parties to litigation might represent nonparties with whom they had a common interest so that the nonparties would be bound by the final decree. The modern class action developed from this equity practice. For an excellent historical treatment, see Stephen Yeazell, From Medieval Group Litigation To The Modern Class Action (1987).

The notion that one can be bound by litigation to which she is not made a party raises significant constitutional concerns, which we will address below. Before we do, it is important to set the stage for detailed consideration of the class action by noting some fundamental policy issues raised by its use.

2. Policy and Ethical Issues

The class action is controversial. The fact that it can bind numerous potential claimants to a single judgment leads some commentators to praise its efficiency. Instead of hundreds of potential cases, the judicial system can handle a large dispute with a single proceeding. Critics note, however, that the single class action is potentially an enormous burden on the court in which it proceeds. Moreover, some note that the class action might actually create litigation that otherwise would not exist.

Consider, for example, a class action on behalf of 1,000,000 consumers allegedly overcharged illegally by a retailer. Assume that the illegal act resulted in an average overcharge of $10.00 per consumer. Without the class action, there will likely be no litigation in this scenario. No consumer will file suit to recover $10.00, even in a small claims court. It is simply not worth the effort. Thus, allowing a class action here creates litigation. Is this an appropriate result for an ostensibly procedural rule?

On the other hand, if the consumers cannot aggregate through the class action, the retailer may be able to engage in illegal behavior without civil consequence.* Some commentators argue that such illegal behavior ought to be addressed by the criminal law or through administrative mechanisms. One problem is that criminal proceedings generally do not result in compensation for those harmed. Does the class action properly fill that void? Some observers answer in the affirmative; one cheers the class action as "one of the most socially useful remedies in history." Abraham Pomerantz, *New Developments in Class Actions—Has Their Death Knell Been Sounded?*, 25 Bus. Lawyer 1259, 1259 (1970). The Supreme Court seems to agree.

> The aggregation of individual claims in the context of a classwide suit is an evolutionary response to the existence of injuries unremedied by the regulatory action of government. Where it is not economically feasible to obtain relief within the traditional framework of a multiplicity of small individual suits for damages, aggrieved persons may be without any effective redress unless they may employ the class-action device.

Deposit Guaranty National Bank v. Roper, 445 U.S. 326, 338–39 (1980).

While the class action, like all civil dispute resolution, fills a socially useful role, it must be used with care. It is subject to abuse, and has been abused both by plaintiffs and defendants. Assume, for example, that the class claim against the retailer is very weak on the merits. If the court permits the class action to proceed, the defendant is facing potential aggregated liability of $10,000,000. No matter how good she considers her chances of winning at trial, the defendant may be reluctant to "roll the dice" and proceed in the face of such a huge potential loss. Thus, the incentive to settle the case may become virtually irresistible, even if the defendant has a strong case on the merits. Focusing on this potential to coerce a settlement on claims that otherwise might be defended vigorously, Professor Handler long ago damned the class action as "legalized blackmail." Milton Handler, *The Shift from Substantive to Procedural Innovations in Antitrust Suits*, 71 Colum. L. Rev. 1, 9 (1971).

Now consider the interest of the class member willing to serve as class representative. As we will see, the rules impose various responsibilities on the representative.

---

* Parties to many contracts agree that their disputes will not be litigated, but be subject to arbitration. As we will study in Chapter 15, arbitration is an alternative to litigation in which the parties choose a neutral person to resolve their dispute, with very limited right to appeal. Increasingly, such arbitration clauses are found in consumer contracts. In addition, many such contracts also have a "class action waiver," by which the parties agree that anyone suing under the contract gives up her right to sue with others, either through joinder or assertion of a class action. As a result, many consumers, with small monetary claims (for example, for a defective product) will (1) not be allowed to sue in court and (2) will be required to assert her claim in arbitration alone, with no co-plaintiffs. Because very few people will actually go to the trouble of arbitrating for a small amount of money, the result of such "procedural" contract provisions may be to insulate the defendant from accountability. The Court has been remarkably receptive to this practice. See, e.g., American Express Co. v. Italian Colors Restaurant, 133 S. Ct. 2304 (2013).

Generally, there is no financial reward for undertaking these responsibilities. If the class action is successful, then, the representative will recover her costs and her individual damages, or about $10.00 in our hypothetical case. Although courts occasionally reward the representative with a bonus payment, such action is rare. It seems, then, that the representative is often motivated by principle, not economics.

The class lawyer, on the other hand, may be motivated by economics, not principle. If the defendant settles the case for several millions of dollars, the lawyer may be in a position to recover a substantial fee award without having to go to trial. Thus, class action litigation can create serious ethical tension. The lawyer must be careful that her own self-interest does not conflict with the interests of her clients, the representative, and the class itself.

The potential abuse of the class action device is not limited to plaintiffs and their lawyers. In some situations, defendants have actually preferred to litigate against a plaintiff class because they may be able to structure a "sweetheart" settlement that binds all class members and thus prevents them from suing separately. In several noteworthy instances, critics charge, defense and plaintiff counsel have struck settlements that are fairly painless to the defendant, which include a significant payment of fees to the class lawyer, and which, by the binding nature of class actions, insulate the defendant from further suit by class members. See generally Bruce Hay & David Rosenberg, *"Sweetheart" and "Blackmail" Settlements in Class Actions: Reality and Remedy*, 75 Notre Dame L. Rev. 1377 (2000).

Sometimes defendants engage in what is called a "reverse auction," which Judge Posner describes as:

> the practice whereby the defendant in a series of class actions picks the most ineffectual class lawyers to negotiate a settlement in the hope that the district court will approve a weak settlement that will preclude other claims against the defendant. * * * The ineffectual lawyers are happy to sell out a class they anyway can't do much for in exchange for generous attorneys' fees, and the defendants are happy to pay generous attorneys' fees since all they care about is the bottom line — the sum of the settlement and the attorneys' fees — and not the allocation of money between the two categories of expense.

Reynolds v. Beneficial National Bank, 288 F.3d 277, 282 (7th Cir. 2002).

Because of these potential abuses, and the seemingly inherent potential conflicts between counsel and the group, class action litigation rules place increased burdens on the court. They force the court to assume administrative tasks to ensure that the class is being adequately represented by counsel and to approve settlements. Courts generally do not have this policing job in other types of litigation. Thus, class litigation has contributed to a metamorphosis of the judge from umpire to case manager. We will discuss the judge's role in approving voluntary dismissal and settlement in Section 4.e below.

After considering several proposals over several years, Congress passed the Class Action Fairness Act in 2005. It substantially relaxes federal subject matter jurisdiction requirements for some (not by any means all) class actions. CAFA was supported generally by large corporate interests who argued that some state court class action judgments evinced bias against national businesses. In passing CAFA, Congress expressly found that "abuses of the class action device" had adversely affected interstate commerce and often resulted in large counsel fees in cases in which class members received little compensation. In particular, Congress singled out "coupon settlements," in which class members received coupons for discounted products "or other awards of little or no value." Congress further found that the purpose underlying diversity of citizenship jurisdiction was thwarted when class actions of "national importance" were kept out of federal court. We will discuss the jurisdictional relaxation of the Act in Section 5 below.

Interestingly, while antagonism may be increasing toward class actions in the United States, "courts around the world have opened their doors to class actions and group litigation." Deborah Hensler, *The Future of Mass Litigation: Global Class Actions and Third-Party Litigation Funding*, 79 GEO. WASH. L. REV. 306, 307 (2011). For example, in 2013, the European Commission published a recommendation on "collective redress," which invited member countries to adopt aggregate mechanisms of dispute resolution for violations of European Union law. In an effort to curb what the Commission considered excesses of the American system, the recommendation limits use of contingent fees and third-party financing, and requires members to opt into the class (rather than fail to opt out). Though few countries have responded with adoption of new provisions, the topic is being debated. In October 2015, legislation in the United Kingdom introduced a "collective action" for enforcement of antitrust laws, to be resolved in a special tribunal. See http://www.collectiveredress.org/collective-redress/reports/ew/overview.

3. Constitutional Considerations

The utility of the class action comes from its binding effect on class members, even though those members are not joined as parties. In other words, the class action, if done correctly, results in "nonparty preclusion" — people who were not parties to the case are bound by the judgment in that case. The leading case on the constitutional problems with binding nonparties through the class action is the 1940 Supreme Court decision in *Hansberry v. Lee.* Before reading that case, however, we note two important predecessors.

Smith v. Swormstedt, 57 U.S. 288 (1854), involved the split of the Methodist Episcopal Church into southern and northern branches over the issue of slavery. Before the split, the denomination had created the "Book Fund," which totaled about $200,000. After the split, preachers in the northern branch held the property. Six representatives of the preachers in the southern branch sued three representatives of the ministers in the north, seeking their share of the property. Although over 5000 preachers were not joined as parties, the Supreme Court held that they were bound by the outcome. It emphasized that such representation was proper "where the parties interested are numerous, and the suit is for an object common to them all." Id. at 302.

Supreme Tribe of Ben-Hur v. Cauble, 255 U.S. 356 (1921), also involved class members with interests identical to those of their representatives. The class challenged a decision by a fraternal benefits organization to reorganize and reduce benefits for its 70,000 members. Such organizations can provide insurance, pension, and other benefits to members, and were especially important before government programs such as social security. In *Ben-Hur*, non-Indiana members sued the organization, purporting to represent all members; the court entered judgment for the defendant. Thereafter, Indiana members sued, arguing that they were not bound by the judgment in the first case, since they could not have invoked diversity of citizenship against the Indiana organization. The Supreme Court held that all members — including the Hoosiers — were bound by the judgment in the first case.

Thus, in *Smith* and *Ben-Hur*, the representatives and the nonparty class members had identical, nonseparable interests. *Hansberry* involved land allegedly subject to a restrictive covenant. You may study such covenants in your course on property. When effective, they bind landowners in the affected area (usually a subdivision). The covenants are of public record and "run with the land," meaning that they bind all persons who acquire land from the original owner. Such covenants are common today to ensure architectural uniformity in neighborhoods, and work as an adjunct to public zoning rules. Before the Supreme Court declared racially restrictive covenants unconstitutional in Shelley v. Kraemer, 334 U.S. 1 (1948), they were also used to exclude members of particular races from buying or renting in an area.

The litigation in *Hansberry* concerned a racially restrictive covenant in a Chicago neighborhood. The case arose before the Court ruled such restrictions unconstitutional in Shelley v. Kraemer, 334 U.S. 1 (1948). By its terms, this particular covenant was not to take effect until signed by the owners of 95 percent of the frontage in the neighborhood. The Hansberrys, who were black, bought a home in the neighborhood. Other owners then sued in Illinois state court to rescind the sale to the Hansberrys because it violated the restrictive covenant. At trial, the Hansberrys argued that only 54 percent of the owners had actually signed, and that, therefore, the covenant never took effect and could not be enforced.

Although the trial court agreed that fewer than 95 percent of the owners had signed the covenant, it rescinded the sale and ordered the Hansberrys to move out of the neighborhood. According to that court, the Hansberrys were bound by the judgment of an earlier class action case, Burke v. Kleiman, 277 Ill. App. 519 (1934). In that earlier case, some homeowners sued a white owner (Kleiman) who had rented to a black tenant (Hall) in violation of the covenant. The *Burke* court enforced the covenant and voided the lease to Hall. In reaching its conclusion, the court had relied on a stipulation offered by the plaintiffs and accepted by the defendants that 95 percent of the owners had signed the covenant. In the *Hansberry* case, the Illinois Supreme Court affirmed the trial court's conclusion that the judgment in *Burke* bound the persons who sought to sell to the Hansberrys. The United States Supreme Court then reviewed the case.

Hansberry v. Lee

311 U.S. 32, 61 S. Ct. 115, 85 L. Ed. 22 (1940)

Mr. Justice Stone delivered the opinion of the Court.

The question is whether the Supreme Court of Illinois, by its adjudication that petitioners in this case are bound by a judgment rendered in an earlier litigation to which they were not parties, has deprived them of the due process of law guaranteed by the Fourteenth Amendment.

* * * [T]he Supreme Court of Illinois concluded in the present case that *Burke v. Kleiman* was a "class" or "representative" suit, and that in such a suit, "where the remedy is pursued by a plaintiff who has the right to represent the class to which he belongs, other members of the class are bound by the results in the case unless it is reversed or set aside on direct proceedings"; that petitioners in the present suit were members of the class represented by the plaintiffs in the earlier suit and consequently were bound by its decree, which had rendered the issue of performance of the condition precedent to the restrictive agreement res judicata, so far as petitioners are concerned. The court thought that the circumstance that the stipulation in the earlier suit that owners of 95 per cent of the frontage had signed the agreement was contrary to the fact, as found in the present suit, did not militate against this conclusion, since the court in the earlier suit had jurisdiction to determine the fact as between the parties before it, and that its determination, because of the representative character of the suit, even though erroneous, was binding on petitioners until set aside by a direct attack on the first judgment.

State courts are free to attach such descriptive labels to litigations before them as they may choose and to attribute to them such consequences as they think appropriate under state constitutions and laws, subject only to the requirements of the Constitution of the United States. But when the judgment of a state court, ascribing to the judgment of another court the binding force and effect of res judicata, is challenged for want of due process it becomes the duty of this Court to examine the course of procedure in both litigations to ascertain whether the litigant whose rights have thus been adjudicated has been afforded such notice and opportunity to be heard as are requisite to the due process which the Constitution prescribes.

It is a principle of general application in Anglo-American jurisprudence that one is not bound by a judgment in personam in a litigation in which he is not designated as a party or to which he has not been made a party by service of process. Pennoyer v. Neff, 95 U.S. 714 [1878]. A judgment rendered in such circumstances is not entitled to the full faith and credit which the Constitution and statute of the United States prescribe; and judicial action enforcing it against the person or property of the absent party is not that due process which the Fifth and Fourteenth Amendments require.

To these general rules there is a recognized exception that, to an extent not precisely defined by judicial opinion, the judgment in a "class" or "representative" suit, to which some members of the class were parties, may bind members of the class or those represented who are not made parties to it. *Smith v. Swormstead; Supreme Tribe of Ben-Hur v. Cauble.*

The class suit was an invention of equity to enable it to proceed to a decree in suits where the number of those interested in the subject of the litigation is so great that their joinder as parties in conformity to the usual rules of procedure is impracticable. Courts are not infrequently called upon to proceed with causes in which the number of those interested in the litigation is so great as to make difficult or impossible the joinder of all because some are not within the jurisdiction or because their whereabouts is unknown * * *. In such cases where the interests of those not joined are of the same class as the interests of those who are, and where it is considered that the latter fairly represent the former in the prosecution of the litigation of the issues in which all have a common interest, the court will proceed to a decree.

It is evident that the considerations which may induce a court thus to proceed, despite a technical defect of parties, may differ from those which must be taken into account in determining whether the absent parties are bound by the decree or, if it is adjudged that they are, in ascertaining whether such an adjudication satisfies the requirements of due process and of full faith and credit. Nevertheless, there is scope within the framework of the Constitution for holding in appropriate cases that a judgment rendered in a class suit is res judicata as to members of the class who are not formal parties to the suit. * * *

It is familiar doctrine of the federal courts that members of a class not present as parties to the litigation may be bound by the judgment where they are in fact adequately represented by parties who are present, or where they actually participate in the conduct of the litigation in which members of the class are present as parties, or where the interest of the members of the class, some of whom are present as parties, is joint, or where for any other reason the relationship between the parties present and those who are absent is such as legally to entitle the former to stand in judgment for the latter.

In all such cases, so far as it can be said that the members of the class who are present are, by generally recognized rules of law, entitled to stand in judgment for those who are not, we may assume for present purposes that such procedure affords a protection to the parties who are represented, though absent, which would satisfy the requirements of due process and full faith and credit. Nor do we find it necessary for the decision of this case to say that, when the only circumstance defining the class is that the determination of the rights of its members turns upon a single issue of fact or law, a state could not constitutionally adopt a procedure whereby some of the members of the class could stand in judgment for all, provided that the procedure were so devised and applied as to insure that those present are of the same class as those absent and that the litigation is so conducted as to insure the full and fair consideration of the common issue. We decide only that the procedure and the course of litigation sustained here by the plea of res judicata do not satisfy these requirements.

The [racially] restrictive agreement did not purport to create a joint obligation or liability. If valid and effective its promises were the several obligations of the signers and those claiming under them. The promises ran severally to every other signer. It is plain that in such circumstances all those alleged to be bound by the agreement would not constitute a single class in any litigation brought to enforce it. Those who sought to secure its benefits by enforcing it could not be said to be in the same class with or represent those whose interest was in resisting performance, for the agreement by its terms imposes obligations and confers rights on the owner of each plot of land who signs it. If those who thus seek to secure the benefits of the agreement were rightly regarded by the state Supreme Court as constituting a class, it is evident that those signers or their successors who are interested in challenging the validity of the agreement and resisting its performance are not of the same class in the sense that their interests are identical so that any group who had elected to enforce rights conferred by the agreement could be said to be acting in the interest of any others who were free to deny its obligation.

It is one thing to say that some members of a class may represent other members in a litigation where the sole and common interest of the class in the litigation, is either to assert a common right or to challenge an asserted obligation. It is quite another to hold that all those who are free alternatively either to assert rights or to challenge them are of a single class, so that any group, merely because it is of the class so constituted, may be deemed adequately to represent any others of the class in litigating their interests in either alternative. Such a selection of representatives for purposes of litigation, whose substantial interests are not necessarily or even probably the same as those whom they are deemed to represent, does not afford that protection to absent parties which due process requires. The doctrine of representation of absent parties in a class suit has not hitherto been thought to go so far. Apart from the opportunities it would afford for the fraudulent and collusive sacrifice of the rights of absent parties, we think that the representation in this case no more satisfies the requirements of due process than a trial by a judicial officer who is in such situation that he may have an interest in the outcome of the litigation in conflict with that of the litigants.

The plaintiffs in the *Burke* case sought to compel performance of the agreement in behalf of themselves and all others similarly situated. They did not designate the defendants in the suit as a class or seek any injunction or other relief against others than the named defendants, and the decree which was entered did not purport to bind others. In seeking to enforce the agreement the plaintiffs in that suit were not representing the petitioners here whose substantial interest is in resisting performance. The defendants in the first suit were not treated by the pleadings or decree as representing others or as foreclosing by their defense the rights of others; and, even though nominal defendants, it does not appear that their interest in defeating the contract outweighed their interest in establishing its validity. For a court in this situation to ascribe to either the plaintiffs or defendants the performance of such functions on behalf of petitioners here, is to attribute to them a power that it cannot be said that they had assumed to exercise, and a responsibility which, in view of their dual interests it does not appear that they could rightly discharge.

Reversed.

Notes and Questions

1. Exactly why did the judgment in *Burke v. Kleiman* not bind the Hansberrys or the person from whom they bought their property?

2. Does *Hansberry* mean that a representative is inadequate anytime a class member disagrees with her? Suppose the representative and the class member agree on the underlying goals of the case, but disagree on litigation strategy. Can the representative be adequate under *Hansberry*? What if they disagree over the remedy to be sought or the court in which to file? At what point does disagreement mean that giving the judgment a binding effect would violate due process?

3. Under standard doctrine, why would the judgment in *Burke v. Kleiman* not have been entitled to issue preclusion on the question of whether the covenant was signed by 95 percent of the homeowners?

4. For most of this course, we have considered the due process ideal to be one in which no one is bound unless joined as a party to litigation and given notice and an opportunity to participate. For example, due process limitations on a state's power to exercise personal jurisdiction require not only that the defendant have minimum contacts with the forum, but that the court not be so grossly inconvenient as to jeopardize her ability to participate in the litigation. As the Court said in *Burger King*, which we read in Chapter 2: "jurisdictional rules may not be employed in such a way as to make litigation 'so gravely difficult and inconvenient' that a party unfairly is at a 'severe disadvantage' to his opponent." As another example, provisions for notice must be aimed at actually informing the defendant so that her opportunity to be heard is meaningful.

In Taylor v. Sturgell, 553 U.S. 880, 894 (2008), which we read in Chapter 11, the Court listed six scenarios in which nonparty preclusion is appropriate. One of those is when a nonparty to the suit was adequately represented by a litigant who shares the same interests. The first example cited by the Court for this scenario is a "properly conducted class action[]."

5. *Hansberry* is not the only case we have read in which the Supreme Court refused on constitutional grounds to bind nonparty absentees. In *Mullane v. Central Hanover Bank*, in Chapter 3 (which was decided after *Hansberry*), the Court held that beneficiaries of a pooled trust fund were entitled to notice before a court could terminate their right to sue the trustee for misfeasance. By notice, the Court envisioned not formal service of process and joinder, but simply notification by first-class mail of the filing of the case. Remember, too, that the Court required this notice only as to those persons whose names and addresses were readily available. As to others, the Court held, notice by publication was acceptable.

While *Mullane* did not involve a class action, the beneficiaries of the pooled fund held similar, relatively small interests. Moreover, the Court clearly did not foresee the participation of all interested persons, explaining that "notice reasonably certain to reach most of those interested in objecting is likely to safeguard the interest of all, since any objection sustained would inure to the benefit of all." 339 U.S. at 319.

Does *Hansberry* countenance binding members of a class even if they receive no notice of the proceedings? Does *Mullane*?

6. Reconsider this language from *Hansberry*:

> "It is one thing to say that some members of a class may represent other members in a litigation where the sole and common interest of the class in the litigation, is either to assert a common right or to challenge an asserted obligation. It is quite another to hold that all those who are free alternatively either to assert rights or to challenge them are of a single class, so that any group, merely because it is of the class so constituted, may be deemed adequately to represent any other of the class in litigating their interests in either alternative."

(a) Professor Yeazell has asked whether the Court meant what it said to be taken literally. "If, as the Court suggested, the validity of a class depends on the subjective desire of the individuals constituting it to assert their rights, classes could consist only of individuals who had, individually, indicated that they wished to assert the rights in question. Because all persons are always free either to assert their claims or not, classes could consist only of volunteers." Stephen Yeazell, From Medieval Group Litigation To The Modern Class Action 234 (1987). If a class action can consist only of volunteers, how useful is it?

(b) Professor Kamp, referring to the same passage from *Hansberry*, says "the language is so sweeping it could apply to and invalidate every class action." Allen Kamp, *The History Behind* Hansberry v. Lee, 20 U.C. Davis L. Rev. 481, 497 (1987). How does the language do so?

(c) Read in the context of *Hansberry*, can the second sentence of the passage above be considered as referring to a case in which class members are in conflict? Such a situation is quite different from a case in which class members share an identical interest but are indifferent as to its vindication.

7. The facts surrounding the *Hansberry* litigation are rich and interesting. Noted playwright, Lorraine Hansberry, was the daughter of the Hansberry in the case. Her best known play, "A Raisin in the Sun," tells the story of an African-American family that moves into a formerly white neighbourhood in Chicago. Mr. Burke, who helped to broker the sale to the Hansberrys, was the husband of Olive Ida Burke, the plaintiff in *Burke v. Kleinman* who had sued to *enforce* the restrictive covenant. Mr. Burke had for many years been active in the homeowners' association and in efforts to ensure enforcement of the restrictive covenant. However, in 1937, Mr. Burke had a falling out with the association. He also acquired a real estate license and may have discovered that there was money to be made in brokering sales to African-Americans. This change of heart did not escape the notice of the trial judge in *Hansberry*, who called Burke a "villain" who turned against the association that "he had lived off for years" and the "arch conspirator" who had "inaugurated" the "fraudulent scheme

and conspiracy" of the defendants. Jay Tidmarsh, *The Story of* Hansberry: *The Foundation for Modern Class Actions, in* Civil Procedure Stories 233, 263 (K. Clermont ed., 2d ed. 2008).

4. Practice Under Federal Rule 23

a. Background

Hansberry clarified (at least to a degree) the constitutionality of binding nonparties in a class action. Fortunately, few cases involve attempts to bind such disparate groups as those involved in the "class" in *Burke v. Kleiman.* Today, most judicial opinions focus on statutes or rules of procedure prescribing standards for the maintenance of class actions. Federal Rule 23 defines class actions in federal courts. It has also influenced rule and statute drafters in most states. In whatever form, though, such rules serve the salutary function of shifting to the outset of litigation the inquiry into whether the conditions for binding class members—including adequacy of representation—are satisfied. This is a far more efficient way to proceed than what we saw in *Hansberry,* where adequacy of representation could not be challenged until after judgment, in a collateral case.

The present version of Rule 23 differs markedly from the rule originally promulgated in 1938. The older rule liberalized prior practice, but suffered from reliance upon the legal relationships among class members that did not promote liberal use. It permitted three types of class actions: (1) "true" class actions, in which the class right was variously described as "joint" or "common"; (2) "hybrid" class actions, in which class rights were "several" and related to specific property; and (3) "spurious" class actions, in which class rights were "several" and involved a common question and in which the class sought common relief. In the words of the Advisory Committee that amended the rule in 1966, these terms were "obscure and uncertain."

The present version of the Rule traces to 1966, and was part of the substantial overhaul of Rules 19, 23, and 24. You will recall from our discussion of Rules 19 and 24 that the 1966 amendments emphasized practicality and pragmatism, and focused on fact patterns rather than legal relationships. Not surprisingly, we will see substantial kinship between parts of Rule 23 and Rules 19 and 24. Rule 23 was amended substantially in 2003 to increase judicial oversight of the class certification process, appointment of class counsel, and settlement or dismissal of class actions. It was redrafted in 2007 as part of a "restyling" of the Rules, and the Advisory Committee on the Civil Rules is considering additional amendments for the future.

We will focus on Rule 23, which governs in federal courts and which has served as the model for most state provisions for class litigation. It bears note, however, that states are free to provide for class action in any way they see fit, and there is significant variation in provisions in different states, particularly because states adopting Federal Rule 23 as a general matter may not have adopted the many changes made to the Federal Rule in recent years. And indeed, in some states, such as Virginia, there is no general provision for class actions at all.

b. Filing and Certification of a Class Action

In a plaintiff class action, the representative(s) institute(s) suit in the usual way: by filing a complaint and arranging for service of process. The complaint, however, notes that the representatives sue on behalf of a class of persons similarly situated. At some point after filing the putative class action, the representative makes a "motion for class certification." In terms of timing, Rule 23(c)(1)(A) provides that the court must determine whether to certify the class action at "an early practicable time." The court will usually entertain written briefs and oral argument on the issue. The admonition that the decision be made "at an early practicable time" does not mean immediately. It is not unusual for the court to address certification several months after the case is filed. In the interim, the parties might be permitted to pursue discovery on issues relevant to whether the case should proceed as a class action. At the hearing, the class representatives have the burden of establishing that the action satisfies requirements for class treatment.

If the court grants certification, Rule 23(c)(1)(B) requires it to "define the class and the class claims, issues, or defenses." This requirement forces the court to be precise early in the proceedings, to ensure that the class and class issues are well defined from the beginning. The order of certification, however, is not cast in stone. Rule 23(c)(1)(C) recognizes that the order "may be altered or amended before final judgment." The conditional nature of certification orders emphasizes the court's continuing duty to monitor the class action. If changes during the course of the litigation make class treatment undesirable or inappropriate, the court can modify the definition or "decertify" the class. Similarly, circumstances may require the court to redefine the class or the issues subject to class litigation.

Moreover, when the court certifies a class, Rule 23(c)(1)(B) requires it to appoint class counsel. This appointment is governed by Rule 23(g), which provides detailed factors for court consideration, including class counsel's experience in handling complex litigation and the resources counsel will be able to commit to representing the class. If more than one lawyer seeks appointment as class counsel, the court "must appoint the applicant best able to represent the interests of the class." If only one lawyer seeks appointment, the court may not appoint her if she does not satisfy the requirements in Rule 23(g).

If the court denies certification, the representative's individual suit stays before the court; although litigation may proceed in that suit, the lawyer's incentive may be sapped if the case involves a monetarily insignificant claim. Thus, denial of class certification is often the "death knell" of the plaintiff's case. On the other hand, if the court certifies a class action, the defendant's incentive to settle the case increases dramatically, because she faces the potential imposition of devastating liability. In many instances, then, the court's decision on certification effectively seals the outcome of the case.

c. *Requirements for Certification Under Rule 23*

Rule 23 provides a two-step process for determining whether a case should proceed as a class action. First, the class must satisfy each of the prerequisites in Rule 23(a). Second, after doing so, the representative must demonstrate that her class falls within one of the three types of class actions recognized by Rule 23(b). Although it is tempting to approach such a detailed rule in a mechanical, checklist fashion, keep the bigger picture in mind, always asking why the drafters included each requirement, especially in Rule 23(a). Specifically, assess whether each requirement is dictated by *Hansberry*, or at least contributes to addressing the due process concern addressed in that case.

In recent years, the Supreme Court has made it increasingly clear that mere allegations that a case qualifies for class status under Rule 23 are not enough. Rather, the class representative must *prove* that the requirements are satisfied. This means "significant proof" and "actual, not presumed, conformance with Rule 23." Wal-Mart Stores, Inc. v. Dukes, 564 U.S. 338 (2011). Production of such evidence may be very expensive, especially when expert testimony is required, as is usually the case in employment discrimination, securities, and antitrust litigation. In Comcast Corp. v. Behrend, 133 S. Ct. 1184, 1434 (2013), the Court held that the class representative must prove at the class certification stage that damages will be subject to class-wide proof.

i. Prerequisites of Rule 23(a)

Rule 23(a) lists four factors as prerequisites to maintenance of a class action. Before addressing them, however, note that the first sentence of the rule presupposes the existence of "a class." It is difficult to state with great precision what factors are relevant to defining a class. Although the representative generally does not need to name every member of the class, she must convince the judge at a very practical level that the court will be able to manage the action. For example, a class definition such as "poor people within the state" or "those interested in world peace" is simply too vague for a court to consider manageable. See, e.g., Lopez Tijerina v. Henry, 48 F.R.D. 274 (D.N.M. 1969).

Counsel should draft the class definition with great care, considering such things as geographic and temporal limitations. The court must be convinced that it can ultimately determine who is in the class. The relief sought may affect a court's insistence on specificity. Generally, if the class seeks monetary relief, the court may require greater specificity, since it ultimately will need to distribute money to individuals. Remember that the judge who certifies a class will have to "define the class and the class claims, issues, or defenses" under Rule 23(c)(1)(B). The representative can help her cause greatly with a relatively precise definition of the class and class issues.

Rule 23(a)(1) embodies what most lawyers and judges call *numerosity*. Note two things about the rule. First, it prescribes no "magic number" which automatically satisfies the requirement. Second, it focuses on more than numbers — the class must be "so numerous that joinder of all members is impracticable." The court thus must consider other factors in addition to mere numbers. For example, geographic dispersion and whether joinder of individual members would destroy diversity of citizenship might affect the court's conclusion on whether the class satisfies 23(a)(1). Some courts may deny certification of what would appear to be a large class when all of the members are citizens and residents of a single state, since the parties could join with relative ease. See, e.g., Utah v. American Pipe & Construction Co., 49 F.R.D. 17 (C.D. Cal. 1969). On the other hand, one court permitted a discrimination class action to proceed with only 19 members, in part because of the individuals' fear of bringing individual claims. Arkansas Education Ass'n v. Board of Education, 446 F.2d 763 (8th Cir. 1971).

Rule 23(a)(2) requires "questions of law or fact common to the class." Though stated in the plural, courts agree that a single common question of law or fact is sufficient. Historically, this *commonality* requirement has been easy to meet and engaged very little judicial discussion. Indeed, unless there were some commonality among class members, it seems unlikely that anyone would even think of a class action. The difficult issue of commonality usually comes up in class actions under Rule 23(b)(3), in which common questions must "predominate."

This attitude changed, however, with the Supreme Court's holding in Wal-Mart Stores, Inc. v. Dukes, 564 U.S. 338 (2011). That decision reversed the Ninth Circuit, which had upheld a class of potentially 1.5 million members. The class consisted of women employees of Wal-Mart, and alleged discrimination on the basis of sex in violation of Title VII and sought injunctive and declaratory relief, punitive damages, and back pay. Wal-Mart permits managers to exercise great discretion in setting pay (within ranges) and promotion, and plaintiffs asserted that the discretion is exercised disproportionately in favor of men, which causes an unlawful disparate impact on women employees. The Court held, five-to-four, that the class failed to satisfy the commonality requirement of Rule 23(a)(2). (The Court also held unanimously that the class could not proceed under a particular provision of Rule 23(b), which we discuss in Section C.4.c.ii, below.)

The majority recognized that Rule 23(a)(2) requires only a single question of law or fact in common to the class, but held that there was none. Saying that all plaintiffs suffered a violation of federal employment law was insufficient, because that law can be violated in different ways. Rather, the members must have suffered the same injury, so "their claims can productively be litigated at once." The substantive law required a showing of a general policy of discrimination and, the Court concluded, plaintiffs had no support for their assertion that Wal-Mart operated under a general policy of discrimination. Decisions were made in a non-centralized way, raising thousands of individualized questions rather than a common practice. Because they could not show an employment practice that "ties all their 1.5 million claims together," plaintiffs failed to demonstrate the existence of a common question under Rule 23(a)(2). *Wal-Mart* shifts the commonality inquiry under Rule 23(a)(2) from whether there are common questions to whether a class action will generate common *answers* that will resolve the litigation.*

Rule 23(a)(3) gives a *typicality* requirement, focusing on whether the representative's claim or defense is typical of that of the rest of the class. This factor is not met, for instance, if the representative suffered a unique harm from the rest of the class members, or if her claim is subject to a defense not available against the rest of the class. Thus, in a class action seeking redress for several harms — e.g., property damage and personal injuries caused by the defendant's acts — the class may have several representatives, one of whom suffered each of the asserted harms.

Finally, Rule 23(a)(4) requires that the *representatives* "fairly and adequately protect the interests of the class." In practice, courts have long concluded that this factor required an assessment not only of the representative, but of her *lawyer*. Rule 23(g)(1)(B) embraces that focus and requires that the person appointed as class counsel must "fairly and adequately represent the interests of the class." The court must be satisfied that the case is driven by the class' claims, and not by the lawyer's desire. The addition of Rule 23(g), which requires the court to appoint class counsel and to consider various factors in so doing, seeks to ensure that the lawyer will be competent and properly motivated to protect the interests of the class.

Notes and Questions

1. The Rule 23(a) factors are not hermetically sealed from one another. Indeed, as the Supreme Court has noted, the latter three factors "tend to merge." General Tel. Co. of the Southwest v. Falcon, 457 U.S. 147, 157 n.13 (1982). Some observers see the requirements of commonality and typicality as ways to ensure that the representative is adequate. Thus, the four prerequisites seem aimed at two major factors: impracticability of joining all interested members and adequacy of representation.

2. If *Burke v. Kleiman* had been brought for certification under Rule 23, which requirements would not have been met?

3. Juana works for Big Co. She claims that Big Co. violated federal employment discrimination law when it refused to promote her because of her national origin. Can she represent a class of persons of the same national origin who allege that Big Co. refused to hire them on that basis? See General Tel. Co. of the Southwest v. Falcon, 457 U.S. 147 (1982). Is the problem with typicality or with commonality or with adequacy of representation?

---

* It is not clear that *Wal-Mart* has resulted in significant change in the practice, at least with regard to employment discrimination cases. See Michael Selmi & Sylvia Tsakos, *Employment Discrimination Class Actions After* Wal-Mart v. Dukes, 48 Akron L. Rev. 803, 804 (2015) ("As a result of *Wal-Mart*, the analysis by the lower courts varies somewhat, but the result are largely the same; to the extent a court would have certified the claim before the Supreme Court decision it will likely still be certified. Moreover, various efforts by defense attorneys to stretch the *Wal-Mart* decision to have claims dismissed even before a certification hearing have largely failed, although those efforts have undeniably escalated in the last several years.").

4. A group of workers claims that the state has not afforded them benefits to which they are entitled under state law. Representative sues on behalf of the group of 750 workers, properly alleging the claim. Representative is subject to deportation from the United States, however, because of a criminal conviction. What argument should the state make to defeat his motion for class certification?

5. Suppose a class sues two defendants who allegedly agreed to charge the same price for their products and thus violated antitrust laws by overcharging for products sold to class members. Can a representative who dealt only with one of the two defendants represent the class?

6. Freezer Co. sells freezers door-to-door. It uses a sales force of 100 persons who go to various neighborhoods and engage in face-to-face conversations with potential customers, telling them about their freezers and offering a discount if the person agrees to purchase a freezer on the spot. Freezer Co. collects money from 500 people but never delivers the freezers. Can the 500 proceed in a class action for fraud? Remember that two elements of a fraud claim would be knowing misrepresentation by the seller and reliance by the buyer. How can these be shown en masse? Suppose Freezer Co. gave each salesperson a standard "pitch" which she memorized and stated to each prospective buyer? How would this affect your answer? See Vasquez v. Superior Court, 484 P.2d 964 (Cal. 1971).

7. Some courts have attempted to impose prerequisites to class certification beyond those mandated by Rule 23. In cases alleging fraud in the trading of investments, for example, some courts required that the representative—as a prerequisite to certification—show "loss causation" (which is a substantive element for securities fraud cases under Rule 10b-5). The Supreme Court rejected that effort in Erica P. John Fund v. Halliburton Co., 563 U.S. 804 (2011). In 2013, the Court rejected another such effort. In Amgen v. Connecticut Retirement Plans, 133 S. Ct. 1184 (2013), a six-to-three decision, the Court held that a showing of "materiality" (another element of the merits in securities fraud cases) is not required for certification.

The Second Circuit reached a different conclusion in a copyright case. In Authors Guild, Inc. v. Google Inc., 721 F.3d 123 (2d Cir. 2013), a class of authors sued Google for copyright infringement for providing "snippets" of millions of copyrighted works. The defendant asserted the defense of fair use under the copyright law. The district judge certified a class action. The Second Circuit ruled that the holding was premature:

> * * * On the particular facts of this case, we conclude that class certification was premature in the absence of a determination by the District Court of the merits of Google's "fair use" defense. Accordingly, we vacate the * * * order certifying the class and remand the cause to the District Court, for consideration of the fair use issues, without prejudice to any future motion for class certification.

721 F.3d at 132. Can this holding be reconciled with the Supreme Court's holdings in *Erica P. John Fund* and *Amgen*?

ii. Types of Class Actions Under Rule 23(b)

Once the prerequisites of Rule 23(a) are met, the representative must demonstrate that the class fits a category in Rule 23(b). Although the rule requires only that the class fit one of the types, it is possible to seek certification of a single class under more than one. Throughout these materials, consider why Rule 23(b) imposes additional requirements for maintenance of a class action. What is the function of Rule 23(b)? What does it add to Rule 23(a)? Does it address the concerns expressed in *Hansberry*?

Rule 23(b)(1) mirrors the language of Rule 19(a)(1)(B). This is not surprising, since, as noted above, the Rules Advisory Committee redrafted the rules together in 1966 to emphasize a pragmatic approach to joinder problems. When the number of persons affected does not preclude it, Rule 19 applies to force joinder of the nonparties. When joinder is impracticable, Rule 23(b)(1) permits a class action to proceed and binds the nonparties through representation.

Rule 23(b)(1) permits class actions in two situations. First, Rule 23(b)(1)(A), like Rule 19(a)(1)(B)(ii), is concerned with the practical effect of a judgment on a party (usually the defendant). Specifically, it permits class litigation where separate actions would create a risk of "establish[ing] incompatible standards of conduct for the party opposing the class." Such cases almost always involve the assertion of common rights in which individual litigation could come to mutually exclusive results. For example, suppose that the reorganization of the fraternal benefits organization in *Ben-Hur* had been challenged in individual litigation. One court might have concluded that the organization could go through with its plan and change member benefits, while another might conclude exactly the opposite. Faced with these judgments, the organization would be able to obey one judgment only by disobeying the other. Similarly, suppose shareholders sue a corporation to force the declaration of a dividend. Individual litigation might result in contradictory orders—one commanding the corporation to declare the dividend and one decreeing that it shall not.

As two scholars note, a "unitary decision is essential" in such cases. Arthur Miller & David Crump, *Jurisdiction and Choice of Law in Multistate Class Actions After* Phillips Petroleum Co. v. Shutts, 96 YALE L.J. 1, 46 (1986). They explain, "it is impossible to reorganize a single fraternal benefits organization in inconsistent ways, or to keep two basketball leagues merged and separate, or to distribute and withhold a dividend." Id. Another example involves numerous claims to a specific res or fund. If the number of claimants is manageable, the stakeholder might use interpleader. If joinder through interpleader is impracticable, the case might proceed as a Rule 23(b)(1)(A) class action. Note that it might be the defendant in this situation who wants the plaintiffs to proceed as a class. Nothing in Rule 23 prohibits a defendant from seeking certification of a plaintiff class.

Rule 23(b)(1)(A) usually involves claims for equitable relief such as an injunction or declaratory judgment. The "incompatible standards of conduct" test generally is not met in a case seeking damages. Assume that a bus crash injures 80 people, who then sue the busline separately. While these individual actions may reach inconsistent results — Plaintiff-1 may lose and Plaintiff-2 may win — the courts do not consider separate actions for damages as subjecting the busline to the "incompatible standards of conduct." McDonnell Douglas Corp. v. United States District Court, 523 F.2d 1083 (9th Cir. 1975). One reason is that such tort damages are individual, and thus are not the identical, shared sort of interest that class members had in *Smith* and *Ben-Hur* and that the investors had in *Mullane.*

Rule 23(b)(1)(B), like Rule 19(a)(1)(B)(i) and Rule 24(a)(2), is concerned that individual actions will, as a practical matter, impair or impede the ability of nonparties to protect their interests. Such cases often involve claims to a limited fund, and are sometimes called "limited fund class actions." Without unitary adjudication, some claimants will recover, while others, winning their judgments later, may have no fund against which to recover. To avoid this wasteful race to the courthouse, Rule 23(b)(1)(B) allows unitary adjudication.

Rule 23(b)(2) prescribes a remedy as well as a test. It is aimed at equitable relief when the nonclass party "has acted or refused to act on grounds generally applicable to the class." For example, a case seeking an order desegregating schools or ending employment discrimination against a particular group could proceed under Rule 23(b)(2). Because Rule 23(b)(2) speaks only of classes seeking injunctive or declaratory relief, it would seem to be an inappropriate vehicle for claiming damages or other monetary remedies. Many Rule 23(b)(2) classes assert employment discrimination. Assume employees sue for violation of federal employment laws because the employer refused to promote them for some improper reason (e.g., discrimination on the basis of national origin). The class seeks equitable relief ordering the defendant to promote them to the higher-paying jobs. These employees might also seek back pay — to compensate them for being employed at lower-than-proper wages for a set period. But back pay is monetary relief. Can the employees seek it in a Rule 23(b)(2) class?

Courts generally concluded that back pay awards were proper in a Rule 23(b)(2) class if the amounts were easily calculable and "flowed naturally" from the equitable relief sought. Some justified their conclusion by referring to back pay as "equitable" relief. Such holdings created tension, however, because Rule 23(b)(3) seems to be aimed at recovery of monetary relief, and requires notice to class members and gives them a right to opt out of the class and sue on their own. So most courts limited recovery of money in Rule 23(b)(2) classes to back pay.

But some courts went much farther, and permitted recovery of individual damages in a Rule 23(b)(2) class. They tried to justify the result by pointing out that the case was "predominately" about equitable relief. The Supreme Court unanimously rejected this practice in *Wal-Mart v. Dukes.* As noted above, *Wal-Mart* involved a class of 1.5 million female employees of Wal-Mart, who alleged gender discrimination. In rejecting the Rule 23(b)(2) class, the Court emphasized two points.

First, the injunctive or declaratory relief sought must be the same for each class member. The Rule "does not authorize class certification when each individual class member would be entitled to a *different* injunction or declaratory judgment against the defendant." In other words, a class action cannot be used to vindicate unique individual equitable claims.

Second, Rule 23(b)(2) does not authorize a class action when "each class member would be entitled to an individualized award of monetary damages." Id. This is true even if the award is of back pay, notwithstanding that back pay may be considered equitable relief. The Rule does not speak of equitable relief, but of injunctive and declaratory relief. Beyond this, the Court hinted that due process requires that class members be given notice and the right to opt out of any class action that is predominantly for money damages. After *Wal-Mart*, then, very few Rule 23(b)(2) classes will be permitted to seek monetary relief. The Rule 23(b)(2) class apparently must seek a single, class-wide injunctive or declaratory remedy.

The Rule 23(b)(3) class action is sometimes called the "damages" class because that tends to be the type of relief sought in such cases. Note the two requirements: common questions must predominate over questions affecting individual class members and the class action must be superior to other methods of adjudication. Obviously, it is not enough that there are common questions; those questions must *predominate.* That does not mean that every issue in dispute must be common. For example, class members may assert the same bases of defendant liability, but have suffered different damages. The court can certify a class action as to liability only. Once that is determined, it may accommodate individual evidence on damages from each class member. Along these lines, read Rule 23(c), (d) and (g), and note the breadth of the court's discretion in administering a class action.

In determining whether the class action is the superior method of resolving the dispute, the obvious question is "superior to what"? Rule 23(b)(3) lists four nonexclusive factors for assessment of this issue. Clearly, though, the rule presupposes a detailed knowledge of the joinder rules and other multiparty litigation.

The Rule 23(b)(3) class action poses the greatest tension between the desire for efficiency and the need for due process. Unlike class members under Rule 23(b)(1) and (b)(2), members of a 23(b)(3) class are held together solely by common facts. Their claims are individual and independent. Thus, the fact that some claimants might win and some might lose creates none of the problems we saw under Rule 23(b)(1) and 23(b)(2). In keeping with the joinder rules, which emphasize packaging along transactional lines, however, the 23(b)(3) class action seeks to maximize efficiency in determining factually related claims en masse.

Because class members are more tangentially related here than in other classes, courts will be especially concerned about adequacy of representation. This concern is manifested in two provisions. First, Rule 23(c)(2)(B) requires notice to individual class members concerning the pendency of a certified Rule 23(b)(3) class action. Second, it also allows members of the Rule 23(b)(3) class to exclude themselves from the class (or, as lawyers say it, to "opt out"). Class members who opt out are not bound by the class judgment. See Rule 23(c)(3).

Rule 23 does not require such notice or the opportunity to opt out if a class is maintained under Rule 23(b)(1) or (b)(2). Because members of a Rule 23(b)(1) and (b)(2) class cannot opt out, those are called "mandatory" class actions. The opt-out provision for Rule 23(b)(3) classes means, as a practical matter, that the class action will rarely work for mass torts in which class members suffer significant damages. In such a case, it is unlikely that a potential plaintiff will forego the right to sue individually.

Clearly, the decision whether a class action should be certified is of enormous importance. In many cases, it is the make-or-break decision. If the class is not certified, the individual representative's claim remains, but, if it is not individually significant, the lawyer's incentive to proceed may be sapped. If the class is certified, the defendant faces such enormous potential liability that the case will almost always be settled. The side that loses the certification battle will probably lose the litigation war. That being the case, the losing side would like to gain appellate review of the certification decision. Unfortunately, as we will discuss in the next chapter, the certification decision — either to grant or deny — is not a "final judgment," and, therefore, under the general rule, is not appealable until final judgment of the entire underlying case. The certification decision is an "interlocutory," not a final, decision.

That general rule against permitting appeal of interlocutory orders is subject to exceptions, however, and one applies to class actions. Rule 23(f) permits a party to seek appellate review of the certification decision, and gives the court of appeals discretion whether to grant such review. We will discuss the factors assessed in this consideration in Chapter 14, Section B.4. One empirical study demonstrates that Rule 23(f) has been used disproportionately to hinder class certification: fifty-two percent of cases in which the court of appeals reviewed certification decisions resulted in reversal of certification, while denials of certification were reversed in only ten percent of the cases. Richard Freer, *Interlocutory Review of Class Action Certification Decision: A Preliminary Empirical Study of Federal and State Experience*, 35 W. St. L. Rev. 13, 19 (2007).

Notes and Questions

1. Suppose an airplane operated by Airline crashes, killing 80 passengers. The individual wrongful death and punitive damages claims on behalf of the 80 passengers will seek a total of $40,000,000. Airline's net worth and applicable insurance pool totals $8,000,000. If a representative seeks to bring a Rule 23(b)(3) class action, the executors of the other passengers killed will probably opt out and sue individually, trying to strike first and recover their damages before the available fund is depleted. Can you articulate an argument for certifying a class under Rule 23(b)(1)(B)?

Some lawyers have argued that cases such as this — in which the aggregate claims vastly exceed the resources available to pay them — satisfy Rule 23(b)(1)(B). In their view, the facts present the "constructive bankruptcy" of the defendant. Absent a class, the race to the courthouse will deprive some claimants of a meaningful opportunity to recover anything. This theory has met with mixed success. In one portion of the massive Dalkon Shield litigation, which involved a defective intrauterine device, a district court certified a nationwide Rule 23(b)(1)(B) class of women seeking punitive damages against the manufacturer. (Indeed, the manufacturer, as defendant, moved for the certification of the plaintiff class.) The district judge noted that the punitive damages claims exceeded $2.3 billion, while the net worth of the defendant was slightly more than $280 million. In his view, these numbers "raise[d] the unconscionable possibility that large numbers of plaintiffs who are not first in line at the courthouse door will be deprived of a practical means of redress." In re Northern District of California "Dalkon Shield" IUD Prods. Liability Litigation, 526 F. Supp. 887, 893 (N.D. Cal. 1981). The Ninth Circuit reversed the class certification. It criticized the district court for not engaging in sufficient factfinding to determine the defendant's actual assets, whether cases had been settled, and the amount of any insurance coverage for the claims. In re Northern District of California, "Dalkon Shield" IUD Prods. Liability Litigation, 693 F.2d 847, 851 (9th Cir. 1982).

The Supreme Court weighed in on the issue in Ortiz v. Fibreboard Corp., 527 U.S. 815 (1999), in which it reversed the certification of a "limited fund" class. There, the parties reached a complicated "Global Settlement Agreement" to settle massive litigation concerning personal injury claims arising from exposure to asbestos. While not ruling out Rule 23(b)(1)(B) class actions, the Court certainly urged caution and did not encourage creativity. To the Court, practice under Rule 23(b)(1) should be limited to the situations recognized when the Rules were adopted.

The Court pointed to three problems with the settlement structured by the parties, and thereby set forth three apparent requirements of any limited fund class. First, the parties must demonstrate the insufficiency of available funds, to be tested by an evidentiary hearing. In *Ortiz*, the parties basically stipulated the amount that was available for payment of claims, without independent valuation of insurance assets. Second, because the class members have no right to opt out, the distribution must be equitable. In *Ortiz*, the Court found that the class as structured excluded "myriad claimants" and, within the group included, did not ensure equitable distribution of funds. Third, the Court was troubled by the fact that the manufacturer spearheading the settlement would retain virtually its entire net worth, since the money for claims would come from insurers. This latter factor, while perhaps not fatal in itself, was another way in which the class departed from the historical use of the limited fund class.

2. In *Comcast Corp. v. Behrend,* the Supreme Court, in a five-to-four decision, reversed certification of a Rule 23(b)(3) class asserting antitrust claims. The majority concluded that the lower courts erred by certifying the class without sufficient validation of the plaintiffs' damages model. The Court explained:

> Respondents' class action was improperly certified under Rule 23(b)(3). By refusing to entertain arguments against respondents' damages model that bore on the propriety of class certification, simply because those arguments would also be pertinent to the merits determination, the Court of Appeals ran afoul of our precedents requiring precisely that inquiry. And it is clear that, under the proper standard for evaluating certification, respondents' model falls far short of establishing that damages are capable of measure-

> ment on a classwide basis. Without presenting another methodology, respondents cannot show Rule 23(b)(3) predominance: Questions of individual damage calculations will inevitably overwhelm questions common to the class.

133 S. Ct. at 1432–1433.

3. In the 1990s and early 2000s, corporate interests asserted that some state courts were particularly friendly to class action plaintiffs. These interests lobbied Congress for legislation permitting defendants to remove class actions to federal court on the basis of minimal diversity and based upon the desire of a single defendant to remove the case (rather than, as is usually required, the effort of all defendants). Congress responded to the lobbying with the Class Action Fairness Act (CAFA), which is discussed in Section 5 below. Assuming that it is more difficult to obtain class certification under Federal Rule 23 than under some state provisions, do the relaxed jurisdictional requirements of the Class Action Fairness Act (including easier provisions for removal to federal court) work a substantive change in procedural guise? Stated another way, if a defendant can force virtually any interstate class action into federal court—where class action certification may be more difficult than in state court—has Congress enacted tort reform without saying so? Is there anything wrong with that?

d. Notice to Class Members of the Pendency of the Action

Read Rule 23(c)(2)(A) and (B). The former permits (but does not require) the court to "direct appropriate notice" to class members in classes certified under Rule 23(b)(1) or (2). In contrast, as we saw above, Rule 23(c)(2)(B) mandates that the court that certifies a Rule 23(b)(3) class "direct to class members the best notice that is practicable under the circumstances, including individual notice to all members who can be identified through reasonable effort." In Eisen v. Carlisle & Jacquelin, 417 U.S. 156 (1974), the Supreme Court held that the cost of such notice must be borne initially by the class representatives. That expense would ultimately be a taxable "cost" of litigation which the losing party would have to pay, but the Court forbade a district court from imposing the cost on the nonclass party at the outset of litigation.

The holding in *Eisen* has thwarted many potential class actions. The facts of *Eisen* demonstrate why. The representative was part of a class of over two million investors alleging violations of federal antitrust and securities laws. Mr. Eisen's personal claim under these federal laws was about $70. To maintain the class action, however, he would have had to pay for individual notice to hundreds of thousands of identifiable class members. Even at the low postal rates of the time, sending this notice would have cost $225,000. Not surprisingly, no potential representative will be willing to put up $225,000 to engage in complex litigation that will, at best, return that cost plus $70 and which, at worst, will return nothing.

You may want to consider whether notice is worth the effort as a practical matter. Although the notice comes from the court, counsel for both sides in the litigation have a hand in drafting it. Plaintiff's counsel usually will want the allegations set out as fact, while the defense will insist that the notice declare that there has been no finding of liability. Often, the result is a notice filled with legalese, unintelligible to the lay person. Professor Miller demonstrated the point by publishing actual responses from persons who had received notice that they were members of a class suing antibiotics manufacturers for alleged violation of antitrust laws. The responses received by the clerk of the court included these:

> Dear Mr. Clerk: I have your notice that I owe you $300 for selling drugs. I have never sold any drugs, especially those you have listed; but I have sold a little whiskey once in a while.
>
> Dear Sir: I received this paper from you. I guess I really don't understand it, but if I have been given one of those drugs, nobody told me why. If it means what I think it does, I have not been with a man in nine years.
>
> Dear Sir: I received your pamphlet on drugs, which I think will be of great value to me in the future. I am unable to attend your class, however.

Arthur Miller, *Problems of Giving Notice in Class Actions*, 58 F.R.D. 313, 322 (1972).

In an effort to deal with such problems, Rule 23(c)(2)(B) instructs the court that the notice must state certain things "clearly and concisely * * * in plain, easily understood language." Specifically, the notice must inform the class members of (1) the nature of the action, (2) the definition of the class, (3) the class claims, issues, or defenses, (4) that a class member may enter an appearance through counsel if she desires, (5) that the court will exclude any class member requesting exclusion, and (6) that the class member will be bound by the judgment if she does not exclude herself (or "opt out").

The notice required by Rule 23(c)(2)(B)—which, as we just saw, informs the class members of various things regarding the pendency of the action—is to be distinguished from notice required when the court approves the settlement or dismissal of a certified class action. We discuss that point in Section (e) below.

Notes and Questions

1. We discussed above why notice is required in the Rule 23(b)(3) class action. But why is it not required in the others? Courts are not required to give notice to members of a Rule 23(b)(1) or (b)(2) class, and nothing in Rule 23 requires that such members be permitted to opt out of the case. (Remember, this is why Rule 23(b)(1) and (b)(2) classes are considered "mandatory" class actions.) Yet they will be bound by the result of the case under Rule 23(c)(3). Is this consistent with *Mullane* and *Hansberry*?

2. What would be the consequence of permitting opt-outs in class actions under Rule 23(b)(1) and 23(b)(2)?

3. Is the requirement in Rule 23(c)(2)(B) that the court give the best notice practicable, "including individual notice to all members who can be identified through reasonable effort," more stringent than *Mullane* would require? Did *Mullane* require

individual notice to such a broad group? Why do you think Rule 23(c)(2)(B) specifies individual notice?

4. Under what circumstances would a court be likely to give notice to class members under Rule 23(c)(2)(A)? What would be the purpose of such notice? Rule 23 is silent as to whether members of a Rule 23(b)(1) or 23(b)(2) class can opt out. Does any provision of Rule 23(c) or 23(d) give the court sufficient discretion to allow a member of such a class to opt out? If not, why would the court give notice to members in those classes? Recall that in *Mullane*, the Court required notice even without a right to opt out.

5. In *Eisen*, the representative might have lessened the cost of notice by trimming the class definition substantially. For example, he might have pursued a class action on behalf of the investors in a particular city. But what would such a narrow class definition do to the attorney's willingness to pursue the case? Moreover, at some point, she risks failing to satisfy numerosity.

6. Should the representative's lawyer be permitted to advance the cost of notice to her client? In *Eisen*, wasn't the attorney the de facto real party in interest in the case? If so, why shouldn't the lawyer be able to come up with the money? Traditionally, rules of professional responsibility have prohibited lawyers from providing financial assistance to a client in connection with litigation. These rules are changing, however, and in some states a lawyer may advance expenses to the client, with the understanding they will be repaid from any recovery for the client. The American Bar Association adopted this position. See ABA Model Rules Of Prof'l Conduct R. 1.8(e)(1) (2002).

Indeed, traditional restrictions on champerty—that is, maintenance of litigation by a third-party—are eroding, which has led to the fascinating prospect that third-party investors may pay millions of dollars in exchange for a share in any recovery by a class. See, e.g., *Have You Got a Piece of this Lawsuit?*, Fortune Magazine 69 (June 13, 2011). Maintaining a class action is expensive. Is there anything wrong with letting plaintiffs sell a piece of the recovery to obtain litigation funding? See generally Jonathan Molot, *The Feasibility of Litigation Markets,* 89 Indiana L.J. 171 (2014); Victoria Shannon, *Harmonizing Third-Party Litigation Funding Regulation*, 36 Cardozo L. Rev. 861 (2015); Symposium, *A Brave New World: The Changing Face of Litigation and Law Firm Practice*, 63 DePaul L. Rev. 233 (2014).

e. Court's Role in Dismissal and Settlement

Read Rule 23(e). Note that the provision applies only when the court is considering settlement, voluntary dismissal, or compromise of claims or issues or defenses "of a certified class." For many years, courts were uncertain whether Rule 23(e) applied when settlement, dismissal or compromise was sought *before* the class action had been certified. The rule is now explicit on the point.

Why should we require court approval of such actions in a certified class action? After all, in non-class cases, the court generally does not need to approve a settlement or voluntary dismissal. The class action is different because the court's role is different. As we have seen, Rules 23(c), (d), and (g) envision a very active role for the judge. She is not simply a neutral umpire reacting to parties' actions. Instead, she plays a vital role in assuring and constantly reassessing whether the class members' interests are being represented adequately. Because of the possible conflict of interest between a class and its counsel, the judge is required to assess the fairness of any settlement or voluntary dismissal independently.

In determining whether to approve a settlement, voluntary dismissal or compromise in a certified class, Rule 23(e)(1) requires the court to give notice to all class members "who would be bound by" the proposed action. Unlike the notice of pendency of the class action, here notice is required in all three types of class actions. The notice is given to solicit members' feedback as to the fairness of the proposed settlement, dismissal or compromise. Under Rule 23(e)(2), the court is required to hold a hearing (usually called a "fairness hearing") and can approve the proposed action only upon finding that it "is fair, reasonable, and adequate." The assessment of whether this standard is satisfied is not necessarily a democratic exercise. Some courts have upheld settlements as fair even though they were opposed by a majority of the class. See, e.g., TBK Partners, Ltd. v. Western Union Corp., 675 F.2d 456 (2d Cir. 1982).

Some courts have shown a surprising willingness to approve some questionable settlements. In Reynolds v. Beneficial National Bank, 288 F.3d 277 (7th Cir. 2002), the court reversed the trial judge's approval of a settlement of millions of claims in a consumer class action. The class consisted of persons for whom H&R Block had filed tax returns and who were entitled to refunds of taxes paid. H&R Block made a loan of the refund amount to the taxpayers. The loans came from Beneficial National Bank, which paid H&R Block for each transaction. The deals allegedly violated various provisions of federal and state law. Though other class actions had not succeeded, counsel for Beneficial had lunch with three solo practitioners to discuss a global settlement of all related claims arising from the arrangements between Beneficial and H&R Block. At the meeting, Beneficial's lawyer "threw out a number" of about $24 million to settle all claims. At the time of the meeting, none of the three solo practitioners had a client who was a member of the class. Undeterred, however, they (joined later by a large law firm) forged a settlement that included claims against H&R Block (even though it was not a defendant in the pending cases). Though the district judge demanded changes in some of the terms of the proposed settlement, the Seventh Circuit held that the judge abused his discretion in approving the settlement. On remand, the district court rejected the settlement. Reynolds v. Beneficial National Bank, 260 F. Supp. 2d 680 (N.D. Ill. 2003).

Suppose it is obvious at the outset that the parties will settle a class action. Can a court then simply presume that the requirements of Rule 23 are satisfied for the limited purpose of permitting settlement negotiations? Although the Rule does not refer to such "settlement classes," some courts would presume the existence of a class to foster settlement. See, e.g., Mars Steel v. Continental Illinois National Bank &

Trust, 834 F.2d 677, 680 (7th Cir. 1987). Critics argued, however, that such a presumption robbed the class of the protection afforded by a judicial determination that the representative is adequate. The Supreme Court resolved the issue in Amchem Products, Inc. v. Windsor, 521 U.S. 591 (1997), in which it held that a settlement class must satisfy all the criteria for certification of a class action under Rule 23(a) and 23(b). Although the fact that a case may settle is relevant in assessing manageability of a class action (since no trial will be required), it is not, by itself, a basis for certifying a class.

As we noted above, the Class Action Fairness Act (CAFA), reflects congressional concern with perceived abuses of class actions, particularly in state courts. In particular, Congress was concerned about "coupon settlements," in which class members received coupons of questionable value and class counsel received significant compensation for engineering a compromise with the defendants. As we will see in the next Section, CAFA applies only to certain interstate class actions. In such cases, however, the Act imposes significant restrictions on counsel fees in coupon class actions.

Under CAFA, if a proposed class settlement would provide for recovery of coupons by class members, an award of attorney's fees must be based upon the "value to class members of the coupons that are redeemed." 28 U.S.C. § 1712(a). This provision is aimed at the fact that many coupons distributed to class members are never redeemed. (Often the coupons are for discounts on products from the very defendant whose product gave rise to the class action.) The court is permitted to receive expert testimony on the "actual value to the class members of the coupons that are redeemed." 28 U.S.C. § 1712(d). The Act contains detailed provisions concerning attorney's fee awards in cases involving awards of coupons and other relief (such as injunctive relief against the defendant), and requires court approval of the fee. 28 U.S.C. § 1712(b) & (c). Moreover, coupon settlements may only be approved after the court holds a hearing and makes a written finding that the settlement is fair, reasonable, and adequate for class members. 28 U.S.C. § 1712(e).

CAFA envisions ongoing oversight by the court in some particulars, but also imposes restrictions on the court's discretion to approve settlements. First, the court may require as part of the settlement of a coupon class action that unclaimed coupons be distributed to charitable or governmental organizations. 28 U.S.C. § 1712(e). Second, the court may approve a settlement in which a class member is required to pay money to class counsel that would result in a net loss to the class member "only if the court makes a written finding that nonmonetary benefits to the class member substantially outweigh the monetary loss." 28 U.S.C. § 1713. This latter provision seems to address those very rare cases in which class members have been required to contribute to costs or attorney's fees in the class action. Third, no class settlement can be approved if it permits greater recovery to some members based solely on geographic proximity to the forum. 28 U.S.C. § 1714. This provision is thought to be consistent with the underlying purpose of diversity of citizenship jurisdiction by prohibiting discrimination based upon citizenship (although the statute does not refer to "citizenship").

5. Subject Matter Jurisdiction

Many class actions brought in federal court invoke federal question jurisdiction. But what if a plaintiff class seeks to invoke diversity of citizenship jurisdiction? Must all members of the class be of diverse citizenship from the defendant? Must all members of the class claim an amount exceeding $75,000?

In *Ben-Hur*, the Supreme Court held that only the representative's citizenship is relevant in determining whether there is complete diversity under *Strawbridge v. Curtiss*. This holding is consistent with the notion that the representative is a formal party, while the class members are not. It is also consistent with the principle of supplemental jurisdiction. Once the representative properly invokes federal court jurisdiction, *Ben-Hur* permitted binding those whose claims were so closely related to the representative as to constitute part of the same case or controversy.

What about assessing the amount in controversy? In Snyder v. Harris, 394 U.S. 332 (1969), the Court held that the claims of class members generally cannot be aggregated in determining the amount in controversy. (Remember from our discussion of diversity of citizenship jurisdiction that multiple plaintiffs may not aggregate their claims to satisfy the amount in controversy requirement, unless they assert a joint, common, or undivided right. Recall also that such rights are rare outside the property context.) On the other hand, supplemental jurisdiction would seem to support class members' claims so long as the representative's claim exceeds $75,000. The Supreme Court rejected this argument (actually, the majority opinion ignored it) in Zahn v. International Paper Co., 414 U.S. 291 (1973). So, under *Snyder* and *Zahn*, the claim of each class member must satisfy the amount in controversy requirement independently.

Obviously, *Ben-Hur* and *Zahn* are completely inconsistent. For determining citizenship, the court looks only to the representative. But in determining amount in controversy, the court looks to every member of the class. Of the two, commentators criticize *Zahn* as the aberration.

Things stood like this for decades, until the supplemental jurisdiction statute, 28 U.S.C. § 1367, was passed in 1990. Almost immediately, commentators argued that the literal terms of §§ 1367(a) and 1367(b) had overruled the result in *Zahn*. Specifically, the former granted supplemental jurisdiction over claims by class members that arose from a common nucleus of operative fact with the representative's claim, and nothing in § 1367(b) removes that grant (because nothing in that section mentions Rule 23). See, e.g., Richard Freer, *Compounding Confusion and Hampering Diversity: Life After* Finley *and the Supplemental Jurisdiction Statute*, 40 Emory L.J. 445 (1991). But it seems that Congress did not intend the result dictated by the literal terms of the statute. In a paragraph of the House Report, which was one part of the legislative history to the statute, there was a one-sentence statement that the legislature did not intend to overrule *Zahn*. Three professors involved in the drafting of the statute explain that the statement in the legislative history "was an attempt to correct the oversight" about the effect of the statutory language. Thomas Rowe,

Stephen Burbank & Thomas Mengler, *Compounding or Creating Confusion About Supplemental Jurisdiction? A Reply to Professor Freer*, 40 EMORY L.J. 943, 960 n.90 (1991).

The possibility that § 1367 had de facto overruled the result in *Zahn* created great uncertainty. Between 1995 and 2005, federal Courts of Appeals split six-to-four on this question (with the majority concluding that *Zahn* had been abrogated). This lamentable state of affairs led the Supreme Court to address the issue in the following case. Interestingly, the opinion resolves two disputes—one a class action (*Allapattah*), one not (*Ortega*). Both raised the question of whether one plaintiff's satisfaction of the amount-in-controversy requirement would permit the jurisdictionally insufficient claims of other plaintiffs to invoke supplemental jurisdiction. One important question in this case is what weight, if any, the Court should give the House Report, which contained the one-sentence disclaimer of any intent to overrule the result in *Zahn*.

Exxon Mobil Corp. v. Allapattah Services

545 U.S. 546, 125 S. Ct. 2611, 162 L. Ed. 2d 502 (2005)

KENNEDY, J. delivered the opinion of the Court.

These consolidated cases present the question whether a federal court in a diversity action may exercise supplemental jurisdiction over additional plaintiffs whose claims do not satisfy the minimum amount-in-controversy requirement, provided the claims are part of the same case or controversy as the claims of plaintiffs who do allege a sufficient amount in controversy. Our decision turns on the correct interpretation of 28 U.S.C. § 1367. The question has divided the Courts of Appeals, and we granted certiorari to resolve the conflict.

We hold that, where the other elements of jurisdiction are present and at least one named plaintiff in the action satisfies the amount-in-controversy requirement, § 1367 does authorize supplemental jurisdiction over the claims of other plaintiffs in the same Article III case or controversy, even if those claims are for less than the jurisdictional amount specified in the statute setting forth the requirements for diversity jurisdiction. * * *

I

In 1991, about 10,000 Exxon dealers filed a class-action suit against the Exxon Corporation in the United States District Court for the Northern District of Florida. The dealers alleged an intentional and systematic scheme by Exxon under which they were overcharged for fuel purchased from Exxon. The plaintiffs invoked the District Court's § 1332(a) diversity jurisdiction. After a unanimous jury verdict in favor of the plaintiffs, the District Court certified the case for interlocutory review, asking whether it had properly exercised § 1367 supplemental jurisdiction over the claims of class members who did not meet the jurisdictional minimum amount in controversy.

[In Allapattah], [t]he Court of Appeals for the Eleventh Circuit upheld the District Court's extension of supplemental jurisdiction to these class members. "We find," the court held, "that § 1367 clearly and unambiguously provides district courts with the authority in diversity class actions to exercise supplemental jurisdiction over the claims of class members who do not meet the minimum amount in controversy as long as the district court has original jurisdiction over the claims of at least one of the class representatives." This decision accords with the views of the Courts of Appeals for the Fourth, Sixth, and Seventh Circuits [citations omitted]. The Courts of Appeals for the Fifth and Ninth Circuits, adopting a similar analysis of the statute, have held that in a diversity class action the unnamed class members need not meet the amount-in-controversy requirement, provided the named class members do. These decisions, however, are unclear on whether all the named plaintiffs must satisfy this requirement [citations omitted].

In [*Ortega*], the Court of Appeals for the First Circuit took a different position on the meaning of § 1367(a). In that case, a 9-year-old girl sued Star-Kist in a diversity action in the United States District Court for the District of Puerto Rico, seeking damages for unusually severe injuries she received when she sliced her finger on a tuna can. Her family joined in the suit, seeking damages for emotional distress and certain medical expenses. The District Court granted summary judgment to Star-Kist, finding that none of the plaintiffs met the minimum amount-in-controversy requirement. The Court of Appeals for the First Circuit, however, ruled that the injured girl, but not her family members, had made allegations of damages in the requisite amount.

The Court of Appeals then addressed whether, in light of the fact that one plaintiff met the requirements for original jurisdiction, supplemental jurisdiction over the remaining plaintiffs' claims was proper under § 1367. The court held that § 1367 authorizes supplemental jurisdiction only when the district court has original jurisdiction over the action, and that in a diversity case original jurisdiction is lacking if one plaintiff fails to satisfy the amount-in-controversy requirement. Although the Court of Appeals claimed to "express no view" on whether the result would be the same in a class action, its analysis is inconsistent with that of the Court of Appeals for the Eleventh Circuit. The Court of Appeals for the First Circuit's view of § 1367 is, however, shared by the Courts of Appeal for the Third, Eighth, and Tenth Circuits, and the latter two Courts of Appeals have expressly applied this rule to class actions [citations omitted].

II

A

The district courts of the United States, as we have said many times, are "courts of limited jurisdiction. They possess only that power authorized by Constitution and statute." In order to provide a federal forum for plaintiffs who seek to vindicate federal rights, Congress has conferred on the district courts original jurisdiction in federal-question cases — civil actions that arise under the Constitution, laws, or treaties of the United States. 28 U.S.C. § 1331. In order to provide a neutral forum for what have come to be known as diversity cases, Congress also has granted district courts original jurisdiction in civil actions between citizens of different States, between U.S. citizens and foreign citizens, or by foreign states against U.S. citizens. § 1332. To ensure that diversity jurisdiction does not flood the federal courts with minor disputes, § 1332(a) requires that the matter in controversy in a diversity case exceed a specified amount, currently $75,000. § 1332(a).

Although the district courts may not exercise jurisdiction absent a statutory basis, it is well established—in certain classes of cases—that, once a court has original jurisdiction over some claims in the action, it may exercise supplemental jurisdiction over additional claims that are part of the same case or controversy. The leading modern case for this principle is Mine Workers v. Gibbs, 383 U.S. 715 (1966). In *Gibbs*, the plaintiff alleged the defendant's conduct violated both federal and state law. The District Court, *Gibbs* held, had original jurisdiction over the action based on the federal claims. *Gibbs* confirmed that the District Court had the additional power (though not the obligation) to exercise supplemental jurisdiction over related state claims that arose from the same Article III case or controversy. ("The federal claim must have substance sufficient to confer subject matter jurisdiction on the court.... Assuming substantiality of the federal issues, there is *power* in federal courts to hear the whole").

We have not, however, applied *Gibbs*' expansive interpretive approach to other aspects of the jurisdictional statutes. For instance, we have consistently interpreted § 1332 as requiring complete diversity: In a case with multiple plaintiffs and multiple defendants, the presence in the action of a single plaintiff from the same State as a single defendant deprives the district court of original diversity jurisdiction over the entire action. The complete diversity requirement is not mandated by the Constitution, or by the plain text of § 1332(a). The Court, nonetheless, has adhered to the complete diversity rule in light of the purpose of the diversity requirement, which is to provide a federal forum for important disputes where state courts might favor, or be perceived as favoring, home-state litigants. The presence of parties from the same State on both sides of a case dispels this concern, eliminating a principal reason for conferring § 1332 jurisdiction over any of the claims in the action. The specific purpose of the complete diversity rule explains both why we have not adopted *Gibbs*' expansive interpretive approach to this aspect of the jurisdictional statute and why *Gibbs* does not undermine the complete diversity rule. In order for a federal court to invoke supplemental jurisdiction under *Gibbs*, it must first have original jurisdiction over at least one claim in the action. Incomplete diversity destroys original jurisdiction with respect to all claims, so there is nothing to which supplemental jurisdiction can adhere.

In contrast to the diversity requirement, most of the other statutory prerequisites for federal jurisdiction, including the federal-question and amount-in-controversy requirements, can be analyzed claim by claim. True, it does not follow by necessity from this that a district court has authority to exercise supplemental jurisdiction over all claims provided there is original jurisdiction over just one. Before the enactment of § 1367, the Court declined in contexts other than the pendent-claim instance to follow *Gibbs*' expansive approach to interpretation of the jurisdictional statutes. The Court took a more restrictive view of the proper interpretation of these statutes in so-called pendent-party cases involving supplemental jurisdiction over claims involving additional parties — plaintiffs or defendants — where the district courts would lack original jurisdiction over claims by each of the parties standing alone.

Thus, with respect to plaintiff-specific jurisdictional requirements, the Court held in Clark v. Paul Gray, Inc., 306 U.S. 583 (1939), that every plaintiff must separately satisfy the amount-in-controversy requirement. Though *Clark* was a federal-question case, at that time federal-question jurisdiction had an amount-in-controversy requirement analogous to the amount-in-controversy requirement for diversity cases. "Proper practice," *Clark* held, "requires that where each of several plaintiffs is bound to establish the jurisdictional amount with respect to his own claim, the suit should be dismissed as to those who fail to show that the requisite amount is involved." The Court reaffirmed this rule, in the context of a class action brought invoking § 1332(a) diversity jurisdiction, in Zahn v. International Paper Co., 414 U.S. 291 (1973). It follows "inescapably" from *Clark*, the Court held in *Zahn*, that "any plaintiff without the jurisdictional amount must be dismissed from the case, even though others allege jurisdictionally sufficient claims."

[The Court then discussed two supplemental jurisdiction cases, *Aldinger* and *Finley*, which we addressed in Chapter 12, Section D.2.]

As the jurisdictional statutes existed in 1989, then, here is how matters stood: First, the diversity requirement in § 1332(a) required complete diversity; absent complete diversity, the district court lacked original jurisdiction over all of the claims in the action. Second, if the district court had original jurisdiction over at least one claim, the jurisdictional statutes implicitly authorized supplemental jurisdiction over all other claims between the same parties arising out of the same Article III case or controversy. Third, even when the district court had original jurisdiction over one or more claims between particular parties, the jurisdictional statutes did not authorize supplemental jurisdiction over additional claims involving other parties.

B

In *Finley* we emphasized that "whatever we say regarding the scope of jurisdiction conferred by a particular statute can of course be changed by Congress." In 1990, Congress accepted the invitation. It * * * enacted § 1367, the provision which controls these cases.

All parties to this litigation and all courts to consider the question agree that § 1367 overturned the result in *Finley*. There is no warrant, however, for assuming that § 1367 did no more than to overrule *Finley* and otherwise to codify the existing state of the law of supplemental jurisdiction. We must not give jurisdictional statutes a more expansive interpretation than their text warrants, but it is just as important not to adopt an artificial construction that is narrower than what the text provides. No sound canon of interpretation requires Congress to speak with extraordinary clarity in order to modify the rules of federal jurisdiction within appropriate constitutional bounds. Ordinary principles of statutory construction apply. In order to determine the scope of supplemental jurisdiction authorized by § 1367, then, we must examine the statute's text in light of context, structure, and related statutory provisions.

Section 1367(a) is a broad grant of supplemental jurisdiction over other claims within the same case or controversy, as long as the action is one in which the district courts would have original jurisdiction. The last sentence of § 1367(a) makes it clear that the grant of supplemental jurisdiction extends to claims involving joinder or intervention of additional parties. The single question before us, therefore, is whether a diversity case in which the claims of some plaintiffs satisfy the amount-in-controversy requirement, but the claims of others plaintiffs do not, presents a "civil action of which the district courts have original jurisdiction." * * *

We now conclude the answer must be yes. When the well-pleaded complaint contains at least one claim that satisfies the amount-in-controversy requirement, and there are no other relevant jurisdictional defects, the district court, beyond all question, has original jurisdiction over that claim. The presence of other claims in the complaint, over which the district court may lack original jurisdiction, is of no moment. If the court has original jurisdiction over a single claim in the complaint, it has original jurisdiction over a "civil action" within the meaning of § 1367(a), even if the civil action over which it has jurisdiction comprises fewer claims than were included in the complaint. Once the court determines it has original jurisdiction over the civil action, it can turn to the question whether it has a constitutional and statutory basis for exercising supplemental jurisdiction over the other claims in the action.

Section 1367(a) commences with the direction that §§ 1367(b) and (c), or other relevant statutes, may provide specific exceptions, but otherwise § 1367(a) is a broad jurisdictional grant, with no distinction drawn between pendent-claim and pendent-party cases. In fact, the last sentence of § 1367(a) makes clear that the provision grants supplemental jurisdiction over claims involving joinder or intervention of additional parties. * * *

If § 1367(a) were the sum total of the relevant statutory language, our holding would rest on that language alone. The statute, of course, instructs us to examine § 1367(b) to determine if any of its exceptions apply, so we proceed to that section. While § 1367(b) qualifies the broad rule of § 1367(a), it does not withdraw supplemental jurisdiction over the claims of the additional parties at issue here. The specific exceptions to § 1367(a) contained in § 1367(b), moreover, provide additional support for our conclusion that § 1367(a) confers supplemental jurisdiction over these claims. Section 1367(b), which applies only to diversity cases, withholds supplemental jurisdiction over the claims of plaintiffs proposed to be joined as indispensable parties under Federal Rule of Civil Procedure 19, or who seek to intervene pursuant to Rule 24. Nothing in the text of § 1367(b), however, withholds supplemental jurisdiction over the claims of plaintiffs permissively joined under Rule 20 (like the additional plaintiffs in [*Ortega*]) or certified as class-action members pursuant to Rule 23 (like the additional plaintiffs in [*Allapattah*]). The natural, indeed the necessary, inference is that § 1367 confers supplemental jurisdiction over claims by Rule 20 and Rule 23 plaintiffs. This inference, at least with respect to Rule 20 plaintiffs, is strengthened by the fact that § 1367(b) explicitly excludes supplemental jurisdiction over claims against defendants joined under Rule 20.

We cannot accept the view, urged by some of the parties, commentators, and Courts of Appeals, that a district court lacks original jurisdiction over a civil action unless the court has original jurisdiction over every claim in the complaint. As we understand this position, it requires assuming either that all claims in the complaint must stand or fall as a single, indivisible "civil action" as a matter of definitional necessity—what we will refer to as the "indivisibility theory"—or else that the inclusion of a claim or party falling outside the district court's original jurisdiction somehow contaminates every other claim in the complaint, depriving the court of original jurisdiction over any of these claims—what we will refer to as the "contamination theory."

The indivisibility theory is easily dismissed, as it is inconsistent with the whole notion of supplemental jurisdiction. If a district court must have original jurisdiction over every claim in the complaint in order to have "original jurisdiction" over a "civil action," then in *Gibbs* there was no civil action of which the district court could assume original jurisdiction under § 1331, and so no basis for exercising supplemental jurisdiction over any of the claims. The indivisibility theory is further belied by our practice—in both federal-question and diversity cases—of allowing federal courts to cure jurisdictional defects by dismissing the offending parties rather than dismissing the entire action. *Clark*, for example, makes clear that claims that are jurisdictionally defective as to amount in controversy do not destroy original jurisdiction over other claims. 306 U.S. at 590 (dismissing parties who failed to meet the amount-in-controversy requirement but retaining jurisdiction over the remaining party). If the presence of jurisdictionally problematic claims in the complaint meant the district court was without original jurisdiction over the single, indivisible civil action before it, then the district court would have to dismiss the whole action rather than particular parties.

We also find it unconvincing to say that the definitional indivisibility theory applies in the context of diversity cases but not in the context of federal-question cases. The broad and general language of the statute does not permit this result. The contention is premised on the notion that the phrase "original jurisdiction of all civil actions" means different things in § 1331 and § 1332. It is implausible, however, to say that the identical phrase means one thing (original jurisdiction in all actions where at least one claim in the complaint meets the following requirements) in § 1331 and something else (original jurisdiction in all actions where every claim in the complaint meets the following requirements) in § 1332.

The contamination theory, as we have noted, can make some sense in the special context of the complete diversity requirement because the presence of nondiverse parties on both sides of a lawsuit eliminates the justification for providing a federal forum. The theory, however, makes little sense with respect to the amount-in-controversy requirement, which is meant to ensure that a dispute is sufficiently important to warrant federal-court attention. The presence of a single nondiverse party may eliminate the fear of bias with respect to all claims, but the presence of a claim that falls short of the minimum amount in controversy does nothing to reduce the importance of the claims that do meet this requirement.

It is fallacious to suppose, simply from the proposition that § 1332 imposes both the diversity requirement and the amount-in-controversy requirement, that the contamination theory germane to the former is also relevant to the latter. There is no inherent logical connection between the amount-in-controversy requirement and § 1332 diversity jurisdiction. After all, federal-question jurisdiction once had an amount-in-controversy requirement as well. If such a requirement were revived under § 1331, it is clear beyond peradventure that § 1367(a) provides supplemental jurisdiction over federal-question cases where some, but not all, of the federal-law claims involve a sufficient amount in controversy. In other words, § 1367(a) unambiguously overrules the holding and the result in *Clark*. If that is so, however, it would be quite extraordinary to say that § 1367 did not also overrule *Zahn*, a case that was premised in substantial part on the holding in *Clark*.

We also reject the argument * * * that while the presence of additional claims over which the district court lacks jurisdiction does not mean the civil action is outside the purview of § 1367(a), the presence of additional parties does. The basis for this distinction is not altogether clear, and it is in considerable tension with statutory text. Section 1367(a) applies by its terms to any civil action of which the district courts have original jurisdiction, and the last sentence of § 1367(a) expressly contemplates that the court may have supplemental jurisdiction over additional parties. So it cannot be the case that the presence of those parties destroys the court's original jurisdiction, within the meaning of § 1367(a), over a civil action otherwise properly before it. Also, § 1367(b) expressly withholds supplemental jurisdiction in diversity cases over claims by plaintiffs joined as indispensable parties under Rule 19. If joinder of such parties were sufficient to deprive the district court of original jurisdiction over the civil action within the meaning of § 1367(a), this specific limitation on supplemental jurisdiction in § 1367(b) would be superfluous. The argument that the presence of additional parties removes the civil action from the scope of § 1367(a) also would mean that § 1367 left the *Finley* result undisturbed. *Finley*, after all, involved a Federal Tort Claims Act suit against a federal defendant and state-law claims against additional defendants not otherwise subject to federal jurisdiction. Yet all concede that one purpose of § 1367 was to change the result reached in *Finley*.

Finally, it is suggested that our interpretation of § 1367(a) creates an anomaly regarding the exceptions listed in § 1367(b): It is not immediately obvious why Congress would withhold supplemental jurisdiction over plaintiffs joined as parties "needed for just adjudication" [Note: now called "a required party"] under Rule 19 but would allow supplemental jurisdiction over plaintiffs permissively joined under Rule 20. The omission of Rule 20 plaintiffs from the list of exceptions in § 1367(b) may have been an "unintentional drafting gap." If that is the case, it is up to Congress rather than the courts to fix it. The omission may seem odd, but it is not absurd. An alternative explanation for the different treatment of Rule 19 and Rule 20 is that Congress was concerned that extending supplemental jurisdiction to Rule 19 plaintiffs would allow circumvention of the complete diversity rule: A nondiverse plaintiff might be omitted intentionally from the original action, but joined later under Rule 19 as a necessary party. The contamination theory described above, if applicable, means this ruse would fail, but Congress may have wanted to make assurance double sure. More generally, Congress may have concluded that federal jurisdiction is only appropriate if the district court would have original jurisdiction over the claims of all those plaintiffs who are so essential to the action that they could be joined under Rule 19.

To the extent that the omission of Rule 20 plaintiffs from the list of § 1367(b) exceptions is anomalous, moreover, it is no more anomalous than the inclusion of Rule 19 plaintiffs in that list would be if the alternative view of § 1367(a) were to prevail. If the district court lacks original jurisdiction over a civil diversity action where any plaintiff's claims fail to comply with all the requirements of § 1332, there is no need for a special § 1367(b) exception for Rule 19 plaintiffs who do not meet these requirements. Though the omission of Rule 20 plaintiffs from § 1367(b) presents something of a puzzle on our view of the statute, the inclusion of Rule 19 plaintiffs in this section is at least as difficult to explain under the alternative view.

And so we circle back to the original question. When the well-pleaded complaint in district court includes multiple claims, all part of the same case or controversy, and some, but not all, of the claims are within the court's original jurisdiction, does the court have before it "any civil action of which the district courts have original jurisdiction"? It does. Under § 1367, the court has original jurisdiction over the civil action comprising the claims for which there is no jurisdictional defect. No other reading of § 1367 is plausible in light of the text and structure of the jurisdictional statute. Though the special nature and purpose of the diversity requirement means that a single nondiverse party can contaminate every other claim in the lawsuit, the contamination does not occur with respect to jurisdictional defects that go only to the substantive importance of individual claims.

It follows from this conclusion that the threshold requirement of § 1367(a) is satisfied in cases, like those now before us, where some, but not all, of the plaintiffs in a diversity action allege a sufficient amount in controversy. We hold that § 1367 by its plain text overruled *Clark* and *Zahn* and authorized supplemental jurisdiction over all claims by diverse parties arising out of the same Article III case or controversy, subject only to enumerated exceptions not applicable in the cases now before us.

C

The proponents of the alternative view of § 1367 insist that the statute is at least ambiguous and that we should look to other interpretive tools, including the legislative history of § 1367, which supposedly demonstrate Congress did not intend § 1367 to overrule *Zahn*. We can reject this argument at the very outset simply because § 1367 is not ambiguous. For the reasons elaborated above, interpreting § 1367 to foreclose supplemental jurisdiction over plaintiffs in diversity cases who do not meet the minimum amount in controversy is inconsistent with the text, read in light of other statutory provisions and our established jurisprudence. Even if we were to stipulate, however, that the reading these proponents urge upon us is textually plausible, the legislative history cited to support it would not alter our view as to the best interpretation of § 1367.

As we have repeatedly held, the authoritative statement is the statutory text, not the legislative history or any other extrinsic material. Extrinsic materials have a role in statutory interpretation only to the extent they shed a reliable light on the enacting Legislature's understanding of otherwise ambiguous terms. Not all extrinsic materials are reliable sources of insight into legislative understandings, however, and legislative history in particular is vulnerable to two serious criticisms. First, legislative history is itself often murky, ambiguous, and contradictory. Judicial investigation of legislative history has a tendency to become, to borrow Judge Leventhal's memorable phrase, an exercise in "'looking over a crowd and picking out your friends.'" Second, judicial reliance on legislative materials like committee reports, which are not themselves subject to the requirements of Article I, may give unrepresentative committee members — or, worse yet, unelected staffers and lobbyists — both the power and the incentive to attempt strategic manipulations of legislative history to secure results they were unable to achieve through the statutory text. * * *

[The Court then concluded that the legislative history as a whole was not clear in indicating a congressional desire to maintain the *Zahn* and *Clark* rules.]

* * * [T]he worst fears of critics who argue legislative history will be used to circumvent the Article I process were realized in this case. The telltale evidence is the statement, by three law professors who participated in drafting § 1367, that § 1367 "on its face" permits "supplemental jurisdiction over claims of class members that do not satisfy section 1332's jurisdictional amount requirement, which would overrule [*Zahn*]. [There is] a disclaimer of intent to accomplish this result in the legislative history.... It would have been better had the statute dealt explicitly with this problem, and the legislative history was an attempt to correct the oversight." Rowe, Burbank, & Mengler, *Compounding or Creating Confusion About Supplemental Jurisdiction? A Reply to Professor Freer*, 40 Emory L.J. 943, 960, n.90 (1991). The professors were frank to concede that if one refuses to consider the legislative history, one has no choice but to "conclude that section 1367 has wiped *Zahn* off the books." Ibid. So there exists an acknowledgment * * * both that the plain text of § 1367 overruled *Zahn* and that language to the contrary in the House Report was a *post hoc* attempt to alter that result. One need not subscribe to the wholesale condemnation of legislative history to refuse to give any effect to such a deliberate effort to amend a statute through a committee report.

In sum, even if we believed resort to legislative history were appropriate in these cases — a point we do not concede — we would not give significant weight to the House Report. * * *

The judgment of the Court of Appeals for the Eleventh Circuit [in *Allapattah*] is affirmed. The judgment of the Court of Appeals for the First Circuit [in *Ortega*] is reversed, and the case is remanded for proceedings consistent with this opinion.

Stevens, J., joined by Breyer, J., dissenting.

The sweeping purpose that the Court's decision imputes to Congress bears no resemblance to the House Report's description of the statute. But this does not seem to trouble the Court, for its decision today treats statutory interpretation as a pedantic exercise, divorced from any serious attempt at ascertaining congressional intent. Of course, there are situations in which we do not honor Congress' apparent intent unless that intent is made "clear" in the text of a statute — in this way, we can be certain that Congress considered the issue and intended a disfavored outcome. * * * But that principle provides no basis for discounting the House Report, given that our cases have never recognized a presumption in *favor* of expansive diversity jurisdiction.

Ginsburg, J., joined by Stevens, J., O'Connor, J., and Breyer, J., dissenting.

Section 1367, all agree, was designed to overturn this Court's decision in *Finley*.

What more § 1367 wrought is an issue on which courts of appeals have sharply divided. * * * The Court today holds that § 1367, although prompted by *Finley*, a case in which original access to federal court was predicated on a federal question, notably enlarges federal diversity jurisdiction. The Court reads § 1367 to overrule *Clark* and *Zahn*, thereby allowing access to federal court by co-plaintiffs or class members who do not meet the now in excess of $75,000 amount-in-controversy requirement, so long as at least one co-plaintiff, or the named class representative, has a jurisdictionally sufficient claim.

The Court adopts a plausibly broad reading of § 1367, a measure that is hardly a model of the careful drafter's art. There is another plausible reading, however, one less disruptive of our jurisprudence regarding supplemental jurisdiction.

[Justice Ginsburg largely adopted the argument discussed by the majority as the "indivisibility theory."]

Notes and Questions

1. The majority opinion concludes that a federal court obtains subject matter jurisdiction differently in federal question and diversity cases. Specifically, federal question jurisdiction is invoked by a *claim*, to which the plaintiff may append other claims eligible for supplemental jurisdiction. In contrast, diversity jurisdiction is invoked by the *case*, so that the presence of any non-diverse opposing party prevents the federal court from taking jurisdiction over any part of the dispute. How does the Court justify the different treatment of these two bases of subject matter jurisdiction? How can any justification be reconciled with Federal Rule 21, which instructs federal district courts to dismiss non-diverse parties (rather than dismissing the entire suit)?

2. After *Allapattah*, supplemental jurisdiction is available to a plaintiff in a diversity case to overcome a lack of amount-in-controversy. It is not available, however, to a plaintiff in a diversity case to overcome a lack of complete diversity. How does the Court justify this disparate treatment? Is any justification possible in light of the fact that both the amount-in-controversy and complete diversity requirements are imposed by statute and not by the Constitution?

3. The Court in *Allapattah* employed a textual approach to statutory interpretation, and refused to look to legislative history when the statutory language was clear. But doesn't a textualist approach lead to a bizarre result in a case involving multiple defendants? Suppose the facts were exactly the same as in *Allapattah* except the plaintiffs asserted their claims against two defendants. As we saw in Chapter 12, Section D, plaintiffs would join two or more defendants in a single case by using Rule 20. On its face, however, § 1367(b) prohibits the exercise of supplemental jurisdiction in a diversity case over claims "against persons made parties under Rule[] * * * 20." Literally, then, the statute appears to overrule *Zahn* and *Clark* if there is one defendant in the case (because then there is no claim against one joined under Rule 20), but not to overrule them if there are multiple defendants. See 4 MOORE'S FEDERAL PRACTICE § 20.07[3]. Does that make any sense? How could a court employing a textualist approach to statutory interpretation avoid such a result?

4. Recall from our discussion of diversity of citizenship jurisdiction that an unincorporated association takes on the citizenship of all its members. Suppose that a partnership of 150 people, who are citizens of Arizona, Nevada, and New Mexico, wants to sue a citizen of New Mexico. If it sued as a partnership, the case would be dismissed for failure to satisfy the complete diversity rule. Assuming that the amount in controversy could be met, could the partnership sue as a class? Whom would you, as counsel, select as representative(s)? See Kerney v. Fort Griffin Fandangel Ass'n, 624 F.2d 717 (5th Cir. 1980).

Note on Jurisdiction Under CAFA

In Section C.2 of this chapter, concerning "Policy and Ethical Issues," we noted that the Class Action Fairness Act (CAFA) was passed in 2005 largely at the behest of large commercial concerns. In a nutshell, businesses concluded that many state courts were too lenient in granting class certification. In an effort to avoid state court, they sought an expansion of federal jurisdiction (both for cases filed by plaintiffs and removed by defendants). The purpose was to get more class actions into federal court and thus to avoid the plaintiff-friendly state courts.

CAFA contains its own jurisdictional provisions in § 1332(d). Section 1332(d)(2) permits federal subject matter jurisdiction based upon minimal diversity between *any* class member and *any* defendant, so long as the matter in controversy exceeds $5,000,000. The amount in controversy is determined by aggregating the claims of all class members.* Thus, the Act avoids the *Zahn* issue altogether by overruling *Snyder v. Harris* and permitting aggregation. The provision for minimal diversity is more liberal than the rule in *Ben-Hur*. Under that case, the representative must be of diverse citizenship from all defendants. Under the Act, jurisdiction is satisfied if

* In discussing removal jurisdiction in Chapter 4, we noted Standard Fire Insurance Co. v. Knowles, 133 S. Ct. 1345 (2013), in which the Court held that the class representative's effort to stipulate that the class would not accept more than $5,000,000 in damages did not bind class members. Accordingly, defendant, upon showing that the amount in fact exceeded $5,000,000, was able to remove the case from state to federal court under CAFA.

any class member—not just the representative—is of diverse citizenship from any defendant.

The jurisdictional statute provides the federal district court with discretion to refuse to hear a case brought under the Act if (1) over one-third but fewer than two-thirds of plaintiff class members and (2) "the primary defendants" are citizens of the state in which the action was filed, based upon specific factors, including whether the claims involve matters of national or interstate interest. It is not at all clear how one defines "primary defendants." Further, the court "shall decline to exercise jurisdiction" in certain circumstances if (1) more than two-thirds of plaintiff class members and (2) at least one defendant from whom significant relief is sought and whose conduct forms a "significant basis" for the claims asserted are citizens of the state in which the action was filed.

The Act also relaxes restrictions on removal of cases from state to federal court. As we studied in Chapter 4, removal permits defendants to have a case originally filed in state court transferred to a federal court. Generally, removal is permitted only if all defendants join in the notice of removal. Moreover, removal is not permitted on the basis of diversity of citizenship jurisdiction if any defendant is a citizen of the forum in which the case is filed. Neither of these restrictions applies in cases removed under CAFA. 28 U.S.C. § 1453(b). Clearly, one purpose of the Act is to allow defendants to get large class actions out of state and into federal court. Some critics of the Act, noting that federal courts may be more stringent than some states in certifying classes (and that a federal certification order is subject to appellate review under Rule 23(f)), argue that Congress has attempted to effect tort reform in the guise of a procedural and jurisdictional statute.

6. Personal Jurisdiction

Must the court in which a class action is pending have in personam jurisdiction over all class members? *Mullane v. Central Hanover Bank*, which we read in Chapter 3, involved a New York statute that established a time limit during which members of a pooled trust fund could sue the trustee for misfeasance. The Supreme Court held, among other things, that the scheme violated due process insofar as it did not provide for individual notice to members whose names and addresses were readily available. Although *Mullane* was not technically a class action, does it help us address the question here?

The Supreme Court addressed the issue more directly in Phillips Petroleum Co. v. Shutts, 472 U.S. 797 (1985). In that case, three representatives brought a Rule 23(b)(3) class action in Kansas state court (Kansas' class action rule was modeled on Federal Rule 23). They purported to represent over 33,000 other owners of royalty interests in gas wells, and sued Phillips Petroleum to recover interest on royalty payments that the company had delayed. The average interest claim of each member of the class was $100. (Remember, amount in controversy is not a problem here. Why?) Each class member was given the notice required by Rule 23(c)(1). About 3,400 opted out, leaving a class of about 28,000. Of those, about 1,000 were Kansas citizens. Defendant argued that the Kansas court could not enter a binding judgment against the other 27,000, since they did not have minimum contacts with Kansas which would satisfy *International Shoe.*

The Supreme Court rejected the argument, and drew a distinction between members of a plaintiff class and defendants in a nonclass suit:

> The purpose of [the "minimum contacts"] test, of course, is to protect a defendant from the travail of defending in a distant forum, unless the defendant's contacts with the forum make it just to force him to defend there. * * *
>
> * * * An adverse judgment by Kansas courts in this case may extinguish the chose in action forever through res judicata. Such an adverse judgment, petitioner claims, would be every bit as onerous to an absent plaintiff as an adverse judgment on the merits would be to a defendant. Thus, the same due process protections should apply to absent plaintiffs: Kansas should not be able to exert jurisdiction over the plaintiffs' claims unless the plaintiffs have sufficient minimum contacts with Kansas.
>
> We think petitioner's premise is in error. The burdens placed by a State upon an absent class-action plaintiff are not of the same order or magnitude as those it places upon an absent defendant. An out-of-state defendant summoned by a plaintiff is faced with the full powers of the forum State to render judgment *against* it. The defendant must generally hire counsel and travel to the forum to defend itself from the plaintiff's claim, or suffer a default judgment. The defendant may be forced to participate in extended and often costly discovery, and will be forced to respond in damages or to comply with some other form of remedy imposed by the court should it lose the suit. The defendant may also face liability for court costs and attorney's fees. These burdens are substantial, and the minimum contacts requirement of the Due Process Clause prevents the forum State from unfairly imposing them upon the defendant.
>
> A class-action plaintiff, however, is in quite a different posture. * * * In sharp contrast to the predicament of a defendant haled into an out-of-state forum, the plaintiffs in this suit were not haled anywhere to defend themselves upon pain of a default judgment. As commentators have noted, from the plaintiffs' point of view a class action resembles a "quasi-administrative proceeding, conducted by the judge." 3B J. Moore & J. Kennedy, Moore's Federal Practice 23.45[4.-5] (1984).
>
> Unlike a defendant in a normal civil suit, an absent class-action plaintiff is not required to do anything. He may sit back and allow the litigation to run its course, content in knowing that there are safeguards provided for his protection. In most class actions an absent plaintiff is provided at least with an opportunity to "opt out" of the class, and if he takes advantage of that opportunity he is removed from the litigation entirely.

We reject petitioner's contention that the Due Process Clause of the Fourteenth Amendment requires that absent plaintiffs affirmatively "opt in" to the class, rather than be deemed members of the class if they do not "opt out." We think that such a contention is supported by little, if any precedent, and that it ignores the differences between class-action plaintiffs, on the one hand, and defendants in nonclass civil suits on the other. Any plaintiff may consent to jurisdiction. The essential question, then, is how stringent the requirement for a showing of consent will be.

We think that the procedure followed by Kansas, where a fully descriptive notice is sent by first-class mail to each class member, with an explanation of the right to "opt out," satisfies due process.

Shutts, 472 U.S. at 807–12.

Notes and Questions

1. How can a state lacking in personam jurisdiction over a class member force her to take an affirmative act (opt out) to avoid being bound by its judgment?

2. Would *Shutts* permit a binding final judgment against plaintiff class members in actions brought under Rule 23(b)(1) or (b)(2)? In a footnote, the Court limited its holding in *Shutts* to plaintiff class actions "concerning claims wholly or predominately for money judgments." The Court would "intimate no view concerning other types of class actions, such as those seeking equitable relief." 472 U.S. at 811–12 n.3.

In *Wal-Mart v. Dukes*, the Court rejected the recovery of monetary relief in a Rule 23(b)(2) class action. It said: "[Rule] 23(b)(2) does not require that class members be given notice and opt-out rights, presumably because it is thought (rightly or wrongly) that notice has no purpose when the class is mandatory, and that depriving people of their right to sue in this manner complies with the Due Process Clause. In the context of a class action predominately for money damages we have held that absence of notice and opt-out violates due process. See [*Shutts*]. While we have never held that to be so where the monetary claims do not predominate, the serious possibility that it may be so provides an additional reason not to read rule 23(b)(2) to include the monetary claims here." 131 S. Ct. at 2559. Thus, while not holding that due process requires notice and the right to opt out anytime a class seeks monetary recovery, the Court certainly tips its hand in that direction.

3. In the same footnote 3 in *Shutts*, the Court indicated that its discussion did not address defendant classes. Indeed, it seems clear that the Court would not permit defendant class actions to bind members of the defendant class over whom the court lacked in personam jurisdiction. Interestingly, in decisions before *Shutts*, several courts permitted actions against defendant classes even though they only had in personam jurisdiction over the representative. See, e.g., Dale Electronics, Inc. v. R.C.L. Electronics, Inc., 53 F.R.D. 531 (D.N.H. 1971); Canuel v. Oskoian, 23 F.R.D. 307 (D.R.I. 1959).

4. Remember that the prevailing party in litigation usually recovers her costs and, in exceptional circumstances, attorney's fees, from the losing party. Suppose that a

plaintiff class action resulted in judgment for the defendant. From whom can the defendant recover costs and, if appropriate, attorney's fees? Is the representative of the plaintiff class solely responsible for these amounts, or may she seek contribution from the class? If the latter, shouldn't the court be required to have in personam jurisdiction over the class members? The Court in *Shutts* dodged the issue, noting that the petitioner had cited no cases involving such a scenario, and saying "the disposition of these issues is best left to a case which presents them in a more concrete way." 472 U.S. at 810 n.2. Because such issues would only arise when the court entered judgment, how should a court address them at the point of class certification?

5. In a part of the *Shutts* opinion not reproduced above, the Court held that a Kansas court could not apply Kansas substantive law to the claims of class members who had no connection with Kansas. This choice of law issue will be especially important in an upper-division course on Conflict of Laws. For our purposes, note that *Shutts* presented the possible use of subclasses. After remand, the trial court could certify subclasses of members to whom the law of a particular state applied. Thus, there could be a subclass consisting of members whose claims are to be governed by Kansas law and another for those whose claims are governed by Missouri law, and so forth.

Chapter 14

Appellate Review

A. Introduction and Integration

Earlier we examined two mechanisms by which judgments can be re-examined. In one, the rendering court reopens and reconsiders the judgment. In federal court, this approach is controlled by Rule 60. In the second, the dissatisfied litigant attacks the judgment collaterally by challenging its validity or enforceability in a second law suit. This approach is constrained by the rules of preclusion and the full faith and credit provisions. This chapter focuses on a third mechanism for reexamining judgments — appellate review.

In an appeal, a litigant seeks review by a different level of the judiciary. An appeal does not include a new trial — it is a review of what happened in the trial court.* Thus, there are no juries and the appellate court does not take evidence. Instead, the appellate court relies on the transcript and other records of the proceedings below. Appellate courts typically sit in multi-judge panels of three or more.

There is no federal constitutional right to appeal in either civil or criminal cases. See Dohany v. Rogers, 281 U.S. 362, 369 (1930); Reetz v. Michigan, 188 U.S. 505, 508 (1903). See John Leubsdorf, *Constitutional Civil Procedure*, 64 TEX. L. REV. 579, 628–31 (1984). Today the federal system and all state courts have some mechanisms for appeal, although not all states permit appeals "of right." In Virginia and West Virginia, for example, appellate review in most civil cases is entirely discretionary, that is, before addressing the merits of the appeal, the appellate court decides whether to hear the appeal at all. See Thomas Marvell, *Appellate Capacity and Caseload Growth*, 16 AKRON L. REV. 43, 72–74 (1982).

* Some states permit litigants to "appeal" by seeking a trial de novo before a different court. Under this system, which is often used for minor criminal offenses, the defendant is tried first before a court of limited jurisdiction, such as a police traffic court, without a jury. If convicted, the defendant may request a trial de novo before a court of general criminal jurisdiction and a jury. In the trial de novo, the prior trial is ignored — there is no review by the second court of the findings or errors of the first court — and the case is treated as an entirely new proceeding. See generally Ludwig v. Massachusetts, 427 U.S. 618 (1976) (upholding the Massachusetts system of trials de novo). This chapter does not address trials de novo.

Why are appeals allowed at all? One book on appellate courts offers the following justifications:

> *First.* Appellate courts provide a means of ensuring that the law is interpreted and applied correctly and uniformly. * * *
>
> *Second.* Appellate courts provide a means for the ongoing development and evolution of the law in the common law tradition. * * *
>
> *Third.* Appellate courts heighten the legitimacy and acceptability of judicial decisions. * * *
>
> *Fourth.* Appellate courts provide a means for the institutional sharing of judicial responsibility for decisions. * * *

Daniel John Meador & Jordana Simone Bernstein, Appellate Courts in the United States 3–5 (1994). A report by the American Bar Association described appeals as "a fundamental element of procedural fairness as generally understood in this country." ABA Comm. On Standards Of Judicial Administration: Standards Relating To Appellate Courts § 3.10 commentary at 12 (1977). Do you agree? Do the justifications for appeals listed above assume that courts of appeals are more likely to be "correct" than trial courts? Is this assumption warranted? Cf. Brown v. Allen, 344 U.S. 443, 540 (1953) (Jackson, J., concurring) ("We are not final because we are infallible, but we are infallible because we are final.").

B. Appellate Jurisdiction in the Federal Courts

1. Section 1291

The federal appellate courts consist of the United States Courts of Appeals, sometimes called circuit courts, and the United States Supreme Court. (The Supreme Court has trial court jurisdiction over cases involving Ambassadors and cases involving disputes between states.) The courts of appeals primarily review district court decisions, although they also have appellate authority over certain decisions of federal regulatory agencies. The United States Supreme Court primarily reviews decisions of the courts of appeals and of the highest state courts. Congress regulates the jurisdiction of both the courts of appeals and the Supreme Court by statute.

The primary statute conferring jurisdiction on the courts of appeals is 28 U.S.C. § 1291, which provides in relevant part:

> The courts of appeals * * * shall have jurisdiction of appeals from all final decisions of the district courts of the United States, * * * except where a direct review may be had in the Supreme Court. * * *

Notice that § 1291 grants an appeal of right in all cases decided by a federal district court. Litigants do not need to persuade the court of appeals that their case warrants review.

The statute nonetheless contains an important qualification — § 1291 only grants appellate jurisdiction over "final decisions." The Supreme Court has explained that "[a] 'final decision' generally * * * ends the litigation on the merits and leaves nothing for the court to do but execute the judgment." Catlin v. United States, 324 U.S. 229, 233 (1945). In other words, "final decision" as used in the statute ordinarily means "final judgment" or "final decree."

Would the following rulings be appealable under § 1291?

(a) The defendant moves to dismiss the complaint for failure to state a claim.

  (i) The court grants the motion.

  (ii) The court denies the motion.

(b) Following a jury verdict, the plaintiff moves for a new trial.

  (i) The court denies the motion and enters judgment for the defendant.

  (ii) The court grants the motion for a new trial.

Many decisions made in the course of litigation are "interlocutory," that is, they come before the end of the case and, thus, are not immediately appealable under § 1291. For example, rulings on motions to transfer, discovery, and the admissibility of evidence are all interlocutory. Does it make sense to require litigants to wait until the case is over before appealing? Isn't there a risk of a waste of resources? Suppose, for example, the district court refuses to dismiss a case for lack of jurisdiction and a full trial ensues. On appeal, the court of appeals rules that the case should have been dismissed. Wouldn't an early appeal have prevented unnecessary trial expenses? Are there some rights that might be irreparably lost if litigants must await a final judgment before appealing? On the other hand, what costs might be saved by requiring parties to await a final decision?

Does allowing early appeals have any positive or negative effects on the administration of justice?

Policies concerning appeals might turn at least in part on the likelihood that the lower court will be reversed. One study found that about 20% of civil judgments were appealed and that of these appeals, about 21% resulted in a reversal. However, reversal rates varied significantly among categories of appeals. For example, jury verdicts for plaintiffs that were appealed were reversed in 33%% of the cases while appealed jury verdict for defendants were reversed in only 12% of cases. Kevin Clermont & Theodore Eisenberg, *Anti-Plaintiff Bias in the Federal Appellate Courts*, 84 JUDICATURE 128 (2000). Another study by the same authors suggests that in particular types of cases, the variations may be even greater. That study concludes that in employment discrimination cases, defendants that appealed won reversals in 44% of cases whereas plaintiffs that appealed won reversals in only 6% of cases. Kevin Clermont & Theodore Eisenberg, *Plaintiphobia in the Appellate Courts: Civil Rights Really Do Differ from Negotiable Instruments*, 2002 U. ILL. L. REV. 947.

Aside from whether early appeals are cost-effective, does allowing early appeals have any positive or negative effects on the administration of justice? It has been argued, for example, that given the relatively low percentage of cases that actually go to trial, pre-trial rulings on pleadings, discovery, and summary judgment are increasingly important and may, for all practical purposes, be dispositive. Without some mechanism of interlocutory appeals, these rulings may essentially be unreviewable. See Adam Steinman, *Reinventing Appellate Jurisdiction*, 48 B.C. L. Rev. 1237 (2007).

2. Collateral Order Doctrine

Suppose that a plaintiff who is too poor to pay a filing fee requests that the court waive the fee, and the court denies the motion. At least from the plaintiff's point of view, the ruling is a final decision, because unless the fee is waived, she will never be able to file, let alone proceed to the merits. Should the ruling on the fee waiver be immediately appealable?

The Supreme Court has recognized that in at least some circumstances, a ruling may be immediately appealable even though there is no final ruling on the merits of the case. The leading case is Cohen v. Beneficial Industrial Loan Corp., 337 U.S. 541 (1949), which we first encountered in the chapter on *Erie*, Chapter 10, Section B.2. The *Erie* issue in that case was whether the federal court was required to apply a state law that obligated plaintiffs in shareholder derivative actions to post a substantial bond. The district court refused to apply state law, and the defendant immediately appealed. Ultimately, the Supreme Court held that state law should be applied in federal court, but before reaching this issue, the Court had to determine whether the appeal was premature. The Court allowed the immediate appeal, explaining:

> The effect of the statute [§ 1291] is to disallow appeal from any decision which is tentative, informal or incomplete. Appeal gives the upper court a power of review, not one of intervention. So long as the matter remains open, unfinished or inconclusive, there may be no intrusion by appeal. But the District Court's action upon this application was concluded and closed and its decision final in that sense before the appeal was taken.
>
> Nor does the statute permit appeals, even from fully consummated decisions, where they are but steps towards final judgment in which they will merge. The purpose is to combine in one review all stages of the proceeding that effectively may be reviewed and corrected if and when final judgment results. But this order of the District Court did not make any step toward final disposition of the merits of the case and will not be merged in final judgment. When that time comes, it will be too late effectively to review the present order, and the rights conferred by the statute, if it is applicable, will have been lost, probably irreparably. * * *
>
> This decision appears to fall in that small class which finally determine claims of right separable from, and collateral to, rights asserted in the action, too important to be denied review and too independent of the cause itself to require that appellate consideration be deferred until the whole case is

> adjudicated. The Court has long given this provision of the statute this practical rather than a technical construction.

Id. at 546.

Cohen has sometimes been described as an "exception" to the final decision rule, but the Court has explained that "[t]he collateral order doctrine is best understood not as an exception to the 'final decision' rule laid down by Congress in § 1291, but as a 'practical construction' of it." Digital Equip. Corp. v. Desktop Direct, Inc., 511 U.S. 863 (1994). The following case considers how far this "practical construction" extends.

Cunningham v. Hamilton County

527 U.S. 198, 119 S. Ct. 1915, 144 L. Ed. 2d 184 (1999)

Justice Thomas delivered the opinion of the Court.

Federal courts of appeals ordinarily have jurisdiction over appeals from "final decisions of the district courts." 28 U.S.C. § 1291. This case presents the question whether an order imposing sanctions on an attorney pursuant to Federal Rule of Civil Procedure 37(a)(4) is a final decision. We hold that it is not, even where, as here, the attorney no longer represents a party in the case.

I

Petitioner, an attorney, represented Darwin Lee Starcher in a federal civil rights suit filed against respondent and other defendants. Starcher brought the suit after his son, Casey, committed suicide while an inmate at the Hamilton County Justice Center. The theory of the original complaint was that the defendants willfully ignored their duty to care for Casey despite his known history of suicide attempts.

A Magistrate Judge oversaw discovery. On May 29, 1996, petitioner was served with a request for interrogatories and documents; responses were due within 30 days after service. See Fed. Rules Civ. Proc. 33(b)(3), 34(b). This deadline, however, passed without compliance. The Magistrate Judge ordered the plaintiff "by 4:00 p.m. on July 12, 1996 to make full and complete responses" to defendants' requests for interrogatories and documents and further ordered that four witnesses — Rex Smith, Roxanne Dieffenbach, and two individual defendants — be deposed on July 25, 1996.

Petitioner failed to heed the Magistrate Judge's commands. She did not produce the requested documents, gave incomplete responses to several of the interrogatories, and objected to several others. Flouting the Magistrate Judge's order, she noticed the deposition of Rex Smith on July 22, 1996, not July 25, and then refused to withdraw this notice despite reminders from defendants' counsel. And even though the Magistrate Judge had specified that the individual defendants were to be deposed only if plaintiff had complied with his order to produce "full and complete" responses, she filed a motion to compel their appearance. Respondent and other defendants then filed motions for sanctions against petitioner.

At a July 19 hearing, the Magistrate Judge granted the defendants' motions for sanctions. In a subsequent order, he found that petitioner had violated the discovery order and described her conduct as "egregious." Relying on Federal Rule of Civil Procedure 37(a)(4), the Magistrate Judge ordered petitioner to pay the Hamilton County treasurer $1,494, representing costs and fees incurred by the Hamilton County Prosecuting Attorney as counsel for respondent and one individual defendant. He took care to specify, however, that he had not held a contempt hearing and that petitioner was never found to be in contempt of court.

The District Court affirmed the Magistrate Judge's sanctions order. The court noted that the matter "[h]ad already consumed an inordinate amount of the Court's time" and described the Magistrate's job of overseeing discovery as a "task assum[ing] the qualities of a full time occupation." It found that "[t]he Magistrate Judge did not err in concluding that sanctions were appropriate" and that "the amount of the Magistrate Judge's award was not contrary to law." The District Court also granted several defendants' motions to disqualify petitioner as counsel for plaintiff due to the fact that she was a material witness in the case.

Although proceedings in the District Court were ongoing, petitioner immediately appealed the District Court's order affirming the Magistrate Judge's sanctions award to the United States Court of Appeals for the Sixth Circuit. The Court of Appeals, over a dissent, dismissed the appeal for lack of jurisdiction. It considered whether the sanctions order was immediately appealable under the collateral order doctrine which provides that certain orders may be appealed, notwithstanding the absence of final judgment, but only when they "are conclusive, ... resolve important questions separate from the merits, and ... are effectively unreviewable on appeal from the final judgment in the underlying action." Swint v. Chambers County Comm'n, 514 U.S. 35, 42 (1995) (citing Cohen v. Beneficial Industrial Loan Corp., 337 U.S. 541, 546 (1949)). In the Sixth Circuit's view, these conditions were not satisfied because the issues involved in petitioner's appeal were not "completely separate" from the merits. As for the fact that petitioner had been disqualified as counsel, the court held that "a non-participating attorney, like a participating attorney, ordinarily must wait until final disposition of the underlying case before filing an appeal." It avoided deciding whether the order was effectively unreviewable absent an immediate appeal but saw "no reason why, after final resolution of the underlying case ... a sanctioned attorney should be unable to appeal the order imposing sanctions."

The Federal Courts of Appeals disagree over whether an order of Rule 37(a) sanctions against an attorney is immediately appealable under § 1291. We granted a writ of certiorari, limited to this question, and now affirm.

II

Section 1291 of the Judicial Code generally vests courts of appeals with jurisdiction over appeals from "final decisions" of the district courts. It descends from the Judiciary Act of 1789 where "the First Congress established the principle that only 'final judgments and decrees' of the federal district courts may be reviewed on appeal." In accord with this historical understanding, we have repeatedly interpreted § 1291 to mean that an appeal ordinarily will not lie until after final judgment has been entered in a case. As we explained in Firestone Tire & Rubber Co. v. Risjord, 449 U.S. 368 (1981), the final judgment rule serves several salutary purposes:

> "It emphasizes the deference that appellate courts owe to the trial judge as the individual initially called upon to decide the many questions of law and fact that occur in the course of a trial. Permitting piecemeal appeals would undermine the independence of the district judge, as well as the special role that individual plays in our judicial system. In addition, the rule is in accordance with the sensible policy of avoiding the obstruction to just claims that would come from permitting the harassment and cost of a succession of separate appeals from the various rulings to which a litigation may give rise, from its initiation to entry of judgment. The rule also serves the important purpose of promoting efficient judicial administration." Id. at 374 (citations and internal quotation marks omitted).

Consistent with these purposes, we have held that a decision is not final, ordinarily, unless it "'ends the litigation on the merits and leaves nothing for the court to do but execute the judgment.'" Van Cauwenberghe v. Biard, 486 U.S. 517, 521–522 (1988) (quoting Catlin v. United States, 324 U.S. 229, 233 (1945)).

The Rule 37 sanction imposed on petitioner neither ended the litigation nor left the court only to execute its judgment. Thus, it ordinarily would not be considered a final decision under § 1291. However, we have interpreted the term "final decision" in § 1291 to permit jurisdiction over appeals from a small category of orders that do not terminate the litigation. "That small category includes only decisions that are conclusive, that resolve important questions separate from the merits, and that are effectively unreviewable on appeal from the final judgment in the underlying action."[4]

Respondent conceded that the sanctions order was conclusive, so at least one of the collateral order doctrine's conditions is presumed to have been satisfied. We do not think, however, that appellate review of a sanctions order can remain completely separate from the merits. In *Van Cauwenberghe*, for example, we held that the denial of a motion to dismiss on the ground of *forum non conveniens* was not a final decision. We reasoned that consideration of the factors underlying that decision such as "the relative ease of access to sources of proof" and "the availability of witnesses" required trial courts to "scrutinize the substance of the dispute between the parties to evaluate what proof is required, and determine whether the pieces of evidence cited by the parties are critical, or even relevant, to the plaintiff's cause of action and to any potential defenses to the action." Similarly, in *Coopers & Lybrand*, we held that a de-

4. Most of our collateral order decisions have considered whether an order directed at a party to the litigation is immediately appealable. E.g., Coopers & Lybrand v. Livesay, 437 U.S. 463, 468–469 (1978). Petitioner, of course, was an attorney representing the plaintiff in the case. It is nevertheless clear that a decision does not automatically become final merely because it is directed at someone other than a plaintiff or defendant. See Richardson-Merrell, Inc. v. Koller, 472 U.S. 424, 434–435 (1985) (rejecting, as outside collateral order doctrine, immediate appeal of order disqualifying counsel). For example, we have repeatedly held that a witness subject to a discovery order, but not held in contempt, generally may not appeal the order.

termination that an action may not be maintained as a class action also was not a final decision, noting that such a determination was enmeshed in the legal and factual aspects of the case.

Much like the orders at issue in *Van Cauwenberghe* and *Coopers & Lybrand*, a Rule 37(a) sanctions order often will be inextricably intertwined with the merits of the action. An evaluation of the appropriateness of sanctions may require the reviewing court to inquire into the importance of the information sought or the adequacy or truthfulness of a response. Some of the sanctions in this case were based on the fact that petitioner provided partial responses and objections to some of the defendants' discovery requests. To evaluate whether those sanctions were appropriate, an appellate court would have to assess the completeness of petitioner's responses. See Fed. Rule Civ. Proc. 37(a)(3) ("For purposes of this subdivision an evasive or incomplete disclosure, answer, or response is to be treated as a failure to disclose, answer, or respond"). Such an inquiry would differ only marginally from an inquiry into the merits and counsels against application of the collateral order doctrine. Perhaps not every discovery sanction will be inextricably intertwined with the merits, but we have consistently eschewed a case-by-case approach to deciding whether an order is sufficiently collateral.

Even if the merits were completely divorced from the sanctions issue, the collateral order doctrine requires that the order be effectively unreviewable on appeal from a final judgment. Petitioner claims that this is the case. In support, she relies on a line of decisions holding that one who is not a party to a judgment generally may not appeal from it. She also posits that contempt orders imposed on witnesses who disobey discovery orders are immediately appealable and argues that the sanctions order in this case should be treated no differently.

Petitioner's argument suffers from at least two flaws. It ignores the identity of interests between the attorney and client. Unlike witnesses, whose interests may differ substantially from the parties', attorneys assume an ethical obligation to serve their clients' interests. This obligation remains even where the attorney might have a personal interest in seeking vindication from the sanctions order. In *Richardson-Merrell*, we held that an order disqualifying an attorney was not an immediately appealable final decision. * * * [S]ee also Flanagan v. United States, 465 U.S. 259, 263–269 (1984) (order disqualifying attorney in criminal case not a "final decision" under § 1291). We explained that "[a]n attorney who is disqualified for misconduct may well have a personal interest in pursuing an immediate appeal, an interest which need not coincide with the interests of the client. As a matter of professional ethics, however, the decision to appeal should turn entirely on the client's interest." *Richardson-Merrell* (citing ABA Model Rules of Professional Conduct 1.7(b), 2.1 (1985)). This principle has the same force when an order of discovery sanctions is imposed on the attorney alone. The effective congruence of interests between clients and attorneys counsels against treating attorneys like other nonparties for purposes of appeal.

Petitioner's argument also overlooks the significant differences between a finding of contempt and a Rule 37(a) sanctions order. "Civil contempt is designed to force the contemnor to comply with an order of the court." Willy v. Coastal Corp., 503 U.S. 131, 139 (1992). In contrast, a Rule 37(a) sanctions order lacks any prospective effect and is not designed to compel compliance. Judge Adams captured the essential distinction between the two types of orders when he noted that an order such as civil contempt

> "is not simply to deter harassment and delay, but to effect some discovery conduct. A non-party's interest in resisting a discovery order is immediate and usually separate from the parties' interests in delay. Before final judgment is reached, the non-party either will have surrendered the materials sought or will have suffered incarceration or steadily mounting fines imposed to compel the discovery. If the discovery is held unwarranted on appeal only after the case is resolved, the non-party's injury may not be possible to repair. Under Rule 37(a), no similar situation exists. The objective of the Rule is the prevention of delay and costs to other litigants caused by the filing of groundless motions. An attorney sanctioned for such conduct by and large suffers no inordinate injury from a deferral of appellate consideration of the sanction. He need not in the meantime surrender any rights or suffer undue coercion."

Eastern Maico Distributors, Inc. v. Maico-Fahrzeugfabrik, G.m.b.H., 658 F.2d 944, 949–950 (3d Cir. 1981) (citation and footnote omitted). To permit an immediate appeal from such a sanctions order would undermine the very purposes of Rule 37(a), which was designed to protect courts and opposing parties from delaying or harassing tactics during the discovery process. Immediate appeals of such orders would undermine trial judges' discretion to structure a sanction in the most effective manner. They might choose not to sanction an attorney, despite abusive conduct, in order to avoid further delays in their proceedings. Not only would such an approach ignore the deference owed by appellate courts to trial judges charged with managing the discovery process, it also could forestall resolution of the case as each new sanction would give rise to a new appeal. The result might well be the very sorts of piecemeal appeals and concomitant delays that the final judgment rule was designed to prevent.

Petitioner finally argues that, even if an attorney ordinarily may not immediately appeal a sanction order, special considerations apply when the attorney no longer represents a party in the case. Like the Sixth Circuit, we do not think that the appealability of a Rule 37 sanction imposed on an attorney should turn on the attorney's continued participation. Such a rule could not be easily administered. For example, it may be unclear precisely when representation terminates, and questions likely would arise over when the 30-day period for appeal would begin to run under Federal Rule of Appellate Procedure 4. The rule also could be subject to abuse if attorneys and clients strategically terminated their representation in order to trigger a right to appeal with a view to delaying the proceedings in the underlying case. While we recognize that our application of the final judgment rule in this setting may require nonparticipating attorneys to monitor the progress of the litigation after their work has ended, the efficiency interests served by limiting immediate appeals far outweigh any nominal monitoring costs borne by attorneys. For these reasons, an attorney's continued participation in a case does not affect whether a sanctions order is "final" for purposes of § 1291.

We candidly recognize the hardship that a sanctions order may sometimes impose on an attorney. Should these hardships be deemed to outweigh the desirability of restricting appeals to "final decisions," solutions other than an expansive interpretation of § 1291's "final decision" requirement remain available. Congress may amend the Judicial Code to provide explicitly for immediate appellate review of such orders. See, e.g., 28 U.S.C. § 1292(a)(1)–(3). Recent amendments to the Judicial Code also have authorized this Court to prescribe rules providing for the immediate appeal of certain orders, see §§ 1292(e), 2072(c), and "Congress' designation of the rulemaking process as the way to define or refine when a district court ruling is 'final' and when an interlocutory order is appealable warrants the Judiciary's full respect." Finally, in a particular case, a district court can reduce any hardship by reserving until the end of the trial decisions such as whether to impose the sanction, how great a sanction to impose, or when to order collection.

For the foregoing reasons, we conclude that a sanctions order imposed on an attorney is not a "final decision" under § 1291 and, therefore, affirm the judgment of the Court of Appeals.

It is so ordered.

JUSTICE KENNEDY, concurring.

This case comes to our argument docket, of course, so that we may resolve a split of authority in the Circuits on a jurisdictional issue, not because there is any division of opinion over the propriety of the underlying conduct. Cases involving sanctions against attorneys all too often implicate allegations that, when true, bring the law into great disrepute. Delays and abuses in discovery are the source of widespread injustice; and were we to hold sanctions orders against attorneys to be appealable as collateral orders, we would risk compounding the problem for the reasons suggested by Justice Thomas in his opinion for the Court. Trial courts must have the capacity to ensure prompt compliance with their orders, especially when attorneys attempt to abuse the discovery process to gain a tactical advantage.

It should be noted, however, that an attorney ordered to pay sanctions is not without a remedy in every case. If the trial court declines to stay enforcement of the order and the result is an exceptional hardship itself likely to cause an injustice, a petition for writ of mandamus might bring the issue before the Court of Appeals to determine if the trial court abused its discretion in issuing the order or denying the stay. In addition, if a contempt order is entered and there is no congruence of interests between the person subject to the order and a party to the underlying litigation, the order may be appealable. In United States Catholic Conference v. Abortion Rights Mobilization, Inc., 487 U.S. 72, 76 (1988), a case involving a nonparty witness, we said: "The right of a nonparty to appeal an adjudication of contempt cannot be questioned. The order finding a nonparty witness in contempt is appealable notwithstanding the absence of a final judgment in the underlying action."

The case before us, however, involves an order for sanctions and nothing more. I join the opinion of the Court and its holding that the order is not appealable under the collateral order doctrine.

Notes and Questions

1. The Court has wrestled with whether various orders constitute final decisions under § 1291. Do you agree with its resolution of the following?

(a) In a series of cases, the Court held that orders granting or denying motions to disqualify counsel are not immediately appealable. See Richardson-Merrell, Inc. v. Koller, 472 U.S. 424 (1985); Flanagan v. United States, 465 U.S. 259 (1984); Firestone Tire & Rubber Co. v. Risjord, 449 U.S. 368 (1981). The Court stressed that these orders can be reviewed effectively on appeal from the final judgment. But consider the situation of a litigant whose lawyer is disqualified. On appeal from the final judgment, would the litigant have to show only that the disqualification was erroneous, or would she also have to show prejudice? As one leading treatise has observed, "Reversal of an otherwise proper judgment without requiring a showing of prejudice would be costly in the extreme, and would be a high price to pay for the abstract desire to protect freedom of choice in representation." 15B Wright & Miller, Federal Practice & Procedure § 3914.21, at 99. On the other hand, if the litigant must show prejudice, then she would presumably have to show that the representation by substitute counsel was not as good as she would have received from original counsel and that this qualitative difference altered the outcome. How likely is it that any litigant could ever make this showing?

(b) In Puerto Rico Aqueduct & Sewer Authority v. Metcalf & Eddy, Inc., 506 U.S. 139 (1993), the defendant, an arm of the government of Puerto Rico, sought to dismiss a suit on grounds that it was immune from suit under the Eleventh Amendment. That Amendment prohibits states from being sued in federal court. The Supreme Court held that the denial of this motion was immediately appealable because a central purpose of Eleventh Amendment immunity is to protect the state from the costs and burdens of trial. This benefit would be effectively lost if a case were erroneously permitted to go to trial. See Mitchell v. Forsyth, 472 U.S. 511, 524–30 (1985) (allowing immediate appeal of order denying an official's claim of absolute or qualified immunity).

(c) In Digital Equipment Corp. v. Desktop Direct, Inc., 511 U.S. 863 (1994), the parties had settled a pending lawsuit and pursuant to the settlement, the plaintiff filed a notice of dismissal. Several months later, the district court granted the plaintiff's motion to vacate the dismissal and rescind the settlement on grounds that the defendant had misrepresented certain facts during the settlement negotiations. The Court held that the defendant could not immediately appeal the district court's grant of the motion to vacate. In reaching this conclusion, the Court focused on whether the decision involved an "important" question that was "effectively unreviewable" upon final judgment. The Court explained that "the third *Cohen* question, whether a right is 'adequately vindicable' or 'effectively reviewable,' simply cannot be answered without a judgment about the value of the interests that would be lost through rigorous application of a final judgment requirement." Id. at 878–79. "Where statutory and constitutional rights are concerned, 'irretrievabl[e] los[s]' can hardly be trivial * * *. But it is one thing to say that the policy of § 1291 to avoid piecemeal litigation should be reconciled with policies embodied in other statutes or the Constitution, and quite another to suggest that this public policy may be trumped routinely by the expectations or clever drafting of private parties." Id. at 879–80. "[A]n agreement's provision for immunity from trial * * * simply does not rise to the level of importance needed for recognition under § 1291." Id. at 878.

(d) In Coopers & Lybrand v. Livesay, 437 U.S. 463 (1978), the Court held that a district court's decision to decertify a class action was not immediately appealable under § 1291. The plaintiffs had argued that decertification was likely to be the "death knell" for the litigation because the individual recovery of each potential class member was too small to provide an incentive for individual litigation. Lower courts had accepted the argument that a "death knell" ruling was immediately appealable. The Supreme Court rejected the death knell doctrine, noting that under that doctrine, appealability would turn on a case by case factual inquiry into whether a ruling was or was not a death knell. The Court further noted that § 1292(b), infra Section B.3, authorizes appeals of interlocutory orders under limited circumstances and the death knell doctrine seemed to be a way to circumvent the limitations of § 1292(b). Subsequent to *Coopers & Lybrand*, and pursuant to 28 U.S.C. § 2072(c), Rule 23(f) was added. That Rule authorizes a court of appeals in its discretion to permit an appeal from a district court order granting or denying class action certification. This rule change effectively overrules the holding of *Coopers & Lybrand*, although the Court's analysis and its approach to the final judgment rule is still applicable in other cases. Rule 23(f) is discussed in Section B.4, infra.

(e) In Moses H. Cone Memorial Hospital v. Mercury Construction Corp., 460 U.S. 1 (1983), the Supreme Court held that an order staying a federal court action pending resolution of a parallel state case was immediately appealable. The Court reasoned that because the state judgment would be binding on the federal court, the plaintiff was "effectively out of court." The Court further explained that the case fell within the "*Cohen* exception." The defendant argued that the ruling on the stay could be reconsidered by the district court because it did not "conclusively determine the disputed question." The Court rejected this argument, explaining: "this is true only in the technical sense that every order short of a final decree is subject to reopening at the discretion of the district judge. * * * He surely would not have made that decision in the first instance unless he had expected the state court to resolve all relevant issues adequately." Id. at 12–13.

(f) In Mohawk Indus., Inc. v. Carpenter, 558 U.S. 100 (2009), the Court held that an order requiring a party to disclose material that it considered protected under the attorney-client privilege is not immediately appealable under the collateral order doctrine. The appealing party had argued that disclosure of privileged material is not effectively reviewable on appeal from final judgment because the privilege protects against not only the use of privileged material at trial but the disclosure of material in the first place. The Court rejected this argument, explaining: "Appellate courts can remedy the improper disclosure of privileged material in the same way they remedy a host of other erroneous evidentiary rulings: by vacating an adverse judgment and remanding for a new trial in which the protected material and its fruits are excluded from evidence." Id. at 109. As to concerns that delayed review might undermine the core purposes of the attorney-client privilege, the Court noted: "Mohawk is undoubtedly correct that an order to disclose privileged information intrudes on the confidentiality of attorney-client communications. But deferring review until final judgment does not meaningfully reduce the *ex ante* incentives for full and frank consultations between clients and counsel." Id. The Court also observed that if confronted with a "particularly injurious or novel privilege ruling" a litigant does have several other options including seeking review under § 1292 or mandamus (discussed below), or defying the order and appealing the punishment for criminal contempt of court.

2. In Will v. Hallock, 546 U.S. 345 (2006), the Supreme Court clarified when denials of claims of immunity from trial are immediately appealable. Reviewing its past cases in which immediate appeals were allowed, the Court explained:

> In each case, some particular value of a high order was marshaled in support of the interest in avoiding trial: honoring the separation of powers, preserving the efficiency of government and the initiative of its officials, respecting a State's dignitary interests, and mitigating the government's advantage over the individual. That is, it is not mere avoidance of a trial, but avoidance of a trial that would imperil a substantial public interest, that counts when asking whether an order is 'effectively' unreviewable if review is to be left until later.

Id. at 352–53. Applying this standard, the Court held that an immediate appeal was not appropriate in *Will.* In that case, the plaintiff had brought Federal Tort Claims Act claim against the federal government and that claim had been dismissed. The plaintiff then brought a claim against individual government agents alleging violations of her constitutional rights. The agents sought to dismiss the case, citing a federal statute that provides that a judgment under the Federal Torts Claims Act "shall constitute a complete bar to any action by the claimant, by reason of the same subject matter, against the employee of the government whose act or omission gave rise to the claim." When the district court denied the motion to dismiss, the defendants sought an immediate appeal. The Court held that the judgment bar at issue in the case was more like a rule of res judicata than immunity and "has no claim to greater importance than the typical defense of claim preclusion" for which an immediate appeal is not available.

3. The denial of a motion for summary judgment is an interlocutory order and is immediately appealable only in the relatively rare circumstance that it meets the criteria of the collateral order doctrine. If the denial of a motion for summary judgment can't be appealed immediately, can it be appealed after a trial on the merits?

In Ortiz v. Jordan, 562 U.S. 180 (2011), the Court held that an appeal of the summary judgment motion following trial came too late. The losing party could, of course, appeal the denial of a motion for judgment as a matter of law, provided that the party made a timely motion both before and after the verdict.

4. Should the denial of a motion to dismiss for lack of personal jurisdiction or for forum non conveniens be appealable immediately? In Van Cauwenberghe v. Biard, 486 U.S. 517 (1988), a criminal defendant was extradited to the United States and upon arrival here was served with civil process. The defendant moved to dismiss, arguing first that under the extradition treaty he was immune from civil process and, second, on grounds of forum non conveniens. The district court refused to dismiss on either ground, and the defendant sought an immediate appeal. The Supreme Court held that the appeal was not proper. Concerning the ruling on immunity from civil process, the Court concluded that this was simply an argument that the district court lacked personal jurisdiction. The Court then explained:

> In the context of due process restrictions on the exercise of personal jurisdiction, this Court has recognized that the individual interest protected is in "not being subject to the binding judgments of a forum with which [the defendant] has established no meaningful 'contacts, ties, or relations.'" *Burger King Corp.*, quoting *International Shoe Co.* Similarly, we believe petitioner's challenge to the District Court's exercise of personal jurisdiction because he is immune from civil process should be characterized as the right not to be subject to a binding judgment of the court. Because the right not to be subject to a binding judgment may be effectively vindicated following final judgment, we have held that the denial of a claim of lack of jurisdiction is not an immediately appealable collateral order.

Id. at 526–27. Isn't one of the purposes of personal jurisdiction "to protect a defendant from the travail of defending in a distant forum"? Phillips Petroleum Co. v. Shutts, 472 U.S. 797, 807 (1985). Can this purpose be vindicated on appeal following a full trial on the merits?

The Court also rejected an immediate appeal of the forum non conveniens ruling, holding that it is not "completely separate from the merits of the action," but requires an evaluation of the "locus of the alleged culpable conduct, often a disputed issue, and the connection of that conduct to the plaintiff's chosen forum." 486 U.S. at 528. See also Lauro Lines s.r.l. v. Chasser, 490 U.S. 495 (1989) (district court denied motion to dismiss on basis of contractual forum-selection clause; no immediate appeal allowed).

5. Section 1291 and the collateral order doctrine of *Cohen* apply only in federal court. In Johnson v. Fankell, 520 U.S. 911 (1997), plaintiff brought a § 1983 action in state court. The court denied the defendant's motion to dismiss on grounds of qualified immunity. Such a denial in federal court would have been immediately appealable. See Note 1(b), supra. The Court held that there was no federal right to an immediate appeal in state court.

3. Section 1292

The collateral order doctrine provides a means by which some interlocutory orders can be appealed. (Remember, "interlocutory" refers to any trial court order that is not a final judgment under § 1291.) In addition to this court-made doctrine, Congress has explicitly authorized immediate appeals of certain interlocutory orders. Section 1292(a)(1) permits the immediate appeal of the grant or denial of an injunction. The statute reflects the reality that the erroneous grant or denial of even a preliminary injunction may result in irreparable harm.

In 1958, Congress established a certification procedure to allow immediate appeal of certain other interlocutory orders. Under § 1292(b) the district court may certify an order for immediate appeal. The criteria for certification are that (1) there is "an order," (2) involving "a controlling question," (3) "of law," (4) "as to which there is substantial ground for difference of opinion," and (5) "that an immediate appeal from the order may materially advance the ultimate termination of the litigation." Once an order has been certified, an application must be filed with the court of appeals for permission to appeal. The court of appeals has discretion whether to grant permission, and one study indicates that permission is granted in fewer than half of the certified cases. See Michael Solimine, *Revitalizing Interlocutory Appeals in the Federal Courts*, 58 Geo. Wash. L. Rev. 1165, 1174 (1990).

Notes and Questions

1. Review § 1292(b), and consider whether the following cases would be proper for certification.

(a) Plaintiff files suit under the Americans with Disabilities Act, 42 U.S.C. § 12101 et seq. Plaintiff's right to recover depends on a difficult and unsettled question of statutory interpretation. Can the district court certify this interpretive question?

(b) The court orders the plaintiff to provide English translations of certain documents produced pursuant to Rule 34. The translations will be quite expensive to procure.

(c) The defendant moves to dismiss a case for lack of personal jurisdiction. The court expresses uncertainty as to whether the defendant really has sufficient contacts, but denies the motion to dismiss.

(d) The district court concludes that it would be more convenient for the litigation to proceed in a different district and orders the case transferred under § 1404(a).

2. In Yamaha Motor Corp. v. Calhoun, 516 U.S. 199 (1996), the Court held that when an order is certified under § 1292(b), the court of appeals can exercise jurisdiction over any question fairly included within the order. Review by the court is not limited to the particular question certified by the district court.

3. Suppose that one ruling in a case is immediately appealable, but other rulings are not. In an appeal of the first ruling, can the court of appeals exercise "pendent appellate jurisdiction" over the other rulings and review them at the same time? In

Swint v. Chambers County Commission, 514 U.S. 35 (1995), the Supreme Court held that at least under the facts of that case, pendent appellate jurisdiction was not proper. There, the rulings concerned different parties and were not "inextricably intertwined." Id. at 51. The Court specifically declined "definitively or preemptively [to] settle here whether or when it may be proper for a court of appeals with jurisdiction over one ruling to review, conjunctively, related rulings that are not themselves independently appealable." Id. at 50–51. The Court suggested that the proper way to resolve the scope of pendent appellate jurisdiction was through the rule making authority under §§ 2072(c) and 1292(e).

4. Rule 23(f)

As noted above, the Supreme Court held in *Coopers & Lybrand* that decisions concerning class certification are not final judgments. In 1998, the Federal Rules of Civil Procedure were amended to add Rule 23(f), which allows interlocutory review of certification decisions. Like § 1292(b), Rule 23(f) gives the court of appeals discretion whether to hear the appeal. However, unlike § 1292(b), Rule 23(f) does not require the district court to certify the appeal, nor does the Rule include any criteria for the court of appeals to use in determining when an immediate appeal is appropriate. Indeed, the Committee Note accompanying Rule 23(f) notes that the court of appeals is given "unfettered discretion whether to permit the appeal." The Supreme Court has yet to decide a case under Rule 23(f), and the circuit courts have been developing their own standards, with some variations among the circuits.

Building on an approach first outlined by the Seventh Circuit in Blair v. Equifax Check Serv., Inc., 181 F.3d 832 (7th Cir. 1999), most courts have focused on three categories of cases in which appeals of class certification decisions would be considered appropriate:

> First, an appeal ordinarily should be permitted when a denial of class status effectively ends the case (because, say, the named plaintiff's claim is not of a sufficient magnitude to warrant the costs of stand-alone litigation). Second, an appeal ordinarily should be permitted when the grant of class status raises the stakes of the litigation so substantially that the defendant likely will feel irresistible pressure to settle. Third, an appeal ordinarily should be permitted when it will lead to clarification of a fundamental issue of law.

Waste Management Holdings, Inc. v. Mowbray, 208 F.3d 288, 293 (1st Cir. 2000). See Newton v. Merrill Lynch, Pierce, Fenner & Smith, Inc., 259 F.3d 154 (3d Cir. 2001); In re Lorazepam & Clorazepate Antitrust Litigation, 289 F.3d 98 (D.C. Cir. 2002); In re Delta Air Lines, 310 F.3d 953 (6th Cir. 2002). See also Prado-Steiman v. Bush, 221 F.3d 1266 (11th Cir. 2000) (adding several factors).

Courts have noted that in considering the first two categories, the court of appeals should "tak[e] into account the discretion the district judge possesses in implementing Rule 23, and the corresponding deferential standard of appellate review." *Blair*, 181 F.3d at 835. Courts have also suggested that the third category "should be restricted to those instances in which an appeal will permit the resolution of an unsettled legal issue that is important to the particular litigation as well as important in itself and likely to escape effective review if left hanging until the end of the case." *Mowbray*, 208 F.3d at 294. At least one circuit has stated that "the standards of Rule 23(f) will rarely be met." In re Sumitomo Copper Litigation, 262 F.3d 134, 140 (2d Cir. 2001).

5. Rule 54(b)

As a result of the liberal joinder rules of the Federal Rules of Civil Procedure, a single case may include multiple parties or claims. It is possible for the court to grant partial summary judgment and dispose of claims involving one party long before the rest of the case is decided. Forcing that party to await the outcome of the entire case before being able to appeal may impose a significant hardship. To address this problem, Rule 54(b) permits the court to enter final judgment as to some claims and thereby make that judgment appealable even though other portions of the case remain unresolved. As the Supreme Court has explained:

> With the Federal Rules of Civil Procedure, there came an increased opportunity for the liberal joinder of claims in multiple claims actions. This, in turn, demonstrated a need for relaxing the restrictions upon what should be treated as a judicial unit for purposes of appellate jurisdiction. Sound judicial administration did not require relaxation of the standard of finality in the disposition of the individual adjudicated claims for the purpose of their appealability. It did, however, demonstrate that, at least in multiple claims actions, some final decisions, on less than all of the claims, should be appealable without waiting for a final decision on *all* of the claims.

Sears, Roebuck & Co. v. Mackey, 351 U.S. 427, 432 (1956) (emphasis in original).

Notes and Questions

1. Read Rule 54(b). Would it permit an immediate appeal in these cases?

(a) The plaintiff brings suit for breach of contract and seeks damages. The court grants the plaintiff's motion for partial summary judgment and holds that the defendant did breach the contract, but the court has not yet determined the amount of damages. Is the ruling on partial summary judgment immediately appealable?

(b) In response to the plaintiff's breach of contract complaint, the defendant files a compulsory counterclaim asserting a claim that the contract in question violates federal antitrust laws. The court grants the plaintiff's motion for summary judgment on the antitrust counterclaim. Is this grant immediately appealable? If the court had denied the plaintiff's motion, would that be immediately appealable?

(c) Two plaintiffs file suit against one defendant. The court dismisses the claim of one of the plaintiffs, but not the other. Is that dismissal immediately appealable? Does the court have to take another step to make it appealable now?

(d) One plaintiff sues a defendant. Later, the plaintiff seeks to amend her complaint to add a second plaintiff. The court refuses to allow joinder of the second plaintiff. Is this ruling immediately appealable?

2. Rule 54(b) requires "more than one claim for relief" or "multiple parties." For these purposes, what is a claim? One treatise explains: "A single claimant presents multiple claims for relief * * * when his possible recoveries are more than one in number and not mutually exclusive or, stated another way, when the facts give rise to more than one legal right or cause of action." 10 Wright & Miller, Federal Practice & Procedure § 2657 at 76–77. How would this apply in the following cases?

(a) A customer is bitten by a poisonous snake in a pet store. She brings a claim for damages against the store alleging negligence, strict liability, and violation of state or federal licensing provisions. The court dismisses the statutory claims.

(b) A prison inmate who is injured by a guard brings suit for damages against the government alleging respondeat superior and negligence in the supervision and training of the guard. The court dismisses the claim based on respondeat superior.

3. Why does Rule 54(b) require that the district court make an express finding "that there is no just reason for delay"? Should the district court's refusal to make such a finding be reviewable?

4. Rule 54(b) vests authority in the district court to permit the appeal. Suppose the court dismisses some but not all of the claims, but refuses to direct entry of final judgment as to those claims. If the plaintiff voluntarily dismisses the remaining claims, can the court's ruling on the other claims be immediately appealed? Courts have split on this issue. Several circuits have held there is no final judgment when unresolved claims are voluntarily dismissed without prejudice, see, e.g., Rabbi Jacob Joseph School v. Province of Mendoza, 425 F.3d 207 (2d Cir. 2005); Marshall v. Kansas City Southern Ry. Co., 378 F.3d 495 (5th Cir. 2004), while the Federal Circuit has rejected a categorical approached and focused on whether there is "evidence of intent to manipulate our appellate jurisdiction." Doe v. United States, 513 F.3d 1348, 1353 (Fed. Cir. 2008).

6. Mandamus

The All Writs Act, 28 U.S.C. § 1651(a), authorizes federal courts to "issue all writs necessary or appropriate in aid of their respective jurisdictions and agreeable to the usages and principles of law." Pursuant to this provision, courts of appeals can issue writs of mandamus, which order a district court to take certain actions, or writs of prohibition, which command a district court not to take some action. Such writs are considered "extraordinary remedies" and are appropriate only where the party seeking issuance of the writ has "no other adequate means to attain the relief he desires" and has carried his "burden of showing that [his] right to issuance of the writ is 'clear and indisputable.'" Kerr v. United States District Court, 426 U.S. 394, 403 (1976).

In Will v. United States, 389 U.S. 90, 95–96 (1967), the Court explained the use of the writ:

> The peremptory writ of mandamus has traditionally been used in the federal courts only "to confine an inferior court to a lawful exercise of its prescribed jurisdiction or to compel it to exercise its authority when it is its duty to do so." While the courts have never confined themselves to an arbitrary and technical definition of "jurisdiction," it is clear that only exceptional circumstances amounting to a judicial "usurpation of power" will justify the invocation of this extraordinary remedy. Thus the writ has been invoked where unwarranted judicial action threatened "to embarrass the executive arm of the Government in conducting foreign relations," where it was the only means of forestalling intrusion by the federal judiciary on a delicate area of federal-state relations, where it was necessary to confine a lower court to the terms of an appellate tribunal's mandate, and where a district judge displayed a persistent disregard of the Rules of Civil Procedure promulgated by this Court. And the party seeking mandamus has "the burden of showing that its right to issuance of the writ is 'clear and indisputable.'"

The use of mandamus is illustrated by Thermtron Products, Inc. v. Hermansdorfer, 423 U.S. 336 (1976). There the district court had remanded a removed case on grounds that the federal docket was too crowded to hear the case, and the defendant sought mandamus. Although remand orders are ordinarily not reviewable on appeal, see 28 U.S.C. § 1447(d), the Supreme Court held that mandamus was appropriate "where the district court has refused to adjudicate a case; and has remanded it on grounds not authorized by the removal statutes." Id. at 353.

Writs of mandamus are not frequently granted. One study found that between 1995 and 2000, courts of appeal granted on average less than one mandamus per circuit per year. Glynn, supra, 77 Notre Dame L. Rev. at 218. As the Supreme Court has explained: "[O]ur cases have answered the question as to the availability of mandamus * * * with the refrain: 'What never? Well, *hardly* ever!'" Allied Chemical Corp. v. Daiflon, Inc., 449 U.S. 33, 36 (1980) (per curiam).

Courts sometimes use mandamus when the right to a jury trial is improperly denied. See *Dairy Queen* and *Beacon Theatres*, supra in Chapter 9, Section B.1.b. Judge Easterbrook has criticized this use:

> Neither *Beacon Theatres* nor *Dairy Queen* answers the question: Why mandamus? * * * Surely the answer is not * * * that there is a constitutional right at stake. Much federal litigation involves constitutional rights, but the nature of the right does not dictate whether review comes in mid-course or at the end of the district court's proceedings. Jury trial is not the most essential of rights, either.

First National Bank of Waukesha v. Warren, 796 F.2d 999, 1002 (7th Cir. 1986). Do you agree?

7. Appealability of Discovery Orders

Discovery orders ordinarily are not "final decisions" for purposes of § 1291. Occasionally, such orders are reviewed as interlocutory appeals under § 1292(b), but usually it will be difficult to show that a discovery order involves a controlling question of law or that an immediate appeal will materially advance the termination of the litigation. Discovery orders are also occasionally reviewed by means of a writ of mandamus. See Schlagenhauf v. Holder, 379 U.S. 104 (1964).

As noted above, in Mohawk Indus., Inc v. Carpenter, 558 U.S. 100 (2009), the Court held that an order denying protection to material allegedly protected under the attorney-client privilege is not immediately appealable under the collateral order doctrine. The Court noted that if confronted with a "particularly injurious or novel privilege ruling," immediate review might be available under § 1292 or by means of mandamus. Cf. Agster v. Maricopa County, 422 F.3d 836 (9th Cir. 2005) (allowing interlocutory appeal of order to produce document claimed to be privileged). See Cassandra Burke Robertson, *Appellate Review of Discovery Orders in Federal Court: A Suggested Approach for Handling Privilege Claims*, 81 Wash. L. Rev. 733 (2006). A further option is to defy the order and be held in contempt of court. Because the courts treat the contempt judgment as a separate proceeding, that judgment is immediately appealable. You will recall that this is the route used in *Hickman v. Taylor* and *Ager*, Chapter 8. There, the lawyers and clients refused to turn over material that they believed was protected from discovery. They were convicted of contempt and ordered to jail by the trial judge. Although they were allowed to appeal immediately, this is obviously a risky mechanism for securing an appeal.

Discovery orders directed at non-parties can present a different set of issues. If the non-party possesses materials that implicate a privilege held by one of the parties, but that don't really implicate the interests of the non-party herself, the non-party may be unwilling to risk a contempt citation in order to appeal immediately. In this situation, courts have allowed an immediate appeal of the discovery order. See Perlman v. United States, 247 U.S. 7 (1918); United States v. Krane, 625 F.3d. 568 (9th Cir. 2010) (holding that *Perlman* survives *Mohawk*).

In extraordinary cases, the Supreme Court has allowed immediate appeals of discovery rulings. In the Watergate Tapes Case, United States v. Nixon, 418 U.S. 683 (1974), the special prosecutor subpoenaed tapes, and the district court ordered President Nixon to produce the material. The President appealed to the court of appeals and then sought review in the Supreme Court. Before the Court could reach the merits, it had to decide whether the immediate appeal of this interlocutory order was proper. The Court allowed the appeal, without requiring that the President first be held in contempt. The Court explained: "To require a President of the United States to place himself in the posture of disobeying an order of the court merely to trigger the procedural mechanism for review of the ruling would be unseemly, and would present an unnecessary occasion for constitutional confrontation between two branches of the Government." Id. at 691–92. A President (or Vice President) who objects to a discovery order is not required to invoke executive privilege to be allowed to appeal immediately. See Cheney v. United States Dist. Court, 542 U.S. 367 (2004).

Any alleged discovery errors can, of course, be included as a basis for appeal from the final judgment. However, it is frequently difficult to get a judgment reversed on grounds of a discovery error because of the harmless error doctrine, discussed in Section D, below.

8. Mechanics and Timing of Filing an Appeal

The Federal Rules of Appellate Procedure require that, in an appeal of a final judgment, notice of appeal be filed with the district court within 30 days after the entry of the judgment or order from which the appeal is taken. The time limit is 60 days when the United States is a party. These temporal limits are set forth in Fed. R. App. P. 4(a) and are also rooted in a statute, 28 U.S.C. § 2107. The time for filing the notice of appeal runs from the date the district court enters judgment. The fact that the district court must still determine and assess costs does not extend the time for appeal. Budinich v. Becton Dickinson & Co., 486 U.S. 196 (1988). This time requirement for filing notice of appeal is jurisdictional, and cannot be waived or extended except as provided by § 2107 and Appellate Rule 4(a)(6). See Bowles v. Russell, 551 U.S. 205 (2007).

In *Budinich,* the Court held that a district court's decision that left unresolved a question of whether a party was entitled to a statutory award of attorney's fees was an appealable "final decision" under § 1291(a). In Ray Haluch Gravel Co. v. Central Pension Fund of International Union of Operating Eng'rs & Participating Employers, 134 S. Ct. 773 (2014), the Supreme Court held that the pendency of a ruling on attorney's fees does not prevent a ruling on the merits from being final and appealable. In that case, the district court entered judgment on the merits and, more than a month later, ruled on contractual attorney's fees. Appellant filed a notice of appeal on both the merits and the ruling regarding fees within 30 days after the fees ruling. The Supreme Court held that the appeal of the merits was not timely because it was more than 30 days after the decision on the merits.

The filing of a notice of appeal does not suspend the effect of a judgment. To prevent the enforceability of a judgment pending the appeal, the appellant may be required to post a "supersedeas bond" guaranteeing that the judgment will be paid if she loses on appeal. See Fed. R. App. P. 8(b). Frequently, the bond must be at least as large as the amount of the judgment plus costs. In one famous case, Pennzoil sued Texaco for breach of contract and won a $10.5 billion jury verdict. To appeal the judgment, Texaco was required to post a bond in excess of $11 billion. Texaco sought unsuccessfully to enjoin the requirement of so large a bond. See Pennzoil Co. v. Texaco, Inc., 481 U.S. 1 (1987). Texaco ultimately filed for bankruptcy and Pennzoil settled for $3 billion. See Douglas Laycock, *The Remedies Issues: Compensatory Damages, Specific Performance, Punitive Damages, Supersedeas Bonds and Abstention*, 9 Litig. Rev. 473 (1990).

9. Appellate Jurisdiction of the United States Supreme Court

The appellate jurisdiction of the Supreme Court, like that of the courts of appeals, is defined by statute. See 28 U.S.C. § 1254. Traditionally there have been two mechanisms available for Supreme Court review—appeal and certiorari. In theory, the difference between these two mechanisms is that an "appeal," where applicable, is available as a matter of right, whereas certiorari review is entirely discretionary. In practice, however, the Court treats jurisdiction over appeals of right as if they were discretionary and will hear such cases only if they present a "substantial" federal question. See Zucht v. King, 260 U.S. 174 (1922). In 1988, Congress abolished virtually all of the Court's mandatory appellate jurisdiction so that now nearly all of the Court's cases fall into the discretionary certiorari category.

The Supreme Court hears oral argument in very few of the cases in which review is sought. Most of the matters disposed of by the Court are handled by order, usually an order denying certiorari—that is, refusing to hear the case. In the October 2014 Term, the Court disposed of 12,521 cases. Of these, most were in forma pauperis filings, which means they were filed by indigent persons. In the 2014 Term, the Court heard oral argument in 75 cases, which generated 66 signed opinions. The Court also issued eight per curiam opinions in cases that were not argued. In deciding which cases to accept for review, the Court relies on the unwritten "Rule of Four," under which certiorari is granted upon the vote of four Justices. In deciding whether to grant certiorari, error below is one factor, but not the only or even the most important factor. The Court also considers the importance of the issue presented, whether there is a split among the circuits on the issue, and whether the issue of interest to the Court is squarely presented by the case or is entangled in factual or state law disputes. See Rules of the Supreme Court of the United States, Rule 10. What does this list tell you about the Court's perception of its role? A decision by the Court not to grant certiorari has no precedential effect, and contrary to the impression sometimes created in the popular press, such a decision indicates nothing about whether the Court agrees with the lower court opinion.

C. Appeals in State Courts

Each state has its own appellate system. All states have a supreme court and most have intermediate courts of appeals, though these courts have different names in different states. Nearly all states permit at least one appeal as a matter of right, though, as noted in Section A above, Virginia and West Virginia do not; in such states, appeal of civil cases is generally in the discretion of the state supreme court.

The timing of appeals in state courts is governed by state law (not by federal statutes such as § 1291). Some states allow appeals under circumstances that the federal courts would not. For example, New York allows an immediate appeal of any order that "grants or refuses a new trial," "involves some part of the merits," or "affects a substantial right." N.Y. Civ. Prac. L. & R. 5701(a)(2)(iii–v). What are the advantages and disadvantages of this approach?

In addition, some states permit mandamus or a similar writ called a writ of prohibition under circumstances that the federal courts would not allow. For example, in *World-Wide Volkswagen*, Chapter 2, the trial court denied the motion to dismiss for lack of jurisdiction, and the defendants immediately sought a writ of prohibition. Similarly, in *Kulko, Burnham*, and *Asahi*, also in Chapter 2, the defendants sought immediate appellate review of the denial of their motions to dismiss by seeking writs of mandate (or "mandamus").

D. Standards of Review

Appellate review involves a reexamination of the judge's rulings in the court below. For that reason, appellate courts will only review issues or objections that were raised at trial and appear on the record — in the pleadings, briefs, or transcripts from the proceeding below. In addition, appellate courts will ordinarily consider only those issues that are raised and argued on appeal — they will not search the record on their own looking for errors. Finally, appellate review is limited by the concept of "harmless error." See Federal Rule 61. Under this doctrine, even where there is error, the appellate court will not reverse the judgment unless the error materially affected the outcome. The Supreme Court has described the harmless error test as follows:

> If, when all is said and done, the conviction is sure that the error did not influence the jury, or had but very slight effect, the verdict and the judgment should stand, except perhaps where the departure is from a constitutional norm or a specific command of Congress. But if one cannot say, with fair assurance, after pondering all that happened without stripping the erroneous action from the whole, that the judgment was not substantially swayed by the error, it is impossible to conclude that substantial rights were not affected. The inquiry cannot be merely whether there was enough to support the result, apart from the phase affected by the error. It is rather, even so, whether the error itself had substantial influence.

Kotteakos v. United States, 328 U.S. 750, 764–65 (1946).

Before reviewing an issue properly before it, an appellate court must determine by what standard to review the decision. Issues of law are reviewed de novo, meaning there is no presumption in favor of the lower court's determination and the appellate court can substitute its view of the law for that of the lower court. In other words, on matters of law, the appellate court gives no deference to the trial judge. In reaching its determination, the appellate court can consider legal precedents that the lower court did not consider or was unaware of. See Elder v. Holloway, 510 U.S. 510 (1994).

In contrast to legal determinations, factual determinations made by the trial judge are reversible only if "clearly erroneous."* See Rule 52(a)(6). The Supreme Court has

* Rulings on some motions — including dismissal for forum non conveniens, see *Piper Aircraft Co. v. Reyno*, Chapter 5, Section F, certification of class actions, see Gulf Oil Co. v. Bernard, 452 U.S. 89, 103 (1981), and discovery sanctions, see National Hockey League v. Metropolitan Hockey Club,

explained that "a finding is 'clearly erroneous' when although there is evidence to support it, the reviewing court on the entire evidence is left with the definite and firm conviction that a mistake has been committed." Anderson v. Bessemer City, 470 U.S. 564, 573 (1985). However,

> [i]f the district court's account of the evidence is plausible in light of the record viewed in its entirety, the court of appeals may not reverse it even though convinced that had it been sitting as the trier of fact, it would have weighed the evidence differently. Where there are two permissible views of the evidence, the factfinder's choice between them cannot be clearly erroneous.

Id. at 513–14.

A more memorable statement of the standard is found in Parts & Electric Motors, Inc. v. Sterling, Electric, Inc., 866 F.2d 228, 233 (7th Cir. 1988): "To be clearly erroneous, a decision must strike us as more than just maybe or probably wrong; it must, as one member of this court recently stated during oral argument, strike us as wrong with the force of a five-week-old, unrefrigerated dead fish."

Appellate courts are even more deferential to findings of fact made by a jury. In federal court, appellate courts must be mindful of the "re-examination clause" of the Seventh Amendment, which provides that "no fact tried by a jury, shall be otherwise re-examined in any Court of the United States, than according to the rules of the common law." Accordingly, on appeal, the appellate court views all evidence, including credibility determinations and inferences, in the light most favorable to the verdict, and must affirm so long as a reasonable fact-finder could have reached that conclusion. FREER, CIVIL PROCEDURE 866.

What about determinations involving the application of law to fact, are these legal or factual? The Supreme Court has acknowledged that there is no easy rule for distinguishing between legal and factual issues. See Pullman-Standard v. Swint, 456 U.S. 273, 288 (1982). Several cases illustrate the problem:

In Bose Corp. v. Consumers Union of United States, Inc., 466 U.S. 485 (1984), Bose sued Consumers Union, claiming that an article published by the defendant constituted trade libel. Under the applicable First Amendment doctrine, the defendant was liable only if it acted with "actual malice," that is, with knowledge of the falsity or with reckless disregard for the truth. The district court found actual malice. In upholding the court of appeals' reversal, the Supreme Court engaged in a de novo review of the record. The Court explained:

> Rule 52(a) applies to findings of fact, including those described as "ultimate facts" because they may determine the outcome of litigation. But Rule 52(a) does not inhibit an appellate court's power to correct errors of law, including those that may infect a so-called mixed finding of law and fact,

---

Inc., 427 U.S. 639, 642 (1976)—are reviewable for "abuse of discretion." The Court has suggested that review for abuse of discretion is comparable to review under the clearly erroneous standard. See Cooter & Gell v. Hartmarx Corp., 496 U.S. 384, 405 (1990).

> or a finding of fact that is predicated on a misunderstanding of the governing rule of law. * * *
>
> A finding of fact in some cases is inseparable from the principles through which it was deduced. At some point, the reasoning by which a fact is "found" crosses the line between application of those ordinary principles of logic and common experience which are ordinarily entrusted to the finder of fact into the realm of a legal rule upon which the reviewing court must exercise its own independent judgment. Where the line is drawn varies according to the nature of the substantive law at issue. Regarding certain largely factual questions in some areas of the law, the stakes — in terms of impact on future cases and future conduct — are too great to entrust them finally to the judgment of the trier of fact.

Id. at 501 & n.17. The Court then went on to apply these principles to the case at hand:

> In a consideration of the possible application of the distinction to the issue of "actual malice," at least three characteristics of the rule enunciated in the *New York Times* case are relevant. First, the common law heritage of the rule itself assigns an especially broad role to the judge in applying it to specific factual situations. Second, the content of the rule is not revealed simply by its literal text, but rather is given meaning through the evolutionary process of common-law adjudication; though the source of the rule is found in the Constitution, it is nevertheless largely a judge-made rule of law. Finally, the constitutional values protected by the rule make it imperative that judges — and in some cases judges of this Court — make sure that it is correctly applied.

Id. at 501–02.

The Court does not always review de novo mixed questions of law and fact. In Pierce v. Underwood, 487 U.S. 552 (1988), the district court held that a legal position taken by the government was not "substantially justified" and therefore the other party was entitled to attorneys fees under the Equal Access to Justice Act. The Supreme Court held that this ruling should not be reviewed de novo even though it was obviously bound up with an assessment of the strength of the government's legal arguments. Similarly, in Cooter & Gell v. Hartmarx Corp., 496 U.S. 384 (1990), the Court held that a district court's finding that a lawyer had violated Rule 11 was subject to the clearly erroneous standard, even where the district court's ruling is based on a determination of whether the lawyer's legal arguments were well grounded.

Notes and Questions

1. Professor Sward has described the role of standards of review as follows:

> Standards of review serve to allocate decision-making responsibility among the various levels of courts in a hierarchial judicial system. A standard of review that calls for considerable deference to trial level decision-makers places

> primary responsibility for resolving disputes in the trial courts. By contrast, a standard of review that allows non-deferential review by appellate courts places primary decision-making authority in appellate courts.

Ellen Sward, *Appellate Review of Judicial Fact-Finding*, 40 KAN. L. REV. 1, 4 (1990). Why do you think the Court chooses to make trial courts the primary decision makers with respect to attorney's fees and Rule 11 enforcement, but not with respect to findings of malice in libel cases?

2. Lower courts have held that the determination of citizenship for purposes of diversity jurisdiction is a mixed question of law and fact for which "clearly erroneous" is the proper standard of review. See, e.g., Rogers v. Bates, 431 F.2d 16 (8th Cir. 1970); Julien v. Sarkes Tarzian, Inc., 352 F.2d 845 (7th Cir. 1965). Under what standard should a court of appeals review a district court finding that a defendant had sufficient contacts for personal jurisdiction? Compare Gulf Ins. Co. v. Glasbrenner, 417 F.3d 353, 355 (2d Cir. 2005) (de novo review), with Home Ins. Co. v. Thomas Industries, Inc., 896 F.2d 1352, 1355 (11th Cir. 1990) (abuse of discretion).

3. Why should appellate courts ordinarily exercise such limited review of factual determinations? Is it that trial courts, having seen the actual presentation of the evidence and witnesses, are more likely to be correct in their determination? Lawyers frequently observe that reading a "cold record" or transcript of a trial can leave a very different impression than seeing the trial live. Is this a reason for deferring to trial courts or for not deferring? Maybe it would be useful to have the court of appeals review the cold record, uninfluenced by the emotion of the live event. What about determinations based entirely on documentary proof in which the evidence is equally available to a court of appeals? See Federal Rule 52(a). Are trial courts any more likely to be correct in their assessment of this evidence? Are "mere facts" simply not important enough for appellate courts to waste their time on? See Mucha v. King, 792 F.2d 602, 605–06 (7th Cir. 1986) (Rule 52(a) "rest[s] on the notions of the proper division of responsibilities between trial and appellate courts * * * rather than just on considerations of comparative accessibility to the evidence").

4. Are there some issues *of law* as to which trial judges are more likely to be correct? Courts of appeals had long held that when federal courts apply state law, district court determinations of the content of that law are entitled to great deference. The justification relied on the fact that district judges who sit in that state and who are usually drawn from the bar of that state are more likely to be correct about the content of state law than are appellate judges. As Justice Rehnquist explained: "A judge attempting to predict how a state court would rule must use not only his legal reasoning skills, but also his experience and perceptions of judicial behavior in that State. It therefore makes perfect sense for an appellate court judge with no local experience to accord special weight to a local judge's assessment of state court trends." Salve Regina College v. Russell, 499 U.S. 225, 241 (1991) (Rehnquist, C.J., dissenting). In *Salve Regina College*, the majority of the Court rejected this argument and held that determinations of state law are subject to de novo review by the court of appeals. The Court explained:

> Independent appellate review of legal issues best serves the dual goals of doctrinal coherence and economy of judicial administration. District judges preside alone over fast-paced trials: Of necessity they devote much of their energy and resources to hearing witnesses and reviewing evidence. Similarly, the logistical burdens of trial advocacy limit the extent to which trial counsel is able to supplement the district judge's legal research with memoranda and briefs. Thus, trial judges often must resolve complicated legal questions without benefit of "extended reflection [or] extensive information."
>
> * * * Perhaps most important, courts of appeals employ multijudge panels, see 28 U.S.C. §§ 46(b) and (c), that permit reflective dialogue and collective judgment. Over 30 years ago, Justice Frankfurter accurately observed: "Without adequate study there cannot be adequate reflection; without adequate reflection there cannot be adequate discussions; without adequate discussion there cannot be that fruitful interchange of minds which is indispensable to thoughtful, unhurried decision and its formulation in learned and impressive opinions."

Id. at 231–32. See Dan Coenen, *To Defer or Not to Defer: A Study of Federal Circuit Court Deference to District Court Rulings on State Law*, 73 MINN. L. REV. 899 (1989). Wouldn't it be valuable to use the collaborative and reflective process of appellate review which the Court praises to review factual determinations?

5. Federal appellate courts do not always review questions of law de novo. In reviewing the actions of administrative agencies, the courts frequently defer to the agency's interpretation of the law. "[I]f the statute is silent or ambiguous with respect to the specific issue, the question for the court is whether the agency's answer is based on a permissible construction of the statute." Chevron, U.S.A. Inc. v. Natural Resources Defense Council, Inc., 467 U.S. 837, 843 (1984). It is not necessary "that the agency construction was the only one it permissibly could have adopted, or even the reading the court would have reached if the question had arisen in a judicial proceeding." Id. at 843 n.11.

6. In Cooper Indus., Inc. v. Leatherman Tool Group, Inc., 532 U.S. 424 (2001), the Court held that decisions of trial courts concerning punitive damages awarded by juries should be reviewed de novo by the court of appeals. The Court noted that in a previous decision, BMW of North America v. Gore, 517 U.S. 559 (1996), it had set forth three factors that courts should use in reviewing punitive damage awards: (1) the degree of reprehensibility of the defendant's misconduct, (2) the disparity between the harm suffered by the plaintiff and the punitive damage award, and (3) the difference between the punitive damages award by the jury and the civil penalties in comparable cases. The Court then considered which level of court — trial or appellate — was better situated to assess each factor. The Court concluded that trial courts had a slight advantage with respect to the first, since it was able to observe credibility first-hand, that both courts were equally well-situated with respect to the second, but that the third factor "which calls for a broad comparison, seems more suited to the expertise of appellate courts." 532 U.S. at 440. The Court concluded that "[c]onsid-

erations of institutional competence therefore fail to tip the balance in favor of deferential appellate review." Id.

7. For a case to be appealable, there must be a live controversy — if the case settles or otherwise becomes moot it cannot be appealed. This proposition is illustrated by Gator.com Corp. v. L.L. Bean, Inc., 398 F.3d 1125 (9th Cir. 2005). There, the district court had dismissed the case for lack of personal jurisdiction. While the case was pending, the parties settled the dispute with the plaintiff agreeing to make a monetary payment to the defendant and to cease certain conduct. However, the settlement did not call for the dismissal of the appeal. Instead, the parties included in the agreement a provision that if the personal jurisdiction dismissal was upheld, the plaintiff would make an additional monetary payment. The court of appeals dismissed the appeal as moot, finding that the underlying dispute had been fully resolved and the "side bet" concerning personal jurisdiction "does not alter the fact that the personal jurisdiction issue is wholly divorced from any live case or controversy." Id. at 1132.

E. Review of Judgments Outside of the Appeal Process

This chapter focuses on the review of judgments by means of an appeal to a higher court. Earlier in the book we have seen two other mechanisms by which a judgment might be reexamined. The first is a collateral attack where a second court declines to enforce a prior judgment because the second court determines that the first judgment is void. See Chapter 6.C.

The second mechanism is to seek to reopen a judgment by means of Rule 60(b). See Chapter 10.C. Rule 60(b)(4) allows a party to seek relief from a judgment if it is "void," but as the Supreme Court has explained, the fact that a judgment is wrong does not make it void. United Student Aid Funds Inc. v. Espinosa, 559 U.S. 260 (2010). The case involved a bankruptcy judgment that discharged the debtor's student loan obligations. Contrary to the requirements of the bankruptcy code, this discharge occurred without the court finding "undue hardship." The creditor received notice of the discharge but did not object. Later, after the creditor sought to collect the discharged debt and the debtor filed a motion to enforce the discharge, the creditor sought to reopen the judgment. The Court held that even though the bankruptcy court's failure to find an undue hardship was "legal error," "the order remains enforceable and binding on [the creditor] because [it] had notice of the error and failed to object or timely appeal." Id. at 275.

> "A judgment is not void," for example, "simply because it is or may have been erroneous." Similarly, a motion under Rule 60(b)(4) is not a substitute for a timely appeal. Instead, Rule 60(b)(4) applies only in the rare instance where a judgment is premised either on a certain type of jurisdictional error or on a violation of due process that deprives a party of notice or the opportunity to be heard. Cf. Chicot County Drainage Dist. v. Baxter State Bank, 308 U.S. 371, 376 (1940). The error United alleges falls in neither category.

> Rule 60(b)(4) strikes a balance between the need for finality of judgments and the importance of ensuring that litigants have a full and fair opportunity to litigate a dispute. Where, as here, a party is notified of a plan's contents and fails to object to confirmation of the plan before the time for appeal expires, that party has been afforded a full and fair opportunity to litigate, and the party's failure to avail itself of that opportunity will not justify Rule 60(b)(4) relief. We thus agree with the Court of Appeals that the Bankruptcy Court's confirmation order is not void.

Id. at 276.

Chapter 15

Alternative Models of Dispute Resolution

A. Introduction and Integration

This book has focused on one system of dispute resolution—the American litigation system. In recent years, this system has come under increasing criticism. Many observers complain that litigation takes too long and is too expensive. In addition, some argue that litigation as practiced in this country does not always produce the best outcomes. The partisan nature of the adversary system may obscure the truth. Moreover, adjudicated outcomes are largely zero-sum, or "winner-take-all." In at least some situations, a compromise in which each side "wins" something may be a more socially desirable outcome.

In this chapter we explore some alternative models of dispute resolution. Some of these are drawn from other cultures, while others are available within our system.

B. Models of Greater Judicial Control

The German Advantage in Civil Procedure

John H. Langbein
52 U. Chi. L. Rev. 823 (1985)

Our lawyer-dominated system of civil procedure has often been criticized both for its incentives to distort evidence and for the expense and complexity of its modes of discovery and trial. The shortcomings inhere in a system that leaves to partisans the work of gathering and producing the factual material upon which adjudication depends.

We have comforted ourselves with the thought that a lawyerless system would be worse. The excesses of American adversary justice would seem to pale by comparison with a literally nonadversarial system—one in which litigants would be remitted to faceless bureaucratic adjudicators and denied the safeguards that flow from lawyerly intermediation.

The German advantage. The main theme of this article is drawn from Continental civil procedure, exemplified for me by the system that I know reasonably well, the West German. My theme is that, by assigning judges rather than lawyers to investigate the facts, the Germans avoid the most troublesome aspects of our practice. But I shall emphasize that the familiar contrast between our adversarial procedure and the supposedly nonadversarial procedure of the Continental tradition has been grossly overdrawn.

I. Overview of German Civil Procedure

There are two fundamental differences between German and Anglo-American civil procedure, and these differences lead in turn to many others. First, the court rather than the parties' lawyers takes the main responsibility for gathering and sifting evidence, although the lawyers exercise a watchful eye over the court's work. Second, there is no distinction between pretrial and trial, between discovering evidence and presenting it. Trial is not a single continuous event. Rather, the court gathers and evaluates evidence over a series of hearings, as many as the circumstances require.

Initiation. The plaintiff's lawyer commences a lawsuit in Germany with a complaint. Like its American counterpart, the German complaint narrates the key facts, sets forth a legal theory, and asks for a remedy in damages or specific relief. Unlike an American complaint, however, the German document proposes means of proof for its main factual contentions. The major documents in the plaintiff's possession that support his claim are scheduled and often appended; other documents (for example, hospital files or government records such as police accident reports or agency files) are indicated; witnesses who are thought to know something helpful to the plaintiff's position are identified. The defendant's answer follows the same pattern. It should be emphasized, however, that neither plaintiff's nor defendant's lawyer will have conducted any significant search for witnesses or for other evidence unknown to his client. Digging for facts is primarily the work of the judge.

Judicial preparation. The judge to whom the case is entrusted examines these pleadings and appended documents. He routinely sends for relevant public records. These materials form the beginnings of the official dossier, the court file. All subsequent submissions of counsel, and all subsequent evidence-gathering, will be entered in the dossier, which is open to counsel's inspection continuously.

When the judge develops a first sense of the dispute from these materials, he will schedule a hearing and notify the lawyers. He will often invite and sometimes summon the parties as well as their lawyers to this or subsequent hearings. If the pleadings have identified witnesses whose testimony seems central, the judge may summon them to the initial hearing as well.

Hearing. The circumstances of the case dictate the course of the hearing. Sometimes the court will be able to resolve the case by discussing it with the lawyers and parties and suggesting avenues of compromise. If the case remains contentious and witness testimony needs to be taken, the court will have learned enough about the case to determine a sequence for examining witnesses.

Examining and recording. The judge serves as the examiner-in-chief. At the conclusion of his interrogation of each witness, counsel for either party may pose additional questions, but counsel are not prominent as examiners. Witness testimony is seldom recorded verbatim; rather, the judge pauses from time to time to dictate a summary of the testimony into the dossier. The lawyers sometimes suggest improvements in the wording of these summaries, in order to preserve or to emphasize nuances important to one side or the other.

Since the proceedings in a difficult case may require several hearings extending across many months, these summaries of concluded testimony—by encapsulating succinctly the results of previous hearings—allow the court to refresh itself rapidly for subsequent hearings. The summaries also serve as building blocks from which the court will ultimately fashion the findings of fact for its written judgment. If the case is appealed, these concise summaries constitute the record for the reviewing court. * * *

Anyone who has had to wade through the long-winded narrative of American pretrial depositions and trial transcripts (which preserve every inconsequential utterance, every false start, every stammer) will see at once the economy of the German approach to taking and preserving evidence. Our incentives run the other way; we pay court reporters by the page and lawyers mostly by the hour.

A related source of dispatch in German procedure is the virtual absence of any counterpart to the Anglo American law of evidence. German law exhibits expansive notions of testimonial privilege, especially for potential witnesses drawn from the family. But German procedure functions without the main chapters of our law of evidence, those rules (such as hearsay) that exclude probative evidence for fear of the inability of the trier of fact to evaluate the evidence purposively. In civil litigation German judges sit without juries * * * ; evidentiary shortcomings that would affect admissibility in our law affect weight or credit in German law.

Expertise. If an issue of technical difficulty arises on which the court or counsel wishes to obtain the views of an expert, the court—in consultation with counsel—will select the expert and define his role. * * *

Further contributions of counsel. After the court takes witness testimony or receives some other infusion of evidence, counsel have the opportunity to comment orally or in writing. Counsel use these submissions in order to suggest further proofs or to advance legal theories. Thus, nonadversarial proof-taking alternates with adversarial dialogue across as many hearings as are necessary. The process merges the investigatory function of our pretrial discovery and the evidence-presenting function of our trial. Another manifestation of the comparative efficiency of German procedure is that a witness is ordinarily examined only once. Contrast the American practice of partisan interview and preparation, pretrial deposition, preparation for trial, and examination and cross-examination at trial. These many steps take their toll in expense and irritation.

Judgment. After developing the facts and hearing the adversaries' views, the court decides the case in a written judgment that must contain full findings of fact and make reasoned application of the law.

II. Judicial Control of Sequence

From the standpoint of comparative civil procedure, the most important consequence of having judges direct fact-gathering in this episodic fashion is that German procedure functions without the sequence rules to which we are accustomed in the Anglo-American procedural world. The implications for procedural economy are large. The very concepts of "plaintiff's case" and "defendant's case" are unknown. In our system those concepts function as traffic rules for the partisan presentation of evidence to a passive and ignorant trier. By contrast, in German procedure the court ranges over the entire case, constantly looking for the jugular—for the issue of law or fact that might dispose of the case. Free of constraints that arise from party presentation of evidence, the court investigates the dispute in the fashion most likely to narrow the inquiry. A major job of counsel is to guide the search by directing the court's attention to particularly cogent lines of inquiry.

Suppose that the court has before it a contract case that involves complicated factual or legal issues about whether the contract was formed, and if so, what its precise terms were. But suppose further that the court quickly recognizes (or is led by submission of counsel to recognize) that some factual investigation might establish an affirmative defense—illegality, let us say—that would vitiate the contract. Because the court functions without sequence rules, it can postpone any consideration of issues that we would think of as the plaintiff's case—here the questions concerning the formation and the terms of the contract. Instead, the court can concentrate the entire initial inquiry on what we would regard as a defense. If, in my example, the court were to unearth enough evidence to allow it to conclude that the contract was illegal, no investigation would ever be done on the issues of formation and terms. A defensive issue that could only surface in Anglo-American procedure following full pretrial and trial ventilation of the whole of the plaintiff's case can be brought to the fore in German procedure.

Part of what makes our discovery system so complex is that, on account of our division into pretrial and trial, we have to discover for the entire case. We investigate everything that could possibly come up at trial, because once we enter the trial phase we can seldom go back and search for further evidence. By contrast, the episodic character of German fact-gathering largely eliminates the danger of surprise; if the case takes an unexpected turn, the disadvantaged litigant can count on developing his response in another hearing at a later time. Because there is no pretrial discovery phase, fact-gathering occurs only once; and because the court establishes the sequence of fact-gathering according to criteria of relevance, unnecessary investigation is minimized. In the Anglo-American procedural world we value the early-disposition mechanism, especially summary judgment, for issues of law. But for fact-laden issues, our fixed-sequence rule (plaintiff's case before defendant's case) and our single-continuous-trial rule largely foreclose it.

The episodic character of German civil procedure * * * has other virtues: It lessens tension and theatrics, and it encourages settlement. Countless novels, movies, plays, and broadcast serials attest to the dramatic potential of the Anglo-American trial.

The contest between opposing counsel; the potential for surprise witnesses who cannot be rebutted in time; the tricks of adversary examination and cross-examination; the concentration of proof-taking and verdict into a single, continuous proceeding; the unpredictability of juries and the mysterious opacity of their conclusory verdicts — these attributes of the Anglo-American trial make for good theatre. German civil proceedings have the tone not of the theatre, but of a routine business meeting — serious rather than tense. When the court inquires and directs, it sets no stage for advocates to perform. The forensic skills of counsel can wrest no material advantage, and the appearance of a surprise witness would simply lead to the scheduling of a further hearing. In a system that cannot distinguish between dress rehearsal and opening night, there is scant occasion for stage fright.

In this business-like system of civil procedure the tradition is strong that the court promotes compromise. The judge who gathers the facts soon knows the case as well as the litigants do, and he concentrates each subsequent increment of factgathering on the most important issues still unresolved. As the case progresses the judge discusses it with the litigants, sometimes indicating provisional views of the likely outcome. He is therefore, strongly positioned to encourage a litigant to abandon a case that is turning out to be weak or hopeless, or to recommend settlement. The loser-pays system of allocating the costs of litigation gives the parties further incentive to settle short of judgment.

III. Witnesses

If we had deliberately set out to find a means of impairing the reliability of witness testimony, we could not have done much better than the existing system of having partisans prepare witnesses in advance of trial and examine and cross-examine them at trial. Jerome Frank described the problem a generation ago:

> [The witness] often detects what the lawyer hopes to prove at the trial. If the witness desires to have the lawyer's client win the case, he will often, unconsciously, mold his story accordingly. Telling and re-telling it to the lawyer, he will honestly believe that his story, as he narrates it in court, is true, although it importantly deviates from what he originally believed.[29] Thus, said Frank, "the partisan nature of trials tends to make partisans of the witnesses."

Cross-examination at trial — our only substantial safeguard against this systematic bias in the testimony that reaches our courts — is a frail and fitful palliative. Cross-examination is too often ineffective to undo the consequences of skillful coaching. Further, because cross-examination allows so much latitude for bullying and other truth-defeating stratagems, it is frequently the source of fresh distortion when brought to bear against truthful testimony. * * *

When we cross the border into German civil procedure, we leave behind all traces of this system of partisan preparation, examination, and cross-examination of witnesses. German law distinguishes parties from witnesses. A German lawyer must

29. Jerome Frank, [Courts On Trial: Myth and Reality in American Justice (1949)].

necessarily discuss the facts with his client, and based on what his client tells him and on what the documentary record discloses, the lawyer will nominate witnesses whose testimony might turn out to be helpful to his client. As the proofs come in, they may reveal to the lawyer the need to nominate further witnesses for the court to examine. But the lawyer stops at nominating; virtually never will he have occasion for out-of-court contact with a witness. Not only would such contact be a serious ethical breach, it would be self-defeating. * * *

No less a critic than Jerome Frank was prepared to concede that in American procedure the adversaries "sometimes do bring into court evidence which, in a dispassionate inquiry, might be overlooked." That is a telling argument for including adversaries in the fact-gathering process, but not for letting them run it. German civil procedure preserves party interests in fact-gathering. The lawyers nominate witnesses, attend and supplement court questioning, and develop adversary positions on the significance of the evidence. Yet German procedure totally avoids the distortions incident to our partisan witness practice.

IV. Experts

The European jurist who visits the United States and becomes acquainted with our civil procedure typically expresses amazement at our witness practice. His amazement turns to something bordering on disbelief when he discovers that we extend the sphere of partisan control to the selection and preparation of experts. In the Continental tradition experts are selected and commissioned by the court, although with great attention to safeguarding party interests. In the German system, experts are not even called witnesses. They are thought of as "judges' aides."

Perverse incentives. At the American trial bar, those of us who serve as expert witnesses are known as "saxophones." This is a revealing term, as slang often is. The idea is that the lawyer plays the tune, manipulating the expert as though the expert were a musical instrument on which the lawyer sounds the desired notes. I sometimes serve as an expert in trust and pension cases, and I have experienced the subtle pressures to join the team—to shade one's views, to conceal doubt, to overstate nuance, to downplay weak aspects of the case that one has been hired to bolster. Nobody likes to disappoint a patron; and beyond this psychological pressure is the financial inducement. Money changes hands upon the rendering of expertise, but the expert can run his meter only so long as his patron litigator likes the tune. Opposing counsel undertakes a similar exercise, hiring and schooling another expert to parrot the contrary position. The result is our familiar battle of opposing experts. The more measured and impartial an expert is, the less likely he is to be used by either side.

At trial, the battle of experts tends to baffle the trier, especially in jury courts. If the experts do not cancel each other out, the advantage is likely to be with the expert whose forensic skills are the more enticing. The system invites abusive cross-examination. * * *

Thus, the systematic incentive in our procedure to distort expertise leads to a systematic distrust and devaluation of expertise. Short of forbidding the use of experts altogether, we probably could not have designed a procedure better suited to minimize the influence of expertise.

The Continental tradition. European legal systems are, by contrast, expert-prone. Expertise is frequently sought. The literature emphasizes the value attached to having expert assistance available to the courts in an age in which litigation involves facts of ever-greater technical difficulty. The essential insight of Continental civil procedure is that credible expertise must be neutral expertise. Thus, the responsibility for selecting and informing experts is placed upon the courts, although with important protections for party interests.

Selecting the expert. German courts obtain expert help in lawsuits the way Americans obtain expert help in business or personal affairs. If you need an architect, a dermatologist, or a plumber, you do not commission a pair of them to take preordained and opposing positions on your problem, although you do sometimes take a second opinion. Rather, you take care to find an expert who is qualified to advise you in an objective manner; you probe his advice as best you can; and if you find his advice persuasive, you follow it.

When in the course of winnowing the issues in a lawsuit a German court determines that expertise might help resolve the case, the court selects and instructs the expert. The court may decide to seek expertise on its own motion, or at the request of one of the parties. The code of civil procedure allows the court to request nominations from the parties — indeed, the code requires the court to use any expert upon whom the parties agree — but neither practice is typical. In general, the court takes the initiative in nominating and selecting the expert.

Preparing the expert. The court that selects the expert instructs him, in the sense of propounding the facts that he is to assume or to investigate, and in framing the questions that the court wishes the expert to address. In formulating the expert's task, as in other important steps in the conduct of the case, the court welcomes adversary suggestions. If the expert should take a view of premises (for example, in an accident case or a building-construction dispute), counsel for both sides will accompany him.

Safeguards. The expert is ordinarily instructed to prepare a written opinion. When the court receives that report, it is circulated to the litigants. The litigants commonly file written comments, to which the expert is asked to reply. The court on its own motion may also request the expert to amplify his views. If the expert's report remains in contention, the court will schedule a hearing at which counsel for a dissatisfied litigant can confront and interrogate the expert.

The code of civil procedure reserves to the court the power to order a further report by another expert if the court should deem the first report unsatisfactory. A litigant dissatisfied with the expert may encourage the court to invoke its power to name a second expert. * * * When * * * a litigant can persuade the court that an expert's report has been sloppy or partial, that it rests upon a view of the field that is not generally shared, or that the question referred to the expert is exceptionally difficult, the court will commission further expertise.

A litigant may also engage his own expert, much as is done in the AngloAmerican procedural world, in order to rebut the court-appointed expert. The court will discount the views of a party-selected expert on account of his want of neutrality, but cases occur in which he nevertheless proves to be effective. Ordinarily, I am told, the court will not in such circumstances base its judgment directly upon the views of the party-selected expert; rather, the court will treat the rebuttal as ground for engaging a further court-appointed expert * * * whose opinion will take account of the rebuttal.

To conclude: In the use of expertise German civil procedure strikes an adroit balance between nonadversarial and adversarial values. Expertise is kept impartial, but litigants are protected against error or caprice through a variety of opportunities for consultation, confrontation, and rebuttal.

The American counterpart. It may seem curious that we make so little use of court-appointed experts in our civil practice, since "[t]he inherent power of a trial judge to appoint an expert of his own choosing is virtually unquestioned" and has been extended and codified in the Federal Rules of Evidence and the Uniform Rules of Evidence (Model Expert Testimony Act). The literature displays both widespread agreement that our courts virtually never exercise this authority, and a certain bafflement about why.

* * * The difficulty originates with the locktight segmentation of our procedure into pretrial and trial compartments, and with the tradition of partisan domination of the pretrial. Until lately, it was exceptional for the judge to have detailed acquaintance with the facts of the case until the parties presented their evidence at trial. By then the adversaries would have engaged their own experts, and time would no longer allow a court-appointed expert to be located and prepared. * * *

V. Shortcomings of Adversary Theory

The case against adversary domination of fact-gathering is so compelling that we have cause to wonder why our system tolerates it. Because there is nothing to be said in support of coached witnesses, and very little to be said in favor of litigation-biased experts, defenders of the American status quo are left to argue that the advantages of our adversary procedure counterbalance these grievous, truth-defeating distortions. "You have to take the bad with the good; if you want adversary safeguards, you are stuck with adversary excesses."

The false conflict. This all-or-nothing argument overlooks the fundamental distinction between fact-gathering and the rest of civil litigation. Outside the realm of fact-gathering, German civil procedure is about as adversarial as our own. Both systems welcome the lawyerly contribution to identifying legal issues and sharpening legal analysis. German civil procedure is materially less adversarial than our own only in the fact-gathering function, where partisanship has such potential to pollute the sources of truth.

Accordingly, the proper question is not whether to have lawyers, but how to use them; not whether to have an adversarial component to civil procedure, but how to prevent adversarial excesses. If we were to incorporate the essential lesson of the German system in our own procedure, we would still have a strongly adversarial civil procedure. We would not, however, have coached witnesses and litigation-biased experts.

Equality of representation. The German system gives us a good perspective on another great defect of adversary theory, the problem that the Germans call "Waffenungleichheit"—literally, inequality of weapons, or in this instance, inequality of counsel. In a fair fight the pugilists must be well matched. You cannot send me into a ring with Muhammed Ali if you expect a fair fight. The simple truth is that very little in our adversary system is designed to match combatants of comparable prowess, even though adversarial prowess is a main factor affecting the outcome of litigation. Adversary theory thus presupposes a condition that adversary practice achieves only indifferently. * * *

Prejudgment. Perhaps the most influential justification for adversary domination of fact-gathering has been an argument put forward by Lon Fuller: Nonadversarial procedure risks prejudgment—that is, prematurity in judgment.

In German procedure counsel oversees and has means to prompt a flagging judicial inquiry; but quite apart from that protection, is it really true that a "familiar pattern" would otherwise beguile the judge into investigating sparingly? If so, it seems odd that this asserted "natural human tendency" toward premature judgment does not show up in ordinary business and personal decision-making, whose patterns of inquiry resemble the fact-gathering process in German civil procedure. Since the decision-maker does his own investigating in most of life's decisions, it seems odd to despair of prematurity only when that normal mode of decision-making is found to operate in a courtroom. * * *

Depth. Fuller's concern about prematurity shades into a different issue: how to achieve appropriate levels of depth in fact-gathering. Extra investment in search can almost always turn up further proofs that would be at least tenuously related to the case. Adversary domination of fact-gathering privatizes the decision about what level of resources to invest in the case. The litigants who are directly interested in the outcome decide how much to spend on search. In German procedure, by contrast, these partisan calculations of self-interest are subordinated, for a variety of reasons. The initiative in fact-gathering is shared with the judge; and the German system of reckoning and allocating the costs of litigation is less sensitive to the cost of incremental investigative steps than in our system where each side pays for the proofs that it orders. On the other hand, the German judge cannot refuse to investigate party-nominated proofs without reason, and this measure of party control greatly narrows the difference between the two systems.

VI. Judicial Incentives

Viewed comparatively from the Anglo-American perspective, the greater authority of the German judge over fact-gathering comes at the expense of the lawyers for the parties. Adversary influence on fact-gathering is deliberately restrained. Furthermore, in routine civil procedure, German judges do not share power with jurors. There is no civil jury.

Because German procedure places upon the judge the responsibility for fact-gathering, the danger arises that the job will not be done well. The American system of partisan fact-gathering has the virtue of its vices: It aligns responsibility with incentive. Each side gathers and presents proofs according to its own calculation of self-interest. This privatization is an undoubted safeguard against official sloth. After all, who among us has not been treated shabbily by some lazy bureaucrat in a government department? And who would want to have that ugly character in charge of one's lawsuit?

The answer to that concern in the German tradition is straightforward: The judicial career must be designed in a fashion that creates incentives for diligence and excellence. The idea is to attract very able people to the bench, and to make their path of career advancement congruent with the legitimate interests of the litigants.

The career judiciary. The distinguishing attribute of the bench in Germany (and virtually everywhere else in Europe) is that the profession of judging is separate from the profession of lawyering. Save in exceptional circumstances, the judge is not an ex-lawyer like his Anglo-American counterpart. Rather, he begins his professional career as a judge.

In Germany judges and lawyers undergo a common preparatory schooling. After completing a prescribed course of university legal education that lasts several years, the young jurist sits a first state examination. After passing this examination satisfactorily, he enters upon an apprenticeship that now lasts two and one-half years. He clerks for judges in the civil and criminal courts, assists in the prosecutor's office, and works in a lawyer's office. At the conclusion of this tour of duty, the young jurist sits a second state examination, remotely akin to our bar examination, which concludes the certification process. Thereafter, the career lines of judge and lawyer diverge.

Recruitment. Although West Germany is a federal state, the state and federal courts comprise an integrated system. The courts of first instance and the first layer of appellate courts are state courts, while the second (and final) layer of appellate jurisdiction operates at the federal level. Thus, even though the basic codes of civil and criminal law and procedure are federal codes, the state courts have exclusive jurisdiction until the final appellate instance. It follows that most judges are state judges; and since appointment to the federal bench is by way of promotion from the state courts, all entry-level recruitment to the bench occurs at the state level.

In each of the eleven federal states, the ministry of justice is responsible for staffing the courts. Entry-level vacancies are advertised and applications entertained from young jurists. The judiciary is a prized career: influential, interesting, secure, and (by comparison with practice of the bar) prestigious and not badly compensated. "[O]nly the graduates with the best examination results have any chance of entering the judicial corps."

Advancement. A candidate who is accepted begins serving as a judge without any prior legal-professional experience, typically in his late twenties. At the outset his position is probationary, although he must be promoted to tenure or dismissed within five years. His first assignment may be to a court of petty jurisdiction * * *, or else he will become the junior member of a collegial chamber of the main court of general jurisdiction * * *, where he can receive guidance from experienced judges.

The work of a German judge is overseen and evaluated by his peers throughout his career, initially in connection with his tenure review, and thereafter for promotion through the several levels of judicial office and salary grades. A judge knows that his every step will be grist for the regular periodic reviews that will fill his lifelong personnel file. His "efficiency rating" is based in part upon objective factors, such as caseload discharge rates and reversal rates, and in part on subjective peer evaluation. The presiding judge of a chamber has special responsibility for evaluating the work of the younger judges who serve with him, but the young judges are rotated through various chambers in the course of their careers, and this reduces the influence of an aberrant rating from any one presiding judge. These evaluations by senior judges pay particular regard to (1) a judge's effectiveness in conducting legal proceedings, including fact-gathering, and his treatment of witnesses and litigants; and (2) the quality of his opinions — his success in mastering and applying the law to his cases.

American contrasts. If I were put to the choice of civil litigation under the German procedure that I have been praising in this article or under the American procedure that I have been criticizing, I might have qualms about choosing the German. The likely venue of a lawsuit of mine would be the state court in Cook County, Illinois, and I must admit that I distrust the bench of that court. The judges are selected by a process in which the criterion of professional competence is at best an incidental value. Further, while decent people do reach the Cook County bench in surprising numbers, events have shown that some of their colleagues are crooks. If my lawsuit may fall into the hands of a dullard or a thug, I become queasy about increasing his authority over the proceedings.

German-style judicial responsibility for fact-gathering cannot be lodged with the Greylord judiciary. Remodeling of civil procedure is intimately connected to improvement in the selection of judges. I do not believe that we would have to institute a German style career judiciary in order to reform American civil procedure along German lines * * *. The difference in quality between the state and federal trial benches in places like Cook County is sufficient to remind us that measures far short of adopting the Continental career judiciary can bring about material improvement.

Cultural differences surely do explain something of why institutional and procedural differences arise in different legal systems. The important question for present purposes is what weight to attach to this factor, and my answer is, "Not much." It is all too easy to allow the cry of "cultural differences" to become the universal apologetic that permanently sheathes the status quo against criticism based upon comparative example. Cultural differences that help explain the origins of superior procedures need not restrict their spread. If Americans were to resolve to officialize the fact-gathering process while preserving the political prominence of the higher bench, we would probably turn initially to some combination of judges, magistrates, and masters for getting the job done. Over time, we would strike a new balance between bench and bar, and between higher and lower judicial office.

Notes and Questions

1. Are there aspects of the German approach that you find particularly appealing? Particularly unappealing? Do you think it would be possible to borrow pieces of the German system without taking the whole system?

2. Professor Reitz has argued that the differences between the United States and Germany is less a result of positive law, and more a function of "legal culture." John Reitz, *Why We Probably Cannot Adopt the German Advantage in Civil Procedure*, 75 IOWA L. REV. 987 (1990). He notes that "on paper," American judges have broader powers than German judges to call expert witnesses, but that power goes largely unused. Id. at 992. Likewise, although the German system permits lawyers to cross-examine witnesses, vigorous cross-examination is relatively rare. Id. at 993. Reitz concludes, "The primacy of cultural definitions over positive law does not mean that change is impossible, but it suggests that the mechanism of change is an important problem." Id. at 994. How much are our models for dispute resolution shaped by our culture and how much can we reshape our culture by reshaping our methods of dispute resolution?

3. Professor Gross has argued that although the German system may be more efficient, "efficiency is a questionable standard for evaluating a system of adjudication." Samuel Gross, *The American Advantage: The Value of Inefficient Litigation*, 85 MICH. L. REV. 734, 756 (1987). First, he notes that defenders of the adversary system argue that it produces greater accuracy than other adjudicative models and in addition "is uniquely respectful of the autonomy of the individual." Id. at 745. Second, he suggests that the inefficiency of our system can be viewed as a strength rather than a weakness: "The inefficiency of our adjudicative system reduces incentives to litigate." Id. at 752. How important is efficiency in a dispute resolution system? Is efficiency a strength or a weakness? What other values are important?

Sempier v. Johnson & Higgins

45 F.3d 724 (3d Cir. 1995)

GARTH, CIRCUIT JUDGE.

On March 9, 1994, the district court granted summary judgment in favor of Johnson & Higgins ("J & H"), the employer of appellant Burt Sempier. Sempier now appeals the district court's grant of summary judgment on his Age Discrimination in Employment Act ("ADEA") claim, 29 U.S.C. § 623 (1988), and the discretionary dismissal of his pendent state law claims. He also raises as error the district court's substitution of a "Bill of Particulars" in place of his interrogatories.

We have jurisdiction pursuant to 28 U.S.C. § 1291 to review the March 9, 1994 final order of the district court. Because the record reflects a genuine issue of material fact regarding whether J & H's asserted nondiscriminatory reasons for discharging Sempier are pretextual, we will reverse the summary judgment entered in favor of J & H. We also conclude that the district court abused its discretion in substituting its own "Bill of Particulars" for Sempier's interrogatories.

[The court describes the circumstances surrounding Sempier's hiring and later firing by the defendant.]

At the outset of the litigation, Sempier served two sets of interrogatories and a series of document requests on J & H. When J & H refused to respond to a substantial portion of the discovery requested, Sempier sought an order from the magistrate judge which would have compelled J & H to respond. The magistrate judge denied Sempier's motion. On appeal, the district court judge vacated the order of denial but remanded the dispute to the magistrate judge without entering an order compelling discovery. On remand, the magistrate judge relieved J & H from answering the original two sets of interrogatories and required that Sempier draft a third set of interrogatories. After J & H refused to answer almost all of these interrogatories, Sempier again sought a second order compelling discovery. The magistrate judge denied Sempier's motion to compel answers and ordered J & H to provide information responding to a "Bill of Particulars" drafted by the court. On appeal, the district court affirmed the magistrate judge's order and added one question of its own to the "Bill of Particulars."

Between November and December 1993, the parties disputed whether J & H had complied with the court's orders to answer the court's questions and to provide documents. In December, Sempier filed additional motions for an order to compel discovery and for partial summary judgment. J & H replied with its motion for summary judgment.

The district court granted J & H's summary judgment motion on the ADEA claim and dismissed the remaining pendent claims without prejudice. * * *

Sempier filed a timely appeal.

[The court concludes that there was conflicting evidence as to whether Sempier was fired because of poor performance or age discrimination. The court reverses the grant of summary judgment.]

VI

In addition to challenging the district court's order which granted summary judgment to J & H, an order which we now hold must be reversed, Sempier also complains that the district court abused its discretion in ruling on his discovery efforts. In so doing, Sempier contends that he was prevented from marshaling additional evidence establishing that J & H's proffered reason for his discharge was pretextual.

We normally do not become involved with "nitty gritty" rulings on discovery matters. Nor do we generally engage in exercises to determine whether a party's interrogatories are relevant or are unduly burdensome. This appeal, however, requires that we review the actions taken by the magistrate judge and the district court judge with respect to discovery sought and answered by the parties. While we will not examine each jot and tittle of the discovery process, it is important to our analysis that some background be furnished.

Sempier's complaint was filed in April 1992. In June 1992, Sempier served his first set of interrogatories and a request for production of documents. In July 1992, Sempier served a second set of interrogatories with a second request for production of documents. Unfortunately, not all of the interrogatories that were served have found their way into the record, and thus, into the appendix. We have examined those that have been reproduced in the appendix, and we find it difficult to understand how the magistrate judge could have condoned the answers given by J & H. Moreover, we are perplexed by the failure of the magistrate judge or the district court judge to compel responsive answers to the interrogatories — almost all of which appear to us to be relevant and directed to the issues of Sempier's employment, performance and relationship with J & H.

For example, Interrogatory No. 36 sought the name of each and every person who had supervision and/or control over Sempier from January 1, 1986 through the termination of Sempier's employment. It also sought, with respect to each such supervisor identified, the job title, the department supervised, the duties and responsibilities of the job, the date on which he or she assumed the supervisory position, and, if the individual was not still employed, the date and reason of termination and the last known address. True, that interrogatory sought as well the date of hire, date of birth and educational background, but those three inquiries, if not deemed relevant in the district court's judgment, could have been excised and the remainder of the interrogatory answered. Yet J & H objected to the interrogatory on the grounds that it was "overbroad, unduly burdensome, and exceeding the scope of permissible discovery." J & H then referred Sempier to a J & H Position Statement which does not even appear to be part of the record.

Again, Interrogatory No. 44 asked J & H if it voluntarily terminated the employment and/or relationship of Sempier with J & H. J & H's response reads: "Defendant refers plaintiff to pages 3 through 17 of the J & H Position Statement." The following interrogatory, Interrogatory No. 45, sought the dates on which the decision to terminate Sempier was made, and J & H's response was "See Interrogatory No. 44." Interrogatory No. 46 sought the factual basis for J & H's decision to terminate Sempier and/or the relationship of Sempier with J & H. The answer given by J & H: "Defendant refers plaintiff to the J & H Position Statement." The other interrogatories which we have reviewed — all seemingly relevant — have been answered in much the same manner. All of J & H's answers disregard the requirements of the Federal Rules of Civil Procedure. See Fed. R. Civ. P. 33(a) (requiring separate and complete answers unless specific objections are provided); 26(b) (defining the scope of discovery) (1993 version).[9]

Without dwelling further on this subject, we observe that the magistrate judge did not compel the answers which Sempier sought. Rather, he relieved J & H from answering the various discovery requests and instructed Sempier to issue a third set of

9. Lead counsel for J & H is apparently the New York law firm of Sullivan & Cromwell. Perhaps this accounts for the lack of familiarity with New Jersey Federal Court practice. We note, however, that J & H has local counsel. It is a matter of concern to us that the discovery practice in this case was so badly abused when at the least, local counsel had to have recognized the need to conform to the standards of discovery practice which have long been established in the District of New Jersey.

interrogatories and a third document request. The latter two discovery requests were no more answered than the earlier ones. In lieu of compelling answers to the third set of interrogatories served by Sempier, the district court instructed J & H to answer a four question "Bill of Particulars."

Against this background, we consider Sempier's arguments. Under the Federal Rules of Civil Procedure and our jurisprudence, district courts have broad discretion to manage discovery. Nonetheless, the district court's discretion has boundaries, and in particular, we frown upon unnecessary discovery limitations in Title VII, and hence ADEA, cases. In such cases, other courts have refused, and now we refuse, "to allow procedural technicalities to impede the full vindication of guaranteed rights." A plaintiff in an ADEA case, as Sempier is here, should not be hamstrung by the district court in limiting his discovery. In substituting a "Bill of Particulars" for those means of discovery authorized by the Federal Rules of Civil Procedure, the district court here far exceeded the outermost limits on its discretion.

Since 1938, civil discovery has been an attorney-initiated, attorney-focused procedure. The vast majority of federal discovery tools operate, when used properly, almost entirely without the court's involvement. See Fed. R. Civ. P. 26(f) (requiring the parties to devise and submit a discovery plan); Fed. R. Civ. P. 30 ("[A] party may take the testimony of any person, including a party, by deposition upon oral examination without leave of court."); Fed. R. Civ. P. 34(b) (production of documents); cf. Fed. R. Civ. P. 35 (providing for physical examinations only by leave of the court); see also William Schwarzer, *The Federal Rules, The Adversary Process, and Discovery Reform*, 50 U. Pitt. L. Rev. 703, 714–16 (1989).

Indeed under the recent amendments to Federal Rule of Civil Procedure 26(a), which became effective December 1, 1993 in the District of New Jersey, a party must provide discovery "without waiting [for] a discovery request." Under this scheme, when civil litigation proceeds smoothly, the parties conduct discovery with minimal interference from and minimal appeal to the court. Through the discovery process, even before the amendments became effective, the attorneys obtain answers to questions that they feel are relevant to the issues if not determinative of the issues. Nowhere in the process is the district court authorized to initiate its own questioning or to seek documents for itself. See John H. Langbein, *The German Advantage in Civil Procedure*, 52 U. Chi. L. Rev. 823, 827–30 (1985) (noting the difference between civil law procedure in which judges initiate the investigation and common law procedure in which the parties conduct the investigation).

When the parties stray from this course, Rule 37 provides the court with tools to give the litigants new and proper bearings. A court may compel answers to interrogatories or deposition questions, compel the production of documents, or conversely, grant protective orders. Fed. R. Civ. P. 37; Fed. R. Civ. P. 26(b)(5)(c). If these measures fail, a court may order facts established, forbid the introduction of evidence, strike the pleadings, file a default judgment, dismiss the action, or hold a party in contempt of court. However, none of the weapons in this formidable arsenal include the wholesale substitution of court-engineered discovery.

The district court was evidently not content with the contents of its discovery arsenal. Rather, it abandoned the structure and command of the Rules to revive a procedural device abandoned in civil practice forty-five years ago. Although still used in criminal matters, a "Bill of Particulars" has not graced the shores of federal civil discovery since the 1950s. Even in criminal matters, a "Bill of Particulars" is not generally considered a discovery device. In this case, it was not only an unwelcome and inappropriate incursion by the district court into the parties' dispute, but it severely trenched upon the Rules of Civil Procedure which have been crafted to provide information as to matters relevant to the issues disputed. Fed. R. Civ. P. 26(b)(1).

Sempier had served his interrogatories in compliance with Federal Rule of Civil Procedure 33. The Rule provides, "[e]ach interrogatory shall be answered separately and fully in writing under oath, unless it is objected to, in which event the objecting party shall state the reasons for objection and shall answer to the extent the interrogatory is not objectionable." J & H believed the interrogatories were objectionable and stated its objections. Sempier sought to compel answers.

The court could have denied the discovery on the ground that it was privileged, burdensome, duplicative, or otherwise outside of the scope of discovery. Fed. R. Civ. P. 26(b). It could have compelled answers and awarded attorney's fees and/or sanctions. Fed. R. Civ. P. 37(b). It did none of these things nor did it comply with its obligation to consider and rule upon each interrogatory to which J & H objected. Rather than rule upon the objections, the district court decided that "[the] Magistrate Judge ... provided a mechanism (Bill of Particulars) for further discovery regarding the precise issue outlined in this Court's September 7, 1993 Order."

The district court may have disliked its obligation to examine each interrogatory and review the magistrate judge's ruling. Regardless of its feelings, the district court, guided only by its own discretion and determination of what is important or relevant, could not rewrite a party's questions and in effect serve its own set of interrogatories. When the court took upon itself to author the questions being asked, it virtually became a participant in the parties' controversy in a manner inconsistent with fundamental conceptions of the role of a judge in our common law system.

In this case, the district court reformulated Sempier's interrogatories into four broad questions about Sempier's performance. The magistrate judge reframed specific requests pertaining to the reasons considered by J & H, and the reasons upon which J & H actually relied to terminate Sempier, into a vague question, "[w]hy were Plaintiff's job responsibilities reassigned?" Pertinent and direct interrogatories, that were propounded by Sempier, sought the dates of conversations regarding Sempier's performance and the names of the participants in those discussions. Those interrogatories were replaced by the district court with a vague and general "Bill of Particulars." Because the district court's questions were, with one exception, general, nonspecific, and broad, the resulting answers, to the extent that they answered the questions at all, were uninformative and of little value. Sempier had good reason to draft specific interrogatories and had a right to expect correspondingly specific answers. The district court's substitution of its own work product denied Sempier this opportunity.

We have examined the Supplemental Bill of Particulars which contains the questions framed by the magistrate judge and the district court judge, and we have examined closely J & H's answers. Those answers can best be described as an attempt, if not to outwit, then to frustrate all legitimate efforts to furnish information to an adversary. Moreover, whereas Federal Rule of Civil Procedure 33 provides that interrogatories must be answered under oath and thus may be evidentiary, there is no such provision in the Federal Rules of Civil Procedure for a "Bill of Particulars." Indeed, there is no provision at all for "Bills of Particulars"—and for good reason. As we have noted, "Bills of Particulars" were replaced by the discovery rules of the Federal Rules of Civil Procedure.

The district court's action was unauthorized by the Federal Rules of Civil Procedure and in violation of the principles of our jurisprudence. The Federal Rules of Civil Procedure, which must obtain Supreme Court and Congressional approval, not only prescribe the procedures to be followed by counsel, but they also prescribe the Rules under which the courts operate. By venturing so far outside the parameters set by the Rules, the court abused its discretion.

Our discussion and holding here does not leave the district court powerless to manage the discovery difficulties presented by this and similar cases. On the contrary, the district court has considerable authority and discretion by which to resolve discovery disputes. Indeed, if discovery has reached an impasse or a nonproductive stage either through counsel's obstinacy, intransigence, or even incompetence, the district court can always, through appropriate intervention, suggest the proper manner in which questions should be asked and the answers furnished. A district court's creativity in this respect is unrestricted, although it cannot, of course, disregard the commands of the Federal Rules of Civil Procedure or, as in this case, substitute a "Bill of Particulars" for a party's relevant discovery. It can, however, always give counsel guidance and direction as to the manner in which discovery should proceed.

If, after an examination of a party's interrogatories, the district court determines that the interrogatories are inappropriate, the court can refuse to compel answers. If a party is unable to draft satisfactory interrogatories after a reasonable time for discovery has concluded, the court can limit further discovery. If the court feels either party was acting in bad faith, it can impose sanctions. Certainly, if a party, without justification, refuses to answer interrogatories in the manner required by Federal Rule of Civil Procedure 33, the court can compel answers under threat of sanctions. Any or all of these options could have been employed in this case. Any and all of these options would have received substantial deference upon review.

VII

We will reverse the summary judgment of the district court dated March 9, 1994 and remand. On remand, the district court is directed to vacate the magistrate judge's order of August 7, 1993 and to vacate its own order of November 3, 1993 which approved and modified a "Bill of Particulars." The district court is also directed to permit and schedule additional appropriate and adequate discovery pursuant to the

Federal Rules of Civil Procedure so that further proceedings, including trial, may be conducted consistent with the foregoing opinion.

Notes and Questions

1. In light of the Langbein article, would you recommend amending the Federal Rules of Civil Procedure to permit judges to do what the magistrate judge attempted to do in *Sempier*? As we saw in Chapter 8, Section D.4, magistrate judges serve as adjuncts to federal district judges. They are appointed by the district judges and serve a term of years. Federal law permits district judges to delegate various tasks to magistrate judges, subject to review by the district judge. 28 U.S.C. § 636. The review provisions are intended to ensure that the ultimate decision-making authority for the case remains with a judge appointed under Article III of the Constitution.

2. Is what the magistrate judge attempted in *Sempier* a reasonable approximation of the German approach to discovery? Or did the judge maintain the basic model of partisanship but simply substituted himself for one of the parties? In other words, did the judge borrow too little?

3. In Gentile v. Missouri Department of Corrections & Human Resources, 986 F.2d 214 (8th Cir. 1993), a prisoner filed an Eighth Amendment claim against prison officials alleging deliberate indifference to his serious medical needs. The prisoner represented himself and requested leave to proceed in forma pauperis under 28 U.S.C. § 1915.*

The case was assigned to a magistrate judge who, after a hearing, granted leave to proceed in forma pauperis. The magistrate judge then conducted a personal investigation into the merits of the plaintiff's claim, holding a series of informal "hearings" at which the magistrate interviewed that plaintiff and defendant's lawyers. Later, the judge held a telephone conference call with plaintiff's physician. The doctor was not put under oath, but the magistrate questioned the doctor extensively about the plaintiff's medical condition and treatment. Ultimately, the magistrate granted summary judgment for the defendant on the basis of the doctor's unsworn statements.

The court of appeals criticized the approach taken by the magistrate judge. It explained that the § 1915 in forma pauperis procedure "does not mean that the participants at trial are to perform different duties from those they would perform if the plaintiff had been able to pay his filing fee. The goal of § 1915 is to put 'the indigent plaintiff on a similar footing with paying plaintiffs.'" The court then said:

> What happened here seems more akin to a civil-law proceeding, in which the judge takes the initiative to determine the truth. The inquisitional method may have something to commend it, but it is not our system. In common-law countries judicial proceedings are adversarial. The judge (or jury) finds

---

* This statute authorizes the court to waive an indigent litigant's fees and costs. It also directs the court to serve process on the indigent's behalf.

> the facts on the basis of evidence properly sworn to and offered by both sides in the customary order.

986 F.2d at 219.

There is a final irony to the case. Although the court of appeals held that it was error for the magistrate judge to rely on the unsworn doctor's statement, it affirmed the grant of summary judgment. The court explained that the defendant's motion for summary judgment had included sworn affidavits and the burden had therefore shifted to the plaintiff "to make a showing of specific factual issues for trial." Id. The court concluded that "[b]ecause the plaintiff did not come forward with enough specific facts to support his deliberate indifference claim, summary judgment was proper." Id. Would unrepresented indigent litigants such as the plaintiff in *Gentile* be better off under a civil-law system?

4. *Managerial Judging.* Notwithstanding *Sempier,* many have argued that the American system has embraced a model of "managerial judging," and becoming more like the civil law system with its emphasis on greater judicial control. See Richard Marcus, *Reining in the American Litigator: The New Role of American Judges*, 27 HASTINGS INT'L & COMP. L. REV. 3, 29–30 (2003). As we saw in Chapter 8, Section E, Rules 11, 16, and 26 foster greater judicial involvement and control of pre-trial proceedings. The same "hands on" approach is found the Manual for Complex Litigation, which is promulgated by the Federal Judicial Center and intended to guide district judges in handling complex cases. It describes in detail techniques for judicial supervision and management of complex cases and explains:

> Although not without limits, the court's express and inherent powers enable the judge to exercise extensive supervision and control of litigation. * * * In planning and implementing case management, the court should keep in mind the goal of bringing about a just resolution as speedily, inexpensively, and fairly as possible. Judges should tailor case-management procedures to the needs of the particular litigation and to the resources available from the parties and the judicial system. Judicial time is the scarcest resource of all: Judges should use their time wisely and efficiently and make use of all available help. Time pressures may lead some judges to believe that they should not devote time to civil case management. Investing time in the early stages of the litigation, however, will lead to earlier dispositions, less wasteful activity, shorter trials, and, in the long run, economies of judicial time and fewer judicial burdens.

FED. JUDICIAL CTR., MANUAL FOR COMPLEX LITIGATION § 10.1 (4th ed. 2004). Many have praised the trend toward managerial judging. See, e.g., Robert Peckham, *The Federal Judge as a Case Manager: The New Role in Guiding a Case from Filing to Disposition*, 69 CAL. L. REV. 770 (1981).

Others, however, are not so enthusiastic. As Professor Elliott notes:

> Opponents of managerial judging * * * argue that litigants are being forced, directly or indirectly, to abandon positions on the merits. To make matters worse, they say, judges are making discretionary procedural decisions early on that ef-

> fectively close off lines of substantive inquiry without benefit of full development and consideration of the merits of the parties' positions. And the "managerial" decisions of these judges are largely immune from appellate review.

Donald Elliott, *Managerial Judging and the Evolution of Procedure*, 53 U. Chi. L. Rev. 306, 314 (1986). See Judith Resnik, *Managerial Judges*, 96 Harv. L. Rev. 374 (1982); Judith Resnik, *Failing Faith: Adjudicatory Procedure in Decline*, 53 U. Chi. L. Rev. 494 (1986).

Professor Elliott offers the following assessment:

> In the long run, * * * the disadvantages that arise from the ad hoc character of managerial judging cannot be eliminated, only reduced. More fundamental reform must proceed by addressing directly the system of incentives that creates the need for managerial judging in the first place. Redesigning incentives with an eye to their effect on the terms of settlements will not only reduce the arbitrariness which is inherent in managerial judging, but will also be more likely than ad hoc intervention by judges to encourage just outcomes. For example, if the existing methods of compensating counsel do in fact create powerful economic incentives for lawyers to act in ways that are not in the best interest of their clients, restructuring the compensation system directly is more likely to be effective than managerial techniques. Similarly, if defendants are encouraged to delay judgment because of rules of law that deny successful litigants the full time-value of money during the pendency of litigation, restructuring the system of incentives is more likely to be successful than is an overlay of counter-incentives imposed on an ad hoc basis by managerial judges.
>
> Reforming procedural incentives to promote just settlements requires a fundamental change in the way that we view civil procedure. Before such changes can be made, we will have to stop thinking of the "pretrial" process as a prelude to trial, and start thinking of it as the "main event"—as the matrix of incentives within which the overwhelming majority of cases are going to be settled by two party-appointed arbitrators (the opposing lawyers).

Elliott, supra, 53 U. Chi. L. Rev. at 335. What changes might go along with thinking of pretrial as the main event?

5. An increase in "managerial judging" and related pretrial dispositions may at least partially explain the decline in the percentage of cases that go to trial. One of the remarkable trends in recent years, best documented in the federal courts, is the "vanishing" civil trial. Fewer than two percent of cases filed in federal district courts will ever go to trial. In most cases, the parties reach settlement. But in many cases, the dispute is adjudicated in the pre-trial phase, for example, through summary judgment. Some cases are ferried out of the litigation system to arbitration or some other form of "alternative" dispute resolution. See, e.g., Alexander Reinert, *The Burdens of Pleading*, 162 U. Pa. L. Rev. 1767, 1769 (2014) ("[T]he federal judiciary has very little experience evaluating the merits of claims. Trials have decreased and cases have been shunted away from federal court by arbitration doctrine.").

C. Models of Non-Judicial Resolution

1. Brief Overview

We have seen that litigation has its critics. The process can be expensive and intrusive, it is a zero-sum game, and it is retrospective. That is, litigation forces the parties to focus on the past — on what happened, rather than on going forward with their lives (either with or without each other). Critics often tout "alternative" dispute resolution (ADR). We put "alternative" in quotation marks because in the past generation the field has become so well entrenched that it is probably best referred to simply as "dispute resolution." See, e.g., Judith Resnik, *Diffusing Disputes: The Public in the Private of Arbitration, the Private in Courts, and the Erasure of Rights*, 124 YALE L.J. 2804, 2805–2806 (2015) ("An increasingly common parlance (crisscrossing the globe) replaces the phrase 'alternative dispute resolution (ADR)' with DR, so as to put courts * * * on a continuum of mechanisms responding to conflicts."). Undoubtedly, your law school has upper-level courses on ADR generally, and probably specialized courses on negotiation, mediation, and arbitration. The well-trained litigator today must be comfortable with litigation and the "alternatives."

The commonest form of ADR is settlement, which results from negotiation. The parties may structure the outcome of the dispute in a way that makes sense for them. In a dispute between businesses that foresee an ongoing relationship, for instance, perhaps a settlement will involve future conduct toward each other. Some disputes settle before anyone files a case. Many times, however, the parties are moved toward serious negotiation because someone has instituted litigation.

The two main models of ADR are mediation and arbitration. In mediation, the parties engage a third party to help them reach a settlement. The mediator is not focused on who is right, but on getting the parties to find common ground. Mediation is the antithesis of the zero-sum game — the goal is to reach accord, rather than to declare a winner and a loser. Though some have suggested that mediation's reliance on communication rather than adversarial confrontation may be more conducive to women, some feminist scholarship has questioned that argument. Trina Grillo, *The Mediation Alternative: Process Dangers for Women*, 100 YALE L.J. 1545, 1608 (1991). And others have criticized mediation as inappropriate when one's rights have been violated. See Albert Alschuler, *Mediation with a Mugger: The Shortage of Adjudicative Services and the Need for a Two-Tier Trial System in Civil Cases*, 99 HARV. L. REV. 1808 (1985).

Arbitration bears more resemblance to litigation. The parties present evidence to a neutral third party in a hearing that looks a great deal like a trial. There is no jury, however, and the arbitrator (or sometimes the panel of arbitrators), unlike a judge, is not employed by the government. Rather, she is paid by the litigants to render a decision — to decide who wins. Proceedings are less formal than litigation and the rules governing admissibility of evidence in court do not apply. Historically, there has been no discovery in arbitration, but this is changing, at least in large-scale disputes between commercial entities. Even there, discovery generally is the result of contract and not of procedural rules. Litigation is public—hearings take place in the courthouse, to which the general public and press have access and pleadings generally are available to the public (often online). In contrast, arbitration is confidential, so the public cannot learn about allegations of wrongdoing made in arbitration. Finally, though judgments in court are subject to appellate review, judicial review of arbitration decisions is very limited.

2. Court-Annexed Versus Contractual ADR

Traditionally, ADR of any type was the result of agreement among the parties. Such "contractual" arbitration is increasingly common today, as we discuss in the next Section. The past generation has seen the expansion of "court-annexed" ADR. With this, the court in which litigation is filed refers the parties to mediation or arbitration. The terms of the relevant statutes and rules can vary greatly from state to state and even from locality to locality. For example, some courts may require (or suggest) that parties whose dispute does not exceed $25,000 must go through mediation or arbitration procedure. Congress has imposed the ADR ethos on the federal courts; every federal district court is required to offer some form of court-annexed ADR.*

The goal of court-annexed ADR is to provide a benchmark, with the hope that it will spur the parties to compromise and settle the case without trial. Should the effort not work, however, parties generally are free to return to the litigation stream and complete the case.

3. Expansion of Contractual Arbitration

Most arbitration is the result of agreement among the parties, which might arise in two ways. First, after a dispute has arisen, the parties may agree to hire an arbitration service and resolve the dispute in the arbitral forum. There are many providers of such services, notably the American Arbitration Association. Second, parties to a contract may include a clause providing that if a dispute arises, they will submit it to arbitration. Such arbitration clauses are thus entered before there is a dispute. They usually specify the manner in which the arbitrator(s) will be chosen and the location of the arbitration hearing.

At common law, courts would not enforce arbitration agreements. The courts saw them as improper private efforts to "oust" courts of jurisdiction. Against this background, Congress passed the Federal Arbitration Act (FAA) in 1925. 9 U.S.C. §§ 1–14. It requires courts to enforce valid arbitration agreements and permits them to stay (suspend) litigation and order the parties to arbitrate. It also provides for judicial enforcement of arbitration awards and for very limited judicial review of arbitral decisions.

When Congress passed the FAA, contractual arbitration provisions were found only in commercial agreements. Thus, "the FAA was originally envisioned by Con-

* The Alternative Dispute Resolution Act of 1998, 28 U.S.C. §§ 651–58, 652(a).

gress as a relatively limited legislation that would govern disputes between commercial parties in federal court."* For over half a century, such agreements were limited to the business-to-business context. Starting in the 1980s, however, the Supreme Court has interpreted the FAA very broadly, which has resulted in its being applied to many more types of disputes. We note three particulars. One, the FAA applies to require state courts (not just federal courts) to enforce valid arbitration provisions. See, e.g., Buckeye Check Cashing, Inc. v. Cardegna, 546 U.S. 440, 445–446 (2006). Two, the Court has required arbitration of various federal statutory claims. Thus, though a law may give the plaintiff a federal right (as, for example, to be free from discrimination on the basis of age), it does not guaranty access to a judicial forum to vindicate that right. See, e.g., Gilmer v. Interstate/Johnson Lane Corp., 500 U.S. 20, 26, 28 (1991). Three, the Court has extended the command of the FAA to contracts of adhesion — that is, to contracts entered without negotiation.

Thus contractual arbitration has moved from the business-to-business context to apply to the vindication of employee, consumer, and other rights. Again, agreeing to arbitration means that one has waived the right to a public forum, to trial by jury, to oversight of proceedings by a professional judicial officer, and to appellate review. Most of us would be surprised to find that we have done that simply by signing or clicking onto any number of agreements, including cellphone contracts, purchases online, and rental and employment agreements.

The Court's expansion of the FAA to contracts of adhesion has given rise to a powerful combination: a contract containing both an arbitration clause and a prohibition of aggregation. In AT&T Mobility LLC v. Concepcion, 563 U.S. 333 (2011), one million consumers signed up for a cellphone plan. As part of the plan, they were to receive a free cellphone. They received the phones, but were each billed $30 as sales tax on the phone. Two of the consumers brought a class action against the phone provider, claiming violation of state consumer-protection and related common law claims. Their contract waived litigation, however, and required them to proceed in arbitration. While there can be class proceedings in arbitration, these consumers encountered another problem — the contract also forbade them from arbitrating together. That is, each person must arbitrate her own claim individually. The fear is that no one will find it worth the effort to file the paperwork and do what must be done in arbitration to recover a mere $30. As Judge Posner famously said, no one but a lunatic or fanatic will undertake such effort for $30. Carnegie v. Household Int'l Inc., 367 F.3d 656, 661 (7th Cir. 2004).

If that is true, however, the defendant is effectively shielded from being called to account (at least in private civil proceedings) for an alleged wrongdoing. Because of that, some states have refused to enforce clauses that prohibit class or aggregate arbitration. But the Court held in *Concepcion* that such state rules are preempted by the FAA. Later cases have been consistent in requiring claimants to proceed indi-

* 31 Moore's Federal Practice §907.01 at 907-3.

vidually. DIRECTV, Inc. v. Imburgia, 136 S. Ct. 463 (2015); American Express Co. v. Italian Colors Restaurant, 133 S. Ct. 2304 (2013).

Again, if individuals will not file arbitration claims, defendants will be free from civil proceedings concerning alleged wrongdoing. Is there anything wrong with that? Can you answer that question without taking a position on the role of civil litigation in the enforcement of law?

Without question, arbitration agreements are increasingly common in the United States, for reasons discussed. Arbitration clauses are also quite common in international commercial transactions. Parties to such deals may be uncomfortable with the judicial options available. In the international arena, one significant advantage of arbitration is that arbitral awards are much easier to enforce than judicial judgments. Over 140 nations including the United States have ratified the United Nations Convention on the Recognition and Enforcement of Foreign Arbitral Awards (the New York Convention). In contrast, there is no similar world-wide treaty on enforcement of judicial judgments.

4. Dispute Resolution Without Adjudication

Arbitration, like litigation, relies on a third-party decision maker. However, most disputes are ultimately settled, that is, resolved by the parties themselves without a dispositive determination by a third party. Though settlement may come as a result of the threat of adjudication, the settlement terms are determined by the parties.

There are a variety of techniques as well as social customs that may facilitate nonjudicial settlement of disputes. In an earlier era, dueling was a socially accepted, if not quite legal, mechanism that accomplished this purpose. It had the virtues of relative speed and finality, though also carried some obvious social costs. Today, mediation is a popular approach. Unlike an arbitrator, a mediator does not decide the dispute, but instead acts as a facilitator to aid the parties in reaching a mutually acceptable solution. In addition to mediation, there may be other cultural practices that facilitate settlement.

The Implications of Apology: Law and Culture in Japan and in the United States

Hiroshi Wagatsuma & Arthur Rosett
20 Law & Soc'y Rev. 461 (1986)

Apology is a social lubricant used every day in on-going human relationships. People constantly utter words of apology in both Japan and the United States, most often to seek indulgence for a minor social breach, to ask for permission to violate conventional rules, or to express sympathetic regret for a mishap. * * *

I. Apology and Culture

* * * We believe * * * that there are real differences in the incidence of apologetic behavior by Japanese and Americans faced with a serious claim that they have injured

another. We are even more confident, however, that there are differences in the significance that is likely to be attached to apologetic behavior or the failure of a person to apologize. These differences in significance are expressive of important cultural assumptions that influence many forms of social interaction and that form a central part of the foundation supporting the structure of the legal system. Studying them should reveal significant information about the formal and informal operation of both the Japanese and American legal systems and about the connections between culturally influenced behavior and the legal processes used to resolve disputes.

We would agree, for example, with [a] recent suggestion that apology in Japan is one of a number of social behaviors that compensate for the weakness of the formal enforcement sanctions of the law. [This] point also can be turned inside out. The availability of social restorative mechanisms like apology obviates formal legal sanction in many cases. In the United States, the relative absence of recognition of apology may be related to the observed tendency of American society to overwork formal legal processes and to rely too heavily on the adjudication of rights and liabilities by litigation. Alternative means of dispute resolution accordingly receive less attention and social support. The relative absence of apology in American law may also be connected to the legal system's historic preoccupation with reducing all losses to economic terms that can be awarded in a money judgment and its related tendency either not to compensate at all or to award extravagant damages for injuries that are not easily reducible to quantifiable economic losses. Finally, the small role of apology or any other personal contact between criminal and victim also seems related to the disquieting tendency in American law to ignore and even abuse the victim during the formal process of criminal prosecution.

IV. Apology as an Admission of the Wrongfulness of the Act

Many Japanese seem to think it is better to apologize even when the other party is at fault, while Americans may blame others even when they know they are at least partially at fault. Americans, as a group, seem more ready to deny wrongdoing, to demand proof of their delict, to challenge the officials' right to intervene, and to ask to speak to a lawyer. Japanese criminal offenders are said to be more ready than Americans to admit their guilt and throw themselves on the mercy of an offended authority. Only when an individual "sincerely" acknowledges his transgression against the standards of the community does the community take him back.

An apology in the Japanese cultural context thus is an indication of an individual's wish to maintain or restore a positive relationship with another person who has been harmed by the individual's acts. When compensation or damages are to be paid to the victim, it is extremely important that the person responsible expresses to the victim his feeling of deep regret and apologizes, in addition to paying an appropriate sum. If a person appears too willing to pay the damages, that willingness may be taken as the sign of his lack of regret. He may be regarded as thinking that money can settle anything and as not being sincerely interested in restoring a positive relationship with his victim. In dealing with those who have offended them, the cultural assumption of social harmony would lead the Japanese to accept the external act of apology at face value and not to disturb the superficial concord by challenging the sincerity of the person apologizing. The act of apologizing can be significant for its own sake as an acknowledgment of the authority of the hierarchical structure upon which social harmony is based. * * *

Sincerity of apology thus has different connotations in the two cultures, with the Americans preoccupied with the problematics of wholeheartedness and the Japanese focused on the more attainable externality of submission to order and return to harmonious relationship. Thus it appears that the Japanese view an apology without an acceptance of fault as being insincere, while an American is more likely to treat an exculpatory explanation as the equivalent of an apology at least to the extent that it is accompanied by a declaration of nonhostile intent in the future.

VI. Legal Aspects of Apology

C. Apology as an Admission

A crucial inhibition to a person making an apology in an American legal proceeding is the possibility that a sincere apology will be taken as an admission: evidence of the occurrence of the event and of the defendant's liability for it. * * * [W]e have been told that Japanese corporations preparing to send their executives to work in the United States have prepared a training program and materials designed to introduce the Japanese to social situations they are likely to find difficult in America. One topic that is discussed in detail for those coming to California is the operation of an automobile, including the appropriate behavior if one is involved in an accident. Along with advice on the handling of insurance, the police, and injuries, the instructions urgently warn the Japanese, "Do not apologize." This advice is considered necessary because, in a parallel situation in Japan, the cultural assumption would be that both sides would immediately apologize to each other, without regard to where fault for the accident might lie. The Japanese advice might be something of an overreaction, for it is not certain that serious adverse consequences will follow in the United States from the tendering of an apology in these circumstances, but many cautious American lawyers and insurance agents might well be tempted to offer similar advice.

D. Apology and Liability: Obligation to Make Compensation and Accept Punishment

In both the Japanese and American cultures, acceptance of responsibility for the hurtful act by making compensatory reparations to the person injured and by accepting punishment for the violation of criminal rules are stronger elements of apology than mere admission of the act itself. An apology without reparation is a hollow form, at least when the injured person has suffered a clear economic loss and when the actor has the capacity to make compensation.

At the same time, punishment and compensation for injury alone probably are an insufficient basis for forgiving the offender. A felon who has served his time or a tort-feasor who has paid the damage judgment is not entitled to be restored to social acceptance without some acknowledgment of guilt and remorse. As we mentioned above, in Japan a person too willing to pay damages may be thought to lack regret.

When industrial pollution, dangerous pharmaceutical drugs, or a commercial aircraft crash cause injury to a large number of people, the company president, as the most senior official of the wrongdoers, is expected to make a public apology, bowing deeply and preferably shedding tears. In such a situation it is important that compensation not be mentioned openly, because it is felt that money does not bring back the dead or restore health. It is important that the company official not appear too eager to settle the matter with money. It also is important that victims not appear too interested in receiving cash payment; they should mourn instead of displaying greed. This behavior reflects multiple layers of consciousness, for the individuals behave as the culture suggests they should while, at the same time, they are entertaining concerns that are quite inconsistent with the externality.

The important point here is that while there are some injuries that cannot be repaired just by saying you are sorry, there are others that can only be repaired by an apology. Such injuries are the very ones that most trouble American law. They include defamation, insult, degradation, loss of status, and the emotional distress and dislocation that accompany conflict. To the extent that a place may be found for apology in the resolution of such conflicts, American law would be enriched and better able to deal with the heart of what brought the controversy to public attention. It would also be relieved of some of the pressure to convert all damages into dollars — a pressure that produces absurdly large punitive damage judgments when a trier of fact sympathetically identifies with the claim of degradation and emotional distress but the economic loss is fictive. More to the point, society at large might be better off and better able to advance social peace if the law, instead of discouraging apologies in such situations by treating them as admissions of liability, encouraged people to apologize to those they have wronged and to compensate them for their losses. Lawsuits may never be filed in such situations.

VII. Formal Apology and Shimatsusho

A striking difference in apologetic behavior in the two legal cultures is the frequency with which a formal, ceremonial apology is tendered in Japan, often by an abject public apology by the senior official of an organization responsible for injury or by a written letter of apology (shimatsusho). For example, following the crash of a Japan Air Lines DC-8 caused by a mentally unstable pilot in 1982, the president of the airline personally called on the bereaved families of the crash victims and was pictured in the press on his knees, bowing in remorseful apology. The ceremony was accompanied by a large cash payment, which apparently obviated litigation of the legal claims arising from the accident. By contrast, American executives whose enterprise has been accused of injury or wrongdoing are thought to be more likely to deny or evade charges of any responsibility and remorse, and even less likely to call on the victims personally and apologize tearfully. The behavior of Union Carbide officials after the Bhophal disaster in 1985 combined an attempt to meet promptly the human problems engendered by the corporation's operations with a desire to avoid admissions of unlimited legal liability. The efforts appear to have satisfied no one.

Although its origins are not clear, it has long been the custom in Japan that a person who breaks a rule should express regret by writing a shimatsusho, or "letter of apology," in lieu of facing an official punishment. These letters are a common and significant aspect of Japanese apology. The practice suggests the use of a formal, written apology as the basis for relieving a wrongdoer from the legal consequences of the misbehavior. A number of examples suggest the range of ways in which a shimatsusho may serve the needs of both the wrongdoer and, equally important, the injured person or the official interested in resolving the hurtful situation without recourse to formal legal sanctions.

During a field study in Japan by one of us, he encountered the case of a sixteen-year-old high school student who took a motorcycle from a parking lot in front of a railway station. Unfortunately for him, the gasoline tank was empty, and he therefore could not start the engine. Undaunted, he rode the cycle downhill without using the motor and was stopped by a policeman. The student had no driver's license, but, since the engine was not running, his act did not legally constitute the offense of driving a motor vehicle without a license. The officer undoubtedly was suspicious of the student's tale of borrowing the motorcycle from a friend, yet he did not want to blow the incident out of proportion by treating it as a theft. Accordingly, the officer summoned the student's father to the station and told the student to sign the following shimatsusho:

> On December 24, 1977, at 1:30 PM, I was found by a police officer while riding on a motorcycle without a driver's license on P Street of Block D of City Z. I was warned by the officer. I regret deeply what I have done and I pledge myself never again to ride a motorcycle without obtaining a driver's license. Please deal with me leniently this time.

Both the student and his father signed the letter, which the police officer kept himself, although it was addressed to the chief of the patrol division. The officers thought that if the student had stolen the motorcycle his father certainly must have discovered this and could be relied on to deal with the boy. If it was not stolen, the father would admonish his son not to drive without a license "In either case," said the officer, "the matter has been dealt with effectively."

VIII. Conclusion

* * * In Japan it is believed that the settlement of any amount of compensation will go smoothly if both parties start out apologizing to each other. This insight—that apology is an important ingredient in resolving conflict—is hardly unique to the Japanese. It is something every eight-year-old knows, yet somehow it tends to be swallowed up during adult American discussions of law and business. Hegland makes this point nicely in discussing a classroom experience:

> In my first year Contracts class, I wished to review various doctrines we have recently studied. I put the following:
>
> In a long term installment contract, seller promises buyer to deliver widgets at the rate of 1,000 a month. The first two deliveries are perfect. However,

in the third month seller delivers only 990 widgets. Buyer becomes so incensed that he rejects deliveries and refuses to pay for the widgets already delivered.

After stating the problem, I asked, "If you were Seller, what would you say?" What I was looking for was a discussion of the various common law theories which would force the buyer to pay for the widgets delivered and those which would throw buyer into breach for canceling the remaining deliveries. In short, I wanted the class to come up with the legal doctrines which would allow Seller to crush Buyer.

After asking the question, I looked around the room for a volunteer. As is so often the case with first year students, I found that they were all either writing in their notebooks or inspecting their shoes. There was, however, one eager face, that of an eight year old son of one of my students. It seems that he was suffering through Contracts due to his mother's sin of failing to find a sitter. Suddenly he raised his hand. Such behavior, even from an eight year old, must be rewarded.

"OK," I said, "What would you say if you were the seller?" "I'd say, 'I'm sorry.'"

The underdevelopment of American legal doctrine based on apology suggests the degree to which other, individualistic values — most notably compensation, declaration of right, punishment, professional self-interest, and administrative convenience — have been elevated at the expense of the restorative capacity of law and social ceremony. The American lawsuit is designed to deal with claims of economic loss; indeed, its lawyer-dominated, adversarial structure is not suited to resolve other kinds of issues. The legal system tends to reduce disputes to the types it is comfortable handling. Claims for personal injury are treated as if the issues is how to put a dollar price on pain and suffering, while claims essentially based on insult and psychic hurt are not dealt with well, if they are recognized at all.

* * * Pragmatic Americans realize that an apology is a potentially useful tool of informal or nonlitigated resolution, even if apology is formal and there is some cause to doubt the wholeheartedness of the person tendering it. A process built around apology and compensation would fit well into a justice system that increasingly seeks to resolve conflicts by settlement, mediation, or alternative methods of dispute resolution, rather than trial.

Notes and Questions

1. Could a more developed mechanism for formal apology exist within our litigation system, or is never having to say you're sorry a necessary corollary of our system? Are there social and legal prerequisites to an effective system of apology? Some lawyers may counsel against a client making any apology for fear it could be used at trial as an admission of liability. Others argue that expressions of remorse and concern can defuse the anger of a victim and make it less likely the victim will sue. See generally Steven Keeva, *Does Law Mean Never Having to Say You're Sorry?*, 85 A.B.A. J. 64

(Dec. 1999); Daniel Shuman, *The Role of Apology in Tort Law*, 83 JUDICATURE 180 (2000); Note, *The Role of Apology in Mediation*, 72 N.Y.U. L. REV. 1165 (1997). Massachusetts and California have enacted statutes making inadmissible "benevolent gestures" offered following an accident. See CAL. GOV'T CODE § 11440.45; MASS. ANN. LAWS ch. 233, § 23D.

2. Following a 1985 airplane crash, Delta Airlines consciously reached out to the victims. It sent employees to be with every family and offered help in arranging funerals, locating personal property that might have survived the crash, and just lending a friendly and sympathetic ear. The result was that far fewer lawsuits were filed than in other similar crashes. But Delta's strategy had another side as well. Where suits were filed, Delta used the information its employees had gathered to reduce recoveries. In one case, a bereaved family member confided to a sympathetic Delta employee that the decedent had had an extra-marital affair. When the family filed suit, Delta pointed to the affair as a reason why the family's claim was not worth as much as they had sought. In another suit, Delta threatened to disclose that the decedent was homosexual. See Ed Bean, *After 137 People Died in Its Texas Jet Crash, Delta Helped Families*, WALL ST. J., Nov. 7, 1986, at 1. Compare this with the description in Wagatsuma and Rosett of Japan Air Lines' response following the crash of its DC-8.

3. The Japanese system of apology is intertwined with other mechanisms of non-judicial dispute resolution, particularly mediation. The traditional model of litigation is that the "winner takes it all." Litigation is seen largely as a zero-sum game in which one side wins and the other loses. Mediation is an important form of alternative dispute resolution (ADR) in which a third party mediator assists the parties in working out a compromise, but the mediator does not impose an outcome. One commentator has explained:

> The availability of suitable third parties who are willing and able to perform this role [of mediator] reduces the need to invoke formal judicial intervention. At the outset, mediation requires the presence of persons who, because of position or personal relationships, command respect and are able to exercise some measure of authority. In other words, to be effective, the mediator must be someone who can command the parties' trust and their obedience to the settlement.
>
> One would thus anticipate that suitable third parties are more readily available in a stable, closely-integrated and hierarchical society like Japan, than in a more geographically mobile, less cohesive society like the United States in which individual autonomy and social equality are emphasized. Societal expectations and habits are equally relevant. The role of the mediator becomes increasingly legitimate for both the mediator and the parties to disputes where there is repeated reliance on third parties to settle disputes. A contrast in police attitudes in Japan and the United States pointed out by David H. Bayley is especially interesting in this respect. Japanese commonly rely on the police for assistance in settling disputes. But despite similar popular demand in the United States, "what is different," says Bayley,

> "is that American police organizations have not adapted willingly to perform this function." Another Japanese example is the mediating service some companies provide for employees involved in traffic accidents. In short, the Japanese may be more successful in avoiding litigation because of social organization and values more conducive to informal dispute resolution through mediation.

John Haley, *The Myth of the Reluctant Litigant*, 4 J. JAPANESE STUDIES 359, 378–79 (1980).

An important point made by Wagatsuma and Rosett is that the goal of the Japanese system is to reestablish social relationships which may have been broken by the dispute. A similar concern is expressed by advocates of mediation. Mediation may offer a vehicle through which human connections can be re-established. Professor Riskin has argued:

> Mediation offers some clear advantages over adversary processing: it is cheaper, faster, and potentially more hospitable to unique solutions that take more fully into account nonmaterial interests of the disputants. It can educate the parties about each other's needs and those of their community. Thus, it can help them learn to work together and to see that through cooperation both can make positive gains. One reason for these advantages is that mediation is less hemmed-in by rules of procedure or substantive law and certain assumptions that dominate the adversary process. * * * [I]n mediation * * * the ultimate authority resides with the disputants. The conflict is seen as unique and therefore less subject to solution by application of some general principle. The case is neither to be governed by a precedent nor to set one. Thus, all sorts of facts, needs, and interests that would be excluded from consideration in an adversary, rule oriented proceeding could become relevant in a mediation. Indeed, whatever a party deems relevant is relevant.

Leonard Riskin, *Mediation and Lawyers*, 43 OHIO ST. L.J. 29, 34 (1982).

One of the advantages of settlement or mediation is that they permit non-binary resolutions in which both sides may get at least some of what they seek. See Carrie Menkel-Meadow, *The Trouble with the Adversary System in a Postmodern, Multicultural World*, 38 WM. & MARY L. REV. 5 (1996). Indeed, in some situations, creative lawyers may be able to construct solutions in which both sides get much of what they seek. As Professor Menkel-Meadow has observed, "settlement offers the opportunity to craft solutions that do not compromise, but offer greater expression of the variety of remedial possibilities in a postmodern world." Carrie Menkel-Meadow, *Whose Dispute Is It Anyway?: A Philosophical and Democratic Defense of Settlement (In Some Cases)*, 83 GEO. L.J. 2663, 2674 (1995). For example, increasingly the problems of discrimination in the workplace stem not from overt discrimination but from more subtle organizational structures. As a result, the resolution of these cases have gone beyond changing formal employment rules and may involve changes to a complex array of practices that impact the "corporate culture," and it is through settlement that changes in these practices can be structured. Susan Sturm, *Second*

Generation Employment Discrimination: A Structural Approach, 101 COLUM. L. REV. 458 (2001).

Mediation has not been universally acclaimed. Professor Grillo has argued:

> It has been said that "[d]isputes are cultural events, evolving within a framework of rules about what is worth fighting for, what is the normal or moral way to fight, what kinds of wrongs warrant action, and what kinds of remedies are acceptable." The process by which a society resolves conflict is closely related to its social structure. Implicit in this choice is a message about what is respectable to do or want or say, what the obligations are of being a member of the society or of a particular group within it, and what it takes to be thought of as a good person leading a virtuous life. In the adversary system, it is acceptable to want to win. It is not only acceptable, but expected, that one will rely on a lawyer and advocate for oneself without looking out for the adversary. The judge, a third party obligated to be neutral and bound by certain formalities, bears the ultimate responsibility for deciding the outcome. To the extent that women are more likely than men to believe in communication as a mode of conflict resolution and to appreciate the importance of an adversary's interests, this system does not always suit their needs.
>
> On the other hand, under a scheme of mediation, the standards of acceptable behavior and desires change fundamentally. Parties are to meet with each other, generally without their lawyers. They are encouraged to look at each other's needs and to reach a cooperative resolution based on compromise. Although there are few restrictions on her role in the process, the mediator bears no ultimate, formal responsibility for the outcome of the mediation. In sum, when mediation is the prototype for dispute resolution, the societal message is that a good person—a person following the rules—cooperates, communicates, and compromises.
>
> The glories of cooperation, however, are easily exaggerated. If one party appreciates cooperation more than the other, the parties might compromise unequally. Moreover, the self-disclosure that cooperation requires, when imposed and not sought by the parties, may feel and be invasive. Thus, rather than representing a change in the system to accommodate the "feminine voice," in actuality, mandatory mediation overrides real women's voices saying that cooperation might, at least for the time being, be detrimental to their lives and the lives of their children. Under a system of forced mediation, women are made to feel selfish for wanting to assert their own interests based on their need to survive.

Trina Grillo, *The Mediation Alternative: Process Dangers for Women*, 100 YALE L.J. 1545, 1607–1608 (1991).

4. Even if mediation is not perfect, is it better for more people more often than litigation? Can't the litigation system be dehumanizing and disempowering? Professor

White describes in detail "Mrs. G.'s" hearing concerning her welfare benefits. Professor White concludes:

> Mrs. G. had a hearing in which all of the rituals of due process were scrupulously observed. Yet she did not find her voice welcomed at that hearing. A complex pattern of social, economic, and cultural forces underwrote the procedural formalities, repressing and devaluing her voice.

Lucie White, *Subordination, Rhetorical Survival Skills, and Sunday Shoes: Notes on the Hearing of Mrs. G*, 38 Buff. L. Rev. 1, 32 (1990).

5. The type of dispute resolution system one favors may depend, at least in part, on one's view of the goal of such a system. Some view the goal as almost entirely private—the peaceful resolution of individual disputes. The government is involved primarily to prevent parties from choosing to resolve disputes through socially costly techniques such as violence. Others take a different view. Professor Owen Fiss has argued:

> Som[e] * * * se[e] adjudication in essentially private terms: The purpose of lawsuits and the civil courts is to resolve disputes, and the amount of litigation we encounter is evidence of the needlessly combative and quarrelsome character of Americans. Or as [Dean Derek] Bok put it, using a more diplomatic idiom: "At bottom, ours is a society built on individualism, competition, and success." I, on the other hand, see adjudication in more public terms: Civil litigation is an institutional arrangement for using state power to bring a recalcitrant reality closer to our chosen ideals. We turn to the courts because we need to, not because of some quirk in our personalities. We train our students in the tougher arts so that they may help secure all that the law promises, not because we want them to become gladiators or because we take a special pleasure in combat.
>
> To conceive of the civil lawsuit in public terms as America does might be unique. I am willing to assume that no other country—including Japan, Bok's new paragon—has a case like *Brown v. Board of Education* in which the judicial power is used to eradicate the caste structure. I am willing to assume that no other country conceives of law and uses law in quite the way we do. But this should be a source of pride rather than shame. What is unique is not the problem, that we live short of our ideals, but that we alone among the nations of the world seem willing to do something about it. Adjudication American-style is not a reflection of our combativeness but rather a tribute to our inventiveness and perhaps even more to our commitment.

Owen Fiss, *Against Settlement*, 93 Yale L.J. 1073, 1089–90 (1984). How might different views about the goals of adjudication affect one's views about the desirability of techniques such as mediation or settlement?

6. There is growing interest in various forms of alternative dispute resolution (ADR). This interest has been reinforced by congressional legislation, passed in 1998, which requires each district court to "authorize, by local rule * * * , the use of alter-

native resolution processes in all civil actions." 28 U.S.C. § 651. These rules may provide for mandatory mediation or arbitration of certain types of disputes.

7. New problems can also generate new forms of dispute resolution. With a growing number of commercial transactions taking place over the internet, often between people in disparate locations, there is increasing attention focused on the creation of an online dispute resolution system for small transactions. See Colin Rule, et al., *Designing a Global Consumer Online Dispute Resolution (ODR) System for Cross-Border Small Value-High Volume Claims — OAS Developments*, 42 U.C.C. L. REV. 221 (2010). eBay India has already launched an online "community court" that sellers can use to challenge negative feedback. Under the system, 21 randomly selected eBay users will review evidence submitted online by both buyer and seller. If a majority of jurors conclude that the feedback was unjustified, the negative comments will be removed.

Table of Cases

[References are to pages]

B

C

D

E

F

G

H

L

M

N

O

T

Table of Scholarly Commentary

[References are to page number]

A

Adams, Charles. World-Wide Volkswagen v. Woodson — *The Rest of the Story*, 72 Neb. L. Rev. 1122 (1993): 19; 61; 244; 463–64

Allen, Michael. *In Rem Jurisdiction from* Pennoyer *to* Shaffer *to the Anticybersquatting Consumer Protection Act*, 11 Geo. Mason L. Rev. 243 (2002): 125

ALI-ABA. Civil Trial Manual: 417

Alschuler, Albert. *Mediation with a Mugger: The Shortage of Adjudicative Services and the Need for a Two-Tier Trial System in Civil Cases*, 99 Harv. L. Rev. 1808 (1985): 851

American Bar Association Comm'n on Standards of Judicial Administration: Standards Relating to Appellate Courts § 3.10 commentary at 12 (1977): 802

American Law Institute. Complex Litigation: Statutory Recommendations and Analysis with Reporter's Study: a Model System for State-to-state Transfer and Consolidation (1994): 260

Arthur, Thomas & Richard Freer. *Grasping at Burnt Straws: The Disaster of the Supplemental Jurisdiction Statute*, 40 Emory L.J. 963 (1991): 734

As Jurors Turn to Google and Twitter, Mistrials Are Popping Up, N.Y. Times, March 1, 2009, at A1: 539

Atkinson, Thomas. *The Real Party in Interest Rule: A Plea for its Abolition*, 32 N.Y.U. L. Rev. 926 (1957): 677

B

Babcock, B. *A Place in the Palladium, Women's Rights and Jury Service*, 61 U. Cin. L. Rev. 1139 (1993): 472

Baxter, William. *Choice of Law and the Federal System*, 16 Stan. L. Rev. 1 (1963): 551

Bean, Ed. *After 137 People Died in Its Texas Jet Crash, Delta Helped Families*, Wall St. J., Nov. 7, 1986, at 1: 860

BELLI, M. 3 MODERN TRIALS §§ 51.67 and 51.68 (2d ed. 1982): 471

Bellia, Anthony. *Federal Regulation of State Court Procedures*, 110 YALE L.J. 947 (2001): 620

BENTHAM, JEREMY. 3 RATIONALE OF JUDICIAL EVIDENCE 579 (1827), *reprinted in* 7 WORKS OF JEREMY BENTHAM 171 (J. Bowring ed. 1843): 655

Black, Hugo. *Address*, 13 MO. B.J. 173 (1942): 543

BLACKSTONE, WILLIAM. 4 COMMENTARIES (1859): 465; 467; 480

Bone, Robert. *The Story of* Connecticut v. Doehr: *Balancing Costs and Benefits in Defining Procedural Rights*, *in* CIVIL PROCEDURE STORIES 159 (K. Clermont ed., 2d ed. 2008): 176

Borchers, Patrick. *Comparing Personal Jurisdiction in the United States and the European Community: Lessons for American Reform*, 40 AM. J. COMP. L. 121 (1992): 143

Borchers, Patrick. *The Origins of Diversity Jurisdiction, The Rise of Legal Positivism, and a Brave New World for* Erie *and* Klaxon, 72 TEX. L. REV. 79 (1993): 550

Borchers, Patrick. *The Problem with General Jurisdiction*, 2001 U. CHI. LEGAL F. 119: 109

Born. *Reflections on Judicial Jurisdiction in International Cases*, 17 GA. J. INT'L & COMP. L. 1, 36 (1987): 95

Branson, David & Andrea Johnson. *Aids Needed for Jury to Understand Instructions*, LEGAL TIMES OF WASHINGTON, March 5, 1984 at A9: 534

Brilmayer, *How Contacts Count: Due Process Limitations on State Court Jurisdiction*, 1980 S. CT. REV. 77, 109–10: 141

Bronsteen, John. *Against Summary Judgment*, 75 GEO. WASH. L. REV. 522 (2007): 514

Buckley, Colin. *Issue Preclusion and Issues of Law: A Doctrinal Framework Based on Rules of Recognition, Jurisdiction and Legal History*, 24 HOUS. L. REV. 875 (1987): 667

Burbank, Stephen. *The Bitter With the Sweet: Tradition, History, and Limitations on Federal Judicial Power — A Case Study*, 75 NOTRE DAME L. REV. 1291 (2000): 5

Burbank, Stephen. *Federal Judgments Law: Sources of Authority and Sources of Rules*, 70 TEX. L. REV. 1551 (1992): 670

Burbank, Stephen. *Interjurisdictional Preclusion, Full Faith and Credit and Federal Common Law: A General Approach*, 71 CORNELL L. REV. 733 (1986): 671

Burbank, Stephen. *The Rules Enabling Act of 1934*, 130 U. PA. L. REV. 1015 (1982): 613

Burbank, Stephen. *Vanishing Trials and Summary Judgment in Federal Civil Cases: Drifting Toward Bethlehem or Gomorrah?* 1 J. EMPIRICAL LEGAL STUD. 591 (2004): 505

Burbank, Stephen, Thomas Rowe & Thomas Mengler. *Compounding or Creating Confusion About Supplemental Jurisdiction? A Reply to Professor Freer*, 40 EMORY L.J. 943, 957 (1991): 734; 786

C

D

E

Handler, Milton. *The Shift from Substantive to Procedural Innovations in Antitrust Suits*, 71 COLUM. L. REV. 1, 9 (1971): 760

HANS, V. & N. VIDMAR, JUDGING THE JURY (1986): 470

HASTIE, R., S. PENROD & N. PENNINGTON, INSIDE THE JURY 140 (1983): 470; 476

Have You Got a Piece of this Lawsuit?, FORTUNE MAGAZINE 69 (June 13, 2011): 782

Hay, Bruce. *Some Settlement Effects of Preclusion*, 1993 U. ILL. L. REV. 21, 49: 663

Hay, Bruce. & David Rosenberg, *"Sweetheart" and "Blackmail" Settlements in Class Actions: Reality and Remedy*, 75 NOTRE DAME L. REV. 1377 (2000): 761

Hay, Peter. *Transient Jurisdiction, Especially Over International Defendants: Critical Comments on* Burnham v. Superior Court of California, 1990 U. ILL. L. REV. 593, 600: 130

Hazard, Geoffrey. *From Whom No Secrets Are Hid*, 76 TEX. L. REV. 1665, 1677–82 (1998): 420

Hazard, Geoffrey. *Indispensable Party: The Historical Origin of a Procedural Phantom*, 61 COLUM. L. REV. 1254 (1961): 731

Hazard, Geoffrey. *Preclusion as to Issues of Law: The Legal System's Interest*, 70 IOWA L. REV. 81 (1984): 667

Hazard, Geoffrey & Myron Moskovitz, *An Historical and Critical Analysis of Interpleader*, 52 CAL. L. REV. 706 (1964): 744

Hensler, Deborah. *The Future of Mass Litigation: Global Class Actions and Third Party Litigation Funding*, 79 GEO. WASH. L. REV. 306, 307 (2011): 762

Hoffman, Lonny & Keith Rowley, *Forum Non Conveniens in Federal Statutory Cases*, 49 EMORY L.J. 1137 (2000): 278

Hoffman, Morris. *10 Trial Mistakes*, 19 THE DOCKET 17 (Spring 1994): 488

Holmes, Oliver Wendell, Jr. *The Path of the Law*, 10 HARV. L. REV. 457, 461 (1897): 551

Holtzoff, Alexander. *The Elimination of Surprise in Federal Practice*, 7 VAND. L. REV. 576, 577 (1954): 372

HUNTER, NAN D. THE POWER OF PROCEDURE: THE LITIGATION OF *JONES V. CLINTON* 172–73 (2002): 347

I

Interim Report of the Committee on Civility of the Seventh Federal Judicial Circuit, 143 F.R.D. 371, 387 (1991): 357; 373–74

J

JAMES, CIVIL PROCEDURE (1965): 728

James, *Right to a Jury Trial in Civil Actions*, 72 YALE L.J. 655, 658–59 (1963): 453

Janutis, Rachel M. *Pulling Venue Up by Its Own Bootstraps: The Relationships Among Nationwide Service of Process, Personal Jurisdiction, and 1391(c)*, 78 ST. JOHN'S L. REV. 37 (2004), 255

Johnstone, A.C. *Peremptory Pragmatism: Religion and the Administration of the* Batson *Rule*, 1998 U. CHI. LEGAL F. 441, 482

Juenger, Friedrich. *The American Law of General Jurisdiction*, 2001 U. CHI. LEGAL F. 141, 164–65: 111

Juenger, Friedrich. *Judicial Jurisdiction in the United States and in the European Communities: A Comparison*, 82 MICH. L. REV. 1195 (1984): 142

K

Kahan, Dan, David Hoffman & Donald Braman. *Whose Eyes Are You Going to Believe?* Scott v. Harris *and the Perils of Cognitive Illiberalism*, 122 HARV. L. REV. 837 (2009): 511

KALMAN, LAURA. LEGAL REALISM AT YALE 21 (1986): 513

Kamp, Allen. *The History Behind* Hansberry v. Lee, 20 U.C. DAVIS L. REV. 481, 497 (1987): 768

Kane, Mary Kay. *Civil Jury Trial: The Case for Reasoned Iconoclasm*, 28 HAST. L.J. 1, 2 (1976): 459

Kane, Mary Kay. *The Golden Wedding Year:* Erie Railroad Company v. Tompkins *and the Federal Rules*, 63 NOTRE DAME L. REV. 671 (1988): 551

Keeva, Steven. *Does Law Mean Never Having to Say You're Sorry?*, 85 A.B.A. J. 64 (Dec. 1999): 859

Kennedy, *Let's All Join In: Intervention under Federal Rule 24*, 57 KY. L.J. 329, 362–63 (1969): 740

KIRP, D., M. YUDOF, & M. FRANKS. GENDER JUSTICE 137 (1986): 477

Koppel, Glenn. *Reflections on the "Chimera" of a Uniform Code of State Civil Procedure: The Virtue of Vision in Procedural Reform*, 58 DEPAUL L. REV. 971 (2009): 7

Koppel, Glenn S. *Toward a New Federalism in State Civil Justice: Developing a Uniform Code of State Civil Procedure Through a Collaborative Rule-Making Process*, 58 VAND. L. REV. 1167 (2005): 7

Kurland, Philip. *The Supreme Court, the Due Process Clause and the In Personam Jurisdiction of State Courts — From* Pennoyer *to* Denckla: *A Review*, 25 U. CHI. L. REV. 569, 584–85 (1958): 38

L

Langbein, John H. *The German Advantage in Civil Procedure*, 52 U. CHI. L. REV. 823 (1985): 831–41; 845

Laycock, Douglas. *The Remedies Issues: Compensatory Damages, Specific Performance, Punitive Damages, Supersedeas Bonds and Abstention*, 9 LITIG. REV. 473 (1990): 821

Lee, Emery & Thomas Willging, *Defining the Problem of Costs in Federal Civil Litigation*, 60 DUKE L.J. 765, 773–774 (2010): 374

LEFLAR, ROBERT, LUTHER MCDOUGAL & ROBERT FELIX. AMERICAN CONFLICTS LAW 102 (4th ed. 1986): 146

Leubsdorf, John. *Constitutional Civil Procedure*, 64 TEX. L. REV. 579, 628–31 (1984): 801

Luneberg, William. *The Opportunity to be Heard and the Doctrines of Preclusion: Federal Limits on State Law*, 31 VILL. L. REV. 81 (1986): 668

M

MADISON, BENJAMIN V., III. CIVIL PROCEDURE FOR ALL STATES (2010): 7

MADISON, BENJAMIN V., III. *Color-Blind: Procedure's Quiet but Crucial Role in Achieving Racial Justice*, 78 U.M.K.C. L. REV. 617 (2010): 5

MADISON, BENJAMIN V., III. *Trial by Jury or by Military Tribunal for Accused Terrorist Detainees Facing the Death Penalty? An Examination of the Principles That Transcend the U.S. Constitution*, 17 U. FLA. J.L. & PUB. POL. 347, 391 (2006): 445–46

Marcus, Richard. *Reining in the American Litigator: The New Role of American Judges*, 27 HASTINGS INT'L & COMP. L. REV. 3, 29–30 (2003): 849

Marcus, Richard. *The Revival of Fact Pleading Under the Federal Rules of Civil Procedure*, 86 COLUM. L. REV. 433, 484–85 (1986): 504

Marcus, Richard. *The Story of* Hickman: *Preserving Adversarial Incentives While Embracing Broad Discovery, in* CIVIL PROCEDURE STORIES 307, 331–33 (K. Clermont, ed. 2004): 408

Marvell, Thomas. *Appellate Capacity and Caseload Growth*, 16 AKRON L. REV. 43, 72–74 (1982): 801

Mashaw, Jerry. *The Supreme Court's Due Process Calculus for Administrative Adjudication in* Mathews v. Eldridge: *Three Factors in Search of a Theory of Value*, 44 U. CHI. L. REV. 28,50 (1976): 155

Matasar, Richard. *A Pendent and Ancillary Jurisdiction Primer: The Scope and Limits of Supplemental Jurisdiction*, 17 U.C. DAVIS L. REV. 103, 150–57 (1983): 682

McCoid, John. *Procedural Reform and the Right to Jury Trial: A Study of* Beacon Theatres, Inc. v. Westover, 116 U. PA. L. REV. 1 (1967): 453

McCoid, John. *A Single Package for Multiparty Disputes*, 27 STAN. L. REV. 707 (1976): 673

MCCORMICK ON EVIDENCE 151 (6th ed. 2006): 389

McFarland, Douglas. *Dictum Run Wild: How Long-Arm Statutes Extended to the Limits of Due Process*, 84 B.U. L. REV. 491 (2004): 145

McFarland, Douglas D. *Supplemental Jurisdiction over Permissive Counterclaims and Set Offs: A Misconception*, 64 MERCER L. REV. 437 (2013): 707

MEADOR, DANIEL JOHN & JORDANA SIMONE BERNSTEIN, APPELLATE COURTS IN THE UNITED STATES 3–5 (1994): 802

Menkel-Meadow, Carrie. *For and Against Settlement: Uses and Abuses of the Mandatory Settlement Conference*, 33 UCLA L. REV. 485 (1985): 424

Menkel-Meadow, Carrie. *The Trouble with the Adversary System in a Postmodern, Multicultural World*, 38 WM. & MARY L. REV. 5 (1996): 861

Menkel-Meadow, Carrie. *Whose Dispute Is It Anyway?: A Philosophical and Democratic Defense of Settlement (In Some Cases)*, 83 GEO. L.J. 2663, 2674 (1995): 861

Mengler, Thomas. *The Demise of Pendent and Ancillary Jurisdiction*, 1990 BYU L. REV. 247: 696

Merrigan, Edward. Erie *to* York *to* Ragan—*A Triple Play on the Federal Rules*, 3 Vand. L. Rev. 711 (1950): 556

Merrill, Thomas. *The Common Law Powers of Federal Courts*, 52 U. Chi. L. Rev. 1, 13–24 (1985): 553

Mezibov, Marc and H. Louis Sirkin. *The Mapplethorpe Obscenity Trial*, 18 Litigation 12 (Summer 1992): 484–88

Miller, Arthur. *The Pretial Rush to Judgment: Are the "Litigation Explosion," "Liability Crisis," and Efficiency Cliches Eroding Our Day in Court and Jury Trial Commitments?*, 78 N.Y.U. L. Rev. 982, 1071 (2003): 503; 513

Miller, Arthur. *Problems of Giving Notice in Class Actions*, 58 F.R.D. 313, 322 (1972): 781

Miller, Arthur & David Crump, *Jurisdiction and Choice of Law in Multistate Class Actions After* Phillips Petroleum Co. v. Shutts, 96 Yale L.J. 1, 46 (1986): 775

Molot, Jonathan. *The Feasibility of Litigation Markets,* 89 Indiana L.J. 171 (2014): 782

Moore's Federal Practice, 161; 186; 192; 203; 207; 214; 263; 333; 338; 339; 342; 350; 354; 367; 426–27; 515; 583; 602; 690; 709; 713; 737; 738; 744; 752; 796; 798; 853

Moore, Karen. *Collateral Attack on Subject Matter Jurisdiction: A Critique of the Restatement (Second) of Judgments*, 66 Cornell L. Rev. 534 (1981): 290–91

Moore, Patricia W. Hatamyar. *The Anti-Plaintiff Pending Amendments to the Federal Rules of Civil Procedure and the Pro-Defendant Composition of the Federal Rulemaking Committees*, 83 U. Cinn. L. Rev. 1083 (2015): 392

Mullenix, Linda S. *Aggregate Litigation and the Death of Democratic Dispute Resolution*, 107 Nw. U. L. Rev. 511 (2013): 266

Mullenix, Linda S. *Discovery in Disarray: The Pervasive Myth of Pervasive Discovery Abuse and the Consequences for Unfounded Rulemaking*, 46 Stan. L. Rev. 1393 (1994): 374

Murphy, Colleen. *Determining Compensation: The Tension Between Legislative Power and Jury Authority*, 74 Tex. L. Rev. 345 (1995): 460

Murphy, Colleen. *Integrating the Constitutional Authority of Civil and Criminal Juries*, 61 Geo. Wash. L. Rev. 723, 739–82 (1993): 460

Murphy, Colleen P. *Judgment as a Matter of Law on Punitive Damages*, 75 Tul. L. Rev. 459 (2000): 531

Murphy, Colleen. *Judicial Assessment of Legal Remedies*, 94 Nw. L. Rev. 153 (1999): 460

Murphy, Colleen. *Misclassifying Monetary Restitution*, 55 SMU L. Rev. 1577 (2002): 458

Mushlin, Michael. *The New Quasi in Rem Jurisdiction: New York's Revival of a Doctrine Whose Time Has Passed*, 55 Brook. L. Rev. 1059 (1990): 124; 146; 179

N

Nadelmann, K.H. *Jurisdictionally Improper Fora, in* XXth Century Comparative And Conflicts Laws: Legal Essays in Honor of Hessel E. Yntema 329 (Nadelman, von Mehren & Hazard, eds. 1961): 126

R

S

Shapiro, David. *The Story of* Celotex: *The Role of Summary Judgment in the Administration of Civil Justice, in* CIVIL PROCEDURE STORIES 359, 376 (K. Clermont ed., 2d ed. 2008): 505

SHAPIRO, D. CIVIL PROCEDURE: PRECLUSION IN CIVIL ACTIONS 77–78 (2001): 634

Shavell, Steven. *Suit, Settlement, and Trial: A Theoretical Analysis Under Alternative Methods for the Allocation of Legal Costs*, 11 J. LEG. STUD. 55, 57–58 (1982): 372

Shreve, Gene. *Preclusion and Federal Choice of Law*, 64 TEX. L. REV. 1209 (1986): 668

SHREVE, GENE & PETER RAVEN-HANSEN. UNDERSTANDING CIVIL PROCEDURE 63 (4th ed. 2009): 124

Shuman, Daniel. *The Role of Apology in Tort Law*, 83 JUDICATURE 180 (2000): 860

Silberman, Linda. *Comparative Jurisdiction in the International Context: Will the Proposed Hague Judgments Convention Be Stalled?* 52 DEPAUL L. REV. 319, 340–41 (2002): 111; 130

Silberman, Linda. Shaffer v. Heitner: *The End of an Era*, 53 N.Y.U. L. REV. 33, 88 (1978): 59

Silver, Charles & Geoffrey Miller. *The Quasi-Class Action Method of Managing Multi-District Litigation: Problems and a Proposal*, 63 VAND. L. REV. 107 (2010): 266

Singer, Joseph. *Legal Realism Now*, 76 CAL. L. REV. 465 (1988): 46

Smith, Allen. Blue Ridge *and Beyond: A* Byrd's *Eye View of Federalism in Diversity Litigation*, 36 TULANE L. REV. 443 (1962): 562

SOBOL, RICHARD. BENDING THE LAW 13 (1991): 391

Solimine, Michael. *The Quiet Revolution in Personal Jurisdiction*, 73 TULANE L. REV. 1 (1998): 145

Solimine, Michael. *Revitalizing Interlocutory Appeals in the Federal Courts*, 58 GEO. WASH. L. REV. 1165, 1174 (1990): 815

Sperlich, Peter. *And Then There Were Six: The Decline of the American Jury*, 63 JUDICATURE 262 (1980): 489

STARR, V. & M. MCCORMICK. JURY SELECTION 522 (1993): 475

Stein, Allan. Erie *and Court Access*, 100 YALE L.J. 1935 (1991): 561; 575

Stein, Allan. *Personal Jurisdiction and the Internet: Seeing Due Process Through the Lens of Regulatory Precision*, 98 NW. U. L. REV. 411 (2004): 132; 139

Stein, Allan. *Styles of Argument and Interstate Federalism in the Law of Personal Jurisdiction*, 65 TEX. L. REV. 689, 751 (1987): 141

Steinman, Adam. *Reinventing Appellate Jurisdiction*, 48 B.C. L. REV. 1237 (2007): 804

Steinman, Joan. *After* Steel Co.: *Hypothetical Jurisdiction in the Federal Appellate Courts*, 58 WASH. & LEE L. REV. 855 (2001): 245

Steinman, Joan. *Postremoval Changes in the Party Structure of Diversity Cases: The Old Law, the New Law, and Rule 19*, 38 U. KAN. L. REV. 864, 950 (1990): 740

Stempel, Jeffrey. *Sanction, Symmetry, and Safe Harbors: Limiting Misapplications of Rule 11 by Harmonizing It with Pre-Verdict Dismissal Devices*, 60 FORDHAM L. REV. 257, 260–61 (1991): 357

T

Twitchell, Mary. *Why We Keep Doing Business with Doing-Business Jurisdiction*, 2001 U. CHI. LEGAL F. 171, 109

U

UNDERWOOD, JAMES. A GUIDE TO FEDERAL DISCOVERY RULES (2d ed. 1985): 411

V

VON MEHREN, ARTHUR. THEORY AND PRACTICE OF ADJUDICATORY AUTHORITY IN PRIVATE INTERNATIONAL LAW: A COMPARATIVE STUDY OF THE DOCTRINE, POLICIES AND PRACTICES OF COMMON—AND CIVIL—LAW SYSTEMS 306 (2003): 280

von Mehren & Trautman. *Jurisdiction to Adjudicate: A Suggested Analysis*, 79 HARV. L. REV. 1121 (1966): 102

W

Wagatsuma, Hiroshi & Arthur Rosett. *The Implications of Apology: Law and Culture in Japan and in the United States*: 854–59

Warren, Charles. *New Light on the History of the Federal Judiciary Act of 1789* (1923), 37 HARV. L. REV. 49, 51–52, 81–88, 108: 545; 550

WARREN, 2 THE SUPREME COURT IN UNITED STATES HISTORY (rev. ed. 1935) 89: 546

Wasserman, Howard M. *Jurisdiction and Merits*, 80 WASH. L. REV. 643 (2005): 367

Wasserman, Howard M. *Jurisdiction, Merits, and Non-Extant Rights*, 56 U. KAN. L. REV. 227 (2008): 367

Wasserman, Howard M. *Jurisdiction, Merits, and Procedure: Thoughts on Dodson's Trichotomy*, 102 NW. U. L. REV. COLLOQUY 215, 220 (2008): 367

Weinstein, Jack. *Considering Jury "Nullification:" When May and Should a Jury Reject the Law to Do Justice*, 30 AM. CR. L. REV. 239 (1993): 489

Weinstein, Jack. *The Ghost of Process: The Fiftieth Anniversary of the Federal Rules of Civil Procedure and* Erie, 54 BROOK. L. REV. 1 (1988): 551

Weinstein, James. *The Early American Origins of Territoriality in Judicial Jurisdiction*, 37 ST. LOUIS U. L.J. 1, 27 (1992): 141

Weintraub, Russell. *A Map Out of the Personal Jurisdiction Labyrinth*, 28 U.C. DAVIS L. REV. 531, 555 (1995): 92

Weintraub, Russell. *An Objective Basis for Rejecting Transient Jurisdiction*, 22 RUTGERS L.J. 611, 615–16 (1991): 129–30

Weintraub, Russell. COMMENTARY ON THE CONFLICT OF LAWS 139 (6th ed. 2010): 81; 124

Weintraub, Russell. *International Litigation and Forum Non Conveniens*, 29 TEX. INT'L L.J. 321, 330–32 (1994): 278; 373

White, Lucie. *Subordination, Rhetorical Survival Skills, and Sunday Shoes: Notes on the Hearing of Mrs. G*, 38 BUFF. L. REV. 1, 32 (1990): 863

Williams, Spencer. *Mass Tort Class Actions: Going, Going, Gone?*, 98 F.R.D. 323, 328–29 (1983): 664

Y

Z

Index

[References are to sections.]